Contracts

Contracts

Cases, Text, and Problems

SECOND EDITION

Charles Calleros
Professor of Law
Sandra Day O'Connor College of Law
Arizona State University
Chapters 1–12 and Appendices

Stephen A. Gerst
Professor Emeritus
Retired Judge, Arizona Superior Court
Chapters 13 and 14

Carolina Academic Press
Durham, North Carolina

ISBN: 978-1-5310-1760-6
eISBN: 978-1-5310-1761-3
LCCN: 2019950625

Carolina Academic Press
700 Kent Street
Durham, NC 27701
Telephone (919) 489-7486
Fax (919) 493-5668
www.cap-press.com

Printed in the United States of America

In loving memory of my parents, Charles and Emily Calleros.
—Charles Calleros

To my "Dodi Li" for her love and support.
—Stephen A. Gerst

Contents

Table of Cases

(Includes only main cases presented for student analysis, not all cases cited, quoted, or used as inspiration for exercises.)

Preface

I. Pedagogy for this Course

This book is designed for use in a course that employs both case analysis and the "problem method." It combines the following features and approaches: text, cases, and problems.

A. Text

In the practice of law, new attorneys are seldom experts in all the laws that apply to their clients' problems. If they immediately waded into the latest judicial decision in the field, they might not fully understand the decision or appreciate the significance of that decision within the larger field of law. To secure a general familiarity with the general topic, so that they can identify issues and develop an effective research strategy, new attorneys typically turn first to a secondary source, such as a treatise or law review article, which will provide basic background information about a field of law and will refer to the most important statutes and judicial decisions. Armed with this general background knowledge, an attorney can then more effectively research and understand the latest law on point in the relevant jurisdiction and can more easily identify issues raised by the facts of a client's case.

To mirror this experience in the practice of law, and to save time for problem-solving, this book presents more text and somewhat fewer judicial opinions than most casebooks of its size. On most topics, statutes and judicial opinions are introduced with text that provides background information. At times, this background text consists of the author's summary of one or more judicial opinions, so that you can spend somewhat less time briefing cases and can spend more time applying the lessons of the cases to new facts. Don't worry; in light of the hundreds of judicial opinions presented in this book and in other first-year courses, you will be presented with seemingly innumerable opportunities to engage in case analysis.

Other text consists of excerpts from books or articles, providing perspective on the topics. These readings typically follow the cases and statutes on a topic, providing historical background, comparisons to approaches in other legal systems, or ideas for reform or innovation within our own legal system.

Chapter 1 is exceptional in its exclusive use of text to provide an overview of sources of contract law, followed by an introduction to some critical concepts through text and problems. That background reading should provide students with the tools needed to dive deeply into the topic of contract formation, explored in Chapters 2–7.

B. Casebook

Like traditional casebooks, this book presents many judicial opinions, most of them developing common law and a few interpreting and applying statutory law. These provide you with repeated opportunities to: (a) learn to read and interpret cases, (b) gain a deep understanding of how judges decide cases and develop the law, and (c) derive legal rules and standards from individual cases and from your synthesis of a series of cases. A few of the opinions are not binding on any court in other cases because they are issued by a trial court, are unpublished, or both; even these opinions, however, tell helpful stories about contracts, conflict, and judicial resolution of conflict.

C. Problem Method

You will fully comprehend the material only if you actively work with the legal principles by applying them to new facts. The many exercises and practice exams scattered throughout the book provide ample opportunity to engage in this analytic process before, during, and after class.

D. Statutory Analysis

This book presents important provisions of Articles 1 and 2 of the Uniform Commercial Code, primarily as enacted by Arizona, California, and Texas, as well as brief references to other statutes. Although several judicial interpretations of statutes are presented, this book frequently explores statutory analysis through the problem method, so that you can experience the intellectual challenge of engaging in original statutory application in light of the text and purpose of the statutes, under the guidance of your professor.

II. Preparing for Class and for Exams

Each professor will have his or her own expectations for class discussion, and you should seek to understand and meet those expectations. In the meantime, the following general guidance might be helpful.

A. Briefing Cases for Class

It's not a tired cliché: You will develop the skills of reading, interpretation, and analysis necessary for lawyering and for success on law school essay exams only if you perform the work of preparing your own case briefs.

If you are fortunate, one or more of your courses will address techniques of briefing cases. Various formats for case briefs might differ in the names assigned to elements of the case brief, or the order in which they are presented, but they do not vary greatly in substance. Following is one reasonable format for a case brief:

1. Identification of the Case

State the case name and authoring court. Identify the context of the case within the casebook: Consult the latest section heading in the book and identify the current topic of study. After you have analyzed the case, identify the role the case plays in the section or chapter.

2. Facts

Summarize the facts that led to the legal dispute. Tell the story in your own words, so that the case comes to life for you, and so that you can summarize the case in class without simply reading from the opinion.

3. Procedural History

Summarize the judicial proceedings in the courts below the court that authored the opinion. At the least, state the disposition of the issue or issues in the lower court or courts.

4. Issue(s) and Holding(s)

State the question or questions addressed by the court, followed by the court's conclusion on each question. Try to state the issue narrowly, incorporating critical facts into the question, so that your holding is grounded in those critical facts.

5. Reasoning

Explain the court's reasons for its conclusions. Among other things, this can include the court's analysis of the law and facts, and its balancing of policy considerations. Note how the court analogizes or distinguishes previous decisions that arguably are controlling or persuasive.

6. Evaluation

Explain your agreement or disagreement with the court's conclusions and reasoning. Feel free to be critical.

7. Synthesis

Explain how this opinion's holding and reasoning compare to those of other assigned opinions that address the same issue.

B. Additional Reading

1. Citations in the Textbook

Notes before or after the cases frequently cite to scholarly articles and additional judicial opinions that shed light on the current topic of study. You might wonder whether you are expected to find and read those cited materials to prepare for class discussion or examinations.

Unless your professor tells you otherwise, you are not expected to read those additional cited materials. Those additional resources are cited partly to verify the accuracy of the textbook's statements about the law. They could also be helpful if a student is interested in digging more deeply into a topic for a separate research project, either for an independent study or work in a law office. It would never hurt to find and read some of these materials for class, but you will seldom have time to do so in your normal preparation for your first-year Contracts course.

Some of the exercises in this book cite to the cases that inspired the facts of the exercises. If so, you need not look up the case, which often will present more complicated facts and legal analysis than does the exercise. You will fulfill the purpose of the exercise by applying the legal rules you have learned to the facts of the exercise, and then joining discussion of the exercise in class.

2. Treatises and Commercial Study Aids

To prepare for exams, you should summarize your course materials in an outline, organizing it around legal rules, and illustrating each rule with one or more one-sentence summaries of cases in which the rule was satisfied or not. You will find that the process of synthesizing cases, as briefly described in Section A.7 above, provides a bridge to outlining. Synthesis and outlining are sophisticated activities that are described in detail in a number of books about the study of law. One such book was written by the primary author of this textbook: Charles Calleros, LAW SCHOOL EXAMS: PREPARING AND WRITING TO WIN (2d ed. 2013).

You might be tempted to buy a commercially available outline of a course and simply study that outline. You will find, however, that doing so would be a poor substitute for composing your own outline, for at least two reasons: (1) the commercial outline will not be tailored to the perspective that your professor brings to the course, and (2) by far the greatest educational benefit of a course outline lies in the process of creating it, which forces you to gain a deep, working knowledge of the material. Reading someone else's outline cannot replace the intellectually demanding process of preparing your own outline, stated with precision but in your own words.

When reviewing course material while preparing your course outline, you might find it helpful to clear up any lingering confusion by consulting a respected treatise in the library or by comparing your summary with that in a commercial outline. This consultation is harmless so long as you begin with your own analysis.

Acknowledgments

I am very grateful to Vera Hamer-Sonn, Suzanne Lynn, and Sunny Larson for technical assistance, our College librarians for library assistance, and the following law students for research assistance or other substantial contributions to various drafts of this book, which has been used in class since Fall 2008: Alison Atwater (Class of 2010), Erin Maupin (Class of 2011), Natalya Ter-Grigoryan (Class of 2011), Jillian Tse (Class of 2011), Nedda Reghabi (Class of 2012), Rebecca Janssen (Class of 2013), Chinedu Orjih (Class of 2013), Edith Cseke (Class of 2013), Kevin Blood (Class of 2013), Kyle Sol Johnson (Class of 2015), Nathan Andrews (Class of 2016), Jennifer Hancock (Class of 2017), Kevin Hanlon (Class of 2017), Stephen Kaneshiro (Class of 2020), Cameron Stanley (Class of 2020), and Christina Jutzi (Class of 2021).

I also thank Professor Stephen Gerst for preparing chapters on third-party rights and on assignment and delegation, added to this book in 2013.

Professor Charles Calleros
Sandra Day O'Connor College of Law at Arizona State University
January 2020

I wish to express my gratitude and appreciation to Professor Charles Calleros and his research assistant, Tim Forsman (Class of 2014), for their assistance and collaboration. I also wish to acknowledge the contributions made by my research assistant, Amanda Jaksich, and by Professor Warren Miller.

Stephen A. Gerst
Professor Emeritus and Retired Judge
January 2020

Acknowledgments

Contracts

Chapter 1

Introduction and Overview

To launch our study of contract law and legal method, this chapter will introduce a number of fundamental concepts. As you work through the chapter, keep in mind the following questions:

- What is a contract, and how does it differ from an agreement?
- What are the sources of contract law, and what methods will we use to study the law?
- What are the basic kinds of exchanges through which parties might create contracts?
- What are the interests potentially protected by contract law, and what are the remedial tools employed by the courts?

I. Overview of Contracts and Sources of Contract Law

A. Agreements and Contracts in Our Society

Before the first day of your Contracts class, consider the range of contracts you have encountered recently. Have you entered into a lease? Have you purchased a product that is warranted to perform to specified standards or that limits your remedy if the warranty is breached? Have you paid tuition to a school in exchange for admission to its course of study? Have you left clothes with a dry cleaning establishment that promised to have the clothes ready by "tomorrow after 5," subject to posted disclaimers of liability for certain kinds of damage to clothes, and with the understanding that you will pay a fee that is displayed on the window or written on a receipt? Along with the legal machinery that enforces them, contracts form the engine of our economy, providing a basis for relying on the promises of others and planning for the future.

We will distinguish between "contracts" and "agreements." The word "agreement" describes the terms to which two or more people have consented. "Contract" describes the terms of an agreement that have legal effect, the terms that a court will enforce. From this distinction, you can infer that two people can agree to some course of action, but it does not follow that their agreement is coextensive with an enforceable "contract." More specifically, (1) some agreements are not contracts at all, and (2) some agreements form contracts but not precisely on the terms to which the parties agreed.

1. Agreements That Are Not Legally Binding Contracts

We will learn that an agreement generally is a binding contract under state law only if it

- is reached through a process of offer and acceptance that reflects an intent to create legal obligations,
- satisfies the requirement of "consideration" or falls within an exception to that requirement,
- is sufficiently definite in its terms to permit a court to fashion a remedy, and
- is not compromised by problems such as illegality or mutual mistake.

Thus, for reasons that we will study, two persons might reach the following *agreements* without creating legally binding *contracts*:

- A: "I want to give you $10,000 next week to help you open your bakery. Are you agreeable to that?" B: "Yes, of course. I agree. Thank you."
- A: "I will sell you a good plot of land for the house you want to build." B: "Great. I agree."
- A: "Shall we see the movie tonight at the 8 p.m. showing? I'll treat for pizza at JJ's Pizzeria if you buy the movie tickets." B: "Perfect. See you at JJ's at 7."
- A: "If you agree to drive the getaway car, I promise to give you 30% of the proceeds of the robbery." B: "You've got a deal."

2. Contract Terms That Vary from the Agreement

Some agreements will result in binding contracts, but the enforceable contract might be different in scope from the terms reached by the parties in their agreement. For example, some parts of the agreement could be unenforceable because they violate public policy. Conversely, the contract might include terms that were not discussed by the parties in their agreement but are implied in law.

Consider, for example, an agreement by a consumer to purchase a gas-powered lawn mower from a retail hardware store. Even if the parties did not discuss the performance of the lawn mower, and even if the mower was not accompanied by a written warranty, the Uniform Commercial Code (UCC), which is described in greater detail in a few pages, will add a warranty to the contract. Specifically, if the parties were silent on this issue, the UCC statutorily supplies an implied warranty that the lawnmower will meet certain minimum standards of "merchantable" quality. *See* U.C.C. § 2-314 (2011). Moreover, assuming that the mower malfunctioned in a way that breached the implied warranty, if a provision in the parties' written agreement purported to relieve the seller of liability for the buyer's personal injury stemming from the breach of warranty, this provision likely will be unenforceable as "unconscionable" under the UCC. *See* U.C.C. § 2-719(3) (2011).

Thus, the legally enforceable contract would include a statutorily implied warranty term that was not expressed in the parties' agreement. On the other hand, the contract likely would *not* include a limitation on liability, because it probably will not meet statutory requirements, even though the parties agreed to it.

B. Sources of Contract Law

1. International, Federal, and State Law

Our legal system belongs to the "common law" family, derived from the English legal system. From time to time, this book will draw a contrast between our common law system and the different legal approaches adopted in "civil law" systems, such as those found throughout much of Europe and Latin America. Even if these occasional references to foreign law are beyond the scope of your course, they should enable you to better critique the common law approach and to resist the tendency to view our legal solutions as the sole and inevitable answers to legal questions.

Some rules of contract law applicable in the United States are found in federal statutes or agency regulations. Others can be found in international treaties entered into by the United States; these have the same force as federal statutes.

For the most part, however, contracts are governed by state law. Although the specific rules often vary from state to state, general principles of contract law and legal method are sufficiently universal and consistent within the United States that we can usually generalize from the judicial decisions of any state, and from some English decisions as well. Moreover, as we shall learn, the UCC provides additional statutory uniformity in contracts for the sale of goods.

2. Enacted Law, Common Law, and Case Law

We have already mentioned one source of contract law, a collection of statutes known as the UCC. We will spend more time, however, studying common law rules, ones created by judges independent of any statutes enacted by a legislature. Once we draw a clear distinction between statutory law and common law, we can then define "case law."

We start with a chart of the branches of a state's government, which shows that each branch of government can contribute to the creation or further development of the law:

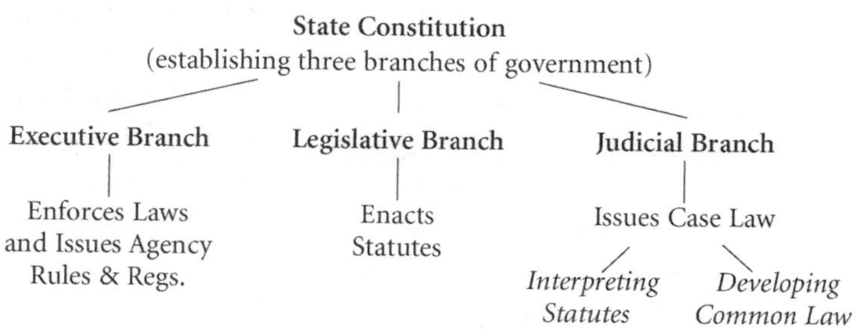

a. Executive Branch Initiatives

Although the executive branch is primarily responsible for enforcement of law, it participates in the formulation and adoption of law as well. In a state's executive branch, for example, the governor can propose legislation, and agencies within the executive branch can issue specific rules and regulations that help implement the more general terms of a statute. Other officials of the executive branch, such as those in the Office of the State Attorney General, will enforce some statutory schemes relating to contracts, such as consumer protection laws, by bringing lawsuits in courts.

Even the federal executive branch has adopted a form of contract law, an international treaty that applies to international sales of goods. In 1983, the U.S. government entered into the United Nations Convention on Contracts for the International Sale of Goods ("CISG"), which was incorporated into our federal law upon ratification by the Senate. This treaty became effective in adopting countries in 1988. It governs contracts between a seller and buyer of goods if their places of business are in different adopting countries, such as a contract between a seller of goods from Mexico and a commercial buyer of those goods in Arizona.

Again, however, this course will refer almost entirely to state laws, and even then almost entirely to the actions of branches of government other than the executive branch. Our focus will be primarily on state common law developed by the courts and secondarily on statutes enacted by state legislatures.

b. The Uniform Commercial Code and Other State Legislation

The legislative branch enacts statutes, some of which govern or affect contractual relations. For example, states have commonly enacted statutes relating to consumer protection, landlord-tenant relationships, and some facets of employment relations. One statutory scheme, however, stands out as an obvious topic for study: Article 2 of the Uniform Commercial Code ("UCC"), which includes dozens of statutory sections governing "transactions in goods."

(1) The Nature of the UCC

Although the UCC is enacted with some variations in all 50 states, it is not a federal law. Instead, it is the product of two private organizations, the American Law Institute (ALI) and the National Conference of Commissioners on Uniform State Laws, which completed their work in 1956 and invited state legislatures to adopt the UCC as part of their state laws.

The UCC is designed to be a relatively comprehensive code, a system of numerous interrelated statutory sections that work together to provide binding law for commercial transactions. We will explore selected provisions of two parts of the UCC: mainly Article 2, whose sections address contracts for sales of goods, and less frequently Article 1, whose sections provide general standards for all commercial transactions within the ambit of the UCC, including the sales contracts addressed in Article 2.

(2) Success in Achieving Uniformity in State Commercial Law

Most of these statutory provisions are "default" rules, ones that supply a rule governing the rights or obligations of parties if the parties did not address that topic in their agreement and devise their own rule. For example, if the parties have not agreed to the time and date of delivery of the goods, the UCC provides that the goods must be delivered in "a reasonable time." *See* U.C.C. § 2-309(1) (2011).

The authors of the UCC were largely successful in achieving uniformity in commercial law in the United States. All 50 states adopted the UCC, although Louisiana excluded Article 2 from its adoption because its French and Spanish roots left it with a pre-existing code system for contracts.

Of the 49 states that adopted Article 2, some of them enacted versions that varied from the original text on a few provisions. Moreover, the courts of each state can independently interpret and apply the provisions of their state's version of the UCC, so two different states can end up with different legal meanings attached to the identical statutory language adopted in both states. Finally, Article 2 of the UCC does not address every issue that might arise in a contract for the sale of goods, and those gaps will be filled by other statutes and the common law of each state, which vary from state to state. Accordingly, the law governing contracts for the sale of goods is not perfectly uniform within the United States. Nonetheless, the UCC provides substantial national uniformity for sales of goods.

(3) Proposed Revisions to the UCC

Shortly after the turn of the century, the ALI proposed new versions of Articles 1 and 2 of the UCC, for adoption by state legislatures. Revised Article 1 (2001) has been adopted by all states, with some variations; it thus is an appropriate subject for current study. Revised Article 2 (2003), however, was mired in controversy and failed to achieve adoption by a significant number of states. In May 2011, the ALI withdrew its proposed revisions to Article 2 and readopted its earlier version. Accordingly, we will study the unrevised, readopted version of Article 2 (2011), which is reproduced in Appendix 1 as it has been enacted in Texas, where it is called "Chapter 2" of the Texas Business and Commerce Code.

c. Common Law and the Restatements

In civil law systems, which originated in Europe and spread to other regions such as Latin America and some countries in Asia, statutory code systems are traditionally and ideally viewed as complete and comprehensive sources of law, covering the entire field of law in several topics, including contracts. True, the language of these codes is necessarily general and must be interpreted and applied by the courts, but civil law judges generally do not openly embrace the role of developing a body of law independent of the codes.

In our common law system, it is true that legislation has primacy over judicial decisions because a statute can modify or replace a point of common law with a different statutory rule. However, in contrast with comprehensive legislative codes in civil law systems, the law of contracts in our common law system was largely created and developed by English and American judges as "common law," expressed in judicial opinions independent of any legislation. Prior to the middle of the nineteenth century, legislation addressing contracts in the United States was viewed as a rare and exceptional overlay to the common law. A statute usually reflected occasional legislative dissatisfaction with an isolated point of common law.

Since then, state and federal legislation and agency regulations have so greatly increased in volume that our current system has become a hybrid of common law and civil law systems. Nonetheless, a substantial amount of contract law is still governed by common law. As noted above, the UCC's provisions focusing on issues of contract law generally apply only to transactions in goods, which leaves the common law (supplemented by other statutes) free to address contracts for services or real estate. Moreover, even for sales of goods, the UCC contains gaps that are filled by the common law, which remains in the background, ready to step in as the applicable law if it is not displaced by statutory law. *See* U.C.C. § 1-103(b) (2001).

For centuries, when statutory law has not addressed an issue of contract law, judges have created common law based on custom, policy, and common sense. They have acted incrementally, defining and developing carefully limited portions of the law as needed to resolve specific disputes brought before them, one case at a time. Today, judges continue to create and further develop the common law, in contracts as well as in other fields of law. They seldom write on a clean slate; instead, they build on the foundation created by previous decisions as a bricklayer might build a wall, brick by brick with each judicial decision in a specific dispute represented by a new brick.

Under the legal doctrine of *stare decisis*, which means to stand by what has been decided, a court within a state will endeavor to decide new cases so that they are consistent with the preceding judicial decisions (the "precedent") of that court or a higher court within that state. In this way, the "bricks" representing new judicial decisions are supported by previously laid bricks, forming a stable, predictable wall of common law. New decisions might extend the reach of previous ones, but they normally will do so in a manner that is consistent with the reasoning of the previous decisions.

Under *stare decisis*, this brickwork of common law will change its direction abruptly only if an appellate court finds very good reason to abandon its previous decisions, or if the legislature decides to do so by enacting an overriding statute.

If one reads and analyzes numerous cases, one can begin to see patterns on this wall of bricks, and can then derive some general rules from groups of cases. The ALI has engaged in such an enterprise by drafting "restatements" of several subjects of the law, including contracts. The Restatement (Second) of Contracts (1981) represents the ALI's second effort in the twentieth century to summarize the common law of contracts in the United States, and sometimes to anticipate emerging developments. When the second edition of this textbook was submitted for editing and printing, the ALI was in the process of drafting and debating a new Restatement of the Law of Consumer Contracts, which might be in final form by the time this textbook is published. The concepts addressed in the draft of this Restatement as of the summer of 2019, however, are already addressed in the second edition of this textbook, through text, cases, and problems.

A court can adopt a provision of a Restatement as part of its common law, thus incorporating the substance of the Restatement into its published judicial opinions; in turn, these opinions are a source of potentially binding "primary law." By itself, however, a Restatement is not a binding source of primary law; rather, it is the ALI's attempt to summarize the common law or to predict or influence its future direction on some topics. It is thus a nonbinding "secondary source" of law.

This book will quote or explain important provisions of the second Restatement to introduce topics that are explored in greater detail in judicial opinions. Nonetheless, we should remember that the judicial opinions came first, and the Restatement simply provides us with a model for generalizing from the cases.

So let's return now to a form of primary law, the judicial decisions published by courts when they resolve disputes. The way in which precedent can guide or sometimes even bind courts in new cases is a complicated matter that you will study in depth in all of your classes, but especially in your class on legal method and writing. For now, it will suffice to introduce the term "case law," and to comment briefly on the relationship between the judicial and legislative branches of government.

d. Case Law

The term "case" can refer to a dispute, real or hypothetical, to which the law can be applied. As you will soon see, this book is filled with real and hypothetical cases of this sort.

More narrowly, you will hear students and professors use the word "case" to refer to the published judicial opinion in which a judge or panel of judges explains the court's resolution of a real dispute. This meaning is carried over to the term "casebook," which is largely a collection of judicial opinions.

Some students and professors use the term "case law" to refer only to judicial decisions that discuss and develop the common law. Judges, however, also interpret and apply statutes to resolve some disputes. Indeed, in the same case a judge might need to address several issues to resolve the dispute, some issues governed by common law and others governed by statutory law such as provisions of that state's enactment of the UCC.

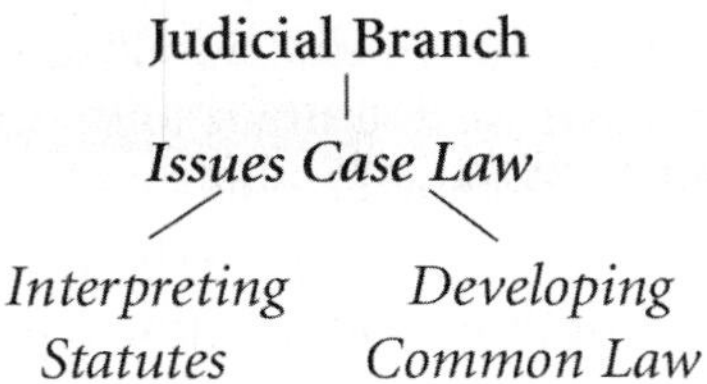

Consequently, we need a term that encompasses all of the precedent created by appellate judges when they publish their judicial opinions resolving specific cases. This book will use the term "case law" to refer to all such judicial precedent, whether a judicial opinion develops common law, interprets statutory law, or does both.

If displeased with the common law, the state legislature can overrule the common law developed by judges and replace it with a different statutory rule. Conversely, a legislature can "codify" a common law rule by adopting that judicial rule in a statute, thus precluding the courts from changing course and abandoning that rule.

True, the courts have their influence on statutory law, because they must interpret the general or ambiguous language of statutes and apply the language to the facts of specific disputes to resolve those disputes. If the legislature of that state is displeased with a judicial interpretation of its statute, however, it can amend the statute to clarify the legislature's intended meaning.

Thus, our body of case law might look predominantly like an enormous wall of bricks, representing the common law, built case by case, brick by brick. At various intervals, groups of common law bricks might be replaced by stonework, representing a statute.

Or a whole section of the brick wall might be replaced with panels of stonework, representing dozens or hundreds of sections of a code addressing a broad topic of the law, just as Article 2 of the UCC addresses contracts for sales of goods. The stonework, however, likely will leave some gaps through which the brick shows through, representing opportunities for common law principles to apply to fill the gaps.

For example, even though the UCC will apply generally to a dispute arising in a sale of goods, if the UCC provides no rule to address a particular issue that arises in that dispute, common law principles will reappear to apply to that issue.

As judges interpret and apply the statutes, they add their judicial gloss to the statutory meaning, perhaps represented by some judicial etching and sculpting of a portion of the stone.

C. The Study of Contract Law

As with most of your first-year classes, you will study Contract Law primarily through case law, by analyzing judicial opinions that explain the court's resolutions of disputes on specific facts. Most of these judicial opinions (or "cases," as they are more commonly called) will discuss common law, but some opinions will interpret the UCC or other statutes.

1. Analyzing Statutes

When not studying common law cases, you might be analyzing the language of a statute or studying a judicial opinion that interprets and applies a statute. Even when judicial interpretations are available to you, remember to start with the statutory language, before turning to the court's interpretation and application.

2. Working with Case Law

Through your orientation sessions or your legal method and writing course, and through experience in each of your "casebook" courses, you will learn the steps of drafting a "case brief" of a judicial opinion as a way of preparing a case for class discussion. Then, as you gain analytic skills, you will learn how to "synthesize" a group of cases that address the same or similar issue by comparing them and seeing a bigger picture from their sum total. Through this process of synthesis, you can derive some general rules from groups of cases, around which you can eventually organize an outline of the law.

3. Applying the Law to New Facts and Gaining Comfort with Legal Uncertainty

Once you have immersed yourself in this thicket of law, your professors will test your understanding and your analytic skills by asking you to apply these legal principles to new sets of facts, not quite like any of those that you studied in the published cases. They will ask you to perform this task both in class and on exams.

You'll soon learn that some questions posed by your professor have certain answers. This will be so if the law is clear and settled and if it applies to the stated facts in a certain, predictable manner. Or it might be so because the application of a legal rule to new facts follows clearly and logically from other rules and applications. You should be able to answer these questions if you have carefully studied assigned judicial opinions and have paid attention in class.

However, the interesting legal questions—ones that parties might plausibly litigate in trial and appellate courts—will have no certain answers. These could be questions about emerging areas of the law that are not yet settled in the courts, where clashing policy considerations support competing conceptions of the law. Or they might be questions in which settled legal rules are applied to facts in the "gray area" between satisfying the elements of the rule and failing to meet its requirements. These are the kinds of questions that might give pause to a judge or jury, leading to much deliberation and ultimately to a choice between two or more equally reasonable conclusions.

When your professors pose questions in these gray areas, your task is not to supply an "answer" so much as to supply a reasoned argument for one side or another, and for both sides if you can. Similarly, your professors might illustrate the limits of a legal rule by repeatedly and incrementally changing the facts until the legal rule in question must lead to a different result; however, the point at which you would reach a different conclusion might be uncertain and debatable. Thus, you might be expected to simply note that the latest set of hypothetical facts would present a stronger or weaker case for satisfaction of the rule, and to explain why.

Accordingly, if your professors pose questions in the gray areas and invite arguments for both sides, but supply no answers to the questions, they are not "hiding the ball" by depriving you of the answers. Your professors are illustrating legal uncertainty and developing your ability to see both sides of reasonably contested legal issues, ones without certain answers. When that is the case, your ability to develop arguments for both sides *is* the solution.

II. Exchanges and Contracts

An enforceable contract requires:

- *Consideration*, in the form of a "*bargained-for exchange*," which in turn contemplates
- *Mutual Assent*, usually through "*offer and acceptance*," on
- *Reasonably Definite Terms*, with
- *No Defenses* to Formation or Enforcement.

Once an enforceable contract is formed, a court often must

- *Interpret* the contract to determine what it requires, and then determine
- whether each party *Performed or Breached*, and
- what *Remedy*, if any, is appropriate.

Each of the italicized terms above encompasses numerous topics and subtopics, which will occupy most of our attention in this course. In addition, we will briefly study some alternative grounds for relief that supplement the paradigm above. As we proceed, we will use this subject matter as a vehicle for developing analytic skills and for gaining familiarity with common law legal method, including case analysis, approaches to statutory interpretation, and policy analysis. Periodically, we will also reflect on ethics and on competing approaches to the law.

To gain an overview to some fundamental concepts and terminology, study the following principles and perform the related exercise.

A. Types of Exchanges

Someone might engage in a current *performance* by delivering goods or services to another, or by refraining from taking some action if the forbearance is valued by another. Alternatively, someone might *promise* you that he or she will engage in a future performance.

Most contracts involve the exchange of *promises*, such as a promise to deliver goods within a week in exchange for a promise to pay for the goods within 30 days after delivery. For future reference, let's call that a *bilateral contract* because both parties owe future performances at the time of contract formation.

Some contracts are formed on the exchange of a *promise for a current performance.* For example, the owner of a home might offer to pay a broker a commission, and the offer might state that the broker can accept this offer only by completing the performance of selling the owner's house. If the broker accepts the offer by finding a buyer for the house, the contract will be formed at the moment of sale to the buyer, and the broker will then have the owner's binding promise to pay the commission. We'll call that a *unilateral contract*, because one party has already fully performed at the moment of contract formation (in this case, the broker), leaving only the other party owing a future performance (in this case, the owner).

In less sophisticated transactions, the parties simply exchange current performances without previous promises to do so, such as by encountering each other at a "flea market" and deciding to trade goods on the spot. Let's call that a *barter transaction* and ponder whether it raises any issues under contract law.

B. Interests Potentially Protected by Contract Law

In defining the interests protected by contract law, we owe a great debt to an influential article by Lon L. Fuller and William R. Perdue, Jr., *The Reliance Interest in Contract Damages:1*, 46 YALE L.J. 52 (1936). To simplify the ideas presented in this article, if someone makes an enforceable promise to you, we can identify three different kinds of interests, sometimes overlapping, that the law might protect:

1. Expectation Interest

You have expectations that the promise will be performed, thus creating a sense of entitlement to the benefits that full performance of the promise will bring. (If you have promised something in return, your full expectations are to perform your own promise and to gain the net benefit of the counter-performance.) Contract law is designed primarily to protect this interest, but the other two interests described below play important roles as well.

2. Reliance Interest

Counting on the performance of the other party's promise, you might change position in reliance on that promise. For example, you might incur expenses preparing to receive the performance, such as by renting warehouse space. Or, if you had exchanged your own promise for the other party's promise, you might incur expenses in beginning your own performance, such as by purchasing materials uniquely suited to this transaction. These out-of-pocket expenses are the simplest kind of reliance.

You might also rely on the other party's promise by passing up a similar opportunity offered by another party, but it could be difficult to prove your losses if the other opportunity or the gains from it are speculative. It's normally much easier to prove your reliance interest by showing receipts for out-of-pocket expenses.

3. Restitution Interest

Counting on the performance of the other party's promise, or acting in other proper circumstances that we will study, you might provide some benefit to the other party, such as by delivering goods or services to the other party while reasonably expecting counter-performance or other compensation. If other party does not compensate you for the benefit, restitution refers to the principle of divesting the other party of the benefit and returning the benefit to you. This principle normally is one of preventing the other party from enjoying the benefit unjustly, so the restitution interest is often measured by the value of the benefit to the other party, the one who received it and must return it, which might be different from the cost you incurred in supplying the benefit.

C. Legal Remedies for Breach of Promise

The school of relational contract theory is associated most closely with the scholarship of Ian MacNeil and Stuart Macaulay. It posits that most contracts take place between parties with established, collaborative relationships, who strive to perform their obligations in good faith and who typically work through disputes in a manner that maintains the relationship for the long term, rather than invoke the legal system in an adversarial manner to vindicate every legal right. *See* Chapin F. Ciminoa, *The Relational Economics of Commercial Contract*, 3 TEX. A&M L. REV. 91, 92, 96–101 (2015); Stewart Macaulay, *Non-Contractual Relations in Business: A Preliminary Study*, 28 AM. SOC. REV. 55, 55 (1963). In addition to acting on a desire to maintain a mutually beneficial relationship with a contracting partner, many people will readily perform their promises simply because they feel morally obligated to do so or because they fear the loss of opportunities to deal with others once their reputation for reliability is tarnished.

In some cases, however, those factors are outweighed by a party's regret over entering into an agreement. If so, the concept of contract has little significance except within a legal system that will recognize and enforce promises in proper circumstances:

> Contracts are incapable of existing in a legal vacuum. They are mere pieces of paper devoid of all legal effect unless they were made by reference to some system of ... law which defines the obligations assumed by the parties to the contract....

Amin Rasheed Shipping Corp. v. Kuwait Ins. Co., [1984] A.C. 50, 65 (HL, Eng.).

We will soon study the requirements for formation of a legally enforceable contract. For the moment, however, let's assume that a court has ruled that an agreement between two parties is an enforceable contract, and let's consider the judicial remedies available for breach of the contract.

1. Specific Enforcement

The clearest way to enforce the other party's promise and to vindicate your expectation interest is to obtain a court order compelling both parties to actually perform as promised. With such enforcement, the court orders the parties to engage in "specific performance." As you will study in greater detail at the end of the semester, this remedy is viewed as extraordinary and discretionary. It is granted infrequently, sometimes due to historical and policy-oriented limitations on this remedy, and sometimes for the practical reason that the time for meaningful performance has passed or because specific performance otherwise is not feasible.

2. Award of Money Damages

An award of "damages" is sometimes known as substitutional relief because it operates as a monetary substitute for actual performance. If the other party has breached some right owed to you, the court might award one or more of three kinds of monetary damages to you:

a. Nominal Damages

This is a symbolic award, for example $1, to show that you proved that the other party breached a right owed to you, even though you could prove no losses or other injury resulting from the breach.

b. Compensatory Damages

These are designed to make you "whole" after an injury, by providing you with an amount of money that compensates for actual losses caused by the other party's breach of your rights. The law measures compensatory damages in different ways for different kinds of claims. The kinds of injuries compensable for a tort, for example, such as for intentional fraud, will differ from the kinds of losses compensable for breach of contract. Even within the field of contract law, compensatory damages might be measured in various ways: usually by expectation interest, designed to place the victim of breach in the same economic position as though the other party had performed as promised. But compensation for breach of promise sometimes is measured by an alternative standard such as reliance interest or by an even more flexible measure designed to prevent injustice. All these measures, however, are designed to make you whole for actual losses caused by the other party's breach of your rights. Restitution might be viewed as yet another measure of compensatory damages, although it does not always coincide with the claimant's losses.

c. Punitive Damages

Punitive damages are "extra-compensatory" because they represent a monetary award in addition to compensation for injury. An award of punitive damages is designed to punish the other party for an especially egregious breach of your rights, and to deter that party and others from behaving in a similar way in the future. U.S. law is well known for allowing juries discretion to award punitive damages for reckless or intentional torts, and some kinds of torts can arise out of contractual relationships. However, except in a very few states, U.S. contract law does not permit an award of punitive damages for a claim that is based solely on breach of contract. We will explore and critique the justifications for this rule in Chapter 12.

Exercise 1 — Elementary Exchanges

1. Barter Transaction

Baker carried a tray of baked goods to Candle-maker's shop and offered to exchange the baked goods for 12 candles standing in a box on Candle-maker's counter. Candle-maker agreed, and they immediately exchanged the items.

Each party may give to the other either a performance or a promise of future performance. When Baker left Candle-maker's shop, what had each party given to the other? What roles, if any, should a body of contract law play in such a transaction?

2. Credit Transactions

On Monday, Baker carried a tray of baked goods to Shoemaker's shop and expressed interest in a pair of sandals.

You can assume the following facts about relative values of products: Standard candles from Candle-maker's shop are so fungible and so widely used and possessed in the village that they are often used as a medium of exchange as well as a consumer good. Assume also that the tray of baked goods normally would exchange for 12 candles and that the sandals, if properly finished, would have exchanged for 15 candles from a willing buyer. Finally, assume that Baker's costs in producing the tray of baked goods, including payment of a salary to himself for his labor, equaled 12 candles.

a. Unilateral Contract

Shoemaker had no sandals available at that time but said she could make a pair in Baker's size by Friday. Baker said, "If you give me the sandals on Friday, I'll give you these baked goods now." Shoemaker replied, "Yes, I'll do that," and took the fresh baked goods. When Baker left Shoemaker's shop, what had each party given to the other? Had the parties formed a contract? What roles, if any, should a body of contract law play in such a transaction? What would be the consequences of not having laws and judicial machinery to perform such roles?

Suppose that Baker returned on Friday and discovered that Shoemaker had eaten the baked goods and had no intention of providing sandals to Baker. What interests might contract law protect, and what kinds of remedies might be available to Baker?

b. Bilateral Contract

Suppose that Shoemaker had no need for baked goods on Monday but needed them on Friday for lunch with friends. On Monday, the parties agreed that Baker would freshly bake and deliver a tray of baked goods on Friday and would exchange them for sandals that Shoemaker would make by Friday at noon. How does this transaction differ from that in ***a.*** above? Should a court enforce this as a valid contract if the shoemaker repudiates it on Tuesday, before either party has changed position in reliance?

III. Summary

- Most contract law resides in state legislation (such as the Uniform Commercial Code) and in common law developed by state courts apart from legislation. Whether developing common law or interpreting statutes, courts create case law when they publish opinions explaining their resolutions of specific disputes brought before them.
- A binding contract can be formed through an agreement in which the parties exchange mutual promises or exchange an immediate performance for a promise. In either case, at least one promise is left to be performed by a party or to be enforced by the courts.
- The legally binding contract can vary from the parties' original agreement if the law adds some mandatory or implied terms to their agreement or if it bars enforcement of other terms of the agreement.
- Courts can enforce promises in a binding contract by ordering the parties to perform, or by providing the monetary equivalent of the performance through an award of compensatory damages. In nearly all states, courts will refuse to award additional punitive damages on a claim based solely on breach of contract.
- Compensatory damages for breach of contract are normally calculated to protect the claimant's expectation interest. With some limitations that we will study later, this means putting the victim of breach in the same economic position as though the contract had been fully performed. In other kinds of claims within the field of contracts, damages will be measured by reliance interest (costs or losses associated with changing position in reliance on the other party's promise) or restitution interest (the value of benefits provided to the other party).

IV. Access to Justice and Alternative Dispute Resolution

Litigation in court with representation by legal counsel is expensive: "If you want to use the civil justice system, you have to have money. If there's less money, you'd have less litigation. But then you'd also have less justice." Binyamin Appelbaum,

"Putting Money on Lawsuits, Investors Share in the Payouts," N.Y. TIMES, Nov. 15, 2010, at A1 (quoting Alan Zimmerman, the founder of a litigation finance company). As one Phoenix attorney observed: "Sometimes clients don't appreciate how expensive it is to prove that they're right."

In some states, including Arizona, a party with a winning claim or defense on a contract claim may benefit from a judicial award of attorney's fees, authorized by the legislature. *See, e.g.*, ARIZ. REV. STAT. ANN. § 12-341.01 (2016). Nonetheless, the risks and immediate costs of litigation typically place a trial and appeal outside the reach of all but very well-funded clients or those with the largest and most promising claims, including class actions in which the claims of many people are combined.

Even though all but a small percentage of legal claims are settled short of full trial, the cost of pretrial legal representation can still be significant. The parties can reduce the cost of litigating a major claim by agreeing to litigate it in a relatively streamlined arbitration proceeding, in which the dispute is heard and adjudicated by one or more arbitrators. Although the parties must pay the arbitrators, the fee of any arbitration association that oversees the arbitration, and other expenses, they might save much more in attorney's fees because arbitration typically will take much less time than litigation in court, resulting in fewer billable hours from the attorneys.

Even the more moderate expense of private arbitration, however, makes it impractical for individual arbitration of a small consumer claim, which might otherwise be joined with other claims in a class action lawsuit or brought without legal counsel in small claims court. Accordingly, compulsory arbitration clauses in standard-form contracts are sometimes viewed as oppressive provisions that invite judicial or legislative intervention, an issue explored in Chapter 9.

Moreover, some clients might prefer the more complete procedural requirements and protections afforded in court or might place more trust in judges and juries than in private arbitrators. Indeed, studies have examined scholarly claims that alternative dispute resolution, such as through mediation or arbitration, might amplify biases in dispute resolution. *See, e.g.*, Gilat J. Bachar & Deborah R. Hensler, *Does Alternative Dispute Resolution Facilitate Prejudice and Bias? We Still Don't Know*, 76 SMU L. REV. 817 (2017).

In sum, for various reasons arbitration cannot provide a complete answer to the problem of the high costs of litigation and legal representation. Consequently, a substantial proportion of our population has inadequate means to gain access to justice. This is a continuing challenge for our profession, one that demands attention, ideas, and efforts from all of us.

Fortunately, most law schools offer a means to chip away at this problem through a variety of opportunities to provide pro bono services under the supervision of volunteer attorneys. Perhaps a new generation of law students and attorneys will find ways to use advancing technology to improve access to justice. *See, e.g.*, Kathleen Elliott Vinson and Samantha A. Moppett, *Digital Pro Bono: Leveraging Technology to Provide Access to Justice*, 92 ST. JOHN'S L. REV. 551 (2018).

Chapter 2

Introduction to Mutual Assent: Basics of Offer and Acceptance

I. Overview

Formation of an enforceable contract requires mutual assent to a transaction with consideration, and with no defenses to formation or enforcement. The topic of mutual assent encompasses a number of issues, such as clear communication of commitment to a proposed deal, acceptance of an offer before the offer has terminated, option contracts, and problems of variation in terms between the offer and acceptance.

The requirements of mutual assent and consideration are interrelated. For example, the Restatement refers to a "bargain," which contemplates an exchange between the parties, and which encompasses both mutual assent and consideration: "[With some exceptions] the formation of a contract requires a bargain in which there is a manifestation of mutual assent to the exchange and a consideration." RESTATEMENT (SECOND) OF CONTRACTS § 17(1) (1981).

This interrelationship between mutual assent and consideration creates a dilemma about which topic to address first. This casebook adopts the following solution: We will first address basic questions about mutual assent related to the objective theory of assent and to the basics of offer and acceptance. That background should be helpful when we next explore the consideration requirement. In turn, our study of consideration should better prepare us to return to mutual assent to explore special problems relating to whether the offer is still open at the time of attempted acceptance.

As we study this material, think about the following questions:

- When a judge or jury seeks to determine a person's intent to enter in a contract, should it endeavor to determine what the person was *actually thinking* at the relevant time, or limit its inquiry to the person's *apparent* intentions as reflected by that person's *outward manifestations*?
- How do we distinguish an offer from preliminary negotiations? Why is a statement more easily interpreted to be an offer if the speaker has included details that limit the speaker's responsibilities under any contract that might be formed?
- Aside from consumer rights under modern statutes, does an advertisement of an item for sale constitute an offer under common law so that a customer can

bind the advertising store by consenting to buy the item at the advertised price? Does it depend on the facts? (If so, does that provide an important insight into the resolution of most legal questions?)

- What kinds of acts or statements qualify as an acceptance? To what extent does it depend on the terms of the offer? In what circumstances must the offeree provide the offeror with notice of the act of acceptance before the contract is formed?
- To what extent can parties to apparently complete negotiations avoid forming a contract through disclaimers or other expressions of intent to avoid forming legal obligations?
- When should a court find lack of contractual intent simply from the context in which an agreement is made? Should contract law impose liability for breaching an agreement to go out on a date or to get married?

II. The Objective Theory of Assent

A. Mutual Assent and Authority

1. The Necessity of Mutual Assent

Let's begin our formal study of contract formation with an introduction to mutual assent: the process of reaching agreement, normally through offer and acceptance. This fundamental requirement of mutual assent is illustrated nicely by two cases, each finding that a party had not agreed to submit future claims to private arbitration and thus had retained her right to bring suit in court.

In the first case, an attorney was permitted to pursue her sex discrimination suit against her law firm in federal court. Although the attorney was a shareholder/director of the incorporated law firm, and although the bylaws of the firm required disputes to be resolved in private arbitration, the attorney had never been presented with a copy of the bylaws and thus had not been aware of the arbitration clause, much less agreed to it. *Kirleis v. Dickie, McCamey & Chilcote, P.C.*, 560 F.3d 156 (3d Cir. 2009).

In the second case, an elderly woman's claims of negligence against her nursing home could proceed in state court, even though her sons had signed identical admission contracts, which provided that future disputes would be submitted to private arbitration. The mother had not agreed to arbitrate her claims, and neither son had the power of attorney to agree to it on her behalf. *Adams Community Care Center, LLC v. Reed*, 37 So. 3d 1155 (Miss. S. Ct. 2010).

2. Actual and Apparent Authority

In *Adams Community Care Center*, the sons lacked authority to bind their mother to the arbitration clause. In many of the cases we study, you might wonder whether an employee is authorized to bind his or her employer to a contract by conveying an offer or acceptance to another on behalf of the employer. In the following two cases, look for either of two kinds of authority by which a party can be bound by its employee or agent: actual or apparent authority. In the first case, is it clear which the court is finding?

European Import Co., Inc. v. Lone Star Co., Inc.

596 S.W.2d 287 (Tex. Civ. App. 1980)

Doyle, Justice.

¶1 ... Lone Star Company, Inc., appellee, brought suit to recover the price of certain liquor and alcoholic beverage merchandise sold to appellant, European Import Company. Appellee also sued appellant, Rose Marie Bagnoli, individually, to recover on her personal guaranty for the company indebtedness.

....

¶2 Evidence showed that Rose Marie Bagnoli was the president and major stockholder of European during 1974. In February or March of 1974, Mrs. Bagnoli was having financial problems with European. She hired one Dr. William L. Blachman in an effort to revive the failing company. Although there was testimony that after several weeks disagreement arose between Mrs. Bagnoli and Dr. Blachman concerning the operation of European's business, it appears that some progress was made toward getting the business "back on its feet." This prosperity was shortlived, however, and amid arguments of who had the authority to place orders for European with appellee and the signing of a guaranty agreement, the company was finally closed by the Internal Revenue Service because of unpaid taxes in November, 1974.

....

¶3 Appellants complain there was no evidence or insufficient evidence to support the jury's finding ... that [European] accepted the merchandise which is the basis of this suit.

¶4 Evidence in the instant case showed that numerous deliveries were made to European, and many invoices for these deliveries bear a stamp from European showing their acceptance. Although Mrs. Bagnoli denies knowing of the goods, Dr. Blachman was associated with the company as an employee and apparently he had authority to negotiate with wholesalers and sign checks. He consulted with Mrs. Bagnoli regarding the business and together they secured bank loans and jointly signed a guaranty agreement. Testimony shows that he increased the gross revenue of the business in the short time he was there and that he brought two other men into the business. There is no evidence that Mrs. Bagnoli limited his authority or terminated his services. She also tendered a check to appellee to pay for the merchandise. We think there was evidence showing a sale, delivery and acceptance. We overrule points of error one, three, four and five.

Robertson v. Alling

237 Ariz. 345, 351 P.3d. 352 (2015)
[paragraphs renumbered from original; footnote omitted]

Justice Timmer, opinion of the Court.

....

I. BACKGROUND

¶ 1 Petitioners ("the Robertson Group") sued neighboring property owners ("the Alling Group") concerning a water line. [After an unsuccessful mediation,] the Alling Group, represented by attorney Mark Sifferman, made a settlement offer requiring acceptance within forty-eight hours. Hours before the offer expired, Robert Grasso, the Robertson Group's attorney, told Sifferman that the Robertson Group needed more time to respond to the offer because one group member had a family emergency. Grasso proposed that the attorneys discuss the offer the next week. Sifferman did not extend the January 31 deadline, and the offer expired.

¶ 2 Sifferman advised his clients of Grasso's request and recommended they "leave the door open" for settlement. Two of the Alling Group members emailed Sifferman on February 4 stating that they and others favored "removing the settlement offer proposed in the mediation." But Sifferman did not read the email and mistakenly thought all his clients were willing to settle on the terms previously conveyed to the Robertson Group.

¶ 3 On February 6, after talking with another attorney at Grasso's law firm, Sifferman sent that attorney an email extending a new settlement offer with terms that mirrored the prior offer but would expire at 5:00 p.m. on February 8. Grasso timely accepted the offer via email. Later, after Grasso's law firm had informed the trial court of the settlement (the "February 8 settlement") and circulated draft settlement documents, Sifferman discovered he had lacked authority to extend the settlement offer. After conferring with his clients, Sifferman made a new settlement offer, which materially varied from the February 8 settlement.

¶ 4 The Robertson Group moved to enforce the February 8 settlement. [The trial court enforced the settlement agreement, but the intermediate court of appeals reversed.]

II. DISCUSSION

....

B. Apparent Authority

¶ 5 The relationship between an attorney and client is governed by agency law principles. *See Panzino*, 196 Ariz. at 447 ¶ 17, 999 P.2d at 203. The Robertson Group concedes, contrary to the trial court's ruling, that Sifferman lacked actual authority to enter into the February 8 settlement. It argues, however, that Sifferman had apparent authority to bind the Alling Group to that agreement.

¶6 An attorney without actual authority to settle a dispute can nevertheless do so if the other party to the agreement "reasonably assumes that the lawyer is authorized to do the act on the basis of the client's (and not the lawyer's) manifestation of such authorization." Restatement (Third) of Law Governing Lawyers § 27; Restatement (Third) of Agency § 3.03 (to same effect). The client "manifests assent or intention through written or spoken words or other conduct." Restatement (Third) of Agency § 1.03. That the client has retained an attorney does not establish apparent authority to settle a dispute. *See United Liquor Co. v. Stephenson*, 84 Ariz. 1, 3, 322 P.2d 886, 887 (1968). The party seeking to enforce the settlement bears the burden of showing that its reliance on the attorney's apparent authority was reasonable. *See Miller v. Mason-McDuffie Co. of S. Cal.*, 153 Ariz. 585, 590, 739 P.2d 806, 811 (1987).

¶7 The undisputed facts establish Sifferman's apparent authority to bind the Alling Group to the February 8 settlement. At the end of the mediation, all members of the Alling Group, after consulting with their attorneys, offered, through the mediator, to settle the lawsuit on specified terms. The attorneys for each side, at the mediator's suggestion, immediately met without their clients to "hash out" the settlement terms. At Grasso's request, Sifferman agreed to leave the offer open for forty-eight hours to enable Grasso to expedite discussions with the Robertson Group's insurers concerning payment of the group's attorney fees. Although the deadline initially requested by Grasso expired, Sifferman confirmed days later that the offer remained available on the same terms, and the Robertson Group accepted it.

¶8 By extending a settlement offer and then leaving Sifferman to finalize the timing and terms, the Alling Group manifested its intention that Sifferman was empowered to conclude the settlement on the terms approved by the Alling Group. The forty-eight-hour deadline was not part of the offer extended by the Alling Group. Rather, Grasso requested the deadline for the benefit of the Robertson Group, Sifferman agreed to it without consulting the Alling Group, and nothing suggested that the deadline was material to the Alling Group. Without a deadline, the offer would have expired after a reasonable time period, unless revoked. 1 Williston on Contracts § 5:2 (4th ed.) (2015). By initially granting Grasso's request for a forty-eight-hour deadline and then effectively extending the offer as "still open" days after the deadline expired, Sifferman acted within his apparent authority to complete the settlement on the terms agreed to by the Alling Group. *Cf.* Restatement (Third) of Law Governing Lawyers § 21(3) (stating that absent client instruction or agreement, "a lawyer may take any lawful measure within the scope of representation that is reasonably calculated to advance a client's objectives as defined by the client").

¶9 In sum, we hold that the Alling Group's actions allowed the Robertson Group to reasonably assume that Sifferman had authority to keep a settlement offer on the table or reoffer the same settlement terms days after the agreement's expiration, and the Robertson Group reasonably relied on the attorney's apparent authority. Therefore, we agree with the trial court that the settlement agreement is binding on the Alling Group.

C. Attorney Fees

¶ 10 The Robertson Group requests attorney fees pursuant to A.R.S. § 12–341.01, which gives courts discretion to award fees "[i]n any contested action arising out of a contract." Because enforcement of the February 8 settlement is such an action, we award the Robertson Group its reasonable attorney fees expended on appeal upon its compliance with ARCAP 21(b).

In *Robertson*, the attorney for the Alling Group clearly lacked *actual* authority from his client to renew the first, expired settlement offer, because some of the Alling Group's members desired to alter the terms of that offer. Nonetheless, the Alling Group was bound by the renewal of the first offer because its members' earlier actions, made known to the Robertson Group, *appeared* to give their attorney authority to reconvey the terms of the first offer. What were those actions?

More generally, in analyzing an issue of contract formation, to what extent should a party be bound by its own apparent intention to enter into a contract, based on a reasonable interpretation of its words and conduct, even if the party's actual, unexpressed intentions at the time—if later proved in some way—were to avoid entering into a contract on those terms? The next section explores this fundamental question.

B. The Standard for Determining Contractual Intent

When both parties have more clearly considered and addressed the terms of a proposed deal, how shall we assess the statements and other forms of communications between the parties? Shall we use a subjective standard, by attempting to divine the actual thoughts and intentions of each party, to determine if they were actually of "the same mind" to form a contract on certain terms? This standard was once prominent in the United States, as reflected by the appearance of the phrase "meeting of the minds" in some of the older cases.

An objective standard will give legal effect to the outward manifestations of the parties, such as their verbal statements and their conduct, without regard to contrary thoughts that they might be actually but secretly holding. In the following case, after the court's review of the facts, try to identify the portions of the opinion in which the court applies a subjective standard and those in which it applies an objective one. On what standard does the court settle?

Note on the Opinion in Lucy v. Zehmer:

Most judicial opinions in your casebooks will be edited by the authors of the casebooks, so that the edited opinions isolate a particular issue discussed by the case. The opinion's discussion of other issues is customarily deleted. Moreover, most published judicial opinions are written by appellate courts, which normally provide a concise summary of the facts, rather than a comprehensive statement of the findings of fact in the trial court or of the underlying evidence.

The next judicial opinion in this book, however, is not edited by the authors of this casebook, except for some trivial deletions of a few words and except for the addition of paragraph numbers to facilitate class discussion. Fortunately, the appellate court included an unusually complete statement of the testimony in the trial court, from the perspective of several parties and witnesses, thus providing you with a full and colorful picture of the events. Try to identify factual matters on which the parties agree and matters on which their testimony reveals factual dispute.

Although the unedited opinion provides you with a vivid image of the dispute, do not be overly distracted by the entertaining facts relating to intoxication and the related legal issue of mental capacity; we will return to that issue later in the semester. Instead, focus now on the facts and discussion relating to any divergence between a party's actual, subjective intent and his objectively expressed intentions. Even with those facts, try not to add excessive detail to your case brief. Instead, summarize the facts by identifying categories or conclusions of facts that seem to be important to the court's analysis and judgment.

Lucy v. Zehmer

196 Va. 493, 84 S.E.2d 516 (1954)
Supreme Court of Appeals of Virginia

Buchanan, J., delivered the opinion of the court.

¶1 This suit was instituted by W. O. Lucy and J. C. Lucy, complainants, against A. H. Zehmer and Ida S. Zehmer, his wife, defendants, to have specific performance of a contract by which it was alleged the Zehmers had sold to W. O. Lucy a tract of land owned by A. H. Zehmer in Dinwiddie county containing 471.6 acres, more or less, known as the Ferguson farm, for $50,000. J. C. Lucy, the other complainant, is a brother of W. O. Lucy, to whom W. O. Lucy transferred a half interest in his alleged purchase.

¶2 The instrument sought to be enforced was written by A. H. Zehmer on December 20, 1952, in these words: "We hereby agree to sell to W. O. Lucy the Ferguson Farm complete for $50,000.00, title satisfactory to buyer," and signed by the defendants, A. H. Zehmer and Ida S. Zehmer.

¶3 The answer of A. H. Zehmer admitted that at the time mentioned W. O. Lucy offered him $50,000 cash for the farm, but that he, Zehmer, considered that the offer was made in jest; that so thinking, and both he and Lucy having had several drinks, he wrote out "the memorandum" quoted above and induced his wife to sign it; that he did not deliver the memorandum to Lucy, but that Lucy picked it up, read it, put it in his pocket, attempted to offer Zehmer $5 to bind the bargain, which Zehmer refused to accept, and realizing for the first time that Lucy was serious, Zehmer assured him that he had no intention of selling the farm and that the whole matter was a joke. Lucy left the premises insisting that he had purchased the farm.

¶4 Depositions were taken and the decree appealed from was entered holding that the complainants had failed to establish their right to specific performance, and dismissing their bill. The assignment of error is to this action of the court.[1]

¶5 W. O. Lucy, a lumberman and farmer, thus testified in substance: He had known Zehmer for fifteen or twenty years and had been familiar with the Ferguson farm for ten years. Seven or eight years ago he had offered Zehmer $20,000 for the farm which Zehmer had accepted, but the agreement was verbal and Zehmer backed out.[2] On the night of December 20, 1952, around eight o'clock, he took an employee to McKenney, where Zehmer lived and operated a restaurant, filling station and motor court. While there he decided to see Zehmer and again try to buy the Ferguson farm. He entered the restaurant and talked to Mrs. Zehmer until Zehmer came in. He asked Zehmer if he had sold the Ferguson farm. Zehmer replied that he had not. Lucy said, "I bet you wouldn't take $50,000.00 for that place." Zehmer replied, "Yes, I would too; you wouldn't give fifty." Lucy said he would and told Zehmer to write up an agreement to that effect. Zehmer took a restaurant check and wrote on the back of it, "I do hereby agree to sell to W. O. Lucy the Ferguson Farm for $50,000 complete." Lucy told him he had better change it to "We" because Mrs. Zehmer would have to sign it too. Zehmer then tore up what he had written, wrote the agreement quoted above and asked Mrs. Zehmer, who was at the other end of the counter ten or twelve feet away, to sign it. Mrs. Zehmer said she would for $50,000 and signed it. Zehmer brought it back and gave it to Lucy, who offered him $5 which Zehmer refused, "You don't need to give me any money, you got the agreement there signed by both of us."

¶6 The discussion leading to the signing of the agreement, said Lucy, lasted thirty or forty minutes, during which Zehmer seemed to doubt that Lucy could raise $50,000. Lucy suggested the provision for having the title examined and Zehmer made the

1. Author's note: In this case, specific enforcement would require the Zehmers to perform as promised by delivering title to the farm, in exchange for Lucy's payment of the purchase price. It is an "equitable" remedy, originally made available by the English Court of Chancery or other courts of equity when the "legal" remedy of money damages under the common law was inadequate to provide full relief. Findings of fact on such equitable claims are typically made by the trial judge without a jury. In *Lucy*, the trial court apparently used a procedure by which the attorneys elicited testimony from the parties and other witnesses in depositions prior to trial, and the trial judge found the facts on the basis of written transcripts of the deposition testimony. Appellate courts usually defer to some extent to the factual findings of the trial judge or jury, who normally had the opportunity to assess the credibility of the witnesses. In Virginia, however, the appellate courts have been comfortable drawing their own factual inferences and conclusions when they have the same documentary evidence as that available to the trial judge. *Brewer v. Brewer*, 199 Va. 753, 102 S.E.2d 303 (1958). The history of law and equity is discussed further in Chapter 4, near the end of Section III.

2. Author's note: As shown in Chapter 7, a typical state "Statute of Frauds" bars enforcement of some kinds of agreements, including contracts for the sale of real estate, unless they are in writing. The statute does not require special formality in the writing, as shown by this court's enforcement of a written agreement scribbled on the back of a restaurant tab.

suggestion that he would sell it "complete, everything there," and stated that all he had on the farm was three heifers.

¶7 Lucy took a partly filled bottle of whiskey into the restaurant with him for the purpose of giving Zehmer a drink if he wanted it. Zehmer did, and he and Lucy had one or two drinks together. Lucy said that while he felt the drinks he took, he was not intoxicated, and from the way Zehmer handled the transaction he did not think he was either.

¶8 December 20 was on Saturday. Next day Lucy telephoned to J. C. Lucy and arranged with the latter to take a half interest in the purchase and pay half of the consideration. On Monday he engaged an attorney to examine the title. The attorney reported favorably on December 31 and on January 2 Lucy wrote Zehmer stating that the title was satisfactory, that he was ready to pay the purchase price in cash and asking when Zehmer would be ready to close the deal. Zehmer replied by letter, mailed on January 13, asserting that he had never agreed or intended to sell.

¶9 Mr. and Mrs. Zehmer were called by the complainants as adverse witnesses. Zehmer testified in substance as follows:

¶10 He bought this farm more than ten years ago for $11,000. He had had twenty-five offers, more or less, to buy it, including several from Lucy, who had never offered any specific sum of money. He had given them all the same answer, that he was not interested in selling it. On this Saturday night before Christmas it looked like everybody and his brother came by there to have a drink. He took a good many drinks during the afternoon and had a pint of his own. When he entered the restaurant around eight-thirty, Lucy was there and he could see that he was "pretty high." He said to Lucy, "Boy, you got some good liquor, drinking, ain't you?" Lucy then offered him a drink. "I was already high as a Georgia pine, and didn't have any more better sense than to pour another great big slug out and gulp it down, and he took one too."

¶11 After they had talked a while Lucy asked whether he still had the Ferguson farm. He replied that he had not sold it and Lucy said, "I bet you wouldn't take $50,000.00 for it." Zehmer asked him if he would give $50,000 and Lucy said yes. Zehmer replied, "You haven't got $50,000 in cash." … They argued "pro and con for a long time," mainly about "whether he had $50,000 in cash that he could put up right then and buy that farm."

¶12 Finally, said Zehmer, Lucy told him if he didn't believe he had $50,000, "you sign that piece of paper here and say you will take $50,000.00 for the farm." He, Zehmer, "just grabbed the back off of a guest check there" and wrote on the back of it. At that point in his testimony Zehmer asked to see what he had written to "see if I recognize my own handwriting." He examined the paper and exclaimed, "Great balls of fire, I got 'Firgerson' for Ferguson. I have got satisfactory spelled wrong. I don't recognize that writing if I would see it, wouldn't know it was mine."

¶13 After Zehmer had, as he described it, "scribbled this thing off," Lucy said, "Get your wife to sign it." Zehmer walked over to where she was and she at first refused to sign but did so after he told her that he "was just needling him [Lucy], and didn't mean a thing in the world, that I was not selling the farm." Zehmer then "took it back over there ... and I was still looking at the dern thing. I had the drink right there by my hand, and I reached over to get a drink, and he said, 'Let me see it.' He reached and picked it up, and when I looked back again he had it in his pocket and he dropped a five dollar bill over there, and he said, 'Here is five dollars payment on it.' ... I said, 'Hell no, that is beer and liquor talking. I am not going to sell you the farm. I have told you that too many times before.'"

¶14 Mrs. Zehmer testified that when Lucy came into the restaurant he looked as if he had had a drink. When Zehmer came in he took a drink out of a bottle that Lucy handed him. She went back to help the waitress who was getting things ready for next day. Lucy and Zehmer were talking but she did not pay too much attention to what they were saying. She heard Lucy ask Zehmer if he had sold the Ferguson farm, and Zehmer replied that he had not and did not want to sell it. Lucy said, "I bet you wouldn't take $50,000 cash for that farm," and Zehmer replied, "You haven't got $50,000 cash." Lucy said, "I can get it." Zehmer said he might form a company and get it, "but you haven't got $50,000.00 cash to pay me tonight." Lucy asked him if he would put it in writing that he would sell him this farm. Zehmer then wrote on the back of a pad, "I agree to sell the Ferguson Place to W. O. Lucy for $50,000.00 cash." Lucy said, "All right, get your wife to sign it." Zehmer came back to where she was standing and said, "You want to put your name to this?" She said "No," but he said in an undertone, "It is nothing but a joke," and she signed it.

¶15 She said that only one paper was written and it said: "I hereby agree to sell," but the "I" had been changed to "We". However, she said she read what she signed and was then asked, "When you read 'We hereby agree to sell to W. O. Lucy,' what did you interpret that to mean, that particular phrase?" She said she thought that was a cash sale that night; but she also said that when she read that part about "title satisfactory to buyer" she understood that if the title was good Lucy would pay $50,000 but if the title was bad he would have a right to reject it, and that that was her understanding at the time she signed her name.

¶16 On examination by her own counsel she said that her husband laid this piece of paper down after it was signed; that Lucy said to let him see it, took it, folded it and put it in his wallet, then said to Zehmer, "Let me give you $5.00," but Zehmer said, "No, this is liquor talking. I don't want to sell the farm, I have told you that I want my son to have it. This is all a joke." Lucy then said at least twice, "Zehmer, you have sold your farm," wheeled around and started for the door. He paused at the door and said, "I will bring you $50,000.00 tomorrow.... No, tomorrow is Sunday. I will bring it to you Monday." She said you could tell definitely that he was drinking and she said to her husband, "You should have taken him home," but he said, "Well, I am just about as bad off as he is."

¶17 The waitress referred to by Mrs. Zehmer testified that when Lucy first came in "he was mouthy." When Zehmer came in they were laughing and joking and she thought they took a drink or two. She was sweeping and cleaning up for next day. She said she heard Lucy tell Zehmer, "I will give you so much for the farm," and Zehmer said, "You haven't got that much." Lucy answered, "Oh, yes, I will give you that much." Then "they jotted down something on paper … and Mr. Lucy reached over and took it, said let me see it." He looked at it, put it in his pocket and in about a minute he left. She was asked whether she saw Lucy offer Zehmer any money and replied, "He had five dollars laying up there, they didn't take it." She said Zehmer told Lucy he didn't want his money "because he didn't have enough money to pay for his property, and wasn't going to sell his farm." Both of them appeared to be drinking right much, she said.

¶ 18 She repeated on cross-examination that she was busy and paying no attention to what was going on. She was some distance away and did not see either of them sign the paper. She was asked whether she saw Zehmer put the agreement down on the table in front of Lucy, and her answer was this: "Time he got through writing whatever it was on the paper, Mr. Lucy reached over and said, 'Let's see it.' He took it and put it in his pocket," before showing it to Mrs. Zehmer. Her version was that Lucy kept raising his offer until it got to $50,000.

¶ 19 The defendants insist that the evidence was ample to support their contention that the writing sought to be enforced was prepared as a bluff or dare to force Lucy to admit that he did not have $50,000; that the whole matter was a joke; that the writing was not delivered to Lucy and no binding contract was ever made between the parties.

¶ 20 It is an unusual, if not bizarre, defense. When made to the writing admittedly prepared by one of the defendants and signed by both, clear evidence is required to sustain it.

¶ 21 In his testimony Zehmer claimed that he "was high as a Georgia pine," and that the transaction "was just a bunch of two doggoned drunks bluffing to see who could talk the biggest and say the most." That claim is inconsistent with his attempt to testify in great detail as to what was said and what was done. It is contradicted by other evidence as to the condition of both parties, and rendered of no weight by the testimony of his wife that when Lucy left the restaurant she suggested that Zehmer drive him home. The record is convincing that Zehmer was not intoxicated to the extent of being unable to comprehend the nature and consequences of the instrument he executed, and hence that instrument is not to be invalidated on that ground. 17 C.J.S., Contracts, § 133 b., p. 483; *Taliaferro v. Emery*, 124 Va. 674, 98 S.E. 627. It was in fact conceded by defendants' counsel in oral argument that under the evidence Zehmer was not too drunk to make a valid contract.

¶ 22 The evidence is convincing also that Zehmer wrote two agreements, the first one beginning "I hereby agree to sell." Zehmer first said he could not remember about that, then that "I don't think I wrote but one out." Mrs. Zehmer said that what he wrote was "I hereby agree," but that the "I" was changed to "We" after that night. The agreement that was written and signed is in the record and indicates no such change. Neither are the mistakes in spelling that Zehmer sought to point out readily apparent.

¶ 23 The appearance of the contract, the fact that it was under discussion for forty minutes or more before it was signed; Lucy's objection to the first draft because it was written in the singular, and he wanted Mrs. Zehmer to sign it also; the rewriting

to meet that objection and the signing by Mrs. Zehmer; the discussion of what was to be included in the sale, the provision for the examination of the title, the completeness of the instrument that was executed, the taking possession of it by Lucy with no request or suggestion by either of the defendants that he give it back, are facts which furnish persuasive evidence that the execution of the contract was a serious business transaction rather than a casual, jesting matter as defendants now contend.

¶24 On Sunday, the day after the instrument was signed on Saturday night, there was a social gathering in a home in the town of McKenney at which there were general comments that the sale had been made. Mrs. Zehmer testified that on that occasion as she passed by a group of people, including Lucy, who were talking about the transaction, $50,000 was mentioned, whereupon she stepped up and said, "Well, with the high-price whiskey you were drinking last night you should have paid more. That was cheap." Lucy testified that at that time Zehmer told him that he did not want to "stick" him or hold him to the agreement because he, Lucy, was too tight and didn't know what he was doing, to which Lucy replied that he was not too tight; that he had been stuck before and was going through with it. Zehmer's version was that he said to Lucy: "I am not trying to claim it wasn't a deal on account of the fact the price was too low. If I had wanted to sell $50,000.00 would be a good price, in fact I think you would get stuck at $50,000.00." A disinterested witness testified that what Zehmer said to Lucy was that "he was going to let him up off the deal, because he thought he was too tight, didn't know what he was doing. Lucy said something to the effect that 'I have been stuck before and I will go through with it.'"

¶25 If it be assumed, contrary to what we think the evidence shows, that Zehmer was jesting about selling his farm to Lucy and that the transaction was intended by him to be a joke, nevertheless the evidence shows that Lucy did not so understand it but considered it to be a serious business transaction and the contract to be binding on the Zehmers as well as on himself. The very next day he arranged with his brother to put up half the money and take a half interest in the land. The day after that he employed an attorney to examine the title. The next night, Tuesday, he was back at Zehmer's place and there Zehmer told him for the first time, Lucy said, that he wasn't going to sell and he told Zehmer, "You know you sold that place fair and square." After receiving the report from his attorney that the title was good he wrote to Zehmer that he was ready to close the deal.

¶26 Not only did Lucy actually believe, but the evidence shows he was warranted in believing, that the contract represented a serious business transaction and a good faith sale and purchase of the farm.

¶27 In the field of contracts, as generally elsewhere, "We must look to the outward expression of a person as manifesting his intention rather than to his secret and unexpressed intention. 'The law imputes to a person an intention corresponding to the reasonable meaning of his words and acts. [13 C.J. 265.]'" *First Nat. Bank v. Roanoke Oil Co.*, 169 Va. 99, 114, 192 S.E. 764, 770.

¶ 28 At no time prior to the execution of the contract had Zehmer indicated to Lucy by word or act that he was not in earnest about selling the farm. They had argued about it and discussed its terms, as Zehmer admitted, for a long time. Lucy testified that if there was any jesting it was about paying $50,000 that night. The contract and the evidence show that he was not expected to pay the money that night. Zehmer said that after the writing was signed he laid it down on the counter in front of Lucy. Lucy said Zehmer handed it to him. In any event there had been what appeared to be a good faith offer and a good faith acceptance, followed by the execution and apparent delivery of a written contract. Both said that Lucy put the writing in his pocket and then offered Zehmer $5 to seal the bargain. Not until then, even under the defendants' evidence, was anything said or done to indicate that the matter was a joke. Both of the Zehmers testified that when Zehmer asked his wife to sign he whispered that it was a joke so Lucy wouldn't hear and that it was not intended that he should hear.

¶ 29 The mental assent of the parties is not requisite for the formation of a contract. If the words or other acts of one of the parties have but one reasonable meaning, his undisclosed intention is immaterial except when an unreasonable meaning which he attaches to his manifestations is known to the other party. Restatement ... of Contracts, Vol. I, § 71, p. 74.

¶ 30 "The law, therefore, judges of an agreement between two persons exclusively from those expressions of their intentions which are communicated between them." Clark on Contracts, 4 ed., § 3, p. 4.

¶ 31 An agreement or mutual assent is of course essential to a valid contract but the law imputes to a person an intention corresponding to the reasonable meaning of his words and acts. If his words and acts, judged by a reasonable standard, manifest an intention to agree, it is immaterial what may be the real but unexpressed state of his mind. 17 C.J.S., Contracts, § 32, p. 361; 12 Am. Jur., Contracts, § 19, p. 515.

¶ 32 So a person cannot set up that he was merely jesting when his conduct and words would warrant a reasonable person in believing that he intended a real agreement, 17 C.J.S., Contracts, § 47, p. 390; Clark on Contracts, 4 ed., § 27, at p. 54.

¶ 33 Whether the writing signed by the defendants and now sought to be enforced by the complainants was the result of a serious offer by Lucy and a serious acceptance by the defendants, or was a serious offer by Lucy and an acceptance in secret jest by the defendants, in either event it constituted a binding contract of sale between the parties.

....

¶ 34 The complainants are entitled to have specific performance of the contracts sued on. The decree appealed from is therefore reversed and the cause is remanded for the entry of a proper decree requiring the defendants to perform the contract in accordance with the prayer of the bill.

Reversed and remanded.

The next case finds no contract because, in addition to the offeror subjectively intending a jest, his jest was obvious to a reasonable person. Synthesize the next case with *Lucy v. Zehmer* by asking how the facts of the two cases differ, thus justifying a different result when applying the same objective standard to facts relating to mutual assent.

Kolodziej v. Mason

774 F.3d 736 (11th Cir. 2014)

Wilson, Circuit Judge:

¶ 1 This case involves a law student's efforts to form a contract by accepting a "million-dollar challenge" that a lawyer extended on national television while representing a client accused of murder....

I.

¶ 2 The current dispute—whether Mason formed a unilateral contract with Kolodziej—arose from comments Mason made while representing criminal defendant Nelson Serrano, who stood accused of murdering his former business partner as well as the son, daughter, and son-in-law of a third business partner. During Serrano's highly publicized capital murder trial, Mason participated in an interview with NBC News in which he focused on the seeming implausibility of the prosecution's theory of the case. Indeed, his client ostensibly had an alibi—on the day of the murders, Serrano claimed to be on a business trip in an entirely different state, several hundred miles away from the scene of the crimes in central Florida. Hotel surveillance video confirmed that Serrano was at a La Quinta Inn (La Quinta) in Atlanta, Georgia, several hours before and after the murders occurred in Bartow, Florida.

¶ 3 However, the prosecution maintained that Serrano committed the murders in an approximately ten-hour span between the times that he was seen on the security camera....

¶ 4 Mason argued that it was impossible for his client to have committed the murders in accordance with this timeline; for instance, for the last leg of the journey, Serrano would have had to get off a flight in Atlanta's busy airport, travel to the La Quinta several miles away, and arrive in that hotel lobby in only twenty-eight minutes. After extensively describing the delays that would take place to render that twenty-eight-minute timeline even more unlikely, Mason stated, "I challenge anybody to show me, and guess what? Did they bring in any evidence to say that somebody made that route, did so? State's burden of proof. If they can do it, I'll challenge 'em. I'll pay them a million dollars if they can do it."

¶ 5 ... [I]n December 2006, NBC featured an edited version of Mason's interview in a national broadcast of its "Dateline" television program. The edited version removed much of the surrounding commentary, including Mason's references to the State's burden of proof, and Mason's statement aired as, "I challenge anybody to show me—I'll pay them a million dollars if they can do it."

¶6 Enter Kolodziej, then a law student at the South Texas College of Law, who had been following the Serrano case. Kolodziej saw the edited version of Mason's interview and understood the statement as a serious challenge, open to anyone, to "make it off the plane and back to the hotel within [twenty-eight] minutes"—that is, in the prosecution's timeline—in return for one million dollars.

¶7 Kolodziej subsequently ordered and studied the transcript of the edited interview, interpreting it as an offer to form a unilateral contract—an offer he decided to accept by performing the challenge. In December 2007, Kolodziej recorded himself retracing Serrano's alleged route, traveling from a flight at the Atlanta airport to what he believed was the former location of the now-defunct La Quinta within twenty-eight minutes. Kolodziej then sent Mason a copy of the recording of his journey and a letter stating that Kolodziej had performed the challenge and requested payment. Mason responded with a letter in which he refused payment and denied that he made a serious offer in the interview.

IV.

¶8 We do not find that Mason's statements were such that a reasonable, objective person would have understood them to be an invitation to contract, regardless of whether we look to the unedited interview or the edited television broadcast seen by Kolodziej. Neither the content of Mason's statements, nor the circumstances in which he made them, nor the conduct of the parties reflects the assent necessary to establish an actionable offer—which is, of course, essential to the creation of a contract.

¶9 ... Even removed from its surrounding context, the edited sentence that Kolodziej claims creates Mason's obligation to pay (that is, "I challenge anybody to show me—I'll pay them a million dollars if they can do it") appears colloquial. The exaggerated amount of "a million dollars"—the common choice of movie villains and schoolyard wagerers alike—indicates that this was hyperbole. As the district court noted, "courts have viewed such indicia of jest or hyperbole as providing a reason for an individual to doubt that an 'offer' was serious." *See Kolodziej v. Mason*, 996 F. Supp. 2d 1237, 1252 (M.D. Fla. 2014) (discussing, in dicta, a laughter-eliciting joke made by Mason's co-counsel during the interview). Thus, the very content of Mason's spoken words "would have given any reasonable person pause, considering all of the attendant circumstances in this case." *See id.*

¶10 Those attendant circumstances are further notable when we place Mason's statements in context. As Judge Learned Hand once noted, "the circumstances in which the words are used is always relevant and usually indispensable." *N.Y. Trust Co. v. Island Oil & Transp. Corp.*, 34 F.2d 655, 656 (2d Cir. 1929); .... Here, Mason made the comments in the course of representing a criminal defendant accused of quadruple homicide and did so during an interview solely related to that representation. Such circumstances would lead a reasonable person to question whether the requisite assent and actionable offer giving rise to contractual liability existed. Certainly, Mason's statements—made as a defense attorney in response to the prosecution's theory against his client—were far more likely to be a descriptive illustration of what that attorney saw as serious holes in the prosecution's theory instead of a serious offer to enter into a contract.

¶ 11 Nor can a valid contract be "inferred in whole or in part from the parties' conduct" in this case. [The court contrasted the extensive negotiations and related actions between the parties in *Lucy v. Zehmer* with the absence of such communications and actions in this case.]

....

¶ 12 ... We could just as easily substitute a comparable idiom such as "I'll eat my hat" or "I'll be a monkey's uncle" into Mason's interview in the place of "I'll pay them a million dollars," and the outcome would be the same. We would not be inclined to make him either consume his headwear or assume a simian relationship were he to be proven wrong; nor will we make him pay one million dollars here.

¶ 13 [The court also found that Mason's challenge was too indefinite to constitute an enforceable offer, and—even assuming the challenge could constitute an offer—the court expressed serious doubts about whether Kolodziej had accepted the offer before it had lapsed through passage of time. The appellate court did not address grounds relied on by the trial court, which were based on the fact that Kolodziej had not performed in response to the original unedited interview, in which Mason directed his challenge solely to the prosecution.]

....

VI.

¶ 14 Just as people are free to contract, they are also free from contract, and we find it neither prudent nor permissible to impose contractual liability for offhand remarks or grandstanding. Nor would it be advisable to scrutinize a defense attorney's hyperbolic commentary for a hidden contractual agenda, particularly when that commentary concerns the substantial protections in place for criminal defendants. Having considered the content of Mason's statements, the context in which they were made, and the conduct of the parties, we do not find it reasonable to conclude that Mason assented to enter into a contract with anyone for one million dollars. We affirm the district court's judgment in favor of Mason and J. Cheney Mason, P.A.

Affirmed.

Exercise 2.1—Applying the Objective Theory

1. The Objective Theory and Manifest Jest

In *Lucy v. Zehmer*, would the result have been different had the evidence shown that Lucy had overheard Zehmer telling his wife that it was just a joke, but that Zehmer otherwise appeared to be serious in his bargaining? Would it have been different if Zehmer had written with a grin that he would sell the farm for $500 when everyone knew that it was worth $50,000?

PepsiCo aired an entertaining television ad, displaying the cool things that consumers could buy with their Pepsi points, which they could collect by buying Pepsi or which they could purchase at $0.10/point. For example, the ad stated that consumers could buy sunglasses for 175 Pepsi points and a leather jacket for 1,450 points. The television ad ended with a depiction of a student landing on the school grounds while piloting a Harrier jet, with text on the screen stating the jet was available for 7,000,000 Pepsi points. A group of investors realized that a Harrier jet was worth $23 million and that they could buy the requisite Pepsi points for $700,000. They sent Pepsi 15 Pepsi points and a check for $700,000, demanding delivery of the Harrier jet. Is PepsiCo bound to do so? What is the issue? Can you articulate arguments for both sides?

2. Objectively Conveying (or Concealing?) Proposed Terms

Imagine that you purchased an electronic device at a retail store. As stated on the outside of the box, the device was accompanied by a booklet, provided by the retailer at the time of sale, that is 143 pages in length and titled "Health and Safety and Warranty Guide." On pp. 97–102, the booklet states that the parties agree to resolve all disputes with the manufacturer in binding arbitration, rather than in the courts, unless the consumer opts out of the arbitration clause within 30 days of purchase. Neither the table of contents nor the index to the booklet has an entry about arbitration or dispute resolution, nor do they indicate that any entry in the book contains terms of the parties' contract. You did not read pp. 97–102 and thus did not opt out of arbitration. Moreover, when you and many other purchasers discover a common defect in the device, you want to combine your claims in a class action in court rather than bear the expense of individual arbitrations. Did you agree to arbitrate your claim about the performance of the electronic device? More specifically, did the manufacturer objectively communicate the arbitration clause to you, as a proposed contract term, so that it became part of the contract? [This problem was inspired by *Noble v. Samsung Electronics, Inc.*, 682 Fed. Appx. 113 (3d Cir. 2017); *see also Norcia v. Samsung Telecommunications America, LLC*, 845 F.3d 1279 (9th Cir. 2018). We will study this issue of adequate notice of proposed terms again in Section VI of this chapter and in Chapters 6 and 9.]

C. The Objective Standard and Unilateral Mistake

1. The Traditional Rule

Although courts will normally employ an objective theory to issues of offer and acceptance, inquiries into a party's actual subjective intent can be relevant to other issues, which we will address in later chapters. What are the benefits and potential problems of using a purely objective standard to assess intent to enter into a contract? For example, what are the pitfalls of adhering to a subjective standard, and how does an objective standard remedy them? Conversely, how would an objective standard apply to a retailer who orders goods from a distributor and accidentally types the quantity "200" in the purchase order when she meant to order 100 or 20?

If you are the only one entertaining a mistake during bargaining, you generally will *not* be relieved of the consequences of that *unilateral* mistake. Under the traditional rule, a court will make an exception and relieve you of your contractual obligations only if the other party caused the mistake or had notice of your mistake during bargaining; even then, you will be denied relief if your mistake relates to some matter for which you assumed the risk, such as poor exercise of your professional judgment rather than a purely clerical error.

Exercise 2.2 — Relief under the Traditional Rule?

In the following problems, you may assume that the non-mistaken party did not cause or contribute to the other party's mistake. Analyze the problems under the branch of the traditional rule that a party is relieved from his or her unilateral mistake if the mistake is apparent to the other party at the time of contract formation.

1. An Extra Zero

For five years, an independent retailer of high fashion has normally ordered 20 pairs of a certain style of designer shoes each month from her regular supplier, with up to 40 pairs ordered in October for holiday sales in November and December. In July, the retailer e-mailed an order for 200 pairs, which the retailer intended to sell to customers at $200/pair. She had intended to order 20 pairs but had absent-mindedly typed an extra zero while thinking about the retail price of the shoes. If the supplier accepts this order, is the retailer bound to purchase 200 pairs?

How would the analysis change if the retailer had intended to order the 200 pairs because she had predicted that a back-to-school fashion trend would increase demand for the shoes tenfold to 200 pairs in August, a prediction that she explained in her order to the supplier? If the supplier sent notice of acceptance for 200 pairs but the retailer learns later that her assumption about increased demand is badly mistaken, does the retailer have grounds for relief from her unilateral mistake?

2. The Contractor's Error

An owner sought bids from several reputable contractors for a major remodeling and repair of a grand old house. Five contractors submitted bids within the range of $105,000 to $111,000. The remaining contractor, Hanson Construction ("HC"), submitted a bid of $96,000, which the owner accepted. HC has since discovered that, for some parts of its master bid on this project, an assistant in the office had mistakenly written in and added up subcontractors' sub-bids from a different and less expensive job, resulting in an error of $11,000. Thus, HC had intended to bid $107,000, and not $96,000. Is HC bound to the bid it communicated? On what does it depend? Try to argue both sides.

---

2. The Modern Trend

Donovan v. RRL Corp.

26 Cal. 4th 261, 27 P.3d 702 (2001)

George, C. J.

¶ 1 Defendant RRL Corporation is an automobile dealer doing business under the name Lexus of Westminster. Because of typographical and proofreading errors made by a local newspaper, defendant's advertisement listed a price for a used automobile that was significantly less than the intended sales price. Plaintiff Brian J. Donovan read the advertisement and, after examining the vehicle, attempted to purchase it by tendering the advertised price. Defendant refused to sell the automobile to plaintiff at that price, and plaintiff brought this action against defendant for breach of contract. The municipal court entered judgment for defendant on the ground that the mistake in the advertisement precluded the existence of a contract. The appellate department of the superior court and the Court of Appeal reversed, relying in part upon Vehicle Code section 11713.1, subdivision (e), which makes it unlawful for an automobile dealer not to sell a motor vehicle at the advertised price while the vehicle remains unsold and before the advertisement expires.

① If supplier accepts order of 200 pairs, retailer is liable for her mistake, since the other party did not contribute to her mistake.
→ Analysis would not change if she sent notice because that was a risk the retailer took on her own judgement.
→ on the other hand, depending on other facts of the case, she may have grounds for an exception bc she sent notice.

② HC is bound to the bid because the mistake was not influenced by the other party.
HC is not bound to the bid because the error was purely clerical & not a risk/poor judgement call on their part.
→ outward manifestation of contract was $96,000, intent irrelevant

① Also on the other hand can consider the supplier could have realized the apparent mistake bc usually orders 20 & 200 is a far jump

② Also depends on location & how long after they caught the error
→ 5 days open bid in CA

ıke did not render a
stake.... [However,]
96, 701, 235 P.2d 7
n of the foregoing
plaintiff in *Kemper*
endant city's public
ce. After discovering
otified the city and
the erroneous bid,
plaintiff's unilateral

or mistake of fact if
of neglect of a legal
cionable, and if the
. 701, 235 P.2d 7.)
ed the bid, and this
plaintiff to perform
2–703, 235 P.2d 7),
gh the city had not
.

) 54 Cal. 2d 380, 6
on of an erroneous
he agency inquired,
d accepted the bid
arty clearly had no
bid.

¶ 5 Consistent with the decisions in *Kemper* and *Elsinore*, the Restatement Second of Contracts authorizes rescission for a unilateral mistake of fact where "the effect of

Exercise 2.3

a) party seeking to be excused was mistaken at time of contract
→ sales clerk mistakenly relayed price of $235,000

b) non-mistaken party had reason to know other party was mistaken
→ partner & sister advised not to buy since they assumed from the price it is not a real diamond
• is this pointing out a mistake?

c) mistaken party did not bear the risk of mistake
→ sales clerk did bear risk

BUT
- clerical error of omitting "per carat"

Debate about unconscionable loss - need to look at the facts to see if loss is huge or not

AND
- outward manifestation of contract to buyer - could not tell intent
- unreasonable to enforce contract bc price difference is unreasonable

V

The judgment of the Court of Appeal is reversed.

The court's fact application in *Donovan*, omitted from the excerpts above, delves deeply into concepts of materiality, basic assumptions, allocation of risk, and unconscionable unfairness, concepts that are best left to later chapters. It suffices here to note that the objective theory of contracts potentially recognizes a contract based on a party's outward manifestations, even if the conveyed intent reflects some clerical or computational error. The traditional rule grants relief from such a unilateral mistake only if the other party caused the mistake, or if the mistake was apparent to the other party at the time of contract formation, thus undermining a finding of mutual contractual intent even under an objective theory.

The modern trend, however, as reflected in the second Restatement and in the case law of California and several other states, provides an additional and potentially broader basis for relief, as outlined in *Donovan*. Moreover, by statute, California has further liberalized grounds for relief for a contractor who submits a bid to a public entity and then reports a mistake within five days after the opening of bids. CAL. PUB. CONTR. CODE § 5103 (2017). Although the contractor cannot withdraw from its contractual obligation absent the consent of the public entity, the contractor can bring an action for "recovery of the amount forfeited, without interest or costs," *id.* § 5101, and need not show that the loss from the mistake is unconscionable, so long as the mistake was material and was "not due to error in judgment or to carelessness in inspecting the site of the work, or in reading the plans or specifications," *id.* § 5103.

Despite these departures from the traditional rule, rescission of a contract for one party's unilateral mistake is far from automatic. If the law routinely precluded contract formation on the basis of mistakes in communication, it would be applying a more subjective standard of intent—based on what a party had actually intended absent the error—rather than adopting an objective approach that frequently binds a party to what he or she mistakenly communicated.

In Chapter 8, we will study the common law requirements for relief for *mutual* mistake of existing fact, shared by both parties at the time of contracting.

Exercise 2.3 — Truly A Gem of a Case

This exercise is based on *DePrince v. Starboard Cruise Services, Inc.*, 163 So. 3d 586 (Fla. App. 2015), described by the court as "truly a gem of a case." *Id.* at 589. The court found several competing tests for unilateral mistake in Florida case law. Although the court was bound by precedent to apply a more demanding test, it appeared to find merit in Florida's Standard Jury Instructions. The relevant jury instruction states the traditional rule supplemented by the modern trend, and thus is "nearly identical" to the second Restatement test. *Id.* at 594. The jury instruction recognizes a defense for unilateral mistake if the mistaken party establishes that: (1) the party seeking to be excused from contract obligations was mistaken at the time of contracting; (2) the non-mistaken party caused the mistake or had reason to know that the other party was mistaken, or the mistake would make it unconscionable to enforce the contract; and (3) the mistaken party did not bear the risk of mistake. *Id.* (citing Fla. Std. Jury Instr. (Civ.) 416.26 (2013)).

To gain familiarity with a modern approach, apply the test in the Florida jury instruction to the facts below, which are simplified from the facts in *DePrince*, and to inferences you fairly draw from the facts. Discuss whether Retailer should be excused from its obligations to Buyer because of its unilateral mistake, and try to develop arguments for both sides. Although we will not study allocation of risk until Chapter 8's discussion of mutual mistake, you can develop common sense arguments about whether Retailer should bear the risk of its mistake, based on whether it was well situated to avoid the mistake.

Facts: Buyer requested a diamond of approximately 20 carats from Retailer, whose sales clerk did not have experience with diamonds of that magnitude. The sales clerk consulted the store's computerized inventory records, which identified a diamond of 20.64 carats in stock at a secure location and which stated a price of $235,000. The sales clerk relayed this information to Buyer, who stated that he would think about it overnight. That evening, Buyer's partner and Buyer's sister, both experts in gemology, advised Buyer not to enter into the contract, because a genuine diamond of that size would be worth at least $2,000,000, so the offered gem must not be a genuine diamond. Ignoring their advice, Buyer returned to Retailer the next morning and entered into a contract to purchase the described diamond for a total price of $235,000. Soon afterward, and prior to delivery of the diamond, a sales manager discovered that the inventory records should have stated a price of $235,000 *per carat*, for a total price of $4,850,400, but the total price and the phrase "per carat" had been omitted through another employee's clerical error. Retailer sought to rescind the contract with Buyer, offering to return Buyer's deposit. Buyer sued for specific enforcement of the contract, and Retailer requested to be excused from its obligation based on its unilateral mistake. You may assume that Retailer's employees have full authority to act on its behalf and that Retailer is responsible for any employee's unilateral mistake, except to the extent that the Florida jury instructions would excuse Retailer from its obligations under the contract because of the mistake.

III. The Offer

A. Expression of Commitment, Creating Power in the Offeree

Mutual assent requires an offer and then acceptance of the offer while the offer is still open. We turn first to the requirements for an offer.

The Restatement defines "offer" as "the manifestation of willingness to enter into a bargain, so made as to justify another person in understanding that his assent to that bargain is invited and will conclude it." RESTATEMENT (SECOND) OF CONTRACTS § 24 (1981). Be prepared to explain the ways in which this definition embraces an objective theory of contracts.

Note a critical point in this definition: An offer gives to the party to whom it is addressed, the "offeree," the power to create the contract ("conclude" the bargain) by assenting to the offer. If the communication from the first party amounts to anything less, then it is not an offer but only a step in preliminary negotiations. For example, if the communication requires further expression of commitment by the purported offeror before a contract can be concluded, then it is not an offer. A good deal of analysis of "offers" lies in distinguishing them from preliminary negotiations.

As with many legal questions, examining all the circumstances provides a better analysis than categorical answers based on labels:

> The general rule is that a price quotation is not an offer, but rather is an invitation to enter into negotiations or a mere suggestion to induce offers by others.... *USEMCO, Inc. v. Marbro Co.*, 60 Md. App. 351, 483 A.2d 88, 93 (1984). However, price quotes, if detailed enough, can amount to an offer creating the power of acceptance; to do so, it must reasonably appear from

the price quote that assent to the quote is all that is needed to ripen the offer into a contract. *Quaker State Mushroom Co. v. Dominick's Finer Foods, Inc.*, 635 F. Supp. 1281, 1284 (N.D. Ill. 1986); ....

Brown Machine, Div. of John Brown, Inc. v. Hercules, Inc., 770 S.W.2d 416, 419 (Mo. Ct. App. 1989).

Exercise 2.4 — Offer or Preliminary Negotiations?

Explain or discuss whether each of the following statements meets the definition of "offer," so that a contract would be formed if the other party said the equivalent of "Yes, I agree." Remember the objective test: To constitute an offer, an expression from the offeror must lead a reasonable person in the position of the offeree to understand that he or she has received the power to create a contract by expressing agreement. The expression meets that standard if the reasonable person would conclude that nothing important is left to negotiate, that the speaker is not just inviting further negotiations, and that the power to create a contract has not otherwise been deferred.

(1) A homeowner, who had just received an estimate from a contractor to paint the home for $3,000, with all other essential terms included, states: "That's way too much. I wouldn't consider paying any more than $2,500 for the whole paint job." Is the homeowner's statement an offer to pay $2,500 for the paint job? (The Contractor probably made an offer, but the homeowner rejected it, so we are now asking whether the homeowner made a counter-offer.)

(2) An unoccupied sidewalk artist, with examples of a single style and size of sketch portraits on display, states to a passerby: "I will complete your portrait, like these, within 10 minutes for $15. How about it?" Offer?

(3) A college student distributes a flyer to neighbors, stating: "I offer to tutor high school students in math." Offer? Is this conclusively an offer because it uses the term "offer"? What would be the possible consequences if this were viewed as an offer?

(4) A homeowner provided each of three contractors with architect's specifications for remodeling her home, requesting each contractor's price to perform the remodeling; the specifications include all essential terms of performance, including timing. Contractor #1 submits a bid stating that he will perform the specified work for $62,000, and he leaves his phone number so that the homeowner can call with her decision. Offer? By whom?

(5) Same as (4) above, except that Contractor #1's bid states "this bid will become a contract after Homeowner signs it on the Acceptance line and when [Contractor #1] thereafter gives notice that he has the time and resources to perform the work." Is the Contractor's bid an offer? Who would be making the first offer?

(6) A distributor of swimming pool vacuums sent a flier to 50 retailers of swimming pool equipment in the region, with a photo of the product and the following statement: "Through a special purchase from the manufacturer, we have Model T-431 Hancock 'Pool-Vac' units available for sale at the highly discounted price of $100/unit." Offer?

(7) Same as (6) above, except that the flier states "offered for sale to you," rather than "available for sale to you." Automatically an offer? Would it more likely be an offer if the

distributor added the following sentence? "We have more of these in stock than we could possibly sell to our best customers this season — we will fill any orders from addressees of this flier if received at our Phoenix office by this Friday at noon."

(8) Same as (6) above, except that the flyer included an additional sentence: "100 units in stock; we will honor orders subject to stock on hand." Offer?

B. Reading Party Communications in Context

In the following case, notice how the court interprets the seller's first response in light of the Buyer's opening inquiry. What term is thus implied in the seller's response, usually missing in a standard price quote? Why is this term critically important, even though the court does not emphasize it in the opinion?

As you read the opinion, do you find yourself regretting that the court refers to the parties by procedural names? You can make sense of the facts by making a chart that associates "appellee" and "appellant" with the name of a party and with its status as buyer or seller.

Fairmount Glass Works v. Crunden-Martin Woodenware Co.

106 Ky. 659, 51 S.W. 196 (Ct. App. 1899)

Hobson, J.

¶ 1 On April 20, 1895, appellee wrote appellant the following letter:

> St. Louis, Mo., April 20, 1895. Gentlemen: Please advise us the lowest price you can make us on our order for ten car loads of Mason green jars, complete, with caps, packed one dozen in a case, either delivered here, or f. o. b. cars your place, as you prefer. State terms and cash discount. Very truly, Crunden-Martin W. W. Co.

¶ 2 To this letter appellant answered as follows:

> Fairmount, Ind., April 23, 1895. Crunden-Martin Wooden Ware Co., St. Louis, Mo. — Gentlemen: Replying to your favor of April 20, we quote you Mason fruit jars, complete, in one-dozen boxes, delivered in East St. Louis, Ill.: Pints $4.50, quarts $5.00, half gallons $6.50, per gross, for immediate acceptance, and shipment not later than May 15, 1895; sixty days' acceptance, or 2 off, cash in ten days. Yours, truly, Fairmount Glass Works. Please note that we make all quotations and contracts subject to the contingencies of agencies or transportation, delays or accidents beyond our control.

¶ 3 For reply thereto, appellee sent the following telegram on April 24, 1895:

> Fairmount Glass Works, Fairmount, Ind.: Your letter twenty-third received. Enter order ten car loads as per your quotation. Specifications mailed. Crunden-Martin W. W. Co.

¶ 4 In response to this telegram, appellant sent the following:

Fairmount, Ind., April 24, 1895. Crunden-Martin W. W. Co., St. Louis, Mo.: Impossible to book your order. Output all sold. See letter. Fairmount Glass Works.

¶5 Appellee insists that, by its telegram sent in answer to the letter of April 23d, the contract was closed for the purchase of 10 car loads of Mason fruit jars. Appellant insists that the contract was not closed by this telegram, and that it had the right to decline to fill the order at the time it sent its telegram of April 24. This is the chief question in the case. The court below gave judgment in favor of appellee, and appellant has appealed, earnestly insisting that the judgment is erroneous.

¶6 We are referred to a number of authorities holding that a quotation of prices is not an offer to sell, in the sense that a completed contract will arise out of the giving of an order for merchandise in accordance with the proposed terms. There are a number of cases holding that the transaction is not completed until the order so made is accepted.... But each case must turn largely upon the language there used. In this case we think there was more than a quotation of prices, although appellant's letter uses the word "quote" in stating the prices given. The true meaning of the correspondence must be determined by reading it as a whole. Appellee's letter of April 20th, which began the transaction, did not ask for a quotation of prices. It reads: "Please advise us the lowest price you can make us on our order for ten car loads of Mason green jars ... State terms and cash discount." From this appellant could not fail to understand that appellee wanted to know at what price it would sell it ten car loads of these jars; so when, in answer, it wrote: "We quote you Mason fruit jars ... pints $4.50, quarts $5.00, half gallons $6.50, per gross, for immediate acceptance; ... 2 off, cash in ten days," it must be deemed as intending to give appellee the information it had asked for. We can hardly understand what was meant by the words "for immediate acceptance," unless the latter was intended as a proposition to sell at these prices if accepted immediately.

¶7 In construing every contract, the aim of the court is to arrive at the intention of the parties. In none of the cases to which we have been referred on behalf of appellant was there on the face of the correspondence any such expression of intention to make an offer to sell on the terms indicated. In *Fitzhugh v. Jones*, 6 Munf. 83, the use of the expression that the buyer should reply as soon as possible, in case he was disposed to accede to the terms offered, was held sufficient to show that there was a definite proposition, which was closed by the buyer's acceptance. The expression in appellant's letter, "for immediate acceptance," taken in connection with appellee's letter, in effect, at what price it would sell it the goods, is, it seems to us, much stronger evidence of a present offer, which, when accepted immediately, closed the contract. Appellee's letter was plainly an inquiry for the price and terms on which appellant would sell it the goods, and appellant's answer to it was not a quotation of prices, but a definite offer to sell on the terms indicated, and could not be withdrawn after the terms had been accepted.

....

Judgment affirmed.

C. An Exercise in Case Synthesis: Are Newspaper Ads Offers?

Suppose a store takes out an ad in a local newspaper, stating that a particular type of product is on sale at a specified attractive price, and a customer enters the store, shows the ad, and says, "I'll buy one." Did the store make an offer with its ad? If so, the customer created a contract by accepting the offer, and the store would be bound to supply the good at the advertised price or be liable for breach of contract.

If the ad was not an offer, however, then the customer would be making the first offer by requesting to purchase the advertised good, and the store would be free to accept or reject the customer's offer. If not bound by its ad, the sales staff could lure customers into the store with an attractive advertised price (the "bait"), brush off attempts by customers to buy the advertised product, and try to persuade the customer to buy a more expensive item (the "switch"). Abusive practices such as this have inspired state consumer-protection legislation, such as those prohibiting misleading advertising or other deceptive practices, or those requiring stores in some circumstances to give "rain checks" when they deplete their stock of advertised goods. *See, e.g.*, David Adam Friedman, *Explaining "Bait-and-Switch" Regulation*, 4 Wm. & Mary Bus. L. Rev. 575 (2013); *Shaw v. CTVT Motors, Inc.*, 232 Ariz. 30, 300 P.3d 907 (Ct. App. 2013) (interpreting Arizona's Consumer Fraud Act).

For now, however, let's focus only on the common law definition of "offer" and determine why the common law did not supply a reliable response to these abusive practices. Analyze each of the two cases below and then compare, or "synthesize," them. They reach different results on the general question of whether a newspaper ad amounted to an offer under the common law. Does that mean that they are legally inconsistent, perhaps because courts in different states developed different tests for an offer? Or do differences in facts of the two cases justify the different results, so that the two courts might have applied the same legal standards? If the latter, can you state a rule about ads as offers that is sufficiently broad to explain the results in both cases? Based on your analysis of the typical price quote, can you explain why the typical newspaper ad should not be reasonably interpreted as an offer to sell under common law? What more is needed to tip the scales in favor of the ad constituting an offer?

Craft v. Elder & Johnston Co.

38 N.E.2d 416 (Ohio Ct. App. 1941)

Barnes, Judge....

¶1 ... On or about January 31, 1940, the defendant, the Elder & Johnston Company, carried an advertisement in the Dayton Shopping News, an offer for sale of a certain all electric sewing machine for the sum of $26 as a "Thursday Only Special." Plaintiff ... alleges that the above publication is an advertising paper distributed in Montgomery County and throughout the city of Dayton; that on Thursday, February 1, 1940, she tendered to the defendant company $26 in payment for one of the machines offered in the advertisement, but that defendant refused to fulfill the offer and has continued to so refuse. The petition further alleges that the value of the machine offered was $175 and she asks damages in the sum of $149 plus interest from February 1, 1940....

¶2 The trial court dismissed plaintiff's petition as evidenced by a journal entry, the pertinent portion of which reads as follows: "Upon consideration the court finds that said advertisement was not an offer which could be accepted by plaintiff to form a contract, and this case is therefore dismissed with prejudice to a new action, at costs of plaintiff." ...

¶3 We will now briefly make reference to some of the authorities. "It is clear that in the absence of special circumstances an ordinary newspaper advertisement is not an offer, but is an offer to negotiate—an offer to receive offers—or, as it is sometimes called, an offer to chaffer." Restatement of the Law of Contracts, Par. 25, Page 31. [Author's note: this refers to the Restatement (First) of Contracts, completed in 1932.]

¶4 Under the above paragraph the following illustration is given, "[A] clothing merchant, advertises overcoats of a certain kind for sale at $50. This is not an offer but an invitation to the public to come and purchase."

¶5 "Thus, if goods are advertised for sale at a certain price, it is not an offer and no contract is formed by the statement of an intending purchaser that he will take a specified quantity of the goods at that price. The construction is rather favored that such an advertisement is a mere invitation to enter into a bargain rather than an offer. So a published price list is not an offer to sell the goods listed at the published price." Williston on Contracts, Revised Edition, Vol. 1, Par. 27, Page 54.

¶6 "The commonest example of offers meant to open negotiations and to call forth offers in the technical sense are advertisements, circulars and trade letters sent out by business houses. While it is possible that the offers made by such means may be in such form as to become contracts, they are often merely expressions of a willingness to negotiate." Page on the Law Contracts, 2d Ed., Vol. 1, Page 112, Par. 84....

¶7 "... [G]enerally a newspaper advertisement or circular couched in general language and proper to be sent to all persons interested in a particular trade or business, or a prospectus of a general and descriptive nature, will be construed as an invitation to make an offer." 17 Corpus Juris Secundum, Contracts, Page 389, §46, Column 2....

¶8 We are constrained to the view that the trial court committed no prejudicial error in dismissing plaintiff's petition.

¶9 The judgment of the trial court will be affirmed and costs adjudged against the plaintiff-appellant. Entry may be prepared in accordance with this opinion.

Geiger, P. J., and Hornbeck, J., concur.

Lefkowitz v. Great Minneapolis Surplus Store

251 Minn. 188, 86 N.W.2d 689 (1957), Minn. S. Ct.

Murphy, Justice.

¶1 This is an appeal from an order of the Municipal Court of Minneapolis.... The order for judgment awarded the plaintiff the sum of $138.50 as damages for breach of contract.

¶2 This case grows out of the alleged refusal of the defendant to sell to the plaintiff a certain fur piece which it had offered for sale in a newspaper advertisement. It appears from the record that ... the defendant published the following advertisement in a Minneapolis newspaper:

> Saturday 9 A.M.... 1 Black Lapin Stole Beautiful, worth $139.50.... $1.00
> First Come First Served

¶3 The record supports the findings of the court that on ... the Saturday[] following the publication of the above-described ad[] the plaintiff was the first to present himself at the appropriate counter in the defendant's store and ... demanded the ... stole so advertised and indicated his readiness to pay the sale price of $1.... [T]he defendant refused to sell the merchandise to the plaintiff....

¶4 The defendant relies principally on *Craft v. Elder & Johnston Co.*... On the facts before us we are concerned with whether the advertisement constituted an offer, and, if so, whether the plaintiff's conduct constituted an acceptance.

¶5 There are numerous authorities which hold that a particular advertisement in a newspaper or circular letter relating to a sale of articles may be construed by the court as constituting an offer, acceptance of which would complete a contract. [citations omitted]....

¶6 The authorities above cited emphasize that, where the offer is clear, definite, and explicit, and leaves nothing open for negotiation, it constitutes an offer, acceptance of which will complete the contract. The most recent case on the subject is *Johnson v. Capital City Ford Co.*, La. App., 85 So. 2d 75, in which the court pointed out that a newspaper advertisement relating to the purchase and sale of automobiles may constitute an offer, acceptance of which will consummate a contract and create an obligation in the offeror to perform according to the terms of the published offer.

¶7 Whether in any individual instance a newspaper advertisement is an offer rather than an invitation to make an offer depends on the legal intention of the parties and the surrounding circumstances. Annotation, 157 A.L.R. 744, 751; 77 C.J.S., Sales, §25b; 17 C.J.S., Contracts, §389. We are of the view on the facts before us that the offer by the defendant of the sale of the Lapin fur was clear, definite, and explicit, and left nothing open for negotiation. The plaintiff having successfully managed to be the first one to appear at the seller's place of business to be served, as requested by the advertisement, and having offered the stated purchase price of the article, he was entitled to performance on the part of the defendant....

Affirmed.

Although statutes and administrative rules now regulate advertising in various ways, the common law applies to the issue of whether a store has made an offer through an advertisement, unless a statute has supplanted the common law in that context. Recall, for example, the PepsiCo television advertisement summarized earlier in this chapter in Exercise 2.1. In addition to determining that the ad was an obvious jest and thus did not reflect or convey serious contractual intent, the court concluded that the ad did not include sufficient detail to constitute an offer under common law. *Leonard v. Pepsico, Inc.*, 88 F. Supp. 2d 116 (1999). The court distinguished *Lefkowitz*, because the Pepsico advertisement: (1) was not "sufficiently definite, because it specifically reserved the details of the offer to a separate writing, the Catalog," and (2) did not contain "any words of limitation, such as 'first come, first served,' " words that would protect the seller from obligations exceeding its ability to perform and thus would reflect the seller's readiness to commit to the advertised deal. *Id.* at 124.

Indeed, the common law and regulatory law might combine in a court's analysis of whether an advertisement constitutes an offer. In *Donovan*, which we encountered earlier in our study of unilateral mistake, the court applied common law principles to find that a car dealer's advertisement to sell a specifically identified car for a certain price constituted an offer, even though further details would not be clarified until the parties signed papers. *Donovan v. RRL Corp.*, 26 Cal. 4th 261, 276, 27 P.3d 702, 712–13 (2001). The court's conclusion was buttressed by a section of the state Vehicle Code that made it a violation for a licensed dealer to fail to sell a vehicle "to a person at the advertised total price ... while the vehicle remains unsold," unless a specified time for the advertised price has elapsed. CAL. VEH. CODE § 11713.1(e) (West Supp. 2018). According to the court, "even though section 11713.1(e) does not alter the applicable common law regarding contractual offers, consumer expectations arising from the statute are relevant in determining whether defendant's advertisement constituted an offer pursuant to governing principles of contract law." *Donovan*, 26 Cal. 4th at 275, 27 P.3d at 712. In sum, the court applied the common law but assessed the reasonable meaning of the advertisement in light of the statute. *Id.* at 273, 27 P.3d at 710–11.

In *Donovan*, the advertisement described a single used vehicle, stated its final price, and identified it by vehicle number. Consequently, the most important further limiting factor in the advertisement would be identification of the one offeree who could bind the seller, to eliminate the possibility that two offerees could bind the seller to supply the same car by both stating their intent to accept. Did the terms of the California Vehicle Code essentially incorporate the equivalent of "first come, first served," by requiring sale at the advertised price to "a person ... while the vehicle remains unsold"? Absent such language, why are common law courts reluctant to imply a term such as "while supplies last" or "first-come, first-served"? Wouldn't the resulting offer empower consumers while limiting the seller's obligation to stock on hand?

IV. The Acceptance

The offer gives to the offeree a power to create a contract by expressing assent, and the acceptance exercises that power. According to the Restatement, "Acceptance of an offer is a manifestation of assent to the terms thereof made by the offeree in a manner invited or required by the offeror." Restatement (Second) of Contracts § 50(1) (1981).

Under both common law and the UCC, acceptance can be manifested in any reasonable manner unless the offer restricts the manner of acceptance. The Restatement, for example, advances the following generalization from case law: "Unless otherwise indicated by the language or the circumstances, an offer invites acceptance in any manner and by any medium reasonable in the circumstances." Restatement (Second) of Contracts § 30(2) (1981). For sales contracts, the UCC provides that "[u]nless otherwise unambiguously indicated by the language or circumstances, (a) an offer to make a contract shall be construed as inviting acceptance in any manner and by any medium reasonable in the circumstances; ..." U.C.C. § 2-206(1) (2011).

On the other hand, the offeror is often known as the "master of the offer." With some exceptions, the offeror can specify who may accept as well as the authorized means of acceptance. For example, the offeror can dictate the means of acceptance by:

1) making it clear that the acceptance must be by return promise (thus limiting formation to a bilateral contract), or must be by full performance (thus limiting formation to a unilateral contract), and
2) requiring notice of acceptance in a certain manner, or by dispensing with notice that might otherwise be required.

The offeror's mastery over the terms of acceptance is not unlimited. In some contexts, for example, state and federal statutes prohibit an offeror from restricting the class of offerees by race or other invidiously discriminatory classifications. Also, an offeror normally cannot specify that your silence will constitute acceptance of the offer; otherwise, you would be saddled with the burden of affirmatively rejecting offers to avoid forming unwanted contracts. Even silence may operate as acceptance, however, when the parties have expressly agreed to such bargaining or through prior conduct have acquiesced to it. Thus, with very limited exceptions, the offeror has wide latitude in specifying the manner of acceptance if the specification is clear.

Conrad v. Hebert

2010 WL 2431461 (Tex. Civ. App. June 17, 2010) (unpublished)

Sherry Radack, Chief Justice.

....

BACKGROUND

¶1 In August 2005, Conrad was driving the car of his parents, Eric and Tammy Hanusch, when he collided with the car driven by the Heberts. The Heberts were injured in the accident. The Hanusches' car involved in the accident was insured by Farmer's Insurance Group ("Farmers").

¶2 On June 5, 2006, the Heberts each sent a letter to April Bossley, Farmers's adjuster, offering to settle their claims. The pertinent portions of the offer letters read as follows:

> I offer to settle the claims I have for the injuries I received resulting from the collision in exchange for payment to me of Robert Conrad's policy limits. Payment must be made to me on or before 5:00 p.m., July 5, 2006. In exchange for payment of policy limits, I will execute a full and complete release in favor of Robert Conrad for all claims I have arising out of the collision. I will also pay all subrogation amounts I may owe with the proceeds. There are no hospital liens. You can make the check payable to Trailblazer Health Enterprises, LLC, and me if you choose.
>
> If payment is not made on or before that date and time, this offer will expire and no further offer will be forthcoming....

¶3 Bossley responded to each of the Heberts by separate letters dated June 14, 2006. Those letters, in pertinent part provided:

> I am extending an offer of $25,000.00, which is our policy limits, to settle your bodily injury claim in exchange for a full and final release.
>
> Please find the enclosed release form for your injury claim. The amount on the release is the total amount of the claim. Upon receipt of this form, we can issue your settlement check....

....

B. Discussion

....

¶4 The Heberts' June 5 offer letters prescribed the precise manner and time of acceptance: "I offer to settle the claims I have ... in exchange for payment to me of ... policy limits. *Payment must be made to me on or before 5:00 p.m., July 5, 2006.* In exchange for payment of policy limits, I will execute a full and complete release ... *If payment is not made on or before that date and time, this offer will expire* and no further offer will be forthcoming." (Emphasis added.) ... The acceptance term of the Heberts' offers [was] clear and unambiguous: it required payment in a specified manner by a specified time, or the offer would expire. Nothing in the remainder of the letter rendered this requirement ambiguous.

¶ 5 It is undisputed that Bossley failed to pay the policy limits by the July 5 deadline. What Bossley did before July 5 was to extend an offer to pay policy limits to each plaintiff in exchange for a prior full and final release of all claims. This did not constitute an acceptance because it did not strictly comply with the offer's acceptance method. *See Williams*, 264 S.W.3d at 236 (providing that one element of enforceable contract is that acceptance be in strict compliance with offer). Although "a different method of acceptance may be effectual where the 'original offeror thereafter manifests his assent to the other party,'" *Padilla* 907 S.W.2d at 460 (quoting *Town of Lindsay*, 502 S.W.2d at 118), that did not happen here: it is undisputed that the Heberts did not respond to Bossley's June 14 letter.

....

¶ 6 Conrad argues that "the letters invited acceptance either by payment or promise to pay." Specifically, he contends that offers "can be accepted either by performance or by promise of performance, where the offeror does not *explicitly* limit the method of acceptance." (Emphasis in original.) However, the offer letters do explicitly limit the method of acceptance by requiring actual payment by the specified deadline. *See id.*

....

¶ 7 We hold that no contract was formed because Conrad failed to accept the offers in strict compliance with their terms.

A. Acceptance by Return Promise

In most transactions, each party desires a commitment by the other before either incurs the expense of performing. Consequently, most contracting parties form bilateral contracts, in which both parties exchange promises of future performance. In the typical bargaining, the offeror states an intention to give his promise or promises to the offeree and will do so if the offeree accepts by giving a return promise or promises.

In many cases, an offer is sufficiently general that it invites acceptance either by a return promise (immediately forming a bilateral contract) or by performance (forming a unilateral contract when the performance by the offeree is complete). In some cases, however, the language or nature of an offer, along with the circumstances surrounding it, make it clear that the offeror is authorizing acceptance only by return promise. If so, under an objective theory of contracts, is it inherent in the nature of a return promise that the offeree must communicate it before acceptance is effective?

Exercise 2.5 — Notice of Acceptance by Return Promise

1. Need for a Bilateral Contract

Explain why the following offer, conveyed over the telephone on Friday by Contractor to Lumberyard, is reasonably interpreted as requiring a return promise as the only authorized means of acceptance: "I'm working on a deadline for the framing on the Crescent Hill project. I'll pay on delivery at the listed price for [specified lumber] if you agree today to deliver the lumber to my work site on Monday between 8 and 9 a.m." If Lumberyard responded, "I don't know, we're really busy; I'll see where we are on Monday morning," and then hung up on Contractor, did Lumberyard accept? Aside from contract formation, would Contractor likely be satisfied with Lumberyard's response?

Suppose that: (1) Contractor immediately called Supplier with the same proposal and received an acceptance over the phone, (2) Supplier delivered the lumber as promised on Monday at 8 a.m. and received its pay at the site, and (3) Lumberyard arrived at the worksite at 8:30 a.m. and unloaded a second load of lumber while Contractor was busy supervising some framing work. Did Lumberyard successfully form a unilateral contract so that Contractor is bound to pay Lumberyard, or can Contractor demand that Lumberyard take its lumber back without pay? Explain fully.

2. Notice of Acceptance

With respect to Contractor's offer to Lumberyard on Friday, does such an offer seem to require communication of the acceptance, or could the manager for Lumberyard accept by writing "okay" on a slip of paper in his office and placing it in the top drawer of his desk (while equivocating over the phone)? What answer is suggested by the objective standard for contract formation? What general rule would you infer about whether acceptance by return promise normally requires that the offeree give notice to the offeror of that acceptance? Can you think of an example in which an offeror overrides such a general default rule by clearly providing otherwise in the offer? We'll see some further nuances in this issue when we discuss the mailbox rule in Chapter 5.

3. Dispensing with Notice of Acceptance in Bilateral Contract Formation

An offer by B to purchase specified assets of X Corporation states "this offer becomes a contract when the Board of Directors for X Corporation approves it." The Board of Directors of X Corporation formally resolved to accept the offer at 10 a.m. on Monday but did not communicate its acceptance to the offeror until Tuesday. In the meantime, the offeror, B, delivered a notice of revocation of the offer on Monday at 2 p.m. Did the Board create a contract on Monday morning, prior to the attempted revocation? If so, why was contract formation not delayed until X Corporation conveyed its return promise on Tuesday?

cancellation

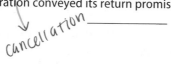

B. Return Promise through Expressive Conduct

Must a party communicate her acceptance verbally, either in writing or orally? Isn't it possible to signal assent through actions other than the use of words?

Exercise 2.6—Acceptance by Return Promise Conveyed by Beginning Performance

Suppose that you break the heel on a shoe that you need to wear to a formal occasion in one hour. Next to your office is a shoe repair shop, and another one is located across the street. You enter the shop next door and you state the following to the manager: "If you agree to repair this shoe within 30 minutes, I'll pay you double your normal rate."

Would a reasonable person in the manager's position believe that: (1) you are looking for an immediate return promise as acceptance of a bilateral contract, or (2) you are willing to wait to see if the manager actually fully performs within 30 minutes, thus forming a unilateral contract on completion of performance while having no obligation to do so?

Suppose that the manager, without speaking a word, smiles and responds to your offer by nodding his head up and down vigorously, taking your shoe, and beginning work on it. Did the manager accept your offer? By what means?

Alternatively, imagine that you stated the same offer, but the manager—without word or other gesture—began working intensely on your shoe right in front of you, apparently beginning a process of repairing the shoe within the requested time limit. What's the best argument that the manager accepted your offer the moment he began working on your shoe within your view? Under that theory, did he form a bilateral or unilateral contract?

In the next case, the buyer's supplemental purchase order included an offer to settle its claim regarding problems with goods delivered in the initial sales contract. What act constituted acceptance of the supplemental purchase order, and why? Why did the seller's claim depend on which act constituted the point of acceptance?

Before reading the opinion, review the discussion of the UCC in Chapter 1. The opinion below quotes section 2206(1)(a) of the California Commercial Code, which is California's enactment of UCC § 2-206 (2011). Remember that relevant portions of the UCC apply to "transactions in goods," UCC § 2-102 (2011), as distinguished from ones primarily involving services or real estate.

M+W Zander, U.S. Op. v. Scott Co. of Cal.

190 Or. App. 268, 276, 78 P.3d 118, 123 (2003)
[with fact summary by the author]

Before Edmonds, Presiding Judge, and Deits, Chief Judge, and Schuman, Judge.

Schuman, J.

¶1 [On August 24, 2001, Plaintiff M+W Zander (M+W) filed suit against Defendant Scott Co. (Scott) for $300,000 owed for construction equipment delivered by M+W. M+W sued not on the original sales contract but on a subsequent modification (in effect, a settlement agreement) offered by Scott through a supplemental purchase order. In that modification, M+W agreed to reduce the price for the goods in light of its late delivery and the poor condition of the equipment, and Scott agreed to release its claims concerning M+W's performance and to pay the reduced price of $911,124.]

¶2 [According to the modification agreement, the payment was due 45 days after the modification, so M+W's cause of action for the unpaid sum of $300,000 accrued at the expiration of that 45-day payment period, and the statute of limitations began to run on that date. Whether M+W filed its lawsuit within the four-year statute of limitations turned on when the modification agreement was formed.]

¶3 [M+W argued that the modification agreement was formed on August 7, 1997, when it signed and returned the supplemental purchase order that had conveyed Scott's offer to settle their dispute. If so, the statute of limitations began to run on the expiration of 45 additional days, on September 21, 1997, and M+W timely filed suit on August 24, 2001.]

¶4 [Scott argued that M+W accepted Scott's settlement offer and formed the modification agreement on June 26, 1997, when M+W "applied the requested discount to Scott's account and billed Scott for the reduced amount." If so, M+W's cause of action accrued when Scott failed to pay on August 11, 1997, and the limitations period expired on August 10, 2001, two weeks before M+W filed suit.]

¶5 [Although this Oregon court applied Oregon procedural law, it honored a provision in the parties' contract in which the parties had chosen California contract law to govern any future dispute arising out of the contract.]

¶6 Contrary to its argument, M+W was not required by the terms of the supplemental purchase order to accept it in writing.

¶7 Section 2206 of the California Commercial Code provides, in part:

> (1) Unless otherwise *unambiguously* indicated by the language or circumstances
>
> (a) An offer to make a contract shall be construed as inviting acceptance in any manner and by any medium reasonable in the circumstances[.]

(Emphasis added.)

¶8 The supplemental purchase order requests written acknowledgment by M+W, stating, "Acknowledgment copy attached please sign reverse side and return within ten days...." The request for a written acknowledgment was not stated in mandatory terms. Thus, written acknowledgment is not *unambiguously* a term or condition of the purchase order. That being the case, acceptance could be made by any reasonable means in the circumstances.

¶9 Both the original and supplemental purchase orders contain the following language: "Seller's acceptance of this purchase order is limited to the terms and conditions hereof, and written confirmation, commencing performance, or making deliveries hereunder constitutes such acceptance...." Under the contract terms, then, M+W ... commenced performance of the modification when it applied the requested discount to Scott's account on June 26, 1997. On that date, the contract, as modified, was fully formed; under M+W's own theory of what "net 45 days" means, Scott's payment was due on August 11, 1997; and Scott's failure to pay on that date put it in breach, thereby beginning the limitations period.

....

¶ 10 ... Nothing tolled the limitations period, which expired at the close of business on August 10, 2001. The trial court did not err in concluding that M+W's action was untimely....

Affirmed.

Exercise 2.7 — Notice of Acceptance in Bilateral Contract Formation

Did the seller accept the buyer's offer in the second purchase order the moment the seller changed the buyer's account in its own unpublished records, to reflect the discounted price that the buyer requested in that order? Or would that form of acceptance be effective only when the seller sent the bill to the buyer, thus notifying the buyer of the adjustment to its account? Can you argue that the buyer dispensed with the usual requirement that it receive notice of acceptance as a prerequisite to formation of a bilateral contract? Or, by crediting the buyer's account, did the seller fully perform its obligations under the second contract, thus forming a unilateral contract? If so, should that affect whether notice of acceptance is normally required?

Exercise 2.8 — Offeror as Master of the Offer

As the offeror, the buyer in *M+W Zander* could have specified that the seller could accept the offer only by signing and returning the attached acknowledgment form, but the buyer did not unambiguously do so when its purchase order form stated "Acknowledgment copy attached please sign reverse side and return within ten days." The court's permissive interpretation of that clause, however, was made significantly easier because the purchase order form also affirmatively identified "commencing performance" as an alternative to "written confirmation" as a means of acceptance.

Suppose that the only relevant language in the purchase order form was the following, taken from *Allied Steel and Conveyors, Inc. v. Ford Motor Co.*, 277 F.2d 907, 909 (6th Cir. 1960): "This purchase order agreement is not binding until accepted. Acceptance should be executed on acknowledgment copy which should be returned to buyer." Does this language unambiguously identify the sole effective means of acceptance, or does it merely express a preference for one method, without displacing the default rule that permits any reasonable means of acceptance, including beginning performance?

Exercise 2.9 — Unequivocal, Unambiguous Acceptance

Although conduct can communicate the equivalent of verbal assent, case law shows that the conduct must be clearly referable to the offer and must be unambiguous so that a reasonable person in the position of the offeror would interpret the conduct as expressing assent to *her* offer.

1. Assent by Emoji?

If A texted the terms of an offer to B, did B accept if she immediately texted a thumbs-up emoji in reply?

2. Commencing Work

The following facts are inspired by those of *White v. Corlies*, 46 N.Y. 467, 469 (1871). Would the conduct of Contractor convey assent, creating a contract? After preliminary negotiations, Owner submitted an offer to Contractor to pay for remodeling of Owner's offices. The written offer stated that Owner would telephone Contractor at 5 p.m. for Contractor's response. Contractor received this offer at noon. He did not respond verbally but immediately purchased materials for the first stage of the remodeling, brought them to his shop, and began working on them, such as by sawing wood to length. These were common materials that Contractor frequently used for various jobs, and the cut length of the lumber was typical. No one else was present in Contractor's workplace. At 3 p.m., Owner telephoned Contractor and revoked her offer before Contractor could say anything other than "hello." Had Contractor already accepted the offer? How many arguments can you state to support the conclusion that Contractor had not yet accepted the offer?

In *Allied Steel*, introduced in Exercise 2.8 above, the moment of contract formation arguably affected the reach of an indemnity clause in a contract for the sale and installation of factory equipment. Explain why the following facts, taken from *Allied*, present a more compelling case for acceptance by conduct than in the case described in the previous paragraph: Before responding in writing to the buyer's offer in its purchase order, the seller arrived at the buyer's factory with the ordered equipment, along with a crew of workers to help install the equipment
and requested entry to deliver and install the eq

3. Continuing Performance

Suppose that an employment contract is term
day trial period. The original contract allowed en
days per year. Six months after the employer f
employer announced that these days off will be un
announcement constitutes an offer to modify the
shows up for work after the announcement wit
should that be interpreted as the employee's ac
contract? What inferences should be drawn from
continuing the employment relationship after the
does not want to accept the offer, is quitting her
expressly stating that she does so without any
Nordstrom, Inc., 755 F.3d 1089, 1093 (9th Cir. 2014)
an employee continues in his or her employme
terms or conditions, he or she has accepted those
change if the original contract was not termina
employee could be fired only for misconduct o
difficult questions presented in such cases, see *L*
1138 (1999). These facts raise issues not only abou
a topic addressed in the next chapter.

Now assume that the employer offered to m
implementing a new grievance resolution procedu
the offer by opting out of it, and authorized employ
to work without having opted out. Should an empl
constitute acceptance? For an affirmative respons
Inc., 735 F.3d 453 (6th Cir. 2013).

Exercise 2.8 → courts are explicit on the sole means.

① I think one way it is the sole means because it doesn't add "or any other method that ensures buyer is made aware" but also the word "should" indicates you prefer this way but will accept others.

Exercise 2.9

① Yes - like a nod, a reasonable person can infer a thumbs up as a yes.
→ may need more facts.

② Contractor had not yet accepted offer because he did not outwardly manifest to buyer to acknowledge. Went off an assumption.

"Please" & "should" vs. "must"
both indicate preferred means of acceptance

Contractor is returning promise, not performance; master of offer is saying that is means of acceptance

C. Acceptance by Full Performance

1. Act and Notice of Acceptance

Our common law of contracts has its roots in English common law; accordingly, much of its content is consistent with principles established in English case law. In the following famous English common law opinion, what sort of acceptance is solicited by the offer in the ad? As you read the opinion, answer the following questions:

- What, precisely, must the offeree do to perform (what is the seller seeking)?
- On what event is the offeror's obligation conditioned?
- Why does the court find it to be an offer, when newspaper ads frequently do not meet common law standards for an offer?
- How does the court respond to the argument that notice of acceptance was a prerequisite to contract formation?

Carlill v. Carbolic Smoke Ball Co.

1 Q.B. 256 (Ct. App. 1893)

¶ 1 The defendants, who were the proprietors and vendors of a medical preparation called "The Carbolic Smoke Ball," inserted in the Pall Mall Gazette of November 13, 1891, and in other newspapers, the following advertisement:

> 100 [£] reward will be paid by the Carbolic Smoke Ball Company to any person who contracts the increasing epidemic influenza, colds, or any disease caused by taking cold, after having used the ball three times daily for two weeks according to the printed directions supplied with each ball. 1000 is deposited with the Alliance Bank, Regent Street, shewing our sincerity in the matter.

....

¶ 2 The plaintiff, a lady, on the faith of this advertisement, bought one of the balls at a chemist's, and used it as directed, three times a day, from November 20, 1891, to January 17, 1892, when she was attacked by influenza. Hawkins, J., held that she was entitled to recover the 100. The defendants appealed.

....

per Lindley, L.J.

¶ 3 ... We are dealing with an express promise to pay 100 in certain events. Read the advertisement how you will, and twist it about as you will, here is a distinct promise expressed in language which is perfectly unmistakable— "100 reward will be paid by the Carbolic Smoke Ball Company to any person who contracts the influenza after having used the ball three times daily for two weeks according to the printed directions supplied with each ball."

¶ 4 We must first consider whether this was intended to be a promise at all, or whether it was a mere puff which meant nothing. Was it a mere puff? My answer to that question is No, and I base my answer upon this passage: "1000 is deposited with the Alliance Bank, shewing our sincerity in the matter." Now, for what was that money deposited or that statement made except to negative the suggestion that this was a mere puff and meant nothing at all? The deposit is called in aid by the advertiser as proof of his sincerity in the matter—that is, the sincerity of his promise to pay this 100 in the event which he has specified. I say this for the purpose of giving point to the observation that we are not inferring a promise; there is the promise, as plain as words can make it.

¶5 Then it is contended that it is not binding. In the first place, it is said that it is not made with anybody in particular. Now that point is common to the words of this advertisement and to the words of all other advertisements offering rewards. They are offers to anybody who performs the conditions named in the advertisement, and anybody who does perform the condition accepts the offer. In point of law this advertisement is an offer to pay 100 to anybody who will perform these conditions, and the performance of the conditions is the acceptance of the offer. That rests upon a string of authorities, the earliest of which is Williams v. Carwardine 4 B. Ad. 621, which has been followed by many other decisions upon advertisements offering rewards.

¶6 ... [Lord Justice Lindley's discussion of notice of acceptance is omitted here, in favor of a clearer exposition of that issue by Lord Justice Bowen, below.]

¶7 We, therefore, find here all the elements which are necessary to form a binding contract enforceable in point of law, subject to two observations. First of all it is said that this advertisement is so vague that you cannot really construe it as a promise—that the vagueness of the language shews that a legal promise was never intended or contemplated. The language is vague and uncertain in some respects, and particularly in this, that the 100 is to be paid to any person who contracts the increasing epidemic after having used the balls three times daily for two weeks....

¶8 ... It strikes me, I confess, that the true construction of this advertisement is that 100 will be paid to anybody who uses this smoke ball three times daily for two weeks according to the printed directions, and who gets the influenza or cold or other diseases caused by taking cold within a reasonable time after so using it; and if that is the true construction, it is enough for the plaintiff.

¶9 It appears to me, therefore, that the defendants must perform their promise, and, if they have been so unwary as to expose themselves to a great many actions, so much the worse for them.

per Bowen, L.J.

I am of the same opinion....

¶10 It was also said that the contract is made with all the world—that is, with everybody; and that you cannot contract with everybody. It is not a contract made with all the world. There is the fallacy of the argument. It is an offer made to all the world; and why should not an offer be made to all the world which is to ripen into a contract with anybody who comes forward and performs the condition? It is an offer to become liable to any one who, before it is retracted, performs the condition, and, although the offer is made to the world, the contract is made with that limited portion of the public who come forward and perform the condition on the faith of the advertisement. It is not like cases in which you offer to negotiate, or you issue advertisements that you have got a stock of books to sell, or houses to let, in which case there is no offer to be bound by any contract. Such advertisements are offers to negotiate—offers to receive offers—offers to chaffer, as, I think, some learned judge in one of the cases has said. If this is an offer to be bound, then it is a contract the moment the person fulfils the condition.

....

¶ 11 Then it was said that there was no notification of the acceptance of the contract. One cannot doubt that, as an ordinary rule of law, an acceptance of an offer made ought to be notified to the person who makes the offer, in order that the two minds may come together. Unless this is done the two minds may be apart, and there is not that consensus which is necessary according to the English law—I say nothing about the laws of other countries—to make a contract. But there is this clear gloss to be made upon that doctrine, that as notification of acceptance is required for the benefit of the person who makes the offer, the person who makes the offer may dispense with notice to himself if he thinks it desirable to do so, and I suppose there can be no doubt that where a person in an offer made by him to another person, expressly or impliedly intimates a particular mode of acceptance as sufficient to make the bargain binding, it is only necessary for the other person to whom such offer is made to follow the indicated method of acceptance; and if the person making the offer, expressly or impliedly intimates in his offer that it will be sufficient to act on the proposal without communicating acceptance of it to himself, performance of the condition is a sufficient acceptance without notification.

....

¶ 12 Now, if that is the law, how are we to find out whether the person who makes the offer does intimate that notification of acceptance will not be necessary in order to constitute a binding bargain? In many cases you look to the offer itself. In many cases you extract from the character of the transaction that notification is not required, and in the advertisement cases it seems to me to follow as an inference to be drawn from the transaction itself that a person is not to notify his acceptance of the offer before he performs the condition, but that if he performs the condition notification is dispensed with. It seems to me that from the point of view of common sense no other idea could be entertained. If I advertise to the world that my dog is lost, and that anybody who brings the dog to a particular place will be paid some money, are all the police or other persons whose business it is to find lost dogs to be expected to sit down and write me a note saying that they have accepted my proposal? Why, of course, they at once look after the dog, and as soon as they find the dog they have performed the condition. The essence of the transaction is that the dog should be found, and it is not necessary under such circumstances, as it seems to me, that in order to make the contract binding there should be any notification of acceptance. It follows from the nature of the thing that the performance of the condition is sufficient acceptance without the notification of it, and a person who makes an offer in an advertisement of that kind makes an offer which must be read by the light of that common sense reflection. He does, therefore, in his offer impliedly indicate that he does not require notification of the acceptance of the offer.

....

Appeal dismissed.

Exercise 2.10 — Questions and Notes on *Carbolic*

1. Newspaper Ad as an Offer

In a normal reward notice, such as the offer of a reward to the person who finds and returns a lost dog, a newspaper ad giving notice of the reward can fairly easily overcome the usual objections to a newspaper ad being reasonably interpreted as an offer. Can you explain why? Can you also explain why the ad for a reward in the *Carbolic* case presented a more difficult issue about whether it constituted an offer? What facts or factual inferences helped to resolve that issue in favor of finding an offer?

2. Notice of Acceptance of Offer for a Unilateral Contract

According to *Carbolic,* when performance is the only invited means of acceptance, what act constitutes acceptance that forms a unilateral contract? Beginning performance? Completion of performance without more? Completion of performance plus notice to the offeror that performance has taken place?

What rule should apply if the offeree does not notify the offeror of the acceptance and the offeror has no other means of learning of the offeree's full performance?

3. Formation of a Contract to Guarantee Payment

As the general contractor on an office project, Ruskin Corp. hired Baimbridge as its carpeting subcontractor. Ruskin sent a letter to J & J in which it offered to pay J & J for carpet if J & J would deliver the carpet to Baimbridge on credit and if Baimbridge failed to pay for the delivered carpet. After J & J delivered carpet for which Baimbridge never paid, J & J demanded payment from Ruskin. Ruskin showed that J & J never communicated its acceptance of its mailed offer to guarantee payment. The court found acceptance nonetheless:

> "In the case of a guaranty agreement, which by its terms does not require notice of acceptance, no such notice is necessary. Sale of goods on credit in reliance on the guaranty is itself sufficient acceptance." *Cobb v. Texas Distribs. Inc.,* 524 S.W.2d 342, 345 (Tex. Civ. App.-Dallas 1975, no writ). J & J shipped carpet to Baimbridge in reliance on that promise. The shipment constituted acceptance of Ruskin's signed offer of April 15, 1997.

The Ruskin Corp. v. J & J Ind., No. 01-98-01261, 1999 WL 1080933 (Tex. Civ. App. Dec. 2, 1999) (unpublished). Following principles stated in the *Carbolic Smoke Ball* case, explain how a contract was formed between Ruskin and J & J, separate from any contract between J & J and Baimbridge. What kind of contract was formed, and what constituted the acceptance? Why was notice of acceptance unnecessary to contract formation?

Exercise 2.11

6: ① Alicia technically did ~~not~~ accept the offer even if she didn't know about it before because she was the one who completed the performance, ∴ closing the contract.

② Marlon's is different bc he submitted info first before hearing offer. ~~[illegible]~~ Alicia found out about offer before returning.

E

local newspaper,
dding band (with
ffice. Alicia found
ght it home, read
ffice the next day.
led to the reward?
e with knowledge

licia has a stronger
in his. What is the
rminative?

an isolated area of
rd, Marlon learned
ffered a reward of
vants to collect the
ull amount offered.

ested act, regardless
ting the act. Would
his less demanding

V. Review of Basic Offer and Acceptance

A. Offers, in the Style of Dr. Seuss

By Alison Atwater, 1L Fall 2007

Listen! Listen! Can you hear? There is an offer very near.
I want to offer, yes I do. I want to offer a contract to you.
I want to offer right away. I want to offer—what do you say?
I'll make an offer with a quote, I'll write it on this great, big note.

Stop right there! You cannot do it. A quote has got no offer to it.
Unless you give a certain limit, a quote has got no offer in it.[4]

4. If a seller was confident of its ability to supply all demand, could it effectively make an offer "to sell any amounts ordered by any buyers who respond to this price quote by October 1"? Can you draft language for a purported "price quote" that would lead a reasonable recipient to believe that the seller is ready to commit to any and all orders, without a stated quantity limitation?

Then here's an offer to change your story: My full-color ad in all its glory!
You cannot offer in an ad. There's too much risk that will be had.[5]
Your ad is seen by way too many; an offer, well, you don't have any!

How about an offer made with laughter? Will it bind us ever after?
It will not bind us, it cannot yoke. You cannot offer with a joke!
No one with reason could thus glean, a serious offer is what you mean.[6]

But surely I do offer well, when I tell you I will gladly sell.
You do not offer well at all! An offer, that, I cannot call.
No power moves from you to me; we won't contract if I agree.[7]

Listen! Listen! What do you say? What if I make you an offer *this* way?
I'll tell you the what and the where and the how, I'll offer to make you a promise right now.
Then it is *you* who can make the decision. Tell me, does *this* offer need more revision?

You've done it, I say! You've done it quite nicely.
This time you've made me an offer precisely.
If I accept now, if I promise too, a contract will form and we'll be through!

Now I can see it—a transfer of power.
Thank you, thank you! We'll contract within the hour.

---

5. Describe the kinds of details that would reduce the seller's risk to the point that an ad would be reasonably interpreted as an offer and not just as an invitation to negotiate. Write the text for such a sample ad.

6. Here, the poem refers to an obvious jest, one "made with laughter," which "no one with reason" would understand to be serious. In a stanza offered by David Blackledge (Class of 2012), however, we remember from *Lucy v. Zehmer* that a secret jest will not prevent contract formation:

> But if you keep your joke so safely hidden,
> How will others know that you are kiddin'?
> The court won't care what's on your mind.
> It's your outward actions that legally bind.

Or this one from Stephen Brookman (Class of 2012):

> You must be clear if the offer's a joke,
> And state up front that it's not real,
> Or an unwelcome contract you'll invoke
> And you'll find out that you've made a deal

7. It would be difficult to flesh this point out in the poem without losing our flow, but one way to explain this part of the poem is to assume that the seller has reserved the right to accept or reject and thus has not given the buyer the power to create a contract, as in this offering from Sara Holyoak (Class of 2012):

> I have made an "offer" to you,
> Just want to add a note or two,
> You may reply by signing this note
> Then I must approve as a matter of rote.

If contract formation is dependent on such approval, such an "offer" is no offer at all; instead, the signed reply would be the first offer.

Exercise 2.12 — Problems for Review

1. Notice of Acceptance

In a few sentences stated in your own words, explain when notice of acceptance is required for effective acceptance, and when it is not. Compose an offer that requires a return promise as acceptance and that explicitly or implicitly specifies a certain mode of expressing the acceptance. Then compose another one that seeks a return promise but dispenses with any requirement that the offeror receive notice of that expression before a contract is formed. Then, compose an offer that requires notice of acceptance, where none would ordinarily be required for the invited contract, before a contract is formed.

2. Newspaper Ad — Walk-in Bathtub

A newspaper ad posted in the Arizona Republic on July 18, 2008 refers to "Walk-in Bathtubs from Independent Living USA." It pictures a bathtub with a side door, all next to the words "safety, dignity, and independence." Other statements in the ad include:

"Save an Additional $500 with this ad * Limited Offer Expires 8/15/08"

"Guaranteed Lowest Prices"

"Models Include: [physical features are listed, as well as] Many Models, Sizes, and Colors for ANY Problem ANY Space Any Décor * Installation Available in ALL 50 States"

"CALL TO PREVENT A FALL * For Details and Live Operator 24/7 Call Now, Toll Free 1-800-560-2476"

Does this ad state an offer under the common law, empowering the reader to accept and bind the store to a certain price, at least in certain circumstances? Argue both sides of that issue if you can. What elements of the ad suggest that it might be an offer? What elements suggest that it should not be interpreted as an offer? List the elements for and against recognizing an offer on either side of the page.

3. Item on Display at Store

How does the analysis differ if, rather than seeing an item displayed in a newspaper ad, you walk into a store and see an item displayed on a shelf, marked with a certain price? Is that an offer that you can accept under common law principles, thus binding the store at that price? What information does the item on the store shelf convey that is not necessarily conveyed in a general newspaper ad, making the display more likely to state an offer? How can you argue that it is not reasonably interpreted as an offer? If the display is not an offer, what other acts would constitute offer and acceptance?

4. Acceptance of Offer in Item Displayed at Store

Assuming the display of a priced item is an offer, what kind of acceptance does it invite? Does a customer accept by selecting an item and putting it in a shopping cart? By taking it to the cashier and tendering payment for it? Why does it matter? If a bottle of carbonated beverage exploded in a shopper's hand and injured her as she placed the bottle in her shopping cart, the shopper could sue the store for breach of implied warranty of merchantability under the UCC, but only if the shopper and the store had formed a contract at that point. *See, e.g., Barker v. Allied Supermarket*, 596 P.2d 870 (Okla. 1979). If you were deciding such a case, would you be motivated more by a desire to do justice in this particular case or a perceived need to develop the law in a coherent manner so that it can be easily applied to future cases?

5. Contract Terms in the Box

Suppose that a consumer purchased a boxed set of computer software at a retail store and was not informed at the time of purchase of any limitations on her rights to use the software. She opened the box at home and discovered for the first time a written licensing agreement inside the box that purports to contractually limit ways in which the consumer can use the software. Has the consumer assented to the licensing agreement under common law? What facts would you add to support a conclusion that the consumer is bound by the licensing agreement, at least if she uses the software? We will revisit this problem after we study UCC § 2-207 in Chapter 6.

6. Communicating Acceptance by Signature and by Action

In late March 2012, Gonzaga University Law Professor Scott Burnham went skydiving. He signed a contract that released any claims against the skydiving company for its negligence. In addition to securing the skydiver's signature, however, the skydiving company inserted the following clause to identify a more colorful signifier of each skydiver's acceptance of the company's terms: "My actual exit or jump out of an airplane will be a physical demonstration of my acceptance and agreement with this Contract." Moreover, the skydiving company routinely photographed each skydiver's jump, as in this photograph of Professor Burnham's jump.

Why would the skydiving company elicit a "physical demonstration" of the skydiver's acceptance when it earlier required the skydiver's signature on the contract? Is the company concerned that a patron might substitute unintelligible scribbling for his signature, thus complicating proof of assent? Could the company address such concerns by taking a photograph of the jump after presenting the skydiver with the contract and its "physical demonstration" clause? Assuming for a moment that the skydiver neglected to sign at all, but had notice of the physical demonstration clause, would the jump constitute acceptance by performance or by return promise?

B. Modifications as Contracts

A modification of a contract, like the initial contract, is effective only if the parties agree to it through offer and acceptance, objectively conveyed. Why did the appellate court find no effective modification of the original contract in the following case?

Douglas v. U.S. Dist. Court for Cent. Dist. of California

495 F.3d 1062 (9th Cir. 2007)

cert. denied sub nom. Talk America, Inc. v. Douglas, 552 U.S. 1242 (2008)

On Petition for Writ of Mandamus to the United States District Court for the Central District of California. D.C. No. CV-06-03809-GAF.

PER CURIAM:

¶ 1 We consider whether a service provider may change the terms of its service contract by merely posting a revised contract on its website.

Facts

¶ 2 Joe Douglas contracted for long distance telephone service with America Online. Talk America subsequently acquired this business from AOL and continued to provide telephone service to AOL's former customers. Talk America then added four provisions to the service contract: (1) additional service charges; (2) a class action waiver; (3) an arbitration clause; and (4) a choice-of-law provision pointing to New York law. Talk America posted the revised contract on its website but, according to Douglas, it never notified him that the contract had changed. Unaware of the new terms, Douglas continued using Talk America's services for four years.

¶ 3 After becoming aware of the additional charges, Douglas filed a class action lawsuit in district court, charging Talk America with violations of the Federal Communications Act, breach of contract and violations of various California consumer protection statutes. Talk America moved to compel arbitration based on the modified contract and the district court granted the motion. Because the Federal Arbitration Act, 9 U.S.C. § 16, does not authorize interlocutory appeals of a district court order compelling arbitration, Douglas petitioned for a writ of mandamus.

Analysis

¶ 4 Because a writ of mandamus is an extraordinary remedy, we have developed five factors that cabin our power to grant the writ:

....

3. "The district court's order is clearly erroneous as a matter of law."

....

Bauman v. U.S. Dist. Court, 557 F.2d 650, 654–55 (9th Cir. 1977).

....

¶ 5 ... Douglas alleges that Talk America changed his service contract without notifying him. He could only have become aware of the new terms if he had visited Talk America's website and examined the contract for possible changes. The district court seems to have assumed Douglas had visited the website when it noted that the contract was available on "the web site on which Plaintiff paid his bills." However, Douglas claims that he authorized AOL to charge his credit card automatically and Talk America continued this practice, so he had no occasion to visit Talk America's website to pay his bills. Even if Douglas had visited the website, he would have had no reason to look at the contract posted there. Parties to a contract have no obligation to check the terms on a periodic basis to learn whether they have been changed by the other side. [footnote omitted] Indeed, a party can't unilaterally change the terms of a contract; it must obtain the other party's consent before doing so. *Union Pac. R.R. v. Chi., Milwaukee, St. Paul & Pac. R.R.*, 549 F.2d 114, 118 (9th Cir. 1976). This is because a revised contract is merely an offer and does not bind the parties until it is accepted. *Matanuska Val Farmers Cooperating Ass'n v. Monaghan*, 188 F.2d 906, 909 (9th Cir. 1951). And generally "an offeree cannot actually assent to an offer unless he knows of its existence." 1 Samuel Williston & Richard A. Lord, A Treatise on the Law of Contracts § 4:13, at 365 (4th ed.1990); *see also Trimble v. N.Y. Life Ins. Co.*, 234 A.D. 427, 255 N.Y.S. 292, 297 (1932) ("An offer may not be accepted until it is made and brought to the attention of the one accepting."). Even if Douglas's continued use of Talk America's service could be considered assent, such assent can only be inferred after he received proper notice of the proposed changes. Douglas claims that no such notice was given.

....

¶ 6 The district court thus erred in holding that Douglas was bound by the terms of the revised contract when he was not notified of the changes. The error reflects fundamental misapplications of contract law and goes to the heart of petitioner's claim. It would alone be sufficient to satisfy the third *Bauman* factor, ...

VI. Internet Contracting

Douglas demonstrates that the objective theory's requirement of actual communication of contract terms applies online as well as in other contexts. Following that principle in another case, the Second Circuit found that consumers were not bound by licensing terms associated with software available on the web, because no reference to the terms was visible on the screen that presented the download prompt; instead, consumers could see a link to the terms only if they happened to scroll down further. *Specht v. Netscape Communications Corp.*, 306 F.3d 17 (2d Cir. 2002).

In yet another case, mutual assent was lacking because a link to "TERMS OF USE"—although visible on the screen without further scrolling—was difficult to see due to the size, color, and placement of the link relative to other colors and content on the screen. *Long v. Provide Commerce, Inc.*, 245 Cal. App. 4th 855, 200 Cal. Rptr. 3d 117 (Ct. App. 2016). Even if the link had been easier to see, the court suggested that mutual assent might still be lacking because the site failed to alert users that they would be contractually bound by the terms if they continued to use the website. *Id.* at 867, 200 Cal. Rptr. at 126–27; *see also Nicosia v. Amazon.com, Inc.*, 834 F.3d 220, 233 (2d Cir. 2016) ("Whether there was notice of the existence of additional contract terms presented on a webpage depends heavily on whether the design and content of that webpage rendered the existence of terms reasonably conspicuous.").

On the other hand, even when a link to contract terms is conspicuously presented to online consumers, and even when consumers must click on an affirmation of agreement to those terms before proceeding with a transaction, nearly all consumers who choose to proceed do so without reading the offered terms. Under the traditional common law approach, a party who communicates assent to an offer is bound to the terms conveyed in the offer, even if the offeree neglected to read them after having an opportunity to do so. Critics argue that a court engages in a fiction when it finds consent in a consumer's apparent adoption of voluminous, unread, standard-form contract terms. *See, e.g.*, Nancy S. Kim, WRAP CONTRACTS: FOUNDATIONS AND RAMIFICATIONS (2013); Margaret Jane Radin, BOILERPLATE: THE FINE PRINT, VANISHING RIGHTS, AND THE RULE OF LAW (2013).

The next case presents the traditional common law approach in an employment context. As you read the analysis, ask yourself whether you agree with the traditional approach or whether you would develop new doctrines to address the reality that very few contracting parties read the terms of click-through agreements in online transactions or study the fine print in many paper transactions.

The decision below was reversed on appeal in 2016, but on a ground other than the issue of assent discussed in the following excerpt. This trial court opinion presents the issue of mutual assent in online contracting in clear and vivid terms.

Mohamed v. Uber Technologies, Inc.

109 F. Supp. 3d 1185 (N.D. Cal. 2015),
rev'd on other grounds, 836 F.3d 1102 (9th Cir. 2016) [footnotes omitted]

Judge Edward Chen:

I. INTRODUCTION

¶ 1 Plaintiff Ronald Gillette began driving for Uber in the San Francisco Bay Area in March 2013. Gillette Docket No. 7 at ¶ 12. Gillette's access to the Uber application was "abruptly deactivated" in April 2014. *Id.* at ¶ 15. According to Gillette, an Uber representative told him he was terminated because " 'something had come up' on his consumer background report." *Id.*

¶ 2 Gillette filed a lawsuit against Uber Technologies on November 26, 2014. *Gillette* Docket No. 1. Gillette's operative complaint alleges putative class claims under [various state and federal statutes regulating employment and credit reporting]. *See Gillette* Docket No. 7 at ¶ 79. Uber filed a motion to compel all of Gillette's claims to individual arbitration pursuant to the terms of its 2013 contract with Gillette. *Gillette* Docket No. 16.

¶ 3 Plaintiff Abdul Mohamed began driving for Uber's black car service in Boston in 2012, and for uberX around October 2014. *Mohamed* Docket No. 1 at ¶ 31. According to Mohamed, his access to the Uber application was terminated around

October 28, 2014, at least in part as a "result of information obtained [by defendants] through [a] Consumer Reporting Agency...." *See id.* at ¶32.

¶4 On November 24, 2014, Mohamed filed suit against Uber Technologies, Rasier LLC, and Hirease, LLC. *Mohamed* Docket No. 1. Mohamed's complaint alleges that these defendants violated numerous laws that "impose certain strictures on employers' use of consumer background reports as a factor in their decisions to hire, promote, reassign, or terminate employees." *See id.* at ¶14.... Hirease filed a joinder in its co-defendants' motion to compel arbitration, contending that Mohamed's putative class claim against it should also be compelled to individual arbitration pursuant to Mohamed's contracts with Uber. *Mohamed* Docket No. 32.

¶5 Having considered the parties' briefs, supplemental briefs, and lengthy oral arguments, the Court ... finds that both Gillette and Mohamed validly assented to be bound to the terms of the various contracts at issue here....

II. BACKGROUND

¶6 Around July 23, 2013, Uber notified its drivers via email that "it was planning on rolling out a Software License and Online Services Agreement ... and Driver Addendum within the next couple of weeks." *Gillette* Docket No. 16-2 (Colman Decl. *Gillette*) at ¶9....

¶7 Once the relevant agreements were finalized, drivers saw the following message when they attempted to log-on to the Uber application:

Colman Decl. *Gillette*, Ex. B. According to Uber, the words "Driver Addendum," "Software License and Online Services Agreement," and "City Addendum" that appear in the picture above were hyperlinks that "a driver could have clicked in order to review [the relevant agreements] prior to hitting 'Yes, I agree.'" Colman Decl. *Gillette* at ¶10. If the driver hit the "Yes, I agree" button, Uber contends that the driver would next see the following screen.

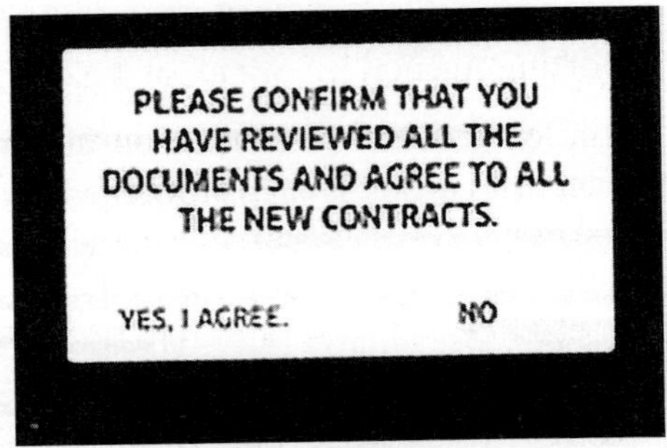

¶ 8 According to Uber's records, Gillette electronically accepted the 2013 Software License and Online Services Agreement (2013 Agreement) on July 29, 2013. Colman Decl. *Gillette* at ¶¶ 11–12. Gillette avers that he does "not recall accepting" the agreements on July 29. Gillette Decl. at ¶ 7. He does not dispute, however, that he continued to drive for UberBlack until April 2014, when Uber allegedly deactivated his account and terminated his employment "without notice or explanation." *Id.* at ¶ 6.

¶ 9 ... On October 3, 2014, Uber claims that Mohamed accepted the 2014 Rasier Software Sublicense & Online Services Agreement (2014 Rasier Agreement) through the same process described above. Colman Decl. *Mohamed* at ¶ 15. He thereafter drove for uberX in Boston. *Mohamed* Docket No. 1 at ¶ 30.

....

¶ 10 It is undisputed that neither Plaintiff received a paper copy of any of the relevant contracts with either Uber or Rasier. *See, e.g.*, *Gillette* Decl. at ¶ 8.... Mohamed's counsel further contends that "Mr. Mohamed's ability to speak and understand English is extremely limited, and an interpreter's assistance has been required to communicate with [him]." *Mohamed* Docket No. 37-2 (Maya Decl.) at ¶ 6. Counsel goes on to state an opinion that "based on conversations with Mr. Mohamed ... if Mr. Mohamed had clicked on a link in the Uber app to open one of the agreements ... he would not have been able to understand the agreement." *Id.* at ¶ 7.

B. The Applicable Contracts

¶ 11 Each of the 2013 and 2014 contracts provide that they will be "governed by California law, without regard to the choice or conflicts of law provisions of any jurisdiction." *See, e.g.*, 2013 Agreement at § 14.1. And each of the contracts also contains an arbitration provision. While there are significant differences between the 2013 Agreement's arbitration provision and the ones contained in each of the 2014 contracts, all of the arbitration provisions share a number of key features. First, each provision requires all disputes not expressly exempted from the scope of the arbitration provision to be resolved in "final and binding arbitration and not by way of court or jury trial." *See, e.g.*, 2013 Agreement at § 14.3(i)....

III. DISCUSSION

¶ 12 The Court's analysis of Uber's motions to compel arbitration will proceed as follows. First, the Court determines whether either Plaintiff validly assented to the terms of the relevant contracts. That is, was an agreement to arbitrate ever formed? ...

A. Plaintiffs Assented to be Bound to the Applicable Contracts

¶ 13 Plaintiffs argue that the arbitration provisions contained in the relevant contracts cannot be enforced against them because they never assented to be bound by those contracts. Put differently, Plaintiffs contend no agreement to arbitrate was ever formed as a matter of law. This argument is rejected.

¶ 14 Plaintiffs initially contend that Uber failed to prove assent by a preponderance of the evidence where it failed to produce signed versions of any contracts, or other "hard evidence" that the Plaintiffs received copies of the contracts and agreed to be bound. This contention is factually incorrect. Uber presented evidence from its business records, including electronic receipts, that indicate that both Gillette and Mohamed clicked the "Yes, I agree" buttons on the Uber application, as depicted in the pictures above. *See* Colman Decl. *Mohamed* at ¶ 13-16; Colman Decl. *Gillette* at ¶ 12. Moreover, it is undisputed that Uber requires drivers to indicate acceptance of the relevant agreements before a driver can continue to use the Uber application, and it is similarly undisputed that both Gillette and Mohamed did, in fact, drive for Uber. Thus, Uber has submitted sufficiently probative evidence that Gillette and Mohamed took some affirmative step to indicate an assent to be bound (*i.e.*, they clicked "Yes, I agree" on two separate application screens). *See Tompkins v. 23andMe, Inc.*, 2014 WL 2903752, at *7 (N.D. Cal. Jun. 25, 2014) (Koh, J.) (holding that an individual's access to a service or website that requires an indication of assent to contractual terms before access to the service or website will be granted was "sufficient evidence that the user clicked 'I Accept' ") (citing *Feldman v. Google, Inc.*, 513 F. Supp. 2d 229, 237 (E.D. Pa. 2007)).

¶ 15 The remaining question, then, is whether the specific manifestation of assent Uber can prove—that Plaintiffs clicked a "Yes, I agree" button that appeared near hyperlinks to the relevant contracts, and then clicked another "Yes, I agree" button on a subsequent application screen—was sufficient to form a legally binding contract under California law. *See Marin Storage & Trucking, Inc. v. Benco Contracting & Eng'g, Inc.*, 89 Cal. App. 4th 1042, 1049–50 (2001) (explaining that "[e]very contract requires mutual assent," and the "existence of mutual assent is determined by objective criteria" designed to measure whether "a reasonable person would, from the conduct of the parties, conclude that there was a mutual agreement"); *see also Windsor Mills, Inc. v. Collins & Aikman Corp.*, 25 Cal. App. 3d 987, 992 (1972) (explaining that California law is clear that "an offeree, regardless of apparent manifestation of his consent, is not bound by inconspicuous contractual provisions of which he is unaware, contained in a document whose contractual nature is not obvious").

¶ 16 Judge Koh recently addressed very similar issues about contract formation in the internet era in a persuasive and comprehensive opinion. *See Tompkins*, 2014 WL 2903752, at *3–9. There, as here, plaintiffs "clicked a box or button that appeared near a hyperlink to the [contract] to indicate acceptance of the [contract]." *Id.* at *8. Judge Koh held that a valid and binding agreement had been formed.

¶ 17 The *Tompkins* court first distinguished between two types of contractual scenarios frequently encountered in the digital realm—"clickwrap" and "browsewrap" agreements. *Id.* at *5–6. "A clickwrap agreement 'presents the user with a message on his or her computer screen, requiring that the user manifest his or her assent to the terms of the license agreement by clicking on an icon.'" *Id.* at *5 (quoting *Specht v. Netscape Commc'ns Corp.*, 306 F.3d 17, 22 n.4 (2d Cir. 2002)). By contrast, the "defining feature of browsewrap agreements is that the user can continue to use the website or its services without visiting the page hosting the browsewrap agreement or even knowing that such a webpage exists." *Id.* at *6 (citation omitted) (emphasis added). Judge Koh explained that courts tend to enforce clickwrap agreements, but not browsewrap agreements. *Id.* at *7; *see also Savetsky v. Pre-Paid Legal Servs., Inc.*, No. 14-cv-3514 SC, 2015 WL 604767, at *3–4 (N.D. Cal. Feb. 12, 2015) (discussing in detail the enforceability of clickwrap and browsewrap agreements).

¶ 18 The *Tompkins* court next considered the situation, presented here, where the actual contract terms were not necessarily presented to the user at the time of formation, but a hyperlink to those terms was conspicuously presented nearby, and the user had to click a button indicating that they agreed to be bound by those hyperlinked terms. The court concluded that such situations "resemble clickwrap agreements, where an offeree receives an opportunity to review terms and conditions and must affirmatively indicate assent. The fact that the [contract was] hyperlinked and not presented on the same screen does not mean that customers lacked adequate notice" of the contract terms. *Id.* at *8. Specifically, the court concluded that users had adequate notice of the contract terms "because courts have long upheld contracts where "'the consumer is prompted to examine terms of sale that are located somewhere else.'" *Id.* (quoting *Fteja v. Facebook*, 841 F. Supp. 2d 829, 839 (S.D.N.Y. 2012)); *see also Swift v. Zynga Game Network, Inc.*, 805 F. Supp. 2d 904, 911–12 (N.D. Cal. 2011) (enforcing arbitration clause where "Plaintiff was provided with an opportunity to review the terms of service in the form of a hyperlink immediately under the 'accept' button"); Mark A. Lemley, *Terms of Use*, 91 Minn. L. Rev. 459, 459–60 (2006) (noting that courts regularly enforce clickwrap agreements, and collecting cases).

¶ 19 Here, it is beyond dispute that Mohamed and Gillette had the opportunity to review the relevant terms of the hyperlinked agreements, and the existence of the relevant contracts was made conspicuous in the first application screen which the drivers were required to click through in order to continue using the Uber application (i.e., driving for Uber). Uber has similarly presented uncontroverted evidence that Mohamed and Gillette clicked "Yes, I Agree." *See* Colman Decl. *Mohamed* at ¶ 13-16;

Colman Decl. *Gillette* at ¶ 12. Thus, Plaintiffs cannot successfully argue that a binding contract was not formed here. *See Tompkins*, 2014 WL 2903752, at *7–9. Whether or not the drivers actually clicked the links or otherwise read the terms of the contracts is irrelevant: Under California law "[a] party cannot avoid the terms of a contract on the ground that he or she failed to read it before signing." *Marin Storage & Trucking, Inc.*, 89 Cal. App. 4th at 1049.

¶ 20 Plaintiffs' remaining arguments regarding contract formation are equally without merit. First, Mohamed appears to argue that he could not legally assent to the contract because he does not sufficiently understand English. Mohamed cites no case law in support of this contention, however, and what case law the Court has found does not support it. As the Seventh Circuit has held:

> [I]t is a fundamental principle of contract law that a person who signs a contract is presumed to know its terms and consents to be bound by them.... [T]he fact that the rules were in German [does not] preclude enforcement of the contract. In fact, a blind or illiterate party (or simply one unfamiliar with the contract language) who signs the contract without learning of its contents would be bound. Mere ignorance will not relieve a party of her obligations.... [A] party who agrees to terms in writing without understanding or investigating those terms does so at his own peril.

Paper Express, Ltd. v. Pfankuch Maschinen GmbH, 972 F.2d 753, 757 (7th Cir. 1992); *see also* Lauren E. Miller, *Note, Breaking the Language Barrier: The Failure of the Objective Theory to Promote Fairness in Language-Barrier Contracting*, 43 Ind. L. Rev. 175, 176 (2009) (arguing against the apparently universal common law rule that "treats non-English speakers the same as people who speak English—they have a duty to read the contract") (citations omitted). As a matter of contract formation, Mohamed is bound by his legal assent.

¶ 21 Plaintiffs also argue that no contract was formed because it is very unlikely that anyone would actually click the hyperlinks presented in the Uber application to actually view Uber's contracts, and that any such review would be particularly difficult on the small screens of drivers' smartphones. This argument misses the mark. As noted above, for the purposes of contract formation it is essentially irrelevant whether a party actually reads the contract or not, so long as the individual had a legitimate opportunity to review it. *Marin Storage & Trucking, Inc.*, 89 Cal. App. 4th at 1049 ("A party cannot avoid the terms of a contract on the ground that he or she failed to read it before signing."). Here, Plaintiffs had the opportunity to read the agreements on their phones, even if doing so would be somewhat onerous. Plaintiffs cite no authority that holds or suggests that mutual assent should not be found on these facts. Therefore the Court finds that valid and binding contracts were formed between the Plaintiffs and Uber/Rasier.

E. The 2013 Agreement's Arbitration Provision is Unenforceable

....

¶ 22 Plaintiffs argue that the 2013 Agreement's arbitration provision is unenforceable in its entirety because it is unconscionable under California law. [After finding contract formation based on mutual assent, the Court refused to enforce the arbitration clause because it found the clause to be so grossly unfair as to be "unconscionable," a doctrine that we will study in Chapter 9. That part of the Court's decision, however, was reversed on appeal.]

Exercise 2.13 — Questions on Notice of Terms

1. The "Somewhat Onerous" Task of Reading Terms on a Smartphone

In paragraph 21 of the edited opinion, the court finds that the drivers had an adequate opportunity to review the proposed contract terms on their smartphones, "even if doing so would be somewhat onerous." When significant terms are presented on paper but buried in fine print, how small or otherwise hidden must the print be to support a conclusion that the proposed terms were not adequately conveyed to a reasonable person under the objective theory of contracts? Would such a conclusion ever be supported when proposed contract terms are conveyed to a smartphone that can adjust the size of displayed text? Would text conveyed in some nonstandard fonts, such as *Brush Script MT*, be so difficult to read on a smartphone that the purported communication would fail the objective test?

As a prelude to Chapter 9's discussion of procedural unconscionability, consider the following question: If one party presents proposed contract terms in a way that makes the terms "somewhat onerous" for the other party to read and understand, and assuming that mutual assent is established, should that difficulty be viewed as at least one relevant factor in a multi-faceted fairness test for enforceability? Should a language barrier to full understanding be viewed as a relevant factor in such a test?

2. Consumer Contracts with Uber — A Tale of Two Cases

Consumers have also challenged Uber's arbitration clauses, disputing whether the contract terms were reasonably presented to consumers when they registered for Uber service on their smartphones. In one case, a court found that a user had adequate notice of the arbitration clause on the following facts: An uncluttered screen invited the consumer to provide payment details and to click on a button to register for service. Appearing below the register button was the sentence, "By creating an Uber account, you agree to the TERMS OF SERVICE & PRIVACY POLICY." Although in small font, the dark print of this sentence contrasted with white background, and the capitalized words — which linked to the contract terms — were in the blue underlined font normally associated with hyperlinks. Although the screen did not require the consumer to separately click through his or her agreement to the contract terms before clicking on the register button, the court found that a consumer registering for service had adequate notice of the terms, including the arbitration clause, and thus had assented to them. *Meyer v. Uber Tech., Inc.*, 868 F.3d 66 (2d Cir. 2017) (applying California contract law).

Ten months later, another court found that Uber had *not* adequately communicated its contract terms to consumers who had registered for Uber service. *Cullinane v. Uber Tech., Inc.*, 893 F.3d 53 (1st Cir. 2018) (applying Massachusetts law). By then, however, Uber had apparently updated its user interface. In that case, the payment page once again included a link to contract terms, but in different form. The phrase, "By creating an Uber account, you are agreeing to the" faintly appeared in grey font over black background. Below that phrase, the hyperlink appeared in a rectangular box with the phrase, "Terms of Service and Privacy Policy," presented in bold white font on black background. When a consumer had entered payment information, the page illuminated a "DONE" button to complete the registration. On these facts, the court found inadequate notice of contract terms, and thus no assent to an arbitration clause, largely for two reasons: (1) the notice of agreement to terms, in grey font on black background, was difficult to notice on a smartphone screen, especially in comparison to other screen content in larger and more contrasting font on the payment page, and (2) although highly visible in bold white font on black background, the phrase in the rectangular box would not be readily recognizable as a link to the terms because it was not in the underlined blue font customary for hyperlinks.

If you synthesize *Meyer* and *Cullinane,* are you satisfied that the factual differences justify the different results? In other words, would the same court, applying the same contract rules, find mutual assent in *Meyer* but not in *Cullinane*? Alternatively, do you conclude instead that the court in *Cullinane* applied a more demanding standard for notice than in *Meyer*? *See also Starke v. SquareTrade, Inc.*, 913 F.3d 279 (2d Cir. 2019) (comparing *Meyer* with other Second Circuit cases).

3. Existing Agreement to Allow Unilateral Modification

Should a court enforce a clause in an existing contract, such as the following section 19, which purports to permit one party to unilaterally change the terms of a contract during the term of the contract, and to bind the other party to the changes without more?

> 19. This Agreement is binding upon you at the time you enroll ... in a Program. We may, from time to time, change this Agreement ... by adding, modifying or deleting any term or condition ("Changed Term"). A Changed Term will be effective upon posting to our Website, although we may provide you notice by other means.

4. Contracts by Computer

Suppose a discount department store chain has entered into a framework agreement with a supplier of a popular product. In the framework agreement, the parties agree to install software that will allow the computer systems of each party to convey assent to future sales contracts, at a unit price that is set for a year but can vary with different ranges of quantities ordered. The department store's computer system will track the sales, returns, and remaining inventory of the product; when the inventory falls to a predesignated level set for that time of year, it will send a purchase order to the supplier's computer system, which will check its own inventory and its outstanding orders from other customers and then will automatically respond whether the supplier can fill the order within the time frame designated in the purchase order.

If the department store's computer sends an order on behalf of the store to purchase 100 units for delivery to a designated retail location within 21 days at the predetermined price, and the supplier's computer responds that the supplier will fill the order within that time frame, have the computers created a sales contract for 100 units? If the department store manager later refuses to take delivery on the ground that the store does not need the product, has the department store breached a contract? If so, is it a contract formed by the computers on one computer's acceptance of the other computer's purchase order? Alternatively, did the department store and the supplier form a sales contract for 100 units by entering into the earlier framework agreement and agreeing at that time to buy and sell at times and quantities to be determined in the future by the operation of software and without further human intervention in the contracting process? *See* CAL. CIV. CODE § 1633.14(a)(1) (West 2011) ("A contract may be formed by the interaction of electronic agents of the parties, even if no individual was aware of or reviewed the electronic agents' actions or the resulting terms and agreements.").

Will the store manager retain the ability to reject shipment and refuse payment if the software adopted by the parties automatically transfers payment from the department store to the supplier once the supplier's computer uses electronic means to confirm the nature, quantity, and location of the goods at the department store's loading dock? For explorations of questions like these, see Scott A. McKinny, Rachel Landy, and Rachel Wilka, *Smart Contracts, Blockchain, and the New Frontier of Transactional Law,* 13 WASH. J.L. TECH. & ARTS 313 (2018), and Mykyta Sokolov, *Smart Legal Contract as a Future of Contract Enforcement*, https://ssrn.com/abstract=3208292 (2018).

Suppose a firm purchased or developed a system of hardware and software with advanced artificial intelligence and then gave it a contracting *objective* — such as maximizing revenue for the firm with respect to sales of a designated product — while enabling it to respond electronically to orders from customers at any time and on any terms consistent with the designated objective, or to initiate such bargaining. If the artificially intelligent system pursues its objective by independently setting or negotiating prices, is it acting as an independent contracting entity? Should the firm be bound by the agreements formed by the artificial intelligence and customers of the firm?

VII. Escape Hatch — Intent Not to Be Bound

A. *Expressed* Intent Not to be Legally Bound

Under the objective theory of contracts, a reasonable person would not interpret another party to be committing to an enforceable contract if that party expressly denied willingness to be legally bound. True, a court would not readily allow a party to escape contractual liability simply by framing a proposal in a way that usurps the court's responsibility to declare and apply the law. For example, assent to the following proposal would not clearly avoid the application of contract law if one of the parties later decided to seek enforcement: "If you agree to pay me $3,000 on completion, I'll paint your house by the end of the month, and let's also agree that state law will not enforce this deal." On the other hand, statements that reflect an intention to delay or avoid commitment can prevent communications from amounting to an offer and acceptance.

Chapter 4, Section V ends with an exploration of letters of intent, in which parties typically do not intend to create a binding contract on the main deal, although they often intend to create some preliminary mutual obligations regarding future negotiations on the main deal. In this chapter, we will explore oral agreements that the parties intend to put in writing, express disclaimers in documents, and social contexts in which parties arguably do not intend legal consequences.

Exercise 2.14 — Oral Contract or Just Preliminary Negotiations Leading to a Written Contract?

> Where it is clearly understood that the terms of a proposed contract, though tentatively agreed on, shall be reduced to writing and signed before it shall be considered as complete and binding on the parties, there is no final contract until that is done.

Universal Products Co., Inc. v. Emerson, 36 Del. 553, 179 A. 387, 394 (1935). This issue is factually oriented, requiring an inquiry into the parties' apparent intentions either to conclude a contract immediately on oral agreement, or to view the oral agreement as tentative until the parties can approve and sign a written agreement. *See R.G. Group, Inc. v. Horn & Hardart Co.*, 751 F.2d 69, 74 (2d Cir. 1984).

Have the parties reached agreement in either of the following fact situations at the conclusion of the quoted dialogue? Why do the facts suggest the possibility of preliminary negotiations rather than an offer and acceptance? In which case is it more likely that the parties concluded a contract, even if at least one of them refuses to sign the written version the next day? Why?

1. Let's See It in Writing First

After X and Y have closed the gaps between their negotiating positions on all the essential terms of a consulting contract, they make the following statements:

> X: "So, do we have a deal on these terms?"
>
> Y: "It looks like we are in agreement, but I'd like to put it down in writing first, take a last look at it, and then sign it."
>
> X: "Yeah, that sounds good. I'll have it typed up today, ready for us to look over and sign tomorrow at 9 a.m. if you are free then."

2. Let's Get Some Written Copies

After X and Y have closed the gaps between their negotiating positions on all the essential terms of a consulting contract, they make the following statements:

> X: "So, do we have a deal on these terms?"
>
> Y: "Yes, we do. Can we get a written copy for our files?"
>
> X: "Sure. I'll have it typed up today, and we can sign the copies tomorrow at 9 a.m."

Exercise 2.15 — Disclaimers in Employee Manuals

An employer's policies in its employee manual might be communicated in such a way that it joins with other writings and oral statements to convey the employers' promises in the employment contract. Specifically, statements in a policy manual about job security, if interpreted to be contractual promises, could override the usual legal presumption that an employment contract of indefinite duration is terminable at the will of either party (which generally means terminable for any reason that does not violate a statute or important public policy).

In 1984, as a matter of common law, the Arizona Supreme Court recognized that statements of policy made by an employer in an employee manual could amount to promises that become incorporated into the employment contract, depending on the specific language and circumstances; consequently, the employer might be legally bound to adhere, for example, to a stated policy that permits the employer to fire the employee only for certain causes rather than at the employer's unrestricted will. *Leikvold v. Valley View Community Hospital,* 141 Ariz. 544, 548, 688 P.2d 170, 174 (1984). The court hastened to add, however, that the employer could avoid such obligations simply by stating "clearly and conspicuously" in the manual "that the manual is not part of the employment contract" and thus that the employer is free to change its discretionary policies at any time. *Id.* A reasonable person reading such a disclaimer would conclude that the policy manual is simply stating current policies, which the employer is voluntarily advancing, but which are not incorporated into the employment contract and thus do not bind the employer.

In 1996, the Arizona legislature enacted "The Employment Protection Act," which superseded common law standards with the following new statutory rules. How does this statute change the analysis of an employee's claim that an employee manual sets forth enforceable promises as part of the employment contract? As a matter of policy, do you prefer the common law rule or the statutory modification? Why?

> ***The Employment Protection Act***
>
> The public policy of this state is that:
>
> 1. The employment relationship is contractual in nature.
> 2. The employment relationship is severable at the pleasure of either the employee or the employer unless both the employee and the employer have signed a written contract to the contrary setting forth that the employment relationship shall remain in effect for a specified duration of time or otherwise expressly restricting the right of either party to terminate the employment relationship. Both the employee and the employer must sign this written contract, or this written contract must be set forth in the employment handbook or manual or any similar document distributed to the employee, if that document expresses the intent that it is a contract of employment, ...

ARIZ. REV. STAT. ANN. § 23-1501 (2016).

B. Accord and Satisfaction

Suppose that Contractor has completed work for Owner, but the two parties have a good-faith dispute about how much is owed to the Contractor under an ambiguous provision of the contract. Contractor believes that $10,000 is due, while Owner believes that only $5,000 is still owed. The contractual deadline for payment will not expire for 30 days.

Owner might try to resolve this dispute by offering to enter into a settlement agreement that compromises their competing claims. Owner could convey this offer in a letter with the following statement: "I propose that we split the difference and agree that a payment of $7,500 will fully satisfy my remaining obligations under our consulting contract. Enclosed is a check for $7,500, which is made available to you only for the purpose of executing this compromise. To express your agreement, simply cash the check within seven days of receipt. Your doing so will show that you agree to $7,500 as full payment of my remaining debt to you. If you are not agreeable to that, please return the uncashed check, and we will resume our negotiations."

Contractor believes that he is owed $10,000. Accordingly, can he cash the check while disclaiming any intent to accept the settlement offer, deposit the $7,500, and continue to press his claim for an additional $2,500?

The majority common law rule responds in the negative: Contractor is bound by the settlement agreement if Contractor cashes the check, even if Contractor had written on the check that he had no intent to accept the offer of settlement. As master of the offer, Owner dictated that cashing the check was the means of expressing assent to the settlement offer, and Owner made the check available only for that purpose.

In fact, Owner could have accomplished the same result under the majority common law rule without the explanatory cover letter. Owner could have sent a check with a conspicuous notation on it that "Cashing this check constitutes acceptance of the amount of the check as full satisfaction of the payor's outstanding debt to the payee." Such a notation would likely convey an offer to settle the dispute regarding the debt, and the cashing of the check would: (1) express acceptance of the settlement offer ("accord") and thus (2) amount to collection of the full remaining debt ("satisfaction"). *See Vance v. Hammer*, 105 Ariz. 317, 319, 464 P.2d 340, 342 (1970). An accord and satisfaction through a negotiable instrument such as a check is now governed by UCC § 3-311 (2002), which largely follows the common law approach.

C. *Context* Reflecting Lack of Intent to be Legally Bound

Even absent an explicit disclaimer, some contexts and circumstances invite an interpretation that limits the reach of contractual promises. For example, courts are hesitant to interpret a doctor's predictions as promises that the medical treatment will bring about a particular result. If a doctor provides treatment and says, "You should have full range of movement and feel normal within a week," a reasonable patient normally would interpret that statement as simply a prediction of recovery, and not a contractual guarantee.

Of course, the provision of medical treatment in exchange for a payment, co-payment, or other consideration gives rise to a contractual relationship, and physicians can give a binding promise to provide a specific result under the common law if they do so very clearly. In the famous "hairy hand" case, for example, the court found that a doctor had stated a contractual promise that patient would return home after three or four days "with a good hand." *Hawkins v. McGee*, 84 N.H. 114, 146 A. 641 (1929). Contracts for medical procedures, however, are seldom interpreted to include promises guaranteeing particular results. *E.g.*, *Anglin v. Kleeman*, 140 N.H. 257, 665 A.2d 747 (1995) (finding that doctor's statement about knee being stronger after an operation, enabling a committed patient to play ball again, was an opinion and not a contractual promise).

In some contexts, mutual commitments are reasonably interpreted as agreements that create no contractual relationships at all. An agreement between two people to go out on a date, for example, normally is intended by both parties to have only social consequences and not legal ones. If such lack of contractual intent would be apparent to a reasonable person in light of all the circumstances, a court will not intervene to enforce the agreement but will leave the parties to sort out their social obligations on their own.

Nonetheless, it is entirely possible for parties to engage in serious bargaining in the context of a social or intimate relationship. It is common knowledge, for example, that parties who are engaged to be married often enter into premarital agreements in all seriousness and often with the representation of legal counsel. Such agreements typically state mutual decisions about the ownership of separate property that each spouse will bring to the marriage and about how property will be divided in the event of dissolution of the marriage. If these agreements otherwise meet common law or special statutory requirements for enforceability, courts will not deny enforcement simply because they arose in an intimate social context.

Exercise 2.16 — Dates or Engagements as Contracts?

1. Jilted at the High School Prom

On rare occasions, small claims courts have found that agreements to take someone on a particularly important and formal date, such as a high school prom, are reasonably interpreted as binding commitments, intended by the parties to have legal consequences. These courts may have been influenced by the fact that the jilted parties in broken prom dates had incurred expenses in preparation for the dates.

In a case from Florida in 1989, a jilted high school student was able to return her prom dress but sought damages to cover the cost of new shoes, flowers, and hair styling. She settled the case for a little more than $80. In 1990, a court awarded another young woman a bit less than $80 to cover her costs when her prom date opted instead to attend a rock concert.

As illustrated by the 1990 case, in the rare event that a court enforces an agreement to attend a social event, it typically limits recovery to the plaintiff's out-of-pocket reliance costs. Can you see why? How would the court put a monetary value on the jilted party's disappointed expectations? What precisely was the benefit of the bargain that the victim of the breach would have enjoyed had the promise been performed, and how would a court put a monetary value on that? (In Chapter 12, we will examine the limited circumstances in which the victim of breach of contract is entitled to damages for emotional distress.)

Do you agree with the settlement in the 1989 prom case and the judge's decision in the 1990 case, or do you believe that the law should have no application in such matters? We can safely assume that nearly all such social disappointments are dealt with privately, and that nearly all of the few claims brought before a court are dismissed. Only the rare cases that result in court enforcement, however, are likely to attract the attention of news media.

2. Denied the Red Carpet Treatment

Suppose that a celebrated actress, nominated for an academy award, agreed to take a popular singer to the awards ceremony and to exclusive parties afterwards. They are merely acquaintances, but their appearing together would generate enhanced publicity for both, and it would help the singer meet powerful industry executives who might help him realize his goal of landing a major movie role. If the actress breaches this commitment and takes another date, should a court enforce her promise by awarding damages to the jilted singer? Or should a court find that a reasonable person would understand that this agreement simply was not intended to have legal consequences and thus is not enforceable at all? Is this hypothetical date closer to a business deal than a purely social date? Should that matter?

As a preview of our study of definiteness and proof of damages, ponder this question: If a court decides to enforce the agreement, could it calculate the singer's expectation interest in the form of the value of the publicity and networking that he lost? Could it and should it calculate the lost profits associated with the additional sales of his musical recordings and tickets to his concerts that the publicity of the red carpet might have generated, and the revenue from any movie roles that the singer might have landed had he accompanied an established Hollywood star to the parties? Should it limit recovery to the singer's out-of-pocket costs in buying or renting an expensive designer tuxedo? (He wasn't sponsored by a designer.)

3. Engagement as Marriage Contract

Most states will enforce prenuptial agreements that divide property rights, at least if certain safeguards are met. More than half of the states have adopted some version of the Uniform Premarital and Marital Agreements Act (2012), which enforces such agreements, even without consideration, if the agreement is in writing and if, among other things, it meets requirements relating to disclosure and an opportunity to obtain legal advice.

But what about the engagement itself? It turns out that the early common law of many states recognized an enforceable contract arising out of an affirmative response to a proposal of marriage. *See, e.g., Burton v. Valentine*, 60 Ariz. 518, 141 P.2d 847 (1943) (affirming jury verdict for breach of contract to marry). For an example of a complaint stating a claim for breach of promise to marry, only slightly edited, see Charles R. Calleros & Kimberly Y.W. Holst, Legal Method and Writing II: Trial and Appellate Advocacy, Contracts, and Correspondence 248–51 (8th ed. 2018).

During the twentieth century, legislatures in many states eliminated the contract claim for breach of an agreement to marry. *E.g.*, Cal. Civ. Code § 43.5 (West 2007) ("No cause of action arises for: … [b]reach of promise of marriage."); *McGrath v. Dockendorf*, 280 Va. 834, 838, 793 S.E. 336, 338 (2016). [But these statutes do not necessarily bar an action to recover gifts made in contemplation of marriage, the success of which could depend on whether the parties intended a token, such as an engagement ring, to be a permanent and unconditional gift or to be conditioned on the marriage going through. *See id.*] A few other states have legislatively confirmed the enforceability of agreements to marry, although some of these statutes limit the remedy for breach. *Compare* Okla. Stat. Ann. tit. 23, § 40 (2011) (leaving damages to the discretion of the jury) *with* Tenn. Code Ann. §§ 36-3-401 to 36-3-404 (LexisNexis 2017) (requiring certain proof of marriage agreement, and limiting remedy in some cases to financial losses).

If you represented a plaintiff in an action to enforce a contract in which the parties agreed to marry, in a state that permitted such an action without limitations on remedies, would you file an action for specific performance if your client demanded that the marriage go forward? How would you try to prove expectation interest if the client instead wanted to get the "benefit of the bargain" in money damages? Should a court or legislature limit recovery to reliance costs, such as the costs of quitting a job and moving?

More fundamentally, in your opinion, should engagements be viewed as enforceable contracts, or as purely social commitments that are not within the reach of the law? Should it depend on factors such as the formality of the engagement, or on whether the jilted party has incurred reliance costs? If you were a judge on the state Supreme Court, would you recognize a claim for breach of an agreement to marry, or would you abandon early common law precedent that recognizes a contract in such cases? As a legislator, would you support a bill that would eliminate a claim for breach of contract to marry that is currently recognized under the state's common law? Would you support a bill that codified a common law claim for breach of contract to marry, while statutorily limiting the recoverable damages?

VIII. Summary

- Although many courts still invoke the phrase "meeting of the minds," which suggests a subjective theory of evaluating contractual intent, the objective theory predominates on the issue of contract formation. Courts or juries will assess intent to enter into a contract on the basis of the parties' outward manifestations.
- An offer is a proposal that expresses such definite commitment to a contract that it gives the offeree the power to create a contract by expressing assent, without the need for further assent from the offeror. Under the objective theory of contracts, a fact-finder will ask how a reasonable person in the position of the offeree would interpret the offeror's statements. If the offer contains terms limiting the offeror's potential obligations and liabilities, it usually is more reasonable to interpret it to reflect a commitment by the offeror to go forward.
- Like other forms of price quote, a newspaper ad usually is too general to amount to an offer; however, nothing prevents an ad from containing all the necessary specificity, limitations on performance, and expressions of commitment to meet the standards for an offer. As with most legal questions, the answer depends on the facts of each case and how the legal rule applies to the facts.
- As the master of the offer, the offeror can dictate—with some limitations—the required manner of acceptance. To some extent, the requirements for acceptance, including whether notice is required before the contract is formed, depend in part on whether the contract is formed as a bilateral contract (by a return promise) or unilateral contract (by the offeree's completed performance), which also may be controlled by the terms of the offer.

- Sometimes conduct can express a return promise, forming a bilateral contract. In all cases, however, the response to an offer will amount to an acceptance only if it is unequivocal and if it unambiguously responds to the offer.
- In some circumstances, parties to an agreement can avoid contract obligations by making it clear that their agreement is not intended to have legal consequences. For example, they might reach preliminary agreement but express the intent to delay contract formation until a more formal document is reviewed and signed or until other parties can approve the deal.
- Based on context, courts usually find that parties who agreed to participate in casual social activities did not intend their agreement to have legal effect. If so, the social agreement will not be viewed as a legally enforceable contract. However, agreements to marry were once viewed as more than purely social obligations and were widely enforced under the common law. Legislatures in some states have eliminated actions for breach of agreement to marry, while facilitating the enforcement of premarital agreements that address the rights and obligations during marriage, such as the division of property. Other states have codified the cause of action for breach of a marriage agreement, often with limitations on remedies.

IX. Perspectives

A. Historical Note on the Objective Theory of Contract Formation

Consideration as Contract: A Secular Natural Law of Contracts
12 TEX. REV. L. & POL. 267–327 (2008) by Nicholas C. Dranias
[footnotes omitted]

....

A. The Rise of the Will Theory of Contracts

The will theory dominated Anglo-American contract law during the latter quarter of the eighteenth and most of the nineteenth century. During the theory's prime, an actual "meeting of the minds" between the parties was regarded as essential to the formation of an enforceable contract. When determining whether the parties' minds met, courts applying the will theory focused on the actual intent of the promisor and the actual understanding of the promisee. Manifestations of agreement were interpreted in conformity with the parties' actual intent and understanding. Accordingly, evidence of "subjective" knowledge and intent was admitted to prove or disprove the existence of such a "meeting of the minds."

....

b. The Objective Theory Dominates ...

Although Judge Learned Hand was declaring victory for the objective theory in 1911, there is little evidence that the theory was widely accepted until the publication of the Restatement (First) of Contracts [in 1932]. Thereafter, an identifiable trend towards acceptance of the objective theory (and the concurrent rejection of the will theory) is evidenced by the holdings of many state supreme courts, including the Minnesota State Supreme Court. Moreover, most states have adopted the Uniform Commercial Code, which has been widely interpreted as upholding the objective theory of contracts. Accordingly, there is a consensus among legal scholars that the objective theory dominates contract law. Many jurists agree. In *Skycom Corp. v. Telstar Corp.*, for example, Justice Easterbrook held, "Walters [one of the defendants] stoutly maintains that he subjectively intended to be bound and he wants to invite a jury to infer the same.... Yet 'intent' does not invite a tour through Walters' cranium, with Walters as the guide."

When compared with such strident assertions, however, some modern legal theorists remain relatively coy about the objective theory's dominance. A comment to the Restatement (Second) of Contracts, for example, states, "The parties to most contracts give actual as well as apparent assent, but it is clear that a mental reservation of a party to a bargain does not impair the obligation he purports to undertake." This coyness is reflected in the fact that many courts continue to use the "meeting of the minds" rhetoric of the will theory, while ostensibly applying the objective theory. Perhaps, it also reflects uncertainty over the objective theory's grasp on contract law. [*Note from Professor Calleros*: Subjective intent may be relevant to post-formation issues, such as interpretation or avoidance for mutual mistake, but the objective standard governs contract formation.]

B. Learning the Law

Reflect on the way you have learned the law of offer and acceptance. If you can analyze whether a newspaper ad is an offer—or if you can at least identify arguments for either side of that issue—did you gain that facility mostly by memorizing a verbal test, or mostly by studying and comparing real and hypothetical cases in which courts found some ads to be offers and others to be only invitations to submit an offer?

One author compares the study of law to the way a child learns to place objects into categories. Robert M. Lloyd, *Zen and the Art of Contract Formation*, 39 J. Leg. Ed. 185 (1989). A child doesn't learn to identify animals as "dogs" by memorizing a verbal definition from a parent. Instead, from a very young age, the child can associate the category of "dog" with certain kinds of animals because a parent has pointed to animals from time to time and remarked, "look at the dog!" After repeated "cases" of seeing and hearing an animal identified as a dog by a parent, the child begins to recognize attributes of animals that qualify as dogs, even though dogs turn out to be quite diverse in size, shape, and color. Similarly, after repeated cases of seeing and hearing an animal that a parent refers to as a "cat," the child learns to distinguish cats from dogs, even though they share some attributes, such as walking on four legs, sporting a tail, and being covered with fur.

These insights about the case method of study will apply as well to our next topic of study, "consideration," and to many other topics in your law school courses.

Exercise 2.17 — Practice Essay Exams

1. Introduction to IRAC — Practice Exam

The following simplified practice exam question is inspired by the more complicated facts of *Donovan v. RRL Corp.*, appearing earlier in this chapter. Take this exam on your own, at a time and place that are free of distractions. Do not review that case now, and do not limit your analysis to its discussion. Although a California statute regarding automobile marketing figured into the analysis of the actual case, for purposes of this examination you can assume that no statutory provisions apply. Moreover, you can apply general common law rules; you are not expected to know any special case law of California or any other jurisdiction.

Most law school essay exams invite a discussion in a form represented by the acronym IRAC. After carefully reading the exam question, you must determine what legal issues are raised by the facts. Issues are questions about how the law applies to the facts, questions over which attorneys could reasonably argue. You will then discuss each issue in a separate IRAC by identifying the **I**ssue, summarizing the **R**ule that helps to resolve the issue, **A**pplying the rule to the facts, and reaching a reasonable **C**onclusion.

If you are not ready to write a full essay answer, limit your analysis to answering the following questions: (1) Which facts raise some uncertainty about whether Riley Motors is legally bound by its newspaper ad, giving rise to a dispute? (2) What legal issues could be reasonably debated by the parties in light of that uncertainty? (3) What specific rule applies to each such issue? (4) With respect to each issue, what factual arguments support and what arguments oppose a finding that Riley is bound by its newspaper ad? Try to find arguments for both sides. You can compare your abbreviated analysis with the full sample answer in Appendix 3.

Practice Exam Question:

On September 14, a local newspaper, the Daily Pilot, ran the following ad placed by Riley Motors, a dealer of new and used cars: "Now at Riley Motors: 2016 Jaguar XJ6; 25,000 miles; great condition; silver. Out it goes for $30,000! Upgrades and extras available at additional cost. Financing available at low rates. Hurry, this will go fast." Jana Donovan read the ad over breakfast and recognized the selling price as a tremendous bargain, quite substantially below market price for a car of that model and condition.

Jana was waiting at Riley Motors when it opened for business on September 14. She found the owner, Rick Riley, and expressed her willingness to write a check for $30,000 to buy the 2016 Jaguar. Rick got red in the face and explained that the purchase price for the 2016 model actually was $50,000, but that he could sell Jana a 2013 Jaguar XJ6, with 40,000 miles, for $30,000. Riley Motors refused to sell the 2016 model for the advertised price.

An examination of the events showed that no one at Riley Motors had intended to advertise the 2016 car for sale at $30,000. A few days earlier, Rick Riley had been in the process of preparing text for a newspaper ad for a 2013 Jaguar XJ6 with an advertised price of $30,000. Rick then learned, however, that his dealership had just acquired the 2016 Jaguar, with only 25,000 miles, and Rick decided to advertise that car instead. In a rush to meet a submission deadline with the newspaper, Rick then changed the description of the car in the advertising text, but he forgot to change the advertised price from $30,000 to $50,000. The Daily Pilot ran the ad as submitted by Riley Motors and as described in the first paragraph above. No one at Riley Motors, however, had ever intended to sell the 2016 Jaguar for $30,000 or to advertise the car for sale at that price.

Jana wants to sue Rick Riley in his capacity as sole owner and manager of Riley Motors. Discuss any claims that might arise in such a suit, but only to the extent that the law and facts raise them as issues subject to reasonable dispute, and only the extent that we have studied them in this chapter. Although the transaction described in the problem is for a sale of goods, you can assume for this question that no provision of the UCC or any other statute applies to the issues, so you exclusively apply common law principles that we have studied in class, consistent with the directive of UCC § 1-103(b) (2001) (unless displaced by provisions of the UCC, common law principles will apply to sales transactions, filling gaps left by the UCC).

2. Previous Midterm Exam

Sophie has built a successful business out of her home, in which she uses recycled materials to manufacture trendy purses, handbags, backpacks, and shoulder bags, all under the trademarked brand name "Sofi-Sacks." Dean, the owner of Earth Friendly Fashions, has been negotiating with Sophie to purchase her business, including her designs, brand name, manufacturing techniques, and proprietary information about suppliers, customers, and pricing. Sophie has also received expressions of interest from James, whom she has not met but who operates a store for clothing and accessories.

On Monday, Sophie and Dean worked late into the night trying to work out the details of a sale of Sophie's business to Dean. Their discussions shifted back and forth between various parts of the deal. By the end of the night, they had written notes on four sheets of paper, each with terms of a different part of the sale, such as brand name on one sheet and manufacturing techniques on another.

At 10 pm, after hours of rejecting each other's proposals and coming closer to common ground, Sophie was confident that she could name terms that were acceptable to her and would be acceptable to Dean. She circled some terms at the bottom of each of the four sheets, showed them to Dean, and had the following conversation:

> *Sophie:* "I'm done for the night. I think you should take these terms and take off with this business."
>
> *Dean:* "Shouldn't we put it all together in a nice, neat document?"
>
> *Sophie:* "Sure. I can do that tomorrow. Right now, I just need to know whether we have a deal, because I have an appointment with another interested buyer tomorrow at lunch, and I need to know whether my business is still for sale or is sold to you."
>
> *Dean:* "Okay, let me take a copy of these pages and think on it tonight and get back to you before noon tomorrow."
>
> *Sophie:* "Good. I'm ready to sell on these terms, so if you agree, let me know tomorrow before 11 am. I'll be on the move, so you'll need to call me on my iPhone. If you approve these terms, just call me and tell me that we have a deal."

Sophie made copies of the four pages with circled terms and gave the originals to Dean. The next day, at 10 am, Dean sent an email to Sophie's email account from his computer, with the subject heading: "Approving Your Proposal." The body of the email stated: "I approve of all the terms on your notes. Let me know when you have combined the terms into a single formal document so that we can check it over, sign it, and get copies. I look forward to carrying your business to new heights."

Sophie opened up and read the email from her iPhone. At lunch, however, the other potential buyer offered Sophie much better terms than she had negotiated with Dean, so she denies any obligation to Dean.

You may assume that the four pages included terms that were sufficiently complete and definite that they constituted an offer from Sophie to sell her business to Dean, and you should not address that topic as an issue. Analyze only whether Dean accepted Sophie's offer. If you identify more than one issue regarding acceptance, analyze each issue in a separate IRAC. Apply general common law principles.

Rather than attempt to write a full essay answer at this point, answer the following questions: (1) Which facts raise some uncertainty about acceptance? (2) What kinds of acceptance problems are raised by the facts? (3) What specific rule applies to each such acceptance issue? (4) With respect to each kind of acceptance problem, what factual arguments support or oppose finding acceptance? Try to find arguments for both sides. You can compare your abbreviated analysis with the full sample answer in Appendix 3.

Chapter 3

Consideration (Bargained-For Exchange)

I. Overview

"No legal system has ever been reckless enough to make all promises enforceable." E. Allan Farnsworth, CONTRACTS § 1.5, at 11 (4th ed. Aspen Publ. 2004). Instead, legal systems have fashioned a variety of doctrines to identify the kinds of promises that justify application of the enforcement mechanisms of the courts. In the common law system, the term "consideration" has been used for several centuries to identify the circumstances in which a promise will be legally enforceable.

The consideration doctrine has been employed to exclude enforcement of a promise so casually made that the promisor ought to be allowed to change his mind without legal consequences. "Words of promise are not enough, there must be something [from the other party] promised 'in consideration' to show that the words are to be taken seriously and that there is substance and meaning to the words." Gary Watt, EQUITY STIRRING : THE STORY OF JUSTICE BEYOND LAW 95 (Hart Pub. Oxford 2009). As you study consideration, ask yourself whether the common law has devised an effective test for distinguishing between promises that deserve enforcement and those whose performance or breach should be left to an individual's conscience.

Dougherty v. Salt

227 N.Y. 200, 125 N.E. 94 (1919)
New York Court of Appeals

Cardozo, J.

¶ 1 The plaintiff, a boy of eight years, received from his aunt, the defendant's testatrix, a promissory note for $3,000, payable at her death or before. Use was made of a printed form, which contains the words "value received." How the note came to be given was explained by the boy's guardian, who was a witness for his ward. The aunt was visiting her nephew.

¶ 2 [After the aunt stated her intention to benefit her nephew, a] blank was then produced, filled out, and signed. The aunt handed the note to her nephew, with these words: "You have always done for me, and I have signed this note for you. Now, do not lose it. Some day it will be valuable."

¶ 3 The trial judge submitted to the jury the question whether there was any consideration for the promised payment. Afterwards, he set aside the verdict in favor of the plaintiff, and dismissed the complaint. The Appellate Division, by a divided court, reversed the judgment of dismissal, and reinstated the verdict on the ground that the note was sufficient evidence of consideration.

¶ 4 We reach a different conclusion. The inference of consideration to be drawn from the form of the note has been so overcome and rebutted as to leave no question for a jury.... The note was the voluntary and unenforcible promise of an executory gift.... The aunt was not paying a debt. She was conferring a bounty. *Fink v. Cox*, 18 Johns. 145, 9 Am. Dec. 191. The promise was neither offered nor accepted with any other purpose.... A note so given is not made for "value received," however its maker may have labeled it. The formula of the printed blank becomes, in the light of the conceded facts, a mere erroneous conclusion, which cannot overcome the inconsistent conclusion of the law.... The plaintiff through his own witness, has explained the genesis of the promise, and consideration has been disproved.... We hold, therefore, that the verdict of the jury was contrary to law, and that the trial judge was right in setting it aside....

¶ 5 The judgment of the Appellate Division should be reversed, and the judgment of the Trial Term modified by granting a new trial, and, as modified, affirmed, with costs in all courts to abide the event.

A. Consideration as a Bargained-For Exchange

In the fourteenth century, the English common law would enforce a promise in an action on "covenant" if the promise was set forth in a formal writing, to which the promisor had affixed the image of a personal stamp, imprinted in hot wax. This formality served as good evidence of the promise. It also showed that the promisor had not made the promise lightly or casually but had committed to it with serious intentions.

Another early form of action, "debt," however, rested not on formalities but on the substantive requirement of one party's prior delivery of a "quid pro quo." For example, a seller would have an action in debt based on his delivery of goods for which the recipient had promised to pay but had failed to pay. In the centuries of judicial decisions that followed, the common law focused increasingly on substance over formality. Eventually, the word "consideration" gained prominence as the term of art denoting this substantive element of contract formation.

Consideration now revolves around an exchange between the parties: a promise for a promise, or a promise for a performance, each "bargained-for" in the sense that each was the inducement for the other. You might say that each promise or performance was given "in consideration" of the other. The word "consideration," however, does not convey a clear image of the elements of the bargain theory. As we shall see, the term "bargained-for exchange" is a more descriptive shorthand term for the analysis now applied by the courts. If you like, you can start with the term "consideration" and then recognize that the current predominant definition of consideration is a "bargained-for exchange."

When you see "bargained-for exchange," you should think of two basic elements:

- an "exchange"
- that is "bargained for."

See Restatement (Second) of Contracts §71 (1981).

1. The Requirement of an Exchange

The modern definition of consideration is satisfied only if two or more parties exchange things, typically a promise or set of promises exchanged for another promise or set of promises. For example, a general contractor could promise to construct an office building according to an architect's specifications in exchange for an owner's promise to make progress payments at various stages of the construction. The parties have formed this bilateral contract on the exchange of promises, and they will both be obligated to perform those promises at specified times in the future.

Sometimes one or more promises are exchanged for a complete performance, such as an owner's promise to pay a reward in exchange for someone's completed performance of finding and returning lost property. In this example, a recipient of the reward offer could accept it by completing the performance of finding and returning the lost property. At that moment, the contract would be formed on the exchange of the completed performance for the promise to pay, so that only the owner's promise to pay the reward must still be performed after contract formation.

The requirement of an exchange, however, *is not satisfied by a promise by one party to make a gift to another.* True, if you actually transfer a gift of personal property to a friend who accepts the gift, the legal right to that property passes to the friend as a matter of property law, and you cannot invoke contract law to reclaim the gift. However, if you have not yet transferred the gift, but have only promised to do so, the common law of contracts generally will not enforce this "gratuitous promise" because it lacks consideration.[1] *See, e.g., Flanders v. Blandy*, 45 Ohio St. 108, 12 N.E. 321 (1887).

2. Reciprocal Inducement — The Exchange Must Be Bargained For

This element of consideration does not require extensive bargaining in the sense of negotiations. A contract can be made with a single proposal on one side and an expression of agreement on the other.

1. In Chapter 4, we will study a limited exception to the refusal to enforce gratuitous promises, in a doctrine popularly called promissory estoppel.

Instead, the term "bargained-for" refers to a relationship between the things exchanged: the parties exchanged one for the other, so that each thing exchanged was an inducement for the other. The promise of a counter-performance need not be the sole or even main inducement for one's own promise, so long as it is a genuine inducement that combines with others. We will study this element of consideration under the label "reciprocal inducement."

3. *Questions to Consider*

While working through this chapter, consider the following questions:

- Why should the common law generally limit enforcement to promises exchanged in a bargain? What policies support such a limitation? What policies support the approach of some civil law countries, like France, which will enforce a one-sided promise to make a gift?
- Does the requirement of a performance or a promise require proof of a "detriment" suffered by the party who gives the performance or promise?
- What kinds of problems might cause an act or forbearance to fall short of a performance?
- What kinds of statements fall short of a valid promise? To what extent can a promise be inferred from conduct and statements on other topics, even though the promise itself is not clearly expressed?
- How does the traditional requirement of a "benefit" in the exchange give way to the more nuanced requirement of reciprocal inducement?
- How does one distinguish an *inducement*, necessary to a bargained-for exchange, from a *motive* for making a gratuitous promise? Doesn't the promisor always have a motive for making every promise, even a promise to give a gift to another person?
- How does the requirement of reciprocal inducement help to explain why courts do not find consideration in a past performance, a conditional gratuitous promise, or a purported consideration that is really a sham?
- Is the consideration requirement satisfied in a one-sided modification of an existing contract? What is the current state of the common law pre-existing duty rule?

B. Comparing Common Law and Civil Law

In light of the common law emphasis on an exchange, our study of consideration will largely be a process of distinguishing one-sided gratuitous promises from certain kinds of exchanges. In civil law countries, by contrast, even gratuitous promises can be legally enforceable if the parties have consented to the transfer and if the transfer is supported by a valid motive or "cause." (In 2016, France reformed its civil code, deleting any mention of the requirement of "cause" and increasing the contrast with the common law consideration doctrine.)

True, in some U.S. states, putting an agreement in writing will create a presumption that the agreement satisfies the consideration requirement. *See, e.g.*, ARIZ. REV. STAT. ANN. §44-121 (2013) ("Every contract in writing imports a consideration."). Nonetheless, presumptions can be rebutted by contrary evidence, just as the false recital of "value received" was rebutted in *Dougherty v. Salt.*

Some have argued that the common law's reluctance to enforce gratuitous promises is based on the view that new wealth is much more likely to be created through exchanges than through the transfer of a promised gift from one to another. Robert A. Hillman & Maureen A. O'Rourke, *Rethinking Consideration in the Electronic Age*, 61 HASTINGS L.J. 311, 320 (2009) (describing this as the most convincing of justifications offered by contracts scholar Lon Fuller). Civil law countries such as France, however, are more concerned with recognizing the moral duty to keep a promise if voluntarily made by one with capacity and autonomy. Barry Nicholas, THE FRENCH LAW OF CONTRACT 118 (2d ed. Clarendon Press Oxford 1992) (referring to the "moral principle that contracts should be observed").

As you study the materials on consideration, ask yourself which approach you favor. Would it be simpler and more satisfying if the common law enforced any promise made with intent to be bound, regardless whether it is part of a bargained-for exchange? Or does the concept of an exchange provide a good test for excluding promises that do not warrant the application of judicial resources and thus are best left to the conscience and good reputation of the promisor?

For reasons that will soon become apparent, consideration as a requirement for contract formation is routinely satisfied in commercial transactions and thus is not frequently litigated. Moreover, we will see in Chapter 6 that the Uniform Commercial Code eliminates the consideration requirement in two narrow contexts. Finally, in Chapter 4 we will study the doctrine of promissory estoppel, which provides a remedy to prevent injustice resulting from foreseeable reliance on a gratuitous promise. Still, when neither promissory estoppel nor a statutory basis for enforcement of a promise applies, consideration remains a fundamental feature in common law countries, and one that helps set our legal system apart from those in civil law countries. Accordingly, it is a topic worthy of serious inquiry.

C. Benefit and Detriment; Exchange with Reciprocal Inducement

Partly because of early forms of action under English common law that predated modern bargain theory (summarized in the Historical Perspective in Part V near the end of this chapter), judges often have equated consideration with a benefit given or detriment suffered by the party on each side of an exchange. *See, e.g.*, *USLife Title Co. of Ariz. v. Gutkin*, 152 Ariz. 349, 354, 732 P.2d 579, 584 (App.

1986). In routine commercial transactions, this rather crude cliché works well enough, even if we attach the ordinary meanings to the terms "benefit" and "detriment." For example, the buyer in a sales transaction provides a tangible benefit to the seller by paying for the goods, and the buyer suffers a tangible detriment by divesting itself of that sum; the same can be said about the seller's delivery of valuable goods to the buyer.

In less routine cases, however, the bargain theory may require a more nuanced analysis than one suggested by the terms "benefit" or "detriment" in the usual sense of those words. Accordingly, the Restatement rejects the notion that consideration requires a "gain, advantage, or benefit" to one party or a "loss, disadvantage, or detriment" to the other. RESTATEMENT (SECOND) OF CONTRACTS § 79(a) (1981). Cases that require this depth of understanding arise infrequently, but they help to illustrate the complete and precise requirements of modern consideration doctrine. One case in point is *Hamer v. Sidway*, litigation arising out of an exchange between family members.

1. *Hamer v. Sidway*

In *Hamer*, an uncle made an announcement at a family celebration in 1869, promising to pay his teenage nephew the sum of $5,000 if the nephew refrained from engaging in certain vices—drinking, using tobacco, swearing, and playing cards or billiards for money—for several years until the nephew reached the age of 21. At this time, it apparently was lawful for the nephew to engage in at least some of these activities between the ages of 16 and 21. *Hamer v. Sidway*, 27 N.E. 256 (N.Y. 1891). It's not certain whether the uncle was requesting a promise or a return performance from the nephew as the means of acceptance; however, the court noted that the nephew "assented thereto" at the celebration, *id.*, suggesting that agreement was reached on their exchange of promises on that day. Moreover, in a letter to the nephew shortly after the nephew completed the performance, the uncle referred to "the promise made to me several years ago." *Id.* Accordingly, let's assume that the uncle and nephew reached agreement through the exchange of promises at the family celebration.[2]

But did their agreement on that day amount to an enforceable contract supported by consideration? In the lawsuit to enforce the uncle's promise to pay $5,000, the defendant (the executor of the uncle's estate) argued that the nephew gave no consideration for that promise. Specifically, the executor argued that the nephew's promised forbearances did not bring any benefit to the uncle, nor did they cause the nephew to suffer any detriment, because his avoiding the designated vices was beneficial to him. *Id.* at 257.

---

2. As discussed in Chapter 8, Section II.A, if we assume that the nephew had not yet reached the age of contractual capacity when the uncle made his promise, he nonetheless could ratify the contract when he reached the age of majority, at the time of completion of his performance.

In its opinion issued in 1891, the New York Court of Appeals (the highest court in the state) rejected the defendant's premise that "benefit" and "detriment"—at least in the usual senses of those words—precisely defined the requirements of consideration. With respect to the necessity of showing a detriment to the nephew, the court stated that it need not "speculate on the effort which may have been required to give up those stimulants." *Id.* The nephew's return promise was for a valid performance (in the form of a forbearance) because he promised to restrict his freedom to engage in legal activities in the future. *Id.* Thus, the nephew was not simply expecting to receive a gift but had promised his own performance. It was not legally significant whether the nephew's performance would be easy or difficult for him, or whether it would cause him to suffer some sort of loss or other detriment in that sense.

The court also hinted at another element of bargain theory. Once the court found that the nephew had performed by restricting his lawful freedom of action, it found it unnecessary to determine whether the uncle benefited from the nephew's forbearance in the usual sense of "benefit." However, the court did recognize that the promises of the uncle and his nephew must be connected to one another in a way that is consistent with the notion that each party's promise was "bargained for." The court quoted an author of a contracts treatise to the effect that the nephew satisfied his half of the consideration requirement if he limited his legal freedom of action "as an inducement for the [uncle's] promise." *Id.*

Thus, to use the modern language of the Restatement, the bargain theory does not require a court to find that each party benefited from the other's performance in some conventional, tangible way, so long as each party genuinely sought the other's promised performance, so that each party was induced by the other's promise to give his own promise or performance. This is what we mean by a promise or performance being "bargained for." RESTATEMENT (SECOND) OF CONTRACTS § 71(2) (1981). This is often known as the requirement of reciprocal inducement. This concept received a great boost from the writings and judicial opinions of Oliver Wendell Holmes more than a century ago. The concept does not often appear in the case law, however, because it is seldom contested in light of the obvious economic inducements in routine commercial transactions.

We will explore the concept of reciprocal inducement further when we reach the case of *Kirksey v. Kirksey*. First, however, let's examine some other facets of *Hamer* and then continue exploring the kinds of performances or promises that can satisfy the requirement of an exchange.

2. Note—Apparent Intention to Make a Legally Binding Promise

In light of the final issue we studied in Chapter 2, you might wonder whether an uncle's proposal in the midst of a family celebration should be reasonably interpreted by the nephew only as a social gesture of the moment, and not as a serious offer containing a proposed promise with legally binding consequences. The result in

Hamer shows that promises in a social or family context can indeed be legally binding if the circumstances reflect such an intention by the parties. In *Hamer*, the court might have found such circumstances in the uncle's sending a signed letter, after the nephew completed his performance, confirming that the uncle viewed the agreement as one that was legally enforceable rather than having only social import.

Exercise 3.1 — Synthesizing *Hamer* with Other Cases, Real and Hypothetical

1. Forbearance from Illegal Activities

In *Hamer*, the New York Court of Appeals emphasized more than once that the nephew had restricted his freedom from engaging in lawful activities. Suppose that an uncle in a contemporary family has promised to pay his nephew $5,000 in five years in exchange for the nephew's promise to refrain from possessing or using an illegal substance such as cocaine for five years. If the nephew performed but the uncle refuses to pay, is the uncle's promise supported by consideration? *Hamer* does not address that question. The most we can say is that our hypothetical case is *different* from the dispute in *Hamer*. If it is different in a legally significant way, the New York Court of Appeals could reach a different result by distinguishing *Hamer* rather than departing from its lessons. Should it? We will return to this question near the end of this chapter, as part of our discussion of the pre-existing duty rule.

2. A Less Fortunate Nephew

This chapter began with a case, *Dougherty v. Salt*, decided by the same court nearly three decades after *Hamer*. In *Dougherty*, an aunt's written promise to pay $3,000 to her nephew was unenforceable because it lacked consideration. Explain why differences in the facts justify different results in the two cases.

II. Elements of Exchange: Performances and Promises

A. Forbearance as a Performance

It seems intuitively obvious that an act such as payment of money, or the promise to engage in such an act, can be a performance or promised performance that can be exchanged in a bargain. The promise to *forbear* from certain activities, however, raised sufficient uncertainty in the minds of reasonable attorneys that it led to litigation in *Hamer v. Sidway*. Nonetheless, in *Hamer* the nephew's promised forbearance from engaging in legal activities provided perfectly good consideration for the uncle's promise to pay money.

1. Forbearance from Asserting a Legal Claim

Another type of forbearance that has occupied the attention of courts is in the form of promising to refrain from asserting a legal claim in exchange for a return promise or performance. Suppose that the legal claim being surrendered is highly doubtful on its merits. For purposes of consideration, does forbearing from asserting such a claim amount to a performance? Would forbearance from asserting a wholly baseless claim amount to consideration? Would it matter if the promise to forbear is written in the promisor's own blood, to show the seriousness of his intent?

Kim v. Son

No. G039818, 2009 WL 597232 (Cal. Ct. App. 2009)
[unpublished and not for citation in California courts] [footnote omitted]

O'Leary, J.

¶1 Jinsoo Kim begins his opening brief by stating, "Blood may be thicker than water, but here it's far weightier than a peppercorn." Kim appeals from the trial court's refusal to enforce a gratuitous promise, handwritten in his friend's own blood, to repay money Kim loaned and lost in two failed business ventures [when Kim invested money in two failed corporate ventures owned by Son]. He faults the trial court for not discussing or deciding in its statement of decision the issue of whether Kim's forbearance (waiting over a year to file a meritless lawsuit against his friend, Stephen Son), supplied adequate consideration for Son's blood-written document. We conclude ... Son's promise to repay the money was entirely gratuitous and unenforceable, even when reduced to blood. Forbearance to sue cannot supply consideration to what the trial court determined was an invalid claim. In the context of this contract dispute, Son's blood was not weightier than a peppercorn.

¶2 ... Here, the purported forbearance to sue cannot be good consideration because Kim's claims against Son were wholly invalid [because Kim had loaned money to corporations for which Son was not personally liable]. As determined by the trial court, any claim [that] Son personally owed Kim money was invalid.... The blood agreement lacked sufficient consideration because it "was not a result of a bargained-for-exchange, but rather a gratuitous promise by [Son] who took personally that [Kim], his good friend, had a failure in his investments that [Son] had initially brought him into."

....

The judgment is affirmed. Respondent shall recover his costs on appeal.

Exercise 3.2 — Kim's Forbearance

See the end of Appendix 2 for a copy of the complaint and the written promise in *Kim v. Son*. Why did Kim's delay in suing Son over Kim's lost investment fail to provide consideration for Son's promise to repay Kim?

If Kim's forbearance did not qualify as a performance, Son's promise was gratuitous. Although stating a gratuitous promise with formality in a signed, sealed document provided a basis for enforcement under common law centuries ago, *Kim v. Son* illustrates that even writing a gratuitous promise in blood, reflecting a serious intent indeed, does not serve as a substitute for modern consideration requirements.

Exercise 3.3 — Taking It Out on Your Contracts Professor

Suppose that you injure me while driving your car, and I threaten to sue you in tort for $50,000 in damages. You make the following offer: You promise to pay me $35,000 in four years, by which time you hope to be making a good income practicing law, if I promise to refrain from asserting my tort claim until then. (In four years, the statute of limitations will bar my tort claim.) I accept that offer, and I perform my promise by refraining from asserting my claim for four years. You then refuse to pay me, asserting that my forbearance from asserting my claim was not a performance that satisfied the consideration requirement (and thus not the subject of an effective promise). If you are correct on that point, your promise would be gratuitous and unenforceable.

If you were developing the common law, in your opinion, should my promise be viewed as one for a valid performance, providing consideration for your promise to pay me in four years, under each of the following assumptions?

(i) You clearly were negligent, so I have a clearly meritorious tort claim against you.

(ii) The facts and law are doubtful from the outset, and we know that I have only a 50% chance of prevailing if my claim goes to trial.

(iii) You and I never collided at all, and I made up a false claim to extract some money from you. We both know that my claim is completely groundless, but you sought to avoid the inconvenience of defending yourself in court, so you agreed to pay the sum I demanded. You later changed your mind and refused to pay on grounds of lack of consideration. (Do I have a legal right to file a claim that I know is groundless? If not, should a court recognize my forbearance from doing so as a valid performance, providing consideration for a promise to pay?)

(iv) We originally had reason to believe and did believe that you were negligent. We reached our settlement agreement, and I did forbear from bringing suit for four years. But you then refused to pay $35,000, because a smart phone video that surfaced after we reached agreement shows clearly that I was solely responsible for the accident, so my claim turned out to be completely invalid on the facts, much to our surprise.

---

2. Uncertainty in the Facts or Law Underlying a Claim

In *Fiege v. Boehm*, Hilda Boehm's promise to forbear from asserting her statutory paternity claim against Louis Fiege was good consideration for Louis's promise to pay medical expenses and child support, even though a blood test later showed that he could not be the father of her child. At the time of contracting (before Louis's blood test), the parties held a good-faith and reasonable belief in the potential validity of Hilda's paternity claim against Louis. *Fiege v. Boehm*, 210 Md. 352, 123 A.2d 316 (1956). Hilda's claim against Louis was potentially valid at the time of contracting because of uncertainty, at the time of contracting, regarding the facts (the identity of the father). Parties frequently settle uncertain claims, with each side normally abandoning some more extreme position in an agreement to compromise.

What was the nature of the uncertainty in the validity of the claim in the next case? Why did the court not find that the Hospitals' claims were completely groundless under controlling law? What test did the court apply to determine whether the forbearance to assert the claim satisfied consideration requirements?

Abbott v. Banner Health Network

239 Ariz. 409, 372 P.3d 933 (2016)
[footnotes omitted and paragraphs renumbered]

¶1 Petitioners are health care providers ("Hospitals") who treated patients ("Patients") injured by third parties. The Hospitals were paid by the Patients' insurer, the Arizona Health Care Cost Containment System ("AHCCCS") [Arizona's Medicaid program], which had negotiated reduced rates with the Hospitals. The Hospitals then recorded liens against the Patients pursuant to A.R.S. § 33–931 and A.R.S. § 36–2903.01(G) for the difference between the amount typically charged for their treatment and the reduced amount paid by AHCCCS. In order to receive their personal injury settlements with the third parties, Patients settled with the Hospitals by paying negotiated amounts to release the liens.

....

¶2 The Patients ... sued to set aside the accord and satisfaction agreements and to recover the amounts paid to release the liens. The Hospitals moved to dismiss the complaint against the settling Patients pursuant to Arizona Rule of Civil Procedure 12(b)(6) for failing to state a claim because the parties had reached an accord and satisfaction....

¶3 The trial court dismissed the Patients' complaint stating, "it is irrelevant whether federal law preempts Arizona law and prohibits hospitals from enforcing statutory liens on AHCCCS accounts ... [because] [a]ccord and satisfaction does not turn on whether Plaintiffs would have prevailed on the merits of the dispute that was settled." The court concluded that the accord and satisfaction agreements were "final and binding regardless of the validity of the underlying claims."

¶5 The court of appeals reversed. *Abbott v. Banner Health Network*, 236 Ariz. 436, 448 ¶37, 341 P.3d 478, 490 (App. 2014). Reasoning that the accord and satisfaction agreements were void because federal law preempts the Arizona laws allowing the liens, *id.* at 438 ¶1, 341 P.3d at 480, the court held that there was not a "good faith dispute about the enforceability of the lien[s]," and therefore the accord and satisfaction agreements lacked both proper subject matter and consideration. *Id.* at 446–47 ¶¶30–33, 341 P.3d at 478, 489.... The court concluded that "[i]f the underlying agreement is prohibited and unenforceable, an accord and satisfaction based on that agreement is also unenforceable." *Id.* at 443 ¶20, 341 P.3d at 485.

....

¶6 Assuming, as noted above, that federal law preempts the Arizona lien statutes, we turn to the validity of the accord and satisfaction agreements. An "accord and satisfaction discharges a contractual obligation or cause of action when the parties agree to exchange something of value in resolution of a claim or demand and then perform on that agreement, the accord being the agreement, and the satisfaction its execution or performance." *Best Choice Fund, LLC v. Low & Childers, P.C.*, 228 Ariz. 502, 510 ¶ 24, 269 P.3d 678, 686 (App. 2011) (quoting *Vance v. Hammer*, 105 Ariz. 317, 319, 464 P.2d 340, 342 (1970)) (internal quotation marks omitted)....

¶ 7 The settlement of a bona fide dispute provides consideration if it is made fairly and in good faith. *Brecht v. Hammons*, 35 Ariz. 383, 389, 278 P. 381, 383 (1929), *disapproved on other grounds*, *Ariz. Pub. Serv. Co. v. S. Union Gas Co.*, 76 Ariz. 373, 382, 265 P.2d 435, 441 (1954). As this Court stated in *Brecht*:

> The settlement of a controversy is valid and binding, not because it is the settlement of a valid claim, but because it is the settlement of a controversy. And when such settlement is characterized by good faith, the court will not look into the question of law or fact in dispute between the parties, and determine what is right. All that it needs to know is, that there was a controversy between the parties, each claiming in good faith rights in himself against the other and that such controversy has been settled.

Id. On the other hand, "the surrender of a claim which is known to be entirely without foundation either in law or at equity does not afford a sufficient consideration for a compromise." *Id.* at 390, 278 P. at 383. If the matter in controversy was fairly considered by the parties to be unsettled at the time of the agreements, the settlement will not be unwound, even if the statutory provision creating the controversy is later determined to be invalid. *Id.* at 390–91, 278 P. at 383 (citing *Bofinger v. Tuyes*, 120 U.S. 198 (1887)). These principles align with the general proposition that settlements of disputed matters are favored by the law and will be upheld if fairly made. *E.g.*, *Brecht*, 35 Ariz. at 390, 278 P. at 383; *Phillips v. Musgrave*, 23 Ariz. 591, 594–95, 206 P. 164, 165 (1922).

....

¶ 8 The Patients argue that the Hospitals' liens asserted under Arizona law are illegal under federal Medicaid law, 42 C.F.R. § 447.15 and 42 U.S.C. § 1396a(a)(25)(C). Further, because they are illegal they cannot constitute a proper subject for an accord and satisfaction, and thus the agreements lack consideration. Under *Brecht*, however, the pertinent question is whether the legality of the liens (that is, whether federal Medicaid law preempts the Arizona laws authorizing the liens) was "settled" at the time of the agreement. The Hospitals argue that since 1984, A.R.S. § 36–2903.01(G)(4) has allowed hospitals to enforce provider-liens under A.R.S. § 33–931 after accepting payment from AHCCCS, and this statute is presumptively valid and constitutional.

¶ 9 Liens such as these have been authorized by Arizona statute for more than thirty years without an Arizona appellate court suggesting that enforcement of such liens is preempted by federal law. Indeed, our courts have found such liens valid and enforceable. *See Blankenbaker v. Jonovich*, 205 Ariz. 383, 388 ¶ 22, 71 P.3d 910, 915 (2003)....

¶ 10 ... Several courts, however, have concluded that settlement proceeds belong to the patient and the federal prohibitions on balance billing apply. [The opinion cites to decisions of the U.S. Court of Appeals for the Sixth Circuit and for the Seventh Circuit, as well as to a decision of the U.S. District Court for the District of Arizona.]

¶ 11 But these cases are not binding on Arizona state courts, and at the time of the accord and satisfaction agreements here, no Arizona appellate court had addressed the enforceability of Arizona's medical lien statutes against third-party settlements obtained by Medicaid patients. Thus, while federal law may preempt state law in situations like these, the issue was not settled in Arizona when these agreements were entered into. The stated public policy in Arizona, as reflected by our statutes, was that such liens were valid.

....

III. CONCLUSION

¶ 20 Based on the bona fide dispute about the enforceability of the liens when the Patients and Hospitals entered into the accord and satisfaction agreements, these agreements were supported by adequate consideration and had a proper subject matter. Consequently, the agreements are valid, and the trial court appropriately granted Hospitals' motion to dismiss. We reverse the court of appeals' opinion and affirm the trial court's dismissal of the complaint and entry of judgment in favor of the Hospitals.

B. Proposing to Exchange a Valid (Not Illusory) Promise

1. Illusory Promises

Let's suppose now that two parties are bargaining for an exchange of promises, to form an immediate bilateral contract. And let's also suppose that each party is purporting to promise a future action or forbearance that without doubt would amount to a performance. The question remains whether the purported promisor really does state a promise to engage in that future performance or instead voices an intention that falls short of a commitment.

To take an obvious example, the following statement does not propose an exchange of promises that would amount to a bargained-for exchange: "If you promise to paint my house next week, I might pay you $3,000 or I might not." If the painter said, "Okay, it's a deal," the parties have agreed to some sort of transaction, but not one with consideration. Sure, painting a house and paying money are good performances, and the painter gave a good promise to paint the house in the future, but the owner neither paid money in return nor promised to do so. As a result, the owner has no enforceable obligations, because she made no promise; moreover, the painter's promise is unenforceable because it is gratuitous.

Of course, the cases that cause uncertainty in the courts raise closer and subtler questions about consideration than does the example of the equivocating homeowner. The next Exercise raises a series of closer questions about whether a party has stated a promise that can help support a bargained-for exchange or has instead voiced only an "illusory promise," which is no promise at all.

To help guide you in your analysis of the problem, consider this colorful explanation of illusory promises by the late contracts scholar Arthur Corbin:

> If what appears to be a promise is an illusion, there is no promise; like the mirage of the desert with its vision of flowing water which yet lets the traveler die of thirst, there is nothing there. By the phrase "illusory" promise is meant words in promissory form that promise nothing; they do not purport to put any limitation on the freedom of the alleged promisor, but leave his future action subject to his own future will, just as it would have been had he said no words at all.

Arthur Linton Corbin, CORBIN ON CONTRACTS § 145, at 211 (one vol. ed. 1952).

The Supreme Court of California has offered a more succinct definition of illusory promise: "[I]f one of the promises leaves a party free to perform or to withdraw from the agreement at his own unrestricted pleasure, the promise is deemed illusory and it provides no consideration." *Mattei v. Hopper*, 51 Cal. 2d 119, 122, 330 P.2d 625, 626 (1958). In *Mattei*, a developer's obligation to purchase commercial property was subject to the condition that the developer first obtain commitments from commercial tenants that satisfied its subjective standards for the kind of tenants suitable for its planned shopping center. This condition did not render the developer's promise illusory, because the developer was still committed to purchase the property if—after evaluating proposed tenants in good faith—it was honestly satisfied with them. *Id.* at 123, 330 P.2d at 627. Can you explain how this promise, which was qualified by a subjective standard of satisfaction, is different from an illusory promise that would allow the developer to "withdraw from the agreement at his own unrestricted pleasure"?

Exercise 3.4—Promises, Real and Illusory

1. Promises Subject to Qualifications

Assume that the following proposals are accepted by the other party. Consider the qualifications or conditions to the promises in the proposed exchanges. Do they render any of the promises illusory? In each case, what are the range of options open to the promisor? Is performance by the promisor left wholly to his or her own discretion? Whenever your analysis is uncertain, identify arguments for both sides.

(i) "If you agree to paint my house, I will pay you $2,000 on completion."

(ii) "If you agree to prepay an additional $1,000 on the amount due, I'll forbear from asserting my remaining claim against you *until I want my money*."

(iii) "If you agree to prepay an additional $1,000 on the amount due, I'll forbear from asserting my remaining claim against you *until economic circumstances require that I collect the money*."

(iv) "I promise to pay you $1,000 for painting the house, *if I feel like I can afford* it at the time for payment."

(v) "In exchange for premium payments, Insurer will pay replacement cost to Insured, *if the house is destroyed in a covered accident.*"

(vi) *Mattei:* "We promise to buy the shopping center *if available commercial tenants meet our personal, subjective standards for this development.*"

2. Forbearance to Assert a Claim until "I Need the Money"

Thomas Beatty (Creditor) is suing Dale Driggs (Guarantor) for failing to pay money primarily owed by Guarantor's cousin, Don Caslin (Buyer).

On December 15, Buyer purchased two rare antique automobiles from a private owner, Creditor, for a total of $200,000. In a self-financing arrangement, Buyer paid $80,000 on delivery and agreed in writing to pay the remainder of the purchase price to Creditor in 12 monthly installments of $10,000 each, beginning January 1.

From January to April, Buyer paid Creditor a total of $40,000 in monthly installments. In late April, however, Buyer suffered unusual losses in his private business, and he failed to pay the installments due on May 1 and June 1. After Creditor threatened to sue for the return of the automobiles, Guarantor and Creditor entered into a written agreement (the Guarantee Agreement) designed to give Buyer time to recover from his temporary financial difficulties. Dated June 6, the Guarantee Agreement refers to the agreement between Creditor and Buyer as the "Credit/Sale Agreement," and it contains the following statement of mutual obligations:

1. Creditor will refrain from asserting his claim against Buyer and from demanding payment on the Credit/Sale Agreement until Creditor needs the money.
2. In the event that Buyer fails to pay all amounts due under the Credit/Sale Agreement upon demand by Creditor, Guarantor will pay those amounts immediately and will pay further installments as they become due under the Credit/Sale Agreement.

On July 1, Creditor asserted that he "needed" his money, and he demanded payment from Buyer of sums due from May through July. Buyer explained that he could not yet pay anything. On July 5, Creditor demanded immediate payment of $30,000 from Guarantor; he also stated that he expects either Buyer or Guarantor to pay the remaining five installments as they become due on the first of each month. Buyer states that he will not be able to make further payments for at least the remainder of this year, and Guarantor hopes to avoid responsibility for the debt.

Did Creditor make only an illusory promise in the Guarantee Agreement, so that Guarantor's promise is gratuitous and unsupported by consideration? Analyze that issue in writing, as though composing the Discussion section of an Office Memorandum. You may assume that this case arises in the fictitious state of Calzona, whose case law includes the following precedent:

Atco Corp. v. Johnson, 155 Calz. 1211, 627 P.2d 781 (1980). In *Atco*, the manager of an automobile repair shop purportedly promised to delay asserting a claim against the owner of an automobile for $900 in repairs. Specifically, he promised to forbear from asserting the claim "until I want the money." In exchange, a friend of the owner promised to act as guarantor of the owner's obligation. *See id.* at 1212, 627 P.2d at 782. The word "want" stated no legal commitment because it permitted the manager at his own discretion to refuse to perform any forbearance at all. Because the manager incurred no obligation, the guarantor's promise was gratuitous and unenforceable. *Id.* at 1213–14, 627 P.2d at 783–84; *accord, Strong v. Sheffield*, 144 N.Y. 392, 39 N.E. 330 (1895) (creditor's assurance that he would not assert his claim until "I want my money" was an illusory promise).

Bonnie v. DeLaney, 158 Calz. 212, 645 P.2d 887 (1982). In *Bonnie*, an agreement for the sale of a house provided that the buyer could cancel the agreement if the buyer "cannot qualify for a 30-year mortgage loan for 90% of the sales price" with any of several banks listed in the agreement. *Id.* at 213, 645 P.2d at 888. In enforcing the agreement against the seller, the court distinguished *Atco Corp.* on the ground that the word "cannot" referred to the buyer's ability to obtain a loan rather than to his desire. Because his ability to obtain a loan was partly controlled by events and decisions outside his control, the promises in the sale agreement were non-illusory and binding. *Id.* at 214–15, 645 P.2d at 889–90.[3]

---

2. *Curing Illusory Promises with Obligations Implied in Fact*

In some of the problems in Exercise 3.4.1 above, a party articulated a purported "promise" but arguably stated no firm commitment, depending on the interpretation given to the spoken or written words. In other cases, consideration is placed in doubt because one of the parties said little or nothing about a critical obligation, so that any promise must be inferred from the parties' actions, their statements on related topics, or other circumstances.

Let's suppose the fact-finder infers a promise from such evidence, finding that a party actually intended to make the promise and in fact communicated it in some way, but failed to clearly express it in words. Such a promise and resulting obligation are "implied in fact." In some cases, an entire contract—consisting of implied promises binding both parties—can be implied in fact.

Implied-in-fact obligations or contracts are real, based on the actual intentions of the parties. They are different from those arising out of express promises or agreements in that implied terms are objectively conveyed by parties through means other than directly through express verbal statements.

True, statutes of frauds—which we will study in Chapter 7—bar enforcement of some kinds of agreements unless the essential terms of the agreement are expressed in writing. And some courts or legislatures might bar enforcement of certain other kinds of agreements unless they are *expressed* in some way, either orally or in writing, rather than implied from conduct or from statements that do not directly address the topic in question. Otherwise, however, a judge or jury can infer implied promises or agreements from conduct of the parties, statements made by the parties on other topics, background information about the parties or their industry, and other relevant circumstances.

---

3. This problem is adapted from a sample office memorandum in Charles R. Calleros and Kimberly Y.W. Holst, Legal Method and Writing I - Predictive Writing 149–52 (8th ed. 2018).

a. Implying an Obligation from all the Circumstances

Implication of an obligation is illustrated nicely in the case of *Merrimac Chemical Co. v. Moore*, 279 Mass. 147, 181 N.E. 219 (1932). Mellenville Corp. owed money on a past due account to Merrimac Co. When told of this by a representative of Merrimac, Moore (a major stockholder of Mellenville) wrote and signed a guaranty: Moore's personal promise to pay Mellenville's debt to Merrimac if Mellenville failed to do so. The parties said nothing about whether Merrimac was considering legal action to collect the debt from Mellenville and would delay doing so as consideration for Moore's guaranty. *Id.* at 149–50, 181 N.E. at 220. And the fact that Merrimac did delay its legal action would not supply consideration for *this* agreement if Moore was bargaining solely for an exchange of *promises* when the parties met. The court nonetheless found consideration. It looked at all the circumstances and found an implied promise on the part of Merrimac to delay for a reasonable time its efforts to collect the past due obligation, in return for Moore's personal guaranty:

> ... No consideration is stated in the written instrument of guaranty signed by the defendant.... The circumstances of the parties and what was said and done at the crucial interview between the defendant and Warren representing the plaintiff constitute the setting from which their purpose must be determined.
>
> They met with a certain common knowledge concerning the financial condition of the Mellenville Products Corporation and its indebtedness to the corporation represented by Warren. That had been discussed at a previous interview. Warren declared that the account due from the Mellenville Products Corporation, in which the defendant was deeply interested, could not go on without some payment. The defendant replied in substance that he was not then inclined to make any money payment on its account, but that he was willing to give his personal guaranty of the account. He caused such guaranty to be written, signed it, and handed it to Warren. The latter took it, inspected it, made no objection to its form or substance, put it in his pocket, and went away.... The guaranty of the defendant was kept by the plaintiff and no action was brought for almost a year against the corporation whose account the defendant had guaranteed. Nothing further was said or done between the parties for a substantial period of time.
>
> The rational construction and the natural import of these words and this conduct, in view of the circumstances known to both the participants in the conversation and the events, are that the defendant signed and delivered the guaranty for the purpose of securing for his corporation immunity for a reasonable time from legal proceedings against it by the plaintiff, and that Warren in behalf of the plaintiff received and accepted that guaranty upon the plainly implied understanding and agreement that such immunity was to be extended to that corporation. Thus there was a valid and binding consideration for the guaranty signed by the defendant.

Merrimac Chemical Co. v. Moore, 279 Mass. 147, 155–57, 181 N.E. 219, 222–23 (1932).

b. Implying an Obligation from Other Terms of the Agreement

In the next case, an agent's promises under a contract were arguably illusory if the contract left it entirely within his discretion whether he would try to market his principal's endorsement, license, or design. (That issue is not undercut by a provision requiring the agent to make an accounting or to take out patents, copyrights, or trademarks, because the Court appears to find that those duties would arise only if the agent first sold a license, endorsement, or design.)

Celebrated jurist Benjamin Cardozo cured this consideration problem by finding that the parties had implicitly intended the agent to assume a certain obligation. Identify the obligation that Justice Cardozo inferred from all the circumstances, thus ensuring that both parties were firmly committed. Be prepared to explain the facts, and the sources of those facts, from which Justice Cardozo inferred the obligation, which the parties had objectively conveyed, even though they failed to address that topic in a specific contract clause.

Wood v. Lucy, Lady Duff-Gordon

222 N.Y. 88, 118 N.E. 214 (1917)
Court of Appeals of New York (highest court in the state)
Appeal from Supreme Court, Appellate Division, First Department.

Cardozo, J.

¶1 The defendant styles herself "a creator of fashions." Her favor helps a sale. Manufacturers of dresses, millinery, and like articles are glad to pay for a certificate of her approval. The things which she designs, fabrics, parasols, and what not, have a new value in the public mind when issued in her name. She employed the plaintiff to help her to turn this vogue into money.

¶2 He was to have the exclusive right, subject always to her approval, to place her indorsements on the designs of others. He was also to have the exclusive right to place her own designs on sale, or to license others to market them. In return she was to have one-half of "all profits and revenues" derived from any contracts he might make. The exclusive right was to last at least one year from April 1, 1915, and thereafter from year to year unless terminated by notice of 90 days.

¶3 The plaintiff says that he kept the contract on his part, and that the defendant broke it. She placed her indorsement on fabrics, dresses, and millinery without his knowledge, and withheld the profits. He sues her for the damages, and the case comes here on demurrer.

¶4 The agreement of employment is signed by both parties. It has a wealth of recitals. The defendant insists, however, that it lacks the elements of a contract. She says that the plaintiff does not bind himself to anything. It is true that he does not promise in so many words that he will use reasonable efforts to place the defendant's indorsements and market her designs. We think, however, that such a promise is fairly to be implied. The law has outgrown its primitive stage of formalism when the precise word was the sovereign talisman, and every slip was fatal. It takes a broader view today. A promise may be lacking, and yet the whole writing may be "instinct with an obligation," imperfectly expressed (Scott, J., in *McCall Co. v. Wright*, 133 App. Div. 62, 117 N. Y. Supp. 775; *Moran v. Standard Oil Co.*, 211 N. Y. 187, 198, 105 N. E. 217). If that is so, there is a contract.

¶5 The implication of a promise here finds support in many circumstances. The defendant gave an exclusive privilege. She was to have no right for at least a year to place her own indorsements or market her own designs except through the agency of the plaintiff. The acceptance of the exclusive agency was an assumption of its duties. *Phoenix Hermetic Co. v. Filtrine Mfg. Co.*, 164 App. Div. 424, 150 N. Y. Supp. 193; [two other citations omitted]. We are not to suppose that one party was to be placed at the mercy of the other. [two citations omitted]. Other terms of the agreement point the same way. We are told at the outset by way of recital that:

¶6 "The said Otis F. Wood possesses a business organization adapted to the placing of such indorsements as the said Lucy, Lady Duff-Gordon, has approved."

¶7 The implication is that the plaintiff's business organization will be used for the purpose for which it is adapted. But the terms of the defendant's compensation are even more significant. Her sole compensation for the grant of an exclusive agency is to be one-half of all the profits resulting from the plaintiff's efforts. Unless he gave his efforts, she could never get anything. Without an implied promise, the transaction cannot have such business "efficacy, as both parties must have intended that at all events it should have." Bowen, L. J., in the *Moorcock*, 14 P. D. 64, 68. But the contract does not stop there. The plaintiff goes on to promise that he will account monthly for all moneys received by him, and that he will take out all such patents and copyrights and trade-marks as may in his judgment be necessary to protect the rights and articles affected by the agreement.

¶8 It is true, of course, as the Appellate Division has said, that if he was under no duty to try to market designs or to place certificates of indorsement, his promise to account for profits or take out copyrights would be valueless. But in determining the intention of the parties the promise has a value. It helps to enforce the conclusion that the plaintiff had some duties. His promise to pay the defendant one-half of the profits and revenues resulting from the exclusive agency and to render accounts monthly was a promise to use reasonable efforts to bring profits and revenues into existence. For this conclusion the authorities are ample. *Wilson v. Mechanical Orguinette Co.*, 170 N.Y. 542, 63 N.E. 550;.... [Eight more precedents omitted]

¶9 The judgment of the Appellate Division should be reversed, and the order of the Special Term affirmed, with costs in the Appellate Division and in this court.

Cuddeback, McLaughlin, and Andrews, JJ., concur. Hiscock, C.J., and Chase and Crane, JJ., dissent.

Exercise 3.5 — Challenges in Curing Illusory Promises

1. No Room for Implication?

Suppose that the contract had addressed Wood's level of efforts with the following term: "Wood will exercise sole discretion regarding whether he will, or the extent to which he will, endeavor to place such endorsements and enter into such contracts on behalf of Lady Duff-Gordon." Could Cardozo have saved that contract? Why does that contract term pose a more serious consideration problem than a case in which the parties omitted any mention of a term, assuming both cases take place in the context of a larger business transaction?

2. Statutory Term Evading Illusory Promise

To place it in context within a code system, turn to Appendix 1 and find section 2.306 of the Texas Business and Commerce Code, which represents the Texas enactment of UCC § 2-306. Suppose a manufacturer promises to supply all of its output of steel rails for the month of November to a buyer for a certain price per ton. Is the manufacturer's promise illusory, because it leaves the manufacturer the option of not running its business and not having any output, at its unfettered discretion? If the manufacturer does not clearly leave itself that option, but simply refers to quantity by its "output," the UCC will define that quantity term. It does the same for a contract term that measures quantity by the buyer's "requirements."

The first subsection of the statute cited above provides the following:

> (a) A term which measures the quantity by the output of the seller or the requirements of the buyer means such actual output or requirements as may occur in good faith, except that no quantity unreasonably disproportionate to any stated estimate or in the absence of a stated estimate to any normal or otherwise comparable prior output or requirements may be tendered or demanded.

If a requirements contract stated no estimated requirements, and if the buyer was new to the business and had no "normal" or "prior" requirements, what statutory language helps to state a minimum obligation, thus avoiding an illusory promise? Under that test, would a promise to buy all of a business' requirements for a stated period be non-illusory even if the business turned out to have no such requirements during the contract term because consumer demand for its products plummeted?

3. Contracts Terminable At Will

Suppose that an agreement provides that "either party may terminate this contract at any time and for any reason." Why does that raise a question about illusory promises? *See, e.g., Soars v. Easter Seals Midwest*, 563 S.W.3d 111, 117–19 (Mo. S. Ct. 2018) (Draper, J., dissenting). To cure the consideration problem at the time of contract formation, what changes in the language of the agreement would you propose? If the quoted language above were the final express agreement on termination, would it be plausible for a court to add an implied-in-fact term that would cure the consideration problem? What kind of implied term would address the problem and be plausibly within the intentions of the parties? What kinds of facts or circumstances might reflect such an intention shared by the parties?

III. Reciprocal Inducement: Is the Exchange Bargained For?

A. Introduction

In the preceding Section II, we focused on the requirement of an exchange and explored the kinds of acts, forbearances, and promises that could form the elements of an exchange. In this section, we address the necessary relationship between the things exchanged.

Under our modern definition of consideration as "bargained-for exchange," the requisite relationship between the things exchanged is captured by the term "bargained-for," otherwise known as the requirement of reciprocal inducement. To use a bilateral contract as an easily articulated example, this requirement of reciprocal inducement is satisfied at the time of contract formation if each party's promise is a genuine inducement for the other party's promise, in other words, if each party seeks the other's promise in exchange for her own. *See* RESTATEMENT (SECOND) OF CONTRACTS §71(2) (1981).

According to an early Arizona decision,

> [t]he parties must understand and be influenced to the particular action by something of value ... recognized by all of them as the moving cause. That which is a mere fortuitous result flowing accidentally from an arrangement, but in no degree prompting the actors to it, is not to be esteemed a legal consideration.

Yuma Nat'l Bank v. Balsz, 28 Ariz. 336, 343, 237 P. 198, 200 (1925).

In an even earlier decision, a Massachusetts court rejected the argument that multiple pledges to an educational institution had each provided consideration for the others' commitment, because each promise to donate—although perhaps given with knowledge of the other promises—was independent of the others, rather than mutual and reciprocal:

> ... The writing given in evidence in this case contains no proof of a contract; there is no mutuality, ... no valuable consideration. It is a promise to give, connected with a similar promise by others to give to the same appropriation and purpose; but these promises are not mutual among the subscribers, so as to make the promise of one, or the performance of it, a consideration for the promise of another. At the most, it was a donation to come into operation at the will of each subscriber, ... and we cannot therefore confirm this verdict, without contradicting a course of decisions in cases where this question has occurred.

Phillips Limerick Academy v. Davis, 11 Mass. 113, 116–17 (1814).

Exercise 3.6 — Independent or Reciprocal Promises

Consider each of the dialogues in paragraphs 1 and 2 below. Which describes a bargained-for exchange, and which does not? What is the material distinction of fact between them? How does that distinction relate to the concept of bargained-for exchange?

1. New Year's Resolutions

Bob and Jan meet for brunch after a wild New Year's Eve party and discuss their resolutions for the New Year:

> Bob: "I promise you this, I'm not going to take another drink for the rest of the year."
>
> Jan: "Good for you. I've decided to quit smoking; I promise you that I won't have another cigarette for the rest of the year."

2. Conditional Resolutions

Bob and Jan meet for brunch after a wild New Year's Eve party and argue about which of them has the most will power and which of them has the most irritating vice. Finally, they decide to take action:

> Bob: "I promise to quit drinking for the rest of the year if you agree to quit smoking for the year."
>
> Jan: "Agreed."

B. Bargained-For Exchange or Conditional Gratuitous Promise?

Imagine that I have purchased a new television set and am willing to part with my old one. I call you on the telephone and say, "I will give you my old television set if you drive over and pick it up." Am I bargaining for your act of hauling away my television set in exchange for giving it to you? Or, am I just promising to give you a gift and merely explaining a limitation on my gift, a condition to it?

Without more facts, a reasonable person probably would interpret my statement as follows: "I'm willing to give you this television set, but I'm not willing to bring the gift to your house, so if you want it, come and get it." If so, my statement would be viewed as a promise to make a gift. Because I am willing to give it to you only if you come to my house to take it away, my promise might be called a "conditional gratuitous promise," which generally is not enforceable but is left to my own conscience and sense of honor.

Can you add facts or statements that would bolster the argument that I am in fact *bargaining* for your performance of picking up the television set and taking it away? Specifically, what facts would support an argument that your act of picking up the television is a genuine inducement for my promise to give it away to you?

1. Spotting the Issue and Analyzing the Facts

In some cases, the difference between an enforceable bargained-for exchange and an unenforceable conditional gratuitous promise can be quite subtle and depend on inferences drawn by the fact-finder. In the next case, what specific issue about consideration is raised by the facts? You will not receive much guidance from the single paragraph at the end of the opinion, announcing the split decision of the court. Therefore, use the facts and your knowledge about the requirements of a bargain to identify the likely basis for the disagreement between Justice Ormond and his fellow justices. If the issue remains elusive after reading the opinion, Exercise 3.7 after the opinion should advance your thinking.

Kirksey v. Kirksey

Supreme Court of Alabama, 8 Ala. 131 (1845)

¶1 ASSUMPSIT by the defendant, against the plaintiff in error. The question is presented in this Court, upon a case agreed, which shows the following facts:

¶2 The plaintiff was the wife of defendant's brother, but had for some time been a widow, and had several children. In 1840, the plaintiff resided on public land, under a contract of lease, she had held over, and was comfortably settled, and would have attempted to secure the land she lived on. The defendant resided in Talladega county, some sixty, or seventy miles off. On the 10th October, 1840, he wrote to her the following letter:

> "Dear sister Antillico—Much to my mortification, I heard, that brother Henry was dead, and one of his children. I know that your situation is one of grief, and difficulty. You had a bad chance before, but a great deal worse now. I should like to come and see you, but cannot with convenience at present.... I do not know whether you have a preference on the place you live on, or not. If you had, I would advise you to obtain your preference, and sell the land and quit the country, as I understand it is very unhealthy, and I know society is very bad. If you will come down and see me, I will let you have a place to raise your family, and I have more open land than I can tend; and on the account of your situation, and that of your family, I feel like I want you and the children to do well."

¶3 Within a month or two after the receipt of this letter, the plaintiff abandoned her possession, without disposing of it, and removed with her family, to the residence of the defendant, who put her in comfortable houses, and gave her land to cultivate for two years, at the end of which time he notified her to remove, and put her in a house, not comfortable, in the woods, which he afterwards required her to leave.

¶4 A verdict being found for the plaintiff, for two hundred dollars, the above facts were agreed, and if they will sustain the action, the judgment is to be affirmed, otherwise it is to be reversed.

....

Ormond, J.

¶5 The inclination of my mind, is, that the loss and inconvenience, which the plaintiff sustained in breaking up, and moving to the defendant's, a distance of sixty miles, is a sufficient consideration to support the promise, to furnish her with a house, and land to cultivate, until she could raise her family. My brothers, however think, that the promise on the part of the defendant, was a mere gratuity, and that an action will not lie for its breach. The judgment of the Court below must therefore be reversed, pursuant to the agreement of the parties [about the facts].

Exercise 3.7 — Questions on *Kirksey* and Reciprocal Inducement

1. Unraveling *Kirksey*

In *Kirksey,* Justice Ormond briefly stated the decision of the Alabama Supreme Court, but only after he revealed his dissenting view. Is it plausible to argue that the act of moving a household 60–70 miles in 1840 could not amount to a performance for an exchange? If not, we can assume that the other justices found a lack of consideration because reciprocal inducement was absent — or at least that's how we might explain the majority decision today.

Do you have any doubt that the brother-in-law's promise of lodging induced Antillico to move her household? If Antillico certainly was induced by the promise of lodging, doesn't the issue narrow to whether the prospect of Antillico moving her household to her brother-in-law's land was an inducement to *him* for *his* promise, thus satisfying the requirement of *reciprocal* inducement? Although the parties agreed on the statement of facts, one can draw different inferences and conclusions from the record about whether it supports a finding of reciprocal inducement.[4] After all, the jury and Justice Ormond found consideration on the facts, while the other justices found no consideration. In any event, we can view this as a close case that could have been resolved in favor of either party, which makes it an excellent vehicle for developing factual arguments for both sides.

2. Advocating in *Kirksey*

After summarizing the issue, holding, and facts of *Kirksey*, try to rationalize its result in terms of reciprocal inducement. Then, try to argue both sides of the issue of reciprocal inducement. For example, in place of the "Reasoning" section of your case brief, you could present your arguments in the following way. In place of the last paragraph of the opinion, draft two opinions: (a) a majority opinion authored by Justice Ormond's fellow justices, explaining in detail why the facts do *not* support a finding that Antillico's actions constituted a performance that her brother-in-law was seeking, so that it was not an inducement for his promise of lodging for Antillico's family, and (b) a dissenting opinion authored by Justice Ormond explaining in detail why the facts do support a jury finding that Antillico's moving her household was an inducement for his promise.

You can state the same legal rule in both opinions, but try to argue the facts differently, partly by emphasizing different facts and by drawing different inferences from the facts.

---

4. As with all published opinions, our analysis is limited by the facts presented in the opinion, the inferences that we can draw from those facts, and perhaps some basic information about the world that is commonly shared in society. One author has thoroughly researched all of the facts surrounding the Kirkseys' transaction and argues that the full story supports different factual and legal arguments than those invited by the parties' spare stipulation of facts. Val D. Ricks, *"Dear Sister Antillico . . .": The Story of Kirksey v. Kirksey*, 94 GEO. L.J. 321 (2006).

3. Appellate Standard of Review

By drawing inferences from the facts, could members of the jury have reasonably found that Antillico and her brother-in-law were reciprocally induced? If so, what is the appropriate scope of appellate review? If this case really turned on questions of factual inference, should the Alabama Supreme Court have deferred to the fact-finding of the jury? Alternatively, in light of the opinion's reference to "a case agreed," did the Supreme Court view its task as one of drawing a legal conclusion from undisputed facts?

4. Assessing *Kirksey*

We can assume that the brother-in-law breached a promise to provide Antillico with a comfortable home until her children were raised. Assuming also that the majority correctly found no consideration for that promise, are you left with a feeling that the consideration doctrine did not do justice in this case? Should the law introduce more flexibility into the consideration doctrine, or supplement it with other doctrines, to protect the interests of parties like Antillico and her family? Remember these questions when we study promissory estoppel and similar doctrines in the next chapter. In the meantime, consider the following observations by commentators from other nations: "Without equity, the law's story becomes all rules and no justice." GARY WATT, EQUITY STIRRING : THE STORY OF JUSTICE BEYOND LAW 45 (Hart Pub. Oxford 2009). On the other hand, "one must balance the advantage of greater justice in individual cases as against the loss of ascertainability and predictability in the application of law and the increase in transaction costs...." Eugen Bucher, ENGLAND AND THE CONTINENT: DISTINGUISHING THE PECULIARITIES OF THE ENGLISH COMMON LAW OF CONTRACT 50 (Tony Weir, trans., Dike Law Books 2009).

5. Promise for a Past Performance

How does the requirement of reciprocal inducement help to explain why the following facts do not amount to a bargained-for exchange? Motivated by altruism, Trang spent many hours helping her friend Cathy prepare for the bar exam. Months after Trang's coaching services ended, and after Cathy discovered that she had passed the bar exam, Cathy promised to pay Trang $1,000 for her many hours of help.

6. IKEA's Proposition to Celebrate Valentine's Day

Recall the offer in the *Carbolic Smoke Ball* case, in Chapter 2, inviting acceptance by engaging in the act of completing a requested performance, sought by the offeror. On February 14, 2013, IKEA published the following ad in an Australian newspaper:

> Free for babies born 9 months from today. To celebrate Valentine's Day, IKEA is offering parents-to-be a free cot if your baby is born on 14 November 2013. Limit of one cot per baby. Proof of birth must be provided. Voucher must be presented to redeem offer. Delivery not included.

The ad includes a picture of a baby's crib, which is further described as made of beech wood, spanning specified dimensions, and normally selling for $99. The ad includes fine print with the following restrictions: "Valid only in South Australia and Western Australia. If stock is unavailable a $99 Gift Card will be issued. Offer valid until 14/12/13." Do you see any other restrictions in the ad?

If limited to its express provisions, does the ad state an unenforceable gratuitous promise to provide a free crib, conditioned on birth of a baby on a specified date? Or is IKEA implicitly seeking a performance on the part of readers in exchange for IKEA's conditional promise? Was IKEA induced by the prospect of couples becoming amorous on Valentine's Day with IKEA furniture partly on their minds, thus generating customer goodwill?

IV. Working with Consideration Concepts

A. Relative Values of the Things Exchanged

1. Equality in Exchange Not Required for Consideration

Although we'll study some mitigating doctrines later in the semester,[5] the consideration requirement did not develop as a mechanism for assuring equality in the exchange. Remember that the court in *Hamer v. Sidway* was not concerned with the amount of effort that the nephew's forbearances might have required, or with the degree to which the uncle was benefitted by the nephew's forbearance. So long as the nephew restricted his lawful activities, and so long as the uncle sought that forbearance in exchange for his promise to pay $5,000, the court was not interested in inquiring whether the nephew's performance was "worth" $5,000. *See also* Restatement (Second) of Contracts § 79(b) (1981) (rejecting any requirement of "equivalence in the values exchanged" if other elements of consideration are met). Thus, the doctrine of consideration allows parties the freedom to strike their own deals, good or bad, and holds them to a deal when they have satisfied the requirements for contract formation.

Yet this conception of consideration must have some limit. Some performances must be so insubstantial that they fail to hold up one end of an "exchange." Could delivery of a tiny peppercorn ever amount to consideration for a return promise? Does payment of Greek currency worth $25 provide consideration for a promise to repay the lender $2,000 plus interest? Does it depend on the circumstances surrounding the transaction?

Batsakis v. Demotsis

226 S.W.2d 673 (Tex. Ct. Civ. App. 1949)

McGill, Justice.

¶ 1 This is an appeal from a judgment of the 57th judicial District Court of Bexar County. [Mr. Batsakis] was plaintiff and [Ms. Demotsis] was defendant in the trial court. The parties will be so designated.

¶ 2 Plaintiff sued defendant to recover $2,000 with interest at the rate of 8% per annum from April 2, 1942, alleged to be due on the following instrument, being a translation from the original, which is written in the Greek language:

> Mr. Batsakis:
>
> I state by my present (letter) that I received today from you the amount of two thousand dollars ($2,000.00) of United States of America money, which

---

5. *See, e.g.*, UCC § 2-302 (2011) (allowing courts to refuse to enforce "unconscionable" contracts or contract clauses). Moreover, even when a lopsided bargain is enforceable at law for money damages, a court can deny the equitable remedy of specific performance on the ground that the exchange is grossly unfair. *See, e.g.*, *McKinnon v. Benedict*, 38 Wis. 2d 607, 157 N.W.2d 665 (1968).

> I borrowed from you for the support of my family during these difficult days and because it is impossible for me to transfer dollars of my own from America.
>
> The above amount I accept with the expressed promise that I will return to you again in American dollars either at the end of the present war or even before in the event that you might be able to find a way to collect them (dollars) from my representative in America to whom I shall write and give him an order relative to this. You understand until the final execution (payment) to the above amount an eight per cent interest will be added and paid together with the principal.
>
> I thank you and I remain yours with respects.
>
> The recipient,
>
> (Signed) Eugenia The. Demotsis.

¶3 Trial to the court without the intervention of a jury resulted in a judgment in favor of plaintiff for $750.00 principal, and interest at the rate of 8% per annum from April 2, 1942 to the date of judgment, totaling $1163.83, with interest thereon at the rate of 8% per annum until paid. Plaintiff has perfected his appeal.

¶4 The answer ... consisted [partly] of a general denial contained in paragraph I thereof, and of paragraph IV, which is as follows:

> IV. That under the circumstances alleged in Paragraph II of this answer, the consideration ... is wanting and has failed to the extent of $1975.00, and defendant ... now tenders ... $25.00 as the value of the loan of money received by defendant from plaintiff, together with interest thereon.
>
> Further, in connection with this plea of want and failure of consideration defendant alleges that she at no time received from plaintiff himself or from anyone for plaintiff any money or thing of value other than, as hereinbefore alleged, the original loan of 500,000 drachmae. That at the time of the loan ... the value of 500,000 drachmae ... in dollars of money of the United States of America, was $25.00....

¶5 The allegations in paragraph II ... were that the instrument sued on was signed and delivered in the Kingdom of Greece on or about April 2, 1942, at which time both plaintiff and defendant were residents of and residing in the Kingdom of Greece, and

> ... That in the circumstances [of occupation of Greece by the Axis Powers] the plaintiff agreed to and did lend to defendant the sum of 500,000 drachmae, which at that time, on or about April 2, 1942, had the value of $25.00 in money of the United States of America. That the said plaintiff, knowing defendant's financial distress and desire to return to the United States of America, exacted of her the written instrument plaintiff sues upon, which was a promise by her to pay to him the sum of $2,000.00 of United States of America money.

....

¶6 Defendant testified that she did receive 500,000 drachmas from plaintiff.... Her testimony clearly shows that the understanding of the parties was that plaintiff would give her the 500,000 drachmas if she would sign the instrument. She testified:

> Q.... who suggested the figure of $2,000.00?
>
> A. That was how he asked me from the beginning. He said he will give me five hundred thousand drachmas provided I signed that I would pay him $2,000.00 American money.

¶7 The transaction amounted to a sale by plaintiff of the 500,000 drachmas in consideration of the execution of the instrument sued on, by defendant. It is not contended that the drachmas had no value. Indeed, the judgment indicates that the trial court placed a value of $750.00 on them or on the other consideration which plaintiff gave defendant for the instrument if he believed plaintiff's testimony. Therefore the plea of want of consideration was unavailing. A plea of want of consideration amounts to a contention that the instrument never became a valid obligation in the first place. *National Bank of Commerce v. Williams*, 125 Tex. 619, 84 S.W.2d 691.

¶8 Mere inadequacy of consideration will not void a contract. 10 Tex. Jur., Contracts, Sec. 89, p. 150; *Chastain v. Texas Christian Missionary Society*, Tex. Civ. App., 78 S.W.2d 728, loc. cit. 731(3), Wr. Ref.

¶9 Nor was the plea of failure of consideration availing. Defendant got exactly what she contracted for according to her own testimony. The court should have rendered judgment in favor of plaintiff against defendant for the principal sum of $2,000.00 evidenced by the instrument sued on, with interest as therein provided. We construe the provision relating to interest as providing for interest at the rate of 8% per annum. The judgment is reformed so as to award appellant a recovery against appellee of $2,000.00 with interest thereon at the rate of 8% per annum from April 2, 1942....

Reformed and affirmed.

In *Batsakis*, the appellate court appears to accept Ms. Demotsis's testimony that Mr. Batsakis agreed to pay only 500,000 drachmae as the loan to Ms. Demotsis, in exchange for her promise to repay $2,000 in U.S. dollars (USD) plus 8% interest, and that she in fact received only 500,000 drachmae from Mr. Batsakis. On those facts, the letter agreement appears to contain a false recital that Ms. Demotsis received $2,000 as the loan principal. It's not clear on what basis the trial court found a loan valued at $750.

If Mr. Batsakis had agreed to loan $2,000 but had delivered only a fraction of that amount, then Ms. Demotsis presumably would argue that Mr. Batsakis had materially breached the contract, thus relieving Ms. Demotsis of her obligation to repay the full $2,000 plus interest, under principles that we will study in Chapter 11. Indeed, Ms.

Demotsis apparently advanced that argument through her attorney's imprecise reference to "failure of consideration." However, Mr. Batsakis had not breached the agreement according to Ms. Demotsis's own testimony that Batsakis agreed to pay her 500,000 drachmae, which she admittedly received. Accordingly, Ms. Demotsis was left to argue that consideration was "wanting" in the exchange of drachmae worth only $25 for a promise to repay $2,000 with interest.

2. *Defining the Floor with Reciprocal Inducement*

Can reciprocal inducement provide a basis for determining whether a something very small in market value provides consideration for something of much greater market value? Suppose that the uncle in *Hamer v. Sidway* had agreed to pay $5,000 to his nephew for a marked-up paperback book that would be priced at less than $1 if sold in a used book store. If all evidence showed that the uncle cared not at all for the book, we could reasonably conclude that the parties had agreed to the transfer of a gift to the nephew, so that the uncle's promise to pay $5,000 is unenforceable. True, the parties had dressed up the gratuitous promise to resemble a bargain. The absence of reciprocal inducement, however, reveals the true nature of the transaction. Sure, the nephew was induced by the uncle's promise to give up the nearly worthless book; however, the inducement was not reciprocal because the prospect of receiving the book was no inducement at all to the uncle in his decision to promise the money.

Add a few facts, however, and one might reasonably conclude that the uncle was induced by the nephew's promise to transfer the book to him, thus making the inducement reciprocal. Would you reach that conclusion, for example, if the book owned and held dearly by the nephew was a gift from his recently deceased father, who had acted out scenes from this very book during playtime with the uncle when they were both children? If the book contained acting notes from the siblings and held great sentimental value to the uncle, but the nephew was reluctant to part with it, is it possible that the uncle might be induced to pay $5,000 for the opportunity to own that book and recall his childhood with his brother? These facts could explain why the uncle might be induced to pay $5,000 for the book even though the general market would still value the book at less than $1.

In sum, courts do not mire themselves in an inquiry into the relative values of the things exchanged when the courts apply the consideration doctrine. Instead, the minimum "value" required for one party's promise or performance can be set by the doctrine of reciprocal inducement. If the facts show that one party genuinely seeks another's promise or performance in exchange for her own promise, then the consideration doctrine requires no further inquiry into the relative values of the things exchanged.

So, then, what is the answer to the question posed earlier about whether a tiny peppercorn can be consideration for a promise to pay money? This tiny morsel meant for a pepper grinder might normally be no inducement at all for a return promise and thus serve only to make a gratuitous promise look a bit like a bargain. However, if I have a great craving for pepper in my bowl of soup on a camping trip, and if you possess the only peppercorn in the camp, isn't it entirely possible that I would be induced to promise to pay you a dollar for the peppercorn held in your hand? If so, we could find consideration in the exchange of a promise to pay money for delivery of a single, tiny peppercorn. In sum, the answer to the peppercorn question is, "it depends"—on the facts of each case.

3. Finding Reciprocal Inducement in an Exchange of Equivalents

In the next case, the bank and some customers agreed to exchange—and did exchange—denominations of currency that were precisely equal in face value. If each party is induced by the other denomination, consideration doctrine is easily satisfied. The customer is induced to exchange bills because he finds smaller bills easier to use. Can you think of a reason for the bank to prefer a larger bill and thus to be reciprocally induced to enter into this exchange?

If the bank, however, asserts that receiving the larger bill was no inducement at all, should we view the transaction in a different analytic framework, one in which the bank engages in the gratuitous service of providing change? Even under that framework, however, is the bank acting gratuitously or is it induced by the prospect of non-account-holders visiting the bank? How do you explain the court's reasoning?

In the following case, the consideration issue is embedded in a civil rights suit under a federal statute that redressed a deficiency in the common law of contracts. Common law rules of offer and acceptance permitted parties to restrict their offers in any way and to reject offers for any reason, including for reasons of racial prejudice. This deficiency in the common law led to legislation shortly after the Civil War banning racial discrimination in contracting. 42 U.S.C. § 1981 (2012).

Barfield v. Commerce Bank, N.A.

484 F.3d 1276 (10th Cir. 2007)

Before Kelly, McConnell, and Holmes, Circuit Judges.

McConnell, Circuit Judge.

¶ 1 Chris Barfield, an African-American man, entered a Commerce Bank branch in Wichita, Kansas, and requested change for a $50 bill. He was refused change on the ground that he was not an account-holder. The next day, Chris Barfield's father, James Barfield, asked a white friend, John Polson, to make the same request from the bank. Mr. Polson was given change, and the teller never asked whether he held an account with the bank. A few minutes later, James Barfield entered the bank, asked for change for a $100 bill, and was told that he would not be given change unless he was an account-holder.

¶ 2 James Barfield then enlisted the help of a white news reporter and his African-American colleague. The two men, separately, visited the bank to request change.

The African-American man was asked whether he was an account holder, and the white man was not.

¶3 The Barfields filed suit under 42 U.S.C. § 1981, alleging racial discrimination in the impairment of the ability to contract....

....

¶4 Originally enacted in the wake of the Civil War, Section 1981(a) states:

> All persons within the jurisdiction of the United States shall have the same right in every State and Territory to *make and enforce contracts*, ... as is enjoyed by white citizens, ...

42 U.S.C. § 1981(a) (emphasis added)....

¶5 All courts to have addressed the issue have held that a customer's offer to do business in a retail setting qualifies as a "phase[ ] and incident[ ] of the contractual relationship" under § 1981....

¶6 The question, then, is whether the Barfields' proposal to exchange money at a bank is a contract offer in the same way as an offer to purchase doughnuts or apple juice. The claim made by the appellees, and accepted by the district court, is that the Barfields' proposed exchange was not a contract because it involved no consideration: "The bank would not have received any benefit or incurred a detriment if it had agreed to change the Barfields' bills." App. at 56. That reasoning, however, departs in several significant ways from our understanding of contract law.

¶7 To determine the contours of a contract, we look to state common law. *Hampton*, 247 F.3d at 1104; 42 U.S.C. § 1988(a). Under Kansas law:

> A contract must be supported by consideration in order to be enforceable. *State ex rel. Ludwick v. Bryant*, 237 Kan. 47, 697 P.2d 858 (1985); *Mitchell v. Miller*, 27 Kan. App. 2d 666, 8 P.3d 26 (2000). 'Consideration is defined as some right, interest, profit, or benefit accruing to one party, or some forbearance, detriment, loss, or responsibility, given, suffered, or undertaken by the other.' 17A Am. Jur. 2d, Contracts § 113, p. 129. A promise is without consideration when the promise is given by one party to another without anything being bargained for and given in exchange for it. 2 Corbin on Contracts § 5.20 (rev. ed. 1995).

Varney Bus. Servs., Inc. v. Pottroff, 275 Kan. 20, 59 P.3d 1003, 1014 (2002). *See also French v. French*, 161 Kan. 327, 167 P.2d 305, 308 (1946) (noting that "inconvenience to the promisee" is valid consideration).

¶8 In the most straightforward sense, the transaction proposed by the Barfields was a contract of exchange: they would give up something of value (a large-denomination bill) in exchange for something they valued more (smaller-denomination bills). It is hard to see why this is not a contract. If two boys exchange marbles, their transaction is a contract, even if it is hard for outsiders to fathom why either preferred the one or the other. Consideration does not need to have a quantifiable financial value:

> [T]he legal sufficiency of a consideration for a promise [does not] depend upon the comparative economic value of the consideration and of what is promised in return, for the parties are deemed to be the best judges of the bargains entered into.... Where a party contracts for the performance of an act which will afford him pleasure, gratify his ambition, please his fancy, or express his appreciation of a service another has rendered him, his estimate of value must be left undisturbed....

In re Shirk's Estate, 186 Kan. 311, 350 P.2d 1, 10 (1960).

¶9 The Bank, however, argues that the proposed exchange was not a contract because it received no remuneration for performing the service of bill exchange. In other words, rather than view the transaction as an exchange of one thing for another, the Bank urges us to treat the transaction as a gratuitous service provided by the Bank, for no consideration. We cannot regard the Bank's provision of bill exchange services as "gratuitous" in any legal sense. Profit-making establishments often offer to engage in transactions with no immediate gain, or even at a loss, as a means of inducing customers to engage in other transactions that are more lucrative; such offers may nonetheless be contractual, and they do not lack consideration. *See Idbeis v. Wichita Surgical Specialists, P.A.*, 279 Kan. 755, 112 P.3d 81, 90 (2005) (holding that unquantifiable consideration, such as an employee's goodwill and professional contacts, is adequate to sustain a contract). If, as is alleged in the complaint, the Bank effectively extends bill exchange services to persons of one race and not the other, that is sufficient to come within the ambit of § 1981.

....

We therefore reverse the district court's dismissal of the Barfield's Section 1981 claim.

Exercise 3.8 — Sham or Genuine Inducement?

Consider how the requirement of reciprocal inducement may be used to distinguish bargained-for exchanges from sham bargains: unenforceable promises to make gifts that are disguised as bargains.

1. $2,000 Discount

John desperately needs to sell his old car so that he can pay some overdue bills. When a potential buyer strikes a hard bargain, John reluctantly agrees to sell his car for $1,000, even though it has a market value of $3,000. Bargained-for exchange?

2. $2,000 Give-Away

Bob owns a car with a market value of $2,000. He announces his intention to give the car to his sister, Alicia, on her birthday in November. Alicia, a first-year law student, insists on promising to pay $1 for Bob's promise to give her the car. The idea sounds silly to Bob, but Alicia insists. Accordingly, Bob promises to transfer title to the car in November, and Alicia promises to pay Bob $1 on delivery. Bargained-for exchange? How is this arguably different from problem 1 above?

3. Fairness in Exchanges

Should courts be more concerned with fairness in an exchange, beyond finding reciprocal inducement and other elements of consideration? If so, would you empower courts to do so through the consideration doctrine or through some separate doctrinal mechanism? We will return to this question when we study unconscionability.

B. The Pre-Existing Duty Rule

1. Promising to Perform the Same Duties Owed in an Existing Contract with the Other Party

We learned in Chapter 2 that a party cannot unilaterally modify an existing contract. A modification is a separate agreement of the parties, normally reached through acceptance of an offer to modify the existing contract.

To constitute a new enforceable contract, must the agreement to modify be supported by consideration, as was the case with the original contract? In other words, is it necessary for both parties to add some new promise or performance, or will a one-sided modification suffice so long as the parties agreed to it?

Alaska Packers' Ass'n v. Domenico

117 F. 99 (9th Cir. 1902)

Ross, Circuit Judge.

¶1 The libel in this case was based upon a contract alleged to have been entered into between the [shipmates] and the appellant corporation on the 22d day of May, 1900, at Pyramid Harbor, Alaska, by which it is claimed the appellant promised to pay each of the [shipmates], among other things, the sum of $100 for services rendered and to be rendered....

¶2 The evidence shows without conflict that on March 26, 1900, at the city and county of San Francisco, the [shipmates] entered into a written contract with the appellants, whereby they agreed to go from San Francisco to Pyramid Harbor, Alaska, and return, on board such vessel as might be designated by the appellant, and to work for the appellant during the fishing season of 1900, at Pyramid Harbor, as sailors and fishermen, agreeing to do "regular ship's duty, both up and down, discharging and loading; and to do any other work whatsoever when requested to do so by the captain or agent of the Alaska Packers' Association." By the terms of this agreement, the appellant was to pay each of the [shipmates] $50 for the season, and two cents for each red salmon in the catching of which he took part.

¶3 The [shipmates] arrived [at Pyramid Harbor] early in April of the year mentioned, and began to unload the vessel and fit up the cannery. A few days thereafter, to wit, May 19th, they stopped work in a body, and demanded of the company's superintendent there in charge $100 for services in operating the vessel to and from Pyramid Harbor, instead of the sums stipulated for in and by the contracts; stating that unless they were paid this additional wage they would stop work entirely, and return to San Francisco. The evidence showed, and the court below found, that it was impossible for the appellant to get other men to take the places of the [shipmates], the place being remote, the season short and just opening; so that, after endeavoring for several days without success to induce the [shipmates] to proceed with their work in accordance with their contracts, the company's superintendent, on the 22d day of May, so far yielded to their demands as to instruct his clerk to copy the contracts executed in San Francisco, including the words "Alaska Packers' Association" at the end, substituting, for the $50 ... payments, respectively, of those contracts, the sum of $100, which document, so prepared, was signed by the [shipmates] before a shipping commissioner whom they had requested to be brought from Northeast Point;.... Upon the return of the [shipmates] to San Francisco at the close of the fishing season, they demanded pay in accordance with the terms of the alleged contract of May 22d, when the company denied its validity, and refused to pay other than as provided for by the contract[] of March 26th....

¶4 On the trial in the court below, the [shipmates] undertook to show that the fishing nets provided by the respondent were defective, and that it was on that account that they demanded increased wages. On that point, the evidence was substantially conflicting, and the finding of the court was against the [shipmates] the court saying:

> The contention of [shipmates] that the nets provided them were rotten and unserviceable is not sustained by the evidence. The defendants' interest required that [shipmates] should be provided with every facility necessary to their success as fishermen, for on such success depended the profits defendant would be able to realize that season from its packing plant, and the large capital invested therein. In view of this self-evident fact, it is highly improbable that the defendant gave [shipmates] rotten and unserviceable nets with which to fish. It follows from this finding that [shipmates] were not justified in refusing performance of their original contract.

112 Fed. 554.

¶5 The evidence being sharply conflicting in respect to these facts, the conclusions of the court, who heard and saw the witnesses, will not be disturbed. [citations omitted]

¶6 The real questions in the case as brought here are questions of law, and, in the view that we take of the case, it will be necessary to consider but one of those. Assuming that the appellant's superintendent at Pyramid Harbor was authorized to make the alleged contract of May 22d, and that he executed it on behalf of the appellant, was it supported by a sufficient consideration? From the foregoing statement of the case, it will have been seen that the [shipmates] agreed in writing, for certain stated compensation, to render their services to the appellant in remote waters where the season for conducting fishing operations is extremely short, and in which enterprise the appellant had a large amount of money invested; and, after having entered upon the discharge of their contract, and at a time when it was impossible for the appellant to secure other men in their places, the [shipmates], without any valid cause, absolutely refused to continue the services they were under contract to perform unless the appellant would consent to pay them more money. Consent to such a demand, under such circumstances, if given, was, in our opinion, without consideration, for the reason that it was based solely upon the [shipmates]' agreement to render the exact services, and none other, that they were already under contract to render....

No new considerati given

....

¶7 ... The circumstances of the present case bring it, we think, directly within the sound and just observations of the supreme court of Minnesota in the case of *King v. Railway Co.*, 61 Minn. 482, 63 N.W. 1105:

> ... [W]here the promise is simply a repetition of a subsisting legal promise[,] [t]here can be no consideration for the promise of the other party, and there is no warrant for inferring that the parties have voluntarily rescinded or modified their contract. The promise cannot be legally enforced, although the other party has completed his contract in reliance upon it.

¶8 In *Lichtenfeld v. Brewing Co.*, 103 Mo. 578, 15 S.W. 844, the court, in holding void a contract by which the owner of a building agreed to pay its architect an additional sum because of his refusal to otherwise proceed with the contract, said:

> It is urged upon us by respondents that this was a new contract. New in what? Jungenfeld was bound by his contract to design and supervise this building. Under the new promise, he was not to do anything more or anything different. What benefit was to accrue to Wainwright? He was to receive the same service from Jungenfeld under the new, that Jungenfeld was bound to tender under the original, contract. What loss, trouble, or inconvenience could result to Jungenfeld that he had not already assumed? No amount of metaphysical reasoning can change the plain fact that Jungenfeld took advantage of Wainwright's necessities, and extorted the promise of five per cent. on the refrigerator plant as the condition of his complying with his contract already entered into.... What we hold is that, when a party merely does what he has already obligated himself to do, he cannot demand an additional compensation therefor; and although, by taking advantage of the necessities of his adversary, he obtains a promise for more, the law will regard it as *nudum pactum*, and will not lend its process to aid in the wrong.

[The court refused to follow decisions from Massachusetts and Michigan, each of which enforced a second contract that changed only one party's duties in relation to an earlier, abandoned contract.]

¶ 9 In addition to the Minnesota and Missouri cases above cited [¶¶ 7–8], the following are some of the numerous authorities holding [contrary to the Massachusetts and Michigan decisions]: [the court cites to 16 cases from various jurisdictions, as well as the writings of four commentators, all of which support this court's view].

¶ 10 It results from the views above expressed that the judgment must be reversed, and the cause remanded, with directions to the court below to enter judgment for the respondent, with costs. It is so ordered.

Exercise 3.9 — Questions on the Pre-Existing Duty Rule

1. Waiver or Rescission

The excerpt below is excised from a passage that appeared between paragraphs 8 and 9 in the preceding edited opinion. In this excerpt, the court reviewed a decision from Massachusetts that found one-sided modifications enforceable on the ground that one party had first voluntarily waived its rights under the original contract and then freely negotiated a new one:

> The Massachusetts cases cited by the court below in support of its judgment commence with the case of *Munroe v. Perkins*, 9 Pick. 305, 20 Am. Dec. 475 [Mass.], which really seems to be the foundation of all of the cases in support of that view. In that case, the plaintiff had agreed in writing to erect a building for the defendants. Finding his contract a losing one, he had concluded to abandon it, and resumed work on the oral contract of the defendants that, if he would do so, they would pay him what the work was worth without regard to the terms of the original contract. The court said that whether the oral contract was without consideration
>
>> "depends entirely on the question whether the first contract was waived. The plaintiff having refused to perform that contract, as he might do, subjecting himself to such damages as the other parties might show they were entitled to recover, he afterward went on, upon the faith of the new promise, and finished the work. This was a sufficient consideration. If Payne and Perkins were willing to accept his relinquishment of the old contract, and proceed on a new agreement, the law, we think, would not prevent it."

Alaska Packers' Ass'n v. Domenico, 117 F. 99, 104–05 (9th Cir. 1902). In *Alaska Packers*, the court appears to reject *Munroe* and similar cases as representing an unpersuasive minority view. But, rather than rejecting the reasoning of these cases, could the court have distinguished them on the facts?

The court in *Alaska Packers* could have distinguished *Munroe* on the basis of a finding that the shipmates had coerced their employer into signing the second contract. What facts might support an inference that the shipmate's employer, although not desiring to modify the contract, had no reasonable choice but to give in to the shipmates' demands and promise an increase in pay? We will return to this question of coercion when we study duress, a ground for rescinding a contract.

Aside from any question of coercion, could the court in *Alaska Packers* have distinguished the "waiver" cases on the simple ground that the parties in *Alaska Packers* had not mutually abandoned their original contract before agreeing to the second one? What facts show that the employer had not agreed with the shipmates to rescind (cancel) the first contract, prior to signing the second contract?

Suppose instead that both the shipmates and their employer had been dissatisfied with the contract negotiated on March 26 and had voluntarily rescinded that contract on May 21, symbolizing their mutual rescission by having representatives of both parties join in tearing up a copy of the March 26 contract. If the parties had then negotiated a new contract from scratch and ended up with the May 22 contract described in *Alaska Packers*, explain why the court could more easily find consideration in the second contract.

2. Change in Duties

Suppose that the shipmates had agreed in the May 22 contract not only to perform their duties under the March 26 contract but also to apply a new coat of paint on the interior of the cabin of the ship, a duty that we will now assume was not included in the March 26 contract. If applying the new paint was an idea advanced by the shipmates and initially resisted by their employer, what finding should a court make to support a conclusion that this additional promise helped to provide consideration for the additional $50 in pay for each shipmate?

In an Arizona decision 77 years after *Alaska Packers*, an employer agreed to pay a salary to a foreman for supervising union employees on a construction project, the estimated cost of which was based on union standards of pay and organization of work spelled out in a collective bargaining agreement with the employees. The employer subsequently agreed to pay the foreman an additional bonus in exchange for the foreman's promise to "use extra efforts to maximize his crew's efficiency," thus producing expected savings on construction costs. *Leone v. Precision Plumbing and Heating of Southern Arizona*, 121 Ariz. 514, 516, 591 P.2d 1002, 1004 (Ct. App. 1979). Did the foreman give consideration for the employer's promise to pay a bonus on top of the salary originally agreed to? What arguments can you make for both sides?

3. Change in Method of Pay

In *Alaska Packers*, it appears that the May 22nd contract increased the shipmates' base pay of $50 to $100 and retained the additional piece work pay of two cents per salmon caught. Suppose, however, that the shipmates in the May 22nd contract had asked for a total pay of $100, without more for salmon caught, in place of the original pay of $50 plus two cents per salmon. Would the new contract, modifying the original one, be supported by new consideration? Would the new contract be supported by consideration if the shipmates promised the same work, and the corporation promised to pay $100 plus two cents per salmon ($50 more than in the original contract), but to pay it 60 days later than called for in the first contract? If the idea for the delay in payment originated with the shipmates, what finding should a court make to assure that this change in the time for payment provided consideration for the additional $50 in pay?

4. Good Faith Dispute about Pre-Existing Duties

Imagine that the original contract in *Alaska Packers* was ambiguous about whether the payment of $50 plus two cents per salmon included loading crates of canned salmon onto trucks, as well as catching and packing the salmon. Suppose the parties settled a good-faith dispute about that issue by entering into a second contract at the cannery, in which the shipmates promise to load the crates onto trucks, and the corporation promised to increase the shipmates' base pay. If the employer later continued to assert that the shipmates were obligated under the first contract to load the crates onto trucks, why is the second contract nonetheless supported by consideration?

5. Unanticipated Circumstances

Following trends in the case law, the second Restatement advances an argument for enforcing a one-sided modification of a contract, agreed to prior to full performance by either side, "if the modification is fair and equitable in view of circumstances not anticipated by the parties when the contract was made...." RESTATEMENT (SECOND) OF CONTRACTS § 89(a) (1981). Do you agree with this limited exception to the Pre-existing Duty Rule?

In *Alaska Packers*, imagine that the trial court had resolved the factual question about the condition of the fishing nets differently and had instead found that the nets had deteriorated to an unexpected degree, making the shipmates' work more difficult than either party had anticipated, leading to an agreement to increase shipmates' pay. Assuming that the appellate court accepted this factual conclusion and assuming that it followed the rule of the Restatement, would these new facts justify enforcement of the modified agreement?

6. Pre-existing Duty to Third Party?

A promises to pay B $500 in return for B's promise to remove junk from B's yard by the end of the month, to improve real estate values in their neighborhood. Soon afterwards, C promises to pay B in exchange for B's promise to remove the same junk from B's yard by the end of the same month. Is C's promise enforceable, or does it lack consideration under the pre-existing duty rule? The courts are split. Let's explore both sides of this divide.

First, apply the pre-existing duty rule, and explain how a court could find that C's promise to B lacks consideration. Next, still applying the pre-existing duty rule, explain why a court might find that B has provided additional consideration to C in the second contract (Hint: Suppose A and B enter into a voluntary rescission. Has B restricted his freedom further by having entered into the agreement with C?). Alternatively, explain why some courts might apply the pre-existing duty rule to a case such as *Alaska Packers* but not to this hypothetical (Hint: To the extent that courts are using the pre-existing duty rule to help guard against coercion, does this third-party hypothetical present much of a risk of coercion in the second contract? Explain).

7. Noncontractual Source of Pre-Existing Duties?

The *Hamer* court repeated several times that consideration can be satisfied by giving up a legal right and that the nephew had a right to engage in the vices from which he promised to abstain (or at least some of them). Suppose that an uncle and nephew agreed today that the uncle would pay his nephew $5,000 if the nephew refrained from buying, selling, possessing, or using cocaine, all actions prohibited by state criminal law, for the next five years. If we define the holding of the *Hamer* decision narrowly, we would conclude that *Hamer* did not decide that such an agreement is supported by consideration. Indeed, the opinion in *Hamer* suggests that such a case would be materially different from *Hamer*. Construct an argument explaining why the new case is distinguishable from *Hamer* and why the New York Court of Appeals should find no consideration in the new case.

---

2. *State of the Pre-Existing Duty Rule*

We will later study the doctrine of duress. If it proves to be a sufficient tool for guarding against coercion between parties to an existing contract, does the consideration doctrine need a pre-existing duty rule? After all, even in the case of a one-sided modification, the original contract was supported by consideration, and the modified contract still reflects an exchange even though one side of the exchange lacks new consideration. For example, if parties A and B exchanged promises of X for Y in the original contract, and if they agreed to modify the original contract so that now A is promising X in exchange for B promising Y + Z, the modified contract still reflects an exchange, does it not?

For sales of goods, Article 2 of the UCC eliminates the pre-existing duty rule: "An agreement modifying a contract within this Article needs no consideration to be binding." UCC § 2-209(1) (2011). For non-sales contracts, such as for services (including employment) or real estate, the pre-existing duty rule articulated by cases such as *Alaska Packers* is alive but not particularly well. Although only a very few states have abandoned the rule for non-sales contracts, many of them will be open to the exception for unanticipated circumstances advanced by the second Restatement.

3. *Applicability of the UCC to Hybrid Contracts*

Because the UCC overrules the pre-existing duty rule for sales of goods, the enforceability of a one-sided modification often will depend on whether it is classified as a sale of goods, rather than a real estate contract or service contract. This classification can be tricky in a hybrid contract such as one that calls for a mix of sales and services. For example, a contract may require a manufacturer to supply goods, install them, and maintain them for a year. The UCC does not state whether it applies to hybrid contracts, so courts have developed judicial rules to classify such contracts. Although approaches vary slightly from state to state, under a typical test the UCC applies to all facets of a contract if it is predominantly one for the sale of goods:

> The test ... is ... whether their predominant factor, their thrust, their purpose, reasonably stated, is the rendition of service, with goods incidentally involved (e.g., contract with artist for painting) or is a transaction of sale, with labor incidentally involved (e.g., installation of a water heater in a bathroom).

Bonebrake v. Cox, 499 F.2d 951, 960 (8th Cir. 1974) (footnotes omitted).

Gross Valentino Printing Co. v. Clarke

120 Ill. App. 3d 907, 458 N.E.2d 1027 (1983)

Goldberg, Justice:

¶ 1 Gross Valentino Printing Company (plaintiff) brought this action against Frederick S. Clarke, doing business as Cinefantastique (defendant) based on an alleged breach of contract. Defendant asserted three affirmative defenses: lack of consideration, fraudulent or innocent misrepresentation, and business compulsion.

¶2 Plaintiff moved for summary judgment. After a hearing, the trial court granted plaintiff's motion and entered judgment of $5,116.20 for plaintiff. Defendant appeals.

¶3 Defendant publishes a magazine. After discussion, in July of 1979, plaintiff sent defendant a letter for printing the magazine including a price quotation of $6,695. Defendant accepted the terms. On August 8, 1979, the parties met to discuss the layout....

....

¶4 Defendant also stated the parties had a telephone conversation on August 14, 1979. Defendant was informed the job "was going to cost more than we thought." Plaintiff's agent told defendant the higher cost was incurred because plaintiff had to "send the stripping out."...

¶5 Defendant also deposed that sometime thereafter plaintiff sent defendant a letter dated August 15, 1979. The letter specified the same work as represented in the parties' earlier contract. However the price was increased to $9,300. Defendant made no objection to this increase until a later date.

¶6 On August 30, 1979, plaintiff delivered the first 5,000 magazines to defendant. Defendant signed the purchase order reflecting the new price and paid plaintiff $4,650 on account of the purchase. Defendant subsequently received the complete shipment of 15,000 magazines. However, on October 28, 1979, defendant informed plaintiff he would not accept the price increase.

I.
Lack of Consideration.

¶7 The parties agree that the sufficiency of defendant's first affirmative defense of lack of consideration depends on the determination of whether the transactions at issue are subject to the Uniform Commercial Code (UCC).... Under the UCC a modification of an existing contract "within this Article needs no consideration to be binding." (Ill. Rev. Stat. 1981, ch. 26, par. 2-209(1).) The parties also agree that the applicability of the UCC depends on the determination of whether they contracted for "goods" or "services."

¶8 The UCC defines "goods" as ... :

> "'Goods' means all things, including specially manufactured goods, which are movable at the time of identification to the contract for sale other than the money in which the price is to be paid, investment securities (Article 8) and things in action. 'Goods' also includes the unborn young of animals and growing crops and other identified things attached to realty as described in the section on goods to be severed from realty (Section 2-107)."

....

¶ 9 In the case at bar, we conclude that the primary subject of the contract was the tangible printed magazines and not "printing services." Defendant's deposition indicates he worked with plaintiff in arriving at the "layout" of the magazine. Furthermore, defendant's deposition indicates he "shopped" for printers based solely on which printer submitted the lowest price estimate. Such an admission suggests that to defendant the "printing services" were largely fungible or interchangeable and were merely incidental to delivery of the final product. It is clear that defendant was simply interested in determining who could get him the magazines, the ultimate product, at the lowest possible price.

¶ 10 Defendant relies on three cases. We find them inapposite to the case at bar: ....

¶ 11 In *For Children, Inc. v. Graphics International, Inc.* (S.D.N.Y. 1972), 352 F. Supp. 1280, the court held damages for breach of a contract for the publishing of "pop-up" children's books were not governed by the UCC. The court indicated the manufacture of pop-up books was "a limited field." (352 F. Supp. 1280, 1284.) Therefore, the publishing at issue in *For Children* was in the nature of a specialty. Such specialized printing requires greater skill and expertise than the simple printing of a magazine as in the case at bar.

¶ 12 In *Curtis Publishing Co. v. Sheridan* (S.D.N.Y. 1971), 53 F.R.D. 642, the court denied summary judgment in an action based on a contract for the publication of books. The court concluded there were disputed facts regarding whether the contract was for goods or services. (53 F.R.D. 642, 643.) However, the court noted that the contract included various responsibilities of the publisher other than printing, such as financing and marketing of the books.

¶ 13 In all of these cases the responsibility of the publisher went beyond the simple printing of the material. Each of the contracts in the cited cases required more independent judgment, skill, and service than the contract in the case at bar. Therefore we hold that the agreement between these parties for printing the magazines was subject to the provisions of the UCC. It follows that proof of consideration was unnecessary. The trial court properly struck the first affirmative defense.

....

III.

Business Compulsion.

¶ 14 Similarly, defendant has failed to allege sufficient facts to sustain the affirmative defense of business compulsion.

¶ 15 For these reasons the summary judgment in favor of plaintiff is affirmed.

V. Historical Perspective on Consideration under Common Law

To help you review this chapter, and to gain additional perspective, consider the following historical summary of the development of the consideration doctrine, with the footnotes omitted:[6]

A. Early Forms of Action under Common Law

1. Early Forms of Action: Debt and Covenant

Beginning with the reign of King Henry II (1154–89), civil actions in the central royal courts in England were limited to claims that fit within recognized forms of action for which the Crown would issue a writ. One of the earliest of these was debt-detinue, which split early in the thirteenth century into separate actions for detinue to recover personal property or its value, and for debt to recover a sum of undisputed amount owed for the delivery of something of value.

Although a forerunner of contract law, the action for debt was not one for breach of promise; rather, it alleged that the defendant wrongfully withheld payment owed for something valuable that had already been delivered to the defendant. Precisely this feature, however, sowed the seeds of the consideration doctrine, because debt required a *quid pro quo*, in the form of the prior delivery of property, services, or loaned money, to support the demand for payment.

A plaintiff could more directly enforce a promise by bringing an action for breach of covenant, without the necessity of showing a *quid pro quo*. By the fourteenth century, however, this writ applied only to promises set forth in a written instrument formalized with a seal. The action on covenant thus could not be used for informal transactions.

---

6. The sources used for this passage include several provisions of the UCC and the Restatement, several judicial opinions, and excerpts from the following treatises, listed in their order of appearance in the footnotes for this excerpt: P.S. Atiyah, The Rise and Fall of Freedom of Contract (Clarendon Press 1979); J.H. Baker, An Introduction to English Legal History (Butterworths 4th ed. 2002); Eugen Bucher, England and the Continent: Distinguishing the Peculiarities of the English Common Law of Contract 50 (Tony Weir, trans., Dike Law Books 2009); Arthur Linton Corbin, Corbin on Contracts (one vol. ed. West Publ. 1980) (1952); E. Allan Farnsworth, Contracts (4th ed. Aspen Publ. 2004); E. Allan Farnsworth, William F. Young, and Carol Sanger, Contracts: Cases and Materials (hereafter, "Cases and Materials") (6th ed. 2001). Oliver Wendell Holmes, Jr., The Common Law (Dover Publ.,1991) (1881); David Ibbetson, A Historical Introduction to the Law of Obligations (1999); F. W. Maitland, Equity Also, The Forms of Action at Common Law: Two Courses of Lectures (A. H. Chaytor and W. J. Whittaker, eds.) (Cambridge Univ. Press, 1910); Charles Rembar, The Law of the Land: The Evolution of Our Legal System (N.Y.: Simon and Schuster 1980); A.W.B. Simpson, A History of the Common Law of Contract (Clarendon Press 1975).

Moreover, the action for debt proved unpopular with plaintiffs, partly because the defendant could adopt the ancient wager of law. Through this procedure, the defendant could defeat the action by producing a sufficient number of compurgators who were willing to support the defendant's sworn denial by swearing an oath in support of the defendant's credibility.

2. *Assumpsit as a Form of Trespass on the Case*

Beginning in the fourteenth century, English courts began to employ a writ of more general application, *trespass on the case*, which could avoid some of the restrictions of debt and covenant. One form of action on the case, *assumpsit*, provided a remedy when the defendant caused damage to the plaintiff's property while lawfully possessing the property (and thus not committing a simple trespass) after undertaking to provide a service. When the King's Bench decided in *Slade's Case* in 1602 that an action in assumpsit could be brought even if debt might otherwise apply, settling a long-simmering debate, the way was clear for assumpsit to supplant debt and its outmoded wager of law.

3. *Assumpsit—Active Harm vs. Failure to Perform*

In the early cases, assumpsit required the defendant to have engaged in misfeasance in the undertaking, actively causing the plaintiff to have suffered a tangible loss or detriment, and providing a forerunner to modern actions in both contracts and tort. In the seminal case of *Humber Ferryman* in 1348, the defendant actively caused the loss of the plaintiff's horse by overloading a ferry after undertaking to carry the horse across a river. In other typical cases, liability in assumpsit was based on the defendant's actively injuring the plaintiff's horse by negligently shoeing the horse after undertaking to shod it.

Eventually, however, assumpsit was applied to nonfeasance, as in the simple failure to perform an undertaking, at least if the plaintiff had still suffered some loss, such as by making prepayment in reliance on the promise. Liability for nonfeasance provided a foundation for the concept of breach of promise.

The road to a theory of contract was further paved in the case of *Lucy v. Walwyn* in 1561, when the courts began imposing liability for breach of promise in a fully executory contract, arising from unperformed mutual promises without previously delivered *quid pro quo* or other detrimental reliance. This significant development, coupled with the boost to assumpsit in *Slade's Case* 41 years later, helped to usher in the modern law of contracts and its consideration requirement.

The term "consideration" emerged gradually. In the sixteenth century, for example, the term *quid pro quo* from the action of debt, and the Roman term *causa* as developed in Canon Law, often competed with the term "consideration" as a way of expressing a required element in an action in assumpsit to enforce a promise. The term "consideration" ultimately prevailed and its requirements evolved to require an exchange, as in the exchange of mutual promises or the exchange of a performance for a promise.

B. Consideration in Modern Contract Law

As a supplement to its consideration doctrine, English legislation still recognizes the modern equivalent of the ancient action of covenant. An authenticating seal is no longer necessary, but English courts will enforce a promise that is set forth in a "deed," without requiring proof of consideration. A deed is defined by statute as a written promise signed before an attesting witness and delivered to the promisee.

In many jurisdictions in the United States, the owner of tangible property can gratuitously convey the property through a written deed accepted by the recipient, but that represents actual change of ownership in the property rather than merely a gratuitous promise to give the property to another. Thus, the formality of recording a gratuitous promise in a sealed instrument or a deed is no longer a basis for enforcement of the promise in in most states of the United States. In some states, setting forth a promise in a signed writing shifts the burden to the defendant to prove lack of consideration, but consideration remains an element of contract formation. Thus, in U.S. consideration doctrine, the substantive requirements of debt and assumpsit have survived to a greater degree than the formalities of the early action of covenant.

Specifically, the *quid pro quo* of debt and the injury or detriment of assumpsit continue to influence the shape of consideration requirements. In fact, some twentieth-century judicial opinions in the United States surprisingly characterize the contract actions before the courts as ones in "assumpsit," harkening back to the historical roots of modern contract claims.

1. Consideration Requires an Exchange

The modern common law consideration doctrine essentially represents an exercise in distinguishing exchanges from gratuitous promises. To be sure, American common law will enforce a gratuitous promise if it satisfies the equitable doctrine of promissory estoppel. That remedy, however, is distinct from the concept of consideration and is limited to cases in which an injury, detriment, or other injustice results from foreseeable reliance on a promise. The consideration doctrine, on the other hand, is satisfied without regard to reliance or equality of the exchange, as long as the promise to be enforced was part of a reciprocally induced exchange.

Growing out of the injury or detriment from the now-obsolete action of assumpsit is the current requirement that each party to a bargain must add a promise or immediate performance to the exchange. Under modern doctrine, however, the performance—or promised performance—need not visit a tangible loss, injury, or detriment on the person providing it, so long as the performance consists of an act or forbearance that the obligor is not already legally obligated to perform, and so long as a promise to engage in such a performance states a non-illusory commitment.

2. Consideration as Bargained-For Exchange

These elements of exchange, however, do not amount to consideration under modern doctrine unless they are linked together in a bargain. According to the

Restatement (Second) of Contracts § 71, "[a] performance or return promise is bargained for if it is sought by the promisor in exchange for his promise and is given by the promisee in exchange for that promise." According to Holmes, the plaintiff need not show that each party received a tangible benefit or profit from the other's promise or performance, so long as each promise or performance was a genuine inducement for the return consideration. A return promise or performance need not be the sole or even primary inducement for the promise, so long as it is *an* inducement, and so long as it is a genuine one rather than a sham.

Accordingly, one who performs the act requested in an offer to pay a reward has not satisfied the consideration requirement if he had no knowledge of the offered reward when he performed; in such a case, he obviously was induced exclusively by other factors to engage in the act. Similarly, a past act cannot be consideration for a subsequent promise because it could not have been induced by a promise that had not yet been formed and communicated.

This requirement of reciprocal inducement, cemented into United States common law doctrine by Justice Holmes in the nineteenth century, could be viewed as consideration's counterpart to *cause*, because it relates to a party's *reason* for contracting. A charitable motivation, however, will not suffice for consideration. Therefore, the common law concept of *inducement* requires more than a charitable desire to benefit someone else with a promised performance. If it were otherwise, the common law would enforce gratuitous promises as well as promises in an exchange.

Similarly, a feeling of love or affection for the other party does not satisfy the requirement of reciprocal inducement. If—motivated solely by love and affection for my son—I promise to buy him a new car, I am still promising to make a gift, and I will not be legally liable if I breach my promise. Some cases and scholars in early English common law took a contrary position, asserting that a promisor's feelings of love and affection for a close relative could serve as consideration for a promise to the relative. Indeed, the centuries-old phrase "good and valuable consideration" was intended to refer to both: (1) "valuable consideration" in the form of goods, services, money or other conventional inducements for a promise and (2) "good consideration" in the form of love and affection for a family member as the motivation for a promise. To the extent that such an extension of consideration was ever recognized, however, it has long been abandoned in the common law.

Of course, the modern definition of consideration is satisfied if the object of your affection promises to perform an act in exchange for your promise. For example, if your child promises to study diligently in college in exchange for your promise to pay the tuition, that reciprocally induced exchange satisfies modern consideration requirements. True, your love for your child likely explains a good deal of the motivation for your promise; nonetheless, if your child's promise to study diligently operates as part of the inducement for your promise, you have formed a bargained-for exchange.

VI. Consideration Reconsidered

Recall our comparison in Section I.B of the common law consideration doctrine, which requires an exchange, with the civil law approach, which permits enforcement of a gratuitous promise. We asked at that time whether the common law's requirement of an exchange was justified.

The distinction between exchanges and gratuitous promises is drawn most sharply in the United States, because English legislation provides a procedure for conveying enforceable gratuitous promises. Would you support legislation in your state that would enforce a gratuitous promise if it is recorded with designated formalities that reflect a serious intent to perform the promise? Legislation of that sort would place the state more in line with civil law jurisdictions and with our common law parent, England.

VII. Summary

- Modern consideration doctrine requires a bargained-for exchange. The exchange can consist of a promise for a return promise or a promise for a completed performance. The performance can consist of an act or forbearance. The exchange is "bargained for" if the parties were reciprocally induced, so that each was seeking the other party's promise or performance in exchange for his own.
- Forbearance from asserting a legal claim is a valid performance if the claim had potential merit at the time of contracting, with the precise requirements varying from state to state.
- A charitable motivation does not satisfy the requirement of an inducement; thus, a one-sided promise to make a gift does not satisfy the consideration requirement.
- In the case of a conditional gratuitous promise, an act by the promisee is not a return performance if it does not induce the promise; instead, it could simply be a convenient way to collect the promised gift.
- In applying the consideration doctrine, courts will not inquire into the relative values of the things exchanged, so long as each thing was a genuine inducement (not necessarily the sole or main inducement) for the other.
- A statement is not a valid promise, but is only an illusory one, if it leaves the promisor free to avoid all obligation at his own whim or discretion. However, a promise that is conditioned on the promisor's good-faith satisfaction with the other party's performance is not illusory, because it obligates the promisor to perform if the other party has met the promisor's subjective standards.
- Courts sometimes avoid apparent consideration problems by finding obligations that are implicit in the parties' conduct, in their statements on other matters, or in other circumstances surrounding the transaction. Such obligations are implied in fact.

- A one-sided modification of an existing contract does not satisfy the consideration requirement under the pre-existing duty rule, because only one party is adding to the pre-existing obligations. The common law pre-existing duty rule is abandoned in the UCC for sales of goods, and some states have relaxed it for other transactions governed by common law.

Exercise 3.10 — Preliminary Analysis of Essay Question

Bob owns the Rhythm Room ("RR" for short), a music club with a capacity of 250 people. Last May, Bob contracted with the "Bad Boys Blues Band" ("BB" for short) for a three-hour concert this December, at a fee of $5,000. The contract requires the Band to be set up in time for a 7:00 p.m. sound check, to perform three hour-long sets between 9:00 p.m. and 1:00 a.m. with two breaks of 30 minutes each, and to remove their equipment from the club by 2:00 a.m. Over the summer, BB released a music CD and a music video, which launched the band into national fame.

In a telephone conversation with BB's agent, Jan Hummer, Bob expressed his good fortune at having BB performing in his small club when it was now being booked for large arenas. Their dialogue continued:

> Jan: Yeah, you showed great judgment in booking this band on the way up, and we haven't lost or replaced any members for two years, so the band is tighter than ever. But the $5,000 fee you agreed to pay us is a small fraction of our current booking fee. Why don't you double that in light of the publicity our band will generate for your club? I'm guessing the local media will want some interviews with our band members, and I can remind the guys to save some time in their schedules for the media.
>
> Bob: You are right that this concert will put our club in a national spotlight, interviews or not. But I'm charging a $20 cover charge now, and the maximum I can charge at the door at a club like this is $30. I can increase your fee to $7,500, but that's the most I can offer. Can you live with that?
>
> Jan: Agreed. You're getting the deal of a century, but that's because you're good at recognizing talent.

You may assume that Bob and Jan have authority to bind the band and the club, and that they reached agreement over the phone to increase the band's fee on the existing, continuing contract, so do not address offer and acceptance. Address only one issue: whether the new agreement between Bob and Jan satisfies consideration requirements. Rather than attempt to write a full essay answer at this point, answer the following questions: (1) Which facts raise some uncertainty about consideration? (2) What kinds of consideration problems are raised by the facts? (3) What specific rule applies to each such consideration problem? (4) With respect to each kind of consideration problem, what factual arguments support or oppose finding consideration? Try to find arguments for both sides. You can compare your abbreviated analysis with the full sample answer in Appendix 3.

Chapter 4

Consideration II: Moral Obligation, Promissory Estoppel, and Obligations Implied in Law

I. Introduction

Although consideration is a fundamental requirement for contract formation in our common-law system, courts have frequently encountered cases in which some remedy seems to be justified, even in the absence of a bargained-for exchange. Compelling facts in such cases have inspired some courts to recognize an expansive view of consideration or to develop supplementary theories of liability. Although the facts of some cases will support a claim in tort, we will limit our exploration in this chapter to theories of liability that are more closely associated with the field of contract law.

As you work through this chapter, consider the following questions:

- When the application of the traditional doctrine to unusual facts seems to deny recovery to a sympathetic or deserving claimant, should a court stretch traditional legal doctrine—or carve out exceptions to it—if necessary to produce a just result? Or should courts preserve the values of certainty and predictability in the law through a relatively formalistic and mechanical theory that does not depend on application of amorphous concepts such as justice or morality?
- If an appellate court is determined to grant recovery in the absence of consideration narrowly defined, should it do so by expanding the definition of consideration so that it encompasses some transactions that do not amount to a bargained-for exchange? Or should it instead develop a supplemental theory of recovery that stands side by side with consideration doctrine?
- If a court develops a supplemental theory of liability, what is the appropriate remedy under the companion theory? As in an action to enforce a contract with consideration, should supplemental theories protect expectation interest? Depending on the nature of the theory or the facts of the dispute, should recovery sometimes be limited to protecting reliance or restitution interest, or some other measure of recovery?

- Should U.S. law impose greater responsibilities during bargaining, such as a universal duty to bargain in good faith, or does the law wisely leave parties largely free of obligations unless and until agreement is reached?

II. Moral Obligation Arising out of Past Performance

Some courts have addressed the question whether the doctrine of consideration should be expanded to support enforcement of a promise given in consideration of a past performance, one completed before the promisor conceived of making the promise. To appreciate why this is a difficult issue, we must first understand why such a transaction does not amount to consideration narrowly defined as a bargained-for exchange. After all, we still do have a promise or performance on each side of the transaction, and the promisor might feel a moral obligation to pay for the other party's past performance, thus providing the promisor with a motivation (inducement?) for making the promise.

Exercise 4.1 — The Problem of a Promise for Past Performance

What is required for a bargained-for exchange, and why do the following facts almost certainly fall short of those requirements? Explain.

Dan and Nancy have always felt extremely grateful for the enormous, marvelous, and memorable wedding cake that Debbie had made for them for their wedding, charging them only $100 for it on that wonderful day. In gratitude for Debbie's contribution to their wedding day memories, on their tenth anniversary, on a Friday, the now well-off Dan and Nancy promised to give Debbie $10,000 because they knew she was struggling to make ends meet. All three agreed to meet at the bank on Monday to arrange for transfer of the funds. On Sunday, however, Dan and Nancy called Debbie to repudiate their promise.

A. The Traditional View: Moral Obligation Does Not Support Consideration

Mills v. Wyman

3 Pick. [20 Mass.] 207 (1825)
Supreme Judicial Court of Massachusetts

¶ 1 This was [a contract action] brought to recover a compensation for the board, nursing, &c., of Levi Wyman, son of the defendant [Seth Wyman], from the 5th to the 20th of February, 1821. The plaintiff [Mills] then lived at Hartford, in Connecticut; the defendant, at Shrewsbury, in this county. Levi Wyman, at the time when the services were rendered, was about 25 years of age, and had long ceased to be a member of his father's family. He was on his return from a voyage at sea, and being suddenly taken sick at Hartford, and being poor and in distress, was relieved by the plaintiff in the manner and to the extent above stated. On the 24th of February, after all the expense had been incurred, the defendant [Seth Wyman] wrote a letter to the plaintiff [Mills], promising to pay him such expenses. There was no consideration for this promise, except what grew out of the relation which subsisted between Levi Wyman and the defendant, and Howe, J., before whom the cause was tried in the court of common pleas, thinking this not sufficient to support the action, directed a nonsuit. To this direction, the plaintiff filed exception.

Parker, C. J.

¶2 General rules of law established for the protection and security of honest and fair-minded men, who may inconsiderately make promises without any equivalent, will sometimes screen men of a different character from engagements which they are bound *in foro conscietiae* to perform. This is a defect inherent in all human systems of legislation. The rule that a mere verbal promise, without any consideration, cannot be enforced by action, is universal in its application, and cannot be departed from to suit particular cases in which a refusal to perform such a promise may be disgraceful.

¶3 The promise declared on in this case appears to have been made without any legal consideration. The kindness and services towards the sick son of the defendant were not bestowed at his request. The son was in no respect under the care of the defendant. He was twenty-five years old, and had long left his father's family. On his return from a foreign country, he fell sick among strangers, and the plaintiff acted the part of the good Samaritan, giving him shelter and comfort until he died. The defendant, his father, on being informed of this event, influenced by a transient feeling of gratitude, promises in writing to pay the plaintiff for the expenses he had incurred. But he has determined to break this promise, and is willing to have his case appear on record as a strong example of particular injustice sometimes necessarily resulting from the operation of general rules.

¶4 It is said a moral obligation is a sufficient consideration to support an express promise; and some authorities lay down the rule thus broadly; but upon examination of the cases we are satisfied that the universality of the rule cannot be supported, [unless the promise revived an obligation that had once been part of a bargain but was extinguished by operation of law, such as through discharge in bankruptcy]....

¶5 A deliberate promise, in writing, made freely and without any mistake, one which may lead the party to whom it is made into contracts and expenses, cannot be broken without a violation of moral duty. But if there was nothing paid or promised for it, the law, perhaps wisely, leaves the execution of it to the conscience of him who makes it....

¶6 These principles are deduced from the general current of decided cases upon the subject, as well as from the known maxims of the common law. The general position, that moral obligation is a sufficient consideration for an express promise, is to be limited in its application, to cases where at some time or other a good or valuable consideration has existed.

¶7 For the foregoing reasons we are all of opinion that the nonsuit directed by the Court of Common Pleas was right, and that judgment be entered thereon for costs for the defendant.

B. Departures from the Traditional View

1. *Consideration in Renewal of an Obligation Discharged by Law*

In portions of the opinion largely omitted from the excerpts above, the *Mills* court conceded that a promise made in recognition of a past performance would be enforceable in a very limited circumstance: when the past performance was once part of a bargained-for exchange between the parties but the promisor's obligation to render her counter-performance was discharged (eliminated) by operation of law, such as by bankruptcy of running of the statute of limitations. In such circumstances, the promisor can renew her obligation by making a new promise to pay for the past performance, or by otherwise affirmatively recognizing the obligation arising out of the past events. *See* Restatement (Second) of Contracts §§ 82, 83 (1981).

For example, suppose that you and I agreed in a bargained-for exchange seven years ago that you would provide consulting services for me in exchange for a payment of $5,000. After you performed your valuable services for me, but before you collected your fee from me, I declared bankruptcy and was able to discharge my debt to you; alternatively, perhaps you allowed the statute of limitations to run before filing suit to collect your fee. At this point—because of the operation of bankruptcy laws or the statute of limitations—I am free of any legal obligation to pay you. On the other hand, I likely would feel a moral obligation to pay you, arising out of our past contractual relationship and your performance. If I now make a new promise to pay you $5,000 for your past consulting work, many courts will enforce that promise, at least if the promise is in writing. The new promise is enforceable in many states not merely because I felt a moral obligation to make the promise, but because I have renewed an obligation that once was part of an enforceable bargained-for exchange.

2. Webb v. McGowin: *Directly Recognizing Moral Obligation*

Case law in some states more squarely rejects the traditional rule of *Mills v. Wyman* and permits enforcement of a new promise arising out of a sense of moral obligation to repay the other party for a past performance, even though the promisor is not merely renewing a promise previously made in the context of a prior bargained-for exchange. Such a case is *Webb v. McGowin*, 27 Ala. App. 82, 168 So. 196, *cert. denied*, 232 Ala. 374, 168 So. 199 (1936). In *Webb*, an employee saved his employer's life by diverting the direction of a falling block of wood, a heroic act that cost the employee to suffer serious permanent injuries. At the time of the incident, the parties had no time to enter into a contract by which the employer could promise to pay the employee if the employee acted to save the employer's life. Afterwards, however, in recognition of the employee's past service, the employer promised to pay the employee a pension for the rest of the employee's life. Unfortunately for the employee, the employer's successors ceased making these payments after the death of the employer.

Even though the employer's promise did not satisfy the requirements of a bargained-for exchange (can you explain why?), the Alabama Court of Appeals enforced the promise. The majority opinion of the Court of Appeals ignored the requirements of a current exchange and reciprocal inducement, while inaccurately asserting that the employer's promise was enforceable under traditional consideration doctrine.

In a concurring opinion, Judge Samford conceded that the court was stretching the usual boundaries of consideration doctrine in the interests of achieving a just result: "[P]erhaps the strict letter of the rule, as stated by judges, though not always in accord, would bar a recovery by plaintiff, but following the principle announced by Chief Justice Marshall..., 'I do not think that law ought to be separated from justice, where it is at most doubtful,' I concur in the conclusions reached by the court." *Webb*, at 86, 168 So. at 199.

In denying review, the Alabama Supreme Court explained that this moral-obligation extension of the consideration doctrine was appropriate because the past act of the promisee had provided a "material and substantial" benefit "to the person" of the promisor. It added that this expanded view of consideration was especially justified if the new promise is given partly in recognition of injuries sustained by the promisee in rendering the past act. *Webb v. McGowin*, 232 Ala. 374, 168 So. 199 (1936).

A few states have followed *Webb*'s lead, and some have even enacted statutes that authorize enforcement of promises based on moral obligation. *See, e.g.*, S.D. CODIFIED LAWS § 53-6-2 (2004) (declaring that "good consideration" lies in "a moral obligation originating in some benefit conferred upon the promisor or prejudice suffered by the promisee"). Still others, however, have clung to the requirement of a bargain, even on facts as compelling as those of *Webb*, such as in *Harrington v. Taylor*, decided nine years after *Webb*. *Harrington v. Taylor*, 225 N.C. 690, 36 S.E.2d 227 (1945). In *Harrington*, Taylor promised to pay Harrington in recognition of Harrington's having previously saved Taylor's life by coming between Taylor and his attacker and deflecting an axe aimed at Taylor's head, resulting in serious injuries to Harrington's hand. In a brief opinion, the North Carolina Supreme Court found no consideration for the promise.

Three decades after *Harrington*, the American Law Institute provided a boost to claims to enforce promises made after receipt of services, with a new section in the second Restatement that supplements its bargain theory. This new section recommends enforcement of a promise "to the extent necessary to prevent injustice," if the promisor made the promise "in recognition of a benefit previously received by the promisor from the promisee." RESTATEMENT (SECOND) OF CONTRACTS § 86(1) (1981). Arizona case law has cited section 86 with approval. *Realty Associates of Sedona v. Valley National Bank of Arizona*, 153 Ariz. 514, 517, 738 P.2d 1121, 1124 (Ct. App. 1986) (citing as well to an Arizona Supreme Court case law from 1924). The Arizona case law, however, is closer to the limited exceptions discussed in Section B.1 above and embraced even in *Mills*: a statute barred enforcement of an agreement with a real estate broker because it was not in writing, but the owner's subsequent written promise to pay the broker for past services could overcome the original defect. *Id.*

Nearly two decades after publication of the second Restatement, the movement to enforce promises outside the context of a bargained-for exchange remained only a minority trend. *See* Kevin M. Teeven, Promises on Prior Obligations at Common Law 115–123 (1998). The traditional view of *Mills v. Wyman*—restricting consideration to the bargain theory—likely will continue to be embraced by the majority of jurisdictions for the foreseeable future. *But cf. id.* at 123 (predicting that other jurisdictions should "eventually" find it attractive to reform their consideration doctrines).

Ironically, the debate over moral obligation theory has limited consequence due to the universal recognition of a separate theory that provides a remedy in appropriate cases under similar circumstances. Benefits provided outside the context of a bargained-for exchange can be analyzed under the doctrine of quasi-contract, which provides restitution to prevent unjust enrichment. We will study quasi-contract in Section IV of this chapter.

Exercise 4.2 — Comparing *Mills* and *Webb*

Which do you prefer: the stability and certainty of the adherence in *Mills* to the strict definition of bargained-for exchange, or the more flexible and expansive standard for consideration in *Webb*, which takes justice into account?

The facts in *Mills* presented a less compelling case for departing from a strict definition of consideration as bargained-for exchange. Would the *Mills* court in Massachusetts have been tempted to adopt a more flexible and expansive standard for consideration if it had instead confronted the facts in *Webb*? Would the *Webb* court in Alabama have postponed its expansion of consideration if it had instead confronted the facts of *Mills*?

III. Promissory Estoppel— Reliance as an Alternative Basis for Relief

A. Perceived Need to Supplement the Consideration Doctrine

Review *Kirksey v. Kirksey* in Chapter 3, an 1845 decision in which the court found no bargained-for exchange. We might explain that decision today as a ruling by the majority that the brother-in-law's promise was gratuitous, based on an implicit finding of lack of reciprocal inducement. Did you find that to be an unjust result, in light of the promise made by the brother-in-law and the trouble, loss, and expense incurred by Antillico in abandoning her homestead and moving her household to his property? If you were a judge on that court, would you have been motivated to find an alternative basis for enforcing a promise in such circumstances, even in the absence of a bargained-for exchange?

1. Adapting Equitable Estoppel to Protect Reliance on a Promise

Late in the nineteenth century, in the common law method of developing the law incrementally, one case at a time, a few courts explored the concept that reliance on a gratuitous promise can justify enforcement of the promise in certain circumstances. The doctrine of equitable estoppel had long been used to preclude a party from asserting a position in court that was inconsistent with a previous factual representation or similar act of that party, on which the other party had relied. Later, courts began extending this concept of estoppel to bind a party to his previously stated *promise*, an application that later gave rise to the term "promissory estoppel." In other words, even though the promise in question was gratuitous and thus not supported by consideration, in certain circumstances the defendant was estopped—or precluded—from asserting lack of consideration as a legal defense to enforcement of the promise.

After studying the following case, be prepared to: (1) explain why the promise was not supported by consideration, and (2) identify the elements for a claim of promissory estoppel, based on the *Ricketts* court's application of estoppel to the facts relevant to that claim.

Ricketts v. Scothorn

57 Neb. 51, 77 N.W. 365 (Neb. 1898)

Sullivan, J.

¶1 In the district court of Lancaster county the plaintiff, Katie Scothorn, recovered judgment against the defendant, Andrew D. Ricketts, as executor of the last will and testament of John C. Ricketts, deceased. The action was based upon a promissory note, of which the following is a copy: "May the first, 1891. I promise to pay to Katie Scothorn on demand, $2,000, to be at 6 per cent. per annum. J. C. Ricketts."

¶2 In the petition the plaintiff alleges that the consideration for the execution of the note was that she should surrender her employment as bookkeeper for Mayer Bros., and cease to work for a living. She also alleges that the note was given to induce her to abandon her occupation, and that, relying on it, and on the annual interest, as a means of support, she gave up the employment in which she was then engaged. These allegations of the petition are denied by the administrator.

¶3 The material facts are undisputed. They are as follows: John C. Ricketts, the maker of the note, was the grandfather of the plaintiff. Early in May—presumably on the day the note bears date—he called on her at the store where she was working. What transpired between them is thus described by Mr. Flodene, one of the plaintiff's witnesses:

> "A. Well, the old gentleman came in there ... early in the morning, and he unbuttoned his vest, and took out a piece of paper in the shape of a note; that is the way it looked to me; and he says to Miss Scothorn, 'I have fixed out something that you have not got to work any more.' He says, none of my grandchildren work, and you don't have to.

Q. Where was she?

A. She took the piece of paper and kissed him, and kissed the old gentleman, and commenced to cry."

¶4 It seems Miss Scothorn immediately notified her employer of her intention to quit work, and that she did soon after abandon her occupation. The mother of the plaintiff was a witness, and testified that she had a conversation with her father, Mr. Ricketts, shortly after the note was executed, in which he informed her that he had given the note to the plaintiff to enable her to quit work; that none of his grandchildren worked, and he did not think she ought to. For something more than a year the plaintiff was without an occupation, but in September, 1892, with the consent of her grandfather, and by his assistance, she secured a position as bookkeeper with Messrs. Funke & Ogden.

¶5 ... The testimony of Flodene and Mrs. Scothorn, taken together, conclusively establishes the fact that the note was not given in consideration of the plaintiff pursuing, or agreeing to pursue, any particular line of conduct. There was no promise on the part of the plaintiff to do, or refrain from doing, anything. Her right to the money promised in the note was not made to depend upon an abandonment of her employment with Mayer Bros., and future abstention from like service. Mr. Ricketts made no condition, requirement, or request. He exacted no quid pro quo. He gave the note as a gratuity, and looked for nothing in return. So far as the evidence discloses, it was his purpose to place the plaintiff in a position of independence, where she could work or remain idle, as she might choose. The abandonment of Miss Scothorn of her position as bookkeeper was altogether voluntary. It was not an act done in fulfillment of any contract obligation assumed when she accepted the note. The instrument in suit, being given without any valuable consideration, was nothing more than a promise to make a gift in the future of the sum of money therein named. Ordinarily, such promises are not enforceable, even when put in the form of a promissory note. [citations omitted]

¶6 But when the payee changes his position to his disadvantage in reliance on the promise, a right of action does arise. McClure v. Wilson, 43 Ill. 356; Trustees v. Garvey, 53 Ill. 401.

¶7 Under the circumstances of this case, is there an equitable estoppel which ought to preclude the defendant from alleging that the note in controversy is lacking in one of the essential elements of a valid contract? We think there is. An estoppel in pais is defined to be "a right arising from acts, admissions, or conduct which have induced a change of position in accordance with the real or apparent intention of the party against whom they are alleged." Mr. Pomeroy has formulated the following definition: "Equitable estoppel is the effect of the voluntary conduct of a party whereby he is absolutely precluded, both at law and in equity, from asserting rights which might, perhaps, have otherwise existed, either of property, of contract, or of remedy, as against another person who in good faith relied upon such conduct, and has been led thereby to change his position for the worse, and who on his part acquires some corresponding right, either of property, of contract, or of remedy." 2 Pom. Eq. Jur. 804.

¶ 8 According to the undisputed proof, as shown by the record before us, the plaintiff was a working girl, holding a position in which she earned a salary of $10 per week. Her grandfather, desiring to put her in a position of independence, gave her the note, accompanying it with the remark that his other grandchildren did not work, and that she would not be obliged to work any longer. In effect, he suggested that she might abandon her employment, and rely in the future upon the bounty which he promised. He doubtless desired that she should give up her occupation, but, whether he did or not, it is entirely certain that he contemplated such action on her part as a reasonable and probable consequence of his gift. Having intentionally influenced the plaintiff to alter her position for the worse on the faith of the note being paid when due, it would be grossly inequitable to permit the maker, or his executor, to resist payment on the ground that the promise was given without consideration. The petition charges the elements of an equitable estoppel, and the evidence conclusively establishes them. If errors intervened at the trial, they could not have been prejudicial. A verdict for the defendant would be unwarranted. The judgment is right, and is affirmed.

Exercise 4.3 — Consideration and Estoppel

1. Absence of Bargained-For Exchange in *Ricketts*

Let's assume that the grandfather in *Ricketts* told Katie something like the following when handing her the written promissory note: "Here's my promise to pay you $5,000, whenever you want the money, and with interest accruing until you do. My other grandchildren don't work, and I hope this gives you the option to quit your work if that's what you choose." If Katie immediately quit her job, why wouldn't that act amount to an acceptance of his offer for a unilateral contract, exchanging his offered promise for her performance of quitting her job (or her forbearance from working)? Can you explain why these facts reflect a gratuitous promise and not a bargained-for exchange?

2. Promised Pension Problem

Employee worked as a bookkeeper for Employer for 40 years at agreed-upon salaries. In 1947, Employer resolved to pay Employee a bonus in the form of a monthly pension upon Employee's retirement, in gratitude for Employee's past services. The promise to pay the pension was unconditional: Employer did not seek Employee's retirement, nor did it require Employee to continue working for any specified period. When Employee retired two years later, was the promise to pay the pension enforceable as part of a bargained-for exchange? Why or why not?

Suppose that Employee had relied on the promise by retiring while still productive in her work, that Employer breached its promise to pay the pension and refused to rehire Employee, and that Employee was unable to secure alternative employment because of widespread discrimination against women over the age of 50. Is the promised pension enforceable? Why and under what theory of relief? (Inspired by the facts of *Feinberg v. Pfeiffer Co.*, 322 S.W.2d 163 (Mo. Ct. App. 1959).)

2. Advancing Promissory Estoppel through the Restatements

Early in the twentieth century, the American Law Institute ("ALI") advanced a rule that made a promise "binding" if the promise induced definite and substantial action or forbearance that the promisor should reasonably have expected, if "injustice can be avoided only by enforcement of the promise." RESTATEMENT (FIRST) OF CONTRACTS § 90 (1932).

Most sections of the Restatements of Contracts are intended to summarize widely established jurisprudence. Section 90, however, more proactively helped to advance an emerging doctrine. Courts that had not yet applied estoppel to promises began to cite to this first Restatement § 90. Some of them even adopted its provisions verbatim, incorporating the Restatement language into the state's common law.

One might question, however, whether a justice-based doctrine like this should be restricted to either enforcing a promise in full or granting no relief at all. In *Ricketts v. Scothorn*, for example, if Katie lost only $500 in salary, and enjoyed a nice rest from work before regaining employment, would some judges hesitate to invoke estoppel if the only available remedy was enforcement of the entire $2,000 promise? Would you? Would you prefer the flexibility to award less than that, perhaps just the $500 of Katie's reliance costs? Would courts feel comfortable providing at least some relief in a greater number of cases if the remedy were more flexible? Would that be a good thing?

The following excerpts from an article on modern promissory estoppel nicely explain the way in which this doctrine departed from consideration theory. It also traces the history of promissory estoppel, from its early form in cases like *Ricketts* and as summarized in the first Restatement to a more flexible form recommended in the second Restatement. As you read the excerpts, pay attention to the changes recommended in the second Restatement.

Marco J. Jimenez, *The Many Faces of Promissory Estoppel: An Empirical Analysis Under the Restatement (Second) of Contracts*

57 UCLA L. Rev. 669 (2010) [footnotes omitted]

This Article examines more than three hundred promissory estoppel cases decided between January 1, 1981, when the Restatement (Second) of Contracts was published, and January 1, 2008, when research for this project began, to explore the manner in which courts conceptualize, decide, and enforce promissory estoppel claims under § 90 of the Restatement (Second) of Contracts. Specifically, because the drafters of the Restatement (Second) made several important changes to § 90 of the Restatement (First) with the intent of making promissory estoppel more available, the role of reliance more prominent, and the remedies awarded to successful litigants more flexible, this Article investigates whether these changes have had their desired effect on promissory estoppel doctrine as reflected in the case law.

The research presented here can be interpreted to support three major claims. First, these data suggest that promissory estoppel is a much more significant theory of promissory recovery than has been previously thought[,] and [it] seems positioned to continue to grow in importance in the coming decades. Second, the data reveal that promissory estoppel cannot be understood exclusively in terms of "promise" or "reliance," as some scholars and judges have suggested. Instead, the data reveal that most judges require the existence of both promise and reliance before allowing a promissory estoppel claim to proceed, although surprisingly few judges require a plaintiff to show that the equitable principle of "justice" has been satisfied. Last, and most significantly, these data reveal that, with respect to remedies, courts tend to treat promissory estoppel actions as traditional breach of contract actions, in that courts generally tend to award the (usually) more generous expectation measure of damages, which is typical in ordinary breach of contract actions, over the (usually) less generous reliance measure of damages, which is often awarded where non-contractual obligations have been breached (such as in tort law)....

....

I. Historical Background

A. Grant Gilmore and the Changing Face of Promissory Estoppel

In 1932, the American Law Institute published the much-anticipated Restatement (First) of Contracts, which contained within its pages two completely different and, some would say, irreconcilable theories of contract law. On the one hand, the relatively innocuous § 75 endorsed the centuries-old, bargain-based theory of contracts in which a promise, to be enforceable, must be supported by "consideration," which was defined as "an act," "forbearance," or "return promise bargained for and given in exchange for the promise." On the other hand, tucked away several pages later, the drafters of the Restatement enshrined in § 90 a completely different and contradictory theory of contractual obligation based on the normative principle of reliance, as opposed to the more settled principle of bargain. This provision, which established what is today commonly referred to as "promissory estoppel," provided:

> A promise which the promisor should reasonably expect to induce action or forbearance of a definite and substantial character on the part of the promisee and which does induce such action or forbearance is binding if injustice can be avoided only by enforcement of the promise.
>
> ....

... [I]t is no easy task to describe how different § 90 was from the prevailing bargain-based theory of consideration, or the challenge that it would, in time, pose to the dominant theory of contractual obligation. Professor Gilmore came close when he colorfully described the differences between § 75 and § 90 as analogous to "matter and anti-matter," "Restatement and anti-Restatement," and, most poignantly, "Contract and anti-Contract." It was the more traditional, consideration-based view that played the starring role of "Contract" opposite the newer, tort-like theory of promissory estoppel, which was left to play the villainous role of "anti-Contract." ...

But what exactly makes these two theories of promissory recovery so different from one another? Here is one explanation: Under the traditional, bargain-based theory of contract, a party who wishes to form a binding contract with another must offer something by way of performance or return promise in exchange for the desired promise. Under this view, because each promisee has given something in exchange for the other's promised performance, when the other party breaches, the promisee may "feel that he has been 'deprived' of something" that belonged to him, and can therefore justifiably demand as a remedy the very thing that was promised to him by way of specific performance or, where that remedy is unavailable, expectation damages.

The justification behind promissory estoppel, however, is entirely different. As one commentator explained, the wrong complained of in a promissory estoppel claim "is not primarily in depriving the plaintiff of the promised reward but in causing the plaintiff to change position to his detriment." Therefore, because the right that the law seeks to protect in a bargain-based contract (the promised performance) is distinct from the right involved in a reliance-based contract (detrimental reliance), the remedies invoked to protect these rights should also be distinct. Thus, rather than protecting the promisee's expectation interest, as would be customary in a bargain-based contract, some commentators and judges have suggested that promissory estoppel damages "should not exceed the loss caused by the change of position, which would never be more in amount, but might be less, than the promised reward." Stated differently, the remedy for promissory estoppel should never exceed what are frequently referred to as "reliance damages."

Although many commentators think about the difference between consideration-based contracts and promissory estoppel in these terms today, as an historical matter, this was simply not true. Instead, "the original Restatement was conceived and drafted primarily in terms of promise," rather than reliance. Therefore, because promissory estoppel was originally conceived of as a promise-based theory of recovery (that also required reliance), rather than a reliance-based theory of recovery (that just so happened to require a promise), it should come as no surprise that Professor Samuel Williston, the Reporter and primary drafter of the Restatement (First) of Contracts, thought that the remedy awarded in promissory estoppel cases should be the same as the remedy awarded for an ordinary breach of contract action. In other words, they should both be protected with the (usually) more generous expectation remedy [full enforcement of the promise].

....

C. A Methodological Challenge to the Empirical View

....

[T]he Restatement (Second) of Contracts was published in 1981 ... and made several important alterations to § 90 with the specific purpose of changing the way judges decided promissory estoppel cases....

What, specifically, were these significant changes? Although a thorough discussion of the differences between the two Restatements has been explored elsewhere, the two most significant changes are worth a brief mention. First, the Restatement (Second) of Contracts dropped the requirement that a promisee's reliance must be of "a definite and substantial character." According to Professor Melvin Eisenberg, the reason for this limitation in the original Restatement rested on "an unstated axiom" of Professor Williston, who believed that "as a matter of contract law any promise that is legally enforceable at all must be enforceable to its full extent (through the award of expectation damages), rather than merely to the extent of the promisee's reliance." Because the expectation remedy was so drastic, Williston reasoned, it should not be lightly awarded to anyone who relied on a promise, but should instead be limited only to those persons whose reliance was of "a definite and substantial character."

Second, the drafters of the Restatement (Second) added a sentence to the end of § 90 that specifically allowed judges, for the first time ever, and in no uncertain terms, to award less than full expectation damages to successful promissory estoppel claimants. Thus, as revised, the Restatement (Second) of Contracts § 90(1) now reads:

> A promise which the promisor should reasonably expect to induce action or forbearance on the part of the promisee or a third person and which does induce such action or forbearance is binding if injustice can be avoided only by enforcement of the promise. The remedy granted for breach may be limited as justice requires.

....

D. The Vindication of Grant Gilmore?

[The article describes a study in which Professor Robert Hillman examined 362 promissory estoppel cases that were decided during a two-year period from July 1, 1994, through June 30, 1996.]

Professor Hillman's claims were echoed by Professor Sidney DeLong who, in a survey of promissory estoppel cases decided between 1995 and 1996, similarly found that "courts rigorously enforce Section 90's requirement that the promise induce actual reliance by the promisee,".... Surprisingly, however, Professor DeLong did find, contrary to Professor Hillman's study, that there was good evidence for the expectation hypothesis ... in that, when plaintiffs did succeed in their promissory estoppel claims, courts tended to award expectation damages rather than reliance damages.

[The author presents his own survey of cases, between 1981 and 2008.]

Conclusion

So what do these data, viewed collectively, tell us about the action of promissory estoppel? First, the prevalence and viability of promissory estoppel has grown in recent decades, both in regard to the number of cases that are being brought and in terms of the success rates of the promissory estoppel actions themselves....

Second, promissory estoppel cannot be thought of exclusively as either a promise-based or reliance-based theory of recovery. Instead, courts have been much more even handed in their approach, usually making sure that a promissory estoppel plaintiff has satisfied both the promise and reliance prongs of the test, although they have been much more hesitant in requiring a showing of injustice before enforcing the promise....

Third, ... the percentage of claimants who receive full contractual damages is much higher than has been previously thought....

Exercise 4.4 — Analysis of the Surveyed Cases

What might explain Professor Jimenez's observations that courts have typically granted full enforcement of the promise as the remedy for promissory estoppel and have spent little time analyzing whether full enforcement is necessary to prevent an injustice? Could it be that most cases that are worth litigating in the courts present facts supporting definite, substantial, and reasonable reliance, so that the injustice of breaching the promise is so plain that it does not require separate discussion and analysis? Or are some courts avoiding an overt analysis of injustice for the same reason that the court in *Mills* rejected a test for consideration that required defining moral obligation? Is it easier to base promissory estoppel on a promise and on foreseeable and substantial reliance, without further analysis of a more amorphous or subjective concept such as injustice? Should injustice nonetheless remain an important part of the test for promissory estoppel, as the most analytically rigorous means of excluding claims based on overly hasty or otherwise unreasonable reliance?

B. Judicial Recognition of Promissory Estoppel as an Affirmative Cause of Action for Damages

The next case, *Newton*, discusses whether promissory estoppel can be wielded as a "sword" and not just defensively as a "shield." Does the opinion, coupled with the exercise that precedes it, enable you to distinguish between those two ways of using estoppel?

It is instructive that in 2009 the lower courts in *Newton* could conclude that state law did not recognize the sort of affirmative cause of action that other state courts had embraced as early as the nineteenth century. As a consequence, the state supreme court was forced to clarify its precedent on that issue, leading the court to an interesting point about the appropriate remedy. The author of this casebook has added a few headings in brackets to help these topics to stand out.

Before studying the opinion, work through the following problems to help you distinguish between different types and applications of estoppel.

Exercise 4.5 — Equitable and Promissory Estoppel; Sword and Shield

What's the difference between the following three applications of estoppel? Which is traditional equitable estoppel and which is promissory estoppel? In which is estoppel used as a shield and in which is it used as a sword to advance an affirmative claim for relief? Explain.

1. The Disputed Property Line

A asked B to confirm that B's hedge defines the boundary line running north to south between their properties. B responded that, yes, the outer header board framing the soil for his hedge lies just a few inches from the outer bounds of his property. Accordingly, A built a six-foot masonry wall, running parallel to B's hedge and header board, with a space of one foot between B's header board and A's wall. B later determined that the property line in fact runs about two feet beyond his header board, so that A's wall slightly encroaches on his property along the entire length of the wall. B sues A, and A brings an estoppel defense. Explain the nature of A's defense and the basis for it.

2. The Late Fee

A's commercial lease provides that A will pay a late fee of $50/day for each day that A is late in paying the monthly rent, which is due on the first of the month. When A notified B in August that he was low on cash but would have plenty on hand to pay the rent by September 10, B responded: "No problem for this month only; I promise that I will not assess any late fee this month, unless you delay past September 10." Relieved, A did not take out a short-term loan to pay the rent on time, and he paid on September 10. B now demands $450 in late fees. A protests. Explain the nature of A's estoppel claim or defense and the basis for it.

3. Uninsured Furniture

B, the owner of a warehouse, had a long-term relationship with A, a retailer of furniture. When A received a special shipment of furniture that exceeded the capacity of his retail showroom, B assured A that B could store the excess furniture in an unused storage shed adjacent to B's warehouse without charge for up to one month and that B would ensure that the furniture was covered by his warehouse insurance policy. Grateful, A refrained from making alternative plans for storage and for insuring the furniture against loss. While stored in B's storage shed, the furniture was stolen, causing A to suffer a loss of $50,000. B had neglected to extend his insurance to cover the contents of the storage shed. A is furious and brings suit against B. Explain the nature of A's estoppel claim and the basis for it.

Newton Tractor Sales, Inc. v. Kubota Tractor Corp.

233 Ill. 2d 46, 906 N.E.2d 520 (2009)

Justice Garman delivered the judgment of the court, with opinion:

¶ 1 Plaintiff-Appellant, Newton Tractor Sales, Inc. (Newton), brought suit against defendants, Kubota Tractor Corporation and Michael Jacobson, a local Kubota representative (collectively, Kubota) on counts of promissory estoppel, common law fraud, and negligent misrepresentation. The circuit court of Fayette County granted summary judgment in favor of Kubota on all three counts. The appellate court affirmed.... On appeal we are asked to determine whether promissory estoppel is a recognized cause of action in Illinois and, if so, whether Newton has sufficiently established a genuine issue of material fact so as to survive Kubota's motion for summary judgment. For the reasons set forth below, we agree with Newton that promissory estoppel is a recognized cause of action in Illinois, reverse the circuit and appellate courts' judgments, and remand the cause for further proceedings.

BACKGROUND

¶2 [In 2002, Newton signed a contract to purchase VTE, a dealership that sold farm equipment and that was authorized to sell Kubota products. The contract obligations were contingent on Newton retaining VTE's authority to sell Kubota products. Kubota's local representative, Jacobson, said that Kubota could not process Newton's application to become an authorized Kubota dealer until Kubota had terminated its existing contract with VTE. Jacobson assured all parties that Newton would become the new Kubota dealer. In reliance on that statement, VTE terminated its existing contract with Kubota, Newton performed the agreement to purchase VTE, and Newton continued selling and servicing Kubota equipment through its new ownership of VTE. Kubota later denied Newton's application for a Kubota dealership.]

....

¶3 The circuit court granted summary judgment in favor of Kubota and Jacobson on all three counts. With respect to count I, the promissory estoppel claim, the circuit court relied on several decisions by the appellate court in deciding that promissory estoppel was not a recognized cause of action under Illinois law....

¶4 Newton filed a notice of appeal seeking reversal of the circuit court's judgment on each of the three counts.... In line with its previous decisions ... the appellate court held that a promissory estoppel claim may be brought only as a defense, and not as a cause of action. Newton then sought leave to appeal in this court.

ANALYSIS

I. Promissory Estoppel

¶5 The doctrine of promissory estoppel is a common law doctrine. This doctrine has been incorporated into the Restatement (Second) of Contracts as section 90. That section provides, in relevant part:

> §90. Promise Reasonably Inducing Action or Forbearance
>
> (1) A promise which the promisor should reasonably expect to induce action or forbearance on the part of the promisee or a third person and which does induce such action or forbearance is binding if injustice can be avoided only by enforcement of the promise. The remedy granted for breach may be limited as justice requires.

Restatement (Second) of Contracts §90(1), at 242 (1981).

¶6 Although section 90 does not expressly refer to "promissory estoppel," that term is widely used in connection with this provision of the Restatement. Restatement (Second) of Contracts §90, Comment a, at 242 (1981). Black's Law Dictionary formulates the doctrine as: "The principle that a promise made without consideration may nonetheless be enforced to prevent injustice if the promisor should have reasonably expected the promisee to rely on the promise and if the promisee did actually rely on the promise to his or her detriment." Black's Law Dictionary 591 (8th ed. 2004).

¶7 ... To establish a claim, the plaintiff must prove that (1) defendant made an unambiguous promise to plaintiff, (2) plaintiff relied on such promise, (3) plaintiff's reliance was expected and foreseeable by defendants, and (4) plaintiff relied on the promise to its detriment. *Quake*, 141 Ill. 2d at 309–10, 152 Ill. Dec. 308, 565 N.E.2d 990.

....

[Discussion of claim as "sword" rather than just a "shield":]

¶8 Quake, decided almost 17 years after *Bank of Marion*, also recognized promissory estoppel as an affirmative cause of action. In *Quake* this court affirmed the appellate court judgment allowing plaintiff's promissory estoppel claim to go forward, recognizing that promissory estoppel is an available theory in the absence of a contract. *Quake*, 141 Ill. 2d at 310, 152 Ill. Dec. 308, 565 N.E.2d 990....

....

[Fashioning a remedy when the promise is imprecise:]

¶9 We next address Kubota's second public policy argument. Kubota has argued that recognizing an affirmative action under promissory estoppel will result in reluctance to enter into commercial negotiations for fear of being obligated to perform contracts that have not been fully negotiated.

¶10 Kubota uses *Quake* to support its argument that promissory estoppel would hinder commercial negotiations. Kubota argues that in *Quake*, a letter of intent at issue was "quite detailed" and included "all the necessary terms of the contractual relationship." In that case, had the court found in favor of the plaintiff on promissory estoppel grounds, ordering the defendant to perform the contract under the terms of the letter of intent might be appropriate. Kubota argues here, however, that the alleged promise made to Newton was merely that Newton "would get the dealership." Kubota contends that enforcing this promise would be impractical, because that promise includes none of the necessary terms of a contractual relationship and does not represent mutual assent.

¶11 Here, we believe that Kubota misunderstands the equitable nature of promissory estoppel. Although the Restatement indicates that "full-scale enforcement by normal remedies is often appropriate," it also contemplates partial enforcement. *See* Restatement (Second) of Contracts § 349, Comment b; § 90, Comment d (1981). Thus, courts may appropriately limit relief to only those damages suffered as a result of justifiably relying on the other party's promise.

¶12 Two cases from our sister state courts demonstrate the application of reliance damages in promissory estoppel cases. In *Hoffman v. Red Owl Stores, Inc.*, 26 Wis. 2d 683, 133 N.W.2d 267 (1965), plaintiff had hoped to open a grocery store and entered into negotiations with a representative of a grocery store chain. Plaintiff was advised to sell his current business and relocate to a location the company thought was better suited for him. Plaintiff sold his store at a busy time of year for tourists and consequently missed an opportunity for profit. Throughout the process, representatives from the grocery chain told the plaintiff that everything was "all set" and ready to go. The deal fell through based on a previously undisclosed condition to which the plaintiff could not agree.

¶ 13 Plaintiff brought a promissory estoppel claim. In that case the Wisconsin Supreme Court adopted section 90 of the Restatement and proceeded to determine whether the trial court awarded the proper damages to the plaintiff. The court did not hold that the plaintiff was entitled to the grocery store franchise based on the original understood terms of the agreement. Rather, citing Corbin on Contracts, the court reasoned that the appropriate measure of damages was plaintiff's expenditures or change of position in reliance on the promise. *Hoffman*, 26 Wis. 2d at 701–02, 133 N.W.2d at 277.

¶ 14 Similarly, the Texas Supreme Court limited the damages of a plaintiff who had hoped to enter into a construction contract. *See Wheeler v. White*, 398 S.W.2d 93 (Tex. 1966). The plaintiff had planned to begin construction of a new apartment building. In reliance on a promised loan by the defendant, the plaintiff proceeded to demolish the buildings that were already on the property. Later, the promised financing was not delivered, and plaintiff brought suit under a theory of promissory estoppel.

¶ 15 In discussing damages the court focused on the harm plaintiff suffered in reliance on the promised loan. "[A]ll that is required to achieve justice is to put the promisee in the position he would have been in had he not acted in reliance upon the promise." *Wheeler*, 398 S.W.2d at 97.

¶ 16 In neither of the above cases did the court order that a contract be specifically performed. Where there has not been mutual assent, and the terms are not sufficient to constitute a contract, damages may appropriately be limited to restoring plaintiff to the position he was in prior to relying, to his detriment, on the promise. Thus, we reject Kubota's concerns that promissory estoppel would somehow undermine preliminary negotiations.

....

¶ 17 For the foregoing reasons, we conclude that promissory estoppel is an affirmative cause of action in Illinois, reverse the judgments of the appellate and circuit courts, and remand to the circuit court for further proceedings consistent with this opinion.

Judgments reversed; cause remanded.

Exercise 4.6—The Promise: Comparing Cases

Compare the following cases, and discuss whether the promise to provide $10,000 in each case is enforceable. Explore any theory that seems plausible, and argue both sides whenever possible. How do the cases differ in their facts and analyses?

Case #1: Disappointed Expectations

Dan's family opens the door to greet Debbie, who is bearing a birthday cake.

Debbie: A special cake for the birthday girl!

Nancy: Hi. Look what just arrived, kids! This looks great. And how is William?

Debbie: Still ill, but he is recovering. He's excited about my plan to open the bakery.

Nancy: Did you get your loan from the bank?

Debbie: Unfortunately, no. All I need is $10,000 to get it started. We'll get it somehow.

Dan: Well, we heard as much, and we'd like to help. Here's a Get Well card for William. And here's a card for you, in gratitude for all you have done for us over the years.

The card reads: "Debbie, good luck with your new bakery. To help you get started, please allow us to make a donation of $10,000. Your friends, [signed] Dan and Nancy."

Debbie: Really? Are you loaning me $10,000?

Nancy: Not a loan. This is a gift. If you are available this coming Monday, let's all meet at the bank at noon and arrange the transfer of funds.

Debbie: I'll be there. Thank you so much. We won't forget this. I'll make you proud with this bakery.

[Later that day ...]

Nancy: [getting off the phone]: That was Doug. The buyer backed out of purchasing that cabin we wanted so much. It's ours for the taking.

Dan: No fooling!! That's great!!

Nancy: But we'll need all of the cash we have on hand.

Dan: Right ... Ohh, shoot....

[The next morning ...]

Debbie *(on the phone):* Hello, Dan. How are you? Oh, hi Nancy. Hey, we've got a conference call! ... Bad news? ... Oh no, you promised to help, and I'm counting on you. I've been working so hard for this dream.... Well, I don't want this to affect our friendship either, but I must hold you to your promise.

Case #2: Reliance

Same as above, except for the final phone call, which goes as follows:

Debbie: Hello, Dan. How are you? Oh, hi Nancy. Hey, we've got a conference call! ... Bad news? ... But, when you promised me the money, I acted immediately. I entered into a lease on Main St. for the bakery, and I just purchased some expensive equipment on credit.... I'll need more than luck. I'm already out $6,000. I'm afraid that I must hold you to your promise or I will be financially ruined.

Case #3: The Estranged Sibling

Charles (on the phone): Hi, John, this is your brother, Charles. (Charles cringes at the response from the other side.) Yes, I know you are still angry with me about missing the

> wedding, and I know that you don't want to see me or speak to me again, but you can't avoid me forever. I have apologized, and now I want to set things right.... Listen, I know that you need $10,000 to open a cafe. I would like to give you $10,000 to get started. If you will just agree to meet me for lunch next Monday at Tomaso's Restaurant, we can go to the bank after lunch to transfer the funds.... You agree? Great, I'll see you Monday.

C. Promises to Charitable Organizations

With some exceptions, courts apply the consideration requirement to promises made to charitable or other nonprofit organizations, such as churches and public universities. Nonetheless, courts are often inclined to stretch to find a bargain, such as by requiring minimal evidence to find a reciprocal commitment by the recipient institution to spend the money in a particular way. *See, e.g., Philomath College v. Hartless*, 6 Or. 158 (1876) (describing judicial tendency to liberally find a reciprocal commitment from the benefited institution). Similarly, when two or more donors have simultaneously donated to the same institution, courts frequently have found consideration by liberally finding that each of them donated in exchange for the reciprocal agreement of the others to commit their resources to the same cause. *See, e.g., Wilson v. First Presby. Church of Savanna*, 56 Ga. 554 (1876) (finding consideration partly in the mutual promises of subscribers to donate and partly in the recipient church's making preparations to construct the building for which the money was donated); *but see Phillips Limerick Academy v. Davis*, 11 Mass. 113 (1814) (finding that multiple subscribers made independent, and not reciprocal, promises to donate).

When consideration is undeniably absent, many courts have stretched to find grounds under promissory estoppel to enforce promises to charities. The second Restatement recommends a more direct approach in such cases. It recommends a rule that dramatically prunes the elements of promissory estoppel in charitable subscriptions by making them binding under promissory estoppel "without proof that the promise induced action or forbearance." RESTATEMENT (SECOND) OF CONTRACTS § 90(2) (1981).

Although section 90(2) may describe the reality in many cases, it's likely that most courts will continue to recite all the usual elements of consideration or promissory estoppel, while applying them loosely to liberally enforce promises to charities. And some courts will apply all the usual requirements of promissory estoppel, even to gratuitous promises to a charity, without any apparent deviation from their ordinary standards of application. *Congregation Kadimah Toras-Moshe v. DeLeo*, 405 Mass. 365, 540 N.E.2d 691 (1989) (rejecting section 90(2)'s abandonment of required proof of reliance).

D. Consideration and Promissory Estoppel: Can They Coexist?

1. Does Promissory Estoppel Undermine Consideration?

The late contracts scholar Grant Gilmore described the doctrines of consideration and promissory estoppel in the First Restatement as "matter and anti-matter," reflecting the "schizophrenia" of the Restatement. Grant Gilmore, THE DEATH OF CONTRACT 60–61 (1974). For a summary of the history of consideration doctrine and a strong critique of the first Restatement's advancement of promissory estoppel, see Eric Alden, *Reversing the Reliance Revolution in Contract*, 93 WASH. L. REV. 1609 (2018).

Can promissory estoppel coexist comfortably with the consideration doctrine, or does it threaten to swallow it up by too easily creating grounds for enforcement of gratuitous promises? Should courts apply promissory estoppel sparingly to avoid this risk? Would you prefer to limit enforcement of promises to those exchanged in bargains that meet the consideration requirement, or is that too restrictive?

While pondering these questions, consider the following summary of the history of law and equity in the common law systems. It should help you understand the relationship between legal rules and the equitable doctrines that sometimes provide flexible alternatives to the general legal rule.

2. A Brief History of Equity Jurisdiction in the Common Law System

In 1066, William the Conqueror claimed the English crown by crossing the English Channel and defeating the English King Harold in the Battle of Hastings. In time, the victorious Normans established central royal courts to create and apply a body of common law. The early King's Court—or the Queen's Court during the reign of a queen—heard criminal cases and those implicating royal interests. The Court of Common Pleas heard civil disputes between private parties, if the claims could be shoehorned into an approved form of action, such as debt or trespass. The jurisdiction of the King's Court later expanded to private civil suits, and the forms of action gradually expanded in scope.

The law developed by these royal courts was known as the "common law" because it applied throughout England and thus largely replaced the local laws dispensed in feudal courts, county courts, and other local courts. Local courts filled some of the legal gaps by continuing to hear claims that did not fall within the forms of actions over which the royal courts exercised jurisdiction.

With respect to claims falling with the jurisdiction of the King's Court and the Court of Common Pleas, a body of common law gradually developed as the courts decided one case after another over the centuries. The resulting rules of general application, however, occasionally worked an injustice when applied to the facts of an unusual case. To address these injustices, a separate system of "equity" law was dispensed by a competing system of equity courts. The Court of Exchequer, for example, split from the King's Court in the twelfth century and exercised equity jurisdiction, common law jurisdiction, or both at various times over the following centuries. Far more claims in equity, however, were heard by the Court of Chancery, led by the Lord Chancellor.

The courts of equity, acting without juries and normally taking evidence in written form, sought to get to the factual heart of a dispute and to correct injustices that might result from application of inflexible common law rules. In extreme cases, they could issue an injunction that ordered a private party to refrain from enforcing the judgment of a common law court. In other cases, they developed claims or remedies that could be applied as alternatives to those available in the common law courts.

Not surprisingly, the common law courts did not gladly acquiesce to equity's exercise of power to intervene in the operation of the common law. In the early centuries, the Chancellor's standing as a religious figure helped to stem opposition. Even when Chancery evolved into a fully secular institution, the King or Queen continued to support equity's restrained intervention in a dual system of common law and equity.

If they hoped to maintain this support, the courts of equity could not afford to overplay their hands. They prudently intervened only when the limits or harshness of the common law failed to achieve justice in exceptional cases. For example, the common law courts provided only the remedy of money damages for breach of contract. This usually sufficed, because it permitted the victim of breach to obtain the money equivalent of the promised performance, so that the victim could purchase similar goods or services from a substitute vendor rather than the breaching party. Consequently, a court of equity normally had no reason to upset or supplement this remedy at law.

In exceptional cases, however, such as in the breach of a contract to sell land or a unique work of art, money damages would not suffice, because an award of money could not enable the victim of breach to buy substitute land of the precise location, or substitute art of the unique character, as that promised but withheld by the breaching party. In such a case, a court of equity sometimes exercised discretion to grant the extraordinary remedy of specific enforcement, ordering the breaching party to perform as promised: to deliver the land or unique object to the victim of the breach in exchange for the contract price.

In this way, the common law courts and the courts of equity worked in complementary fashion, described by English scholar Gary Watt as "constructive opposition." Watt compares this constructive opposition to an archer's hands: they work together to hit the target, but one hand pushes against the bow and the other hand pulls on the bowstring. Gary Watt, EQUITY STIRRING : THE STORY OF JUSTICE BEYOND LAW 76 (2009).

According to Watt, the equitable defense of estoppel derived its name from the word *estouppail* in old French, referring to a bung of twisted cloth used to plug a flow of liquid. Thus, estoppel could be invoked in a court of equity to figuratively stop up the mouth of the other party when he pleaded common law rules that would work an injustice. *Id.* at 106. If a landowner protested the encroachment of a neighbor's wall onto his property, the neighbor's claim of equitable estoppel could stop the landowner's plea if the landowner had provided inaccurate information about the boundaries to the neighbor, who then relied on that information when setting the location of the wall. By the early twentieth century in the United States, a claim of *promissory* estoppel could bring relief to one who had relied on a gratuitous *promise*, in effect stopping the defendant from pleading lack of consideration as a defense to enforcement of a promise.

Other equitable claims, defenses, and remedies will make their appearances at various stages of our study of contracts. However, they are no longer part of a separate system of law dispensed by a court system that competes for jurisdiction with courts of law. In England, the common law and equity courts were placed under central administration pursuant to the Judicature Acts of 1873 and 1875. In America, legal and equitable rules have long been merged in federal courts and most state systems, so that a single court applies claims and defenses that had their roots in early common law and equity.

Exercise 4.7 — Matter and Anti-Matter?

Recall Grant Gilmore's charge that consideration and promissory estoppel represent "matter and anti-matter" and reflect a schizophrenic approach to contract law. Do you agree? Or do these doctrines work in complementary fashion? To use Watts' metaphor, do they represent the two hands of the archer, working together in constructive opposition to hit the target of justice?

Should promissory estoppel at least be restricted in its scope and applied judiciously to avoid excessive interference with the usual requirement of consideration? Alternatively, should the common law system abandon the doctrine of bargained-for exchange and return to a system that enforces any promise — even gratuitous — made with certain formalities, such as in a signed, notarized writing? How would you reform the consideration doctrine if you could do so with the stroke of a pen?

E. Perspective — Divergence in English and U.S. Approaches to Promissory Estoppel

Recall the issue addressed by *Newton Tractor Sales* in Subsection B above: Can a claimant wield a claim of promissory estoppel as a sword to support an award of damages, and not just as a shield to defend against the other party's claim for relief? Although courts in both England and the United States developed promissory estoppel from centuries-old English principles of equitable estoppel, the common law parent and child diverged on the use of promissory estoppel as an affirmative claim for damages.

Equitable estoppel, protecting reliance on representations of existing fact, is properly limited to defensive use, as a shield. *Newton Tractor Sales, Inc. v. Kubota Tractor Corp.*, 23 Ill. 2d 46, 56, 906 N.E. 2d 520, 526 (2009) (distinguishing traditional "equitable estoppel," as is it is commonly called in the United States, from promissory estoppel). With limited exceptions, England has retained this limitation for promissory estoppel, while all but a few U.S. jurisdictions have allowed promissory estoppel to operate either as a defensive shield or as an affirmative claim for relief, depending on the circumstances.

Which approach do you prefer? Does the English approach appropriately prevent promissory estoppel from undermining the consideration doctrine's limitations on enforcement of promises? Or does the U.S. approach provide the affirmative remedy needed to correct injustices that sometimes result from the application of consideration doctrine to gratuitous promises?

IV. Obligations Implied in Law

As we learned toward the end of Chapter 3, a promise or agreement that is implied in fact is an actual one that was intended by the parties and objectively conveyed by them in light of all the circumstances, although not expressed by them in specific terms. In contrast, an obligation or contract *implied in law* is one constructed by the courts in certain circumstances to advance legal policy, even in the absence of a promise or agreement intended by the parties.

To take a simple example, both the UCC and the common law imply an obligation of good faith in the performance and enforcement of a contract. UCC § 1-304 (2001); *see* RESTATEMENT (SECOND) OF CONTRACTS § 205 (1981) (reflecting duty of good faith and fair dealing implied at common law). This obligation might track the parties' actual intentions in the vast majority of agreements. The nearly universal implication of this duty, however, usually without an inquiry into the facts or circumstances of each agreement, suggests that common law and legislation impose it as a matter of law. This is particularly clear under the UCC, which will not enforce an agreement by the parties to disclaim the implied duty of good faith. UCC § 1-302(b) (2001).[1] The content of this duty of good faith is explored in Chapter 10.

A. Quasi-Contract (Constructive Contract or One Implied in Law)

When an entire contract is implied *in law*, it is commonly known as a *quasi-contract*. Another name, *constructive contract*, is less commonly used but is instructive nonetheless.

When lawyers or judges use the terms "interpretation" and "construction" with precision, they can distinguish obligations that were intended by the parties from ones that are recognized by courts as a matter of legal policy. When a judge or jury *interprets* the parties' agreement, for example, it is primarily exploring the facts in an effort to determine the parties' actual or apparent intentions. When a judge *construes* the contract, however, she is going beyond the parties' intentions and is instead constructing contract terms based on legal policies.[2]

---

1. The UCC does, however, permit parties to agree to standards by which performance of this duty will be measured, so long as those standards are not "manifestly unreasonable." UCC § 1-302(b) (2001).

2. One can use the terms "statutory interpretation" and "statutory construction" with equal precision to draw a similar distinction in the context of judges attempting to determine legislative intent or, falling short in that endeavor, construing statutes in light of general policy considerations.

Thus, a quasi-contract (one that is implied in law) is a ground for relief constructed from legal policies related to justice and equity, rather than one based on bargaining of the parties. It is not an actual contract, but a claim for relief that you might place somewhere near the boundary between contract and tort. Our study of quasi-contract will explore only a few short trails of doctrine within a substantial field of law that occupies an entire Restatement. RESTATEMENT (THIRD) OF RESTITUTION & UNJUST ENRICHMENT (2011).

You'll soon see that the elements for a claim under quasi-contract are proof of *unjust enrichment*. See whether you can glean the contents of that test from the following Arizona decision, and consider the following questions. What is the difference between: (1) an express contract, (2) a contract implied in fact, and (3) a contract implied in law? What remedy does the court grant for a claim under quasi-contract? How is that measured, how does the court limit it, and how does it compare with the usual measure for breach of an actual contract?

Pyeatte v. Pyeatte

135 Ariz. 346, 661 P.2d 196 (Ct. App. 1982)

Corcoran, Judge.

¶1 This is an appeal by the husband from an award of $23,000 in favor of the wife as ordered in a decree of dissolution. Two issues are before us: (1) The validity of an oral agreement entered into by the husband and wife during the marriage, whereby each spouse agreed to provide in turn the sole support for the marriage while the other spouse was obtaining further education; and, (2) whether the wife is entitled to restitution for benefits she provided for her husband's educational support in a dissolution action which follows closely upon the husband's graduation and admission to the Bar. The word "agreement" is used as a term of reference for the stated understanding between the husband and wife and not as a legal conclusion that the agreement is enforceable at law as a contract.

¶2 The husband, H. Charles Pyeatte (appellant), and the wife, Margrethe May Pyeatte (appellee), were married in Tucson on December 27, 1972. At the time of the marriage both had received bachelors degrees. Appellee was coordinator of the surgical technical program at Pima College. Appellant was one of her students. In early 1974, the parties had discussions and reached an agreement concerning postgraduate education for both of them.

¶3 Appellee testified that they agreed she "would put him through three years of law school without his having to work, and when he finished, he would put [her] through for [her] masters degree without [her] having to work."

¶4 Appellant concedes the existence of an agreement. Although there was a claim by appellant that his agreement with appellee was qualified by certain contingencies, there is substantial evidence in the record to support the findings made by the trial court after the trial:

> The Court is of the opinion that there was a definite agreement that the respondent [appellant] would pay for the support of petitioner [appellee] while the petitioner [appellee] obtained her master's degree without her having to work. The Court is further of the opinion that there was no contingency expressed or implied that this would not be carried out or enforced in the event of a divorce. Petitioner [appellee] carried out her part of the agreement in supporting the respondent [appellant] while he obtained his law degree.

¶5 Appellant attended law school in Tucson, Arizona, from 1974 until his graduation. He was admitted to the State Bar shortly thereafter.

¶6 During appellant's first two years of law school appellee supported herself and appellant on the salary she earned at Pima College. During the last year, appellee lost her job, whereupon savings were used to support the couple. Although each spouse contributed to the savings, a significant amount was furnished by appellee.

¶7 After appellant's admission to the Bar, the couple moved to Prescott, Arizona, where appellant was employed by a law firm. Both parties realized that appellant's salary would not be sufficient to support the marriage and pay for appellee's education for a masters degree simultaneously. Appellee then agreed to defer her plans for a year or two until her husband got started in his legal career. In the meantime, she obtained part-time employment as a teacher.

¶8 In April, 1978, appellant told appellee that he no longer wanted to be married to her, and in June of 1978, she filed a petition for dissolution. Trial was had in March of 1979, and a decree of dissolution was granted. At the time of the trial, there was little community property and no dispute as to division of any community or separate property. Spousal maintenance was neither sought by nor granted to appellee.

¶9 The trial court determined that there was an agreement between the parties, that appellee fully performed her part of that agreement, that appellant had not performed his part of the agreement, and that appellee had been damaged thereby.

¶10 Based on appellee's expert testimony on the cost of furthering her education, in accordance with the agreement, the trial court awarded judgment of $23,000 against appellant as damages for breach of contract, with additional directions that the judgment be payable through the court clerk on a quarterly basis in a sum of not less than ten percent of appellant's net quarterly income.

....

¶11 On appeal, appellant argues that the agreement did not rise to the level of a binding contract because, among other things, the terms thereof were not definite and could not be legally enforced.

¶12 Appellee advances three ... grounds upon which the trial court's award should be upheld:

> 1. The agreement between the parties was a binding contract. Appellant's failure to perform after appellee had fully performed her obligations renders appellant liable in damages.
>
> 2. Appellant's education was obtained through the exhaustion of the community resources. Appellee argues that her financing of appellant's education was an extraordinary expenditure and that the trial court's award should be sustained as a lien upon appellant's separate estate to the extent of those expenditures pursuant to A.R.S. § 25-318.
>
> 3. If the agreement is not enforceable as a binding contract, appellee is nevertheless entitled to restitution in quantum meruit to prevent appellant's unjust enrichment because he received his education at appellee's expense.

We will address each argument in turn.

The Contract Claim

¶ 13 [As presented in Chapter 7, the court finds that the contract is too indefinite to enforce.]

Statutory Reimbursement under A.R.S. § 25-318

¶ 14 [The court rejected this claim, which is outside the scope of our course.]

The Restitution Claim

¶ 15 Appellee's last contention is that the trial court's award should be affirmed as an equitable award of restitution on the basis of unjust enrichment. She argues that appellant's education, which she subsidized and which he obtained through the exhaustion of community assets constitutes a benefit for which he must, in equity, make restitution. This narrow equitable issue is one of first impression in this court. We first addressed the broad outlines of the problem in *Wisner*, but in the context of significantly different facts and legal theories. Our recognition of the disparate considerations involved in a case such as the one before us led us to limit our holding in *Wisner* to its facts. 129 Ariz. at 341, 631 P.2d at 123.

¶ 16 Restitution is available to a party to an agreement where he performs services for the other believing that there is a binding contract.

When Restitution for Services is Granted.

> A person who has rendered services to another or services which have inured to the benefit of another … is entitled to restitution therefor if the services were rendered
>
> ….
>
> (b) To obtain the performance of an agreement with the other therefor, not operative as a contract, or voidable as a contract and avoided by the other

> party after the services were rendered, the one performing the services erroneously believing because of a mistake of fact that the agreement was binding upon the other....

Restatement of Restitution § 40(b) at 155 (1937).

¶ 17 In order to be granted restitution, appellee must demonstrate that appellant received a benefit, that by receipt of that benefit he was unjustly enriched at her expense, and that the circumstances were such that in good conscience appellant should make compensation. *John A. Artukovich & Sons v. Reliance Truck Co.*, 126 Ariz. 246, 614 P.2d 327 (1980); Restatement of Restitution § 1 at 13 (1937). In *Artukovich*, the Supreme Court discussed unjust enrichment.

> Contracts implied-in-law or quasi-contracts, also called constructive contracts, are inferred by the law as a matter of reason and justice from the acts and conduct of the parties and circumstances surrounding the transactions ... and are imposed for the purpose of bringing about justice without reference to the intentions of the parties....
>
> Restatement of Restitution § 1 provides, "A person who has been unjustly enriched at the expense of another is required to make restitution to the other." Comment (a) to that section notes that a person is enriched if he received a benefit and is unjustly enriched if retention of that benefit would be unjust. Comment (b) defines a benefit as being any form of advantage....
>
> ....
>
> Unjust enrichment does not depend upon the existence of a valid contract, ... nor is it necessary that plaintiff suffer a loss corresponding to the defendant's gain for there to be valid claim for an unjust enrichment....

126 Ariz. at 248, 614 P.2d at 329.

¶ 18 A benefit may be any type of advantage, including that which saves the recipient from any loss or expense. *See Artukovich, supra*. Appellee's support of appellant during his period of schooling clearly constituted a benefit to appellant. Absent appellee's support, appellant may not have attended law school, may have been forced to prolong his education because of intermittent periods of gainful employment, or may have gone deeply into debt. Relieved of the necessity of supporting himself, he was able to devote full time and attention to his education.

¶ 19 The mere fact that one party confers a benefit on another, however, is not of itself sufficient to require the other to make restitution. Retention of the benefit must be unjust.

¶ 20 Historically, restitution for the value of services rendered has been available upon either an "implied-in-fact" contract or upon quasi-contractual grounds. D. Dobbs, Remedies § 4.2 at 237 (1973); 1 Williston, Contracts § 3 and 3A at 10–15 (3d ed. 1957). An implied-in-fact contract is a true contract, differing from an express contract only insofar as it is proved by circumstantial evidence rather than by express written or oral terms. *United States v. O. Frank Heinz Construction Co.*, 300 F. Supp.

396 (D.C. Ill. 1969); *Plumbing Shop, Inc. v. Pitts*, 67 Wash. 2d 514, 408 P.2d 382, 383 (1965). In contrast, a quasi-contract is not a contract at all, but a duty imposed in equity upon a party to repay another to prevent his own unjust enrichment. The intention of the parties to bind themselves contractually in such a case is irrelevant. 1 Williston, Contracts § 3A at 12–15 (3d ed. 1957). To support her claim for restitution on the basis of an implied-in-fact contract, appellee must demonstrate the elements of a binding contract. For the reasons we have previously discussed, we cannot find the necessary mutual assent or certainty as to the critical terms of the agreement sufficient to establish such a contract. *See also Osborn v. Boeing Airplane Co.*, 309 F.2d 99 (9th Cir. 1962).

¶ 21 Restitution is nevertheless available in quasi-contract absent any showing of mutual assent. While a quasi-contractual obligation may be imposed without regard to the intent of the parties, such an obligation will be imposed only if the circumstances are such that it would be unjust to allow retention of the benefit without compensating the one who conferred it. *See Williston, supra.* One circumstance under which a duty to compensate will be imposed is when there was an expectation of payment or compensation for services at the time they were rendered.

> [A]n obligation to pay, ordinarily, will not be implied in fact or by law if it is clear that there was indeed no expectation of payment, that a gratuity was intended to be conferred, that the benefit was conferred officiously, or that the question of payment was left to the unfettered discretion of the recipient.

Osborn v. Boeing Airplane Co., 309 F.2d at 102.

¶ 22 Although we found that the spousal agreement failed to meet the requirements of an enforceable contract, the agreement still has importance in considering appellee's claim for unjust enrichment because it both evidences appellee's expectation of compensation and the circumstances which make it unjust to allow appellant to retain the benefits of her extraordinary efforts.

¶ 23 We next address the question of whether restitution on the basis of unjust enrichment is appropriate in the context of the marital relationship. No authority is cited to the court in support of the proposition that restitution as a matter of law is inappropriate in a dissolution proceeding. In *Wisner*, we observed that "[i]n our opinion, unjust enrichment, as a legal concept, is not properly applied in the setting of a marital relationship." 129 Ariz. at 341, 631 P.2d at 123. Our observation was directed to the wife's claim in that case for restitution for the value of her homemaking services during the couple's 15-year marriage and for the couple's reduced income during the husband's lengthy training period. Where both spouses perform the usual and incidental activities of the marital relationship, upon dissolution there can be no restitution for performance of these activities. *Ibid.* Where, however, the facts demonstrate an agreement between the spouses and an extraordinary or unilateral effort by one spouse which inures solely to the benefit of the other by the time of dissolution, the remedy of restitution is appropriate.

. . . .

¶24 A number of jurisdictions have addressed the issue of restitution in the context of the marital relationship. The cases which have dealt with the issue involve two factual patterns: (1) The first group consists of those cases in which the couples had accumulated substantial marital assets over a period of time from which assets the wife received large awards of property, maintenance and child support. The courts have refused to apply the theory of restitution on the basis of unjust enrichment in each of these cases. (2) The second group consists of those cases in which the parties are divorced soon after the student spouse receives his degree or license and there is little or no marital property from which to order any award to the working spouse.

¶25 In the first group the courts have consistently refused to find a property interest in the husband's education, degree, license or earning capacity or to order restitution in favor of the wife. Because restitution is a matter of equity, the circumstances of these cases preclude at the outset any basis for a finding of inequitable circumstances sufficient to support restitution inasmuch as the wife in each case had received substantial awards of the marital assets and was seeking, in addition to those assets, a property interest in the husband's education, degree, license or earning capacity. Because the property award itself is largely the product of the education, degree, license or earning capacity in which the wife sought a monetary interest, the courts hold that the wife realized her "investment" in the husband's education by having received the benefits of his increased earning capacity during marriage and by receipt of an award of property upon its dissolution. *Wisner, supra*; *Lucas v. Lucas*, 27 Cal. 3d 808, 166 Cal. Rptr. 853, 614 P.2d 285 (1980), *overruling in part on other grounds*, *Aufmuth v. Aufmuth*, 89 Cal. App. 3d 446, 152 Cal. Rptr. 668 (1979); [three other citations omitted].

....

¶26 The second group presents the more difficult problem of the "working spouse" claiming entitlement to an equitable recovery where there is little or no marital property to divide and therefore the conventional remedies of property division or spousal maintenance are unavailable. The emerging consensus among those jurisdictions faced with the issue in this factual context is that restitution to the working spouse is appropriate to prevent the unjust enrichment of the student spouse. *See Inman v. Inman*, 578 S.W.2d 266 (Ky. 1979); *DeLa Rosa v. DeLa Rosa*, 309 N.W.2d 755 (Minn. 1981); *Hubbard v. Hubbard*, 603 P.2d 747 (Okl. 1979); *Lundberg v. Lundberg*, 107 Wis. 2d 1, 318 N.W.2d 918 (1982); *Contra*, *In re Marriage of Graham*, 194 Colo. 429, 574 P.2d 75 (1978). [*Discussion of the* Hubbard *case is omitted.*]

¶27 The Minnesota Supreme Court in *DeLa Rosa* similarly affirmed an award of restitution to the wife for the financial support she provided her husband while he attended medical school, in a dissolution which occurred shortly after the husband's graduation.

> The case at bar presents the common situation where one spouse has foregone the immediate enjoyment of earned income to enable the other to pursue

> an advanced education on a full-time basis. Typically, this sacrifice is made with the expectation that the parties will enjoy a higher standard of living in the future. Because the income of the working spouse is used for living expenses, there is usually little accumulated marital property to be divided when the dissolution occurs prior to the attainment of the financial rewards concomitant with the advanced degree or professional license. Furthermore, the working spouse is not entitled to maintenance ... as there has been a demonstrated ability of self-support. The equities weigh heavily in favor of providing a remedy to the working spouse in such a situation ....

309 N.W.2d at 758.

[Discussion is omitted of the *Inman* case and an Arizona precedent that decided a similar case but did not address the issue of restitution under quasi-contract.]

¶ 28 The record shows that the appellee conferred benefits on appellant—financial subsidization of appellant's legal education—with the agreement and expectation that she would be compensated therefor by his reciprocal efforts after his graduation and admission to the Bar. Appellant has left the marriage with the only valuable asset acquired during the marriage—his legal education and qualification to practice law. It would be inequitable to allow appellant to retain this benefit without making restitution to appellee. However, we need not decide what limits or standards would apply in the absence of an agreement. Commentators have discerned in various statutory enactments and the developing case law a renewed and expanded recognition of marriage's economic underpinnings. *See Comment, The Interest of the Community in a Professional Education*, 10 Calif. W.L. Rev. 590 (1974); Erickson, *Spousal Support Toward the Realization of Educational Goals: How the Law Can Ensure Reciprocity*, 1978 Wis. L. Rev. 947. By our decision herein, we reject the view that the economic element necessarily inherent in the marital institution (and particularly apparent in its dissolution) requires us to treat marriage as a strictly financial undertaking upon the dissolution of which each party will be fully compensated for the investment of his various contributions. When the parties have been married for a number of years, the courts cannot and will not strike a balance regarding the contributions of each to the marriage and then translate that into a monetary award. To do so would diminish the individual personalities of the husband and wife to economic entities and reduce the institution of marriage to that of a closely held corporation.

The Measure of Recovery

¶ 29 Generally, ... the trial court in each case must make specific findings as to whether the education, degree or license acquired by the student spouse during marriage involved an unjust enrichment of that spouse, the value of the benefit, and the amount that should be paid to the working spouse. A variety of methods of computing the unjust enrichment may be employed in ascertaining the working spouse's compensable interest in the attainment of the student spouse's education, degree or license.

¶ 30 The award to appellee should be limited to the financial contribution by appellee for appellant's living expenses and direct educational expenses. *See DeLa Rosa v. DeLa Rosa*, 309 N.W.2d 755.

¶ 31 Under the agreement between the parties, the anticipated [value of the husband's promised performance] may [be] a lesser amount than the benefit conferred by appellee on appellant. In that event, the award to appellee should be limited to the [lesser] amount of [her husband's promised support while she earned her master's degree]. Appellee should not recover more than the benefit of her bargain. Restatement of Restitution, § 107, Comment b, at 449 (1937).

....

¶ 32 The portion of the judgment in the amount of $23,000 is reversed and remanded for proceedings in accordance with this opinion.

B. The Elements of Quasi-Contract: Unjust Enrichment

1. Enrichment

The Supreme Court of Arkansas applied quasi-contract to grant a remedy to a physician who rendered emergency medical care to the unconscious victim of a streetcar accident, after being summoned by a bystander. *Cotnam v. Wisdom*, 83 Ark. 601, 104 S.W. 164 (1907). Because the accident victim was unconscious and unattended by a friend or relative, the physician had no opportunity to enter into a bargained-for exchange for medical services. For the same reason, the accident victim could not even engage in speech or conduct that conveyed a promise to pay on which the physician could rely for purposes of promissory estoppel.

Nonetheless, the *Cotnam* court awarded compensation to the physician against the deceased victim's estate on a claim of quasi-contract, requiring proof of *unjust enrichment*. The first element of this claim is enrichment: a benefit provided by the plaintiff to the defendant. For quasi-contract, we are not using the term "benefit" in a nuanced way, or even avoiding it altogether, as is sometimes necessary when critiquing the usefulness of "benefit" and "detriment" for precise analysis of consideration issues. *See, e.g.*, Restatement (Second) of Contracts § 79(a) (1981) (rejecting benefit and detriment as requirements for consideration); *Hamer v. Sidway* (as analyzed in Chapter 3, Section I.C). Rather, for quasi-contract, we mean benefit in its usual sense: a measurable benefit that represents something of value transferred to the defendant.

Exercise 4.8 — Enrichment: Benefit Transferred to the Defendant in Saving a Life ... or Not

In *Cotnam v. Wisdom*, we can assume that the physician capably performed an operation that stood a chance of saving the accident victim's life. Nonetheless, the victim died without regaining consciousness. Was the victim enriched by the physician's actions?

2. *Injustice*

In the absence of an actual contract or promissory estoppel, transferring a benefit to another will not justify a remedy unless it would be unjust for the defendant to retain the benefit without compensating the plaintiff for it. Otherwise, an unemployed painter could make a habit of painting houses while their owners are out of town and then could demand payment for the enhanced value of the house when the owners return. Just as the law generally does not recognize a power in an offeror to dictate that silence is acceptance of his offer, an officious person who forces benefits on others is not deserving of quasi-contractual relief. As stated in a case quoted in *Pyeatte*, enrichment normally is not unjust and thus does not require compensation if "it is clear that there was indeed no expectation of payment, that a gratuity was intended to be conferred, that the benefit was conferred officiously, or that the question of payment was left to the unfettered discretion of the recipient." *Osborn v. Boeing Airplane Co.*, 309 F.2d 99, 102 (9th Cir. 1962).

a. Expecting Compensation or Donating Benefit?

At a minimum, enrichment is *unjust* only if the plaintiff was expecting compensation for the benefit at the time of providing it; allowing the defendant to keep the benefit without paying for it cannot be unjust if the plaintiff had intended to convey it as a gift. In many states, for example, a court applying common law principles will presume that a person who rendered emergency assistance to another intended to do so gratuitously, perhaps out of a sense of sympathy or civic duty. If so, the service was provided without expectation of compensation, so that the recipient justly retains the enrichment without paying for it.

The presumption of gratuitous emergency services can be rebutted by evidence to the contrary, such as evidence that the service was unusually burdensome or that the person providing it normally charges for such services professionally and was not under a legal or professional obligation to provide the service gratuitously. In *Cotnam v. Wisdom*, for example, the physician expected compensation for services for which he had professional training and for which he routinely charged in his daily work, especially because he was summoned in his professional capacity. The result would be different today in states with legislation that requires physicians to provide medical treatment without charge in emergency circumstances while limiting their liability for mistakes.

b. Reasonably Expecting Compensation

Merely expecting or hoping for compensation for goods or services, however, won't justify compensation. The expectation must be reasonable. Normally, this standard is easily met if the parties reasonably thought they had formed a contract and were bound to perform by transferring benefits to each other. If one of the parties performed in this way, but the other party withheld counter-performance, the contract might turn out to be unenforceable due to some defect in its formation, such as indefiniteness or mutual mistake. If so, the performing party would still have a good claim for unjust enrichment, having transferred a benefit to the other party with the reasonable expectation of receiving compensation for it. A reasonable belief that the other party was contractually bound to provide compensation is a particularly strong basis for injustice when the other party retains the benefit while withholding the compensation.

The circumstances that support a reasonable expectation of compensation are varied, however, and raise more difficult questions when the benefit is provided outside the context of a perceived contract to provide them. In some cases, reasonable expectation of compensation might be provided by some pre-existing personal or business relationship between the parties that suggests that the benefit would be welcomed, even though the parties had not specifically bargained for it.

Even in the absence of such a pre-existing relationship, the circumstances might suggest that the recipient clearly would welcome the benefit and be willing to pay for it. The physician in *Cotnam*, for example, did not impose himself on the accident scene in a meddlesome manner; he was summoned to it in his capacity as a professional who customarily charged for his provision of medical services. Moreover, he presumably reasonably believed that the accident victim would have enthusiastically welcomed—and bargained for—the physician's emergency medical services, if only he had possessed the capacity to do so. The victim's receiving, while unconscious and dying, the benefit of an operation that might have saved his life is a far cry from his receiving an unsolicited coat of paint on his house while on vacation.

Exercise 4.9 — Quasi-Contract in *Pyeatte, Mills,* or *Webb*?

1. Injustice: Reasonable Expectation of Compensation

Why is *Pyeatte* such a strong case for quasi-contract? Aside from the benefit of supporting her husband through law school, why was that enrichment so clearly unjust? Stated otherwise, why was it easy for the appellate court to conclude that Margrethe reasonably expected compensation when she provided that support?

2. Moral Obligation Compared with Quasi-Contract

Review the cases on moral obligation, *Mills* and *Webb*, discussed earlier in Section II. Do the facts of either of these cases support a claim for restitution under quasi-contract?

C. The Remedy for Quasi-Contract: Restitution

As explained in *Pyeatte*, the usual remedy in quasi-contract is *restitution* of the benefit to the plaintiff: a monetary award representing the value of the benefit that the plaintiff had provided to the defendant. The policy underlying quasi-contract is to avoid unjustly enriching the defendant; the remedy thus seeks to take the enrichment away from the defendant and return it to the plaintiff.

This award of restitution may be different from the plaintiff's reliance costs in providing the benefit, as well as different from the plaintiff's expectations arising out of any promise from the defendant if they were acting in a perceived contractual relationship. Instead, the proper measure is the reasonable value of the benefit received by the defendant.

Indeed, in some cases, the restitution awarded may even be different than the value of the benefit *to the plaintiff*, because the policy of unjust enrichment arguably is best advanced by taking from the defendant an amount that represents the extent to which *the defendant* gained from the benefit. That perspective makes perfect sense, for example, when the plaintiff transferred a benefit to the defendant, who then sold it to another, thus increasing his wealth by a definite, liquidated amount.

But, even if the value to the defendant is the theoretical ideal for measuring the restitution interest, some cases will present practical problems of valuation. In *Cotnam*, for example, how would a jury place a value on the increased chances of survival that the operation provided to the accident victim? Moreover, if the operation had been successful, should a jury be allowed to measure the benefit by the value of the life preserved? The court in *Cotnam* decided to measure the benefit provided by the physician by the amount that the victim normally would have paid for such medical services, thus avoiding the imprecision of the first question posed above. In a case in which services did save a life, the valuation approved in *Cotnam* also avoids an award that is wildly disproportionate to the efforts that provided the benefit.

Exercise 4.10 — Measuring Restitution in *Pyeatte*

On remand in *Pyeatte*, how would you calculate the restitution interest? What measure does the appellate court allow? Assume the following facts relating to the years that H. Charles attended law school: (1) Margrethe contributed $60,000 of her earnings and savings to tuition payments and living expenses for H. Charles, (2) Margrethe performed more than her normal share of household chores because H. Charles was busy going to class and studying nearly every waking hour, and (3) by going to law school H. Charles enhanced his earning power by $40,000/year for the first three years after law school.

Notice the court's admonition in ¶ 31 that restitution cannot exceed Margrethe's expectation interest. In other words, if she provided H. Charles with more support through three years of law school than she expected to derive from his supporting her through one or two years in a master's program, the level of support she expected from H. Charles would form a ceiling for her restitution interest. But, in light of the appellate court's finding that her expectation interest was too indefinite to enforce, how can the trial court determine the ceiling for restitution?

V. Liability Arising from Failed Negotiations

Outside the United States, some countries will impose liability for precipitously breaking off negotiations after raising expectations that a deal was near. In contrast, if parties in the United States seek a contractual relationship but fail to reach agreement, it is unlikely that either will be liable to the other for the failed negotiations.

As we will learn in Chapter 8, the implied duty of good faith does not attach to negotiations prior to contract formation. Nonetheless, in exceptional cases, behavior during failed negotiations may give rise to liability under traditional theories associated with the field of contract law: promissory estoppel, quasi-contract, or breach of a pre-existing contract to negotiate the main deal.

A. Promissory Estoppel

Normally, promissory estoppel provides a remedy only if the claimant relied on an unconditional subsidiary promise made by the other party during bargaining. *See, e.g., Hoffman v. Red Owl Stores, Inc.*, 26 Wis.2d 683, 133 N.W.2d 267 (1965) (promise during bargaining that a franchise would be forthcoming if certain capital could be raised). Mere reliance on the normal give and take of negotiations will not give rise to a claim for relief. In nearly all cases, a party's expenses in negotiations—such as preparing complicated proposals, performing research, or traveling to negotiation sites—are viewed as routine costs of doing business.

B. Quasi-Contract

Quasi-contract might provide a stronger basis for damages if the claimant had revealed some valuable information to the other party in the course of unsuccessful negotiations. The other party cannot solicit the claimant's valuable ideas and then allow negotiations to fall apart for the purpose of evading any obligation to compensate for the ideas, especially if information conveyed was the main subject of the proposed contract. For example, if an architect provided some preliminary architectural plans during negotiations, and the owner abandoned negotiations simply to use those plans without paying for them, the architect would have a fairly good claim for restitution. Still, retaining enrichment during negotiations will be unjust only if the party providing the benefit reasonably expected compensation for it. In many cases, that party expected nothing in return for an informative bid or proposal except an increased chance of landing a contract, which was never guaranteed.

C. Pre-Existing Contract to Negotiate Main Contract; Letters of Intent

A party will more surely be liable for failed negotiations if she breaches a pre-existing binding contract to negotiate the main deal in a certain manner. If a party breaches obligations under such an agreement, causing negotiations on the main deal to fail or to become more costly, she could be liable for breach of the pre-existing contract.

In some commercial contexts, such as the sale of a business, bargaining obligations may be included in a preliminary agreement, often called a "letter of intent." As described by Phoenix attorneys James P. O'Sullivan and May Lu, a letter of intent demonstrates the parties' belief that their interests are sufficiently compatible to warrant further investment of time and resources in the final negotiation of the main deal. Ms. Lu analogizes it to a successful match on a dating web site: A letter of intent reflects the parties' preliminary determination that their assets and interests are likely to lead to mutually satisfactory terms, warranting serious and often exclusive negotiations toward the main deal. During this "courtship," the parties will "ask the tough questions" and reveal sensitive information. Whether the parties will ultimately conclude the main deal in a "marriage" is uncertain, but signing a letter of intent demonstrates that the parties have serious intentions.

Although the letter of intent will not express agreement on the main deal, it typically will include mutual obligations regarding further negotiations: For example, it may set forth mutual promises to negotiate in good faith for a designated period of time; to maintain confidentiality about information revealed and even about the fact of the negotiations; to negotiate exclusively with one another for the designated period, or to pay a "break-up fee" if a party decides to deal with another; to disclose certain kinds of information; and to submit disputes arising out of the letter of intent to negotiation and conciliation prior to resorting to litigation.

Many provisions of the letter of intent will be nonbinding terms identifying the general outline of a deal which the parties hope to make more definite over the course of the "courtship." The mutual promises regarding the process of negotiations, however, when conveyed in a document reached through offer and acceptance, will constitute an enforceable contract regarding the negotiation process.

The damages for breach of a promise to bargain in a certain manner may be uncertain because of doubts about whether the parties would have concluded the main deal even if both had fully performed all bargaining obligations. If so, a court might be inclined to limit damages to provable reliance costs.

Conversely, if the parties are not careful to specify that parts of the letter of intent are nonbinding, the document could give rise to unexpected litigation or liability. If the parties do not yet wish to be bound to an agreement on the main deal, for example, their letter of intent should expressly disclaim final agreement on the main deal. In one case, a preliminary document contained so much detail and so little disclaimer that the jury found an enforceable contract for casino management and awarded $10,000,000 against a party that had abandoned the deal and had argued unsuccessfully that the document was only an unenforceable "agreement to agree." *Pavone v. Kirke*, 801 N.W.2d 477, 489–91 (Iowa 2011).

For an interesting discussion of various stages of preliminary documents in Chinese commercial culture, see *Rockefeller Tech. Inv. (Asia) v. Changzhou Sinotype Tech. Co.*,

24 Cal. App. 5th 115, 124 (2018). The parties' intentions about the binding or nonbinding nature one of these expressions of preliminary negotiations could be complicated by differences in legal cultures. *See id.* at 124–26 (describing differing positions about the enforceability of a preliminary document variously referred to as a *bei wang lu* or an MOU).

VI. Summary, Review, and Exam-Taking

A. Summary

- Although some states have expanded consideration doctrine to enforce promises made in recognition of a moral obligation arising out of a previous act, most courts limit consideration to a bargained-for exchange. All states nonetheless permit recovery in circumstances beyond a bargained-for exchange; as a formal matter, however, they do so largely through separate theories of recovery, such as promissory estoppel and quasi-contract, the latter sometimes known as a constructive or implied-in-law contract.
- Both promissory estoppel and quasi-contract are designed to remedy an injustice, stemming from foreseeable and detrimental reliance on a promise or from the unjust retention of a benefit. The remedy for unjust enrichment is restitution of the reasonable value of the benefit, while the remedy for promissory estoppel may vary as needed to address the injustice.
- Precontractual liability in the United States is generally limited to cases in which unusual actions or statements before or during unsuccessful negotiations for a contract give rise to traditional claims—such as promissory estoppel, quasi-contract, or breach of a contract to bargain in a certain manner.

B. General Guidance on Essay Exams

Review Chapters 3 and 4 and prepare your own outline of their content, organized around general legal topics and around legal rules that you have derived from the material. Illustrate the rules with one-sentence case summaries that explain in a nutshell why the rule was or was not satisfied in each case.

The first of the following practice exams raises issues relating only to a claim of quasi-contract. The second practice exam presents issues on topics covered in Chapters 3 and 4 of this book. Take the exams, using the following format: First, read the question carefully to understand the facts and to identify issues that are raised by the facts. To identify issues, determine which legal questions the opposing sides could reasonably debate, in light of the law and how the law would apply to the facts.

Next, for each issue that you have spotted, discuss the issue in a separate "IRAC," arguing both sides whenever possible. Each IRAC should include:

- the **I**ssue,
- a summary of the applicable legal **R**ule,
- an **A**pplication of the law to the facts, and
- a **C**onclusion (if the issue is debatable, either conclusion is fine)

Do not start your exam with a restatement of the facts; instead, wait until the "A" of IRAC to analyze the facts in relation to a legal rule. Normally the first words of your exam answer should be a brief statement of the first issue that you will discuss.

Do not spend time discussing a legal rule unless it is relevant to an issue that might reasonably be in dispute.

Exercise 4.11 — Practice Exams

1. Practice Exam on Quasi-Contract

Essay Question — Suggested Time Allocation: 40 minutes.

While jogging one morning, realtor Maria Reyes came upon the victim of an auto accident that had occurred a few minutes earlier. The victim was unconscious and was bleeding profusely from a severed artery. Reyes saved the victim's life by flagging down a motorist and by applying direct pressure to the severed artery during the 10-minute ride to the hospital. A paramedic would have charged $600 for providing a similar lifesaving technique. Reyes's clothes were covered with blood, but they washed clean. Reyes herself was shaken and exhausted for a few hours after the incident. A week or so later, after learning that the victim was an attorney with substantial earning power, Reyes demanded compensation from the victim.

Assume that no statute is relevant; apply only common law rules. Discuss only quasi-contract. Discuss the potential liability of the accident victim to Reyes, and — in a general fashion — discuss the appropriate remedy. After identifying the issues about quasi-contract raised by the facts, discuss each issue separately. For each issue, state the legal rule that helps to resolve the issue, and apply that rule to the facts, arguing both sides when possible. Reach a conclusion, even if either of two competing conclusions would be reasonable. For a sample answer, see Appendix 3 of this book.

2. Practice Exam — *Kirksey* Revisited

For this practice exam, I have used the facts of *Kirksey v. Kirksey* as the general basis for the facts in the question; however, don't look to that case for help on this exam — it won't be helpful. Instead, use your own understanding of contemporary law to identify and discuss issues relating to any topic addressed in Chapters 3 and 4 of this book.

Essay Question — Suggested Time Allocation: 60 minutes.

When Bradford learned that his brother Henry had passed away, leaving a wife, Antillico, and three children, Bradford wrote the following letter to Antillico:

> I feel absolutely awful that I was out of the country and missed Henry's funeral. I should be there with you now to help you get through this difficult period, but I'm afraid that the harvest season compels me to spend every waking hour in the fields;

> I really have more land here than I can tend myself. Without Henry's income, I can't imagine how you will keep up the mortgage payments on your house and make ends meet. You know that I want nothing but the best for the family of my beloved brother, so if you move your household to my estate, I will let you and the children live in our comfortable guest house until the children are grown and off on their own. You know that I have no family of my own, so it will be no trouble to have you all here; on the contrary, you will be most welcome. You probably should sell your house, regain whatever equity you have built up in it, and be done with that obligation.

Distraught over Henry's death and desperate to find a secure place for her children, Antillico spent $1,000, nearly all of her savings, in hiring a company to move her household goods several hundred miles to Bradford's property, where he made his guest house available to Antillico and her children. In her haste, rather than selling her house, Antillico simply abandoned it, defaulting on the mortgage, and losing her equity in the house as she allowed the bank to foreclose and sell the house for the amount owed to the bank on the mortgage.

Antillico and her children lived comfortably on Bradford's land; they neither paid rent to Bradford nor provided him with any significant services or other benefits. After two years, Bradford saw an opportunity to rent his guest house to workers who helped him tend his land, and he ordered Antillico and her children to leave. With nowhere to go and with little money and a bad credit history, Antillico sues Bradford for money damages. You may assume that Bradford breached a promise to provide Antillico with a comfortable guest house until her children were grown. Do not discuss whether Antillico breached any promise; focus only on her claims against Bradford.

Discuss any claims for relief that you have studied in Chapters 3 and 4 (Consideration and Alternative Theories of Relief) but only if they are raised by these facts. In addition to discussing the basis for relief, discuss the measure of recovery that would be appropriate, but only at the most general level. Try to discuss both sides of each issue or subissue that you discuss. For a sample answer, see Appendix 3 of this book.

Chapter 5

Mutual Assent II: Termination of Offers under Common Law

I. Introduction

A reply to an offer cannot create a contract unless it conveys acceptance while the offer is still open. In this chapter, we will explore several ways in which offers can terminate under the traditional common law. In the next chapter, we will address some innovations under the UCC for sales contracts. As you work through this chapter, consider the following questions:

- If an act can terminate an offer, when is the termination effective: when the act is taken or when the other party receives notice of the act? How does this question relate to the mailbox rule?
- In close cases, should the law find termination of offers fairly easily, so that fewer contracts are formed, or should it apply a demanding test for termination, maximizing the number of contracts that are formed?
- What is an option contract? In what circumstances will a statement be interpreted as a promise not to revoke an offer, and in what circumstances will such a promise be implied?
- What is the common law mirror-image rule?

II. Termination Through Death of Offeror or Offeree

A. Death After Contract Formation

If parties enter into a contract during their lifetimes, the contract may still be perfectly effective and enforceable even if one of them dies before performance is complete (while the contract is still "executory"). True, contracts that call for unique personal services will be terminated after their formation if a person who is essential to a remaining performance dies before the contract is completed. Many contractual duties, however, can be performed by the estate of the deceased, such as buying or selling goods or real estate, or paying for services that improve property of the estate.

B. Death Before Offer Is Accepted

The death of either the offeror or an offeree prior to acceptance, however, terminates the offer to that offeree. Thus, if the offeree dies before acceptance, a representative of the offeree cannot thereafter accept on behalf of the estate (unless the offer had effectively made the estate, through its representative, an alternative offeree in the event of the offeree's death).

Similarly, if the offeror dies prior to acceptance, the offeree no longer has the power to create a contract by communicating acceptance to the offeror's estate. In either case, of course, the surviving party or the representative of the deceased's estate can reiterate the original offer and begin bargaining anew.

The Restatement reflects the majority position that an offer terminates at the moment of the death of the offeror. In a departure from an objective theory of contracts, this rule applies even if the offeree does not receive notice of the death until after she has communicated her intent to accept. *See generally* RESTATEMENT (SECOND) OF CONTRACTS § 48 (1981).

Exercise 5.1 — Death and the Unilateral Contract

Owner's apartment complex, which Owner plans to sell, badly needs a new coat of paint and likely will not sell at a reasonable price until both the interior and exterior are painted. After Owner solicited bids from several painters, Contractor submitted a written offer to paint the complex with specified paint within a month for a fee of $50,000, stating that he could start in 10 days. Owner then met Contractor briefly on Saturday and stated the following counter-offer:

> I would have accepted your bid, but I need to change the timing before we strike a deal. I would like the job done for a potential buyer who will visit next Saturday, but no other contractor is available right away, so I can't get a commitment to finish it on time, and I can assume you can't commit today either. So, here's my proposition to you: if you can manage to fit this into your schedule this week, and if you get this job done by 5 p.m. on Friday, I'll pay you $55,000 Friday evening. I'll be gone all week on business, but I'll return late on Friday and see whether you have come through.

Contractor replied *"Sounds good,"* and the two shook hands and parted ways. On Monday, Owner died in a tragic accident while traveling to a meeting. Contractor, who did not learn of Owner's death until the following week, sent a crew to Owner's apartment complex on Tuesday. The crew worked all week and completed the painting by Friday at 2 p.m.

Does Owner's estate owe Contractor $55,000 on an enforceable contract? Explain why the result might depend on the kind of acceptance that Owner's offer authorized. If no witnesses overheard the parties' conversation during their meeting on Saturday, how would Contractor prove the nature of the bargaining? Does this raise any possible ethical questions when you interview Contractor in your initial meeting with him, or when you help him prepare his testimony prior to arbitration?

If an enforceable contract was not formed, does Contractor have any other claim that might provide compensation for the work? If so, how would the remedy differ?

III. Termination Through Lapse: Specified Time or Reasonable Time

An unaccepted offer does not last indefinitely, even if the parties remain alive and have not actively terminated the offer through revocation or rejection. The offer eventually will "lapse," terminating simply through the passage of an appropriate period of time. A positive response to a lapsed offer will not create a contract, although it might convey a new offer.

The lapse period can be specified by the offeror, the master of the offer. If the offeror has not specified a lapse term, it will lapse in a reasonable time. What period of time is "reasonable" depends on all the circumstances, including such factors as the nature of the transaction; the mode by which the offer was transmitted or by which it requests the acceptance be conveyed; and the speed with which these parties have communicated in previous transactions, if any.

It might be difficult to determine precisely when a lapse term expires, but not so hard to determine whether an acceptance is conveyed prior to that expiration. For example, it would be difficult to determine the precise hour and date in January on which a reasonable time elapses, but it might be easy to determine from all the circumstances that—whatever the precise moment of lapse—an attempted acceptance on January 25 comes too late.

Exercise 5.2 — Vagueness or Ambiguity in Lapse Terms

1. Interpreting a Specified Time

A specified lapse term in the offer does not necessarily end uncertainty about the period before lapse. If the offer specifies an imprecise lapse term, such as "To accept, you must promptly sign and return this form," the specified term "promptly" requires a degree of contextual interpretation similar to that required for the default term of "reasonableness."

Ambiguity can appear even when lapse terms appear at first glance to specify a lapse period with a definite term. For example, what are the possible meanings of an offer e-mailed from a business in California that requires the offeree, a business in New York, to "respond today"?

2. Defining a "Reasonable" Time

Which of the following offers is likely to lapse in less than a week after receipt by the offeree, if no lapse term is specified? Which is most likely to persist for a week or more before lapsing? Explain.

- An offer to sell a large parcel of land for the development of a supermarket at a recently appraised price, at a time of stable land prices but relatively weak sales, communicated in a regularly mailed letter to a prospective buyer with whom the owner has been negotiating intermittently over the course of two months.
- An offer to sell a crop of apples at the current wholesale market price, now being harvested over a two-day period in Watsonville, California. The offer is conveyed to a grocery store chain by e-mail, on a day when storms in the states of Oregon and Washington have possibly caused damage to crops there, yet to be determined.

- A written bid by a contractor to repair the roof of a house by a date two weeks from the bid date, after a storm that created great demand for repairs of roofs on residential and commercial buildings.

IV. Termination Through Revocation by the Offeror

Under U.S. common law, an offeror can revoke, or withdraw, the offer any time before it is accepted, unless the offeror has made an enforceable promise to hold the offer open in an option contract. Absent an option contract, the only question is whether the offeror has effectively revoked before the offeree has effectively accepted. Some special timing problems under the mailbox rule will be addressed soon. First, however, let's study cases discussing the clarity and manner with which the revocation is communicated

A. Revocation through Verbal Expression

An offeror can revoke an offer most surely and simply by delivering to the offeree the message, "I revoke my offer," while referring to an offer of a certain date or description. If the offer had been conveyed to the general public, such as through posted fliers or newspaper or radio ads, so that the identity of individual offerees is unknown, the offeror can revoke by publishing a notice of revocation in a medium equal or better to the method of publicizing the offer. *See, e.g.*, RESTATEMENT (SECOND) OF CONTRACTS § 46 (1981).

Suppose, however, that the offeror's post-offer communications suggest a change of heart but do not clearly state an intention to revoke, leading the offeree to wonder whether the offeror is still committed to the offer. Do such expressions of doubt or indecision amount to a revocation?

In the following case, the offeror did not make an enforceable promise to hold its offer open for a designated period, because—as stated rather cryptically in the first paragraph—the offeree paid no consideration for such an option contract. Consequently, the only issue was whether the offeror revoked before the offeree accepted. Does the court appear to require an unambiguous notice of revocation before the offer is terminated?

Hoover Motor Exp. Co. v. Clements Paper Co.

193 Tenn. 6, 241 S.W.2d 851 (1951)

Tomlinson, Justice.

¶ 1 On November 19, 1949 Hoover Motor Express Company, Inc. made and delivered to Clements Paper Company a written offer with reference to the purchase of certain real estate. There was no consideration paid for the offer. On January 20,

1950, Clements Paper Company made a written acceptance of that offer. Hoover refused to go forward with the transaction and Clements Paper Company brought suit for specific performance or, in the alternative, for damages. Hoover defended on the ground that it had withdrawn the offer before its acceptance.

¶2 The Chancellor and the Court of Appeals concurred in sustaining the bill of Clements Paper Company and ordered a reference to the master for ascertainment of damages....

¶3 All are agreed that in order to convert into a contract an offer for which no consideration was paid there must be an acceptance of that offer before it is withdrawn. The Chancellor found that Clements had shown by a preponderance of the evidence that Hoover had breached "the written contract entered into by and between the parties." Implicit in such conclusion is the finding that Hoover had not withdrawn the offer before its acceptance. The Court of Appeals expressly found that the offer had not been withdrawn before acceptance. There was, therefore, a concurrent finding of the two Courts upon that controlling question of fact.

¶4 If there is any material evidence to sustain the above stated concurrent finding of fact then this Court is bound thereby not only as to that finding but as well to an inference or conclusion reasonably drawn from the evidence that it is a fact. *Conaway v. New York Life Ins. Co.*, 171 Tenn. 290, 295, 102 S.W.2d 66. Therefore, since we cannot consider the case de novo, we must look to the evidence most favorable to Clements and determine from it whether there is therein any material evidence in support of this concurrent finding or any testimony that reasonably supports an inference or conclusion that the offer had not been withdrawn before its acceptance on January 20.

¶5 Clements was represented in this transaction by its Vice-President, Mr. Williams. He wrote the letter of January 20, 1950 accepting the offer. It is not contended in behalf of Clements that there was any acceptance prior to that date. Williams closes that letter with this statement: "We are ready to comply with our part of this agreement and are calling on you to do the same." The statement just quoted suggests the thought that its author, Mr. Williams, realized at the time he wrote the letter that something previously had occurred which caused him to anticipate that Hoover might not "comply" by going forward with its prior offer, Mr. Williams' letter of acceptance notwithstanding. This is important in that it throws light upon the construction placed by Williams upon a phone conversation had on January 13, 1950 by him with Hoover.

¶6 Williams had been authorized by Clements Paper Company some time in December to accept the written offer made by Hoover on November 19. It would, therefore, have been a simple matter for him then to have written the letter of acceptance which he finally wrote on January 20. The record leaves no doubt of the fact that Williams intended to accept the offer provided he could not get from Hoover a substantially better trade that he, Williams, had in mind. He, therefore, withheld acceptance and undertook on several occasions to get in touch with Hoover for the purpose of procuring, if he could, that better trade. Fortunately for Williams, in so far as the keeping alive of the offer is concerned, he never got around to conveying to Hoover the changes or additions he had in mind. But he did take a step to that end on January 13, 1950 by phoning Hoover with the idea of promoting his proposition. It is upon the legal effect that must be given that phone conversation, *as testified to by Williams*, that the outcome of this case must depend. If it can be given a construction which reasonably supports the concurrent finding mentioned that construction must be given.

¶ 7 Mr. Williams testified that he got Mr. Hoover on the phone on January 13 and "told him that we were ready to go through with it and I would like to discuss it with him." The matter which he testifies that he wanted to discuss with Mr. Hoover was whether Hoover would permit Clements to retain an easement for certain purposes through the property which Hoover had offered to buy.

¶ 8 Williams testifies that in reply to Williams' statement that he, Williams, wanted to discuss the offer with Hoover that Hoover replied "Well, I don't know if we are ready. We have not decided, we might not want to go through with it."

¶ 9 Williams made several other statements in his testimony as to what Hoover said in this phone conversation. The following are quotations from Williams' testimony: "He said he thought they might not go through with it."

¶ 10 Q. After you had talked to him on January 13, on the telephone, that is Mr. Eph Hoover, Jr., he indicated to you that he had made other plans or in some way "indicated" to you that the company had made other plans? A.... He said that he didn't think they were going through with the proposal and that he would call me on January 17 [and] [t]hat they had other plans in mind and he would let me know. He was not sure if he was going through with the original proposition.

¶ 11 Q. Did he definitely refuse to positively commit himself on January 13 that he would go through with it? A. That is right.... It was a very short discussion. Frankly, I was very much shocked when I heard from him that they didn't plan to go through with it. I had made my plans and had gone to the extent of having this elevation made.

[Hoover did not call Williams after the January 13 phone conversation.]

¶ 12 The interpretation which Mr. Williams placed upon what Hoover said to him in the phone conversation of January 13 is stated in Clements' bill of complaint as follows: "This was the first information, suggestion or intimation that complainant had received that the defendant would not or might not carry out its agreement or offer."

¶ 13 Our problem is reduced to answering the question as to whether there can reasonably be placed upon the above quoted testimony of Williams a construction that prevents the statements of Hoover, as testified to by Williams, from amounting to a withdrawal on January 13 of the offer before it was attempted on January 20 to accept it. This is true because "the continued existence of the offer until acceptance is, however, necessary to make possible the formation of the contract." 12 American Jurisprudence, page 531.

¶ 14 Although there is no Tennessee case deciding the point, in so far as we can find, the general rule is that express notice, in so many words, of withdrawal before acceptance of an offer of the character we have here is not required. In 55 American Jurisprudence, page 488, under a discussion of "Termination of Offer," there appears in the text, supported by reference to decisions, this statement: "It is sufficient to constitute a withdrawal that knowledge of acts by the offerer inconsistent with the continuance of the offer is brought home to the offeree."

¶ 15 In *Coleman v. Applegarth*, 68 Md. 21, 11 A. 284, 287, quoting with approval from the English case of *Dickinson v. Dodds*, L.R. 2 Ch.Div. 463, it is said:

> That being the state of things, it is said that the only mode in which Dodds could assert that freedom (freedom from the offer) was by actually and distinctly saying to Dickinson, "Now I withdraw my offer." It appears to me that there is neither principle nor authority for the proposition that there must be an express and actual withdrawal of the offer, or what is called a retraction. It must, to constitute a contract, appear that the two minds were as one, at the same moment of time; that there was an offer continuing up to the time of the acceptance. If there was not such a continuing offer, then the acceptance comes to nothing.

¶ 16 Applying to the undisputed testimony as furnished by Williams the rule clearly stated in all the authorities from which we have above quoted—and we find none to the contrary—we think it must be concluded that Hoover's written offer of November 19 was withdrawn on January 13 thereafter prior to its attempted acceptance on January 20, and that the concurrent finding of the Chancellor and the Court of Appeals to the contrary is not supported by any material evidence. There can be no doubt as to it being a fact that on January 13 knowledge was brought home to Williams that Hoover no longer consented to the transaction. There was, therefore, no offer continuing up to the time of the attempted acceptance on January 20.

¶ 17 We have been greatly concerned over the fact that the above stated conclusion which we have felt compelled to reach is contrary to the concurrent findings of two very able Courts and we have long pondered the question presented. It is our feeling that the disagreement between our Court and these Courts is due to the fact that the Chancellor and the Court of Appeals and counsel for Clements Paper Company mistakenly failed to give effect to the general rule that express notice, in so many words, of withdrawal of an offer of the character we have here is not required. Apparently, in so far as a close search reveals, our Courts of Tennessee have not heretofore been presented a case in which that rule was applicable.

¶ 18 The decree of the Court of Appeals and of the Chancellor will be reversed and the cause remanded for entry of a decree in keeping with this opinion. All costs in all Courts will be adjudged against Clements Paper Company.

Exercise 5.3 — Questions and Notes on *Hoover*

1. Standard of Appellate Review on Factual Matters

Notice that the Tennessee Supreme Court carefully justified its decision to reach a conclusion that differed from that reached by both the trial court and the intermediate court of appeals. How did the Tennessee Supreme Court defend its overturning the conclusions of two lower courts on a matter that appears largely factual in nature? Should the majority of the court in *Kirksey v. Kirksey* (Chapter 3) have explained why it drew factual inferences contrary to those drawn by the jury in that case?

2. Expressions of Doubt or Indecision

The second Restatement summarizes the common law by stating that an offer is terminated when "the offeree receives from the offeror a manifestation of an intention not to enter into the proposed contract." RESTATEMENT (SECOND) OF CONTRACTS § 42 (1981). The question remains: How readily should courts or properly instructed juries conclude that an offeror's words or conduct manifested a withdrawal of commitment?

Why did the Tennessee Supreme Court find that Hoover's statement of indecision amounted to a revocation? We learned in Chapter 2 that a proposal is not an offer unless it clearly conveys commitment to a binding contract, and that a response is not an acceptance unless it unequivocally and unambiguously conveys assent to the offer. Is it inconsistent for courts to find a revocation on the basis of expression of indecision rather than a clear statement of withdrawal? Or do all of those doctrinal approaches fit into a consistent framework?

3. Lapse?

Hoover delivered its offer on November 19. If the parties had not spoken over the phone on January 13, would the offer have lapsed by the time Clement attempted to accept on January 20? Construct a statement by Hoover that (a) does not revoke any outstanding offer, (b) rejects Williams's request for an easement, and (c) reiterates the original offer, thus extending the lapse period.

B. Revocation Through Conduct (and Communicated by a Third Party)

The *Hoover* court rejected the position that revocation requires "express notice, in so many words, of withdrawal of an offer." In other words, one can revoke without using the words "I am revoking my offer on this deal." Hoover did so by expressing doubt or indecision about his continuing commitment to his earlier offer.

Still, Hoover communicated his revocation through verbal communication, so we should hesitate to say that Hoover implied a revocation through conduct. Perhaps one could argue that he implied the revocation through his statements on other topics. It's probably more accurate, however, to say that Hoover expressly and specifically addressed the topic of revocation or continuing offer but used verbal expression that conveyed equivocation about whether he was still committed to the offer. The court developed and applied a rule about the legal effect of such a statement.

A better example of *implied* revocation is provided by the case of *Dickinson v. Dodds*. In this nineteenth century English case, John Dodds offered in writing, on Wednesday, to sell real estate to George Dickinson for £800. Before Dodd's offer would have lapsed, Dickinson's agent, Berry, delivered a note to Dodds on Friday, communicating Dickinson's intention to accept. The Court of Appeal, Chancery Division, however, found that Dodds had agreed on Thursday to sell the same land to Allan, and that Dodd's offer to Dickinson had been revoked when Dickinson learned later on Thursday of this occurrence. *Dickinson v. Dodds*, 2 Ch. Div. 463 (1876).

Thus, an offer—and the corresponding power of acceptance—is terminated not only when an offeror verbally expresses an intention to withdraw from the proposed contract, but also when "the offeror takes definite action inconsistent with an intention to enter into the proposed contract...." Restatement (Second) of Contracts § 43 (1981).

The *Dickinson* case, however, presented a second difficulty. Assuming that Dodds's transaction with Allan amounted to conduct that manifested an intention to revoke the offer to Dickinson, at what point would the revocation be effective? A purely subjective standard might find the offer revoked at the moment of Dodd's commitment to Allan, even before Dickinson learned of it. Indeed, the judges' opinions did resort to some language, such as "of the same mind between the two parties," which reminds us of a subjective standard. However, the judges undoubtedly were aware even in 1876 that an outward manifestation was needed under an objective standard for issues of contract formation, because they emphasized that Dickinson had received notice of Dodds's bargaining with Allan.

Certainly, the revocation would have been objectively conveyed to Dickinson if he had been present during Dodds's transaction with Allan and had witnessed this conduct inconsistent with a continuing offer to him. On the facts of the case, however, the court was satisfied with indirect notification: On Thursday, Dickinson had received notice of the revocation through his trusted agent, Berry, who testified that he "knew" of the transaction between Dodds and Allan. This holding of *Dickinson v. Dodds* is reflected in a Restatement provision that summarizes the common law as recognizing a revocation when "the offeree acquires reliable information" of the "definite action inconsistent with an intention to enter into the proposed contract." *Id.*

Exercise 5.4—Questions on *Dickinson*

1. Conduct Inconsistent with a Continuing Offer

Suppose that Dodds manufactured handsome horse-drawn carriages and had three completed carriages of the same design in stock. If he had made an offer to sell one to Dickinson on Wednesday, would an agreement to sell one to Allan on Thursday have any effect on the offer to Dickinson? What feature of the subject matter in *Dickinson v. Dodds* affects the interpretation of Dodds's conduct?

We will study conditions in greater depth later in the semester, but you can imagine now that a promise may be conditioned on some future event, such as "I promise to pay you a bonus of 10% in the event that you complete the work at least one week before the scheduled deadline." On the original facts of *Dickinson v. Dodds*, in which Dodds made an offer on Wednesday to sell specified land to Dickinson, can you think of any way that accurate news of Dodds's contract on Thursday to sell the land to Allan might still be consistent with a continuing offer to Dickinson? Is this possible consistency, however, too speculative to affect the analysis of revocation?

2. Reliable Information of the Offeror's Inconsistent Conduct

Notice that both in *Dickinson* and in the Restatement summary, the revocation is initiated by a definite act of the offeror. If Dodds had never negotiated with Allan, and if Berry had transmitted to Dickinson a false rumor of an agreement between Dodds and Allan, that case would be distinguishable from *Dickinson v. Dodds* and would present a weak basis for finding revocation.

But if Dodds in fact had reached agreement with Allan, how reliable must the information be to give proper notice of the fact to Dickinson? Would the revocation be effective if an accurate story of the agreement with Allan had been relayed to Dickinson not by his trusted agent but by the town's notorious practical joker? What if it had been relayed by Berry, who had overheard it in a tavern, from a conversation between two people with whom Berry was not acquainted? Would it be enough that Berry, a trusted agent, had reasonably assessed the source of information and was himself convinced of its accuracy?

C. Option Contracts — Enforceable Promises Not to Revoke

In some European or other civil law countries, an offer is normally irrevocable for a reasonable period of time, or it becomes irrevocable during the lapse term if one is stated. As we learned in Sections A and B above, however, an offer normally is revocable under the common at any time before acceptance.

Under the common law, moreover, a lapse term does no more than state the time at which the offer will terminate through passage of time; it does not protect the offer from revocation. Prior to acceptance, the offer might terminate before the end of the lapse period through active revocation by the offeror, or by some other means such as the death of a party.

1. *Irrevocable Offers in a Common Law System*

Even in common law countries, an offer may be irrevocable for a certain period in limited circumstances. First, legislation in some states may require certain kinds of offers to remain open and irrevocable for a specified period, such as offers to provide services to a government entity in a competitive bid process. More generally, the common law will hold an offer open if the offeror has promised not to revoke the offer, and if the facts support a ground for enforcement of the promise.

We have already explored grounds for enforcing a promise under the common law: consideration for the promise, or reliance on the promise in circumstances giving rise to promissory estoppel. The offer in *Dickinson v. Dodds* serves as a good illustration for review. The court found that Dodds had promised to Dickinson to hold his offer open until Friday 9 a.m., but it also found that this promise was a "mere *nudum pactum*" (a naked pact) that "did not bind Dodds." In other words, the promise not to revoke the offer was an unenforceable gratuitous promise, so Dodds could still revoke his offer at any time before acceptance. Similarly, in the *Hoover* case, in which the court found an effective revocation, the court's opinion specifically states in the first paragraph that "[t]here was no consideration paid for the offer" by Clements (even if we assume that Hoover had promised to hold the offer open).

Like other kinds of promises, a promise not to revoke an offer will be enforceable if it is supported by consideration, or by reliance giving rise to promissory estoppel. The combination of a promise and grounds for enforcement creates an *option contract* that can be viewed as separate from the proposed underlying exchange and subsidiary to it.

2. Offer, Promise Not to Revoke, and Option Contract

Imagine, for example, an offer by Dodds on Wednesday to sell land to Dickinson for $800,000, represented by the following:

Offer: Proposed exchange of Promise to sell land *for* Promise to pay $800,000.

Now, imagine a separate promise by Dodds to hold the offer open until Friday at 9 a.m., represented by the second line in our representation:

Offer: Proposed exchange of Promise to sell land for Promise to pay $800,000.
\
Offer includes promise not to revoke offer until Friday 9 a.m.

In light of the offeror's assurance that the offer will remain open until Friday at 9 a.m., we know at least that the offer will not lapse before then. However, the promise not to revoke will not prevent revocation before Friday unless we find a basis for enforcement, such as the following example of consideration:

Offer: Proposed exchange of Promise to sell land for Promise to pay $800,000.
\
Offer includes promise not to revoke offer until Friday 9 a.m., exchanged for promise to pay $500, or for actual payment of $500, on Wednesday.

Alternatively, the promise not to revoke might be enforceable under promissory estoppel:

> ***Offer:*** Proposed exchange of Promise to sell land for Promise to pay $800,000.
>
> \
>
> *Offer includes promise not to revoke offer until Friday 9 a.m., on which the offeree foreseeably relies, creating an injustice that can be remedied only by enforcing the promise not to revoke.*

In either of these last two examples, we have an option contract: a separate enforceable obligation to hold open the offer to sell the land for $800,000. We do not yet have a contract for the sale of the land, and we don't know if the offer to sell will be accepted prior to lapse, but we know that the offer to sell cannot be effectively revoked prior to Friday at 9 a.m.

Because the promise to hold the offer open is subsidiary to the main proposed transaction, and because option contracts can serve a useful function, some courts tend to be a bit relaxed in their scrutiny of consideration for the promise not to revoke. *See, e.g.*, Restatement (Second) of Contracts § 87(1)(a) (1981) (asserting that an option contract can be found if an offer is in a signed writing and "recites a purported consideration for the making of an offer"). One might speculate as well that the level of reliance and injustice required for promissory estoppel might be somewhat relaxed when the offeree is seeking only enforcement of the subsidiary promise not to revoke the offer.

Exercise 5.5 — Option Contract Puzzles

1. Where's the Promise?

The first element of an option contract is a promise not to revoke. In *Dickinson v. Dodds*, in the same signed writing in which Dodds offered to sell the land, he wrote: "This offer to be left over until Friday, 9 ... a.m." The court assumed that the phrase "to be left over" conveyed a promise not to revoke. Do you agree, or would you interpret it to be merely a statement that the offer will lapse on Friday morning if not accepted or revoked before then? Do you interpret each of the following to be a lapse term, a promise not to revoke, or a combination of both?

(i) To accept, you must respond by Friday noon.

(ii) I promise not to revoke before Friday noon.

(iii) This offer lapses on Saturday at noon, and I promise not to revoke before Friday at noon.

(iv) This offer is good until Friday at noon.

2. Where's the Consideration?

In the illustrations set forth in Subsection 2 above, why do we need the $500 or reliance as a basis for enforcing the promise not to revoke the offer? Why doesn't the $800,000 from the offeree constitute consideration for the promise not to revoke?

Suppose that Dickinson was not interested in Dodds's offer, and Dodds added a clear promise not to revoke with the following explanation: "Look, if you agree to perform some reasonable research on this property and to give it some serious thought, I'll keep this offer open to you exclusively until Friday morning; I think you'll see the value of this proposal if you look into it." If Dickinson had said, "Okay," would Dodds's promise be enforceable? Explain.

Suppose that Dodds had promised not to revoke, but without the explanation immediately above. In reliance on the promise not to revoke, Dickinson decided to give the offer serious consideration, and he expended $200 researching the property prior to Friday morning. Would Dickinson have an option to buy until Friday morning?

3. What's the Difference?

Owner agreed to lease its office building to Dentist for $2,000/month. The lease agreement provides that Dentist has the option of purchasing the office building at any time during the term of the lease for $800,000 minus rent paid by Dentist up to the time of the sale. After the commencement of the lease, but before Dentist has exercised the purchase option, Owner notified Dentist that it no longer is willing to sell the building. Can Dentist nonetheless exercise the option? How is this different from the illustrations in Subsection 2 above, as underscored by the question in the first paragraph of Exercise 5.5(2) immediately above?

4. What's the Reason?

If Dodds had taken consideration on Wednesday morning for his promise not to revoke his offer before Friday morning, and if Dodds then died on Wednesday night, Dodds's offer to sell the land would not terminate on his death, and Dickinson would be able to accept the offer on Thursday. Explain why this should be so, even though death of the offeror prior to acceptance normally terminates a simple offer, even before the offeree receives notice of the death. For a hint, reread the first paragraph of Section II.B of this chapter.

D. Option Contracts Based on Implied Promises Not to Revoke

In Section C above, we assumed that the offeror accompanied the offer with an express statement about the duration of the offer. We addressed issues about whether the express statement should be interpreted as only a lapse term or as a promise not to revoke, and whether any promise not to revoke was enforceable on the basis of consideration or promissory estoppel.

But let's now assume that the offeror made no statement about holding the offer open, so that we have no express promise not to revoke. Can the offeree use promissory estoppel to hold the offer open if the offeree relies on the offer itself, and not on any separate promise to hold the offer open?

What's the difference between relying on either of the following statements:

- "I promise to pay you $5,000 on December 1. I require nothing in return. This will enable you to quit work." You rely before December 1.

- "I will pay you $3,000 if you agree to paint my house." (Precise legal effect: "If you accept my offer by giving me your promise to paint my house, you will then have my promise to pay you $3,000.") You rely before accepting. Did you rely on a promise?

If you rely only on an offer, rather than on an unconditional promise, should it matter whether the offeror is looking for acceptance in the form of a completed return performance (forming a unilateral contract) or a return promise (forming a bilateral contract)? We will explore these issues now. However, you might want to start with this hint: These questions can be analyzed entirely with principles that we have already studied: promissory estoppel, and promises that are implied in fact.

Before you study this topic in depth, ask yourself whether you feel different levels of sympathy for the offerees in the following hypotheticals. If so, explain why. To what extent was each offeree forced to act in reliance on the offer before accepting the offer and creating a binding contract? To what extent did either offeree have the power to bind the offeror before engaging in the slightest reliance?

(i) Owner offered to pay $2,000 to Contractor to build a slatted roof over Owner's back porch, to provide shade for the porch. Owner emphasized that she was asking for a return performance to form a unilateral contract, because her written offer stated: "To accept this offer, you must build the roof according to the attached specifications; no contract is formed until you complete the construction." The offer said nothing about whether the offer was irrevocable. After Contractor had measured the porch, purchased suitable lumber and paint, sawed some of the lumber to length, brought these and other materials to the work site, and constructed the frame and the supporting beams for the roof, Owner stepped out on the back porch and revoked her offer.

(ii) In early October, Law Firm, located in Los Angeles, mailed an offer to Graduate, who resides in Tempe, proposing to pay Graduate a starting salary of $80,000/year to work at the firm beginning November 1. The letter ended by saying: "We hope to hear soon that you have accepted our offer. My phone number, email address, and mailing address are all set forth at the bottom of this letter." Ecstatic, Graduate gave her landlord notice that she would be terminating the lease at the end of the month, placed a security deposit and first month's rent on an available apartment in Los Angeles, hired a moving company to move her belongings to Los Angeles, and began studying the area of law in which she would practice with the firm. Once she was certain that all these details were in place or in progress, she began composing an email message accepting the offer. Before she finished composing it, however, the hiring partner of Law Firm called to tell her that it was revoking its offer because of financial problems within the firm.

1. *Reliance on an Offer for a Unilateral Contract (or on an Implied Promise Not to Revoke)*

In a Southwestern version of a classic hypothetical about the Brooklyn Bridge, imagine that I am seeking to determine whether you are able to walk across the Mill Avenue Bridge in Tempe in 30 minutes.

I offer to pay you $100, making it clear that you can accept the offer and create a contract only by actually walking across the entire length of the bridge in 30 minutes, sometime before 5 p.m. tonight. By 4:25 p.m., you have paid a cab $10 to take you to the entrance of the Mill Ave. Bridge, and you have just taken your first steps on the bridge. At 4:40 p.m., you are about halfway across the bridge when I drive up in my car, roll down the window, and say "I revoke my offer."

By 4:40 p.m., have you accepted my offer for a unilateral contract? If at 4:35 p.m., after you had walked only a third of the length of the bridge, you had grown tired and turned back, would you be liable for breach of contract?

Assuming again that you are determined to walk across the entire bridge within 30 minutes, if I made no promise to hold the offer open, the normal rules of contract formation would permit me to revoke at any time before acceptance, right? If so, does that result bother you? If so, why?

If you are bothered by my asserted right to revoke when you are halfway across, can you find an option contract in this case based on theories of implied promise and promissory estoppel? State your explanation in writing.

a. Restatement § 45

Courts have protected reliance on an offer for a unilateral contract in limited circumstances, inspiring the influential section 45 of both the first and second Restatements of Contracts. Section 45 advances a rule that recognizes an option contract if an offer invites the offeree "to accept by rendering a performance and does not invite a promissory acceptance," and if the offeree has begun the invited performance. RESTATEMENT (SECOND) OF CONTRACTS § 45 (1981).

How does this summary of the common law apply to the questions posed in illustrations (i) and (ii) appearing on page 190? In the Mill Ave. hypothetical, if an option contract is created at 4:25 p.m., does that mean that you are then obligated to continue to cross the bridge, or that I am obligated at 4:25 to pay you $100, or neither?

b. Applying the Familiar Principle of Promissory Estoppel

Why do we need a new doctrine to deal with option contracts for offers for unilateral contracts? Why can't we just routinely apply the doctrine of *promissory* estoppel to protect your reliance on my *offer* to pay you $100?

For the answer, review the discussion of promissory estoppel in Chapter 4, and recall the promise made by the grandfather to his granddaughter, Katie, to pay her $2,000. The grandfather gave his promise to Katie without conditions; indeed, he even physically transferred possession to her of a written symbol of the promise, a promissory note. She had his promise literally in hand, and she relied on that promise, creating an injustice to her when the promise was not performed.

But, in the Mill Ave. Bridge case, did I give you a promise to pay you $100 when I made my offer? Didn't I *propose* to give you my promise to pay *if* you first performed by crossing the bridge? Until you accept my offer by completing that performance, you do not yet have my promise to pay you $100: "an offer for an exchange is not meant to become a promise until a consideration has been received, either a counter-promise or whatever else is stipulated." *James Baird Co. v. Gimbel Bros.*, 64 F.2d 344, 346 (1933) (opinion by Learned Hand). If I have not yet given you an express promise on which to rely, promissory estoppel does not routinely apply to our case, at least not without another analytic step.

Can we think of another way to invoke our established doctrine of promissory estoppel to create an option contract? A hint is provided in comment b to section 45 of the First Restatement, which explained that the main offer for a unilateral contract "includes as a subsidiary promise, necessarily implied, that if part of the requested performance is given, the offeror will not revoke his offer." RESTATEMENT (FIRST) OF CONTRACTS § 45 comm. b (1932) (*quoted in Drennan v. Star Paving Co.*, 51 Cal. 2d 409, 414, 333 P.2d 757, 760 (Cal. 1958)).

Of course, if the offeror expressly reserved the right to revoke, that would leave no room to imply a promise to hold the offer open. However, if circumstances do support implication of a promise not to revoke, then promissory estoppel principles can be applied to determine whether reliance on the implied promise should be protected.

Can you explain why it makes sense to imply a promise not to revoke an offer for a unilateral contract? Return to the case of the Mill Ave. Bridge on page 191 and to the question about Owner and Contractor in paragraph (i) on page 190. In each of those cases, do you see language and circumstances from which you would find an implied promise not to revoke the offer once the offeree has begun to perform? If so, you can apply promissory estoppel to the facts to determine what remedy you might award, if any, for reliance on the implied promise.

Section 45 of the Restatement suggests a fairly inflexible approach to this issue, similar to that of the first Restatement's treatment of promissory estoppel: the only remedy is full enforcement of the implied promise not to revoke (by creating an option contract that makes the offer irrevocable for a reasonable time), and that relief is triggered under section 45 only if the offeree engages in the definite and substantial reliance of beginning performance.

What acts constitute "beginning performance" in each of the hypothetical cases? Did you begin performance in the bridge case by paying for the cab ride to the bridge, or is that only preparation for performance? Did the Contractor begin performance by buying the lumber and sawing some of it to length, or is that only preparation if the lumber can be used for other jobs?

The questions don't matter much if we free ourselves of the language of section 45 of the Restatement and simply apply the flexible standards of modern promissory estoppel to the reliance on the *implied promise* not to revoke. If the reliance is substantial (such as beginning performance) and the injustice is great (as it would be if I revoke when you are midway across the bridge), then full enforcement of the promise not to revoke would be necessary to avoid injustice; that would create an option contract and give you the opportunity to earn the $100. On the other hand, if reliance is small (taking the cab to the bridge) and the injustice is slight (my revoking before you have started crossing), then perhaps injustice can be avoided by awarding a small amount of money, such as the $10 cab fare.

But it's not clear that courts will free themselves of the rather inflexible language of the influential section 45, so a cautious application of this doctrine will require a finding that the offeree for a unilateral contract relied to the extent of actually beginning performance. Greater flexibility is suggested not only by the approach of implying a promise and applying modern promissory estoppel, as described above, but also by Restatement (Second) of Contracts § 87. Analysis of that section, however, will be taken up in Subsection 2 below.

Exercise 5.6 — The Real Estate Broker

Apply either section 45 of the Restatement, or apply doctrines of implied promises and promissory estoppel, or apply both, to the following facts. Write your answer in IRAC form.

Owner offered to pay a 5% commission to Broker if Broker succeeded in finding a willing and able purchaser for Owner's desert mansion at a price of no less than $2 million. The offer made it clear that Broker was not under any obligation to find such a buyer, and that a contract would not be formed unless and until Broker completed performance by securing the signature of a financially sound buyer on a sale contract. (If formed, the contract for a commission would, by its terms, make Owner's obligation to pay contingent on the sale closing.) Over the course of a few days, Broker studied the features of the property, appraised it to arrive at an asking price of $2.3 million, and listed the property at that price. Within a short time after listing the property, Broker received expressions of interest from two potential buyers. Before Broker could arrange to show the property to either of them, however, Broker received an e-mail from Owner expressing Owner's intentions to revoke the offer of a commission. At that moment, does Broker have an option contract under the doctrine of section 45, or has Owner effectively revoked the offer? If Broker has an option contract, what are Broker's legal rights in such an option? What remedy, if any, would you award to Broker if you applied a flexible approach based on general principles of estoppel?

---

2. *Reliance on an Offer for a Bilateral Contract*

In the next case, where a subcontractor made an offer for a bilateral contract, the court refers to "the analogous problem of an offer for a unilateral contract." But are they analogous on this issue? Only in special circumstances?

a. The Difficulty of Implying a Promise Not to Revoke

Refer again to the hypothetical cases in paragraphs (i) and (ii) on page 190. Were you equally ready to grant relief in both cases? Why was the Graduate's pre-acceptance reliance completely unnecessary in the second case?

Can you think of any context in which an offeree for a bilateral contract must rely before conveying a return promise and binding the offeror? Is the following case an example, or could the general contractor have protected itself in other ways, so that its reliance does not create an injustice?

Drennan v. Star Paving Co.

51 Cal. 2d 409, 333 P.2d 757 (Cal. 1958)

Traynor, J.

¶ 1 Defendant appeals from a judgment for plaintiff in an action to recover damages caused by defendant's refusal to perform certain paving work according to a bid it submitted to plaintiff.

¶ 2 On July 28, 1955, plaintiff, a licensed general contractor, was preparing a bid on the "Monte Vista School Job" in the Lancaster school district. Bids had to be submitted before 8 p.m. Plaintiff testified that it was customary in that area for general contractors to receive the bids of subcontractors by telephone on the day set for bidding and to rely on them in computing their own bids. Thus on that day plaintiff's secretary, Mrs. Johnson, received by telephone between 50 and 75 subcontractors' bids for various parts of the school job. As each bid came in, she wrote it on a special form, which she brought into plaintiff's office. He then posted it on a master cost sheet setting forth the names and bids of all subcontractors. His own bid had to include the names of subcontractors who were to perform one-half of one per cent or more of the construction work, and he had also to provide a bidder's bond of 10 per cent of his total bid of $317,385 as a guarantee that he would enter the contract if awarded the work.

¶3 Late in the afternoon, Mrs. Johnson had a telephone conversation with Kenneth R. Hoon, an estimator for defendant. He gave his name and telephone number and stated that he was bidding for defendant for the paving work at the Monte Vista School according to plans and specifications and that his bid was $7,131.60. At Mrs. Johnson's request he repeated his bid. Plaintiff listened to the bid over an extension telephone in his office and posted it on the master sheet after receiving the bid form from Mrs. Johnson. Defendant's was the lowest bid for the paving. Plaintiff computed his own bid accordingly and submitted it with the name of defendant as the subcontractor for the paving. When the bids were opened on July 28th, plaintiff's proved to be the lowest, and he was awarded the contract.

¶4 On his way to Los Angeles the next morning plaintiff stopped at defendant's office. The first person he met was defendant's construction engineer, Mr. Oppenheimer. Plaintiff testified: "I introduced myself and he immediately told me that they had made a mistake in their bid to me the night before, they couldn't do it for the price they had bid, and I told him I would expect him to carry through with their original bid because I had used it in compiling my bid and the job was being awarded them. And I would have to go and do the job according to my bid and I would expect them to do the same."

¶5 Defendant refused to do the paving work for less than $15,000. Plaintiff testified that he "got figures from other people" and after trying for several months to get as low a bid as possible engaged L & H Paving Company, a firm in Lancaster, to do the work for $10,948.60.

¶6 The trial court found on substantial evidence that defendant made a definite offer to do the paving on the Monte Vista job according to the plans and specifications for $7,131.60, and that plaintiff relied on defendant's bid in computing his own bid for the school job and naming defendant therein as the subcontractor for the paving work. Accordingly, it entered judgment for plaintiff in the amount of $3,817 (the difference between defendant's bid and the cost of the paving to plaintiff) plus costs.

¶7 Defendant contends that there was no enforceable contract between the parties on the ground that it made a revocable offer and revoked it before plaintiff communicated his acceptance to defendant.

¶8 There is no evidence that defendant offered to make its bid irrevocable in exchange for plaintiff's use of its figures in computing his bid. Nor is there evidence that would warrant interpreting plaintiff's use of defendant's bid as the acceptance thereof, binding plaintiff, on condition he received the main contract, to award the subcontract to defendant. In sum, there was neither an option supported by consideration nor a bilateral contract binding on both parties.

¶9 Plaintiff contends, however, that he relied to his detriment on defendant's offer and that defendant must therefore answer in damages for its refusal to perform. Thus the question is squarely presented: Did plaintiff's reliance make defendant's offer irrevocable?

¶10 Section 90 of the Restatement of Contracts states: "A promise which the promisor should reasonably expect to induce action or forbearance of a definite and substantial character on the part of the promisee and which does induce such action or forbearance is binding if injustice can be avoided only by enforcement of the promise." This rule applies in this state. *Edmonds v. County of Los Angeles,* 40 Cal.2d 642, 255 P.2d 772; [four additional case citations, and two citations to articles are omitted].

¶11 Defendant's offer constituted a promise to perform on such conditions as were stated expressly or by implication therein or annexed thereto by operation of law. (See 1 Williston, Contracts [3d ed.], §24A, p. 56, §61, p. 196.) Defendant had reason to expect that if its bid proved the lowest it would be used by plaintiff. It induced "action ... of a definite and substantial character on the part of the promisee."

¶12 Had defendant's bid expressly stated or clearly implied that it was revocable at any time before acceptance we would treat it accordingly. It was silent on revocation, however, and we must therefore determine whether there are conditions to the right of revocation imposed by law or reasonably inferable in fact. In the analogous problem of an offer for a unilateral contract, the theory is now obsolete that the offer is revocable at any time before complete performance. Thus section 45 of the Restatement of Contracts provides: "If an offer for a unilateral contract is made, and part of the consideration requested in the offer is given or tendered by the offeree in response thereto, the offeror is bound by a contract, the duty of immediate performance of which is conditional on the full consideration being given or tendered within the time stated in the offer, or, if no time is stated therein, within a reasonable time." In explanation, comment *b* states that the "main offer includes as a subsidiary promise, necessarily implied, that if part of the requested performance is given, the offeror will not revoke his offer, and that if tender is made it will be accepted. Part performance or tender may thus furnish consideration for the subsidiary promise. Moreover, merely acting in justifiable reliance on an offer may in some cases serve as sufficient reason for making a promise binding (see §90)."

¶ 13 Whether implied in fact or law, the subsidiary promise serves to preclude the injustice that would result if the offer could be revoked after the offeree had acted in detrimental reliance thereon. Reasonable reliance resulting in a foreseeable prejudicial change in position affords a compelling basis also for implying a subsidiary promise not to revoke an offer for a bilateral contract.

¶ 14 The absence of consideration is not fatal to the enforcement of such a promise.... Reasonable reliance serves to hold the offeror in lieu of the consideration ordinarily required to make the offer binding. In a case involving similar facts the Supreme Court of South Dakota stated that

> we believe that reason and justice demand that the doctrine [of section 90] be applied to the present facts. We cannot believe that by accepting this doctrine as controlling in the state of facts before us we will abolish the requirement of a consideration in contract cases, in any different sense than an ordinary estoppel abolishes some legal requirement in its application. We are of the opinion, therefore, that the defendants in executing the agreement [which was not supported by consideration] made a promise which they should have reasonably expected would induce the plaintiff to submit a bid based thereon to the Government, that such promise did induce this action, and that injustice can be avoided only by enforcement of the promise.

Northwestern Engineering Co. v. Ellerman, 69 S.D. 397, 408 [10 N.W.2d 879]; [second citation omitted]; *cf. James Baird Co. v. Gimbel Bros.*, 64 F.2d 344.

¶ 15 When plaintiff used defendant's offer in computing his own bid, he bound himself to perform in reliance on defendant's terms. Though defendant did not bargain for this use of its bid neither did defendant make it idly, indifferent to whether it would be used or not. On the contrary it is reasonable to suppose that defendant submitted its bid to obtain the subcontract. It was bound to realize the substantial possibility that its bid would be the lowest, and that it would be included by plaintiff in his bid. It was to its own interest that the contractor be awarded the general contract; the lower the subcontract bid, the lower the general contractor's bid was likely to be and the greater its chance of acceptance and hence the greater defendant's chance of getting the paving subcontract. Defendant had reason not only to expect plaintiff to rely on its bid but to want him to. Clearly defendant had a stake in plaintiff's reliance on its bid. Given this interest and the fact that plaintiff is bound by his own bid, it is only fair that plaintiff should have at least an opportunity to accept defendant's bid after the general contract has been awarded to him.

¶ 16 It bears noting that a general contractor is not free to delay acceptance after he has been awarded the general contract in the hope of getting a better price. Nor can he reopen bargaining with the subcontractor and at the same time claim a continuing right to accept the original offer. (*See R. J. Daum Const. Co. v. Child,* 122 Utah 194 [247 P.2d 817, 823].) In the present case plaintiff promptly informed defendant that plaintiff was being awarded the job and that the subcontract was being awarded to defendant.

[The court further held that the subcontractor could not be relieved of its unilateral mistake in calculating its paving bid, because the error was not so obvious that the general contractor had notice of the mistake when it accepted the bid.]

The judgment is affirmed.

Exercise 5.7 — Dissenting Opinion

The result in *Drennan* is not inevitable, even in the subcontractor context. The *Drennan* opinion itself cites to *James Baird Co. v. Gimbel Bros.*, which refused to protect a general contractor's reliance on a subcontractor's offer for a bilateral contract in similar circumstances. Write a dissenting opinion in *Drennan* in which you argue in favor of following the example of *James Baird Co.* Explain the various ways in which the contractor in *Drennan* could have protected itself had it bargained differently, thus undermining the need to imply a promise not to revoke in the subcontractor's offer. Hint: Ironically, paragraph 8 of the *Drennan* decision suggests the possibilities.

---

b. The Restatement (Second) and *Drennan*

As a supplement to section 90 of the Second Restatement, which protects reliance on a gratuitous promise, section 87(2) takes inspiration from *Drennan* and supports the protection of reliance on an *offer*—even an offer for a bilateral contract—when necessary to avoid injustice.

As applied to an offer for a unilateral contract, this section is uncontroversial and indeed offers welcome flexibility as an alternative to the more mechanical provisions of section 45. As applied to an offer for a bilateral contract, however, this section must be viewed with great caution. As illustrated by the hypothetical case of the graduate and the law firm in paragraph (ii) at the bottom of page 190, only rarely will an offeree foreseeably rely on an offer for a bilateral contract before binding the offeror, because she normally can accept and create a contract without delay by communicating a return promise. Even the circumstances of the *Drennan* case will not move all courts to find an injustice, as illustrated by Judge Learned Hand's opinion in *James Baird Co.*

An Arizona court purported to approve and apply the *Drennan* decision; however, it found that the subcontractor had made an *express promise* to maintain its bid as "good" for 30 days, so the court arguably was applying simple promissory estoppel under section 90 of the second Restatement. *Double AA Builders, LTD. v. Grand State Construction L.L.C.*, 210 Ariz. 503, 506–08, 114 P.3d 835, 838–40, ¶¶ 13–26 (Ct.

App. 2005); *see also id.* at 507, 114 P.3d at 839, ¶16 (identifying cases from six other states that are purportedly in accord with *Drennan*).

Perhaps reliance prior to acceptance of an offer for a bilateral contract would be justified if the offeror had specified an unusually demanding mode of communication of acceptance, such as: "You can accept this offer to sell you my ranch only by traveling to Paris and calling me by cell phone from the sidewalk outside Café de Flore on the Boulevard St. Germain."

In the usual case, however, communicating a return promise is a simple matter, and pre-acceptance reliance is unnecessary.

Exercise 5.8 — Past Exam [Suggested Time: 20 minutes]

Contractor solicited bids from subcontractors for the downtown Baron Hotel project. One day before Contractor's own master bid to Baron Hotels was due, Pathway Co. submitted its subcontractor bid for all the carpeting and other floor covering in the hotel. Pathway's bid of $950,000 was the lowest bid for floor covering. Contractor incorporated Pathway's bid into Contractor's master bid for the construction of the new hotel, helping to make Contractor's master bid the lowest master bid submitted to Baron Hotels.

After Baron Hotels accepted Contractor's master bid, thus creating a binding contract with Contractor, Contractor began notifying all its subcontractors that it had the master contract and that it was accepting the subcontractor bids. Before Contractor could accept Pathway's bid, however, Pathway notified Contractor that Pathway was revoking its bid because it had accepted an offer on a different project that would occupy its full capacity during the relevant time period. Contractor notified Pathway that it was accepting Pathway's bid and that it considered Pathway to be contractually bound. Hiring a replacement for Pathway would cost Contractor $100,000 more than Pathway's bid.

You may assume that each subcontractor bid to Contractor amounted to an offer for a bilateral contract to supply specified services to Contractor, that none of these bids had lapsed during relevant times, that none of these bids contained an express promise not to revoke, and that Pathway did not make any mistake in its bid. Discuss one issue only, *which has not yet been decided in the relevant state*: Does Contractor have a legal basis under common law to bind Pathway to its bid? Fully describe and critique the legal theory supporting Contractor's claim. To fully discuss and critique the rule, you will need to refer to the facts. However, once you have identified the legal theory and argued for and against it, you need not further apply the legal rule to the facts to reach a conclusion in this case. Just fully discuss the "R" in IRAC and not the whole IRAC. Try to argue both for and against Contractor's claim, in separate paragraphs of your answer. For a sample answer, see Appendix 3.

E. Back to the Forest

Lest we lose sight of the forest while examining individual trees, let's regain our bearings in our current exploration. We are studying ways in which offers can terminate under the common law. We began this inquiry by studying death of a party and then lapse of the offer. We then lingered for quite some time on termination of offers through revocation by the offeror, which included discussion of express or implied promises not to revoke.

It's now time to move to another way in which an offer may terminate through the action of one of the parties: rejection of the offer by the offeree, who later changes his mind and wishes to accept.

V. Termination Through Rejection by the Offeree

Rejection of an offer by the offeree normally terminates the offer, so that the offeree is no longer empowered to create a contract by changing his mind and expressing assent. True, after terminating the offer through rejection, either party can begin bargaining anew by making a new offer. Indeed, as discussed below, the rejection can itself state a counter-offer on new terms.

A. The Common Law Mirror-Image Rule

Under the common law, even if the offeree responds with apparent assent, if the offeree simultaneously adds, deletes, or changes any of the terms of the offer, then the offeree's response normally is interpreted as an implicit rejection, which terminates the offer. Typically, this implicit rejection by the original offeree also communicates a counter-offer on its terms, to which the other party (originally the offeror, but now the offeree on the counter-offer) can respond.

This common law "mirror-image" rule requires the terms in the acceptance to match those in the offer. It can create problems in sales of goods, when commercial entities routinely respond to each other with print forms whose standard terms vary from each other. Accordingly, the UCC overrides the common law mirror-image rule for sales of goods. We will study the UCC approach in the next chapter, but let's first examine the common law mirror-image rule, which still applies to contracts for services and real estate in most states.

Exercise 5.9 — Acceptance or Rejection?

In each of the following cases, did the homeowner accept the contractor's offer? Or had the homeowner previously terminated the contractor's offer through the homeowner's own rejection of it? If the homeowner rejected, the parties might still reach agreement with further discussion, but focus for now on the legal effect of the homeowner's initial response.

1. The Quick Change of Mind

Contractor offered to repair Homeowner's air conditioning unit for $600. Homeowner responded: "No, that's too much." When Contractor walked toward his truck to leave, making it clear that he was not going to lower the fee, Homeowner quickly reversed herself and firmly declared: "I accept your bid."

2. The Attempt to Negotiate

Contractor offered to repair Homeowner's A/C for $600. Homeowner responded: " I can pay you $500." When Contractor did not reply to this but started walking toward his truck, Homeowner feared that she might not find another available contractor for several days, so she quickly added: "Okay, I'm good for $600."

3. The Grumbling Offeree

Contractor offered to repair Homeowner's A/C for $600. Homeowner responded: "Ok, I accept, but I think you are overcharging."

---

1. Rejection v. Clarification or Suggestion

The mirror-image rule is not completely unforgiving: A positive response to an offer might appear at first glance to add a term to the offer, but on reflection a court might find that the response was merely clarifying a term that was implicit in the offer from the outset. If so, the response is an acceptance even under the demanding requirements of the mirror-image rule. In other cases, an acceptance might more clearly refer to a new term, but it might be interpreted as (i) accepting the offer on precisely the terms of the offer, and then (ii) requesting a gratuity or a modification of the contract just formed. This would be an acceptance on the terms of the offer, without violating the mirror-image rule, with no obligation on the parties to reach agreement on other proposed terms.

In each of the following cases, is the response to the offer a rejection, or is it an unconditional acceptance on the terms of the offer, perhaps supplemented with expression of terms that were implied in the offer, or supplemented with a request for further bargaining on a second contract?

Fairmount Glass Works v. Crunden-Martin Woodenware Co.

106 Ky. 659, 51 S.W. 196 (1899)

[Chapter 2, Section III presents a longer excerpt of this case, where the facts show that the seller offered to sell "ten car loads of Mason fruit jars, complete" in various sizes and prices that could be selected by the buyer.]

It is insisted for [the seller] that [the buyer's response] was not an acceptance of the offer as made; that the stipulation, "The jars and caps to be strictly first-quality goods," [in the buyer's response] was not in [the seller's] offer; and that, it not having been accepted as made, [the seller] is not bound. But it will be observed that [the seller] declined to furnish the goods before it got this letter, and in the correspondence with [the buyer] it nowhere complained of these words as an addition to the contract. Quite a number of other letters passed, in which the refusal to deliver the goods was placed on other grounds, none of which have been sustained by the evidence. [The buyer] offers proof tending to show that these words, in the trade in which parties were engaged, conveyed the same meaning as the words used in [the seller's] letter, and were only a different form of expressing the same idea. [The seller's] conduct would seem to confirm this evidence.

Ardente v. Horan

117 R.I. 254, 366 A.2d 162 (1976)
Supreme Court of Rhode Island

Doris, Justice.

¶1 Ernest P. Ardente, the plaintiff, brought this civil action in Superior Court to specifically enforce an agreement between himself and William A. and Katherine L. Horan, the defendants, to sell certain real property. The defendants filed an answer together with a motion for summary judgment pursuant to Super. R. Civ. P. 56. Following the submission of affidavits by both the plaintiff and the defendants and a hearing on the motion, judgment was entered by a Superior Court justice for the defendants. The plaintiff now appeals.

¶2 In August 1975, certain residential property in the city of Newport was offered for sale by defendants. The plaintiff made a bid of $250,000 for the property which was communicated to defendants by their attorney. After defendants' attorney advised plaintiff that the bid was acceptable to defendants, he prepared a purchase and sale agreement at the direction of defendants and forwarded it to plaintiff's attorney for plaintiff's signature. After investigating certain title conditions, plaintiff executed the agreement.

¶3 Thereafter plaintiff's attorney returned the document to defendants along with a check in the amount of $20,000 and a letter dated September 8, 1975, which read in relevant part as follows:

> My clients are concerned that the following items remain with the real estate: a) dining room set and tapestry wall covering in dining room; b) fireplace fixtures throughout; c) the sun parlor furniture. I would appreciate your confirming that these items are a part of the transaction, as they would be difficult to replace.

¶4 The defendants refused to agree to sell the enumerated items and did not sign the purchase and sale agreement. They directed their attorney to return the agreement and the deposit check to plaintiff and subsequently refused to sell the property to plaintiff. This action for specific performance followed.

¶5 In Superior Court, defendants moved for summary judgment on the ground that the facts were not in dispute and no contract had been formed as a matter of law. The trial justice ruled that the letter quoted above constituted a conditional acceptance of defendants' offer to sell the property and consequently must be construed as a counteroffer. Since defendants never accepted the counteroffer, it followed that no contract was formed, and summary judgment was granted.

....

¶6 Summary judgment is a drastic remedy and should be cautiously applied; nevertheless, where there is no genuine issue as to any material fact and the moving party is entitled to judgment as a matter of law, summary judgment properly issues. *Ladouceur v. Prudential Ins. Co.*, 111 R.I. 370, 302 A.2d 801 (1973). On appeal this court is bound by the same rules as the trial court. *Cardente v. Travelers Ins. Co.*, 112 R.I. 713, 315 A.2d 63 (1974). With these rules in mind we address ourselves to the facts.

....

¶7 The trial justice proceeded on the theory that the delivery of the purchase and sale agreement to plaintiff constituted an offer by defendants to sell the property. Because we must view the evidence in the light most favorable to the party against whom summary judgment was entered, in this case plaintiff, we assume as the trial justice did that the delivery of the agreement was in fact an offer.

....

¶8 The question we must answer next is whether there was an acceptance of that offer. The general rule is that where, as here, there is an offer to form a bilateral contract, the offeree must communicate his acceptance to the offeror before any contractual obligation can come into being. A mere mental intent to accept the offer, no matter how carefully formed, is not sufficient. The acceptance must be transmitted to the offeror in some overt manner. *Bullock v. Harwick*, 158 Fla. 834, 30 So.2d 539 (1947); *Armstrong v. Guy H. James Constr. Co.*, 402 P.2d 275 (Okl. 1965); 1 Restatement Contracts § 20 (1932). *See generally* 1 Corbin, Contracts § 67 (1963). A review of the record shows that the only expression of acceptance which was communicated to defendants was the delivery of the executed purchase and sale agreement accompanied by the letter of September 8. Therefore it is solely on the basis of the language used in these two documents that we must determine whether there was a valid acceptance. Whatever plaintiff's unexpressed intention may have been in sending the documents is irrelevant. We must be concerned only with the language actually used, not the language plaintiff thought he was using or intended to use.

¶9 There is no doubt that the execution and delivery of the purchase and sale agreement by plaintiff, without more, would have operated as an acceptance. The terms of the accompanying letter, however, apparently conditioned the acceptance upon the inclusion of various items of personalty. In assessing the effect of the terms of that letter we must keep in mind certain generally accepted rules. To be effective, an acceptance must be definite and unequivocal. "An offeror is entitled to know in clear terms whether the offeree accepts his proposal. It is not enough that the words of a reply justify a probable inference of assent." 1 Restatement Contracts § 58, comment a (1932). The acceptance may not impose additional conditions on the offer, nor may it add limitations. "An acceptance which is equivocal or upon condition or with a limitation is a counteroffer and requires acceptance by the original offeror before a contractual relationship can exist." *John Hancock Mut. Life Ins. Co. v. Dietlin*, 97 R.I. 515, 518, 199 A.2d 311, 313 (1964). *Accord*, *Cavanaugh v. Conway*, 36 R.I. 571, 587, 90 A. 1080, 1086 (1914).

¶ 10 However, an acceptance may be valid despite conditional language if the acceptance is clearly independent of the condition. Many cases have so held. Williston states the rule as follows:

> Frequently an offeree, while making a positive acceptance of the offer, also makes a request or suggestion that some addition or modification be made. So long as it is clear that the meaning of the acceptance is positively and unequivocally to accept the offer whether such request is granted or not, a contract is formed.

1 Williston, Contracts § 79 at 261–62 (3d ed. 1957).

¶ 11 Corbin is in agreement with the above view. 1 Corbin, *supra*, § 84 at 363–65. Thus our task is to decide whether plaintiff's letter is more reasonably interpreted as a qualified acceptance or as an absolute acceptance together with a mere inquiry concerning a collateral matter.

¶ 12 In making our decision we recognize that, as one text states, "The question whether a communication by an offeree is a conditional acceptance or counter-offer is not always easy to answer. It must be determined by the same common-sense process of interpretation that must be applied in so many other cases." 1 Corbin, *supra* § 82 at 353.

¶ 13 In our opinion the language used in plaintiff's letter of September 8 is not consistent with an absolute acceptance accompanied by a request for a gratuitous benefit. We interpret the letter to impose a condition on plaintiff's acceptance of defendants' offer. The letter does not unequivocally state that even without the enumerated items plaintiff is willing to complete the contract. In fact, the letter seeks "confirmation" that the listed items "are a part of the transaction." Thus, far from being an independent, collateral request, the sale of the items in question is explicitly referred to as a part of the real estate transaction. Moreover, the letter goes on to stress the difficulty of finding replacements for these items. This is a further indication that plaintiff did not view the inclusion of the listed items as merely collateral or incidental to the real estate transaction.

¶ 14 A review of the relevant case law discloses that those cases in which an acceptance was found valid despite an accompanying conditional term generally involved a more definite expression of acceptance than the one in the case at bar. *E.g., Moss v. Cogle*, 267 Ala. 208, 101 So.2d 314 (1958); [five other cited cases are omitted].

¶ 15 Accordingly, we hold that since the plaintiff's letter of acceptance dated September 8 was conditional, it operated as a rejection of the defendants' offer and no contractual obligation was created.

The plaintiff's appeal is denied and dismissed, the judgment appealed from is affirmed and the case is remanded to the Superior Court.

Exercise 5.10 — Avoiding the Mirror-Image Rule

1. New Terms, or Implied in the Offer?

Suppose that the letter dated September 8 in *Ardente* had not mentioned furniture, tapestries, or fireplace fixtures but had stated: "My clients are concerned that all landscaping remain with the real estate. The trees and flowering shrubs are an important source of the property's charm." If the offer had not addressed this topic, would the September 8 response violate the mirror-image rule?

2. Rejection or Acceptance and Solicitation?

Redraft the letter of September 8 in the *Ardente* case so that it asks about acquiring the furniture and tapestry but still accepts the offer to sell the real estate.

---

2. Rejection and Termination through Variance

Construct a timeline of the communications in the following case, and summarize the essential content of the communication at each point of your timeline. Where can you find an offer? An acceptance? This dispute arose well before special UCC rules governing responses that vary the terms of an offer, so apply the common-law mirror-image rule to this early sale of goods.

Minneapolis & St. Louis Railway Co. v. Columbus Rolling-Mill Co.

119 U.S. 149 (1886)

¶ 1 This was an action by a railroad corporation established at Minneapolis, in the state of Minnesota, against a manufacturing corporation established at Columbus, in the state of Ohio. The petition alleged that on December 19, 1879, the parties made a contract by which the plaintiff agreed to buy of the defendant, and the defendant sold to the plaintiff, 2,000 tons of iron rails, of the weight of 50 pounds per yard, at the price of $54 per ton gross, to be delivered free on board cars at the defendant's rolling-mill in the month of March, 1880, and to be paid for by the plaintiff in cash when so delivered. The answer denied the making of the contract. It was admitted at the trial that the following letters and telegrams were sent at their dates, and were received in due course, by the parties, through their agents:

¶ 2 *December 5, 1879. Letter from plaintiff to defendant:* "Please quote me prices for … 2,000 to 5,000 tons 50-lb. iron rails, March, 1880, delivery."

¶ 3 *December 8, 1879. Letter from defendant to plaintiff:* "Your favor of the fifth inst. at hand.… For iron rails, we will sell 2,000 to 5,000 tons of 50-lb. rails for fifty-four ($54) dollars per gross ton, for spot cash, F. O. B. cars at our mill, March delivery, subject as follows: In case of strike among our workmen, destruction of or serious damage to our works by fire or the elements, or any causes of delay beyond our control, we shall not be held accountable in damages. If our offer is accepted, shall expect to be notified of same prior to December 20, 1879."

¶ 4 *December 16, 1879. Telegram from plaintiff to defendant:* "Please enter our order for twelve hundred tons rails, March delivery, as per your favor of the eighth. Please reply."

¶ 5 *December 16, 1879. Letter from plaintiff to defendant:* "Yours of the 8th came duly to hand. I telegraphed you to-day to enter our order for twelve hundred (1,200) tons 50-lb. iron rails for next March delivery, at fifty-four dollars, ($54,) F.O.B. cars at your mill. Please send contract. Also please send me templet of your 50-lb. rail…".

¶ 6 December 18, 1879. Telegram from defendant to plaintiff, received same day: "We cannot book your order at present at that price."

¶ 7 *December 19, 1879. Telegram from plaintiff to defendant:* "Please enter an order for two thousand tons rails as per your letter of the [eighth]. Please forward written contract. Reply."

¶ 8 *December 22, 1879. Telegram from plaintiff to defendant:* "Did you enter my order for two thousand tons rails, as per my telegram of December 19th? Answer."

¶ 9 After repeated similar inquiries by the plaintiff, the defendant, on January 19, 1880, denied the existence of any contract between the parties.

¶ 10 The jury returned a verdict for the defendant, under instructions which need not be particularly stated; and the plaintiff alleged exceptions, and sued out this writ of error.

Mr. Justice Gray, after making the foregoing statement of the case, delivered the opinion of the court:

¶ 11 The rules of law which govern this case are well settled. As no contract is complete without the mutual consent of the parties, an offer to sell imposes no obligation until it is accepted according to its terms. So long as the offer has been neither accepted nor rejected, the negotiation remains open, and imposes no obligation upon either party—the one may decline to accept, or the other may withdraw his offer; and either rejection or withdrawal leaves the matter as if no offer had ever been made. A proposal to accept, or an acceptance, upon terms varying from those offered, is a rejection of the offer, and puts an end to the negotiation, unless the party who made the original offer renews it, or assents to the modification suggested. The other party, having once rejected the offer, cannot afterwards revive it by tendering an acceptance of it. *Eliason* v. *Henshaw*, 4 Wheat. 225; [citations to four other cases omitted]....

¶12 The defendant, by the letter of December 8th offered to sell to the plaintiff 2,000 to 5,000 tons of iron rails on certain terms specified, and added that if the offer was accepted the defendant would expect to be notified prior to December 20th. This offer, while it remained open, without having been rejected by the plaintiff or revoked by the defendant, would authorize the plaintiff to take, at his election, any number of tons not less than 2,000, nor more than 5,000, on the terms specified. The offer, while unrevoked, might be accepted or rejected by the plaintiff at any time before December 20th.

¶13 Instead of accepting the offer made, the plaintiff, on December 16th, by telegram and letter, referring to the defendant's letter of December 8th, directed the defendant to enter an order for 1,200 tons on the same terms. The mention, in both telegram and letter, of the date and the terms of the defendant's original offer, shows that the plaintiff's order was not an independent proposal, but an answer to the defendant's offer, a qualified acceptance of that offer, varying the number of tons, and therefore in law a rejection of the offer. On December 18th, the defendant, by telegram, declined to fulfill the plaintiff's order. The negotiation between the parties was thus closed, and the plaintiff could not afterwards fall back on the defendant's original offer. The plaintiff's attempt to do so, by the telegram of December 19th, was therefore ineffectual, and created no rights against the defendant....

Judgment affirmed.

Exercise 5.11 — Questions on *Rolling-Mill*

1. Offer by Seller

What factors lead to the conclusion that the mill's letter of December 8 is an offer, rather than just preliminary negotiations in the form of a price quote?

2. Drafting to Avoid Rejection

As representative for the railway company, redraft the December 16 telegram so that it explores the possibility of a purchase and sale of 1,200 tons of rails, while avoiding acceptance or rejection of the mill's offer.

3. Effect of Option Contract

If the parties had entered into a separate option contract making the seller's offer irrevocable until December 20, should a rejection prior to that date be treated as terminating the offer? If not, what should the seller argue if the seller had sold remaining current stock to another buyer on December 18 after having received a rejection on December 16 from the railway company?

VI. Timing Problems—The Mailbox Rule

A. The Problem

When two parties are bargaining in person or in a conversation over the phone, the communication is instantaneous. In such a setting, the formation of a contract may depend on whether the offeror voices a revocation a split second before the offeree voices acceptance.

When other forms of communication are used, such as mail through the postal service, a gap appears between the time a message is dispatched by one party and the time that it is received by the other. While an acceptance is in transit, what is the effect of an intervening revocation or rejection voiced over the telephone? To take another example, if a revocation is mailed first and then an acceptance is mailed, which is given effect?

The answer depends on whether mailed communications are effective on dispatch or on receipt. What answer is most consistent with an objective theory of contract formation?

B. The General Rule

In light of the application of an objective theory under the common law, it should not surprise you that courts find that revocations and rejections are effective only when they are received (not necessarily when they are actually opened and read, but when their contents have been delivered and are available to the recipient).

In a partial departure from a purely objective theory, however, the courts in most states follow the "mailbox rule" for dispatch of acceptances, dating from the English case of *Adams v. Lindsell*, 107 Eng. Rep. 250 (Kings Bench 1818). As explained by the New York Court of Appeals in a later American case:

> We understand the rule to be, that where an offer is made by one party to another when they are not together, the acceptance of it by that other must be manifested by some appropriate act. It does not need that the acceptance shall come to the knowledge of the one making the offer before he shall be bound.... Thus a letter received by mail containing a proposal may be answered by letter by mail, containing the acceptance. And in general, as soon as the answering letter is mailed, the contract is concluded. Though one party does not know of the acceptance, the manifestation thereof is put in the proper way of reaching him.

White v. Corlies, 46 N.Y. 467, 469 (1871). Indeed, the mailed acceptance is effective on dispatch even if the letter is lost in the mail and never reaches the offeror. *See, e.g.*, Restatement (Second) of Contracts § 63(a) (1981).

Wouldn't it be simpler to recognize the effectiveness of all communications on receipt, absent some contrary intention expressed by the bargaining parties? In your opinion, does the mailbox rule fulfill some important policy when it gives the offeree immediate knowledge of the formation of a contract but leaves the offeror potentially in a state of uncertainty while the acceptance might be in transit, or even lost?

If you have misgivings about the mailbox rule, are they eased by the following mitigating factors?

- A letter of acceptance is effective on posting only if it is properly addressed and posted, and only if acceptance by a mailed letter is within the modes of acceptance expressly or implicitly authorized by the offer. (In what circumstances would acceptance by mail be implicitly authorized or excluded?)
- As master of the offer, the offeror can override the mailbox rule by specifying that acceptance must be made in some mode of instantaneous communication or that acceptance will be effective only on receipt.
- If the parties have an option contract, so that the offer is irrevocable for a certain period, the mailbox rule does not apply in most states, so that a mailed acceptance is not effective until delivered.
- If an offeree's conflicting communications (such as a telephoned rejection followed by mailed acceptance) could lead to reliance by the offeror and to an injustice if the mailbox rule applies, then a court might refrain from applying the mailbox rule, often through the doctrine of equitable estoppel.

See generally RESTATEMENT (SECOND) OF CONTRACTS §§ 40, 63, 66 (1981).

C. Range of Application of the Mailbox Rule

The quotation from *White v. Corlies* in Section B above appears to state a general rule that would apply not just to mailed acceptances, but to any manifestation of acceptance that is "put in a proper way" so that it will reach the offeror in a reasonable time "in the usual course of events." *White v. Corlies*, 46 N.Y. 467, 469 (1871); *see also* RESTATEMENT (SECOND) OF CONTRACTS § 63(a) (1981) (summarizing the law to find an acceptance when a manifestation in any "medium invited by an offer ... is put out of the control of the offeree's possession").

In practice, however, most courts will be cautious in extending the mailbox rule to other modes of communication. Nonetheless, they are likely to do so whenever the communication shares important characteristics of mail by post, including a delay between dispatch and receipt, and inability—or very limited ability—to retrieve the message once it is dispatched. Does e-mail sometimes share these characteristics? For arguments that the mailbox rule should apply to e-mail communications, see Valerie Watnick, *The Electronic Formation of Contracts and the Common Law "Mailbox Rule,"* 56 BAYLOR L. REV. 175 (2004), and Paul Fasciano, *Internet Electronic Mail: A Last Bastion for the Mailbox Rule*, 25 HOFSTRA L. REV. 971 (1997). *See also Szollosy v. Hyatt Corp.*, 396 F. Supp. 2d 159, 164, n. 11 (D. Conn. 2005) (applying mailbox rule to faxing of acceptance, after analogizing modern forms of electronic communication to mail).

Exercise 5.12 — Applying the Mailbox Rule

1. The Basics

In the following problems, none of the mailed offers restricts the means of acceptance, so that either a mailed or e-mailed response is a reasonable means of acceptance. Apply the mailbox rule to the following sequences of events:

a. Acceptance or Revocation?

(1) A mails an offer to B.

(2) B mails an acceptance.

(3) A sends an e-mail revoking the offer.

(4) B receives the e-mailed revocation.

(5) A receives the acceptance.

b. Acceptance or Revocation (#2)?

(1) A mails an offer to B.

(2) A mails a revocation.

(3) B mails an acceptance.

(4) B receives the revocation.

(5) A receives the acceptance.

c. Acceptance or Rejection?

(1) A sends an offer to B.

(2) B mails a rejection.

(3) B changes his mind and e-mails an acceptance.

(4) A receives the acceptance.

(5) A receives the mailed rejection.

d. Acceptance or Rejection (#2)?

(1) A mails an offer to B.

(2) B mails an acceptance.

(3) B changes his mind and e-mails a rejection, which does not mention the letter of acceptance.

(4) A receives the rejection.

(5) A later receives the mailed acceptance.

Analyze the events above, before adding (6).

(6) Alternatively, in addition to the above facts, suppose that A immediately contracted with C at step 4 in reliance on B's apparent rejection, but now B wants to enforce any contract that was formed with A.

e. Acceptance or Rejection (#3)?

(1) A mails an offer to B.

(2) B mails a rejection.

(3) B changes his mind and mails an acceptance.

(4) A receives the rejection.

(5) A later receives the acceptance.

2. Mailbox Rule?

On Wednesday Seller called Buyer on the phone and made the following offer: "I will sell you my car for $2,000 cash. If you want it, call me at my office before next Wednesday." Before hanging up, Buyer replied that he would consider the offer seriously. One hour after Buyer received the offer, Buyer mailed a letter to Seller's office address that said: "I accept your offer to sell your car to me. I'll bring the cash by your office early next week." On Thursday Seller called Buyer; before Buyer could say anything about his desire to purchase the car, Seller expressed her intention to revoke. Seller received Buyer's letter on Friday. Contract?

VII. Summary

- Consistent with the objective theory of contract formation, offers, acceptances, revocations, and rejections normally are not effective until communicated to the other party. In two departures from this standard,
  - a simple offer (one that is fully revocable) terminates at the moment of the death of the offeror or offeree, even before notice to the other party, and
  - when mail or similar means of acceptance is authorized, the acceptance is effective on dispatch, and—as established in Chapter 2—an offer for a unilateral contract is accepted on completion of the requested performance even if the offeror has not received immediate notice of that act.
- Under the common law, courts traditionally have been cautious before finding that parties entered into a contractual relationship, as suggested by their requiring an unambiguous offer and acceptance. Indeed, manifestations by the offeror must reflect clear commitment throughout the time the offer is pending; thus, a statement of equivocation about the offeror's continuing commitment to the offer can revoke the offer. Conduct by the offeror inconsistent with a continuing offer, if conveyed to the offeree, can similarly terminate the offer.

- An option contract is a pending offer accompanied by an enforceable promise not to revoke the offer. Such a promise may be implied if the circumstances reflect a mutual expectation that the offeree would be protected from revocation while the offeree is in the process of performing a substantial act of acceptance, which normally is the case only with an offer for a unilateral contract. Whether express or implied, the promise not to revoke can be enforceable if the offeree pays consideration for it or relies on it in circumstances that give rise to promissory estoppel. Of course, providing the offeree with an option does not bind the parties to the main contract, which will be formed if the offeree exercises the option by accepting the offer for the main exchange.
- Under the common law mirror-image rule, a purported acceptance is only a rejection and a counter-offer if it does not match the terms of the offer, unless the new terms were implicit in the offer, or unless they are reasonably interpreted as the subject of separate inquiries after an acceptance on the terms of the offer. The next chapter explores the UCC's departure from this rule.

Chapter 6

UCC Innovations in Mutual Assent

I. Introduction

Chapters 2 and 5 explored issues of mutual assent under the judicially developed common law, with only occasional references to statutes that displaced or confirmed the common law approach. In contrast, this chapter is devoted almost entirely to selected provisions of the UCC, to show how it has modified or abandoned common law rules in an attempt to adapt the law to business realities in sales of goods.

These statutory provisions, of course, are subject to interpretation by courts, and this chapter includes two substantial judicial opinions that discuss the potential application of UCC § 2-207, as well as excerpts from several other opinions. However, this chapter predominantly employs the problem method to prompt the reader to engage in original statutory analysis, interpretation, and application to facts, so that our attention is focused intensely on the statutory language itself, without the mediation of a judge.

A. State Enactment of the UCC

Once again, review the discussion of the UCC in Chapter 1, pages 6–7. Then, consult Appendix 1 and study the Texas legislature's enactment of the following sections of the UCC:

2-102 and 2-104

2-204(1)&(2)

2-205 through 2-207

You'll notice that the Texas enactment of the UCC uses a slightly different system to name or number parts of the code. For one thing, the Texas enactment sensibly refers to major divisions of the UCC as "chapters" rather than "articles" as the UCC calls them. Regarding sections within these major divisions, the Texas enactment uses a period after the chapter number rather than a hyphen, and it uses different numbering and lettering for subsections. So, for example, UCC § 2-207(2)(a) is enacted in Texas as Texas Business & Commerce Code § 2.207(b)(1). In contrast, the California Commercial Code simply removes the hyphen from the UCC section, as in Cal. Com. Code § 2207(2)(a) for UCC § 2-207(2)(a). Arizona's enactment of the

UCC, on the other hand, precedes the UCC section number with "47," which corresponds with the volume of the Arizona Revised Statutes that deals with commercial law, and it moves the hyphen so that it separates the volume number from the UCC digits. For example, UCC § 2-101 is codified in the Arizona Revised Statutes as section 47-2101. The Arizona codification also uses different numbering and lettering for subsections.

For purposes of class discussion and exams, you presumably will refer to the sections and subsections as set forth in the UCC. To cite to the UCC in a brief to a court, however, or to otherwise prepare for the practice of law, you should become accustomed to finding UCC provisions in their official codification in the relevant state.

B. The UCC's Relationship to the Common Law

Recall that Article 2 of the UCC, which applies to transactions in goods, does not address every issue that might arise in contracts for the sale of goods. With respect to issues arising in a sale of goods but not addressed by the UCC, the UCC simply incorporates the underlying common law, as it may be modified in turn by other statutes in effect in the state. UCC § 1-103(b) (2001). This approach applies, for example, to the definition of an offer in a sales transaction:

> Article two of the Uniform Commercial Code governs transactions involving the sale of goods. U.C.C. § 2-102 (1977). Because the term "offer" is not defined in the code, the common law definition remains relevant. U.C.C. § 1-103. An offer is made when the offer leads the offeree to reasonably believe that an offer has been made. *Gilbert & Bennett Manufacturing Co. v. Westinghouse Electric Corp.*, 445 F. Supp. 537, 545 (D. Mass. 1977). Restatement (Second) of Contracts § 24 (1981) defines "offer" as "the manifestation of willingness to enter into a bargain, so made as to justify another person in understanding that his assent to that bargain is invited and will conclude it."

Brown Machine, Div. of John Brown, Inc. v. Hercules, Inc., 770 S.W.2d 416, 418–19 (Mo. Ct. App. 1989).

Moreover, with respect to issues specifically addressed by the UCC, some UCC provisions set forth rules that are substantially the same as rules that have developed in most states under the common law.

Some UCC provisions, however, depart from the common law and supersede it for sales contracts. In some cases, the UCC abandons a common law rule that its drafters believed did not reflect the way that buyers and sellers actually operate in the real world. The UCC is thus a strong example of the jurisprudential approach of "legal realism," reflecting an attempt to resolve disputes, solve problems, and fill gaps in contracts in a manner that meets the needs of those engaged in commerce in goods.

While working through this chapter, consider the following questions about the UCC:

- In what way does section 2-205 provide an additional statutory basis for enforcing a merchant's written and signed promise not to revoke an offer to sell, even if the common law requirement of consideration or promissory estoppel is not satisfied?
- In what ways do sections 2-204 and 2-206 largely adopt general common law principles of offer and acceptance? In what ways do they seem to depart from common law principles?
- How does section 2-207(1) reject or modify the common law mirror-image rule?
- If a contract is formed under section 2-207(1), how does section 2-207(2) modify common law principles regarding formation of a second agreement to modify the first one?

II. Option Contracts—"Firm Offers" under UCC § 2-205

We learned earlier that an offer may become irrevocable under the common law if a promise not to revoke (expressed or implied) is supported by consideration or by substantial reliance. For sales of goods, the UCC offers a third and supplementary way to create an option contract: a "firm offer" to buy or sell goods. UCC § 2-205 (2011). Find the Texas enactment of this UCC section in Appendix 1 so that you become accustomed to finding UCC provisions in a state code. Study each clause carefully, word for word:

> Sec. 2.205 FIRM OFFERS
>
> An offer by a merchant to buy or sell goods in a signed writing which by its terms gives assurance that it will be held open is not revocable, for lack of consideration, during the time stated or if no time is stated for a reasonable time, but in no event may such period of irrevocability exceed three months; but any such term of assurance on a form supplied by the offeree must be separately signed by the offeror.

Exercise 6.1—Dissecting Section 2-205

1. Elements of a Firm Offer under Section 2-205

List all the requisites of a firm offer under the UCC, in a bullet point list, as they are set forth in the statute, before the first comma appears. What is the definition of a "merchant"? Find Texas Business and Commerce Code § 2.104(a) in Appendix 1.

2. Effect of Meeting the Elements of a Firm Offer

If the elements of a firm offer are present, list or describe the parameters of the rights or duties that are created by the statute, as set forth in the section before the semi-colon.

3. Separate Signature

Compose a set of facts that would trigger the final proviso to the section, requiring a separate signature next to the promise not to revoke. What's the purpose of this clause? Would it be satisfied by placing initials next to the promise not to revoke, in addition to signing fully at the end of the offer? *See* U.C.C. § 1-201(37) (2001) (find the Texas enactment of this section in Appendix 1 or find another state's version on the web).

4. Firm Offer, or Revocable?

Gallery Owner made a written offer to Consumer to sell an original painting for $10,000 in 10 monthly installments of $1,000 each; the written and signed form says that the offer is irrevocable for five days. Consumer gave no consideration for the promise not to revoke and did not rely on the promise. Is the promise not to revoke enforceable?

Suppose instead that Gallery Owner gave the same form to Consumer, not yet signed by Gallery Owner, and Consumer signed it once at the bottom, thus making an offer to buy the painting. Gallery Owner did not accept immediately because she had promised to give another potential buyer first rights to purchase paintings from this artist. A term in the middle of the form says that Consumer is holding the offer open for five days. Gallery Owner gave no consideration for this promise. Before Gallery Owner relied in any way, Consumer attempted to revoke the offer. Consumer is new to the art world. Can Gallery Owner enforce Consumer's promise to hold the offer open? How many reasons support your answer?

5. Promise to Hold Offer Open for More Than Three Months

A merchant signed a written offer to sell goods, which includes a promise to hold the offer open for four months. Without more, can the offeree enforce the promise not to revoke for four months? Is it enforceable for some other length of time? Is it binding for four months if the offeree paid $100 for the promise not to revoke?

III. Basic Standards for Contract Formation: UCC §§ 2-204, 2-206(1)(a)

Subsections 1–3 of UCC § 2-204 set forth basic standards for formation of a sales contract. Those provisions are codified in Texas as subsections (a)–(c) of the Texas Business and Commerce Code § 2.204:

> Sec. 2.204. FORMATION IN GENERAL.
>
> (a) A contract for sale of goods may be made in any manner sufficient to show agreement, including conduct by both parties which recognizes the existence of such a contract.

(b) An agreement sufficient to constitute a contract for sale may be found even though the moment of its making is undetermined.

(c) Even though one or more terms are left open a contract for sale does not fail for indefiniteness if the parties have intended to make a contract and there is a reasonably certain basis for giving an appropriate remedy.

We will postpone our study of indefiniteness, addressed in the third subsection above, until Chapter 7. In the meantime, UCC §2-206(1)(a) adds a familiar point to the basic standards, as codified in the Texas Code as subsection 2.206(a)(1):

Sec. 2.206. OFFER AND ACCEPTANCE IN FORMATION OF CONTRACT.

(a) Unless otherwise unambiguously indicated by the language or circumstances

(1) an offer to make a contract shall be construed as inviting acceptance in any manner and by any medium reasonable in the circumstances;....

Subsection (a) states a narrow version of the common law rule that an offeror may restrict the means of acceptance. The Code recognizes such a restriction only if the offeror had "unambiguously" indicated it.

Assuming no such restriction, section 2.204(a) of the Texas Code embraces the common law rule that contractual intent can be inferred from conduct of the parties. As explored in Chapter 2, for example, if one party communicates a verbal offer and does not restrict acceptance to a verbal response, the other party might convey an acceptance through conduct rather than through words. To take it further, is it possible to infer contractual intent from the conduct of both parties, neither of whom verbally expressed an offer or acceptance?

European Import Co., Inc. v. Lone Star Co., Inc.

596 S.W.2d 287 (Tex. Civ. App. 1980)

Doyle, Justice.

¶1 ... Lone Star Company, Inc., appellee, brought suit to recover the price of certain liquor and alcoholic beverage merchandise sold to appellant, European Import Company....

¶2 Testimony elicited during the trial showed European Import Company was a package liquor retailer operating several stores in Houston in 1974. Lone Star Company is a liquor wholesaler and entered into numerous transactions with European during 1974 to supply European with alcoholic beverage. During the trial, appellee introduced into evidence unpaid invoices covering these transactions. Mr. Raymond Hairell, testifying on behalf of appellee, explained the invoices and the accounting procedures for Lone Star. These invoices totaled $98,621.99 which was the amount set forth in appellee's pleadings and found by the jury to be due.

¶3 At the conclusion of the testimony six special issues were submitted to the jury which found (1) that European Import Company never ordered the disputed merchandise; (2) that Lone Star delivered the merchandise to European; (3) that European accepted the goods; (4) that the amount due for these goods was $98,621.99; .... Based upon these answers the court rendered judgment for [Lone Star]....

....

¶4 Appellants contend ... that a sale is a contract and as such must comply with certain provisions of the Texas Business & Commerce Code contained in chapter two on Sales. Pursuant to § 2.204 thereof, a contract for sale of goods may be made in any manner sufficient to show agreement, including conduct by both parties; and under § 2.206, an offer to make a contract shall be construed as inviting acceptance in any manner and by any medium reasonable in the circumstances.

¶5 The jury in answer to special issue number one found that European Import Company did not order the merchandise made the basis of this suit. If the goods were not ordered, then the conduct of the parties must be examined to see if there was an acceptance of appellee's shipment of the goods so as to constitute a contract by the parties' conduct.

¶6 Appellants cite two cases for their argument that if the goods have not been ordered there is no sale. *Johnson v. Gattegno*, 267 S.W. 740 (Tex. Civ. App.-El Paso 1924, no writ); *Farley v. Clark Equipment Company*, 484 S.W.2d 142 (Tex. Civ. App.-Amarillo 1972, writ ref. n. r. e.). In neither of these cases are the facts parallel to the facts in our case. However, both cases set forth the general rule pertaining to liability for the retention of unordered goods. In the *Johnson* case the court stated that:

> "... it must be shown that, after learning of the unauthorized delivery, he in some manner evidenced an intention to appropriate them or ratify the delivery. This may be shown by the retention of the goods after he learned of their receipt and in various other ways."

....

¶7 In every case examined by this court addressing the issue of liability for unordered goods, the courts have held the defendants liable for such goods if they were received and appropriated to their use and were of the value specified in the account. *Masterson v. F. W. Heitmann & Co.*, 38 Tex. Civ. App. 476, 87 S.W. 227 (San Antonio 1905, writ ref'd); *Johnson v. Gattegno*, *supra*.

....

¶8 ... We think there was evidence showing a sale, delivery and acceptance.

IV. Acceptance by Words or Conduct under UCC § 2-206

Subsections 1 and 2 of UCC § 2-206 are codified as subsections (a) and (b) in the Texas enactment:

> Sec. 2.206. OFFER AND ACCEPTANCE IN FORMATION OF CONTRACT.
>
> (a) Unless otherwise unambiguously indicated by the language or circumstances
>
> (1) an offer to make a contract shall be construed as inviting acceptance in any manner and by any medium reasonable in the circumstances;
>
> (2) an order or other offer to buy goods for prompt or current shipment shall be construed as inviting acceptance either by a prompt promise to ship or by the prompt or current shipment of conforming or non-conforming goods, but such a shipment of non-conforming goods does not constitute an acceptance if the seller seasonably notifies the buyer that the shipment is offered only as an accommodation to the buyer.
>
> (b) Where the beginning of a requested performance is a reasonable mode of acceptance an offeror who is not notified of acceptance within a reasonable time may treat the offer as having lapsed before acceptance.

Exercise 6.2 — Interpreting UCC § 2-206

As explored in Section III of this chapter, subsection (a)(1) of the Texas Business and Commerce Code (subsection (1)(a) of the UCC version) states a general approach that should strike you as consistent with common law principles. What, precisely, does section (a)(2) provide? Dissect it, outline it, or state its terms in bullet point fashion. Can you explain it as an example of an application of general principles to a specific fact situation? Can you analogize those general principles to common law rules with which you are familiar?

What is the meaning and purpose of subsection (b) (subsection 2 of the UCC version)? Is its reference to lapse of the offer analytically imprecise? If so, how would you reword this section?

Exercise 6.3 — Applying UCC § 2-206

1. Reprise on *Allied v. Ford*

Recall the case of *Allied Steel and Conveyors, Inc. v. Ford Motor Co.*, discussed in Exercises 2.8 and 2.9 in Chapter 2, Section IV.B. The court found that Allied manifested its acceptance (in the form of a return promise) through the expressive conduct of arriving at Ford's factory with the ordered machinery and with employees who were ready to install the machinery in Ford's factory.

Suppose that Allied had arrived to install the machinery in response to Ford's purchase order, but that both parties soon discovered that Allied had brought the wrong machinery.

Would Allied's conduct on its first visit still have manifested an intention to accept, even though it had mistakenly brought the wrong goods? Why else would it have gone to the trouble of sending out a truck to the work site with heavy machinery and employees? If so, what are Allied's obligations? Does this help you understand the statute's reference to "acceptance ... by the prompt or current shipment of ... nonconforming goods"?

2. Acceptance or Accommodation?

Seller, the manufacturer of a vaccine, provided price quotes to potential pharmaceutical buyers, clearly informing recipients that it was not making an offer, and inviting the potential buyers to place orders on Seller's web site. Buyer, learning in advance about a price increase due to take place on May 20, placed an order on Seller's web site for 1,000 vials of vaccine on May 19 at the lower price then effective, checking the box for speedy, higher-priced delivery. Seller's computer system immediately provided Buyer with a tracking number, and stated that Seller would review Buyer's order promptly, to determine whether it would fill Buyer's order.

Within 24 hours, Seller shipped 50 vials of the vaccine to Buyer; as the goods were placed in transit, Seller e-mailed to Buyer a message explaining it stood ready to ship the bulk of Buyer's order at the new, increased price if Buyer chose to place a new order at that price, and that Seller had shipped a small portion of the order at the earlier price to serve Buyer's immediate needs. When the shipment of 50 vials arrived a day later, Buyer accepted and paid for that shipment, but it insisted that Seller was bound to deliver the remaining 950 vials of vaccine at the price that was effective on May 19. Identify any offer, acceptance, or counter-offer in these facts. Under the terms of UCC § 2-206, is Seller bound by contract to deliver the remaining 950 vials at the lower price effective on May 19? [Problem based on *Corinthian Pharmaceutical Systems, Inc. v. Lederle Laboratories*, 724 F. Supp. 605 (S.D. Ind. 1989).]

3. Manifestation of Acceptance?

On the morning of June 22, the owner of an outdoor entertainment complex, Leah Harris, faxed a purchase order to Skyworks, Inc., for prompt shipment of 10 cases of model #26 "Star Wars" sky rockets for Harris's July 4th music and fireworks show. When Skyworks received the purchase order, it had no "Star Wars" sky rockets left in stock, but it promptly shipped comparable rockets. On June 25, United Parcel Service, an independent delivery service, delivered 10 cases of model #14 "Razzle Dazzle" sky rockets to Harris. Attached to one case was an invoice from the shipper, Skyworks, and a copy of Harris's June 22 purchase order for the Star Wars sky rockets. Contract? If Harris doesn't want Razzle Dazzle sky rockets, what are Skyworks's obligations? How could Skyworks have limited its obligations?

4. Discharge of Contract Formed?

Assume the same purchase order as in question 3 above. This time, however, Skyworks had "Star Wars" sky rockets in stock, and it internally approved the order for processing and shipping. It arranged for slow carriage, partly by rail, beginning on the afternoon of June 22, resulting in delivery on July 2, just in time for set up for the big fireworks show. Harris refused delivery, however, because she had heard nothing from Skyworks and had ordered sky rockets from another supplier on June 28, accepting delivery of that order earlier in the day on July 2. Is Harris obligated to pay for the goods shipped by Skyworks? How could Skyworks have reduced uncertainty about its rights and Harris's duties?

V. UCC § 2-207 and the Battle of the Forms

A. Review: the Common Law Mirror-Image Rule and the Last-Shot Doctrine, in the *Battle of the Forms*

Recall the common law mirror-image rule, discussed in Chapter 5, Section V. Although the mirror-image rule provides a clear and certain requirement for acceptances, it can operate in an arbitrary manner when buyers and sellers communicate with standard forms that contain preprinted "boilerplate" terms that conflict with one another. To understand the complaints about this arbitrariness in the common law, let's begin our exploration of this topic by imagining a pre-UCC case.

1. The Offer (Pre-UCC Battle of the Forms)

Imagine a transaction set in 1960, prior to a state's adoption of the UCC, so that general common law principles would control. Let's assume that a buyer prepared an offer on a written purchase order form for 10 pool tables at the seller's quoted price by signing the form and by writing in the quantity, price, and place of delivery in the blanks of the standard form:

Purchase Order

Rockin Pool & Billiards

333 W. Central Ave.

River City, Iowa 22222

P.O. # 37114 Date: 9-2-60

TO: Rollin Mfg. Co.

FOR: 10 #6 Pro-slate pool tables, ready to play

Price: $1,000/table x 10 = $10,000

Location for delivery or services: address above by 9-30

1. Prices or fees exceeding $1,000 are payable 30 days after delivery of goods or completion of services.

....

Signed, for Rockin Pool & Billiards: *Moe Rockin*

If the seller simply signed the purchase order and returned a copy of it, or if the seller sent a note stating, "We accept your order #37114, dated 9/2/60," then a contract would be formed under the common law mirror-image rule.

2. *Counter-Offer under the Common Law*

Frequently, however, the seller would respond by signing and sending a statement of acceptance on its own acknowledgment form, perhaps filling in the terms peculiar to this order:

Acknowledgment
Rollin Mfg. Co.
76 Trouble St.
Detroit, Michigan 12121

Ack. # 1010621

Date: 9-5-60

TO: Rockin Pool & Billiards

FOR: 10 #6 Pro-slate pool tables, PO # 37114

Price: $10,000 total

Status: In stock—will deliver to your site & set up 9-19

1. Prices payable at time of delivery and installation.

2. Seller makes no warranties, express or implied.

3. Any disputes arising out of this transaction will be adjudicated in binding arbitration under the rules and procedures of the Michigan Manufacturer's Arbitration Assoc.

. . . .

Signed, for Rollin Mfg.:

Susan Rollin

The parties might have thought that they had an agreement, because they had paid attention only to the terms that they typed in the blanks of their submitted forms. The common law mirror-image rule, however, likely would hold that the seller made only a counter-offer because her acknowledgment form contained pre-printed terms that conflict with pre-printed terms on the buyer's form. If one of the parties backed out after the acknowledgment was delivered, neither party would have any obligations under the common law because no contract was formed.

3. *The "Last Shot" Rule under Common Law*

But the result could seem even more arbitrary if the parties believed they had formed a contract and then performed. Because the seller sent the last written communication, it had the "last shot" at proposing the terms of the transaction. If it later delivered the pool tables, by that conduct it would reiterate the counter-offer stated in its acknowledgment form. If the buyer accepted the delivery, by that conduct it would manifest acceptance of the seller's counter-offer, and a contract would be formed on the seller's terms.

A dispute probably would erupt when the pool tables were fully installed and the seller demanded payment at that moment, even though the buyer was accustomed to paying within 30 days after delivery. Because the seller's acknowledgment form fired the "last shot," the seller's terms would control under common law rules.

4. *UCC Rejects the Common Law*

This kind of misunderstanding will not arise when parties sign the same written document in a major deal. It may become less common in smaller deals as parties express assent to the same terms electronically on a web site, or through e-mail exchanges without conflicting standard terms riding on the coattails of the e-mail messages.

At the time of the drafting of the UCC, however, the "battle of the forms" illustrated above was a common occurrence, and the common law rules were viewed by the drafters as inadequate to the needs and practices of typical buyers and sellers. In response, the UCC superseded the common law rules in this "battle of the forms" and offered a new solution in section 2-207.

B. Introduction to the Terms of Section 2-207

The UCC addresses the battle of the forms in section § 2-207, entitled "Additional terms in acceptance or confirmation." It is codified in the California Commercial Code without that descriptive title:

> 2207.
>
> (1) A definite and seasonable expression of acceptance or a written confirmation which is sent within a reasonable time operates as an acceptance even though it states terms additional to or different from those offered or agreed upon, unless acceptance is expressly made conditional on assent to the additional or different terms.
>
> (2) The additional terms are to be construed as proposals for addition to the contract. Between merchants such terms become part of the contract unless:
>
> (a) The offer expressly limits acceptance to the terms of the offer;
>
> (b) They materially alter it; or
>
> (c) Notification of objection to them has already been given or is given within a reasonable time after notice of them is received.
>
> (3) Conduct by both parties which recognizes the existence of a contract is sufficient to establish a contract for sale although the writings of the parties do not otherwise establish a contract. In such case the terms of the particular contract consist of those terms on which the writings of the parties agree, together with any supplementary terms incorporated under any other provisions of this code.

Exercise 6.4 — Purposes of the Three Major Subsections of Section 2-207

Study the terms of UCC § 2-207, and briefly describe the general purpose of each subsection. What general issue is each subsection designed to address? Take care to link each subsection to its corresponding issue and subissues, without mixing in the standards of other subsections.

C. Focus on Subsection 1 of UCC § 2-207

CBS, Inc. v. Auburn Plastics, Inc.

67 A.D.2d 811, 413 N.Y.S.2d 50 (1979)

MEMORANDUM:

....

In our view then, plaintiff's purchase orders constituted offers to buy the molds, and defendant's acknowledgements of those orders represented its acceptance of the offers. While the acknowledgements incorporate the conditions contained in the price quotations and therefore conflict with the terms of the offers with respect to the mold acquisition charge, the acknowledgements are nonetheless operable as acceptances since they are not expressly made conditional on plaintiff's assent to the different terms (Uniform Commercial Code, § 2-207, subd. 1; *see C. Itoh & Co. (America) Inc. v. Jordan Intern. Co.*, 7 Cir., 552 F.2d 1228, 1235; ...).

....

Order unanimously affirmed, with costs.

Exercise 6.5 — Identifying and Analyzing the Elements of Subsection 1

Closely study each clause of the first subsection of section 2207 set forth prior to Exercise 6.4, except that you should momentarily set aside the phrase "or a written confirmation that is sent within a reasonable time," which we will soon address separately. Focus on the circumstances in which an expression of acceptance operates as an acceptance, including attention to the proviso in the final clause beginning with "unless." Outline these elements of focus in bullet-point format, such as the following:

Under California Commercial Code § 2207(1), an expression of acceptance operates as an acceptance if it is:

- ..., and
- ...,
- even if it...,
- but not if....

As you learn more about each element, add a definition, description, or illustration.

For sales contracts, in what way does the first subsection override the common law? If the final proviso applies, draw an analogy to the common law to characterize the legal effect of such a response to the offer.

Brown Machine, Div. of John Brown, Inc. v. Hercules, Inc.

770 S.W.2d 416 (Mo. Ct. App. 1989)

Stephan, Judge.

....

¶1 Under subsection (1) an offeree's response to an offer operates as a valid acceptance of the offer even though it contains terms additional to, or different from, the terms of the offer unless the "acceptance is expressly made conditional" on the offeror's assent to the additional or different terms. Where the offeree's acceptance is made "expressly conditional" on the offeror's assent, the response operates not as an acceptance but as a counter offer which must be accepted by the original offeror. *Falcon Tankers, Inc. v. Litton Systems, Inc.*, 355 A.2d 898, 906 (Del. Super. 1976). Restatement (Second) of Contracts § 59 (1981) expresses it succinctly: "[A]n offeree's reply which purports to accept an offer but makes acceptance conditional on the offeror's assent to terms not contained in the original offer is effective as a counteroffer rather than acceptance."

¶2 The general view held by the majority of states is that, to convert an acceptance to a counter offer under UCC § 2-207(1), the conditional nature of the acceptance must be clearly expressed in a manner sufficient to notify the offeror that the offeree is unwilling to proceed with the transaction unless the additional or different terms are included in the contract. *See* Annot. "What Constitutes Acceptance 'Expressly Made Conditional' Converting it to Rejection and Counteroffer under UCC § 2-207(1)", 22 ALR 4th 939, 948–49 (1983) and cases cited therein. The conditional assent provision has been construed narrowly to apply only to an acceptance which clearly shows that the offeree is unwilling to proceed absent assent to the additional or different terms. *Id.*; *see Challenge Machinery Co. v. Mattison Machine Works*, 138 Mich. App. 15, 359 N.W.2d 232, 235 (1984), *citing Idaho Power Co. v. Westinghouse Electric Corp.*, 596 F.2d 924 (9th Cir.1979);....

¶3 We find nothing in Brown Machine's acknowledgment of February 5, 1976, which reflects its unwillingness to proceed unless it obtained Hercules' assent to the additional and different terms in Brown Machine's acknowledgment, ... which contained the indemnity provision. Brown Machine's acknowledgment was not "expressly made conditional" on Hercules' assent to the additional or different terms as provided for under § 2-207(1). Acceptance will be considered a counteroffer only if the acceptance is expressly made conditional on assent to the additional terms....

Section 2-207 imprecisely refers to "a written confirmation" in the same clause as "expression of acceptance." According to the first clause of the statute, both operate "as an acceptance." A confirmation, however, normally refers to confirmation of an existing agreement. *See* U.C.C. § 2-207 comm. 1 (2011). A confirmation thus comes too late to operate as the "acceptance" in the original agreement. The drafters probably should have addressed confirmations in a separate sentence, explaining that—even though a confirmation contains an additional or different term—it does not repudiate or otherwise upset the agreement previously formed, unless it conditions the confirming party's performance of the pre-existing agreement on acceptance of its new terms.

The following opinion finds that invoices sent by a seller after contract formation confirmed the existing agreement without undermining it, even though each confirming invoice contained an additional term. The additional term will have some legal significance, but we will address that issue in Subsection D below, when we focus on the second subsection of section 2-207.

Office Supply Store.com v. Kansas City School Bd.

334 S.W.3d 574 (Mo. Ct. App. 2011)

....

¶ 1 Both Missouri and California have adopted § 2-207 of the pre-2003 Uniform Commercial Code (the "UCC"), which provides:

> (1) A definite and seasonable expression of acceptance or a written confirmation which is sent within a reasonable time operates as an acceptance even though it states terms additional to or different from those offered or agreed upon, unless acceptance is expressly made conditional on assent to the additional or different terms.
>
> ....

§ 400.2-207, RSMo; Cal. Comm. Code § 2207.

¶ 2 Under § 2-207 as adopted in both Missouri and California, Office Supply's invoices were effective to confirm the parties' agreement to a purchase transaction, despite the inclusion in the invoices of an additional forum selection term [selecting the California courts for resolution of any disputes arising out of the contract]....

Exercise 6.6—Section 2-207(1): Contract on the Forms?

B sent a signed, written offer to purchase goods from S, with payment 30 days after delivery. The offer says nothing about warranties or dispute resolution. Consult UCC § 2-314, as enacted in Texas in Appendix 1, to confirm that a sale by a merchant includes an implied warranty of "merchantability" unless the seller has effectively disclaimed it in the agreement pursuant to UCC § 2-316.

Purchase Order #23231
B [name & address]

We will buy x goods at Y price.

1. On all orders, payment will be made within 30 days after delivery.

. . . .

Signed . . .

Answer the following questions about the legal effect of S's response to B's offer.

1. Acceptance in Face of Varying Terms?

S immediately sent a signed acknowledgment form that says, "We accept your order #23231" Printed terms on the form describe a mandatory arbitration clause, a disclaimer of warranties, and a requirement of payment on delivery. Contract under section 2-207(1)?

Acknowledgment #99988
S [name & address]

We accept your order #23231

1. Payment is due on delivery.

2. Delivered goods come with no warranties, express or implied. Seller specifically disclaims the implied warranty of merchantability.

3. Any dispute arising out of this sale must be arbitrated under the rules of the American Arbitration Association.

. . . .

Signed . . .

---

2. Expression of Acceptance?

Alternatively, S immediately sent an acknowledgment form that says "We have received your order #23231; we will consider it as soon as possible," rather than "We accept your order." Printed terms on the form describe a mandatory arbitration clause, a disclaimer of warranties, and a requirement of payment on delivery. Contract under section 2-207(1)?

Acknowledgment #99988
S [name & address]

We have received your order #23231; we will consider it as soon as possible.

1. Payment is due on delivery.

2. Delivered goods come with no warranties, express or implied. Seller specifically disclaims the implied warranty of merchantability.

3. Any dispute arising out of this sale must be arbitrated under the rules of the American Arbitration Association.

. . . .

3. Conditional Acceptance

S immediately sent a signed acknowledgment form that says, "We accept your PO# 23231," but the acknowledgment also states, "This acceptance is conditioned on your agreement to the terms on this acknowledgment." Contract under section 2-207(1)?

Acknowledgment #99988
S [name & address]

We accept your PO# 23231. This acceptance is conditioned on your agreement to the terms on this acknowledgment.

1. Payment is due on delivery.

2. Delivered goods come with no warranties, express or implied. Seller specifically disclaims the implied warranty of merchantability.

3. Any dispute arising out of this sale must be arbitrated under the rules of the American Arbitration Association.

. . . .

---

4. Still Actively Negotiating

S and B are negotiating a contract through email exchanges and have reached agreement on most terms, but they have reached a stalemate on terms of payment. S has insisted on payment in advance, and B has insisted on payment 30 days after delivery. B then broke off the email exchanges and mailed a purchase order to S on its form, which calls for payment 30 days after delivery. S sent an acknowledgment form that expressed acceptance of B's purchase order; however, Seller wrote "14 days prior to shipment date" in the blank on its form for "Terms of Payment." Did the parties reach an agreement under section 2-207(1)?

D. Focus on Subsection 2 of UCC § 2-207

Closely study each clause of subsection (2) of California Commercial Code § 2207:

> (2) The additional terms are to be construed as proposals for addition to the contract. Between merchants such terms become part of the contract unless:
>
> (a) The offer expressly limits acceptance to the terms of the offer;
>
> (b) They materially alter it; or
>
> (c) Notification of objection to them has already been given or is given within a reasonable time after notice of them is received.

1. *Significance of Merchant Status of Both Parties*

Office Supply Store.com v. Kansas City School Bd.

334 S.W.3d 574 (Mo. App. 2011)

....

¶ 1 Under § 2-207 as adopted in both Missouri and California, Office Supply's invoices were effective to confirm the parties' agreement to a purchase transaction, despite the inclusion in the invoices of an additional forum selection term. But the additional term did not thereby become part of the parties' contract. It does not appear that the School District would be deemed a "merchant" of office supplies under the UCC definition. *See* § 400.2-104(1), RSMo; Cal. Comm. Code § 2104(1). If the School District is not a "merchant," under § 2-207(2) the additional forum-selection term stated in Office Supply's invoice must be construed simply as a proposal for an addition to the contract. There is no evidence that the School District agreed to the forum selection clause, and Office Supply's attempted reliance on it must accordingly fail. *See Klocek v. Gateway, Inc.*, 104 F. Supp. 2d 1332, 1341 (D. Kan. 2000) (applying Missouri and Kansas law; finding that "Standard Terms" delivered by seller to non-merchant buyer with shipment of computer "did not become part of the parties' agreement unless plaintiff expressly agreed to them").

¶ 2 Even if the School District were deemed a "merchant," to our knowledge every court presented with the issue has found that a forum selection clause included in a confirmatory writing constitutes a material alteration of the underlying contract; under § 2-207(2)(b), the forum selection clause accordingly cannot become part of the contract absent some indicia of the parties' agreement to the term. [citations omitted]

Exercise 6.7 — Identifying and Analyzing the Elements of Subsection 2

In subsection 2, what is a transaction that is "between merchants"? (*See* UCC § 2-104 by looking up the Texas counterpart in Appendix 1.) What are the special rules for finding mutual assent to modify the existing contract if both parties are merchants? In a transaction in which at least one party is not a merchant, the first sentence of subsection (2) still applies, but the special rules for assent in the remainder of subsection (2) do not apply, so that normal rules for mutual assent in the UCC and the common law would apply. How do those differ from the special rule in UCC § 2-207(2) about a modification between merchants?

2. Additional Terms That Would Materially Alter the Contract Formed under Subsection 1

The Official Comment to UCC § 2-207 suggests that a materially altering term is one that would result in "surprise or hardship if incorporated without express awareness of the other party." UCC § 2-207 cmt. 4 (2011). Comment 4 provides examples of such terms, including a clause disclaiming UCC implied warranties in transactions in which such warranties would be the norm, a seller's right to cancel the remainder of a contract for any delay by the buyer in paying an invoice, and other terms that define significant rights or obligations and that depart from reasonable standards or usages in the trade. *Id.* Does the notion of "surprise" refer to departures from norms or past dealings of the parties, and "hardship" to a term that imposes a substantial burden on one party? We will study implied terms, including UCC implied warranties, in Chapter 10.

The Official Comment also provides examples of additional terms that would not result in surprise or hardship and therefore could be automatically incorporated into the contract between merchants absent some objection by the other party. UCC § 2-207 cmt. 5 (2011). The Comment refers to a clause slightly enlarging the excuse from performance allowed by the UCC for unexpected changes in circumstances, as well as clauses that expand or limit rights or obligations within a range that is reasonable and consistent with trade usage. *Id.*

Exercise 6.8 — Determining Whether Additional or Different Terms Are Added to the Contract That Was Formed under Subsection 1

1. Construct an outline of subsection (2) in bullet point format, such as the following:

(2) If the parties reached agreement under subsection (1):

- Any additional terms in the acceptance are viewed as . . . .
- If one of the parties is not a merchant, this . . . will be viewed as accepted, and the additional terms thus will become part of the contract, only if . . . .
- If both parties are merchants, this . . . will be viewed as automatically accepted, and the additional terms will become part of the contract, unless . . . .

2. Terms of the Contract in Consumer Transaction

Assume: (1) S immediately sent a signed acknowledgment form that says, "We accept your order"; (2) B is not a merchant, but a consumer; and (3) B does not respond to S's acknowledgment form. Which of the printed terms becomes part of the contract?

B [name, address, and date]

S [name and address]

Please send x goods at the advertised price of Y. Please send invoice for payment within 30 days after delivery. . . . .

Acknowledgment #99988

S [name & address]

We accept your order dated....

1. Payment is due on delivery.

2. Delivered goods come with no warranties, express or implied. Seller specifically disclaims the implied warranty of merchantability.

3. Any dispute arising out of this sale must be arbitrated under the rules of the American Arbitration Association.

....

---

3. Terms of the Contract between Merchants

Assume: (1) S immediately sent a signed acknowledgment form that says, "We accept your order"; (2) both parties are merchants; and (3) B does not respond to S's acknowledgment form. Which of the printed terms on S's acknowledgment form becomes part of a contract? If you need more facts, what factors might be relevant to an analysis of materiality? The inclusion of one or more of S's terms in the contract can be viewed as a modification of the contract that was recognized under section 2-207(1). Does section 2-207(2) recognize this modification on facts that would not amount to an agreement to modify under common law? How?

Purchase Order #23231

B [name & address]

We will buy x goods at Y price.

1. On all orders, payment will be made within 30 days after delivery.....

Acknowledgment #99988

S [name & address]

We accept your order #23231

1. Payment is due on delivery.

2. Delivered goods come with no warranties, express or implied. Seller specifically disclaims the implied warranty of merchantability.

3. Any dispute arising out of this sale must be arbitrated under the rules of the American Arbitration Association.

....

[no response by B]

---

4. *Treatment of Different Terms under Subsection 2*

UCC § 2-207 refers only to "additional" terms in its second subsection, even though its first subsection refers to both additional and different terms. Did the drafters intend "different" as well as "additional" terms in the acceptance to operate as proposals to modify the terms of the contract formed under the first paragraph? If not, what happens to the different terms if a contract is formed by an acceptance with different terms? Consider the following different answers to this question.

Oakley Fertilizer, Inc. v. Continental Ins. Co.

276 S.W.3d 342, 348 n.4 (Mo. App. 2009)

....

We note that, although U.C.C. § 2-207(2) only expressly references "additional" terms and § 2-207(1) holds that an acceptance is valid even when it contains "terms additional to or different from those offered," Missouri courts have held that the applicability of U.C.C. § 2-207(2) does not turn upon a characterization of the varying terms of an acceptance as "additional" or "different." ... Accordingly, the different risk of loss term contained in Buyer's acceptance is assessed under U.C.C. § 2-207(2).

....

Northrop Corp. v. Litronic Industries

29 F.3d 1173 (7th Cir. 1994)

....

¶ 1 The Code does not explain, however, what happens [in subsection 2] if the offeree's response contains different terms (rather than additional ones) within the meaning of section 2-207(1). There is no consensus on that question.... *See* James J. White & Robert S. Summers, Uniform Commercial Code 33–36 (3d ed. 1988); John E. Murray, Jr., "The Chaos of the 'Battle of the Forms': Solutions," 39 Vand. L. Rev. 1307, 1354–65 (1986). We know there is a contract because an acceptance is effective even though it contains different terms; but what are the terms of the contract that is brought into being by the offer and acceptance? One view is that the discrepant terms in both the nonidentical offer and the acceptance drop out, and default terms found elsewhere in the Code fill the resulting gap. Another view is that the offeree's discrepant terms drop out and the offeror's become part of the contract. A third view, possibly the most sensible, equates "different" with "additional" and makes the outcome turn on whether the new terms in the acceptance are materially different from the terms in the offer—in which event they operate as proposals, so that the offeror's terms prevail unless he agrees to the variant terms in the acceptance—or not materially different from the terms in the offer, in which event they become part of the contract.

....

¶2 Unfortunately, the Illinois courts—whose understanding of Article 2 of the UCC is binding on us because this is a diversity suit governed, all agree, by Illinois law—have had no occasion to choose among the different positions on the consequences of an acceptance that contains "different" terms from the offer. We shall have to choose. ....

¶3 The Uniform Commercial Code, as we have said, does not say what the terms of the contract are if the offer and acceptance contain different terms, as distinct from cases in which the acceptance merely contains additional terms to those in the offer. The majority view is that the discrepant terms fall out and are replaced by a suitable UCC gap-filler.... Our own preferred view—the view that assimilates "different" to "additional," so that the terms in the offer prevail over the different terms in the acceptance only if the latter are materially different, has as yet been adopted by only one state, California. *Steiner v. Mobil Oil Corp.*, 20 Cal. 3d 90, 141 Cal. Rptr. 157, 569 P.2d 751, 759 n. 5 (1977)....

¶4 Because Illinois in other UCC cases has tended to adopt majority rules, [citation omitted], and because the interest in the uniform nationwide application of the Code—an interest asserted in the Code itself (*see* § 1-102)—argues for nudging majority views, even if imperfect (but not downright bad), toward unanimity, we start with a presumption that Illinois, whose position we are trying to predict, would adopt the majority view. We do not find the presumption rebutted. The idea behind the majority view is that the presence of different terms in the acceptance suggests that the offeree didn't really accede to the offeror's terms, yet both parties wanted to contract, so why not find a neutral term to govern the dispute that has arisen between them? ... And if the offeror doesn't want to do business other than on the terms in the offer, he can protect himself by specifying that the offeree must accept all those terms for the parties to have a contract. UCC § 2-207(2)(a)....

What are the full implications of the court's final clause in the excerpt above? In one Arizona case, the buyer's offer specified that it could be accepted only on its terms, but the seller responded with varying terms. Because of offeror's restriction on acceptance, the courts applied the common law mirror-image rule and last-shot doctrine rather than section 2-207: they held that the seller's response constituted a counter-offer, which the buyer accepted through its conduct. *Salt River Project Agr. Imp. and Power Dist. v. Westinghouse Elec. Corp.*, 143 Ariz. 437, 444–45, 694 P.2d 267, 274–75 (Ct. App. 1984), *analysis adopted by Salt River Project Agr. Imp. and Power Dist. v. Westinghouse Elec. Corp.*, 143 Ariz. 368, 374, 694 P.2d 198, 204 (1984), *overturned on other grounds, Phelps v. Firebird Raceway, Inc.*, 210 Ariz. 403, 111 P.3d 1003 (2005).

E. Focus on Subsection 3 of UCC § 2-207

Closely study each clause of subsection (3) of California Commercial Code § 2207:

> (3) Conduct by both parties which recognizes the existence of a contract is sufficient to establish a contract for sale although the writings of the parties do not otherwise establish a contract. In such case the terms of the particular contract consist of those terms on which the writings of the parties agree, together with any supplementary terms incorporated under any other provisions of this code.

Consider the circumstances in which subsection (3) applies. What two issues does this subsection address, and what solutions does it provide?

Notice that the second part of subsection 3 addresses the content of the contract, a topic primarily addressed in Chapter 10 of this book. The first sentence, however, addresses a form of contract formation.

Exercise 6.9 — Performance and Dispute

1. Construct an outline of subsection (3) using a bullet point format such as the following:

(3) If the parties did not reach agreement under subsection (1),

- nonetheless, they could form . . . ;
- if so, the terms of . . . would be:
- . . . ., and
- . . . .

2. Equivocation, Performance, and Dispute

Assume: (1) S's acknowledgment form contains the additional and different terms and says, "We have received your order #23231; we will consider it as soon as possible," rather than, "We accept your order." (2) B does not respond to S's acknowledgment; and (3) S delivers the goods and B accepts delivery, but a dispute immediately arises over the time of payment and the quality of the goods. What are the terms of the contract that relate to the dispute? What subsection of UCC § 2-207 addresses this question?

Acknowledgment #99988
S [name & address]

We have received your order #23231; we will consider it as soon as possible.

1. Payment is due on delivery.
2. Delivered goods come with no warranties, express or implied. Seller specifically disclaims the implied warranty of merchantability.
3. Any dispute arising out of this sale must be arbitrated under the rules of the American Arbitration Association.

....

[no verbal response, but parties begin performing]

---

3. Condition, Performance, and Dispute

Assume: (1) although the acknowledgement purports to accept the offer, it also states: "This acceptance is conditioned on your agreement to the terms on this acknowledgment"; (2) B does not respond to S's acknowledgment; and (3) S delivers the goods and B accepts delivery, but a dispute immediately arises over the time of payment and the quality of the goods. What are the terms of the contract that relate to the dispute?

Acknowledgment #99988

S [name & address]

We accept your PO #23231. This acceptance is conditioned on your agreement to the terms on this acknowledgment.

1. Payment is due on delivery.

2. Delivered goods come with no warranties, express or implied. Seller specifically disclaims the implied warranty of merchantability.

3. Any dispute arising out of this sale must be arbitrated under the rules of the American Arbitration Association.

....

[no verbal response, but parties begin performing]

Exercise 6.10 — Knock-Out Doctrine as Applied to Conflicting Confirmations

A and B orally agreed over the phone that B will sell a large truck to A; neither party mentioned warranties. A immediately mailed a written confirmation of the oral agreement that included the following clauses: "B warrants that the truck can safely haul full loads in severe weather conditions." On the same day, B mailed a written confirmation to A that included: "B makes no warranty on the truck." Each party received the other's confirmation two days later. What warranties, if any, does the contract provide? What specific provisions of section 2-207 are you applying?

F. Terms Disclosed After Delivery

After a buyer paid for a computer in a telephone credit card transaction, the computer arrived and the buyer found inside the box a five-page statement of "terms of the agreement," which buyer had never seen or heard before and which included a disclaimer of seller's warranties and limitation on the seller's liabilities. How might UCC § 2-207 apply?

Step-Saver Data Systems, Inc. v. Wyse Technology

939 F.2d 91 (3d Cir. 1991) [footnotes omitted]

Before Sloviter, Chief Judge, and Cowen and Wisdom, Circuit Judges.

Wisdom, Circuit Judge:

¶ 1 The "Limited Use License Agreement" printed on a package containing a copy of a computer program raises the central issue in this appeal. The trial judge held that the terms of the Limited Use License Agreement governed the purchase of the package, and, therefore, granted the software producer, The Software Link, Inc. ("TSL"), a directed verdict on claims of breach of warranty brought by a disgruntled purchaser, Step-Saver Data Systems, Inc. We disagree with the district court's determination of the legal effect of the license, and reverse and remand the warranty claims for further consideration. Step-Saver raises several other issues, but we do not find these issues warrant reversal. We, therefore, affirm in all other respects.

I. FACTUAL AND PROCEDURAL BACKGROUND

....

¶ 2 As a result of advances in micro-computer technology, Step-Saver developed and marketed a multi-user system. With a multi-user system, only one computer is required. Terminals are attached, by cable, to the main computer. From these terminals, a user can access the programs available on the main computer.

¶ 3 After evaluating the available technology, Step-Saver selected a program by TSL, entitled Multilink Advanced, as the operating system for the multi-user system. Step-Saver selected WY-60 terminals manufactured by Wyse, ... Step-Saver began marketing the system in November of 1986, and sold one hundred forty-two systems mostly to law and medical offices before terminating sales of the system in March of 1987. Almost immediately upon installation of the system, Step-Saver began to receive complaints from some of its customers.

¶ 4 Step-Saver, in addition to conducting its own investigation of the problems, referred these complaints to Wyse and TSL, and requested technical assistance in resolving the problems. After several preliminary attempts to address the problems, the three companies were unable to reach a satisfactory solution, and disputes developed among the three concerning responsibility for the problems. As a result, the problems were never solved. At least twelve of Step-Saver's customers filed suit against Step-Saver because of the problems with the multi-user system.

¶ 5 ... Step-Saver [alleged] breach of warranties by both TSL and Wyse and intentional misrepresentations by TSL. The district court's actions during the resolution of this second complaint provide the foundation for this appeal.

¶ 6 On the first day of trial, the district court specifically agreed with the basic contention of TSL that the form language printed on each package containing the Multilink Advanced program ("the box-top license") [was part of the contract].

....

II. THE EFFECT OF THE BOX-TOP LICENSE

....

¶7 ... From August of 1986 through March of 1987, Step-Saver purchased and resold 142 copies of the Multilink Advanced program [from TSL]. Step-Saver would typically purchase copies of the program in the following manner. First, Step-Saver would telephone TSL and place an order. (Step-Saver would typically order twenty copies of the program at a time.) TSL would accept the order and promise, while on the telephone, to ship the goods promptly. After the telephone order, Step-Saver would send a purchase order, detailing the items to be purchased, their price, and shipping and payment terms. TSL would ship the order promptly, along with an invoice. The invoice would contain terms essentially identical with those on Step-Saver's purchase order: price, quantity, and shipping and payment terms. No reference was made during the telephone calls, or on either the purchase orders or the invoices with regard to a disclaimer of any warranties.

¶8 Printed on the package of each copy of the program, however, would be a copy of the box-top license. The box-top license contains five terms relevant to this action:

(1) The box-top license provides that the customer has not purchased the software itself, but has merely obtained a personal, non-transferable license to use the program.

(2) The box-top license, in detail and at some length, disclaims all express and implied warranties except for a warranty that the disks contained in the box are free from defects.

(3) The box-top license provides that the sole remedy available to a purchaser of the program is to return a defective disk for replacement; the license excludes any liability for damages, direct or consequential, caused by the use of the program.

(4) The box-top license contains an integration clause, which provides that the box-top license is the final and complete expression of the terms of the parties's [sic] agreement.

(5) The box-top license states: "Opening this package indicates your acceptance of these terms and conditions. If you do not agree with them, you should promptly return the package unopened to the person from whom you purchased it within fifteen days from date of purchase and your money will be refunded to you by that person."

¶9 The district court, without much discussion, held, as a matter of law, that the box-top license was [incorporated into the parties' contract]. Because the district court decided the questions of contract formation and interpretation as issues of law, we review the district court's resolution of these questions de novo.

¶10 Step-Saver contends that the contract for each copy of the program was formed when TSL agreed, on the telephone, to ship the copy at the agreed price. The box-top license, argues Step-Saver, was a material alteration to the parties' contract which did not become a part of the contract under UCC § 2-207....

¶ 11 ... Finding that UCC § 2-207 best governs our resolution of the effect of the box-top license, we then consider whether, under UCC § 2-207, the terms of the box-top license were incorporated into the parties's [sic] agreement.

A. Does UCC § 2-207 Govern the Analysis?

....

¶ 12 To understand why the terms of the license should be considered under § 2-207 in this case, we review briefly the reasons behind § 2-207. Under the common law of sales, and to some extent still for contracts outside the UCC, an acceptance that varied any term of the offer operated as a rejection of the offer, and simultaneously made a counteroffer. This common law formality was known as the mirror image rule, because the terms of the acceptance had to mirror the terms of the offer to be effective. If the offeror proceeded with the contract despite the differing terms of the supposed acceptance, he would, by his performance, constructively accept the terms of the "counteroffer", and be bound by its terms. As a result of these rules, the terms of the party who sent the last form, typically the seller, would become the terms of the parties' contract. This result was known as the "last shot rule".

¶ 13 The UCC, in § 2-207, rejected this approach. Instead, it recognized that, while a party may desire the terms detailed in its form if a dispute, in fact, arises, most parties do not expect a dispute to arise when they first enter into a contract. As a result, most parties will proceed with the transaction even if they know that the terms of their form would not be enforced. The insight behind the rejection of the last shot rule is that it would be unfair to bind the buyer of goods to the standard terms of the seller, when neither party cared sufficiently to establish expressly the terms of their agreement, simply because the seller sent the last form. Thus, UCC § 2-207 establishes a legal rule that proceeding with a contract after receiving a writing that purports to define the terms of the parties' contract is not sufficient to establish the party's consent to the terms of the writing to the extent that the terms of the writing either add to, or differ from, the terms detailed in the parties' earlier writings or discussions. In the absence of a party's express assent to the additional or different terms of the writing, section 2-207 provides a default rule that the parties intended, as the terms of their agreement, those terms to which both parties have agreed, along with any terms implied by the provisions of the UCC.

¶ 14 The reasons that led to the rejection of the last shot rule, and the adoption of section 2-207, apply fully in this case. TSL never mentioned during the parties' negotiations leading to the purchase of the programs, nor did it, at any time, obtain Step-Saver's express assent to, the terms of the box-top license. Instead, TSL contented itself with attaching the terms to the packaging of the software, even though those terms differed substantially from those previously discussed by the parties. Thus, the box-top license, in this case, is best seen as one more form in a battle of forms, and the question of whether Step-Saver has agreed to be bound by the terms of the box-top license is best resolved by applying the legal principles detailed in section 2-207.

[Question from the author: What part of section 2-207 is the court apparently applying to conclude that the box-top license is a proposal to modify an existing contract? What is the existing contract and when was it formed, according to the apparent assumption of the court?]

B. Application of § 2-207

¶ 15 TSL advances several reasons why the terms of the box-top license should be incorporated into the parties's [sic] agreement under a § 2-207 analysis. First, TSL argues that the parties's [sic] contract was not formed until Step-Saver received the package, saw the terms of the box-top license, and opened the package, thereby consenting to the terms of the license. TSL argues that a contract defined without reference to the specific terms provided by the box-top license would necessarily fail for indefiniteness. Second, TSL argues that the box-top license was a conditional acceptance and counter-offer under § 2-207(1). Third, TSL argues that Step-Saver, by continuing to order and use the product with notice of the terms of the box-top license, consented to the terms of the box-top license.

1. Was the contract sufficiently definite?

[In a portion of the opinion that is presented in the next chapter, the court finds that the contract would be sufficiently definite to enforce without the box-top license.]

2. The box-top license as a counter-offer?

¶ 16 [The court rejected the argument that the box-top license, which appeared only after delivery, constituted a counter-offer under the proviso to UCC § 2-207(1).]

¶ 17 TSL has raised a number of public policy arguments focusing on the effect on the software industry of an adverse holding concerning the enforceability of the box-top license. We are not persuaded that requiring software companies to stand behind representations concerning their products will inevitably destroy the software industry. We emphasize, however, that we are following the well-established distinction between conspicuous disclaimers made available before the contract is formed and disclaimers made available only after the contract is formed. When a disclaimer is not expressed until after the contract is formed, UCC § 2-207 governs the interpretation of the contract, and, between merchants, such disclaimers, to the extent they materially alter the parties' agreement, are not incorporated into the parties' agreement.

. . . .

C. The Terms of the Contract

[The court had earlier noted that it "is undisputed that Step-Saver never expressly agreed to the terms of the box-top license."]

¶ 18 Under section 2-207, an additional term detailed in the box-top license will not be incorporated into the parties' contract if the term's addition to the contract would materially alter the parties' agreement. Step-Saver alleges that several representations made by TSL constitute express warranties, and that valid implied warranties were also a part of the parties' agreement.... [W]e must conclude that adding the disclaimer of warranty and limitation of remedies provisions from the box-top license would, as a matter of law, substantially alter the distribution of risk between Step-Saver and TSL. Therefore, under UCC § 2-207(2)(b), the disclaimer of warranty and limitation of remedies terms of the box-top license did not become a part of the parties' agreement.

¶ 19 Based on these considerations, we reverse the trial court's holding.... Because the warranty disclaimer and limitation of remedies terms would materially alter the parties's [sic] agreement, these terms did not become a part of the parties's [sic] agreement. We remand for further consideration the express and implied warranty claims against TSL.

....

UCC § 2-207 addresses selected issues in the formation, content, and performance of contracts for the sale of goods. Section 2-105(1) generally defines "goods" as "things ... which are movable." The parties in *Stepsaver* agreed that the computer program was in the form of "goods" so that the UCC would apply to the dispute, presumably because the program was sold in a tangible form, such as a CD-ROM, to facilitate transfer of the program to the user's computer. The court further appeared to view the accompanying license as an incidental adjunct to the physical product.

Would section 2-207 apply to a copy of computer software downloaded from a website, without the delivery of any physical product? For a negative response, see Lorin Brennan, *Why Article 2 Cannot Apply to Software Transactions*, 38 DUQUESNE L. REV. 459 (2000); *see also* Robert W. Gomulkiewicz, *Is the License Still the Product?*, 60 ARIZ. L. REV. 425 (2018) (discussing applicability of common law of contracts, federal copyright law, and federal patent law to end-user licensing agreements). Moreover, a transaction on a website will more likely present *all* relevant terms and require agreement to them prior to check-out, payment, and downloading, thus avoiding the issues addressed in section 2-207 (while perhaps raising others discussed in Chapter 2 if the link to the terms was not reasonably visible).

With respect to issues governed by state contract law, such as contract formation and content, the common law—rather than the UCC—would apply if the software and its licensing agreement are not "goods." However, is that relevant to the outcome in *Step-Saver*? Wouldn't Judge Wisdom have reached the same conclusion under common law rules, even more easily, on the facts of *Step-Saver*? If the parties had formed their contract over the telephone (or at the latest with the delivery of the invoice in response to the purchase order), under common law wouldn't a new term inside the delivered box come too late to be part of the contract? If so, at most it would constitute an offer to modify that contract, as would an additional term in a confirmation under UCC § 2-207(2). Under common law, couldn't the recipient of the box avoid adding that term to the contract simply by refraining from affirmatively agreeing to the new term, regardless of its materiality? (The same would be true under UCC § 2-207(2), regardless of the materiality of a proposed additional term, if one of the parties was not a merchant.)

In other words, although *Step-Saver* provides an excellent review of the UCC provisions that we have studied, Judge Wisdom's exclusion of the terms inside the box was not a function of any modifications of the common law by section 2-207. Instead, as the next case illustrates through contrast, Judge Wisdom's conclusion stems from the absence of any suggestion in *Step-Saver* that the offeror had specified an unusual means of acceptance that would have delayed contract formation until the box-top license was in the buyer's hands.

On the other hand, if an offeror desired to unambiguously specify a special procedure for acceptance, one that delayed contract formation until a buyer has an opportunity to read terms packed inside a delivered box, both the common law and UCC § 2-206(a)(1) presumably would honor that specified means of acceptance.

In the next case, what procedure for contract formation does Judge Easterbrook approve? How was the process for acceptance communicated to the offeree?

Hill v. Gateway 2000, Inc.

105 F.3d 1147 (7th Cir.), *cert. denied*, 522 U.S. 808 (1997)

Easterbrook, Circuit Judge.

¶1 A customer picks up the phone, orders a computer, and gives a credit card number. Presently a box arrives, containing the computer and a list of terms, said to govern unless the customer returns the computer within 30 days. Are these terms effective as the parties' contract, or is the contract term-free because the order-taker did not read any terms over the phone and elicit the customer's assent?

¶2 One of the terms in the box containing a Gateway 2000 system was an arbitration clause. Rich and Enza Hill, the customers, kept the computer more than 30 days before complaining about its components and performance. They filed suit in federal court arguing, among other things, that the product's shortcomings make Gateway a racketeer (mail and wire fraud are said to be the predicate offenses), leading to treble damages under RICO for the Hills and a class of all other purchasers. Gateway asked the district court to enforce the arbitration clause; the judge refused, writing that "[t]he present record is insufficient to support a finding of a valid arbitration agreement between the parties or that the plaintiffs were given adequate notice of the arbitration clause." ...

....

¶3 *ProCD, Inc. v. Zeidenberg*, 86 F.3d 1447 (7th Cir.1996), holds that terms inside a box of software bind consumers who use the software after an opportunity to read the terms and to reject them by returning the product.... The district court concluded in *ProCD* that the contract is formed when the consumer pays for the software; as a result, the court held, only terms known to the consumer at that moment are part of the contract, and provisos inside the box do not count. Although this is one way a contract could be formed, it is not the only way: "A vendor, as master of the offer, may invite acceptance by conduct, and may propose limitations on the kind of conduct that constitutes acceptance. A buyer may accept by performing the acts the vendor proposes to treat as acceptance." *Id.* at 1452. Gateway shipped computers with the same sort of accept-or-return offer ProCD made to users of its software....

¶4 Plaintiffs ask us to limit *ProCD* to software, but where's the sense in that? *ProCD* is about the law of contract, not the law of software. Payment preceding the revelation of full terms is common for air transportation, insurance, and many other endeavors. Practical considerations support allowing vendors to enclose the full legal terms with their products. Cashiers cannot be expected to read legal documents to customers before ringing up sales. If the staff at the other end of the phone for direct-sales operations such as Gateway's had to read the four-page statement of terms before taking the buyer's credit card number, the droning voice would anesthetize rather than enlighten many potential buyers. Others would hang up in a rage over the waste of their time. And oral recitation would not avoid customers' assertions (whether true or feigned) that the clerk did not read term X to them, or that they did not remember or understand it. Writing provides benefits for both sides of commercial transactions. Customers as a group are better off when vendors skip costly and ineffectual steps such as telephonic recitation, and use instead a simple approve-or-return device. Competent adults are bound by such documents, read or unread. For what little it is worth, we add that the box from Gateway was crammed with software. The computer came with an operating system, without which it was useful only as a boat anchor. *See Digital Equipment Corp. v. Uniq Digital Technologies, Inc.*, 73 F.3d 756, 761 (7th Cir.1996). Gateway also included many application programs. So the Hills' effort to limit ProCD to software would not avail them factually, even if it were sound legally—which it is not.

....

¶5 At oral argument the Hills propounded still another distinction: the box containing ProCD's software displayed a notice that additional terms were within, while the box containing Gateway's computer did not. The difference is functional, not legal. Consumers browsing the aisles of a store can look at the box, and if they are unwilling to deal with the prospect of additional terms can leave the box alone, avoiding the transactions costs of returning the package after reviewing its contents. Gateway's box, by contrast, is just a shipping carton; it is not on display anywhere....

¶6 Perhaps the Hills would have had a better argument if they were first alerted to the bundling of hardware and legal-ware after opening the box and wanted to return the computer in order to avoid disagreeable terms, but were dissuaded by the expense of shipping. What the remedy would be in such a case—could it exceed the shipping charges?—is an interesting question, but one that need not detain us because the Hills knew before they ordered the computer that the carton would include some important terms, and they did not seek to discover these in advance. Gateway's ads state that their products come with limited warranties and lifetime support. How limited was the warranty—30 days, with service contingent on shipping the computer back, or five years, with free onsite service? What sort of support was offered? Shoppers have three principal ways to discover these things. First, they can ask the vendor to send a copy before deciding whether to buy. The Magnuson–Moss Warranty Act requires firms to distribute their warranty terms on request, 15 U.S.C. § 2302(b)(1)(A); the Hills do not contend that Gateway would have refused to enclose the remaining terms too. Concealment would be bad for business, scaring some customers away and leading to excess returns from others. Second, shoppers can consult public sources (computer magazines, the Web sites of vendors) that may contain this information. Third, they may inspect the documents after the product's delivery. Like Zeidenberg, the Hills took the third option. By keeping the computer beyond 30 days, the Hills accepted Gateway's offer, including the arbitration clause.

¶ 7 .... The decision of the district court is vacated, and this case is remanded with instructions to compel the Hills to submit their dispute to arbitration.

If Judge Easterbrook's analysis is sound in theory, it underscores the factual issue of whether Gateway adequately communicated the mandatory means of acceptance to the Hills. Why didn't the court require a statement by Gateway's agent on the phone that the shipping box would contain the complete terms of Gateway's offer and that the Hills could reject the offer by returning the computer for a full refund? *Cf. DeFontes v. Dell, Inc.*, 984 A.2d 1061 (R.I. 2009) (adopting *ProCD* but finding insufficient notice to the buyers that they would be bound by terms in the box).

Exercise 6.11—Safeguards for *ProCD* Approach

Imagine that you are a justice on a state court of last resort, considering whether to adopt the *ProCD/Gateway* view of contract formation. Alternatively, imagine that you are a state legislator, considering whether to support a bill that would codify the approach in *ProCD* and *Gateway*. What factual predicates would you require before adopting a rule that recognized the vendor's ability to delay acceptance until the buyer had opened the goods at home or office, discovered detailed terms, and then made a decision about whether to accept the offer or return the goods? If those factual predicates were satisfied, would you require the vendor to pay the cost of return shipping if the customer decided to reject the vendor's offer after reading the full set of terms in the delivered box?

G. Reform and Reflection

1. Assessment of UCC § 2-207

After working through section 2-207, what is your opinion on whether the UCC improves on the common law rules in domestic sales of goods? If you are skeptical about the merits of section 2-207, take heart; you are in good company:

> Current § 2-207 is irreparably fraught with problems and inconsistencies. Cases and commentators are hopelessly divided on when it should be applied, how it should be applied, and how it should be interpreted. To paraphrase Winston Churchill, § 2-207 has proven to be a riddle, packed in a puzzle, wrapped in a mystery, inside an enigma, surrounded by a conundrum.

Corneill A. Stephens, *Escape from the Battle of the Forms: Keep it Simple, Stupid*, 11 Lewis & Clark L. Rev. 233, 253 (2007).

2. UN Convention on Contracts for the Int'l Sale of Goods

The United Nations Convention on Contracts for the International Sale of Goods (1980) ("CISG"), appears at first glance to adopt features of UCC § 2-207. In the end, however, it operates almost entirely like the common law mirror-image rule. CISG art. 19 (1980). The CISG would apply, for example, to a sale of goods between a party in the United States and a party in Mexico, unless the parties agreed to opt out of this international law. *Id.* art. 1, 6. Do you prefer the simpler mirror-image rule, or do you applaud section 2-207's efforts to avoid the frequently arbitrary results of the mirror-image rule and related last-shot doctrine?

3. ALI Principles of the Law of Software Contracts

The American Law Institute has recommended a set of principles favoring enforcement of box-top or shrinkwrap licenses accompanying software, similar to the ruling in *ProCD* and *Gateway*, but only if certain safeguards are in place. ALI, Principles of the Law of Software Contracts § 2.02, pg. 121 (2010). In its Summary Overview of this topic, the ALI addresses the issue of terms accompanying software that can be copied once removed from its shrinkwrap:

> ... [I]n the case of shrinkwrap, a right to return the software for a reasonable period of time makes sense if transferees have no access to the terms prior to opening the software package. Otherwise, transferees have no opportunity to accept or reject the terms after opening the package and reviewing the terms. However, transferees who open the package can easily make and keep a copy of the software before returning it. Further, monitoring the transferee to detect such conduct is not feasible. Instead of an unconditional right to return opened software, § 2.02 of these Principles therefore adopts a disclosure strategy: To ensure enforcement of their standard form, software transferors should disclose terms on their website prior to a transaction and should give reasonable notice

> of and access to the terms upon initiation of the transfer, whether initiation is by telephone, Internet, or selection in a store. Shrinkwrap transferees, therefore, would have an opportunity to read terms and accept or reject them before making a commitment or, at least, before opening the software package. Transferees should be able to return opened software only if opening the package is the only way to see the terms accompanying the package.

Id. at TOPIC 2: STANDARD-FORM TRANSFERS OF GENERALLY AVAILABLE SOFTWARE; ENFORCEMENT OF THE STANDARD FORM, Summary Overview, pp. 116–17.

The published "Principles," however, are not primary law and indeed should be viewed as more tentative than the summaries of rules in the ALI's Restatement projects. Moreover, software increasingly is downloaded directly from websites, rather than from physical copies of software that are literally wrapped in plastic shrinkwrap. Nonetheless, the Principles suggest an alternative to delaying the acceptance until after goods are delivered: the burden should be on the vendor to provide access to all terms prior to the purchase. How does this compare with Judge Easterbrook's listing of options open to buyers?

4. *Poetic Relief*

Another poem by Alison Atwater will help guide us through the maze of section 2-207, or at least to entertain us while we sift its contents. Once again with apologies to Dr. Seuss, this one places section 2-207 in the role of the Grinch.

The Tale of Two-Oh-Seven

By Alison Atwater, 1L Fall 2007

Way down in the Code, in the dark depths so scary,
Lives a terrible beast all grizzled and hairy.
He hates all tradition, he hates it a bunch.
It's said that he'll eat common law for his lunch.

Now everyone knows, oh yes, everyone knows,
How a contract is formed—and here's how it goes:
Offer, acceptance, it couldn't be clearer;
The two parts must match like a face in the mirror.

But old Two-Oh-Seven, with a sinister smile
Said, "I'll make those law students think for awhile."
"I'll throw in a wrench, oh, isn't this fun?
I'll throw it right here in my Subsection One."

"All those students, they're thinking an offer's rejected
If in the acceptance new terms are injected."
"'Additional,' 'different,' are the words that I'll use
So the parties can have any terms that they choose."

"A contract will form, never mind the additions.
Yes, oh yes! Yes! I do love these provisions!"
Now old Two-Oh-Seven, his heart black as coal,
Decided he wasn't quite done with his goal.

He thought up another, more mean little twist
And added it in with a flick of his wrist.
"'Written confirmation' They never will get.
It means an agreement that's already met."

"The parties just want something formal in writing;
Oh, *this* makes my subsection really quite biting!"
He added some limits like "definite" and "season,"
And allowed the contract to fail for only one reason:

"If a party accepts but on some condition,
He'll find no contract—No! He'll just find perdition!"
And then Two-Oh-Seven danced a neat little jig
And decided he wasn't quite done with this gig.

"It's not quite enough; no, I'm really not through.
I think I'll put more here in Subsection Two."
"Those law students, aaah—they all think they see,
But the one who will fire the *last* shot is *me*!"

He took those new terms—the "additions" alone—
And decided they'd be a contract of their own.
It wasn't a normal contract he devised.
"I'll make it work different! They'll be so surprised!"

"This contract will form without even a word.
It will form soon unless an objection is heard."
"It will form without letters or emails ethereal,
'Less the change that is made be deemed quite material."

"It will form without couriers that need to be hired,
'Less the first contract says its own terms are required."
"But something's still missing," the old beast decided.
"Aha! *Here's* one thing that should be provided":

"It will be so tricky and misunderstood
If this subsection's only for merchants with goods!"[1]
"*Now* those law students, they'll never recall
Which law to use—no, they'll not know at all.

1. Even though article 2 generally applies to all transactions in goods, some provisions are limited only to merchants. Except for the first sentence of the subsection, for example, § 2-207(2) is limited to transactions between merchants.

And on the exam they'll think they're home free.
They'll never remember my Subsection Three!"
So that mean Two-Oh-Seven, he thought up another
Nasty, horrid provision to rival the other.

"What if an express contract's not formed?" he now wondered,
"Though the money's been paid and the goods are all plundered?"
"I suppose that those parties can contract here as well,
But I'll look at their writings—I'll put them through hell."

"Any terms that are found where they do not agree
I'll throw out and replace with my own UCC."
"Now," said Two-Oh-Seven as he grew rather tired,
"I think these 1Ls are sufficiently mired."

"After all this hard work, I need a vacation—
Somewhere I can party with much jubilation."
"I'll sit and relax—I think that's quite wise—
'Till Article Two I decide to revise."[2]

VI. Summary

- Under UCC § 2-205, with some limitations, the formality of a merchant's signed writing supplements consideration as an alternative basis for enforcing a merchant's promise not to revoke an offer.
- Sections 2-204 and 2-206 largely adopt common law principles of contract formation, allowing the offeror to dictate the means of acceptance, if stated unambiguously, but otherwise permitting acceptance in any reasonable way. In a specific application of these principles, section 2-206(2) states that an offer to buy goods for prompt shipment is accepted either with the seller's promise to ship promptly or with the act of actually promptly shipping. Prompt shipment constitutes acceptance even if the shipped goods are non-conforming, unless notice from the seller excludes that interpretation of the act of shipping. If acceptance is accomplished through the act of shipping, and if the circumstances reflect a need by the buyer to receive notice that shipment has begun, failure of the seller to provide notice of shipment within a reasonable time can justify canceling the contract.
- Section 2-207(1) modifies the common law mirror-image rule by recognizing contract formation even when the response to an offer varies the terms of the offer, subject to some limitations. Under the majority rule, *different* (conflicting) terms in the offer and acceptance fall out, and any resulting gap is filled by a UCC default term. *Additional* terms in the acceptance are viewed as proposals to modify

2. In 2003 the American Law Institute indeed revised article 2 of the UCC, including provisions relating to the so-called battle of the forms. State legislatures, however, rejected the ALI's proposed revisions, and the ALI in 2011 reverted to its original version of article 2, including section 2-207.

the contract formed under subsection 1. If one of the parties is a consumer, this proposal must be accepted under normal rules of mutual assent before the additional terms are added to the contract. If both parties are merchants, the additional terms can be added automatically to the contract, unless precluded by the offer or by objection, or unless they would materially alter the contract.

- If a response to an offer varies the terms of the offer and does not result in acceptance under section 2-207(1), subsection 3 provides that conduct—such as partial performance by the parties—may establish an implied-in-fact contract, whose terms will be those on which the writings agree, supplemented by default terms of the UCC.

Exercise 6.12—Practice Exams[3]

The following essay exams do not ask for arguments on both sides of a close question. Instead, they ask for a detailed explanation, in IRAC format, of relevant provisions of the law and how the law applies to facts to reach certain conclusions.

1. Q1—40 minutes

On January 7, Seller received from Buyer a mailed offer, on a printed form, to buy factory machine parts. On the first line of the form, directly after the printed term "Purchase order form," Buyer had written the following message by hand: "10 #BK-1000 machine parts, at your current catalog price, for delivery at our Newtown factory within 30 days." The purchase order form said nothing about dispute resolution or warranties.

On January 7, Seller sent a printed acknowledgment form, with a copy of the purchase order attached, with the handwritten message: "Your attached order is accepted, conditioned on your agreement to the printed terms on this form." Among the printed terms on the form were provisions: (1) requiring private arbitration of any dispute arising out of the transaction, and (2) disclaiming all express and implied warranties. Buyer did not respond, Seller shipped the machine parts within two weeks, and Buyer accepted delivery of the parts a few days later, paying for them on delivery.

When Buyer installed a few of the parts later that week, however, the parts did not perform properly, slowing down the production line. Buyer threatened to bring suit in state court unless Seller replaced the goods with nondefective ones. Seller denied any liability and asserted that Buyer had waived its right to bring suit in court. For each issue raised by these facts, explain in detail how applicable legal rules apply to the facts. If this leads to certain conclusions, you need not argue both sides. Do not discuss federal arbitration law.

2. Q2—40 Minutes

On January 7, Seller received from Buyer a mailed offer on a printed form to buy factory machine parts. On the first line of the form, directly after the printed term "Purchase order form," Buyer had written the following message by hand: "10 #BK-1000 machine parts, guaranteed to process 1,000 units per hour, at your current catalog price, for delivery at our Newtown factory within 30 days." The purchase order form said nothing about dispute resolution.

3. These practice exams, as well as the answers to them in Appendix 3, also appear in Charles R. Calleros, Law School Exams: Preparing and Writing to Win (2d ed. 2013).

On January 7, Seller sent a printed acknowledgment form, with a copy of the purchase order attached, with the handwritten message: "Your attached order is accepted. Expect delivery within two weeks." Among the printed terms on the form was a provision requiring private arbitration of any dispute arising out of the transaction. On the same day that Buyer received the acknowledgment form, Buyer read the form and sent an e-mail to Seller stating: "We object to mandatory private arbitration and reserve the right to bring any legal claims in state court."

Seller shipped the machine parts within two weeks, and Buyer accepted delivery of the parts a few days later, paying for them on delivery. When Buyer installed a few of the parts later that week, however, the parts did not perform properly, resulting in the processing of only 500 units per hour. Buyer threatened to bring suit in state court unless Seller replaced the goods with nondefective ones. Seller asserted that Buyer had waived its right to bring suit in court and that any dispute must be resolved through private arbitration.

Fully discuss whether the parties formed a contract and whether it requires disputes to be resolved in private arbitration. You may assume that both parties are merchants and that this is a transaction in goods to which the UCC applies, and thus you need not discuss those matters. Focus your answer on analyses that provide you with clear conclusions to the issues, but fully explain how you arrive at your conclusions through the law and the facts.

Chapter 7

Completeness and Formality in Contract Formation

I. Overview

This chapter will focus on two potential obstacles to enforcement of an agreement: indefiniteness and failure to satisfy the statute of frauds. These issues lie on a spectrum of problems ranging from:

- incomplete agreements in which some terms must still be negotiated, or
- agreements whose terms are spelled out with imperfect clarity or detail, to
- agreements that may be complete except for the absence of a written record.

As you study this chapter, consider the following questions:

- How does the requirement of definiteness relate to issues of mutual assent? How does it relate to practical concerns about a court's ability to enforce a contract?
- What is an "agreement to agree," and why does it present a particularly difficult issue of indefiniteness?
- In what ways do UCC provisions help to overcome indefiniteness problems in contracts for sales of goods?
- Why do statutes of frauds require some kinds of agreements to be in writing as a prerequisite to enforcement? Do statutes of frauds create as many problems as they solve?
- What kind of written document is sufficient to satisfy a statute of frauds?
- What are the judicial mitigating doctrines that permit relief even if the claimant has failed to satisfy a statute of frauds? Do they represent judicial intrusion into the legislative sphere if the statutes do not explicitly set forth mitigating doctrines? Do they instead reflect recognition of the imperfect nature of statutes of frauds and the need for equitable mitigation?

II. Definiteness

An agreement is not enforceable unless it is sufficiently definite to reflect commitment to a contract and unless it provides a court with a reasonable basis for devising a remedy.

A. Indefiniteness at Either of Two Stages

Lack of definiteness and detail in a party's proposal can suggest that the party is not ready to make an offer and instead is simply inviting negotiations. For example, the statement "I will sell you a house that meets all your needs," sounds like an enthusiastic commitment to make a deal, but no reasonable person would believe that the seller is ready to commit to the sale of some house yet to be identified at an unspecified price and location. This statement would reasonably be interpreted as simply inviting an expression of interest from a prospective buyer so that information can be exchanged and can lay the groundwork for a much more specific and detailed offer.

Even if the parties reach agreement through an appropriately detailed offer and acceptance, a dispute during performance might focus attention on a topic that is not addressed clearly in the contract, or perhaps is not addressed at all. If the court has no reasonable basis for determining the scope of the parties' rights and duties relating to that topic, then it cannot develop a remedy for breach, and thus cannot enforce the obligation.

We first encountered *Pyeatte v. Pyeatte* in Chapter 4, when exploring quasi-contract as a theory of relief. We now return to this case to examine why the express contract was too indefinite to enforce, thus necessitating resort to quasi-contract.

Pyeatte v. Pyeatte

135 Ariz. 346, 661 P.2d 196 (Ct. App. 1983)

Corcoran, Judge.

¶ 1 This is an appeal by the husband from an award of $23,000 in favor of the wife as ordered in a decree of dissolution. Two issues are before us: (1) The validity of an oral agreement entered into by the husband and wife during the marriage, whereby each spouse agreed to provide in turn the sole support for the marriage while the other spouse was obtaining further education; and, (2) whether the wife is entitled to restitution for benefits she provided for her husband's educational support in a dissolution action which follows closely upon the husband's graduation and admission to the Bar. The word "agreement" is used as a term of reference for the stated understanding between the husband and wife and not as a legal conclusion that the agreement is enforceable at law as a contract. [Other facts are set forth in Chapter 4, Section IV.A, including the agreement between Margrethe and H. Charles that she would support him through law school, after which he would support her through a graduate master's program.]

1. The Contract Claim

¶2 Although the terms and requirements of an enforceable contract need not be stated in minute detail, it is fundamental that, in order to be binding, an agreement must be definite and certain so that the liability of the parties may be exactly fixed.... In *Savoca Masonry Co. v. Homes and Son Construction Co.*, 112 Ariz. 392, 542 P.2d 817 (1975), the court found that a contractual relationship based upon an oral agreement did not exist between a general contractor and a subcontractor because "[o]nly the price and work involved were agreed upon; other provisions which might in the end have proven critical were not [agreed upon]." 112 Ariz. at 395, 542 P.2d at 820.

¶3 Upon examining the parties' agreement in this instance, it is readily apparent that a sufficient mutual understanding regarding critical provisions of their agreement did not exist. For example, no agreement was made regarding the time when appellee would attend graduate school and appellant would be required to assume their full support. Both parties concede that appellee could not have begun her masters program immediately after appellant's graduation because his beginning salary was not sufficient to provide both for her education and the couple's support. Appellee told appellant she was willing to wait a year or two until he "got on his feet" before starting her program. Nothing more definite than that was ever agreed upon. Furthermore, although appellee agreed to support appellant while he attended law school for three years, no corresponding time limitation was placed upon her within which to finish her education. Even if we assume that the agreement contemplated appellee's enrolling as a full-time student, the length of time necessary to complete a masters degree varies considerably depending upon the requirements of the particular program and the number of classes an individual elects to take at one time. Such a loosely worded agreement can hardly be said to have fixed appellant's liability with certainty.

¶4 The agreement lacks a number of other essential terms which prevent it from becoming binding. Appellee's place of education is not mentioned at all, yet there are masters programs available throughout the country. Whether or not they would be required to relocate in another state should she choose an out-of-state program was not agreed upon. Appellant testified at trial that "that particular problem was really never resolved." Nor was there any agreement concerning the cost of the program to which appellee would be entitled under this agreement. There can be several thousand dollars' difference in tuition, fees, and other expenses between any two masters programs depending upon resident status, public versus private institutions, and other factors. Appellant testified that at the time of the "contract," neither he nor his wife had any idea as to the specific dollar amounts that would be involved.

¶5 Since the trial court found that there was no "contingency expressed or implied" regarding the enforceability of the agreement in the event of a dissolution, the appellant asserts that the absence of such a mutual understanding further demonstrates the lack of specificity. A resolution of that issue is not necessary for a determination of this case.

¶6 Appellee urges us to enforce this agreement because contracts should be interpreted, whenever reasonable, in such a way as to uphold the contract, and that this is particularly true where there has been performance by one party. We are aware of these general legal concepts, and also note that reasonableness can be implied by the courts when interpreting agreements. *Shattuck v. Precision-Toyota, Inc.*, 115 Ariz. 586, 566 P.2d 1332 (1977); *Employer's Liability Assurance Corp. v. Lunt*, 82 Ariz. 320, 313 P.2d 393 (1957); *Malcoff v. Coyier*, 14 Ariz. App. 524, 484 P.2d 1053 (1971).

¶7 The court's function, however, cannot be that of contract maker. *Savoca Masony Co. v. Homes and Son Construction Co., supra.* Nor can the court create a contract simply to accomplish a purportedly good purpose. *Stearns-Roger Corp. v. Hartford Accident and Indemnity Co.*, 117 Ariz. 162, 571 P.2d 659 (1977). Our review of the record persuades us that the essential terms and requirements of this agreement were not sufficiently definite so that the obligations of the parties to the agreement could be determined.

¶8 A party will not be subjected to a contractual obligation where the character of that obligation is so indefinite and uncertain as to its terms and requirements that it is impossible to state with certainty the obligations involved. *Aztec Film Productions v. Tucson Gas and Electric Co.*, 11 Ariz. App. 241, 243, 463 P.2d 547, 549 (1969).

¶9 Based on its ruling that the agreement was enforceable, the trial court awarded appellee $23,000, the amount established by expert testimony as necessary to further her education in accordance with the agreement. On the basis of our determination that the agreement in this case is unenforceable, there can be no recovery for amounts necessary to further appellee's education.

¶10 Having decided that the agreement was not enforceable for the reasons stated above, we need not consider appellant's other arguments regarding that issue.

[Author's note: Nonetheless, the court found that Margrethe was entitled under quasi-contract to restitution of the reasonable value of her supporting her husband through law school. Even so, the court stated that Margrethe should not be awarded restitution interest that exceeded what she would have recovered under an enforceable contract: "Appellee should not recover more than the benefit of her bargain."]

Exercise 7.1 — The Cost of a Master's Degree

Did the *Pyeatte* court persuasively conclude that H. Charles's promise to Margrethe was too indefinite to enforce, thus necessitating relief under quasi-contract? Taking into consideration all the facts and reasonable inferences, could you interpret their agreement to identify a course of study that was sufficiently certain that a court could calculate the value of H. Charles's promise to support Margrethe in that educational pursuit? Or would the court be "making a contract" for the parties if it fixed "a reasonable master's program" based on all the circumstances?

Why was Margrethe's expectation interest impossible to define, but her restitution interest relatively easy to calculate? On the other hand, if Margrethe's expectation interest was impossible to define, how could it be used as a ceiling to limit recoverable restitution, as dictated by the court?

B. Curing Indefiniteness

If the remedy for a claim is flexible, such as recovery necessary to prevent injustice under promissory estoppel, indefiniteness in the expectation interest will not necessarily hinder recovery under other measures. For a discussion of this point, review the *Newton Tractor Sales* case, at paragraphs 10–16, in Chapter 4, Section III.B.

Moreover, if the parties are beyond the stage of offer and acceptance and clearly have intended to enter into a contract, a court will not lightly let the contract fail for lack of definiteness. Instead, it will take reasonable measures to clarify a contract term that is implicated in a dispute. Within some limits, indefiniteness can be cured, sometimes by the parties themselves, sometimes by external events, and sometimes by the court or by statute.

1. *Specification or Other Clarifying Events*

Sometimes an offer will not state a definite term on some topic, such as precise quantity or subject matter, but will authorize the offeree, in the acceptance, to clarify that term within a specified range. Recall, for example, that the offer by the steel mill in the *Rolling-Mill* case (Chapter 5, Section V) did not itself state a definite quantity of goods but permitted the offeree to clarify the quantity in the acceptance by ordering within the range of 2,000 to 5,000 tons of rails.

Recall as well the offer to sell 10 car loads of Mason fruit jars in the *Fairmount* case, Chapter 2, Section III. The seller's offer left indefinite both the precise date of delivery and the mix of sizes and associated prices of jars. Consider the various ways in which the court found that this indefiniteness could be cured by specifications in the acceptance, with a little help from custom in the trade:

> Appellant also insists that the contract was indefinite, because the quantity of each size of the jars was not fixed, that 10 car loads is too indefinite a specification of the quantity sold, and that appellee had no right to accept the goods to be delivered on different days. The proof shows that "10 car loads" is an expression used in the trade as equivalent to 1,000 gross, 100 gross being regarded a car load. The offer to sell the different sizes at different prices gave the purchaser the right to name the quantity of each size, and, the offer being to ship not later than May 15th, the buyer had the right to fix the time of delivery at any time before that. [citations to three precedents omitted].

Fairmount Glass Works v. Crunden-Martin Woodenware Co., 51 S.W. 196, 198 (1899).

An indefinite term in the offer and acceptance can also be made definite by later events not within the control of the parties but contemplated in the agreement. For example, the parties might have tied a wage increase in an employment contract to changes in a government cost-of-living index. For another example, recall that—unless the parties have agreed otherwise—the UCC defines the quantity in an output or requirements contract in part as "such actual output or requirements as may occur in good faith." UCC § 2-306 (2011). Although the quantity term in such a contract is not known with precision at the time of contract formation, it will become definite during performance as a party generates requirements or output in good faith operation of its business.

2. *Judicial Gap-Filling under Common Law*

a. Gap-Filling and Interpretation

If a missing term is not filled by party specification or other events contemplated by the offer or the agreement, a court must determine whether it can fill the gap through interpretation or the application of general default standards. In *Wood v. Lucy, Lady Duff-Gordon* (Chapter 3, Section II.B.2) for example, Justice Cardozo avoided a consideration problem by finding an obligation on the part of Wood to use reasonable efforts to place endorsements and create income, an implied obligation inferred from the nature of the transaction and from various provisions of the parties' agreement.

Even without such guidance from other terms in the contract, Courts will normally feel comfortable using a standard of reasonableness to fill gaps in minor terms. Imagine, for example, that a contract omits any term relating to timing of performance, not because the parties had tried and failed to agree about timing, but because the parties had not viewed timing as critically important and had simply neglected to address it during negotiations. In those circumstances, if a dispute about timing later arose, a court likely would find that implication of a "reasonable time" would be consistent with custom and with the parties' apparent intentions. The court in *Pyeatte*, for example, might have enforced the agreement if the parties had spelled out Margrethe's program of study and the only remaining uncertainty was the delay required before H. Charles could earn a sufficient salary to begin supporting Margrethe in her studies.

Similarly, if the parties have addressed a topic but have used an ambiguous term, courts will do their best to interpret the term, so that obligations can be defined and enforced. As set forth in the immediately preceding subsection, for example, the *Fairmount* court used custom in the trade to find that the term "ten car loads" of fruit jars meant the quantity of 1,000 gross.

Common sense suggests some obvious limits to judicial implication and interpretation to fill gaps and clarify essential terms, especially in transactions governed by common law. As stated by the court in *Pyeatte*, although "reasonableness can be implied by the courts when interpreting agreements," a court will not act as "contract maker." If an agreement fails to specify the location of real estate or its price, for example, and if other evidence does not reflect the parties' likely intentions, a court normally will not fill that gap by implying a "reasonable parcel of land" to be sold at a "reasonable price."

In sum, in transactions governed by common law, essential terms are not easily left to gap-filling based on general habits of others in the market or industry. As we will soon see, the UCC more liberally fills gaps in contracts for the sale of goods, although even its statutory cures for indefiniteness are not unlimited.

Starland v. Fusari

2015 WL 1220218 (D.N.J. Mar. 17, 2015)

(not for publication in F. Supp. or for citation) [footnotes omitted]

Linares, District Judge.

I. BACKGROUND

¶1 Plaintiff, Wendy Starland (hereinafter "Plaintiff"), commenced this action in 2010 against Rob Fusari (hereinafter "Fusari") and Rob Fusari Productions, LLC (collectively "Defendants"), for breach of contract and breach of fiduciary duty. Both breaches stem from Plaintiff and Defendants' agreement that Plaintiff would find, and both Parties would develop, a specific musical artist (the "Strokes Girl"). These efforts later led to the discovery and development of the artist currently known as "Lady Gaga," yet Plaintiff was never compensated for her contribution to the "artist project." The facts of this case have previously been articulated by the Court and synthesized in this Court's recent Opinion and Order granting in part Plaintiff's motion for entry of judgment, denying the motion for a constructive trust, and denying Defendants' motion for remittitur. (*See* ECF No. 553). Thus, suffice it to say that after a jury trial held in November of 2014, the jury returned a verdict in favor of Plaintiff on both causes of action and for the full amount which Plaintiff sought in damages [$7,340,696.50 in the amended judgment].

....

III. DISCUSSION

A. Judgment as a Matter of Law: Breach of Contract

¶2 ... Defendants argue the following terms were absent or vague: 1) time for performance; 2) duration of the agreement; 3) treatment of expenses incurred; and 4) revenue derived from songs written without the Plaintiff.

¶3 However, the law generally and in New Jersey does not favor voiding a contract for vagueness. *See* E. Allen Farnsworth, Contracts § 3.27 at 208–09 (2d ed. 1990). A contract may also be sufficiently certain even though one party has discretion to choose between material terms. *Kleckner v. Mutual Life Ins. Co.*, 822 F.2d 1316, 1319 (3d Cir. 1987). In line with these propositions, Plaintiff responds by claiming each of Defendants aforementioned "absent" terms, were immaterial either based on the facts of this case or in light of Plaintiff's testimony at trial, where the jury reasonably inferred a meeting of the minds. Indeed, at trial Plaintiff stated Defendant, Rob Fusari's offer relevant to their contract was the following:

> "You know, Wendy, I am looking for a girl under the age of 25 who could be the female equivalent to the lead singer of The Strokes, somebody who is edgy and bold and confident and charismatic, and somebody most importantly that you can't take your eyes off of. And if you find this person and deliver her to me, then I would approve her. If I approve her, I will sign her to my production company.
>
> When I sign her to my production company, we will develop her together. We will write songs for her, produce the album, and then shop it around to all of the, you know, use my team to shop it around to all of the record labels and publishing companies to see if we can get her a deal. And if we can get her a deal, any revenues that results from that artist project will be split 50/50 between us.
>
> And in the meantime, we will write songs for her, you know, and we will have a lot of songs ready for her for when you hopefully find her."

(Tr. 11/6/2014 27:20–29:4). Thus, with this testimony in mind, which the jury clearly found credible, the jury reasonably inferred this specific offer was made to Plaintiff, and when she performed by bringing Stefani Germanotta to Defendant, she was entitled to a 50/50 split of "any revenues that result[ed] from that artist project." (citation omitted).

¶4 The "time for performance" term that Defendants claim is indefinite, is in fact a moot issue because when Fusari deemed Stefani Germanotta was the "Strokes girl" he was looking for under his contract with Plaintiff and began working with her, it was clear that Plaintiff performed within an acceptable time period. The "duration" term Defendants refer to as vague, is contrary to Plaintiff's recount that she was to receive 50% of any revenues from the contract. Despite Defendants' reading of case law in this District, the variable (here, any revenues) to which the percentage rate (50%) is applied in a contract, "need not be determined at the time of contracting for the contract to be enforceable." *Lo Bosco v. Kure Eng'g Ltd.*, 891 F. Supp. 1020, 1026 (D.N.J. 1995).

¶5 Defendants' next argument that the contract was silent regarding "expenses" fails because Defendants produced no evidence at trial as to what specific expenses were incurred, nor any evidence that expenses were an essential term to the contract. Lastly, the fact that the contract was not specific as to which albums or songs Plaintiff was entitled to revenues on is unmoving to the Court in light of the jury's damages award. That is, the jury found that *all* albums and songs were deemed to be included in the "artist project" under the contract....

---

b. Special Problems of Agreements to Agree

Complete omission of a critical term in a contract presents a potentially serious problem of indefiniteness, because it may reflect a failure to reach final agreement on the term. In most contexts, parties place great importance on such terms as price, quantity, and description of the subject matter, so a failure to include such terms in the agreement raises strong suspicions that the parties reached a deadlock in negotiations on those terms. Problems of indefiniteness that undermine the assumption of mutual assent are particularly difficult to overcome.

Indefiniteness of this nature is made explicit in so-called "agreements to agree," in which the parties address a topic but resolve to postpone negotiations on the topic until a later date. If the parties later fail to agree, and if that term must be clarified to resolve a dispute, the contractual admission of incomplete negotiations on the topic often leaves the court with little choice but to find no agreement on that term. Unless the "agreement to agree" identifies some objective basis for determining the final term that the parties had obligated themselves to negotiate, the court will rule that the contract is not enforceable, lest the court breach the maxim that it should not create a contract for the parties. After all, if the parties specifically addressed the issue and resolved to negotiate further, the missing term can hardly be viewed as a minor and inadvertent omission subject to gap-filling with a term of reasonableness.

Exercise 7.2 — Agreement to Agree to What?

A commercial lease sets the monthly rent at $2,000 for 10 years, and it provides the lessee with an option to extend the lease for another five years when the initial 10-year term expires. The rent for the extended five-year term, if any, is governed by one of the following agreements to agree. If you were the judge, and if the parties did not successfully negotiate the second-term rent in the agreements below, would you enforce any of these alternative provisions in the commercial lease? If so, with what remedy?

(i) If and when Lessee exercises the option for a five-year extension, the Parties will renegotiate the rent, taking changes in economic conditions into their consideration.

(ii) If and when Lessee exercises the option for a five-year extension, the Parties will adjust rent according to changes in comparable rents since the beginning of the initial term of lease.

(iii) Rent for the five-year optional extension will be negotiated in good faith by the Parties if and when Lessee exercises the option.

---

3. Curing Indefiniteness under the UCC

a. General Standards under UCC § 2-204

Recognizing that buyers and sellers of goods frequently transact business in a relatively hurried and informal manner, the UCC tolerates omission of a wide range of terms in the agreement, standing ready to supply statutory default terms to fill the gaps. The UCC's standard for definiteness is set forth in section § 2-204(3), quoted and applied in the following case.

Step-Saver Data Systems, Inc. v. Wyse Technology

939 F.2d 91 (3d Cir. 1991)

Wisdom, Circuit Judge:

[As set forth in Chapter 6, Section IV.F, the court found that the "box-top license" was excluded from the contract under UCC § 2-207, raising the question of whether the contract was sufficiently definite to enforce without the excluded terms.]

¶ 1 TSL argues that the parties intended to license the copies of the program, and that several critical terms could only be determined by referring to the box-top license. Pressing the point, TSL argues that it is impossible to tell, without referring to the box-top license, whether the parties intended a sale of a copy of the program or a license to use a copy. TSL cites *Bethlehem Steel Corp. v. Litton Industries* in support of its position that any contract defined without reference to the terms of the box-top license would fail for indefiniteness.

¶ 2 From the evidence, it appears that the following terms, at the least, were discussed and agreed to, apart from the box-top license: (1) the specific goods involved; (2) the quantity; and (3) the price. TSL argues that the following terms were only defined in the box-top license: (1) the nature of the transaction, sale or license; and (2) the warranties, if any, available. TSL argues that these two terms are essential to creating a sufficiently definite contract. We disagree.

¶ 3 Section 2-204(3) of the UCC provides:

> Even though one or more terms are left open a contract for sale does not fail for indefiniteness if the parties have intended to make a contract and there is a reasonably certain basis for giving an appropriate remedy.

¶ 4 Unlike the terms omitted by the parties in *Bethlehem Steel Corp.*, the two terms cited by TSL are not "gaping holes in a multi-million dollar contract that no one but the parties themselves could fill." First, the rights of the respective parties under the federal copyright law if the transaction is characterized as a sale of a copy of the program are nearly identical to the parties' respective rights under the terms of the box-top license. Second, the UCC provides for express and implied warranties if the seller fails to disclaim expressly those warranties. Thus, even though warranties are an important term left blank by the parties, the default rules of the UCC fill in that blank.

¶ 5 We hold that contract was sufficiently definite without the terms provided by the box-top license.

---

b. UCC Gap-Fillers

As noted in *Step-Saver*, the UCC provides a whole batch of default terms that stand ready to fill gaps left in the parties' agreement. Here are a few examples:

- § 2-305 (supplying a "reasonable price" if the parties omit price but intended to reach agreement)
- § 2-306 (providing default definitions for "output" and "requirements," and for duties in an exclusive dealing arrangement)
- § 2-307 (stating that the goods must be delivered in a single delivery unless otherwise agreed)
- § 2-308 (identifying the place of delivery as seller's place of business in most cases unless otherwise agreed)
- § 2-309 (specifying that the time for performance is a "reasonable time" unless otherwise agreed)
- § 2-310 (providing that "payment is due at time and place at which the buyer is to receive the goods" unless otherwise agreed)
- § 2-312 (implying a warranty of good title unless excluded by specific language or clear circumstances)
- § 2-314 (implying a warranty of merchantability in a sale by a merchant of such goods, unless excluded or modified under § 2-316)
- § 2-315 (implying a warranty of fitness for a particular purpose in certain circumstances, unless excluded or modified under § 2-316)

The greatest deviation from common law standards appears in the first example above, section 2-305. For one thing, the fee for a service, or the price for purchasing or renting real property, would normally be viewed as a critically important term under the common law, a term that a judge would ordinarily be very reluctant to fill with a "reasonable" fee, price, or rent. The UCC's statutory gap-filling with a "reasonable price" is apparently based on a legal realist premise that parties to sales agreements often intend to go forward with their transaction even if price has not been mentioned, perhaps on the assumption that the parties are accustomed to paying and receiving the general market price for goods when none is specifically negotiated.

Even more surprising, section 2-305 goes so far as to rescue failed *agreements to agree* on the price, supplying a reasonable price at the time of delivery if "the price is left to be agreed by the parties and they fail to agree." UCC § 2-305(b) (2011). This statutory gap-filler overcomes a particularly difficult type of indefiniteness, one that reflects the parties' awareness of a term and their failure to successfully negotiate it.

The first line of section 2-305 provides needed grounding: "The parties *if they so intend* can conclude a contract for sale even though the price is not settled." (italics added). If the absence of a price term is accompanied by credible evidence that the parties did not intend to reach agreement without a price term, then even the liberal provisions of section 2-305 will not save the deal.

III. Statutes of Frauds— The Requirement of a Written Agreement

A. Overview

As illustrated by *Starland v. Fusari* earlier in this chapter, many oral agreements, if they can be proved with credible testimony, are perfectly enforceable. In *Starland*, the woman who discovered "Lady Gaga" was awarded more than $7 million on an oral agreement with a producer to split the revenue that his production company earned in promoting the recording star.

According to various "statutes of frauds," however, a few kinds of agreements are generally not enforceable unless reduced to a writing signed by the party resisting enforcement.

Three issues can potentially arise in the attempt to enforce any oral agreement that arguably falls within a statute of frauds:

i. Does an agreement fall within one of the categories for which the statute requires a writing?

ii. If yes, is the agreement memorialized in a signed writing that is sufficient to satisfy the statute's mandate?

iii. If the agreement falls within the statute but does not satisfy its writing requirement, is the party seeking enforcement nonetheless entitled to a remedy based on exceptions, or mitigating doctrines, to the statute of frauds?

Long-standing statutes of frauds enacted in the states are patterned at least loosely after a now largely repealed Act of English Parliament of 1677. Although statutes of frauds were designed to prevent enforcement of nonexistent oral contracts advanced through fraudulent testimony, they can also help to undermine genuine intentions when a party resists enforcement of a seriously intended oral agreement on the ground that it was not reduced to writing. To balance these competing pressures, courts tend to minimize the impact of statutes of frauds, by: (i) narrowly interpreting the categories of contracts that fall within the statute, (ii) interpreting the writing requirement to require only the essential terms of the agreement, allowing other terms to be proved through other means, and (iii) providing equitable relief from the operation of the statute when the party seeking performance has partly performed, has otherwise created grounds for estoppel by engaging in certain kinds of reliance, or at least is deserving of restitution for benefits conferred under the oral agreement.

B. Example of Coverage: Arizona's Statute of Frauds

The typical statute of frauds requires a written contract for such transactions as sales of real estate, agreements for services that cannot be performed in one year, and agreements to guarantee the debt of another. They also typically apply to certain sales of goods, although that provision is superseded (or in some states supplemented) by the later enacted UCC § 2-201 (2011). Arizona's general statute of frauds—which was taken from provisions in the California and Texas statutes of frauds—provides an illustration:

> ARIZ. REV. STAT. ANN. § 44-101 (2017). Statute of frauds
>
> No action shall be brought in any court in the following cases unless the promise or agreement upon which the action is brought, or some memorandum thereof, is in writing and signed by the party to be charged, or by some person by him thereunto lawfully authorized:
>
> 1. To charge an executor or administrator upon any promise to answer for any debt or damages due from his testator or intestate out of his own estate.
> 2. To charge a person upon a promise to answer for the debt,. default or miscarriage of another.
> 3. To charge a person upon any agreement made upon consideration of marriage, except a mutual promise to marry.
> 4. Upon a contract to sell or a sale of goods or choses in action of the value of five hundred dollars or more,.... [supplemented by Arizona's UCC statute of frauds].
> 5. Upon an agreement which is not to be performed within one year from the making thereof.
> 6. Upon an agreement for leasing for a longer period than one year, or for the sale of real property or an interest therein. Such agreement, if made by an agent of the party sought to be charged, is invalid unless the authority of the agent is in writing, subscribed by the party sought to be charged.
> 7. Upon an agreement authorizing or employing an agent or broker to purchase or sell real property, or mines, for compensation or a commission.
> 8. Upon an agreement which by its terms is not to be performed during the lifetime of the promisor, or an agreement to devise or bequeath any property, or to make provision for any person by will.
> 9. Upon a contract, promise, undertaking or commitment to loan money or to grant or extend credit, or a contract, promise, undertaking or commitment to extend, renew or modify a loan or other extension of credit involving both an amount greater than two hundred fifty thousand dollars and not made or extended primarily for personal, family or household purposes.

In addition, Arizona's enactment of the UCC statute of frauds applies to agreements "for the sale of goods for the price of five hundred dollars or more." ARIZ. REV. STAT. ANN. § 47-2201(A) (2017).

Judicial treatment of category 4 of Arizona's general statute of frauds, "an agreement which is not to be performed within one year," provides a good example of judicial efforts to interpret the scope of the statute narrowly:

> Under Arizona law, contracts which are not to be performed within one year from the making of the contract must be in writing. Ariz. Rev. Stat. § 44-101. The one-year provision of the statute of frauds is narrowly construed. John D. Calamari & Joseph M. Perillo, *Contracts* § 19-17 (3d ed. 1987). The mere possibility that performance can be completed within one year—even if not contemplated by the parties—is usually sufficient to remove the agreement from the statute of frauds.... *Healey v. Coury,* 162 Ariz. 349, 353, 783 P.2d 795, 799 (App.1989) (statute requires impossibility of performance within a year). The fact that performance is completed in more than a year is immaterial. *Healey v. Coury,* 162 Ariz. at 353, 783 P.2d at 799.

Western Chance No. 2, Inc. v. KFC Corp., 957 F.2d 1538, 1541 (9th Cir. 1992).

C. Satisfying the Writing Requirement

1. Arizona's General Statute of Frauds

If an agreement falls within a general statute of frauds, it is not enforceable unless it is memorialized in a written document, or a combination of related documents, signed by the party against whom enforcement is sought.[1] The written document need not set forth all the terms of the agreement, and thus can leave some terms for proof by testimony, so long as the document contains the "essential terms" and shows that the parties reached a final agreement; a document recording ongoing negotiations does not suffice.

Under those standards, the written documents in *Western Chance*, cited in the previous paragraph, were insufficient to satisfy the statute of frauds for two reasons. From the following passage, identify and explain those reasons:

> Western Chance also contends that the oral agreement is evidenced by sufficient memoranda. Specifically, it argues that two letters sent by Robinson's office attest to KFC's grant of [exclusive rights to develop the Tucson market]. To satisfy the statute of frauds, a memorandum must state with reasonable certainty the identity of the parties, the subject matter of the agreement, and the essential terms. John D. Calamari & Joseph M. Perillo, *Contracts* § 19-29 (3d ed. 1987). It also must be signed by the party to be charged. *Id.* at § 19-31. The parties need not intend the writing to be

1. An Arizona statute governing real estate broker agreements, as a supplement to its companion provision in the general Arizona statute of frauds, exceptionally provides that such agreements are not enforceable unless signed by *all* parties. ARIZ. REV. STAT. ANN. § 32-2151.02(A) (2005) (as interpreted in *Young v. Rose*, 230 Ariz. 433, 286 P.3d 518 (Ct. App. 2012)).

> the full and final expression of their agreement; an informal letter setting forth the required information can suffice. *Custis v. Valley Nat'l Bank,* 92 Ariz. 202, 205–06, 375 P.2d 558, 561 (1962). Unless the memorandum is intended to be the complete expression of the parties' agreement, parol evidence [such as oral testimony] may be admitted to explain its terms. *Crone v. Amado,* 69 Ariz. 389, 397, 214 P.2d 518, 523 (1950). However, parol evidence cannot be used to cure a deficient memorandum. [citation omitted]
>
> The letters from Robinson's office do not state the central term of the alleged oral agreement; they do not intimate that Western Chance's presence in Tucson would be exclusive. The letters did speak of Western Chance's options "for the City of Tucson," and expressed KFC's interest in "working with (Western Chance) regarding the city of Tucson." At no point do the letters refer to an exclusive territory. Moreover, one letter states that Western Chance's "option is tentative until all paper work is cleared and we can submit your application to our Executive Committee for final approval." The district court properly found as a matter of law that the extrinsic evidence submitted by Western Chance could not cure this fatal deficiency. *See Custis v. Valley Nat'l Bank,* 92 Ariz. at 206, 375 P.2d at 561.

2. Arizona's UCC Statute of Frauds

For a sale of goods, the UCC statute of frauds is particularly lax about the terms that must be in writing. As adopted in Arizona, it requires only:

> some writing sufficient to indicate that a contract for sale has been made between the parties and signed by the party against whom enforcement is sought or by his authorized agent or broker. A writing is not insufficient because it omits or incorrectly states a term agreed upon but the contract is not enforceable under this subsection beyond the quantity of goods shown in such writing.

Ariz. Rev. Stat. Ann. § 47-2201(A) (2017) (enacting UCC § 2-201(1) (2011)).

Indeed, between merchants, even if the writing is not signed by the party against whom enforcement is sought, that party may be deemed to have adopted a sufficient writing signed by the party seeking enforcement:

> Between merchants if within a reasonable time a writing in confirmation of the contract and sufficient against the sender is received and the party receiving it has reason to know its contents, it satisfies the requirements of subsection (1) of this section against such party unless written notice of objection to its contents is given within ten days after it is received.

Ariz. Rev. Stat. Ann. § 47-2201(B) (2017) (enacting UCC § 2-201(2) (2011)).

The next excerpt discusses the general requirements under UCC § 2-201(1), as enacted in Arizona.

Koenen v. Royal Buick Co.

162 Ariz. 376, 783 P.2d 822 (1989)

....

¶1 Royal Buick next argues that the purchase order fails to satisfy the requirements of the statute of frauds. A.R.S. § 47-2201(A) provides that:

> [A] contract for the sale of goods for the price of five hundred dollars or more is not enforceable ... unless there is some writing sufficient to indicate that a contract for sale has been made between the parties and signed by the party against whom enforcement is sought or by his authorized agent or broker. A writing is not insufficient because it omits or incorrectly states a term agreed upon but the contract is not enforceable under this subsection beyond the quantity of goods shown in such writing.

¶2 A.R.S. § 47-2201 is identical to § 2-201 of The Uniform Commercial Code (UCC). In interpreting this section of the UCC, we look to other states. This provision has been interpreted to mean that a contract for sale need not contain all material terms and that such material terms as are included need not be precisely stated. The writing need only afford a basis for believing that offered oral evidence rests on a real transaction. *Howard Constr. Co. v. Jeff-Cole Quarries, Inc.*, 669 S.W.2d 221, 227 (Mo. App. 1983). This interpretation follows UCC § 2-201, Official Comment One, which states in part:

> The required writing need not contain all the material terms of the contract and such material terms as are stated need not be precisely stated. All that is required is that the writing afford a basis for believing that the offered oral evidence rests on a real transaction.... The only term which must appear is the quantity term which need not be accurately stated but recovery is limited to the amount stated. The price, time and place of payment or delivery, the general quality of the goods, or any particular warranties may all be omitted.

¶3 The statute of frauds does not require that the writing contain the price. Courts have consistently held that the statute of frauds is satisfied so long as the writing evidences a contract for the sale of goods, is signed by the party against whom enforcement is sought, and specifies a quantity. *See, e.g., Alaska Indep. Fishermen's Mktg. Ass'n v. New England Fish Co.,* 15 Wash. App. 154, 157–59, 548 P.2d 348, 351 (1976).

¶4 Royal Buick argues that because neither price nor availability were set forth in the purchase order and the possibility existed that Royal Buick might not receive a GNX for sale, the agreement contained impermissibly "futuristic" language. *See* J. White & R. Summers, *Uniform Commercial Code* §§ 2–4 (3d ed. 1988); *Conaway v. Twentieth Century Corp.*, 491 Pa. 189, 200–01, 420 A.2d 405, 411 (1980). In *Conaway,* the writings contained the words "plan," "offer," and "tentative stages," and the trial court concluded that the writings were part of ongoing negotiations rather than a contract.

¶5 In this case, the purchase order was signed by Koenen and by Yalen and Sager of Royal Buick. The quantity specified was one GNX Regal. In addition, there was sufficient evidence for the trial court to determine that the purchase order indicated that a contract for sale had been created. The purchase order included the type of vehicle, optional equipment ("loaded"), and noted receipt of a $500 down payment. The purchase order was sufficient to indicate that a contract for sale existed between Koenen and Royal Buick.

....

---

3. *Electronic Signature Laws*

The federal Electronic Signatures in Global and National Commerce Act (ESIGN Act), 15 U.S.C. §§7001–7006 (2009 & Supp. 2018), and the state Uniform Electronic Transactions Act (UETA) provide that a saved and retrievable electronic record, with symbols intended to operate as an electronic signature, will satisfy the requirements in other laws that a document be memorialized in a signed writing if the parties have consented to transacting business electronically. For an example of one state's version of UETA, see CAL. CIV. C. §§1633.1–1633.17 (West 2011 & Supp. 2019).

Even when a transaction took place prior to the effective date of electronic signature statutes, some courts have found that email messages could satisfy the statute of frauds, without regard to the absence of a handwritten signature. *E.g.*, *Lamle v. Mattel, Inc.*, 394 F.3d 1355, 1362 (Fed. Cir. 2005) (email ending with typed phrase, "Best regards Mike Bucher," satisfied requirement of statute of frauds of a signed writing); *Cloud Corp. v. Hasbro, Inc.*, 314 F.3d 289, 295–96 (7th Cir. 2002). Will courts next recognize that text messages on smartphones can satisfy the statute of frauds? *See St. John's Holdings, LLC v. Two Electronics, LLC*, 2016 WL 1460477, at *9, not reported in N.E.3d (Mass. Land Ct. 2016) (finding that responsive text message ending with typed name, "Tim," satisfied statute of frauds), *aff'd*, 94 N.E.3d 880 (table) (2017).

D. Exceptions or Mitigating Doctrines

1. *Exceptions to a State's General Statute of Frauds*

The introduction to this unit on the statute of frauds mentioned mitigating doctrines of part performance, estoppel, and unjust enrichment. These doctrines may overlap, as described in *Owens v M.E. Schepp Ltd. Partnership*, 218 Ariz. 222, 182 P.2d 664 (2008).

A typical statute of frauds does not itself set forth exceptions based on these equitable doctrines. Accordingly, ask yourself whether a judicial exception to the statute of frauds, based on equity, is an appropriate exercise of judicial authority, or whether it constitutes—in the words of one early critic—"a parasite, strangely coddled and nurtured by judges, who have allowed themselves from time to time to be carried away by prejudice from ... special circumstances." Jesse W. Lilienthal, *Judicial Repeal of the Statute of Frauds*, 9 HARV. L. REV. 455 (1896).

The next case examines estoppel as a means of avoiding the statute of frauds.

Munoz v. Kaiser Steel Corp.

156 Cal. App. 3d 965, 203 Cal. Rptr. 345 (1984)
[footnotes omitted]

Kaufman, Acting Presiding Justice.

¶1 Anthony Munoz (plaintiff) filed an amended complaint against Kaiser Steel Corporation (Kaiser or defendant) alleging one cause of action for breach of an oral employment contract for a minimum of three years.... Defendant's motion for summary judgment was granted as to the cause of action for breach of contract on the basis of the statute of frauds....

¶2 Plaintiff appeals contending that the trial court erred in granting defendant's motions for summary judgment and nonsuit.

Facts

....

¶3 In March 1979 plaintiff was living in the State of Texas with his wife and two children. In a period of about six months plaintiff had been laid off from two separate jobs, the last of which he had held for about five months. Plaintiff had decided to seek more stable employment in the Southern California area. He had been born in California and raised in Redlands and his parents and a brother were living in that area.

¶4 Plaintiff came to Southern California and sought job interviews. On March 14, 1979, unsolicited, he dropped into the personnel department at Kaiser Steel Corporation in Fontana, explained his qualifications and asked whether a job might be available. He was informed by the personnel department that there was. He was given an interview with Mr. Steritz, the coke plant superintendent, following which he was tentatively hired as a labor foreman at a salary of $1,800 per month pending management confirmation. Although Mr. Steritz made no specific statement concerning the duration of employment and did not tell plaintiff his employment would last three years or any other specific time, Mr. Steritz stated to plaintiff that he "would be trained for at least three years." Assertedly, plaintiff understood this statement to mean that he was assured employment with defendant for a minimum of three years.

¶5 Plaintiff returned to Texas and on or about May 1, 1979, was informed by telephone that his employment was confirmed. He commenced work for Kaiser on May 7, 1979. Then, in the words of counsel: "At that point my client does two things: He decides to permanently move to California and he sells his home. He sold his home in Dallas, Texas. He comes to Highland, California, and purchases a new home." Plaintiff's Texas home had been purchased for approximately $27,500 and was sold for approximately $57,000. The purchase price of the house in Highland, California, was approximately $60,000, and the down payment of approximately $5,000 came from the proceeds of sale of the house in Texas. Plaintiff's monthly mortgage payments in Texas had been approximately $267; his monthly mortgage payments on the Highland house were approximately $607 exclusive of taxes and insurance. Counsel's opening statement indicated that some months after his discharge from employment at Kaiser, plaintiff was unable to pay the mortgage payments on the Highland house and "lost it."

¶6 Plaintiff received approximately three weeks of on the job training in the position as labor foreman. Although plaintiff was apparently not informed of it, his supervisor expressed some dissatisfaction with his performance and he was soon transferred to another job known as "top foreman." Plaintiff continued in that job until he was discharged on or about October 31, 1979. On November 9, 1979, Mr. Steritz wrote a letter to plaintiff explaining the reason for his termination and providing him a reference for use in seeking other employment. The letter read in part: "As I told you when you left, Tony, you were not being let go because of any particular fault on your part. Kaiser Steel is and will be in a period of contraction, which includes the lay off of many experienced supervisors from the discontinued facilities. In order to learn the Coke Plant operation starting from ground zero as you did, it takes a minimum of two to three years before you can compete with experienced personnel. I realized this when I hired you, and had things been otherwise we would have given you time to mature in your experience."

¶7 After being terminated at Kaiser, plaintiff diligently sought other employment. Although he obtained some part-time, temporary work at odd jobs, he was not successful in securing full-time employment until about June 1981 when he went to work as a state police officer at Chico State University. He commenced this action March 10, 1980.

The Summary Judgment

....

¶8 If plaintiff's alleged cause of action for breach of contract is barred by the statute of frauds, the summary judgment was properly granted; otherwise not. We conclude it was.

¶9 Civil Code section 1624 provides in pertinent part: "The following contracts are invalid, unless the same, or some note or memorandum thereof, is in writing and subscribed by the party to be charged or by his agent: [¶] 1. An agreement that by its terms is not to be performed within a year from the making thereof;...."

¶10 Plaintiff alleged and asserted both in his deposition and in counsel's opening statement an oral employment contract for a minimum of three years. Thus, by its terms, the employment contract claimed by plaintiff was not to be performed within a year from its making and comes within the purview of section 1624, subdivision 1, of the Civil Code. (*See Ruinello v. Murray* (1951) 36 Cal. 2d 687, 688–689, 227 P.2d 251;....)

¶ 11 The only remaining question in review of the summary judgment is whether or not there existed a triable issue of fact as to defendant's being estopped to assert the statute of frauds. While in most instances the existence of an estoppel is a question of fact, summary judgment is appropriate if no estoppel could exist as a matter of law. (*State of California v. Haslett Co.* (1975) 45 Cal. App. 3d 252, 256, 119 Cal. Rptr. 78.)

¶ 12 The law governing the existence of an estoppel to assert the statute of frauds is succinctly and accurately summarized in *Ruinello v. Murray* (1951) 36 Cal. 2d 687, 689, 227 P.2d 251: "Plaintiff contends that he has alleged sufficient facts to estop defendant from relying on the statute of frauds. There can be no estoppel unless plaintiff will suffer unconscionable injury or defendant will be unjustly enriched if the oral contract is not enforced." (*Monarco v. Lo Greco*, [1950] 35 Cal. 2d 621, 623–624 [220 P.2d 737] and cases there cited.) Plaintiff has not alleged facts that meet either of these conditions.

¶ 13 "To state a cause of action based on unconscionable injury it is not enough to allege that plaintiff gave up existing employment to work for defendant. (*Murdock v. Swanson* [1948] 85 Cal. App. 2d 380, 385 [193 P.2d 81]; ...) He must set forth his rights under the contract given up and show that they *were so valuable that unconscionable injury would result from refusing to enforce the oral contract* with defendant. (*See, e.g., Seymour v. Oelrichs* [1909] 156 Cal. 782, 792...." (Emphasis added.)) The touchstone under California law is unjust enrichment of the party to be estopped or unconscionable injury to the other party.... *Ruinello v. Murray, supra*, 36 Cal. 2d 687, 689, 227 P.2d 251.

¶ 14 Here, as a matter of law, there is neither. Plaintiff was employed by defendant from May 7 until October 31, 1979, and received a salary of $1,700 a month for his services during that time. No contention is made that plaintiff was not reasonably and adequately compensated during the time he was employed by defendant. "No unjust enrichment results when the promisee has received the reasonable value of his services." (*Ruinello v. Murray, supra*, 36 Cal. 2d 687, 690, 227 P.2d 251.)

¶ 15 Nor would the evidence support an estoppel. Contrary to an allegation in plaintiff's pleadings, he did not relinquish existing employment to accept the job with Kaiser. He was unemployed at the time, having lost two jobs within a period of about six months in Texas. Plaintiff had grown up in the Redlands area, his parents and brother were living in that area and he sought employment only in Southern California because "I wanted to come back to where I was born and raised."

¶ 16 Plaintiff estimated his expenses in moving from Texas to California at about $2,000. He sold his house in Texas for approximately $57,000 and purchased a comparable house in Highland for approximately $60,000. The mortgage payment on the Highland home exclusive of taxes and insurance was approximately $607 a month whereas the mortgage payment on the Texas home had been approximately $267 a month. However, plaintiff realized a substantial profit and apparently a substantial cash sum from the sale of the Texas house.

....

¶ 17 Plaintiff's reliance on *Seymour v. Oelrichs, supra*, 156 Cal. 782, 106 P. 88, is entirely misplaced. In that case the plaintiff had given up a secure job as Captain of Detectives in the Police Department of the City and County of San Francisco to accept a position with the defendant in reliance on defendant's promise to reduce the oral agreement to writing. (156 Cal. at pp. 785–786, 795–800, 106 P. 88.)

¶ 18 Plaintiff's reliance on *Alaska Airlines v. Stephenson* (9th Cir. 1954) 217 F.2d 295, 298, is unwarranted for essentially the same reason. In that case the court decided to apply Alaskan law, but finding none on point, it adopted section 90 of the Restatement of Contracts dealing with promissory estoppel. The court noted that promissory estoppel is principally utilized as a substitute for consideration but that the same principle could apply to eliminate the necessity of a writing under the statute of frauds if the additional factor of a promise to reduce the contract to writing were present. Finding that factor present and also finding the plaintiff had given up his right to another job in reliance on the oral agreement, it was held that the statute of frauds would not bar recovery. Here, there is no claim or evidence that defendant ever promised to reduce the oral agreement to writing, nor is there any evidence that plaintiff gave up secure, existing employment to go to work for Kaiser. On the contrary, the evidence establishes plaintiff was unemployed and had been unable to maintain stable employment in Texas.

¶ 19 Plaintiff's reliance on ... *Bondi v. Jewels by Edwar Ltd.* (1968) 267 Cal. App. 2d 672, 73 Cal. Rptr. 494 on the issue of estoppel is also unwarranted.... *Bondi* involved an oral agreement with an alleged duration of "so long as plaintiff should satisfactorily perform." (*Bondi, supra*, at p. 674, 73 Cal. Rptr. 494.) As the court in *Bondi* expressly recognized, such a contract is for an indefinite duration, may be performed within one year, and does not come within the statute of frauds as embodied in Civil Code section 1624, subdivision 1. (267 Cal. App. 2d at pp. 676–677, 73 Cal. Rptr. 494, and cases there cited.)

¶ 20 Neither is section 139 of the Restatement of Contracts Second of aid to plaintiff. It reads in part: "(1) A promise which the promisor should reasonably expect to induce action or forbearance on the part of the promisee or a third person and which does induce the action or forbearance is enforceable notwithstanding the Statute of Frauds if injustice can be avoided only by enforcement of the promise...."

¶ 21 It could well be argued that, as a matter of law, Kaiser could not reasonably have expected Mr. Steritz's statement that plaintiff "would be trained for at least three years" to be relied on by plaintiff as a promise of employment for a minimum term of three years. However, we do not deem it necessary to resolve that question. As we have indicated, the law is clear in California that to avoid the bar of the statute of frauds the plaintiff must demonstrate either unconscionable injury to himself or herself or unjust enrichment to the defendant. (*Ruinello v. Murray, supra*, 36 Cal. 2d 687, 689, 227 P.2d 251, and cases there cited.) While so far as we are informed no appellate case has discussed the applicability of section 139 of the Restatement of Contracts Second to California law, we interpret the prerequisite in section 139 that "injustice can be avoided only by enforcement of the promise" as meaning essentially the same thing substantively as the cited California authorities mean by their requirement of unjust enrichment to the defendant or unconscionable injury to the plaintiff.

....

Conclusion and Disposition

¶ 22 As a matter of law, the oral employment contract asserted by plaintiff is unenforceable on account of the statute of frauds as embodied in subdivision 1 of Civil Code section 1624.... With no triable issue of material fact existing and with a complete defense established by the statute of frauds, the summary judgment and nonsuit were properly granted. The judgment is therefore affirmed as to both orders.

---

2. Exceptions to Arizona's UCC Statute of Frauds

Even if a sale of goods for a price of $500 or more does not meet the UCC's minimal requirements for a written memorandum, the UCC provides for several mitigating doctrines, as set forth by Arizona's version:

> A contract which does not satisfy the requirements of subsection A of this section but which is valid in other respects is enforceable:
>
> 1. If the goods are to be specially manufactured for the buyer and are not suitable for sale to others in the ordinary course of the seller's business and the seller, before notice of repudiation is received and under circumstances which reasonably indicate that the goods are for the buyer, has made either a substantial beginning of their manufacture or commitments for their procurement; or
> 2. If the party against whom enforcement is sought admits in his pleading, testimony or otherwise in court that a contract for sale was made, but the contract is not enforceable under this provision beyond the quantity of goods admitted; or
> 3. With respect to goods for which payment had been made and accepted or which have been received and accepted (section 47-2606).

ARIZ. REV. STAT. ANN. § 47-2201(C) (2017) (enacting U.C.C. § 2-201(3) (2011)). Subsections (1) and (3) owe much to the traditional part-performance exception. Subsection (2) makes it clear that—under the UCC Statute of Frauds—the absence of a writing is no defense once the party resisting enforcement admits in court to the existence of an oral contract.

Exercise 7.3 — Exceptions and Mitigating Doctrines

As they admired a vintage car at a car show, the car's owner (Owner) orally agreed to sell the car to a car collector (Collector) for $60,000, with delivery and payment due in one week. When Collector asked for a written memorandum of the agreement, Owner responded: "Don't worry, I know all about these kinds of sales. An oral agreement to sell a used car is perfectly enforceable in this state. Our handshake is as good as a 10-page written contract." They exchanged business cards, shook hands, and departed. Collector then quickly sold three other cars at slight losses to raise money for the $60,000 vintage car. Owner, however, sold the vintage car to another buyer for $70,000 and denies having agreed to sell it to Collector. Collector had not yet paid Owner any money.

Collector seeks to collect money damages in the enforcement of the oral agreement, or at least to recover $6,000 in reliance costs and losses incurred in selling his other cars. Collector cannot satisfy the writing requirement under the UCC Statute of Frauds. Do any of the exceptions under UCC § 2-201(3) provide him a way to avoid operation of the statute? Assuming that Collector could establish the relevant facts, would you interpret the UCC to permit application of traditional estoppel theory, such as that which mitigates the general statutes of frauds in most states, or should UCC § 2-201(3) be viewed as the exclusive source of exceptions for the UCC statute of frauds? If the traditional estoppel argument is available to Collector, would you grant relief based on equitable estoppel in this case? If so, on what factual basis, and what relief would you provide?

IV. Summary

- An agreement is not enforceable if it is so indefinite that a court cannot determine whether a party breached or cannot fashion a remedy for breach. In fact, indefiniteness in the offer can raise questions about whether an agreement was reached at all. "Agreements to agree" raise questions about definiteness at this early stage of mutual assent.
- Gap-filling provisions in the UCC, including one that liberally cures missing price terms, help to cure indefiniteness in contracts for the sale of goods.
- State statutes of frauds are designed to prevent fraudulent claims of oral contracts in certain kinds of transactions. However, they can bar enforcement of oral agreements intended by the parties to be enforceable. Consequently, courts tend to interpret the statutes narrowly and to recognize equitable mitigating doctrines.

V. Review

It may have occurred to you that the same set of facts could raise issues about

- whether the parties reached agreement,
- whether any such agreement is sufficiently definite to enforce, and
- whether any agreement reached by the parties satisfies the statute of frauds.

The following judicial opinion is unpublished and therefore cannot be cited in a brief to a court in many states. Nonetheless, it provides a good example of a court's at least partial analysis of each of these three overlapping issues. Try to identify the passage in the opinion that relates to each of the issues listed in bullet points above. If you were presenting the analysis as an exam answer, could you separate your discussion of some of the issues more distinctly, placing each more clearly in a separate IRAC? In what order would you discuss the issues?

Carimati di Carimate v. Ginsglobal Index Funds

2009 U.S. Dist. Lexis 96641, 2009 WL3233538 (C.D. Cal. Sept. 30, 2009) [unpublished] [footnotes omitted]

....

¶ 1 Defendants contend that this Court should grant their motion to dismiss Plaintiff's breach of contract claim because Plaintiff has failed to prove that a contract was formed.... As will be discussed, *infra*, the terms of the MOU [Memorandum of Understanding] as modified by the February emails could create an enforceable agreement [for equal sharing of future earnings in their joint venture].

¶ 2 [The parties had agreed in the MOU to application of Delaware law to any dispute arising out of the transaction.] Defendants contend that because the February emails fail to satisfy Delaware's Statute of Frauds, Plaintiff's breach of contract action is barred. Delaware's Statute of Frauds, 6 Del. C. § 2714(a), requires that agreements "not to be performed within the space of one year ... be reduced to writing, or some memorandum, or notes thereof, are signed by the party to be charged therewith, or some other person thereunto by the party lawfully authorized in writing." ...

¶ 3 Defendants ... argue that the February emails fail to satisfy the Statute of Frauds because they do not confirm a definitive agreement, but merely "reflect an exchange of preliminary information and invitation to further discussion." (Motion to Dismiss at 13.) Plaintiff argues that the February emails contain the identifying factors and material terms necessary to satisfy the Statute of Frauds. Delaware caselaw appears silent on the issue. In their motion, Defendants rely on *Oracle Corp. v. Falotti*, 187 F. Supp. 2d 1184 (N.D. Cal. 2001), where, under California law, the court determined that an email failed to satisfy the Statute of Frauds because it was silent as to how long the Plaintiff was to be employed by Defendant, a term material to Plaintiff's breach of contract claim. *Oracle*, 187 F. Supp. 2d. at 1205. Defendants also rely on *Hugh Symons Group, plc. v. Motorola Inc.*, 292 F.3d 466 (5th Cir. 2002), where the Court held that the email failed to satisfy Texas's Statute of Frauds because it pertained to information "being exchanged between parties, one of whom is developing a product not yet in production" and because "there [was] no language expressing or contemplating a final agreement." *Hugh Symons*, 292 F.3d 466, 470.

¶ 4 Here, in response to Plaintiff's February 18, 2008 email confirming Plaintiff's understanding on passing worldwide sales through HIG, Defendant Ginsberg responded, "Yes I agree with your comments re splitting all future initiatives using

Hindsight Investment entity—no problem." (FAC Ex. 4.) The email signatures clearly identify the parties. Unlike in *Oracle* or *Hugh Symons*, Defendant Ginsberg's email that he "agreed" with Plaintiff's comments regarding "splitting all future initiatives" appears to indicate both language expressing a final agreement so as to satisfy the Statute of Frauds, and mutual assent that would lead an objectively reasonable person to conclude that the parties intended to be bound by those terms. Furthermore, shortly after the February emails were exchanged, Defendant Ginsberg allegedly sent Plaintiff an encouraging email indicating he was pleased with the work Plaintiff had been doing pursuant to their new agreement, also indicating mutual assent to the terms proposed by the February emails in conjunction with the MOU. (FAC Ex. 5.) In *Lamle v. Mattel, Inc.*, 394 F.3d 1355 (Fed. Cir. 2005), the Court made clear that "if a court ... can plainly determine from the memorandum the identity of the parties to the contract, the nature of its subject matter and its essential terms, the memorandum will be held to be adequate [with respect to the Statute of Frauds]." *Lamle*, 394 F.3d at 1361 (applying California law).

¶5 Moreover, the equal sharing agreement embodied in the MOU and February emails contains the elements essential to create an enforceable contract. Delaware courts will not enforce an agreement that is indefinite as to a material or essential term. [citation omitted]. Defendants rely on a Delaware court ruling that held that "price is an essential ingredient in every contract." *Raisler Sprinkler Co. v. Automatic Sprinkler Co.*, 36 Del. 57, ... (Del. Super. Ct. 1934). However, ... "the question of what is an essential term is often a question of fact involving a determination of each party's intent to be bound and thus must frequently be decided by a jury." *Pantzer v. Shields Devel. Co.*, 660 F. Supp. 56, 60 (D. Del. 1986).

¶6 Clearly, how much Plaintiff would earn as a result of dealings with the Hindsight Product is an essential component of the contract. Defendants argue that the contract formed by the MOU and February emails is unenforceable because Plaintiff's fee is "legally indefinite" and "nothing more to agree at a later time." (Motion to Dismiss at 14.) As discussed, *supra*, the MOU clearly states that Plaintiff and Defendant "shall enter into an equal fee sharing arrangement." (FAC Ex.1.) The February emails reference Plaintiff's understanding that the proceeds from his future initiatives would be "divided as agreed." (FAC Ex. 3, pp. 30–31.) While, the February emails indicate an ongoing discussion between Plaintiff and Defendant Ginsberg regarding the proceeds from past initiatives, Defendant confirmed in a February 19, 2008 email that he "agree[d] with [Plaintiff's] comments re splitting all future initiatives." (FAC Ex. 4.)

For the foregoing reasons, I DENY Defendant's motion to dismiss the first cause of action.

Chapter 8

Grounds for Avoidance

I. Overview and Form of Relief

We have already seen that an agreement generally will not be enforceable if it is unsupported by consideration, if it is too indefinite to enforce, or if it violates a statute of frauds. In such a case, neither party can use the courts to obtain expectation interest, the value of the unperformed promise of the other party. Still, in some cases of this type, quasi-contract could be available to grant restitution of a benefit conferred by a party who partially or fully performed on the assumption that the agreement was enforceable. (Recall *Pyeatte v. Pyeatte*, in which the wife supported her husband through law school, pursuant to an indefinite contract.)

Closely related are several defenses to contract enforcement that we will group under the label "grounds for avoidance." In these cases, the parties appeared to strike a definite bargain with mutual assent, and they satisfied formal requirements such as the statute of frauds. Nonetheless, the integrity of the mutual assent might be questioned, and important policies could be undermined, if a court finds a serious problem relating to the parties' mutual assumptions during bargaining or to the status or behavior of one of the parties at that time. If so, the court may *avoid* the contract, which means to annul it.

In a different context, when parties mutually agree to *rescind* their agreement, they essentially enter into a second agreement to annul the first one. In so doing, they "abrogate [the contract] and undo it from the beginning; that is, not merely to release the parties from further obligation to each other in respect to the subject of the contract, but to annul the contract and restore the parties to the relative positions which they would have occupied if no such contract had ever been made." *Reed v. McLaws*, 56 Ariz. 556, 562–63, 110 P.2d 222, 225 (1941). The effect is the same when the court *avoids* the contract at the behest of a party because of a defect such as misrepresentation during bargaining. Indeed, as will become apparent in this chapter, many courts use the word "rescission" interchangeably with "avoidance" to refer to a court's action to "undo" a contract because of a defect during formation.

If only one party wants to avoid the contract, and he has grounds for doing so, he can bring an action in court for avoidance or rescission. Alternatively, he could refuse to perform, wait to be sued for breach of contract, and assert grounds for avoidance as a defense to the contract suit. Either way, the court will avoid the contract only on certain grounds, such as the following ones within the scope of our study in this chapter: lack of capacity, duress, misrepresentation, and mistake.

Although these grounds for avoidance vary greatly in nature, the relief is nearly always the same: the court attempts to return the parties to their precontractual status quo. This is accomplished by avoiding the contract and awarding restitution to each party in the amount of any benefit each has given to the other party while performing the agreement.

As you study these grounds for avoidance, keep in mind the following questions:

- Does the ground for avoidance employ a bright-line test that is predictable in its application or a more flexible test that introduces uncertainty and unpredictability into the analysis?
- What effect, if any, does the existence of a confidential relationship between the parties play in formulating the applicable legal standard?
- When does simple non-disclosure of a material fact amount to a form of misrepresentation that justifies avoidance?
- What's the difference between the remedy of avoidance and that of reformation?

In roughly the first half of this chapter, the text will summarize the law and ask you to apply or analyze that law in exercises. For roughly the second half, this chapter returns to a case method, in which the law is largely presented through judicial opinions, supplemented as usual with the problem method in the form of exercises and practice exams.

II. Incapacity

One of the most fundamental defects that can block enforcement of a contract is lack of contractual capacity of one of the parties. Contractual incapacity may be in the form of status as a minor or possession of a mental illness or defect.

A. Infancy

1. Capacity Defined

State statutes tend to follow a bright-line rule setting the age of general contractual capacity at 18, regardless whether a younger person is mature, emancipated, and experienced, and regardless whether a minor appeared to the other party to be 18 or older. For centuries the age of contractual capacity was 21, but state legislatures lowered it to 18 after the conscription of 18-year-olds for military service in Vietnam spurred a constitutional amendment lowering the voting age to 18. Andrew Schwartz, *Old Enough to Fight, Old Enough to Swipe: A Critique of the Infancy Rule in the Federal Credit Card Act*, 2011 UTAH L. REV. 407, 409–20 (2011).

Many states, however, provide that certain kinds of contracts are enforceable, even when entered into by a minor. Conversely, the federal Credit CARD Act of 2009 reinstates the age of capacity of 21 for credit card contracts, although it also abandons the bright-line test by permitting issuance of a credit card account to a younger applicant if the applicant submits financial information demonstrating an independent ability to make payments on the account. *Id.* at 423–25 (critiquing the Credit Card Accountability Responsibility and Disclosure (Credit CARD) Act of 2009, Pub. L. No. 111-24, § 301, 123 Stat. 1734, 1748).

2. *Avoidance and Restitution, or Ratification*

If a minor lacks general contractual capacity, a contract with the minor is not absolutely void. Instead, it generally is "voidable," meaning that the minor has the option of either avoiding the contract, or performing and enforcing it.

a. Avoiding the Contract

Unless the contract comes within a statutory or common law exception, a minor has the option of avoiding the contract any time before reaching the age of contractual capacity, or even for a reasonable time afterwards if she hasn't yet ratified the contract. When the minor expresses an intention to avoid, we sometimes say that the minor "disaffirms" the contract.

If the minor exercises her option to disaffirm the contract, a court will avoid the contract and will grant restitution to the parties. For example, if the minor purchased a car on credit, the minor would return the car and would recover her down payment. Depending on the jurisdiction, other adjustments may be made to account for depreciation, rental value, or damage to the car in such a case. If the other party provided the minor with a necessity, the minor will normally keep the necessity and be bound to pay restitution of the reasonable value of the necessity (which might be less than the contract price).

b. Ratifying the Contract

The minor might decide that the contract is a good one, and she has the option of performing and enforcing it. Indeed, the minor will be contractually bound to perform if she ratifies the contract after reaching the age of contractual capacity. After this time, she can ratify the contract by expressly acknowledging the contract, by making payments to the other party or by affirmatively accepting performance from the other party, or merely by failing to disaffirm the contract within a reasonable time while retaining the goods or services supplied by the other party.

Again, a different rule applies to credit card accounts under the federal Credit CARD Act of 2009. If an applicant does not meet the requirements of that statute, a credit card agreement with that applicant is void and unenforceable, and not merely voidable at the option of the applicant. *Id.* at 423 (citing to section 301 of the federal Credit CARD Act of 2009).

Exercise 8.1 — Bright-Line Tests

What are the merits or shortcomings of the bright-line test for general contractual capacity at the age of 18? Would you prefer a rule that permits minors to contract if they are emancipated or otherwise can demonstrate economic independence?

For credit card contracts, do you support the federal Credit CARD Act's approach of raising the age of capacity to 21 but then abandoning the bright-line test, permitting those under the age of capacity to take out a credit card if they can prove financial independence? What are the merits or shortcomings of this approach?

B. Mental Illness or Defect

1. Incapacity, and Avoidance or Ratification

Even a temporary mental illness, injury, or other impairment may give the mentally impaired person an option to avoid a contract if the person suffered from the mental impairment at the time of contracting. Under the traditional rule, the impaired person will lack contractual capacity at the time of contracting if he was unable at that time to understand the nature and the consequences of his actions, regardless of whether he objectively appeared to be fully mentally competent.

Courts are apt to be less forgiving of a person who claims lack of contractual capacity because of voluntary intoxication rather than a mental illness or injury. For example, the Restatement opines that a contract entered into by such a person is not voidable at that person's option unless the other party *had reason to know* that the intoxication was sufficient to rob the person of his mental capacity. *See* RESTATEMENT (SECOND) OF CONTRACTS § 16(a) (1981).

If a person had been adjudicated to be mentally incompetent before the contract was formed, a contract with that person is void and unenforceable, not just voidable at the option of the person lacking capacity. Otherwise, the rules for disaffirming or ratifying the contract are similar to those for infancy, although a person with a permanent mental illness or defect might need to act through a guardian. If the contract is disaffirmed, the court will avoid it and grant restitution. Again, if a mentally incompetent person is furnished necessities, he will keep the necessities and be liable for restitution of the reasonable value.

Exercise 8.2 — "High as a Georgia Pine"

Review the facts regarding A.H. Zehmer's intoxication and bargaining in *Lucy v. Zehmer*, Chapter 2, Section II.C. Do you agree with the court's conclusion that Zehmer was not so intoxicated as to lack contractual capacity? If you were Zehmer's counsel, would you have conceded that point in oral argument, as stated by the court in paragraph 21 of the opinion?

---

2. *Trend to Expand Test for Mental Incapacity*

Under the majority rule, an adult lacks capacity to enter into a contract only if he or she cannot understand the nature and the consequences of the transaction. In a minority trend, a few states add a second and alternative ground for incapacity, which the Restatement describes in the following manner: the party is unable "to act in a reasonable manner in relation to the transaction and the other party has reason to know of his condition." RESTATEMENT (SECOND) OF CONTRACTS § 15(1)(b) (1981). Under this minority trend, a party could avoid a contract for lack of capacity, even if he understood the burdensome terms of a contract, if a mental disease rendered him unable to resist entering into the contract. *See* Carl S. Bjerre, *Mental Capacity as Metaphor*, 18 INT'L J. FOR THE SEMIOTICS OF LAW 101, 131–40 (2005).

The Restatement's embrace of the progressive trend provides a good illustration of a characteristic of the Restatement that you should keep in mind. Most provisions of the Restatement attempt to summarize common law approaches that are adopted in most or all states. A few provisions, however, represent the American Law Institute's support for progressive trends that do not yet have majority support, some of which may never gain widespread support.

Exercise 8.3 — Merits of the Volitional Test

Why do you believe that the progressive, volitional branch of the mental capacity test has not been more widely adopted? Does that test require overly difficult line-drawing between one who is unable to resist entering into a bad deal because of a mental illness and one who is merely impulsive and should be held to his contracts? If you were a state supreme court justice, would you expand your state's common law to include this expanded test for mental incapacity?

III. Duress and Undue Influence

Recall the case of *Alaska Packers' Ass'n v. Domenico* in Chapter 3, in which a one-sided modification of a contract was unenforceable because it lacked consideration under the pre-existing duty rule. To what extent do modifications of unperformed contracts also raise the possibility of coercion in agreeing to the modification?

Totem Marine Tug & Barge, Inc. v. Alyeska Pipeline Service Co.

584 P.2d 15 (Alaska S. Ct. 1978)

Burke, Justice.

¶1 This appeal arises from the superior court's granting of summary judgment in favor of defendants-appellees Alyeska Pipeline Services, et al., in a contract action brought by plaintiffs-appellants Totem Marine Tug & Barge, Inc., Pacific, Inc., and Richard Stair. The following summary of events is derived from the materials submitted in the summary judgment proceedings below.

¶2 Totem is a closely held Alaska corporation which began operations in March of 1975. Richard Stair, at all times relevant to this case, was vice-president of Totem. In June of 1975, Totem entered into a contract with Alyeska under which Totem was to transport pipeline construction materials from Houston, Texas, to a designated port in southern Alaska, with the possibility of one or two cargo stops along the way. In order to carry out this contract, which was Totem's first, Totem chartered a barge (The "Marine Flasher") and an ocean-going tug (the "Kirt Chouest"). These charters and other initial operations costs were made possible by loans to Totem from Richard Stair individually and Pacific, Inc., a corporation of which Stair was principal stockholder and officer, as well as by guarantees by Stair and Pacific.

¶3 By the terms of the contract, Totem was to have completed performance by approximately August 15, 1975. From the start, however, there were numerous problems which impeded Totem's performance of the contract. For example, according to Totem, Alyeska represented that approximately 1,800 to 2,100 tons of regular uncoated pipe were to be loaded in Houston, and that perhaps another 6,000 or 7,000 tons of materials would be put on the barge at later stops along the west coast. Upon the arrival of the tug and barge in Houston, however, Totem found that about 6,700 to 7,200 tons of coated pipe, steel beams and valves, haphazardly and improperly piled, were in the yard to be loaded. This situation called for remodeling of the barge and extra cranes and stevedores, and resulted in the loading taking thirty days rather than the three days which Totem had anticipated it would take to load 2,000 tons. The lengthy loading period was also caused in part by Alyeska's delay in assuring Totem that it would pay for the additional expenses, bad weather and other administrative problems.

¶4 The difficulties continued after the tug and barge left Houston. It soon became apparent that the vessels were travelling more slowly than anticipated because of the extra load. In response to Alyeska's complaints and with its verbal consent, on August 13, 1975, Totem chartered a second tug, the "N. Joseph Guidry." When the "Guidry" reached the Panama Canal, however, Alyeska had not yet furnished the written amendment to the parties' contract. Afraid that Alyeska would not agree to cover the cost of the second tug, Stair notified the "Guidry" not to go through the Canal. After some discussions in which Alyeska complained of the delays and accused Totem of lying about the horsepower of the first tug, Alyeska executed the amendment on August 21, 1975.

¶ 5 By this time the "Guidry" had lost its preferred passage through the Canal and had to wait two or three additional days before it could go through. Upon finally meeting, the three vessels encountered the tail of a hurricane which lasted for about eight or nine days and which substantially impeded their progress.

¶ 6 The three vessels finally arrived in the vicinity of San Pedro, California, where Totem planned to change crews and refuel. On Alyeska's orders, however, the vessels instead pulled into port at Long Beach, California. At this point, Alyeska's agents commenced off-loading the barge, without Totem's consent, without the necessary load survey, and without a marine survey, the absence of which voided Totem's insurance. After much wrangling and some concessions by Alyeska, the freight was off-loaded. Thereafter, on or about September 14, 1975, Alyeska terminated the contract. Although there was talk by an Alyeska official of reinstating the contract, the termination was affirmed a few days later at a meeting at which Alyeska officials refused to give a reason for the termination.

¶ 7 Following termination of the contract, Totem submitted termination invoices to Alyeska and began pressing the latter for payment. The invoices came to something between $260,000 and $300,000. An official from Alyeska told Totem that they would look over the invoices but that they were not sure when payment would be made perhaps in a day or perhaps in six to eight months. Totem was in urgent need of cash as the invoices represented debts which the company had incurred on 10-30 day payment schedules. Totem's creditors were demanding payment and according to Stair, without immediate cash, Totem would go bankrupt. Totem then turned over the collection to its attorney, Roy Bell, directing him to advise Alyeska of Totem's financial straits. Thereafter, Bell met with Alyeska officials in Seattle, and after some negotiations, Totem received a settlement offer from Alyeska for $97,500. On November 6, 1975, Totem, through its president Stair, signed an agreement releasing Alyeska from all claims by Totem in exchange for $97,500.

¶ 8 On March 26, 1976, Totem, Richard Stair, and Pacific filed a complaint against Alyeska, which was subsequently amended. In the amended complaint, the plaintiffs sought to rescind the settlement and release on the ground of economic duress and to recover the balance allegedly due on the original contract....

¶ 9 ... [P]laintiffs contended that the purported release was executed under duress in that Alyeska wrongfully terminated the contract; that Alyeska knew that Totem was faced with large debts and impending bankruptcy; that Alyeska withheld funds admittedly owed knowing the effect this would have on plaintiffs and that plaintiffs had no alternative but to involuntarily accept the $97,500 in order to avoid bankruptcy. Plaintiffs maintained that they had thus raised genuine issues of material fact such that trial was necessary, and that Alyeska was not entitled to judgment as a matter of law. Alyeska disputed the plaintiffs' assertions.

¶ 10 On November 30, 1976, the superior court granted the defendant's motion for summary judgment. This appeal followed.

....

II

¶ 11 As was noted above, a court's initial task in deciding motions for summary judgment is to determine whether there exist genuine issues of material fact. In order to decide whether such issues exist in this case, we must examine the doctrine allowing avoidance of a release on grounds of economic duress.

¶ 12 This court has not yet decided a case involving a claim of economic duress or what is also called business compulsion. At early common law, a contract could be avoided on the ground of duress only if a party could show that the agreement was entered into for fear of loss of life or limb, mayhem or imprisonment. 13 Williston on Contracts, § 1601 at 649 (3d ed. Jaeger 1970). The threat had to be such as to overcome the will of a person of ordinary firmness and courage. *Id.*, § 1602 at 656. Subsequently, however, the concept has been broadened to include myriad forms of economic coercion which force a person to involuntarily enter into a particular transaction. The test has come to be whether the will of the person induced by the threat was overcome rather than that of a reasonably firm person. *Id.*, § 1602 at 657.

¶ 13 At the outset it is helpful to acknowledge the various policy considerations which are involved in cases involving economic duress. Typically, those claiming such coercion are attempting to avoid the consequences of a modification of an original contract or of a settlement and release agreement. On the one hand, courts are reluctant to set aside agreements because of the notion of freedom of contract and because of the desirability of having private dispute resolutions be final. On the other hand, there is an increasing recognition of the law's role in correcting inequitable or unequal exchanges between parties of disproportionate bargaining power and a greater willingness to not enforce agreements which were entered into under coercive circumstances.

....

¶ 14 ... [The element of coercion] is further explained as follows:

> In order to substantiate the allegation of economic duress or business compulsion, the plaintiff must go beyond the mere showing of reluctance to accept and of financial embarrassment. There must be a showing of acts on the part of the defendant which produced these two factors. The assertion of duress must be proven by evidence that the duress resulted from defendant's wrongful and oppressive conduct and not by the plaintiff's necessities.

W. R. Grimshaw Co., *supra*, 111 F. Supp. at 904.

¶ 15 As the above indicates, one essential element of economic duress is that the plaintiff show that the other party by wrongful acts or threats, intentionally caused him to involuntarily enter into a particular transaction. Courts have not attempted to define exactly what constitutes a wrongful or coercive act, as wrongfulness depends on the particular facts in each case. This requirement may be satisfied where the alleged wrongdoer's conduct is criminal or tortious but an act or threat may also be considered wrongful if it is wrongful in the moral sense. Restatement of Contracts, § 492, comment (g); *Gerber v. First National Bank of Lincolnwood*, 30 Ill. App. 3d 776, 332 N.E.2d 615, 618 (1975);....

¶ 16 In many cases, a threat to breach a contract or to withhold payment of an admitted debt has constituted a wrongful act. *Hartsville Oil Mill v. United States*, 271 U.S. 43, 49 ... (1926); *Austin Instrument, Inc. v. Loral Corp.*, 29 N.Y.2d 124, ... 272 N.E.2d 533, 535 (1971);.... Implicit in such cases is the additional requirement that the threat to breach the contract or withhold payment be done in bad faith. *See Louisville Title Insurance Co. v. Surety Title & Guaranty Co.*, 60 Cal. App. 3d 781, 132 Cal. Rptr. 63, 76, 79 (1976); Restatement (Second) of Contracts, § 318 comment (e).

¶ 17 Economic duress does not exist, however, merely because a person has been the victim of a wrongful act; in addition, the victim must have no choice but to agree to the other party's terms or face serious financial hardship. Thus, in order to avoid a contract, a party must also show that he had no reasonable alternative to agreeing to the other party's terms, or, as it is often stated, that he had no adequate remedy if the threat were to be carried out. *First National Bank of Cincinnati v. Pepper*, 454 F.2d 626, 632-33 (2d Cir. 1972); *Austin Instrument, supra*, 324 N.Y.S.2d at 25, 272 N.E.2d at 535;.... What constitutes a reasonable alternative is a question of fact, depending on the circumstances of each case. An available legal remedy, such as an action for breach of contract, may provide such an alternative. *First National Bank of Cincinnati, supra*; *Austin Instrument, supra*; *Tri-State Roofing, supra*. Where one party wrongfully threatens to withhold goods, services or money from another unless certain demands are met, the availability on the market of similar goods and services or of other sources of funds may also provide an alternative to succumbing to the coercing party's demands. *Austin Instrument, supra*; *Tri-State Roofing, supra*. Generally, it has been said that "(t)he adequacy of the remedy is to be tested by a practical standard which takes into consideration the exigencies of the situation in which the alleged victim finds himself." *Ross Systems*, 173 A.2d at 262. *See also First National Bank of Cincinnati, supra* at 634; Dalzell, *Duress By Economic Pressure I*, 20 N. Carolina L. Rev. 237, 240 (1942).

¶ 18 An available alternative or remedy may not be adequate where the delay involved in pursuing that remedy would cause immediate and irreparable loss to one's economic or business interest. For example, in *Austin Instrument, supra*, ... duress was found in the following circumstances: A subcontractor threatened to refuse further delivery under a contract unless the contractor agreed to modify the existing contract between the parties. The contractor was unable to obtain the necessary materials elsewhere without delay, and if it did not have the materials promptly, it would have been in default on its main contract with the government. In each case such default would have had grave economic consequences for the contractor and hence it agreed to the modifications. In both, the courts found that the alternatives to agreeing to the modification were inadequate (*i.e.*, suing for breach of contract or obtaining the materials elsewhere) and that modifications therefore were signed under duress and voidable.

¶ 19 Professor Dalzell, in *Duress By Economic Pressure II*, 20 N. Carolina L. Rev. 340, 370 (1942), notes the following with regard to the adequacy of legal remedies where one party refuses to pay a contract claim:

> Nowadays, a wait of even a few weeks in collecting on a contract claim is sometimes serious or fatal for an enterprise at a crisis in its history. The business of a creditor in financial straits is at the mercy of an unscrupulous debtor, who need only suggest that if the creditor does not care to settle on the debtor's own hard terms, he can sue. This situation, in which promptness in payment is vastly more important than even approximate justice in the settlement terms, is too common in modern business relations to be ignored by society and the courts.

¶ 20 This view finds support in *Capps v. Georgia Pacific Corporation*, 253 Or. 248, 453 P.2d 935 (1969). There, the plaintiff was owed $157,000 as a commission for finding a lessee for defendant's property but in exchange for $5,000, the plaintiff signed a release of his claim against defendant. The plaintiff sued for the balance of the commission, alleging that the release had been executed under duress. His complaint, however, was dismissed. On appeal, the court held that the plaintiff had stated a claim where he alleged that he had accepted the grossly inadequate sum because he was in danger of immediately losing his home by mortgage foreclosure and other property by foreclosure and repossession if he did not obtain immediate funds from the defendant....

III

¶ 21 Turning to the instant case, we believe that Totem's allegations, if proved, would support a finding that it executed a release of its contract claims against Alyeska under economic duress. Totem has alleged that Alyeska deliberately withheld payment of an acknowledged debt, knowing that Totem had no choice but to accept an inadequate sum in settlement of that debt; that Totem was faced with impending bankruptcy; that Totem was unable to meet its pressing debts other than by accepting the immediate cash payment offered by Alyeska; and that through necessity, Totem thus involuntarily accepted an inadequate settlement offer from Alyeska and executed a release of all claims under the contract. If the release was in fact executed under these circumstances, we think that under the legal principles discussed above that this would constitute the type of wrongful conduct and lack of alternatives that would render the release voidable by Totem on the ground of economic duress....

....

¶ 22 Our examination of the materials presented by Totem in opposition to Alyeska's motion for summary judgment leads us to conclude that Totem has made a sufficient factual showing as to each of the elements of economic duress to withstand that motion. There is no doubt that Alyeska disputes many of the factual allegations made by Totem and drawing all inferences in favor of Totem, we believe that genuine issues of material fact exist in this case such that trial is necessary.... Therefore, we hold that the superior court erred in granting summary judgment for appellees and remand the case to the superior court for trial in accordance with the legal principles set forth above.

A. Physical Duress

It should come as no surprise that a contract is subject to avoidance if a person was physically compelled to express assent, such as if the other party literally twisted the person's arm behind his back, nearly breaking it, until the person signed a contract. Grounds for avoidance are also obvious when apparent assent is compelled under a credible *threat* of imminent physical harm, such as if the other party held a gun to the victim's head and threatened to shoot if the victim did not sign. *See* Daniel P. O'Gorman, *"Sign or Die!": The Threat of Imminent Physical Harm and the Doctrine of Duress*, 85 TENN. L. REV. 423 (2018). Of course, such actions would constitute torts and crimes, so avoidance of the contract and restitution of benefits transferred should be the least of the aggressor's worries.

B. Economic Duress

Compulsion may also come in the form of threatening a party's economic interests. Duress in the commercial world often comes in the form of business compulsion stemming from withholding performance under an existing contract, or a threat to do so. For example, a vendor in an existing contract might engage in economic duress by threatening to withhold goods or services due under the contract, unless the other party agrees to modify the existing contract to increase the vendor's pay.

1. The Pre-Existing Duty Rule Is an Imperfect Tool to Control Coerced Modifications

If such a modification increased the vendor's pay without requiring more goods or services from the vendor, then it would not be supported by consideration, and it would violate the pre-existing duty rule if the jurisdiction has retained that rule. However, consideration is not required for a modification of a contract for a sale of goods. U.C.C. § 2-209(1) (2011). Moreover, even if the transaction is one for services governed by common law, and even if the jurisdiction takes the pre-existing duty rule seriously, lack of consideration for the modification might be difficult to prove if the vendor cleverly agreed to change its performance in some inexpensive way while extracting a promise to pay significantly more money. Finally, if a party releases a contract claim in exchange for money, as in *Totem*, such a settlement agreement would not run afoul of the pre-existing duty rule if the agreed payment lies within a range of good-faith dispute about the amount owed under the original contract.

Consequently, the pre-existing duty rule of the consideration doctrine is not always an effective tool for denying enforcement to modifications extracted through an improper threat. The doctrine of duress can address this kind of problem more directly. Still, the courts must take care not to upset a modification when a party voluntarily agreed to increase the pay of a vendor and then later changed his mind and insincerely complained to the court that a threat by the vendor compelled the modification.

2. *The Test for Economic Duress*

"It is well established that an agreement is voidable due to duress when 'a party's manifestation of assent is induced by an improper threat by the other party that leaves the victim no reasonable alternative.'" *Balogh v. Balogh*, 134 Haw. 29, 44, 332 P.3d 631, 646 (2014) (quoting *Standard Fin. Co., Ltd. v. Ellis*, 3 Haw. App. 614, 621, 657 P.2d 1056, 1061 (1983)).

a. Improper Threat

Outside of an existing contractual relationship, it is not improper to threaten to take your business elsewhere if the other party doesn't agree to your terms for a proposed contract, even if the other party has a pressing economic need for your goods, services, or money. Similarly, according to the court in *Balogh*, in the context of an agreement to divide marital property, "[a] threat of divorce does not constitute an improper threat since the party making it has the legal right to seek a divorce."

In contrast, a threat to breach an existing, valid contract to extract greater compensation or to reduce one's contractual obligation is normally viewed as "improper." One might argue that a contracting party enjoys the option of either performing a contract or paying damages, but a breach of contract leads to civil liability, and a threat to breach is generally viewed as wrongful for purposes of applying the duress doctrine. If the improper threat overcame the victim's free will, compelling the victim to agree to new terms, the victim of duress will have the option to avoid the new contract.

b. Overcoming Free Will

The threat overcomes the complaining party's free will if the threat leaves the party with no reasonable alternative except to agree to the modification and then to turn to the court later for avoidance. A good illustration is provided by the case of *Austin Instrument, Inc. v. Loral Corp.*, 29 N.Y.2d 124, 272 N.E.2d 533 (1971). In the first contract in that case, Loral, a general contractor, agreed to pay Austin, a subcontractor, a substantial sum of money for 23 precision gear components on which Austin had been the lowest bidder. According to Loral, when Loral later requested that Austin bid on a second contract for more of the gear parts, Austin stated that it would cease deliveries of parts still owed on the first contract unless Loral awarded the second contract to Austin on all of the gear parts, and unless Loral agreed to increase Austin's pay under the first contract. This threat by Austin had some bite to it because Loral was under contract with the U.S. Navy to use the gear parts to construct radar sets for the Navy on a strict time schedule. *Id.* at 128–29, 272 N.E.2d at 534.

Loral stood firm and demanded that Austin perform the first contract, but Austin stopped delivery on that contract. Loral reacted by searching for an alternative supplier of the parts for the first contract so that it could meet its obligations to the Navy and then could sue Austin for any increased costs associated with purchasing from a substitute supplier. *Id.* at 129, 272 N.E.2d at 534–35.

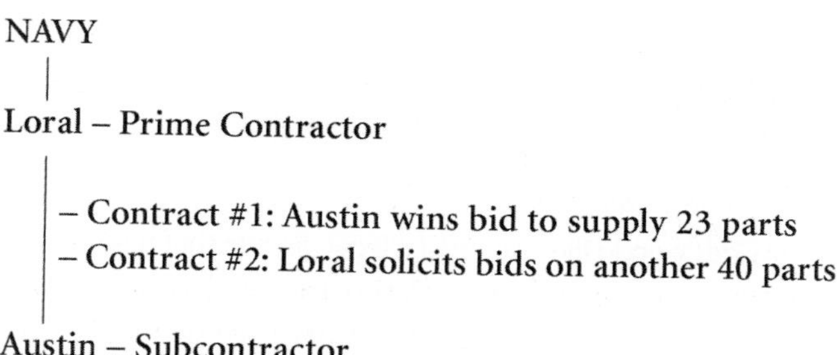
NAVY
Loral – Prime Contractor
– Contract #1: Austin wins bid to supply 23 parts
– Contract #2: Loral solicits bids on another 40 parts
Austin – Subcontractor

Loral did not contact every available supplier, but it did contact all 10 of its vendors that were preapproved for these sophisticated precision gear parts, and it learned that none of them could deliver the parts in time to meet Loral's obligations to the Navy. Breaching its commitments to the Navy was not a reasonable option for Loral, because its contract with the Navy provided for cancellation of the whole contract on any breach by Loral, and it entitled the Navy to recover contractually specified damages for any delay in delivery. Moreover, Loral's asking the Navy for extra time was not a reasonable option, because such a request could damage Loral's credibility as a reliable contractor, and it was impractical in light of uncertainty about how soon any of the substitute suppliers could complete deliveries of the parts promised by Austin under the first contract. In sum, Loral had little choice but to agree to Austin's demands as a means of obtaining the needed gear parts and meeting its obligations to the Navy. *Id.* at 131–33, 272 N.E.2d at 536–37.

After receiving delivery of all the goods under both contracts with Austin, Loral attempted to recoup some of its additional costs by withholding the final installment of payment on the second contract, leading to a lawsuit by Austin and a counterclaim by Loral. The trial court and the intermediate court of appeals found no duress and enforced Loral's promise to increase the pay to Austin on the first contract. *Id.* at 130, 272 N.E.2d at 535.

A four-justice majority of the New York Court of Appeals reversed the lower courts and decided that Austin's improper threat indeed overcame Loral's free will in light of all the circumstances. Loral had resisted Austin's threat and pursued every reasonable alternative, but in the end had no reasonable option but to agree to the terms of Austin's proposed second contract. In those circumstances, Loral could avoid the second agreement, canceling the increase in prices for the parts under the first contract. *Id.* at 131–34, 272 N.E.2d at 536–37.

Three justices joined in a dissent that credited evidence in the record tending to show that the parties renegotiated the first contract to respond to Austin's dissatisfaction with Loral's cooperation under that contract, and that Austin had not stopped deliveries in breach of that contract but as part of a customary vacation period contemplated by the parties. The dissenters also believed that the trial court's finding of no duress was supported by evidence that Loral could have and should have contacted additional potential suppliers before claiming duress. *Id.* at 134–35, 272 N.E.2d at 537–38 (Bergan, J., dissenting).

Exercise 8.4 — Duress and the Pre-Existing Duty Rule

1. Uncertain Outcomes and Essay Exams

Austin v. Loral provides a good illustration of a legal dispute that has no certain answer. True, a bare majority of justices in the state's court of last resort found duress, thus dictating the result in this case. After applying the law to the facts, however, fewer than half of the total number of judges in all the courts at all levels found a good claim for duress. Thus, before the highest court rendered its decision, it would be folly to say that one result or another was the "correct result" in this close case. In such cases, the role of the lawyer and the law student is not to somehow "know the right answer," because there is no single "right answer" to the question posed in the case. Instead, the role of the lawyer or law student is to understand the issues and to work with the law and the facts to construct arguments for a client and to anticipate arguments from the opposing counsel. A similar task awaits the law student in the typical law school essay exam, which frequently presents a close case on the law and facts, which has no single "correct answer," and which provides rich opportunities to present arguments for both sides of the case.

2. Pre-Existing Duty Rule Not a Factor

Provide two reasons why the second agreement between Austin and Loral, the one that Loral signed under duress, did not violate the pre-existing duty rule. The absence of that rule as a means of challenging the enforceability of the second contract left only duress as a ground for avoidance.

3. Striking Seamen

Review the *Alaska Packers' Association* case, Chapter 3, Section IV.B. If the court had not applied the pre-existing duty rule, would it have avoided the contract for duress? What facts are relevant to that question?

4. Practice Exam

The following is loosely based on real events: Members of the rock group Led Zeppelin assaulted and battered one of the employees of Bill Graham, a celebrated promoter of rock music concerts from 1965 until his death in a helicopter crash in 1991. At their next major concert for Bill Graham Productions, the musicians in Led Zeppelin stalled before going on stage. While thousands of fans chanted and stomped impatiently, an agent for Led Zeppelin told Graham that the band would not go on stage until Graham signed a document that: (1) obligated Bill Graham Productions to indemnify Led Zeppelin and its members if they incurred any liability arising out of the assault and battery, and (2) obligated the band to perform an encore number if the audience demanded more music.

The existing contract did not guarantee an encore number at the end of the regular 90-minute set, and Graham liked the idea of a guaranteed encore. However, the prospect of an encore was inconsequential compared to Graham's distaste for the indemnity clause. Accordingly, he initially refused to sign the agreement. However, he soon signed when Led Zeppelin carried through its threat to remain backstage and when impatient audience members demanded the band ever more loudly. Graham was greatly concerned about the consequences of canceling the concert, including lost profits after refunding tickets, a general loss of reputation in the industry, and even the possibility of a riot.

Later, Graham disavowed the indemnity clause. Is the signed indemnity agreement enforceable? Discuss each issue in a separate IRAC, and argue both sides when possible.

C. Undue Influence in Special Circumstances

In special circumstances, pressure during bargaining can establish grounds for avoidance even if the test for duress is not strictly met.

The standards for avoidance are relaxed, for example, if the parties are in a confidential relationship (such as priest and parishioner, or husband and wife in some circumstances) or a fiduciary relationship (such as attorney and client, or more generally, principal and agent). In such relationships, a subordinate party may place unusual trust and confidence in the dominant party. In a confidential relationship, bargaining characterized by inappropriate pressure from the dominant party, or by other abuse of the trust placed by one party in the other, may be viewed as "undue influence" that establishes grounds for avoidance.

Similarly, a party who takes advantage of an infirmity or weakness of the other party during bargaining, such as negotiating a contract with a sick or injured person, can create grounds for avoidance on the basis of undue influence if inappropriate pressure is placed on the weaker party or if the result of the bargaining is unfair.

In some states, once the party seeking avoidance establishes a confidential relationship, the burden of proof shifts to the other party to establish that the transaction was fair and not the result of exploitation of the first party's weakened state or subordinate status.

Because a confidential relationship provides an enhanced basis for challenging an unfair agreement, a court will not conclude that every close relationship amounts to a confidential one. In one case, for example, a court found no confidential relationship between a brother and sister, because the sister was capable and not dependent on her brother, even though the brother transacted some business for his sister, who had some physical limitations. *In re Scott's Estate*, 455 Pa. 429, 432, 316 A.2d 883, 885 (1974).

Exercise 8.5 — Deathbed Contract

While in her final illness, with only days or even hours to live, a widow — Antillico — gratefully recognized the arrival of her son, Able. Antillico had often sought out Able, the elder and better educated of her two children, for advice on financial matters. After Able spoke gently but persuasively and persistently to Antillico for 30 minutes, Able convinced Antillico that her house would be best managed by Able and that her estate needed more liquidity in the form of cash. Accordingly, Antillico summoned all of her remaining strength to sign a contract that Able had prepared, which sold Antillico's house to Able for 15% less than its market value in cash. This contract would take that house out of the property that was owned by Antillico and that would be distributed through Antillico's will to both of her children, but it would add the proceeds of the sale to the estate. The executor of Antillico's will, seeking to implement Antillico's true wishes and to protect both beneficiaries under the will, wants to avoid the contract prepared by Able, so that the house can be sold for a higher price, with those proceeds being split between the two children. Is this a good case for avoidance?

IV. Misrepresentation

A. Introduction: Distinguishing Tortious Fraud, Breach of Warranty, and Avoidance for Misrepresentation

We will study avoidance for misrepresentation in this chapter and breach of warranty in Chapter 10. We will not study the tort of fraud at all, beyond a brief mention in this introduction.

To help you place the current topic in proper context, let's begin by comparing the general characteristics of these three types of claims before we address avoidance for misrepresentation. The following hypothetical facts will provide a vehicle for our comparisons:

Agreement between the Promoter and Lessor:

In August, a promoter for a popular musical group negotiated with the lessor of Stanton Hall, a concert hall, to lease Stanton Hall for a musical performance in November. The promoter emphasized that the legal seating capacity was important, particularly in relation to the fee for Stanton Hall and its staffing. In response, the lessor stated that Stanton Hall would have a seating capacity of 4,000, and he provided a seating chart that showed 3,000 seats on the main floor and 1,000 seats in the balcony.

After comparing the seating capacity with the costs and with the estimated demand for tickets, the promoter reached agreement with the lessor. The lessor, however, had provided inaccurate information about the seating. Because the balcony did not meet state or city fire codes, it had been closed for seating for decades. The extensive renovations necessary to meet fire codes were prohibitively expensive. On the concert date, the balcony was not open, so available seating numbered 3,000 seats, but the demand for the concert exceeded 4,000 tickets.

1. *Tort: Fraud*

Tort liability for misrepresentation requires proof of fault on the part of the misrepresenting party. For example, let's assume that the lessor knowingly lied about the seating capacity to secure an agreement at a desired fee, because he gambled that the promoter would not sell more than 3,000 tickets. If the promoter relied on that intentional falsehood, then the lessor could be liable in tort for fraud.

2. *Breach of Warranty*

Breach of contract, however, does not require the kind of fault or culpability associated with most torts. If the lessor warranted in the contract that Stanton Hall would have a seating capacity of 4,000, then the lessor normally would be liable for breach of contract if Stanton Hall in fact had less than the promised capacity on the concert date, even if the lessor had been innocently mistaken about the seating capacity.

For example, suppose that the lessor was a third-party contractor who planned to rent Stanton Hall, make it available to the promoter for a higher fee, and provide supplies and staffing for the concert. Further, suppose that the lessor genuinely thought that Stanton Hall had seating for 4,000. If the lessor promised a hall with 4,000 seats in a valid contract, the lessor must deliver such a hall on the performance date or—with very few exceptions—be liable for breach of contract. The fact that the lessor was ignorant about the problem with balcony seating and had innocently misrepresented the seating capacity to the promoter would normally be irrelevant to the promoter's liability for breach of contract.

If the balcony remained closed on the performance date without any accommodation from the lessor, and if the promoter discovered the problem too late to move the concert to another hall, then the promoter likely would hold the concert at Stanton Hall, pay the fee to the lessor, sell 1,000 fewer tickets than expected, and sue the lessor for lost profits. On such a claim, the promoter is not avoiding the contract; instead, the promoter is performing the contract and is enforcing it against the lessor.

3. *Avoidance for Misrepresentation*

Assume the same facts as in Subsection 2 above, except that the promoter learned of the problem with the balcony in September, at which time both parties discovered that the balcony was permanently closed. If the promoter had time to move the concert to a nearby hall with 4,000 seats, the promoter likely would seek to avoid the contract with the lessor. Once that contract was avoided, the promoter would be released from any obligation to rent Stanton Hall, and the promoter would be entitled to restitution of any deposit that the promoter had paid to the lessor, along with any increased costs associated with procuring the replacement hall.

The promoter could avoid the contract for even an innocent misrepresentation by the lessor during bargaining. If the lessor had represented during bargaining that the hall would have a capacity of 4,000, and if the promoter had relied on that material fact, then the promoter would be entitled to avoidance if the representation of fact turns out to be inaccurate, even though the lessor had genuinely believed during bargaining that Stanton Hall had a seating capacity of 4,000. Moreover, these grounds for *avoidance* could be established on the basis of statements made in preliminary negotiations and would not depend on an express warranty of 4,000 seats in the contract.

In sum, a party can avoid the contract by showing a:

- *misrepresentation* during bargaining of
- a *material fact* on which the victim
- *justifiably relied.*

Avoidance is an equitable remedy, so courts will sometimes adopt the flexible approach of assessing the elements of the claim as a whole. For example, if the misrepresentation is egregious, the court might be satisfied with a relatively weak showing on one of the other elements, such as justifiable reliance. Examples of this flexibility are explored in Subsection C below.

B. Misrepresentation During Bargaining

1. Three Kinds of Misrepresentation

A misrepresentation can take the form of an affirmative falsehood, a half-truth, or active concealment. However, with some exceptions, simple nondisclosure does not amount to a misrepresentation.

a. Affirmative Falsehood

The clearest form of misrepresentation is an affirmative statement that turns out to be false. As mentioned earlier, the speaker's knowledge of the inaccuracy is not a prerequisite for avoidance. For example, if a buyer relied on the seller's representation about the interior square footage of a house for sale, and the house turned out to have 30% less square footage, the buyer could avoid the contract for a material misrepresentation of fact, even though the seller was innocently mistaken about the square footage.

Many persons who appeared in the outrageous *Borat* movie comedy, however, were victims of intentional misrepresentations. Employees of the production falsely represented to these persons that comedian Sasha Baron Cohen was a Kazakhstani television reporter filming a documentary about American culture. After they signed a "Standard Consent Agreement," the recipients of these misrepresentations were then filmed in humiliating circumstances and featured in a movie set for full release by Twentieth Century Fox. *See* Russell Korobkin, *The Borat Problem in Contract Law: Fraud, Assent, and Standard Forms*, 101 CALIF. L. REV. 51, 54–55 (2013).

Misrepresentation can also come in subtler forms. By explaining why the facts of a case established no misrepresentation, one court identified in *dicta* two forms of misrepresentation in addition to an affirmative falsehood:

> There is no allegation of any false statement or representation, or of the uttering of a half truth which may be tantamount to a falsehood. There is no intimation that the defendant by any means prevented the plaintiff from acquiring information as to the condition of the house.

Swinton v. Whitinsville Savings Bank, 311 Mass. 677, 678, 42 N.E.2d 808 (1942).

Thus, a misrepresentation may come in the form of a half-truth or active concealment, as well as a false statement.

b. Half-Truth

A half-truth is a statement that addresses a topic but provides less than all of the information known by the speaker relating to that topic. If the speaker leaves out important information on the topic, the incomplete statement may be as misleading as a falsehood.

In one case, for example, the seller of dwellings accurately represented that the dwellings had been rented as apartments. The seller also provided accurate statements of the income and expenses of the rental units. The seller neglected to tell the buyer, however, that the dwelling had been converted into rental units in violation of zoning ordinances. Although the seller's statements about the past rental income and expenses were accurate in themselves, the seller conveyed a false impression by addressing the topic of rentals but failing to tell the whole story. *Kannavos v. Annino*, 356 Mass. 42, 247 N.E.2d 708 (1969).

c. Active Concealment

The *Swinton* court also referred to the act of preventing the other party from discovering important information about a transaction. This sort of *active concealment* is treated as a misrepresentation just as though the concealing party had uttered a falsehood.

Suppose, for example, that the seller of a car used a pretext to divert a prospective car buyer away from a hill during a test drive, to prevent the buyer from discovering that the car operated sluggishly while climbing even moderate inclines. This sort of active concealment is a form of misrepresentation.

d. Nondisclosure Generally Is Not a Misrepresentation

The *Swinton* court, however, distinguished active concealment from a party's simple failure to disclose information known to that party: "The charge is … mere failure to reveal, with nothing to show any peculiar duty to speak." *Swinton v. Whitinsville Savings Bank*, 311 Mass. 677, 678, 42 N.E. 2d 808 (1942). Thus, so long as a party does not actively mislead the other, and does not actively impede the other's ability to discover information, keeping one's knowledge to oneself generally is not a misrepresentation.

This rule is a product of the American tradition of *caveat emptor*, in which each party is expected to act diligently to protect its own interests, such as by asking probing questions and conducting its own thorough investigations. By rejecting a general duty to disclose, courts create incentives for parties to acquire knowledge, because the parties are permitted to exploit that knowledge without a general duty to disclose it to their counterparts in negotiation:

> If you offer a low price for some good to its owner, you are not obliged to tell him that you think the good is underpriced—that he does not realize its market value and you do. You are not required to be an altruist, to be candid, to be a good guy. You are permitted to profit from asymmetry of information. If you could not do that, the incentive to discover information about true values would be blunted. It is an example of the traditional economic paradox that private vice can be public virtue.

Richard A. Posner, *Let Us Never Blame a Contract Breaker*, 107 MICH. L. REV. 1349, 1357–58 (2009).

The rule against liability for nondisclosure, however, is softened by exceptions. For example, a traditional basis for a duty to disclose material facts is revealed in the *Swinton* court's explanation of the absence of a duty in that case:

> There is nothing to show any fiduciary relation between the parties, or that the plaintiff stood in a position of confidence toward or dependence upon the defendant. So far as appears the parties made a business deal at arm's length.

Swinton v. Whitinsville Savings Bank, 311 Mass. 677, 678, 42 N.E.2d 808 (1942). As stated more affirmatively:

> Although the general rule is that "one party to a transaction has no duty to disclose material facts to the other," an exception to this rule is made when the parties are in a fiduciary relationship with each other. *Klein v. First Edina National Bank*, 293 Minn. 418, 421, 196 N.W.2d 619, 622 (1972). "'A fiduciary relation exists when confidence is reposed on one side and there is resulting superiority on the other; and the relation and duties in it need not be legal but may be moral, social, domestic, or merely personal.'" *Kennedy*

> *v. Flo-Tronics, Inc.*, 274 Minn. at 331, 143 N.W.2d at 830 (*quoting Stark v. Equitable Life Assurance Society*, 205 Minn. 138, 145, 285 N.W. 466, 470 (1939)).

Midland Nat. Bank of Minneapolis v. Perranoski, 299 N.W.2d 404, 413 (Minn. 1980).

Thus, a party could have a duty to disclose material facts during bargaining if the other party would place an unusual degree of trust in her, typically because of a personal or professional relationship. In such a relationship, the parties are not bargaining "at arm's length," with each taking care to protect his or her own interests by acting cautiously and skeptically and by making all prudent inquiries; instead, one party may be letting his guard down and placing exceptional trust in the other.

Other factors can also give rise to a duty to disclose:

> When a party becomes aware, however, that another is "operating under a mistaken perception of a material fact," then it also has a duty to disclose if it has made "a partial or ambiguous statement that requires additional disclosure to avoid misleading the other party," or if it "possesses superior knowledge, not readily available to the other."

B. Lewis Productions, Inc. v. Angelou, No. 06 Civ. 6390(DLC), slip. op. at 6 (S.D.N.Y. April 22, 2008) (unpublished opinion quoting *Remington Rand Corp. v. Amsterdam-Rotterdam Bank, N.V.*, 68 F.3d 1478, 1484 (2d Cir.1995)); *see Warner Constr. Corp. v. City of Los Angeles*, 2 Cal. 3d 285, 294, 466 P.2d 996, 1001 (1970) (duty to disclose if the defendant knows that facts accessible only to the defendant are not reasonably discoverable by the plaintiff); Restatement (Second) of Contracts § 161(b) (1981) (duty to disclose when necessary to correct a mistake of the other party and act in good faith).

Additionally, under a modern trend, many states have imposed a duty to disclose material facts in negotiations for sales of real estate, or at least for sales of dwellings. *See, e.g., Isaacs v. Bishop*, 249 S.W.3d 100, 114 n.14 (Tex. App. 2008) (citing to Texas cases); *Condon v. Kunse*, 208 Ga. App. 856, 858, 432 S.E.2d 266, 269 (1993) (in Georgia, recognizing duty to disclose in sales of residential housing, but not in sale of farmland); *Hill v. Jones*, 151 Ariz. 81, 725 P.2d 1115 (Ct. App. 1986) (finding seller's duty to disclose termite damage in dwelling as a matter of common law).

These exceptions, however, serve to highlight the general rule: a party generally does not have a duty to disclose even material facts during bargaining. Moreover, some states have resisted the trend to add real estate transactions to the traditional exceptions to this rule. New York is one such state, yet the intermediate appellate court in the next case developed a narrower exception to caveat emptor. What is the scope of the exception? To what extent is the majority's ruling facilitated by the procedural posture of the case and the flexibility of equitable remedies? Does the majority sensibly advance the common law in an incremental manner, or do you agree with the dissent?

Stambovsky v. Ackley

572 N.Y.S.2d 672, 169 A.D.2d 254 (S. Ct. App. Div. 1991)

Rubin, J.

¶ 1 Plaintiff, to his horror, discovered that the house he had recently contracted to purchase was widely reputed to be possessed by poltergeists, reportedly seen by defendant seller and members of her family on numerous occasions over the last nine years. Plaintiff promptly commenced this action seeking rescission of the contract of sale. Supreme Court [the trial court in N.Y.] reluctantly dismissed the complaint, holding that plaintiff has no remedy at law in this jurisdiction.

¶ 2 The unusual facts of this case, as disclosed by the record, clearly warrant a grant of equitable relief to the buyer who, as a resident of New York City, cannot be expected to have any familiarity with the folklore of the Village of Nyack. Not being a "local", plaintiff could not readily learn that the home he had contracted to purchase is haunted.... [N]o divination is required to conclude that it is defendant's promotional efforts in publicizing her close encounters with these spirits which fostered the home's reputation in the community. In 1989, the house was included in a five-home walking tour of Nyack and described in a November 27th newspaper article as "a riverfront Victorian (with ghost)." The impact of the reputation thus created goes to the very essence of the bargain between the parties, greatly impairing both the value of the property and its potential for resale. The extent of this impairment may be presumed for the purpose of reviewing the disposition of this motion to dismiss the cause of action for rescission (*Harris v City of New York*, 147 AD2d 186, 188-189) and represents merely an issue of fact for resolution at trial.

¶ 3 While I agree with Supreme Court that the real estate broker, as agent for the seller, is under no duty to disclose to a potential buyer the phantasmal reputation of the premises and that, in his pursuit of a legal remedy for fraudulent misrepresentation against the seller, plaintiff hasn't a ghost of a chance, I am nevertheless moved by the spirit of equity to allow the buyer to seek rescission of the contract of sale and recovery of his down payment. New York law fails to recognize any remedy for damages incurred as a result of the seller's mere silence, applying instead the strict rule of caveat emptor. Therefore, the theoretical basis for granting relief, even under the extraordinary facts of this case, is elusive if not ephemeral.

....

¶ 4 ... [W]ith respect to transactions in real estate, New York adheres to the doctrine of caveat emptor and imposes no duty upon the vendor to disclose any information concerning the premises (*London v Courduff*, 141 AD2d 803) unless there is a confidential or fiduciary relationship between the parties (*Moser v Spizzirro*, 31 AD2d 537, *affd* 25 NY2d 941; ... or some conduct on the part of the seller which constitutes "active concealment" (*see, 17 E. 80th Realty Corp. v 68th Assocs.*,—AD2d— [1st Dept, May 9, 1991] [dummy ventilation system constructed by seller]; *Haberman v Greenspan*, 82 Misc 2d 263 [foundation cracks covered by seller])....

¶5 Caveat emptor is not so all-encompassing a doctrine of common law as to render every act of nondisclosure immune from redress, whether legal or equitable. "In regard to the necessity of giving information which has not been asked, the rule differs somewhat at law and in equity, and while the law courts would permit no recovery of damages against a vendor, because of mere concealment of facts under certain circumstances, yet if the vendee refused to complete the contract because of the concealment of a material fact on the part of the other, equity would refuse to compel him so to do, because equity only compels the specific performance of a contract which is fair and open, and in regard to which all material matters known to each have been communicated to the other" (*Rothmiller v Stein*, 143 NY 581, 591-592 [emphasis added]).... Common law is not moribund. *Ex facto jus oritur* (law arises out of facts). Where fairness and common sense dictate that an exception should be created, the evolution of the law should not be stifled by rigid application of a legal maxim.

¶6 The doctrine of caveat emptor requires that a buyer act prudently to assess the fitness and value of his purchase and operates to bar the purchaser who fails to exercise due care from seeking the equitable remedy of rescission (*see, e.g., Rodas v Manitaras*, 159 AD2d 341). For the purposes of the instant motion to dismiss the action pursuant to CPLR 3211 (a) (7), plaintiff is entitled to every favorable inference which may reasonably be drawn from the pleadings (*Arrington v New York Times Co.*, 55 NY2d 443; 442; ...), specifically, in this instance, that he met his obligation to conduct an inspection of the premises and a search of available public records with respect to title. It should be apparent, however, that the most meticulous inspection and the search would not reveal the presence of poltergeists at the premises or unearth the property's ghoulish reputation in the community. Therefore, there is no sound policy reason to deny plaintiff relief for failing to discover a state of affairs which the most prudent purchaser would not be expected to even contemplate (*see, Da Silva v Musso*, 53 NY2d 543, 551).

¶7 The case law in this jurisdiction dealing with the duty of a vendor of real property to disclose information to the buyer is distinguishable from the matter under review.... No case has been brought to this court's attention in which the property value was impaired as the result of the reputation created by information disseminated to the public by the seller (or, for that matter, as a result of possession by poltergeists).

¶8 Where a condition which has been created by the seller materially impairs the value of the contract and is peculiarly within the knowledge of the seller or unlikely to be discovered by a prudent purchaser exercising due care with respect to the subject transaction, nondisclosure constitutes a basis for rescission as a matter of equity. Any other outcome places upon the buyer not merely the obligation to exercise care in his purchase but rather to be omniscient with respect to any fact which may affect the bargain. No practical purpose is served by imposing such a burden upon a purchaser. To the contrary, it encourages predatory business practice and offends the principle that equity will suffer no wrong to be without a remedy.

....

¶9 In the case at bar, defendant seller deliberately fostered the public belief that her home was possessed. Having undertaken to inform the public-at-large, to whom she has no legal relationship, about the supernatural occurrences on her property, she may be said to owe no less a duty to her contract vendee. It has been remarked that the occasional modern cases which permit a seller to take unfair advantage of a buyer's ignorance so long as he is not actively misled are "singularly unappetizing" (Prosser, Torts § 106, at 696 [4th ed 1971]). Where, as here, the seller not only takes unfair advantage of the buyer's ignorance but has created and perpetuated a condition about which he is unlikely to even inquire, enforcement of the contract (in whole or in part) is offensive to the court's sense of equity. Application of the remedy of rescission, within the bounds of the narrow exception to the doctrine of caveat emptor set forth herein, is entirely appropriate to relieve the unwitting purchaser from the consequences of a most unnatural bargain.

¶10 Accordingly, the judgment of the Supreme Court, New York County ... should be modified, on the law and the facts, and in the exercise of discretion, and the first cause of action seeking rescission of the contract reinstated, without costs.

Smith, Justice (dissenting).

....

¶11 [I]f the doctrine of caveat emptor is to be discarded, it should be for a reason more substantive than a poltergeist....

Exercise 8.6 — Lack of General Duty to Disclose

1. Duty of Good Faith and Fair Dealing

The universally recognized duty of good faith is summarized in the Restatement: "Every contract imposes upon each party a duty of good faith and fair dealing in its performance and its enforcement." Restatement (Second) of Contracts § 205 (1981). For sales of goods, the UCC similarly provides that "[e]very contract or duty within this Act imposes an obligation of good faith in its performance or enforcement." U.C.C. § 1-203 (2001). Under the UCC, "good faith ... means honesty in fact and the observance of reasonable commercial standards of fair dealing." U.C.C. §§ 1-201(20), 2-103(1)(b) (2001). The version of the UCC adopted in Arizona and a few other states, however, retains only the subjective "honesty in fact" branch of the good-faith test for non-merchants. *See, e.g.*, Ariz. Rev. Stat. Ann. § 47-1201(20) (2017).

Assuming that "good faith" means at least "honesty in fact," why doesn't this implied term obligate every party to disclose all known important facts during bargaining? Read the Restatement and UCC provisions again. Why should the common law and the UCC limit the contexts in which the implied duty of good faith operates?

One author observes that Chinese law — in contrast to U.S. law — extends the duty of good faith to actions of the parties prior to contract formation; the author attributes the different legal approaches to cultural and political differences and to differences in legal traditions. Chunlin Leonhard, *A Legal Chameleon: An Examination of the Doctrine of Good Faith in Chinese and American Contract Law*, 25 CONN. J. INT'L L. 305, 317–20, 323–28 (2010).

2. Policy and Personal Ethics

Would you favor a legal rule that requires full disclosure of all important facts during bargaining, in all contexts? What are the policy arguments in favor of such an approach, and what are the arguments in favor of retaining the general rule against a duty to disclose? In your personal dealings, are you inclined to disclose all important facts to the other party during bargaining? Would it be appropriate to engage in such disclosure when you are negotiating on behalf of a client, if the law does not require disclosure?

---

2. Material Misrepresentation

A court will avoid a contract for misrepresentation during bargaining only if the offending party misrepresented a material fact. A fact is material if it is important to the bargaining, such as by affecting the outcome of the bargaining in some non-trivial way. If a misrepresented fact did not influence a party's decision to enter into the contract, and if it did not affect the terms to which the party would agree, then it was immaterial to the bargaining, and avoidance is not justified.

For example, suppose that the seller of a used car lied during bargaining by falsely stating that the previous owner of the car had attended the same high school as the buyer. That misrepresentation might have been a good "ice-breaker," helping the seller to establish a rapport with the buyer; however, it would not be material if it had no influence on the outcome of the negotiations.

In what some might view as a closer case, the South Dakota Supreme Court affirmed the trial court's denial of a home buyer's request for avoidance. A South Dakota statute requires sellers of real estate to affirmatively disclose important facts known to the seller by responding to dozens of questions on a disclosure form, including a final question that asks about "any other material facts or problems." S.D. Codified L. 43-4-44 (Supp. 2018). The Court affirmed the trial court's denial of avoidance based on its conclusion that the seller was not required to appreciate and disclose the existence of "a snake problem" after the seller had seen only one snake in the house during 30 years of ownership. *McCollam v. Cahill*, 766 N.W.2d 171, 175 ¶10 (2009).

Exercise 8.7 — Disclosure of Material Facts

Suppose that you are a sales agent in a state that imposes an affirmative duty to disclose all material facts in sales of residential dwellings. You know a good deal about the houses that you have listed for sale, but you are not always certain which information is material and thus must be disclosed. Some states provide a checklist of topics to address in a disclosure statement; however, the checklist might not be exclusive and could invite disclosure of other material facts not addressed in the checklist.

For example, would a death in the house be a material fact? Would it matter if the death was from natural causes, suicide, homicide by an intruder, or homicide by a family member after a domestic quarrel? Assume that the death had occurred a year earlier and that it had no effect at all on the habitability or appearance of the house. Assume also, however, that—if informed of the death—the average buyer would react emotionally and would require a 5% decrease in the price before agreeing to buy. If state legislation generally requires full disclosure of material facts in real estate transactions, but does not specifically address whether such disclosure requirements extend to a death on the property, how would you interpret and apply the general disclosure statute to the facts stated above? Is the death a "material" fact?

By statute, the Arizona legislature has barred any action against a seller or lessor of real property, such as for "termination or rescission," for failure to disclose during bargaining that a person had died on the property, that a felony had been committed there, that the property had been owned or occupied by someone diagnosed with or exposed to H.I.V., or that a sex offender resides in the vicinity. ARIZ. REV. STAT. ANN. § 32-2156 (2018); *see also* N.Y. REAL PROP. LAW § 443-a (McKinney 2015) (similar provision, but not addressing sex offender in vicinity); Cal. Civ. Code § 1710.2 (West Supp. 2018) (A seller is not liable for nondisclosure of an occupant's death occurring more than three years prior, or an occupant's death from or affliction with HIV/AIDS, but may be liable for affirmative misrepresentation in response to questions about deaths.). Beyond simple nondisclosure, suppose that a seller in Arizona actively conceals one of these designated facts, or affirmatively misrepresents the absence of one of these facts. Would the Arizona statute bar a civil action? *See Lerner v. DMB Realty, LLC*, 234 Ariz. 397, 322 P.3d 909 (Ct. App. 2014) (statute does not bar an action for active concealment or affirmative misrepresentation regarding the presence of a level one sex offender in the vicinity, leaving question of materiality for the jury).

---

3. Misrepresentation of Fact, Not Opinion

A party seeking avoidance for misrepresentation must show that the other party misrepresented a fact, not merely a matter of opinion, during bargaining. Sellers or vendors of services, for example, are entitled to engage in a reasonable amount of "sales puffing," in which they laud their goods, properties, or services with assertions such as "This is a beautiful car, inside and out," or "This is a great neighborhood for kids," or "Our cleaning service will make your house sparkle again."

The author is reminded of a sales pitch from the owner of Don Weir's Music City in San Francisco (who was widely known by customers as "Weird Weir"), when he showed the author's high school buddy a used Fender Twin Reverb guitar amplifier and exclaimed, "Man, this thing really SCREAMS!" If the buyer later complained that the amplifier did not produce the kind of ear-splitting sound for which he had hoped, it's extremely unlikely that a court would find a misrepresentation of fact in Mr. Weir's exuberant statement. Such boasting during a sales pitch is reasonably interpreted as a statement of opinion, which the buyer ought to take with a grain of salt rather than placing reliance on it.

The justification for excluding opinions from misrepresentation claims appears in an early Arizona case, in which the buyer of cattle complained that the seller had exaggerated the general quality and value of the cattle:

> Misrepresentations as to value cannot ordinarily constitute fraud because they are generally to be regarded as mere expressions of opinion or "trader's talk" involving a matter of judgment and estimation as to which men may differ. It has been held that such representations may, under certain circumstances, be nonactionable even when made with intent to deceive, and with knowledge of their falsity, and *a fortiori* they are not actionable where made in honest ignorance. Where the parties deal at arm's length with equal means of knowledge, it is obvious that there can be no redress for misrepresentations as to value, because in such a case the hearer should investigate and judge for himself. He has no right to rely upon the speaker's representations as to value, and if he does so and suffers injury it is his own folly, for which the law will grant no relief, and this is especially true where the relation of the parties is antagonistic, or where the hearer has made an investigation before acting, or knows that the speaker is relying upon information from another, or the matter is one of public record.

Sorrells v. Clifford, 23 Ariz. 448, 458–59, 204 P. 1013, 1016–17 (1922).

The passage from *Sorrells v. Clifford* shows that some elements of an action for misrepresentation can overlap. A misrepresentation may be classified as a statement of mere opinion rather than one of fact partly because it does not provide a solid basis for justifiable reliance, the element discussed in the next section. This point was made nearly 80 years after *Sorrells*, although in a different legal context:

> [I]t is clear that the assertion by Papa John's that it makes a "Better Pizza." is a general statement of opinion regarding the superiority of its product over all others. This simple statement, "Better Pizza.," epitomizes the exaggerated advertising, blustering, and boasting by a manufacturer upon which no consumer would reasonably rely.... Consequently, it appears indisputable that Papa John's assertion "Better Pizza." is non-actionable puffery.

Pizza Hut v. Papa John's Int'l, 227 F.3d 489, 498 (5th Cir. 2000) (rejecting Pizza Hut's claim of false advertising under the Lanham Act).

4. *Justifiable Reliance*

a. Reliance

A party is not entitled to avoidance unless he relied on a misrepresentation. In the *Sorrells* case, the buyer also claimed that the seller had overstated the number of cattle with the seller's brand that could be found on the range. The court concluded, however, that the buyer had not relied on any misrepresentation as to the quantity of cattle that the buyer would be acquiring:

[The buyer], as an experienced cattle man, familiar with the methods of ascertaining approximately the number of cattle ranging on the range at large in any given brand, pursued these methods, and, from all that can be known, relied upon the results of his investigation rather than upon the representations of the defendant. [The buyer] also says:

> While the law is as stated in the cases cited by appellant, it is equally the law that, if the buyer, instead of investigating as fully as he might, made only a partial investigation, and relied in part on the representations of the adverse party, and was deceived by such representation to his injury, he is not precluded from maintaining action for such deceit

—and cites in support thereof *Meland v. Youngberg*, 124 Minn. 446, 145 N. W. 167, Ann. Cas. 1915B, 775. That case ... also says:

> But, if the buyer undertakes to investigate and determine the entire matter for himself, and is afforded a full and fair opportunity therefor, and in fact does make such investigation, and is permitted to make it as full and complete as he chooses, and he accepts the property after such investigation, the authorities are practically unanimous that he cannot ... assert that he relied upon the representations of the adverse party.

Sorrells v. Clifford, 23 Ariz. 448, 459–60, 204 P. 1013, 1017 (1922).

b. Justifiable

Furthermore, even if a party relied on a misrepresentation of material fact, she will be entitled to avoidance only if her reliance was justified. As explored in the previous section, some misrepresentations are such obvious exaggerations or statements of opinion that no reasonable person would rely on them. Moreover, even if a representation is not plainly misleading on its face, if the victim of the misrepresentation could easily have discovered the facts with a prudent investigation of her own, she may not be justified in relying on the statements of a person with whom she is bargaining at arm's length.

Nonetheless, as explored in greater detail in the next section, courts apply the requirement of justifiable reliance, as well as other elements of misrepresentation, in a flexible manner.

C. Discretion in Applying the Equitable Remedy of Avoidance

Courts have analyzed misrepresentation claims in a flexible manner. They sometimes apply a relaxed standard for one element if the facts strongly support another element of the claim, or if special circumstances justify relaxing the standard for one or more elements. This flexibility could stem from—or at least be related to—the discretionary nature of the equitable remedy of avoidance, or rescission:

> Rescission is an equitable remedy that operates to extinguish a contract that is legally valid but must be set aside due to fraud, mistake, or for some other reason to avoid unjust enrichment.... Rescission of a contract is an equitable remedy used as a substitute for monetary damages when such damages would not be adequate.... Whether to grant rescission lies within the trial court's discretion....
>
> ... The trial court does not abuse its discretion if some evidence reasonably supports the trial court's decision.

Isaacs v. Bishop, 249 S.W.3d 100, 109–110 (Tex. App. 2008) (citations omitted).

In one case, for example, a client at a dance studio purchased more than $31,000 in dance lessons, partly in reliance on her instructor's lavish praise of her dancing skills and her aptitude for becoming an accomplished dancer, even though she had trouble "hearing the beat." The instructor's representations arguably were falsehoods or at least half-truths; however, the dance studio sensibly argued that the instructor's praise amounted to statements of opinion, rather than fact, and thus could not support a claim for avoidance. The court overcame this objection and treated the instructor's praise as it would statements of fact, because the instructor had superior knowledge about the aptitude of dance students, thus justifying the student's reliance on statements that otherwise might be viewed as sales puffing. Although the court did not clearly make this point, its relaxing of the rule about statements of opinion was also justified by a fiduciary duty owed by the instructor: the instructor was already under contract with the student when he made the representations that induced the subsequent contracts, and the contract already in force arguably obligated the instructor to provide accurate and honest feedback, or at least to act in good faith when expressing his assessment of his client's aptitude for further progress. *See Vokes v. Arthur Murray, Inc.*, 212 So. 2d 906 (Fla. App. 1968).

The discretion exercised by judges in avoidance claims is well illustrated by the degree of diligence that courts demand of claimants when determining whether a claimant's reliance on a misrepresentation is justified. Compare the very different tones and results of the following two cases on that issue. What circumstances might move a court to be more or less demanding on the question of reasonableness of reliance?

Isaacs v. Bishop

249 S.W.3d 100 (Tex. App. 2008)

Opinion by Chief Justice Morriss:

....

¶ 1 Bishop purchased real and personal property known as the Hallsville Dragway (the track) from Isaacs, with Isaacs providing purchase-money financing. Isaacs' attorney, R.G. Schleier, after negotiations between the parties, prepared the documents for the sale, including the promissory note that later became one focal point of the later dispute.

....

¶2 When Isaacs began looking for a way to foreclose, he found violations of what turned out to be—to Bishop's surprise—a hair-trigger default provision in the promissory note. There is evidence that Schleier changed the promissory note at Isaacs' direction to insert that provision, a provision the jury later found to have been fraudulently added. Isaacs began foreclosure proceedings. Evidence suggested that the track had been making a profit for Bishop until Isaacs began his campaign to cause Bishop's fiscal ruin and that bankruptcy ultimately resulted from that campaign.

....

¶3 ... Bishop contends first that the trial court abused its discretion by denying his election to rescind the purchase....

....

¶4 Some evidence and a jury finding established that Bishop was at least partly responsible for the fraud perpetrated on him. Evidence suggested that, before Bishop signed the promissory note prepared by Schleier—who Bishop knew had a history as Isaacs' lawyer—Bishop did have, but failed to make use of, an opportunity to read the note. The jury found that Isaacs committed fraud and was seventy percent responsible for the damages, but that Bishop was thirty percent responsible. Some authority suggests that a negligent party may not obtain rescission; substantial authority exists that unclean hands will preclude such relief. *See Schenck*, 803 S.W.2d 361.

¶5 We conclude from the record that the trial court's ruling was within the scope of its equitable authority. We overrule this contention of error. [But Bishop was entitled to damages and attorney's fees on other claims.]

Kannavos v. Annino

356 Mass. 42, 247 N.E.2d 708 (1969)

Cutter, Justice.

....

¶1 Kannavos and his wife acquired 11 Ingersoll Grove from the vendors (who are the trustees of Annino Realty Trust) on June 28, 1965. Kannavos and Bellas bought 71–73 and 79 Ingersoll Grove from the vendors on July 12, 1965. The situation as to each purchase is substantially the same.

....

¶2 Mrs. Annino (who at all pertinent times "was authorized to act and did act on behalf of ... Annino Realty Trust") had bought the Ingersoll Grove properties in 1961 and 1962. At that time there was a single family house on each property. Each house was, under the Springfield zoning ordinance, in a Residence A district, where multi-family uses are prohibited. This zoning has remained in effect at all times since 1961. Despite the zoning provisions, Mrs. Annino converted each single family house into a multi-family apartment building. Each was furnished and rented as a multi-family dwelling. All the work of conversion was done "without obtaining any building permit," as each trustee of the realty trust knew. Each trustee also knew that the use of the buildings for multi-family purposes was in violation of the zoning ordinance.

¶ 3 In 1965 Kenneth F. Foote was retained as real estate broker "to try to sell the properties." He caused advertisements, of which the following is an example, to appear in Springfield newspapers: "Income gross $9,600 yr. in lg. single house, converted to 8 lovely, completely furn. (includ. TV and china) apts. 8 baths, ideal for couple to live free with excellent income. By apt. only. Foote Realty." Each advertisement clearly advertised, in some form of words, the particular property as being income property of multi-family use.

¶ 4 Kannavos, a self-employed hairdresser, about thirty-eight years old, read one advertisement. He "wanted to acquire some income real estate." He got in touch with Foote, who showed him the 11 Ingersoll Grove property and gave him income and expense figures obtained from Mrs. Annino. Kannavos executed a purchase agreement to buy 11 Ingersoll Grove. The vendees had no lawyer representing them with respect to the negotiations, the agreement, or the final closing. An attorney representing a mortgagee, under a mortgage obtained by the vendees, drew and recorded the papers used at the closing, at which the vendors were also represented by an attorney "to check the adjustments." [Kannavos was an immigrant with a high school education who spoke English as a second language].

. . . .

¶ 5 In the present cases, the defect in the premises related to a matter of public regulation, the zoning and building ordinances. Its applicability to these premises could have been discovered by these vendees or by the vendees' counsel if, acting with prudence, they had retained counsel, which they did not. The bank mortgagee's counsel presumably was looking only to the protection of the bank's security position. Nevertheless, where there is reliance on fraudulent representations or upon statements and action treated as fraudulent, our cases have not barred plaintiffs from recovery merely because they "did not use due diligence . . . (when they) could readily have ascertained from . . . records" what the true facts were. See *Yorke v. Taylor*, 332 Mass. 368, 373, 124 N.E.2d 912. There this court allowed rescission because of the negligent misrepresentation, innocent but false, of the current assessed value of the property being sold. Here the representations made by the advertising and the vendors' conduct and statements in effect were that the property was multi-family housing suitable for investment and that the housing could continue to be used for that purpose. Because the vendors did as much as they did do, they were bound to do more. Failing to do so, they were responsible for misrepresentation. . . .

We hold that the vendors' conduct entitled the vendees to rescind. [affirming rescission by the trial court]

Exercise 8.8 — Practice Exam: *Fiege v. Boehm* Revisited

The facts of the following exam question are loosely based on *Fiege v. Boehm*, discussed briefly in Chapter 3, Section II.A. The consideration analysis in that opinion does not apply to this question, however, which raises only one or more claims addressed in this chapter.

Essay Question. Suggested Time Allocation: 40 minutes

Hilda and Louis had dated three times over the course of two months. Louis engaged in sexual relations with Hilda once, on July 2. Hilda also had sexual relations once with Jason, on July 4. She discovered in August that she was pregnant, with conception taking place sometime within first week of July. Hilda did not know then whether Louis or Jason was the father, but she decided to ask Louis for support, because Louis had a handsome income and could provide support with much greater ease than could Jason, who had meager savings and had been laid off from work recently. Louis and Hilda met in August in a coffee shop, the first time they had seen each other since July 2. After a few minutes of inconsequential small talk, Hilda informed Louis that she was pregnant, told him that she expected him to provide support in exchange for her surrendering her good-faith claim under the state's paternity statute, and presented him with a short written contract setting forth her proposal. Louis asked Hilda whether she was sure that she was pregnant but did not ask her whether she had engaged in sexual relations with any other man. Hilda showed Louis a physician's report confirming her pregnancy and identifying the time of conception as sometime in the first week of July. Hilda offered no other information, so Louis is unaware of her intimacy with Jason. Hilda and Louis both signed the agreement at the coffee house. They both are adults with contractual capacity. Tests later showed that Jason, and not Louis, is the father. You may assume an offer and acceptance with consideration. Discuss only whether Louis can avoid the contract for some form of misrepresentation. Discuss each issue or subissue separately, and argue both sides whenever possible.

V. Mutual Mistake of Fact

Review the topic of relief for unilateral mistake, Chapter 2, Section II.C. Let's now assume that *both* parties harbored a mistaken assumption of fact during bargaining and learned of the mistake only after contract formation. If one party now regrets the bargain, in what circumstances will a court avoid the contract on the ground of mutual mistake?

A. "A Different Creature"

Sherwood v. Walker and others

66 Mich. 568, 33 N.W. 919 (1887)

Morse, J.

¶1 Replevin for a cow. Suit commenced in justice's court; judgment for plaintiff; appealed to circuit court of Wayne county, and verdict and judgment for plaintiff in that court. The defendants bring error, and set out 25 assignments of the same.

....

¶2 May 5, 1886, plaintiff went out to Greenfield, and saw the cattle. A few days thereafter, he called upon one of the defendants with the view of purchasing a cow, known as "Rose 2d of Aberlone." ... He requested defendants to confirm the sale in writing, which they did by sending him the following letter:

> "WALKERVILLE, May 15, 1886.
>
> "T.C. Sherwood, President, etc.-DEAR SIR: We confirm sale to you of the cow Rose 2d of Aberlone, lot 56 of our catalogue, at five and half cents per pound, less fifty pounds shrink. We inclose herewith order on Mr. Graham for the cow. You might leave check with him, or mail to us here, as you prefer.
>
> "Yours, truly, HIRAM WALKER & SONS."

....

¶3 On the twenty-first of the same month the plaintiff went to defendants' farm at Greenfield, and presented the order and letter to Graham, who informed him that the defendants had instructed him not to deliver the cow. Soon after, the plaintiff tendered to Hiram Walker, one of the defendants, $80, and demanded the cow. Walker refused to take the money or deliver the cow. The plaintiff then instituted this suit. After he had secured possession of the cow under the writ of replevin, the plaintiff caused her to be weighed by the constable who served the writ, at a place other than King's cattle-yard. She weighed 1,420 pounds.

¶4 It appears from the record that both parties supposed this cow was barren and would not breed, and she was sold by the pound for an insignificant sum as compared with her real value if a breeder. She was evidently sold and purchased on the relation of her value for beef, unless the plaintiff had learned of her true condition, and concealed such knowledge from the defendants. Before the plaintiff secured the possession of the animal, the defendants learned that she was with calf, and therefore of great value, and undertook to rescind the sale by refusing to deliver her. The question arises whether they had a right to do so. The circuit judge ruled that this fact did not avoid the sale and it made no difference whether she was barren or not. I am of the opinion that the court erred in this holding. I know that this is a close question, and the dividing line between the adjudicated cases is not easily discerned. But it must be considered as well settled that a party who has given an apparent consent to a contract of sale may refuse to execute it, or he may avoid it after it has been completed, if the assent was founded, or the contract made, upon the mistake of a material fact, such as the subject-matter of the sale, the price, or some collateral fact materially inducing the agreement; and this can be done when the mistake is mutual. [Court cites to four cases and two treatises].

¶ 5 If there is a difference or misapprehension as to the substance of the thing bargained for; if the thing actually delivered or received is different in substance from the thing bargained for, and intended to be sold, then there is no contract; but if it be only a difference in some quality or accident, even though the mistake may have been the actuating motive to the purchaser or seller, or both of them, yet the contract remains binding. "The difficulty in every case is to determine whether the mistake or misapprehension is as to the substance of the whole contract, going, as it were, to the root of the matter, or only to some point, even though a material point, an error as to which does not affect the substance of the whole consideration." *Kennedy v. Panama, etc., Mail Co., L.R.* 2 Q.B. 580, 587....

¶ 6 It seems to me, however, in the case made by this record, that the mistake or misapprehension of the parties went to the whole substance of the agreement. If the cow was a breeder, she was worth at least $750; if barren, she was worth not over $80. The parties would not have made the contract of sale except upon the understanding and belief that she was incapable of breeding, and of no use as a cow. It is true she is now the identical animal that they thought her to be when the contract was made; there is no mistake as to the identity of the creature. Yet the mistake was not of the mere quality of the animal, but went to the very nature of the thing. A barren cow is substantially a different creature than a breeding one.... If the mutual mistake had simply related to the fact whether she was with calf or not for one season, then it might have been a good sale, but the mistake affected the character of the animal for all time, and for its present and ultimate use. She was not in fact the animal, or the kind of animal, the defendants intended to sell or the plaintiff to buy. She was not a barren cow, and, if this fact had been known, there would have been no contract. The mistake affected the substance of the whole consideration, and it must be considered that there was no contract to sell or sale of the cow as she actually was. The thing sold and bought had in fact no existence. She was sold as a beef creature would be sold; she is in fact a breeding cow, and a valuable one. The court should have instructed the jury that if they found that the cow was sold, or contracted to be sold, upon the understanding of both parties that she was barren, and useless for the purpose of breeding, and that in fact she was not barren, but capable of breeding, then the defendants had a right to rescind, and to refuse to deliver, and the verdict should be in their favor.

¶7 The judgment of the court below must be reversed, and a new trial granted, with costs of this court to defendants.

Sherwood, J., (dissenting.)

¶8 I do not concur in the opinion given by my brethren in this case....

....

¶9 It is claimed that a mutual mistake of a material fact was made by the parties when the contract of sale was made.... [Justice Sherwood agreed with the legal rule announced by the majority regarding mutual mistake of fact.]

....

¶10 The only pretense for avoiding this contract by the defendants is that they erred in judgment as to the qualities and value of the animal.... The judgment should be affirmed.

B. Affecting Substance, Not Just Value or Quality

Because mutual mistake does not result from one party's culpability, as in the case of misrepresentation, the *Sherwood* court appears to require the mistaken fact to be more than merely "material." How important must the subject of the mistake be to justify avoidance? The majority and dissent in *Sherwood* agree on the legal rule. How do they differ on the application of the rule to the facts?

What degree of importance, beyond simple materiality, does the following Arizona decision require for avoidance for mutual mistake?

Renner v. Kehl

150 Ariz. 94, 722 P.2d 262 (1986) (In Banc)

Gordon, Vice Chief Justice.

¶1 This Petition for Review was granted in order to determine the measure of damages available to the plaintiff upon rescission of a land contract. We have jurisdiction pursuant to Ariz. Const. art. 6 § 5(3) and Rule 23, Ariz. R. Civ. App. P., 17 A A.R.S.

¶2 In 1981 the petitioners, defendants below, acquired from the State of Arizona agricultural development leases covering 2,262 acres of unimproved desert land near Yuma. The petitioners made no attempt to develop the property themselves, but instead decided to sell their interest in the land. The respondents, plaintiffs below, were residents of the state of Washington interested in the large scale commercial cultivation of jojoba. The respondents and their agent, who was familiar with commercial jojoba development, were shown the petitioners' property and became interested in purchasing it. The property appeared to be ideal for the respondents' purposes; the soil and climate were good and both parties were of the opinion that sufficient water was available beneath the land to sustain jojoba production. The respondents made it clear that they were interested in the property only for jojoba production and required adequate water supplies.

¶3 The respondents decided to buy the leases and on June 5, 1981, executed a Real Estate Purchase Contract to that effect. Respondents agreed to pay $222,200 for the leases, and paid petitioners $80,200 as a down payment, the remainder to be paid in annual installments. In November of 1981 respondents began development of the property for jojoba production. As part of the development process the respondents had five test wells drilled, none of which produced water of sufficient quantity or quality for commercial jojoba cultivation. After spending approximately $229,000 developing the land respondents determined that the aquifer underlying the property was inadequate for commercial development of jojoba. At this point the project was abandoned and the respondents sued to rescind the purchase contract. The petitioners counterclaimed for the balance of payments due under the contract.

¶4 The case was tried before the court between October 25 and October 27, 1983, and the trial court entered Findings of Fact, Conclusions of Law, and an Order on January 9, 1984. The court found that the respondents were entitled to rescission based on mutual mistake of fact and failure of consideration, and ordered the respondents to reassign the lease to the petitioners. The petitioners were ordered to pay the respondents $309,849.84 ($80,200 representing the down payment and $229,649.48 representing the cost of developing the property) together with costs and attorney's fees.

¶5 The petitioners appealed to the court of appeals, which affirmed the trial court by memorandum decision. *Renner v. Kehl*, 1 CA-CIV 7749 (filed December 17, 1985). The petitioners raise the same arguments before this Court, viz., that rescission was not justified, or if rescission was appropriate petitioners are not liable for consequential damages.

RESCISSION

¶6 Mutual mistake of fact is an accepted basis for rescission. *Amos Flight Operations, Inc. v. Thunderbird Bank*, 112 Ariz. 263, 540 P.2d 1244 (1975); *Mortensen v. Berzell Investment Co.*, 102 Ariz. 348, 429 P.2d 945 (1967). *See* Restatement (Second) of Contracts § 152. In Arizona a contract may be rescinded when there is a mutual mistake of material fact which constitutes "an essential part and condition of the contract." *Mortensen v. Berzell Investment Co.*, 102 Ariz. at 350, 429 P.2d at 947. The trial court found that the sole purpose of the contract was to enable respondents to grow jojoba, which depends upon an adequate water supply. The trial court specifically found that "There would have been no sale if both sellers and buyers had not believed it was possible to grow jojoba commercially on the leased acres. . . ." and that "[b]ased upon the factual data available, all parties were of the opinion that there would be sufficient good quality water for commercial jojoba production, and that it would be close enough to the surface that it would be economically feasible to pump it for irrigation of large acreages." Consequently, the trial court concluded that "[p]laintiffs are entitled to rescind the purchase agreement because of the mutual mistake of fact...." The belief of the parties that adequate water supplies existed beneath the property was "a basic assumption on which both parties made the contract," Restatement (Second) of Contracts § 152 comment b, and their mutual mistake "ha[d] such a material effect on the agreed exchange of performances as to upset the very bases of the contract." *Id.* comment a. The contract was therefore voidable and the respondents were entitled to rescission.

[In a footnote, the court noted that the parties did not allocate the risk of mistake to the buyer, and that rescission was not precluded by the parties' failure to inspect or test for groundwater.]

C. Allocation of Risk: Bargaining with Awareness of Uncertainty about the Subject Matter

Aluminum Co. of America v. Essex Group, Inc.

499 F. Supp. 53 (W.D. Penn. 1980)

Teitelbaum, District Judge.

....

¶1 Essex next argues that ALCOA may not be relieved of the consequences of the mistake because it assumed or bore the risk of the market. Essex relies on both Restatements and on a variety of cases fairly typified by ... *McNamara Const. of Manitoba Ltd. v. United States*, 509 F.2d 1166 (Ct. Cl. 1963), and *Flippin Materials Co. v. United States*, 312 F.2d 408 (Ct. Cl. 1963). *McNamara Construction* involved a fixed price construction contract which was upset by extensive labor strife. The Court of Claims denied the contractor relief from its extra costs, holding, *inter alia*, that the contractor had been aware of the risk of labor trouble when it entered the contract; that the contract expressly provided for delay caused by strikes; and that in the absence of some further express provision the contractor bore the risk of the cost of strikes and labor cost increases. The court declared: "What we have in this case is a risk which is known to both parties and results from human inability to predict the future. The authorities are unanimous in distinguishing such risks from *bona fide* mutual mistakes of fact." *Id.* at 1168.

¶2 In *Flippin Materials Co. v. United States, supra*, the plaintiff sought relief from unexpected costs it suffered in a contract to quarry limestone from a mountain and to process it into aggregate. The costs derived from the presence of unexpected amounts of waste material at the quarry site. The Court of Claims held that the plaintiff could not claim relief on a mutual mistake theory because the contract clearly put the risk of unknown subsurface conditions on the plaintiff. The contract offer made the government's geological findings available to the bidders and it further provided:

> GC-2 SITE INVESTIGATION AND REPRESENTATIONS:
>
> The contractor acknowledges that he has satisfied himself as to the nature and location of the work, the general and local conditions, particularly those bearing upon ... conformation and condition of the ground, the character, quality and quantity of surface and subsurface materials to be encountered ... and all other matters which can in any way affect the work or the cost thereof under this contract. Any failure by the contractor to acquaint himself with all the available information concerning these conditions will not relieve him from responsibility for estimating properly the difficulty or cost of successfully performing the work. *Id.* at 415.

The court declared that relief for mutual mistake is not available "if the contract puts the risk of such a mistake on the party asking reformation ... or normally if the other party, though made aware of the correct facts, would not have agreed at the outset to the change...." *Id.*

¶ 3 The Restatements and these cases reveal four facets of risk assumption and risk allocation under the law of mistake. First, a party to a contract may expressly assume a risk. If a contractor agrees to purchase and to remove 114,000 cubic yards of fill from a designated tract for the landowner at a set price "regardless of subsurface soil and water conditions" the contractor assumes the risk that subsurface water may make the removal unexpectedly expensive.

¶ 4 Customary dealing in a trade or common understanding may lead a court to impose a risk on a party where the contract is silent. Often the result corresponds to the expectation of both parties, but this will not always be true. *See* Berman, *Excuse for Nonperformance in the Light of Contract Practices in International Trade*, 63 Colum. L. Rev. 1413, 1420–24 (1963). At times legal rules may form the basis for the inferred common understanding....

¶ 5 Third, where neither express words nor some particular common understanding or trade usage dictate a result, the court must allocate the risk in some reasoned way. Two examples from the Restatement 2d of Contracts § 296 illustrate the principle. A farmer who contracts to sell land may not escape the obligation if minerals are discovered which make the land more valuable. And in the case of the sale of fill stated above, if there is no express assumption of the risk of adverse conditions by the contractor, he may still bear the risk of losing his expected profits and suffering some out of pocket losses if some of the fill lies beneath the water table. These cases rest on policies of high generality. Contracts are—generally—to be enforced. Land sales are—generally—to be treated as final.

¶ 6 Fourth, where parties enter a contract in a state of conscious ignorance of the facts, they are deemed to risk the burden of having the facts turn out to be adverse, within very broad limits. Each party takes a calculated gamble in such a contract. Because information is often troublesome or costly to obtain, the law does not seek to discourage such contracts. Thus if parties agree to sell and purchase a stone which both know may be glass or diamond at a price which in some way reflects their uncertainty, the contract is enforceable whether the stone is in fact glass or diamond. If, by contrast, the parties both mistakenly believe it to be glass, the case is said not to be one of conscious ignorance but one of mutual mistake. Consequently the vendor may void the contract.

Estate of Martha Nelson v. Rice

198 Ariz. 563, 12 P.3d 238 (Ct. App. 2000)

Espinosa, Chief Judge.

¶1 Plaintiff/appellant the Estate of Martha Nelson, through its copersonal representatives Edward Franz and Kenneth Newman, appeals from a summary judgment in favor of defendants/appellees Carl and Anne Rice in the Estate's action seeking rescission or reformation of the sale of two paintings to the Rices. The Estate argues that these remedies are required because the sale was based upon a mutual mistake. The Estate also contends that enforcing the sale "contract" would be unconscionable. We affirm.

Facts and Procedural History

¶2 We view the evidence and all reasonable inferences therefrom in the light most favorable to the party opposing the summary judgment. *Hill-Shafer Partnership v. Chilson Family Trust*, 165 Ariz. 469, 799 P.2d 810 (1990). After Martha Nelson died in February 1996, Newman and Franz, the copersonal representatives of her estate, employed Judith McKenzie-Larson to appraise the Estate's personal property in preparation for an estate sale. McKenzie-Larson told them that she did not appraise fine art and that, if she saw any, they would need to hire an additional appraiser. McKenzie-Larson did not report finding any fine art, and relying on her silence and her appraisal, Newman and Franz priced and sold the Estate's personal property.

¶3 Responding to a newspaper advertisement, Carl Rice attended the public estate sale and paid the asking price of $60 for two oil paintings. Although Carl had bought and sold some art, he was not an educated purchaser, had never made more than $55 on any single piece, and had bought many pieces that had "turned out to be frauds, forgeries or ... to have been [created] by less popular artists." He assumed the paintings were not originals given their price and the fact that the Estate was managed by professionals, but was attracted to the subject matter of one of the paintings and the frame of the other. At home, he compared the signatures on the paintings to those in a book of artists' signatures, noticing they "appeared to be similar" to that of Martin Johnson Heade. As they had done in the past, the Rices sent pictures of the paintings to Christie's in New York, hoping they might be Heade's work. Christie's authenticated the paintings, Magnolia Blossoms on Blue Velvet and Cherokee Roses, as paintings by Heade and offered to sell them on consignment. Christie's subsequently sold the paintings at auction for $1,072,000. After subtracting the buyer's premium and the commission, the Rices realized $911,780 from the sale.

¶4 … [The Estate settled its claim against its contractor, McKenzie-Larson.] During 1997, the Rices paid income taxes of $337,000 on the profit from the sale of the paintings, purchased a home, created a family trust, and spent some of the funds on living expenses.

¶5 The Estate sued the Rices in late January 1998, alleging the sale contract should be rescinded or reformed on grounds of mutual mistake and unconscionability. In its subsequent motion for summary judgment, the Estate argued the parties were not aware the transaction had involved fine art, believing instead that the items exchanged were "relatively valueless, wall decorations." In their opposition and cross-motion, the Rices argued the Estate bore the risk of mistake,…. The trial court concluded that, although the parties had been mistaken about the value of the paintings, the Estate bore the risk of that mistake….

….

Mutual Mistake

¶6 … A party seeking to rescind a contract on the basis of mutual mistake must show by clear and convincing evidence that the agreement should be set aside. *Emmons v. Superior Court*, 192 Ariz. 509, 968 P.2d 582 (App. 1998). A contract may be rescinded on the ground of a mutual mistake as to a "'basic assumption on which both parties made the contract.'" *Renner v. Kehl*, 150 Ariz. 94, 97, 722 P.2d 262, 265 (1986), *quoting* Restatement (Second) of Contracts § 152 cmt. b (1979). Furthermore, the parties' mutual mistake must have had "'such a material effect on the agreed exchange of performances as to upset the very bases of the contract.'" *Id.*, quoting Restatement § 152 cmt. a. However, the mistake must not be one on which the party seeking relief bears the risk under the rules stated in § 154(b) of the Restatement. *Emmons*; Restatement § 152.

¶7 In concluding that the Estate was not entitled to rescind the sale, the trial court found that, although a mistake had existed as to the value of the paintings, the Estate bore the risk of that mistake under § 154(b) of the Restatement, citing the example in comment a. Section 154(b) states that a party bears the risk of mistake when "he is aware, at the time the contract is made, that he has only limited knowledge with respect to the facts to which the mistake relates but treats his limited knowledge as sufficient." In explaining that provision, the Washington Supreme Court stated, "In such a situation there is no mistake. Instead, there is an awareness of uncertainty or conscious ignorance of the future." *Bennett v. Shinoda Floral, Inc.*, 108 Wash. 2d 386, 739 P.2d 648, 653–54 (1987); *see also State Farm Fire & Cas. Co. v. Pacific Rent-All, Inc.*, 90 Hawaii 315, 978 P.2d 753 (1999).

¶8 The Estate contends neither party bore the risk of mistake, arguing that § 154 and comment *a* are not applicable to these facts. In the example in comment a, the risk of mistake is allocated to the seller when the buyer discovers valuable mineral deposits on property priced and purchased as farmland. Even were we to accept the Estate's argument that this example is not analogous, comment c clearly applies here and states:

> Conscious ignorance. Even though the mistaken party did not agree to bear the risk, he may have been aware when he made the contract that his knowledge with respect to the facts to which the mistake relates was limited. If he was not only so aware that his knowledge was limited but undertook to perform in the face of that awareness, he bears the risk of the mistake. It is sometimes said in such a situation that, in a sense, there was not mistake but "conscious ignorance."

¶9 Through its personal representatives, the Estate hired two appraisers, McKenzie-Larson and an Indian art expert, to evaluate the Estate's collection of Indian art and artifacts. McKenzie-Larson specifically told Newman that she did not appraise fine art. In his deposition, Newman testified that he had not been concerned that McKenzie-Larson had no expertise in fine art, believing the Estate contained nothing of "significant value" except the house and the Indian art collection. Despite the knowledge that the Estate contained framed art other than the Indian art, and that McKenzie-Larson was not qualified to appraise fine art, the personal representatives relied on her to notify them of any fine art or whether a fine arts appraiser was needed. Because McKenzie-Larson did not say they needed an additional appraiser, Newman and Franz did not hire anyone qualified to appraise fine art. By relying on the opinion of someone who was admittedly unqualified to appraise fine art to determine its existence, the personal representatives consciously ignored the possibility that the Estate's assets might include fine art, thus assuming that risk. *See Klas v. Van Wagoner*, 829 P.2d 135, 141 n. 8 (Utah App. 1992) (real estate buyers not entitled to rescind sale contract because they bore risk of mistake as to property's value; by hiring architects, decorators, and electricians to examine realty, but failing to have it appraised, purchasers executed sale contract knowing they "had only 'limited knowledge' with respect to the value of the home"). Accordingly, the trial court correctly found that the Estate bore the risk of mistake as to the paintings' value.

¶10 The Estate asserts that the facts here are similar to those in *Renner*, in which real estate buyers sued to rescind a contract for acreage upon which they wished to commercially grow jojoba after discovering the water supply was inadequate for that purpose. The supreme court concluded that the buyers could rescind the contract based upon mutual mistake because both the buyers and the sellers had believed there was an adequate water supply, a basic assumption underlying formation of the contract. The parties' failure to thoroughly investigate the water supply did not preclude rescission when "the risk of mistake was not allocated among the parties." 150 Ariz. at 97 n. 2, 722 P.2d at 265 n. 2. The Estate's reliance on *Renner* is unavailing because, as stated above, the Estate bore the risk of mistake based on its own conscious ignorance.

¶11 Furthermore, under Restatement § 154(c), the court may allocate the risk of mistake to one party "on the ground that it is reasonable in the circumstances to do so." In making this determination, "the court will consider the purposes of the parties and will have recourse to its own general knowledge of human behavior in bargain transactions." Restatement § 154 cmt. d. Here, the Estate had had ample opportunity to discover what it was selling and failed to do so; instead, it ignored the possibility that the paintings were valuable and attempted to take action only after learning of their worth as a result of the efforts of the Rices. Under these circumstances, the Estate was a victim of its own folly and it was reasonable for the court to allocate to it the burden of its mistake.

. . . .

Affirmed.

Exercise 8.9 — Allocating and Assuming Risk

1. Allocating Risk on the Basis of Agreement or Circumstances

By assuming the risk of being mistaken in its assumptions, a party can be held to a bargain, even if both parties shared the mistaken assumption at the time of contract formation. Parties can expressly allocate the risk of mistaken assumptions to one of the parties in the contract, thereby undercutting any claim by that party for avoidance for mutual mistake. For example, a contract could provide that "No warranties are made about the presence of groundwater in the Property, and Buyer assumes the risk of inadequate groundwater for its purposes." Even if inadequate groundwater would be extremely unusual in this area, and would run contrary to the parties' assumptions, such a contract provision would preclude avoidance for mutual mistake (unless the clause itself was unenforceable because, for example, it was included in the contract through fraud or duress).

In the absence of such a specific allocation of risk, a court might still find that all the terms of the contract and other circumstances, taken as a whole, reflects an agreement to allocate the risk of a mistaken assumption to one party. In a dispute over the sale of a home, for example, the risk of mutual mistake about the adequacy of the home's septic tank was allocated to the buyer largely on the basis of a general contract clause stating that the buyer agreed to accept the property "in its present condition." *Lenawee County Bd. Of Health v. Messerly*, 417 Mich. 17, 32-33, 331 N.W.2d 203, 210-11 (1982).

Often, one or both parties are held to have assumed the risk of mistaken assumptions simply because they chose to proceed in the face of uncertainty about existing facts, when they knew that their knowledge was incomplete. In *Rice*, for example, the estate chose to proceed with its sales in the face of factual uncertainty that it fully appreciated.

What was the estate's "conscious ignorance" in *Rice*? Did the parties both share an assumption about the paintings, or was it understood that they were both taking a gamble and pitting each one's judgment against the other's? What facts support one conclusion or another?

In the *Renner* case, the parties had not tested the property for ground water, but the parties concluded that the land contained sufficient ground water, based on "the factual data available." What kind of data would be sufficiently convincing to rebut any argument that the buyer proceeded in conscious ignorance of the amount of ground water available? Are you persuaded that *Renner* and *Rice* are distinguishable on this point?

2. The Diamond in the Rough

The following facts are inspired by a case that mostly discussed the absence of fraud, but that provides an opportunity to discuss mutual mistake of fact: *Wood v. Boynton*, 64 Wis. 265, 25 N.W. 42 (1885). Alice found an unusual rock. Knowing that it might be worthless but wondering whether it might contain a semi-precious gem, Alice took the rock to a jeweler, Bryce. Bryce accurately and honestly stated that the rock could contain a valuable gem, might amount to a cheap but pretty paperweight if cut and polished, or might be completely worthless and thus a complete waste of time to cut and polish. When Alice asked how much it would cost to appraise it, Bryce replied that he would charge $10 to make several cuts with a special saw to determine the nature of the rock. Alice declined to spend $10 on an appraisal and asked whether Bryce would purchase the rock for $5. Bryce considered the proposed price for a few moments, paid $5 for the rock, and put it aside. That evening, he cut into the rock and discovered that it contained an uncut diamond, which was worth $1.5 million when fully faceted and polished.

Can Alice avoid the contract, return the $5, and recover the gem after providing restitution for the reasonable value of Bryce's cutting and polishing the diamond? Alternatively, if Bryce had cut into the rock and found it to be completely worthless, could he avoid the contract, return the worthless rock, and reclaim his $5?

3. Refusing to Assume the Risk

If a party did not wish to assume the risk of uncertainty about the subject matter of a contract, and did not wish to rely on its ability to avoid the contract for mutual mistake of fact, it could allocate responsibility to the other party to stand behind an assumption, perhaps with a warranty or a condition. For example, a contract might provide that "Seller warrants that the Property contains [specified measure] of groundwater." If this warranty turns out to be inaccurate, the seller could be liable in damages for breach of contract. Alternatively, to encourage the seller to agree to such a warranty, the contract might limit the buyer's remedy for breach of warranty to cancellation of the contract and restitution.

For another example, the parties in Exercise 2 above might agree that "This sale is predicated on the rock having a value of no more than $50. In the event that the rock is determined to have a greater value, Buyer will share equally with Seller any enrichment beyond $50 realized by Buyer from his ownership or resale of any part of the rock."

If you were the lawyer for the estate in *Rice*, what sort of standard-form clause might you insert in a simple contract that buyers would be asked to sign when they purchased any of the many items of framed art offered for sale at prices ranging from $10–$100?

4. Mistake about Madoff and Marital Assets

After nearly 30 years of marriage, Steven Simkin and his wife, Laura Blank, both attorneys, divorced. In performance of a settlement agreement that called for an "equitable distribution" of the couple's property, Steven paid $6,250,000 to Laura while retaining the couple's main residence and various financial accounts. One of the financial accounts retained by Steven as part of the property division was a brokerage account maintained by Bernard L. Madoff Investment Securities. Steven successfully withdrew some money from his Madoff account to pay part of the settlement with Laura. However, the remainder of his account with Madoff eventually proved to be nearly worthless because it was part of Madoff's fraudulent Ponzi scheme, in which Madoff deposited investors' money in a bank account, fabricated reports of successful investment of the funds, converted some of the funds to his own use, and retained some of the invested funds in the bank account to cover occasional investor withdrawals—until investors learned of the fraud and all clamored for return of their investments. Steven wishes to avoid his settlement agreement with Laura and to gain restitution of $2,700,000 of the money he paid to Laura under that agreement, on the ground that they entered into that agreement under a mutual mistake regarding the existence of a legitimate investment account with Madoff. Develop arguments for both sides. The intermediate appellate court ordered avoidance, but the state's high court reinstated the trial court's dismissal of Steven's action. *Simkin v. Blank*, 19 N.Y.3d 46 (2012).

D. Awarding Restitution when the Contract Is Avoided

How is the restitution interest calculated? What adjustments are made if a buyer must return land but has enjoyed the benefit of using the land and has made improvements on the land? Let's revisit *Renner v. Kehl*, in which a buyer agreed to purchase desert land for cultivation of jojoba plants.

Renner v. Kehl

150 Ariz. 94, 722 P.2d 262 (1986) (In Banc)

Gordon, Vice Chief Justice.

[continued from Section V.B of this Chapter]

DAMAGES

....

¶ 7 ... When a party rescinds a contract on the ground of mutual mistake he is entitled to restitution for any benefit that he has conferred on the other party by way of part performance or reliance. Restatement (Second) of Contracts § 376. Restitutionary recoveries are not designed to be compensatory; their justification lies in the avoidance of unjust enrichment on the part of the defendant. D. Dobbs, Remedies § 4.1 p. 224 (1973). Thus the defendant is generally liable for restitution of a benefit that would be unjust for him to keep, even though he gained it honestly. *Id*; Restatement (Second) of Contracts § 376 comment a. The issue we must now address is the proper measure of the restitutionary interest.

¶ 8 The first step determining the proper measure of restitution requires that the rescinding party return or offer to return, conditional on restitution, any interest in property that he has received in the bargain. Restatement (Second) of Contracts § 384(1)(a). In Arizona this includes reimbursement for the fair market value of the use of the property. With respect to land contracts we have noted that "[i]t is of course essential to justify the rescinding of a contract that the rescinding party offer to place the other in status quo, and this includes the offer to credit the vendors with a reasonable rental value for the time during which the land was occupied." *Mortensen v. Berzell Investment Co.*, 102 Ariz. at 351, 429 P.2d at 948. Earlier we stated that "[t]he offer to surrender possession of property received under the contract need not be unqualified, but may be made conditional upon the vendor's restitution of amounts paid on the contract, less proper allowances in respect of vendee's use of the premises." *Mahurin v. Schmeck*, 95 Ariz. 333, 341, 390 P.2d 576, 581 (1964). Thus the respondents were obliged to return the land to the petitioners in exchange for their down payment, and in addition to pay the petitioners the fair rental value of the land for the duration of their occupancy.

¶ 9 However, to avoid unjust enrichment the petitioners must pay the respondents a sum equal to the amount by which their property has been enhanced in value by the respondents' efforts. The Restatement (Second) of Contracts § 376 provides that "[i]f [a party] has received and must return land ... he may have made improvements on the land in reliance on the contract and he is entitled to recover the reasonable value of those improvements.... The rule stated in this section applies to avoidance on any ground, including ... mistake...." comment a. The reasonable value of any improvements is measured by "the extent to which the other party's property has been increased in value or his other interests advanced." Restatement (Second) of Contracts § 371(b). Thus the petitioners must pay to the respondents that amount of money which represents the enhanced value of the land due to the respondents' development efforts. In short, the respondents are entitled to their down payment, plus the amount by which their efforts increased the value of the petitioners' property, minus an amount which represents the fair rental value of the land during their occupancy. They are not entitled to the $229,649.84 expended upon development, because that would shift the entire risk of mistake onto the petitioners, which is incompatible with equitable rescission.

CONCLUSION

¶ 10 The respondents were entitled to rescind the contract, but may not recover the costs of developing the land in the form of consequential damages. The respondents are entitled to restitution of their down payment and any amount by which the value of the land was enhanced, but in turn the respondents must pay petitioners the fair rental value of the tenancy. Accordingly, the trial court is affirmed in part and reversed in part and the court of appeals' decision is approved in part and vacated in part. The case is remanded to the trial court for further proceedings not inconsistent with this opinion.

Exercise 8.10—Cost of Providing Benefits versus Value to Recipient

The *Renner* court approved restitution to the buyers of their down payment. It also approved restitution to the sellers of their possession of the land and the reasonable rental value of buyer's use of the land. It held, however, that the buyers were not entitled to restitution of the roughly $230,000 that they expended on improvements to the land. With respect to those improvements, the buyers were entitled only to an amount representing the enhanced value of the land, the amount to which the sellers were benefited by the improvements.

What's the difference between the reasonable value of improvements to the land and the amount expended to make those improvements? Why is it not surprising that the former is less than the latter in *Renner*?

E. Related Doctrines

1. *Discharge of Obligations Due to Unexpected Post-Formation Events*

Complementing mutual mistake of fact are two other means of avoiding contract obligations, which we will examine in Chapter 11: (1) impossibility (or impracticability) of performance and (2) frustration of purpose. In some circumstances, impossibility will excuse the nonperformance of an obligation that has unexpectedly become impossible or commercially impracticable to perform, and frustration of purpose will excuse the nonperformance of a contract whose fundamental purposes have been unexpectedly undermined by the events.

Although these doctrines can overlap with mutual mistake of fact, our study will focus on two mutually exclusive time frames. Mutual mistake of fact normally is based on mutual misunderstanding about essential facts existing at the time of contract formation. In contrast, the doctrines of impossibility and frustration of purpose most frequently apply to unexpected events (the risk of which was not allocated to either party) that occur *after* contract formation.

2. *Reformation for Fraud or Clerical Error*

Take care as well to distinguish: (1) *avoidance* (or rescission, as many courts put it) for mutual mistake of fact from (2) *reformation* of a contract. In a typical claim for reformation, the parties have reached an agreement with no misunderstandings about the facts relating to their transaction. The need for reformation occurs when someone translates the final agreement to another medium and then—either through fraud or clerical error—changes the terms of the actual agreement in the new medium.

For example, suppose that Buyer orally agreed to purchase lot 183 from Seller in a new housing development. In Seller's office, they discussed and reached a final agreement on all the terms for the sale contract, taking notes along the way. Although both parties initialed the notes, Seller suggested that Buyer go out to lunch while Seller's office typed up a more formal contract for signature after lunch. After lunch, Buyer and Seller signed the formal contract, while failing to notice that the contract identified the lot for sale as 184, rather than the lot 183 that the parties had earlier agreed to. When Buyer pointed this out a few days later, Seller—recognizing that lot 184 was less desirable and more difficult to sell than lot 183—argued that the latest and most formal signed document superseded all previous representations or agreements and represented the parties' final enforceable contract.

If Buyer can prove to a court that the parties had in fact agreed to transfer ownership of lot 183 and that the signed document's reference to lot 184 was simply a clerical error that went unnoticed by the parties, a court likely will "reform" the contract. The court will reform the final written document by ordering it to be changed to refer to lot "183," so that it reflects the parties' actual agreement. If the Seller had intentionally and fraudulently changed the lot number in the final document, while hiding the change from Buyer, the case for reformation will be even more compelling.

Reformation thus contemplates enforcement of the parties' actual agreement, which they reached without laboring under any mistake, but which was reduced to writing imperfectly, requiring correction prior to enforcement. In contrast, avoidance for mutual mistake results in cancelation of the contract, because the parties' initial agreement was the product of mutually mistaken assumptions of material fact.

VI. Summary

Problems during formation can provide grounds for avoidance even if an agreement appears to be formed through mutual assent and with consideration. As you review this chapter, consider the following sampling of points:

- Economic duress requires not only an improper threat but also an overcoming of a party's free will, which requires a showing that the party seeking relief did not cave in to the demands too easily but resisted them until it was clear that it had no reasonable alternative but to agree to the proposal.
- Misrepresentation of fact can be based on an affirmative falsehood, a half-truth, or active concealment, but not on simple failure to disclose facts except in special relationships, certain kinds of transactions, or other exceptional circumstances.
- A party can establish grounds for avoidance on the basis of even an innocent misrepresentation. Moreover, if a serious misrepresentation is established, the court has some flexibility in the strictness with which it applies the requirements of justifiable reliance and misrepresentation of fact rather than opinion.
- To establish grounds for avoidance, a misrepresentation must be of a *material* fact, but mutual mistake must relate to an existing fact of even greater significance, one that goes to the *basis* or the *essence* of the contract.
- Avoidance contemplates cancellation of the contract with restitution of any benefits that have been transferred to the other party, and with any adjustments necessary to return the parties to their precontractual status quo.
- Reformation is the judicial action of revising a written document so that it accurately reflects the actual agreement of the parties—reached by them without duress, misrepresentation, or mistake—when the written document fails to reflect that actual agreement because of clerical error or fraud.

Exercise 8.11 — Past Exam Question

The following exam question raises two general issues, each of which may arise from any of the materials studied in this course up to this point, including but not limited to topics in this chapter.

Suggested Time Allocation: 35 minutes

John King, a contractor specializing in excavation, entered into a written agreement with Dell Developers ("DD") to excavate "all soil, rock, and other material" in a large area for an underground parking garage. DD agreed to pay a fee of $60,000 for the excavation.

After excavating six feet of soil at one end of the structure, King's crew encountered large structures of rock, quite unusual for that area. They soon determined that these rock structures ran through most of the excavation site. No one on either King's crew or DD's staff had discussed the amount of expected rock during negotiations, because the amount of rock in that area, to the depth of the excavation site, was normally insignificant. Although King could have conducted tests of the soil before entering into the contract, he had not done so because no one had encountered problems with unusual amounts of rock in that area previously. After the rock was encountered, representatives for both parties expressed genuine shock at the size and number of the boulders and sheets of rock. King can excavate the site with his normal crew and equipment. However, he will need an extra two weeks and an additional $20,000 in pay to complete the excavation while maintaining a reasonable profit. Without these changes, he cannot complete the work without sustaining a substantial loss.

A. Assume first that King asked whether he could have the additional time and money but DD's CEO rejected the request, stating, "I'm sorry. We too expected this to be a routine excavation. But that's your problem. Stick to the contract." King wants to avoid the contract to be relieved of further obligations under this contract. Identify a single theory for avoidance that would best suit King's purposes, and discuss it fully in IRAC form. To the extent possible, argue both sides so that King understands the weaknesses as well as the strengths of his legal position.

B. Alternatively, assume now that King stated his willingness to perform as promised, but also mentioned his belief that he had a right to avoid. Without making threats of any kind, King then requested the additional time and payment. DD's CEO stated, "Well, I want to do what's fair." Accordingly, both parties cheerfully signed a writing in which DD agreed to provide the additional time and pay requested by King, and they attached this writing to the original contract. With respect to King's promised performance, the new writing referred to the original contract's statement of King's excavation obligations, specifying that only the terms regarding timing and pay were modified. Soon afterwards, DD's CEO changed her mind and retracted her decision to grant additional time and pay, before any reliance by King on the new agreement. In IRAC form or any other organization that best suits your answer, identify and discuss the single issue that is most clearly raised by these facts about the enforceability of the second agreement to grant additional time and pay to King. You may assume that there are no issues or problems with offer and acceptance or the parol evidence rule, and you should not discuss those.

Chapter 9

Non-Enforcement of Contract Obligations for Illegality, Violations of Public Policy, or Unconscionability

I. Overview

"Contract provisions are unenforceable if they violate legislation or other identifiable public policy." *1800 Ocotillo, LLC v. The WLB Group, Inc.*, 219 Ariz. 200, 202, 196 P.3d 222, 224 (2008). Illegality generally refers to direct violations of the law, whereas a violation of public policy refers to more general inconsistencies with important policies underlying the law. In either case, enforcement of the offending contract or clause would harm the public interest, which often outweighs the parties' private expectation, reliance, and restitution interests. *See id.*

Unconscionability, on the other hand, denies enforcement on the basis of sharp practices and an unfair exchange, which may harm only a party to the private bargaining relationship. In contrast to problems with legality and public policy, unconscionability does not require a contravention of broader public interests.

As you study these materials, think about the following questions:

- When does a contract or a clause violate the policy underlying a statute, even though it does not directly violate the terms of the statute? How should a court weigh the policy violation against policies favoring freedom of the parties to agree to contract terms of their choosing?
- What remedies are available to a court if it finds a contract or clause to be illegal, to violate public policy, or to be unconscionable?
- What is unconscionability and how does it relate to other doctrines of contract law, like mutual assent, consideration, public policy, and grounds for avoidance?

II. Direct Illegality

A. Illegality in Contract Formation, Performance, or Enforcement

The most direct form of illegality is presented by a contract that is identified by a statute as unenforceable. The California Civil Code, for example, provides that "[e]very contract in restraint of the marriage of any person, other than a minor, is void." CAL. CIV. CODE § 1669 (West 2011). Another California statute addresses an issue that is explored later in this chapter: it provides that, with some exceptions, "every contract by which anyone is restrained from engaging in a lawful profession, trade, or business of any kind is to that extent void." CAL. BUS. & PROF. CODE § 16600 (West 2008). An Alabama statute provides that contracts calling for the payment of interest beyond that permitted by related statutory provisions "are usurious and cannot be enforced except as to the principal." ALA. CODE 1975 § 8-8-12 (LexisNexis 2002). An Arizona statute provides that certain kinds of contractors, if unlicensed at the time of entering into a contract for certain kinds of services, cannot "maintain any action in any court of the state for collection of compensation for the performance" of such services. ARIZ. REV. STAT. ANN. § 32-1153 (2008). In statutes such as these, the legislature in effect is directing the judicial branch of government to refrain from enforcing all or part of an agreement that falls within the statutory definition.

More frequently, as a matter of common law, a court will refuse to enforce an agreement not because a statute refers specifically to nonenforcement of certain kinds of agreements, and not even because any law specifically prohibits the agreement itself, but simply because the contract contemplates actions that would violate a statute or other regulatory law. An obvious example would be an agreement between a buyer and seller of illegal drugs or an agreement to engage in gambling activities prohibited by statute. Those actions violate criminal statutes, so an agreement to engage in those actions would be unenforceable, regardless of whether a statute specifically addresses the enforceability of such contracts.

For example, a federal statute makes it a crime to "transfer a human organ for valuable consideration for use in human transplantation if the transfer affects interstate commerce." 42 U.S.C. § 274e(a) (2006). Those who violate this statute would not only face a fine or imprisonment, they would meet certain rejection if they sought to enforce an agreement to engage in the prohibited exchange.

In some cases, the conflict with a criminal or other regulatory statute might be uncertain, so that the illegality is established only after a court interprets the terms of the statute and those of the arguably conflicting agreement. For example, would an agreement between two unmarried, cohabiting partners contemplate a violation of the state's prostitution statute if it provided that the parties would share their earnings, divide the household chores, and provide one another with "mutually desired love, affection, and intimacy"?

B. Non-Enforcement of Illegal Contracts or Clauses

1. Restitution or No Judicial Assistance?

The traditional judicial response to an action to enforce a directly illegal contract is to dismiss the action and to leave the parties where it found them, without even granting restitution of benefits that might have been transferred by one party to another under their agreement. Suppose, for example, that a gambler placed a bet in an illegal gaming enterprise, won 10 times the amount of his bet, and sought to enforce the other party's agreement to pay his winnings. Because the gaming was illegal, the agreement to pay his winnings on the bet would be unenforceable. Moreover, not only would the court deny the gambler's claim for the tenfold winnings; it typically would deny him even restitution of the bet that he had placed. Judges have been reluctant to soil their hands by entertaining the suit long enough even to return the parties to their precontractual status quo with restitution. As explained by one court: "It is not for the sake of a party, but for the sake of the law itself, that a court refuses to be made use of for the enforcement of illegal contracts and leaves the parties where it finds them." *Del Rey Realty Co. v. Fourl*, 44 Cal. App. 2d 399, 403, 112 P.2d 649, 651 (1941) (quoting 6 Cal. Juris. 6).

Landi v. Arkules

172 Ariz. 126, 835 P.2d 458 (Ariz. App. 1992)

....

¶ 1 We find that defendants' theory of substantial compliance does not validate the contract. Neither Moorehead nor David Arkules were licensed. Neither was qualified to act as an heir finder in Arizona.

D. [Non-enforcement of the Contract]

¶ 2 Having rejected defendants' arguments that they were not required to be licensed and that they had substantially complied with the licensing statute, we turn to the underlying issue: is the contract unenforceable because defendants were not licensed as required by law?

¶ 3 We believe that the contract is unenforceable. Defendants' performance of the contract involved the unlawful act of conducting a private investigation without a license. A.R.S. § 32-2410. The failure to obtain a license, permit, or certificate does not invalidate every contract as contrary to public policy. *See Mountain States Bolt*, 116 Ariz. 123, 568 P.2d 430. However, the regulation of private investigators is so infused with important public policy considerations that a contract to perform investigations is, in the absence of a license, unenforceable.

¶ 4 The public policy behind licensing and regulating private investigators is apparent from the Legislature's enactments. Qualifications for licensing are set forth by statute and include the applicant's good moral character and prior investigative experience. A.R.S. § 32-2412(A). The statute imposes specific duties on licensees with respect to the confidentiality and accuracy of information and the disclosure of investigative reports to the client. A.R.S. § 32-2425. A license may be suspended or revoked for a wide range of misconduct, including acts of dishonesty or fraud, aiding the violation of a court order, or soliciting business for an attorney. A.R.S. § 32-2427.

¶ 5 The Legislature's concern for the protection of the public from unscrupulous and unqualified investigators is apparent. This concern for the public's protection precludes enforcement of an unlicensed investigator's fee contract. *Shorten v. Milbank*, 170 Misc. 905, 11 N.Y.S.2d 387 (1939), *aff'd*, 256 App. Div. 1069, 12 N.Y.S.2d 583 (1939). The courts will not participate in a party's circumvention of the legislative goal by enforcing a fee contract to provide regulated services without a license. *Cf. Hall v. Bowman*, 88 Ariz. 409, 357 P.2d 149 (1960) (courts will not become party to collection of fees by unlicensed cemetery lot salesman).

¶ 6 For the above reasons, we affirm the trial court's judgment finding this agreement unenforceable as contrary to public policy.

V. [Denial of Restitution]

¶ 7 Defendants finally argue that even if the agreement is unenforceable, this court should allow the defendants to recover on an equitable claim for relief they label "quantum meruit." Quantum meruit is actually a measure of damages, not a remedy. Recovery under quantum meruit is based on the value of services rendered [restitution]. The claim for relief is for unjust enrichment. Dan B. Dobbs, *Handbook on the Law of Remedies* ("*Dobbs on Remedies*") § 4.2, at 232–39 (1973).

....

¶ 8 ... [E]quitable relief is not available when recovery at law is forbidden because the contract is void as against public policy. Professor Dobbs stated in *Dobbs on Remedies* § 13.5, at 994–97 that:

> The rule is that a contract whose formation or performance is illegal is, subject to several exceptions, void and unenforceable. But this is not all, for one who enters into such a contract is not only denied enforcement of his bargain, *he is also denied restitution for any benefits he has conferred under the contract....*
>
> The rule against restitution applies not only to contracts that involve a direct violation of the law by both parties, but also to contracts involving conduct deemed unconscionable or morally improper. In effect, the "*clean hands" approach is applied to deny not only enforcement but also restitution where the claimant's conduct is either illegal or immorally motivated....*
>
> ....
>
> If restitution were granted, this may in some situations, prove tantamount to enforcement. At the very least, it would provide a floor or cushion on which an illegal actor might fall back, sure that if his illegal conduct were

> not challenged, he could profit by it, and that if it were challenged, he could at least get his money or property back. This would no doubt encourage such illegal contracts. In quite a few situations, then, it seems proper to deny both enforcement of the bargain on a contract basis and restitution. Though a denial of restitution leads, as in both the examples given above, to unjust enrichment, this has generally been deemed a less weighty consideration than the policy of discouraging illegal bargains.

(Emphasis added; footnotes omitted). *See also* Restatement of Restitution § 140 and comment.

¶ 9 Although Landi may have been benefitted by the defendants' services, equity will not allow defendants to obtain compensation when the services were performed under an illegal contract. The purpose of the licensing statute is to avoid unscrupulous and unqualified persons from performing investigative services. This public policy would be undermined if defendants were assured of receiving compensation for their services despite their unlicensed status. We agree with the trial court and affirm on this issue.

¶ 10 For the foregoing reasons, we affirm the trial court's judgment and its denial of the motion for a new trial. We further grant Landi his request for reasonable attorney's fees on appeal pursuant to Arizona Rules Civil Appellate Procedure Rule 21 and A.R.S. § 12-341.01(A).

In line with the *Landi* decision are cases that deny even restitution to a contracting party who provided legal services without a license to practice law in the state. *E.g.*, *Morrison v. West*, 30 So. 3d 561 (Fla. Ct. App. 2010).

A different issue would be raised if a statute or ordinance required certain kinds of contractors to be licensed solely to raise revenue through licensing fees and for other purely administrative purposes, rather than to prevent fraud, incompetence, or other harm to the public in the delivery of important services within the jurisdiction. *Orlinoff v. Campbell District Court of Appeal*, 91 Cal. App. 2d 382, 385, 205 P.2d 67, 69 (1949) (stating in dictum, "[i]t is uniformly held that where the licensing provisions are for revenue only the contracts of unlicensed persons are not void").

Moreover, courts have recognized an exception to the denial of restitution if one party to an illegal contract does not share equally in the illegality—is not in *pari delicto*. A party, for example, who was ignorant of the illegality, whose role in the illegal conduct was minor, or who withdrew from the illegal enterprise before its aims were accomplished, might prevail on a claim for restitution of benefits transferred under the agreement, or sometimes even for enforcement of the agreement. *See Straley v. Universal Uranium and Milling Corp.*, 289 F.2d 370 (9th Cir. 1961) (remanding for findings relevant to claim of restitution of consideration paid by innocent buyer in illegal securities transaction).

Even if a party is in *pari delicto*, in other exceptional circumstances a court might grant restitution or even enforce the contract. For example, a court might enforce a technically illegal contract if the violation of the law was slight—so that the policy of the law was not greatly offended—and if non-enforcement would cause a party to suffer a substantial forfeiture. *See, e.g., Asdourian v. Araj*, 38 Cal. 3d 276, 696 P.2d 95 (1985) (citing to other California cases, and enforcing contract over Justice Mosk's dissent).

More commonly, a court sometimes can enforce the lawful parts of an otherwise illegal contract through severance of the illegal provisions.

2. Enforcement after Severance of Illegal Provision

If a severable provision of a contract is illegal, and if enforcement of the remainder of the contract would be consistent with the parties' intentions and interests, a court may strike out the illegal clause and enforce the rest of the contract.

In the next opinion, *Booker v. Robert Half Int'l, Inc.*, an employee brought a statutory civil rights claim for employment discrimination. Unlike a contract claim, this civil rights claim can result in an award of punitive damages beyond compensatory damages, to help vindicate important policies underlying civil rights statutes.

A contract issue remains, however, because the employer and the employee had agreed in their employment contract to waive their right to litigate employment-related claims in a jury trial in court and to instead resolve them in private arbitration without the possibility of punitive damages. As you brief this case, consider the following questions:

- Which party wants to avoid the arbitration clause and litigate in court?
- What is the specific argument for avoiding the arbitration clause in *Booker*?
- What issue must the court resolve to determine whether the entire arbitration clause is void for illegality or violation of public policy?
- What factors does the court consider in resolving that issue?
- How is the analysis influenced by a federal statute, the Federal Arbitration Act, which favors enforcement of arbitration agreements?

Booker v. Robert Half International, Inc.

413 F.3d 77 (D.C. Cir. 2005)

Roberts, Circuit Judge.

. . . .

¶ 1 In this case an employee sued his employer for racial discrimination under the District of Columbia Human Rights Act, D.C. Code §§ 2-1401 et seq. ("DCHRA"), and the employer sought to compel arbitration pursuant to an arbitration clause in the employment agreement. The arbitration clause was unenforceable as written because it precluded an award of punitive damages, which are available under the D.C. statute. The existence of an express severability clause in the agreement, the fact that the agreement is otherwise valid and enforceable, and a "healthy regard for the federal policy favoring arbitration," *Gilmer*, 500 U.S. at 26 ... (*quoting Moses H. Cone Mem. Hosp. v. Mercury Constr. Corp.*, 460 U.S. 1, 24 ... (1983)), lead us to affirm the decision below, severing the ban on punitive damages and compelling arbitration.

I.

¶ 2 From April 1996 to February 2001, Timothy R. Booker worked for Robert Half Int'l, Inc. ("RHI"). Before starting his job at RHI, Booker signed an employment agreement containing the arbitration clause at the heart of this dispute. The clause states in relevant part:

> Any dispute or claim arising out of or relating to Employee's employment ... shall be submitted to arbitration pursuant to the commercial arbitration rules of the American Arbitration Association. This Agreement shall be governed by the [Federal] Arbitration Act.... The parties agree that punitive damages may not be awarded in an arbitration proceeding required by this Agreement.

Employment Agreement ¶ 18.

¶ 3 The agreement also contained a severability clause, providing that "[t]he provisions of this Agreement are severable. If any provision is found by any court of competent jurisdiction to be unreasonable and invalid, that determination shall not affect the enforceability of other provisions." *Id.* ¶ 13.

¶ 4 On April 24, 2001, Booker filed suit against RHI in District of Columbia Superior Court, alleging racial discrimination and wrongful constructive discharge in violation of the DCHRA....

¶ 5 Over the opposition of Booker and amicus curiae the Equal Employment Opportunity Commission, the district court granted RHI's motion [to dismiss the court action and to compel private arbitration]....

¶ 6 ... The district court ... declined Booker's invitation to strike down the arbitration clause in its entirety. Looking instead to the agreement's severability clause, District of Columbia contract law, and the federal policy favoring enforcement of agreements to arbitrate, the court concluded that the remainder of the arbitration clause was enforceable despite the invalid punitive damages provision. Accordingly, the district court severed the punitive damages bar and compelled arbitration. *Id.* at 19–25. Booker appeals.

II.

....

¶ 7 B. The parties do not dispute that the arbitration agreement's bar on punitive damages is unenforceable as applied to Booker's claim under the DCHRA. *See, e.g., Hadnot v. Bay, Ltd.*, 344 F.3d 474, 478 & n. 14 (5th Cir. 2003) (arbitration agreement's bar on punitive damages unenforceable in Title VII case). Booker contends, however, that the district court erred in severing the punitive damages provision and enforcing the remainder of the agreement....

....

¶ 8 Under the [Federal Arbitration Act], arbitration "is a matter of consent, not coercion." *Volt Info. Scis., Inc. v. Bd. of Trs. of Leland Stanford Jr. Univ.*, 489 U.S. 468, 479 ... (1989). Compelling Booker to arbitrate with the bar on punitive damages severed is entirely consistent with the intent to arbitrate he manifested in signing the employment agreement in the first place. As the Eighth Circuit recently explained in a similar case, "[w]e do not believe that the severance of the provision limiting punitive damages diminishes [the claimant's] contractual intent to arbitrate because excluding the provision only allows her the opportunity to arbitrate her claims under more favorable terms than those to which she agreed." *Gannon v. Circuit City Stores, Inc.*, 262 F.3d 677, 682-83 (8th Cir. 2001).

¶ 9 C. Booker next argues that enforcing the remainder of the arbitration clause contravenes the federal policy interest in ensuring the effective vindication of statutory rights. He contends that responding to illegal provisions in arbitration agreements by judicially pruning them out leaves employers with every incentive to "overreach" when drafting such agreements. If judges merely sever illegal provisions and compel arbitration, employers would be no worse off for trying to include illegal provisions than if they had followed the law in drafting their agreements in the first place. On the other hand, because not every claimant will challenge the illegal provisions, some employees will go to the arbitral table without all their statutory rights.

....

¶ 10 ... Decisions striking an arbitration clause entirely often involved agreements without a severability clause, *see, e.g., Perez*, 253 F.3d at 1286, or agreements that did not contain merely one readily severable illegal provision, but were instead pervasively infected with illegality, *see, e.g., Graham Oil*, 43 F.3d at 1248–49; *Hooters v. Phillips*, 173 F.3d 933, 938–39 (4th Cir. 1999). Decisions severing an illegal provision and compelling arbitration, on the other hand, typically considered agreements with a severability clause and discrete unenforceable provisions, *see, e.g., Morrison*, 317 F.3d at 675; *Gannon*, 262 F.3d at 680.

¶ 11 A critical consideration in assessing severability is giving effect to the intent of the contracting parties. *See, e.g., Frankenmuth Mut. Ins. Co. v. Escambia County*, 289 F.3d 723, 728–29 (11th Cir. 2002).... If illegality pervades the arbitration agreement such that only a disintegrated fragment would remain after hacking away the unenforceable parts, *see, e.g., Graham Oil*, 43 F.3d at 1248–49, the judicial effort begins to look more like rewriting the contract than fulfilling the intent of the parties.... Thus, the more the employer overreaches, the less likely a court will be able to sever the provisions and enforce the clause, a dynamic that creates incentives against the very overreaching Booker fears.

¶ 12 We agree with the district court that severing the punitive damages bar and enforcing the arbitration clause was proper here. Not only does the agreement contain a severability clause, but Booker identifies only one discrete illegal provision in the agreement.... This one unenforceable provision does not infect the arbitration clause as a whole. The district court did not unravel "a highly integrated" complex of interlocking illegal provisions, *Graham Oil*, 43 F.3d at 1248, but rather removed a punitive damages bar that appears to have been grafted onto an intact and functioning framework, for the AAA commercial rules—incorporated by reference in the clause—already contain provisions on remedies that do not prohibit punitive damages. *See* Commercial Rules 43–48. Indeed, by severing a remedial component of the arbitration clause, the district court removed a provision generally understood as not being essential to a contract's consideration, and thus more readily severable. *See* 15 Corbin on Contracts § 89.10, at 659 (rev. ed. 2003); Williston on Contracts § 19:69, at 543 (4th ed. 1998) (citing Restatement (Second) of Contracts §§ 183 & cmt. a, 184). *See also Hadnot*, 344 F.3d at 478 (rejecting argument that bar on punitive damages in arbitration clause is integral to overall employment agreement and accordingly cannot be severed).

....

¶ 13 By invoking the severability clause to remove a discrete remedial provision, the district court honored the intent of the parties reflected in the employment agreement, which included not only the punitive damages bar but the explicit severability clause as well. In doing so, the court was also faithful to the federal policy which "requires that we rigorously enforce agreements to arbitrate." *Mitsubishi Motors*, 473 U.S. at 626 (citation omitted). For these reasons, ... the judgment of the district court is Affirmed.

In another case, a court enforced an arbitration agreement after severing a clause that shifted a bank's costs and fees of litigation to the prevailing consumer. *Barras v. Branch Banking and Trust Co.*, 685 F.3d 1269, 1283 (11th Cir. 2012); *see also Serpa v. California Surety Investigations, Inc.*, 215 Cal. App. 4th 695, 709–10 (Cal. App. 2013) (enforcing arbitration after severing a clause that required each party to bear its attorney's fees, contrary to a state fair employment statute, which authorized an award of fees to a prevailing plaintiff).

Do these cases stand in contrast to the reasoning in *Landi* that courts should discourage the drafting of illegal provisions by denying other benefits of the contract when refusing enforcement of the illegal provision? One explanation lies in the policy of the Federal Arbitration Act (FAA) to reverse the hostility toward arbitration agreements that courts exhibited a century ago. In response, one author argues—against the grain of judicial decisions—that the FAA's provisions favoring enforcement of arbitration agreements do not require liberal severance of unenforceable clauses and enforcement of the remainder of the arbitration agreement; instead, he argues that the FAA views an arbitration agreement as either fully enforceable or not enforceable at all. Imre S. Szalai, *A New Legal Framework for Employee and Consumer Arbitration Agreements*, 19 CARDOZO J. CONFLICT RESOL. 653 (2018). This chapter discusses the FAA in greater detail in Section IV.B.2.

III. Violations of Public Policy

A. Overview

Even if a contract does not strictly violate the terms of a criminal or regulatory statute, it might nonetheless contravene important public policies underlying the statute or other law. In such a case, although the parties to the contract will escape punishment under the statute, they will not be able to enforce the contract if the policies offended by the contract outweigh the policy of respecting the parties' freedom of contract. *See 1800 Ocotillo, LLC v. The WLB Group, Inc.*, 219 Ariz. 200, 202, 196 P.3d 222, 224 (2008). Throughout the remainder of this chapter, you should consider whether public policy or concerns over fairness are sufficiently serious that they outweigh "ancient concepts of freedom of contract." *M/S Bremen v. Zapata Off-Shore Co.*, 407 U.S. 1, 12 (1972); *see, e.g.*, *Mueller v. Apple Leisure Corp.*, 880 F.3d 890, 895 (7th Cir. 2018) (consumers of vacation package were bound to forum selection clause because they "pointed to no public interest to justify setting aside the contractual choice of forum").

B. Agreement to Share Earnings in Unmarried Cohabitation

Sometimes a case will raise a range of questions regarding direct illegality or violation of public policy. Suppose, for example, that an unmarried couple agreed to live together as an intimate, romantic couple, to allocate responsibility for the household work, and to share the income and property that either of them earns and accumulates. When the relationship ended, one party claimed half of the very substantial income and assets earned and invested over the years by the other party. The property of the unmarried couple was not governed by the state's community property laws, so the party claiming a share of the income sought to enforce the parties' agreement.

A number of issues might be raised in such a lawsuit. For example, does the state still have a statute that criminalizes unmarried intimate cohabitation, a fairly common statute in many states until legislatures began to repeal them in the last half of the twentieth century? If such a statute had not yet been repealed and was still "on the books," would a court deny enforcement of the contract on the ground of direct illegality, even if the statute had long fallen into disuse and no longer reflected popular sentiments?

If the state no longer criminalizes unmarried intimate cohabitation, does the cohabitation agreement violate state criminal prostitution statutes to the extent that it contemplates the sharing of income in exchange for sexual relations? To the extent that the agreement does not directly violate the terms of the prostitution statute, would it violate the underlying policies of that statute, policies against inducing sexual favors with payments or promises of money? Would it violate the policies underlying marriage laws and community property statutes, which promote the institution of marriage? If some parts of the agreement do violate public policy, are other parts severable and enforceable?

The following early case under English law helps to introduce the issue, although it does not have the last word.

Walker v. Perkins, Administrator

97 Eng. Rep. 985 (1764)

Sarah Walker brought an action upon a bond. It recites, that ... William Perkins (the intestate) and Sarah Walker had agreed to live together, therefore he had agreed to find her meat, drink, washing, and lodging, &c. and to leave her an annuity of 60£ a year, if he quitted her, or she outlived him.... But if she should leave him, or go to another man, then he should not be obliged to provide for her any longer, or to leave her any annuity. [Walker outlived Perkins and sues to enforce Perkins' obligation as a debt of his estate.]

Lord Mansfield—It is the price of prostitution, ... for if she becomes virtuous, she is to lose the annuity. It appears clearly, upon the condition, that the bond is illegal and void.

Judgment for the defendant.

A more contemporary analysis of this issue is provided by the so-called "palimony" suits, the first and most famous of which was brought by Michelle Triola Marvin, who was the live-in partner of the late actor Lee Marvin and who had taken Lee Marvin's last name.

Marvin v. Marvin

18 Cal. 3d 660, 557 P.2d 106 (1976) (In Bank) [footnotes omitted]

Tobriner, Justice.

¶1 During the past 15 years, there has been a substantial increase in the number of couples living together without marrying. Such nonmarital relationships lead to legal controversy when one partner dies or the couple separates. Courts of Appeal, faced with the task of determining property rights in such cases, have arrived at conflicting positions.... We take this opportunity to resolve that controversy and to declare the principles which should govern distribution of property acquired in a nonmarital relationship.

¶2 We conclude: (1) The provisions of the Family Law Act do not govern the distribution of property acquired during a nonmarital relationship; such a relationship remains subject solely to judicial decision. (2) The courts should enforce express contracts between nonmarital partners except to the extent that the contract is explicitly founded on the consideration of meretricious sexual services. (3) In the absence of an express contract, the courts should inquire into the conduct of the parties to determine whether that conduct demonstrates an implied contract, agreement of partnership or joint venture, or some other tacit understanding between the parties. The courts may also employ the doctrine of quantum meruit, or equitable remedies such as constructive or resulting trusts, when warranted by the facts of the case.

¶3 In the instant case plaintiff and defendant lived together for seven years without marrying; all property acquired during this period was taken in defendant's name. When plaintiff sued to enforce a contract under which she was entitled to half the property and to support payments, the trial court granted judgment on the pleadings for defendant, thus leaving him with all property accumulated by the couple during their relationship. Since the trial court denied plaintiff a trial on the merits of her claim, its decision conflicts with the principles stated above, and must be reversed.

1. The factual setting of this appeal.

¶4 Since the trial court rendered judgment for defendant on the pleadings, we must accept the allegations of plaintiff's complaint as true, determining whether such allegations state, or can be amended to state, a cause of action....

¶5 Plaintiff avers that in October of 1964 she and defendant "entered into an oral agreement" that while "the parties lived together they would combine their efforts and earnings and would share equally any and all property accumulated as a result of their efforts whether individual or combined." Furthermore, they agreed to "hold themselves out to the general public as husband and wife" and that "plaintiff would further render her services as a companion, homemaker, housekeeper and cook to ... defendant."

¶6 Shortly thereafter plaintiff agreed to "give up her lucrative career as an entertainer [and] singer" in order to "devote her full time to defendant ... as a companion, homemaker, housekeeper and cook;" in return defendant agreed to "provide for all of plaintiff's financial support and needs for the rest of her life."

¶7 Plaintiff alleges that she lived with defendant from October of 1964 through May of 1970 and fulfilled her obligations under the agreement. During this period the parties as a result of their efforts and earnings acquired in defendant's name substantial real and personal property, including motion picture rights worth over $1 million. In May of 1970, however, defendant compelled plaintiff to leave his household. He continued to support plaintiff until November of 1971, but thereafter refused to provide further support.

....

2. Plaintiff's complaint states a cause of action for breach of an express contract.

¶8 In *Trutalli v. Meraviglia* (1932) 215 Cal. 698, 12 P.2d 430 we established the principle that nonmarital partners may lawfully contract concerning the ownership of property acquired during the relationship. We reaffirmed this principle in *Vallera v. Vallera* (1943) 21 Cal. 2d 681, 685, 134 P.2d 761, 763, stating that "If a man and woman [who are not married] live together as husband and wife under an agreement to pool their earnings and share equally in their joint accumulations, equity will protect the interests of each in such property."

¶ 9 In the case before us plaintiff, basing her cause of action in contract upon these precedents, maintains that the trial court erred in denying her a trial on the merits of her contention....

¶ 10 Defendant first and principally relies on the contention that the alleged contract is so closely related to the supposed "immoral" character of the relationship between plaintiff and himself that the enforcement of the contract would violate public policy. He points to cases asserting that a contract between nonmarital partners is unenforceable if it is "involved in" an illicit relationship.... A review of the numerous California decisions concerning contracts between nonmarital partners, however, reveals that the courts have not employed such broad and uncertain standards to strike down contracts. The decisions instead disclose a narrower and more precise standard: a contract between nonmarital partners is unenforceable only *to the extent* that it *explicitly* rests upon the immoral and illicit consideration of meretricious sexual services.

....

¶ 11 Although the past decisions hover over the issue in the somewhat wispy form of the figures of a Chagall painting, we can abstract from those decisions a clear and simple rule. The fact that a man and woman live together without marriage, and engage in a sexual relationship, does not in itself invalidate agreements between them relating to their earnings, property, or expenses. Neither is such an agreement invalid merely because the parties may have contemplated the creation or continuation of a nonmarital relationship when they entered into it. Agreements between nonmarital partners fail only to the extent that they rest upon a consideration of meretricious sexual services....

¶ 12 The three cases cited by defendant which have *declined* to enforce contracts between nonmarital partners involved consideration that *was* expressly founded upon ... illicit sexual services. In *Hill v. Estate of Westbrook*, *supra*, 95 Cal. App. 2d 599, 213 P.2d 727, the woman promised to keep house for the man, to live with him as man and wife, and to bear his children; the man promised to provide for her in his will, but died without doing so. Reversing a judgment for the woman based on the reasonable value of her services, the Court of Appeal stated that "the action is predicated upon a claim which seeks, among other things, the reasonable value of living with decedent in meretricious relationship and bearing him two children.... The law does not award compensation for living with a man as a concubine and bearing him children." ...

....

¶ 13 The decisions in the *Hill* and *Updeck* cases thus demonstrate that a contract between nonmarital partners, even if expressly made in contemplation of a common living arrangement, is invalid only if sexual acts form an inseparable part of the consideration for the agreement.... The Court of Appeal opinion in *Hill*, however, indicates that even if sexual services are part of the contractual consideration, any *severable* portion of the contract supported by independent consideration will still be enforced.

....

¶ 14 ... We need not treat nonmarital partners as putatively married persons in order to apply principles of implied contract, or extend equitable remedies; we need to treat them only as we do any other unmarried persons.

....

¶ 15 The argument that granting remedies to the nonmarital partners would discourage marriage must fail;.... Although we recognize the well-established public policy to foster and promote the institution of marriage (*see Deyoe v. Superior Court* (1903) 140 Cal. 476, 482, 74 P. 28), perpetuation of judicial rules which result in an inequitable distribution of property accumulated during a nonmarital relationship is neither a just nor an effective way of carrying out that policy.

....

¶ 16 [W]e base our opinion on the principle that adults who voluntarily live together and engage in sexual relations are nonetheless as competent as any other persons to contract respecting their earnings and property rights. Of course, they cannot lawfully contract to pay for the performance of sexual services, for such a contract is, in essence, an agreement for prostitution and unlawful for that reason. But they may agree to pool their earnings and to hold all property acquired during the relationship in accord with the law governing community property; conversely they may agree that each partner's earnings and the property acquired from those earnings remains the separate property of the earning partner. So long as the agreement does not rest upon illicit meretricious consideration, the parties may order their economic affairs as they choose, and no policy precludes the courts from enforcing such agreements.

¶ 17 In summary, we believe that the prevalence of nonmarital relationships in modern society and the social acceptance of them, marks this as a time when our courts should by no means apply the doctrine of the unlawfulness of the so-called meretricious relationship to the instant case. As we have explained, the nonenforceability of agreements expressly providing for meretricious conduct rested upon the fact that such conduct, as the word suggests, pertained to and encompassed prostitution. To equate the nonmarital relationship of today to such a subject matter is to do violence to an accepted and wholly different practice.

¶ 18 We are aware that many young couples live together without the solemnization of marriage, in order to make sure that they can successfully later undertake marriage. This trial period, preliminary to marriage, serves as some assurance that the marriage will not subsequently end in dissolution to the harm of both parties. We are aware, as we have stated, of the pervasiveness of nonmarital relationships in other situations.

¶19 The mores of the society have indeed changed so radically in regard to cohabitation that we cannot impose a standard based on alleged moral considerations that have apparently been so widely abandoned by so many. Lest we be misunderstood, however, we take this occasion to point out that the structure of society itself largely depends upon the institution of marriage, and nothing we have said in this opinion should be taken to derogate from that institution. The joining of the man and woman in marriage is at once the most socially productive and individually fulfilling relationship that one can enjoy in the course of a lifetime.

¶20 We conclude that the judicial barriers that may stand in the way of a policy based upon the fulfillment of the reasonable expectations of the parties to a nonmarital relationship should be removed. As we have explained, the courts now hold that express agreements will be enforced unless they rest on an unlawful meretricious consideration. We add that in the absence of an express agreement, the courts may look to a variety of other remedies in order to protect the parties' lawful expectations.

¶21 The courts may inquire into the conduct of the parties to determine whether that conduct demonstrates an implied contract or implied agreement of partnership or joint venture (*see Estate of Thornton* (1972) 81 Wash. 2d 72, 499 P.2d 864), or some other tacit understanding between the parties.... Finally, a nonmarital partner may recover in quantum meruit for the reasonable value of household services rendered less the reasonable value of support received if he can show that he rendered services with the expectation of monetary reward. (*See Hill v. Estate of Westbrook, supra*, 39 Cal. 2d 458, 462, 247 P.2d 19.)

....

The judgment is reversed and the cause remanded for further proceedings consistent with the views expressed herein.

In *Marvin*, the Court did not reject the defendant's argument that an agreement to share earnings with a partner outside of marriage might in some circumstances violate the public policy underlying California's community property laws, if it diluted the community property to which the defendant's spouse was entitled. However, the defendant, Lee Marvin, was divorced from his wife, Betty, who had an opportunity to fully assert her community property interests in the divorce action.

On remand in *Marvin*, the plaintiff, Michelle Triola Marvin, failed to prove an express or implied contract or to establish a right to restitution based on quasi-contract. The trial court nonetheless granted Michelle judgment for $104,000 for economic rehabilitation. The Court of Appeals vacated this award, agreeing with Lee Marvin's contention that "the challenged award is outside the issues of the case as framed by the pleadings of the parties ... and furthermore lacks any basis in equity or in law."

Ten years after *Marvin*, the Arizona Supreme Court "agree[d] with the court in *Marvin* ... in that 'homemaking' severable from the meretricious relationship can support an implied agreement as between two parties." *Carroll v. Lee*, 148 Ariz. 10, 14, 712 P.2d 923, 927 (1986) (suit for partition of jointly held property acquired during cohabitation).

Exercise 9.1 — Cohabitation with a Married Partner

While A is married to B, A maintains a separate residence (the "apartment") for part-time cohabitation with a lover, C. A and C enter into an agreement in which A agrees to pay all of the rent on the apartment and to share 20% of A's earnings with C, in exchange for C's maintaining the apartment and providing A with general companionship. State statutes criminalizing adultery and unmarried cohabitation have long been repealed.

Although A and C were engaged in mutually desired sexual relations, their agreement does not specifically make sexual relations part of the consideration for either party's obligations. Can you argue that the agreement nonetheless violates the terms of a statutory scheme commonly found in state codes, or violates the policies underlying the statutes, and thus would be unenforceable even under the rules of *Marvin v. Marvin*?

C. Surrogacy Contracts

1. Background, and Questions to Ponder

In a true surrogate mother contract, the surrogate mother agrees for compensation to carry the fertilized egg of another woman in her womb, to obtain specified prenatal care, and—if the pregnancy goes full term to birth—to surrender custody of the newborn baby to the other parties to the contract, the prospective parents. A "true" surrogate, or "gestational carrier," is not the biological mother of the child, although she has been biologically intertwined with it for nine months. A prospective parent might be biologically related to the baby, depending on whether sperm or egg came from the prospective parent or another source.

In a partial surrogacy contract, similar mutual promises are exchanged, but the woman is carrying a fetus created from her own ovum, which was artificially inseminated. In this case, the surrogate in fact is biologically related to the infant, so it is something of a misnomer to call her a "surrogate" mother. For simplicity, however, we will use the term "surrogate" in both cases.

Suppose that the surrogate refuses to surrender custody after birth. Can the person or couple who hired the surrogate enforce the surrogacy contract? Should it matter whether the defendant is a true or partial surrogate? If the contract is enforceable, can the plaintiffs secure specific performance in the form of a court order transferring parental rights to the contracting couple, or would the court limit their recovery to substitutional relief in the form of money damages? If the latter, how would a judge or jury assess the damage suffered in such a case? Is contract law well suited to resolve this type of conflict?

2. *Selling One's Baby*

In April 2006, a Wisconsin father was arrested for attempting to sell his 18-month-old baby, apparently to raise money to make improvements on his house. The prospective adoptive parents wanted to follow legal adoption procedures. They called police when the father instead said that he would simply deliver the girl to them for $7,000. Prosecutors charged him with unauthorized adoption placement. Similarly, in 2011 the California Court of Appeals affirmed the convictions of three persons for selling or attempting to sell a baby, in violation of a 1901 statute criminalizing slavery and the selling or buying of "any person." *People v. Loos*, 2011 WL 3918956 (Cal. Ct. App. 2011) (unpublished).

Exercise 9.2 — Enforcement of Surrogacy Contracts

In all of the questions below, assume that the prospective parents who hired the surrogate are seeking to enforce the surrogate's contractual promise to relinquish custody of the baby and all parental rights after delivery of the baby.

1. Is Surrogacy the Same as Baby-Selling?

Absent legislation that directly addresses surrogacy contracts, should a court find that a surrogacy contract is unenforceable because it directly violates laws in a manner similar to the "baby-selling" episode described above? Or could the parties avoid any direct violation of law simply by agreeing that the parties will follow all necessary adoption procedures? Should it matter whether the "surrogate" is in fact the biological mother, carrying a fetus created from her own ovum through artificial insemination, or is a full surrogate who did not supply the ovum? Should state legislatures enable the prospective parents to formally adopt the child while it is a viable embryo in gestation, so that they have undisputed parental rights when the child is born?

2. Does a Surrogate Contract Violate Public Policy?

If the contract does not violate the letter of a regulatory statute, should a court refuse to enforce a surrogacy contract on the basis of a more general violation of important public policies, such as those underlying adoption statutes and related objections to child custody being determined on the basis of contractual obligation rather than the best interests of the child? Should a court refuse to enforce such contracts on the ground that they violate public policies protecting the personal dignity of the surrogate mother and opposing the exploitation of the economically needy? Again, should it matter whether the "surrogate" is in fact the biological mother, carrying a fetus created from her own ovum through artificial insemination, or is a full surrogate?

3. Remedies in the Event of Violation of Law or Public Policy

If the contract is not enforceable, should a court at least grant restitution of all or part of the compensation paid to the surrogate mother? If the surrogacy contract is not enforceable, does that mean that the surrogate mother necessarily retains custody, or should some other legal framework resolve the dispute rather than contract law? The following two early cases, both decided in 1993, help to define the issues and arguments.

In re Baby M

109 N.J. 396, 537 A.2d 1227 (1993)

Willentz, C.J.

¶ 1 In this matter the Court is asked to determine the validity of a contract that purports to provide a new way of bringing children into a family. For a fee of $10,000, a woman agrees to be artificially inseminated with the semen of another woman's husband; she is to conceive a child, carry it to term, and after its birth surrender it to the natural father and his wife. The intent of the contract is that the child's natural mother will thereafter be forever separated from her child. The wife is to adopt the child, and she and the natural father are to be regarded as its parents for all purposes. The contract providing for this is called a "surrogacy contract," the natural mother inappropriately called the "surrogate mother."

¶ 2 We invalidate the surrogacy contract because it conflicts with the law and public policy of this State. While we recognize the depth of the yearning of infertile couples to have their own children, we find the payment of money to a "surrogate" mother illegal, perhaps criminal, and potentially degrading to women. Although in this case we grant custody to the natural father, the evidence having clearly proved such custody to be in the best interests of the infant, we void both the termination of the surrogate mother's parental rights and the adoption of the child by the wife/stepparent. We thus restore the "surrogate" as the mother of the child....

¶ 3 We find no offense to our present laws where a woman voluntarily and without payment agrees to act as a "surrogate" mother, provided that she is not subject to a binding agreement to surrender her child. Moreover, our holding today does not preclude the Legislature from altering the current statutory scheme, within constitutional limits, so as to permit surrogacy contracts. Under current law, however, the surrogacy agreement before us is illegal and invalid.

....

¶ 4 If the Legislature decides to address surrogacy, consideration of this case will highlight many of its potential harms. We do not underestimate the difficulties of legislating on this subject. In addition to the inevitable confrontation with the ethical and moral issues involved, there is the question of the wisdom and effectiveness of regulating a matter so private, yet of such public interest. Legislative consideration of surrogacy may also provide the opportunity to begin to focus on the overall implications of the new reproductive biotechnology—in vitro fertilization, preservation of sperm and eggs, embryo implantation and the like. The problem is how to enjoy the benefits of the technology—especially for infertile couples—while minimizing the risk of abuse. The problem can be addressed only when society decides what its values and objectives are in this troubling, yet promising, area.

The judgment is affirmed in part, reversed in part, and remanded for further proceedings consistent with this opinion.

In New Jersey, *Baby M* does not bar a biological birth mother from voluntarily surrendering her parental rights and placing her child for adoption. However, she is not bound by a prior agreement to do so and thus can express her intentions after the birth. *See Matter of Adoption of a Child by DMH*, 135 N.J. 473, 641 A2d 235 (citing both *Baby M* and adoption statute in determining whether birth mother had intentionally abandoned her parental rights and responsibilities), *cert. denied*, 513 U.S. 967 (1994).

How should the calculus change if one party to a surrogacy contract is a true surrogate, not biologically related to the child?

Johnson v. Calvert

5 Cal. 4th 84, 851 P.2d 776, *cert. denied*, 510 U.S. 874 (1993)
[footnotes omitted]

Panelli, Justice. [Lucas, C.J., and Mosk, Baxter, and George, JJ., concur.]

¶ 1 In this case we address several of the legal questions raised by recent advances in reproductive technology. When, pursuant to a surrogacy agreement, a zygote formed of the gametes of a husband and wife is implanted in the uterus of another woman, who carries the resulting fetus to term and gives birth to a child not genetically related to her, who is the child's "natural mother" under California law? ... We conclude that the husband and wife are the child's natural parents, and that this result does not offend ... public policy.

FACTS

¶ 2 Mark and Crispina Calvert are a married couple who desired to have a child. Crispina was forced to undergo a hysterectomy in 1984. Her ovaries remained capable of producing eggs, however, and the couple eventually considered surrogacy. In 1989 Anna Johnson heard about Crispina's plight from a coworker and offered to serve as a surrogate for the Calverts.

¶ 3 On January 15, 1990, Mark, Crispina, and Anna signed a contract providing that an embryo created by the sperm of Mark and the egg of Crispina would be implanted in Anna and the child born would be taken into Mark and Crispina's home "as their child." Anna agreed she would relinquish "all parental rights" to the child in favor of Mark and Crispina. In return, Mark and Crispina would pay Anna $10,000 in a series of installments, the last to be paid six weeks after the child's birth. Mark and Crispina were also to pay for a $200,000 life insurance policy on Anna's life.

¶ 4 The zygote was implanted on January 19, 1990. Less than a month later, an ultrasound test confirmed Anna was pregnant.

¶ 5 Unfortunately, relations deteriorated between the two sides. Mark learned that Anna had not disclosed she had suffered several stillbirths and miscarriages. Anna felt Mark and Crispina did not do enough to obtain the required insurance policy. She also felt abandoned during an onset of premature labor in June.

¶ 6 In July 1990, Anna sent Mark and Crispina a letter demanding the balance of the payments due her or else she would refuse to give up the child. The following month, Mark and Crispina responded with a lawsuit, seeking a declaration they were the legal parents of the unborn child. Anna filed her own action to be declared the mother of the child, and the two cases were eventually consolidated. The parties agreed to an independent guardian ad litem for the purposes of the suit.

¶ 7 The child was born on September 19, 1990, and blood samples were obtained from both Anna and the child for analysis. The blood test results excluded Anna as the genetic mother. The parties agreed to a court order providing that the child would remain with Mark and Crispina on a temporary basis with visits by Anna.

¶ 8 At trial in October 1990, the parties stipulated that Mark and Crispina were the child's genetic parents. After hearing evidence and arguments, the trial court ruled that Mark and Crispina were the child's "genetic, biological and natural" father and mother, that Anna had no "parental" rights to the child, and that the surrogacy contract was legal and enforceable against Anna's claims. The court also terminated the order allowing visitation. Anna appealed from the trial court's judgment. The Court of Appeal for the Fourth District, Division Three, affirmed. We granted review.

DISCUSSION

Determining Maternity Under the Uniform Parentage Act [and the Parties' Agreement]

....

¶ 9 Disregarding the presumptions of paternity that have no application to this case, then, we are left with the undisputed evidence that Anna, not Crispina, gave birth to the child and that Crispina, not Anna, is genetically related to him. Both women thus have adduced evidence of a mother and child relationship as contemplated by the Act. (Civ. Code, §§ 7003, subd. (1), 7004, subd. (a), 7015; Evid. Code, §§ 621, 892.) Yet for any child California law recognizes only one natural mother, despite advances in reproductive technology rendering a different outcome biologically possible.

¶ 10 We see no clear legislative preference in Civil Code section 7003 as between blood testing evidence and proof of having given birth.... This ambiguity, highlighted by the problems arising from the use of artificial reproductive techniques, is nowhere explicitly resolved in the Act. [Author's note: Thus, the UPA, adopted by California, does not resolve the issue arising in this case.]

¶ 11 Because two women each have presented acceptable proof of maternity, we do not believe this case can be decided without enquiring into the parties' intentions as manifested in the surrogacy agreement. Mark and Crispina are a couple who desired to have a child of their own genetic stock but are physically unable to do so without the help of reproductive technology. They affirmatively intended the birth of the child, and took the steps necessary to effect in vitro fertilization. But for their acted-on intention, the child would not exist. Anna agreed to facilitate the procreation of

Mark's and Crispina's child. The parties' aim was to bring Mark's and Crispina's child into the world, not for Mark and Crispina to donate a zygote to Anna. Crispina from the outset intended to be the child's mother. Although the gestative function Anna performed was necessary to bring about the child's birth, it is safe to say that Anna would not have been given the opportunity to gestate or deliver the child had she, prior to implantation of the zygote, manifested her own intent to be the child's mother. No reason appears why Anna's later change of heart should vitiate the determination that Crispina is the child's natural mother.

¶ 12 We conclude that although the Act recognizes both genetic consanguinity and giving birth as means of establishing a mother and child relationship, when the two means do not coincide in one woman, she who intended to procreate the child—that is, she who intended to bring about the birth of a child that she intended to raise as her own—is the natural mother under California law.

¶ 13 Our conclusion finds support in the writings of several legal commentators. (*See* Hill, *What Does It Mean to Be a "Parent"? The Claims of Biology As the Basis for Parental Rights*, *supra*, 66 N.Y.U. L. Rev. 353; Shultz, *Reproductive Technology and Intent-Based Parenthood: An Opportunity for Gender Neutrality* (1990) Wis. L. Rev. 297 [Shultz];....) Professor Hill, arguing that the genetic relationship per se should not be accorded priority in the determination of the parent-child relationship in the surrogacy context, notes that "while all of the players in the procreative arrangement are necessary in bringing a child into the world, the child would not have been born but for the efforts of the intended parents.... [¶] ... [T]he intended parents are the first cause, or the prime movers, of the procreative relationship." (Hill, *op. cit. supra*, at p. 415, emphasis in original.)

....

¶ 14 Moreover, as Professor Shultz recognizes, the interests of children, particularly at the outset of their lives, are "[un]likely to run contrary to those of adults who choose to bring them into being." (Shultz, *op. cit. supra*, at p. 397.) Thus, "[h]onoring the plans and expectations of adults who will be responsible for a child's welfare is likely to correlate significantly with positive outcomes for parents and children alike." (*Ibid.*)....

¶ 15 In deciding the issue of maternity under the Act we have felt free to take into account the parties' intentions, as expressed in the surrogacy contract, because in our view the agreement is not, on its face, inconsistent with public policy.

....

¶ 16 Anna urges that surrogacy contracts violate several social policies. Relying on her contention that she is the child's legal, natural mother, she cites the public policy embodied in Penal Code section 273, prohibiting the payment for consent to adoption of a child. She argues further that the policies underlying the adoption laws of this state are violated by the surrogacy contract because it in effect constitutes a prebirth waiver of her parental rights.

¶ 17 We disagree. Gestational surrogacy differs in crucial respects from adoption and so is not subject to the adoption statutes. The parties voluntarily agreed to participate in in vitro fertilization and related medical procedures before the child was conceived; at the time when Anna entered into the contract, therefore, she was not vulnerable to financial inducements to part with her own expected offspring. As discussed above, Anna was not the genetic mother of the child. The payments to Anna under the contract were meant to compensate her for her services in gestating the fetus and undergoing labor, rather than for giving up "parental" rights to the child. Payments were due both during the pregnancy and after the child's birth. We are, accordingly, unpersuaded that the contract used in this case violates the public policies embodied in Penal Code section 273 and the adoption statutes. For the same reasons, we conclude these contracts do not implicate the policies underlying the statutes governing termination of parental rights. (*See* Welf. & Inst. Code, § 202.)

¶ 18 It has been suggested that gestational surrogacy may run afoul of prohibitions on involuntary servitude. (*See* U.S. Const., Amend. XIII; Cal. Const., art. I, § 6; Pen. Code, § 181.) … We see no potential for that evil in the contract at issue here, and extrinsic evidence of coercion or duress is utterly lacking. We note that although at one point the contract purports to give Mark and Crispina the sole right to determine whether to abort the pregnancy, at another point it acknowledges: "All parties understand that a pregnant woman has the absolute right to abort or not abort any fetus she is carrying. Any promise to the contrary is unenforceable." We therefore need not determine the validity of a surrogacy contract purporting to deprive the gestator of her freedom to terminate the pregnancy.

¶ 19 Finally, Anna and some commentators have expressed concern that surrogacy contracts tend to exploit or dehumanize women, especially women of lower economic status. Anna's objections center around the psychological harm she asserts may result from the gestator's relinquishing the child to whom she has given birth. Some have also cautioned that the practice of surrogacy may encourage society to view children as commodities, subject to trade at their parents' will.

¶ 20 We are all too aware that the proper forum for resolution of this issue is the Legislature, where empirical data, largely lacking from this record, can be studied and rules of general applicability developed. However, in light of our responsibility to decide this case, we have considered as best we can its possible consequences.

¶ 21 We are unpersuaded that gestational surrogacy arrangements are so likely to cause the untoward results Anna cites as to demand their invalidation on public policy grounds. Although common sense suggests that women of lesser means serve as surrogate mothers more often than do wealthy women, there has been no proof that surrogacy contracts exploit poor women to any greater degree than economic necessity in general exploits them by inducing them to accept lower-paid or otherwise undesirable employment. We are likewise unpersuaded by the claim that surrogacy will foster the attitude that children are mere commodities; no evidence is offered to support it. The limited data available seem to reflect an absence of significant adverse effects of surrogacy on all participants.

¶22 The argument that a woman cannot knowingly and intelligently agree to gestate and deliver a baby for intending parents carries overtones of the reasoning that for centuries prevented women from attaining equal economic rights and professional status under the law. To resurrect this view is both to foreclose a personal and economic choice on the part of the surrogate mother, and to deny intending parents what may be their only means of procreating a child of their own genetic stock. Certainly in the present case it cannot seriously be argued that Anna, a licensed vocational nurse who had done well in school and who had previously borne a child, lacked the intellectual wherewithal or life experience necessary to make an informed decision to enter into the surrogacy contract.

Constitutionality of the Determination That Anna Johnson Is Not the Natural Mother

¶23 Anna argues at length that her right to the continued companionship of the child is protected under the federal Constitution. [The Court rejects these arguments].

....

The judgment of the Court of Appeal is affirmed.

Arabian, Justice, concurring to opinion by Panelli, Justice.

¶24 I concur ... [but] decline to subscribe to the dictum in which the majority find surrogacy contracts "not ... inconsistent with public policy."

....

¶25 The multiplicity of considerations at issue in a surrogacy situation plainly transcend traditional principles of contract law and require careful, nonadversarial analysis. For this reason, I do not think it wise for this court to venture unnecessarily into terrain more appropriately cleared by the Legislature in the first instance.... The New Jersey Supreme Court echoed similar cautionary tones in *Matter of Conroy* (1985) 98 N.J. 321, 486 A.2d 1209: "As an elected body, the Legislature is better able than any other single institution to reflect the social values at stake. In addition, it has the resources and ability to synthesize vast quantities of data and opinions from a variety of fields and to formulate general guidelines that may be applicable to a broad range of situations." (*Id.*, 486 A.2d at pp. 1220–1221; *accord*, *Matter of Guardianship of Hamlin* (1984) 102 Wash. 2d 810, 821–822, 689 P.2d 1372, 1378–1379.)

¶26 Clearly, this court should not avoid proper resolution of the issue before it.... Nevertheless, I would not move beyond the available legal mechanism into such socially and morally uncharted waters....

Kennard, Justice, dissenting.

....

¶ 27 ... The majority's resort to "intent" to break the "tie" between the genetic and gestational mothers is unsupported by statute, and, in the absence of appropriate protections in the law to guard against abuse of surrogacy arrangements, it is ill-advised. To determine who is the legal mother of a child born of a gestational surrogacy arrangement, I would apply the standard most protective of child welfare—the best interests of the child.

....

¶ 28 The determination of a question of parental rights to a child born of a surrogacy arrangement was before the New Jersey Supreme Court in *Matter of Baby M.* (1988) 109 N.J. 396, 537 A.2d 1227, a case that received worldwide attention. But in the surrogacy arrangement at issue there the woman who gave birth to the child, Marybeth Whitehead, had been impregnated by artificial insemination with the sperm of the intending father, William Stern. Whitehead thus provided the genetic material and carried the fetus to term. This case is different, because here those two aspects of the female role in reproduction were divided between two women. This process is known as "gestational" surrogacy, to distinguish it from the surrogacy arrangement involved in *Baby M.*

IV. POLICY CONSIDERATIONS

¶ 29 .... [Justice Kennard reviews policy considerations, such as those raised by Anna and discussed by the majority]. Whether surrogacy contracts are viewed as personal service agreements or agreements for the sale of the child born as the result of the agreement, commentators critical of contractual surrogacy view these contracts as contrary to public policy and thus not enforceable....

....

V. MODEL LEGISLATION

¶ 30 The debate over whom the law should recognize as the legal mother of a child born of a gestational surrogacy arrangement prompted the National Conference of Commissioners on Uniform State Laws to propose the Uniform Status of Children of Assisted Conception Act....

....

¶ 31 In its key components, the proposed legislation provides that "a woman who gives birth to a child is the child's mother" (USCACA, § 2) unless a court has approved a surrogacy agreement before conception (USCACA, § 5, 6). In the absence of such court approval, any surrogacy agreement would be void. (USCACA, § 5, subd. (b).) If, however, the arrangement for gestational surrogacy has court approval, "the intended parents are the parents of the child." (USCACA, § 8, subd. (a)(1).)

....

¶ 32 The USCACA offers predictability in delineating the parentage of children born of gestational surrogacy arrangements. Under the model legislation, if enacted, there would never be a question as to who has the legal responsibility for a child born of a gestational surrogacy arrangement: If the couple who initiated the surrogacy had complied with the provisions of the legislation, they would be the child's legal parents. If they had not, the rights and responsibilities of parenthood would go to the woman who gave birth to the child and her spouse.

¶ 33 Because California Legislature has not enacted the Uniform Status of Children of Assisted Conception Act, its provisions were not followed in this case.

VI. THE UNIFORM PARENTAGE ACT

¶ 34 The only California statute defining parental rights is the Uniform Parentage Act (hereafter also UPA). (*See* Civ. Code, § 7000 et seq.). The Legislature enacted the UPA to abolish the concept of illegitimacy and to replace it with the concept of parentage. (Adoption of Kelsey S. (1992) 1 Cal. 4th 816, 828, 4 Cal. Rptr. 2d 615, 823 P.2d 1216.) The UPA was never intended by the Legislature to govern the issues arising from new reproductive technologies such as gestational surrogacy.... Thus, the UPA by its terms cannot resolve the conflict in this case.

VII. ANALYSIS OF THE MAJORITY'S "INTENT" TEST

¶ 35 Faced with the failure of current statutory law to adequately address the issue of who is a child's natural mother when two women qualify under the UPA, the majority breaks the "tie" by resort to a criterion not found in the UPA—the "intent" of the genetic mother to be the child's mother.

....

¶ 36 Next, the majority offers as its third rationale the notion that bargained-for expectations support its conclusion regarding the dispositive significance of the genetic mother's intent.... But the courts will not compel performance of all contract obligations. For instance, even when a party to a contract for personal services (such as employment) has wilfully breached the contract, the courts will not order specific enforcement of an obligation to perform that personal service. (§ 3390; *see* 11 Witkin, Summary of Cal. Law, *supra*, Equity, § 59, p. 736.) The unsuitability of applying the notion that, because contract intentions are "voluntarily chosen, deliberate, express and bargained-for," their performance ought to be compelled by the courts is even more clear when the concept of specific performance is used to determine the course of the life of a child. Just as children are not the intellectual property of their parents, neither are they the personal property of anyone, and their delivery cannot be ordered as a contract remedy on the same terms that a court would, for example, order a breaching party to deliver a truckload of nuts and bolts.

....

¶ 37 [The dissent explains that enforcement of the agreement would be less objectionable if the agreement were undertaken under the conditions of the model legislation on assisted conception, not enacted in California.]

....

CONCLUSION

. . . .

¶ 38 . . . I would reverse the judgment of the Court of Appeal, and remand the case to the trial court for a determination of disputed parentage on the basis of the best interests of the child.

---

3. *Common Law of Contracts or Legislated Solutions?*

Are issues about the enforcement of surrogacy contracts easily resolved by the courts as a matter of common law, or would the public be better served if legislatures answered these questions? Two decades after the decision in *Johnson v. Calvert*, the California legislature provided that gestational surrogacy contracts with a true surrogate, such as that in *Johnson*, are presumptively valid if they meet certain statutory requisites. CAL. FAM. CODE § 7962 (Supp. 2018).

In contrast, in 1989, Arizona joined a few other states in statutorily prohibiting surrogate contracts: "No person may enter into, induce, arrange, procure or otherwise assist in the formation of a surrogate parentage contract." ARIZ. REV. STAT. ANN. § 25-218(A) (West 2017). However, because another provision of the statute placed the biological mother at a disadvantage compared to the biological father in claiming parental status of the child born of the non-biologically related surrogate mother, the Arizona Court of Appeals held that at least part of the Arizona statute—and maybe all of it—is unconstitutional as a violation of equal protection. *Soos v. Superior Court*, 182 Ariz. 470, 897 P.2d 1356 (Ct. App. 1994). In a concurring opinion, one member of the appellate panel explained why surrogacy contracts are a legitimate subject of state concern and regulation:

> Preliminarily, the state, in principle, may indeed seek to regulate or even to prohibit surrogacy. It has a legitimate interest in preventing the mercenary trafficking in babies, i.e., rent-a-womb services and the buying and selling of eggs. It also has a legitimate concern to avoid the emotional disruption in the gestational mother likely to result from taking the child from her . . . , as well as the child's denigration as an object of profit. These constitute compelling reasons in principle why regulation or prohibition in this area may be appropriate. *See* W. Wagner, "The Ethical and Legal Implications of Hired Maternity," 35 American Journal of Jurisprudence 187 (1990).

Id. at 475, 897 P.2d at 1361 (Gerber, J., *concurring*).

Do you agree with these concerns? Should the weighing of these concerns be left to courts, rather than legislatures? One scholar raises his own concerns about judicial assessment of public policy objections to contracts addressing intimate relations and formation of families, such as surrogacy agreements and the cohabitation agreements explored in Section III.B. He worries about the uncertainty and unpredictability of enforcement when courts weigh public policy considerations, and he fears that a robust public policy defense will not only interfere with private autonomy generally but will especially burden sexual minorities by selectively disfavoring their agreements. Kaiponanea T. Matsumura, *Public Policing of Intimate Agreements*, 25 YALE J.L. & FEMINISM 159, 190–204 (2013). Professor Matsumura argues that courts should moderate their interference with contracts addressing intimate relations and family formation in light of Supreme Court recognition that private decisions on these matters are worthy of constitutional protection. Kaiponanea T. Matsumura, *Consent to Intimate Regulation*, 96 N.C. L. REV. 1013, 1046–47 (2018).

4. Is Uniform Legislation Needed?

Although state legislation can increase certainty regarding enforceability of surrogacy contracts in that state, it can still leave a patchwork of standards across state lines. In extreme contrast to the California legislation facilitating gestational surrogacy contracts, legislation in Michigan and New York not only bars enforcement of surrogacy agreements but authorizes civil or criminal penalties for entering into a surrogacy contract for compensation, or for assisting in the contract formation. N.Y. DOM. REL. L. §§ 122, 123 (McKinney 2010); MICH. COMP. L. ANN. 722.855, 722.859 (2011 & Supp. 2018). A few other legislatures have taken a middle position, barring the enforcement of surrogacy agreements without imposing criminal penalties. *See* Sital Kalantry, *Should Compensated Surrogacy Be Permitted or Prohibited?*, Cornell Law School research paper No. 17-41, at 35–37, n. 47 (Sept. 2017), http://ssrn.com/abstract=3039011 (identifying various approaches taken by states as of 2017); *see also id.* at 23, Table 3 (classifying surrogacy laws by country); *Raftopol v. Ramey*, 299 Conn. 681, 713–16, 12 A.3d 783, 801–04 (2011) (reviewing the approaches of many states as of 2010).

Do we need uniform legislation to provide consistency across state lines? Or should the judicial or legislative responses to this issue be allowed to vary with local policies? *See, e.g.*, Eric A. Feldman, *Baby M Turns 30: The Law and Policy of Surrogate Motherhood*, 44 AM. J.L. & MED. 7 (2018) (arguing for a more uniform regulatory approach).

A model law advanced by the American Bar Association would enforce agreements for surrogacy services exchanged for reasonable compensation. MODEL ACT GOVERNING ASSISTED REPROD. TECH. § 802(1) (2008). For more on surrogacy contracts and on the model law proposed by the ABA, see Charles P. Kindregan Jr., *Considering Mom: Maternity and the Model Act Governing Assisted Reproductive Technology*, 17 J. GENDER, SOC. POL'Y & L. 601 (2009). For an argument in favor of uniform legislation based on British law, see Austin Caster, *Don't Split the Baby: How the U.S. Could Avoid Uncertainty and Unnecessary Litigation and Promote Equality by Emulating the British Surrogacy Law Regime*, 10 CONN. PUB. INT. L.J. 139 (2010).

5. *Disposition of Frozen Embryos*

If a couple has created frozen embryos from their own sperm and ova for possible future implantation, they might enter into an agreement to use the embryos only if both parties later consent. If they later divorce and disagree about disposition of the embryos, a party not wishing to use the embryos could invoke the agreement and withhold consent for use of the embryos. *See Bilbao v. Goodwin*, 217 A.3d 977 (Conn. 2019) (enforcing agreement to discard stored pre-embryos on divorce, and reviewing approaches in other states). Effective in 2018, however, an Arizona statute governing distribution of property in divorce proceedings provides in part that a couple's frozen embryos will be awarded "to the spouse who intends to allow the in vitro human embryos to develop to birth." ARIZ. REV. STAT. § 25-318.03.A.1 (ch. 128, 2018). It further provides that this statutory disposition will override an agreement between the parties, *id.* § 25-318.03.B, and any resulting child will be deemed not to be the child of the nonconsenting spouse, who will have no parental rights or obligations, *id.* § 25-318.03.D. As a legislator, would you support or oppose such legislation? For discussion of this and related questions, see I. Glenn Cohen, *The Right Not to Be a Genetic Parent?*, 81 S. CAL. L. REV. 1115 (2008).

D. Noncompetition Agreements

1. *Balancing the Interests of Various Stakeholders*

Noncompetition agreements (traditionally called covenants not to compete) provide an interesting illustration of public policy constraints on enforceability, because they require the balancing of several competing policies. All of the following kinds of restraints on competition appear in the case law, although the employee non-competition agreement is the most common.

a. Three Types of Agreements

Employee Non-Competition Agreement: As part of the employment contract, an employee agrees not to compete with the employer after the employee leaves the firm. This non-competition clause typically restricts the employee from engaging in certain kinds of business activities for a specified time and within a specified geographic area.

Sale of Business Noncompetition Agreement: As part of the agreement to sell a business, the seller agrees not to compete with the business that is being transferred to the buyer. Again, this agreement typically restricts designated business activities of the seller for a specified time and within a specified geographic area.

Equity Forfeiture Agreement: This kind of agreement applies to an employee who has an equity interest in a firm, such as a shareholder in the firm. Unlike a simple noncompetition agreement, it does not contractually obligate the departing member of a firm to refrain from competition. It does discourage competition, however, by forcing a departing employee to forfeit all or part of the employee's equity interest in the firm if the former employee chooses to compete with the firm in specified ways.

b. Public Policy Implications for Each Type of Agreement

A noncompetition agreement in the sale of a business typically is fair and consistent with public policy and thus is enforceable, for the following reasons:

> When a business is sold, the value of that business's goodwill usually figures significantly into the purchase price. The buyer therefore deserves some protection from competition from the former owner.... A restraint accompanying the sale of a business is necessary for the buyer to get the full goodwill value for which it has paid.

Valley Medical Specialists v. Farber, 194 Ariz. 363, 368, 982 P.2d 1277, 1282 (1999).

In some states, forfeiture agreements are similarly viewed as more benign than simple employee non-competition agreements because they provide the departing employee with some choice. Consequently, they are more readily enforced in some states than are employee noncompetition agreements, at least if the shareholder has departed voluntarily. *See, e.g., Morris v. Schroder Capital Mgt. Int'l*, 7 N.Y.3d 616, 859 N.E.2d 503 (2006) (enforcing forfeiture agreement with officer of financial firm, without regard to reasonableness, so long as the employee's departure is voluntary); *see also Fearnow v. Ridenour, Swenson, Cleere & Evans, P.C.*, 213 Ariz. 24, 138 P.3d 723 (2006) (adopting California's position that a reasonable forfeiture agreement with a departing attorney is enforceable, even though a non-competition agreement would not be enforced against an attorney).

A non-competition agreement in an employment contract, however, raises more serious questions of public policy relating to mandatory restraints on the departing employee's ability to maintain a livelihood and to provide services to the public. Both the common law and state and federal statutes have long prohibited certain restraints on trade and anti-competitive behaviors. Even though employee non-competition agreements typically do not violate the strict terms of such laws, they offend the policies underlying the laws. An employee noncompetition agreement not only restricts the employee's ability to make a living and thus to avoid the need for state-supported economic assistance, it also reduces the number of providers of goods and services from which the public can choose, and it could result in higher prices if competition is reduced to a substantial degree.

On the other hand, even though an employer has no justification for complaining about general competition from other purveyors of goods or services, in some circumstances it could have legitimate reasons for restricting a former employee's competition. For example, the former employee might have enjoyed access to valuable trade secrets and client lists, as well as the opportunity to develop relationships with the employer's clients. Moreover, although an employer should expect that any employee will develop general skills and knowledge over the course of months or years of employment, if an employer has invested substantial resources in providing specialized training for the employee, the employee could be a formidable competitor at the employer's expense.

For reasons such as these, countervailing public policies provide some support for employee non-competition agreements. These policies are reflected in common law doctrines that impose liability for certain kinds of unfair competition or breaches of an employee's duty of loyalty, and they are more generally reflected in legislation such as federal copyright and patent statutes, which encourage innovation by granting limited monopoly rights to innovators. Competition by a former employee normally would not directly violate any of these laws, but it could harm an employer's legitimate interests in a way that implicates the policies underlying the laws, thus providing some legal justification for enforcing employee noncompetition agreements, in addition to the general policy favoring freedom of contract.

c. Rule of Reasonableness for Employee Noncompetition Agreements

California has legislatively balanced these interests strongly in favor of employees, by statutorily forbidding employee noncompetition agreements, with limited exceptions, even though broadly permitting non-competition agreements connected with the sale of a business or its goodwill. CAL. BUS. & PROF. CODE §§ 16600–16601 (West 2017); *see Edwards v. Arthur Andersen LLP*, 44 Cal. 4th 937, 189 P.3d 285 (2008) (discussing the history of these provisions). Indeed, an employer in California commits a misdemeanor by requiring an employee to enter into a noncompetition agreement that the employer knows to be unenforceable. CAL. LAB. CODE §§ 432.5, 433 (West 2011). A few other states have also adopted legislation that broadly prohibits employee noncompetition agreements.

In most states, however, employee noncompetition agreements are governed by common law rules that strike a more balanced approach. The competing interests of the employee, the employer, and the public have spawned a judicial rule of reasonableness to assess whether an employee noncompetition agreement violates public policy or instead is enforceable to protect an employer's legitimate interests. *Amex Distributing Co., Inc. v. Mascari*, 150 Ariz. 510, 514–15, 724 P.2d 596, 600–601 (1986).

To justify a noncompetition agreement, the employer must first demonstrate that the departing employee had access to trade secrets, customer lists, extraordinary training, or other facets of employment that justify protecting the employer from the departing employee's competition. An employer cannot complain about competition that arises from the ordinary skill and experience that a departing employee had routinely acquired in the workplace. *Behnke v. Hertz Corp.*, 70 Wis. 2d 818, 822, 235 N.W.2d 690, 693 (1975).

Assuming that the employer has legitimate interests to protect, most courts will nonetheless deny enforcement of a noncompetition agreement if any of the following kinds of restrictions in the agreement are greater than reasonably necessary to protect the legitimate interests: (1) the scope of the employee's activities that are restricted, (2) the period for which the competition is restricted, and (3) the geographic area within which the employee's activities are restricted. *See generally Farber*, 194 Ariz.

at 370–71, 982 P.2d at 1284–85 (assessing the reasonableness of these three features of the agreement in the context of competition by a departing physician, restrictions on which were given special scrutiny for reasonableness). In addition, the court will consider the public interest, such as the availability of services and service providers to the public. *See id.* at 371, 982 P.2d at 1285.

For example, suppose that an employee's work with the employer provided the employee with access to client lists and with the opportunity to develop good relationships with clients. A non-competition agreement could reasonably prohibit the former employee from engaging in the same kind of business within the geographic area that serves those former clients. This restriction would reasonably balance the employer, employee, and public interests, but only if it was limited to a period of time necessary to enable the firm to reestablish its relationship to the clients and neutralize the competitive edge that the former employee had secured through its previous employment with the firm. If that and other threats to the employer's legitimate interests would dissipate in six months or a year, then a non-competition restriction for two years would be unreasonable.

Some trade secrets are so central to a company's profitability and brand association, however, that an employer's legitimate interest in protecting such a secret may endure for decades. Because it is highly unlikely that a court would enforce a non-competition agreement for so many years, an employer should consider an alternative means of protecting a trade secret that does not quickly become obsolete. A dispute in 2010, for example, revealed that the manufacturer of Thomas' brand English Muffins disclosed to only seven employees the trademarked secret to creating the air pockets in its muffins. To protect this secret, it required selected employees to enter into nondisclosure agreements as part of their employment contracts. An obligation of nondisclosure would not prevent an employee from taking a job with a competitor so long as the employee kept the secret. Because such an obligation does not restrict a former employee's ability to secure gainful employment, public policy normally should not demand the same time limitations that apply to noncompetition agreements.

Finally, the employer's burden of establishing its legitimate interests may be greater in some courts and in some circumstances if the former employee did not leave voluntarily but was fired by the employer. *See, e.g., Wrigg v. Junkermier, Clark, Campanella, Stevens, P.C.*, 362 Mont. 496, 265 P.3d 646 (2011) (reasoning that employer can prevent competition by retaining a good employee and that it need not fear competition from an employee who is fired for incompetence, absent the employee's access to trade secrets or customer lists). Courts in some states apply a more rigid rule in favor of such employees: "New York courts will not enforce a non-competition provision in an employment agreement where the former employee was involuntarily terminated." *SIFCO Indus., Inc. v. Advanced Plating Techs.*, Inc., 867 F. Supp. 155, 157 (S.D.N.Y. 1994).

d. Elevated Public Interest in Professions in Which Client Choice Is Critically Important

The public interest associated with a few professions is strong enough to engender special judicial antagonism to non-competition agreements in those professions. For example, partly because of the importance attached to a client's interest in representation by the lawyer of the client's choosing, an employee non-competition agreement imposed by a law firm on a departing lawyer is never enforceable in some states ("per se unenforceable") or is subject to special scrutiny in others. *See Farber*, 194 Ariz. at 368–69, 982 P.2d at 1282–83 (stating in dictum that such agreements are not enforceable in Arizona, based on state rules of professional conduct, because the agreements adversely affect both an attorney's professional autonomy and unrestricted choice by clients).[1]

For similar reasons, non-competition agreements between medical offices and departing physicians are typically subjected to special scrutiny, even where not viewed as per se unenforceable:

> We therefore conclude that the doctor-patient relationship is special and entitled to unique protection. It cannot be easily or accurately compared to relationships in the commercial context. In light of the great public policy interest involved in covenants not to compete between physicians, each agreement will be strictly construed for reasonableness.

Id. at 369, 982 P.2d at 1283 (reserving in footnote 1 the question whether a physician's non-competition agreement should be viewed as per se unenforceable, a question unnecessary to decide because the agreement was found to be unreasonable when subjected to strict scrutiny), *see also* TEX. BUS. & COM. CODE § 15.50(b) (2011) (permitting enforcement of non-competition agreement against a physician, but only if strict and specific requirements are met).

2. Revision of Unreasonable Non-Competition Agreements

a. Three Competing Approaches

If an unreasonable employee non-competition agreement restricts the former employee's activities to a greater degree than is necessary to protect the employer's legitimate interests, a court could simply deny enforcement, as it would deny enforcement of any illegal contract or contract provision. *See Central Adjustment Bureau, Inc. v. Ingram*, 678 S.W.2d 28, 36 (1984) ("At one time the majority of courts employed [this] rule."). This traditional all-or-nothing approach has the benefit of

---

1. Courts are split on whether to enforce *equity forfeiture* agreements on an attorney who voluntarily departs from a law firm. *See Fearnow v. Ridenour, Swenson, Cleere & Evans, P.C.*, 213 Ariz. 24, 28–31, 138 P.3d 723, 727–30 (2006) (citing to cases reflecting the split and adopting the California approach of enforcing such agreements if they are reasonable).

exerting pressure on the employer to draft restrictions on competition that are clearly reasonable: the employer knows that it will be denied all enforcement of the non-competition clause if any facet of it (activities restricted, duration, or geographic scope) is found to be unreasonable.

On the other hand, in light of the competing policies affecting non-competition agreements, including those supporting the employer's restrictions, some courts are reluctant to deny all enforcement of an unreasonably broad clause, at least in the absence of bad faith on the part of the employer. At the opposite end of the spectrum of the traditional all-or-nothing approach is a willingness of some courts to freely revise an unreasonable non-competition clause, cutting it down to a reasonable scope and then enforcing it as rewritten. For example, if a non-competition clause were otherwise reasonable but had a duration of two years when six months of protection from competition would have served the employer's legitimate interests, a court that exercised maximum flexibility would replace the term "two years" with the term "six months" and then enforce the clause as modified. *See id.* at 37 (affirming trial judge's enforcement of a non-competition clause in an employment agreement after reducing its duration and the scope of prohibited client contacts).

This maximally flexible modification approach is subject to at least two criticisms. First, it permits the court to rewrite the parties' contract, substituting the court's own revision for the parties' actual agreement. Second, it could encourage an employer to write the broadest possible non-competition clause, secure in the knowledge that either the employee will comply with the broad restrictions without challenge or a court will revise the clause to make it reasonable and enforceable. A court can hope to discourage such abuse by denying all enforcement if the employer drafted restrictions that the employer knew would be unreasonable, hoping that the employee would not challenge them. *See id.* Nonetheless, the employer would have less incentive to aim for clearly reasonable restrictions than it would in a state that retained the traditional all-or-nothing approach.

As a middle ground between the traditional approach and the one allowing all necessary modification, courts in some states, such as Arizona, adopt the "blue-pencil rule," which liberally permits severance of unreasonably broad noncompetition provisions and enforcement of the remainder. Under the blue-pencil rule, a court will attempt to cut an unreasonably broad noncompetition clause down to reasonable and enforceable size, but only if it can do so by striking out unreasonable provisions, allowing it to enforce the reasonable terms remaining in the parties' original agreement, if the remaining terms could sensibly stand alone, and even then only if the parties' agreement reflects an intent to permit the court to sever unreasonable provisions and selectively enforce the remainder of the noncompetition clause. *See, e.g., Valley Medical Specialists v. Farber*, 194 Ariz. 363, 982 P.2d 1277 (1999) (en banc).

For example, suppose that a noncompetition clause restricted a former employee's competition in "Arizona and California," but the employer had legitimate business interests to protect only in Arizona, and the parties' contract included a provision authorizing a court to strike out unreasonable provisions and enforce the remainder.

In these circumstances, an Arizona court could use the "blue-pencil" approach to strike out the words "and California," leaving a reasonable and enforceable geographic scope of "Arizona." Striking out unreasonably broad terms in this manner allows the court to maintain that it is not "rewriting" the parties' contract but instead is simply severing and refusing to enforce discrete provisions that violate public policy.

Exercise 9.3 — Applying the Blue-Pencil Rule

Julia started her career as the production manager for an ice cream manufacturer in Oregon but later assumed the position of assistant sales manager for Sabor, a Phoenix-based manufacturer and distributor of corn, flour, and whole wheat tortillas. For Sabor, Julia developed valuable relationships with numerous retail clients, such as grocery stores and restaurants, in Phoenix and immediately surrounding cities. After a falling out with the sales manager for Sabor, Julia voluntarily quit and now seeks a position with a competing manufacturer and distributor of tortillas, Del Sol, which distributes its goods to retail clients both in Phoenix and its surrounding cities and in Tucson, 110 miles to the southeast. Del Sol has offered Julia well-paying positions either in the sales department or in production and quality control.

Julia's agreement with the Sabor includes the following provisions:

> **IX. Noncompetition.** For a period of three years after termination of employment with Sabor, Employee may not accept employment with any other manufacturer or distributor of tortillas, or engage in the sale or marketing of tortillas for any other business, in the Cities of Phoenix, Chandler, Guadalupe, Gilbert, Glendale, Mesa, Scottsdale, Tempe, and Tucson, Arizona.
>
> **X. Severability.** If a court finds any portion of the noncompetition clause in section IX above to be unreasonably broad, it may, consistent with the parties' intentions, enforce only that portion of the clause that is reasonable and is consistent with public policy.

If Sabor threatens to enforce the noncompetition clause, would it bar Julia from accepting employment with Del Sol? Assume that a judge would find that: (1) the maximum reasonable duration is one year; (2) because of her relationships with purchasing managers of Sabor's clients, it is reasonable to restrict Julia from marketing and selling tortillas but she should not be restricted from working in other capacities, such as production and quality control; and (3) all the cities in the list are within Sabor's distribution area except Tucson. Can you modify the clause, using the blue pencil rule, so that it is reasonable and enforceable? If so, as modified, to what extent would the clause limit Julia's opportunities with Del Sol?

Suppose that, rather than listing cities, section IX of the contract restricted the former employee's activities "in the State of Arizona," and Julia accepted a position with Del Sol to market its tortillas to stores and restaurants in Phoenix and Tucson. Can you use the blue-pencil rule to cut the geographic scope down to a single city and at least enjoin Julia's activities in Phoenix?

Do you think that the blue-pencil rule is arbitrary and formalistic, or is it a sound application of severance principles and a good compromise between the traditional all-or-nothing approach and the trend to rewrite the contract to make it reasonable and enforceable?

b. Step-Down Provisions and the Blue-Pencil Rule

In a state that adopts the blue-pencil rule, can the drafter of a contract gain the benefits of judicial revision by inserting a number of grammatically severable step-down provisions—ranging from the broadest possible scope to a clearly reasonable scope—and by inviting a court to strike out the provisions that are unreasonably broad and to enforce the next broadest provision? If you were a judge confronted with such a noncompetition agreement, how would you respond? Would it depend on whether the employer appeared to draft the agreement in a good-faith belief that any of the step-down provisions might be found to be reasonable?

Read the following article excerpt, which defines the issue raised by "step-down" provisions, and then the federal district court's decision in *Compass Bank v. Hartley*. Under the approach of *Compass Bank*, in what circumstances will courts enforce an agreement with step-down provisions?

Non-Compete Agreements with Step-Down Provisions—Will Arizona Courts Enforce Them?

By Ali J. Farhang and Ray K. Harris,
Dec. 2005 Ariz. Atty. 26 [footnotes omitted]

A client walks into your office, throws an employment agreement on your desk and asks, "Is the covenant not to compete in there enforceable?"

After fixing the damage to your desktop "filing system" caused by the flight of the agreement, you skim to the non-compete section and identify what is referred to as a "step-down provision." The non-compete provides alternative time and area restrictions. But which one applies?

You are aware that a covenant not to compete must be reasonably limited as to time and territory. You also recall that Arizona courts have repeatedly approved use of the blue-pencil rule, whereby a court is empowered to cross out overbroad, unreasonable provisions in an agreement, while keeping in place less onerous, enforceable provisions.

Whether you are representing the employee or employer, the client's next question is obvious: "Which provisions are enforceable?" The client also asks, "Is there any way a court will find the entire covenant void?"

The answers are not obvious, and you finally give the response learned on the first day of law school: "It depends."

A covenant not to compete is generally enforceable as long as it is no broader than necessary to protect an employer's legitimate business interests. The burden is on the employer to prove the extent of its protectable interests. If an employer cannot do so, the entire covenant will be deemed unenforceable.

Employers continue to use non-competition clauses regularly. In an effort to take advantage of Arizona's adoption of the blue-pencil rule, Arizona employers frequently include step-down provisions within their non-competition clauses. By including grammatically separate restraints, the employer attempts to guarantee at least some protection. There is no definitive test to determine which provisions are enforceable. Indeed, for a number of reasons, a court could actually find the entire non-compete void.

....

What Do "Step-Down Provisions" Look Like?

A hypothetical step-down provision might provide:

1. NONCOMPETITION. For the **TIME PERIOD** set forth in paragraph 2, Employee shall not, directly or indirectly, own, manage, operate, participate in or finance any business venture that competes with the Company within the **AREA,** set forth in paragraph 3.

2. TIME PERIOD. **TIME PERIOD** for purposes of paragraph 1 shall mean the period beginning as of the date of Employee's employment with the Company and ending on the date of death of the employee; provided, however, that if a court determines that such period is unenforceable, **TIME PERIOD** shall end five (5) years after the date of termination; provided, however, that if a court determines that such period is unenforceable, **TIME PERIOD** shall end six (6) months after the date of termination.

3. AREA. **AREA** for purposes of paragraph I shall mean: the planet Earth, provided however, if a court determines such a geographic scope is unenforceable, **AREA** shall mean the United States; provided however, if a court determines such a geographic scope is unenforceable, **AREA** shall mean the City of Tucson.

4. In the event any provision of the Agreement is deemed unenforceable, it shall be severed and the balance of the Agreement shall be enforced.

Compass Bank v. Hartley

430 F. Supp. 2d 973, 981 (D. Ariz. 2006)

....

In light of these cases, the Court finds under limited circumstances carefully crafted ... step-down provisions are a permissible application of Arizona's blue-pencil rule, if they permit a Court to cross-out some unreasonable sections in favor of more reasonable ones without rewriting them.... [S]tep down provisions provide the parties with several scenarios that may be found reasonable. In this sense, it affords parties an opportunity to contemplate several options at the time the contract is signed. If a court subsequently finds the covenant unreasonable and uses the step-down provision to amend the covenant, such a modification is not significant because it has already been contemplated. Thus, there was a meeting of the minds at the initiation of the contract with regard to the alternatives presented by the step-down provision. On the other hand, if the alternatives presented are indefinite and inconsistent with the underlying provision, and are not easily severable from unreasonable provisions, there is no meeting of the minds and the covenant is invalid. That is not the case here. The step-down provision includes a narrow duration range of 1–2 years and a reasonable geographical scope of 25–50 miles. The agreement was drafted in good faith and is an acceptable application of Arizona's blue-pencil law.

Based on the foregoing, the covenant is saved by the step-down provisions allowing the Court to limit its duration to one-year and a scope of 25 miles.

Exercise 9.4 — Good Faith, Reasonableness, and Blue Pencils

Would the step-down provisions set forth in the article immediately before *Compass Bank* satisfy the test of good faith adopted by the court in *Compass Bank*? Consider the differences among provisions that, at the time of contracting, the employer: (1) knows are reasonable, (2) reasonably and in good faith believes might be approved as reasonable, and (3) knows are certainly unreasonable and unenforceable. Which of these kinds of provisions did the court find in *Compass Bank*? Would the court have enforced a reasonable step-down provision if the broadest alternative provision set a duration of 10 years and geographic scope of 500 miles, and the employer knew at the time of contracting that those restrictions were clearly unreasonable?

---

3. *Legislative Intervention*

Statutes in California and Texas have modified common law treatment of noncompetition clauses, albeit in different directions.

a. Texas — Restoring Traditional Common Law

A provision of the Texas Business and Commercial Code codifies the common law rule of reasonableness as a means of assessing a noncompetition agreement's conformity with public policy. In addition, the statute briefly addresses threshold issues of contract formation. By doing so, it appears at first glance to erect additional requirements for enforcement of an employee noncompetition agreement. As explained by the excerpt below, however, the legislature intended to return to a more expansive approach to contract formation for noncompetition agreements by overruling intervening case law that had taken a more restrictive approach. Consider how you could redraft the code provision so that it more clearly conveyed the legislative intent found by the court.

Sheshunoff Mgt. Serv., L.P. v. Johnson

209 S.W.3d 644 (Tex. S. Ct. 2006)

Justice Willett delivered the opinion of the Court, in which Justice Hecht, Justice Brister, Justice Green, and Justice Johnson joined.

....

II. Discussion

¶ 1 The Covenants Not to Compete Act (Act) states:

> [A] covenant not to compete is enforceable if it is ancillary to or part of an otherwise enforceable agreement at the time the agreement is made to the extent that it contains limitations as to time, geographical area, and scope of activity to be restrained that are reasonable and do not impose a greater restraint than is necessary to protect the goodwill or other business interest of the promisee.

Tex. Bus. & Com. Code § 15.50(a).

....

¶ 2 Cumulatively, this legislative history indicates that (1) in 1989 and 1993 the Legislature wanted to expand the enforceability of covenants not to compete beyond that which the courts had allowed, (2) in 1989 the Legislature specifically wanted to ensure that covenants could be signed after the employment relationship began so long as the agreement containing the covenant was supported by new consideration, and (3) in 1993 the Legislature specifically wanted to make clear that covenants not to compete in the at-will employment context were enforceable....

¶ 3 As best we can tell, the language in the current version of the Act making reference to the agreement "at the time the agreement is made" was included in the 1993 amendment to maintain the rule, recognized in the 1989 version of the Act, that a covenant could be signed after the date that employment began so long as the new agreement was supported by independent consideration.... There is no indication in the legislative history of the 1993 amendment of an intent to reduce the enforceability of covenants not to compete; all of the legislative history is to the contrary.

....

¶ 4 ... [T]he statute's core inquiry is whether the covenant "contains limitations as to time, geographical area, and scope of activity to be restrained that are reasonable and do not impose a greater restraint than is necessary to protect the goodwill or other business interest of the promisee." Tex. Bus. & Com. Code § 15.50(a)....

---

b. California—Legislatively Abrogating the Balancing Test

As noted earlier, California legislation has rejected the rule of reasonableness in favor of a per se prohibition of employee noncompetition agreements. The next case discusses this statutory rule and its limited exceptions.

Edwards v. Arthur Andersen LLP

44 Cal. 4th 937, 189 P.3d 285 (2008) [footnotes omitted]

....

A. Section 16600

¶ 1 Under the common law, as is still true in many states today, contractual restraints on the practice of a profession, business, or trade, were considered valid, as long as they were reasonably imposed.... This was true even in California.... However, in 1872 California settled public policy in favor of open competition, and rejected the common law "rule of reasonableness," when the Legislature enacted the Civil Code. (... Bus. & Prof. Code, § 16600....) Today in California, covenants not to compete are void, subject to several exceptions discussed briefly below.

¶ 2 Section 16600 states: "Except as provided in this chapter, every contract by which anyone is restrained from engaging in a lawful profession, trade, or business of any kind is to that extent void." The chapter excepts noncompetition agreements in the sale or dissolution of corporations (§ 16601), partnerships (*ibid.*; § 16602), and limited liability corporations (§ 16602.5). In the years since its original enactment as Civil Code section 1673, our courts have consistently affirmed that section 16600 evinces a settled legislative policy in favor of open competition and employee mobility. (*See D'sa v. Playhut, Inc.* (2000) 85 Cal. App. 4th 927, 933, 102 Cal. Rptr. 2d 495.) The law protects Californians and ensures "that every citizen shall retain the right to pursue any lawful employment and enterprise of their choice." (*Metro Traffic Control, Inc. v. Shadow Traffic Network* (1994) 22 Cal. App. 4th 853, 859, 27 Cal. Rptr. 2d 573.) It protects "the important legal right of persons to engage in businesses and occupations of their choosing." (*Morlife, Inc. v. Perry* (1997) 56 Cal. App. 4th 1514, 1520, 66 Cal. Rptr. 2d 731.)

¶ 3 This court has invalidated an otherwise narrowly tailored agreement as an improper restraint under section 16600 because it required a former employee to forfeit his pension rights on commencing work for a competitor. (*Muggill v. Reuben H. Donnelley Corp.* (1965) 62 Cal. 2d 239, 242–243, 42 Cal. Rptr. 107, 398 P.2d 147 ...);.... *Muggill* held that, with exceptions not applicable here, section 16600 invalidates provisions in employment contracts and retirement pension plans that prohibit "an employee from working for a competitor after completion of his employment or imposing a penalty if he does so [citations] unless they are necessary to protect the employer's trade secrets [citation]." (*Muggill*, at p. 242, 42 Cal. Rptr. 107, 398 P.2d 147.) In sum, following the Legislature, this court generally condemns noncompetition agreements. (*See, e.g., Armendariz v. Foundation Health Psychcare Services, Inc.* (2000) 24 Cal. 4th 83, 123, fn. 12, 99 Cal. Rptr. 2d 745, 6 P.3d 669 [such restraints on trade are "largely illegal"].)

¶ 4 Under the statute's plain meaning, therefore, an employer cannot by contract restrain a former employee from engaging in his or her profession, trade, or business unless the agreement falls within one of the exceptions to the rule. (§ 16600.)

Andersen, however, asserts that we should interpret the term "restrain" under section 16600 to mean simply to "prohibit," so that only contracts that totally prohibit an employee from engaging in his or her profession, trade, or business are illegal. It would then follow that a mere limitation on an employee's ability to practice his or her vocation would be permissible under section 16600, as long as it was reasonably based.

¶ 5 Andersen contends that some California courts have held that section 16600 (and its predecessor statutes, Civil Code former sections 1673, 1674, and 1675) are the statutory embodiment of prior common law, and embrace the rule of reasonableness in evaluating competitive restraints. (*See, e.g., South Bay Radiology Medical Associates v. Asher* (1990) 220 Cal. App. 3d 1074, 1080, 269 Cal. Rptr. 15 (*South Bay Radiology*) [§ 16600 embodies common law prohibition against restraints on trade];....

¶ 6 As Edwards observes, however, the cases Andersen cites to support a relaxation of the statutory rule simply recognize that the statutory exceptions to section 16600 reflect the same exceptions to the rule against noncompetition agreements that were implied in the common law. For example, *South Bay Radiology* acknowledged the general prohibition against restraints on trade while applying the specific partnership dissolution exception of section 16602 to the facts of its case. (*South Bay Radiology, supra*, 220 Cal. App. 3d at p. 1080, 269 Cal. Rptr. 15.).... [The Court rejected an approach reflected in nonbinding case law from state and federal intermediate appellate courts, which would have recognized an exception to section 16600 for agreements that imposed less than complete restraints on the practice of a trade or profession.]

¶ 7 We conclude that Andersen's noncompetition agreement was invalid. As the Court of Appeal observed, "The first challenged clause prohibited Edwards, for an 18-month period, from performing professional services of the type he had provided while at Andersen, for any client on whose account he had worked during 18 months prior to his termination. The second challenged clause prohibited Edwards, for a year after termination, from 'soliciting,' defined by the agreement as providing professional services to any client of Andersen's Los Angeles office." The agreement restricted Edwards from performing work for Andersen's Los Angeles clients and therefore restricted his ability to practice his accounting profession.... The noncompetition agreement that Edwards was required to sign before commencing employment with Andersen was therefore invalid because it restrained his ability to practice his profession....

....

DISPOSITION

¶ 8 We hold that the noncompetition agreement here is invalid under section 16600, and we reject the narrow-restraint exception urged by Andersen. Noncompetition agreements are invalid under section 16600 in California, even if narrowly drawn, unless they fall within the applicable statutory exceptions of sections 16601, 16602, or 16602.5....

Exercise 9.5 — Revisiting the Rule of Reasonableness

1. Assessing *Edwards*

Do you support the California approach of broadly prohibiting employee noncompetition agreements by statute? Study the description of the noncompetition agreement in paragraph 7 of *Edwards*. Would all or part of this agreement likely fail a judicial test based on reasonableness, or did section 16600 operate to disallow an agreement that would have been enforced in most other jurisdictions? You may assume that the noncompetition agreement had no geographic limitations, except that it was limited to providing professional services to clients associated with Andersen's Los Angeles office during a certain prior period.

2. Noncompetition Agreements for Low-wage Workers

Studies show that employers are increasingly requiring noncompetition agreements in low-skill, low-wage employment, preventing these employees from earning higher wages offered by competing firms. If employees do not have access to legal counsel and thus remain in place, noncompetition agreements in this context could suppress the wages of low-income workers, shielding employers from entirely *fair* competition between firms for the services of employees with only general skills.

While not restricting employee noncompetition agreements as broadly as has California, some states have considered or adopted legislation invalidating noncompetition agreements in low-wage employment. *See, e.g.*, 820 ILL. COMP. STAT. 90/10 (2016). At the federal level, a Senate bill would prohibit noncompetition agreements with hourly employees covered by the Fair Labor Standards Act, while allowing employers to protect their trade secrets. Freedom to Compete Act, S. 124, 116th Cong. (2019). Do you support this legislative approach?

Alternatively, is the judicial rule of reasonableness adequate to regulate such agreements, invalidating them if the employee has not acquired trade secrets, received highly specialized training, or developed valuable relationships with clients? Even if unenforceable under a rule of reasonableness, would a noncompetition agreement discourage many employees from switching jobs because they assume that they are legally bound? Would you support legislation that both: (1) invalidates noncompetition agreements for some or all kinds of employees, and (2) imposes a criminal penalty on an employer who imposes an employee noncompetition agreement that the employer knows to be unenforceable?

3. No-Hire Agreements between Firms

In the absence of a noncompetition agreement between an employer and an employee, should a court invalidate an agreement between the employer and another firm in which the other firm agrees not to hire the employee after the employee leaves the first employer? *See Pittsburgh Logistics Systems, Inc., v. Beemac Trucking, LLC*, 202 A.3d 801, 2019 Pa. Super. 13 (2019) (en banc) (over a dissent, the majority holding that the clause violated public policy as a restraint on trade).

Exercise 9.6 — Practice Exam

Suggested time: 1 hour

Bug Busters (which you can refer to as "BB" if you like) is a new pest control company that offers monthly pesticide services to residences and businesses within the City of Phoenix, Arizona. By the end of its first year of operation, January to December 2017, Bug Busters had gained a large share of the pest control market in Phoenix, and it was poised to reproduce that success in the adjoining southeast cities of Tempe, Chandler, and Mesa in the second year, with plans in later years to expand to other cities surrounding Phoenix.

Jill Lee graduated from the A.S.U. School of Business with honors in May 2016 and worked as a junior investment counselor at an investment firm for a few months before joining Bug Busters at its inception. She worked at Bug Busters throughout its first year of operations. Her duties in the office included working with others to maintain inventory, to solicit new accounts, to organize billing procedures, and to maintain good customer relations with existing accounts. When other employees were unavailable, she even applied pesticides at customers' offices or residences on an emergency basis.

At the end of Bug Busters' first year of operations, December 31, 2017, Lee resigned from her post at Bug Busters. She immediately secured financial backing and opened her own pest control company, "Roach Raiders" ("RR," for short, if you like), with its base of operations on the southern edge of the City of Scottsdale, situated just east of Phoenix and north of Tempe. Lee quickly set up operations, hired a small staff, and set about soliciting customers in south Scottsdale and all of the adjacent City of Tempe.

To help get started, Lee also immediately and successfully solicited some clients of Bug Busters located in an adjacent area of Phoenix with whom she had developed good relations while working at Bug Busters. Had she waited an additional year before opening Roach Raiders, office and field procedures would have changed sufficiently, and relationships with customers and suppliers would have dissipated sufficiently, that any success that Lee enjoyed would have been due solely to her own efforts rather than to training and experience at Bug Busters.

As soon as Bug Busters learned of Lee's new business, in January 2018, it brought suit to enforce the following conspicuous non-competition clause in the employment agreement that Lee had entered into at the commencement of her employment with Bug Busters (Lee is identified as "Employee"):

If Employee terminates his/her employment with Bug Busters for any reason, Employee will not work in any capacity in the pest control trade within the Phoenix metropolitan area for a period of two years.

Early in the suit, the court denied Bug Busters' request for a temporary restraining order (preliminary injunctive relief), preferring to delay any relief until the full facts could come out at trial. It is now nearly two years after Lee terminated her employment with Bug Busters, and the trial court has finally set the trial for January 2020, at which time money damages will be the only possible relief.

You may assume that the employment agreement was formed by the parties with consideration and through voluntary offer and acceptance and that it is sufficiently definite to enforce. You may also assume that a court would interpret "Phoenix Metropolitan area" to mean not just the City of Phoenix, but the surrounding cities and towns as well. Fully discuss all facets of the question of whether the quoted clause is unenforceable for violation of public policy, and discuss the approaches that a court might take to address any problem with enforceability. Do not otherwise discuss remedies; for example, do not discuss damages.

Apply general common law principles. Organize your response around IRAC. Be sure to argue both sides of the facts, or explore competing legal approaches, when appropriate. Do not simply restate the facts in narrative form; for each issue, link relevant facts to a legal rule when you argue them.

IV. Unconscionability

A. Overview

1. Origins and Scope

Even if a contract provision does not violate law or public policy, it could be so unfair to one of the parties that a court will refuse to enforce it on the ground that it is "unconscionable." Courts have long exercised equitable discretion to deny *specific* enforcement on the ground that the party seeking enforcement engaged in sharp practices during bargaining or performance, or that the bargain was unfairly lopsided in favor of that party. The judicially developed doctrine of unconscionability, however, permits a court to deny all enforcement of a contract or contract clause, even denying compensatory damages.

The doctrine of unconscionability did not reach full bloom until it was included in UCC § 2-302, set forth here as codified in Arizona:

> 47-2302. Unconscionable contract or clause
>
> A. If the court as a matter of law finds the contract or any clause of the contract to have been unconscionable at the time it was made the court may refuse to enforce the contract, or it may enforce the remainder of the contract without the unconscionable clause, or it may so limit the application of any unconscionable clause as to avoid any unconscionable result.
>
> B. When it is claimed or appears to the court that the contract or any clause thereof may be unconscionable the parties shall be afforded a reasonable opportunity to present evidence as to its commercial setting, purpose and effect to aid the court in making the determination.

The doctrine of unconscionability, however, is not limited to transactions in goods governed by the UCC. Some jurisdictions recognized its equivalent under common law before the UCC came into force. *See, e.g., Williams v. Walker-Thomas Furniture Co.*, 350 F.2d 445, 448–49 (D.C. Cir. 1965) (denying enforcement to an unconscionable repossession clause in a sales contract).

Indeed, rather than adopt section 2-302, which applies only to sales of goods, the California legislature instead codified the doctrine of unconscionability more generally in its civil code, legislatively making the doctrine potentially applicable to any kind of contract in California. CAL. CIV. CODE § 1670.5 (2011); *see also* RESTATEMENT (SECOND) OF CONTRACTS § 208 (1981) (summarizing a common law principle of unconscionability).

Notice the flexibility of the remedy in the last two clauses of the first paragraph of the UCC's unconscionability provision. The first of those clauses, referring to enforcement of "the remainder of the contract," appears to liberally authorize a court to sever an unconscionable clause and to enforce the remainder, if the remainder can sensibly stand alone, arguably without requiring an expression of the parties' intent to permit such severance. *See, e.g., Barras v. Branch Banking and Trust Co.*, 685 F.3d 1269 (11th Cir. 2012) (UCC permits severance of unconscionable cost-and-fee-shifting provision and enforcement of remainder of arbitration agreement, when remainder of agreement could stand separately, even if party seeking severance had waived its rights under the severance clause in the agreement).

The final clause of the first paragraph of section 2-302 refers in the alternative to "limit[ing] the application of any unconscionable clause." Does that passage permit a court to *modify* an unconscionable provision, thus "rewriting" the clause to moderate its effect? Or should this passage be interpreted to refer to just another type of severance, in the sense of refraining from applying some facet of a contract provision?

2. *Test for Unconscionability*

a. Cumulative Effect of Relevant Factors

The modern doctrine of unconscionability provides a basis for refusing enforcement of all or part of an agreement even in the absence of traditional grounds for rescission or non-enforcement. Unconscionability is triggered by the cumulative effect of a combination of lesser kinds of problems related to the status and the behavior of the parties and the lopsided nature of the bargain. For example, imagine the following facts:

- Although both parties had contractual capacity, one party had substantially greater bargaining power, allowing it to exploit an advantage over the weaker party, who may have had lesser education, experience, and resources.
- Although neither party engaged in duress, the party with significantly greater bargaining power made a "take-it-or-leave-it" proposal to the other party, so that the terms of the proposal "adhered" to the agreement, creating a "contract of adhesion," which was not subject to negotiation.
- Although neither party engaged in misrepresentation, and though the parties objectively conveyed all the terms in their offer and acceptance, the one who drafted the agreement engaged in sharp or oppressive practices, such as hiding harsh terms in fine print, taking advantage of a language barrier, drafting a provision in complex language that would be difficult for an average reader to understand, or using aggressive sales tactics.

- Although the resulting bargain is supported by consideration and does not violate law or public policy, it is substantially lopsided in favor of one party, either in the general fairness of the exchange or in the inclusion of oppressive terms that work solely to the disadvantage of the other party.

If all these factors were present, the unconscionability of the agreement or a provision would be fairly clear. In these cumulative circumstances, a court very likely would refuse to enforce all or part of the agreement, even though the agreement does not lack consideration, even though the parties objectively and voluntarily expressed acceptance, and though neither party lacked capacity or was the victim of misrepresentation or other cause for avoidance.

The factors supporting a finding of unconscionability, however, must have been present at the time of contract formation. *See* U.C.C. § 2-302(1) (2011) ("unconscionable at the time it was made"); RESTATEMENT (SECOND) OF CONTRACTS § 208 (1981) (same). Unconscionability is not a ground for avoiding an obligation that was fair at the time of contracting but that later became unduly burdensome due to changes in the market or other subsequent events.

The elements of unconscionability are most likely to appear in consumer transactions, in which a firm has much greater bargaining power and can impose its terms in a standard-form adhesion contract. Nonetheless, even an experienced businessperson such as the late music promoter Bill Graham can fall victim to an unconscionable clause or contract. *See Graham v. Scissor-Tail, Inc.*, 28 Cal. 3d 807, 623 P.2d 165 (1981). In *Graham*, the celebrated promoter of rock music concerts at Fillmore West in the 1960s, "for all his asserted stature in the industry, was ... reduced to the humble role of 'adherent.'" *Id.* at 818, 623 P.2d at 171–72. The musicians' union was sufficiently strong that Graham could not hire any high-profile musical act except through the union's standard-form agreement, which was not negotiable except on minor terms, and which unconscionably named the union itself as the arbitrator of all disputes between Graham and the musician. *Id.* at 818–19, 821, 623 P.2d at 172, 178.

b. Procedural and Substantive Unconscionability

In 1965, a seminal case succinctly defined unconscionability as "absence of meaningful choice on the part of one of the parties together with contract terms which are unreasonably favorable to the other party." *Williams v. Walker-Thomas Furniture Co.*, 350 F.2d 445, 449 (D.C. Cir. 1965). A critic of the UCC unconscionability provision advanced the dual elements of this definition by referring to the categories of "procedural" and "substantive" unconscionability. Arthur Allen Leff, *Unconscionability and the Code—The Emperor's New Clause*, 115 U. PA. L. REV. 485, 533–540 (1967). As summarized 35 years later by a federal court applying California law:

> When assessing procedural unconscionability, we consider the equilibrium of bargaining power between the parties and the extent to which the contract clearly discloses its terms.... A determination of substantive unconscionability, on the other hand, involves whether the terms of the contract are unduly harsh or oppressive.

Circuit City Stores, Inc. v. Adams, 279 F.3d 889, 893 (9th Cir.), *cert. denied*, 535 U.S. 1112 (2002). Some courts use the term "oppression" in the context of procedural unconscionability as well, referring to oppressive bargaining behavior and the extent to which the weaker party can avoid such oppression by opting out of a term or by dealing instead with competitors of the stronger party. *E.g.*, *Morris v. Redwood Empire Bancorp*, 128 Cal. App. 4th 1305, 1319–20 & n.6, 27 Cal. Rptr. 3d 797, 807 & n.6 (2007) (lack of alternative sources of supply are relevant to question of "oppression" in procedural unconscionability).

A contract is not unconscionable simply because one party has the bargaining power to negotiate a good deal for herself. An official comment to UCC § 2-302 states that "the principle is one of oppression and unfair surprise and not of disturbance of allocation of risks because of superior bargaining power." U.C.C. § 2-302 cmt. 1 (2011). The UCC comments are not part of the statutory provisions enacted by state legislatures, but they can be helpful guides to interpretation, like any secondary source.

Courts are likely to agree with comment 1's statement that unequal bargaining power alone does not give rise to unconscionability. *See, e.g., Seekings v. Jimmy GMC of Tucson, Inc.*, 130 Ariz. 596, 602, 638 P.2d 210, 216 (1981) (no unconscionability because seller did not use its "superior bargaining position to oppress or unfairly surprise" the buyers). An imbalance in bargaining power, however, can lead to procedural unconscionability if a party uses its superior power to engage in sharp practices. For example, if the stronger party is able to present non-negotiable terms in a take-it-or-leave-it proposal, resulting in an "adhesion" agreement, this factor alone may establish a minimal degree of procedural unconscionability in many courts.

The courts and commentators are split on whether a finding of unconscionability must be based on both procedural and substantive elements. "The prevailing view is that these two elements must *both* be present in order for a court to exercise its discretion to refuse to enforce a contract or clause under the doctrine of unconscionability." *Stirlen v. Supercuts, Inc.*, 51 Cal. App. 4th 1519, 1533, 60 Cal. Rptr. 2d 138, 145 (1997). Many of the courts that take this position will allow a strong showing on one branch to compensate for a minimal showing on the other branch. *E.g.*, *Tillman v. Commercial Credit Loans, Inc.*, 362 N.C. 93, 102–03, 655 S.E.2d 362, 370 (2008); *see also* RESTATEMENT OF THE LAW OF CONSUMER CONTRACTS § 5(b) (tent. draft Apr. 18, 2019) (reflecting this approach in consumer contracts).

A requirement of both procedural and substantive unconscionability can be defended by the potential conflict between unconscionability and more traditional contract doctrines if a contract could be avoided on the basis of a single branch of the doctrine. The consideration doctrine, for example, is not concerned with the equality of the exchange. Consequently, that traditional doctrine arguably would be fundamentally altered or eroded if a court could refuse to enforce an agreement solely on grounds that an exchange is "lopsided." Moreover, if a court could refuse to enforce all or part of an agreement solely on the basis of procedural factors short of traditional grounds for avoidance, doctrines such as duress and misrepresentation arguably would be obsolete.

Despite these considerations, some courts have concluded that a single branch of unconscionability is sufficient to grant relief, at least if the showing on that branch is exceptionally strong: "Therefore, we conclude that ... a claim of unconscionability can be established with a showing of substantive unconscionability alone, especially in cases involving either price-cost disparity or limitation of remedies." *Maxwell v. Fidelity Financial Services, Inc.*, 184 Ariz. 82, 89–90, 907 P.2d 51, 58–59 (1995) (leaving open the question whether procedural problems alone could establish unconscionability); *see also Balogh v. Balogh*, 134 Haw. 29, 41, 332 P.3d 631, 643 (2014) (both branches are required unless the substantive unconscionability is so outrageous that it alone justifies nonenforcement).

The *Maxwell* case provides an excellent discussion of the procedural and substantive provisions of UCC's section on unconscionability.

Maxwell v. Fidelity Financial Services, Inc.

184 Ariz. 82, 907 P.2d 51 (1995) [footnotes omitted]

Feldman, Chief Justice.

....

FACTS AND PROCEDURAL HISTORY

¶ 1 The facts, taken in the light most favorable to Maxwell, against whom summary judgment was granted, are that in December 1984, Elizabeth Maxwell and her then husband, Charles, were approached by Steve Lasica, a door-to-door salesman representing the now defunct National Solar Corporation (National). Lasica sold the Maxwells a solar home water heater for a total purchase price of $6,512. Although National was responsible for installation, the unit was never installed properly, never functioned properly, and was eventually declared a hazard, condemned, and ordered disconnected by the City of Phoenix. Thus, although the unit may have been intrinsically worthless, the question of unconscionability is determined as of the time the contract was made. A.R.S. § 47-2302.

¶ 2 Financing for the purchase was accomplished through a loan to the Maxwells from Fidelity Financial Services, Inc. (Fidelity). The sale price was financed for a ten-year period at 19.5 percent interest, making the total cost nearly $15,000.

¶3 At the time of the transaction, Elizabeth Maxwell earned approximately $400 per month working part-time as a hotel maid and her husband earned approximately $1,800 per month working for the local paper. At Fidelity's request, an appraisal was made of the Maxwells' South Phoenix home, where they had resided for the preceding twelve years. The appraisal showed that the Maxwells lived in a modest neighborhood, that their 1,539 square foot home was in need of a significant amount of general repair and maintenance, and that its market value was approximately $40,000.

¶4 In connection with the financing transaction, Elizabeth Maxwell signed numerous documents, including a loan contract, a deed of trust, a truth-in-lending disclosure form, and a promissory note and security agreement. The effect of these documents was not only to secure the deferred purchase price with a lien on the merchandise sold, but also to place a lien on Maxwell's house as additional security for payment on the water heater contract. The forms and their terms were unambiguous and clearly indicated that Maxwell was placing a lien on her house. Included in the consumer credit contract between Maxwell and Fidelity was a clause expressly stating that Fidelity was subject to all claims by and defenses that Maxwell could assert against National.

[After making payments for 3 1/2 years, Maxwell rolled the balance of the first loan over into a second loan with Fidelity in 1988.]

¶5 Maxwell continued to make payments until 1990, when she brought this declaratory judgment action seeking, inter alia, a declaration that the 1984 contract was unenforceable on the grounds that it was unconscionable. [The trial court granted summary judgment for Fidelity, and the appellate court affirmed.]

....

DISCUSSION

A. Unconscionability

1. Is the determination of unconscionability for the trier of fact or for the court to decide?

¶6 Maxwell contends that the determination of whether a contract is unconscionable is for the trier of fact. We find no support for this position given that Arizona law, which is consistent with the law in every other jurisdiction that has ruled on this issue, clearly provides that the determination of unconscionability is to be made by the court as a matter of law. *See* A.R.S. §47-2302.

¶7 Obviously, the court cannot make its determination without first making factual findings upon which to base its legal analysis. *See* A.R.S. §47-2302(B). Therefore, when it is claimed that the contract is unconscionable, the parties must be given an opportunity to present evidence of its commercial setting, purpose, and effect to aid the court in making the determination. *Id.*

¶8 Such factual findings do not, however, convert the determination on unconscionability from one that is a matter of law as applied to those facts to one that is in whole a matter of fact.... Nor is it required that in every instance a judge hold a separate, formal evidentiary hearing to determine the contract's commercial setting, purpose, and effect. Our statute only requires a reasonable opportunity to present evidence; on a developed record, such opportunity may be equally well afforded at the hearing on a motion for summary judgment. [citations omitted] In this case, however, neither Fidelity's motion for summary judgment, Maxwell's response thereto, nor the trial court's ruling addressed the merits of the unconscionability claim;....

2. The test for unconscionability

¶9 The court of appeals found the 1984 contract valid because Maxwell "failed to raise a material issue of fact that the agreement evidenced by [the contract documents] was beyond her reasonable expectations or was unconscionable." It is not clear why the court of appeals applied the test of "reasonable expectations".... This court previously has noted the rule that "reasonable expectations" and unconscionability are two distinct grounds for invalidating or limiting the enforcement of a contract and has stated that "even if [the contract provisions are] consistent with the reasonable expectations of the party" they are unenforceable if they are oppressive or unconscionable. *Broemmer v. Abortion Serv. of Phoenix*, 173 Ariz. 148, 151, 840 P.2d 1013, 1016 (1992) (*quoting Graham v. Scissor-Tail, Inc.*, 28 Cal. 3d 807, 171 Cal. Rptr. 604, 611–12, 623 P.2d 165, 172–73 (1981)).

¶10 This court has not previously had occasion to discuss the requisite elements of unconscionability under Arizona's adoption of the Uniform Commercial Code (U.C.C.). Because Maxwell raises this issue and because resolution hinges on whether the 1984 contract may be unconscionable, we turn to an examination of unconscionability under A.R.S. § 47-2302.

3. The history of unconscionability

¶11 Traditionally, equity courts recognized the defense of unconscionability in denying [specific] relief to plaintiffs who were guilty of unconscionable conduct. *See* Dan B. Dobbs, 2 Law of Remedies 703 (2d ed. 1993). Because barring relief was a matter of the chancellor's discretion, equity never developed a clear set of rules for analyzing claims of unconscionability. *See id.* Additionally, in equity unconscionability served as a remedial doctrine, limiting a party's remedies without truly affecting its substantive legal rights. *Id.* at 704. However, the enactment of an unconscionability defense under U.C.C. Article 2 changed that. The rule as it now exists is largely substantive, working primarily as a defense both in law and in equity and applying to claims for damages as well as specific performance. *Id.* at 704–05.

¶12 Although U.C.C. § 2-302 recognized and codified the amorphous equitable doctrine, it did little to provide a set of rules for analyzing claims of unconscionability. Also lacking in the statutory recognition of unconscionability is a definition of that term. Courts and respected commentators alike have grappled with defining and applying unconscionability under the Code since its adoption. To this day, both groups remain divided on the proper method for doing so, though they share some common ground on defining such a test.

¶ 13 Within this common area, the elements of unconscionability can be ascertained to fulfill the Code's obvious intent of protecting against unconscionable contracts while not unnecessarily denying parties the benefit of their bargain. Although no litmus test exists, the cases do provide a reasonable, workable analysis.

4. Divisions of unconscionability under the U.C.C.

¶ 14 This court previously has acknowledged that the unconscionability principle involves an assessment by the court of

> whether, in the light of the general commercial background and the commercial needs of the particular trade or case, the clauses involved are so one-sided as to be unconscionable under the circumstances existing at the time of the making of the contract.... The principle is one of the prevention of oppression and unfair surprise ... not of disturbance of allocation of risks because of superior bargaining power.

Seekings v. Jimmy GMC of Tucson, Inc., 130 Ariz. 596, 602, 638 P.2d 210, 216 (1981) (citations omitted). This somewhat circular articulation of the principle, however, is not readily applicable to the infinite variety of cases that may involve the doctrine of unconscionability.

¶ 15 The framework upon which the vast majority of courts construct their analysis consists of the well recognized division of unconscionability into substantive and procedural parts. *See, e.g.*, James J. White & Robert S. Summers, 1 Uniform Commercial Code 204, n. 8 and cases cited therein;.... Professor Dobbs provides the following explanation of the difference between these two types:

> Procedural or process unconscionability is concerned with "unfair surprise," fine print clauses, mistakes or ignorance of important facts or other things that mean bargaining did not proceed as it should. Substantive unconscionability is an unjust or "one-sided" contract. Substantive unconscionability is important in two ways. First, substantive unconscionability sometimes seems sufficient in itself to avoid a term in the contract. Second, substantive unconscionability sometimes helps confirm or provide evidence of procedural unconscionability.

Dobbs, *supra* at 706 (footnote omitted). This dichotomy evolved from a distinction made by the late Professor Leff in his oft-cited article *Unconscionability and The Code—The Emperor's New Clause*, 115 U. Pa. L. Rev. 485, 487 (1967). In his article, Professor Leff distinguished between "bargaining naughtiness" (procedural unconscionability) and overly harsh terms (substantive unconscionability). *Id.*

¶ 16 Over the years, courts have refined the two divisions of unconscionability and identified several factors that are indicative of each. Procedural unconscionability was well-explained in *Johnson v. Mobil Oil Corp.*:

> Under the procedural rubric come those factors bearing upon ... the real and voluntary meeting of the minds of the contracting party: age, education, intelligence, business acumen and experience, relative bargaining power, who drafted the contract, whether the terms were explained to the weaker party, whether alterations in the printed terms were possible, whether there were alternative sources of supply for the goods in question.

415 F. Supp. 264, 268 (E.D. Mich. 1976) (internal quotations omitted). As Professors White and Summers have noted, procedural unconscionability bears a strong resemblance to its "common-law cousins" of fraud and duress. WHITE & SUMMERS, *supra* at 204.

¶ 17 Substantive unconscionability concerns the actual terms of the contract and examines the relative fairness of the obligations assumed. *Resource Management Co. v. Weston Ranch & Livestock Co.*, 706 P.2d 1028, 1041 (Utah 1985). Indicative of substantive unconscionability are contract terms so one-sided as to oppress or unfairly surprise an innocent party, an overall imbalance in the obligations and rights imposed by the bargain, and significant cost-price disparity. *Id.* (citations and internal quotations omitted).

¶ 18 We believe these authorities provide useful illustrations of both divisions of unconscionability under the U.C.C., although we do not restrict applicability of the doctrine to the factors outlined.

5. Application

¶ 19 The point of agreement by courts on the substantive-procedural elements also marks a point of departure in analyzing claims of unconscionability. *See generally* WHITE & SUMMERS, supra at 218–20. Many courts, perhaps a majority, have held that there must be some quantum of both procedural and substantive unconscionability to establish a claim, and take a balancing approach in applying them. *Id.* at 219.... Other courts have held that it is sufficient if either is shown. *See, e.g., Gillman v. Chase Manhattan Bank, N.A.*, 73 N.Y.2d 1, 537 N.Y.S.2d 787, 794, 534 N.E.2d 824, 829 (1988) ("While determinations of unconscionability are ordinarily based on the court's conclusion that both the procedural and substantive components are present..., there have been exceptional cases where a provision of the contract is so outrageous as to warrant holding it unenforceable on the ground of substantive unconscionability alone.") (citing State v. Wolowitz, 96 A.D.2d 47, 468 N.Y.S.2d 131 (1983)). In addition to the numerous courts holding that either procedural or substantive unconscionability is sufficient [footnote citing to cases omitted], the leading commentators in this field have also endorsed this position. *See* WHITE & SUMMERS, *supra* at 220 (advocating the sufficiency of excessive price alone).

¶ 20 Indeed, it has long been recognized that gross disparity in terms may satisfy the standard for unconscionability by itself. *See Marks v. Gates*, 154 F. 481, 483 (9th Cir. 1907) (inadequacy of consideration sufficient ground for withholding specific performance if it is so gross as to render the contract unconscionable).

¶ 21 ... Additional evidence that the dual requirement position is more coincidental than doctrinal is found within the very text of the statute on unconscionability, which explicitly refers to "the contract or *any clause* of the contract." A.R.S. § 47-2302 (emphasis added). Conspicuously absent from the statutory language is any reference to procedural aspects. That the U.C.C. contemplated substantive unconscionability alone to be sufficient is the most plausible reading of the language in § 47-2302, given that the Code itself provides for per se unconscionability if there exists, without more, a substantive term in the contract limiting consequential damages for injury to the person in cases involving consumer goods. *See* A.R.S. § 47-2719(C). It is wholly inconsistent to assert that unconscionability under § 47-2302 requires some procedural irregularity when unconscionability under § 47-2719 clearly does not.

¶ 22 Therefore, we conclude that under A.R.S. § 47-2302, a claim of unconscionability can be established with a showing of substantive unconscionability alone, especially in cases involving either price-cost disparity or limitation of remedies. If only procedural irregularities are present, it may be more appropriate to analyze the claims under the doctrines of fraud, misrepresentation, duress, and mistake, although such irregularities can make a case of procedural unconscionability. *See Resource Management Co.*, 706 P.2d at 1043. However, we leave for another day the questions involving the remedy for procedural unconscionability alone.

¶ 23 We conclude further that this case presents a question of at least substantive unconscionability to be decided by the trial court. From the face of it, we certainly cannot conclude that the contract as a whole is not unconscionable, given the $6,500 price of a water heater for a modest residence, payable at 19.5 percent interest, for a total time-payment price of $14,860.43. These facts present at least a question of grossly-excessive price, constituting substantive unconscionability.... This contract is made even more harsh by its security terms, which, in the event of non-payment, permit Fidelity not only to repossess the water heater but foreclose on Maxwell's home. The apparent injustice and oppression in these security provisions not only may constitute substantive unconscionability but also may provide evidence of procedural unconscionability. *See* Dobbs, *supra* at 706–07 (*citing Williams v. Walker-Thomas Furniture Co.*, 350 F.2d 445 (D.C. Cir. 1965)).

¶ 24 Under the U.C.C. as enacted in A.R.S. § 47-2302, the court may "refuse enforcement of the contract altogether." Dobbs, *supra* at 705;.... The present factual record, before the statutorily required evidentiary hearing, certainly contains some evidence that the entire 1984 contract, including sale price, security provisions, and remedies, is unenforceable....

....

CONCLUSION

¶ 25 We are not satisfied from the state of this record that Fidelity had a meaningful opportunity to present evidence on the commercial setting, purpose, and effect of the 1984 contract, as required by A.R.S. §47-2302. The trial court expressly based its decision entirely on the doctrine of novation without addressing the fundamental question of unconscionability in the manner required by statute.

¶26 In his special concurrence, Justice Martone would have us hold that both the 1984 and 1988 contracts are unconscionable as a matter of law. Certainly, on the present record, before an evidentiary hearing, both contracts appear to be unconscionable. But we do not reach that final conclusion for good reason. The unconscionability finding is for the trial judge to make, after the evidentiary hearing contemplated by A.R.S. §47-2302. The opportunity to present evidence, according to the statute, "shall" be extended when it "appears to the [trial court] that a contract may be unconscionable."

....

¶27 Indeed, after the evidence is in, it may be possible to say, as Justice Martone does, that Fidelity "took advantage of a limited person living on the margin of human existence," intending "to extract" unfair profits from this "marginal person." *Id.* If appropriate at all, such a colorful description is better reserved until after the trial judge invokes the provisions of A.R.S. §47-2302 and hears evidence on the commercial setting, purpose, and effect of the contracts.

¶28 Therefore, we vacate the court of appeals' opinion, reverse the trial court's judgment, and remand to the trial court for proceedings consistent with this opinion and A.R.S. §47-2302.

Moeller, V.C.J., and Corcoran and Zlaket, JJ., concur.

Martone, Justice, concurring in the judgment.

¶29 I would hold that the 1984 contract and the 1988 contract are unconscionable as a matter of law. As the majority acknowledges, a declaration of unconscionability under A.R.S. §47-2302(A) is a legal conclusion to be made by the court. And the evidence referred to in §47-2302(B) "is for the court's consideration, and not the jury's." U.C.C. §2-302, Cmt. 3 (1962). The facts as outlined by the majority lead to one inescapable conclusion: one of unconscionability. If these contracts are not unconscionable as a matter of law, what contract would be?

¶30 The majority refuses to hold these contracts unconscionable as a matter of law because it says Fidelity did not have an opportunity to present evidence "on the commercial setting, purpose, and effect of the 1984 contract." *Ante*, at 93, 907 P.2d at 62. The majority argues that "neither Fidelity's motion for summary judgment [nor] Maxwell's response ... addressed the merits of the unconscionability claim." *Ante*, at 87, 907 P.2d at 56. But they did....

¶31 On the undisputed facts, the commercial setting, purpose and effect of the contracts are tragically plain. The commercial setting: a "now defunct" entity, *ante*, at 84, 907 P.2d at 53, took advantage of a limited person living on the margin of human existence. The purpose: to extract "$17,000" from a "hotel maid" who earned

"$400 per month." *Id.* at 84–85, 907 P.2d at 53–54. The effect: to subject a marginal person to the risk of loss of her home, all for a hot water heater that "was never installed properly, [and] never functioned properly." *Id.* at 84, 907 P.2d at 53.

¶ 32 I would remand this case to the trial court for entry of judgment in favor of Maxwell....

Exercise 9.7 — Questions on *Maxwell*

1. Decision to Remand

Do you agree with Justice Martone that the existing record satisfies the requirements of the second paragraph of section 2-207 and that Maxwell is entitled to relief without further fact-finding on remand? Or did the majority appropriately remand to the trial court for further assessment?

2. Factual Arguments

Imagine that the *Maxwell* case arose in a state that requires proof of both procedural and substantive unconscionability. On remand, what facts would help to establish each branch of unconscionability? If you represented Fidelity, what counter-arguments could you make? If you represented Fidelity would you advise your client to settle prior to the hearing on remand in the trial court? On what terms?

3. Class and Unconscionability

Should a consumer or businessperson be free to make a terrible deal and remain obligated to perform it? Or do you welcome unconscionability as an appropriately balanced tool that permits courts to intervene in grossly unfair contracts?

Should courts be particularly attentive to the situation of contracting parties living "at the margin," as Elizabeth Maxwell is described by Justice Martone? Or would such an approach lead to paternalism and unwarranted assumptions about the capabilities of people with lesser educational and economic status than enjoyed by judges?

4. Unconscionability Based on Substance Alone

Was it necessary for the court to reach its decision that substantive unconscionability alone can suffice to preclude enforcement of a contract? On remand, if not on the original record, isn't it likely that the trial court would find that all the contracts signed by the Maxwells were adhesion contracts, not subject to negotiation? Should the Supreme Court have adopted a more conventional approach, by holding that the presence of an adhesion contract alone provides a minimal level of procedural unconscionability, which could be combined with strong evidence of substantive unconscionability? On the question of procedural unconscionability, which party would benefit from a showing that the home solicitation was accompanied by high-pressure sales tactics, as is typical in such sales, but that the Maxwells had a legal right to withdraw from the initial sale contract during a cooling-off period of several days? *See* Trade Regulation Rule Concerning Cooling-Off Period for Sales Made at Homes or at Certain Other Locations, 80 Fed. Reg. 1329-34 (Jan. 9, 2015) (amending 16 C.F.R. pt. 429).

5. Unfairness in the Main Exchange or in Auxiliary Terms

Some argue that judicial intervention is justified only when gross unfairness lies in an auxiliary term, such as one relating to dispute resolution or limitations on remedies, because the disadvantaged party might not scrutinize such a subsidiary term or might be ill equipped to effectively assess it. In contrast, each party presumably has focused attention on the main elements of exchange, such as the price or fee for goods or services of a certain description, and arguably should be held to that bargain even if, for example, one party foolishly paid an inflated price or agreed to provide a service at a fee that will produce a loss. On this reasoning, the counterpart to unconscionability doctrine in the reformed French Civil Code provides relief only if an auxiliary term, and not the main exchange, creates a significant imbalance in the total rights and obligations of an adhesion contract. C. Civ. art. 1171 (Fr. rev. 2016). The UCC's provisions on unconscionability, however, do not restrict the kinds of terms that can produce an unconscionable bargain. Which approach do you support? For more on these contrasting views, see Charles R. Calleros, *U.S. Unconscionability and Article 1171 of the New French Civil Code: Achieving Balance in Statutory Regulation and Judicial Intervention*, 45 Ga. J. Int'l Comp. L. 259 (2017).

B. Unconscionability and Mandatory Arbitration Clauses

With increasing frequency, both commercial and consumer contracts include clauses that require the parties to submit any disputes to private arbitration for final resolution, subject only to limited judicial review. Compared to litigation in court, arbitration can provide relatively quick and streamlined adjudication of claims, thus allowing parties to reduce the number of hours billed by their attorneys.

An agreement to arbitrate, however, represents the waiver of a fundamental right to litigate in court, usually before a jury. *See, e.g.,* U.S. Const. amend. VII (preserving the right to a jury trial in suits "at common law" in federal court, as distinguished from those seeking purely equitable relief). Moreover, arbitration generates costs and fees, including the salaries of the arbitrators. Accordingly, the cost of arbitration can easily exceed the value of a small consumer claim or the means of an individual employee.

As illustrated by the *Booker* case in Section II (discussing severability), mandatory arbitration clauses in employment contracts are frequently challenged on grounds of unconscionability or violation of public policy, particularly if they restrict important remedies or place greater burdens on the employee than on the employer. *See, e.g., Circuit City Stores, Inc. v. Adams*, 279 F.3d 889, 893–94 (9th Cir.), *cert. denied*, 535 U.S. 1112 (2002) (discussing asymmetrical arbitration provisions). In a more commercial context, the holder of a franchise successfully challenged a mandatory arbitration clause because the parent company had much greater bargaining power and had drafted the nonnegotiable contract, because the arbitration clause required the franchise holder to arbitrate any claim it brought but permitted the parent company to bring an action in court in limited circumstances, and because the clause required arbitration in Boston, near the headquarters of the parent company, thus imposing a disproportionate economic burden on the franchise holder, an individual of limited means residing in California. *Nagrampa v. Mailcoups, Inc.*, 469 F.3d 1257 (9th Cir. 2006).

1. *Judicial Reaction to Class Action Waivers in Arbitration Clauses*

The economic barrier to fully litigating modest claims can be overcome in court when the claims of many plaintiffs can be joined in a single proceeding, as in a class action. *See* Fed. R. Civ. P. 23 (stating requisites for class actions in federal court and serving as a model for similar rules in many states). Arbitration clauses, however, frequently include provisions that preclude claimants from aggregating claims with other claimants in arbitration. Moreover, these arbitration clauses, coupled with class action waivers, typically appear in standard-form adhesion contracts, which by definition are not subject to negotiation. *AT&T Mobility LLC v. Concepcion*, 563 U.S. 333, 346–47 (2011) ("the times in which consumer contracts were anything other than adhesive are long past").

When standard-form adhesion contracts include mandatory arbitration clauses that bar aggregation of claims, plaintiffs with small individual contract claims have frequently brought unconscionability challenges to the class action waivers, or to the arbitration clauses as a whole. The challenges to the class action waivers have hit a wall: a wall erected by a federal statute, as interpreted by the Supreme Court.

2. *Application of the Federal Arbitration Act*

The enforcement of arbitration agreements between parties within the United States, in transactions involving commerce, is governed largely by the Federal Arbitration Act (FAA). 9 U.S.C. § 2 (2006). The FAA reflects policies of favoring enforcement of arbitration agreements and arbitration awards. *See id.* at §§ 2–9 (providing for broad enforcement of arbitration agreements, implementation of arbitration, and enforcement of awards).

On the other hand, the FAA permits courts to refuse enforcement of arbitration agreements "upon such grounds as exist at law or in equity," so long as the grounds apply to any contract and do not single out arbitration agreements for special judicial scrutiny or hostility. *Id.* at § 2 (limiting grounds to those available "for the revocation of any contract"). As illustrated by several of the cases cited in this chapter, courts have interpreted the FAA to permit application of unconscionability analysis to arbitration agreements.

Still, even if a state law defense to enforcement applies on its face equally to all contracts, is it possible that it operates in a way that imposes special burdens on arbitration agreements, contrary to the central policy of the FAA? Prior to 2011, California courts applied a special unconscionability test for class action waivers in consumer contracts, denying enforcement

> when the waiver is found in a consumer contract of adhesion in a setting in which disputes between the contracting parties predictably involve small amounts of damages, and when it is alleged that the party with the superior bargaining power has carried out a scheme to deliberately cheat large numbers of consumers out of individually small sums of money.

Discover Bank v. Superior Court, 36 Cal. 4th 148, 162–63, 113 P.3d 1100, 1110 (2005).

The *Discover Bank* unconscionability test does not discriminate on its face against arbitration because it "applies equally to class action litigation waivers in contracts without arbitration agreements as it does to class arbitration waivers in contracts with such agreements." *Id.* at 165–66, 113 P.3d at 1112. Nonetheless, by applying a broader form of unconscionability to class action waivers in all kinds of litigation, thus enabling class actions in arbitration, does this state law violate the FAA's policies of encouraging streamlined arbitration as an alternative to judicial litigation?

In a sharply split decision, the U.S. Supreme Court answered affirmatively, finding that the FAA preempted the *Discover Bank* unconscionability test, preventing its application to class action waivers in arbitration. *AT&T Mobility LLC v. Concepcion*, 563 U.S. 333 (2011). In the plurality opinion, Justice Scalia reasoned that state law permitting a class action in arbitration—when the parties had agreed to waive class arbitration—would frustrate the policies of the FAA, partly because "class arbitration sacrifices the principal advantage of arbitration—its informality—and makes the process slower, more costly, and more likely to generate procedural morass than final judgment." The FAA does permit class arbitration, but only if the parties affirmatively agreed to it; a contract's silence on the question of class arbitration is not sufficient. *Stolt-Nielsen S. A. v. Animal Feeds Int'l Corp.*, 559 U.S. 662 (2010). In 2019, over vigorous dissents, the Supreme Court further held that an ambiguous contract provision was insufficient to support class arbitration, because the lower court's method of resolving the ambiguity against the drafter was based on policy considerations rather than evidence of mutual intentions. *Lamps Plus, Inc. v. Varela*, 139 S. Ct. 1407 (2019) (plurality opinion).

The Supreme Court has applied the holding of *AT&T* to the employment context, rejecting an argument that the right to concerted activity under the National Labor Relations Act superseded the FAA's policy of upholding class-action waivers in arbitration. *Epic Systems Corp. v. Lewis*, 138 S. Ct. 1612 (2018). In contrast, the 2010 Dodd-Frank Wall Street Reform and Consumer Protection Act more directly supersedes the FAA by prohibiting mandatory arbitration agreements in certain contexts in the financial industry. 18 U.S.C.A. §§ 1514A(e), 1639c(e) (2018).

Consider also the Supreme Court's decision in *American Express Co. v. Italian Colors Restaurant*, 570 U.S. 228 (2013). In *Italian Colors*, the Supreme Court held that the FAA required enforcement of a class action waiver in a commercial arbitration agreement, even though merchants complained that the cost of any one of them proving its individual federal anti-trust claim would exceed the potential recovery, thus preventing the effective vindication of federal rights. Indeed, an expert's economic analysis alone would greatly exceed the value of an individual claim. *Id.* at 231–32. Justice Scalia, writing for the majority, distinguished precedent protecting the vindication of federal rights, holding that a claimant was not deprived of a statutory remedy simply because the cost of developing evidence or otherwise proving the claim exceeds the value of the claim. *Id.* at 234–36.

In *Italian Colors*, however, the Court left open the possibility that unaffordable "filing and administrative fees attached to arbitration" might preclude access to arbitration and might provide a valid basis for a state law defense to an arbitration clause. *Id.*; *see also Torres v. Simpatico, Inc.*, 781 F.3d 963 (8th Cir. 2015) (engaging in this analysis but finding no proof of inability to pay arbitrators' fees). Do filing fees and arbitrators' fees constitute a gateway expense that is meaningfully distinguishable from the costs of proving one's case?

For a critical review of Supreme Court jurisprudence on FAA preemption of state contract defenses to arbitration clauses, see J. Maria Glover, *Disappearing Claims and the Erosion of Substantive Law*, 124 YALE L.J. 3052 (2015).

3. Unconscionability Still Applies When It Does Not Disfavor Arbitration

AT&T appears to permit application of general standards of unconscionability to factors other than a class action waiver. *See, e.g., Sonic-Calabasas A, Inc. v. Moreno*, 57 Cal. 4th 1109, 311 P.3d 184 (2013) (even after *AT&T*'s ruling about class-action waivers, an arbitration agreement "may be unconscionable if it is otherwise unreasonably one-sided in favor of the employer"); *Davis v. TWC Dealer Group, Inc.*, 41 Cal. App. 5th 662, 254 Cal. Rptr. 3d 443 (2019) (arbitration agreement was unconscionable on the basis of a high degree of procedural unconscionability combined with moderate substantive unconscionability).

Although splitting arbitration costs equally between the parties sounds fair on its face, courts have viewed such a provision as a factor in substantive unconscionability when one party could easily pay for all costs, while the risk of paying half the costs could discourage the other party from vindicating an important right. *E.g., Gabriel v. Island Pac. Acad., Inc.*, 140 Haw. 325, 336–39, 400 P.3d 526, 537–40 (2017) (based on teacher's salary and cost of arbitration, finding that arbitration agreement was unconscionable because it required equal splitting of arbitration fees on civil rights claim).

For an example of an arbitration clause that survived scrutiny under unconscionability standards, see *Day v. CTA, Inc.*, 324 P.3d 1205 (Mont. 2014). In *Day*, the Montana Supreme Court applied general unconscionability standards, but enforced the arbitration clause because it was not contained in an adhesion agreement and was not oppressive, the clause was conspicuous and clear, the party challenging it was an experienced securities attorney who could understand the consequences of an arbitration agreement, and the arbitration clause was within that party's reasonable expectations in the circumstances.

Under an alternative analysis, at least one state scrutinizes arbitration clauses as waivers of the right to bring suit in court, applying a general rule that all waivers of important rights must be clearly established:

> The right to a civil jury trial is guaranteed by the New Jersey Constitution, N.J. Const. art. I, ¶ 9, and conferred by the New Jersey Consumer Fraud Act, *see Allstate N.J. Ins. Co. v. Lajara*, 222 N.J. 129, 147, 151, 117 A.3d 1221 (2015).... Our state-law jurisprudence makes clear "that when a contract contains a waiver of rights—whether in an arbitration or other clause—the waiver 'must be clearly and unmistakably established.'" *Atalese, supra*, 219 N.J. at 444, 99 A.3d 306 (quoting *Garfinkel v. Morristown Obstetrics & Gynecology Assocs.*, 168 N.J. 124, 132, 773 A.2d 665 (2001)). Under state contract law, no greater burden is placed on an arbitration agreement than other agreements waiving constitutional or statutory rights. *Atalese, supra*, 219 N.J. at 443–44, 447, 99 A.3d 306 (collecting non-arbitration-clause cases requiring clear and unambiguous contractual language to achieve waiver of rights).

Morgan v. Sanford Brown Inst., 225 N.J. 289, 308–09, 137 A.3d 1168, 1180 (2016). Accordingly, although "no magical language is required," the New Jersey courts require a mandatory arbitration agreement to explain that it amounts to a waiver of the right to sue in court. *Id.* at 309–10, 137 A.3d at 1180–81. In light of studies that reveal that many consumers and employees do not fully understand the implications of mandatory arbitration, do you approve of this approach? Alternatively, should failure to explain the effect of an arbitration clause be considered as one factor in an analysis of procedural unconscionability?

Do the New Jersey requirements for establishing "all waivers of important rights" apply to arbitration agreements in a neutral fashion, thus avoiding preemption by the FAA, or would these requirements succumb to preemption under the reasoning of *AT&T*?

Exercise 9.8 — Modifying FAA Preemption

1. Will Congress Intervene?

On September 20, 2019, the House of Representatives passed the Forced Arbitration Injustice Repeal Act (FAIR Act), H.R. 1423, 116th Cong. (2019). The purpose of the FAIR Act is to prohibit agreements that (1) compel arbitration of future employment, consumer, antitrust, or civil rights disputes, or (2) interfere with the right to participate in class or collective actions. *Id.* § 2. The Senate is not expected to pass the bill.

If such a bill is enacted, state regulation of unconscionable arbitration clauses—and FAA preemption of that regulation—would be superseded in the designated categories because the new federal law would independently invalidate predispute arbitration agreements within those categories in all cases, regardless of their unconscionability under state law. Do you favor such categorical preclusion of arbitration agreements in these contexts, or does this approach intrude excessively on arbitration and freedom of contract? Would you prefer a middle ground, one that modified the FAA only to the extent of overruling *AT&T*, so that the FAA would permit state law and federal labor law to strike down contractual prohibitions on class actions in arbitration in proper circumstances? Or do you think that the current case law strikes the right balance and should be left undisturbed?

2. Administrative Action

During the Obama administration, an executive order and administrative regulations barred pre-dispute mandatory arbitration in several narrowly defined contexts. On July 31, 2014, for example, President Obama signed an executive order on "Fair Pay and Safe Workplaces," forbidding major federal contractors from requiring employees to agree, prior to a dispute, to mandatory arbitration of claims of sexual assault or harassment. Exec. Order 13,673 § 6, 79 Fed. Reg. 45,309, 45,314 (July 31, 2014). In 2016, administrative agencies prohibited pre-dispute mandatory arbitration in connection with federal student loans, nursing home contracts, and class actions against providers of financial services. In 2017, President Trump or members of his administration repealed Obama's executive order and the prohibition in connection with financial services, postponed the effective date of the regulation of student loans, and took steps to repeal the regulation of nursing home contracts.

Do you support regulation of arbitration by the executive order and by agency regulation, or should the scope of the FAA be a matter left to Congress? Do you support state or federal legislation or administrative regulation that would prohibit agreements precluding employees from disclosing any claims or settlements for sexual harassment or sexual assault in the workplace?

C. Overlap between Unconscionability and Other Doctrines

In some contexts, unconscionability claims may overlap with other grounds for avoiding a contract provision. This overlap is suggested by the following discussion of unconscionability, which encompasses at least two theories that can also stand alone as independent defenses to enforcement: contravention of public policy (addressed earlier in this chapter) and violation of reasonable expectations (addressed in Chapter 10):

> All of these formulations point to the central idea that unconscionability doctrine is concerned not with "a simple old-fashioned bad bargain" (*Schnuerle v. Insight Communications Co.* (Ky. 2012) 376 S.W.3d 561, 575 (*Schnuerle*)), but with terms that are "unreasonably favorable to the more powerful party" (8 Williston on Contracts (4th ed. 2010) § 18.10, p. 91). These include "terms that impair the integrity of the bargaining process or otherwise contravene the public interest or public policy; terms (usually of an adhesion or boilerplate nature) that attempt to alter in an impermissible manner fundamental duties otherwise imposed by the law, fine-print terms, or provisions that seek to negate the reasonable expectations of the nondrafting party, or unreasonably and unexpectedly harsh terms having to do with price or other central aspects of the transaction."

Sonic-Calabasas A, Inc. v. Moreno, 57 Cal. 4th 1109, 1145, 311 P.3d 184, 203 (2013). Indeed, this passage's reference to hidden terms and to the integrity of the bargaining process suggests a third area of overlap, addressed in Chapter 2: the possibility that terms are so thoroughly hidden that they have not been objectively conveyed to the other party and thus are not even included in the bargaining and the contract.

1. Lack of Mutual Assent in Hidden Contract Terms

a. Manifestation of Assent without Reading or Understanding

Under the objective theory of contract formation, an offeree who expresses assent is not bound to terms that the offeror failed to reasonably communicate during bargaining. *See, e.g., National Fed'n of the Blind v. The Container Store, Inc.*, 904 F.3d 70 (1st Cir. 2018) (store did not convey that an arbitration agreement, or any other contract terms, were associated with customers' signing up to participate in a loyalty program); *Specht v. Netscape Commc'ns Corp.*, 306 F.3d 17 (2d Cir. 2002) (web user would not see link to terms associated with downloading software unless they had scrolled down below the screen displaying the download button).

On the other hand, if an offeree had a reasonable opportunity to examine terms, and the offeree manifested assent to them, the offeree is bound to the terms regardless of whether he or she read or understood them: "It will not do for a man to enter into a contract, and, when called upon to respond to its obligations, to say that he did not read it when he signed it, or did not know what it contained." *Upton v. Tribilcock*, 91 U.S. 45, 50 (1875). Accordingly, in the excerpts of the *Uber* case presented in Chapter 2, the court found that an Uber driver had effectively expressed assent to proposed contract terms posted on the Internet, even if he had not viewed the terms before manifesting assent by "clicking through," even though reading the terms on the screen of a smartphone would be somewhat "onerous," and even though the driver spoke little English and might not have understood the arbitration clause had he read it. *See also Paper Express v. Pfankuch Maschinen GmbH*, 972 F.2d 753 (7th Cir. 1992) (U.S. firm was bound by a forum-selection clause written in the German language; it could have secured a translation prior to agreeing); Uri Benoliel & Shmuel I. Becher, *The Duty to Read the Unreadable*, 60 B.C.L. REV. 2255 (2019).

In the face of such unforgiving standards for mutual assent, parties complaining that they had insufficient notice of contract terms, or could not understand them, should also raise an unconscionability challenge to the provisions. Even when obstacles to finding, reading, or understanding proposed terms are not sufficient to negate a party's apparent assent to the terms under the objective theory of contracts, those obstacles can be significant factors in an analysis of procedural unconscionability. If combined with substantive unconscionability, they provide a potential basis for refusing to enforce all or part of the contract.

In a controversial application of the traditional rule governing mutual assent, the majority of a federal appellate panel bound an employee to an arbitration clause contained in an English-language written agreement signed by the employee, even though the employee spoke only Spanish and though the translation *arranged by the employer* turned out to be faulty:

> Morales, in essence, requests that this Court create an exception to the objective theory of contract formation where a party is ignorant of the language in which a contract is written. We decline to do so. In the absence of fraud, the fact that an offeree cannot read, write, speak, or understand the English language is immaterial to whether an English-language agreement the offeree executes is enforceable.

Morales v. Sun Constructors, Inc., 541 F.3d 218, 222 (3d Cir. 2008); *cf. Ballesteros v. Am. Standard Ins. Co. of Wis.*, 226 Ariz. 345, 248 P.3d 193 (2011) (*en banc*) (in light of objective standard, statutory requirement that insurer offer certain coverage by written notice did not require translation into Spanish).

In *Morales*, the dissent presented a compelling but unavailing argument that the facts of this case justified a departure from the traditional rule:

> No one disputes that Sun asked Hodge [another employee] to translate the Employment Agreement for Morales, who did not read English. And no one disputes that Hodge failed to translate the arbitration clause in the Agreement. On this basis, I disagree with my colleagues' conclusion that the parties here manifested mutual assent to the arbitration clause of the Agreement, and I would therefore affirm the District Court's decision.

Id. at 224 (Fuentes, J., dissenting).

Which reasoning do you find to be more persuasive on the facts of this case, that of the majority of the three-member appellate panel, or that of the lone dissenter?

A California statute provides that a business that "negotiates primarily in Spanish, Chinese, Tagalog, Vietnamese, or Korean," must provide a translation of "every term and condition" of the final agreement in the language of negotiation, with respect to several kinds of consumer contracts. CAL. CIV. CODE § 1632 (as amended 2015). Would you support more widespread adoption of such statutes, and would you extend them to employment contracts?

The *Morales* court did not address unconscionability. Assuming that the attorneys for Morales did not raise unconscionability as a basis for avoiding the arbitration clause, did they miss the opportunity to launch a second attack against the clause? Even if the problem with the employer-selected translator did not exclude that clause for lack of mutual assent, surely it would have been a factor strongly supporting procedural unconscionability, especially when combined with the presumably adhesive nature of the contract. If that procedural unconscionability were coupled with substantive problems in the arbitration clause, the clause could be unenforceable under the unconscionability doctrine, even if the clause had been objectively conveyed to Morales. Would it be enough if the procedural problems were coupled with a requirement in the arbitration clause that the employee pay half of the arbitration costs up to a maximum employee share of $5,000, leaving remaining costs to be paid by the employer, which has vastly greater resources?

b. Terms on Ticket Stubs or Other Surprising Places

If you receive an admission ticket for entrance to a theater, does the fine print on the back of the ticket state terms that become part of your contract with the theater? If the terms state that you agree to relieve the theater of liability for the negligence of its employees, would you be bound by those terms?

Assume that the ticket was provided to you—or that a sample was on display—before you completed your transaction at the box office, so that it was conveyed to you during contract formation. Nonetheless, if the box office employee did not bring the fine print on the back of the ticket to your attention, would you be on notice that some of the terms of your contract were expressed on the back of your ticket stub? Or would you assume that the only purpose of the ticket was to grant you admission and identify the location of your reserved seat?

From common experience, should you be expected to look for such terms, because the average person is aware that most ticket stubs have terms on the back? Even if so, if the print was too fine for the average person to read in the dim lighting of the theater, and if you could not read it, would the ticket fail to convey the terms to you?

If the theater did not adequately convey these contract terms to you during contract formation—either because the terms were conveyed to you after the contract was formed or because they were hidden from the view of a reasonable patron—then the terms would not be included in the contract under an objective theory of contract formation. Unless the theater adequately communicated certain proposed terms to you prior to your acceptance, so that a reasonable person would understand that the offer contained those terms, then any resulting contract would not contain those terms.

On the other hand, let's assume that the terms were objectively conveyed to a reasonable person in your position, but you did not bother to read the terms on the back of your ticket stub because you were anxious to get to your seat, or you did not exert the effort needed to read and comprehend complicated language set in fine print. Under those assumptions, the terms on the back of ticket stub likely would not be excluded for lack of mutual assent; however, the timing and method of communicating these contract terms could be a factor in assessing procedural unconscionability if you sought to invoke unconscionability as a ground for non-enforcement. *Cf. Carnival Cruise Lines, Inc. v. Shute*, 499 U.S. 585 (1991) (clause on cruise line ticket, stating that parties agreed to litigate all disputes in Florida, was reasonable and enforceable under federal admiralty law, when passengers conceded that they had adequate notice of this contract term).

Similar problems of notice can arise in other contexts, such as tickets for a parking space issued at the entrance of a parking garage, terms in fine print on the back of a restaurant menu, or terms on a website that arguably are not adequately brought to your attention. In all these contexts, you might challenge the contract terms both for lack of mutual assent and for unconscionability. In a close case of hidden contract terms, unconscionability might provide a back-up claim if the facts did not support your claim of lack of mutual assent.

c. "Accord and Satisfaction" Clause on a Check

Suppose that you believe in good faith that a client owes you $3,000 by January 1 on an existing contract obligation, but the client believes in good faith that the amount owed by January 1 under the contract is only $2,000. If the client offered to settle this dispute by paying you $2,500, and if you accepted that offer of settlement, your voluntary settlement agreement would be supported by consideration and would end any further obligation owed to you by the client once the client performed by paying the $2,500.

Suppose instead that no settlement negotiations took place, but the client sent you a check for $2,500 on December 1, and the check includes the following statement on the front or back: "Cashing this check amounts to acceptance of the sum of this check as full satisfaction of the debt currently owed by the payor to the payee." If you cashed this check, would you be bound by the terms on the check, or could you still demand the additional $500 that you claim is owed?

Under common law, such a clause on a check was viewed as an offer of settlement, which you accepted (under the terms of the offer) if you cashed it. If you were not agreeable to the terms of settlement, you would be expected to leave the check uncashed and repeat your demand for payment of $3,000 by January 1, thus maintaining your dispute with the client. If you instead cashed the check, the common law viewed you as having entered into an *accord* (agreement) that resulted in *satisfaction* (full payment) of the debt owed to you. Accord and satisfaction through the cashing of checks is now governed by UCC § 3-311 (2002), which sets forth a more complicated statutory framework but which maintains a similar analysis for most contexts.

But suppose you cashed the check without full awareness of the terms on the check or their legal effect? Once again, you could try to challenge the terms on the check both on grounds of lack of mutual assent and on grounds of unconscionability. A court might ask whether the check adequately conveyed the offer of settlement at all, perhaps because it was in overly fine print so that a reasonable person would not have noticed it. Alternatively, even if you had actually noticed the clause on the check, or if you should have noticed it, it could be objectionable if it was written in confusing language, or if it was obviously printed on every check so that you weren't sure whether it applied to your transaction. These factors might help support a finding of procedural unconscionability, which could combine with substantive unconscionability if the proposed "settlement" was substantially lopsided in favor of the creditor.

Exercise 9.9 — Accord and Satisfaction

Landlord believed reasonably and in good faith that Tenant owed $1,200 in rent to Landlord at the end of the month, according to their lease agreement. Tenant believed reasonably and in good faith that she owed only $1,000, because she asserted the right to deduct $200 for a plumbing repair that she had arranged after the Landlord had failed to attend to it within 24 hours of notice of the problem. Tenant offered to pay $1,100 in total rent for the month, and Landlord accepted the offer. Is Landlord nonetheless legally entitled to accept the $1,100 and later demand an additional $100? For example, can Landlord argue that Tenant had a pre-existing duty to pay $1,200 and that the Landlord received no consideration for agreeing to accept less? Explain. Assuming no consideration problems, can the Tenant bind the Landlord to a settlement agreement by delivering a check to Landlord for $1,100, if the check included a printed clause in fine print stating that cashing the check amounted to acceptance of the check as full satisfaction of the Tenant's current debt to Landlord? What should Tenant do to maximize the chances that Landlord's cashing the check will be viewed as acceptance of an offer of settlement?

---

2. Public Policy—Releases from Liability (Exculpatory Clauses)

Businesses that enter into contracts with members of the public will often use those contracts to limit their future liability in tort. For example, the owner of a bungee-jumping enterprise or horseback riding stables might require patrons to sign an agreement that relieves the owner of liability for the negligence of any of its employees that causes injury to the patron. Such an "exculpatory clause" might be viewed as a promise by the patron to refrain from bringing a negligence claim against the owner or its employees, which—along with a fee from the patron—is exchanged for the service or entertainment. Viewed slightly differently, a contract clause can establish that the patron agreed to assume certain risks, thus supporting an affirmative defense of assumption of the risk in a subsequent tort action brought by the patron.

A prospective release from liability for future torts is potentially inconsistent with public policy underlying tort law, which is designed to encourage the exercise of due care and to provide compensation for injuries caused by the failure to exercise due care. Consequently, some exculpatory clauses could be unenforceable for violation of public policy. In assessing an agreement's conflict with public policy, courts will consider a variety of factors, including the nature of the service or activity for which the patron contracted and the degree of culpability sought to be excused in the clause.

On grounds of public policy, many states will refuse to enforce waivers for any degree of fault, including simple negligence, if the contract involves the provision of necessities, such as housing, medical services, or food. Thus, many states now will refuse to enforce a clause in a residential lease that purports to excuse a landlord for negligent maintenance of common areas. *Cf. 1800 Ocotillo, LLC v. The WLB Group, Inc.*, 219 Ariz. 200, 202–03, 196 P.3d 222, 224–25 (2008) (discussing statutes that declare indemnity provisions in certain professions to violate public policy, but finding that a *limitation* on liability did not eliminate the defendant's incentive to take precautions).

In some states, legislation may provide additional force to this public policy challenge to an exculpatory clause. For example, a California statute provides that a contract is "against the policy of the law" if its object is to "exempt anyone from responsibility for his own ... violation of law, whether willful or negligent." CAL. CIV. CODE ANN. § 1668 (West 1985). As judicially interpreted, this statute prohibits only exculpatory clauses in transactions that implicate the public interest. *Tunkl v. Regents of Univ. of Cal.*, 60 Cal. 2d 92, 383 P.2d 441 (1963) (*In Bank*). In *Tunkl*, the Court invalidated an exculpatory clause in a hospital's admission agreement for patients, because medical treatment is a "crucial necessity"; hospitals are a type of business "suitable for, and a subject of, public regulation"; the hospital held itself out as broadly serving "members of the public who qualified for their research and training facilities"; and the gross imbalance of bargaining power resulted in an adhesion contract through which the patient "completely placed himself in the control of the hospital," thus subjecting "himself to the risk of its carelessness." *Id.* at 101–02, 383 P.2d at 446–47.

On the other hand, a clause excusing an operator's simple negligence will be enforceable in many states if the operator is providing a non-essential service, such as recreation or entertainment. Reducing the operator's risks of liability could allow it to reduce the fee for the service and to allow more people to enjoy the activity. If you choose to engage in a non-essential activity, such as horseback riding, bungee-jumping, or sky diving, the public policy underlying tort law will not be offended in most states if you contractually assume the risk of simple negligence on the part of the operator or its employees.

Still, even in the context of a non-essential activity, such as recreation, most states will refuse to enforce a clause that seeks to relieve an operator from liability for greater culpability, such as recklessness or an intentional tort. The conflict between such a clause and the public policy underlying tort law—or perhaps even criminal law—is too great to permit enforcement of the exculpatory clause. You might ask whether the same analysis should apply to the intermediate culpability of gross negligence.

Even if the clause does not violate public policy, it might be subject to challenge for unconscionability. For example, suppose that a clause seeks to excuse the operator of a recreational facility for gross negligence, and suppose that a state court decides that such a clause does not violate public policy, although it was a very close question. The clause's release of liability for relatively high culpability nonetheless could be viewed as a harsh provision that establishes a degree of substantive unconscionability. That, in turn, might be combined with procedural unconscionability if the release was not subject to negotiation and perhaps was even hidden in fine print in the middle of numerous terms. In such a case, can you envision a court finding an exculpatory clause to be unconscionable even though not a violation of public policy?

For more reading on this issue, see Scott J. Burnham, *Are you free to contract away your right to bring a negligence claim?*, 89 CHI.-KENT. L. REV. 379 (2014).

Miller v. The Sunapee Difference, LLC

918 F.3d 172 (1st Cir. 2019) [footnotes omitted]

Barron, Circuit Judge.

¶ 1 Thomas Jackson Miller collided with unmarked snowmaking equipment while skiing at the Mount Sunapee Resort in 2015 in Sunapee, New Hampshire. Soon thereafter, he brought a tort suit under New Hampshire law against the resort's owner, The Sunapee Difference, LLC ("Mount Sunapee"), in the District of New Hampshire. Mount Sunapee moved for a judgment on the pleadings under Federal Rule of Civil Procedure 12(c), and the District Court granted the motion after treating it, under Federal Rule of Civil Procedure 12(d), as a motion for summary judgment. Miller now appeals that judgment, which we affirm.

I.

¶ 2 Miller visited the Mount Sunapee Resort in 2015 following a large snowfall. Before taking to the slopes, he purchased a lift ticket. The dispute on appeal concerns the import of what was printed on that ticket.

¶ 3 The front of the lift ticket displayed the following text in 4.3-point font:

> **LIABILITY RELEASE**
>
> Skiing, snowboarding, and other winter sports are inherently dangerous and risky with many hazards that can cause injury or death. As purchaser or user of this ticket, I agree, as a condition of being allowed to use the facilities of the Mount Sunapee resort, to freely accept and voluntarily assume all risks of property damage, personal injury, or death resulting from their inherent or any other risks or dangers. **I RELEASE MOUNT SUNAPEE RESORT**, its parent companies, subsidiaries, affiliates, officers, directors, employees and agents **FROM ANY AND ALL LIABILITY OF ANY KIND INCLUDING NEGLIGENCE** which may result from conditions on or about the premises, operation of the ski area or its facilities [sic] or from my participation in skiing or other winter sports, accepting for myself the full and absolute responsibility for all damages or injury of any kind which may result from any cause. Further I agree that any claim which I bring against Mount Sunapee Resort, its officers, directors, employees or agents shall be brought only in Federal or State courts in the State of New Hampshire. I agree my likeness may be used for promotional purposes.
>
> ....

(emphasis in original).

....

¶ 4 The lift ticket itself is essentially a large sticker with a peel-off backing.... On the face of that peel-off backing, the following text appears in red font that is larger than the text on the front of the ticket itself:

> STOP [a red octagon image similar to a traffic-control "stop sign"]
>
> YOU ARE RELEASING THIS SKI AREA FROM LIABILITY
>
> By removing this peel-off backing and using this ticket, you agree to be legally bound by the LIABILITY RELEASE printed on the other side of this ticket. If you are not willing to be bound by this LIABILITY RELEASE, please return this ticket with the peel-off backing intact to the ticket counter for a full refund.

¶ 5 While skiing at the Mount Sunapee resort after purchasing such a lift ticket and affixing it to his clothing..., Miller struck an unmarked "snow gun holder" that was concealed by snow. The "holder" is a mounting post for snowmaking guns and is "essentially a steel pipe protruding from the ground." No snowmaking gun was in the holder at the time of the accident.

¶ 6 Miller suffered serious leg injuries in the collision. In 2016, he brought a single negligence claim against Mount Sunapee under New Hampshire law in the District of New Hampshire, invoking diversity jurisdiction under 28 U.S.C. § 1332(a), to recover for the injuries that resulted from his collision with the unmarked and unpadded piece of snowmaking equipment. Miller's complaint alleged that Mount Sunapee was liable for his injuries because, among other things, it "failed to mark or warn skiers of the pipe, or otherwise mitigate its danger to skiers, by, for example, padding it or making it visible to skiers."

¶ 7 Mount Sunapee moved for judgment on the pleadings, pursuant to Federal Rule of Civil Procedure 12(c). Mount Sunapee argued in its motion that the liability release printed on Miller's lift ticket barred Miller's claim.... The District Court then ruled for Mount Sunapee on the basis of the release. Miller now appeals.

II.

¶ 8 "Although New Hampshire law generally prohibits a plaintiff from releasing a defendant from liability for negligent conduct, in limited circumstances a plaintiff can expressly consent by contract to assume the risk of injury caused by a defendant's negligence." *Allen v. Dover Co-Recreational Softball League*, 148 N.H. 407, 807 A.2d 1274, 1281 (N.H. 2002). For such a contract to be enforceable, the party seeking to enforce it must show that (1) it does "not violate public policy;" (2) "the plaintiff understood the import of the agreement or a reasonable person in his position would have understood the import of the agreement;" and (3) "the plaintiff's claims were within the contemplation of the parties when they executed the contract." *Dean v. MacDonald*, 147 N.H. 263, 786 A.2d 834, 838 (N.H. 2001).

A.

¶9 [In Section II.A, the court affirmed the trial court's conclusion, as a matter of law, that the parties mutually assented to the release of liability because Miller indisputably had a reasonable opportunity to read the release when purchasing the lift ticket.]

B.

¶10 [In Section II.B, the court interpreted the release and determined that it was sufficiently broad to encompass his accident.]

C.

¶11 We turn, then, to Miller's contention that the release is unenforceable because it is against public policy. Under New Hampshire law, "[a] defendant seeking to avoid liability must show than an exculpatory agreement does not contravene public policy; i.e., that no special relationship existed between the parties and that there was no other disparity in bargaining power." *McGrath v. SNH Dev., Inc.*, 158 N.H. 540, 969 A.2d 392, 396 (N.H. 2009) (quoting *Barnes*, 128 N.H. at 106). Moreover, as the New Hampshire Court explained in *McGrath*, an exculpatory agreement has been found to be against public policy "if, among other things, it is injurious to the interests of the public, violates some public statute, or tends to interfere with the public welfare or safety." *Id.*

¶12 But, McGrath explains that "[t]he fact that an exculpatory agreement waives the right to bring a negligence action arising out of an activity that is regulated by statute is not determinative of a public policy violation." *Id.* And while Miller attempts to argue that this liability release is against public policy—and thus unenforceable—because it would free Mount Sunapee from what he contends is a statutorily imposed duty on operators of ski areas to warn skiers of snowmaking equipment on the slopes, we are not persuaded.

¶13 Miller does point to N.H. Rev. Stat. Ann. § 225-A:23, but that statute's plain terms make clear that it does not, on its own, impose any such duty. The statute refers only to a different set of duties on ski area operators, including marking trail difficulty levels and warning skiers "by use of a trail board" located at the base of the mountain of "snow grooming or snow making operations [that] are routinely in progress." N.H. Rev. Stat. Ann. § 225-A:23....

¶14 Miller separately contends that the liability release is unenforceable on public policy grounds because Mount Sunapee operates the Mount Sunapee resort on New Hampshire state land and, "unlike the operator of a private ski area, is charged with a duty of public service, pursuant to which it must allow public access to the Mount Sunapee Ski resort." Miller then notes that, per the commentary to the Restatement (Second) of Torts § 496B, liability releases that "relate[] to the ... performance of any part of [a public] duty ... will not be given effect." Restatement (Second) of Torts § 496B, cmt. g.

¶ 15 But, under New Hampshire law, "the fact that [a] ski area is available for public use is not dispositive of a special relationship" that might give rise to the sort of public duty contemplated by § 496B. *McGrath*, 969 A.2d at 397; *see Barnes*, 509 A.2d at 154 (explaining that the public duties contemplated by the commentary to § 496B of the Restatement arise out of the existence of a special relationship). And Miller identifies no authority to suggest that the rule is otherwise applicable simply because a privately-run ski area that is open to the public is also on publicly owned land. We thus agree with the District Court that Miller supplies no basis for concluding that the special relationship he must identify under McGrath exists.

D.

¶ 16 We turn, finally, to Miller's contention that the release does not bar his claim under New Hampshire law that Mount Sunapee's conduct vis-à-vis the snowmaker with which he collided was not merely negligent but reckless. To support this contention, Miller points to *Perry v. SNH Development*, No. 2015-CV-00678, 2017 N.H. Super. LEXIS 32 (N.H. Sup. Ct. Sept. 13, 2017), a New Hampshire Superior Court case that held that liability releases do not bar claims of recklessness under New Hampshire law. But, even assuming that Perry correctly states New Hampshire law, we find, like the District Court, that Miller has failed to provide a basis upon which a jury could supportably find Mount Sunapee to have been reckless.

¶ 17 Conduct rises to the level of "recklessness" under New Hampshire law "if it 'would lead a reasonable man to realize, not only that his conduct creates an unreasonable risk of physical harm to another, but also that such risk is substantially greater than that which is necessary to make his conduct negligent.'" *Boulter v. Eli & Bessie Cohen Found.*, 166 N.H. 414, 97 A.3d 1127, 1132 (N.H. 2014) (quoting Restatement (Second) of Torts § 500 (1965)). Thus, conduct is "reckless" where "the known danger ceases to be only a foreseeable risk which a reasonable person would avoid, and becomes in the mind of the actor a substantial certainty." *Thompson v. Forest*, 136 N.H. 215, 614 A.2d 1064, 1068 (N.H. 1992) (quoting W.P. Keeton et al., Prosser & Keeton on the Law of Torts § 8, at 36 (5th ed. 1984)).

¶ 18 [The court affirmed the trial court's conclusion that the record contained no evidence to support a finding of recklessness.]

III.

¶ 19 For the foregoing reasons, the judgment below is *affirmed*.

Exercise 9.10 — Exculpatory Clauses and Ethics

1. Critiquing *Miller*

Write a short dissenting opinion for the preceding case, briefly presenting the ground you believe is strongest for reversing summary judgment.

2. Preschool Exculpatory Clause

A "Bright Eyes Preschool" contract in Tempe, Arizona, included the following provision in the same, very small print as all other provisions of the contract:

> I. Limitations — Parent agrees to indemnify and hold harmless BEP, its officers, directors, instructors, employees, agents, and each of them, from and against any and all claims, demands, losses, attorney's fees, costs, damages, actions, suits, or proceedings arising allegedly or in reality out of the acts or omissions of Child and the participation of Child in any activity at the School. Parent further agrees to a limitation of damages not to exceed the sum of $300.00 for any and all damages, claims, costs, attorney's fees, injuries, or loss caused or occasioned by any acts of negligence or omissions of ordinary care committed or omitted by BEP, its officers, directors, instructors, employees, or agents related to any BEP activity.

The contract is not subject to negotiation, but the parents may choose instead to enroll their children in other local preschools that do not have similar contract provisions. Is the Limitations clause void on the ground that it is contrary to public policy? If not, is it unenforceable on grounds of unconscionability? How would it apply to a case in which an instructor negligently allowed your four-year-old child and another four-year-old to quarrel with pointed scissors in their hands, resulting in serious injuries to both?

3. Professional Responsibility

Suppose that a client asked you to draft an employee noncompetition clause or an exculpatory clause with terms so extreme that you were certain that it would be unenforceable because it would violate public policy or would be viewed as unconscionable. When you explained your analysis to your client, he responded: "I know that's probably not enforceable, but maybe we'll get lucky with a court that values my freedom to contract. Anyway, most of my employees [or patrons] will just read the provision and follow it, because they won't know it's unenforceable."

What would you do? Should you draft the clause and charge your usual fee for it, with or without some accompanying advice? Would it be unethical to assist your client in his effort to exploit others with an unenforceable contract clause? For more reading on this issue, see Charles A. Sullivan, *The Puzzling Persistence of Unenforceable Contract Clauses*, 70 Ohio St. L.J. 1127, 1169 (2009); Paul Carrington, *Unconscionable Lawyers*, 19 Ga. St. U.L. Rev. 361 (2002); *cf.* N.Y. St. Bar Ass'n, *Topic:... Surrogate Parenting Contracts. Preparation of Such Contracts...*, N.Y. Eth. Op. 584 (Dec. 15, 1987) (distinguishing between drafting an agreement that is unenforceable and one that would assist the client in violating a regulatory law prohibiting surrogacy contracts); Alaska Eth. Op. No. 84-4 (June 5, 1984) (permitting an attorney to draft a surrogate mother contract, with appropriate counseling, if its enforceability is uncertain, but not if the agreement is "illegal").

V. Summary

As you outline this area of law, keep in mind the following points:

- Violations of law or public policy require a conflict with the public interest, but unconscionability focuses on unfairness in the bargain and the bargaining between the parties.

- Unlike the grounds for rescission in the previous chapter, violation of law or public policy results in non-enforcement of a contract, or of a contract clause, without even restitution in many cases.
- To determine whether the remainder of a contract is enforceable after a clause is struck down for violation of law or public policy, or for unconscionability, look for indications that the parties intended the unenforceable clause to be severable from the rest of the contract, and determine whether the remainder of the contract is a logical, viable exchange.
- Even in the absence of violations of law or public policy, all or part of an agreement may be unenforceable if elements of procedural and substantive unconscionability combine to establish gross unfairness. In some states, unconscionability may be established on the basis of substantive factors alone.
- Consider how several doctrines might all be invoked as separate challenges to a clause, such as lack of mutual assent, violation of public policy, and unconscionability.

Exercise 9.11 — Issue-Spotting Exercise

According to news reports, Jesse Dimmick broke into the home of Jared and Lindsay Rowley in 2009, displayed a knife, and offered them an unspecified sum of money if the Rowleys harbored him from the police. The Rowleys orally agreed to hide Dimmick, fed him snacks, and then escaped and informed authorities when Dimmick fell asleep. Police arrested Dimmick after a shoot-out in which Dimmick suffered gunshot wounds that required his hospitalization. While later serving a sentence in prison, Dimmick sued the Rowleys for breach of their agreement to hide him from police, demanding $235,000 in damages. What defenses to enforcement of the alleged contract would you raise on behalf of the Rowleys?

Exercise 9.12 — Exam Questions

1. Q1 — Suggested time allocation — 25 minutes

For the following question set in a fictional state, you can assume that the summaries about state and federal law in the first two paragraphs below were accurate at all times relevant to the facts, which are set in 2017. Although the described transaction is a sale of goods so that the UCC generally applies to the transaction, you may assume the following without discussing it: the UCC does not supply an answer to the question posed by the question below, so the UCC will incorporate common law rules. You can assume that the state courts in the jurisdiction have adopted prevailing common law principles of contract law, which you should apply.

* * * *

Calzona is a state in the United States that has passed state legislation fully legalizing cannabis (commonly known as marijuana) for both medical and recreational use. The state legislation licenses growers to produce cannabis plants, and it regulates and taxes the wholesale and retail sale of cannabis in various forms.

Federal law still criminalizes the growing, processing, sale, possession, and use of cannabis. During the Obama administration, federal officials announced that they would allow experimentation in state laws and would not enforce federal law in states that had legalized cannabis, such as Calzona. Under the Trump administration, new Attorney General Jeff Sessions announced that he opposed legalization of cannabis and emphasized that cannabis is still illegal under federal law. However, his Justice Department has not yet moved to enforce federal laws regarding cannabis in states like Calzona, and a Justice Department task force reporting to the new A.G. declined to recommend such enforcement.

Elegant Edibles, Inc. ("EE" for short), located in Calzona, buys cannabis plants from growers, processes the usable parts of the plants, and creates and packages edible forms of cannabis ("edibles" for short) for recreational use. EE sells its edibles in bulk to retailers for resale to the public. Its business is booming.

Hemp House ("HH" for short) is a retailer of cannabis products with a single retail shop in Calzona. HH entered into a written contract with EE to purchase $50,000 worth of edibles from EE, payment 30 days after delivery.

EE timely delivered the full quantity of high-quality edibles that conformed to the contract specifications. When payment was due, however, HH refused to pay any part of EE's invoice for the edibles. EE did not breach the contract, but HH argues that the entire contract is unenforceable and that EE is not even entitled to return of the remainder of the delivered edibles.

Fully discuss whether EE is entitled to any relief under this contract. Address only one defense to enforcement, arguing both sides to the extent possible.

2. Q2—Suggested Time Allocation: 50 minutes

Ada Jones was hired in January as the sales manager for Sun Power ("SP" for short), a firm solely owned and established in 2000 by multimillionaire Rick Boone. SP specializes in manufacturing and installing solar energy systems in homes and commercial buildings.

When Rick hired Ada, the two of them discussed the terms of her employment over a long lunch. During lunch, Rick showed Ada some sample provisions from several standard contracts of which he approved. Ada selected the provisions that she preferred on each topic. They did not reach final agreement during lunch, and Rick said that his assistant would put the selected provisions together in a proposed written contract, which they could sign the next day. In Rick's office the next day, Rick signed the four-page written contract, and offered it to Ada for her signature. Ada asked "Does this contain all the terms that I requested over lunch?" Rick responded, "Yes, all the terms you requested are in the contract." With that, Ada signed the contract without reading it.

The written contract did in fact contain all of the terms that Ada had requested over lunch, revised as she had requested. However, it also contained a few other standard-form clauses that Rick has included in all his contracts since starting his business in 2000, including a mandatory arbitration clause. This arbitration clause appeared in the middle of the final page of the contract, two paragraphs above the signature lines, in the same size and style print as the rest of the contract. It provided that the parties would submit any dispute arising out of the contract to mandatory private arbitration before a panel of all three arbitrators from "Employment ARB" ("ARB" for short). ARB is a local partnership of three arbitrators who are retired employment-law attorneys, two of whom had worked for firms representing employers and one of whom had represented employees.

The arbitration clause provided that the costs of arbitration would be divided equally between SP and the employee. The clause did not specify the costs of arbitration, but—in the average employment dispute—the costs would amount to about $12,000, largely consisting of the fees for the three members of the arbitration panel. Of course, any party wishing to be represented by an attorney would separately arrange for that representation.

On June 30, Rick gave Ada her paycheck for the final two weeks of the month and then fired Ada and replaced her with a less experienced employee, Bob, who had worked for Ada on the sales team. Rick explained that it was simply a cost-cutting measure in the face of the economic downturn. Ada, who cannot find other employment in the current economy, has evidence that she was the victim of sex discrimination, in violation of a state anti-discrimination statute. After she exhausted procedures with the applicable government agency that helps administer the statute, Ada dug into her savings to hire an attorney, and she sued SP in state Superior Court, solely under the state anti-discrimination statute. The anti-discrimination statute provides for an award of reasonable attorney's fees to the prevailing party, which a plaintiff can recover after obtaining relief in any dispute resolution forum and at any stage. The statute also overrides usual rules of civil procedure by providing that questions of discrimination and the damages from discrimination must be decided by the jury and cannot be decided by the judge on summary judgment.

SP moved the court to dismiss Ada's court action on the basis of the mandatory arbitration clause in the employment contract. Ada is now preparing to respond to that motion and is trying to develop arguments that the arbitration clause in the employment contract (or perhaps the whole contract), is unenforceable, so that she can proceed with her statutory discrimination claim. Fully discuss any such arguments, but limit your discussion to possible grounds for rescission or non-enforcement of the arbitration clause (or the whole contract), or obstacles to establishing such grounds (topics covered in this chapter and in Chapter 8). For each such ground, identify the issue, summarize the applicable law, apply the law to the facts, and reach a conclusion, arguing both sides when possible. You may assume that Rick at all times acted on behalf of SP, so that his actions are binding on SP.

Chapter 10

Content of the Contract: Parol Evidence Rule and Interpretation

I. Overview

We have been studying legal rules governing the formation of enforceable contracts. Soon we will study the legal rules defining the consequences of failing to perform contractual obligations.

In this chapter, however, we will emphasize the rules that the parties created themselves: the obligations that they framed and to which they agreed. A court cannot determine whether a party performed or breached its obligations unless it first determines the scope of those obligations. To provide a memorable example, the issue addressed by a federal court in one case in this chapter is "What is Chicken?" (Was the seller obligated to deliver only young, tender fryers and broilers, or could it satisfy its obligations by delivering older, tougher, stewing chicken?)

As we explore the content of these contractual obligations, consider these questions:

- Which of the parties' terms, promises, or agreements made it into the final contract? This issue arises in a special way if the parties put their agreement in a final writing, thus triggering the parol evidence rule.
- What implied-in-law terms will be added to the parties' agreement?
- What is the meaning of a contract term to which the parties agreed? We will study a variety of rules and techniques that courts use to determine the meaning of terms stated by the parties.

II. Parol Evidence Rule

A. Introduction

Imagine that you walk into a dry-cleaning shop to drop off some clothes to be cleaned. As you approach the shop, you see a sign in the window advertising a discount price for laundry service for shirts. You know other prices for dry cleaning from recent experience with this shop, or you can discover them by asking a quick question. As you enter the store, you see a sign disclaiming liability for damage to buttons on clothing left for dry cleaning. Before you leave, an employee provides you with a receipt for clothing left with her, and she tells you that the garments will be "ready tomorrow after 5 p.m."

You have a contract with the dry-cleaning shop. The dry-cleaning shop has an obligation to return your clothes after having applied a cleaning technique to them, and you have an obligation to pay the normal rates charged by the shop. No single written document reflects all these terms; instead, you can piece terms together from a number of sources, including signs posted by the shop, oral statements made by you and the employee, understandings based on your previous transactions in the shop, and possibly even some implied terms based on general customs in the community.

When parties have reduced the final terms of their contract into a signed, written document, however, the common law *parol evidence rule* gives special weight to these written terms, sometimes to the exclusion of notes and oral statements made prior to the signing of the written document. If the contract does not fall within the ambit of an applicable statute of frauds, it need not be in writing to be enforceable; an oral agreement would be perfectly enforceable. Nonetheless, once the parties take the step of stating their final agreement in written form, the parol evidence rule will give special weight to those written terms.

Imagine, for example, that on January 9, two parties negotiated the terms of a commercial lease. A commercial tenant wanted to lease a small space at a shopping center to sell snacks, soft drinks, tobacco products, and similar items. The lessor first demanded rent of $500/month plus a percentage of the tenant's net profits. After failing to agree on a suitable percentage, however, the parties shifted their discussions to a flat monthly rental payment. The tenant was willing to pay the $1,000/month rent desired by the lessor only if the tenant could acquire the exclusive rights to sell soft drinks at the shopping center. The lessor, in turn, demanded that the tenant promise not to sell tobacco products.

Throughout these negotiations, the parties repeatedly responded to constantly changing demands and counter-offers. At some point, after resolving their differences, they put their final terms into a written document, and they expressed their offer and acceptance on January 10 by signing the document, one party signing after the other.

We could depict the various counter-proposals, tentative agreements, accepted terms, and abandoned terms in a sort of funnel that ultimately was merged into the final written agreement:

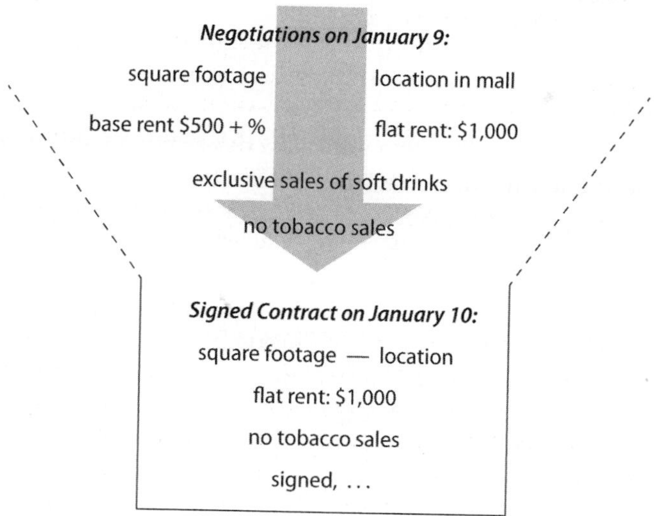

The parol evidence rule requires a court in some circumstances to give effect to the terms in the final written document signed on January 10—represented by the box above—and to exclude evidence of other previously discussed terms—represented by the terms in the funnel above the box.

The word "parol" might remind you of "oral," and indeed the parol evidence rule largely excludes testimony about oral statements made by the parties prior to or simultaneously with the signing of the final written agreement. The rule, however, can also exclude written notes or agreements made prior to signing the final written document. After all, the latest agreement between the parties on any given subject matter can modify and replace earlier agreements, oral or written, on that subject matter. Thus, you can define "parol evidence" as written documents made prior to the signing of the final written agreement, or testimony about oral statements made prior to or simultaneously with the signing.

B. Integrated Writings, and Levels of Integration

The common law parol evidence rule is triggered only when the parties have set forth some or all of their final agreement on a transaction into written form. In legal terminology, such a writing is called an "integrated writing," or a "written integration," or an "integrated agreement" because it integrates the earlier negotiated terms into a written document.

We will soon discover that the parol evidence rule operates with greater strength if the written agreement is *completely* integrated rather than just *partially* integrated. Thus, the admissibility of evidence about the terms of an agreement, and perhaps ultimately the outcome of the case, often turns on whether a written agreement is completely or only partially integrated.

1. Partial Integration and the Parol Evidence Rule

A written document is a *partial integration* if it states only some, and not all, of the terms of the parties' final agreement on a transaction. Under the parol evidence rule, a partially integrated writing will not block evidence tending to show that the final agreement includes terms absent from the written integration. After all, by definition, the partially written integration does not record all of the parties' final agreement. Consequently, a party could offer testimony about oral statements the parties made prior to signing the partial written integration, and this testimony might establish terms that the parties had included in their total final agreement but had decided to leave to memory rather than incorporating them into the writing.

Suppose, for example, that an employer and an employee signed an employee manual on March 20, signifying their agreement to the employee manual as a statement of *some* of the terms of their final employment contract. We can imagine that the employee manual addresses topics that apply to all employees, such as paid holidays, sick leave, vacation leave, and grounds for firing an employee. But some other terms of the employment contract, such as the specific job assignment and pay scale of this newly hired employee, are not stated in the employee manual but are reflected in oral statements and other written notes or e-mail messages. A court likely would rule that the signed employee manual was a partial written integration, because it was intended by the parties to record some—but not all—of the terms of their final agreement with respect to the employment of the employee.

For further discussion, let's suppose that the employee manual, signed on March 20, provides for two weeks of paid vacation time but says nothing about the employee's pay scale.

a. Excluding Parol Evidence that Contradicts the Partial Integration

Under the parol evidence rule, a court would *not* permit the employee to introduce testimony of statements made on March 19, or notes written on March 19, tending to show that the parties agreed to provide the employee with *three* weeks of paid vacation. Such evidence would contradict the terms of the partial but final written agreement signed by the parties on March 20, a written integration that superseded any contrary terms that the parties discussed before signing the written integration. Under the parol evidence rule, the court does not want the jury to be exposed to such evidence; the danger is too great that the testimony will confuse the jury or invite them to ignore the final written terms for improper reasons.

b. Admitting Parol Evidence of Consistent, Supplemental Terms

The parol evidence rule, however, would permit admission of evidence of oral statements or written documents—even ones predating the March 20 written integration—tending to establish facts regarding the employee's salary or job assignment, which are not addressed in the employee manual. Because the signed employee manual was only a partial integration, meaning that it recorded only some of the terms of the parties' final agreement, other terms of that agreement are reflected in other statements or documents. Thus, so long as those other statements or documents do not contradict any terms of the signed partial integration, the parol evidence rule would not exclude them.

In other words, so long as the parol evidence tends to establish terms that are consistent with, and supplemental to, the terms of the signed partial integration, the evidence is admissible (or at least the parol evidence rule is not a basis for exclusion). Admission of the evidence, of course, does not necessarily establish facts. If the employer and employee dispute the content of their oral discussions about the employee's job assignment and salary, for example, the court would admit their conflicting testimony on that topic, and the fact-finder (whether the judge or the jury) would assess the credibility of the witnesses and determine which version of events to accept as fact.

2. Complete Integration and the Parol Evidence Rule

Let's return now to the written commercial lease agreement, signed by a different pair of parties on January 10, and let's assume that the parties intended it to record *all* of the terms of their transaction regarding the lease. In other words, the parties intended the written integration to be the complete and exclusive statement of the parties' lease agreement.

a. Excluding Parol Evidence of Contradictory or Supplemental Terms

Such a complete integration triggers the parol evidence rule in full force. A court will exclude parol evidence tending to prove any term of the lease not found in the written, signed, completely integrated lease agreement. Specifically, the court will exclude parol evidence not only of terms that contradict the written lease agreement, but also of additional terms that are consistent with that complete integration and that would only supplement it. Thus, if the January 10 written lease says nothing about granting the commercial tenant an exclusive right to sell soft drinks in the shopping mall, the parol evidence rule would exclude testimony of statements made on January 9 tending to show that the parties agreed to such an exclusive license. After all, a written agreement about a lease signed on January 10 could modify, abandon, or otherwise supersede an earlier agreement on the same subject matter.

Because a *complete integration* is intended to be the *complete* and *exclusive* statement of the parties' agreement, it "occupies the field" of that transaction. Admission of parol evidence of other terms relating to that transaction would be inconsistent with the complete and exclusive nature of the written agreement. Again, the parol evidence rule reflects the view that the jury should not even hear such evidence, lest it influence the jury in some improper way.

b. Admitting Evidence of Terms Relating to Other Transactions

Of course, it's always possible that the tenant and lessor entered into an agreement relating to a completely separate and independent transaction on January 9, prior to signing the lease agreement. For example, suppose that—while considering the lease—the tenant noticed that the lessor had a used truck for sale, and the parties quickly reached a written agreement on January 9 for the purchase and sale of the truck, with delivery of title and payment to take place by February 1.

If the lessor later refused to sell the truck, and the tenant sued to enforce the January 9 written agreement for sale of the truck, we might imagine the lessor invoking the parol evidence rule to exclude evidence of the January 9 agreement. But, the parol evidence rule would bar the January 9 document only if it related to the lease transaction and thus was superseded by the completely integrated lease signed on January 10. Because the agreement to sell the truck presumably was completely separate from the lease agreement, those two agreements can stand side by side, both perfectly provable and enforceable, without the later one replacing and superseding the earlier one. The agreement to sell the truck could be called "collateral" to the complete integration that is asserted as a bar to admission of the parol evidence.

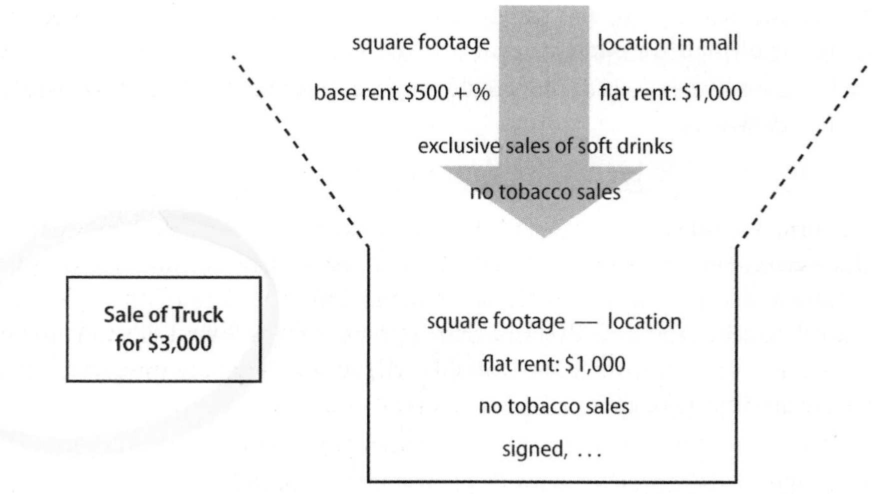

True, it is possible that the truck was indeed related to the negotiations for the lease, perhaps because it was identified as equipment that could help the vendor run his business in the leased premises. If so, the discussion on January 9, or even a written agreement on January 9, relating to the sale of the truck might be viewed as part of the subject matter encompassed by the completely integrated lease agreement signed on January 10. If so, the signed written lease—which says nothing about the sale of a truck or other equipment for the leased premises—would be viewed as rescinding and abandoning the previous agreement to include the sale of a truck as part of the lease:

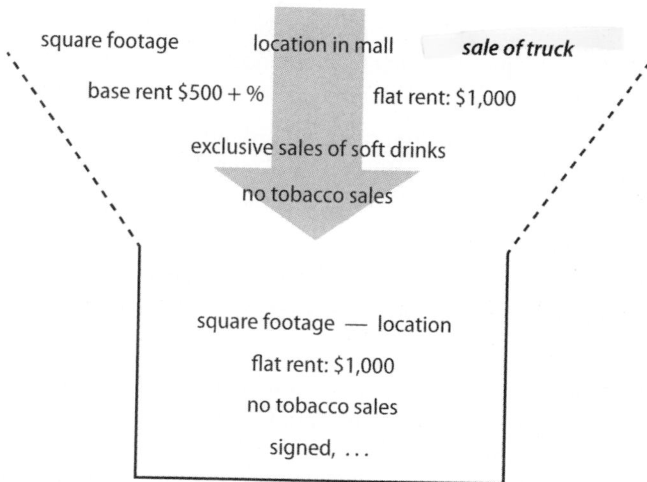

The competing arguments illustrated by the two charts above are similar to those in the case that inspired the example of the lease agreement, *Gianni v. R. Russel & Co.*, 281 Pa. 320, 126 A. 791 (1924). In that case, the final lease agreement said nothing about an exclusive license to sell soft drinks. Because the court found that the written lease agreement was a complete integration, the tenant sought to prove the exclusive license as part of a separate oral agreement, independent of the lease transaction. That line of argument was doomed, however, because an exclusive license to sell soft drinks would normally be viewed as part of the commercial lease agreement and not part of a separate transaction. The tenant further undermined his case by arguing that he agreed to refrain from selling tobacco products in exchange for the exclusive license. Because the obligation to refrain from selling tobacco *was* in the written lease, any quid pro quo for that promise (the exclusive license) would certainly also be in the lease rather than in a separate agreement relating to an independent transaction.

Accordingly, because the exclusive license did not make it into the written lease, it must not have been part of the final agreement; if it had been part of an earlier agreement, the parties must have abandoned it by the time they signed the written lease. As explained by the court, "[a]s the written lease is the complete contract of the parties, and since it embraces the field of the alleged oral contract, evidence of the latter is inadmissible under the parol evidence rule." *Id.* at 324–25, 126 A. at 792.

Exercise 10.1 — Excluding Prior or Contemporaneous Agreements under the Parol Evidence Rule

Apply the parol evidence rule to the following problems, and explain your answer:

1. Complete Integration

The court finds that a document titled "Lease Agreement" is a complete integration of the parties' agreement to lease a small commercial space in a shopping mall. The lease provides that Landlord will maintain specified common areas of the premises, but it says nothing about Landlord's liability for negligence in such maintenance. The lease also provides that Tenant will pay $500/mo. in base rent plus 5% of Tenant's gross revenue each month.

a. If Tenant's sales are disappointing, can Landlord introduce testimony tending to show that, prior to signing the written lease, the parties agreed that Tenant would pay a flat rent of $1,000 per month?

b. Can Tenant introduce testimony that, prior to signing the written lease, the parties agreed that Landlord would sell her car to Tenant for $3,000? Would it matter if Tenant's business was a pizzeria and Tenant mentioned during negotiations of the lease that Tenant was looking for a used car for pizza delivery?

c. Can Landlord introduce testimony tending to show that, prior to signing the written lease, the parties orally agreed that Landlord would not be liable to Tenant for his negligence in maintaining the common areas?

2. Partial Integration

Assume the same facts as in problem 1, except that the court finds that the parties intended the written document to be only a partial integration of their lease agreement. Now address questions 1–3 under this new assumption.

---

3. *Determining the Level of Integration*

Recall that an integrated writing is a written and signed document that records at least some of the parties' final agreement in some transaction. If it is a complete integration, it records all of the parties' agreement on that subject matter and thus is the exclusive statement of the parties' agreement.

As Subsections 1 and 2 above illustrate, in some cases the admissibility of parol evidence will depend on whether the court is deferring to a partially integrated writing or a completely integrated one. How does the court go about determining the level of integration and then applying the parol evidence rule?

Procedurally, the court will hold hearings outside the presence of the jury to determine the level of integration and to decide whether parol evidence is admissible or excludable. If parol evidence is excluded, the jury will never hear it. In a "bench trial" without a jury, if the judge excludes parol evidence, the judge will then ignore that evidence when later finding the facts.

This still leaves questions, however, about the standards a court should use to find the level of integration. As described in the next subsection, the parties can specify the level of integration in the written agreement itself. If that assistance is lacking or inconclusive, the judge must determine whether to consider the parol evidence in assessing the level of integration of the written agreement.

a. Merger Clause Establishing Complete Integration

Whether a written document is an integrated writing at all, and whether it is completely or only partially integrated, is a matter of the expressed intentions of the parties. The best way for the parties to establish that a written agreement is completely integrated is to include a provision in the contract stating just that. Not surprisingly, such a provision is often called an "integration clause." Even more commonly it's called a "merger clause," because it states the parties' intentions to merge all of the prior promises, agreements, and representations in this transaction into the written agreement, so that the written agreement supersedes all those previous discussions and occupies the entire field of that subject matter. A typical merger clause might state something like the following:

> XII. Complete Agreement. This Licensing Agreement is the complete and exclusive statement of the parties' agreement relating to the subject matter herein, and it supersedes all prior or contemporaneous agreements, promises, or representations regarding that subject matter.

Faced with such a provision in a written agreement signed by both parties, a judge will find that the written agreement is completely integrated, unless evidence shows that the agreement, or the merger clause, was the product of fraud or mistake. Because the written agreement is completely integrated, the judge will exclude parol evidence regarding alleged terms that lie within the subject matter of this transaction but do not appear in the complete integration, even if that evidence seeks only to prove additional terms that are consistent with the written agreement and would supplement it rather than contradict it. Remember, a completely integrated agreement by definition is the exclusive statement of the terms of the parties' agreement on that transaction, so it occupies the entire field of that subject matter.

But a merger clause such as the one stated above does not eliminate the possibility of litigation about the application of the parol evidence rule. Can you explain why?

As we learned in Section 2.b above, even a completely integrated written agreement does not exclude parol evidence relating to an earlier agreement that addresses a separate and independent transaction into which these same parties entered prior to signing the completely integrated agreement. The completely integrated writing supersedes only matters relating to the subject matter of *that* agreement. A party is free to prove a separate agreement between the parties, outside the subject matter of the complete integration, even though it was formed prior to the integrated writing.

However, this begs the question: What topics are outside the subject matter of the parties' completely integrated agreement? In the *Gianni* case, it was fairly easy to conclude that the vendor's alleged exclusive license to sell soft drinks was within the subject matter of the completely integrated commercial lease, but even the slight ambiguity on that topic fueled litigation at both the trial and appellate levels.

You can imagine a closer question about collateral agreements. For example, suppose that Vincent and Sophie on January 14 signed a completely integrated agreement, with a merger clause, for the sale of Vincent's celebrated restaurant to Sophie, with the transfer scheduled to take place in March. On January 7, one week prior to signing this agreement, they had signed a written agreement for the sale of Vincent's kitchen equipment, tables, chairs, plates, and silverware to Sophie (the agreement for the "sale of goods"). Between January 7 and January 14, Vincent and Sophie attempted to negotiate a contract for the consulting services of Vincent for the first six months of Sophie's operation of the restaurant, and they even reached some tentative agreements on some of the terms of consulting, but they ultimately abandoned the consulting arrangement by January 14. The agreement for the sale of the restaurant says nothing about the sale of goods or continuing obligations of Vincent to act as a consultant.

Now, imagine that Vincent is negotiating in February to sell the kitchen equipment and other goods to another buyer, and that he is denying any obligations to provide future consulting services to Sophie, contrary to Sophie's demands. If the merger clause in the completely integrated agreement for the sale of the restaurant said only that it superseded promises and agreements relating to "the subject matter herein," would that answer the question of whether the parol evidence rule excludes the written agreement for the sale of goods or testimony seeking to establish the consulting agreement? Are each of these within the subject matter of the completely integrated agreement to sell the restaurant so that they are superseded by it, or can Sophie prove them as agreements relating to separate and independent transactions?

An attorney who anticipated these problems could avoid disputes about the application of the parol evidence rule by defining the subject matter that is occupied by the agreement signed on January 14. For example, the merger clause could specifically state that the subject matter of the January 14 agreement encompasses any promises or agreements regarding services related to the restaurant (so that it supersedes any tentative agreements on such topics, which would be viewed as abandoned).

Moreover, the merger clause could specifically state that the subject matter of the January 14 agreement does not encompass the sale of equipment or supplies that are not affixed to the real property (so that the January 14 agreement would not supersede the sales agreement signed on January 7, which Sophie could separately prove and enforce). Compared to a standard merger clause, one that is tailored to the transaction would more certainly avoid costly litigation over the application of the parol evidence rule.

Exercise 10.2 — Drafting a Merger Clause

Draft a merger clause for the January 14 agreement between Vincent and Sophie. Ensure that it will permit admission of the January 7 written sales agreement but that it supersedes the discussions about consulting agreements and thus will not permit admission of testimony designed to prove a consulting agreement.

---

b. Establishing the Level of Integration in the Absence of a Merger Clause

In the absence of a statement in the contract about the level of integration, the court must determine from other evidence whether the writing is a partial integration, a complete integration, or no integration at all. If presented with terms scribbled on the back of a restaurant tab, should the court find them to represent preliminary notes that do not reflect any final agreement at all, even though the signatures of both parties can be found on the tab? If the parties intended to express a final agreement on that restaurant tab, did they intend that writing to express all of the terms of their agreement, or only some of them?

In the early part of the twentieth century, contracts scholar Samuel Williston espoused the traditional view that the court should answer these questions by looking only at the face of the written document. Applying this approach, if a formal, 10-page, signed document appeared to address all the kinds of terms that normally would accompany such a transaction, the court likely would rule that the signed document was intended by the parties to be a completely integrated writing, and the court would apply the parol evidence rule accordingly. On the other hand, a signed employee manual that addressed only policies relating generally to all employees, and failing to identify a specific employee's job description and salary, would likely be viewed as only a partial integration of that employee's final employment agreement; even if the signed manual purported to express final terms of the employment agreement, a judge likely would infer that it did not contain *all* of the terms to which the parties agreed.

The written agreement in the *Gianni* case provides an illustration of this approach. In the absence of a merger clause, the court applied the Willistonian approach prevailing at that time, which called for determining the level of integration of the lease agreement simply by examining the face of the agreement:

> The writing must be the entire contract between the parties if parol evidence is to be excluded, and to determine whether it is or not the writing will be looked at, and if it appears to be a contract complete within itself, "couched in such terms as import a complete legal obligation without any uncertainty as to the object or extent of the engagement, it is conclusively presumed that the whole engagement of the parties, and the extent and manner of their undertaking, were reduced to writing."

Gianni v. R. Russel & Co., 281 Pa. 320, 323, 126 A. 791, 792 (1924) (quoting *Seitz v. Brewers' Refrigerating Machine Co.*, 141 U. S. 510, 517 (1891), and finding a completely integrated agreement).

By mid-century, however, the view of contracts scholar Arthur Corbin began to gain favor. Under this now-prevailing view, a court can consider all relevant evidence—including the offered parol evidence of prior statements and alleged agreements—to determine whether the parties intended a written agreement to be a complete or partial integration. Thus, if the parties orally expressed an intention during negotiations to reach an oral agreement, and to record only some of the more complicated provisions in writing, parol evidence of this intention could persuade a court that the written document—which has no merger clause—was intended to be only a partial integration. If the judge reached that conclusion, he or she would then permit the jury to hear testimony regarding the terms that were left to oral agreement, leaving it to the jury to determine whether the parties in fact included those terms in their full agreement.

In the next case, the court appears to find a *partial* integration, but only after discussing tests that are normally associated with the issue of whether a collateral agreement lies outside the subject matter of a *complete* integration. Are those two approaches just opposite sides of the same coin? In other words, is it possible in some cases to view agreement "B" either as: (1) a completely integrated agreement whose subject matter does not encompass the topic of the prior agreement "A" or (2) as a partially integrated agreement that is not contradicted by the consistent additional terms in the prior agreement "A"? If so, why is it nonetheless easier to use the framework of partial integration to admit the parol evidence in the next case?

Masterson v. Sine

68 Cal. 2d 222, 436 P.2d 561 (1968)

Traynor, Chief Justice.

¶1 Dallas Masterson and his wife Rebecca owned a ranch as tenants in common. On February 25, 1958, they conveyed it to Medora and Lu Sine by a grant deed "Reserving unto the Grantors herein an option to purchase the above described property on or before February 25, 1968" for the "same consideration as being paid heretofore plus their depreciation value of any improvements Grantees may add to the property from and after two and a half years from this date." Medora is Dallas' sister and Lu's wife. Since the conveyance Dallas has been adjudged bankrupt. His trustee in bankruptcy and Rebecca brought this declaratory relief action to establish their right to enforce the option.

....

¶2 The court ... determined that the parol evidence rule precluded admission of extrinsic evidence offered by defendants to show that the parties wanted the property kept in the Masterson family and that the option was therefore personal to the grantors and could not be exercised by the trustee in bankruptcy.

....

¶3 ... The trial court erred, however, in excluding the extrinsic evidence that the option was personal to the grantors and therefore non-assignable.

¶4 When the parties to a written contract have agreed to it as an "integration"—a complete and final embodiment of the terms of an agreement—parol evidence cannot be used to add to or vary its terms.... When only part of the agreement is integrated, the same rule applies to that part, but parol evidence may be used to prove elements of the agreement not reduced to writing....

¶5 The crucial issue in determining whether there has been an integration is whether the parties intended their writing to serve as the exclusive embodiment of their agreement. The instrument itself may help to resolve that issue. It may state, for example, that "there are no previous understandings or agreements not contained in the writing," and thus express the parties' "intention to nullify antecedent understandings or agreements." (*See* 3 Corbin, Contracts (1960) §578, p. 411.) Any such collateral agreement itself must be examined, however, to determine whether the parties intended the subjects of negotiation it deals with to be included in, excluded from, or otherwise affected by the writing. Circumstances at the time of the writing may also aid in the determination of such integration....

....

¶6 In formulating the rule governing parol evidence, several policies must be accommodated. One policy is based on the assumption that written evidence is more accurate than human memory. (*Germain Fruit Co. v. J. K. Armsby Co.* (1908) 153 Cal. 585, 595, 96 P. 319.) This policy, however, can be adequately served by excluding parol evidence of agreements that directly contradict the writing. Another policy is based on the fear that fraud or unintentional invention by witnesses interested in the outcome of the litigation will mislead the finder of facts.... McCormick has suggested that the party urging the spoken as against the written word is most often the economic underdog, threatened by severe hardship if the writing is enforced. In his view the parol evidence rule arose to allow the court to control the tendency of the jury to find through sympathy and without a dispassionate assessment of the probability of fraud or faulty memory that the parties made an oral agreement collateral to the written contract, or that preliminary tentative agreements were not abandoned when omitted from the writing. (*See* McCormick, Evidence (1954) §210.) He recognizes, however, that if this theory were adopted in disregard of all other considerations, it would lead to the exclusion of testimony concerning oral agreements whenever there is a writing and thereby often defeat the true intent of the parties. (*See* McCormick, *op. cit. supra*, §216, p. 441.)

¶7 Evidence of oral collateral agreements should be excluded only when the fact finder is likely to be misled. The rule must therefore be based on the credibility of the evidence. One such standard, adopted by section 240(1)(b) of the Restatement of Contracts, permits proof of a collateral agreement if it "is such an agreement as might *naturally* be made as a separate agreement by parties situated as were the parties to the written contract." (Italics added; *see* McCormick, Evidence (1954) §216, p. 441; *see also* 3 Corbin, Contracts (1960) §583, p. 475, §594, pp. 568–69; 4 Williston, Contracts (3d ed. 1961) §638, pp. 1039–45.) The draftsmen of the Uniform

Commercial Code would exclude the evidence in still fewer instances: "If the additional terms are such that, if agreed upon, they would *certainly* have been included in the document in the view of the court, then evidence of their alleged making must be kept from the trier of fact." (Com. 3, § 2-202, italics added.)

¶ 8 The option clause in the deed in the present case does not explicitly provide that it contains the complete agreement, and the deed is silent on the question of assignability. Moreover, the difficulty of accommodating the formalized structure of a deed to the insertion of collateral agreements makes it less likely that all the terms of such an agreement were included. (*See* 3 Corbin, Contracts (1960) § 587; 4 Williston, Contracts (3d ed. 1961) § 645; 70 A.L.R. 752, 759 (1931); 68 A.L.R. 245 (1930).) The statement of the reservation of the option might well have been placed in the recorded deed solely to preserve the grantors' rights against any possible future purchasers and this function could well be served without any mention of the parties' agreement that the option was personal. There is nothing in the record to indicate that the parties to this family transaction, through experience in land transactions or otherwise, had any warning of the disadvantages of failing to put the whole agreement in the deed....

¶ 9 [Over a spirited dissent, the majority concluded that the parol evidence of a restriction on the repurchase option did not contradict the repurchase option, because it did no more than rebut a presumption that the repurchase option would be unrestricted and assignable.]

¶ 10 In the present case defendants offered evidence that the parties agreed that the option was not assignable in order to keep the property in the Masterson family. The trial court erred in excluding that evidence.

The judgment is reversed.

Fifty years after the California Supreme Court's decision in *Masterson v. Sine*, the Arizona Court of Appeals analyzed the scope of a contract that clearly constituted a complete integration. *Dunn v. FastMed Urgent Care PC*, 245 Ariz. 35, 424 P.3d 436 (Ct. App. 2018). The following summary of the facts and conclusions in that case serve as a helpful follow-up to *Masterson*:

In May 2015, Dunn, a physician, entered into an agreement with FastMed Urgent Care in which he: (1) committed to sell his interest in Urgent Cares of America to FastMed for $1,000,000, (2) agreed not to compete with FastMed for five years after the sale, and (3) agreed that disputes regarding the sale agreement would be litigated in Delaware under Delaware law. [The sale of Dunn's interest, and his joining with other physicians in the sale of their interests, was accomplished in two agreements, but for the sake of simplicity, this summary will refer to the "May sale agreement" as a single transaction and agreement.]

In June 2015, Dunn entered into an employment agreement with FastMed, but the parties soon decided to part ways and in September 2015 they entered into a separation agreement. This separation agreement provided that any disputes arising out of it would be litigated in Arizona under Arizona law, and it also incorporated a noncompetition clause that the parties had included in the June employment agreement, one that required Dunn to refrain from competing with FastMed for six months after his departure from FastMed.

When Dunn accepted employment with a competing medical center in August 2016, the six-month noncompetition clause in the September separation agreement had already expired, but the five-year clause in the May sale agreement had not. Dunn brought an action in Arizona Superior Court for declaratory relief, arguing that the September 2015 separation agreement superseded the May 2015 sale agreement, so that he was bound only by the shorter noncompetition clause, and so that the September agreement's selection of the Arizona forum and Arizona law applied.

Dunn drew the court's attention to an integration clause in the September 2015 separation agreement, which clearly identified that agreement as a complete integration:

> Entire Agreement. This Separation Agreement constitutes the full understanding and entire agreement between you and the Company and, when effective, supersedes any other agreements of any kind, whether oral or written, formal or informal....

Dunn, 245 Ariz. at 39, n.2, 424 P.3d 440 n.2. Accordingly, Dunn argued that the parties had abandoned the five-year noncompetition clause and the selection of a Delaware forum and law, both of which appeared in the earlier sale agreement.

Despite the breadth of the integration clause in the September separation agreement, the court invoked the rule that even a complete integration will supersede only prior agreements that are within the scope of the complete integration, and not those that stand separately, outside the subject matter of the complete integration. *Id.* at 39 ¶ 14, 424 P.3d 440 ¶ 14 (citing to Restatement (Second) of Contracts § 213 & cmt. c (1981)).

The court concluded that the September 2015 separation agreement, by its own description, served the limited purpose of settling matters relating to the end of Dunn's employment with FastMed, which did not encompass the topic of the May 2015 agreement in which Dunn agreed to sell his interest in a competing medical clinic to FastMed. The two agreements related to wholly different transactions, which could stand side by side without the later one superseding the previous one.

Indeed, you might recall from the discussion of noncompetition clauses in Chapter 9 that the buyer of a business and its goodwill has a particularly great interest in noncompetition from the seller, allowing enforcement of a broader noncompetition clause in the sale of a business than would be permissible in the employment context. Consequently, we can understand how the different noncompetition clauses in the May and September agreements could serve different purposes, with a duration of five years for one and only six months for the other.

In sum, the May and September contracts constituted separate transactions addressing different subject matters, so that the May agreement did not fall within the scope of the completely integrated September agreement and thus was not superseded by it. Both agreements were fully operational and enforceable, including their noncompetition agreements and forum selection clauses. Because the parties' dispute concerned Dunn's obligations under the five-year noncompetition clause of the May sale agreement, which also included a clause selecting a Delaware forum and Delaware law, the trial court had dismissed Dunn's action for declaratory judgment, so that he could refile in Delaware. The Court of Appeals affirmed.

Exercise 10.3 — Is the Parol Evidence Rule Worth Keeping?

We will soon study the plain-meaning rule, which is a branch of the parol evidence rule. The policy reasons underlying the plain-meaning rule, as stated in a 1990 decision of the New York Court of Appeals, offer justifications for the parol evidence rule in general:

> A familiar and eminently sensible proposition of law is that, when parties set down their agreement in a clear, complete document, their writing should as a rule be enforced according to its terms. Evidence outside the four corners of the document as to what was really intended but unstated or misstated is generally inadmissible to add to or vary the writing. [citations omitted]. That rule imparts "stability to commercial transactions by safeguarding against fraudulent claims, perjury, death of witnesses ... infirmity of memory ... [and] the fear that the jury will improperly evaluate the extrinsic evidence." (Fisch, New York Evidence § 42, at 22 [2d ed].) Such considerations are all the more compelling in the context of real property transactions, where commercial certainty is a paramount concern.

W.W.W. Associates, Inc. v. Giancontieri, 77 N.Y.2d 157, 162–63, 566 N.E.2d 639, 642 (1990).

Civil law systems, however, manage very well without a parol evidence rule. Similarly, the United Nations Convention on Contracts for the International Sale of Goods has no parol evidence rule; instead, it provides that "A contract of sale ... may be proved by any means, including witnesses," C.I.S.G. art. 11 (1980), and — in determining intent or meaning — "due consideration is to be given to all relevant circumstances of the case, including the negotiations," C.I.S.G. art. 8(3) (1980).

Which approach do you favor? Is the parol evidence rule an effective tool for preventing fraudulent testimony, or does it promote fraud by excluding evidence relevant to the parties' intentions? Is it necessary to provide some certainty in commerce? Or should we abandon it, allow the jury to hear all relevant evidence, and trust the jury to sort it all out competently?

C. Purposes for Which the Parol Evidence Rule Does Not Bar Admission of Evidence

1. Subsequent Agreements

Most fundamentally, remember that the parol evidence rule bars admission only of prior written statements, and of oral statements made either before or at the same time as signing the written integration. A major justification for the rule is the recognition that the latest written agreement can modify or replace previous statements or agreements regarding the same transaction.

By the same reasoning, the written integration itself can be modified or replaced by an agreement *subsequent* to its signing, if that subsequent agreement meets other requirements of enforceability. Moreover, as we will study in the next chapter, a subsequent statement may operate as a waiver of rights under an existing contract. Accordingly, the parol evidence rule has no application to promises, agreements, or waivers made after the signing of the written integration.

The party advancing rights under a subsequent statement must still prove that the statement in fact was made and that it has some legal effect. The limited point made here is that the parol evidence rule does not bar admission of the evidence.

2. Parol Evidence of Conditions Precedent or Defects in Formation

Even statements made prior to the signing of the integrated agreement are admissible to show that the written integration is not deserving of the protection of the parol evidence rule. This may be the case if the written agreement never took effect or because it was the product of a defect in contract formation, such as misrepresentation, duress, or mutual mistake.

With respect to a contract never taking effect, some courts will relax the parol evidence rule to admit evidence of a prior or contemporaneous oral condition precedent to the effectiveness of the written agreement, so long as the oral condition does not contradict language in the written integration. For example, some courts will allow a party to prove that, just before signing a written agreement for the lease of restaurant space, the parties orally agreed that the lease agreement would not take effect unless the lessee received a franchise from Heavenly Fried Chicken, Inc., prior to the starting date of the lease.

All courts will consider parol evidence tending to show a defect in contract formation that provides grounds for avoidance or reformation, such as misrepresentation or mistake. Imagine, for example, that credible evidence showed that the parties in the *Gianni* case agreed to the exclusive license, that they intended that term to be in the written lease, and that the term had been inadvertently omitted from the written agreement through a clerical error that neither party noticed at the signing. If presented with such an offer of proof, a court should consider this evidence in an action by Gianni for reformation of the contract.

In fact, readers of the *Gianni* case often wonder whether the parties did agree to the exclusive license, perhaps in exchange for the ban on selling tobacco as asserted by the tenant, and whether the lessor fraudulently omitted that term from the written lease, hoping that the tenant would not notice the omission at the signing. Credible evidence of such fraud would be admissible and would provide good support for an action to reform the contract to include the exclusive license.

The opinion in *Gianni* gives no indication whether the tenant tried to establish clerical error or fraud. However, the facts of the case would pose difficulties for the tenant. The tenant received a copy of the written lease prior to the signing, and he admitted that two persons—including his daughter—read its terms to him prior to the signing. It would be difficult for Gianni to prove an error of omission, or his reliance on fraudulent statements, when he had secured the assistance of two people to confirm the terms of the written document. *Gianni*, 281 Pa. at 322, 126 A. at 791.

Exercise 10.4—False Disclaimers

1. False Assurances

Suppose that the parties in *Gianni* both knew that the written lease omitted mention of the exclusive license, but that—just prior to the signing of the lease—the lessor orally assured the tenant that their recent oral agreement for the license was fully enforceable under the law and need not appear in the written lease. Should the judge consider evidence of that assurance by the landlord in assessing whether to apply the parol evidence rule? In these circumstances, how would you argue for admission of testimony about the alleged oral agreement for an exclusive license? *Cf.* Chapter 7, Exercise 7.3.

2. Merger Clause Disclaiming Fraud

Suppose that the parties have signed a completely integrated agreement whose merger clause includes a statement that "the parties to this contract agree and warrant that neither of them has relied on any statements or representations other than those contained in this written Agreement." Statements of this nature were included in consent agreements signed by persons who appeared in the outrageous *Borat* comedy movie, after in fact relying on oral statements that the titular character, Borat, was a foreign news reporter filming a documentary about American culture; indeed, one scholar has characterized the issue created by clauses of this kind as the "Borat problem." Russell Korobkin, *The Borat Problem in Contract Law: Fraud, Assent, and Standard Forms,* 101 CALIF. L. REV. 51 (2013). Should such a clause preclude admission of evidence that a party reasonably relied on an oral misrepresentation? Would the clause constitute a waiver or surrender of any claim based on misrepresentation? Should a court permit proof that this clause of the contract simply is not accurate and that a party did rely on a misrepresentation? The Restatement appears to answer in the affirmative. RESTATEMENT (SECOND) OF CONTRACTS § 218(1) (1981) ("A recital of fact in an integrated agreement may be shown to be untrue."). Case law, however, is mixed. *See* Korobkin, *supra*; Shelby D. Green, *Contesting Disclaimer-of-Reliance Clauses by Efficiency, Free Will, and Conscience: Staving Off Caveat Emptor*, 2 TEX. A&M L. REV. 1 (2014).

Can you distinguish the following two cases based on the brief summaries in the parenthetic explanations? *Compare Hill v. Jones*, 151 Ariz. 81, 83, 725 P.2d 1115, 1117 (Ct. App. 1986) (admitting parol evidence to show fraud by the seller of a home, even though the integration clause stated that no party was bound by any representation outside the written contract) *with Castle v. Barrett-Jackson Auction Co.*, 229 Ariz. 471, 276 P.3d 540 (Ct. App. 2012) (giving conclusive effect to clause in an auction contract stating that the auction company had made no representations about item sold by the seller at auction).

---

3. *Parol Evidence as an Aid to Interpretation*

The parol evidence rule does not exclude evidence designed to explain the meaning of terms in the written integration. Such evidence does not offend the policies underlying the rule, because the evidence does not seek to contradict or even supplement the terms of the written integration. Instead, it respects the terms in the written integration and simply helps to interpret them. Thus, if the term "net profits" is not defined in the written agreement, and if it could reasonably be interpreted in more than one way, then either party could introduce relevant evidence of statements made during negotiations, previous transactions between these parties, or custom in the industry to help determine the meaning intended by the parties at the time of contract formation.

How can a court determine whether parol evidence is really advanced for the purpose of explaining a term in a written agreement or is offered instead to supplement the written integration with a new term, or even to contradict a term in the written agreement? For example, could the tenant in *Gianni* introduce testimony of oral statements about an exclusive license to sell soft drinks as a means of helping the court interpret a provision in the lease authorizing him to "sell soft drinks, snack items, and sundries, but not tobacco products"? Or should that be viewed as an attempt to add a new term to a completely integrated agreement?

The courts have applied different versions of a test for determining whether parol evidence is offered for a permissible purpose. These range from the "four corners" version of the "plain-meaning rule" to a much more flexible approach that recognizes that the parties might have attached an unusual meaning to a word. In a jury trial, the court will typically apply its test in a hearing outside the presence of the jury, to determine whether the evidence will later be admitted in the trial and thus presented to the jury.

a. The Traditional Plain-Meaning Rule

Under the plain-meaning rule, a contract term needs no interpretation if it has a single, clear, and unambiguous meaning on its face. In such a case, parol evidence that is offered to establish a different meaning would contradict the unambiguous contract term rather than help to explain its meaning.

Under the strongest version of this plain-meaning rule, the court does not consider the offered parol evidence—such as testimony about prior negotiations—to determine whether the contract term is ambiguous and in need of interpretation. Instead, the judge confines his or her review to the "four corners of the contract." If, after reviewing the entire written integration on its face, the contract term in question has a single, clear, unambiguous meaning, then the court will give the term that objective meaning and will not allow the fact-finder (the judge or the jury) to consider the parol evidence for the purpose of determining whether some other meaning is plausible.

This traditional approach is still followed by many courts, as shown by this excerpt from a Wisconsin Supreme Court decision, which uses the term "extrinsic evidence" to refer to evidence outside the written integration:

> The lodestar of contract interpretation is the intent of the parties. In ascertaining the intent of the parties, contract terms should be given their plain or ordinary meaning. If the contract is unambiguous, our attempt to determine the parties' intent ends with the four corners of the contract, without consideration of extrinsic evidence.

Huml v. Vlazny, 293 Wis.2d 169, 197, 716 N.W.2d 807, 820 (2006) (citations omitted).

By now you may have discerned that this highly objective approach is not as straightforward as it sounds, because it does not explain how a judge should determine whether a contract term has a single, clear, unambiguous meaning. Is the judge expected to simply apply his or her own understanding of language? Should the judge consult a dictionary to determine whether it lists more than one popular definition for a word? If so, does a secondary definition lie so far beyond the bounds of mainstream usage that the primary definition qualifies as the single "plain meaning" of the word? Should the judge consider the meaning given to that contract term by a reasonable person in the industry rather than an average person in the general population?

As a judge begins to consult external sources to confirm the lack of ambiguity, his or her approach strays from the strict limitations of the "four corners" version of the plain-meaning rule. Nonetheless, if the judge consults a dictionary, or even if the judge takes evidence of trade usage, he or she can plausibly characterize the approach as a version of the plain-meaning rule. The judge is still consulting objective evidence to determine whether some broad population finds the term to have a single, clear, unambiguous meaning.

If the judge instead finds an ambiguity, so that a term might have two or more generally accepted alternative meanings, then the judge will admit parol evidence offered by a party to show the parties' intentions to adopt one of those generally accepted meanings. It's possible that the other party would introduce other parol evidence tending to show the parties' intentions to adopt a different one of the generally accepted meanings. It will be up to the finder of fact to determine how much credence to give to any of the admitted evidence.

Under the traditional plain meaning rule, a finding of ambiguity does not permit admission of parol evidence of any asserted meaning. Instead, the court will admit parol evidence only if it tends to show one of the generally accepted multiple meanings of the term in question.

b. Modern Trend to Reject the Plain-Meaning Rule

Earlier in this chapter, we noted a split between Williston and Corbin over the scope of evidence that a judge should consider in determining the level of integration of an agreement. In addition, they held conflicting views about the scope of the evidence that a judge should consider in determining whether a contract term is ambiguous and requires interpretation. Williston embraced the four-corners and plain-meaning rules discussed above, but Corbin favored a rule more liberally permitting consideration of the parol evidence of the surrounding circumstances, not only to determine the level of integration but also to determine whether a term in the contract requires interpretation. *See Darner Motor Sales, Inc. v. Universal Underwriters Ins. Co.*, 140 Ariz. 383, 393, 682 P.2d 388, 398 (1984) (In Banc) (citing to the contrasting views of Williston and Corbin).

Some courts have followed a modern trend favoring Corbin's views and rejecting the restrictions of the plain meaning rule. They recognize the possibility that the parties to the written agreement used a term in an unusual way, even though the judge, the general population, or a reasonable person in the industry might view the term as unambiguously having a single, standard meaning.

These courts will consider parol evidence to determine whether it's plausible that the parties intended a contract term to have some special meaning other than the term's usual objective meaning. If the evidence shows that both parties might have intended their words to have the unusual meaning advanced by one party, these courts will allow the fact-finder to consider the parol evidence in determining the meaning of the contract term in question.

The rationale for this approach is explained by Justice Traynor in a 1968 decision of the California Supreme Court:

> If words had absolute and constant referents, it might be possible to discover contractual intention in the words themselves and in the manner in which they were arranged. Words, however, do not have absolute and constant referents. "A word is a symbol of thought but has no arbitrary and fixed meaning like a symbol of algebra or chemistry,...." [citation omitted]. The meaning of particular words or groups of words varies with the "... verbal context and surrounding circumstances and purposes in view of the linguistic education and experience of their users and their hearers or readers (not excluding judges).... A word has no meaning apart from these factors; much less does it have an objective meaning, one true meaning." (Corbin, *The Interpretation of Words and the Parol Evidence Rule* (1965) 50 Cornell L.Q. 161, 187.) Accordingly, the meaning of a writing "... can only be found by interpretation in the light of all the circumstances that reveal the sense in

> which the writer used the words. The exclusion of parol evidence regarding such circumstances merely because the words do not appear ambiguous to the reader can easily lead to the attribution to a written instrument of a meaning that was never intended." [citations omitted].
>
> Although extrinsic evidence is not admissible to add to, detract from, or vary the terms of a written contract, these terms must first be determined before it can be decided whether or not extrinsic evidence is being offered for a prohibited purpose. The fact that the terms of an instrument appear clear to a judge does not preclude the possibility that the parties chose the language of the instrument to express different terms. That possibility is not limited to contracts whose terms have acquired a particular meaning by trade usage, but exists whenever the parties' understanding of the words used may have differed from the judge's understanding.
>
> Accordingly, rational interpretation requires at least a preliminary consideration of all credible evidence offered to prove the intention of the parties. [citations omitted]. Such evidence includes testimony as to the "circumstances surrounding the making of the agreement ... including the object, nature and subject matter of the writing ..." so that the court can "place itself in the same situation in which the parties found themselves at the time of contracting." [citations omitted]. If the court decides, after considering this evidence, that the language of a contract, in the light of all the circumstances, is "fairly susceptible of either one of the two interpretations contended for," [citations omitted] extrinsic evidence relevant to prove either of such meanings is admissible.

Pacific Gas & Elec. Co. v. G. W. Thomas Drayage & Rigging Co., 69 Cal. 2d 33, 38–40, 442 P.2d 641, 644–46 (1968).

If we constructed a continuum with the four-corners version of the plain-meaning rule at the left end, the modern approach would lie at the right end of the continuum:

PE Only if Contract Is Ambiguous on Its Face			**Consider Entire Context**
4 Corners	*Dictionary*	*Trade Usage*	*Special Meaning of Parties*

A judge applying the plain meaning rule will not admit parol evidence to explain meaning if the contract term is unambiguous and requires no interpretation. In an extreme version of this approach, the judge will limit the search for ambiguity to the face of the contract (staying within its four corners) and will determine whether the term has a single plain meaning based on the judge's own linguistic training, perhaps with the aid of a dictionary.

Some judges, however, will ask whether the term might have a special meaning in a population relevant to the transaction, such as a meaning based on trade usage within an industry of which both parties are members. A judge taking this middle ground might still characterize his or her approach as consistent with a plain meaning rule, although the judge is admitting that the objective meaning attached to a term might depend on the population that is consulted. Once a judge has opened that door, the modern approach kicks it open further by taking the position that the relevant population consists of the particular parties to the contract, and the ultimate question is whether the term might have been given a special or unusual meaning by them.

Even the modern approach has its limits. If a contract term normally would have a standard, objective meaning, and if a party seeks to prove that the parties intended instead to give the term an unusual meaning, a court adopting the liberal approach will require the parol evidence to pass a sort of "laugh test." After considering all the evidence concerning the context of the agreement, the court will permit the jury to hear the parol evidence only if the asserted nonstandard interpretation of a contract term seems plausible in light of all the evidence. If a litigant asserts that the parties used the terms "payment is due no later than February 1" to mean that payment is due any time before the end of the calendar year, or that the parties used the term "$10,000,000 U.S." to mean five million U.S. dollars, only the most convincing parol evidence of special context or prior negotiations will persuade the judge that this is anything other than a brazen attempt to contradict a written term of the contract, rather than explain its meaning.

Thus, even under the modern approach, if the proponent's theory of interpretation is patently absurd, the court will exclude the parol evidence and give the contract term its usual objective meaning. The court will often explain this result by stating that the parol evidence simply did not satisfy a test of relevance to the question of interpreting the contract term. This limitation helps to show how the modern approach does not completely abandon all features of the plain-meaning rule; it simply represents a highly flexible approach to that rule, and thus lies on the opposite end of the continuum from the strictest version of that rule, the four-corners sub-rule.

Arizona is among the states that have embraced the modern approach. The earliest indication of the modern approach in Arizona probably appears in *Smith v. Melson, Inc.*, 135 Ariz. 119, 121, 659 P.2d 1264, 1266 (1983) ("contract should be read in light of the parties' intentions as reflected by their language and in view of all the circumstances."). It was reinforced in passing a year later in *Darner Motor Sales, Inc. v. Universal Underwriters Ins. Co.*, 140 Ariz. 383, 393, 682 P.2d 388, 398 (1984) (In Banc). It was not until 1993, however, that the Arizona Supreme Court explained its position in detail in the following case.

Taylor v. State Farm Mutual Automobile Insurance Co.

175 Ariz. 148, 854 P.2d 1134 (1993) (In Banc)

Feldman, Chief Justice.

¶1 Bobby Sid Taylor petitions us to review a decision reversing a jury verdict in his favor in a bad faith claim against State Farm Mutual Automobile Insurance Co. He argues that the court of appeals erroneously held that his bad faith claim was barred by a release he signed in 1981. We granted review because the case raises important issues in the area of contract and insurance law. We have jurisdiction pursuant to Ariz. Const. art. VI, § 5(3), and Ariz. R. Civ. App. P. 23.

FACTS AND PROCEDURAL HISTORY

....

¶2 ... [Taylor released "all contractual rights, claims, and causes of action he has or may have against STATE FARM under the policy of insurance ... in connection with the collision ... and all subsequent matters."] The judge [found] that the release was ambiguous and that therefore parol evidence was admissible at trial to aid in interpreting the release. A second judge, who presided at trial, also denied State Farm's motion for directed verdict based on the release. Having been instructed on the interpretation of the release, the jury returned a verdict in favor of Taylor for compensatory damages of $2.1 million. The court also awarded Taylor $300,000 in attorney fees.

¶3 The court of appeals reversed, holding that the release agreement was not ambiguous and therefore the judge erred by admitting parol evidence to vary its terms. *Taylor v. State Farm Mut. Auto. Ins. Co.*, No. 1 CA-CV 9908 (Sep. 17, 1991) (mem. dec.). Based on the agreement's "four corners," the court held that "it clearly release[d] all policy contract rights, claims, and causes of action that Taylor has or may have against State Farm." *Id.* at 20. According to the court, because the release should have been strictly enforced, there was no basis for Taylor's bad faith claim. *Id.* We believe the court's decision both incorrectly applies settled legal principles and raises unsettled issues of contract interpretation.

DISCUSSION

¶4 Much of the dispute in this case centers on the events that surround the drafting of the release and the inferences that can be drawn from those events. As noted, the trial court found that the release was ambiguous and admitted extrinsic evidence to aid in its interpretation. The court of appeals found no ambiguity. *Taylor*, mem. dec. at 20, 23. In resolving this issue, we must address the scope and application of the parol evidence rule in Arizona and decide whether, under these facts, the trial court properly admitted extrinsic evidence to interpret the release.

A. Legal principles

The application of the parol evidence rule has been the subject of much controversy and scholarly debate....

¶5 Interpretation is the process by which we determine the meaning of words in a contract. *See* Restatement § 200. Generally, and in Arizona, a court will attempt to enforce a contract according to the parties' intent. *See Darner*, 140 Ariz. at 393, 682 P.2d at 398; [other citations omitted]. "The primary and ultimate purpose of interpretation" is to discover that intent and to make it effective. 3 Corbin § 572B, at 421 (1992 Supp.). The court must decide what evidence, other than the writing, is admissible in the interpretation process, bearing in mind that the parol evidence rule prohibits extrinsic evidence to vary or contradict, but not to interpret, the agreement. *See* 3 Corbin § 543, at 130–34. These substantive principles are clear, but their application has been troublesome.

1. Restrictive view

¶6 Under the restrictive "plain meaning" view of the parol evidence rule, evidence of prior negotiations may be used for interpretation only upon a finding that some language in the contract is unclear, ambiguous, or vague. E. Allan Farnsworth, Farnsworth on Contracts § 7.12, at 270 (1990) ("Farnsworth"). Under this approach, "if a writing, or the term in question, appears to be plain and unambiguous on its face, its meaning must be determined from the four corners of the instrument without resort to extrinsic evidence of any nature." Calamari & Perillo, *supra* § 3-10, at 166–67; *cf.* Gottsfield, *supra*, at 388–89. Thus, if the judge finds from the face of a document that it conveys only one meaning, parol evidence is neither considered nor admitted for any purpose. The danger here, of course, is that what appears plain and clear to one judge may not be so plain to another (as in this case), and the judge's decision, uninformed by context, may not reflect the intent of the parties.

2. Corbin view

¶7 Under the view embraced by Professor Corbin and the Second Restatement, there is no need to make a preliminary finding of ambiguity before the judge considers extrinsic evidence. 3 Corbin § 542, at 100–05 (1992 Supp.); Restatement § 212 cmt. b; Farnsworth § 7.12, at 272; Gottsfield, *supra*, at 384. Instead, the court considers all of the proffered evidence to determine its relevance to the parties' intent and then applies the parol evidence rule to exclude from the fact finder's consideration only the evidence that contradicts or varies the meaning of the agreement. 3 Corbin § 542, at 100–01 (1992 Supp.). According to Corbin, the court cannot apply the parol evidence rule without first understanding the meaning the parties intended to give the agreement. *Id.* To understand the agreement, the judge cannot be restricted to the four corners of the document. Again, even under the Corbin view, the court can admit evidence for interpretation but must stop short of contradiction. *See* 3 Corbin § 574, at 371–72; Gottsfield, *supra*, at 386–87, 392.

3. Arizona view

¶8 Writing for a unanimous court in *Smith v. Melson*, Inc., 135 Ariz. 119, 121–22, 659 P.2d 1264, 1266–67 (1983), Chief Justice Holohan expressly committed

Arizona to the Corbin view of contract interpretation. [citations omitted]. We have not, however, fully explored *Melson*'s application. *See Gottsfield, supra*, at 378. We have held that a court may consider surrounding circumstances, including negotiation, prior understandings, and subsequent conduct, but have not elaborated much further. *Darner*, 140 Ariz. at 393, 682 P.2d at 398; *see also Burkons*, 168 Ariz. at 351, 813 P.2d at 716; *Melson*, 135 Ariz. at 122, 659 P.2d at 1267.

¶ 9 According to Corbin, the proper analysis has two steps. First, the court considers the evidence that is alleged to ... illuminate the meaning of the contract language, or demonstrate the parties' intent. *See* 3 Corbin § 542, at 100–01 (1992 Supp.). The court's function at this stage is to eliminate the evidence that has no probative value in determining the parties' intent. *Id.* The second step involves "finalizing" the court's understanding of the contract. *Id.* at 100. [In the second step, the judge or jury determines the parties' intended meaning based on the evidence that the judge found to be admissible after undertaking the first step.]

¶ 10 Even during the first step, the judge may properly decide not to consider certain offered evidence because it does not aid in interpretation but, instead, varies or contradicts the written words. *See id.* at 101. This might occur when the court decides that the asserted meaning of the contract language is so unreasonable or extraordinary that it is improbable that the parties actually subscribed to the interpretation asserted by the proponent of the extrinsic evidence. *See id.* "The more bizarre and unusual an asserted interpretation is, the more convincing must be the testimony that supports it." 3 Corbin § 579, at 420. At what point a judge stops "listening to testimony that white is black and that a dollar is fifty cents is a matter for sound judicial discretion and common sense." *Id.*

¶ 11 When interpreting a contract, nevertheless, it is fundamental that a court attempt to "ascertain and give effect to the intention of the parties at the time the contract was made if at all possible." *Polk*, 111 Ariz. at 495, 533 P.2d at 662; [other citations omitted]. If, for example, parties use language that is mutually intended to have a special meaning, and that meaning is proved by credible evidence, a court is obligated to enforce the agreement according to the parties' intent, even if the language ordinarily might mean something different. See Restatement § 212 cmt. b, illus. 3 & 4. The judge, therefore, must avoid the often irresistible temptation to automatically interpret contract language as he or she would understand the words. This natural tendency is sometimes disguised in the judge's ruling that contract language is "unambiguous." *See* 3 Corbin § 543A, at 159 (1992 Supp.). Words, however, are seldom so clear that they "apply themselves to the subject matter." Restatement § 214 cmt. b. On occasion, exposition of the evidence regarding the intention of the parties will illuminate plausible interpretations other than the one that is facially obvious to the judge. *See id.* Thus, ambiguity determined by the judge's view of "clear meaning" is a troublesome concept that often obstructs the court's proper and primary function in this area—to enforce the meaning intended by the contracting parties. *See* 3 Corbin § 542, at 122–24; *Gottsfield, supra*, at 385.

¶ 12 Recognizing these problems, we are hesitant to endorse, without explanation, the often repeated and usually over-simplified construct that ambiguity must exist before parol evidence is admissible. We have previously criticized the ambiguity prerequisite in the context of non-negotiated agreements. [citations omitted]. Moreover, a contract may be susceptible to multiple interpretations and therefore truly ambiguous yet, given the context in which it was negotiated, not susceptible to a clearly contradicting and wholly unpersuasive interpretation asserted by the proponent of extrinsic evidence. In such a case, it seems clear that a court should exclude that evidence as violating the parol evidence rule despite the presence of some contract ambiguity. Finally, and most important, the ambiguity determination distracts the court from its primary objective—to enforce the contract as intended by the parties. Consequently, although relevant, contract ambiguity is not the only linchpin of a court's decision to admit parol evidence.

¶ 13 The better rule is that the judge first considers the offered evidence and, if he or she finds that the contract language is "reasonably susceptible" to the interpretation asserted by its proponent, the evidence is admissible to determine the meaning intended by the parties. *See* Restatement § 215 cmt. b; *see also Pacific Gas & Elec. Co. v. G.W. Thomas Dray. & Rigging Co.*, 69 Cal. 2d 33, 69 Cal. Rptr. 561, 564, 566, 567–68, 442 P.2d 641, 644, 645–46 (1968); [footnote omitted] *cf.* Melson, 135 Ariz. at 121, 659 P.2d at 1266 ("A contract should be read in light of the parties' intentions as reflected by their language and in view of all the circumstances."). The meaning that appears plain and unambiguous on the first reading of a document may not appear nearly so plain once the judge considers the evidence. In such a case, the parol evidence rule is not violated because the evidence is not being offered to contradict or vary the meaning of the agreement. To the contrary, it is being offered to explain what the parties truly may have intended. We believe that this rule embodies the concepts endorsed by Corbin and adopted by this court ten years ago in *Melson*. Other courts more recently have expressed approval of the position taken by Corbin and the Restatement (Second) of Contracts. [citations omitted].

¶ 14 A judge may not always be in a position to rule on a parol evidence objection at first blush, having not yet heard enough relevant evidence on the issue. If this occurs, the judge might, for example, admit the extrinsic evidence conditionally, reserve ruling on the issue until enough relevant evidence is presented, or, if the case is being tried to a jury, consider the evidence outside the jury's presence. *See, e.g.*, Ariz. R. Evid. 103(c), 104(b), 104(c), 105. Because the judge is in the best position to decide how to proceed, we leave this decision to his or her sound discretion. As noted also, the judge need not waste much time if the asserted interpretation is unreasonable or the offered evidence is not persuasive. A proffered interpretation that is highly improbable would necessarily require very convincing evidence. In such a case, the judge might quickly decide that the contract language is not reasonably susceptible to the asserted meaning, stop listening to evidence supporting it, and rule that its admission would violate the parol evidence rule. *See* 3 Corbin § 542, at 112; § 579, at 420.

We now apply these principles to the facts of this case.

B. Was the release so clear that the trial judge erred in admitting extrinsic evidence to interpret it?

¶ 15 Taylor released "all *contractual* rights, claims, and causes of action he ha[d] or may have against STATE FARM under the policy of insurance ... in connection with the collision ... and *all subsequent matters.*" *See* Appendix (emphasis added). Taylor argued that the bad faith claim sounds in tort and was therefore neither covered nor intended to be covered by the language releasing "all contractual" claims....

¶ 16 It is true that bad faith has its genesis in contract. *See Rawlings v. Apodaca*, 151 Ariz. 149, 153–54, 726 P.2d 565, 569–70 (1986). Our cases show, however, that the precise legal character of a bad faith claim may depend on the context of the discussion.... Despite the contractual origin of an insurance bad faith claim, the seminal Arizona decision on the subject, less than six months old at the time State Farm and Taylor made the agreement, declared that such conduct is a tort. *Noble*, 128 Ariz. at 190, 624 P.2d at 868 (Feb. 17, 1981). [Later cases] "demonstrate the uninterrupted recognition that bad faith has components of both tort and contract." ... In fact, State Farm implicitly recognizes the dual nature of Taylor's bad faith claim by conceding its tortious quality for purposes of its statute of limitations argument. *See* State Farm's Opening Brief to Court of Appeals at 36–37 (alleging that Taylor's bad faith claim is barred by the tort statute of limitations). State Farm also abandons the claim's contractual side in arguing that attorney fees should not have been awarded. *Id.* at 49–50.

C. Was the parol evidence for the jury?

¶ 17 Whether contract language is reasonably susceptible to more than one interpretation so that extrinsic evidence is admissible is a question of law for the court. *See Leo Eisenberg & Co., Inc. v. Payson*, 162 Ariz. 529, 532–33, 785 P.2d 49, 52–53 (1989). We have concluded in the preceding section that the language of the agreement, illuminated by the surrounding circumstances, indicates that either of the interpretations offered was reasonable. Because interpretation was needed and because the extrinsic evidence established controversy over what occurred and what inferences to draw from the events, the matter was properly submitted to the jury. [citations omitted]. The trial judge, therefore, instructed the jury as follows:

> ... [State Farm] has alleged the affirmative defense of release. In this regard, [State Farm] contends that the agreement ... was intended by the parties thereto to, among other things, release [State Farm] from all bad faith claims.
>
> ... Whether the parties intended the bad faith claims to be released is for you to determine. If you find that the parties to said agreement intended thereby that [State Farm] be released from bad faith claims, then your verdict must be for [State Farm].
>
> ....

> A release is to be construed according to the intent of the parties to it. This intention is to be determined by what was within the contemplation of the parties when the release was executed, which, in turn, is to be resolved in the light of all of the surrounding facts and circumstances under which the parties acted.

Reporter's Transcript, Mar. 12, 1987, at 184–85. [footnote omitted]. The instruction states the issue quite clearly. So instructed, the jury resolved the release issue in Taylor's favor. [footnote omitted]. We leave that resolution undisturbed.

Corcoran, Justice, specially concurring:

¶ 18 I concur with the opinion—but without enthusiasm.... I fear that this opinion makes this court the supreme court of arguments "that white is black and that a dollar is fifty cents"—to use the colorful words of Professor Corbin.

Exercise 10.5 — Interpretation or Contradiction?

Analyze the following questions under both the plain meaning rule and under a legal approach that more liberally allows parties to prove that they used a term in an unusual way, to mean something other than its usual meaning.

Assume that a written provision in an integrated agreement provides that Seller will sell gravel to Buyer at the rate of "$100/ton." Seller bills Buyer at the rate of $100 for every short ton, which equals 2,000 lbs.

(1) Can Buyer introduce extrinsic evidence of prior negotiations tending to show that the parties meant "$100/ton" to mean $100 for every long ton, which equals 2,240 lbs.?

(2) Can Buyer introduce extrinsic evidence tending to show that the parties used the word "ton" to serve as shorthand for one full truckload in a truck owned by Seller that turns out to hold almost 3,160 lbs.?

(3) In a domestic transaction in the United States, should the court admit extrinsic evidence of bargaining context to determine whether the parties both used the term "$100" to mean two hundred dollars in American currency? Can you think of any circumstances surrounding the transaction that could convince a judge that such an interpretation is plausible so that the jury should hear the parol evidence?

---

c. The UCC Parol Evidence Rule

According to comment 1(b) to UCC § 2-202, the UCC parol evidence rule does not require an ambiguity before parol evidence is admissible to help the fact-finder interpret the meaning of contract terms. Under that interpretation, the parol evidence rule for transactions in goods rejects the plain-meaning rule.

Study Arizona's enactment of section 2-202 copied below. After you examine its text, determine to what extent it seems to be consistent with the common law parol evidence rule that we have explored so far.

47-2202. Final written expression: parol or extrinsic evidence

Terms with respect to which the confirmatory memoranda of the parties agree or which are otherwise set forth in a writing intended by the parties as a final expression of their agreement with respect to such terms as are included therein may not be contradicted by evidence of any prior agreement or of a contemporaneous oral agreement but may be explained or supplemented:

1. By course of performance, course of dealing or usage of trade (section 47-1303); and

2. By evidence of consistent additional terms unless the court finds the writing to have been intended also as a complete and exclusive statement of the terms of the agreement.

4. *The Reasonable Expectations Doctrine*

Along with the modern trend to reject the plain-meaning rule, the "reasonable expectations" doctrine offers a tool for liberally avoiding restrictions imposed by the parol evidence rule. Only a few courts have considered and adopted it, however, and they have applied it mostly to standard-form insurance contracts.

a. Traditional Rule

The best way to explain this doctrine is to begin with the traditional rule that a party is bound by terms to which he or she expressed assent, regardless of whether that party read or understood all the terms in the agreement: "It will not do for a man to enter into a contract, and, when called upon to respond to its obligations, to say that he did not read it when he signed it, or did not know what it contained." *Upton v. Tribilcock*, 91 U.S. 45, 50 (1875).

For example, suppose that a consumer signed an insurance contract without reading all its terms and later discovered that the written contract includes a term that is unpleasantly surprising to the consumer in light of expectations raised during negotiations. The traditional parol evidence rule will not permit the party to contradict that term with a different one that was more consistent with ideas exchanged during prior negotiations. The written integration supersedes those prior discussions, because some of the ideas exchanged in the prior discussion might have been abandoned in the final written agreement. True, a court may admit parol evidence to help interpret a term that appears in the insurance contract, and the court likely will construe ambiguities against the drafter of the contract (the insurer) if the evidence relevant to interpretation is inconclusive; however, that won't help a consumer who is hurt by every conceivable interpretation of a harsh term. It's also true that parol evidence can be admitted to show that an insurance agent fraudulently induced the consumer to enter into the contract through misrepresentations of fact; however, the statements of the agent might not have been sufficiently specific and inaccurate to support such a claim. Indeed, the agent might have simply remained silent about a harsh term.

b. Modern Trend

The modern reality is that consumers often sign standard-form contracts of adhesion (ones that are not subject to negotiation) in circumstances in which we would not reasonably expect them to take the time and effort to read and understand every provision before signing. Instead, the consumer typically relies on the other party's agent to explain the general scope and purposes of the document, or the consumer signs without such guidance on the assumption that the document contains the usual kinds of terms that might fall within a normal range for such agreements. If the standard-form contract contains some term that would be greatly surprising to the average consumer, the consumer would expect the agent, form, or website to point it out and to specially invite the consumer to read it and understand it before signing. Otherwise, the written document might not comport with the consumer's reasonable expectations.

Under the "reasonable expectations" doctrine, a consumer can avoid the application of a surprising term in a standard-form contract in some circumstances. Specifically, the consumer would be permitted to use parol evidence to show the circumstances surrounding the making of the contract, including the stated purposes and goals of the contract. After all, it is a fiction to say that the parties discussed various potential terms and then abandoned some of them in the final written agreement; the language of a standard-form adhesion contract was never subject to negotiation, so the prior discussions consisted solely of explanations of the non-negotiable terms.

To take an extreme example, suppose that an insurance agent explained the general purposes, types of coverage, and policy limits for an automobile insurance contract, and then referred generally to a section of exclusions from coverage. The consumer signed the contract without reading any of the provisions. One of the provisions excluded all coverage for property damage and personal injury if the car involved in an accident had not been "maintained in every way strictly according to the schedule recommended in the owner's manual distributed with the automobile, regardless whether failures or delays in maintenance had any relationship to the accident in question." If this means that coverage for injuries resulting from faulty brakes would be excluded if the insured was slightly late in scheduling a recommended oil change, this exclusion would certainly be outside the expectations of a reasonable consumer who was informed of the general nature and purposes of the insurance contract. Under a reasonable expectations doctrine, these circumstances will justify admitting parol evidence of the circumstances surrounding the contract formation, to establish the reasonable expectations of the consumer.

Once the parol evidence rule is relaxed and the reasonable expectations of the consumer are established, courts vary in the ways in which they will give effect to the reasonable expectations. The Restatement takes the position that a term in a standard-form contract should simply drop out of the contract if the party presenting the contract had reason to believe that the other party would not have assented to the contract if he or she had known that it contained the term. Restatement (Second) of Contracts § 211(3) (1981).

This approach urges a fairly radical departure from traditional common-law principles. For standard-form adhesion contracts, this recommended rule appears to abandon the traditional view that a party is bound to the terms in a contract that she has signed, regardless of whether she read or understood all of the terms. Moreover, to the extent that this doctrine permits the surprised party to eliminate an express term from the final, signed contract, on the basis of reasonable expectations established through parol evidence, the doctrine represents a substantial departure from the parol evidence rule.

Because this doctrine departs so sharply from traditional rules, it is limited to standard-form adhesion contracts; it represents only a recent trend in the law; and it is generally applied cautiously by the few courts that have experimented with it. For example, in the next case, *Darner*, the Arizona Supreme Court boldly adopted the reasonable expectations doctrine and then cautiously used it only to bolster other grounds for avoiding a surprising term in an insurance contract, grounds such as estoppel and reformation for mistake.

Perhaps the *Darner* court applied the doctrine in a limited manner because the party seeking relief in *Darner* was not a consumer, but a commercial lessor of automobiles. A more compelling case for full application of the reasonable expectations doctrine is presented in cases with "unsuspecting consumers in weak bargaining positions faced with daunting, standardized contracts from large companies in superior bargaining positions." *Southwest Pet Products, Inc. v. Koch Industries, Inc.*, 107 F. Supp. 2d 1108, 112 (D. Ariz. 2000) (citing to other cases applying Arizona law), *rev'd on other grounds*, Nos. 00-15930, 00-16015, slip op. at 3 (9th Cir. 2002) (unpublished) (affirming the district court's ruling that the facts did not support application of the reasonable expectations doctrine).

Exercise 10.6 — Unconscionability Compared

To what extent does the reasonable expectations doctrine overlap with the unconscionability doctrine that we encountered in Chapter 9? If a standard-form adhesion contract contained a harsh or surprising term, wouldn't those facts tend to show a combination of procedural and substantive unconscionability? *See, e.g., Wofford v. M.J. Edwards & Sons Funeral Home, Inc.*, 490 S.W. 3d 800, 817 (Tenn. Ct. App. 2015) (in discussing unconscionability, positing that an adhesion contract is unenforceable if its terms exceed the reasonable expectations of an ordinary person). Why introduce a controversial new doctrine when litigants and courts can use the well-established and widely accepted unconscionability doctrine, coupled with the argument that the parol evidence rule should not apply to an unconscionability challenge? Is it likely that the reasonable expectations doctrine could provide relief in a case in which the facts do not support a claim for unconscionability?

c. The Reasonable Expectations Doctrine in Arizona

Darner Motor Sales, Inc. v. Universal Underwriters Ins. Co.

140 Ariz. 383, 682 P.2d 388 (1984) (In Banc)

Feldman, Justice.

....

FACTS

¶ 1 Darner Motors is in the automobile sales, service and leasing business.... Darner purchased a Universal "U-Drive policy" through Doxsee [Universal's agent]. This policy insured Darner Motors and the lessees of its cars for automobile liability risk. [After Darner was liable for a lessee's accident, a dispute arose over the scope of coverage of the Universal umbrella policy.]

....

¶ 2 After considerable discovery, Universal and Doxsee moved for summary judgment, contending that there was no genuine issue of fact and that they were entitled to judgment as a matter of law. The motion was granted and judgment entered against Darner Motors. The court of appeals affirmed; pointing out that Darner Motors had not claimed that the umbrella policy was ambiguous, the court held that the insured's failure to read the policy prevented recovery on any theory, even though the contents of the policy did not comport with the representations of the insurance agent and those same representations were a part of the reason that the insured failed to read the policy.

¶ 3 The court of appeals stated that under Arizona law an insured who had received a copy of an unambiguous policy could not "expand the insurer's liability beyond the terms of the ... policy issued...." We believe this statement is too broad, though we acknowledge that the law is, at best, confused on this subject. In an attempt to bring some clarity and logic to the question, we have reviewed our cases and will discuss each of the theories advanced by Darner Motors. Before doing so, however, we must consider the inherent nature of an insurance contract and of the issues presented by the fact situation before us.

CONTRACT LAW AND INSURANCE POLICIES

¶ 4 Since this is an appeal from summary judgment, we must view the facts in the light most favorable to the party against whom judgment was taken. *Gulf Insurance Co. v. Grisham*, 125 Ariz. 123, 124, 613 P.2d 283, 284 (1980). Taking the facts in that light, the question we must decide is whether the courts will enforce an unambiguous provision contrary to the negotiated agreement made by the parties because, after the insurer's representations of coverage, the insured failed to read the insurance contract which was in his possession. [footnote omitted] ...

¶ 5 If we continue to look at an insurance policy as a contract between the insured and insurer, the ... problem is simply the application of the parol evidence rule. The traditional view of the law of contracts is that a written agreement adopted by the parties will be viewed as an integrated contract which binds those parties to the terms expressed within the four corners of the agreement. Thus, the parties may not vary or expand the agreement by introducing parol evidence to show understandings or antecedent agreements which are in some way contrary to the terms of the contract. Restatement (Second) of Contracts § 215. This rule is applied with varying degrees of exactitude to insurance policies. Cases from this state reflect that attitude. [citations omitted].

¶ 6 When faced with harsh or illogical results, such as those produced by application of the parol evidence rule to most insurance contracts, the law usually reacts by recognizing exceptions which permit courts to avoid injustice. The ambiguity rule is, of course, one of those exceptions. Others, advanced with varying success, are the doctrines of waiver and estoppel. In our view, a better rationale is to be found by application of established principles of contract law. In so doing, however, we must remember that the usual insurance policy is a special kind of contract. It is largely adhesive; some terms are bargained for, but most terms consist of boilerplate, not bargained for, neither read nor understood by the buyer, and often not even fully understood by the selling agent. In contracts, as in other fields, the common law has evolved to accommodate the practices of the marketplace. Thus, in insurance law, as in other areas of contract law, the parol evidence rule has not been strictly applied to enforce an illusory "bargain" set forth in a standardized contract when that "bargain" was never really made and would, if applied, defeat the true agreement which was supposedly contained in the policy. *Sparks v. Republic National Life Insurance Co.*, 132 Ariz. at 537, 647 P.2d at 1135. *See also Zuckerman v. Transamerica Insurance Co.*, 133 Ariz. at 144, 650 P.2d at 446.

¶ 7 *Sparks* and *Zuckerman* reflect this court's attempt to bring some degree of logic and predictability into the field of insurance. What is needed, however, is recognition of a general rule of contract law. We believe that the current formulation of the Restatement (Second) of Contracts contains a workable resolution of the problem. The Restatement approach is basically a modification of the parol evidence rule when dealing with contracts containing boiler-plate provisions which are not negotiated, and often not even read by the parties.

> Standardized Agreements
>
> (1) Except as stated in Subsection (3), where a party to an agreement signs or otherwise manifests assent to a writing and has reason to believe that like writings are regularly used to embody terms of agreements of the same type, he adopts the writing as an integrated agreement with respect to the terms included in the writing.

> (2) Such a writing is interpreted wherever reasonable as treating alike all those similarly situated, without regard to their knowledge or understanding of the standard terms of the writing.
>
> (3) Where the other party has reason to believe that the party manifesting such assent would not do so if he knew that the writing contained a particular term, the term is not part of the agreement.

Restatement (Second) of Contracts § 211.

¶ 8 We believe that the comments to this section of the Restatement support the wisdom of the rule formulated. Comment (a) points out that standardization of agreements is essential

> to a system of mass production and distribution. Scarce and costly time and skill can be devoted to a class of transactions rather than to details of individual transactions.... Sales personnel and customers are freed from attention to numberless variations and can focus on meaningful choice among a limited number of significant features: transaction-type, style, quantity, price, or the like. Operations are simplified and costs reduced, to the advantage of all concerned.

¶ 9 Subsections (1) and (2) of § 211 reflect the reality of the marketplace. Thus, those who make use of a standardized form of agreement neither expect nor desire their customers "to understand or even to read the standard terms." *Id.* comment (b). On the other hand, customers "trust to the good faith of the party using the form [and] ... understand that they are assenting to the terms not read or not understood, subject to such limitations as the law may impose." *Id.* The limitations that the law may impose are that standard terms may be superseded by separately negotiated or added terms (§ 203), they are construed against the draftsman (§ 206), and they are subject to the overriding obligation of good faith (§ 205) and to the power of the court to refuse to enforce an unconscionable contract or term (§ 208). *Id.* comment (c). [footnote omitted].

¶ 10 Subsection (3) of § 211 is the Restatement's codification of and limitation on the "reasonable expectation" rule as applied to standardized agreements. The comment reads as follows:

> Although customers typically adhere to standardized agreements and are bound by them without even appearing to know the standard terms in detail, they are not bound to unknown terms which are beyond the range of reasonable expectation.... [An insured] who adheres to the [insurer's] standard terms does not assent to a term if the [insurer] has reason to believe that the [insured] would not have accepted the agreement if he had known that the agreement contained the particular term. Such a belief or assumption

> may be shown by the prior negotiations or inferred from the circumstances. Reason to believe may be inferred from the fact that the term is bizarre or oppressive, from the fact that it eviscerates the non-standard terms explicitly agreed to, or from the fact that it eliminates the dominant purpose of the transaction. The inference is reinforced if the adhering party never had an opportunity to read the term, or if it is illegible or otherwise hidden from view. This rule is closely related to the policy against unconscionable terms and the rule of interpretation against the draftsman.

Id. comment (f). We believe the analysis contained in the comments to the cited sections in the Restatement is a sensible rationale for interpretation of the usual type of insuring agreement. [In an omitted footnote, the court states that this analysis could apply to other kinds of standard-form consumer contracts as well.]

¶ 11 This treatment of insurance law is neither radical nor new. All that is new in the "changed" Restatement is the articulation of the rule. Some cases long ago recognized the underlying principles....

¶ 12 Thus, not all the cases have been decided on the "four corners" hypothesis. Missing has been the articulation or formulation of some general rule to explain results of many past cases and to provide a pragmatic, honest approach to the resolution of future disputes. Hopefully, the adoption of § 211 of the Restatement as the rule for standardized contracts will provide greater predictability and uniformity of results—a benefit to both the insurance industry and the consumer....

¶ 13 The general rule of contract interpretations adopted by the Restatement and based on Corbin's viewpoint is a modern view which takes into account the realities of present day commercial practice. *See*, Trakman, *Interpreting Contracts: A Common Law Dilemma*, 59 Canadian Bar Review 241 (1981). The rule which we adopt today for interpretation of standardized contracts recognizes modern commercial practice by business entities which use automated equipment to effect a large volume of transactions through use of standardized forms. It parallels the general rule which applies to all contracts by attempting to discover the intent of the parties, in so far as intent existed, and attempts to ascertain the real agreement so far as it was expressed or conveyed by implication. However, it recognizes that most provisions of standardized agreements are not the result of negotiation; often, neither customer nor salesperson are aware of the contract provisions. The rule adopted today recognizes reality and the needs of commerce; it allows businesses that use such forms to write their own contract. It charges the customer with knowledge that the contract being "purchased" is or contains a form applied to a vast number of transactions and includes terms which are unknown (or even unknowable); it binds the customer to such terms. However, the rule stops short of granting the drafter of the contract license to accomplish any result. It holds the drafter to good faith and terms which are conscionable; it requires drafting of provisions which can be understood if the customer does attempt to check on his rights; it does not give effect to boilerplate terms which are contrary to either the expressed agreement or the purpose of the transaction as known to the contracting parties. From the standpoint of the judicial system, the rule recognizes the true origin of standardized contract provisions, frees the courts from having to write a contract for the parties, and removes the temptation to create ambiguity or invent intent in order to reach a result.

¶ 14 The rule does not set a premium on failure to read. Those who negotiate their transactions will be held to the same rules as have previously obtained with regard to the duty to read. The rule which we adopt applies to contracts (or parts of contracts) made up of standardized forms which, because of the nature of the enterprise, customers will not be expected to read and over which they have no real power of negotiation. [footnote omitted].

¶ 15 To apply the old rule and interpret such contracts according to the imagined intent of the parties is to perpetuate a fiction which can do no more than bring the law into ridicule. To those troubled by the change in the law, we point out that the fundamental change occurred first in business practice. The change in legal analysis does no more than reflect the change in methods of doing business. To acknowledge standardized contracts for what they are—rules written by commercial enterprises—and to enforce them as written, subject to those reasonable limitations provided by law, is to recognize the reality of the marketplace as it now exists, while imposing just limits on business practice. These, we think, have always been the proper functions of contract law.

¶ 16 We turn, then, to the facts of this case. We have adopted a rule of law which, in proper circumstances, will relieve the insured from certain clauses of an agreement which he did not negotiate, probably did not read, and probably would not have understood had he read them. Does this case present a proper circumstance? If so, by what process is this to be accomplished? How is the restatement rule to be given effect?

EQUITABLE ESTOPPEL

....

¶ 17 The majority rule is considered to be "that the doctrines of waiver and estoppel are not available to bring within the coverage of an insurance policy risks not covered by its terms, or expressly excluded therefrom." *Annot.* 1 A.L.R.3d 1149, 1147 (1965)....

¶ 18 The "majority rule" is eroding. *See* 16C Appelman, *supra*, § 9166 at 153–58, § 9167 at 162–65 (1981). Given our view of contract theory and the policy considerations in *Sparks* and *Zuckerman*, there are strong reasons to recognize a rule which allows an insured to raise the issue of estoppel to establish coverage contrary to the limitations in the boiler-plate policy when the insurer's agent had represented the coverage as greater than the language found in the printed policy. The fact that the insured has not read the insurance policy "word for word" is not, as a matter of law, an absolute bar to his theory of estoppel. *See Northwestern National Ins. Co. v. Chambers*, 24 Ariz. 86, 94, 206 P. 1081, 1084 (1922) (disapproving of the rule of caveat emptor in insurance transactions). It is for the trier of fact to determine whether, under circumstances such as this, the appellant had a duty to read. [citations omitted].

¶ 19 The facts of the case at bench are within the exception to interpretation contained in subsection (3) to Restatement (Second) of Contracts, § 211. The coverage limits for lessees were separately negotiated. The standard boilerplate definition of the word "insured," excluding lessees, was not bargained for, not written by and not read by the parties. It need not be allowed to "undercut the dickered deal." We therefore adopt the rationale of the New Jersey Supreme Court in Harr [citations omitted] and recognize equitable estoppel as a device to prevent enforcement of those boiler-plate terms of the insurance contract which are more limited than the coverage expressly agreed upon by the parties. As applied to this case, the rule adopted means simply that if the fact finder determines that Darner and Doxsee did agree upon lessee's coverage in limits of 100/300, and if, by justifiably relying on Doxsee's assurances or for some other justifiable reason, Darner was unaware of the limitation in the umbrella policy, Universal would be estopped to assert the definitional exclusion which eliminates Darner's lessee from the class of persons insured. Thus, we do not limit the assertion of estoppel by the insured to cases in which an insurance policy has not been delivered prior to the loss....

REFORMATION

....

¶ 20 ... According to Universal, Darner was simply mistaken about the extent of coverage under his umbrella policy. Darner avers that, if so, this resulted from Doxsee's failure to properly explain the terms of the policy. There is no dispute that Darner told Doxsee he was concerned about having only 15/30 coverage for lessees. There is clearly a factual dispute regarding Doxsee's appreciation of Darner's concern. Arguably, Doxsee had knowledge of Darner's "mistaken" understanding of the agreement....

¶ 21 The same disputed material facts which demand trial on the merits regarding the estoppel remedy can also be marshaled under the reformation theory. Under the provisions of Restatement (Second) of Contracts, § 211 the form provisions at variance with the bargained deal or contrary to the dominant purpose of the transaction are "not part of the agreement." They should be eliminated, so that the bargains made will be realized. The written agreement may be reformed to state the true agreement. Accordingly, summary judgment on reformation was error....

¶ 22 For the foregoing reasons we vacate the decision of the court of appeals and reverse the trial court's summary judgment as to the counts of equitable estoppel, reformation of the contract, negligent misrepresentation and fraud. Because of this disposition of the substantive matters, the court of appeals' award of attorney's fees is vacated.

Gordon, V.C.J., and Hays, J., concur.

Cameron, Justice, specially concurring:

¶ 23 I concur in the majority decision and opinion and write only because I believe the dissent incorrectly characterizes the opinion and could lead to a misinterpretation of the holding of the majority.

¶ 24 First, I do not believe that the opinion adopts "virtually every minority position." The majority opinion adopts the rule of the Restatement (Second) of Contracts, § 211 (1981), and applies to form provisions the same general rules of contract law which we have recently applied to all contracts. *Smith v. Melson*, 135 Ariz. 119, 659 P.2d 1264 (1983).

....

Holohan, Chief Justice, dissenting:

¶ 25 With the stated purpose of reviewing the clarity and consistency of a large body of Arizona law dealing with insurance coverage, the court by this decision proceeds to overrule the major part of past precedent on the subject. Having overruled the past precedent, the court then proceeds to adopt virtually every minority position taken by any court or text writer in the United States....

¶ 26 The court's decision is based on the fact, at least as found by the majority, that people do not read their insurance policies, and, if they do, they don't understand them anyway. Apparently the group encompassed within the court's protection includes not only the ordinary citizen but also the successful sophisticated businessman such as the plaintiff in this case....

....

¶ 27 Under today's decision it appears that we have come full circle in the development of the law on contracts. Oral contracts were largely the method used in early times. To avoid the disputes which arose out of misunderstandings in oral agreements, the written contract became preferred. In modern commercial practice the written contract is not only preferred, it is essential. It is designed to eliminate disputes, and it is intended to establish some certitude in setting out the agreement of the parties. These concepts may be basic, but they are largely ignored in today's decision because an insured is not allowed to help write the contract. A debtor doesn't write the mortgage or deed of trust or most any other type of financing document, but until now the signing of the document bound the borrower to the terms of the agreement.

¶ 28 Whatever evil the majority is attempting to eliminate, the remedy advanced is like decapitation to cure dandruff—a cure that is far worse than the disease.

Three years after *Darner*, the Arizona Supreme Court explained *Darner* and synthesized it with other cases:

> … As a synthesis of the cases and authorities demonstrates, Arizona courts will not enforce even unambiguous boilerplate terms in standardized insurance contracts in a limited variety of situations:
>
> 1. Where the contract terms, although not ambiguous to the court, cannot be understood by the reasonably intelligent consumer who might check on his or her rights, the court will interpret them in light of the objective, reasonable expectations of the average insured (*see Bogart*, *supra*; *Wainscott v. Ossenkop*, 633 P.2d 237 (Alaska 1981) (application of "resident of same household" definition, while not technically ambiguous, defeats reasonable expectations of spouse));
>
> 2. Where the insured did not receive full and adequate notice of the term in question, and the provision is either unusual or unexpected, or one that emasculates apparent coverage (*see Zuckerman*, *supra*);
>
> 3. Where some activity which can be reasonably attributed to the insurer would create an objective impression of coverage in the mind of a reasonable insured (*see Sparks*, *supra*);
>
> 4. Where some activity reasonably attributable to the insurer has induced a particular insured reasonably to believe that he has coverage, although such coverage is expressly and unambiguously denied by the policy (*see Darner*, *supra*).

Gordinier v. Aetna Cas. & Sur. Co., 154 Ariz. 266, 272, 742 P.2d 277, 283 (1987). The Arizona Court of Appeals has applied the reasonable expectations doctrine to an arbitration clause challenged by purchasers of homes. *Harrington v. Pulte Home Corp.*, 211 Ariz. 241, 119 P.3d 1044 (Ct. App. 2005) (holding that the clause was not unconscionable and did not violate reasonable expectations). Should Arizona courts apply this novel doctrine beyond adhesion standard-form insurance or consumer contracts?

d. Relevance of the Reasonable Expectations Doctrine

Could the reasonable expectations doctrine provide a good solution to click-through agreements on the Internet, which link to contract terms that Internet users almost never take the time to read? If so, those who click through without reading the terms could assume that the linked terms are normal or reasonable for agreements of that type, and any bizarre terms that would be patently out of place for such an agreement would drop out of the contract, unless the website brought that term to the user's attention for specific assent.

Based on this and similar scenarios, the reasonable expectations doctrine provides an appealing solution to the disconnect between traditional contract doctrine and the reality that consumers simply do not read the standard terms of contracts into which they enter. *See, e.g.*, John E. Murray, *The Judicial Vision of Contract: The Constructed Circle of Assent and Unconscionability*, 52 Duq. L. Rev. 263, 273 (2014)

("The solution to the printed clause dilemma that would encompass most of the unconscionability cases is a general recognition of the reasonable expectations concept.").

With few exceptions, however, the reasonable expectations doctrine has failed to gain traction with the courts. *See* Eric A. Zacks, *The Restatement (Second) of Contracts §211: Unfulfilled Expectations and the Future of Modern Standardized Consumer Contracts*, 734 WM. & MARY BUS. L. REV. 733, 757-60 (2016). In most cases, consumers will be held to the terms presented to them and to which they voluntarily assented, unless they can strike down objectionable terms based on unconscionability or violation of public policy.

III. Summary Judgment and Parol Evidence

Because a full trial, not to mention appellate litigation, is expensive, summary judgment is an important stage for litigating contract claims or defenses. If a contract claim can survive summary judgment, earning the plaintiff a full trial on the facts, the defendant may be ready to settle the claim to avoid the cost of a full trial and the risk of being held liable for greater damages than the amount of a reasonable settlement offer. Of course, if the defendant secures summary judgment on one or more claims, it avoids both liability and trial on those claims.

A. The Role of the Parol Evidence Rule in Summary Judgment

The parol evidence rule plays an important role in a claimant's ability to successfully resist a defendant's motion for summary judgment based on interpretation of the contract. Under the most widely adopted civil procedure rule for summary judgment, the defendant can defeat a contract claim at that stage by showing that: (1) the parties do not genuinely dispute any facts that are material to the issue of contract interpretation and (2) the judge can interpret the contract in the defendant's favor as a matter of law. *See, e.g.*, FED. R. CIV. P. 56. If preliminary evidentiary showings by the parties—such as documents, sworn affidavits, or transcribed deposition testimony—establish that the parties do not dispute material facts, then no jury trial is necessary, and the judge can interpret the contract as a "matter of law." If the judge interprets the contract in a way that establishes full performance by the defendant, the claim for breach of contract is dismissed at that early stage.

Admissible parol evidence in the form of conflicting testimony about statements made prior to contract formation creates a question of fact that is not appropriately resolved by the judge at the summary judgment stage. Therefore, if the plaintiff can produce affidavits that represent admissible evidence creating a question of fact about contract interpretation, the claim will survive summary judgment and will be tried before a jury, or before the judge, with full presentation of the evidence—or the defendant will settle to avoid the costs of such litigation.

It follows that a contract claimant seeking to survive a motion for summary judgment will benefit from the admission of parol evidence, thus helping to create issues of fact for the jury. The claimant can pave the way for admission, for example, by showing that parol evidence is necessary to explain the meaning of written terms, or perhaps by showing that the evidence tends to establish the terms of a separate and independent contract that is not within the subject matter of the written integration.

Conversely, the party moving for dismissal of the contract claim on summary judgment will seek to invoke the parol evidence rule to exclude parol evidence, providing the opportunity to persuade the judge to interpret the contract in the moving party's favor as a matter of law without a full trial. Thus, the party moving for summary judgment will hope that the nonmoving claimant's parol evidence, supporting the claimant's interpretation, will be viewed as an inappropriate attempt to contradict the terms of the final written agreement. This burden on the moving party, of course, is more difficult to shoulder in Arizona, which largely rejects the plain meaning rule and which allows the judge to admit parol evidence tending to show that the parties attached an unusual meaning to a written term.

B. Finding a Material Dispute of Fact Regarding Contract Interpretation

In the following case, the buyer of a used automobile would be entitled to additional rights under a federal statue if the used car dealer was also a party to the service contract to which the buyer and the manufacturer clearly were parties. This case nicely illustrates that the buyer can escape summary judgment simply by showing a dispute of fact that requires a full trial on an issue of contract interpretation.

The court examined parol evidence in the form of offered testimony, and also in the terms of the service contract *application*, which should be viewed as parol evidence if it was not attached to the final service contract or otherwise joined to that contract. A traditional parol evidence rule might have excluded the buyer's parol evidence, because the final service contract, narrowly defined, arguably contained no evidence at all that the dealer was a party to that contract; consequently, terms in the application and testimony about oral statements showing that the dealer was a party to the service contract could be viewed as adding a new term to that contract or even contradicting its written terms. As we have seen, however, Arizona's liberal approach allows admission of parol evidence to show that the parties intended contracts terms to have an unusual meaning, thus permitting the buyer to establish a genuine issue of fact for trial.

Is the liberal approach necessary to reach a just and accurate interpretation of the parties' intentions? Or does the traditional plain-meaning rule advance efficiency by saving on litigation costs, increasing certainty, and encouraging parties to draft contract terms with an eye to their objective meaning in the general population? For an article advancing the latter argument, see Alan Schwartz & Robert E. Scott, *Contract Theory and the Limits of Contract Law*, 113 Yale L.J. 541, 568–90 (2003). What is your view after reading the next case?

Johnson v. Earnhardt's Gilbert Dodge, Inc.

212 Ariz. 381, 132 P.3d 825 (2006) (En Banc)
[paragraphs renumbered from the original]

Ryan, Justice.

¶1 [The court reviews implied warranties, as well as the limited ability of car dealers to disclaim the warranties, found under both the UCC and additional state statutes governing the sale of automobiles.]

¶2 The statutory ability to limit the implied warranty is subject to an important caveat. Under the [federal] Magnuson Moss Warranty Act..., if a used car dealer enters into a service contract with the purchaser at the time of sale or ninety days thereafter, no limitation on an implied warranty of merchantability is permitted. 15 U.S.C. §2308(a). Under such circumstances, the terms of the service contract govern the duration of the implied warranty of merchantability. *See id.* §2308(b).

¶3 We address ... whether the used car dealer here entered into a service contract with the purchaser....

I

¶4 In May 2000, Brenda Johnson purchased a used 1997 Kia Sportage "AS IS" from Earnhardt's Gilbert Dodge, Inc. ("Earnhardt"). The sales agreement expressly limited the implied warranty of merchantability to fifteen days or five hundred miles, whichever occurred first. In the same transaction, Johnson, through Earnhardt, applied to purchase a DaimlerChrysler service contract. Both Earnhardt's Finance Manager and Johnson signed the application. Johnson paid an amount in addition to the purchase price of the vehicle for the service contract. The service contract was subsequently issued to Johnson by DaimlerChrysler.

¶5 Johnson experienced mechanical problems with the Kia in June 2000, April 2001, and May 2001. These problems were not resolved to Johnson's satisfaction....

¶6 When Earnhardt refused to accept return of the vehicle, Johnson filed suit in superior court.... The superior court granted Earnhardt's motion for summary judgment, finding that Johnson had not entered into a service contract with Earnhardt.

¶7 Johnson appealed. A divided court of appeals reversed the trial court's grant of summary judgment....

II

....

¶8 Under Arizona's parol evidence rule, "[w]here ... an ambiguity exists on the face of [a] document or the language admits of differing interpretations, parol evidence is admissible to clarify and explain the document." *Standage Ventures, Inc. v. State*, 114 Ariz. 480, 482, 562 P.2d 360, 362 (1977); [other citation omitted]. The court may also admit evidence to determine the intention of the parties if "the judge ... finds that the contract language is 'reasonably susceptible' to the interpretation asserted by its proponent." *Taylor v. State Farm Mut. Auto. Ins. Co.,* 175 Ariz. 148, 154, 854 P.2d 1134, 1140 (1993).

C

¶ 9 ... We agree with the court of appeals that the superior court erred in granting summary judgment against Johnson....

¶ 10 In considering Earnhardt's motion for summary judgment, the superior court stated that Congress intended the phrase "enters into" to apply only to parties. Because it granted the motion, the court must therefore have implicitly concluded that Earnhardt was not a party to the service contract.

¶ 11 "Summary judgment is appropriate only if no genuine issues of material fact exist and the moving party is entitled to judgment as a matter of law." *Wells Fargo Bank v. Ariz. Laborers, Teamsters & Cement Masons Local No. 395 Pension Trust Fund,* 201 Ariz. 474, 482, ¶ 14, 38 P.3d 12, 20 (2002) (citing Ariz. R. Civ. P. 56(c); *Orme School v. Reeves,* 166 Ariz. 301, 309, 802 P.2d 1000, 1008 (1990))....

¶ 12 We agree that a service contract that merely obligates a third party to provide services has not been "entered into" by the dealer, even when sold by the dealer. We also assume that to be the case even if the third party (such as DaimlerChrysler) has contractual arrangements with the dealer requiring the dealer to provide the service. In this case, however, language in the documents comprising the transaction, combined with parol evidence, both supports and undermines the conclusion that Earnhardt itself entered into the service contract. This evidence raises a question of fact as to whether Earnhardt was a party to the service contract.

¶ 13 First, the service contract contains conflicting language about who was a party to the service contract. Some language in the contract supports the proposition that only Johnson and DaimlerChrysler are parties to the service contract. For example, the service contract defines "you, your" to mean "the Plan purchaser." It defines "we, us, our" as "DaimlerChrysler Corporation." And, the contract states that "[t]his Plan is a service contract between you and us" and "[w]e are solely responsible (liable) for fulfillment of the provisions of the Plan."

¶ 14 Other language, however, supports the proposition that Earnhardt is also a party to the service contract. The service contract application contained an express signed promise from Earnhardt that it would "provide service to [Johnson] in accordance with the provisions of the service contract DaimlerChrysler will issue to the purchaser." A reasonable consumer in Johnson's position could interpret this language as meaning that Earnhardt was obligated under the service contract to provide service to Johnson. *See Darner Motor Sales, Inc. v. Universal Underwriters Ins. Co.,* 140 Ariz. 383, 389–90, 682 P.2d 388, 394–95 (1984) (recognizing the doctrine of reasonable expectations in contract law).

¶ 15 Parol evidence also supports finding Earnhardt a party to the contract. In her response to Earnhardt's motion for summary judgment, Johnson provided an affidavit stating in relevant part:

> At the time I purchased this extended warranty/service contract, it was explained to me that I was purchasing Earnhardt's extended warranty and that Chrysler was the "administrator" of the warranty. The way it was explained to me was that I could always bring the Kia into Earnhardt's for repair at no charge but that I just had to call Chrysler first. I understood this to mean that the warranty I was buying from Earnhardt's was Chrysler and Earnhardt's joint extended warranty.
>
> It was never explained to me that I was buying a Chrysler warranty only. To the contrary, when I asked the question about extra warranty protection, I was told there were numerous extended warranties on the market but that I wanted to buy a "specific one," the one "we do with Chrysler."

¶ 16 Such parol evidence is admissible to determine the intention of the parties because the conflicting language in the documents comprising the transaction is reasonably susceptible to the interpretation that Earnhardt is a party to the contract. *See Taylor*, 175 Ariz. at 154, 854 P.2d at 1140.

....

¶ 17 The conflicting language of the service contract and the service contract application, along with the parol evidence, creates sufficient questions of fact for Johnson's case to survive summary judgment on the issue of whether Earnhardt entered into the service contract....

V

¶ 18 For the foregoing reasons, we vacate the decision of the court of appeals, reverse the superior court's grant of summary judgment, and remand this case to the superior court for further proceedings consistent with this opinion.

Exercise 10.7 — Examining a Motion for Summary Judgment

The chapter on motions for summary judgment in a legal writing text ends with a sample motion for summary judgment, addressing a contract claim as well as other claims. Charles R. Calleros & Kimberly Y.W. Holst, *Legal Method and Writing II: Trial and Appellate Advocacy, Contracts, and Correspondence* (8th ed. 2018). If your library has a copy of this book, glance through this sample motion and its supporting materials to get a flavor for the contents of this petition to a court.

IV. Implied Obligations

A. Implied Obligations and the Parol Evidence Rule

We have previously addressed both obligations implied in fact, which are ones intended by the parties even though not verbalized, and those implied in law, which are imposed by courts or legislatures as a matter of legal policy. Should either kind of implied obligation fall within the restrictions of the parol evidence rule?

1. Obligations Implied in Fact

Evidence of an implied-in-fact obligation presumably should be excluded by the parol evidence rule on the same ground on which express statements or agreements are excluded. The final written agreement of the party can modify, replace, or otherwise supersede earlier agreements on the same subject matter, and that should include prior agreements implied in fact as well as prior express agreements.

Remember the implication in fact of an obligation on Wood's part to use reasonable efforts to place endorsements in *Wood v. Lucy, Lady Duff-Gordon*, in Chapter 3? We can now fully appreciate the manner in which Justice Cardozo found the implied duty: he limited his search to the face of the contract itself. By inferring the implied obligation from other provisions of the written contract, Justice Cardozo avoided offending the parol evidence rule, which would have excluded parol evidence admitted for the purpose of supplementing a completely integrated agreement.

2. Obligations Implied in Law

In Chapter 4, we encountered a type of implied-in-law obligation: the quasi-contractual obligation to grant restitution, to avoid unjust enrichment. We have referred in passing to the obligation of good faith, implied in every contract, which is discussed further below. Also discussed below are warranty obligations that are implied in law, most notably under the UCC for sales of goods.

The parol evidence rule has no application to implied-in-law obligations. Implied-in-law obligations are not prior agreements that are superseded by the final agreement of the parties. They are obligations added to the final written agreement (and to any previous agreements) as a matter of legal policy.

B. Implied Obligation of Good Faith

1. Introduction

Exercise 8.6 in Chapter 8 summarizes the obligation of good faith that is imposed by the UCC for sales of goods and nearly universally implied by the common law for other transactions. This implied obligation is a duty to exercise good faith in the performance and enforcement of a contract. U.C.C. § 1-304 (2001); RESTATEMENT (SECOND) OF CONTRACTS § 205 (1981).

As we learned in Chapter 8, it does not apply to contract formation, or at least not to the extent of imposing a general duty of full disclosure during negotiations. Even when applied to the parties' performance of a contract, the duty of good faith is limited by the recognition that each party must live with risks allocated to it by the contract. Moreover, depending on the state and context, it normally does not constitute a free-standing basis for a claim of breach of contract; instead, it helps to provide standards for performing obligations or invoking rights reflected in the terms of the parties' agreement. In so doing, it can help to establish a party's breach of an agreed term.

The Restatement's formulation of the duty suggests both a subjective and objective component. It summarizes the common law as imposing a duty of both: (1) "good faith," which is typically associated with subjective honesty, and (2) "fair dealing," which suggests a more objective standard of fair play. RESTATEMENT (SECOND) OF CONTRACTS § 205 (1981).

The UCC more clearly embraces both subjective and objective components, because it defines good faith as both "honesty in fact" and reasonableness, U.C.C. § 1-201(20) (2001) (general definition of "good faith"); U.C.C. § 2-103(1)(b) (2011) (merchant's good faith). In its enactment of Article 1 of the UCC, however, the Arizona legislature omitted the requirement of objective reasonableness for non-merchants, ARIZ. REV. STAT. ANN. § 47-1201(20) (2005), leaving only a good-faith duty of "honesty in fact" for non-merchants.

These very general standards, however, provide little useful guidance in specific cases. Some scholarly commentators have proposed approaches to finding bad faith or even specific categories of bad faith, but these recommendations often differ sharply. *See, e.g.*, Randy E. Barnett, *The Richness of Contract Law: An Analysis and Critique of* CONTEMPORARY THEORIES OF CONTRACT LAW, *by Robert A. Hillman*, 97 MICH. L. REV. 1413, 1413–17 (1999) (summarizing debate between Professors Robert Summers and Steve Burton about the content of good faith).

The following excerpt is from a Supreme Court decision that mainly addressed preemption of state law by federal law. Along the way, however, the Court had occasion to discuss the vagueness of the doctrine of good faith and the question whether it is implied in fact and thus subject to express exclusion by the parties, or is imposed by law without possibility of exclusion.

Northwest, Inc. v. Ginsberg

134 S. Ct. 1422 (2014)

¶ 1 While most States recognize some form of the good faith and fair dealing doctrine, it does not appear that there is any uniform understanding of the doctrine's precise meaning. "[T]he concept of good faith in the performance of contracts 'is a phrase without general meaning (or meanings) of its own.'" *Tymshare, Inc. v. Covell*, 727 F. 2d 1145, 1152 (CADC 1984) (Scalia, J.) (quoting Summers, "Good Faith" in *General Contract Law and the Sales Provisions of the Uniform Commercial Code*, 54 Va. L. Rev. 195, 201 (1968)); *see also* Burton, *Breach of Contract and the Common Law Duty to Perform in Good Faith*, 94 Harv. L. Rev. 369, 371 (1980). Of particular importance here, while some States are said to use the doctrine "to effectuate the intentions of parties or to protect their reasonable expectations," *ibid.*, other States clearly employ the doctrine to ensure that a party does not "'violate community standards of decency, fairness, or reasonableness.'" *Universal Drilling Co., LLC v. R & R Rig Service, LLC*, 2012 WY 31, 37, 271 P. 3d 987, 999; [five additional citations omitted] Restatement (Second) of Contracts §205, Comment a (1979). *See also* Summers, *The General Duty of Good Faith—Its Recognition and Conceptualization*, 67 Cornell L. Rev. 810, 812 (1982).

¶2 Whatever may be the case under the law of other jurisdictions, it seems clear that under Minnesota law, which is controlling here, ... the implied covenant must be regarded as a state-imposed obligation. Respondent concedes that under Minnesota law parties cannot contract out of the covenant. *See* Tr. of Oral Arg. 33–34; *see also In re Hennepin Cty. 1986 Recycling Bond Litigation*, 540 N.W. 2d 292, 502 (Minn. 1995); [two further citations omitted]. And as a leading commentator has explained, a State's "unwillingness to allow people to disclaim the obligation of good faith ... shows that the obligation cannot be implied, but is law imposed." 3A A. Corbin, Corbin on Contracts §654A, p. 88 (L. Cunningham & A. Jacobsen eds. Supp. 1994).... Minnesota law holds that the implied covenant applies to "every contract," *In re Hennepin Cty., supra*, at 502, with the notable exception of employment contracts. *Hunt v. IBM Mid America Employees Fed. Credit Union*, 384 N. W. 2d 853, 857–858 (Minn. 1986). The exception for employment contracts is based, in significant part, on "policy reasons," *id.*, at 858.... When the application of the implied covenant depends on state policy, a breach of implied covenant claim cannot be viewed as simply an attempt to vindicate the parties' implicit understanding of the contract.

Although the full parameters of the implied duty of good faith are uncertain, a few applications or exclusions are well established, at least in some jurisdictions. One exclusion is mentioned in passing in *Northwest*, for which it cites to *Hunt*: Courts generally do not imply a duty of good faith to limit an employer's grounds for terminating an employment contract. In most jurisdictions, an employer's freedom to discharge an employee may be restricted by the terms of the parties' contract, expressed or implied in fact, but—absent exceptional circumstances—generally not by a duty of good faith implied in law. Nonetheless, the implied duty of good faith should apply to other terms of the employment contract. *See, e.g., Nolan v. Control Data Corp.*, 243 N.J. Super. 420, 429, 579 A.2d 1252, 1257 (App. Div. 1990). Texas courts appear to be more generally cautious and selective in implying a duty of good faith and fair dealing. *Barrow-Shaver Resources Co. v. Carrizo Oil & Gas, Inc.*, No.

17-0332, 2019 WL 2668317, **12–16 (June 28, 2019) (unpublished but citing to numerous published decisions).

Another case illustrates unusual circumstances justifying a very narrow exception to the duty of good faith. *Moran v. Erk*, 11 N.Y.3d 452, 901 N.E.2d 187 (2008). In *Moran*, the court refused to recognize an implied limitation of good faith in a clause permitting either party to terminate a real estate contract on the advice of that party's attorney, because enforcing the good-faith obligation would require an inquiry that would intrude on attorney-client confidentiality.

In yet another context the implied duty of good faith is well established and clearly defined in many jurisdictions: An insurer has a duty to act in good faith to respond to insurance claims in a manner that provides the security for which the insured bargained. Indeed, some states find that an insurer's breach of this duty constitutes a tort and not just a breach of the insurance contract.

The following excerpt from a judicial opinion summarizes an insurer's duty to use good faith in processing a claim from the insured:

> In every insurance contract is an implied covenant of good faith and fair dealing, the breach of which is a tort. *Deese v. State Farm Mut. Auto. Ins. Co.*, 172 Ariz. 504, 506, 838 P.2d 1265, 1267 (1992). The covenant of good faith and fair dealing requires an insurer "to play fairly with its insured." *Zilisch v. State Farm Mut. Auto. Ins. Co.*, 196 Ariz. 234, 237, ¶ 20, 995 P.2d 276, 279 (2000) (quoting *Rawlings v. Apodaca*, 151 Ariz. 149, 154, 726 P.2d 565, 570 (1986)). The insurer owes the insured "some duties of a fiduciary nature," including "[e]qual consideration, fairness and honesty." *Zilisch*, 196 Ariz. at 237, ¶ 20, 995 P.2d at 279 (quoting *Rawlings*, 151 Ariz. at 155,726 P.2d at 571). When there is a coverage question, an insurance company breaches its duty of good faith and fair dealing if it "intentionally denies, fails to process or pay a claim without a reasonable basis." *Zilisch*, 196 Ariz. at 237, ¶ 20, 995 P.2d at 279 (quoting *Noble v. Nat'l Am. Life Ins. Co.*, 128 Ariz. 188, 190, 624 P.2d 866, 868 (1981)). Further,
>
> > The carrier has an obligation to immediately conduct an adequate investigation, act reasonably in evaluating the claim, and act promptly in paying a legitimate claim. It should do nothing that jeopardizes the insured's security under the policy. It should not force an insured to go through needless adversarial hoops to achieve its rights under the policy. It cannot lowball claims or delay claims hoping that the insured will settle for less. Equal consideration of the insured requires more than that.
>
> *Zilisch*, 196 Ariz. at 238, ¶ 21, 995 P.2d at 280.

Lennar Corp. v. Transamerica Ins. Co., 227 Ariz. 238, 256 P.3d 635 (Ct. App. 2011).

Many states also recognize a breach of the duty of good faith, and additionally view it as a tort, if an insurer willfully fails to settle a third-party's claim in a reasonable manner, thus exposing the insured to liability to the third party exceeding the insured's policy limits. *E.g.*, *Comunale v. Traders & General Ins. Co.*, 328 P.2d 198 (Cal. 1958).

One court explained the nature of the insurer's duty, both in the context of third-party claims and first-party claims from the insured:

> ... We [have] held that the insurer, when determining whether to settle a claim, must give at least as much consideration to the welfare of its insured as it gives to its own interests. The governing standard is whether a prudent insurer would have accepted the settlement offer if it alone were to be liable for the entire judgment. [citation omitted] The standard is premised on the insurer's obligation to protect the insured's interests in defending the latter against claims by an injured third party.
>
> The implied covenant imposes obligations not only as to claims by a third party but also as to those by the insured.... For the insurer to fulfill its obligation not to impair the right of the insured to receive the benefits of the agreement, it again must give at least as much consideration to the latter's interests as it does to its own.

Egan v. Mutual of Omaha Ins. Co., 24 Cal. 3d 809, 818–19, 620 P.2d 141, 145 (1979) (citations omitted), *cert. denied*, 445 U.S. 912 (1980); *see also Rawlings v. Apodaca*, 151 Ariz. 149, 156–57, 726 P.2d 565, 572–73 (1986) (the insurer must give equal consideration to the insured's legitimate interests, so the insurer breaches the duty when it deprives the insured of the very security for which it contracted, such as when the insurer resists a claim that is not fairly debatable).

Outside the context of insurance contracts, however, the standards for good faith remain fairly vague and flexible. The best we can do is to examine specific applications of the doctrine in various contexts. The next two cases provide that opportunity.

2. Opportunistic Behavior in the Context of a Contractual Relationship

The following opinion by Judge Richard Posner explains why the duty of good faith operates robustly in the performance of a contract, after the parties have established a contractual relationship, but not during contract formation. The opinion also does much to further our understanding of the content of the duty, even if a concise definition remains elusive.

Judge Posner is famous for his economic analysis of the law. Can you detect the influence of "law and economics" in his reasoning? Do you agree that the obligation of good faith should potentially extend to protect a sophisticated party from its own failure to consult its contract years after signing it? Should exploitation of the other party's inattention about its contract rights and obligations be viewed as bad faith?

Market Street Assoc. Ltd. v. Frey

941 F.2d 588 (7th Cir. 1991)

Posner, Circuit Judge.

¶ 1 Market Street Associates Limited Partnership and its general partner appeal from a judgment for the defendants, General Electric Pension Trust and its trustees, entered upon cross-motions for summary judgment in a diversity suit that pivots on the doctrine of "good faith" performance of a contract. *Cf.* Robert Summers, "*Good Faith" in General Contract Law and the Sales Provisions of the Uniform Commercial Code*, 54 Va. L. Rev. 195, 232–43 (1968). Wisconsin law applies common law rather than Uniform Commercial Code, because the contract is for land rather than for goods, UCC § 2-102; Wis. Stat. § 402.102, and because it is a lease rather than a sale and Wisconsin has not adopted UCC art. 2A, which governs leases....

....

¶ 2 [Market Street Associates, as assignee from the original lessee, was leasing commercial property from the General Electric Pension Trust under a 25-year lease that commenced in 1968. In 1988, Market Street Associates wished to purchase the property, to facilitate securing financing for needed improvements. It inquired about purchasing the property, but it rejected the pension trust's asking price of $3,000,000 as far too high. Market Streets Associates then noticed that section 34 of the lease would permit it to purchase the property at 1968 market prices plus 6% per annum if Market Streets Associates requested financing from the pension trust for improvements on the property and if negotiations over financing failed. Market Street Associates requested financing for needed improvements, but the pension trust summarily denied the request because it did not consider investments of less than $7,000,000. Market Streets Associates then invoked section 34 of the lease to demand sale of the property to it at much less than its 1988 market price. The trial court granted summary judgment for the pension trust, partly on the ground that Market Streets Associates breached its implied duty of good faith by the manner in which it took advantage of section 34, without reminding the pension trust of the terms of that section.]

....

¶ 3 ... So we must consider the meaning of the contract duty of "good faith." The Wisconsin cases are cryptic as to its meaning though emphatic about its existence, so we must cast our net wider.... The particular confusion to which the vaguely moralistic overtones of "good faith" give rise is the belief that every contract establishes a fiduciary relationship. A fiduciary is required to treat his principal as if the principal were he, and therefore he may not take advantage of the principal's incapacity, ignorance, inexperience, or even naïveté....

¶ 4 But it is unlikely that Wisconsin wishes, in the name of good faith, to make every contract signatory his brother's keeper, especially when the brother is the immense and sophisticated General Electric Pension Trust, whose lofty indifference to small (= < $7 million) transactions is the signifier of its grandeur. In fact the law contemplates that people frequently will take advantage of the ignorance of those with whom they contract, without thereby incurring liability. Restatement (Second) of Contracts § 161, comment d. The duty of honesty, of good faith even expansively conceived, is not a duty of candor. You can make a binding contract to purchase something you know your seller undervalues. *Laidlaw v. Organ*, 15 U.S. (2 Wheat.) 178, 181 n. 2 ... (1817); [three citations omitted]; Anthony T. Kronman, *Mistake, Disclosure, Information, and the Law of Contracts*, 7 J. Legal Stud. 1 (1978). That of course is a question about formation, not performance, and the particular duty of good faith under examination here relates to the latter rather than to the former. But even after you have signed a contract, you are not obliged to become an altruist toward the other party and relax the terms if he gets into trouble in performing his side of the bargain. *Kham & Nate's Shoes No. 2, Inc. v. First Bank*, 908 F.2d 1351, 1357 (7th Cir. 1990). Otherwise mere difficulty of performance would excuse a contracting party—which it does not. [citations omitted].

¶ 5 But it is one thing to say that you can exploit your superior knowledge of the market—for if you cannot, you will not be able to recoup the investment you made in obtaining that knowledge—or that you are not required to spend money bailing out a contract partner who has gotten into trouble. It is another thing to say that you can take deliberate advantage of an oversight by your contract partner concerning his rights under the contract. Such taking advantage is not the exploitation of superior knowledge or the avoidance of unbargained-for expense; it is sharp dealing. Like theft, it has no social product, and also like theft it induces costly defensive expenditures, in the form of overelaborate disclaimers or investigations into the trustworthiness of a prospective contract partner, just as the prospect of theft induces expenditures on locks. *See generally* Steven J. Burton, *Breach of Contract and the Common Law Duty to Perform in Good Faith*, 94 Harv. L. Rev. 369, 393 (1980).

¶ 6 ... Before the contract is signed, the parties confront each other with a natural wariness. Neither expects the other to be particularly forthcoming, and therefore there is no deception when one is not. Afterwards the situation is different. The parties are now in a cooperative relationship the costs of which will be considerably reduced by a measure of trust. So each lowers his guard a bit, and now silence is more apt to be deceptive. [citation omitted]

¶ 7 Moreover, this is a contract case rather than a tort case, and conduct that might not rise to the level of fraud may nonetheless violate the duty of good faith in dealing with one's contractual partners and thereby give rise to a remedy under contract law. *Burton, supra*, at 372 n. 17. This duty is, as it were, halfway between a fiduciary duty (the duty of utmost good faith) and the duty merely to refrain from active fraud.... It would be quixotic as well as presumptuous for judges to undertake through contract law to raise the ethical standards of the nation's business people. The concept of the duty of good faith like the concept of fiduciary duty is a stab at approximating the terms the parties would have negotiated had they foreseen the circumstances that have given rise to their dispute. The parties want to minimize the costs of performance. To the extent that a doctrine of good faith designed to do this by reducing defensive expenditures is a reasonable measure to this end, interpolating it into the contract advances the parties' joint goal.

¶ 8 It is true that an essential function of contracts is to allocate risk, and would be defeated if courts treated the materializing of a bargained-over, allocated risk as a misfortune the burden of which is required to be shared between the parties (as it might be within a family, for example) rather than borne entirely by the party to whom the risk had been allocated by mutual agreement. But contracts do not just allocate risk. They also (or some of them) set in motion a cooperative enterprise, which may to some extent place one party at the other's mercy. "The parties to a contract are embarked on a cooperative venture, and a minimum of cooperativeness in the event unforeseen problems arise at the performance stage is required even if not an explicit duty of the contract." *AMPAT/Midwest, Inc. v. Illinois Tool Works, Inc., supra*, 896 F.2d at 1041. The office of the doctrine of good faith is to forbid the kinds of opportunistic behavior that a mutually dependent, cooperative relationship might enable in the absence of rule. " 'Good faith' is a compact reference to an implied undertaking not to take opportunistic advantage in a way that could not have been contemplated at the time of drafting, and which therefore was not resolved explicitly by the parties." *Kham & Nate's Shoes No. 2, Inc. v. First Bank, supra*, 908 F.2d at 1357. The contractual duty of good faith is thus not some newfangled bit of welfare-state paternalism or [citation omitted] the sediment of an altruistic strain in contract law, and we are therefore not surprised to find the essentials of the modern doctrine well established in nineteenth-century cases, a few examples being *Bush v. Marshall*, 47 U.S. (6 How.) 284, 291 ... (1848); [three more citations from 1868 to 1886 are omitted].

¶ 9 The emphasis we are placing on postcontractual versus precontractual conduct helps explain the pattern that is observed when the duty of contractual good faith is considered in all its variety.... At the formation of the contract the parties are dealing in present realities; performance still lies in the future. As performance unfolds, circumstances change, often unforeseeably; the explicit terms of the contract become progressively less apt to the governance of the parties' relationship; and the role of implied conditions—and with it the scope and bite of the good-faith doctrine—grows....

¶ 10 ... The dispositive question in the present case is simply whether Market Street Associates tried to trick the pension trust and succeeded in doing so. If it did, this would be the type of opportunistic behavior in an ongoing contractual relationship that would violate the duty of good faith performance however the duty is formulated. There is much common sense in Judge Reynolds' conclusion that Market Street Associates did just that. The situation as he saw it was as follows. Market Street Associates didn't want financing from the pension trust (initially it had looked elsewhere, remember), and when it learned it couldn't get the financing without owning the property, it decided to try to buy the property. But the pension trust set a stiff price, so Orenstein decided to trick the pension trust into selling at the bargain price fixed in paragraph 34 by requesting financing and hoping that the pension trust would turn the request down without noticing the paragraph. His preliminary dealings with the pension trust made this hope a realistic one by revealing a sluggish and hidebound bureaucracy unlikely to have retained in its brontosaurus's memory, or to be able at short notice to retrieve, the details of a small lease made twenty years earlier. So by requesting financing without mentioning the lease, Market Street Associates might well precipitate a refusal before the pension trust woke up to paragraph 34. It is true that Orenstein's second letter requested financing "pursuant to the lease." But when the next day he received a reply to his first letter indicating that the pension trust was indeed oblivious to paragraph 34, his response was to send a lulling letter designed to convince the pension trust that the matter was closed and could be forgotten. The stage was set for his thunderbolt: the notification the next month that Market Street Associates was taking up the option in paragraph 34. Only then did the pension trust look up the lease and discover that it had been had.

¶ 11 The only problem with this recital is that it construes the facts as favorably to the pension trust as the record will permit, and that of course is not the right standard for summary judgment. The facts must be construed as favorably to the nonmoving party, to Market Street Associates, as the record permits.... When that is done, a different picture emerges....

¶ 12 On this [alternative] interpretation of the facts there was no bad faith on the part of Market Street Associates. It acted honestly, reasonably, without ulterior motive, in the face of circumstances as they actually and reasonably appeared to it. The fault was the pension trust's incredible inattention, which misled Market Street Associates into believing that the pension trust had no interest in financing the improvements regardless of the purchase option. We do not usually excuse contracting parties from failing to read and understand the contents of their contract; and in the end what this case comes down to—or so at least it can be strongly argued—is that an immensely sophisticated enterprise simply failed to read the contract. On the other hand, such enterprises make mistakes just like the rest of us, and deliberately to take advantage of your contracting partner's mistake during the performance stage (for we are not talking about taking advantage of superior knowledge at the formation stage) is a breach of good faith. To be able to correct your contract partner's mistake at zero cost to yourself, and decide not to do so, is a species of opportunistic behavior that the parties would have expressly forbidden in the contract had they foreseen it. The immensely long term of the lease amplified the possibility of errors but did not license either party to take advantage of them.

¶ 13 The district judge jumped the gun in choosing between these alternative characterizations. The essential issue bearing on Market Street Associates' good faith was Orenstein's state of mind, a type of inquiry that ordinarily cannot be concluded on summary judgment, and could not be here.... To decide what Orenstein believed, a trial is necessary....

[Therefore, the trial court erred in granting summary judgment for the pension trust, and the case is reversed and remanded for trial.]

3. *Refraining from Impeding the Other Party's Realization of the Benefits of the Contract, even when Consistent with Express Contract Terms*

Although the implied obligation of good faith is difficult to define comprehensively and with specificity, one generalization about the obligation is fairly safe to state: A party violates the duty of good faith when it takes actions that frustrate the other party's ability to realize the fruits of the contract, for which it bargained.

This branch of the obligation of good faith includes the implied duty of cooperation and nonhindrance. That duty requires each party to avoid hindering the other party in its performance, and in some cases requires each party to affirmatively facilitate the other party's performance. We will study duties of cooperation and nonhindrance in Chapter 11.

The scope of such a duty can vary with the nature of the contract and the degree to which the express terms of the contract grant one party freedom to act. A difficult issue arises, for example, when the contract expressly permits one party to exercise discretion over a matter that affects the other party's opportunities to enjoy the full benefits of the contract. If the contract does not expressly limit that discretion, to what extent should the implied duty of good faith restrict it?

The North Dakota Supreme Court addressed this question in a case in which the UCC statutorily supplied a duty of good faith and fair dealing:

> In this case, the contracts did not provide a specific date for the rejection of the potatoes, but accorded significant discretion to Cavendish to reject them "at any time." When one party to a contract "has the power to make a discretionary decision without defined standards," the implied covenant of good faith and fair dealing applies to protect the parties' reasonable expectations. *Speedway SuperAmerica, LLC v. Tropic Enters., Inc.*, 966 So. 2d 1, 3 (Fla. Dist. Ct. App. 2007).... "[U]nder an agreement that appears by word or silence to invest one party with a degree of discretion in performance sufficient to deprive another party of a substantial proportion of the agreement's value, the parties' intent to be bound by an enforceable contract raises an implied obligation of good faith to observe reasonable limits in exercising that discretion, consistent with the parties' purpose or purposes in contracting." *Centronics Corp. v. Genicom Corp.*, 562 A.2d 187, 193 (N.H. 1989).

Cavendish Farms, Inc., v. Mathiason Farms, Inc., 2010 N.D. 236 ¶ 14, 792 N.W. 2d 500, 506 ¶ 14, (2010).

Of course, if the agreement expressly defines the scope of a right or power to a party in specific terms, the implied duty of good faith ordinarily cannot negate that express term. *Carma Developers (California), Inc., v. Marathon Development California, Inc.*, 2 Cal. 4th 342, 372–73, 826 P.2d 710, 726–28 (1992). Perhaps a party could challenge the express term on grounds of unconscionability, violation of public policy, or other infirmity. The implied duty of good faith, however, is better suited to curbing behavior that the parties have addressed in only general terms or have not addressed at all. By filling the gap, the implied obligation of good faith relieves the parties of the cost of anticipating and drafting against every conceivable instance of abusive behavior.

County of La Paz v. Yakima Compost Co., Inc.

224 Ariz. 590, 233 P.3d 1169 (Ct. App. 2010)
[paragraph numbers changed from the original]

Timmer, Chief Judge.

¶ 1 This breach-of-contract action arises from performance of a contract between the County of La Paz (the "County") and Yakima Compost Company, Inc. and Yakima Company, Inc. (collectively "Yakima") in which Yakima agreed to receive and process sewer sludge on county land for twenty-five years. The County appeals from a $9.2 million judgment entered after a jury returned a verdict in the form of special interrogatories in favor of Yakima.... For the reasons that follow, we affirm.

BACKGROUND

¶ 2 On September 17, 2002, the County and Yakima executed the Regional Sludge Drying Facility Operation Agreement (the "Agreement"), which permitted Yakima to receive sewage sludge from wastewater treatment facilities located inside and outside Arizona and process it by solar drying on county land for an initial period of twenty-five years. The Agreement recited that the sludge drying facility would be located temporarily on a county landfill, the facility would be relocated within three years, and the County was "diligently pursuing acquisition of a permanent site." Among other provisions, the Agreement required Yakima to provide a closure plan to the County for approval prior to operation, furnish the County a $1 million performance bond (the "Bond") within sixty days, and comply with all local, state, and federal environmental laws.

....

DISCUSSION

....

¶ 3 The County next argues the trial court erred by denying its motion for JMOL because Yakima breached the Agreement by failing to timely submit the Bond, closure plan, and aquifer permit, thereby permitting the County to terminate the Agreement and negating the counterclaim. Yakima responds, and the trial court agreed, that whether Yakima breached the Agreement was an issue of fact for the jury, and we should defer to the jury's finding. [Evidence showed that the County delayed approval of Yakima's closure plan, which in turn prevented Yakima from securing the required bond. Although the contract did not expressly limit the County's discretion in determining whether to approve Yakima's closure plan, Yakima argues that the implied duty of good faith and fair dealing should impose some limitation on that discretion].

....

¶ 4 The law implies a covenant of good faith and fair dealing in every contract. *Wells Fargo* Bank *v. Ariz. Laborers, Teamsters & Cement Masons Local No. 395 Pension Trust Fund*, 201 Ariz. 474, 490, ¶ 59, 38 P.3d 12, 28 (2002). Among other things, a party breaches this covenant by exercising discretion afforded under the contract for a reason beyond the risks assumed by the other party. *Id.* at 492, ¶ 66, 38 P.3d at 30 (citations omitted). Whether a party breached the covenant is a question of fact for the jury. *Id.* at 493, ¶¶ 69–70, 38 P.3d at 31.

¶ 5 Citing *Southwest Savings and Loan Association v. SunAmp Systems, Inc.*, 172 Ariz. 553, 558–59, 838 P.2d 1314, 1319–20 (App. 1992), the County contends its actions could not constitute a breach of the covenant of good faith and fair dealing because the Agreement permitted the County to seek termination in certain circumstances, and the County did not act "for a reason beyond the risks" that Yakima assumed. In *Southwest Savings*, we considered whether a lender acted in bad faith when it froze and later terminated a borrower's line of credit upon realizing the primary guarantor had invalidly bound community assets. *Id.* at 554–55, 838 P.2d at 1315–16. Recognizing that our supreme court had found "in a variety of contexts that a contracting party may exercise a retained contractual power in bad faith," we characterized the issue as:

> [W]hether the jury might reasonably have found that [the lender] wrongfully exercised [its contractual] power "for a reason beyond the risks" that [the borrower] assumed in its loan agreement or for a reason inconsistent with [the borrower's] "justified expectations."

Id. at 559, 838 P.2d at 1320 (citation omitted). Thereafter, we noted the evidence was undisputed that the lender acted solely out of a financial interest, not "out of spite, ill will, or any other non-business purpose." *Id.* Thus, we concluded the lender did not act contrary to the borrower's justified expectations. *Id.* at 561, 838 P.2d at 1322. Finding the jury's verdict was not supported by sufficient evidence, we remanded the case for entry of JMOL in favor of the lender on the borrower's bad faith claim. *Id.* at 563, 838 P.2d at 1324.

¶ 6 Unlike the situation in Southwest Savings, the parties here disputed whether the County exercised its discretion for reasons beyond the risks assumed by Yakima. Although Yakima assumed the risk the County would act to further its legitimate interests under the Agreement, sufficient evidence exists to support a conclusion that the County exercised its discretion merely to force a termination of the Agreement due to a change of heart regarding the wisdom of the Agreement—a risk not assumed by Yakima. For example, the jury could have concluded that the County delayed its approval of the closure plan to prevent Yakima from timely posting the Bond, thereby placing Yakima in breach of the Agreement. First, evidence was presented at trial demonstrating the County's remorse about the Agreement and a desire to be free of it. Mark Patterson, an unsuccessful candidate for the La Paz County Board of Supervisors, testified that Supervisor Gene Fisher told him in 2004, "Mr. Willett [Yakima's president] was nothing more than a shit broker and that the County was going to do anything they could to get out of the contract." According to Patterson, Fisher "stated that Mr. Willett was not a businessman that he wanted in La Paz County." Patterson also testified that Fisher "indicated that Supervisor Edey was on [b]oard with him against [Yakima] ... [but] that he reversed his decision and voted for [the Agreement]." Supervisor Howe sent the trial court judge a letter dated May 27, 2003 stating that the situation "has been highly politicized and objectively compromised by County Officials and staff" and that the delay in posting the Bond was attributable to the County's failure to timely approve a closure plan. Given this record, we conclude the jury could have reasonably found the County wrongfully exercised its contractual power for "a reason beyond the risks" that Yakima assumed. *Id.* at 559, 838 P.2d at 1320.

[Affirmed]

Exercise 10.8 — Impeding the Other Party's Realization of the Benefits of the Contract

1. Termination of Employment at Will

An employment contract permits an employer to terminate the contract at any time and for any reason, on one week's notice. The contract also provides that any employee who works for at least 10 years will become eligible for generous severance pay on departure, the amount of which is based on total years in service and ending salary. After an employee had worked diligently for two weeks short of 10 years, the employer fired him solely to prevent the employee from earning severance pay. Did the employer violate any express or implied obligation? Even in a state that generally declines to recognize an implied good-faith restriction on the termination of an at-will employee, do these facts pose exceptional circumstances that lie outside the risks reasonably assumed by an employee, even one whose contract is terminable "at will"? (Ignore any statutory regulation of severance pay; analyze the contract issue only.)

2. Termination of Life for Spite

In a written separation agreement, Husband promised to pay Wife $2,000/month in support payments until "the death of Wife or Husband or [until] Wife's remarriage." The agreement specifically states that it "constitutes the entire understanding of the parties," and that "[n]o oral settlements or prior written matter extrinsic to this Agreement shall have any force or effect." Three years after signing the separation agreement, Husband committed suicide. As a result, Wife received $1,300/month in death benefits under a pension plan, but Husband's estate terminated the support payments. Wife sues Husband's estate for the difference. How can you argue on behalf of Wife that Husband's estate is liable for Husband's breach of contract? *Wilmington Trust Co. v. Clark,* 424 A.2d 744 (Md. Ct. App. 1981).

C. Implied Warranties

A warranty is a promise that goods, real estate, or services will meet certain standards of quality or will have other promised characteristics. They can be expressed, implied in law, and—less commonly—implied in fact.

1. Warranties Implied as a Matter of Common Law

Courts have occasionally recognized implied-in-law warranties in non-sales contexts. In contracts for the sale of dwellings by homebuilders, for example, many courts have recognized implied warranties that the dwellings are "habitable," as a matter of common law. *See, e.g., Richards v. Powercraft Homes, Inc.*, 139 Ariz. 242, 678 P.2d 427 (1984) (in face of split of authority, deciding that implied warranty of workmanship and habitability extends to secondary purchasers of homes).

2. Implied Warranties Imposed by Statute

The early common law did not recognize implied warranties in sales of goods. *See, e.g., Warren Glass-Works Co. v. Keystone Coal Co.*, 65 Md. 547, 5 A. 253, 256 (Ct. App. 1886) (no implied warranty of merchantability or fitness for a particular purpose under the common law). But sales of goods are now governed by the UCC, which imposes implied warranties in certain circumstances, unless validly disclaimed by the parties. The UCC's status as a "code" means that its various sections are designed to work together as a cohesive system. Carefully study the following sections of the Arizona Commercial Code or find their counterparts in the Texas Business and Commerce Code in Appendix 1, and then apply them to the questions in the following Exercises 10.9 through 10.11.

47-2104. Definitions: "merchant"; "between merchants"; "financing agency"

A. "Merchant" means a person who deals in goods of the kind or otherwise by his occupation holds himself out as having knowledge or skill peculiar to the practices or goods involved in the transaction or to whom such knowledge or skill may be attributed by his employment of an agent or broker or other intermediary who by his occupation holds himself out as having such knowledge or skill.

47-2313. Express warranties by affirmation, promise, description, sample

A. Express warranties by the seller are created as follows:

1. Any affirmation of fact or promise made by the seller to the buyer which relates to the goods and becomes part of the basis of the bargain creates an express warranty that the goods shall conform to the affirmation or promise.

2. Any description of the goods which is made part of the basis of the bargain creates an express warranty that the goods shall conform to the description.

3. Any sample or model which is made part of the basis of the bargain creates an express warranty that the whole of the goods shall conform to the sample or model.

B. It is not necessary to the creation of an express warranty that the seller use formal words such as "warrant" or "guarantee" or that he have a specific intention to make a warranty, but an affirmation merely of the value of the goods or a statement purporting to be merely the seller's opinion or commendation of the goods does not create a warranty.

47-2314. Implied warranty: merchantability; usage of trade

A. Unless excluded or modified (section 47-2316), a warranty that the goods shall be merchantable is implied in a contract for their sale if the seller is a merchant with respect to goods of that kind. Under this section the service for value of food or drink to be consumed either on the premises or elsewhere is a sale.

B. Goods to be merchantable must be at least such as:

1. Pass without objection in the trade under the contract description; and

2. In the case of fungible goods, are of fair average quality within the description; and

3. Are fit for the ordinary purposes for which such goods are used; and

4. Run, within the variations permitted by the agreement, of even kind, quality and quantity within each unit and among all units involved; and

5. Are adequately contained, packaged, and labeled as the agreement may require; and

6. Conform to the promises or affirmations of fact made on the container or label if any.

C. Unless excluded or modified (section 47-2316), other implied warranties may arise from course of dealing or usage of trade.

47-2315. Implied warranty: fitness for particular purpose

Where the seller at the time of contracting has reason to know any particular purpose for which the goods are required and that the buyer is relying on the seller's skill or judgment to select or furnish suitable goods, there is unless excluded or modified under section 47-2316 an implied warranty that the goods shall be fit for such purpose.

47-2316. Exclusion or modification of warranties

A. Words or conduct relevant to the creation of an express warranty and words or conduct tending to negate or limit warranty shall be construed wherever reasonable as consistent with each other; but subject to the provisions of this chapter on parol or extrinsic evidence (section 47-2202) negation or limitation is inoperative to the extent that such construction is unreasonable.

B. Subject to subsection C of this section, to exclude or modify the implied warranty of merchantability or any part of it the language must mention merchantability and in case of a writing must be conspicuous, and to exclude or modify any implied warranty of fitness the exclusion must be by a writing and conspicuous. Language to exclude all implied warranties of fitness is sufficient if it states, for example, that "there are no warranties which extend beyond the description on the face hereof".

C. Notwithstanding subsection B of this section:

1. Unless the circumstances indicate otherwise, all implied warranties are excluded by expressions like "as is", "with all faults" or other language which in common understanding calls the buyer's attention to the exclusion of warranties and makes plain that there is no implied warranty; and

2. When the buyer before entering into the contract has examined the goods or the sample or model as fully as he desired or has refused to examine the goods there is no implied warranty with regard to defects which an examination ought in the circumstances to have revealed to him; and

3. An implied warranty can also be excluded or modified by course of dealing or course of performance or usage of trade.

D. Remedies for breach of warranty can be limited in accordance with the provisions of this chapter on liquidation or limitation of damages and on contractual modification of remedy (sections 47-2718 and 47-2719).

47-2719. Contractual modification or limitation of remedy

A. Subject to the provisions of subsections B and C of this section and of section 47-2718 on liquidation and limitation of damages:

1. The agreement may provide for remedies in addition to or in substitution for those provided in this chapter and may limit or alter the measure of damages recoverable under this chapter, as by limiting the buyer's remedies to return of the goods and repayment of the price or to repair and replacement of non-conforming goods or parts; and

2. Resort to a remedy as provided is optional unless the remedy is expressly agreed to be exclusive, in which case it is the sole remedy.

B. Where circumstances cause an exclusive or limited remedy to fail of its essential purpose, remedy may be had as provided in this title.

C. Consequential damages may be limited or excluded unless the limitation or exclusion is unconscionable. Limitation of consequential damages for injury to the person in the case of consumer goods is prima facie unconscionable but limitation of damages where the loss is commercial is not.

Exercise 10.9 — Overview Questions on Implied Warranties, Disclaimers, and Limitations on Liability

1. Merchantability as Contrasted with Fitness for a Particular Purpose

In your notes, explain in writing the difference between the two kinds of warranties *implied* by the UCC and cited above. What circumstances trigger the implied warranty in each case? If the basis for the implied warranty is established, what obligation is created by each warranty?

2. Disclaimer of Warranties as Contrasted with Limitation on Remedies

In your notes, explain in writing the difference between a disclaimer of warranties and a contractual limitation on remedies. What kind of limitation does each one impose? Which one of them would be invoked to show that the contract would not be breached, and which would be invoked to minimize the consequences of breach?

Exercise 10.10 — Which UCC Warranty Might Apply, and Does it?

Buyer needed some generic replacement parts for 10 outdated and temperamental McKenna Model 37B sorting machines. Using a catalogue from Seller, a supplier with better prices than McKenna, Buyer wanted to order the appropriate replacement parts. Identify and apply the warranty provisions of the UCC that would apply to the following facts, and identify any other issues that might arise:

1. The Case of the Query and Response

In an e-mail exchange, Buyer asked about compatibility of Seller's parts with the McKenna Model 37B, and Seller responded by identifying certain parts from its catalogue that Seller said are compatible with the McKenna Model 37B sorting machine. Buyer ordered those parts, Seller accepted Buyer's offer and shipped those parts, but the delivered machine parts—although in perfect working order and compatible with all modern sorting machines—are not compatible with the McKenna Model 37B.

2. The Case of the Sample Sent

Buyer asked Seller to send samples of certain parts that would be compatible with its McKenna machines. From its distribution warehouse in Buyer's region, Seller sent one sample each of two requested replacement parts. Because the samples were compatible with the McKenna Model 37B, Buyer ordered 10 each of these parts, and Seller accepted and shipped. The delivered goods were in perfect working order but were not compatible with the Model 37B.

3. The Case of the Buyer's Selection

Using Seller's catalogue and its accurate description of machine parts (which description says nothing about McKenna machines), Buyer selected and ordered certain machine parts by catalogue number and stated no other requirements. Buyer intended to use the parts on the McKenna Model 37B sorting machines. Seller accepted and shipped, and the delivered goods were in perfect working order, but the parts turned out not to be compatible with the outdated Model 37B.

4. The Case of the Seller's Selection

Buyer ordered 10 each of the following generic machine parts at Seller's "current catalogue price." Buyer's order did not specify any parts by catalogue number but requested Seller "to select and supply three-tiered set of sorting screens, for use in the McKenna Model 37B sorting machine." Seller sent a brief note of acceptance but then sent parts that—although in perfect working order—were not compatible with the McKenna Model 37B sorting machine.

5. The Case of the Warped Screens

Buyer ordered sorting screens for use in the McKenna Model 37B sorting machine. Seller delivered screens compatible with the Model 37B. Some of the screens were warped, however, causing the machinery to operate inefficiently.

6. The Case of the Stored Screens

Buyer ordered 100 sets of sorting screens, which it intended to store in its warehouse, ready for use as replacements screens for its 10 sorting machines. Seller accepted and shipped 100 sets of screens that were in perfect condition and were compatible with Buyer's sorting machines, but the screens were packaged in flimsy material that made it impossible to stack the screens in the warehouse more than six feet high without risking a toppling of the stack and causing damage to the screens and injury to employees.

Exercise 10.11 — Disclaimers and Limitations on Liability

What UCC provisions would apply to the following facts, and how would they apply?

1. The Case of the Malfunctioning Machinery

For $10,000, Seller sold factory machinery to Buyer with the following clause set forth just above the signature line of a single-page contract, in the same typeface as the other contract clauses:

> "XII. The goods described in this contract are sold with no express or implied warranties. Buyer assumes all risks of defects or imperfections."

After Buyer examined the factory machinery on delivery, Buyer properly installed the machinery and discovered after one day of operation that the machinery was subject to frequent stoppages of the production line because of "logjams" caused by substandard operation of moving parts in the machinery. If left unrepaired, the machinery would cause Buyer to operate at a loss. Repair of the defective parts would cost $1,000. Assuming no misrepresentation or mutual mistake justifying avoidance of the contract, who should pay the bill for the repairs?

2. The Case of the True Lemon

For $25,000, Seller sold a new car to Buyer with a "limited express warranty," which warrants the automobile against defects for three years but limited the buyer's remedy for breach of that warranty to repair or replacement of defective parts, or to damages of $1,500, at the seller's option. B noticed within one day that the automobile did not run smoothly: it responded slowly to the gas pedal, and then only with a jerk as it zoomed forward, and the ride was bumpy even on smooth roads. The seller's service department examined the car and determined that the car was a true "lemon" with numerous manufacturing defects that mostly stemmed from a slight imperfection in the framing of the car. It would be easier to replace the entire car than to repair it, which would require rebuilding it from the ground up. Accordingly, Seller exercised its option under the sales contract to pay Buyer $1,500 in damages. How would you argue on B's behalf for a fuller remedy? (For purposes of this course, you can analyze this solely under the UCC provisions cited prior to these exercises, as adopted in Arizona. For future reference, you should know that other state and federal laws can affect warranties in sales and financing of automobiles. *See, e.g., Johnson v. Earnhardt's Gilbert Dodge, Inc.*, 212 Ariz. 381, 132 P.3d 825 (2006) (*En Banc*)).

3. The Case of the Consequential Losses

For $20,000, S sold a new car to B with a "limited express warranty," which warranted the automobile against defects for three years but limited the buyer's remedy for breach of that warranty to the repair or replacement of defective parts, and to damages for incidental and consequential losses, but with remedies for all consequential losses limited to $5,000. Unknown to either buyer or seller, the new car suffered from a defect in its steering mechanism that would cost $1,000 to repair. While driving home, B was seriously injured when the defect in the steering mechanism caused the car to veer off the road and into a tree. B's medical costs and lost wages (a form of consequential losses) will exceed $300,000. (You may assume that B has medical and disability insurance but that at least $100,000 of these consequential losses will not be covered by insurance.) Using only UCC provisions, how can B argue that damages for consequential losses are not limited to $5,000?

4. The Case of the Damaging Drill Bit

John entered a hardware store to purchase a power drill for use at home. He explained to a sales clerk that he needed a drill that can safely and effectively bore a hole into concrete. The sales clerk recommended without qualification the B&L #300 speed drill with drill bits, all packaged in a colorful cardboard box containing drill bits and an instruction manual. John bought the drill, inserted one of the drill bits, and attempted to use it to bore into the concrete floor of his garage. Although the drill and its drill bits were properly manufactured, the B&L #300 is not suitable for drilling into concrete, but is suitable only for the normal purposes of drilling into wood. Because of the mismatch between the drill's design and the use to which John put it, the drill failed to drill into the concrete cleanly. Instead, it gouged out a chip of concrete and flung it into John's face, severely injuring his left eye. The instruction manual concludes with the following statement, in normal print: "The manufacturer will repair or replace any defective parts, at its option. This warranty is in lieu of all other warranties, either express or implied, and it states the full scope of the manufacturer's liability." Can John sue the manufacturer or the hardware store in contract for damages resulting from his personal injury? (Tort theories of recovery would also be relevant but need not be explored in this course.) Does it matter whether the outside of the packaging included the conspicuous statement "Limited Warranty Inside"?

V. Contract Interpretation

A. Overview of Interpretation and Construction

You might recall this discussion of interpretation and construction in Chapter 4, Section IV.A: When lawyers or judges use the terms "interpretation" and "construction" with precision, they can distinguish obligations that were intended by the parties from ones that are recognized by courts as a matter of legal policy. When a judge or jury interprets the parties' agreement, for example, it is primarily exploring the facts in an effort to determine the parties' actual or apparent intentions. When it construes the contract, however, it is going beyond the parties' intentions and is instead constructing contract terms based on legal policies.

Parties often dispute the meaning of contract terms because a word or phrase is ambiguous, lending itself to different possible meanings. Although a section of definitions in the contract can minimize disputes over the meaning of words and phrases, other kinds of ambiguity can arise from sentence structure or punctuation.

Careful drafting can avoid expensive disputes and litigation. When ambiguities remain, courts will use tools of interpretation and rules of construction to define the parties' contractual rights and duties.

B. Interpretation

1. *Intrinsic Evidence*

When engaged in the process of interpreting a written agreement, a judge or jury should begin with terms of the agreement itself. The express terms of the agreement are sometimes called *intrinsic* evidence of the parties' intended meaning. Even if parol evidence is admissible to help explain the meaning of terms in a written agreement, priority should be given to intrinsic evidence. When intrinsic evidence is considered, the term in dispute should be analyzed not in isolation, but in the context of all the terms of the agreement. The manner in which the same word or phrase is used elsewhere in the agreement, for example, could shed light on its meaning in the disputed context.

In the next case, *Yakima*, the court gives effect to its "plain reading" of the express contract terms. We first encountered *Yakima* in Section IV.B.3 of this chapter, while exploring the implied obligation of good faith. Notice how the court—when presenting its "plain reading" of the terms of the contract—also draws support from a dictionary definition and from precedent, *Wagenseller*, whose discussion of good faith further supports the *Yakima* court's interpretation of the express contract terms.

County of La Paz v. Yakima Compost Co., Inc.

224 Ariz. 590, 233 P.3d 1169 (Ct. App. 2010)
[paragraph numbers changed from the original]

Timmer, Chief Judge

[The facts and procedural history are set forth in this opinion's earlier appearance of this chapter, in Section IV.B.3.]

DISCUSSION

. . . .

2. Right of termination without cause

¶ 1 The County argues ... the County had an absolute right under sections 6 and 18(B) of the Agreement to terminate the Agreement regardless of whether it made any effort to secure a permanent site for the sludge drying facility within a three-year period, thereby obviating the counterclaim. Yakima responds, and the trial court agreed, the jury properly interpreted sections 6 and 18(B) as permitting termination of the Agreement only if the County was unsuccessful in securing a permanent site after making a diligent effort to do so. We review the trial court's interpretation of the Agreement de novo as a matter of law. *Burke v. Voicestream Wireless Corp. II*, 207 Ariz. 393, 395, ¶ 11, 87 P.3d 81, 83 (App. 2004).

¶ 2 After reciting that the location of the sludge drying facility will be relocated after three years, section 6 of the Agreement provides, in relevant part, as follows:

> The County is diligently pursuing acquisition of a permanent site for the Sludge Drying Facility. Upon finalization of such acquisition[,] Yakima shall proceed to obtain all necessary permits and approvals for relocation and operation of the Sludge Drying Facility to the permanent site[,] and shall relocate the Sludge Drying Facility as expeditiously as possible once such permits and approvals are obtained. If the County does not succeed in acquiring a permanent site within three (3) years after execution of this Agreement, the County may terminate this Agreement pursuant to Section 18 below.

Section 18(B) of the Agreement permits the County to terminate the Agreement "if it has not acquired a permanent site for the Sludge Drying Facility as of the date that is three (3) years after execution of this Agreement." The crux of the parties' dispute is whether section 6 imposed on the County an obligation to diligently seek a permanent site throughout the three-year period.

¶ 3 We construe the meaning of a contract provision from the language the parties used and in view of all circumstances. *Smith v. Melson, Inc.*, 135 Ariz. 119, 121, 659 P.2d 1264, 1266 (1983). We give words their ordinary meaning and interpret the contract "so as to make it effective and reasonable." *Phelps Dodge Corp. v. Brown*, 112 Ariz. 179, 181, 540 P.2d 651, 653 (1975). Applying these principles, we decide the trial court correctly rejected the County's argument.

¶ 4 A plain reading of section 6 reveals the County was obligated for a minimum of three years to seek a permanent site for the sludge drying facility. Section 6 provides that the County has the right to terminate the Agreement "[i]f the County does not succeed in acquiring a permanent site within three (3) years." The word "succeed" contemplates the County would expend effort to acquire a permanent site. *See* Webster's II New College Dictionary 1127 (3d ed. 2005) (defining "succeed" as, among other things, "[t]o accomplish something desired or intended"); *see also Wagenseller v. Scottsdale Memorial Hosp.*, 710 P.2d 1025, 1038, 147 Ariz. 370, 383 (1985) (holding the covenant of good faith and fair dealing implied in every contract "requires that neither party do anything that will injure the right of the other to receive the benefits of their agreement"). Section 6 defines the duration of the effort as three years. Thus, as a matter of law, the Agreement imposed an obligation on the County to actively seek a permanent site, and the trial court correctly rejected the County's contention that it could terminate the Agreement at the end of three years even if it made no effort to acquire a site.

[Affirmed]

2. Extrinsic Evidence

Extrinsic evidence is evidence relating to statements, conduct, or customs outside the terms of the express agreement. It may consist, for example, of testimony about the parties' negotiations leading up to contract formation, admissible to help explain the meaning of a term that requires interpretation.

Three other kinds of extrinsic evidence are especially noteworthy: course of performance, course of dealing, and trade usage. *See, e.g.*, U.C.C. § 1-303 (2001).

a. Course of Performance

Course of performance relates to the manner in which the parties began performing the contract in question before a dispute broke out. If one party's early performance is met without objection by the other party, then this mutually agreeable course of performance is particularly strong evidence of the parties' shared intent about the obligations imposed by their agreement.

For example, if a distributor is bound by contract to deliver a specified quantity of goods to a retailer "each month" during a year, and if the retailer without complaint accepted deliveries during the final few days of each month for first five months of performance, the retailer's conduct is consistent with the distributor's interpretation of the contract to permit delivery of each month's goods at any time before the expiration of that month. If the retailer now insists that, for the remaining months, the contract requires delivery at the beginning of each month, that position would be undermined by the retailer's conduct during the first five months of the contract.

b. Course of Dealing

Course of dealing relates to the parties' previous transactions with each other. If they developed a pattern of interpreting or performing in a certain manner in previous transactions, that pattern might shed light on their interpretation of the current agreement. This past course of dealing is not as potentially telling as evidence of how the parties began performing the agreement in dispute (course of performance), or of their statements during negotiations of the agreement in dispute, but it has the persuasive value of relating to transactions between the parties to the dispute.

To borrow from the previous example, suppose the parties had concluded and performed five contracts over the previous five years, each one requiring delivery of specified goods to the retailer "each month" over a year. Suppose further that, over the course of those five contracts, the retailer had always accepted delivery from the distributor during any week of a month, including the end of the month, without complaint. If the parties now enter into a sixth contract with the same terms, one can infer that the parties are satisfied with their course of dealing over the previous five years, and that they intend the term "each month" in the new contract to permit delivery at any time during a month.

c. Trade Usage

Trade usage refers to ways in which a contract term is customarily used in the industry of which both parties are members. If the parties are knowledgeable about the industry, and if the term is frequently used in a certain way in that industry, then one might infer that the parties—as members of that trade—had the customary meaning in mind when reaching their agreement. This generally is not as reliable an indicator of intent as course of performance, prior negotiations, or course of dealing; however, it is a potentially useful form of extrinsic evidence.

C. Rules of Construction

Terms may be added to, or subtracted from, the parties' agreement to further legal policy. For example, a court may add an implied-in-law term such as the duty of good faith, or it may strike a severable and illegal term from the agreement. *See, e.g.*, U.C.C. § 1-304 (2001) (an obligation of good faith is implied in every sales contract); U.C.C. § 2-718(1) (2011) ("a term fixing unreasonably large liquidated damages is void as a penalty").

Other rules of construction can help a court to resolve an ambiguity remaining in the contract after tools of interpretation have been applied. For example, once parties have clearly expressed their intentions to form a contract, a court will prefer an interpretation that permits the contract to go forward. Thus, as a matter of policy, courts normally will prefer an interpretation that "gives a reasonable, lawful and effective meaning to all the terms," rather than one that "leaves a part unreasonable, unlawful, or of no effect." Restatement (Second) of Contracts § 203(a) (1981).

If an ambiguity remains after application of tools of interpretation, courts frequently apply the doctrine of *contra proferentem* to resolve the ambiguity against the party who drafted the contract term. This rule of construction furthers a policy of providing clear notice of contract terms to the non-drafting party. It does so by giving the sole drafter of a non-negotiable contract an incentive to draft clearly. If the sole drafter uses a term that is reasonably susceptible to two different meanings, that drafting party assumes the risk that a court will later give effect to the meaning advanced by the opposing party.

Careful courts will remember to apply *contra proferentem* and all rules of construction only when an ambiguity remains after first seeking the parties' intended meaning through the process of interpretation:

> Defendant argues that the term "cohabitation" should be construed against plaintiff, as the drafter of the judgment of divorce. Our Supreme Court has held, however, that the rule of *contra proferentem*, *i.e.*, that ambiguities are to be construed against the drafter of the contract, should only be applied if all conventional means of contract interpretation, including the consideration of relevant extrinsic evidence, have left the finder of fact unable

> to determine what the parties intended their contract to mean. *Klapp v. United Ins. Group Agency, Inc.*, 468 Mich. 459, 470–471, 474 ... (2003). Because the trial court relied on conventional rules of contract interpretation, construing the term "cohabitation" against plaintiff as the drafter of the judgment was unnecessary.

Smith v. Smith, 278 Mich. App. 198, 200 n.1, 748 N.W.2d 258, 259 n.1 (2008).

Courts sometimes apply *contra proferentem* more readily to standard-form, non-negotiable insurance contracts:

> This court is committed to the rule that a contract of insurance prepared and phrased by the insurer is to be construed liberally in favor of the insured and strictly against the insurer, where the meaning of the language used is doubtful, uncertain or ambiguous.

Almadova v. State Farm Mut. Auto. Ins. Co., 133 Ariz. 81, 84, 649 P.2d 284, 287 (1982) (quoting *Fireman's Fund Insurance Co. of San Francisco v. Boyd*, 45 So. 2d 499, 500–01 (Fla. 1950)); *accord*, *Faruque v. Provident Life & Acc. Ins. Co.*, 31 Ohio St. 3d 34, 38, 508 N.E.2d 949, 952 (1987) (quoting and citing precedent).

Interestingly, two years after *Almadova*, the Arizona Supreme Court lamented that courts have used *contra proferentem* too readily as a convenient device to resolve ambiguities in insurance contracts, thus avoiding a more searching inquiry into the nature of insurance contracts and the problems they pose. *Darner Motor Sales, Inc. v. Universal Underwriters Ins. Co.*, 140 Ariz. 383, 389, 682 P.2d 388, 394 (1984).

A more recent decision in an insurance dispute adopted an interpretation favoring the insured party—resulting in coverage for a loss—not through simple application of *contra proferentem*, but by preferring a non-technical, non-legalistic interpretation: "The language in the Liberty Mutual policies may be interpreted according to its plain and ordinary meaning, as one untrained in law or business would understand it." *Desert Mt. Properties Ltd. Partnership v. Liberty Mutual Fire Ins. Co.*, 225 Ariz. 194, 201, 236 P.3d 421, 428 (Ct. App. 2010).

D. Interpretation, Construction, and the Parol Evidence Rule

A quick review of the parol evidence rule will help set the stage for approaches to choosing between competing meanings of an ambiguous term. If the following summary is difficult to follow, you may want to review Section II of this chapter.

To a great extent the parol evidence rule is inapplicable to the processes of interpretation and construction of contracts. Because rules of *construction* are based on legal policy rather than on prior statements of the parties, they do not trigger the parol evidence rule at all. Similarly, two kinds of interpretation are outside the reach of the rule. Analysis of *intrinsic evidence* as a tool of interpretation is perfectly consistent with the parol evidence rule, because the rule favors resort to the terms on the face of the final written agreement. Moreover, evidence of extrinsic evidence in the form of course of performance does not implicate the parol evidence rule because performance of the agreement in question occurs after the signing of the written integration and thus can modify or help explain the written agreement.

The parol evidence rule is implicated, however, by extrinsic evidence of statements or conduct of the parties prior to signing the final written agreement. The parol evidence rule will exclude such evidence if it is used to add a new term to a completely integrated writing, or to contradict the terms of any integrated writing, partial or complete.

Parol evidence, such as prior negotiations, will be admitted to help explain the meaning of a term that found its way into an integrated writing. The question remains, however, whether the court views the parol evidence as helping to explain the meaning of a term in the final written agreement, or as violating the parol evidence rule by contradicting the written integration or by adding a new term to a complete integration.

If the court applies the strictest form of the plain-meaning rule, it will admit the parol evidence as an interpretive aid only if the term in dispute is ambiguous on its face, in the context of all the intrinsic evidence within the four corners of the written agreement. If the court follows the modern trend, however, it will more liberally admit the extrinsic evidence to support any meaning that the parties might have plausibly intended, even if they attached an unusual meaning to the term. Moreover, the UCC parol evidence rule will permit a written sales contract to be supplemented, and not just explained, by evidence of course of dealing and trade usage, as well as course of performance. U.C.C. § 2-202(a) (2011).

E. *Frigaliment*: A Case Study in Contract Interpretation

As you read and carefully brief the next case, make a note of the different kinds of evidence that the court considers as it interprets the contract.

In class, you should consider discussing *intrinsic* evidence first, even though the court delays its discussion of an important argument based on intrinsic evidence. What are the arguments concerning intrinsic evidence in *Frigaliment*? Why weren't they conclusive for one side or another?

What different kinds of *extrinsic* evidence supported other arguments by the parties? For purposes of class discussion, label these different kinds of evidence in your notes so that you can easily jump from one to another.

Frigaliment Importing Co., Ltd. v. B.N.S. Int'l Sales Corp.

190 F. Supp. 116 (S.D.N.Y. 1960)

Friendly, Circuit Judge.

¶ 1 The issue is, what is chicken? Plaintiff says "chicken" means a young chicken, suitable for broiling and frying. Defendant says "chicken" means any bird of that genus that meets contract specifications on weight and quality, including what it calls "stewing chicken" and plaintiff pejoratively terms "fowl." Dictionaries give both meanings, as well as some others not relevant here. To support its, plaintiff sends a number of volleys over the net; defendant essays to return them and adds a few serves of its own. Assuming that both parties were acting in good faith, the case nicely illustrates Holmes' remark "that the making of a contract depends not on the agreement of two minds in one intention, but on the agreement of two sets of external signs—not on the parties' having meant the same thing but on their having said the same thing." The Path of the Law, in Collected Legal Papers, p. 178. I have concluded that plaintiff has not sustained its burden of persuasion that the contract used "chicken" in the narrower sense.

¶2 The action is for breach of the warranty that goods sold shall correspond to the description, New York Personal Property Law, McKinney's Consol. Laws, c. 41, §95. Two contracts are in suit. In the first, dated May 2, 1957, defendant, a New York sales corporation, confirmed the sale to plaintiff, a Swiss corporation, of

> US Fresh Frozen Chicken, Grade A, Government Inspected, Eviscerated 2½–3 lbs. and 1½–2 lbs. each all chicken individually wrapped in cryovac, packed in secured fiber cartons or wooden boxes, suitable for export
>
> 75,000 lbs. 2½–3 lbs.... .... @$33.00
>
> 25,000 lbs. 1½–2 lbs.... .... @$36.50
>
> per 100 lbs. FAS New York
>
> scheduled May 10, 1957 pursuant to instructions from Penson & Co., New York.
>
> [*Ftnt. 1*: The Court notes a contract provision stating agreement to settle any dispute by arbitration in the New York Produce Exchange; it treats the parties' failure to avail themselves of arbitration as a subsequent agreement eliminating that clause of the contract.]

¶3 The second contract, also dated May 2, 1957, was identical save that only 50,000 lbs. of the heavier "chicken" were called for, the price of the smaller birds was $37 per 100 lbs., and shipment was scheduled for May 30. The initial shipment under the first contract was short but the balance was shipped on May 17. When the initial shipment arrived in Switzerland, plaintiff found, on May 28, that the 2½–3 lbs. birds were not young chicken suitable for broiling and frying but stewing chicken or "fowl"; indeed, many of the cartons and bags plainly so indicated. Protests ensued. Nevertheless, shipment under the second contract was made on May 29, the 2½–3 lbs. birds again being stewing chicken. Defendant stopped the transportation of these at Rotterdam.

¶4 This action followed. Plaintiff says that, notwithstanding that its acceptance was in Switzerland, New York law controls. *Rubin v. Irving Trust Co.*, 1953, 305 N.Y. 288, 305, 113 N.E.2d 424, 431; defendant does not dispute this, and relies on New York decisions. I shall follow the apparent agreement of the parties as to the applicable law. [The *Rubin* case applies the "center of gravity" approach, by which "the {contract} law of the State which has the most significant contacts with the matter in dispute will be applied."]....

¶5 Defendant notes that the contract called not simply for chicken but for "US Fresh Frozen Chicken, Grade A, Government Inspected." It says the contract thereby incorporated by reference the Department of Agriculture's regulations, which favor its interpretation; I shall return to this after reviewing plaintiff's other contentions.

¶6 The first hinges on an exchange of cablegrams which preceded execution of the formal contracts. The negotiations leading up to the contracts were conducted in New York between defendant's secretary, Ernest R. Bauer, and a Mr. Stovicek, who was in New York for the Czechoslovak government at the World Trade Fair. A few days after meeting Bauer at the fair, Stovicek telephoned and inquired whether defendant would be interested in exporting poultry to Switzerland. Bauer then met with Stovicek, who showed him a cable from plaintiff dated April 26, 1957, announcing that they "are buyer" of 25,000 lbs. of chicken 2½–3 lbs. weight, Cryovac packed, grade A Government inspected, at a price up to 33 cents per pound, for shipment on May 10, to be confirmed by the following morning, and were interested in further offerings. After testing the market for price, Bauer accepted, and Stovicek sent a confirmation that evening. Plaintiff stresses that, although these and subsequent cables between plaintiff and defendant, which laid the basis for the additional quantities under the first and for all of the second contract, were predominantly in German, they used the English word "chicken"; it claims this was done because it understood "chicken" meant young chicken whereas the German word, "Huhn," included both "Brathuhn" (broilers) and "Suppenhuhn" (stewing chicken), and that defendant, whose officers were thoroughly conversant with German, should have realized this. Whatever force this argument might otherwise have is largely drained away by Bauer's testimony that he asked Stovicek what kind of chickens were wanted, received the answer "any kind of chickens," and then, in German, asked whether the cable meant "Huhn" and received an affirmative response....

¶7 Plaintiff's next contention is that there was a definite trade usage that "chicken" meant "young chicken." Defendant showed that it was only beginning in the poultry trade in 1957, thereby bringing itself within the principle that "when one of the parties is not a member of the trade or other circle, his acceptance of the standard must be made to appear" by proving either that he had actual knowledge of the usage or that the usage is "so generally known in the community that his actual individual knowledge of it may be inferred." 9 Wigmore, Evidence (3d ed. § 1940) 2464. Here there was no proof of actual knowledge of the alleged usage; indeed, it is quite plain that defendant's belief was to the contrary. In order to meet the alternative requirement, the law of New York demands a showing that "the usage is of so long continuance, so well established, so notorious, so universal and so reasonable in itself, as that the presumption is violent that the parties contracted with reference to it, and made it a part of their agreement." *Walls v. Bailey*, 1872, 49 N.Y. 464, 472–473.

¶8 Plaintiff endeavored to establish such a usage by the testimony of three witnesses and certain other evidence. Strasser, resident buyer in New York for a large chain of Swiss cooperatives, testified that "on chicken I would definitely understand a broiler." However, the force of this testimony was considerably weakened by the fact that in his own transactions the witness, a careful businessman, protected himself by using "broiler" when that was what he wanted and "fowl" when he wished older birds. Indeed, there are some indications, dating back to a remark of Lord Mansfield, *Edie v. East India Co.*, 2 Burr. 1216, 1222 (1761), that no credit should be given "witnesses to usage, who could not adduce instances in verification." 7 Wigmore, Evidence (3d ed. 1940), § 1954; [other citation omitted]. While Wigmore thinks this goes too far, a witness' consistent failure to rely on the alleged usage deprives his opinion testimony of much of its effect. Niesielowski, an officer of one of the companies that had furnished the stewing chicken to defendant, testified that "chicken" meant "the male species of the poultry industry. That could be a broiler, a fryer or a roaster," but not a stewing chicken; however, he also testified that upon receiving defendant's inquiry for "chickens," he asked whether the desire was for "fowl or frying chickens" and, in fact, supplied fowl, although taking the precaution of asking defendant, a day or two after plaintiff's acceptance of the contracts in suit, to change its confirmation of its order from "chickens," as defendant had originally prepared it, to "stewing chickens." Dates, an employee of Urner-Barry Company, which publishes a daily market report on the poultry trade, gave it as his view that the trade meaning of "chicken" was "broilers and fryers." In addition to this opinion testimony, plaintiff relied on the fact that the Urner-Barry service, the Journal of Commerce, and Weinberg Bros. & Co. of Chicago, a large supplier of poultry, published quotations in a manner which, in one way or another, distinguish between "chicken," comprising broilers, fryers and certain other categories, and "fowl," which, Bauer acknowledged, included stewing chickens. This material would be impressive if there were nothing to the contrary. However, there was, as will now be seen.

¶9 Defendant's witness Weininger, who operates a chicken eviscerating plant in New Jersey, testified "Chicken is everything except a goose, a duck, and a turkey. Everything is a chicken, but then you have to say, you have to specify which category you want or that you are talking about." Its witness Fox said that in the trade "chicken" would encompass all the various classifications. Sadina, who conducts a food inspection service, testified that he would consider any bird coming within the classes of "chicken" in the Department of Agriculture's regulations to be a chicken. The specifications approved by the General Services Administration include fowl as well as broilers and fryers under the classification "chickens." Statistics of the Institute of American Poultry Industries use the phrases "Young chickens" and "Mature chickens," under the general heading "Total chickens." and the Department of Agriculture's daily and weekly price reports avoid use of the word "chicken" without specification.

¶10 Defendant advances several other points which it claims affirmatively support its construction. Primary among these is the regulation of the Department of

Agriculture, 7 C.F.R. §70.300–70.370, entitled, "Grading and Inspection of Poultry and Edible Products Thereof" and in particular 70.301 which recited:

> Chickens. The following are the various classes of chickens:
>
> (a) Broiler or fryer ...
>
> (b) Roaster ...
>
> (c) Capon ...
>
> (d) Stag ...
>
> (e) Hen or stewing chicken or fowl ...
>
> (f) Cock or old rooster ...

¶ 11 Defendant argues, as previously noted, that the contract incorporated these regulations by reference. Plaintiff answers that the contract provision related simply to grade and Government inspection and did not incorporate the Government definition of "chicken," and also that the definition in the Regulations is ignored in the trade. However, the latter contention was contradicted by Weininger and Sadina; and there is force in defendant's argument that the contract made the regulations a dictionary, particularly since the reference to Government grading was already in plaintiff's initial cable to Stovicek.

¶ 12 Defendant makes a further argument based on the impossibility of its obtaining broilers and fryers at the 33 cents price offered by plaintiff for the 2½–3 lbs. birds. There is no substantial dispute that, in late April, 1957, the price for 2½–3 lbs. broilers was between 35 and 37 cents per pound, and that when defendant entered into the contracts, it was well aware of this and intended to fill them by supplying fowl in these weights. It claims that plaintiff must likewise have known the market since plaintiff had reserved shipping space on April 23, three days before plaintiff's cable to Stovicek, or, at least, that Stovicek was chargeable with such knowledge. It is scarcely an answer to say, as plaintiff does in its brief, that the 33 cents price offered by the 2½–3 lbs. "chickens" was closer to the prevailing 35 cents price for broilers than to the 30 cents at which defendant procured fowl. Plaintiff must have expected defendant to make some profit—certainly it could not have expected defendant deliberately to incur a loss.

¶ 13 Finally, defendant relies on conduct by the plaintiff after the first shipment had been received. On May 28 plaintiff sent two cables complaining that the larger birds in the first shipment constituted "fowl." Defendant answered with a cable refusing to recognize plaintiff's objection and announcing "We have today ready for shipment 50,000 lbs. chicken 2½–3 lbs. 25,000 lbs. broilers 1½–2 lbs.," these being the goods procured for shipment under the second contract, and asked immediate answer "whether we are to ship this merchandise to you and whether you will accept the merchandise." After several other cable exchanges, plaintiff replied on May 29 "Confirm again that merchandise is to be shipped since resold by us if not enough pursuant to contract chickens are shipped the missing quantity is to be shipped within ten days stop we resold to our customers pursuant to your contract chickens grade A you have to deliver us said merchandise we again state that we shall make you fully responsible for all resulting costs." [*Ftnt. 2*: These cables were in German; the words "chicken," "broilers" and, on some occasions, "fowl," were in English.]

¶ 14 Defendant argues that if plaintiff was sincere in thinking it was entitled to young chickens, plaintiff would not have allowed the shipment under the second contract to go forward, since the distinction between broilers and chickens drawn in defendant's cablegram must have made it clear that the larger birds would not be broilers. However, plaintiff answers that the cables show plaintiff was insisting on delivery of young chickens and that defendant shipped old ones at its peril.... There is little force in [Defendant's position] in view of plaintiff's immediate and consistent protests.

¶ 15 When all the evidence is reviewed, it is clear that defendant believed it could comply with the contracts by delivering stewing chicken in the 2½–3 lbs. size. Defendant's subjective intent would not be significant if this did not coincide with an objective meaning of "chicken." Here it did coincide with one of the dictionary meanings, with the definition in the Department of Agriculture Regulations to which the contract made at least oblique reference, with at least some usage in the trade, with the realities of the market, and with what plaintiff's spokesman had said. Plaintiff asserts it to be equally plain that plaintiff's own subjective intent was to obtain broilers and fryers; the only evidence against this is the material as to market prices and this may not have been sufficiently brought home. In any event it is unnecessary to determine that issue. For plaintiff has the burden of showing that "chicken" was used in the narrower rather than in the broader sense, and this it has not sustained.

This opinion constitutes the Court's findings of fact and conclusions of law. Judgment shall be entered dismissing the complaint with costs.

Exercise 10.12 — Fictitious Transcript for *Frigaliment*

What are the apparent purposes of the questions in the following fictitious direct and cross examinations of the expert witnesses on trade usage in *Frigaliment*? Were the purposes achieved? What questions would you ask on cross examination of Weininger?

Witness: Strasser

Direct Examination by Buyer

Q Mr. Strasser, what is your present occupation?

A I'm a broker of goods for export to a chain of Swiss firms.

Q Where is your principal place of business?

A New York.

Q Are you familiar with the poultry industry?

A Yes. I've been dealing in poultry for 10 years.

Q In your opinion, is there an established meaning of the word "chicken" in the industry?

A Yes. On "chicken," I would definitely understand a broiler.

Q No further questions, Your Honor.

Cross Examination by Seller

Q Mr. Strasser, do you have occasion to supply chicken to Swiss customers who want to purchase only broilers, and have no need for stewing chickens?

A Sure.

Q On those occasions, you order those chickens from domestic producers for export, do you not?

A That's right.

Q When you want to ensure that you supply your Swiss customers with broilers, do you ask the producers for broilers?

A Yes, and when I want older, stewing chicken, I ask for fowl.

Q Thank you.

Witness: Niesielowski

Direct Examination by Buyer

Q What is your present occupation?

A President of Perfect Poultry Co.

Q What is the relationship of your company to B.N.S. Intn'l Sales Co.?

A We sell chicken to them in bulk for their export business.

Q In your opinion, is there an established meaning of the word "chicken" in the poultry industry?

A Sure.

Q What is it?

A "Chicken" means a broiler, a fryer or a roaster.

Q Does it mean stewing chicken?

A No.

Q What term would you use to describe stewing chicken?

A I'd just say "stewing chicken." In fact, after I found out that B.N.S. was looking for stewing chicken, I asked them to change the confirmation from "chicken" to "stewing chicken."

Q Thank you. That's all.

Cross Examination by Seller

Q Sir, when you received the order from B.N.S. for "chicken," how did you discover that B.N.S. was looking for stewing chicken?

A Well, I called them up and asked whether they wanted fowl or frying chickens.

Q Did you think such a clarification necessary because a broker or buyer might use the term "chicken" to include stewing chicken?

A Yes, that's why I asked.

Witness: Dates

Direct Examination by Buyer

Q Mr. Dates, what is your present occupation?

A I'm the managing editor for Urner-Barry Co.; we publish a daily market report on the poultry trade.

Q In your opinion, is there an established meaning for the word "chicken" in the poultry industry?

A Yes.

Q What kind of poultry does it include?

A Chicken means broilers and fryers.

Q Do your published quotations reflect that narrow definition of chicken?

A Yes they do. We have a category called "chicken" comprised of broilers, fryers & some similar kinds of chicken; and we have a separate category for fowl.

Q In what category do you place stewing chicken?

A That's fowl.

Q Thank you.

Cross Examination by Seller — No questions, Your Honor. [Why no cross-examination?]

Witness: Weininger

Direct Examination by Seller

Q Mr. Weininger, what is your current occupation?

A I operate a chicken eviscerating plant in New Jersey.

Q How long have you been working in the poultry industry?

A Fifteen long years.

Q In your opinion, is there an established meaning of the word "chicken" in that industry?

A Yes. "Chicken" is everything except a goose, a duck, and a turkey. Everything is a chicken, but then you have to specify which category you want or that you are talking about.

Q Thank you.

Cross Examination by Buyer — [What line of questioning would you recommend?]

F. Choosing Between Competing Meanings and Between Objective and Subjective Intent

If a court applies a strict version of the plain-meaning rule, and if it believes that a written term in dispute has a single, clear meaning on the face of the contract, it will deem the parties to have intended that meaning and will give the term that plain meaning. In that case, extrinsic evidence will not even be admitted as an aid to interpretation, because the judge has concluded that the term in question does not require interpretation, after examining intrinsic evidence within the four corners of the contract.

Let's assume, however, that a court finds ambiguity on the face of the contract, or that it does not limit itself to a plain-meaning rule, so that it more liberally admits extrinsic evidence of the parties' expressions about the meaning each of them personally attached to a term. The broadly objective meaning of the term—the one held by a reasonable person in the general population, or perhaps in the parties' trade—will not be irrelevant, but its role in the analysis of intended meaning may vary with the circumstances.

Indeed, in some circumstances a court may even take evidence of a party's unexpressed subjective intent regarding the meaning of a term. Although a purely objective standard is generally applied to questions of offer and acceptance, subjective intent may still be relevant in other inquiries, including contract interpretation. Thus, a liberal court may receive evidence of meaning at varying levels on an objective scale, leading finally to evidence of subjective intent:

Broadly Objective: meaning held by a reasonable person in the general population;

Intermediate Objective: meaning held by reasonable person in the relevant trade;

Objective in Particular Context: meaning held by reasonable people in position of these parties

Subjective Meaning Shared by Both Parties: even if not revealed during contracting

One general guide adopted by many courts is based on an analysis of fault. *See generally* RESTATEMENT (SECOND) OF CONTRACTS § 201 (1981). For example, suppose that Party A can prove that at all relevant times he subjectively attached an unusual meaning to a contract term, one that would not be held by a reasonable member of the general population or the population in the trade. Suppose further that Party B has always been unaware of the unusual meaning held by Party A, and that Party B subjectively intended the term to mean something very similar to the broadly objective meaning of the term. In these circumstances, a court likely would give effect to the more broadly accepted meaning held by Party B.

In the example in the preceding paragraph, even if the court does not apply a plain meaning rule, it would likely find that Party A was at fault in not clearing up the confusion about how the parties should use the term in question. Because Party A's intended meaning departed from the generally accepted meaning of the term, Party A should have known that Party B likely attached a different meaning (the broadly accepted objective meaning), should have pointed out this discrepancy to Party B, and should have attempted to specifically negotiate a provision that would have more clearly given effect to Party A's preferred meaning.

G. Deference to One Party's Interpretation

To what extent will a court honor an agreement by the parties that one of them has the sole authority to interpret ambiguous language in the contract? Can you see parallels between the following opinion and earlier ones that used the obligation of good faith to limit contractual exercises of discretion?

Han v. United Continental Holdings, Inc.

762 F.3d 598 (7th Cir. 2014)

Manion, Circuit Judge.

¶1 Hongbo Han filed a putative class action against United Continental Holding, Inc., United Air Lines, Inc., and Mileage Plus Holdings LLC (hereinafter "United"), alleging that the defendant breached the terms of its frequent-flyer program, the "MileagePlus Program." Specifically, Han maintained that United breached the MileagePlus Program contract by crediting him for "mileage" determined by the distance between the airports, instead of the number of miles the airplanes actually flew (including such things as weather diversions and landing delays). The district court dismissed Han's complaint with prejudice and he now appeals. We affirm.

....

II.

¶2 Han maintains that because United drafted the contract, the ambiguity in the MileagePlus Program Rules must be interpreted in his favor. *See* ... *Gassner v. Raynor Mfg. Co.*, 948 N.E.2d 315, 328 (Ill. App. Ct. 2011) ("the risk of ambiguity and lack of clarity is [placed] on the drafting party"). He also argues that language from other sections of United's web page supports his view that "mileage" means the actual miles flown by the airplane, as opposed to the actual distance-in-miles between the airports. For instance, Han cites to the "Premier Status" qualification requirements, listed on United's web page, where United states that "[Premier qualifying miles] are based on the number of paid flight miles traveled and the fare purchased." He also points to a "Promotion Page" contained on United's web page which, according to Han's complaint, states that "flight miles" are "determined by the purchased ticket routing."

Compl. ¶ 23. Han argues that this language shows that the MileagePlus Program Rules contract is not only ambiguous, but that his reading of the contract is the better one.

¶ 3 Han's argument, though, ignores the plain language of the MileagePlus Program Rules which unequivocally states that "United has the sole right to interpret and apply the Program Rules." Under Illinois law, "a court must give meaning and effect to every part of the contract." *Cress v. Recreation Servs., Inc.*, 795 N.E.2d 817, 852 (Ill. App. Ct. 2003).... More specifically, we have recognized that under Illinois law, "a contract can vary from the norm by including language which indicates that one of the parties is to have discretion to interpret and apply the contract." *Herzberger v. Standard Ins. Co.*, 205 F.3d 327, 330 (7th Cir. 2000). However, the interpretation must be based on "'grounds which are reasonable and just.'" *Id.* (quoting *Muka v. Estate of Muka*, 517 N.E.2d 673, 677 (Ill. App. Ct. 1987));.... Accordingly, because the MileagePlus Program Rules gave United discretion to interpret the terms of that contract, to state a breach of contract claim Han must allege an interpretation of that contract that is unreasonable. Merely alleging that the term is ambiguous and pointing to extrinsic evidence which could support his interpretation of the contract is not enough.

¶ 4 Han, however, does not claim that United's interpretation of the term "mileage," as used in the Program Rules, is unreasonable; rather, he argues that his view is the better one, or at a minimum that the contract is ambiguous. But to avoid dismissal, Han needs to plausibly allege that United's interpretation of the contract is unreasonable. United interprets "mileage" for flights as the total distance-in-miles between the airports. As a matter of law, this interpretation is not unreasonable. Rather, it is entirely reasonable for an airline to use a standard measure of miles for all flights between the same airports. It is quicker, cheaper, easier, and more predictable, and allows customers to readily determine the number of miles they will earn per flight. Conversely, Han's interpretation of "mileage" as the total distance flown to arrive at the destination airport would require an airline to track the exact miles for every flight flown and to credit customers' accounts based on that information. While it might be possible for an airline to do that, that does not make United's interpretation of mileage as the actual distance between airports an unreasonable interpretation of the contract. Nor does any of the language from other parts of United's website render its interpretation of "mileage" in the Mileage-Plus Program Rules unreasonable.

We affirm.

Exercise 10.13 — "What Is Chicken?" Reprised

In the following problems, assume that the parties are a domestic buyer and seller within the United States. Assume also that the court has found the word "chicken" to be ambiguous and in need of interpretation, although different courts have different standards for finding ambiguity. If you see arguments for both sides, state them before explaining which interpretation you would choose as a judge.

1. Battle of the Subjective Intentions

Dictionaries provide various definitions of the word "chicken," in line with the relatively imprecise meaning of that word held by most members of the general population. Most buyers and sellers in the relevant domestic industry, however, use the word "chicken" to mean any kind of chicken, including older stewing chicken, and not just premium "broilers and fryers." Although the parties did not discuss this issue at the time of contracting, extrinsic evidence shows that — at all relevant times — Buyer subjectively intended the word "chicken" to mean only broilers and fryers, and Seller subjectively adopted a meaning consistent with usage in the trade (any kind of chicken). Buyer and Seller are both members of this trade, but Buyer did not realize that Seller used the word "chicken" to mean any kind of chicken. Which party's meaning should prevail and why?

2. Tipped Off about Other Party's Meaning

Suppose the same facts as in Subsection 1 above, but add admissible evidence showing that Seller overheard Buyer talking to an assistant during a break, showing that Buyer understood the word "chicken" to mean only broilers and fryers. Buyer did not raise this issue during negotiations, because Buyer erroneously thought that the word "chicken" was understood in the trade as only premium broilers and fryers, unless the contract specifically permitted other kinds of chicken. Seller, confident that "chicken" is generally interpreted to mean any kind of chicken, did not correct Buyer's mistake or address the issue during negotiations for fear that Buyer would insist on a contract term that would clearly require delivery of only broilers and fryers. Which party's meaning should prevail?

3. Contest Prize

Regional managers of a restaurant chain orally announced a region-wide contest for their wait-staff. The employee who sold the most beer in the region during a stated time period would win a prize that phonetically sounded like "a new Toy-Yota." Assuming that they were competing for a new car or light truck, the wait-staff worked exceptionally hard to sell beer during the relevant time period, until one waitress emerged as the winner. The manager of that restaurant blindfolded the victorious waitress, led her to the parking lot, and removed the blindfold to reveal a brand new toy doll depicting the character Yoda from *Star Wars*. She was not amused and brought suit. Did the parties form a contract? If so, what kind of contract, and when was the offer accepted? Assuming they formed a contract, how should the court interpret the oral word or phrase stated by the managers as the prize?

4. Agreement in Subjectively Held Meanings

Suppose the same facts as in Subsection 1 above, except that extrinsic evidence shows that, at the time of contracting, both parties subjectively used the word "chicken" to mean only broilers and fryers. Seller later found it to be onerous to supply only broilers and fryers at the contract price, and it later discovered the broader meaning of "chicken" in the trade, so Seller asks the court to give effect to the objective meaning as reflected by trade usage. Which party's current position should prevail?

Exercise 10.14 — Ambiguity in Proper Names

1. "Peerless" had a Peer

Buyer and Seller entered into a contract for the purchase and sale of a cargo of cotton that would arrive later in the year from Bombay to Liverpool on the ship named Peerless. Unknown to either party, it turned out that two ships named Peerless were scheduled to carry cotton from Bombay to Liverpool, one in October and one in December. Extrinsic evidence showed that Buyer had used the name "Peerless" to mean the ship that sailed in October, and Seller had used the name "Peerless" to mean the ship that sailed in December. Buyer needed the cotton in October and refused to take delivery of the cotton arriving in December. Neither party realized that the other party was attaching a different meaning to the name "Peerless," and neither ship was better known in the trade as the one bringing cotton from Bombay. In other words, the proper name "Peerless" had no objective meaning that would distinguish between the two ships. What's a court to do? [taken from *Raffles v. Wichelhaus*, 159 Eng. Rep. 375 (1864)].

2. A "Capital" Idea

Client, who is a relatively unsophisticated trader in the stock market, sent an email to his stock-broker ("Broker"), requesting that the broker immediately purchase 100 shares of "Capital" on Client's account. Extrinsic evidence shows that Client meant 100 shares of stock in Capital Bank, the only stock known to him with the name of "Capital." Broker bought 100 shares of stock in Capital Trust, because — although Broker was familiar with Capital Bank — the stock in Capital Trust was on broker's mind because of recent news about it possibly being undervalued and a good bargain. The Capital Bank stock rose and the Capital Trust stock fell sharply. On learning that he was the new owner of 100 shares of losing stock, Client sued Broker for procuring the wrong stock. What arguments would you make on behalf of both parties? What would you decide as judge?

Exercise 10.15 — Drafting Contracts in Plain English

A simple contract should: (1) introduce the parties to the contract, (2) if appropriate, recite any background facts that explain the motivations of the parties and thus help to explain their bargain, (3) define the parties' rights and obligations by setting forth their mutual promises, and (4) signify each party's agreement to the terms of the contract.

The following contract is written in antiquated jargon. Parts of the contract are taken from the contract interpreted in *McMichael v. Price*, 58 P.2d 549 (Okla. 1936). Contract language from formbooks provided further inspiration. Simplify all or part of the structure and language of the contract so that it expresses the terms of the parties' agreement in plain English. Feel free to use subject headings, section numbers, and paragraphing.

Compare your revision with the sample Requirements Contracts in Appendix 2 of the casebook. Glance through the other sample contracts in Appendix 2.

REQUIREMENTS CONTRACT

This contract for the purchase and sale of sand entered into on this, the 15th day of October 20xx, by and between Sooner Sand Co., a general partnership of which Harley T. Price and W. M. McMichael are partners, hereinafter known as the party of the first part, and Bassi Distributing Co. a joint venture of Bassi Trucking Co. and Hardcore Rock & Gravel, Inc., hereinafter known as the party of the second part, Witnesseth:

Whereas, the party of the first part is engaged in the business of selling and shipping sand from Phoenix to various customers in the State of Arizona but has not developed markets outside of Arizona and desires to supply sand wholesale to a distributor with customers outside the state; and

Whereas, the party of the second part has an established business in Phoenix selling and shipping sand to various customers in several states outside Arizona, including California, Nevada, Utah, and Colorado, and desires a stable source of supply of sand for that business;

Now, therefore, in consideration of the mutual covenants herein contained, and other good and valuable consideration the receipt of which is hereby acknowledged, the parties hereby represent, warrant, affirm, promise, covenant, and agree that the said party of the first part will, upon receipt of periodic written orders submitted by the said party of the second part, furnish all of the sand which the said party of the second part requires for shipment to various and sundry points outside of the State of Arizona, for a period of five (5) years from the date hereinabove, said sand to be of a grade and quality at least equal in quality and comparable with the sand of various grades sold by other sand companies in the City of Phoenix, Arizona; furthermore, the said party of the second part agrees to pay as payment and compensation for said sand so furnished a sum per ton which represents sixty percent (60%) of the current market price per ton of concrete at the place of destination of said shipment.

In witness whereof, the said parties have hereunto set their hands and seals the day and year first above written.

[signatures]

VI. Summary

- Use the parol evidence rule to determine what evidence will be admitted to help determine the terms of a final written agreement.
- Exclude parol evidence that contradicts the terms of the integrated writing.
- If the agreement is completely integrated, also exclude evidence of consistent additional terms that are within the subject matter of the complete integration.

- Nonetheless, admit evidence for the purpose of showing grounds for rescission or reformation, such as illegality, fraud, or mutual mistake.
- Admit parol evidence to help explain the meaning of a term in the integrated writing, but only if it is advanced for interpretation, rather than to contradict the written term or to add a new term to a complete integration. Whether it is deemed to be for interpretation may depend on whether a plain-meaning rule is applied or a more contemporary, flexible approach.
- To the parties' agreement, add implied obligations, such as the duty of good faith and implied warranties.
- Interpret the parties' agreement by determining the parties' intended meaning, first by looking at intrinsic evidence (the words of the agreement) and then with extrinsic evidence such as prior negotiations, course of performance, course of dealing, and trade usage.
- If ambiguity remains after tools of interpretation are applied, resolve the ambiguity by applying rules of construction such as *contra proferentem.*
- If the parties attached different meanings to a contract term, use the plain meaning rule to give effect to the objective meaning, or use a fault analysis to choose between the two meanings. In the rare case of absence of fault, objective meaning, and any other basis for choosing between two offered meanings, courts sometimes find that no contract was formed.
- If the parties attached the same subjective meaning to a contract term, give effect to that meaning, even if it departs from the objective meaning, if the court rejects the plain meaning rule and applies a contemporary, flexible approach.
- To avoid disputes, draft contracts in plain English and with precision.

Exercise 10.16 — Past Exams

1. Q1 — 60 minutes {You can write a more sophisticated answer to the questions below, particularly Part A, after you have studied conditions in Chapter 11; however, this question primarily addresses issues from Chapter 10}.

The following is an excerpt from a completely integrated agreement between Owner and Landscaper ("O" and "L" for short, if you like), for sophisticated landscaping at the exterior of O's new office building. O's legal staff drafted the provisions, contained in a document titled "Landscaping Agreement" ("LA" for short, if you like).

> Owner and Landscaper agree to the following reciprocal promises:
>
> 1. Performance of Landscaping Duties: Landscaper will complete the Landscaping detailed in the attached specifications no later than December 3.
>
> 2. Payment: On December 4, Owner will pay a fee of $100,000 to Landscaper, but only in the event that Landscaper has completed performance as required in section 1. Owner may withhold payment until it has an opportunity to inspect and to certify completion.

L's crew fell slightly behind schedule by December and were forced to work through the night of December 3. They completed performance exactly to specifications by 6 a.m. on December 4. At 8 a.m. on December 4, O inspected the work, approved the quality of the work, but did not approve its timing. O stated that he had sent an employee to the worksite at midnight, and the employee reported that L had not yet completed work. Because L did not complete the project by midnight of December 3, O now refuses to pay anything.

L sues O for withheld payment. O responds that O's duty to pay never arose because L did not meet the contractual deadline. O suffered no actual damages due to the completion of construction on December 4 rather than December 3.

Answer the questions in section A, below, and sections B.1 and B.2, on the next page, taking time to plan your answer before writing.

A. Entitlement to Construction Fee

Assume for this question that the parties did not discuss the terms of the LA prior to signing it. The judge, therefore, must interpret the contract solely on the basis of the text of sections 1 and 2 on the face of the contract. In a single IRAC, discuss whether O is obligated to pay the landscaping fee to L or whether O instead is entitled to cancel that obligation. Summarize any helpful rules of interpretation or construction, apply those rules to the facts, and reach a reasonable conclusion. When you argue the facts, try to argue both sides, each time advocating a different interpretation and explaining how that interpretation would operate under the facts.

B. Admission of Parol Evidence

Assume for this part B only that: (1) the court has interpreted the contract term "no later than December 3" to be an express condition of O's duty to pay anything to L, and that (2) L offers to testify that the parties had the following conversation a few minutes prior to signing the contract:

> O: "This December 3d deadline is important to me. We need to get this office complex open for business. So, I'm going to inspect on the morning of December 4, and if this project is not complete according to specifications, you don't get a dime.
>
> L: "I understand. Until what time do I have on December 3, in case we are running late?"
>
> O: "Heck, I don't care if you work all through the night. I won't get to the worksite to inspect till 8 a.m. on December 4, so just make it happen by then."

Respond to the following prompts, adopting the assumption in each prompt.

1. Assume for this part that the court is located in a state that follows a strong version of the Plain Meaning Rule. In IRAC format, explain why the judge likely will not allow the jury to hear testimony of O's oral description of the deadline for performance prior to signing of the contract. Do not argue the other side. State the relevant elements of the rules, apply them to the facts, and state the conclusion.

2. Assume for this part that the court is located in a state (like Arizona or California) that has rejected the Plain Meaning Rule. In IRAC format, present your best argument that the judge will allow the jury to hear testimony about O's oral description of the deadline for performance prior to signing of the contract. Do not argue the other side. Explain the rule, apply it to the facts, and reach the conclusion.

2. Q2—90 minutes {Suggested time allocation—30 minutes to study the facts, to identify the three issues, and to plan your answers; and an average of 20 minutes each to write out each of your three answers. If you have not yet studied liquidated damages in Ch. 12, you can skip Question 1 at the end of this exam and can deduct 20 minutes from your time.}

Grower ("G") owns a large tract of land, which he calls "Terra" and on which he desired to grow wine grapes for sale to winemakers. Terra is accessible from a road along its southern edge and from two roads running north and south along the east and west sides. It also has the advantage of a natural spring in the northeast corner, providing a natural supply of water that could be pumped to irrigation channels when rainwater is insufficient. Terra is uneven in grade, and is dotted with brush and small boulders, so G hired Conway Construction ("CC") to clear and grade 75% of the surface of Terra, which would be sufficient acreage of vines for G's plans.

G selected CC for the job in large part because CC had worked on many vineyards and was familiar with soils suitable for growing grapes. When G and CC inspected Terra together, they sifted through their fingers some soil from the center of Terra, with G stating that the soil had the sandy consistency and good drainage that is ideal for the kinds of wine grapes that G planned to grow. CC agreed completely with G's assessment. They signed a contract soon after that inspection. Three days later, G left a sample of the soil at a lab for complete analysis of its chemical content; he had not previously analyzed or tested the soil in that way, and the results would enable him to order fertilizer with the optimum mix of nutrients for his soil.

Following are excerpts of the contract between G and CC [with the parties and the property identified by the names used above for convenience]:

Recitals:

1. G desires that a portion of Terra be graded to facilitate the planting of vineyards. To enable further work to be performed in time for planting in season, completion of grading within 30 days of formation of this contract is essential.

2. CC has experience in moving earth and removing boulders, has experience with preparing ground for rows of grape vines, and is available to work solely on this project beginning 11 days after contract formation.

Mutual Rights and Obligations:

I. Within 30 days after formation of this contract, CC will grade 75% of Terra to an even grade, moving earth and removing vegetation and rock as needed for cultivation of grapes. CC will grade the portion of Terra that G designates for G's vineyard in the exercise of G's sole discretion. G will communicate this designation to CC within 10 days after formation of this contract, leaving CC at least 20 days to complete performance on time.

II. When CC has completed the work specified in section I, G will pay CC $60,000 minus any deductions for delay, as provided in section III.

III. If CC has not completed grading within 30 days after contract formation, CC will be liable to G in the amount of $3,000 for each day of delayed completion of performance, up to a maximum of $60,000. G may deduct any such liquidated damages from the sum that is owed to CC under section II.

On signing the contract, CC estimated that the job would normally take no longer than 15 days, perhaps a few days more if bad weather slowed the work. A hill of giant boulders sat on the northwest corner of Terra, adjacent to the spring in the northeast corner, but those two geographic features covered only 10% of Terra, and the remainder of Terra consisted mostly of small hills and depressions of soil that could easily be graded. Additionally, a number of shrubs, small boulders, and large rocks were widely scattered over Terra. Removal of those added substantially to CC's work, but he nonetheless could complete all the work within about 15 days if he used nearly all his equipment and his full crew of employees. CC therefore scheduled the grading work to start on the 11th day after contract formation, the day after the deadline for G's designation of the portion to be graded.

The timing of planting was important to producing a full crop within three years, so that delays could be costly to G, although to a degree that was very difficult to calculate. For example, a delay in grading of 20 days could possibly cause a loss to G of up to $60,000, which was an average of $3,000 per day. However, the consequences of delay would not grow uniformly with each day of delay. For example, if the grading were delayed by only five days, G normally could make up that lost time by spending an extra $1,000/day for the next 10 days to speed up the next stages of preparation for planting and to catch up to the original schedule. If CC missed the deadline by 30 days, however, G likely would not be able to make up that lost time and likely would miss the next spring planting season altogether, with ultimate losses averaging much more than $3,000/day for the 30 days delay.

By the end of the eighth day after signing the contract, G had inspected Terra several times and had developed a preliminary plan for designating the portion to be graded: all of Terra running east to west, starting at the southern end and leaving the northern 25% of Terra ungraded. G planned to revisit his plan the next day, to consider whether to move at least some of the vineyard closer to the source of water at the spring on the north end, although that idea was complicated by his desire not to place vines within the shadow of the adjacent hill of boulders. In any event, he was on schedule for communicating a final designation to CC by the tenth day.

On the ninth day, however, the lab reported to G its analysis of the soil, revealing that Terra's soil contained unusually large concentrations of naturally occurring arsenic. The high levels of this toxic element made Terra unsuitable for growing wine grapes. G abandoned his plans to cultivate grapes on Terra, and he currently has no other need to grade the surface of Terra.

G contemplated negotiating a rescission with CC, such as by offering to pay CC $6,000 to rescind the contract. However, G soon came up with a different idea. G decided to modify his preliminary designation of the part of Terra that would be graded. He drew a plan that started the grading above the southern edge, leaving a portion of Terra ungraded at that end, and then including the 5% of Terra sitting in the northwest corner for grading, so that some vineyards would be close to the spring to the south and west of the spring. Because the northwest corner was covered with the hill of giant boulders, G recognized that CC could not complete the removal of boulders before the deadline, so that CC's costs of performance would exceed the contract fee for grading, especially after deductions to the fee for delay, even if only a few days of delay. G hoped that CC would ask to rescind the contract.

G conveyed this designation to CC, explaining that he wanted to maximize the acreage of vineyards that would lie adjacent to the spring. CC was astonished. It made sense to maximize the amount of vineyard that would stand close to the water source, but he was shocked that G would expect him to undertake the formidable task of removing the hill of boulders. With G's designation, CC calculated that performance of the contract would be financially untenable: By using all his resources, renting some heavier equipment, and working his employees overtime, with good weather he probably could clear and grade the land with only a 5-day delay, but it would cost him more than $60,000 in expenses to achieve that result, and he would not even receive his full fee anyway, because G would deduct $15,000 for a delay of 5 days. CC wants to know more about his options.

* * * *

Assume that all the above facts are revealed and available for analysis. Assume that the parties formed the contract with consideration and mutual assent, so do not discuss contract formation. Also, do not discuss impossibility or frustration of purpose. Discuss the three questions set forth below. Use IRAC organization (Issue, Rule, Application to Facts, Conclusion). Argue both sides to the extent possible (even if one side seems stronger, try to find factual arguments for the other side as well). Present the law and analyze the facts to the greatest depth that time allows, but only to the extent that they are relevant to the issue.

1. Assuming for this question only that G's designation is valid so that CC would not be able to complete performance on time, fully discuss whether section III of the contract is enforceable (because, if it is not enforceable, G will be required to prove his actual damages after mitigating them). You can apply generally accepted common law principles without critiquing them or comparing them to alternatives (in other words, this question is not asking you to critique the common law rule on policy grounds).

2. Fully discuss the single strongest ground on which CC could seek to invalidate G's designation of the land to be graded.

3. Assuming for this part only that G's designation is invalid, and that CC asserts his right to earn the contract fee by grading land south of the spring and the hill of boulders, fully discuss the single strongest ground on which G might base an action to avoid the contract with CC.

Chapter 11

Duties, Conditions, Performance, and Breach

I. Overview

Let's assume now that we have an enforceable contract and that the court has determined its meaning. This chapter will explore the legal effect of certain kinds of contract terms and actions by the parties. As we study this material, think about the following questions:

- How do conditions qualify or limit a duty, and when is a contract provision interpreted to be a condition rather than a duty?
- What are constructive conditions, and how do they qualify or limit a duty?
- What is the "material breach" rule, and how does it relate to constructive conditions and the "substantial performance" doctrine?
- How can a breaching party recover part of its expectation interest by substantially performing a divisible part of a contract, while still remaining liable for offsetting damages?
- How does the UCC "perfect tender" rule differ from the common law "material breach" and "substantial performance" rules?
- How does one party's breach of an implied duty of cooperation excuse the other party's nonperformance of a duty?

II. Duties and Express Conditions

A. Basic Definitions

Enforceable promises create contractual duties, also called contractual obligations. A condition is a qualification to, or limitation on, a contractual duty. The condition will identify an event, the occurrence of which triggers the duty, or terminates or modifies the duty, depending on the type of condition. The duty is accordingly "conditional" or "contingent," and the event that satisfies the condition is sometimes called a "contingency."

1. Conditions Subsequent

If a currently owed contractual duty is subject to a "condition *subsequent*," the occurrence of the designated event will terminate or modify the duty. Suppose, for example, that Grower has undertaken a contractual obligation to grow, harvest, and deliver a crop from a specified field to Buyer, but the contract includes a condition subsequent providing that Grower's duty will terminate if a designated type of weather event destroys the crop. Suppose further that the crop is growing well but is still immature when a severe hailstorm destroys the crop. If that occurrence is one of the designated events that satisfies the condition subsequent, Grower's duties to Buyer are discharged (terminated), and Grower will not be liable for breach of contract for failing to deliver the mature crop. The contract undoubtedly also provides that Buyer pays nothing if Grower cannot deliver.

Depending on the precise nature of Grower's obligation, a court might reach the same result by applying the common law doctrine of impossibility, which is explored at the end of this chapter. An express condition subsequent in the contract, however, will more clearly and surely relieve Grower from further duties.

Of course, the hailstorm will visit losses on Grower, because Buyer will not be obligated to pay for Grower's incomplete performance; nonetheless, the condition subsequent will shield Grower from liability for Buyer's losses, including Buyer's lost profits. Either party might have taken out insurance to shift the risk of loss to an insurer, but our concern here is with the use of conditions to allocate the risks between the parties by placing limits on duties.

2. Conditions Precedent

A "condition *precedent*" is one whose satisfaction precedes the triggering of a duty. In contrast to a condition subsequent, a condition precedent attaches its contingency to a duty that lies dormant until the condition is satisfied. Even after formation of the contract that creates the contingent duty, that duty will not arise unless the condition precedent is first satisfied. If the specified event occurs, the condition precedent is satisfied, the restriction on the duty disappears, and the party owing the duty must perform.

All remaining examples of express conditions in this chapter will illustrate conditions *precedent*.

B. Express Conditions in Operation

1. An Express Condition May Qualify All Duties in the Contract

Imagine a bilateral contract in which Subcontractor has agreed to perform specified paving work, and Contractor has agreed to pay Subcontractor $30,000 for the paving work, all expressly conditioned on Contractor successfully securing the master contract for Owner's project. The mutual promises in this paving subcontract—performing paving work for payment of money—give rise to contractual duties. Both parties are bound to their promises and the resulting duties the moment they exchange these promises in an offer and acceptance. The promises are not illusory, because the awarding of the master contract to Contractor is subject to factors outside the control of either party. All promises on both sides, however, are qualified by a condition precedent, which imposes a limitation on the duties:

SC's Duty to Perform Paving ←→ GC's Duty to Pay SC's Fee

/ Condition: but only if GC is awarded Master Contract \

Consequently, if Contractor does not land the master contract from Owner, the duties in the existing contract between Contractor and Subcontractor will never arise. Instead, they will be discharged. That means that the duties are dissolved and will have no further legal effect. The parties created a contract, but they can walk away from it without further duties or liability if the condition precedent is not satisfied:

~~SC's Duty to Perform Paving~~ ←→ ~~GC's Duty to Pay SC's Fee~~

Condition not satisfied: GC is not awarded Master Contract

On the other hand, if the required event takes place, the condition is satisfied and it no longer operates as a potential barrier to the duties. Thus, if Contractor is awarded the master contract, the condition is satisfied, and Contractor and Subcontractor are bound to perform the paving subcontract:

SC's Duty to Perform Paving ←→ GC's Duty to Pay SC's Fee

Condition satisfied: GC is awarded Master Contract

2. An Express Condition May Limit Only Some of the Duties in a Contract

A condition can qualify fewer than all duties in a contract. For example, imagine an insurance contract in which Insurer and Insured agree that: (1) Insured will pay monthly premiums to Insurer, and (2) Insurer will compensate Insured for certain kinds of losses, but only if the losses are caused by an event defined in the contract as a "covered event."

Insured's obligation to pay premiums arises immediately and is not subject to the condition. Insurer is also bound by the contract immediately on reaching agreement, so it must stand ready to perform. Its duty under the contract, however, will arise only if the condition is satisfied.

Insured's Duty to Pay Premiums ←→ *Insurer's Duty to Compensate for Loss*
\ Conditioned on covered loss

If Insured suffers a loss caused by a "covered event," Insurer's duty to compensate arises and must be performed. Otherwise, Insurer's duty never arises, and it might never pay a penny on the contract. Insurer's promise is not illusory, because whether Insured suffers a loss from a covered event is not within Insurer's complete control (although it might have some influence, such as by requiring Insured to take certain safety precautions).

In some cases, fewer than all of one party's duties are subject to a condition. For example, imagine that Distributor has agreed to deliver 50 unassembled units of dining room furniture to Retailer's showroom, in return for payment of $20,000. During negotiations, Retailer expressed a willingness to pay an additional $1,000 if Distributor assigned an employee to assemble two dining room tables and 12 matching chairs for display purposes. Distributor could not guarantee the availability of such service on the delivery date, so the parties agreed that Retailer would pay Distributor $20,000 for delivery of the unassembled furniture, with payment of an additional $1,000 conditioned on Distributor providing the desired assembly on the date of delivery.

Distributor's Duty to Deliver 50 units ←→ Retailer's Duty to Pay $20,000 and *Duty to Pay $1,000*
Conditioned on Assembly /

Distributor has no obligation to provide the desired assembly. If it manages to do so, however, it will satisfy the condition, and Retailer's duty to pay an additional $1,000 will arise.

3. Conditions of Satisfaction

In some contracts, one party's obligation is expressly conditioned on the other party's first performing in a manner that is deemed to be satisfactory. For example, Contractor and Owner might agree that Contractor will construct an office building in four phases, in return for Owner's making progress payments at various intervals. One part of the contract obligates Owner to make the first progress payment of $30,000, but only on the condition that Contractor has first completed the foundation in a satisfactory manner.

As with Distributor in the previous example, satisfaction of the condition in this case lies in the hands of the party who will gain compensation if the condition is satisfied. The challenge remains, however, to define the event on which Owner's payment depends. How is satisfactory performance defined and determined? By whose standards should it be determined?

The parties could expressly define these matters in the contract. They could agree that the Owner will pay only if Contractor completes the foundation in a manner that would be satisfactory to a reasonable person in the industry, or in a satisfactory manner based on the Architect's expert application of prevailing standards in the industry, or to the satisfaction of the Architect according to the Architect's particular and subjective professional standards.

If the contract does not define the express condition of satisfaction, a court normally will interpret it to set forth an objective standard of satisfaction, requiring reasonable quality as generally accepted in the industry. For example, if the contract between Owner and Contractor conditions payment on completion of the foundation in a satisfactory manner, a court almost certainly will interpret that to require completion of the foundation according to contract specifications while meeting standards of quality that would be applied by a reasonable person in the industry.

Without express direction from the parties, a court will not infer that the parties intended a subjective standard of satisfaction except in unusual cases, such as when the circumstances strongly point to the necessity of satisfying one party's personal taste and fancy. For example, imagine that a contract calls for Supplier to deliver fresh fruit and vegetables to the highly rated Restaurant "Sophia," celebrated for the use of the finest, freshest ingredients by its chef, Sophia Cremini. Let's suppose also that this context is well known to the supplier and that the contract further states that the restaurant will accept delivery and pay for the produce "if and only if Chef Cremini approves of its quality." A court might well interpret that condition to allow the chef to apply her subjective, highly personal standards of satisfaction for her cuisine, even though that departs from general industry standards for top-notch restaurants, and even though the contract did not clearly specify whether Chef Cremini's approval would be governed by a subjective or an objective standard of satisfaction.

This example, however, is intended to illustrate the exceptional case. Absent specific direction in the contract, a condition of satisfaction will normally be interpreted as requiring satisfactory performance under an objective standard.

a. Condition of Subjective Satisfaction of a Party

In the following case, the buyer's duty to accept a portrait and pay for it was conditioned on his satisfaction with the portrait. The court interpreted this condition to require subjective satisfaction based on the buyer's personal tastes. What facts support that exceptional interpretation, rather than one requiring satisfactory performance under the usual objective standards of a reasonable person? Why was the buyer's promise not illusory?

Gibson v. Cranage

39 Mich. 49 (1878)

Marston, J.

¶1 Plaintiff in error brought assumpsit to recover the contract price for the making and execution of a portrait of the deceased daughter of defendant. It appeared from the testimony of the plaintiff that he at a certain time called upon the defendant and solicited the privilege of making an enlarged picture of his deceased daughter. He says "I was to make an enlarged picture that he would like, a large one from a small one, and one that he would like and recognize as a good picture of his little girl, and he was to pay me."

¶2 The defendant testified that the plaintiff was to take the small photograph and send it away to be finished, "and when returned if it was not perfectly satisfactory to me in every particular, I need not take it or pay for it. I still objected and he urged me to do so. There was no risk about it; if it was not perfectly satisfactory to me I need not take it or pay for it."

¶3 There was little if any dispute as to what the agreement was. After the picture was finished it was shown to defendant who was dissatisfied with it and refused to accept it. Plaintiff endeavored to ascertain what the objections were, but says he was unable to ascertain clearly, and he then sent the picture away to the artist to have it changed.

¶4 On the next day he received a letter from defendant reciting the original agreement, stating that the picture shown him the previous day was not satisfactory and that he declined to take it or any other similar picture, and countermanded the order.... When the picture was afterwards received by the plaintiff from the artist, he went to see defendant and to have him examine it. This defendant declined to do, or to look at it, and did not until during the trial, when he examined and found the same objections still existing.

....

¶5 The contract ... was an express one. The plaintiff agreed that the picture when finished should be satisfactory to the defendant, and his own evidence showed that the contract in this important particular had not been performed....

¶6 Artists or third parties might consider a portrait an excellent one, and yet it prove very unsatisfactory to the person who had ordered it and who might be unable to point out with clearness or certainty the defects or objections. And if the person giving the order stipulates that the portrait when finished must be satisfactory to him or else he will not accept or pay for it, and this is agreed to, he may insist upon his right as given him by the contract. [citations omitted]

The judgment must be affirmed with costs.

Exercise 11.1 — Good Faith and Opportunity to Cure

Was the seller foolish to incur so much risk in this contract? Was the seller apparently willing to accept this risk to make a sale with a reluctant buyer? How would the seller attempt to prove that a portrait in fact met the buyer's subjective standards, so that the buyer must purchase it?

Assuming that the first painting was deficient according to the buyer's subjective standards, can you nonetheless critique the buyer's behavior when rejecting each version of the painting? Can you recommend any legal safeguards to protect the seller's interests in these circumstances? Turn to Appendix 1 and compare the modern rights and duties for sales of goods at TEX. BUS. & COM. CODE §§ 2.508 (seller's limited right to attempt cure of defects), 2.605 (buyer's waiver of defects in goods for failure to specify the nonconformity) (2005).

C. Avoiding Forfeiture from Non-Satisfaction of a Condition

1. The Power of Conditions

Express conditions are powerful tools. If the condition is not satisfied, one party's duty is discharged and need not be performed. That's not a problem for the insured in an insurance contract, who is content to pay premiums to allocate the risk of catastrophic loss to the insurer; the insured normally is happy to avoid suffering a covered loss and thus to avoid triggering the insurer's duty to pay. It's not even a big problem for the supplier whose produce failed to satisfy the condition of subjective satisfaction of the picky chef, because the supplier likely can sell the produce to another restaurant whose standards are less demanding.

In contrast, Contractor—from our earlier illustration—has gone to great effort and expense to lay the foundation for Owner's office building. Contractor needs the first progress payment from Owner to pay its bills and to finance the next phase of construction. If Contractor's work on the foundation fails to meet the condition of satisfaction in the contract, and if the condition permits Owner to withhold all payment for the foundation, Contractor could suffer a significant forfeiture. After going to great expense to construct the foundation, Contractor could forfeit all contractual right to compensation for the first phase of construction by failing to satisfy the condition of satisfaction.

2. Strict Satisfaction of Conditions

Moreover, courts normally apply express conditions literally and strictly. Unless the condition precedent is strictly satisfied, the contingent duty never arises. *See, e.g., Luttinger v. Rosen*, 164 Conn. 45, 316 A.2d 757 (1972). In *Luttinger*, duties in a real estate contract were discharged because the condition of qualifying for bank financing at no more than 8½% was not satisfied by the buyer qualifying for bank financing at 8¾%, even though the seller offered to make up the difference.

Suppose, for example, that Owner's duty to pay the first progress payment was expressly "conditioned on completion of Phase I no later than October 31, precisely according to Architect's specifications, as certified by Architect."

Contractor's Duty to Lay Foundation by Oct. 31

↕

Owner's Duty to Pay $30,000

\ Conditioned on Contractor completing by 10/31

Suppose further that Contractor failed to meet the precise terms of this condition because it did not complete the foundation until November 1, and even then the architect correctly found that the foundation departed from specifications in a very minor way, requiring a correction that Contractor completed on November 2. Because Contractor did not complete construction of the foundation by October 31, Contractor did not strictly satisfy the condition, and Contractor could forfeit all compensation for a now perfect foundation.

To avoid such forfeiture, some courts might try to interpret the express condition loosely and find that it was in fact satisfied with completion of construction within a few days of October 31, but the language in the example above hardly lends itself to such a loose interpretation. Other courts might strain to avoid the forfeiture by relaxing the norm that express conditions must be strictly and fully satisfied, but Contractor cannot count on a court adopting such a forgiving approach, which flies in the face of the nature and purpose of an express condition. To cover all the bases, some courts might consider providing Contractor with restitution of the reasonable value of its work; however, the Contractor is not clearly entitled to quasi-contractual relief, because it arguably could not have reasonably expected compensation for work that was subject to an express condition that is not satisfied.

In sum, if an express condition is not strictly satisfied, and if the party who is benefited by the condition does not waive rights under the condition, the other party most likely will lose rights to counter-performance.

3. *Substantial Performance of Duties*

Because of the harsh consequences of such a forfeiture stemming from an express condition, courts will not lightly interpret a contract provision to impose an express condition at all. If the requirement to meet the architect's specifications by October 31 were only a duty assigned to Contractor, and not an express condition to Owner's duty to pay, then the consequences of a minor departure from those requirements normally would be much less severe.

For example, suppose that the contract includes the following two provisions:

> Section 9. Contractor must complete Phase I no later than October 31, precisely according to Architect's specifications, as certified by the Architect.

Section10. Owner will pay Contractor $30,000 on satisfactory completion of Phase I.

Without clear language of condition, a court would interpret these clauses to state mutual promises without express conditions. Under that interpretation, section 10 simply states the timing of the payment to Contractor. Let's also assume that completion precisely by October 31 is not critically important to the Owner, which explains why the contract does not contain a stipulation that "time is of the essence."

Now let's suppose that Contractor completed construction on November 2, which caused Owner to suffer $500 in losses due to the two-day delay. Contractor would be guilty of a minor breach of contract because of the delay, and Owner would have a claim against Contractor for $500 for those damages. We will learn later in the chapter, however, that Owner's duty to pay the Phase I progress payment of $30,000 would still arise because Contractor substantially performed its duties, and because Owner's obligation was not expressly conditioned on completion of the foundation by October 31. Contractor undoubtedly substantially performed by October 31, so Owner must pay the progress payment, although Owner could probably delay making the payment until November 2, in light of the wording of Owner's obligations under section 10 of the contract.

Consequently, Contractor would not suffer forfeiture of the entire progress payment if the requirement of completion by October 31 is interpreted to be its duty, and not an express condition to payment. Contractor will be liable for minor damages due to the delay, but that is an easy pill to swallow compared to forfeiting the entire progress payment.

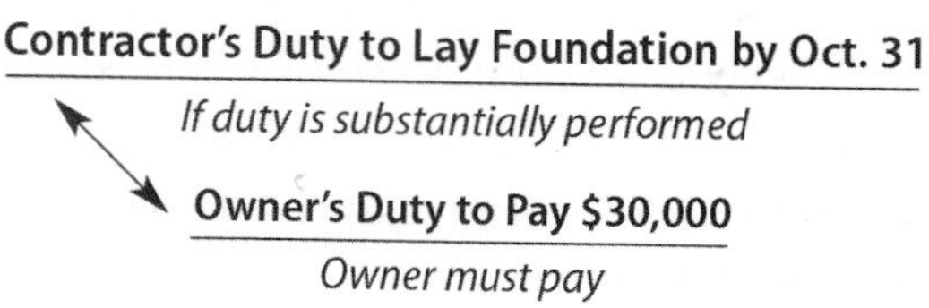

4. *Interpretation of Term as Express Condition Disfavored*

In light of the power of conditions, courts normally favor an interpretation that imposes duties without express conditions. They usually will find an express condition in a contract—particularly if forfeiture could result—only if the parties use unambiguous language of condition. Examples of such language of condition include "on the condition that," "in the event that," "provided that," "if, but only if," "only if," or perhaps simply "if" when the language around it supports the conclusion that the parties meant to make a duty of counter-performance conditional. In case of doubt, as a matter of legal policy, courts will tend to construe ambiguous language as stating only duties, free of express conditions that could cause oppressive forfeiture.

If the parties in our example used clear language of condition, then the court would have no choice but to find that timing was critically important to the parties, so that they intended to make Owner's duty to pay expressly contingent on completion by October 31. In those circumstances, some courts might still depart from traditional approaches if necessary to avoid a serious forfeiture. A liberal court might do so by finding the condition to be satisfied, and thus finding that the duty to pay arises, even if Contractor did not strictly satisfy the condition, but came up a bit short. Such flexibility represents a fairly radical departure from traditional doctrine, however, so Contractor should not count on it. If Contractor is not prepared to suffer the consequences of failing to strictly satisfy express conditions, it should not agree to them and should pass up a job with overly demanding contract terms.

Exercise 11.2 — Duty or Condition

1. Interpretation and Construction of Ambiguous Term

A contract requires Contractor to complete Phase I of construction no later than October 31. It also requires Owner to pay Contractor $30,000 on November 1, "subject to completion of Phase I of construction by October 31." Is the meaning of this provision debatable? If you have no other evidence of contractual intent, how would you interpret or construe the statement of Owner's duty? Is it an express condition, excusing payment if Contractor fails to complete Phase I until November 2? If not, what meaning would you give it?

2. Drafting

Draft three different versions of provisions that call for the purchase or sale of real estate for $500,000, according to the requirements stated below. Don't try to introduce antiquated legal language into your drafting; just use plain English to concisely state the desired obligations:

a. Mutual Obligations

Draft provisions that obligate the parties to buy and sell on February 1, and that obligate Buyer to secure financing by January 1.

b. Mutual Obligations and Condition

Draft provisions that obligate the parties to buy and sell on February 1, that obligate Buyer to make best efforts to secure financing within specified terms by January 1, and that expressly condition all obligations to buy and sell on Buyer securing such financing by January 1.

c. Condition and Mutual Obligations?

Draft provisions that obligate the parties to buy and sell, and that condition all obligations on Buyer obtaining financing by January 1, but that do not expressly obligate Buyer to make certain efforts to obtain financing by January 1. Do these provisions make Buyer's duty to buy the real estate illusory? To avoid that conclusion, would some duty likely be implied in fact or in law if not expressed?

III. Constructive Conditions

Let's assume now that the parties have entered into a bilateral contract with mutual promises but no express conditions. Even in the absence of express conditions, courts normally will recognize *constructive conditions*, implied in law. As discussed below, constructive conditions are "softer" than express conditions, and are satisfied more easily.

A. Common Law Doctrines of Constructive Conditions, Substantial Performance, and Material Breach

1. The Legal Basis for Constructive Conditions

In light of the modern conception of consideration as a bargained-for exchange with reciprocal inducement, courts recognize that promises in a bilateral contract are dependent on one another. Let's suppose that you and I agree that you will paint my house next week and that I will pay you $2,000 on your completion of the work. I am promising to pay you $2,000 only because I expect you to first paint my house. If you breach the contract and fail to paint my house, I will hope that the law permits me to withhold payment.

For centuries the common law has supported my expectations by implying a condition. *See Kingston v. Preston*, 99 Eng. Rep. 437 (1772). Because the condition is implied in law, as a matter of legal policy, it is known as a "constructive condition." Thus, even though our contract contains only mutual promises, without any express condition, my contractual obligation to pay you is *constructively* contingent on your first performing your obligation to me. If you fail to satisfy that *constructive condition*, my obligation to pay you does not arise.

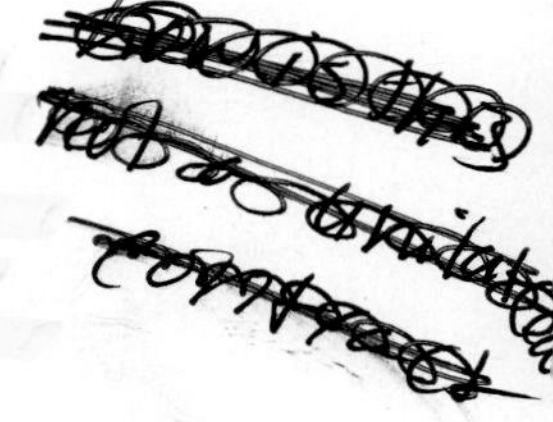

We could change the direction of the constructive condition by agreeing that I will pay your fee in advance. In that case, your obligation to paint my house will be constructively contingent on my first paying you the requisite amount, even in the absence of an express condition.

2. Satisfying Constructive Conditions

The event that satisfies a constructive condition is a party's performance of a contractual obligation. Because constructive conditions are implied from the interdependent nature of reciprocal promises, however, they are applied less strictly than are express conditions. A party can satisfy a constructive condition by *substantially performing* his own obligations, while remaining liable for any damages stemming from the minor delay or defects in performance. Once substantial performance takes place, the other party's duty of counter-performance arises.

3. Substantial Performance, Material Breach, and Minor Breach

If a party *materially breaches* its contractual obligation, it has not substantially performed. Consequently, it has not satisfied the constructive condition to the other party's performance and is not entitled to that counter-performance.

Contractor's Duty to Lay Foundation by Oct. 31

Material breach → Constructive condition not satisfied

~~Owner's Duty to Pay $30,000~~

→ Owner's duty does not arise

On the other hand, if the party has substantially performed, and has committed only a *minor breach*, then she has satisfied the constructive condition and is entitled to counter-performance. The other party, of course, retains a claim for damages for the minor breach, but that party cannot withhold his own performance.

For example, let's imagine that Contractor was contractually obligated to construct the foundation for an office building by October 31 and that Owner was obligated to make a progress payment of $30,000 to Contractor on November 1, without any express conditions. On October 31, Contractor announced completion of the foundation and presented a bill for $30,000. Owner, however, noticed a small deviation from the architect's plans, one that cannot now be "cured" (fixed) except at prohibitive cost. On the other hand, the deviation will not affect the building in any way and will increase the costs of other contractors' work by a mere $500–$1,000, which will eventually be charged to Owner.

Contractor's deviation from the plans would almost certainly amount to only a minor breach. Therefore, Owner would be obligated to render counter-performance by making the progress payment, while retaining a claim for damages for the minor breach. If the minor deviation later results in increased costs to Owner, Owner can send a bill to Contractor for those damages and will have a legal right to recover them. Indeed, if the amount of damages was certain at the time of breach (such as $600), Owner likely would be entitled to deduct those damages from the progress payment, but the damages are uncertain in the hypothetical above.

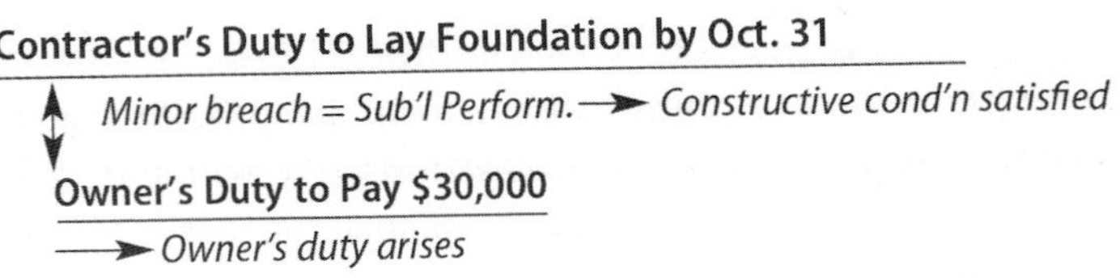

4. Cancellation and Cure

In contrast, if a party has materially breached the whole contract and fails to cure the breach, the victim of breach can withhold its own remaining counter-performance, cancel the contract, and sue for damages. Indeed, if the breaching party is performing so badly that its continued performance might cause great damage, the victim of the breach might need to terminate the contract when the breach becomes material, just to mitigate the damages.

For example, if you agree to paint the interior of my house for $2,000 but then begin to apply the wrong color in a substandard manner while repeatedly spilling paint on my carpet, I should assert my right to fire you immediately, before you ruin my whole house. Let's suppose that it costs me $150 to get a professional cleaning service to get the paint out of my carpet and that a reasonable substitute painter paints the interior of my house in proper fashion for $2,200. In light of your material breach, I will not be obligated to pay your fee, and I will have a contract claim against you for $350 stemming from the damage to my carpet and for the increased cost of hiring another painter to perform the job.

Still, if a breach can reasonably be corrected within critical time constraints, the victim of even a material breach normally should not immediately cancel the contract but may temporarily suspend performance while providing the breaching party with an opportunity to "cure" the breach. For example, imagine that Contractor completed the foundation for the office building on the due date but deviated from the architect's specifications in a manner that would adversely affect the construction of the building. Let's also suppose that the foundation can be corrected within a few days at an expense of $3,000 and that this brief delay will cause Owner to suffer only minor inconvenience and expense. If Contractor breached through some reasonable mistake, and not because it is incapable of performing well, the law in most states would require Owner to permit Contractor a reasonable opportunity to cure the breach before Owner cancels the contract. Then, if Contractor expended the resources to promptly correct the defect, it will have substantially performed, will no longer be in material breach, and will be entitled to its progress payment. The Owner will retain a claim for any damages that resulted from the delay in completing the foundation, and Owner can delay its payment of the Contractor's fee until Contractor successfully cures the breach.

If circumstances do not permit time for a cure, or if the material breaching party fails to cure within a reasonable time, the other party may treat the breach as "total," terminate the contract and his own remaining obligations, and sue for damages.

5. Breach by Repudiation

Sometimes a party will breach by "repudiation," by announcing that it will not perform all or part of its contractual obligations. We will assume now that the repudiation takes place at the time that performance is due, and we will later address the significance of a repudiation of obligations before the performance is due. If a party whose performance is due repudiates all its obligations, it is in total breach, which obviously allows the other party to withhold its own counter-performance and to sue the breaching party for damages.

If the breaching party repudiates only part of its obligations under a contract that contains no express condition, then the victim's right to cancel the contract will depend on whether a minor or material part of the contract has been repudiated. For example, if Contractor completes the foundation on time but announces that it cannot clean up the work site as called for in the contract, Owner will not be entitled to withhold the progress payment for this repudiation of a minor part of Contractor's duties. Instead, it must pay the progress payment while charging Contractor with the cost of hiring another contractor to clean up the work site.

6. Distinguishing Between Minor and Material Breach

In light of the legal significance of a breach being material, rather than only minor, much depends on the criteria for distinguishing between the two. The first and second Restatements have offered a list of five or six factors that may be relevant to this determination, depending on the facts available in each case. RESTATEMENT (SECOND) OF CONTRACTS § 241 (1981); RESTATEMENT (FIRST) OF CONTRACTS § 275 (1932).

Section 275 of the first Restatement is quoted in the next case. Notice that it states that the six listed "circumstances" are "influential" in determining whether a breach is material. Similarly, the second Restatement does not purport to offer a bright-line test, but states that its five "circumstances are significant." RESTATEMENT (SECOND) OF CONTRACTS § 241 (1981).

Accordingly, you should not treat either list of factors as a statement of a "rule" that necessarily should be quoted and applied in totality. *See id.* cmt. a (the standard of materiality is "necessarily imprecise and flexible," so section 241 states "circumstances, not rules"). Instead, you should gain a general understanding of the kinds of considerations that are captured in the list of factors, so that you get a feel for the kinds of facts that might be relevant to a determination whether a breach is material. These factual categories comport with general common sense, so advocates (or students taking an essay exam) should feel free to argue any factor that might suggest that a breach is, or is not, so substantial that the victim of the breach should have a right to cancel the contract.

Walker & Co. v. Harrison

347 Mich. 630, 81 N.W.2d 352 (1957)

Smith, Justice.

¶ 1 This is a suit on a written contract. The defendants are in the dry-cleaning business. Walker & Company, plaintiff, sells, rents, and services advertising signs and billboards. These parties entered into an agreement pertaining to a sign. The agreement is in writing and is termed a "rental agreement." It specifies in part that:

> The lessor agrees to construct and install, at its own cost, one 18'9" high x 8'8" wide pylon type d.f. neon sign with electric clock and flashing lamps.... The lessor agrees to and does hereby lease or rent unto the said lessee the

> said SIGN for the term, use and rental and under the conditions, hereinafter set out, and the lessee agrees to pay said rental....
>
> (a) The term of this lease shall be 36 months....
>
> (b) The rental to be paid by lessee shall be $148.50 per month for each and every calendar month during the term of this lease;....
>
> (d) Maintenance. Lessor at its expense agrees to maintain and service the sign together with such equipment as supplied and installed by the lessor to operate in conjunction with said sign under the terms of this lease; this service is to include cleaning and repainting of sign in original color scheme as often as deemed necessary by lessor to keep sign in first class advertising condition and make all necessary repairs to sign and equipment installed by lessor....

¶ 2 At the "expiration of this agreement," it was also provided, "title to this sign reverts to lessee." This clause is in addition to the printed form of agreement and was apparently added as a result of defendants' concern over title, they having expressed a desire "to buy for cash" and the salesman, at one time, having "quoted a cash price."

¶ 3 The sign was completed and installed in the latter part of July, 1953. The first billing of the monthly payment of $148.50 was made August 1, 1953, with payment thereof by defendants on September 3, 1953. This first payment was also the last. Shortly after the sign was installed, someone hit it with a tomato. Rust, also, was visible on the chrome, complained defendants, and in its corners were "little spider cobwebs." In addition, there were "some children's sayings written down in here." Defendant Herbert Harrison called Walker for the maintenance he believed himself entitled to under subparagraph (d) above. It was not forthcoming. He called again and again. "I was getting, you might say, sorer and sorer.... Occasionally, when I started calling up, I would walk around where the tomato was and get mad again. Then I would call up on the phone again." Finally, on October 8, 1953, plaintiff not having responded to his repeated calls, he telegraphed Walker that:

> You Have Continually Voided Our Rental Contract By Not Maintaining Signs As Agreed As We No Longer Have A Contract With You Do Not Expect Any Further Remuneration.

¶ 4 Walker's reply was in the form of a letter. After first pointing out that "your telegram does not make any specific allegations as to what the failure of maintenance comprises," and stating that "We certainly would appreciate your furnishing us with such information," the letter makes reference to a prior collateral controversy between the parties, "wondering if this refusal on our part prompted your attempt to void our rental contract," and concludes as follows:

> We would like to call your attention to paragraph G in our rental contract, which covers procedures in the event of a Breach of Agreement. In the event

> that you carry out your threat to make no future monthly payments in accordance with the agreement, it is our intention to enforce the conditions outlined under paragraph G through the proper legal channels. We call to your attention that your monthly rental payments are due in advance at our office not later than the 10th day of each current month. You are now approximately 30 days in arrears on your September payment. Unless we receive both the September and October payments by October 25th, this entire matter will be placed in the hands of our attorney for collection in accordance with paragraph G which stipulates that the entire amount is forthwith due and payable. [*An omitted footnote sets forth paragraph G, which states the parties' agreement that any missed payment by Harrison would be deemed a breach of the entire agreement, permitting Walker & Co. to cancel the contract, retrieve the sign, and claim all remaining rents due under the entire contract.*]

¶5 No additional payments were made and Walker sued in assumpsit for the entire balance due under the contract, $5,197.50, invoking paragraph (g) of the agreement. Defendants filed answer and claim of recoupment, asserting that plaintiff's failure to perform certain maintenance services constituted a prior material breach of the agreement, thus justifying their repudiation of the contract and grounding their claim for damages. The case was tried to the court without a jury and resulted in a judgment for the plaintiff. The case is before us on a general appeal.

¶6 Defendants urge upon us again and again, in various forms, the proposition that Walker's failure to service the sign, in response to repeated requests, constituted a material breach of the contract and justified repudiation by them. Their legal proposition is undoubtedly correct. Repudiation is one of the weapons available to an injured party in event the other contractor has committed a material breach. But the injured party's determination that there has been a material breach, justifying his own repudiation, is fraught with peril, for should such determination, as viewed by a later court in the calm of its contemplation, be unwarranted, the repudiator himself will have been guilty of material breach and himself have become the aggressor, not an innocent victim.

¶7 What is our criterion for determining whether or not a breach of contract is so fatal to the undertaking of the parties that it is to be classed as "material"? There is no single touchstone. Many factors are involved. They are well stated in section 275 of Restatement of the Law of Contracts in the following terms:

> In determining the materiality of a failure fully to perform a promise the following circumstances are influential:
>
> (a) The extent to which the injured party will obtain the substantial benefit which he could have reasonably anticipated;
>
> (b) The extent to which the injured party may be adequately compensated in damages for lack of complete performance;

(c) The extent to which the party failing to perform has already partly performed or made preparations for performance;

(d) The greater or less hardship on the party failing to perform in terminating the contract;

(e) The willful, negligent or innocent behavior of the party failing to perform;

(f) The greater or less uncertainty that the party failing to perform will perform the remainder of the contract.

¶8 We will not set forth in detail the testimony offered concerning the need for servicing. Granting that Walker's delay (about a week after defendant Herbert Harrison sent his telegram of repudiation Walker sent out a crew and took care of things) in rendering the service requested was irritating, we are constrained to agree with the trial court that it was not of such materiality as to justify repudiation of the contract, and we are particularly mindful of the lack of preponderant evidence contrary to his determination.... The trial court ... held as follows:

> Now Mr. Harrison phoned in, so he testified, a number of times. He isn't sure of the dates but he sets the first call at about the 7th of August and he complained then of the tomato and of some rust and some cobwebs. The tomato, according to the testimony, was up on the clock; that would be outside of his reach, without a stepladder or something. The cobwebs are within easy reach of Mr. Harrison and so would the rust be. I think that Mr. Bueche's argument that these were not materially a breach would clearly be true as to the cobwebs and I really can't believe in the face of all the testimony that there was a great deal of rust seven days after the installation of this sign. And that really brings it down to the tomato. And, of course, when a tomato has been splashed all over your clock, you don't like it. But he says he kept calling their attention to it, although the rain probably washed some of the tomato off. But the stain remained, and they didn't come. I really can't find that that was such a material breach of the contract as to justify rescission. I really don't think so.

¶9 Nor, we conclude, do we. There was no valid ground for defendants' repudiation and their failure thereafter to comply with the terms of the contract was itself a material breach, entitling Walker, upon this record, to judgment.

¶10 [The court affirmed the trial court's award of all rentals due under the contract, pursuant to paragraph G of the contract, minus what Walker would have spent servicing the sign for the remainder of the contract.]

The following case outlines how section 241 of the second Restatement works with a companion section to emphasize the opportunity for even a materially breaching party to cure the breach, unless allowing such an opportunity is not feasible or would be counter-productive.

Frazier v. Mellowitz

804 N.E.2d 796 (Ind. App. 2004) [footnotes omitted]

....

¶1 [T]he six-factor analysis from the Restatement of Contracts was altered in the Restatement (Second) of Contracts (1981). Specifically, Murray on Contracts, § 167 (2d Rev. ed.1974), provides in relevant part:

> ... The new structure in the Restatement (Second) apparently requires a determination of materiality of failure to perform exclusive of any question of delay in performance. If the determination of materiality is made as to a particular failure to perform, the effect is to suspend the duty of the injured party (assuming there is time remaining for a possible cure). If the time for cure expires (determined by the "circumstances" set forth in the "delay" section), the uncured material failure to perform or offer to perform has the effect of discharging the duty of the injured party.

¶2 ... Accordingly, under the original Restatement of Contracts, once a material breach occurs, the injured party is immediately discharged from any further obligation to perform under the contract. But under the Restatement (Second) of Contracts, an injured party is not discharged from his duty to perform unless (1) the breach is material, and (2) it is too late for performance or an offer to perform to occur. In particular, the Restatement (Second) of Contracts (1981) provides:

> § 241. Circumstances Significant in Determining Whether a Failure Is Material
>
> In determining whether a failure to render or to offer performance is *material*, the following circumstances are significant:
>
> (a) the extent to which the injured party will be deprived of the benefit which he reasonably expected;
>
> (b) the extent to which the injured party can be adequately compensated for the part of that benefit of which he will be deprived;
>
> (c) the extent to which the party failing to perform or to offer to perform will suffer forfeiture;
>
> (d) the likelihood that the party failing to perform or to offer to perform will cure his failure, taking account of all the circumstances including any reasonable assurances;
>
> (e) the extent to which the behavior of the party failing to perform or to offer to perform comports with standards of good faith and fair dealing.

(Emphasis added).

¶3 And Section 242 provides:

> In determining *the time after which a party's uncured material failure to render or to offer performance discharges the other party's remaining duties to render performance* under the rules stated in §§ 237 and 238, the following circumstances are significant:

(a) those stated in § 241;

(b) the extent to which it reasonably appears to the injured party that delay may prevent or hinder him in making reasonable substitute arrangements;

(c) the extent to which the agreement provides for performance without delay, but a material failure to perform or to offer to perform on a stated day does not itself discharge the other party's remaining duties unless the circumstances, including the language of the agreement, indicate that performance or an offer to perform by that day is important.

(Emphasis added).

¶ 4 Additionally, Comment a. to § 242 regarding "cure" states:

Ordinarily there is some period of time between suspension and discharge, and during this period a party may cure his failure. Even then, since any breach gives rise to a claim, a party who has cured a material breach has still committed a breach, by his delay, for which he is liable in damages. *Furthermore, in some instances timely performance is so essential that any delay immediately results in discharge and there is no period of time during which the injured party's duties are merely suspended and the other party can cure his default.*

(Emphasis added).

Exercise 11.3 — Conditions and Constructive Conditions

1. The Risk of Guessing about Material Breach

By wrongly guessing that Walker & Co. had committed a material breach, Harrison committed the first breach by withholding payment and giving notice of canceling the contract, which amounted to a total breach by repudiation. In light of the flexibility and indeterminacy of the test for determining material breach, a party or its attorney should hesitate to find a material breach by the other party in a close case. If you were counseling Harrison when it became dissatisfied with the service provided by Walker & Co., what course of action would you have advised?

2. Past Exam Questions Inviting Drafting

a. Incentive Clause

The owner of an apartment complex ("O") is negotiating an agreement with a contractor ("C") to paint the exterior of all the apartment units, for a fee of $20,000. C has identified February 15 as earliest date that he could guarantee completion, although he says that the project might be completed earlier if conditions are ideal. O's needs are met with a completion date of February 15; however, she would benefit if the painting is completed by February 1. To encourage C to work quickly, O is contemplating negotiating a provision that would award C a bonus of $2,000 for completion by 5 p.m. on February 1 but would leave O free of any obligation to pay any part of this bonus unless C completes by precisely that date and time and no later. Draft a short sample contract clause in plain English, or explain the kind of clause that would meet O's needs. [This question can be answered in two sentences. Just state in plain language what happens in each of two events. In the next chapter, you can ask whether such a clause might in some circumstances create an unenforceable penalty for completion after February 1.]

b. Lesson Learned

It's time to hire a contractor to paint the outside of Owner's storefront, and Owner remembers what happened 10 years ago: Owner's contract then included two simple promises: the painting contractor promised to paint all exposed surfaces on the storefront with a particular type and color paint, and Owner promised in return to pay the painter $2,500. During performance, however, the contractor declined to paint some hard-to-reach areas just under the roofline. These unpainted areas constituted only 1% of the total surface area, and they were visible only from certain angles. Still, the unpainted areas clearly constituted exposed surfaces of the storefront, so the contractor admitted that he was in breach and was not willing to cure it, and Owner had a nasty dispute with him about whether Owner could withhold the entire payment until the contractor completed the performance.

This time, Owner has hired a different painting contractor, and Owner wants the right to withhold the entire payment until the contractor completes the task of painting every inch of exposed surface of the storefront. Owner has partially drafted a contract, section 2 of which already describes the obligations of "Contractor," including a clear description of the total surface to be painted. Owner now seeks your advice on avoiding the problem he encountered 10 years ago. Explain what legal principles created a problem for Owner 10 years ago, and then draft a clause that addresses the problem, or describe the kind of clause that will meet owner's needs.

B. Sales of Goods: The UCC Perfect-Tender Rule

The pre-UCC law exempted sales from the substantial-performance/material-breach rule and instead required sellers to satisfy constructive conditions strictly, as though the buyer's counter-performance were subject to an express condition. Under this "perfect tender rule," if the seller's delivery deviated in any way from the contract terms, even if only to a minor degree, the buyer could reject delivery:

> In the nineteenth century, sellers were required to deliver goods that complied exactly with the sales agreement. *See Filley v. Pope*, 115 U.S. 213, 220 ... (1885) (buyer not obliged to accept otherwise conforming scrap iron shipped to New Orleans from Leith, rather than Glasgow, Scotland, as required by contract); *Columbian Iron Works & Dry-Dock Co. v. Douglas*, 84 Md. 44, 47, 34 A. 1118, 1120–1121 (1896) (buyer who agreed to purchase steel scrap from United States cruisers not obliged to take any other kind of scrap). That rule, known as the "perfect tender" rule, remained part of the law of sales well into the twentieth century. By the 1920's the doctrine was so entrenched

> in the law that Judge Learned Hand declared "(t)here is no room in commercial contracts for the doctrine of substantial performance." *Mitsubishi Goshi Kaisha v. J. Aron & Co., Inc.*, 16 F.2d 185, 186 (2d Cir. 1926).

Ramirez v. Autosport, 88 N.J. 277, 284, 440 A.2d 1345, 1348 (1982). This "perfect tender" rule is retained in the UCC with respect to a buyer's initial acceptance or rejection of delivery in a contract calling for a single delivery. At that stage, the buyer has the right to reject the entire shipment if the goods "fail *in any respect* to conform to the contract." U.C.C. § 2-601(a) (2011) (italics added).

To remind yourself of their place within a state code system, find the Texas enactments of UCC §§ 2-601, 2-711 in Appendix 1. Consulting the Texas statutes either in the Appendix or below, find the statutory language that describes the options available to a buyer as alternative responses to a nonconforming delivery, and find the provisions that establish that a buyer who rejects nonconforming goods can cancel the contract with respect to those goods.

> Sec. 2.601. BUYER'S RIGHTS ON IMPROPER DELIVERY.
>
> Subject to the provisions of this chapter on breach in installment contracts (Section 2.612) and unless otherwise agreed under the sections on contractual limitations of remedy (Sections 2.718 and 2.719), if the goods or the tender of delivery fail in any respect to conform to the contract, the buyer may
>
> (1) reject the whole; or
>
> (2) accept the whole; or
>
> (3) accept any commercial unit or units and reject the rest.
>
> ....
>
> Sec. 2.711. BUYER'S REMEDIES IN GENERAL; BUYER'S SECURITY INTEREST IN REJECTED GOODS.
>
> (a) Where the seller fails to make delivery or repudiates or the buyer rightfully rejects or justifiably revokes acceptance then with respect to any goods involved, and with respect to the whole if the breach goes to the whole contract (Section 2.612), the buyer may cancel and whether or not he has done so may in addition to recovering so much of the price as has been paid....

As with the common law, a victim of breach need not assert his rights to the fullest. Section 2-601 permits the Buyer to accept all or part of a non-conforming delivery, while retaining a claim for damages. Nonetheless, section 2-601 authorizes the buyer to reject the entire delivery for *any* nonconformity.

Although the buyer cannot reject the delivery for a pretextual complaint made in bad faith, in most states it remains true that a seller fails to satisfy constructive conditions to counter-performance if it commits even a minor breach in its delivery of goods. *Y & N Furniture, Inc. v. Nwabuoku*, 190 Misc. 2d 402, 403, 734 N.Y.S.2d 382, 384 (N.Y. Civ. Ct. 2001) (subject to a requirement of good faith, buyer may reject goods for even a "trivial" deviation from contract specifications).

Still, the UCC softens the perfect tender rule, which never escaped criticism and which may seem especially inappropriate to modern commerce. Although the UCC retains the perfect-tender rule with respect to the initial delivery of goods in a non-installment contract, it embraces a version of the material-breach rule for several other contexts. For example, if the buyer has initially accepted delivery of the goods and later discovers a non-conformity, the buyer can then reject the goods ("revoke acceptance" in confusing UCC terminology) only in certain circumstances and only if the delivery's "non-conformity *substantially* impairs its value to him." U.C.C. § 2-608(1) (2011) (italics added). *See, e.g., Colonial Dodge, Inc. v. Miller* 420 Mich. 452, 458–59, 362 N.W.2d 704, 706–07 (1984) (finding substantial impairment).

Moreover, the UCC perfect tender rule does not apply to sales contracts that call for two or more deliveries in installments. In that context, the UCC adopts a material breach doctrine by permitting the buyer to reject delivery only if the delivery "substantially impairs the value of that installment," U.C.C. § 2-612(2) (2011), and by finding a breach of the whole contract only if non-conformity in one or more installments "substantially impairs the value of the whole contract," U.C.C. § 2-612(3) (2011).

Finally, even when the perfect tender rule applies, the UCC mitigates it in three ways. First, the obligation of the buyer to reject goods only for good-faith dissatisfaction includes a duty to act in a commercially reasonable manner, at least for merchant buyers. U.C.C. § 2-103(1)(b) (2011) (defining merchant's duty of good faith to include the "observance of reasonable commercial standards of fair dealing"); *see Alden Press, Inc. v. Block and Co.*, 173 Ill. App. 3d 251, 258, 261, 527 N.E.2d 489, 493, 495 (jury can test rejection under a standard of reasonableness, as well as subjective good faith) (1988); *cf.* ARIZ. REV. STAT. ANN. 47-1201(20) (2005) (In Arizona's UCC, the general definition of good faith, which applies to non-merchants, requires only "honesty in fact"). Indeed, several commentators and the courts of at least one state interpret the UCC's requirement of good faith to permit the buyer to reject only for a nonconformity that is "substantial," at least in some circumstances. *See D.P. Tech. Corp. v. Sherwood Tool, Inc.*, 751 F. Supp. 1038, 1042 (D. Conn. 1990) (citing Connecticut case law that adopts the approach of scholars White & Summers and stating that a buyer's rejection for insubstantial delay that causes no damage "is arguably not in good faith").

Second, the perfect tender rule in the UCC is a default rule subject to contrary agreement by the parties regarding delivered but slightly non-conforming goods. Moreover, some courts will stretch a bit to find an implied agreement by the parties to prohibit rejection for minor nonconformities, perhaps based on past practices of the parties or custom in the industry. *T. J. Stevenson & Co., Inc. v. 81,193 Bags of Flour*, 629 F.2d 338, 356 n.33 (5th Cir. 1980).

Third, the UCC permits sellers to cure the breach with a conforming delivery if the time for performance has not yet expired, and even for a reasonable time after expiration of the time for performance in certain circumstances. U.C.C. § 2-508 (2011).

Thus, the UCC retains the perfect-tender rule only in a limited context. Nonetheless, when it applies to an uncured minor breach, it stands in stark contrast to the common law substantial-performance/material-breach doctrine. It also contrasts with the U.N. Convention on Contracts for the International Sale of Goods, which permits a buyer to reject delivery of goods in an international sale only for a "fundamental breach," which requires a substantial deprivation of the buyer's expectations. CISG art. 25, 46, 49 (1980).

In the next case, the court applies the perfect tender rule in a manner consistent with the contract's description of a special style of "high-end" golf course. Does the evidence also establish that the sod would conform to the contract only if it met the subjective standards of a representative for the developer of the golf course? If so, consider how these two factors might reinforce each other.

Williams v. Medalist Golf, Inc.

910 F.3d 1041 (8th Cir. 2018) (some paragraphing modified)

Kelly, Circuit Judge.

¶ 1 Chris Williams, doing business as Cane Creek Sod, appeals the district court's grant of summary judgment in favor of Medalist Golf, Inc. Upon careful consideration of the issues presented, we affirm the judgment of the district court.

I

¶ 2 Williams operates Cane Creek, which supplies, grows, and delivers sod. Medalist specializes in building high-end golf courses. Medalist's project manager, Todd Tilton, sought sod bids for the Gary Player Designed Golf Course, which Medalist agreed to build at Big Cedar Lodge for Ozarks Golf and Hunt Club, LLC. When requesting a bid from Cane Creek, Tilton informed Mark Woodard, a Cane Creek employee, that the sod was for use on a "high-end golf course for a very important client." ...

....

¶ 3 On February 23 and 24, representatives for Medalist and Cane Creek signed the GSA [Grass Supplier Agreement]. Under the document's title, the GSA states, "Job: Gary Player Designed Golf Course at Big Cedar Lodge." In relevant part, the GSA provides that Cane Creek "guarantees the quality and specification of the materials provided to" Medalist.... Williams testified that he understood the provision of the

GSA stating that Cane Creek "guarantees the quality and specification of the materials provided" to mean that he "was guaranteeing that they were going to get Meyer Zoysia and that it would be the quality that satisfied the customer," and if the customer was not satisfied, then Cane Creek "would fix it."

¶ 4 [After inspecting the Cane Creek field from which the purchased sod would be harvested, the director of agronomy for the golf course instructed Medalist to reject the sod for failure to meet the quality standards for a Gary Player designed golf course. Williams brought suit against Medalist for breach of contract.]

....

¶ 5 Medalist argues that Cane Creek's breach of contract claim fails as a matter of law because it tendered nonconforming goods. Under Mo. Ann. Stat. § 400.2-601, if goods tendered by a seller "fail in any respect to conform to the contract, the buyer may," among other things, "reject the whole." Goods are conforming "when they are in accordance with the obligations under the contract." § 400.2-106(2). Additionally, under § 400.1-304, "[e]very contract or duty [governed by Missouri's UCC] imposes an obligation of good faith in its performance and enforcement."

¶ 6 The crux of Medalist's argument is that because Ozarks Golf determined that the quality of Cane Creek's sod was unacceptable for use in the Gary Player-designed golf course, there is no issue of material fact as to whether Williams tendered conforming goods. We agree that Williams is unable to show that there is a genuine dispute of material fact as to whether his Meyer Zoysia sod satisfied the quality requirements of the Gary Player-designed golf course. Williams testified that he understood he "was guaranteeing that they were going to get Meyer Zoysia and that it would be the quality that satisfied the customer." The GSA also states that Cane Creek "guarantees the quality and specification of the materials" it provides to Medalist and that the "Gary Player Designed Golf Course at Big Cedar Lodge" is the "Job."

¶ 7 Williams does not claim that Bohn acted in bad faith when he determined that Cane Creek's Meyer Zoysia did not meet the quality standards of the project. Rather, he argues that rejection of his Meyer Zoysia was wrongful because (1) outside expert testimony showed that his sod was high quality, weed free, and healthy; (2) the Missouri Department of Agriculture inspected his sod and found no noxious weed contaminates; and (3) the superintendent of another golf course that purchased some of Cane Creek's Meyer Zoysia to resod some tee boxes was satisfied with that sod.

¶ 8 But even with the benefit of all reasonable inferences to be drawn from these facts, Williams does not establish that Cane Creek provided goods conforming to the agreement—the agreement contemplated sod that would satisfy the quality standards of the Gary Player-designed golf course specifically, not the quality standards of golf courses more generally.

¶ 9 Because Williams cannot show that Medalist wrongfully rejected the sod, Medalist was entitled to summary judgment on Williams's breach of contract claim.

C. Divisibility—Partial Recovery by a Materially Breaching Party under Common Law

Let's return to transactions governed by the common law material breach rule, such as construction contracts. Can the materially breaching party demand recovery for partial performance, notwithstanding that the breaching party fell short of substantial performance of the whole contract? As we will discover in Chapter 12, if the victim of the breach has canceled the contract and sued the materially breaching party for damages, the value of the breaching party's partial performance normally will reduce the damages owed by the breaching party.

In the presumably rare case in which the enrichment provided by the materially breaching party more than cancels out any losses suffered by the victim of breach, the victim has no incentive to bring suit. Moreover, the materially breaching party cannot sue on the whole contract for withheld payment because it did not satisfy constructive conditions. Under the modern trend, nonetheless, some courts will award restitution to the breaching party "for any benefit ... in excess of the loss" caused by the breach. Restatement (Second) of Contracts § 374(1); *see also* Restatement (Third) of Restitution and Unjust Enrichment§ 36(1) (2011) (recommending restitution "as necessary to prevent unjust enrichment"). It is not clear, however, whether this has yet attained the status of a prevailing rule in the courts. In particular, "many jurisdictions" still deny restitution to a party whose material breach was "willful or deliberate" in a way that undermines that party's "equitable posture." *Id.* cmt. b.

The more universally accepted doctrine of divisibility will permit a materially breaching party to recover the contract rate for partial performance, whether acting as plaintiff or defendant after failing to substantially perform the entire contract. The breaching party must demonstrate that the contract is divisible so that the court can treat the substantially performed portion of the contract as a separate contract with its own constructive conditions.

1. *Entire or Divisible Contract?*

Suppose that a construction contract, without any express conditions, calls for several phases of construction and that the contractor has completed one or more phases but has not substantially performed the entire contract. If the contract is viewed as a single set of dependent promises, then the contractor has committed a material breach of that contract, and the victim of the breach can cancel the contract and withhold its counter-performance.

On the other hand, if the contractor can establish that the larger contract consists of several smaller exchanges, each with its own set of matching, interdependent promises, then the contractor might persuade a court to divide the contract into sections for purposes of applying the substantial-performance/material-breach doctrine.

2. An Illustration of Divisibility

Imagine, for example, that Owner contracts with Contractor to install three small swimming pools at various areas of its sprawling apartment complex, which is still under construction. The contract calls for construction of the swimming pools at $20,000 each for a total of $60,000. Let's suppose that Contractor had completed the first swimming pool, had completed half of the second swimming pool (by excavating the pit, installing basic plumbing, and pouring the concrete shell for the pool), and had not yet begun working on the third swimming pool, when Contractor abandoned the project to take a much more profitable job.

Total Fee: $60,000

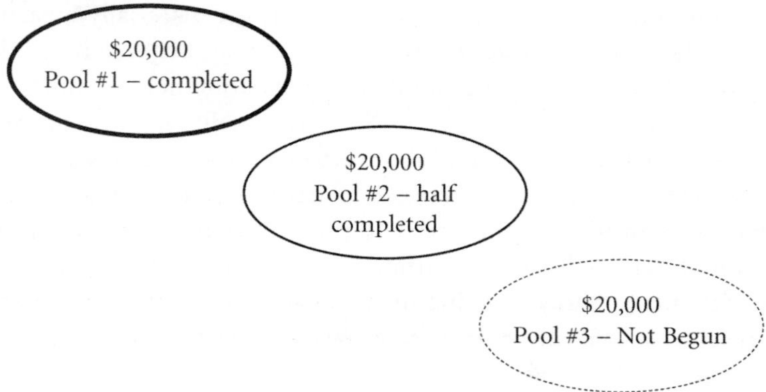

If the entire project of three pools is viewed as a single, indivisible contract, it's certain that a court would find that Contractor failed to substantially perform the entire contract and thus did not satisfy constructive conditions to demanding payment of the contract price of $60,000. Owner could cancel its obligations toward Contractor because of Contractor's material breach of the whole contract. Some courts might grant Contractor restitution of the reasonable value of its partially completed work; however, many courts would be inclined to deny such quasi-contractual recovery in light of Contractor's deliberate breach.

If Contractor can establish that the contract is divisible into three separate parts, however, each with its own set of corresponding, dependent promises, then a court likely would apply the substantial-performance/material-breach analysis to each of the three pools separately:

- Contractor fully constructed pool #1, has thus satisfied constructive conditions to counter-performance, and is entitled to $20,000 for that pool.
- Contractor did not substantially construct pool #2 (because it was only half finished and was unusable) and thus did not satisfy constructive conditions to payment.

- Contractor did not begin pool #3 and thus did not satisfy constructive conditions to payment.

Contractor has abandoned the project, so Owner will hire a different contractor to complete the project and can sue Contractor for any resulting damages. Nonetheless, if the contract is divisible in the manner described above, Owner would be obligated to pay Contractor $20,000 for swimming pool #1.

For example, if a substitute contractor charged Owner $45,000 to finish swimming pool #2 and to construct swimming pool #3, then Owner will end up paying $5,000 more for all three swimming pools than it had expected to pay in its initial contract with Contractor, and it will have a claim against Contractor for those damages. Owner's net payment to Contractor will be $15,000: $20,000 for the first swimming pool, minus $5,000 for damages caused by Contractor's failure to complete the other two pools.

3. Factors Supporting or Undermining Divisibility

The hypothetical contract described above is divisible because the contract described three separate construction projects with separate consideration for each one, and because Owner received full value (on one part of the contract) for completion of one swimming pool. If either of these conditions were absent, the contract would not be divisible, and Contractor would be found to be in material breach of the entire contract, with no right to payment of the contract rate on any of the swimming pools.

For example, suppose that the contract called for a total of $60,000 for three swimming pools of slightly different sizes, shapes, and descriptions, without specifying the fee for each one. The contract likely would be indivisible, because it probably would be impossible for the court to determine the contract rate for completion of swimming pool #1.

Moreover, even if the contract specified a certain payment for each swimming pool, the contract would not be divisible if Owner would not receive substantial value unless all three swimming pools were completed. For example, suppose that Owner had hired Contractor to complete all three swimming pools in time for its heavily advertised grand opening on May 1. Suppose further that Contractor abandoned the project in April, leaving Owner insufficient time to schedule a substitute contractor to complete the pools in time for the grand opening. Contractor's completion of only one of the swimming pools would leave Owner with one completely undeveloped space and one very unsightly half-completed pool, creating eyesores that would ruin the grand opening. In those circumstances, a court likely would treat the contract as a single, indivisible contract for completion of all three pools, even if the contract allocated separate payment for each pool. In that case, Contractor would be liable for a material breach of the whole contract and would not have satisfied constructive conditions to counter-performance.

Exercise 11.4 — Divisibility

1. Incomplete Delivery of Logs

A contractor entered into a contract to drive 20,000 feet of logs down a river to a lumber mill. The contract specified payment at a rate of $x for each thousand feet of logs delivered to the mill. The contractor had successfully delivered 15,000 feet of logs to the mill and had driven the remaining 5,000 feet of logs 90% of the distance to the mill when its equipment failed, causing the remaining logs to float irretrievably past the mill. The mill was able to meet its commitments to six customers for cut lumber but was forced to default on two other accepted purchase orders because of the contractor's failure to deliver the remaining 5,000 feet of lumber.

The contractor is liable to the mill for its failure to deliver 5,000 feet of logs. Can it recover at the contract price for the 15,000 feet delivered? Can it additionally recover for its partial performance of driving the remaining 5,000 feet of logs nearly to its destination, before its equipment failed? [Based loosely on *Gill v. Johnstown Lumber Co.*, 151 Pa. 534, 25 A. 120 (1892).]

2. Past Exam Question

In January, with the consent of his corporate client, Michael Lee hired Laura Padilla, an experienced appellate litigator in a solo practice, to argue the appeal on a case that Lee had tried in the trial court, winning a multimillion dollar judgment for the client. Lee was busy with other trial litigation, and he knew that Padilla would be as effective as anyone in town in protecting the judgment on appeal. The agreement between Padilla and Lee obligates Padilla to: (1) review the trial record, (2) study the opponent's opening brief, (3) perform necessary legal research, (4) write the answering brief, which was due in March, and (5) orally argue the case before the appellate panel of judges in an argument scheduled for May. The agreement also obligates Lee to collect from the client and pay to Padilla $200/hour for her work on the appeal.

Padilla studied the trial record, taking copious notes on portions of the trial transcript and other documents and records relevant to the issues on appeal. She also took careful notes on the opponent's opening brief and researched the law thoroughly, again taking careful notes on the research. Just as she was beginning to prepare an outline for the brief, however, Padilla notified Lee that a sudden illness would preclude Padilla from performing any further work on the case. At that point, Padilla had already performed about 60% of her total estimated hours on the project.

After asking Padilla to reconsider and getting a firmly negative response, Lee — still working full-time on other litigation — hired an experienced appellate litigator, Marcia Beck, to write the brief, which was due in one week, and to orally argue the appeal. Beck got a valuable head start from Padilla's notes, which Padilla provided, but Beck needed to duplicate some of Padilla's work, and she charged a premium rate for the last-minute assignment.

Although Padilla hastened her recovery by ceasing work during her illness, you may assume that her illness did not excuse her from performing her contractual obligations under any legal doctrine or any provision of the contract. Thus, Padilla has breached the contract. Padilla nonetheless wants compensation for the hours that she worked before she terminated her work on the project. If Padilla is entitled to any compensation, you may assume that Lee can claim some damages against her that he could offset against the compensation, but do not discuss Lee's damages.

Discuss only the question whether Padilla is entitled to recover any amounts for the work that she performed. You need not actually calculate damages (and I have not given you sufficient information to do so); instead, simply discuss the measure of recovery for Padilla, if any, in more general terms, and discuss any prerequisites to her getting such relief. As always, discuss discrete issues separately, and for each issue state a rule, apply the rule to the facts, arguing both sides whenever possible, and reach a reasonable conclusion. You may assume that no statutes apply to this question. Assume, for example, that Padilla is an independent contractor, so that statutes that commonly govern the payment of wages to employees do not apply.

IV. Excusing or Waiving Non-Satisfaction of Conditions

A. Excusing Non-Satisfaction of Conditions

In some circumstances, the non-satisfaction of a condition—whether express or constructive—may be excused. If so, a court will treat the contract as though the condition had been satisfied, thus triggering the obligations that were subject to the condition.

1. Breach of a Duty of Cooperation and Non-Hindrance

Some contracts expressly provide that one party will affirmatively facilitate the other party's performance, or at least will refrain from hindering the other party's performance. For example, insurance contracts typically expressly require the insured to cooperate with the insurer when the insurer undertakes its contractual obligation to defend against a liability claim. *See, e.g., Belz v. Clarendon America Ins. Co.*, 158 Cal. App. 4th 615, 625, 69 Cal. Rptr. 3d 864, 869 (2007) ("A standard cooperation clause provides that the insured will cooperate with the insurer in the investigation, settlement, or defense of a claim or suit."); *Arizona Property and Cas. Ins. Guar. Fund v. Helme*, 153 Ariz. 129, 136–37, 735 P.2d 451, 458–59 (1987) (insurer complained that insured parties breached their duty of cooperation under a "standard cooperation clause" because they "were obviously willing to say anything to save their personal backsides").

In other cases, a duty of cooperation is implied from the nature of the contract and all the circumstances. Like any breach of a contractual duty, a breach of the duty of cooperation may give rise to a claim for damages, such as for increased costs of performance. In one case, a contractor could recover damages for extra expenses in constructing practice bombs, because the Navy breached its implied duty to cooperate by failing to promptly deliver tail assemblies necessary to the contractor's manufacturing process. *Kehm Corp. v. United States*, 93 F. Supp. 620 (Ct. Cl. 1950).

More on point for this section, however, my breach of a duty to cooperate with you can excuse your failure to perform and thus excuse your failure to satisfy constructive conditions to counter-performance. In other words, even if you do not perform your contractual duties to me, you might still have a claim against me for payment under the contract, if my failure to cooperate prevented you from performing.

a. Hindering the Other Party's Performance

Arising out of the implied duty of good faith in the performance of a contract is an implied duty to refrain from hindering or preventing the other party's ability to perform and thus to satisfy constructive conditions and trigger counter-performance.

To take an extreme example, suppose that Ford and Allied have agreed that Allied will deliver and install factory machinery at the Ford factory during the first week of September. When Allied arrived with the machinery each day during that week, however, Ford each time turned Allied away, preventing Allied from performing. If Allied later sued for its lost earnings on the contract, Ford might have the nerve to argue that its duty to pay never arose because Allied never installed the machinery and thus failed to satisfy its constructive condition to payment. Of course, Ford's argument would fail. A court would find that Allied failed to satisfy its constructive condition solely because Ford prevented Allied from performing, thus breaching Ford's implied duty of non-hindrance. In these circumstances, the court would excuse Allied's failure to satisfy the constructive condition, and it would find Ford to be the breaching party.

In the following case, an elderly man's breach of an implied duty of non-hindrance or non-prevention excused a caretaker's failure to satisfy constructive conditions, permitting the caretaker to sue for counter-performance notwithstanding his own failure to substantially perform. In addition, the first and final paragraphs address civil procedure issues about concise pleading in complaints and about the court's displeasure with a brief that addressed matters unnecessary to the resolution of the dispute.

Barron v. Cain

216 N.C. 282, 4 S.E.2d 618 (1939)

Barnhill, J.

¶1 The purpose of the complaint is to state, in a plain and concise manner, plaintiff's cause of action so as to disclose the issuable facts and to give the defendant notice of the relief to which the plaintiff supposes himself entitled, and should contain all the facts which the defendant should know to make his defense and which the court should know in order to grant the desired relief. McIntosh, p. 87. It must contain a plain and concise statement of the facts constituting a cause of action without unnecessary repetition. C. S., 506 (2). The material, essential or ultimate facts upon which the right of action is based, and not collateral or evidential facts which are only to be used to establish the ultimate facts, should be stated. The plaintiff is to obtain relief only according to the allegations in his complaint and, therefore, he should allege all of the material facts, but not the evidence upon which he relies to prove them. Irrelevant, redundant and evidential matter should be omitted and unnecessary repetition should be avoided. In actions for damages, when necessary, the plaintiff should allege facts by way of aggravation to increase the damages. McIntosh, p. 389. If there are conditions precedent to plaintiff's right of recovery to be performed by him, such performance should be alleged or sufficient reasons given for failure to perform. If the plaintiff relies upon an implied contract or agreement, the circumstances giving rise to such implied agreement should be stated.

....

¶2 The plaintiff sets forth that the defendant, a man 85 years of age, grand-uncle of the plaintiff, in 1932 induced the plaintiff to go and live with and care for him during his life, upon an understanding that plaintiff, at the death of the defendant, would be well paid for his services; that the plaintiff, pursuant thereto, did move to the home of the defendant and live with him until September, 1938, rendering services for the comfort, welfare and best interest of the defendant; that his failure to continue to live with the defendant during his life was due to no fault of the plaintiff but was caused by the wrongful conduct of the defendant in assaulting the plaintiff with a deadly weapon, running him off of the premises and threatening to do him great bodily harm if he returned; and that he has been substantially damaged thereby.

¶3 As the plaintiff alleges a contractual agreement to live with and render service to the defendant for and during the natural life of the defendant, before he can recover it is necessary for him to allege in his complaint, and prove at the hearing, that his failure to do so was caused by the wrongful acts of the defendant. Although the performance by the plaintiff of the whole of his promise may be a condition precedent to the liability of the defendant to perform on his part, still the plaintiff's failure to perform will not discharge the defendant if the latter prevented the performance. In such case, the plaintiff is discharged from further performance and may recover damages for the breach, or recover on the *quantum meruit* for his part performance. Clark on Contracts (Ed. 1904), p. 468. The law implies a promise by the party to pay for what has been thus received and allows him to recover any damage he has sustained by reason of the breach, for this is exact justice. McCurry v. Purgason, 170 N.C. 463, 87 S.E. 244; Hayman v. Davis, 182 N.C. 563, 109 S.E. 554.

¶4 In paragraph No. 6, the plaintiff alleges that during the seven years he lived with the defendant the defendant was constantly under the influence of liquor and that notwithstanding the indignities, lonesomeness and inconvenience to which the plaintiff was subjected by reason thereof, he remained with and was at all times ready, able and willing to serve the defendant until his death in compliance with the understanding between him and the defendant. In paragraph No. 5 the plaintiff alleges that while the defendant was under the influence of liquor he was disagreeable and subjected the plaintiff to abuse and every manner of indignity, notwithstanding which, the plaintiff, in compliance with his agreement, continued to live with and serve the defendant....

¶5 In paragraph No. 7, plaintiff alleges that the defendant assaulted him with a deadly weapon and ordered him to leave, and sets out the essential facts in relation thereto. He further alleges that he was forced to leave the home of the defendant for fear of bodily harm. These allegations are essential to the plaintiff's cause of action for the purpose of disclosing the alleged reason why the plaintiff has not complied, on his part, with the alleged agreement. Having alleged an agreement to serve defendant during his lifetime and having admitted in his complaint his noncompliance, it is essential to his alleged cause of action that he set forth the wrongful conduct of defendant which caused the breach through no fault of the plaintiff.

¶6 [The court affirmed the trial court's judgment in favor of the plaintiff caretaker, but it ordered that the defendant be charged only one half the printing costs of the plaintiff's brief because the brief contained lengthy discussion of evidence not necessary to the issues at hand.]

The judgment below is Affirmed.

---

b. Failing to Facilitate the Other Party's Performance

Some contracts can be interpreted to impose an express or implied obligation to affirmatively facilitate the other party's performance. For example, if you agree to paint my portrait, unless we agreed that you would do so from a photograph, our agreement undoubtedly would include an obligation on my part to sit for you and follow your instructions for a reasonable time, to permit you to sketch and paint my likeness. That duty of active cooperation on my part—if not expressed—might be implied in fact, or it could be implied in law as an adjunct of my duty of good faith.

If I breached this duty and failed to sit for you for more than a few minutes, you might be robbed of your ability to paint my portrait, so that you would be prevented from satisfying the constructive condition to your demanding payment from me. My breach of my duty to cooperate, however, would excuse your failure to satisfy constructive conditions, thus triggering my duty to pay you (with an offset for the expenses you save by not having to paint my portrait, as discussed in Chapter 12).

For a sale of goods, the UCC addresses this issue by protecting a party's rights when it has been deprived of necessary cooperation from the other party, such as the other party's failure to specify particulars of performance that have been left to that party to determine. U.C.C. § 2-311(3) (2011). As set forth in Arizona's enactment of UCC § 2-311(3):

> 47-2311. <u>Options and cooperation respecting performance</u>
>
> ....
>
> C. Where such specification would materially affect the other party's performance but is not seasonably made or where one party's cooperation

is necessary to the agreed performance of the other but is not seasonably forthcoming, the other party in addition to all other remedies:

1. Is excused for any resulting delay in his own performance; and

2. May also either proceed to perform in any reasonable manner or after the time for a material part of his own performance treat the failure to specify or to cooperate as a breach by failure to deliver or accept the goods.

Exercise 11.5 — The Case of the Fidgety Model

Paul agreed to paint Laura's portrait for $1,000, not from a photograph but with her sitting for the portrait. When Laura sat for Paul, he required her to sit for long hours on the first day. Laura was bored, often required repeated coaching to stay in pose, and complained often that she needed a short break to stretch or make a quick phone call. At the end of the first day, Paul announced that he would need Laura to pose similarly for two more days. Laura responded, "You're kidding. Why are you so slow? Do you need some caffeine, or something? I'll do it, but I'm not going to be a happy camper." Paul, insulted and exasperated by Laura's comments and behavior, abandoned the project and sued Laura for his fee (minus expenses saved by not finishing the painting). Present Laura's response, and evaluate the merits of Paul's likely reply. *Cf. Godburn v. Meserve*, 130 Conn. 723, 37 A.2d 235 (1944) (elderly woman was demanding and cranky with caretakers who abandoned their duties and sued for the house that the woman had promised to leave for them in her will).

---

2. *Preventing Satisfaction of an Express Condition*

Even the failure of an express condition can be excused if one party wrongfully prevented it from being satisfied. If all obligations in a real estate contract, for example, are conditioned on the buyer securing financing on certain terms, a court would imply an obligation on the part of the buyer to use at least good-faith efforts to try to obtain the financing. If the buyer failed to secure financing, she could argue that the condition failed and she would not be required to buy the property. However, if the condition failed because she did not attempt to secure financing, when she could have qualified for it, then failure of the condition likely will be excused, and the buyer will be liable in damages for failing to purchase the real estate at the contract price.

B. Waiver and Estoppel

1. *Waiver of Material Breach and Non-Satisfaction of a Constructive Condition*

If a material breach remains uncured, the victim of the breach can still waive rights to cancel the contract, subject to a duty to mitigate damages. For example, suppose that you have agreed to paint both the inside and outside of my house for $4,000. Suppose further that you show up with the paint for the exterior of the house, and it turns out to be inferior in quality compared to the paint called for in the contract, so that I likely will need a new exterior paint job 25% sooner than if you had purchased the correct, premium paint. You refuse to return with the correct paint, because you have purchased all the non-conforming paint, which was mixed to match the custom color of the exterior of the house.

Let's assume that your breach is indisputably material, and that I thus could fire you, cancel the contract, and hire someone else to apply the correct paint. Alternatively, however, I could opt to waive those rights and to retain you on the project, while retaining my claim for damages for the shorter expected life of the exterior paint job. If you rely on my announced waiver by applying the paint you purchased and employing an assistant to begin painting the interior, I likely would be barred by estoppel from retracting my waiver, and I would be precluded from firing you for the non-conforming paint.

Sometimes a party can *implicitly* waive the right to cancel a contract for material breach. For example, suppose that Buyer in a year-long installment contract is unambiguously entitled to deliveries on the first day of each month for a year, but Seller has delivered in the third or fourth week of each month during the first six months of the contract. Suppose further that each of these delays in delivery is a material breach of that installment, and that the repeated delays amount to a material breach of the whole contract (UCC § 2-612 refers to breach of an installment contract that results in "substantial" impairment). If Buyer has nonetheless repeatedly accepted the late deliveries for the first six months without complaint, Buyer's conduct might communicate a waiver of its right to cancel the contract for late deliveries.

Buyer could reinstate its rights under the contract by giving clear notice retracting its waiver with respect to future deliveries, which Buyer now insists must arrive on the first of each month. Such a notice could reinstate Buyer's contract rights unless Seller has relied on the previous waivers in a way that affects its future ability to deliver on time. Such reliance by Seller could give rise to an estoppel, which would prevent Buyer from retracting its waiver.

These principles of waiver, retraction, and estoppel apply to contracts beyond sales of goods, as suggested by the common law context described in the first example, regarding the house-painting contract. Nonetheless, the principles are summarized nicely in the UCC for transactions in goods, as set forth in Arizona's enactment of UCC § 2-209(5), which refers to an "executory" part of a contract, or a part that is yet to be performed:

> 47-2209. Modification, rescission and waiver
>
> ....
>
> E. A party who has made a waiver affecting an executory portion of the contract may retract the waiver by reasonable notification received by the other party that strict performance will be required of any term waived, unless the retraction would be unjust in view of a material change of position in reliance on the waiver.

2. *Waiver of Non-Satisfaction of an Express Condition*

Even an *express condition* can be waived by the party who would benefit from the condition. For example, suppose that Owner's obligation to pay Contractor is expressly conditioned on Contractor's completing construction by October 31. If Contractor announced in the final week of October that construction could not be completed before November 2 except at great cost, Owner might respond that he will accept construction that is completed by November 2 and will pay the contract rate minus any damages caused by the delay. If Owner does not retract this waiver prior to October 31, Contractor will be relieved of the burdens of the original condition and will be entitled to payment—minus actual damages caused by delay—if it completes the construction by November 2. Moreover, once Contractor relies on Owner's statement of waiver, estoppel will prevent Owner from retracting the waiver.

How did the school board waive a condition precedent in the following case? Try to identify all the grounds on which the court could reject the school board's position.

Haake v. Board of Educ. for Township High Sch. Glenbard Dist. 87

399 Ill. App. 3d 121, 925 N.E.2d 297 (2010)

Justice Schostok delivered the opinion of the court:

¶1 This case presents the question of whether a school board can decrease the health insurance benefits provided to [107] retirees under certain collective bargaining agreements, after the expiration of those agreements. On January 22, 2009, the trial court entered judgment in favor of the plaintiffs here (all retired teachers) on that issue. The school board appeals, raising various arguments that ... some of the plaintiffs do not qualify for the benefits in any case. We affirm.

....

Should 23 of the Plaintiffs be Excluded from the Early Retirement Benefits?

¶2 Lastly, the defendant contends that judgment should be entered in its favor as to 23 of the plaintiffs, because they did not properly qualify for the benefits at issue under the Earlier Contracts. Specifically, the defendant claims that, although the 23 plaintiffs met the other eligibility requirements contained in the Earlier Contracts, those contracts also imposed the requirement that the teachers participate in a separate plan, the Teachers' Retirement System Early Retirement Option (ERO). (The ERO is set out in a portion of the Pension Code (hereinafter Teachers' Retirement System Act or Act) (40 ILCS 5/16-101 et seq. (West 2008)).) The ERO imposed different and additional age and experience qualifications, beyond those necessary under the collective bargaining agreements in effect between the defendant and the GEA, and the 23 plaintiffs do not meet these additional requirements. The plaintiffs argue that participation in the ERO was not a condition of participation in the early retirement plan established by the Earlier Contracts. The plaintiffs also argue that even if participation in the ERO had been a condition precedent to participation in the defendant's early retirement plan, the defendant waived this argument, both by failing to raise it as an affirmative defense in its answer, and by voluntarily approving the participation of the 23 plaintiffs in its early retirement plan.

....

¶3 It is well established that a party's failure to raise an affirmative defense in its answer forfeits a defendant's ability to argue that defense. *Larkin v. Sanelli*, 213 Ill. App. 3d 597, 602, 157 Ill. Dec. 681, 572 N.E.2d 1145 (1991). Even more telling, however, are the defendant's voluntary actions indicating an intent to waive ERO participation as a requirement for participation in its own early retirement plan, if indeed there was such a requirement. It is undisputed that the defendant approved all of the plaintiffs, including the 23 plaintiffs at issue here, for participation in its early retirement plan. If any of the plaintiffs were in fact ineligible because they had not chosen to participate in the ERO, the defendant could have denied those persons' applications for early retirement. A party may waive a provision placed in a contract for its benefit by conduct establishing that it does not intend to insist on compliance with the provision. *Caisse Nationale de Credit Agricole v. CBI Industries, Inc.*, 90 F.3d 1264, 1275 (7th Cir.1996). Such waiver may include waiver of a condition precedent. *LaSalle National Bank v. Metropolitan Life Insurance Co.*, 18 F.3d 1371, 1375 (7th Cir. 1994). The defendant's approval of early retirees who were not ERO participants was conduct unambiguously indicating that the defendant did not intend to insist that all early retirees also be participants in the ERO.

¶4 The defendant argues that it should not be held to have waived compliance with this condition, because it did so based on the mistaken belief that participation in the ERO was not required. The defendant cites to *Breckenridge v. Cambridge Homes, Inc.*, 246 Ill. App. 3d 810, 817, 186 Ill. Dec. 425, 616 N.E.2d 615 (1993), a case holding that a mistake of fact can negate the intent necessary for waiver. But the defendant's mistake was one of law: when it approved the plaintiffs for participation in its early retirement plan, it interpreted the contract as the plaintiffs do, to mean that participation in the ERO was not necessary. Its misinterpretation of its own contract (if it was a misinterpretation) cannot be excused as a mistake of fact. Rather, it appears that the defendant has changed its mind about what the contract says and now seeks to be excused from performing as it said it would.

¶5 Moreover, where one party to a contract simply fails to ascertain whether another has complied with a condition precedent to that contract, it may not excuse its actions on the basis of ignorance. Parties are "presumed to know those things which reasonable diligence on their part would bring to their attention," and hence the lack of diligence cannot defeat the application of waiver. *Whalen v. K-Mart Corp.*, 166 Ill. App. 3d 339, 344, 116 Ill. Dec. 776, 519 N.E.2d 991 (1988); *see also Strauss v. Sullivan*, 991 F.2d 800 (7th Cir. 1993) (table) (where party has the ability to determine whether a condition precedent has been met but fails to do so through lack of diligence, it has waived the condition precedent). Through the approval process, the defendant had the power to determine whether applicants for early retirement met the plan's requirements. It cannot now disclaim the manner in which it exercised that power. For all of these reasons, we find that the defendant has forfeited the application of the alleged condition precedent that it now seeks to raise. The trial court did not err in holding that benefits could not be denied to the 23 plaintiffs on the basis of the "Teachers' Retirement System Early Retirement Plan" language in section 9.05.04 of the Earlier Contracts.

....

Affirmed.

Exercise 11.6

1. Mistake of Fact

Suppose that the *Haake* case had instead presented these facts: The school board had initially accepted the 23 retiring teachers into its early retirement program because of a reasonable clerical error that mistakenly listed these teachers as qualified participants in the state ERO. When the clerical error came to light, the school board promptly sought to exclude the 23 teachers from the school district's early retirement program because they did not qualify for the state ERO and thus—under the terms of the relevant contracts—did not satisfy a condition precedent for participation in the school district's program. Should the court's analysis of waiver come out differently?

2. Waiver of Incomplete Payment?

Owner indisputably owes Contractor $10,000 for completed work but has not paid despite two requests by Contractor. Finally, Owner offered to pay Contractor $9,000 within 24 hours in exchange for Contractor's promise to accept $9,000 as full satisfaction of the claim. Contractor immediately accepts this offer. This agreement should not be recognized as an enforceable settlement agreement for the following reason: Owner's duty was not subject to good-faith dispute; therefore, Owner's promise to pay $9,000 was within Owner's pre-existing duty, robbing the agreement of consideration. *See Foakes v. Beer*, 9 App. Cas. 605 (Eng. H.L. 1884). If, however, Owner *pays* the $9,000 and Contractor accepts that payment and provides Owner with a full release, the parties have proceeded beyond mere agreement. By accepting the part payment and providing the release, has Contractor effectively waived the right to receive the remaining $1,000? Alternatively, could the transaction be viewed as a completed gift from Contractor to Owner of $1,000? *See* Merton L. Ferson, *The Rule in Foakes v. Beer*, 31 YALE L.J. 15 (1921) (critiquing *Foakes* and its American counterpart as "patently absurd" to the extent that they apply the pre-existing duty rule to a creditor's actual receipt of part payment and delivery of a release to the debtor, rather than to an unperformed agreement to do so).

V. Anticipatory Breach and Demands of Assurance of Performance

A. Anticipatory Breach

Imagine that your wedding is planned for March 1. In December, you hired your favorite band—Cacophony—to perform at the reception. In January, however, that band announced that it was forced to cancel its performance at your wedding because it had an opportunity to go on tour as the opening act for a famous band. You and your fiancé acknowledged Cacophony's repudiation of the contract, stated your intention to cancel your contract with Cacophony, and scrambled to hire a comparable band—Barely Awake—at a comparable price for the reception. As Barely Awake was setting up for the reception, Cacophony arrived, announced that the tour had ended early, and stated its intention to perform for the reception and collect its pay. It explained that its time for performance had not yet come and gone, so it never breached the contract and should not have been replaced. If Cacophony is correct in its analysis, you are now bound to pay two bands for the same reception.

1. Anticipatory Breach by Repudiation or Inability to Perform

Modern law will not accept Cacophony's explanation but will instead protect your interests. In January, when Cacophony clearly expressed its intent to repudiate the contract, Cacophony was immediately in total breach of the contract, even though its time for performance was still months away. The law calls this an *anticipatory breach*, one that is effective prior to the time for the breaching party's performance. Just as would be the case with a material breach that takes place when performance is due, you could cancel your obligations to Cacophony in January, make plans to hire a substitute band for the March wedding, and sue Cacophony immediately for any damages that result (such as a higher cost for the substitute band).[1]

This particular anticipatory breach is by repudiation. In another case, the anticipatory breach might result from prospective inability to perform, as when a firm declares bankruptcy and begins plans to liquidate its assets prior to the time for performance.

---

1. This rule of anticipatory breach is subject to a puzzling exception: If the victim of anticipatory breach has already fully performed and is only awaiting payment of money in several installments, the victim of breach cannot sue immediately for all future installments due—even though the other party has repudiated all payment obligations—but must wait until the due date for each payment has come and gone. This may explain why the lessor/seller of the advertising sign in *Walker and Co. v. Harrison* (Section III.A.6 in this chapter) included an acceleration clause in its contract, thus contractually imposing liability on Harrison for all future rents due when Harrison failed to :make payments and then repudiated.

2. *Canceling for Anticipatory Breach*

In the example of the wedding reception, the band anticipatorily repudiated all of its obligations, allowing you to treat it as a total anticipatory breach of the contract. You would have the same right to cancel the contract if the band repudiated a material part of its obligations, such as by saying that it could perform only from 6–7 p.m., rather than 6–11 p.m. as agreed. If the band repudiated a minor part of its contract, such as by announcing that it required 15-minute breaks each hour rather than the 10-minute breaks earlier agreed to, then the couple would not be able to cancel the contract, although they might retain a claim for damages if this adjustment required them to alter their reception agenda in minor ways.

3. *Interpreting a Statement as Repudiation*

Because a prospective repudiation can operate as a total or material breach prior to the time of performance, a court will not lightly interpret a statement to be a repudiation. If a statement could reasonably be interpreted instead as grumbling about the difficulty of a future performance or as an inquiry about the possibility of entering into a mutual modification or rescission of the contract, that interpretation will usually be favored over a finding of repudiation. Consequently, the recipient of an ambiguous communication regarding the other party's future performance should not precipitously cancel her own obligations without first asking for clarification.

Exercise 11.7 — The Case of the Actor's Demands

Comedy Company was under contract with Theater to perform December 10–12 for 50% of the gross receipts. In August, Comedy Company's manager sent a letter to Theater stating in relevant part, "In light of our popularity at the moment, placing us in high demand, we are having great difficulty imagining performing for less than 60% of the gross proceeds in December. Enclosed is a signed modification to our contract, increasing our share accordingly. Please respond promptly." Assuming that Theater is not willing to increase Comedy Company's share, how should it react? Did Comedy Company repudiate the contract? [Based loosely on *Berstein v. Meech*, 29 N.E. 255 (N.Y. 1891).]

---

4. *Options in Responding to Repudiation*

The recipient of an unambiguous anticipatory repudiation need not accept the repudiation and treat it as an immediate total breach of the contract. Instead, subject to her duty to mitigate damages, she could waive her right to cancel her obligations and could insist that both parties perform the contract as agreed. If she maintains this position and does not thereafter cancel the contract, both parties will be obligated to perform as scheduled in the contract, and performance or breach will be established on the due dates. If the recipient's performance is due first, however, she can suspend that performance until the repudiating party retracts its repudiation or performs.

On the other hand, if maintaining the contract would be foolish and would likely increase the injury resulting from the breach, then the recipient of the repudiation should mitigate damages by canceling the contract and making substitute arrangements. The wedding couple, for example, should not seek to maintain its contract with Cacophony if that band is adamant that it will be on tour and unable to perform at the wedding reception. Rather than suffer through the reception without the desired musical group, the couple should accept the reality that Cacophony's repudiation will not be retracted, should cancel that contract, and should hire a substitute band.

For sales of goods, the UCC summarizes the options of the recipient of a total or material anticipatory repudiation, as set forth here in Arizona's enactment of UCC § 2-610:

> 47-2610. Anticipatory repudiation
>
> When either party repudiates the contract with respect to a performance not yet due the loss of which will substantially impair the value of the contract to the other, the aggrieved party may:
>
> 1. For a commercially reasonable time await performance by the repudiating party; or
>
> 2. Resort to any remedy for breach (section 47-2703 or 47-2711), even though he has notified the repudiating party that he would await the latter's performance and has urged retraction; and
>
> 3. In either case suspend his own performance or proceed in accordance with the provisions of this chapter on the seller's right to identify goods to the contract notwithstanding breach or to salvage unfinished goods (section 47-2704).

5. *Retraction of Repudiation*

Similarly, the repudiating party can retract its repudiation, and thus preserve its rights and obligations under the contract, but only if it does so before other events make its repudiation final. In the most extreme example, once the time for performance has passed, it's too late to retract the repudiation; the repudiation coupled with the passing of the due date gives the victim of the breach full rights to cancel the contract and to claim damages for total breach.

Alternatively, even before the due date of performance, once the recipient of the repudiation has acknowledged the repudiation and canceled the contract, or once the recipient has relied on the repudiation, the repudiating party loses its right to retract the repudiation. At that point, the victim of the breach has full rights to cancel the contract. These common law principles are carried over to sales of goods in the UCC in section 2-611, as set forth here in Arizona's enactment:

47-2611. Retraction of anticipatory repudiation

A. Until the repudiating party's next performance is due he can retract his repudiation unless the aggrieved party has since the repudiation cancelled or materially changed his position or otherwise indicated that he considers the repudiation final.

....

C. Retraction reinstates the repudiating party's rights under the contract with due excuse and allowance to the aggrieved party for any delay occasioned by the repudiation.

How clearly must a repudiating party express her intent to retract the repudiation? If anything less than great clarity were required, could a statement of remorse or apology for repudiating the contract be confused with a retraction? Can one retract a repudiation by expressing a desire to once again proceed with the transaction, but only on different terms?

Ratliff v. Hardison

219 Ariz. 441, 199 P.3d 696 (2008)
[paragraphs renumbered from the original]

Espinosa, Judge.

¶1 In this contract action, Daniel Hardison, Sr. appeals from the trial court's order granting partial summary judgment in favor of appellee Alvin Ratliff on his complaint for damages arising from Hardison's breach of his agreement to purchase Ratliff's farm. For the reasons below, we affirm.

Facts and Procedural History

¶2 In January 2006, Hardison entered into a contract to purchase 1,020 acres of farmland in Cochise County from Ratliff for $3,500,000 and deposited $100,000 of that amount in escrow as earnest money. The agreement provided an escrow closing date of August 1, 2006. Both parties to the transaction were represented by real estate broker Earl Moser.

....

¶3 On July 22, Hardison left Ratliff the following telephone message:

> What I'd like to do, Buddy, is buy that section of deeded land and section of state land, and offer you an additional $1.5 million on top of the $100,000 we've given you. We're sorry about the offer, but we're—we're really negative in what we see around here. I just thought (indiscernible) and maybe we can negotiate, and arm wrestle or whatever it takes, and see if we can make a deal, maybe not....

At his deposition, Hardison testified that, "toward the end of July," he had decided not to purchase "the farm" and notified both Ratliff and his banker of that decision as well. After escrow did not close on August 1, Ratliff's attorney sent Hardison a letter demanding that the sale close by August 9, stating that if it did not, litigation would follow.

¶4 On August 9, Hardison and Ratliff spoke on the telephone and Hardison said he still wanted to purchase the land, but he wished to re-negotiate the terms of purchase, at a reduced price or to buy only a portion of the land, which Ratliff refused. During another conversation with Ratliff on August 15, Hardison stated he was unable to close on the farm. He said he still wanted to purchase it, but was too "chicken shit" to go through with the deal because of uncertainties in farming and the real estate market and his inability to sell another property he owned.

....

¶5 In September 2006, Ratliff sued Hardison, seeking damages for breach of contract.... Hardison now appeals the trial court's July 2007 order granting partial summary judgment in favor of Ratliff. In that order, the court found Hardison had repudiated the contract....

Discussion

¶6 As stated above, we view the facts in the light most favorable to the party against whom summary judgment was entered. *See Andrews*, 205 Ariz. 236, ¶12, 69 P.3d at 11. Applying this standard, we agree with the trial court that no genuine issue of material fact exists as to whether Hardison had anticipatorily repudiated the contract. We also agree that no reasonable person could conclude Hardison had subsequently retracted his repudiation....

a. Anticipatory Repudiation

¶7 A party anticipatorily repudiates a contract when he or she provides a "positive and unequivocal manifestation" that the party will not perform when his or her duty to perform arises. *Diamos v. Hirsch*, 91 Ariz. 304, 307, 372 P.2d 76, 78 (1962). Hardison argues "the facts available do not establish beyond any issue of fact that Hardison gave a 'clear and unequivocal' manifestation of intent to breach or repudiate the agreement." Rather, he maintains, he only attempted to modify the contract or warn that he might be unable to close escrow.... That characterization, however, is not supported by the record and, indeed, is contradicted by Hardison's own explanation of his July 2006 actions, which the trial court considered in ruling on the competing motions for summary judgment.

¶8 Hardison testified at his deposition that before the closing, he had attempted to re-negotiate the contract, but Ratliff had "told [him] that he wasn't willing to negotiate." He further stated that, "kind of toward the end of July," he decided the "smartest thing [he] could do" would be to sacrifice the $100,000 earnest money and "[elect] to say [he] wouldn't buy it." Hardison further testified he had called Ratliff and "told him [he] had decided not to purchase the farm." In his subsequent conversations with Ratliff, Hardison affirmed not once, but several times his ongoing intention not to perform. During the August 15 telephone call, Hardison said, "I'm not capable of closing," "[w]e're just not capable," "if my property had ... sold, I would have [been able to perform]," and, "[w]ell Buddy, I can't perform. That's—that's it."

....

b. Retraction of Repudiation

¶ 9 Hardison contends that even if he repudiated the contract, he subsequently retracted his repudiation. Hardison correctly notes that Arizona law allows for the retraction of an anticipatory repudiation. *See Kammert Bros. Enters., Inc. v. Tanque Verde Plaza Co.*, 102 Ariz. 301, 306–07, 428 P.2d 678, 683–84 (1967). However, he fails to develop his argument that, in this case, he did so. Hardison merely asserts that his August 22 telephone conversation with Ratliff constituted a retraction because Hardison said he still wanted to purchase the land. He then suggests that because following that call Ratliff continued to discuss the deal and urge performance, the retraction was effective. This argument is unpersuasive and, as a matter of law, incorrect. *See id.* at 306, 428 P.2d at 683 (non-breaching party may urge performance after repudiation and "should not be penalized for his [or her] efforts to make the other party live up to his [or her] end of the bargain"); *see also United Cal. Bank*, 140 Ariz. at 281, 681 P.2d at 433.

¶ 10 Hardison has not cited, nor have we found, any Arizona authority regarding the clarity and specificity required for a retraction of repudiation. And the Restatement of Contracts does not define what is necessary for an act or statement to constitute "adequate" communication of a retraction. *See* Restatement (Second) of Contracts § 256 cmt. b (1981) ("It is not necessary for the repudiator to use words in order to retract his statement. Conduct, such as an offer of performance, may be adequate to convey the idea of retraction to the injured party."). Ratliff cites a California decision holding that a retraction of a repudiation "must be clear and unequivocal." *Pichignau v. City of Paris*, 264 Cal. App. 2d 138, 70 Cal. Rptr. 147, 149 (1968). Other courts and authorities that have considered this issue have adopted this standard. *See Vahabzadeh v. Mooney*, 241 Va. 47, 399 S.E.2d 803, 805 (1991); 92 C.J.S. Vendor and Purchase § 406 (2000) ("To be effective, a retraction of a repudiation of a land sale contract must be clear, definite, absolute, and unequivocal in evincing the repudiator's intention to honor his or her obligations under the contract."). [Footnote 1: We note this standard is also consistent with the law governing retraction of [repudiation] in the sale of goods under the U.C.C. as adopted by Arizona. *See* A.R.S. § 47-2611(B) ("Retraction may be by any method which clearly indicates to the aggrieved party that the repudiating party intends to perform....") (emphasis added)]. We find the reasoning of these courts instructive.

....

¶ 11 Additionally, allowing a less than clear and unequivocal statement to serve as a retraction of a repudiation could yield harsh results for both repudiators and injured parties. Anticipatory repudiators who express remorse for their prospective breaches could find themselves unwittingly re-bound to a contract under which they are incapable of performing and surprised by substantial damages from a party who did not act to mitigate losses.... Similarly, injured parties who understand an ambiguous retraction to be a mere expression of remorse could find themselves in breach when they make other arrangements to cover the repudiator's breach. *Cf. Comment, A Suggested Revision of the Contract Doctrine of Anticipatory Repudiation*, 64 YALE L.J. 85, 94 (1954) (criticizing contract doctrine whereby injured party who re-contracts to fulfill duty to mitigate, but does not affirmatively accept repudiation, could be left with two contracts if repudiator reinstates initial contract). A standard requiring clear and unequivocal retractions of repudiations both prevents these results and provides identical burdens of proof in breach and finality in dealings. *See Vahabzadeh*, 399 S.E.2d at 805; *Alderson*, 96 P. at 889.

¶ 12 Hardison failed to clearly and unequivocally retract his repudiation. During the August 9 telephone call, well after the contracted closing date, he stated he still wanted to buy the land, but he attempted to negotiate new terms for its purchase. Hardison did not renounce his repudiation or articulate that he would like once again to be bound by the initial agreement. Rather, he affirmed that he wanted to obtain the land, but was unwilling to meet his obligation to pay for it. As a matter of law, this is not a positive and unequivocal statement of his desire to once again abide by the contract, nor is it a retraction at all. *See Kammert Bros. Enters.*, 102 Ariz. at 307, 428 P.2d at 684 (seller's refusal to abide by original contract price constitutes a breach).

¶ 13 Nor did the August 30 letter retract the repudiation and reinstate the contract.... He did not offer to perform under the contract, but rather assured Ratliff that if he provided a document giving Hardison an unconditional right to rescind the contract, he would advise him whether he still wished to perform. This was not a retraction because Hardison did not affirmatively renounce his repudiation and commit himself to the contract and meeting his obligations under it.

....

Disposition

¶ 14 The trial court's grant of partial summary judgment in favor of Ratliff is affirmed.

B. Assurance of Performance

Imagine that your client, Seller, is scheduled to ship goods to Buyer on June 1 but receives information in April that Buyer has been increasingly late in paying invoices from other suppliers. Buyer has not yet failed to perform its contract with Seller, nor has it repudiated its obligations to Seller; therefore, Seller has no legal right to cancel its own obligations. Still, Seller likely feels insecure about shipping goods to a buyer whose solvency and ability to pay are placed in question.

In such a quandary, Seller should seek to clarify the situation to the best of its ability. Seller might start by calling Buyer on the phone and asking for an explanation. If that conversation is not reassuring but still fails to provide Seller with grounds to cancel the contract, Seller remains in a sort of legal limbo unless it can force the issue through other means.

1. Assurance of Performance in Sales of Goods

The UCC introduced a helpful innovation on this issue, by providing a means for an insecure party to clarify the other party's ability and willingness to perform, and to cancel the contract if adequate assurance is not given. U.C.C. §2-609 (2011). As set forth in Arizona's enactment of section 2-609(1) and (4), this doctrine enables an insecure party to force the other party to provide an adequate assurance of performance or be subject to cancellation of the contract:

> 47-2609. Right to adequate assurance of performance
>
> A. A contract for sale imposes an obligation on each party that the other's expectation of receiving due performance will not be impaired. When reasonable grounds for insecurity arise with respect to the performance of either party the other may in writing demand adequate assurance of due performance and until he receives such assurance may if commercially reasonable suspend any performance for which he has not already received the agreed return.
>
> ....
>
> D. After receipt of a justified demand failure to provide within a reasonable time not exceeding thirty days such assurance of due performance as is adequate under the circumstances of the particular case is a repudiation of the contract.

Thus, if a party has reasonable grounds to question the other party's willingness or ability to perform in the future, it can suspend its own performance, demand adequate assurance in writing, and finally cancel the contract if the other party does not provide an adequate assurance in a reasonable time, not to exceed 30 days. In other words, section 2-609 provides the insecure party a means with which to force the other party to either demonstrate that it will perform or be deemed to have anticipatorily repudiated.

The Official Comment to section 2-609 of the UCC makes clear that reasonable grounds for insecurity may arise from the other party's failure to fully perform in transactions other than the current contract in question. The Comment provides two examples: (1) a buyer falling behind on its payments to a seller on contracts other than the current one in question, and (2) a seller making defective deliveries of precision parts to other buyers when the contract in question calls for the same kind of precision parts intended for immediate use on delivery. U.C.C. § 2-609 cmt. 3 (2011).

The adequacy of the other party's assurance may depend on that party's reputation and its relationship with the insecure party. A trusted, long-term partner in commercial transactions might satisfy its burden by providing a credible explanation that the current basis for insecurity will be corrected promptly and will not affect performance under the parties' contract. In other circumstances, more may be required. For example, a buyer who has failed to pay its accounts to several sellers, and who does not have a track record for reliability, might need to show documentation from its bank—perhaps showing the approval of a loan or the recent infusion of assets from accounts receivable—to establish its ability to satisfy its current accounts payable and to perform on its contract with the insecure seller.

2. *Common-Law Extension to Non-Sales Disputes*

This UCC innovation is a useful tool and likely will be embraced by courts for contracts governed by common law, as well as for sales of goods. *See* Restatement (Second) of Contracts § 251 (1981) (recommending this doctrine, without the requirement of a written demand of assurance, and without limiting the reasonable time for giving assurance to 30 days). As explained by one court:

> ... In application, section 2-609 successfully implements the laudatory objectives of quieting the doubt a party fearing repudiation may have, mitigating the dilemma flowing from that doubt, and offering the nonbreaching party the opportunity to interpose timely action to deal with the unusual development. [citations omitted].
>
> Indeed, UCC 2-609 has been considered so effective in bridging the doctrinal, exceptional and operational gap related to the doctrine of anticipatory breach that some States have imported the complementary regimen of demand for adequate assurance to common-law categories of contract law.... [citations omitted].
>
> Commentators have helped nudge this development along. They have noted that the problems redressed by UCC 2-609 are not unique to contracts for sale of goods, regulated under a purely statutory regime. Thus, they have cogently identified the need for the doctrine to be available in exceptional and qualifying common-law contractual settings and disputes because of similar practical, theoretical and salutary objectives (*e.g.*, predictability, definiteness, and stability in commercial dealings and expectations). [citations omitted].

Norcon Power Partners, L.P. v. Niagara Mohawk Power Corp., 92 N.Y.2d 458, 464–65, 705 N.E.2d 656, 660 (1998) (applying the doctrine of section 2-609 to the long-term commercial non-sales contract before it, without deciding whether it would apply to other non-sales contexts).

VI. Discharge of Obligations in Light of Events Taking Place After Contract Formation

In Chapter 8, we encountered grounds for avoiding a contract based on the parties' mutual mistake about facts as they existed at the time of contracting. In Chapter 9, we studied unconscionability, which addresses gross unfairness that existed at the time of contracting.

A party may also seek to have its obligations discharged (canceled) based on unanticipated events that take place after contract formation, traditionally known as *force majeure* (superior force). Two types of post-contract-formation disruptions may justify excusing a party's failure to perform, thus relieving it of liability for breach: an unexpected event that either: (1) impedes a party's ability to perform or (2) destroys the purpose for the performance.

In some cases, excuse for *force majeure* can relate to facts existing at the time of contract formation, thus overlapping with mutual mistake of fact. Our study, however, will focus on post-formation changes in circumstances.

A. Early Departures from Strict Liability

The early English common law generally held parties strictly liable for breaching their contractual promises. If a party promised to perform a certain act or to bring about certain results, and if the promise was otherwise enforceable, the promisor could not escape the obligation simply because the promise had become difficult or even impossible to perform or because the reason for contracting and performing had disappeared. The party seeking excuse should have negotiated an escape clause in the contract to limit his obligation. *E.g.*, *Paradine v. Jane*, 82 Eng. Rep. 897 (K.B. 1647) (tenant was bound to pay rent even though a foreign prince had ousted him from the premises during a civil war, undermining the reason for paying rent).

Eventually, however, two doctrines emerged to provide relief from an obligation based on post-contractual changes in circumstances: (1) impossibility of performance, such as when performance has become illegal because of supervening law or when the promisor had promised to perform a personal service but has since died, and (2) frustration of purpose, when the reason for contracting has unexpectedly ceased. In the next two cases, distinguish the nature of the excuse for impossibility from that of the excuse for frustration of purpose.

1. Impossibility

In the famous English case of *Taylor v. Caldwell*, 122 Eng. Rep. 310 (Q.B. 1863), the court applied evolving common law to excuse the owner of a concert hall from its obligation to make the premises available for a series of concerts. Destroyed by fire the night before the first concert, the concert hall had "ceased to exist, without fault of either party."

Noting that the parties had not anticipated such an event and thus had not expressly allocated the risk in their contract, the court nonetheless recognized an "implied condition" to the contractual obligations. The court relied on precedent excusing an estate from performing the personal services of a promisor, such as "painting a picture," when that task has become "impossible to be performed" because the promisor had died or lost her sight. It then cited to authority that had extended that precedent to personal property that had been destroyed after formation of the contract and prior to performance.

Applying these principles to the facts, the court held that "both parties are excused, the plaintiffs from taking the gardens and paying the money, the defendants from performing their promise to give the use of the Hall and Gardens and other things."

Ontario Deciduous Fruit Growers' Assoc. v. Cutting Fruit Packing Co.

134 Cal. 21, 66 P. 28 (1901)

Gray, C.

¶ 1 [A grower agreed in writing to the sale of peaches of a designated variety, grade, and quantity grown from specified orchards. The trial court found that the grower established an excuse for its failure to deliver the full quantity of the designated goods.]

¶ 2 ... [I]n an ordinary year the orchards referred to [in the contract] would have produced sufficient fruit to carry out the contract, but before it was fully grown the season turned unusually dry and hot, and hot winds impaired the quantity and quality of the fruit to such an extent that it was impossible for plaintiff to furnish, from the orchards of its stockholders in the said districts mentioned in the contract, a quantity of fruit equal to one half of the minimum amount agreed to be furnished.

....

¶ 3 In the case at bar, the sale having been of specific varieties of fruit growing and to be grown on specific orchards, and the orchards having been so far affected by the extraordinary drought that they did not produce sufficient fruit of the varieties named to comply with the contract, the plaintiff could be compelled to perform the contract only so far as it was possible for it to do so. It could not be made to perform impossibilities, nor was it liable in damages, by way of counterclaim or otherwise, for a failure to comply with its contract resulting from [a *force majeure*] not attributable to any fault on the part of said plaintiff....

The judgment and order should be affirmed.

At some point, a continuing drought might become the norm, rather than an unexpected supervening event, so that a grower should be expected to consider scarce water resources in its calculations. Also, note the significance in *Ontario* that the parties had agreed to the supply of peaches from a particular source that was "affected by extraordinary drought." Eleven years later, the Oklahoma Supreme Court distinguished *Ontario* on the ground that a grower had agreed to deliver onions of specified varieties from any source and not exclusively from a particular growing area that had produced an insufficient quantity of onions to fulfill the contract. *A.L. Jones & Co. v. Cochran*, 33 Okla. 431, 126 P. 716 (1912). It was not impossible for the grower to procure and supply the onions from *some* available source, even though at a higher cost to the grower.

2. Frustration of Purpose

In another famous English case, *Krells v. Henry*, 2 KB 740 (1903), a lessee agreed to pay premium rent for daytime use of a suite that the lessor had advertised as providing a good view of coronation processions, scheduled to take place on two days in June. When the processions subsequently were postponed, undermining the reason for the lease, the court excused the lessee from paying rent due on the suite (and, implicitly, excused the lessor from keeping the suite available for that lessee).

Although it was clearly *possible* for the lessee to pay the rent, the court extended the rule of *Taylor v. Caldwell* to a different kind of change in circumstances:

> [W]e have to ask ourselves whether the object of the contract was frustrated by the non-happening of the coronation and its procession on the days proclaimed ... the subject of the contract was rooms to view the coronation procession, and was so to the knowledge of both parties.... It is not essential to the application of the principle of Taylor v. Caldwell that the direct subject of the contract should perish or fail to be in existence at the date of performance of the contract. It is sufficient if a state of things or condition expressed in the contract and essential to its performance perishes or fails to be in existence at that time.

Lord Justice Williams noted that the coronation processions taking place on the days of the rental was "in the contemplation of both parties, the foundation of the contract." Lord Justice Romer, on the other hand, wondered whether the parties might have contemplated a postponement of the coronation or a change in its course away from the view of the suite, and thus whether "that risk was undertaken" by the lessee. But he ultimately adopted Justice Williams's conclusions and explanations.

Would the implementation of Brexit frustrate the purpose of a 25-year commercial lease in England, thus discharging the obligation of the tenant—an agency of the European Union—to continue leasing the premises? For a negative response and a thorough review of the English law of frustration, see *Canary Wharf v. European Medicines Agency* [2019] EWHC 335 (Ch).

B. Modern Doctrines of Excuse for Frustration of Purpose and Impracticability

1. *Frustration of Purpose*

In the next case, notice that the tenant suffered no impediment in paying the rent or using the premises for lawful purposes, so it was not arguing that performance of its obligation was impossible; instead, it complained that a change in the law frustrated the particular purpose—known by both parties—for its entering into the lease. Which one or more of the four stated elements for frustration of purpose was missing?

Next Gen Capital, LLC v. Consumer Lending Assoc., LLC

234 Ariz. 9, 316 P.3d 598 (Ct. App. 2013) [footnotes omitted]

Portley, Judge:

¶ 1 Consumer Lending Associates, L.L.C. ("CLA") challenges the summary judgment granted in favor of Next Gen Capital, L.L.C. ("Next Gen") on a breach of lease claim. Finding no genuine dispute of material fact or legal error, we affirm the judgment.

BACKGROUND

¶ 2 CLA, a Nevada company, is engaged in the business of transferring money, whether by cashing checks or making short-term loans. CLA entered into a commercial lease in Arizona in June 2007 with the predecessor to Next Gen. The five-year lease contained a provision that limited CLA's primary use of the premises to short-term loans and check cashing, and its ancillary use to money transfers.

¶ 3 CLA was operating under statutes authorizing "deferred presentment companies," colloquially known as "payday loans" pursuant to Arizona Revised Statutes ("A.R.S.") sections 6-1251 to -1263. The statutes authorizing payday loans, however, expired on July 1, 2010, by its sunset provision. 2000 Ariz. Sess. Laws, ch. 141, § 3 (2d Reg. Sess.); A.R.S. § 6-1263 ("The deferred presentment licensing program established by this chapter ends on July 1, 2010 pursuant to § 41-3102."). Upon expiration of the authorizing statute, CLA promptly vacated the premises. Next Gen demanded that CLA pay rent due through the end of the lease term, but CLA refused and claimed the lease had terminated "by operation of Arizona law."

¶ 4 Next Gen sued CLA for breach of contract and claimed damages. CLA answered and asserted defenses, including frustration of purpose and failure to mitigate damages. Next Gen subsequently moved for summary judgment and argued that CLA was liable for unpaid rent and related charges until the end of the lease term. After briefing and argument, the superior court granted the summary judgment motion.

¶ 5 ... The court ... entered judgment awarding Next Gen $144,899.06 in damages, plus interest, attorneys' fees and costs.

DISCUSSION

I.

¶ 6 CLA argues that the doctrine of frustration of purpose excuses its breach. Because the issue is a question of law, we review it de novo....

¶ 7 We recognize that the doctrine of frustration of purpose is "essentially an equitable doctrine." *Id.* Moreover, long ago we recognized that the doctrine "has been severely limited to cases of extreme hardship so as not to diminish the power of parties to contract, and have required proof from the party seeking to excuse himself that the supervening frustrating event was not reasonably foreseeable." *Garner v. Ellingson*, 18 Ariz. App. 181, 183, 501 P.2d 22, 24 (1972) (citing *Lloyd v. Murphy*, 153 P.2d 47, 50 (Cal. 1944).

¶ 8 In *7200 Scottsdale Road General Partners*, we examined Restatement (Second) of Contracts § 265 (1981), "particularly comment a," to determine whether the party claiming frustration of purpose has demonstrated that the duty has been discharged. 184 Ariz. at 347–48, 909 P.2d at 414–15. Following the comments to § 265, we found four requirements that must exist before relief may be granted for frustration of purpose. *Id.* at 348, 909 P.2d at 415. First, the frustrated purpose "must have been a principal purpose of that party" and must have been so within the understanding of both parties. *Id.* (quoting Restatement (Second) of Contracts § 265 cmt. a (1981)). Second, the frustration "must be so severe that it is not to be regarded as within the risks assumed under the contract." *Id.* (quoting Restatement (Second) of Contracts § 265 cmt. a (1981)). Third, "the non-occurrence of the frustrating event must have been a basic assumption [on which the contract was made]." *Id.* (quoting Restatement (Second) of Contracts § 265 cmt. a (1981)). And, finally, "relief will not be granted if it may be inferred from either the language of the contract or the circumstances that the risk of the frustrating occurrence, or the loss caused thereby, should properly be placed on the party seeking relief." *Id.* (citing Restatement (Second) of Contracts § 265 cmts. b & c (1981)).

¶ 9 Here, the superior court found that CLA could not satisfy the third requirement because it knew or should have known that the statute it was operating under would expire on July 1, 2010. We agree.

¶ 10 When CLA entered into the lease in 2007, the statute authorizing the payday loan business stated it would expire on July 1, 2010. A.R.S. § 6-1263. CLA, as a result, had notice that, absent further legislative action, it could not continue to operate past that date. *See Pioneer Trust & Sav. Bank v. Zonta*, 393 N.E .2d 548, 551 (Ill. App. Ct. 1979) ("The parties are presumed to know the law at the time the lease is made."); *see also Hoff v. Sander*, 497 S.W.2d 651, 653 (Mo. Ct. App. 1973) ("In the eyes of the law plaintiffs did know of the zoning restrictions [and] are therefore precluded from contending they, or defendant, were mistaken about the permissible use of the premises."). Moreover, the lease did not acknowledge the scheduled expiration of the payday loan statute or otherwise allow the lease to terminate if the law expired as it was intended to when the provisions became law. And, there was no intervening legislative action that extended or continued the law past July 1, 2010.

¶ 11 It is clear that it was reasonably foreseeable in 2007 that CLA would have to end its payday loan operation in Arizona by July 1, 2010. Although the parties could have contracted around the statute, they did not. Under the circumstances, the frustration of purpose doctrine does not apply. *See Mohave Cnty. v. Mohave–Kingman Estates, Inc.*, 120 Ariz. 417, 422–23, 586 P.2d 978, 983–84 (1978) (holding frustration of purpose inapplicable because the risk of a change in the zoning ordinance was reasonably foreseeable and one defendant could have contracted against it); *see also City of Miami Beach v. Championship Sports, Inc.*, 200 So. 2d 583, 586–87 (Fla. Dist. Ct. App. 1967) (holding a lessee liable for rent in the absence of evidence that a disabling injury to a boxer was unanticipated). Consequently, the superior court did not err when it determined that the frustration of purpose doctrine did not allow CLA to escape its obligation under the lease.

....

We affirm the judgment granted to Next Gen.

The court in *Next Gen* might have cited to a Texas case decided more than a century earlier, *Houston Ice & Brewing Co. v. Keenan*, 88 S.W. 197, 198 (Tex. S. Ct. 1905) (publishing and adopting the intermediate appellate court's opinion). In *Houston Ice*, premises were leased exclusively for "the saloon business," but this business became illegal during the term of the lease when the population of the county voted to prohibit the sale of liquor. *Id.* at 198 (quoting from opinion of intermediate appellate court). The lessee, however, was not excused from its obligations to pay rent because it had assumed the risk of this illegality: the lessee should have anticipated and contracted against the risk of such a vote, because the county had conducted the vote pursuant to a "Local Option Statute" that the legislature had enacted prior to the lease. *Id.* at 198, 201.

Note that some kinds of intervening law might do more than frustrate the purpose of a contract; it might also render performance practically impossible and render the contract illegal. For example, suppose that a legislature prohibited the manufacture, purchase, sale, prescription, and possession of a previously lawful pain-killing drug, imposing criminal penalties for violation of this provision. A pre-existing contract between a distributor and a manufacturer for future purchase and sale of the drug would not merely be frustrated in its purpose; neither party could perform its duties without subjecting itself to criminal liability. Although the parties would have the raw capacity to perform, the legal prohibition of performance should be viewed as rendering performance impossible; moreover, as explored in Chapter 9, the contract would become unenforceable for illegality. Should that have been the result in *Next Gen* in light of the provision in the lease limiting *Next Gen*'s primary use to short-term loans and check cashing?

Exercise 11.8 — Questions on Frustration of Purpose

1. Distinguishing *Next Gen* from *Krells*

Assume for a moment that *Krells v. Henry* and *Next Gen* were decided by the same court in the same year. Can you distinguish them on the facts? Was the expiration and non-extension of the law in *Next Gen* more foreseeable to the parties than postponement of the procession in *Krells*? If so, how does that affect the analysis of frustration of purpose?

2. Judicially Allocating the Risk in the Absence of Contractual Allocation

In place of the test applied by the courts, some commentators have argued that the risk should be borne by the party who is in the best position to avoid the unexpected event or to insure against it, advancing economic efficiency. This approach arguably would lead to a different result in *Taylor v. Caldwell*, because the lessor was in possession of the concert hall and thus was in the best position to protect it from destruction by fire. Such a rule, without regard to other factors, would put the lessor on notice that it should contractually provide that its obligations would terminate if the hall was destroyed, should take extra care to protect the premises, or should insure against liability to the lessee as well as property damage.

How would such a rule apply in *Next Gen*? Was CLA in the best position to monitor the continuing legality of its own business and thus to negotiate an escape clause if it desired to avoid the risk of the legislature's decision to allow the authorizing legislation to expire? If so, was the court considering the economic efficiency rationale without making it an explicit factor, or does the Restatement rule simply point to the same conclusion in some cases, for different reasons?

3. Legislative Change

Suppose that the authorizing legislation in *Next Gen* had not been subject to a sunset provision. Instead, the legislature unexpectedly repealed the legislation during the term of the lease. Would the court then hold that continuation of the legislation was a basic assumption on which the parties contracted, or would it find that CLA should have foreseen the possibility of legislative repeal of controversial legislation?

Let's continue to suppose that the authorizing legislation did not have a sunset provision and instead the legislature affirmatively repealed existing legislation during the term of the lease. Next Gen then announced that it was terminating the lease to cease CLA's payday lending operations. CLA protested and sued for specific enforcement of Next Gen's promise to make the premises available to CLA for its payday lending operations. What defense would Next Gen offer to establish that its promise to lease the premises is not enforceable?

---

2. Impracticability — The Successor to Strict Impossibility

a. Evolution and Current Shape of the Doctrine

The common law doctrine of impossibility has evolved to permit an excuse for nonperformance if an unexpected event has rendered performance "impracticable," even though not strictly impossible. *See, e.g.*, RESTATEMENT (SECOND) OF CONTRACTS § 261 (1981). A standard based on impracticability permits a party to be excused from nonperformance if an unexpected change of circumstances makes performance excessively burdensome even though not strictly impossible.

In a bankruptcy case citing California law, for example, Anchor had agreed to produce glass containers at CPI's Lavington factory for purchase by Encore. Although the court found that Anchor's performance had been rendered strictly impossible by CPI's sale of its Lavington factory, it noted in passing the greater scope of modern excuse doctrine under the impracticability standard:

> "Impossibility means not only strict impossibility but impracticability because of extreme and unreasonable difficulty, expense, injury or loss involved." *See* Restatement (First) of Contracts §454 (1932); *see also* ... *City of Vernon v. City of Los Angeles*, 45 Cal. 2d 710, 290 P.2d 841, 845–47 (1955) (holding that a thing is impossible in legal contemplation when it can only be done at an excessive and unreasonable cost).

In re Anchor Glass Container Corp., 245 B.R. 765, 772 (M.D. Fla. 2006). The following excerpts from the West Virginia Supreme Court trace the doctrine's evolution from absolute contractual liability for nonperformance, to initially very limited and then broader grounds for excuse from obligations based on impossibility, and finally to modern impracticability:

Waddy v. Riggleman

216 W. Va. 250, 606 S.E.2d 222 (2004)

Davis, Justice:

A. Overview of the Doctrine of Impossibility

¶1 A statement of the doctrine of impossibility was set out by this Court in 1909 as follows: "If a party by contract charge himself with an obligation possible to be performed, he must make it good, unless performance is rendered impossible by the act of God, the law, or the other party. Unforeseen difficulties, however great, will not excuse him." Syl. pt. 4, *McCormick v. Jordon*, 65 W. Va. 86, 63 S.E. 778 (1909). Rules such as this one announced in *McCormick* were developed in the common law to alleviate, to a limited degree, the harsh results obtained from the strict rule of absolute contractual liability by providing, under certain limited circumstances, an excuse from performance of a contract. *See McGinnis v. Cayton*, 173 W. Va. 102, 110–11 n. 11, 312 S.E.2d 765, 774 n. 11 (1984) ... [*s*]*ee also Opera Co. of Boston, Inc. v. Wolf Trap Found. for Performing Arts*, 817 F.2d 1094, 1097 (1987) ("The doctrine of impossibility of performance as an excuse or defense for a breach of contract was for long smothered under a declared commitment to the principle of sanctity of contracts.... The growth of commercial activity in the nineteenth century, however, made this rigidity of the doctrine of impossibility both 'economically and socially unworkable,'... and ... the English courts recognized these changed conditions and, relying largely on civil law precedents, relaxed the constraints on the doctrine ...)." (internal citations omitted) (footnote omitted)).

¶2 In modern times, the rule of impossibility has undergone further relaxation.... The modern rule, the rule of impracticability, is identified in the Restatement (Second) of Contracts as "Discharge by Supervening Impracticability," and is described as follows:

> Where, after a contract is made, a party's performance is made impracticable without his fault by the occurrence of an event the non-occurrence of which was a basic assumption on which the contract was made, his duty to render that performance is discharged, unless the language or the circumstances indicate the contrary.

§261 (1979). It has been observed that "[m]ost of the more recent cases follow this approach." James P. Nehf, Corbin on Contracts §74.2, at 15 (Rev. ed. 2001) (hereinafter referred to as "Corbin on Contracts"). *See, e.g., United States v. Winstar Corp.*, 518 U.S. 839, 904, ... 964 (1996) ... ; *Cazares v. Saenz*, 256 Cal. Rptr. 209, 212 & n. 7, 208 Cal. App. 3d 279, 285 & n. 7 (1989)....

¶3 Following this modern trend, we now adopt the Restatement (Second) of Contracts §261 and hold that, under the doctrine of impracticability, a party to a contract who claims that a supervening event has prevented, and thus excused, a promised performance must demonstrate each of the following: (1) the event made the performance impracticable; (2) the nonoccurrence of the event was a basic assumption on which the contract was made; (3) the impracticability resulted without the fault of the party seeking to be excused; and (4) the party has not agreed, either expressly or impliedly, to perform in spite of impracticability that would otherwise justify his nonperformance. *See O'Hara v. State*, 218 Conn. 628, 637, 590 A.2d 948, 953....

¶4 Although the present rule is less strict than its inflexible ancestor, it, nevertheless, remains a difficult standard to meet.

> Substituting the term "impracticability"—instead of the historical usage of "impossibility"—better expresses the extent of the increased legal burden that is required. That is, while it remains difficult to prove that something is impracticable, that legal excuse is broader than having to prove that something is impossible.... While impracticability embraces situations short of absolute impossibility, mere increase in difficulty is not enough.

30 Williston on Contracts §77:1, at 277–78.

....

b. Impracticability Under the UCC

The UCC has adopted the impracticability standard for sales of goods, as represented by this excerpt from the Texas Business and Commerce Code:

> Sec. 2.615. EXCUSE BY FAILURE OF PRESUPPOSED CONDITIONS.
>
> Except so far as a seller may have assumed a greater obligation ... :
>
> (1) Delay in delivery or non-delivery in whole or in part by a seller ... is not a breach of his duty under a contract for sale if performance as agreed has been made impracticable by the occurrence of a contingency the non-occurrence of which was a basic assumption on which the contract was made....

TEX. BUS. & COM. CODE § 2.615 (enacting U.C.C. § 2-615); *see also* RESTATEMENT (SECOND) OF CONTRACTS § 261 (1981) (reflecting similar test for non-sales contracts, and stating a factor that is implicit in the UCC: the supervening event must not be the fault of the party seeking relief). Although the statute refers solely to excuse for a seller's nonperformance, the UCC may in limited circumstances excuse a buyer's nonperformance as well, applying the reasoning of UCC § 2-615 and perhaps the terms of other UCC sections. U.C.C. § 2-615 cmt. 9 (1981).

A court will not easily find that nonoccurrence of a contingency was "a basic assumption on which the contract was made." U.C.C. § 2-615(a). "A rise or collapse in the market," for example, "is exactly the type of business risk which business contracts made at fixed prices are intended to cover." U.C.C. § 2-615 cmt. 4. Better examples of qualifying contingency would be "war, embargo, local crop failure, unforeseen shutdown of major sources of supply or the like" that severely disrupt a party's source of supply, *id.*, in a way that is beyond the control of the party seeking relief, *id.* at cmt. 5.

Indeed, even with a qualifying contingency, courts will not lightly excuse nonperformance of contractual obligations on grounds of impracticability. An increase in the cost of performance, for example, does not make performance impracticable unless it "alters the essential nature of the performance." U.C.C. § 2-615 cmt. 4. Thus, when the contract did not specify an exclusive route, wartime closure of the Suez Canal did not render shipment of wheat from the United States to Iran commercially impracticable:

> The goods shipped were not subject to harm from the longer, less temperate Southern route. The vessel and crew were fit to proceed around the Cape. Transatlantic was no less able than the United States to purchase insurance to cover the contingency's occurrence.... The only factor operating here in appellant's favor is the added expense, allegedly $43,972.00 above and beyond the contract price of $305,842.92, of extending a 10,000 mile voyage by approximately 3,000 miles. While it may be an overstatement to say that increased cost and difficulty of performance never constitute impracticability, to justify relief there must be more of a variation between expected cost and the cost of performing by an available alternative than is present in this case,

> where the promisor can legitimately be presumed to have accepted some degree of abnormal risk, and where impracticability is urged on the basis of added expense alone.

Transatlantic Financing Corp. v. United States, 363 F.3d 312, 319 (D.C. Cir. 1966).

Should a labor strike and related picketing at the work site be viewed as a qualifying contingency that renders a subcontractor's performance impracticable? Should courts provide a categorical answer to that question, or should the answer depend on the particular circumstances of each case?

Mishara Constr. Co. v. Transit-Mixed Concrete Co.

365 Mass. 122, 310 N.E.2d 363 (1974)
[additional paragraph breaks added]

Reardon, Justice.

. . . .

¶1 The plaintiff Mishara Construction Company, Inc. (Mishara) was the general contractor under contract with the Pittsfield Housing Authority for the construction of Rose Manor, a housing project for the elderly. In September, 1966, the plaintiff negotiated with the defendant Transit-Mixed Concrete Corp. (Transit) for the supplying of ready-mixed concrete to be used on the project. An agreement was reached that Transit would supply all the concrete needed on the project at a price of $13.25 a cubic yard, with deliveries to be made at the times and in the amounts as ordered by Mishara. . . .

¶2 Performance under this contract was satisfactory to both parties until April, 1967. In that month a labor dispute disrupted work on the job site. Although work resumed on June 15, 1967, a picket line was maintained on the site until the completion of the project in 1969. Throughout this period, with very few exceptions, no deliveries of concrete were made by Transit notwithstanding frequent requests by Mishara. After notifying Transit of its intention, Mishara purchased the balance of its concrete requirements elsewhere. Mishara sought in damages the additional cost of concrete incurred by virtue of the higher price of the replacement product, as well as the expenses of locating an alternate source.

. . . .

¶3 The remainder of the plaintiff's exceptions relate to the proffered defence of the impossibility of performance. Objection was made to the introduction of all evidence regarding the existence of a picket line at the job site and the difficulty which Transit did encounter or might have encountered in attempting to make deliveries through that picket line. Furthermore, Mishara requested an instruction that Transit "was required to comply with the contract regardless of picket lines, strikes or labor difficulties." As a result Mishara would have completely withdrawn the question of impossibility resulting from the picket line from the jury. We are asked to decide as matter of law and without reference to individual facts and circumstances that "picket lines, strikes or labor difficulties" provide no excuse for nonperformance by way of impossibility. This is too sweeping a statement of the law and we decline to adopt it.

¶4 The excuse of impossibility in contracts for the sale of goods is controlled by the appropriate section of the Uniform Commercial Code, G.L. c. 106, §2-615. That section sets up two requirements before performance may be excused. First, the performance must have become "impracticable." Second, the impracticability must have been caused "by the occurrence of a contingency the non-occurrence of which was a basic assumption on which the contract was made." This section of the Uniform Commercial Code has not yet been interpreted by this court. Therefore it is appropriate to discuss briefly the significance of these two criteria.

¶5 With respect to the requirement that performance must have been impracticable, the official Code comment to the section stresses that the reference is to "commercial impracticability" as opposed to strict impossibility. G.L. c. 106, §2-615, comments 3–4. This is not a radical departure from the common law of contracts as interpreted by this court. Although a strict rule was originally followed denying any excuse for accident or "inevitable necessity," *e.g., Adams v. Nichols*, 19 Pick. 275 (1837), it has long been assumed that circumstances drastically increasing the difficulty and expense of the contemplated performance may be within the compass of "impossibility." *See Rowe v. Peabody*, 207 Mass. 226, 233–234, 93 N.E. 604 (1911) (dictum); *Fauci v. Denehy*, 332 Mass. 691, 696–697, 127 N.E.2d 477 (1955). By adopting the term "impracticability" rather than "impossibility" the drafters of the Code appear to be in accord with Professor Williston who stated that "the essence of the modern defense of impossibility is that the promised performance was at the making of the contract, or thereafter became, impracticable owing to some extreme or unreasonable difficulty, expense, injury, or loss involved, rather than that it is scientifically or actually impossible." Williston, Contracts (Rev. ed.) §1931 (1938). *See* Restatement: Contracts, §454 (1932); Corbin, Contracts, §1339 (1962).

¶6 The second criterion of the excuse, that the intervening circumstance be one which the parties assumed would not occur, is also familiar to the law of Massachusetts. *Baetjer v. New England Alcohol Co.*, 319 Mass. 592, 600, 66 N.E.2d 798 (1946).... The rule is essentially aimed at the distribution of certain kinds of risks in the contractual relationship. By directing the inquiry to the time when the contract was first made, we really seek to determine whether the risk of the intervening circumstance was one which the parties may be taken to have assigned between themselves.

¶7 It is, of course, the very essence of contract that it is directed at the elimination of some risks for each party in exchange for others. Each receives the certainty of price, quantity, and time, and assumes the risk of changing market prices, superior opportunity, or added costs. It is implicit in the doctrine of impossibility (and the companion rule of "frustration of purpose") that certain risks are so unusual and have such severe consequences that they must have been beyond the scope of the assignment of risks inherent in the contract, that is, beyond the agreement made by the parties. To require performance in that case would be to grant the promisee an advantage for which he could not be said to have bargained in making the contract. "The important question is whether an unanticipated circumstance has made performance of the promise vitally different from what should reasonably have been within the contemplation of both parties when they entered into the contract. If so, the risk should not fairly be thrown upon the promisor." Williston, Contracts (Rev. ed.) § 1931 (1938).

¶ 8 The emphasis in contracts governed by the Uniform Commercial Code is on the commercial context in which the agreement was made. The question is, given the commercial circumstances in which the parties dealt: Was the contingency which developed one which the parties could reasonably be thought to have foreseen as a real possibility which could affect performance? Was it one of that variety of risks which the parties were tacitly assigning to the promisor by their failure to provide for it explicitly? If it were, performance will be required. If it could not be so considered, performance is excused. The contract cannot be reasonably thought to govern in these circumstances, and the parties are both thrown upon the resources of the open market without the benefit of their contract.

¶ 9 With this backdrop, we consider Mishara's contention that a labor dispute which makes performance more difficult never constitutes an excuse for nonperformance. We think it is evident that in some situations a labor dispute would not meet the requirements for impossibility discussed above. A picket line might constitute a mere inconvenience and hardly make performance "impracticable." Likewise, in certain industries with a long record of labor difficulties, the nonoccurrence of strikes and picket lines could not fairly be said to be a basic assumption of the agreement. Certainly, in general, labor disputes cannot be considered extraordinary in the course of modern commerce. *See* Restatement: Contracts, § 461, illustration 7 (1932).

¶ 10 Admitting this, however, we are still far from the proposition implicit in the plaintiff's requests. Much must depend on the facts known to the parties at the time of contracting with respect to the history of and prospects for labor difficulties during the period of performance of the contract, as well as the likely severity of the effect of such disputes on the ability to perform. From these facts it is possible to draw an inference as to whether or not the parties intended performance to be carried out even in the face of the labor difficulty. Where the probability of a labor dispute appears to be practically nil, and where the occurrence of such a dispute provides unusual difficulty, the excuse of impracticability might well be applicable. Thus in discussing the defence of impossibility, then Chief Judge Cardozo noted an excuse would be provided "conceivably in some circumstances by unavoidable strikes." *Canadian Industrial Alcohol Co. Ltd. v. Dunbar Molasses Co.*, 258 N.Y. 194, 198, 179 N.E. 383, 384 (1932). The many variables which may bear on the question in individual cases were canvassed by Professor Williston in Williston, Contracts (Rev. ed.) § 1951A (1938), and he concluded that the trend of the law is toward recognizing strikes as excuses for nonperformance.

¶ 11 We agree with the statement of the judge in *Badhwar v. Colorado Fuel & Iron Corp.*, 138 F. Supp. 595, 607 (S.D.N.Y. 1955), *affd.* 245 F.2d 903 (2d Cir. 1957), on the same question: "Rather than mechanically apply any fixed rule of law, where the parties themselves have not allocated responsibility, justice is better served by appraising all of the circumstances, the part the various parties played, and thereon determining liability." Since the instructions requested by the plaintiff and the exclusion of the evidence objected to would have precluded such a factual determination, the requests were more properly refused, and the evidence was properly admitted.

Exceptions overruled.

Exercise 11.9 — Drafting to Allocate the Risk of Contingencies

1. Drafting Against Foreseen Events

If the parties actually foresee the possibility of a disruptive change in circumstances, they ought to expressly allocate the risk of loss stemming from such an event, rather than litigate it later under default standards in the law. In an age of climate change and more volatile weather patterns, is it now more foreseeable that previously rare weather events might adversely affect contract performance? At what point is it foreseeable that drought conditions will make it extremely burdensome to grow certain crops at a designated volume in a particular geographic location? To state it differently, at what point is it unrealistic to suppose that adequate and inexpensive water resources formed a basic assumption of such a contract?

Parties to a contract for the supply of crops could supersede the legal default rule by erecting a standard of the parties' own choosing. To take two extremes on the spectrum, the contract could provide that the seller will be strictly liable for any delay in delivery, regardless of impediments to performance, or conversely will be excused for delay or other nonperformance on terms more forgiving than would be provided by the legal default rules.

Suppose, for example, that a seller has agreed to deliver goods to the Port of Houston within a seven-day window within a season that in previous decades would not normally present a significant risk of weather delays. Would it nonetheless be prudent for the parties to negotiate a clause addressing possible weather delays? Find a partner in class, assign the roles of buyer and seller, and negotiate a clause that addresses the parties' rights or liabilities if severe weather forces the seller to deliver outside the seven-day window.

2. Drafting Against Unforeseeable Events

Under default rules, a party will most likely enjoy excuse for nonperformance if an adverse change in circumstances was truly unforeseeable, so that a court would not expect the parties to have addressed the contingency in the contract. Nonetheless, would it be possible to negotiate a clause that allocates the risk of disruptive contingencies generally, whether specifically foreseen or not? After concluding the negotiations under exercise 1 above, attempt to negotiate a second clause that addresses other contingencies in a more general manner.

VII. Summary

- An express condition qualifies a contractual duty and generally must be strictly satisfied to remove the contingency from the duty. Because this could result in forfeiture, contract language will generally be interpreted to state only mutual duties rather than express conditions unless the condition is clearly expressed.
- Duties arising out of mutual, dependent promises—without express conditions—give rise only to constructive conditions, which can be satisfied by substantial performance, meaning performance without material breach.
- Repudiation or other uncured material breach permits the victim of breach to cancel the contract, withhold his own performance, and sue for damages. The victim of the breach, however, has the option of treating the breach as minor and going forward with the contract, although exercising this option would be foolish if it tends to inflate damages rather than mitigate them.
- If a contract is divisible, a breaching party can claim the contract fee for substantial performance of any divisible part, while still remaining liable for damages for the breach.
- The non-satisfaction of express or constructive conditions can be excused if the party benefited by the condition either waives the non-satisfaction, or if that party wrongfully prevented the condition from being satisfied.
- An anticipatory breach, such as by anticipatory repudiation, constitutes an immediate total breach, giving the other party the right to cancel immediately and to sue for damages.
- Reasonable insecurity about the other party's willingness or ability to perform in the future, short of receipt of a repudiation, can be treated as a repudiation if the other party does not provide an adequate assurance after a demand for such an assurance.
- A party may be relieved from liability for nonperformance if unexpected events render the performance impracticable or frustrate the purpose of the contract for that party, but only if the risk of the event was not allocated to the party seeking relief.

Exercise 11.10—Exam Question

1. Q1—Suggested Time Allocation: 30 minutes

Expert Excavation, Inc. ("EE") entered into a contract with General Contractor ("GC") to excavate a parcel of land in preparation for the construction of an underground parking garage. The contract called for excavation to take place during the month of January, before other subcontractors began the next phase of construction starting on February 1.

Near the end of the first day of work, January 2, EE discovered a mass of large boulders below the surface of the site. EE's contract with GC clearly and expressly allocated the risk of any such difficulties in excavation to EE, regardless how unexpected.

On finding the rocky substrata, EE halted work, called GC, and left the following voicemail:

> This is Expert Excavation. We ran into unexpected rock formations at the excavation site. I understand that the contract makes us responsible for this, but to finish on time I would need to hire extra crew, rent special equipment, work extra hours, and take a loss of $10,000. The only sensible solution is for you to give me an extra week and an extra $5,000. With that, I can probably break even, and we'll get this job done. To confirm, just text back the word, "yes."

GC texted back the word, "No." GC then sent an e-mail to EE's office, stating that GC was terminating its contract with EE and that EE should remove its equipment from the worksite immediately. GC then hired another subcontractor, who was fully informed of the rocky substrata and who agreed to complete the excavation work by the end of January, for $20,000 more than EE's total contract fee. (GC intends to claim the extra $20,000 as damages that EE must pay to GC in GC's contract claim against EE; however, calculation of damages is not an issue for discussion.)

You can assume that the contract between EE and GC is fully enforceable, with no defects in contract formation, and the contract's allocation of risk eliminates any defense based on mistake. Moreover, GC and EE did not agree to modify their contract, so you should not discuss any issues that might have arisen from such a modification, such as duress or pre-existing duty. Discuss only two questions:

A. Did GC have a right to terminate its contract with EE? In your issue, state the specific ground on which GC would rely. Argue both sides.

B. If GC had consulted you prior to sending the e-mail terminating the contract, what alternative course of action could you have advised, to best protect GC's position? (This need not fully follow IRAC format, and you need not argue both sides.)

2. Q2—Suggested Time Allocation: 50 minutes [*Until you study the next chapter, you will not be able to fully discuss issues of remedies raised in this question. If you take this exam after studying Chapter 12, add 10 minutes to your time, and discuss all the issues.*]

On November 1, Sonia and Jonathan ("SJ" for short) hired their favorite local band—"Rave"—for their wedding reception in three months, scheduled for Saturday, February 9. Their written contract called for Rave to perform for four hours during the wedding reception, for a fee of $8,000.

In mid-November, a performance by Rave posted on the Youtube Internet site caused a sensation, catapulting the band from a top local band to a nationally known musical act. Over the Thanksgiving weekend, SJ bumped into Rave's booking agent ("BA" for short) at a party and had the following conversation:

> SJ: Congratulations on Rave's new fame. We are just thrilled to have them for our wedding in February.
>
> BA: Yeah, well, I really hope they can still keep that date. We are fielding offers now from all over the country, and we aren't booking weddings or small clubs any longer.

Our current asking rate is $40,000 for a Saturday night concert.

SJ: We trust you are not saying that the band is canceling on us.

BA: Now, I didn't exactly say that. But, let's be realistic. Everything has changed for them. It wouldn't hurt for you to cover all your bases and have a replacement band ready.

What are SJ's legal rights at this moment and what are their options? You may assume that the contract between SJ and Rave is perfectly enforceable and that BA has full authority to represent Rave.

Analyzing the Conversation: For any legal issue that the facts raise (I intended to raise one issue with the limited facts above), identify the issue, summarize the applicable legal rule, and apply the rule to the facts to reach a conclusion, arguing both sides if possible.

Looking to the Future: After discussing any such legal issue, discuss and compare what course or courses of action SJ might pursue to assert their contract rights or achieve their goals. If any of those options or remedies can be developed in IRAC form, feel free to do so. Otherwise, feel free to discuss them in any efficient manner. For these options or remedies, which look to the future, you can speculate on the facts a bit, or fill in your own potential facts as examples, when necessary to illustrate a point.

Chapter 12

Remedies

I. Introduction—Vindicating the Expectation Interest

We have come full circle. At the beginning of the course, we briefly discussed the ways in which contract law can protect various interests. Since then we learned that quasi-contract protects the restitution interest, based on the benefit received by the party who was unjustly enriched. We also learned that promissory estoppel may be used to enforce a promise, thus protecting expectation interest, but also that a modest injustice might be remedied with a lesser remedy, such as out-of-pocket reliance costs.

In this chapter, we will explore ways to remedy a breach of contract based on a bargained-for exchange. Although a party occasionally will ask for reliance or restitution interest to remedy a breach of contract (perhaps because it's easier to prove in some cases), most courts normally will not allow an award based on either of those interests to exceed the expectation interest. Therefore, this chapter will focus on defining remedies that vindicate the expectation interest of the victim of a breach.

The expectation interest is often defined as the benefit of the bargain. The claimant's expectations can be protected with an order compelling actual performance of contractual obligations or with an award of money that puts the victim of breach in the economic position it would have enjoyed had the contractual obligations been performed.

As we explore these issues, keep in mind the following questions:

- What are the limitations on specific enforcement?
- How are money damages calculated?
- Why are punitive damages unavailable for breach of contract, and how do you tell whether a "liquidated damages" clause in a contract is punitive and thus unenforceable?
- What other limitations are imposed on damages for breach of contract?

II. Specific Performance

A. Specific Enforcement Defined

A court can directly protect expectation interests by specifically enforcing the parties' obligations. This is essentially injunctive relief that orders the breaching party to actually perform its obligations as promised in the contract. To avoid placing the victim of breach in a better position than if the contract had been performed, the court's order will also direct the victim of the breach to perform at the appropriate time as well.

For example, suppose that I promised to sell land to you for $100,000, and you promised to pay after I deliver title. Before the performance date, the market value of land increased to $150,000, and I repudiated the contract. Naturally, you are disappointed, because you made a good deal that would have earned you profit of $50,000.

If you had contracted for this land solely as an investment for resale, you might be content to sue for your lost profits of $50,000. If you valued the land itself, however, you might prefer specific performance. An order specifically enforcing the agreement would require me to transfer title to you and would require you to pay me the purchase price of $100,000. You would realize your expectation interest by paying $100,000 and receiving land now worth $150,000.

B. Limitations on Specific Performance

The preceding discussion assumed that the victim of breach is entitled to specific enforcement as an alternative to money damages. In fact, however, specific enforcement is relatively rarely granted. Aside from some practical limitations, specific enforcement is sharply limited in common law countries because courts view this remedy as both *extraordinary* and *discretionary*.

1. *Specific Relief Is Extraordinary*

The early English common law courts generally granted only the "legal" relief of money damages. A separate system of equity courts offered specific relief; however, in deference to the common law courts, they did so only when the legal relief of money damages was inadequate to remedy the breach of contract. Although legal and equitable claims are now largely merged into a unified body of common law and applied by the same court, the early characteristics of equitable relief persist.

Money damages are viewed as adequate in most transactions, because the breaching party's performance normally can be purchased on the market from a substitute supplier. If the market price for substitute performance is higher than the contract price, the difference can be awarded to the victim of the breach in money damages. Thus, breach of an obligation to supply generic goods, or to provide commercially available services, can be remedied adequately by an award of money damages, and the extraordinary relief of specific enforcement would normally be unnecessary and inappropriate.

A plot of land, however, is viewed as unique if only because of its singular location. A buyer who had contracted for the land solely to sell it for a profit might not seek specific performance, because money damages would fully meet that buyer's economic goals. If the buyer valued the land itself and sought specific performance, however, the minimum prerequisite of the inadequacy of money damages would be met by the uniqueness of the land. *Woliansky v. Miller,* 135 Ariz. 444, 446, 661 P.2d 1145, 1147 (Ct. App. 1983). The buyer could persuasively complain that an award of money damages would enable him or her to buy *other*, comparable land, but not real estate with the unique location and other qualities of the land bargained for.

Would the legal remedy of money damages ever be inadequate to a seller of real property when the buyer fails to purchase? In one case, a seller demanded specific performance of a contract for the sale of the home, demanding that the buyer retain the house and pay the purchase price. The South Dakota Supreme Court affirmed the trial court's grant of specific performance for the seller based on the buyers' having diminished the value of the house to a degree that would be difficult to quantify:

> The trial court granted specific performance partially because of the evidence of damage and deterioration to the property while in [the buyers'] possession. The court also found that [the buyers] had created a perception in the community that the property had a "snake problem." The court determined that this irrevocable perception substantially affected the marketability of the house. Because the court was not able to quantify damages, [the seller] lacked an adequate remedy at law. The trial court did not abuse its discretion in awarding Cahill specific performance.

McCollam v. Cahill, 2009 S.D. 34 ¶ 15, 766 N.W.2d 171, 177 ¶ 15 (2009).

The requisite inadequacy of damages would be present as well in a contract for unique services, such as the performance of a famous or uniquely talented artist. Similarly, the requirement of inadequacy is satisfied in a contract to deliver unique goods such as an original and singular work of art or, in one case, a uniquely trained horse, *Morris v. Sparrow*, 287 S.W.2d 583 (Ark. 1956).

The UCC slightly liberalizes the traditional requirement that goods must be unique to establish the inadequacy of money damages: "Specific performance may be decreed where the goods are unique *or in other proper circumstances*." U.C.C. § 2-716(1) (2011) (italics added). A victim of breach seeking specific performance of a contract to supply goods thus has the opportunity to show that money damages would be inadequate because the undelivered goods, although not strictly unique, cannot as a practical matter be replaced through a substitute transaction, perhaps because of a lack of an established market for similar goods.

Why was the legal remedy inadequate in the following case?

Houseman v. Dare

405 N.J. Super. 538, 966 A.2d 24 (App. Div. 2009)

Grall, J.A.D....

¶1 ... [T]he [trial] court found that Houseman established an oral agreement under which she was to obtain possession and ownership of the dog. Despite that finding and solely on the ground that Dare had possession of the dog at that time, the court awarded Dare possession and Houseman the dog's stipulated value.

¶2 The court's conclusion that specific performance is not, as a matter of law, available to remedy a breach of an oral agreement about possession of a dog reached by its joint owners is not sustainable. The remedy of specific performance can be invoked to address a breach of an enforceable agreement when money damages are not adequate to protect the expectation interest of the injured party and an order requiring performance of the contract will not result in inequity to the offending party, reward the recipient for unfair dealing or conflict with public policy. *See Stehr v. Sawyer,* 40 N.J. 352, 357, 192 A.2d 569 (1963); [citations to three other cases omitted]; Restatement (Second) of Contracts §§ 357, 358, 360, 364, 365 (1981).

¶3 Specific performance is generally recognized as the appropriate remedy when an agreement concerns possession of property such as "heirlooms, family treasures and works of art that induce a strong sentimental attachment." *Id.* at § 360 comment b. That is so because money damages cannot compensate the injured party for the special subjective benefits he or she derives from possession....

¶4 The special subjective value of personal property worthy of recognition by a court of equity is sentiment explained by facts and circumstances—such as the party's relationship with the donor or prior associations with the property—that give rise to the special affection. *See* ... Pomeroy, Specific Performance of Contracts §§ 12, 34 (3d ed. 1926). In a different context, this court has recognized that pets have special "subjective value" to their owners. *Hyland v. Borras,* 316 N.J. Super. 22, 25, 719 A.2d 662 (App. Div. 1998) (concluding that the owner of an injured dog was entitled to recover costs of treatment that exceeded replacement cost); *see also Pitney v. Bugbee,* 98 N.J.L. 116, 120, 118 A. 780 (Sup. Ct. 1922) (noting the importance of the "companionship" of animals to humans in concluding that a bequest to the Society for Prevention of Cruelty to Animals was exempt from tax as a transfer to a benevolent and charitable organization). Courts of other jurisdictions have considered the special subjective value of pets in resolving questions about possession. *See, e.g., Morgan v. Kroupa,* 167 Vt. 99, 702 A.2d 630, 633 (1997) (affirming a decision awarding possession of a dog to a person who found the lost pet, "diligently attempted to locate the dog's owner and responsibly sheltered and cared for the animal for over a year").

¶5 There is no reason for a court of equity to be more wary in resolving competing claims for possession of a pet based on one party's sincere affection for and attachment to it than in resolving competing claims based on one party's sincere sentiment for an inanimate object based upon a relationship with the donor. *See Burr, supra,* 101

N.J. Eq. at 626, 138 *A.* 876. In both types of cases, a court of equity must consider the interests of the parties pressing competing claims for possession and public policies that may be implicated by an award of possession. *Cf. Juelfs v. Gough,* 41 P.3d 593, 597 (Alaska 2002) (approving modification of a property settlement agreement providing for shared possession of a dog because the arrangement assumed cooperation between the parties that did not exist); *Akers v. Sellers,* 114 Ind. App. 660, 54 N.E.2d 779, 779–80 (1944) (speculating that the interests of the pet might be different but finding the evidence adequate to support an award of possession to the wife, rather than husband, on the ground that the husband had given her the dog)....

¶6 We conclude that the trial court erred by declining to consider the relevance of the oral agreement alleged on the ground that a pet is property. Agreements about property jointly held by cohabitants are material in actions concerning its division. *Olson v. Stevens,* 322 N.J. Super. 119, 123, 730 A.2d 432 (App. Div. 1999). They may be specifically enforced when that remedy is appropriate.

¶7 Houseman's evidence was adequate to require the trial court to consider the oral agreement and the remedy of specific performance. The special subjective value of the dog to Houseman can be inferred from her testimony about its importance to her and her prompt effort to enforce her right of possession when Dare took action adverse to her enjoyment of that right. Her stipulation to the dog's intrinsic monetary value cannot be viewed as a concession that the stipulated value was adequate to compensate her for loss of the special value given her efforts to pursue her claim for specific performance at trial. *See Burr, supra,* 101 N.J. Eq. at 629, 138 A. 876 (concluding that a payment made on demand to avoid loss of an heirloom did not bar a claim for possession based on an assertion that money damages were inadequate). And, Dare did not establish that an order awarding specific performance would be harsh or oppressive to him, reward Houseman for unfair conduct or violate public policy. *See Stehr, supra,* 40 N.J. at 357, 192 A.2d 569; *Marioni, supra,* 374 N.J. Super. at 599, 866 A.2d 208. To the contrary, assuming an oral agreement that Dare breached by keeping the dog after a visit, an order awarding him possession because he had the dog at the time of trial would reward him for his breach.

¶8 Recognizing that the trial court is in the best position to evaluate the equities implicated by Houseman's request for possession of the dog..., we remand for further proceedings on the existence of an oral agreement about ownership and possession of the dog and the propriety of specific performance.

¶9 [W]e ... reverse and remand to the trial court that part of the judgment awarding Dare possession of the dog and Houseman $1500 for her interest in the pet for further proceedings in conformity with this opinion.

Most commercial services are not unique and can be replaced with a substitute service purchased with the help of an award of money damages. In the following case, however, a court allowed an allegation of the uniqueness of architectural plans for a home to survive a motion to dismiss. On remand, what facts can you imagine that might support a finding that the legal remedy is inadequate?

Sokoloff v. Harriman Estates Development Corp.

96 N.Y.2d 409, 415, 754 N.E.2d 184, 188 (N.Y. 2001)

....

¶ 1 We also reject Harriman's assertion that specific performance is an inappropriate remedy because the architectural plans are not unique and a dollar value can be placed on the purchase of replacement plans. In general, specific performance will not be ordered where money damages "would be adequate to protect the expectation interest of the injured party" (Restatement [Second] of Contracts § 359 ...).

¶ 2 The decision whether or not to award specific performance is one that rests in the sound discretion of the trial court. In determining whether money damages would be an adequate remedy, a trial court must consider, among other factors, the difficulty of proving damages with reasonable certainty and of procuring a suitable substitute performance with a damages award (*see,* Restatement [Second] of Contracts § 360). Specific performance is an appropriate remedy for a breach of contract concerning goods that "are unique in kind, quality or personal association" where suitable substitutes are unobtainable or unreasonably difficult or inconvenient to procure (*see, id.,* comment *c*).

¶ 3 In this case, plaintiffs have alleged that "[t]he architectural plans and drawings are unique in that they are based upon a design conceived by the plaintiffs," and that without specific performance they "would have to change their requirements" as to the design of their new home. These allegations are sufficient to withstand a motion to dismiss for failure to state a cause of action. Whether money damages would adequately compensate plaintiffs for loss of these allegedly unique architectural plans is a matter to be resolved at a later stage, not on a motion to dismiss the complaint.

Some services are more clearly unique, including those of a chef, portrait artist, or musician with singular talent or celebrity. If such an artist breached a contract to apply his or her unique skills, the inadequacy of money damages would be readily established. Other limitations, however, almost certainly would bar specific relief, as discussed in the next subsection.

2. *Specific Relief is Discretionary*

Even if the legal remedy is inadequate, the victim of breach *is not entitled* to a decree of specific enforcement as a matter of right. *Woliansky v. Miller,* 135 Ariz. 444, 446, 661 P.2d 1145, 1147 (App. 1983). This equitable remedy lies within the discretion of the trial judge. This discretion stems from the traditional flexibility of equity practice in early English law and is retained for sales contracts in the UCC's statement that specific performance "*may* be decreed...." U.C.C. §2-716(1) (2011) (italics added).

For example, the judge will specifically enforce a contract only if he or she is persuaded that specific relief is consistent with fairness and equity. Recall the statement in *Houseman v. Dare* that a court will specifically enforce a contract only if the legal remedy is inadequate and if specific enforcement "will not result in inequity to the offending party, reward the recipient for unfair dealing or conflict with public policy."

For example, if the victim of breach has himself engaged in some unfair or unseemly practices in the formation, performance, or enforcement of the contract, the judge might exercise discretion to deny specific relief to that party, even though that party did not breach the contract or provide other grounds for avoidance of the contract. By coming to the court with "unclean hands," the victim of breach is not deserving of specific relief and should be limited to his legal remedy of money damages. *See Queiroz v. Harvey*, 220 Ariz. 273, 205 P.3d 1120 (2009) (dishonesty by agent for the buyer during real estate transaction is imputed to the buyer, resulting in "unclean hands" barring specific enforcement).

Substantive unfairness in the exchange can also spur a judge to exercise discretion to deny specific enforcement. The victim of breach might have used greater bargaining power to negotiate a lopsided exchange in its favor, a winning deal that it now wants to enforce. The contract still has consideration, and it might not be sufficiently oppressive to be unconscionable, so it is enforceable at law for money damages. Nonetheless, the court might exercise its discretion to deny specific performance and limit the remedy to money damages, simply because the exchange is uneven. *Cf. McKinnon v. Benedict*, 38 Wis.2d 607, 157 N.W.2d 665 (1968) (denying specific enforcement of lopsided exchange; money damages not sought).

A court will also be reluctant to compel services that are highly personal in nature. The court would not hesitate to order ministerial acts, such as by ordering a seller to deliver a deed to property or an architect to deliver completed plans, conditioned on buyer paying the contract price for it. But ordering more extensive or sophisticated personal services would be difficult for a court to supervise, might raise objections based on the Thirteenth Amendment's prohibition of involuntary servitude, and could be inappropriate if it forces now hostile parties to work together. Ironically, the uniqueness of services—such as the performance of a uniquely talented artist—helps to satisfy the requirement of inadequacy of legal damages but also raises difficulties that counsel restraint in specific performance.

When specific performance of unique services is inappropriate, a court could exercise its discretion in either of two ways: (1) denying specific relief and leaving the victim of breach to her legal remedy of money damages, or (2) granting specific relief in the form of a *negative* injunction.

For example, if a famous musician repudiates a contract to perform a concert, it is highly unlikely that a court will decree specific performance and order the musician to work her magic by playing the piano to the best of her considerable abilities. The court might, however, enjoin the musician from performing in another concert for another party at that same time and date. Such a negative injunction does not pose the kinds of problems that would be raised by an order affirmatively compelling the musician to perform the contract to which the musician originally agreed.

In Chapter 2, we studied *Lucy v. Zehmer* for its discussion of the objective theory of contract formation. The subject matter of the contract was a unique plot of real estate, so the legal remedy of money damages would be viewed as inadequate. Nonetheless, the state Supreme Court addressed the question of whether the trial court correctly withheld equitable relief as a matter of sound judicial discretion.

Lucy v. Zehmer

196 Va. 493, 84 S.E.2d 516 (1954)

[The facts of this case are set forth in detail in Chapter 2.]

....

¶1 Defendants contend further, however, that even though a contract was made, equity should decline to enforce it under the circumstances. These circumstances have been set forth in detail above. They disclose some drinking by the two parties but not to an extent that they were unable to understand fully what they were doing. There was no fraud, no misrepresentation, no sharp practice and no dealing between unequal parties. The farm had been bought for $11,000 and was assessed for taxation at $6,300. The purchase price was $50,000. Zehmer admitted that it was a good price. There is in fact present in this case none of the grounds usually urged against specific performance.

¶2 Specific performance, it is true, is not a matter of absolute or arbitrary right, but is addressed to the reasonable and sound discretion of the court. *First Nat. Bank v. Roanoke Oil Co., supra*, 169 Va. at p. 116, 192 S.E. at p. 771. But it is likewise true that the discretion which may be exercised is not an arbitrary or capricious one, but one which is controlled by the established doctrines and settled principles of equity; and, generally, where a contract is in its nature and circumstances unobjectionable, it is as much a matter of course for courts of equity to decree a specific performance of it as it is for a court of law to give damages for a breach of it. *Bond v. Crawford*, 193 Va. 437, 444, 69 S.E.(2d) 470, 475....

¶3 The complainants are entitled to have specific performance of the contracts sued on. The decree appealed from is therefore reversed and the cause is remanded for the entry of a proper decree requiring the defendants to perform the contract in accordance with the prayer of the bill.

Reversed and remanded.

3. Practical Limitations

In Chapter 7, we examined one practical obstacle to enforcement that frequently applies with special force to specific enforcement: indefiniteness in contract terms. In some cases, a contract may be sufficiently definite to permit the judge or jury to calculate damages, but not sufficiently definite to support a decree of specific performance.

For example, suppose the following facts: A contract obligated the seller to sell a condominium at the price of $300,000. The seller repudiated the contract when the market value of the condominium units rose to $350,000 prior to performance. In the buyer's contract action, the judge determined that the contract was hopelessly ambiguous about which of two condominium units was promised to the buyer, but the evidence showed that both of these units had a market price of $350,000 at the time of the repudiation and the time of judgment. In these circumstances, the judge likely would find the agreement to be too indefinite to specifically enforce, but could easily award $50,000 in damages.

Another practical consideration—timing—eliminates specific enforcement as a viable option in some cases. If performance by one party has value only if provided by a due date, an action for specific enforcement will be meaningless after that due date. If the caterer for a wedding reception failed to show up for the reception, for example, an action for specific performance the day after the reception would be meaningless. Only an action for damages would be meaningful at that date.

III. Money Damages

A. Overview

1. Compensatory Damages to Vindicate Expectation Interest

Section III.C.2 of Chapter 1 listed three types of damage awards: nominal, compensatory, and punitive. Later in this chapter, we will examine possible policy reasons for the nearly universal rule precluding punitive damage awards for claims based solely on breach of contract. Furthermore, this section will assume that: (1) a breach of contract has caused actual injury so that the victim of breach is entitled to compensatory damages, not just to an award of nominal damages, and (2) the victim has not sought, or is not entitled to, specific relief and is demanding money damages as the sole remedy.

Compensatory damages can be measured in various ways, both within the field of contract law, and across different fields of law, from tort claims to statutory civil rights claims. Within the field of contract law, compensatory damages can be measured by expectation, restitution, or reliance interests. Because an action for breach of contract is primarily designed to vindicate expectation interests, this section will focus on that measure of damages.

2. General Measure of Damages Protecting Expectation Interest

In general, a victim of breach is entitled to damages in the amount of

1) *direct losses* caused by the breach: the difference between the value of the promised performance and the performance actually delivered, if any; plus

2) *incidental and consequential losses* that indirectly result because of the victim's needs in relation to the contract and his need to react to the breach. Incidental costs are transactional costs associated with reacting to a breach, such as the cost of contacting substitute suppliers or negotiating substitute contracts. Consequential losses can be viewed as part of the unavoidable "domino effect" of a breach, such as the profits lost during the unavoidable delay in finding a substitute supplier.

Sometimes the other party's breach, or the victim's reasonable reaction to it, will enable the victim of breach to avoid incurring expenses that the victim would have incurred had the contract been performed. To avoid putting the victim in a position better than if the contract had been performed, these savings must be deducted from the damage award—or at least the court must take care to consider these savings when calculating the losses. The same is often true of earnings that are made possible only because the other party's breach freed the victim of the breach to allocate time to another income-earning opportunity. We will refer to these savings as costs and losses avoided:

3) *Costs avoided* are the costs of his own remaining performance, which the victim need not incur when the other party's material breach permits the victim to cancel the contract; and

4) *Losses avoided* are gains from a substitute transaction made possible only because of the breach of the initial contract.

We'll find that the duty to mitigate damages will lead to deduction of costs and losses that *could have been avoided* through reasonable actions, even if they were not avoided by the victim of breach.

We will address each of these categories in detail soon. For the moment, however, let's get a basic, working knowledge of these concepts with some illustrations and problems.

3. Illustrations

For example, recall the breach posed in Section II.A: a seller repudiated a contract to sell land at the price of $100,000 after the market price of the land increased to $150,000. The buyer's direct loss in value is $150,000: the difference between the value of the land promised ($150,000) and the value of the land delivered (nothing, because no land was delivered). If the seller repudiated before the buyer had paid anything, then the buyer can avoid the cost of her own performance because she can cancel the contract and avoid paying the $100,000 contract price. Thus, an award of damages of $50,000 would put her in the same economic position as though the contract had been performed: when added to the $100,000 that she had expected to pay for the land but now can retain, the buyer now has $150,000 to buy substitute land.

Direct loss ($150,000)—Costs Avoided ($100,000) = Damages ($50,000)

In another case, the direct loss in value and the costs avoided might be less than the entire expected performance of each party. For example, suppose that Contractor repudiated a contract to construct three swimming pools at Owner's apartment complex after Contractor had completed two of the pools and after Owner had paid $60,000 in progress payments out of a total contract fee of $90,000. The direct loss is the value of the third pool, the value of the promised performance that was not delivered. Let's assume that value is $35,000 based on the cost of hiring another contractor to construct the third pool. If Owner withholds the remaining payment of $30,000, as it is entitled to do, its cost avoided would be $30,000. Accordingly, an award of $5,000 will put Owner in as good a position as though the contract had been performed.

Direct loss ($35,000)—Costs Avoided ($30,000) = Damages ($5,000)

A further example will illustrate *consequential losses.* For a fee of $400,000, Allied promised to deliver factory machinery to Ford, and to install it in place of the existing machinery on November 12, so that the factory is shut down for only one day for the installation. The machinery delivered and installed on November 12, however, was defective and did not operate properly. Allied returned on November 13 and successfully installed machinery that operated perfectly. Ford paid the contract price (and thus did not avoid the cost of its own performance), but it notified Allied that it would calculate its damages and demand payment from Allied. Ford later calculated that it suffered damages in the form of $30,000 in lost profits because of the extra day that its factory was shut down. Ford suffered no direct loss in value because Allied eventually delivered and installed machinery that conformed to the contract requirements. The delay, however, caused Ford to suffer consequential losses stemming from its need for working machinery to operate its factory.

Direct loss ($0) + Consequential losses ($30,000) = Damages ($30,000)

In a similar example, imagine that a merchant sold a used car, for a price of $18,000, with a hidden defect in its steering mechanism, and without any disclaimer of the implied warranty of merchantability. Let's suppose that—if the defect were known—the value of the car would be recognized as diminished by $1,000, perhaps based on the cost to repair the defect, and thus would be worth only $17,000. The direct loss in value—based on the difference between the car as promised and the car as delivered—is $1,000.

Direct loss in value ($1,000) = Damages ($1,000)

But suppose the defect remained hidden until the new owner lost control of the car, crashed into a tree, destroyed the car, and suffered $100,000 in injuries that are not covered by insurance, all as a direct consequence of the defect in the steering. In an action for breach of warranty, the main component of damages will be the consequential losses stemming from the destruction of the car ($17,000 loss) and the personal injury ($100,000):

Direct loss ($1,000) + Consequential losses ($117,000) = Damages ($118,000)

Finally, let's examine the role of loss avoided. Returning to the Ford and Allied hypothetical, imagine that after the original machinery had been removed and sold for scrap, Allied installed its defective machinery, could not repair it and so simply removed it, declined to take any pay, and repudiated its obligations under the contract. And let's suppose that Ford could have hired a substitute supplier to install working machinery for a fee of $425,000 within two additional days ($25,000 higher than the fee of $400,000 in the contract with Allied). We could categorize the additional expenditure of $25,000 as a direct loss in value since it was an expenditure required to secure the contractually required machinery. The main component of recovery against Allied would be $60,000 in lost profits caused by two days' delay in procuring a substitute, during which time the factory was stopped beyond the one-day stoppage set aside for installation. But imagine that Ford—acting unreasonably—decided to simply allow its factory to remain idle for 10 days before securing substitute machinery, thus piling up $300,000 in lost profits. Ford would not be entitled to an award of all its losses. Instead, a court would deduct the losses that Ford could have avoided through a substitute transaction, thus awarding damages as though Ford had mitigated its losses.

Direct loss ($25K) + Consequential losses ($300K)—loss that could have been avoided ($240K) = $85K

Alternatively, one could simply limit consequential losses to those that were unavoidable:

Direct loss ($25,000) + consequential losses ($60,000) = $85,000

Exercise 12.1—Basic Damages Calculations

1. The Case of the Moving Market Price

S agreed to sell real estate to a buyer for $100,000. S backed out of the deal when S realized that she had made a bad deal, because the market price of S's land rose to $110,000 by the time of performance. Neither party had performed yet. What are Buyer's loss in value and cost avoided, and what are Buyer's damages?

Now assume that the market value of the land fell to $90,000 after contract formation, and Buyer backed out when he learned that he had made a bad deal. Neither party had performed yet. What are S's loss in value, cost avoided, and damages?

2. Fired from the Fiesta Bowl

Employer repudiated an agreement to hire Student for four days to assist with traffic at Fiesta Bowl events. Employer had promised to pay Student $600. Had Student worked at the Fiesta Bowl events, he would have incurred $50 in expenses in purchasing a uniform and in taking public transportation to and from work. After the repudiation, Student found an alternative job with a catering company, for the same week, within walking distance of his apartment and requiring no purchase of uniform. This substitute job paid $400 for the same four days of full-time work. Student would not have been able to work both jobs. What are student's damages?

3. The Case of the Stymied Structure

Contractor agreed to construct an office building for Owner for $10 million and expected to spend $9 million in labor and materials. Assume that Contractor has no substitute job available to it during this time period and thus is not able to avoid loss through a substitute transaction.

a. Owner Repudiated Prior to Reliance

Owner repudiated before Contractor began construction or expended any money on labor or materials. What are Contractor's damages?

b. Owner Repudiated After Contractor's Reliance

Owner repudiated after Contractor had spent $500,000 on labor and materials. Owner had not yet paid Contractor anything. What are Contractor's damages?

c. Owner Repudiated and Contractor Continued Construction

Owner repudiated after Contractor had spent $100,000 on labor and materials. For purposes of this question only, assume that Owner repudiated because a collapse in the economy made it clear that the office building would not be economically viable for the foreseeable future. After receiving the repudiation, however, Contractor continued working on the building, ultimately expending an additional $400,000 in labor and materials before the absentee Owner discovered the continued construction and was able to exclude Contractor from the work site. Owner had not yet paid Contractor anything. What are Contractor's damages?

d. Contractor Repudiated After Beginning Construction

Contractor repudiated and quit in the middle of constructing the building. The building would have cost Owner $10 million under the original contract. Owner has paid the original contractor $6 million before the breach, and she must pay a substitute contractor another $5 million to finish the building, for a total of $11 million. What are Owner's damages?

4. The Case of the Abandoned Project

Developer contracted with Contractor for the construction of an office building for a total bid price of $20,000,000. Contractor knew that Developer planned to sell the office building upon completion. Developer can prove that it could sell the completed building to Bank for $22,000,000. Before beginning work or receiving any pay, Contractor repudiated the contract. Developer is unable to find a substitute contractor with the required capacity and expertise, and Developer reasonably abandons the project. Developer has no liability to Bank. What damages can Developer recover from Contractor?

5. The Case of the Unfinished Factory

Owner hired Contractor to construct a factory for $10,000,000. One month before the date of completion, Contractor had been paid the full $10,000,000 and had substantially completed the factory but had not yet completed installation of all the equipment necessary to normal operation of the factory. At that time, Contractor willfully breached the construction contract by leaving the factory unfinished and by transferring its crew and equipment to another, more important project, and it clearly informed Owner that it could not return for at least a month. Owner was unable to operate the unfinished factory and suffered $800,000 in lost profits while it waited a month before Contractor returned and completed the construction. Rather than waiting for Contractor, Owner could have immediately hired another contractor to complete the installation for about $100,000. In that event, completion of construction probably would have been delayed no more than a week, causing Owner to suffer $200,000 in lost profits. What damages may Owner recover from Contractor?

B. Other Employment: Loss Avoided or Expected Additional Earnings?

1. *Loss Avoided Through a True Substitute Contract*

In Exercise 12.1 above, the "Fiesta Bowl" problem made clear that Student could not have worked both the original job with the Fiesta Bowl and the employment with the caterer. This is typically the case with fulltime employment, because most people simply do not have the physical capacity to work two fulltime jobs, and because the timing of the jobs often would conflict in any event.

Thus, in the Fiesta Bowl problem, the job with the caterer was a true "substitute" for the repudiated Fiesta Bowl employment contract and was made possible only because the Fiesta Bowl contract had been breached. Accordingly, in the damages calculation, the loss in value should be offset by earnings from the catering contract as loss avoided. Otherwise, Student would end up better off economically than if the Fiesta Bowl contract had been performed.

2. *Excess Capacity*

But suppose that a party could have worked more than one job or project at the same time, so that a second job or project is not a substitute for the canceled one. This could easily be the case for an employee who had planned to work two part-time jobs, or for a contractor whose capacity is not fully occupied by the first contract or can be expanded to some extent when additional work becomes available. When this is the case, the earnings from the second job or project should not be deducted as loss avoided, because the employee or contractor expected to work both jobs at the same time. In such cases, protecting that expectation interest requires awarding loss in value from the breached contract without deducting wages earned from the second contract.

3. *Deduction for Loss That Could Have Been Avoided*

Now, let's return to the assumption that an employee or contractor would have been fully committed by the job or project that is canceled because of the other party's breach, so that he or she could not have taken on additional work except for the breach. After the breach, suppose that substitute employment was available, but the employee or contractor rejected it. Should a court deduct the earnings that the employee or contractor could have earned by taking the substitute work?

An affirmative answer supports policies of encouraging productive behavior and mitigating losses. Consequently, as a general rule, such potential earnings will be deducted if the work was comparable to the work for which the employee or contractor had earlier contracted, or for which it was normally trained and prepared to undertake. Indeed, if such substitute work was available and reasonably discoverable, the earnings should be deducted from the damage award even if the employee or contractor did not know about it, if the employee or contractor failed to make reasonable efforts to search for it.

In the case of a contractor, for whom some risk of loss is present in any job because of uncertainty in costs, potential earnings in a substitute job will not be deducted if the contractor rejected the substitute project because of excessive risk. Moreover, an employee generally will not suffer a deduction of wages that could have been earned from substitute employment that is substantially outside the range of his or her normal work or training.

The Restatement summarizes the general approach on this issue with a test that deducts substitute earnings that could have been earned by the victim of breach, except in the clearest cases of inappropriate substitute employment: "[D]amages are not recoverable for loss that the injured party could have avoided without undue risk, burden or humiliation." RESTATEMENT (SECOND) OF CONTRACTS § 350(1) (1981). Thus, an employee can decline substitute employment, without a deduction in the employee's damage award, if the job would be unduly difficult because it lies substantially outside the employee's skill set or physical or emotional comfort level. On the other hand, if the employee or contractor actually takes the substitute employment, any net earnings will be deducted by most courts, regardless whether the employee could have rejected the substitute job without deduction.

In the next case, how does the standard applied by the California Supreme Court compare to the Restatement test? How does the analysis of the dissent differ from that of the majority?

Parker v. Twentieth Century-Fox Film Corp.

3 Cal. 3d 176, 474 P.2d 689 (1970) [footnotes omitted]

Burke, Justice.

¶ 1 Defendant Twentieth Century-Fox Film Corporation appeals from a summary judgment granting to plaintiff the recovery of agreed compensation under a written contract for her services as an actress in a motion picture. As will appear, we have concluded that the trial court correctly ruled in plaintiff's favor and that the judgment should be affirmed.

¶ 2 Plaintiff is well known as an actress, and in the contract between plaintiff and defendant is sometimes referred to as the "Artist." Under the contract, dated August

6, 1965, plaintiff was to play the female lead in defendant's contemplated production of a motion picture entitled "Bloomer Girl." The contract provided that defendant would pay plaintiff a minimum "guaranteed compensation" of $53,571.42 per week for 14 weeks commencing May 23, 1966, for a total of $750,000. Prior to May 1966 defendant decided not to produce the picture and by a letter dated April 4, 1966, it notified plaintiff of that decision and that it would not "comply with our obligations to you under" the written contract.

¶ 3 By the same letter and with the professed purpose "to avoid any damage to you," defendant instead offered to employ plaintiff as the leading actress in another film tentatively entitled "Big Country, Big Man" (hereinafter, "Big Country"). The compensation offered was identical, as were the 34 numbered provisions or articles of the original contract. Unlike 'Bloomer Girl,' however, which was to have been a musical production, "Big Country" was a dramatic "western type" movie. "Bloomer Girl" was to have been filmed in California; "Big Country" was to be produced in Australia. Also, certain terms in the proffered contract varied from those of the original. Plaintiff was given one week within which to accept; she did not and the offer lapsed. Plaintiff then commenced this action seeking recovery of the agreed guaranteed compensation.

....

¶ 4 As stated, defendant's sole defense to this action which resulted from its deliberate breach of contract is that in rejecting defendant's substitute offer of employment plaintiff unreasonably refused to mitigate damages.

¶ 5 The general rule is that the measure of recovery by a wrongfully discharged employee is the amount of salary agreed upon for the period of service, less the amount which the employer affirmatively proves the employee has earned or with reasonable effort might have earned from other employment.... However, before projected earnings from other employment opportunities not sought or accepted by the discharged employee can be applied in mitigation, the employer must show that the other employment was comparable, or substantially similar, to that of which the employee has been deprived; the employee's rejection of or failure to seek other available employment of a different or inferior kind may not be resorted to in order to mitigate damages....

¶ 6 In the present case defendant has raised no issue of *reasonableness of efforts* by plaintiff to obtain other employment; the sole issue is whether plaintiff's refusal of defendant's substitute offer of "Big Country" may be used in mitigation....

¶ 7 Applying the foregoing rules to the record in the present case, with all intendments in favor of the party opposing the summary judgment motion—here, defendant—it is clear that the trial court correctly ruled that plaintiff's failure to accept defendant's tendered substitute employment could not be applied in mitigation of damages because the offer of the "Big Country" lead was of employment both different and inferior, and that no factual dispute was presented on that issue. The mere circumstance that "Bloomer Girl" was to be a musical review calling upon plaintiff's talents as a dancer as well as an actress, and was to be produced in the City of Los Angeles, whereas "Big Country" was a straight dramatic role in a "Western Type" story taking place in an opal mine in Australia, demonstrates the difference in kind between the two employments; the female lead as a dramatic actress in a western style motion picture can by no stretch of imagination be considered the equivalent of or substantially similar to the lead in a song-and-dance production.

¶ 8 Additionally, the substitute "Big Country" offer proposed to eliminate or impair the director and screenplay approvals accorded to plaintiff under the original "Bloomer Girl" contract..., and thus constituted an offer of inferior employment. No expertise or judicial notice is required in order to hold that the deprivation or infringement of an employee's rights held under an original employment contract converts the available "other employment" relied upon by the employer to mitigate damages, into inferior employment which the employee need not seek or accept. (*See Gonzales v. Internat. Asst. of Machinists*, *supra*, 213 Cal. App. 2d 817, 823–824, 29 Cal. Rptr. 190;....)

....

The judgment is affirmed.

....

Sullivan, Acting Chief Justice (dissenting).

¶ 9 The basic question in this case is whether or not plaintiff acted reasonably in rejecting defendant's offer of alternate employment. The answer depends upon whether that offer (starring in "Big Country, Big Man") was an offer of work that was substantially similar to her former employment (starring in "Bloomer Girl") or of work that was of a different or inferior kind. To my mind this is a factual issue which the trial court should not have determined on a motion for summary judgment. The majority have not only repeated this error but have compounded it by applying the rules governing mitigation of damages in the employer-employee context in a misleading fashion. Accordingly, I respectfully dissent.

¶ 10 The familiar rule requiring a plaintiff in a tort or contract action to mitigate damages embodies notions of fairness and socially responsible behavior which are fundamental to our jurisprudence. Most broadly stated, it precludes the recovery of damages which, through the exercise of due diligence, could have been avoided. Thus, in essence, it is a rule requiring reasonable conduct in commercial affairs. This general principle governs the obligations of an employee after his employer has wrongfully repudiated or terminated the employment contract. Rather than permitting the employee simply to remain idle during the balance of the contract period, the law requires him to make a reasonable effort to secure other employment. He is not obliged, however, to seek or accept any and all types of work which may be available. Only work which is in the same field and which is of the same quality need be accepted.

¶ 11 Over the years the courts have employed various phrases to define the type of employment which the employee, upon his wrongful discharge, is under an obligation to accept. Thus in California alone it has been held that he must accept employment which is "substantially similar" ... "comparable employment" ... employment "in the same general line of the first employment" ... "equivalent to his prior position" ... "employment in a similar capacity" ... employment which is "not ... of a different or inferior kind...."

¶ 12 [T]he phrase ["Not of a different or inferior kind"] is a serviceable one and my concern is not with its use as the standard but rather with what I consider its distortion.

¶ 13 The relevant language excuses acceptance only of employment which is of a *different kind*. (*Gonzales v. Internat. Assn. of Machinists*, *supra*, 213 Cal. App. 2d 817, 822, 29 Cal. Rptr. 190).... It has never been the law that the mere existence of *differences between two jobs in the same field is sufficient*, as a matter of law, to excuse an employee wrongfully discharged from one from accepting the other in order to mitigate damages. Such an approach would effectively eliminate any obligation of an employee to attempt to minimize damage arising from a wrongful discharge. The only alternative job offer an employee would be required to accept would be an offer of his former job by his former employer.

¶ 14 Although the majority appear to hold that there was a difference "in kind" between the employment offered plaintiff in "Bloomer Girl" and that offered in "Big Country" (opn. at p. 10), an examination of the opinion makes crystal clear that the majority merely point out differences between the two *films* (an obvious circumstance) and then apodi[cti]cally assert that these constitute a difference in the *kind* of *employment*. The entire rationale of the majority boils down to this: that the "mere circumstances" that "Bloomer Girl" was to be a musical review while "Big Country" was a straight drama "demonstrates the difference in kind" since a female lead in a western is not "the equivalent of or substantially similar to" a lead in a musical. This is merely attempting to prove the proposition by repeating it. It shows that the vehicles for the display of the star's talents are different but it does not prove that her employment as a star in such vehicles is of necessity different *in kind* and either inferior or superior.

¶ 15 I believe that the approach taken by the majority (a superficial listing of differences with no attempt to assess their significance) may subvert a valuable legal doctrine. The inquiry in cases such as this should not be whether differences between the two jobs exist (there will always be differences) but whether the differences which are present are substantial enough to constitute differences in the *kind* of employment or, alternatively, whether they render the substitute work employment of an *inferior kind*.

....

¶ 16 It is not intuitively obvious, to me at least, that the leading female role in a dramatic motion picture is a radically different endeavor from the leading female role in a musical comedy film. Nor is it plain to me that the rather qualified rights of director and screenplay approval contained in the first contract are highly significant matters either in the entertainment industry in general or to this plaintiff in particular. Certainly, none of the declarations introduced by plaintiff in support of her motion shed any light on these issues.

¶ 17 I believe that the judgment should be reversed so that the issue of whether or not the offer of the lead role in "Big Country, Big Man" was of employment comparable to that of the lead role in "Bloomer Girl" may be determined at trial.

Exercise 12.2 — Deduction for Jobs Not Taken?

1. Fired from Full-Time Employment

College hired Instructor to teach mathematics for two semesters, and to be in residence on campus full time with full faculty governance rights and responsibilities (such as voting rights and committee assignments), at a salary of $100,000. After the first semester, College wrongfully discharged Instructor, after having paid only $50,000 of the $100,000 annual salary. Applying the Restatement test, what are Instructor's damages in the following circumstances?

a. Offer to Teach Mathematics Full Time

A comparable college, Campus Tech, offered to hire Instructor to teach mathematics as a full-time visiting member of the faculty, with limited office privileges and no faculty governance rights or responsibilities, for the second semester at a salary of $40,000.

Suppose (i) Instructor accepted the offer and earned the salary, or alternatively

(ii) Instructor declined the offer and remained unemployed during the second semester.

b. Offer to Teach History Full Time

A comparable college offered to pay Instructor $40,000 to teach history courses full time during second semester.

Suppose (i) Instructor accepted the offer, spent many hours preparing to teach a course outside the field of mathematics, and earned the salary, or alternatively

(ii) Instructor declined the offer and remained unemployed during the second semester, because Instructor's academic training is not in the field of history.

2. Fired from Part-Time Employment

Assume the facts in problem 1(a)(i) above along with the following further facts. Instructor had originally been employed by College as a part-time adjunct, and he would have had the desire and capacity to teach at other schools as well, even if his contract with College had not been terminated mid-year. College had scheduled Instructor's mathematics classes in the morning, and Campus Tech had scheduled Instructor's mathematics classes in the afternoon during the second semester. In Instructor's suit against College, should a court deduct Instructor's earnings at Campus Tech? Explain.

C. Measuring Direct Loss in Value in Construction Contracts

1. Cost to Complete or Diminution in Value?

In Exercise 12.1, in problems positing a contractor's breach of a construction project, the facts of some of the problems invited you to define the owner's loss in value by the cost of hiring a substitute contractor to repair, replace, rebuild, or complete the work, which we can call the "cost to complete" or "cost of completion." In other cases, the better or only means of measuring the owner's loss in value is the diminution in value: the difference between the value of the promised construction and the value of the construction as delivered.

Justice Cardozo offered the following advice in choosing between these two measures of direct loss in value:

> It is true that in most cases the cost of replacement is the measure. [citation omitted] The owner is entitled to the money which will permit him to complete, unless the cost of completion is grossly and unfairly out of proportion to the good to be attained. When that is true, the measure is the difference in value.

Jacob & Youngs v. Kent, 230 N.Y. 239, 244, 129 N.E. 889, 891 (1921). In that case, a contractor inadvertently installed pipe of a different brand than called for in the contract, although it was of equal quality. Justice Cardozo rejected the argument that the owner was entitled to the relatively great cost of removing the existing pipe from the finished building and replacing it with the conforming pipe; instead, the owner was entitled to the difference in value between the conforming pipe and the installed pipe, which was "nominal or nothing." *Id.*

2. Diminution in Market Value or Personal Value?

When diminution in value is the proper measure, it is usually measured by the difference between the market value of the construction as promised and the market value of the construction as delivered. In an appropriate case, however, should a court permit a jury to measure the diminution in value as measured by the owner's more subjective personal loss in value, even if the general market would not recognize as great a diminution in value?

Under the second Restatement, the expectation interest of a victim of breach of contract consists partly of "the loss in value to him of the other party's performance" caused by the breach. Restatement (Second) of Contracts § 347(a) (1981). The phrase "value to him" suggests that personal valuation is relevant. When it more specifically addresses damages for "defective or unfinished construction," the second Restatement refers to the possibility of damages based on "diminution in the market price of the property," or the reasonable cost of completing construction or curing defects if that "is not clearly disproportionate to the probable loss in value to him." *Id.* § 348(2) (1981). As a preface, however, that section states that one of those alternative measures would apply if "the loss in value *to the injured party* is not proved with sufficient certainty." *Id.* (emphasis added).

In what circumstances will a court be persuaded that the owner has proved "the loss in value to the injured party"? It is likely that some courts will permit a measure based on diminution in more subjective, personal value only if supported by compelling facts.

Exercise 12.3 — Measuring Direct Loss in Value

1. Cost to Complete v. Diminution in Market Value

Contractor agreed to construct a building for Owner for $10 million and expected to spend $9 million in labor and materials. Contractor finished the building and was paid the $10 million originally agreed to, but tests later revealed that Contractor had put lower-rated insulation in the walls and roof than the contract required, saving Contractor $100,000 in costs. It would cost Owner $2 million to hire someone to dig into the walls, add the required insulation, and patch up the work. On the other hand, in light of the slight increase in cooling and heating costs, the building's market value (based on resale value or increased costs of operation over time) is diminished by only $1 million because of the lesser insulation. What are Owner's damages? Should the result change if Owner could prove that Contractor intentionally and fraudulently installed lesser insulation to save costs and then tried to conceal its breach? Should policies favoring energy conservation play any role in the court's decision?

2. Diminution in Personal or Market Value?

Garland Coal & Mining Co. breached a contractual promise to restore land on the farm of Willie and Lucille Peevyhouse after strip-mining the land for coal over five years and paying $100,000 for that right. Mr. Peevyhouse had lived on the farm his entire life. Restoring the land would have cost $29,000, but the restoration would have increased the market value of the affected land by only $300. On the Peevyhouses' claim for $25,000 in damages, a jury awarded $5,000 to the Peevyhouses. Did the trial court properly allow the jury to consider an award beyond the diminution in market value of $300? Was the jury's award defensible on a plausible legal theory, even if it is both more than the diminution in market value and less than the cost of completion? [Facts taken from *Peevyhouse v. Garland Coal & Mining Co.*, 382 P.2d 109 (Okla. 1962), *cert. denied*, 375 U.S. 906 (1963).]

3. *Peevyhouse* Revisited

Four decades after the *Peevyhouse* decision, many landowners leased land to corporations for extraction of oil and natural gas, but only after insisting on clauses obligating the firms to restore land that is disrupted by exploration and extraction. If a firm breached such an obligation to restore, would the landlords be assured of full compensation, if not specific performance?

Or might they suffer the same fate as the Peevyhouses, depending on the evidence and the law applied by the court? Is it just a matter of doing a better job of proving loss in market value of the land? *See* Judith L. Maute, *Peevyhouse v. Garland Coal & Mining Co. Revisited: The Ballad of Willie and Lucille*, 89 N.W.U.L. Rev. 1341, 1446–55 (1995) (suggesting that the Peevyhouses could not afford legal counsel who could match the skills and resources available to the coal company's legal counsel).

Assume that you are negotiating an exploration and extraction lease on behalf of one of the landowners described in the previous paragraph. Describe the kinds of provisions you would you draft to protect the landowners' interests.

D. Limitations on Compensatory Damages

1. Mitigation

The previous discussions of costs avoided and losses avoided provided several illustrations of the rule encouraging mitigation of damages: The victim of breach will recover only for damages that were not reasonably avoidable. If the victim of breach incurs additional damages that it reasonably could have avoided, the court will not include those additional damages in the award.

In analyzing the reasonableness of mitigation efforts, courts will consider any difficult circumstances imposed on the victim by the breach. To avoid a deduction of damages suffered, a victim of breach need act only reasonably, not heroically, to minimize losses.

2. Certainty

Courts will not allow juries to award compensatory damages based on mere speculation about the consequences of a breach. An award must be supported by evidence that proves damages with reasonable certainty.

As a specific application of this general standard, many courts adopted a traditional rule barring a new business from claiming damages for lost profits because a new business does not have a track record of past profits from which future expected profits could be estimated with reasonable certainty. This inflexible rule has begun to give way to a more flexible approach, as described in the next case.

Rancho Pescado, Inc. v. Northwestern Mutual Life Ins. Co.

140 Ariz. 174, 680 P.2d 1235 (Ct. App. 1984) [footnotes omitted]

....

¶ 1 Until recently, the majority rule in this country prohibited a jury's verdict of damages for lost profits of a new business. [citations to 5 cases and one article omitted]. These cases were generally decided on the basis that loss of profits from a new business was merely speculative and incapable of being ascertained with the requisite degree of certainty. *See Evergreen Amusement Corp. v. Milstead,* 206 Md. 610, 112 A.2d 901 (1955). Such reasoning is supported by the generally accepted rule of contract law that damages are not recoverable unless they are reasonably certain. 5 Corbin on Contracts §§ 1021–1022 (1964); Restatement of Contracts § 331 (1932).

¶ 2 Recent cases have eroded the once generally accepted rule against awarding damages for lost profits to a new business. The modern trend is to allow recovery for such lost profits if they can be proven with reasonable certainty. *See, e.g.... Chung v. Kaonohi Center Co.,* 62 Hawaii 594, 618 P.2d 283 (1980); ... *Vickers v. Wichita State University, Wichita,* 213 Kan. 614, 518 P.2d 512 (1974);.... [seven other citations omitted] In *Chung,* the Hawaii Supreme Court reasoned that, "it would be grossly unfair to deny a plaintiff meaningful recovery for lack of a sufficient 'track record' where the plaintiff has been prevented from establishing such a record by defendant's actions." 618 P.2d at 291. And, in *Vickers,* the Kansas Supreme Court noted that to preclude recovery "as a matter of law merely because a business is newly established would encourage those contracting with such a business to breach their contracts." 213 Kan. at 620, 518 P.2d at 517. The reasoning of these cases is highly persuasive....

¶ 3 Thus, the issue becomes whether the evidence introduced by Rancho Pescado, when considered in a light most favorable to upholding the jury verdict, established a reasonably certain factual basis for computation of lost profits. With reference to the evidence concerning lost profits, the principle is well established that once the fact of damages has been shown, the amount of damages may be established with proof of a lesser degree of certainty than required to establish the fact of damages. [citation omitted]. However, there still must be a reasonable basis in the evidence for the trier of fact to fix computation when a dollar loss is claimed. [citation omitted]. The evidence required to prove loss of future profits depends on the individual circumstances of each case. [citations omitted]. While absolute certainty is not required, the court or jury must be guided by some rational standard in making an award.

¶ 4 In determining whether a plaintiff has met its burden of proof, courts have considered the profit history from a similar business operated by the plaintiff at a different location, [citations omitted] and the profit history from the business in question if it was successfully operated by someone else before the plaintiff took over. *General Electric Supply Co. v. Mt. Wheeler Power, Inc.,* 94 Nev. 766, 587 P.2d 1312 (Nev. 1978). Neither method was available for use in the instant case. However, as is the case with an established business, *Lininger v. Dine Out Corp.,* 131 Ariz. 160, 639 P.2d 350 (App. 1981), reasonable certainty may be provided when the plaintiff devises some reasonable method of computing his net loss.

¶ 5 In the instant case, Rancho Pescado had the burden of proving with reasonable certainty the fact that it could raise catfish in the canal and that it could thereafter market them at a profit as well as proving with reasonable certainty how much profit it would have realized....

¶ 6 Initially, we note that various experts testified that catfish farming is an extremely risky business, even for experienced farmers. According to the United States Department of Agriculture estimates, the failure rate is approximately ninety-five percent....

¶ 7 It is not reasonably certain from the record that Frosty Fish would have actually been able to market all of Rancho Pescado's production. For instance, Frank Mateljan, Frosty Fish's president, testified that Frosty Fish typically distributed only one thousand pounds of catfish per week, an amount far below that which Rancho Pescado contemplated producing....

¶ 8 In conclusion, we view the evidence as a whole as amounting to nothing more than conjecture and speculation. The picture which emerges is one of an intelligent and enterprising individual who had an ambitious idea to take advantage of existing waterways to raise and sell catfish. However, the evidence is insufficient to prove that he would have succeeded in this highly risky industry. Although he had apparently done quite a bit of research into the catfish industry in general, his experiments on behalf of Rancho Pescado were woefully inadequate. Perhaps most damaging to Rancho Pescado's case is the lack of any conclusive evidence that it could have successfully marketed such large quantities of catfish. It is well settled that conjecture or speculation cannot provide the basis for an award of damages. The evidence must make an approximately accurate estimate possible. *Earle M. Jorgensen Co. v. Tesmer Manufacturing Co., supra.* We are of the opinion that the jury did not have sufficient evidence to make a rational judgment as to the fact that Rancho Pescado would have been successful and if so as to the amount of lost future profits. Thus, the trial court properly granted Northwestern's motion for judgment notwithstanding the verdict.

---

3. *Foreseeable Losses*

Even if the victim of breach proves damages with reasonable certainty, the jury will be permitted to award only those damages that were fairly within the risks contemplated by the parties. In other words, damages are recoverable only if they were foreseeable at the time of contracting. This foreseeability test frequently applies to consequential losses, such as lost profits, as illustrated by the celebrated and seminal English decision of *Hadley and Another v. Baxendale and Others*, 9 Ex. 341, 156 Eng. Rep. 145 (1854).

The following description of the *Hadley* case, taken from a legal writing text, is based partly on the court's opinion and partly on additional facts found in Richard Danzig and Geoffrey R. Watson, THE CAPABILITY PROBLEM IN CONTRACT LAW 48–90 (2d ed. 2004).

> The dispute between the Hadleys and Baxendale began as a business transaction during an economic boom in the midst of England's industrial

revolution. Operators of a flour mill in Gloucester entered into a contract with a carrier for the transportation of a broken engine shaft to a manufacturer in Greenwich, on the other side of England.

The operators of the mill, the Hadleys, were anxious to transport the broken shaft to the manufacturer as quickly as possible; the failure of the shaft had halted the milling of corn, and the broken shaft would serve as a model for the manufacture of a new shaft. An employee of the carrier, Pickford and Co., promised that the shaft would be delivered to the manufacturer within two days after the date that the carrier took possession of the shaft. For this, the mill operators paid 2£ 4s. The carrier could have transported the shaft as promptly as promised had it immediately used available means of land transportation. Presumably to reduce costs, however, it held the shaft for several days in London before loading it onto a canal barge along with a shipment of iron that was bound for the same manufacturer. As a consequence, the carrier delivered the shaft to the manufacturer on the seventh day after the carrier received it, resulting in an additional delay of five days during which the mill was stopped.

... [At trial,] the jury awarded the mill operators 50£ in a compromise verdict that became the judgment of the trial court.

The carrier appealed to the Court of Exchequer. The carrier ultimately persuaded a panel of three judges on this appellate court to reverse the judgment of the trial court and to grant a new trial on the ground that the trial judge had given the jury excessive latitude in awarding damages for lost profits.

In the appellate court's written opinion, the authoring judge explained that a jury may award only those damages that would flow naturally from the breach of such a contract or that would be reasonably within the contemplation of the parties because of special circumstances communicated at the time of contracting. The appellate judges assumed that the mill would ordinarily have spare shafts with which to keep running; consequently, they concluded that lost profits stemming from an idle mill would not be the natural consequence of the breach of the contract for prompt carriage. Whether the possibility of lost profits would nonetheless have been in the contemplation of the parties would depend on whether, at the time of contracting, the mill operators had communicated to the carrier the special circumstances that the broken shaft was the mill's only shaft and that the mill would be idle in its absence.

The appellate court concluded that the mill operators had informed the carrier only that they operated a mill and that the article to be transported was the broken shaft of a mill. On this premise, the appellate court held that the trial judge should not have allowed the jury to consider any lost profits in its calculation of damages.

Charles R. Calleros & Kimberly Y.W. Holst, LEGAL METHOD AND WRITING I: PREDICTIVE WRITING 15–17 (8th ed. 2018) [footnotes omitted].

This foreseeability limitation on contract damages likely imposes a stricter limitation than does the "proximate cause" limitation for tort damages, because breach of contract normally is less blameworthy than is tortious conduct. When a breach of warranty of goods causes "injury to person or property," however, the UCC provides that the buyer may recover damages "proximately resulting" from the breach, apparently referring to the less restrictive limitation on damages associated with tort law. U.C.C. § 2-715(2)(b) (2011).

4. Damages for Emotional Distress

No one disputes that a breach of contract will often result in aggravation to the victim of the breach. Nonetheless, breach of contract is considered to be a normal risk of entering into contracts, and damage awards are generally limited to the economic consequences of breach. If the inconvenience associated with breach can be translated into incidental economic losses, such as the cost of searching for a substitute supplier, then it can be recovered in damages. Pain and suffering in the form of emotional distress, however, is generally not recoverable, in contrast to its more frequent appearance as a component of damages in a tort claim.

In exceptional cases, however, damages for emotional distress will be recoverable for breach of contract, even in the absence of any tort. Some contracts, such as those for provision of funeral and burial services, are designed to protect emotional security rather than economic interests. One does not buy a casket, flowers, and burial plot for resale at a profit but for the peace of mind that comes from saying goodbye to a loved one in a loving, respectful manner. An egregious breach of contract by a funeral parlor will foreseeably cause emotional distress precisely because the purpose of the contract was to help soothe the fragile emotions of grief-stricken survivors. Consequently, it is not surprising that many courts will award damages for emotional distress caused by a callous breach of a contract for funeral services.

Consistent with the funeral cases, some courts have treated the availability of damages for emotional distress as an application or a special branch of the general foreseeability requirement. They typically find that liability for emotional distress is not a risk assumed by the parties in most contracts, but they recognize an exception if the very nature of the contract makes such injury likely in the event of breach. *See, e.g., Farmers Ins. Exch. v. Henderson*, 82 Ariz. 335, 313 P.2d 404 (1957).

In the next case, a California Court of Appeal opened the door for damages for emotional distress by reversing a grant of summary judgment in favor of the breaching parties. What test does it apply to this issue?

Wynn v. Monterey Club

111 Cal. App. 3d 789, 168 Cal. Rptr. 878 (Ct. App. 1980)
[footnotes and some citations omitted]

Compton, J.

¶ 1 Plaintiff ... appeals from a summary judgment entered in favor of defendants who are owners and operators of the Rainbow and the Monterey Clubs. The latter are card clubs licensed by the City of Gardena. We reverse.

....

¶ 2 Plaintiff's wife is a compulsive gambler who apparently attempted unsuccessfully to cure her problem by membership in an organization known as Gamblers Anonymous. It appears that she, as well as her propensities, were known to the defendants. She was afforded check cashing privileges at the club.

¶ 3 During the latter part of 1973, plaintiff's wife suffered heavy losses while gambling at the two clubs. She cashed $1,750 worth of checks which were dishonored because of insufficient funds.

¶ 4 It is conceded that her gambling debts were not chargeable to plaintiff's and wife's community property. The wife's gambling problems, however, did place a severe strain on their marriage.

....

¶ 5 Plaintiff contacted defendant Lochhead, one of the general partners in the operation of the two clubs, by telephone and discussed the problem of his wife's indebtedness. According to plaintiff an agreement was reached whereby plaintiff would undertake to satisfy his wife's debts to the two clubs in exchange for defendants' promise to deny his wife access to the clubs and deny her any further check cashing privileges.

....

¶ 6 Plaintiff, during the ensuing year, paid the obligation in full. During that period and for approximately another year thereafter the wife apparently refrained from gambling. In May of 1977, however, plaintiff learned that his wife was again gambling and cashing checks at the defendants' clubs. She apparently had suffered losses of approximately $30,000 and had begun to borrow money from friends to cover those losses.

¶ 7 According to plaintiff the marriage was destroyed and he commenced an action for dissolution. He contemporaneously filed the instant action.

....

¶ 8 Defendants ... moved for summary judgment which was granted on condition that defendants refund to plaintiff the $1,750 plus interest from December of 1974.

¶ 9 [The appellate court found an enforceable contract, rejecting the Club's argument that the agreement violated public policies underlying a state statute prohibiting discriminatory or arbitrary exclusion of patrons from places of public accommodation.]

¶ 10 The remaining question, and one which neither of the parties has addressed, is whether the type of damage claimed by plaintiff is compensable beyond the return of the initial consideration, i.e., the $1,750....

¶ 11 As previously noted, plaintiff's claim to damages rests on his assertion that defendants' breach of the contract led to a destruction of the marriage with resultant financial, physical and emotional harm to plaintiff. The issue of financial loss is a matter of proof within the confines of the general rule requiring proof of foreseeable damages which flow from a breach of contract. (*Hadley v. Baxendale*, 9 Ex. 341, 156 Eng. Rep., p. 145; Civ. Code, § 3300.)

¶ 12 As for compensating plaintiff for physical or emotional harm it is clear that, under the circumstances, such harm was reasonably foreseeable and was, in contemplation of the contracting parties, likely to result from a breach of the contract. Defendants were well aware of the wife's propensities and the impact that her gambling was having on plaintiff personally and the marriage in particular. They well knew that plaintiff's motivation in entering into the contract was to preserve the tranquility of the marriage and plaintiff's emotional well-being.

¶ 13 The traditional rule, however, has been that damages are not recoverable for mental suffering resulting from a breach of contract. [citations omitted]

¶ 14 On the other hand it was stated in *Westervelt v. McCullough* (1923) 68 Cal. App. 198, at pages 208-209, "Whenever the terms of a contract relate to matters which concern directly the comfort, happiness, or personal welfare of one of the parties, or the subject matter of which is such as directly to affect or move the affection, self-esteem, or tender feelings of that party, he may recover damages for physical suffering or illness proximately caused by its breach." (Italics added.) [additional citations omitted]

¶ 15 In *Windeler v. Scheers Jewelers* (1970) 8 Cal. App. 3d 844, the Court of Appeal approved an award for physical injury growing out of the breach of a bailment contract involving jewelry with great sentimental value. The "physical" injury consisted of headaches, loss of sleep and general nervousness.

¶ 16 The traditional rule was further eroded in *Crisci v. Security Ins. Co.* (1967) 66 Cal. 2d 425, where the Supreme Court permitted recovery of damages for mental suffering in the case of bad faith refusal of an insurer to settle a claim against its insured in violation of a covenant of fair dealing. The court in *Crisci* did, however, treat the insured's cause of action as sounding in tort as well as contract.

....

¶17 In the case at bench, plaintiff's cause of action does not sound in tort. Defendants' duty arose from the contract obligation. Hence we must determine whether plaintiff's claim to damages for emotional distress are compensable as a result of a breach of contract.

. . . .

¶18 [W]e have no difficulty in concluding that the only limitation on plaintiff's recovery in this case is the language of Civil Code section 3300 which provides: "For the breach of an obligation arising from contract, the measure of damages, except where otherwise expressly provided by this code, is the amount which will compensate the party aggrieved for all the detriment proximately caused thereby, or which, in the ordinary course of things, would be likely to result therefrom." (Italics added.)

¶19 In *Leavy v. Cooney* (1963) 214 Cal. App. 2d 496, pure mental and emotional suffering was held to be compensable in a breach of contract case. There it was held that the contracting parties contemplated that a breach of the contract would result in "humiliation and embarrassment" to the plaintiff.

¶20 In the case at bench, our analysis is that, for purposes of determining the propriety of a summary judgment, the contract was a lawful contract which by its nature put the defendants on notice that a breach thereof would result in emotional and mental suffering by the plaintiff as well as other forms of compensable damage. In light of that conclusion it is patent that the defendants in moving for summary judgment did not negate the presence of triable issues of fact.

¶21 The judgment is reversed and the matter is remanded to the trial court with directions to vacate its order granting defendants' motion for summary judgment and to enter a new and different order denying the same.

E. Preclusion of Punitive Damages and Penalty Clauses

The preceding subsections have explored the measure of compensatory damages for actual injury stemming from breach of contract. The common law, however, has long precluded courts from awarding punitive damages for breach of contract.

Furthermore, the common law precludes courts from enforcing an agreement by the parties to impose liability for damages in the event of a breach of contract, if those agreed damages are punitive rather than compensatory. When the parties' agreement on stipulated damages represents their reasonable estimate of the actual losses that will be suffered by a party in the event of a future breach, the clause is viewed as compensatory in nature, and it is deemed to be an enforceable "liquidated damages" clause. In contrast, when the clause imposes a penalty on a breaching party, over and above compensation for anticipated actual losses, then it is deemed to be a "penalty clause," which is unenforceable for violation of public policy.

If the damages clause is not enforced, the victim of breach still retains a remedy. However, in the absence of enforceable liquidated damages, the victim of breach must prove her actual damages rather than rely on the amount agreed to in the damages clause. That may be difficult, because she likely insisted on the damages clause at the time of contracting precisely because she anticipated that actual damages would be difficult to prove in the event of breach.

1. *The Rules*

The following excerpt from an article summarizes the rules regarding damage awards calculated by the court and regarding court enforcement of a contract clause in which the parties have set damages in the event of a future breach. In Sections 2 and 5 below, another excerpt of this article and an opinion by Judge Posner present a law-and-economics argument defending the rules against punitive damages and against penalty clauses. Both also introduce critiques of this economic argument.

Charles R. Calleros, *Punitive Damages, Liquidated Damages, and Clauses Pénales in Contract Actions: A Comparative Analysis of the American Common Law and the French Civil Code*
32 Brooklyn J. Int'l L. 67 (2006)
[footnotes omitted; with minor text added]

....

I. Punitive Damages and Liquidated Damages in the United States

A. Legal Rules and Tests

Juries in the United States have discretion under the common law to award punitive damages for egregiously tortious conduct, defined in most states as a tort committed with at least reckless disregard for the rights of others....

All but a handful of states, however, follow some version of the traditional common law rule denying punitive damages for breach of contract, subject only to a few exceptions. Under the traditional rule, punitive damages are not available for even a deliberate breach of contract, with the possible exceptions of a breach of promise to marry; ... and a breach of contract that also constitutes, or is accompanied by, either a breach of fiduciary duty or a tort for which punitive damages are recoverable.

....

The antipathy in the United States toward punitive damages [for breach of contract] extends to a claim based on a liquidated damages clause to which the parties agreed in their contract. In general, courts in the United States will not enforce such clauses if they are designed to impose a penalty for breaching the contract, rather than to fix compensatory damages at a reasonable estimate of actual injury. The traditional common law test in the U.S. is a prospective one: courts will enforce a liquidated damages clause if, at the time of contracting, (1) actual damages in the event of breach would be difficult estimate, often because they would be difficult to calculate even after they occur, and (2) the liquidated damages represent a reasonable estimate of the damages that would flow from a breach. Under the modern trend, the liquidated damages may be upheld if they are reasonable in light of either the anticipated injury, viewed prospectively, or the actual injury caused by breach, viewed retrospectively. Moreover, under the modern approach, the difficulty of estimating or later calculating actual damages is not a separate element of the test but is a factor in the assessment of the reasonableness of the parties' estimation....

If liquidated damages clearly satisfy the prospective test, they are enforceable even though the actual injury caused by breach is unexpectedly greater or lower, or—in some courts—even though the victim of breach unexpectedly suffers no loss at all from the breach. Still, a great disparity between the liquidated damages and the actual harm suffered by breach may help raise doubts about the integrity of the parties' estimate and may lead to particularly careful scrutiny of the clause under the prospective test. At bottom, the court must determine whether the evidence suggests that the parties, at the time of contracting, were less concerned with fixing uncertain damages than with compelling performance with an *in terrorem* penalty clause.

Dobson Bay Club II DD, LLC v. La Sonrisa de Siena, LLC

239 Ariz. 132, 366 P.3d 1022 (2016)

[footnotes omitted; paragraph numbers changed from the original]

Brown, Judge:

¶1 [Dobson Bay defaulted on a bank loan of approximately $29 million. The lending bank, Canadian Imperial, assigned its rights under the loan to La Sonrisa, which sought foreclosure on property securing the loan. Dobson Bay secured new financing and paid the outstanding loan balance to La Sonrisa. However, Dobson Bay disputed other charges demanded by La Sonrisa, including a contractually stipulated late charge of 5% of the amount past due, amounting to a late charge of approximately $1.4 million.]

¶2 ... Article IV of the promissory note included a late-fee provision, which stated:

> If any installment payable under this Note (including the final installment due on the Maturity Date) is not received by Lender prior to the calendar day after the same is due (without regard to any applicable cure and/or notice period), Borrower shall pay to Lender upon demand an amount equal to the lesser of (a) five percent (5%) of such unpaid sum or (b) the maximum amount permitted by applicable law to defray the expenses incurred by Lender in handling and processing such delinquent payment and to compensate Lender for the loss of the use of such delinquent payment, and such amount shall be secured by the Loan Documents.

The promissory note also provided that in the event of default, Dobson Bay would pay default interest plus costs of collection including reasonable attorneys' fees. The deed of trust further stated that if a foreclosure proceeding were initiated, Dobson Bay would pay attorneys' fees, trustee's fees, and costs related to the foreclosure.

....

¶3 ... The trial court granted partial summary judgment in favor of La Sonrisa under Arizona Rule of Civil Procedure 54(b), finding that the late fee was enforceable as liquidated damages because it reasonably forecasted the harm caused by default and the harm was otherwise difficult to accurately estimate. Dobson Bay timely appealed.

DISCUSSION

¶4 Summary judgment is appropriate if there is no genuine dispute as to any material fact and the moving party is entitled to judgment as a matter of law. Ariz. R. Civ. P. 56(a). We review a superior court's grant of summary judgment de novo. *Link v. Pima Cty.*, 193 Ariz. 336, 340, ¶12, 972 P.2d 669, 673 (App. 1998)....

A. Enforceability of Liquidated Damages Provisions

....

¶5 The principal reason parties include liquidated damages provisions within contracts is to avoid proof and other calculation issues involved in litigating what a reasonable damage award would be in the event a breach occurs, especially when the amount in controversy is small. *See Roscoe–Gill v. Newman*, 188 Ariz. 483, 485, 937 P.2d 673, 675 (App. 1996); *see also Mech. Air Eng'g Co. v. Totem Constr. Co.*, 166 Ariz. 191, 193, 801 P.2d 426, 428 (App. 1989) (explaining that a "liquidated damage clause promotes enterprise by increasing certainty and by decreasing risk-exposure, proof problems, and litigation costs"); Restatement (Second) of Contracts § 356(1) (1981) ("Restatement"). Whether a liquidated damages provision is enforceable depends upon the particular circumstances of each case. *See Pima Sav. and Loan Ass'n v. Rampello*, 168 Ariz. 297, 300, 812 P.2d 1115, 1118 (App. 1991).

¶6 Arizona courts have generally followed the test described in the Restatement of Contracts to determine whether a contractual provision that establishes an amount of damages in advance is reasonable, and therefore enforceable. As explained in *Larson-Hegstrom & Associates v. Jeffries*, an agreement setting the amount of damages in advance of a breach is an unenforceable penalty unless (1) the amount fixed is a reasonable forecast of just compensation for harm caused by the breach, and (2) the harm caused is "incapable or very difficult of accurate estimation." 145 Ariz. 329, 333, 701 P.2d 587, 591 (App. 1985) (citing Restatement (First) of Contracts § 339 (1932)). In 1981, the test was reframed as follows:

> Damages for breach by either party may be liquidated in the agreement but only at an amount that is reasonable in the light of the anticipated or actual

> loss caused by the breach and the difficulties of proof of loss. A term fixing unreasonably large liquidated damages is unenforceable on grounds of public policy as a penalty.

Restatement § 356(1).

¶ 7 The Restatement's revised framing of the inquiry is consistent with the "compensatory, not punitive" objective of contract remedies. *See* Restatement § 356 cmt. a. A contractual provision "fixing unreasonably large liquidated damages," which clearly exceed compensatory damages, "is unenforceable on grounds of public policy as a penalty." Restatement § 356(1). Thus, the touchstone of a liquidated damages clause is reasonableness. *See Wasserman's Inc. v. Twp. of Middletown*, 137 N.J. 238, 645 A.2d 100, 107 (1994) ("Two of the most authoritative statements concerning liquidated damages are contained in the Uniform Commercial Code and the Restatement (Second) of Contracts, both of which emphasize reasonableness as the touchstone.").

¶ 8 ... [W]hether a fixed damages amount is so unreasonable as to constitute a penalty involves the consideration of two factors—(1) the anticipated or actual loss caused by the breach, and (2) the difficulties of proof of loss. *Id.* at cmt. b.

B. Anticipated or Actual Loss

¶ 9 "[T]he amount fixed is reasonable to the extent that it approximates the loss anticipated at the time of the making of the contract, even though it may not approximate the actual loss." *Id.* Likewise the inverse is true: "The amount fixed is reasonable to the extent that *it approximates the actual loss that has resulted from the particular breach*, even though it may not approximate the loss that might have been anticipated under other possible breaches." *Id.* (emphasis added). But, if there is no actual loss, or if the actual loss is both easily quantified and not commensurate with the liquidated damages, then the prescribed fixed damages amount will be deemed a penalty. *See id.*

¶ 10 La Sonrisa presented evidence of the reasonableness of the late fee through the declaration of its financing expert, Mitchel Medigovich, who opined generally that a borrower's failure to timely pay "diminishe[s] if not damage[s]" the economic interests of the lender. To minimize this damage, "a predetermined late fee subsidizes the expense of hiring and training loan counselors assigned to call the borrower, of making a field visit to the borrower or engaging in other activities necessary to get the borrower to pay the debt." Medigovich also explained that other secondary costs may be incurred. For example, a lender may be deprived of the ability to reinvest expected cash payments and may also be placed at "great risk" of defaulting on its own financial obligations when the funding for those obligations is contingent on timely payment from the borrower. Medigovich explained further that the lender may suffer reputational harm from an increase in non-performing loans such that depositors may mistrust the institution and seek to withdraw their deposits. The Federal Reserve Board requires that depository institutions maintain minimum capital reserves, and a borrower's failure to timely pay a substantial balloon payment on a large commercial loan may cause the lender's capital reserves to fall below the regulatory requirements. In consideration of these various risks to the lender, Medigovich ultimately opined that a late fee included as part of a loan is not a penalty, but reimbursement "for expenses and lost opportunities that are impossible to quantify at loan inception[.]"

....

¶ 11 ... Medigovich's opinion about the reasonableness of the late fee is simply irrelevant to this transaction. It is undisputed that La Sonrisa purchased the promissory note from Canadian Imperial after Dobson Bay had defaulted. Thus, at the time of La Sonrisa's acquisition, no damage was speculative or difficult to calculate. La Sonrisa purchased the known debt repayment obligation of Dobson Bay: a distressed product whose value was, by the time of La Sonrisa's purchase, fixed. As a result, nothing in the record suggests La Sonrisa was exposed to any risks of reputational harm, regulatory noncompliance, the inability to fulfill its own financial obligations, or any of the other possible harms Medigovich referenced that could be caused by a borrower's breach, because by the time La Sonrisa entered the picture, Dobson Bay was already in default and all losses, whether incurred by Canadian Imperial or La Sonrisa, were calculable to a degree of reasonable certainty. Therefore, with respect to both Canadian Imperial and La Sonrisa, we conclude as a matter of law that neither the anticipated nor actual losses reasonably approximate the $1.4 million late fee....

....

C. Difficulty of Proof of Loss

¶ 12 ... La Sonrisa acquired the note post-default and immediately initiated foreclosure proceedings knowing it would incur readily calculable damages such as attorneys' fees, trustee's fees, interest, and default interest on the note. Rather than suffering broad institutional losses, which may be difficult to fully ascertain and calculate, La Sonrisa's losses are easily quantified to a degree of near certainty. *See* ... *In re Mkt. Ctr. E. Retail Prop., Inc.*, 433 B.R. 335, 364, 367 (Bankr. D.N.M. 2010) (concluding that damages incurred through foreclosure proceedings (consisting of interest, attorneys' fees, and minimal administrative costs) were not difficult to calculate on a breach for failure to pay a final balloon payment and, because "there would be little or no more administrative expenses in handling and processing delinquent payments," the 5% late fee provided for in the contract constituted an unenforceable penalty).

D. Combination of Factors

¶ 13 Deciding whether the fixed 5% late fee is a penalty turns upon the combination of the two factors discussed above. "If the difficulty of proof of loss is great, considerable latitude is allowed in the approximation of anticipated or actual harm. If, on the other hand, the difficulty of proof of loss is slight, less latitude is allowed in that approximation." Restatement § 356 cmt. b.

¶ 14 Both factors cut sharply against La Sonrisa. First, La Sonrisa has presented no evidence that the $1.4 million late fee reasonably approximated the anticipated losses that would have resulted from Dobson Bay's failure to make the balloon payment in a timely manner generally, much less the actual losses suffered by La Sonrisa. Second, the difficulty of proving loss is not great. As a result of Dobson Bay's breach, La Sonrisa is entitled to compensation for the losses it incurred, which, according to the promissory note and deed of trust, consist of default interest, attorneys' fees and related costs, and trustee's fees. Dobson Bay has challenged whether, on legal grounds, La Sonrisa is entitled to recover all those losses, but that dispute does not alter that the losses are easy to calculate. Applying the factors set forth in Restatement § 356 to these specific circumstances, enforcement of the late-fee provision would serve only punitive purposes rather than compensatory. Therefore, the trial court erred in entering partial summary in favor of La Sonrisa and denying Dobson Bay's motion for partial summary judgment.

CONCLUSION

¶ 15 We hold, as a matter of law, that absent unusual circumstances the imposition of a flat 5% late-fee on a balloon payment for a conventional, fixed-interest rate loan is not enforceable as liquidated damages, and that Medigovich's declaration is insufficient to generate a triable issue of fact as to the reasonableness of the 5% late-fee. We therefore vacate the trial court's entry of partial summary judgment in favor of La Sonrisa, and remand for further proceedings, including entry of partial summary judgment in favor of Dobson Bay on its claim for declaratory relief on liquidated damages. Both parties request awards of attorneys' fees pursuant to Arizona Revised Statutes section 12–341.01. In our discretion, we award reasonable attorneys' fees and costs on appeal to Dobson Bay subject to its compliance with Arizona Rule of Civil Appellate Procedure 21(c).

---

2. Policy Justifications

Charles R. Calleros, *Punitive Damages, Liquidated Damages, and Clauses Pénales in Contract Actions: A Comparative Analysis of the American Common Law and the French Civil Code*
32 Brooklyn J. Int'l L. 67 (2006) [footnotes omitted]

....

B. Historical Roots and Policy Justifications in the Common Law

....

2. Policy Justifications for the Rule Against Punitive Damages and Penalties

....

With assistance from the efficient breach doctrine, the policy of deterrence may help to explain the tort/contract dichotomy in the availability of punitive damages in the United States. Because reckless or intentional torts by their very nature offend community values, and because they often cause their victims to suffer significant physical or emotional injuries, legal rules that tend to deter such conduct, such as the availability of punitive damage awards, are viewed as appropriate in the common law system. The efficient breach doctrine, on the other hand, argues that some kinds of contract breaches will benefit the community and should be permitted, or even encouraged, rather than deterred with extracompensatory damages.

The most easily defended efficient breach is one that achieves Pareto optimality by leaving some entities better off because of the breach while leaving no party in a worse position than if the contract had been performed. For an illustration, suppose that Pierce Construction Co. of Desert City is hired to excavate the site for a new parking garage at Mercado Shopping Center, with a completion date of August 1, earning Pierce an estimated $20,000 in profit after payment of materials, labor, and other expenses. The contract included a clause requiring Pierce's personal supervision and prohibiting Pierce from assigning his duties to a subcontractor.

After Pierce bound itself to Mercado but before commencement of performance, Upstart Development Co. received the final permits and financing needed to begin construction on an upscale boutique shopping center on the edge of the city, around a picturesque array of huge boulders. Anxious to break ground immediately and recognizing that Pierce was uniquely qualified to perform the complicated grading and excavation around the boulders, Upstart offered Pierce a lucrative contract to perform that work, which would earn Pierce an estimated $60,000 profit. Pierce, however, did not have the capacity to complete both the Mercado contract and the Upstart project by August 1, and Upstart remained firm on the completion date, fearing that any delay would disrupt parking during the onset of the holiday shopping season in early November. If Pierce repudiated the Mercado contract, Mercado could hire another perfectly well qualified contractor to perform its rather routine excavation, but only at a fee of $10,000 above Pierce's fee under the original contract because of extra costs associated with the short notice, causing Mercado to suffer $10,000 in damages.

In these circumstances, the community would benefit if Pierce (1) breached the contract with Mercado, (2) voluntarily paid (or was compelled to pay) $10,000 in compensatory damages to Mercado, and (3) reallocated its resources to the Upstart project. With the $10,000 in damages, Mercado would realize its expectation of securing timely and competent excavation without expending any more of its own resources than it had originally bargained to pay Pierce. Indeed, because contract remedies thus protect the expectation interest of the victim of breach, Mercado theoretically should be "*indifferent* between performance and breach." [footnote cites to Robert Cooter and Thomas Ulen, Law and Economics 226 (3d ed. 2000)]. In turn, having abandoned the Mercado contract, Pierce would have the opportunity to put its unique capabilities to full use in a new project that will boost its profits by $40,000, for a net gain of $30,000 additional profits after paying $10,000 in compensation to Mercado. Theoretically, Mercado is no worse off than if Pierce had performed its contract, Pierce is better off for having breached that contract, and the greater income to Pierce and the advancement of the Upstart project likely will have further multiplier effects on the local economy.

Pierce will have an economic incentive to breach his contract with Mercado if he is confident that, in a suit by Mercado to secure damages for Pierce's breach of contract, a court would award only Mercado's compensatory damages in the amount of Mercado's expectation interest, $10,000 in this case. If the law instead would permit a jury to award additional and substantial punitive damages for Pierce's intentional breach, Pierce would face the risk of total liability that exceeded the additional profit earned on the Upstart project, and Pierce likely would turn down the Upstart project to avoid that risk.

In sum, according to the efficient breach theory, the welfare of the community will be enhanced if the law does not permit the threat of punitive damages to deter parties in Pierce's position from breaching. By extension, concerns about efficient allocation of resources would also support a rule that denies enforcement of contract clauses that go beyond liquidating compensatory damages and that contemplate penalties large enough to deter efficient breaches.

Although the efficient breach theory is the dominant contemporary justification offered for the unavailability of punitive damages for contract breaches, it has attracted criticism on a number of grounds. Most obviously, not all breaches are economically efficient. The suppliers of water in *White v. Benkowski* breached the water supply contract not to reallocate the water resources to a more valuable use, but to maliciously harass the other parties, with whom the suppliers had been embroiled in an escalating series of personal squabbles. [footnote cites to *White v. Benkowski*, 155 N.W.2d 74, 75 (Wis. 1974)].

Exercise 12.4 — Malicious Breach of Contract

In light of the discussion above, why shouldn't the law permit punitive damages in the limited case of a malicious breach of contract, undertaken for the purpose of causing harm to the other party? Is it easier to just draw a bright line between contract and tort and encourage the plaintiff to plead and prove a tort when the breaching party acts maliciously?

---

3. *Critiques of the Rule Against Freely Negotiated Penalty Clauses*

Aside from the complaint that the rule against punitive damages and penalty clauses applies even to malicious breaches that do not maximize efficiency, some have argued that the rule is unnecessary to achieve economic efficiency. Because the parties can negotiate a rescission of the first contract, the availability of punitive damages or enforcement of penalty clauses will not prevent a party from withdrawing from a contract to reallocate resources to a more efficient and profitable use. That party can earn greater profit in a competing opportunity simply by negotiating a voluntary release from the other party, while reaping some of the additional profit even after paying the other party for the release. Of course, the availability of punitive damages or the enforcement of a penalty clause will put the other party in the driver's seat in those negotiations, forcing the party who seeks the release to share some of the additional profit that it will earn in the competing opportunity.

For example, let's return to the hypothetical case of Pierce Construction Co., which will earn a net additional profit of $30,000, even after paying compensatory damages of $10,000 to Mercado, if it breaches its contract with Mercado to take advantage of a more lucrative contract with Upstart. If Pierce bore the risk of being liable for $40,000 in punitive damages, or if the law would permit enforcement of a $40,000 penalty clause, one might momentarily assume that Pierce would not breach but would leave its resources in their relatively inefficient use in the Mercado project. In these circumstances, however, Pierce and Mercado could both earn extra profits by negotiating a rescission of their contract, so that Pierce would not be in breach of the contract and could reallocate its resources without risking a penalty for breach. Because Pierce cannot afford to risk a penalty (in our hypothetical legal regime, where penalties are enforceable), Mercado would have sufficient bargaining power to require Pierce to pay more than its $10,000 expectation interest before Mercado agreed to rescind the contract. For example, if Mercado demanded $25,000 for the rescission ($15,000 more than its actual damages stemming from Pierce leaving the project), Pierce would still have an incentive to join in this rescission, because Pierce would still earn an additional $15,000 in profit by reallocating its resources from the Mercado project to Upstart. Moreover, Mercado would have an incentive to refrain from striking too hard a bargain: If it demanded $40,000 or more for the rescission, Pierce presumably would choose to perform the less demanding contract with Mercado rather than pay for a release, thus robbing Mercado of the opportunity to earn a share of the additional profit offered by the Upstart project.

In sum, because the parties could bargain for a rescission of the contract, thus eliminating any liability for penalties, a legal rule that permitted punitive damages or that enforced contractual penalty clauses would not prevent efficient breaches. Such a rule would simply force the party contemplating breach to share the extra profits of the competing opportunity as the price for a release from the first contract.

In the next case, Judge Posner shines a similarly critical light on the rule against enforcement of freely negotiated penalty clauses, before conceding that his court has no authority to change Illinois law on the topic. What does he mean when he states that an enforceable penalty clause can further the parties' interests by providing "an earnest of performance"?

Lake River Corp. v. Carborundum Co.

769 F.2d 1284 (7th Cir. 1985)

Posner, Circuit Judge.

¶ 1 This diversity suit between Lake River Corporation and Carborundum Company requires us to consider questions of Illinois commercial law, and in particular to explore the fuzzy line between penalty clauses and liquidated-damages clauses.

¶ 2 [Lake River entered into a contract with Carborundum to package and distribute goods, "Ferro Carbo," which Carborundum manufactured and shipped to Lake River.

After a drop in the market, Carborundum breached the contract by failing to ship contractually guaranteed quantities to Lake River, which then sought to enforce a contract clause requiring Carborundum to pay Lake River its full contract fee, even though Lake River avoided substantial costs because it had packed and distributed less than the minimum quantity required by the contract.]

¶3 The hardest issue in the case is whether the formula in the minimum-guarantee clause imposes a penalty for breach of contract or is merely an effort to liquidate damages. Deep as the hostility to penalty clauses runs in the common law, *see Loyd, Penalties and Forfeitures*, 29 Harv. L. Rev. 117 (1915), we still might be inclined to question, if we thought ourselves free to do so, whether a modern court should refuse to enforce a penalty clause where the signator is a substantial corporation, well able to avoid improvident commitments. Penalty clauses provide an earnest of performance. The clause here enhanced Carborundum's credibility in promising to ship the minimum amount guaranteed by showing that it was willing to pay the full contract price even if it failed to ship anything.

¶4 On the other side it can be pointed out that by raising the cost of a breach of contract to the contract breaker, a penalty clause increases the risk to his other creditors; increases (what is the same thing and more, because bankruptcy imposes "deadweight" social costs) the risk of bankruptcy; and could amplify the business cycle by increasing the number of bankruptcies in bad times, which is when contracts are most likely to be broken. But since little effort is made to prevent businessmen from assuming risks, these reasons are no better than makeweights.

¶5 A better argument is that a penalty clause may discourage efficient as well as inefficient breaches of contract. Suppose a breach would cost the promisee $12,000 in actual damages but would yield the promisor $20,000 in additional profits. Then there would be a net social gain from breach. After being fully compensated for his loss the promisee would be no worse off than if the contract had been performed, while the promisor would be better off by $8,000. But now suppose the contract contains a penalty clause under which the promisor if he breaks his promise must pay the promisee $25,000. The promisor will be discouraged from breaking the contract, since $25,000, the penalty, is greater than $20,000, the profits of the breach; and a transaction that would have increased value will be forgone. On this view, … penal damages could … deter some efficient breaches.

¶6 But this overlooks the earlier point that the willingness to agree to a penalty clause is a way of making the promisor and his promise credible and may therefore be essential to inducing some value-maximizing contracts to be made. It also overlooks the more important point that the parties (always assuming they are fully competent) will, in deciding whether to include a penalty clause in their contract, weigh the gains against the costs—costs that include the possibility of discouraging an efficient breach somewhere down the road—and will include the clause only if the benefits exceed those costs as well as all other costs.

¶ 7 On this view the refusal to enforce penalty clauses is (at best) paternalistic—and it seems odd that courts should display parental solicitude for large corporations. But however this may be, we must be on guard to avoid importing our own ideas of sound public policy into an area where our proper judicial role is more than usually deferential. The responsibility for making innovations in the common law of Illinois rests with the courts of Illinois, and not with the federal courts in Illinois. And like every other state, Illinois, untroubled by academic skepticism of the wisdom of refusing to enforce penalty clauses against sophisticated promisors, ... continues steadfastly to insist on the distinction between penalties and liquidated damages. *See, e.g., Bauer v. Sawyer*, 8 Ill. 2d 351, 359–61, 134 N.E.2d 329, 333–34 (1956);....

¶ 8 To be valid under Illinois law a liquidation of damages must be a reasonable estimate at the time of contracting of the likely damages from breach, and the need for estimation at that time must be shown by reference to the likely difficulty of measuring the actual damages from a breach of contract after the breach occurs. If damages would be easy to determine then, or if the estimate greatly exceeds a reasonable upper estimate of what the damages are likely to be, it is a penalty. *See, e.g., M.I.G. Investments, Inc. v. Marsala*, 92 Ill. App. 3d 400, 405–06, 47 Ill. Dec. 265, 270, 414 N.E.2d 1381, 1386 (1981).

¶ 9 The distinction between a penalty and liquidated damages is not an easy one to draw in practice but we are required to draw it and can give only limited weight to the district court's determination. Whether a provision for damages is a penalty clause or a liquidated-damages clause is a question of law rather than fact,....

¶ 10 Mindful that Illinois courts resolve doubtful cases in favor of classification as a penalty..., we conclude that the damage formula in this case is a penalty and not a liquidation of damages, because it is designed always to assure Lake River more than its actual damages. The formula ... is invariant to the gravity of the breach. When a contract specifies a single sum in damages for any and all breaches even though it is apparent that all are not of the same gravity, the specification is not a reasonable effort to estimate damages; and when in addition the fixed sum greatly exceeds the actual damages likely to be inflicted by a minor breach, its character as a penalty becomes unmistakable. *See M.I.G. Investments, Inc. v. Marsala, supra*, 92 Ill. App. 3d at 405–06, 47 Ill. Dec. at 270, 414 N.E.2d at 1386; ... 5 Corbin on Contracts § 1066 (1964). This case is within the gravitational field of these principles even though the minimum-guarantee clause does not fix a single sum as damages.

¶ 11 [The court then demonstrated that the contract's damages clause would provide Lake River with a much bigger damages remedy than needed to compensate it for lost profits, especially if the breach occurred early in the contract term, before Lake River had incurred substantial expenses in performing its obligations. In this case, Carborundum breached after it had delivered 55% of the Ferro Carbo. The damages clause would provide Lake River with more than twice the amount needed to compensate it for its actual losses, including lost profits.]

....

¶ 12 The fact that the damage formula is invalid does not deprive Lake River of a remedy. The parties did not contract explicitly with reference to the measure of damages if the agreed-on damage formula was invalidated, but all this means is that the victim of the breach is entitled to his common law damages. *See, e.g.*, Restatement, Second, Contracts § 356, comment a (1981). In this case that would be the unpaid contract price of $241,000 minus the costs that Lake River saved by not having to complete the contract (the variable costs on the other 45 percent of the Ferro Carbo that it never had to bag). The case must be remanded to the district judge to fix these damages.

¶ 13 The judgment of the district court is affirmed in part and reversed in part, and the case is returned to that court to redetermine both parties' damages in accordance with the principles in this opinion. The parties may present additional evidence on remand, and shall bear their own costs in this court....

Affirmed in part, reversed in part, and remanded.

Exercise 12.5 — Application and Assessment of the Rule Against Penalties

1. Liquidated Damages Clause or Penalty?

Which of the following is more likely to be an enforceable liquidated damages clause and why? Which is more likely to be an unenforceable penalty clause and why? The clause appears in a contract between the owners of a shopping center and a contractor for completion of work on a new parking structure. At the time of contracting, the owners predicted that it would be difficult to ever ascertain and prove the precise amount of revenue that the owners would lose if construction of the parking structure were delayed; however, the parties' best rough estimate when contracting was that the owners would lose approximately $20,000 in lost profits for every day of delay beyond the contractual due date of October 31. They also predicted that the contractor would complete the work either just in time for opening the structure to shoppers on November 1 if everything went perfectly, or up to a week late if difficulties arose in the work.

Clause #1: The clause states that the contractor will be liable for damages of $175,000 for any delay in completion beyond October 31, regardless of the length of the delay. The contractor completed construction of the parking structure late in the day on November 3.

Clause #2: The clause states that the contractor will be liable for damages of $20,000 for each day of delay in completion of work, up to a total of $140,000. The contractor completed construction of the parking structure late in the day on November 3. The owner suffered only $20,000 in damages from that delay, however, because a downturn in the economy suppressed retail shopping, leaving plenty of open parking at the shopping center during the delay except for a single busy day and evening on a Saturday.

2. Damages for Failure to Pay

A union, acting as the certified representative of employees, successfully negotiated a collective bargaining agreement with a group of employers, thus avoiding a strike or lock-out. Among other things, the agreement requires the employers to make payments into a fund for employee pensions and other benefits. It also provides that any employer who fails to pay into the fund on schedule will owe both the late payment and "an additional amount of ten (10%) percent of the amount due in liquidated damages for failure to pay in accordance with this Agreement." One employer delayed making a required payment to the union fund for eight months, leading the union to follow up with correspondence and personal visits to the employer, and to use other funds to maintain insurance that would have been funded by the employer. At the time of the delayed payment, the prevailing interest rate was substantially less than 10% per annum. Is the damages clause enforceable, or should the court require the union to prove its actual losses? Develop arguments for both sides. [Facts taken from *United Order of Am. Bricklayers and Stone Masons Union No. 21 v. Thorleif Larsen & Son, Inc.*, 519 F.2d 331 (7th Cir. 1975).]

3. Should Courts Enforce Penalty Clauses Even Though Punitive Damages Are Unavailable?

The French Civil Code does not permit courts to award punitive damages for breach of contract in the absence of a penalty clause in the contract. C. Civ. art. 1131-2 (Fr., rev. 2016). In deference to the autonomy of the parties, however, it directs courts to enforce penalty clauses agreed to by the parties. C. Civ. art. 1231-5 (Fr., rev. 2016). Do you prefer this approach or that of U.S. law?

F. UCC Remedies

The UCC includes provisions consistent with the common law principles stated above, as well as a few that add some additional flexibility in proving damages. Therefore, a quick tour through UCC remedies provisions will serve both as a review of fundamental concepts and as a way of digging a little deeper in the context of a sale of goods. If this section feels a little repetitive to you, that's a good sign; it means that you have assimilated the basic concepts under common law and are recognizing them in the UCC, with a few statutory variations sprinkled in.

1. Recovery Limited to Compensation

We can start where we left off with common law principles: the exclusion of punitive damages and penalty clauses. The UCC authorizes only compensatory awards in the absence of a contractual damages clause. Moreover, as shown by Arizona's enactment of UCC § 2-718(1), if the parties include a liquidated damages clause in a contract for a sale of goods, its enforceability is governed by standards similar to modern trends in the common law:

> 47-2718. Liquidation or limitation of damages; deposits
>
> A. Damages for breach by either party may be liquidated in the agreement but only at an amount which is reasonable in the light of the anticipated

or actual harm caused by the breach, the difficulties of proof of loss, and the inconvenience or non-feasibility of otherwise obtaining an adequate remedy. A term fixing unreasonably large liquidated damages is void as a penalty.

....

2. *Buyer's Compensatory Damages for Seller's Breach*

a. Buyer's Direct Loss in Value When Goods Are Accepted

Let's first assume that the buyer has accepted delivery of goods that do not conform to contract requirements, but the buyer wishes to keep the goods and to go forward with the contract by paying for the goods, while giving prompt notice of defects and retaining a claim for damages for the diminution in value. The basic measure of the buyer's direct loss in value is captured nicely in the UCC provision for damages to the buyer for the seller's breach of warranty. In most cases, the measure of such damages is the familiar amount of the difference in value between the goods as promised and the goods as delivered: "the difference at the time and place of acceptance between the value of the goods accepted and the value they would have had if they had been as warranted." U.C.C. § 2-714(2) (2011). Following is Arizona's enactment of section 2-714, divided into subsections A–C, rather than 1–3 as in the UCC:

> 47-2714. Buyer's damages for breach in regard to accepted goods
>
> A. Where the buyer has accepted goods and given notification (subsection C of section 47-2607) he may recover as damages for any non-conformity of tender the loss resulting in the ordinary course of events from the seller's breach as determined in any manner which is reasonable.
>
> B. The measure of damages for breach of warranty is the difference at the time and place of acceptance between the value of the goods accepted and the value they would have had if they had been as warranted, unless special circumstances show proximate damages of a different amount.
>
> C. In a proper case any incidental and consequential damages under section 47-2715 may also be recovered.

For an example of application of subsection B (as it is codified in Arizona), suppose that a shipment of 20 pairs of shoes to a retailer is not genuine leather, as warranted, and thus has a resale value that is $50/pair less than if they had been as promised. The buyer's loss in value is $50/pair x 20 = $1,000. Assuming the buyer had accepted the goods and paid for them, the buyer has no cost avoided.

The flexibility of the UCC shows through in a proviso to the subsection, which adds: "unless special circumstances show proximate cause of a different amount." This reference to proximate cause matches up with a reference in the next subsection to additional recovery for incidental and consequential damages, U.C.C. § 2-714(3)

(2011), which could include injury to person or property proximately caused by breach of warranty, U.C.C. § 2-715(2)(b) (2011).

The first subsection of section 2-714 provides an even more general and flexible articulation of direct loss in value due to general nonconformities in an accepted delivery: "the loss resulting in the ordinary course of events from the seller's breach as determined in any manner which is reasonable." U.C.C. § 2-714(1) (2011).

b. Buyer's Direct Loss in Value for Non-Delivered Goods

Carefully study the following provisions of Arizona's enactment of UCC §§ 2-711, 2-712, 2-713:

> 47-2711. Buyer's remedies in general; ....
>
> A. Where the seller fails to make delivery or repudiates or the buyer rightfully rejects or justifiably revokes acceptance then with respect to any goods involved, and with respect to the whole if the breach goes to the whole contract (section 47-2612), the buyer may cancel and whether or not he has done so may in addition to recovering so much of the price as has been paid:
>
> 1. "Cover" and have damages under section 47-2712 as to all the goods affected ... ;
>
> 2. Recover damages for non-delivery as provided in this chapter (section 47-2713).
>
> ....
>
> 47-2712. "Cover"; buyer's procurement of substitute goods
>
> A. After a breach within section 47-2711 the buyer may "cover" by making in good faith and without unreasonable delay any reasonable purchase of or contract to purchase goods in substitution for those due from the seller.
>
> B. The buyer may recover from the seller as damages the difference between the cost of cover and the contract price together with any incidental or consequential damages as hereinafter defined (section 47-2715), but less expenses saved in consequence of the seller's breach.
>
> C. Failure of the buyer to effect cover within this section does not bar him from any other remedy.
>
> ....
>
> 47-2713. Buyer's damages for non-delivery or repudiation
>
> A. Subject to the provisions of this chapter with respect to proof of market price (section 47-2723), the measure of damages for non-delivery or repudiation by the seller is the difference between the market price at the time when the buyer learned of the breach and the contract price together with any incidental and consequential damages provided in this chapter

(section 47-2715), but less expenses saved in consequence of the seller's breach.

....

The buyer's loss in value when the seller fails to deliver the goods at all is either: (1) the market price of the non-delivered goods *when the buyer learned of the breach*, under UCC § 2-713(1), or (2) the "cost of cover," meaning the cost of substitute goods, under UCC § 2-714(2), if the buyer makes a substitute purchase on the market without delay. If the seller repudiates prior to the delivery date, the market price remedy is set at the time the buyer learns of that repudiation, on the assumption that the buyer can promptly enter into a contract for substitute goods, before the price rises further. Because the buyer normally would not have paid for goods that were not delivered or were rightfully rejected, the unpaid contract price represents cost avoided and should be deducted from either the market price or the cost of cover.

For a simple example, suppose the following facts: The seller repudiated a contract to supply ten bicycles at a contract price of $200 each, before the buyer had paid any part of the purchase price. The bicycles have a market price of $250 at the time of the repudiation, and the buyer was able to "cover" at that market price by purchasing substitute bicycles for $250 each, so that the loss in value would be the same under either a market price or cover price measure: $250/bicycle x 10 = $2,500. The buyer's cost avoided is the contract price of $200/bicycle x 10 = $2,000, which the buyer need not pay in light of the seller's repudiation. The resulting damages are $50/bicycle x 10 = $500:

Loss in value ($250 x 10 = $2,500)—cost avoided ($200 x 10 = $2,000) = Damages ($500)

The same measures apply if the buyer covered on the market after justifiably rejecting delivered goods. U.C.C. § 2-711(1) (2011).

If the buyer has already paid some of the contract price for goods that are not delivered or are rightfully rejected, then the buyer can also recover that payment. The easiest way to show this in the damages equation is to reduce the amount of cost avoided. For example, if the buyer had paid 25% of the purchase price ($500) in advance, only $1,500 of the cost of the buyer's performance would be avoided because of the seller's breach:

Loss in value ($250 x 10 = $2,500)—cost avoided ($150 x 10 = $1,500) = Damages ($1,000)

In many cases in which a buyer seeks the cover price remedy under section 2-712, the buyer was not able to make a substitute purchase at the market price; instead, in the scramble to react to the breach, the buyer purchased substitute goods at a price higher than the theoretical market price at that time. That higher price results in greater damages than the market price remedy under section 2-713. Nonetheless, the higher cover price remedy is permitted so long as the buyer covered "in good faith and without unreasonable delay" and made a "reasonable purchase." U.C.C. § 2-712(1) (2011).

Exercise 12.6 — Covering with Cow Hides

Seller is a meat packer that accumulates cow hides as a byproduct of its business. Buyer is a broker that purchases cow hides and resells them at a profit to tanneries. On January 1, Buyer and Seller agreed that Seller would sell its entire output of cow hides to Buyer during the year at a price of $10/hide. By March 1, the market price of cow hides had risen to $20/hide and gave every indication of rising further. On March 1, Seller stopped deliveries and repudiated the contract. Because Buyer had resale commitments to tanneries throughout the year, it turned to other sources of supply after Seller repudiated the contract. Because it had limited storage facilities and because the hides deteriorate over time, Buyer purchased substitute hides from other suppliers in increments over the remaining months of the year, as the price rose steadily further and leveled off at $30/hide in November. Between March and December 31, Buyer had purchased 10,000 substitute hides at an average price of $26/hide. Buyer can prove that Seller's output between March 1 and December 31 would have been approximately 10,000 hides. What are Buyer's damages for Seller's breach? What UCC provisions provide support for either party? What issues arise? [Problem based loosely on *Laredo Hides Co., v. H & H Meat Products Co.,* 513 S.W.2d 210 (Tex. Civ. App. 1974).]

---

c. Buyer's Incidental and Consequential Damages

Study the terms of Arizona's enactment of UCC § 2-715:

47-2715. Buyer's incidental and consequential damages

A. Incidental damages resulting from the seller's breach include expenses reasonably incurred in inspection, receipt, transportation and care and custody of goods rightfully rejected, any commercially reasonable charges, expenses or commissions in connection with effecting cover and any other reasonable expense incident to the delay or other breach.

B. Consequential damages resulting from the seller's breach include:

1. Any loss resulting from general or particular requirements and needs of which the seller at the time of contracting had reason to know and which could not reasonably be prevented by cover or otherwise; and
2. Injury to person or property proximately resulting from any breach of warranty.

We earlier defined *incidental damages* as the cost of reacting to a breach, such as the cost of finding a substitute supplier. As you can see from the first subsection above, the UCC confirms that definition and provides examples.

In our discussion of common law principles, we referred to *consequential damages* as losses accumulating in a "domino effect" from a breach, such as lost profits flowing from a work stoppage caused by the breach. We also learned of foreseeability limitations from the case of *Hadley v. Baxendale*, which permitted recovery of damages only if they naturally flowed from the breach, or were within the contemplation of the parties because special circumstances had been communicated at the time of contracting. Similarly, the UCC provides that a buyer may recover as consequential damages "any loss resulting from the general or particular requirements and needs of which the seller at the time of contracting had reason to know." U.C.C. § 2-715(2)(a) (2011). In a reference to a duty to mitigate, the UCC also recognizes that such losses should be limited to those that were unavoidable, because consequential losses are limited to those "which could not reasonably be prevented by cover or otherwise." *Id.*

Finally, as stated earlier, the UCC recognizes a less demanding foreseeability limitation when a breach of warranty causes the kind of harm usually associated with a tort. It permits consequential damages for "injury to person or property proximately resulting from any breach of warranty." U.C.C. § 2-715(2)(b) (2011).

3. *Seller's Remedy on Buyer's Breach*

a. Action for the Price

Specific performance for a *buyer* under the UCC was discussed in Section II of this chapter. If a buyer has accepted delivery of goods but has failed to pay for them, the *seller* can demand the equivalent of specific performance by demanding that the buyer perform by paying the price. U.C.C. § 2-709 (2011) (entitled "Action for the Price"). Although a suit for payment of money sounds more like a suit for damages, an action for the price is consistent with specific performance, because it contemplates that both parties will fully perform: Seller has delivered conforming goods, and buyer will take the goods and pay the contract price, thus relieving Seller of the tasks of recovering and reselling the goods.

b. Seller's Loss in Value from Buyer's Wrongful Non-Acceptance

Study the following excerpts from Arizona's enactment of UCC §§ 2-706, 2-708, 2-710:

> 47-2706. <u>Seller's resale including contract for resale</u>
>
> A.... the seller may resell the goods concerned or the undelivered balance thereof. Where the resale is made in good faith and in a commercially reasonable manner the seller may recover the difference between the resale price and the contract price together with any incidental damages allowed under the provisions of this chapter (section 47-2710), but less expenses saved in consequence of the buyer's breach.
>
> ....
>
> 47-2708. <u>Seller's damages for non-acceptance or repudiation</u>
>
> A.... the measure of damages for non-acceptance or repudiation by the buyer is the difference between the market price at the time and place for tender and the unpaid contract price together with any incidental damages provided

in this chapter (section 47-2710), but less expenses saved in consequence of the buyer's breach.

....

47-2710. Seller's incidental damages

Incidental damages to an aggrieved seller include any commercially reasonable charges, expenses or commissions incurred in stopping delivery, in the transportation, care and custody of goods after the buyer's breach, in connection with return or resale of the goods or otherwise resulting from the breach.

If the buyer repudiates the contract prior to delivery, or wrongfully rejects the delivery, and has not paid for the goods, the seller's direct loss in value is measured by the contract price that the buyer has withheld. The seller's cost or loss avoided (represented by cancellation of the seller's obligation to transfer the goods to the buyer) would be measured by either: (1) the market price of the goods *at the time and place for tender*, under UCC § 2-708, or (2) the resale price if the seller has engaged in a "cover" transaction by reselling the goods, under UCC § 2-706.

Suppose, for example, that the buyer wrongfully rejected a shipment of 10 bicycles priced at $200 each under the contract. Suppose further that the market price of the bicycles had dropped to $150 by that time, and that the seller could resell the bicycles for $150 each if it chose to cover on the market. The seller's damages would be:

Loss in Value ($200 x 10 = $2,000)—Cost or Loss Avoided ($150 x 10 = $1,500) = Damages ($500)

In the scramble to react to the buyer's breach, however, a seller might engage in a resale for something less than the theoretical market price, such as $125 for each bicycle, thus resulting in a smaller deduction from damages for loss avoided, and producing greater damages under the "cover" remedy than under the market price formulation. This greater measure of damages will be permitted so long as the resale is made "in good faith and in a commercially reasonable manner." U.C.C. § 2-706(1) (2011).

c. Seller's Incidental (but not Consequential) Damages

The UCC permits the Seller to recover incidental damages, which it describes as "any commercially reasonable charges, expenses or commissions incurred in stopping delivery, in the transportation, care and custody of goods after the buyer's breach, in connection with return or resale of the goods or otherwise resulting from the breach." U.C.C. § 2-710 (2011). The UCC does not provide for the award of consequential damages to a seller who is the victim of breach. This might reflect an assumption that a seller will not suffer consequential losses from a buyer's failure to pay money owed on a contract; if nonpayment adversely affects the seller's cash flow, it can always borrow money from its bank and recover interest on the judgment against the buyer. Was this assumption sound during the credit crisis beginning in 2008?

d. Seller's Recovery for Lost Volume in Sales

Recall in Subsection *b* above that the proceeds from the resale of wrongfully rejected goods normally would constitute loss avoided and should be deducted from the damage award. But that assumes that the resale is a true substitute transaction.

In some cases, the seller had plenty of stock on hand and would have sold the same model of goods to other buyers in addition to the sale to the buyer under the first contract. In those circumstances, the market price remedy might be inadequate to provide the seller with appropriate compensation. This problem is addressed in UCC § 2-708, set forth here as enacted in Arizona:

> 47-2708. Seller's damages for non-acceptance or repudiation
>
> A.... the measure of damages for non-acceptance or repudiation by the buyer is the difference between the market price at the time and place for tender and the unpaid contract price....
>
> B. If the measure of damages provided in subsection A of this section is inadequate to put the seller in as good a position as performance would have done then the measure of damages is the profit (including reasonable overhead) which the seller would have made from full performance by the buyer, together with any incidental damages provided in this chapter (section 47-2710), due allowance for costs reasonably incurred and due credit for payments or proceeds of resale.

For example, imagine that Buyer #1 repudiates a contract for the purchase and sale of 10 bicycles at a contract price of $200 each, and that the market price for the bicycles remains steady at $200 each. The seller would have no damages under section 2-708(1) (subsection A in the Arizona codification), based on the difference between the contract price and the market price, because the seller retains bicycles worth as much as the contract fee that has been withheld. Similarly, the seller would have no damages under section 2-706(1) if it did in fact resell the 10 bicycles later that day at $200 each to Buyer #2.

If the seller has hundreds of such bicycles in stock, however, and if the seller is constantly selling these bicycles to various buyers, Buyer #1's repudiation represents 10 fewer bicycles sold that week than if that buyer had performed. Seller's expectation was to sell 10 bicycles to Buyer #1 in the morning and another 10 bicycles to Buyer #2 later that day, along with other sales. Moreover, the seller presumably makes some profit on the sale of each bicycle, based on the difference between costs and revenue.

For example, let's suppose that the total costs attributable to producing and selling each bicycle is $175, leaving the seller with $25 in profit. If the market price remedy is inadequate, because the market price has remained steady at the contract price, the UCC will allow the seller to recover its lost profit from Buyer #1. UCC § 2-708(2) (2011) (subsection B in Arizona). Under that measure, the seller's loss in value would not be zero but would be $25 x 10 = $250.

Exercise 12.7 — The Buyer Backs Out

Seller agreed to deliver packaging materials, which are readily available on the market, to Buyer for a price of $10,000. What are Seller's remedies under each of the following situations?

(i) Buyer accepted delivery of the goods but refused to pay.

(ii) Buyer repudiated the agreement on the morning of the delivery date, when the market price of the goods had dropped to $9,000. Seller scrambled to sell the goods to another buyer before the market price dropped further. The average market price remained at $9,000 while Seller attempted to sell the goods. Still, after a reasonable search for buyers, the best the Seller could do was sell the packaging materials for $8,500 to a local buyer. Seller incurred an additional $300 in costs in locating and negotiating a deal with the substitute buyer on short notice, but it saved $200 in transportation costs because the substitute buyer was closer to its warehouse than the original buyer.

(iii) Buyer repudiated the agreement on the morning of the delivery date, while the market price for the goods remained steady at $10,000. Seller has a large inventory, and it easily sold the goods to another regular customer for $10,000; indeed, it would have made that sale even if Buyer had taken its delivery. Seller's full costs in producing, storing, and delivering the goods, including reasonable overhead, are $9,500.

---

e. No Advantage in Cover at Bargain Price

If the victim of breach, either a buyer or a seller, engages in a substitute purchase or sale that is better for that party than the market price, then the market price measure will provide greater damages than the cover price remedy. For example, suppose that the contract price for goods is $10,000, the market price had risen to $11,000 when the seller repudiated, and the buyer was able to make a substitute purchase at $10,500, saving $500 compared to the market price. The buyer's cover price remedy is $500 ($10,500 — $10,000) but buyer might wish to pursue the market price remedy of $1,000 ($11,000 — $10,000). However, a comment to the UCC provision for the buyer's market price remedy states that the buyer should not enjoy this luxury but should be limited to the damages set by the cover transaction. U.C.C. § 2-713 cmt. 5 (2011).

The seller would be in the same position if the buyer wrongfully rejected delivery when the market price had fallen from $10,000 to $9,000, and the seller succeeded in reselling the goods for $9,500 (and let's assume that lost volume recovery would not apply or would be no greater than $500). The seller would prefer to recover its market price remedy of $1,000, and the UCC provisions for sellers' remedies contain no text or comments that preclude this choice. Nonetheless, the seller would likely be limited to its lesser cover price remedy by the general principle that damages should award expectation interest rather than provide a windfall. *See* U.C.C. § 1-305(1) (2001) (remedies should be liberally construed to put victim of breach in as good a position as if the contract had been performed).

The seller would be in a different position if it claimed its market price remedy at the time of breach and then held the goods in question for a substantial period of time, selling for a higher price only after the market for those goods had recovered. In that case, the seller could argue that it had not enjoyed a windfall stemming from a fortuitous resale at the time of breach; instead, it had claimed its market price damages and then held the goods as an investment, while exposing itself to the risk of a continuing fall in prices.

IV. Alternative Remedies for Breach—Reliance, Restitution, and Disgorgement

A. Measuring the Remedy for Breach by the Reliance or Restitution Interest

As illustrated in Exercise 1 in Chapter 1, a victim of breach of contract normally will prefer expectation interest over reliance or restitution interest because the claimant on a contract claim typically had negotiated a profitable deal and thus created high expectations. The victim of breach might seek or be limited to reliance costs or restitution interest if one of those is easily proved and calculated and if the expectation interest is difficult to quantify.

Alternatively, the victim of breach might seek reliance or restitution interest if it had negotiated a losing deal, so that those interests exceed the victim's expectation interest. It is rare for the other party to breach a contract that clearly favors the breaching party. When that occurs, however, will the victim of the breach be entitled to recover its restitution or reliance interest, to avoid the consequences of having negotiated a losing deal?

Example 1: For example, suppose that Contractor agrees to provide services to Owner for a fee of $50,000. If Contractor's performance will require expenditure of $40,000 in materials and labor and will enrich Owner by $45,000, Owner could have second thoughts about the deal and might repudiate the contract before preparation for construction begins. If so, Contractor's reliance interest is zero, its net restitution interest after performance would be $5,000 ($45,000 minus the cost avoided of $40,000), and its net expectation interest is $10,000 ($50,000 minus cost avoided). In its claim for breach of contract, Contractor will claim its expectation interest.

In contrast, in the highly unusual circumstance that Owner had paid in advance and *Contractor had repudiated* prior to beginning performance, Owner's reliance and restitution interests—each is $50,000—would exceed its expectation interest. Owner's expectation interest would be a loss of $5,000, translating to a recovery of only $45,000 (Loss in value of $45,000—zero cost avoided).

Example 2: But suppose that Contractor was a poor negotiator or calculator of costs and agreed to perform the same work for $35,000. Contractor will regret entering into this deal because its expectation is to suffer a loss, earning only $35,000 after expending $40,000 in performance costs. Owner, in contrast, stands to gain value of $45,000 while paying only $35,000 for it, and thus is highly unlikely to repudiate this contract. If Owner repudiated and paid nothing after Contractor completed performance, Contractor's reliance and restitution interests would exceed its expectation interest. (If Owner breached obligations of cooperation that caused Contractor to suffer additional recoverable losses aside from the Owner's failure to pay, then the contract fee would not reflect Contractor's full expectation interest. However, our simple example, in which the unpaid fee is the sole loss to Contractor, helps to illustrate the point about relative values of fundamental interests.)

If the party to a losing contract is the victim of breach, should that party be entitled to recover a reliance or restitution interest that exceeds expectation interest? The responses to this and similar hypotheticals tend to vary.

In Example #1 above, if Owner had paid in advance and Contractor had surprisingly repudiated prior to performance, most courts would grant restitution of the full amount of Owner's advance payment even though that would exceed the Owner's expectation interest by $5,000, and even though its restitution interest equates with its reliance interest. *See* Eric G. Andersen, *The Restoration Interest and Damages for Breach of Contract*, 53 MARYLAND L. REV. 1, 7, 18–19 (1994).

In Example #2, however, if Owner had breached by failing to pay after Contractor had completed performance, Contractor's recovery would be limited to its expectation interest of $35,000 rather than its reliance interest of $40,000. *See id.* at 13–14 & nn. 43–46 (citing to numerous cases and secondary sources). After all, the reliance interest is a component of Contractor's expectation of losing $5,000 through full performance, and that $40,000 cost of performance is a component of Contractor's calculations during bargaining, so it makes sense to give Contractor precisely what it bargained for rather than greater costs of performance. *See generally id.* at 30–31 (presenting views of E. Allan Farnsworth). Contractor's *restitution* interest of $45,000 is not similarly part of the calculus of the expectation interest, and the unjust enrichment of Owner presents a more compelling case for restitution of that enrichment. Nonetheless, most courts would again limit Contractor's recovery to its expectation interest for its full performance. *See id.* at 7, 17–18; RESTATEMENT (SECOND) OF CONTRACTS § 373(2) (1981).

The differing results on these extremes of either advance payment by Owner prior to counter-performance, or full performance by Contractor prior to payment, may stem partly from the certainty of the contract fee that is paid or withheld, compared to any other relevant calculation. Ordering restitution or payment of the fee is a simple solution, and each of those solutions is supported by *some* reasonable principle even if not by a single consistent principle.

In other contexts, however, the law has been "conflicting and confused." *Id.* at 16, 18. In example #2, if Contractor had performed only partially prior to Owner's repudiation, then an award to Contractor of the contract rate would require calculation of costs avoided, lending some uncertainty to the expectation interest and reducing its attractiveness as a ceiling to a claim for restitution interest. Accordingly, the second Restatement of Contracts recommends permitting a victim of breach who has partially performed to choose restitution interest as remedy. Restatement (Second) of Contracts§ 373(1) (1981).

The third Restatement of Restitution and Unjust Enrichment, however, contemplates imposing the contract rate as a ceiling on restitution, and reducing recovery of reliance costs by the loss that the victim of breach would have suffered after full performance if proved with reasonable certainty by the breaching party. Restatement (Third) of Restitution and Unjust Enrichment § 38(2) & cmt. b (2011). Consistent with this view, some courts persist in recognizing expectation interest as a ceiling to recovery of reliance or restitution interests, even if expectation interest is uncertain. An example, albeit in a different context, is provided by *Pyeatte v. Pyeatte*, explored in Chapter 4 of this book. After Margrethe had fully performed by supporting H. Charles through law school, H. Charles failed to support her through a master's degree program, so the court permitted her to recover her restitution interest on a claim of quasi-contract. Nevertheless, the court warned that this recovery could not exceed her expectation interest, even though the court had also ruled that the contract was not enforceable because her expectation interest was too indefinite to calculate! *Pyeatte v. Pyeatte*, 135 Ariz. 346, 357, 661 P.2d 196, 207 (Ct. App. 1982).

B. Disgorgement of the Breaching Party's Profits

Since Chapter 1, we have assumed that contract law primarily protects the expectation interest of the victim of breach, measured by that party's losses, including the victim's failure to realize gains expected from full performance. An award of restitution rests on a wholly different basis, but it stems from benefits conferred on the defendant *by the plaintiff's actions.*

In contrast, the remedy of disgorgement divests the breaching party of profits that it realized as a result of its own opportunistic breach, not consisting of benefits provided by the nonbreaching party (and thus not implicating the traditional restitution interest). *See* Melvin A. Eisenberg, *The Disgorgement Interest in Contract Law*, 105 Mich. L. Rev. 559 (2006). This novel, alternative remedy received a boost from the third Restatement of Restitution and Unjust Enrichment, which recommends making available "restitution of the profit realized by the promisor as a result" of the promisor's "deliberate breach of contract," if the legal remedy of money damages is inadequate. Restatement (Third) of Restitution and Unjust Enrichment § 39(1) (2011). The Restatement defines profits resulting from the breach as those "resulting in gains to the defendant (net of potential liability in damages) greater than" the gains the defendant would have earned from performing the contract. *Id.* § 39(2).

When the "defendant's profits from breach ... exceed the provable loss to the claimant," the Restatement concedes that this novel remedy runs contrary to "the usual presumptions of contract law." *Id.* cmt. a. Although the Restatement denies that disgorgement introduces a punitive element to the remedy for breach, it states an intention "to make breach unprofitable." *Id.* at cmt. e. Nonetheless, it arguably departs from ordinary contract remedies no more than does specific enforcement, which prevents or cures breach by compelling performance. Because disgorgement is not available under the Restatement test except when damages would be inadequate, it mirrors a fundamental prerequisite to specific performance. Moreover, because it is an equitable remedy, a court could exercise the same discretion to withhold it in proper cases that it exercises when determining whether to grant specific performance. Under the Restatement, a court typically would award disgorgement "after the fact" to provide protection "that specific performance would have given ahead of time" had it been practical to do so. *Id.* at cmt. c, d.

The following Supreme Court case addresses enforcement of the terms of an interstate compact, a context that is legally distinguishable from enforcement of a private contract. Nonetheless, the majority's embrace of the Restatement's disgorgement remedy, and the skepticism voiced by the dissenting opinions, undoubtedly reflect more widespread debates about the wisdom of adopting this remedy for private contracts.

Kansas v. Nebraska

135 S. Ct. 1042 (2015)

[footnotes omitted]

Justice Kagan delivered the opinion of the Court.

....

I

¶ 1 The Republican River originates in Colorado; crosses the northwestern corner of Kansas into Nebraska; flows through much of southwestern Nebraska; and finally cuts back into northern Kansas. Along with its many tributaries, the river drains a 24,900-square-mile watershed, called the Republican River Basin. The Basin contains substantial farmland, producing (among other things) wheat and corn.

¶ 2 During the Dust Bowl of the 1930's, the Republican River Basin experienced an extended drought, interrupted once by a deadly flood. In response, the Federal Government proposed constructing reservoirs in the Basin to control flooding, as well as undertaking an array of irrigation projects to disperse the stored water. But the Government insisted that the three States of the Basin first agree to an allocation of its water resources. As a result of that prodding, the States negotiated and ratified the Republican River Compact; and in 1943, as required under the Constitution, Art. I, § 10, cl. 3, Congress approved that agreement. By act of Congress, the Compact thus became federal law. *See* Act of May 26, 1943, ch. 104, 57 Stat. 86.

. . . .

II

¶3 The Constitution gives this Court original jurisdiction to hear suits between the States. *See* Art. III, § 2. Proceedings under that grant of jurisdiction are "basically equitable in nature." *Ohio v. Kentucky*, 410 U. S. 641, 648 … (1973).

. . . .

¶4 Two particular features of this interstate controversy further distinguish it from a run-of-the-mill private suit and highlight the essentially equitable character of our charge. The first relates to the subject matter of the Compact and Settlement: rights to an interstate waterway. The second concerns the Compact's status as not just an agreement, but a federal law.

. . . .

¶5 [W]e agree with the Master's conclusion that Nebraska "knowingly exposed Kansas to a substantial risk" of receiving less water than the Compact provided, and so "knowingly failed" to comply with the obligations that agreement imposed.… Nebraska recklessly gambled with Kansas's rights, consciously disregarding a substantial probability that its actions would deprive Kansas of the water to which it was entitled. *See* Tr. 1870 (Aug. 23, 2012) (Master's statement that Nebraska showed "reckless indifference as to compliance back in '05 and '06").

¶6 After determining that Kansas lost $3.7 million from Nebraska's breach, the Special Master considered the case for an additional monetary award. Based on detailed evidence, not contested here, he concluded that an acre-foot of water is substantially more valuable on farmland in Nebraska than in Kansas. That meant Nebraska's reward for breaching the Compact was "much larger than Kansas' loss, likely by more than several multiples." Report 178. Given the circumstances, the Master thought that Nebraska should have to disgorge part of that additional gain, to the tune of $1.8 million. In making that recommendation, he relied on his finding—which we have just affirmed—of Nebraska's culpability. *See id.*, at 130. He also highlighted this Court's broad remedial powers in compact litigation, noting that such cases involve not private parties' private quarrels, but States' clashes over federal law. *See id.*, at 131, 135; *supra*, at 6–9.

¶7 Nebraska (along with the dissent) opposes the Special Master's disgorgement proposal on the ground that the State did not "deliberately act[ ]" to violate the Compact. Reply Brief for Nebraska 33; *see* post, at 6–7. Relying on private contract law, Nebraska cites a Restatement provision declaring that a court may award disgorgement in certain cases in which "a deliberate breach of contract results in profit to the defaulting promisor." Restatement (Third) of Restitution and Unjust Enrichment § 39(1) (2010) (Restatement); *see* Reply Brief for Nebraska 32. Nebraska then points out that the Master, even though finding a "knowing" exposure of Kansas to significant risk, rejected the idea that "Nebraska officials [had] deliberately set out to violate the Compact." Brief for Nebraska 16 (quoting Report 111). Accordingly, Nebraska concludes, no disgorgement is warranted.

¶ 8 But that argument fails to come to terms with what the Master properly understood as the wrongful nature of Nebraska's conduct. True enough, as the Master said, that Nebraska did not purposefully set out to breach the Compact. But still, as he also found, the State "knowingly exposed Kansas to a substantial risk" of breach, and blithely proceeded. Report 130. In some areas of the law and for certain purposes, the distinction between purposefully invading and recklessly disregarding another's rights makes no difference.... And indeed, the very Restatement Nebraska relies on treats the two similarly. It assimilates "deliberate[ness]" to "conscious wrongdoing," which it defines as acting (as Nebraska did) "despite a known risk that the conduct ... violates [another's] rights." Restatement § 39, Comment f; *id.*, § 51(3). Conversely, the Restatement distinguishes "deliberate[ness]" from behavior (not akin to Nebraska's) amounting to mere "inadvertence, negligence, or unsuccessful attempt at performance." *Id.*, § 39, Comment f.

¶ 9 And whatever is true of a private contract action, the case for disgorgement becomes still stronger when one State gambles with another State's rights to a scarce natural resource. From the time this Court began to apportion interstate rivers, it has recognized part of its role as guarding against upstream States' inequitable takings of water. And as we have noted, that concern persists even after States enter into a compact: This Court may then exercise remedial authority to ensure compliance with the compact's terms—thus preventing a geographically favored State from appropriating more than its share of a river. *See supra*, at 8. Indeed, the formation of such a compact provides this Court with enhanced remedial power because, as we have described, the agreement is also an Act of Congress, and its breach a violation of federal law. *See supra*, at 8–9; *Porter*, 328 U. S. 395 ... (exercising equitable power to disgorge profits gained from violating a federal statute). Consistent with those principles, we have stated that awarding actual damages for a compact's infringement may be inadequate, because that remedy alone "would permit [an upstream State] to ignore its obligation to deliver water as long as it is willing" to pay that amount. *Texas v. New Mexico*, 482 U. S., at 132. And as the Solicitor General noted in argument here, "[i]t is important that water flows down the river, not just money." Tr. of Oral Arg. 24. Accordingly, this Court may order disgorgement of gains, if needed to stabilize a compact and deter future breaches, when a State has demonstrated reckless disregard of another, more vulnerable State's rights under that instrument.

¶ 10 ... [T]he higher value of water on Nebraska's farmland than on Kansas's means that Nebraska can take water that under the Compact should go to Kansas, pay Kansas actual damages, and still come out ahead. That is nearly a recipe for breach—for an upstream State to refuse to deliver to its downstream neighbor the water to which the latter is entitled. And through 2006, Nebraska took full advantage of its favorable position, eschewing steps that would effectively control groundwater pumping and thus exceeding its allotment. In such circumstances, a disgorgement award appropriately reminds Nebraska of its legal obligations, deters future violations, and promotes the Compact's successful administration. *See Porter*, 328 U. S., at 400 ...

("Future compliance may be more definitely assured if one is compelled to restore one's illegal gains"). We thus reject Nebraska's exception to the Master's proposed remedy.

B

....

¶ 11 We ... agree with both the Master and Kansas that disgorgement need not be all or nothing. *See, e.g.*, 1 D. Dobbs, Law of Remedies § 2.4(1), p. 92 (2d ed. 1993) ("Balancing of equities and hardships may lead the court to grant some equitable relief but not" the full measure requested); Restatement § 39, Comment i; *id.*, § 50, Comment a; *National Security Systems, Inc. v. Iola*, 700 F. 3d 65, 80–81, 101–102 (CA3 2012).... So if partial disgorgement will serve to stabilize a compact by conveying an effective message to the breaching party that it must work hard to meet its future obligations, then the Court has discretion to order only that much. *Cf. Kansas v. Colorado*, 533 U. S. 1, 14 ... (2001) (concluding that a master "acted properly in carefully analyzing the facts of the case and in only awarding as much prejudgment interest as was required by a balancing of the equities").

¶ 12 And we agree with the Master's judgment that a relatively small disgorgement award suffices here....

¶ 13 We are thus confident that in approving the Master's recommendation for about half again Kansas's actual damages, we award a fair and equitable remedy suited to the circumstances.

¶ 14 For related reasons, we also reject Kansas's request for an injunction ordering Nebraska to comply with the Compact and Settlement. Kansas wants such an order so that it can seek contempt sanctions against Nebraska for any future breach. *See* Brief for Kansas 36–44. But we agree with the Master that Kansas has failed to show, as it must to obtain an injunction, a "cognizable danger of recurrent violation." *United States v. W. T. Grant Co.*, 345 U. S. 629, 633 ... (1953). As just discussed, Nebraska's new compliance measures, so long as followed, are up to the task of keeping the State within its allotment. And Nebraska is now on notice that if it relapses, it may again be subject to disgorgement of gains—either in part or in full, as the equities warrant. That, we trust, will adequately guard against Nebraska's repeating its former practices.

....

¶ 15 ... Accordingly, we adopt all of the Special Master's recommendations.

It is so ordered.

Justice Scalia, concurring in part and dissenting in part.

¶ 16 I join Justice Thomas's opinion. I write separately to note that modern Restatements—such as the Restatement (Third) of Restitution and Unjust Enrichment (2010), which both opinions address in their discussions of the disgorgement remedy—are of questionable value, and must be used with caution. The object of the original Restatements was "to present an orderly statement of the general common law." Restatement of Conflict of Laws, Introduction, p. viii (1934). Over time, the Restatements' authors have abandoned the mission of describing the law, and have chosen instead to set forth their aspirations for what the law ought to be. Keyes, *The Restatement (Second): Its Misleading Quality and a Proposal for Its Amelioration*, 13 Pepp. L. Rev. 23, 24–25 (1985). Section 39 of the Third Restatement of Restitution and Unjust Enrichment is illustrative; as Justice Thomas notes, post, at 8 (opinion concurring in part and dissenting in part), it constitutes a " 'novel extension' " of the law that finds little if any support in case law. Restatement sections such as that should be given no weight whatever as to the current state of the law, and no more weight regarding what the law ought to be than the recommendations of any respected lawyer or scholar. And it cannot safely be assumed, without further inquiry, that a Restatement provision describes rather than revises current law.

Justice Thomas, with whom Justice Scalia and Justice Alito join, and with whom The Chief Justice joins as to Part III, concurring in part and dissenting in part.

....

¶ 17 The Special Master nevertheless recommended disgorgement because Nebraska "knowingly exposed Kansas to a substantial risk" of noncompliance. Report 130. He rested this recommendation on the Restatement (Third) of Restitution and Unjust Enrichment § 39 (2010). *See* Report 130–134. That section proposes awarding disgorgement when a party's profits from its breach are greater than the loss to the other party. The remedy is thought necessary because one party may "exploit the shortcomings" of traditional damages remedies by breaching contracts when its expected profits exceed the damages it would be required to pay to the other party. Restatement (Third) of Restitution § 39, Comment b, at 649. In other words, the remedy "condemns a form of conscious advantage-taking" and seeks to thwart an "opportunistic calculation" that breaching is better than performing. *Ibid.*

¶ 18 This Court, however, has never before relied on § 39 nor adopted its proposed theory of disgorgement. And for good reason: It lacks support in the law. One reviewer of § 39 has described it as a "novel extension" of restitution principles that "will alter the doctrinal landscape of contract law." Roberts, *Restitutionary Disgorgement for Opportunistic Breach of Contract and Mitigation of Damages*, 42 Loyola (LA) L. Rev. 131, 134 (2008). And few courts have ever relied on § 39. The sheer novelty of this proposed remedy counsels against applying it here.

¶ 19 In any event, § 39 opines that disgorgement should be available only when a party deliberately breaches a contract. This makes sense. If disgorgement is an antidote for "efficient breach," then it need only be administered when "conscious advantage-taking" and "opportunistic calculation" are present. But as noted above, the Master expressly found that no deliberate breach occurred. Report 130. The Master's reliance on § 39 was accordingly misplaced.

V. Alternative Procedures for Securing Remedies

After failing to resolve a contract dispute through demands and negotiation, the victim of breach normally has the right to bring a contract claim in the state trial court of general jurisdiction, unless the amount of the claim is sufficiently low that it belongs in a court of limited jurisdiction, such as a small claims court. The suit may be filed in, or removed to, a federal trial court if the parties reside in different states or nations or if the dispute raises a question of federal law. All the cases in this book consist of opinions authored by appellate courts, or occasionally by trial courts, in such litigation.

Alternative means of dispute resolution, however, are becoming increasingly popular. Parties who are attempting to negotiate a settlement prior to litigation, for example, may seek the assistance of a neutral third party in voluntary mediation.

Two other examples of dispute resolution are presented here as illustrations: (1) private arbitration of international commercial disputes, pursuant to agreement by the parties, in place of litigation in court, and (2) a statutory scheme designed to resolve disputes concerning residential building defects prior to litigation in court.

A. International Commercial Arbitration

We encountered arbitration clauses in a negative light in our explorations of illegality and unconscionability in Chapter 9, because some consumer and employment contracts include abusive or lopsided arbitration provisions. In international commercial transactions, however, arbitration of disputes between business firms has gained popularity. Arbitration provides several advantages over litigation in court: a more streamlined trial procedure, restricted appellate review, confidentiality in the proceedings, neutrality of the forum, and the ability of the parties to choose arbitrators who are experts in the industry.

1. A Brief History

A century ago, many courts were hostile to agreements by the parties to submit their disputes to private arbitration. If one of the parties later ignored that agreement and filed a claim in court, the other party could invoke the parties' earlier agreement to arbitrate their disputes. Many courts, however, viewed the arbitration agreement as an improper attempt to oust the court of its jurisdiction to hear the dispute and would refuse to defer to arbitration.

The judicial hostility toward arbitration agreements largely ended with state and national arbitration legislation that advanced a policy favoring arbitration and directed courts to honor written arbitration agreements. In 1925, for example, Congress enacted the Federal Arbitration Act (FAA), 9 U.S.C. §§ 1–16, which applies to written arbitration agreements in maritime transactions or those "involving commerce."

By far the biggest boost to international arbitration came in 1958 with the U.N. Convention on the Recognition and Enforcement of Foreign Arbitral Awards, adopted by the United States and more than 150 other countries. Article II(3) of the Convention directs courts to refer the parties to arbitration if they have agreed in writing to arbitrate their dispute, unless the arbitration agreement is "null and void, inoperative or incapable of being performed." Once the arbitration tribunal issues its award after completion of arbitration, Article V of the Convention directs courts in adopting countries to enforce the award subject only to narrow exceptions such as ones relating to the validity of the arbitration agreement or fundamental deficiencies in the arbitration proceeding or the award. Implementation of the New York Convention in the United States is addressed in 9 U.S.C. §§ 201–08.

Because Latin American countries were initially reluctant to adopt the New York Convention, the United States and several Latin American countries entered into the Inter-American Convention on International Commercial Arbitration, commonly known as the Panama Convention. It is implemented in the United States through 9 U.S.C. §§ 301–07. The sometimes overlapping relationship between the two Conventions in the United States is discussed in Danielle Dean & Chelsea Masters, *"In the Canal Zone": the Panama Convention and its Relevance in the United States Today*, 2 The Arbitration Brief 90 (2012).

2. Laws, Rules, and Contract Provisions Relating to Arbitration

a. National Arbitration Laws

The operative provisions of the New York Arbitration Convention cover only four pages in the original document. The Convention addresses only the most basic principles, leaving the details of arbitration to national arbitration laws and institutional arbitration rules. The FAA, for example, empowers a court to appoint arbitrators if a party resisting arbitration fails to do so, 9 U.S.C. § 5, and it authorizes arbitrators to summon witnesses, 9 U.S.C. § 7.

The FAA, however, was enacted nearly a century ago, before Congress could be expected to understand the various ways in which a national law might advance arbitration if difficulties or disputes arise. Many nations have adopted as their national arbitration law a version of the more modern Model Law on International Commercial Arbitration promulgated in 1985 and amended in 2006 by the U.N. Commission on International Trade Law (UNCITRAL). The UNCITRAL Model Arbitration Law sets forth 36 articles addressing topics such as the composition of the arbitral tribunal, the grounds and procedures for challenging arbitrators, interim measures with the arbitral tribunal or in court, and the conduct of the main arbitral proceedings.

b. Rules of Arbitration Procedure

Most of the procedural rules in the Model Arbitration Law are default rules, ready to apply if the parties have not agreed to their own procedural rule on a topic. Because arbitration is a private mechanism that arises from the parties' agreement, the parties are free to define the procedure for arbitration. They could do this by negotiating specific procedural rules, but such a negotiation would be terribly time-consuming and would result in an exceedingly long arbitration agreement. If the parties desire to implement their arbitration on their own ("ad hoc" arbitration), they could incorporate into their arbitration agreement the arbitration rules already drafted by an institution. One such set of rules are the model rules of arbitration procedure promulgated in 1976 and revised in 2010, once again by UNCITRAL. The UNCITRAL Arbitration Rules are more detailed than the model national law. The parties could incorporate that body of procedural rules into their arbitration agreement, subject to any departures from those rules to which the parties specifically agree.

Rather than engage in ad hoc arbitration, however, parties typically agree to hire a designated arbitration institution to implement their arbitration proceedings. If so, they are agreeing to the procedural rules of that institution, subject again to any specific departures from those rules that the parties spell out in their agreement. For example, the parties could agree to arbitration with the International Court of Arbitration of the International Chamber of Commerce (ICC), headquartered in Paris. In so doing, they are agreeing to arbitration under the ICC Rules of Arbitration.

c. The Arbitration Agreement

The parties may agree to arbitration either before or after a dispute arises. Most typically, however, they agree to arbitration in a clause within their main commercial contract, sometimes called the container contract, because it contains the arbitration agreement as well as the commercial exchange between the parties. Accordingly, the parties typically agree to arbitration long before any dispute arises, and indeed at a time when the parties hope that their transaction will go smoothly.

In addition to a statement that the parties agree to submit disputes arising out of the contract to binding arbitration, the written arbitration agreement should designate:

- the main location or "seat" of the arbitration, which will identify the national arbitration law that will apply to support the arbitration;
- the arbitration institution that will implement the arbitration with its procedural rules;
- the language of arbitration; and
- the contract law that will govern any dispute.

Sample Arbitration Clause:

> 23. Dispute Resolution—The parties agree to submit any dispute arising out of this Sales Contract to binding arbitration, seated in Paris, France, with the ICC International Court of Arbitration and its procedural rules. The arbitration tribunal must conduct the proceedings in English and apply the contract laws applicable in New York, USA, including the U.N. Convention on Contracts for the International Sale of Goods.

The parties' agreement about dispute resolution need not be limited to arbitration. If they wish, they can agree that they must resort to other means of dispute resolution, such as negotiations and mediation, prior to filing a claim in arbitration.

B. California's Right to Repair Act

In 2002, the California legislature responded to concerns about the costs of construction defects litigation and its impact on the costs of residential construction. In a compromise between consumer advocates and the building industry, it enacted the Right to Repair Act. CAL. CIV. CODE §§ 896–938 (as amended 2015). Among other things, this legislation:

- sets forth construction standards and mandates a minimum warranty for individual dwellings, CAL. CIV. CODE §§ 896–897, 900; and
- sets forth procedures for resolution of consumer complaints *prior to litigation*, emphasizing repair of defects and both voluntary and mandatory mediation at different stages. CAL. CIV. CODE §§ 910–933.

In 2015, Arizona adopted similar right-to-repair legislation. Ariz. Rev. Stat. §§ 12-1361 to 12-1366.

The following opinion by the California Supreme Court addresses the extent to which the California Right to Repair Act's statutory rights, obligations, and procedures displace common law causes of action. In so doing, it addresses the economic loss rule, which limits recovery under common law to contract remedies, thus excluding a tort action for negligent construction, when a builder's defective construction results only in diminution of value to that house or in repair costs ("economic loss") and does not result in personal injury or in damage to property other than the defective construction. In such a case, the Act supersedes a common law action in contract by requiring resort to a prelitigation dispute resolution process prior to bringing an action in court. Does that statutory requirement extend as well to cases in which the homeowner has a tort claim for damage to property other than the defective construction itself?

McMillin Albany LLC v. Superior Court of Kern County

4 Cal. 5th 241, 408 P.3d 797 (2018)

Liu, J.

¶ 1 In *Aas v. Superior Court* (2000) 24 Cal. 4th 627, 632 (*Aas*), this court held that the economic loss rule bars homeowners suing in negligence for construction defects from recovering damages where there is no showing of actual property damage or personal injury. We explained that requiring a showing of more than economic loss was necessary to preserve the boundary between tort and contract theories of recovery, and to prevent tort law from expanding contractual warranties beyond what home builders had agreed to provide. (*Id.* at pp. 635–636; *see Seely v. White Motor Co.*

(1965) 63 Cal. 2d 9, 18.) We emphasized that the Legislature was free to alter these limits on recovery and to add whatever additional homeowner protections it deemed appropriate. (*Aas*, at pp. 650, 653.)

¶2 Two years later, spurred by *Aas* and by lobbying from homeowner and construction interest groups, the Legislature passed comprehensive construction defect litigation reform. (Stats. 2002, ch. 722, principally codified at Civ. Code, §§ 895–945.5 (commonly known as the Right to Repair Act, hereafter the Act); all further unlabeled statutory references are to the Civil Code.) The Act sets forth detailed statewide standards that the components of a dwelling must satisfy. It also establishes a prelitigation dispute resolution process that affords builders notice of alleged construction defects and the opportunity to cure such defects, while granting homeowners the right to sue for deficiencies even in the absence of property damage or personal injury.

¶3 We are asked to decide whether the lawsuit here, a common law action alleging construction defects resulting in both economic loss and property damage, is subject to the Act's prelitigation notice and cure procedures. The answer depends on the extent to which the Act was intended to alter the common law—specifically, whether it was designed only to abrogate *Aas*, supplementing common law remedies with a statutory claim for purely economic loss, or to go further and supplant the common law with new rules governing the method of recovery in actions alleging property damage. Based on an examination of the text and legislative history of the Act, we conclude the Legislature intended the broader displacement. Although the Legislature preserved common law claims for personal injury, it made the Act the virtually exclusive remedy not just for economic loss but also for property damage arising from construction defects. The present suit for property damage is therefore subject to the Act's prelitigation procedures, and the Court of Appeal was correct to order a stay until those procedures have been followed.

....

¶4 The list of recoverable damages in section 944 and the list of exceptions in section 943 have different consequences for recovery of economic losses, personal injury damages, and property damages:

¶5 *Economic Loss.* As noted, before the Act, tort recovery of purely economic losses occasioned by construction defects was forbidden by this court's decision in *Aas*. (*Aas*, *supra*, 24 Cal. 4th at p. 632.) Section 944 now specifies that various forms of economic loss are recoverable in an action under the Act. (§ 944 [listing among recoverable damages "the reasonable value of repairing any violation of the standards set forth in this title, the reasonable cost of repairing any damages caused by the repair efforts, ... the reasonable cost of removing and replacing any improper repair by the builder, reasonable relocation and storage expenses, lost business income if the home was used as a principal place of a business licensed to be operated from the home, [and] reasonable investigative costs for each established violation...."].) Consequently, a party suffering economic loss from defective construction may now bring an action to recover these damages under the Act without having to wait until the defect has caused property damage or personal injury. Were there any doubt, section 942 makes clear that "[i]n order to make a claim for violation of the" Act's standards, "[n]o further showing of causation or damages is required to meet the burden of proof regarding a violation of a standard."

¶6 *Personal Injury*. In contrast, personal injury damages are not listed as a category recoverable under the Act. (§944.) This omission places personal injury claims outside the scope of section 943, subdivision (a), which makes an action under the Act the exclusive remedy for those damages listed in section 944. To make the point even clearer, the Legislature also included personal injury claims in a list of claims that are exempt from the exclusivity of the Act. (§§931 [listing any action for "personal injuries" among the causes of action not covered by the Act], 943, subd. (a) ["this title does not apply to ... any action for ... personal injury ..."].) Thus, common law tort claims for personal injury are preserved.

¶7 *Property Damage*. As with economic losses, the Act expressly includes property damages resulting from construction defects among the categories of damages recoverable under the Act. (§944 [a homeowner may recover "the reasonable cost of repairing and rectifying any damages resulting from the failure of the home to meet the standards"]; *see* §896 [the Act applies to "recovery of damages arising out of, or related to" construction defects].) This places claims involving property damages within the purview of section 943, subdivision (a), which makes a claim under the Act the exclusive way to recover such damages. And unlike personal injury claims, negligence and strict liability claims for property damages are not among the few types of claims expressly excepted from section 943's exclusivity. (§943, subd. (a); *see* §931 [noting claims for personal injury, but not property damage, fall outside the Act's coverage].)

¶8 To sum up this portion of the statutory scheme: For economic losses, the Legislature intended to supersede *Aas* and provide a statutory basis for recovery. For personal injuries, the Legislature preserved the status quo, retaining the common law as an avenue for recovery. And for property damage, the Legislature replaced the common law methods of recovery with the new statutory scheme. The Act, in effect, provides that construction defect claims not involving personal injury will be treated the same procedurally going forward whether or not the underlying defects gave rise to any property damage.

....

¶9 Finally, the Van Tassels argue that the presumption against abrogation of the common law requires an express statement that the Legislature intended to displace existing remedies. It does not. (*Ante*, at p. 5.) Moreover, both sides agree that the Legislature in passing the Act sought to abrogate the common law, even though the text contains no express statement of that intent. They differ only in degree: The Van Tassels contend that the Legislature sought only to overrule the common law limits on recovery identified in *Aas*, whereas McMillin contends that the Legislature went further in supplanting certain common law claims with statutory ones. As explained above, we agree with McMillin's reading of the Act.

. . . .

¶ 10 The legislative history of the Act confirms that displacement of parts of the existing remedial scheme was no accident, but rather a considered choice to reform construction defect litigation.

¶ 11 First, language in the Legislature's analyses of the Act's effects reflects an intent that the Act would govern not only no damage cases, but cases where property damage had resulted. The Act's standards were designed so that "except where explicitly specified otherwise, liability would accrue under the standards regardless of whether the violation of the standard had resulted in actual damage or injury." (Sen. Com. on Judiciary, Analysis of Sen. Bill No. 800 (2001–2002 Reg. Sess.) as amended Aug. 28, 2002, p. 4.) Both halves of this intended application are significant: Liability under the standards would attach even in the absence of actual damage, thus effectively abrogating *Aas*. And liability under the standards would also attach in cases of actual damage; in other words, the Legislature anticipated that passage of the Act would result in standards that governed liability even when violation of the standards *had* resulted in property damage. The Legislature thus recognized and intended that claims under the Act would cover territory previously in the domain of the common law.

¶ 12 Second, the Act "establishes a mandatory process prior to the filing of a construction defect action," with the "major component of this process" being "the builder's absolute right to attempt a repair prior to a homeowner filing an action in court." (Sen. Com. on Judiciary, Analysis of Sen. Bill No. 800 (2001–2002 Reg. Sess.) as amended Aug. 28, 2002, p. 5.) These purposes, the creation of a mandatory prelitigation process and the granting of a right to repair, would be thwarted if we were to read the Act to permit homeowners to continue to sue as before at common law, without abiding by the procedural requirements of the Act, for construction defect claims involving damages other than economic loss.

¶ 13 Third, although there is no doubt that the Act had the intended effect of overriding *Aas*'s limits on construction defect actions, that effect was treated in both the Assembly and Senate as one consequence of the overall reform package, not as the principal goal of the Act....

¶ 14 In sum, the legislative history confirms what the statutory text reflects: the Act was designed as a broad reform package that would substantially change existing law by displacing some common law claims and substituting in their stead a statutory cause of action with a mandatory prelitigation process.

. . . .

CONCLUSION

¶ 15 We affirm the judgment of the Court of Appeal and remand for further proceedings not inconsistent with this opinion.

VI. Summary

- Specific enforcement is not a matter of right to a victim of breach. Even when it is a practical option, this equitable relief is available only when the legal remedy of money damages is inadequate, and even then it is left to the broad discretion of the trial judge.
- Money damages will normally be measured to protect expectation interest, by awarding an amount that places the victim of breach in the same economic position as though the contract had been performed.
- To accomplish this, the court should add or subtract any of the following components that are present in the case: Direct loss in value + incidental and consequential losses – costs or losses avoided (or that could have been avoided).
- Net gains from another transaction, however, are not deducted as loss avoided if it is not a true substitute transaction made possible only because of the breach, and if the victim's expectations thus were to earn income from both sources. (Example: Contractor does not deduct net profits from a second construction job taking place at the same time as the canceled project, if the Contractor could have and would have taken on both jobs at the same time and earned profit on both.)
- The victim of breach can recover only those damages that were foreseeable in light of information known at the time of contracting and that were proved with reasonable certainty (with greater need for certainty in proof of the fact of damages than the precise amount).
- In all but a few states, punitive damages are not allowed for even a deliberate breach of contract, and a damages clause in the contract will not be enforced if it imposes a penalty for breach rather than providing, as liquidated damages, a reasonable estimate of the uncertain damages that would be caused by a future breach.
- Damages for emotional distress are not recoverable except in rare cases in which the nature of the contract and the breach make it particularly foreseeable that emotional distress would be a consequence of breach, such as in breach of a contract with a funeral parlor, where the central purpose of the contract is to ease the survivors' grief and to protect their fragile emotions.

For sales of goods, the UCC applies principles compatible with the common law:

- If a seller repudiates or otherwise fails to deliver, the buyer may ask the court to exercise discretion to grant specific enforcement if money damages would be inadequate. Similarly, if the buyer has accepted goods but failed to pay the contract price, the seller can bring an action for the price.
- A buyer may accept and pay for nonconforming goods and recover the diminution in value as money damages.

- If the seller repudiates or otherwise fails to deliver or if the buyer rightfully rejects delivery, or if the buyer repudiates or wrongfully rejects the goods, the victim of breach can recover the difference between: (1) the contract price and (2) the market price of the goods or the price of substitute goods in a reasonable cover transaction. An aggrieved seller can recover such damages if #1 is higher; an aggrieved buyer can recover such damages if #2 is higher. An aggrieved seller, however, can alternatively recover lost profits if resold goods represent lost volume rather than a true substitute transaction.
- Buyers are entitled to foreseeable and unavoidable consequential losses, and buyers and sellers are entitled to reasonable incidental losses. Both must deduct costs or losses avoided.

Exercise 12.9 — Exam Questions

The following five exam questions may raise issues explored in any chapter of this book.

1. Q1: 50 minutes

After reading the following statement of facts, respond to each of the two problems (A & B) at the end of this question. For each problem, identify one or more issues, and for each issue summarize the applicable rule, apply the rule to the facts while trying to argue both sides, and reach a reasonable conclusion.

Debbie Driggs ("DD") owns a home on several acres in a remote area near a canyon and river, where desert grasses, shrubs, and small trees become an extreme fire hazard in the early, dry summer months. The landscaping immediately around DD's home consists of rock, gravel, and cacti, and she has a small swimming pool with a cement patio in the back of the house, on the south side. Most of her property, however, remains undeveloped, covered with grasses, and dotted with shrubs and an occasional small tree, all of which grows naturally in the canyon area.

To help firefighters save her home in the event of a brush fire, DD periodically hires a contractor to clear the natural growth within 60 feet of her home and its landscaping. This buffer zone of cleared land helps protect the home from flying sparks cast off by an approaching brush fire, making it easier for firefighters to save the home by dropping water or fire retardant chemicals on it from the air.

In 2011, winter rains and hot weather in the spring produced a tinderbox of tall dry grasses dotted with small dry shrubs on DD's property as the summer fire season approached. Because she had not cleared it for a few years, the growth presented an extreme fire hazard, so DD hired Kelly Contracting ("KC") to mow the grass and remove the shrubs within 60 feet of her home and landscaping.

KC measured the area to be cleared and presented a written estimate to DD that stated "mowing or clearing 4,000 square yards of grass and shrubs @ $0.25/sq. yd. = $1,000, work to be completed by June 5." You may assume that this estimate constituted an offer, which DD accepted by signing it at the bottom, forming a valid contract.

KC sent a crew of workers and equipment to clear growth on DD's property all day long on June 4, clearing about 80% of the brush and grasses around the house, leaving the 20% on the west side of the house uncleared. KC did not return on June 5. In response to DD's calls, KC notified DD by telephone at the end of the day on June 5 that KC had diverted all its resources to the other end of the canyon, where a brush fire was threatening several residential areas, and where brush clearing was urgently needed and would earn KC unusually high fees. KC said that it could come back to finish the work on DD's property, but only after it had attended to the more urgent needs at the other end of the canyon, and KC could not predict when that would be.

A. During the phone conversation late on June 5, KC requested that DD pay 80% ($800) of the total contract fee for the work completed. Discuss whether KC is entitled to payment on the contract for the work it completed, arguing both sides of the question if possible. Do not discuss possible recovery under quasi-contract.

B. For purposes of this question only, assume that after June 5 DD could find a substitute contractor to complete the clearing work only at a cost of $0.50 per square yard. She therefore left the work undone and waited for KC to complete the work. By June 10, high winds blowing from the west had helped the fire on the other end of canyon work its way to DD's vicinity, forcing her to evacuate. That night, it burned the high grass and shrubs on the west side of DD's home, with brisk winds causing showers of burning sparks to fly onto the sides and roof of DD's home. Although crews had dropped water on the home earlier in the day, during daylight hours, the assault of sparks and burning embers succeeded in igniting the house, which burned to the ground during the night. All but $40,000 of the resulting loss of the house and personal property is covered by insurance. DD sues KC for the $40,000 in uninsured losses, which she can document with certainty. Discuss whether KC is liable to DD for these $40,000 in losses, arguing both sides of the question if possible.

2. Q2: 80 minutes

John Kiting, doing business as Kiting Inc., owns and manages a sprawling luxury resort hotel, named Shangrila, in the fictitious state of Calzona. The guest rooms are scattered over a huge surface area, around swimming pools and other common areas, and connected by walkways, with lush landscaping throughout.

Kiting's business manager negotiated a five-year contract between Kiting Inc. and Cutting Edge Landscaping Service (CELS) for comprehensive landscaping services for the resort. In return for payment of $100,000 per year, CELS had agreed in a written, signed document entitled "Landscaping Agreement" to maintain all of Kiting's existing landscaping "in keeping with the high standards at Shangrila."

Several months after CELS began performing its contract, the landscaping at Shangrila was thriving and beautiful, and the hotel was exceedingly popular. The hotel was nearly filled to capacity at all times, with most rooms reserved many months in advance.

Kiting, however, was extremely unhappy with CELS's performance, because CELS used portable gas-powered leaf blowers to clear leaves off of the extensive network of walkways throughout the hotel grounds. Kiting abhorred these devices, because they were noisy and kicked up dust into the air. He also knew that the gasoline powered engines on the leaf blowers produced emissions that contributed to pollution. When CELS employees used these devices, Kiting often noticed that hotel guests took the long way around the area being worked on, to avoid the noise and dust. The leaf blowers also struck Kiting as supremely inconsistent with the beauty, serenity, and care for the environment that Kiting saw as a theme for his resort. Because the landscaping at Shangrila was so extensive, CELS had employees working on some portion of the grounds every day, with a leaf blower being used somewhere on the ground—at least for a few minutes—nearly every day.

Kiting called Robert Cruz, the owner of CELS, and demanded that CELS cease using gas-powered leaf blowers while performing the landscaping contract. He insisted that employees use brooms and leaf rakes instead. Cruz rejected these demands, explaining accurately that gas-powered leaf blowers were used routinely throughout the industry in Calzona, that replacing leaf blowers with brooms and rakes would reduce CELS's efficiency and increase costs (and thus reduce his profits from $20,000 to $10,000 each year), and that CELS employees felt that the leaf blowers made them feel cool and powerful but would find brooms and rakes to be demeaning in comparison.

Kiting has consulted you, his attorney, to discuss his options. He wishes that he had hired Gentle Touch Landscaping Co. (GTLC), which prides itself in quiet, environmentally friendly landscaping methods, and which is still available at the same fees charged by CELS.

During his interview with you, Kiting asserts the following: Before signing the Landscaping Agreement in his office on behalf of his company, Kiting explained to Robert Cruz, owner of CELS, that Kiting was a great believer in protecting the environment, and in harmony, serenity, and balance in nature. He added that Shangrila reflected that philosophy in many ways. Kiting then stated that he expected CELS to refrain from using "the infernal gas-powered leaf blowers" in performing the contract, to which Cruz said "no problem," shortly before both signed.

Kiting seems perfectly credible in his description of this conversation, but Cruz denies these statements and you note that the written "Landscaping Agreement" says nothing about what equipment CELS must or must not use, even though it otherwise states the duties of both parties in great detail in 20 sections over four pages. The written agreement contains no merger clause and does not otherwise mention anything about the completeness of the agreement.

Fully discuss Kiting's rights under the Landscaping Agreement relevant to Kiting's desires to exclude leaf blowers, including whether Kiting can introduce evidence of the alleged oral agreement to refrain from using leaf blowers, and the remedies or other options that might be available to Kiting if he can prove that term. (With respect to judicial remedies, I haven't given you facts from which you can actually calculate damages, but—if you assume a breach by CELS at some point in your answer—you can include a discussion of judicial remedies at a general level.)

You can assume that Kiting and Cruz have authority to enter into contracts on behalf of their companies. You may assume that the Agreement was validly entered into with offer and acceptance and consideration, without any defects in its formation, so you should not discuss those issues. You may refer to Landscaping Agreement as "LA" if you like.

3. Q3, with Three Question Prompts: 90 minutes

Masahiro Sato, an experienced chef and businessman, opened up his new Sushi Restaurant, *Sato's Sushi*, between an ice cream parlor and a coffee shop in a small grouping of three commercial tenants (the "strip mall"). This small strip mall is owned by Jill Dell, and it sits adjacent to a larger shopping mall that features a popular *Gracy's* department store.

For the first year of operation beginning in January 2018, Sato negotiated a month-to-month lease while he determined whether the sushi restaurant would succeed. Due to Sato's vision, culinary artistry, and hard work, and due to the restaurant's location close to *Gracy's*, Sato's restaurant was indeed a rousing success from the first month of operation. By December, he was on course for earning expected net profits for the year amounting to $150,000, which would be 25% of expected gross revenue of $600,000.

On December 2, 2018, Dell drafted, signed, and offered to Sato a new, two-page, written five-year lease (the "new Lease"), which would commence January 1, 2019. Section 2 of the new Lease required Sato to pay Dell a base rent of $1,000 each month ($500 below the market rate of $1,500 if this were the total rent), plus a payment at year end of 2% of Sato's gross revenue for the year. Section 10 of the new Lease also required Sato to stay "open for business from at least noon until midnight, at least six days each week, if revenue accruing each month from shorter hours will not adequately supplement the base rent."

Sato signed the lease just before opening the restaurant at noon on December 2, after a busy night at the restaurant on December 1. Before signing, Sato objected to the terms in sections 2 and 10, in the following conversation with Dell:

> Sato: "You want 2% of my revenue on top of the base rent? I know this is a great location, but this is crazy. If this provision had applied to the current year, it would have doubled the base rent by the end of the year. Let's delete that clause right now."
>
> Dell: "Hey, you're making good money, and you seem to recognize that this great location has made it all possible. I deserve a piece of this money machine. This is my only offer. Take it or leave it."
>
> Sato: "Yeah, you know I won't leave now that my restaurant is a big hit here. But what's this clause in section 10 about staying open until midnight if you need more revenue? Everyone in this suburb eats dinner between 5:30 and 8:30; it doesn't pay for me to keep a staff past 9. Cross this section out."
>
> Dell: "Sorry, my attorney won't let me change this form lease. You're already working shorter hours than either of the other shops in my mall. The ice cream shop runs from noon to midnight, and the coffee house runs from 8 a.m. to midnight! Anyway, I'm hoping this clause won't ever apply to your popular dinner place. Just sign and keep making lots of money."

Sato signed and hurried to open his restaurant for the day.

Dell knew something at the December 2 signing that Sato did not: *Gracy's* had declared bankruptcy and would be selling out its inventory during December 2018, closing the store on December 31. This story had been reported briefly on the local television news the previous evening, and the local newspaper had reported the story in its morning edition on December 2. Dell had heard and confirmed this news; however, Sato had been too busy to follow the news. Dell knew that *Gracy's* departure would hurt business at her entire strip mall, and she wanted to retain *Sato's Sushi*, which was the strongest of the three businesses in the strip mall and which stood a chance of continuing to generate substantial revenue.

As shoppers flocked to *Gracy's* during its December closeout sales, *Sato's Sushi* did great business. As the new Lease commenced in January 2019, however, and as the old *Gracy's* space stood empty, Sato's revenue fell steeply. Dell invoked clause 10 and demanded that Sato keep the restaurant open until midnight every night. Sato refused to do so, asserting that section 10 wasn't triggered. He conceded that he might generate modest additional revenue for Dell with the extra hours, but he noted that the expenses of staying open late likely would exceed the small amount of additional revenue, so that Sato's own profits might decrease. He couldn't be sure, but he wasn't willing to risk late-night losses.

Fully and separately discuss in IRAC form each of the issues that are raised by the three questions below, taking care to argue both sides when feasible. Before you begin analyzing and writing, carefully read all three questions, so that you understand how the problem is divided into stages and so that you limit your discussion in each stage. You may assume that none of the issues is governed by a statute and that you can apply general common law principles.

1. Discuss any ground or grounds that Sato might reasonably assert in court to avoid or otherwise deny enforcement of the new Lease in its entirety, so that Sato would not be further obligated to Dell and would be free to move his restaurant to another location.

2. Assume for purposes of this part only that Sato's arguments in #1 above are rejected, so that the new Lease is found to be generally enforceable. Without repeating any of the theories or claims discussed in #1 above, discuss a different ground that Sato could reasonably assert to establish that section 10 of the new Lease is not enforceable.

3. Assume for purposes of this part only that Sato's arguments in both #1 and #2 above are rejected, and that section 10 is found to be triggered by the drop in revenue, so that Sato is found to be in breach of section 10, because he has at all times operated *Sato's Sushi* only from noon until 9 p.m. six nights each week. Assume further that Dell treats this as a minor breach and thus does not cancel the lease. After Sato repeatedly rejected Dell's demands, Dell sues Sato in late December 2019 for specific performance — to begin January 2020 — of section 10 for the remainder of the five-year lease (at times when section 10's terms are still triggered) and for money damages for the share of additional revenue that would have been paid to Dell at the end of 2019 if Sato had stayed open till midnight during the year. Discuss the success or difficulties that Dell likely will encounter in pursuing these two remedies. You may assume that the new Lease contains no provisions about remedies.

4. Q4: 25 minutes

Federal law and the law of State X criminalize the possession or sale of marijuana. Newly developed synthetic chemicals affect people in a way that is quite similar to the effect of marijuana when the chemicals are sprayed on dried herbs and smoked. Boomer Products, a manufacturer/distributor in State X, has sprayed these chemicals on herbs and sold the product as incense under the brand name "Cloud," with a warning label that the product is "not for human consumption." It is well know that consumers, mostly college students, have purchased Cloud as a form of "legal marijuana," for the purpose of smoking it and getting "high."

On November 1, the State X legislature passed a statute that prohibited the possession or sale of products containing the synthetic chemicals in question (such as Cloud), effective January 1. The State X Attorney General announced that businesses should sell or otherwise dispose of such products over the next two months, because they will violate state law beginning on January 1. Sales of Cloud skyrocketed at this news, as consumers of the product rushed to purchase the product while it was still available. In the meantime, Cloud remains completely unregulated for its labeled use under all relevant laws through the end of the calendar year. If it was sold for purposes of smoking through a pipe or in a cigarette, it would not be illegal to sell or possess before the new year, but it would be regulated by federal agencies in various ways.

On November 3, Boomer Products agreed to sell its remaining stock of Cloud to Water Pipe World (WPW), a retail chain of stores in State X that sells various forms of pipes, cigarette papers, and tobaccos or other herbs for smoking. Their contract called for delivery to WPW stores within one week and payment of a total of $50,000 to Boomer Products by December 3.

By December 13, WPW had sold all its stock of Cloud, making a nice profit, but it had not paid Boomer Products any of the $50,000 contract price. On December 13, WPW announced that it was not legally obligated to pay Boomer Products and would not do so.

Identify the single best basis for WPW avoiding liability to Boomer Products for breach of contract, and discuss that issue fully in IRAC form, arguing both sides to the extent possible.

5. Q5: 60 minutes

State X owns four acres of undeveloped land ("the Land") overlooking the ocean at Sea Cliff state beach and park. State X employees mow the wild grass on the Land once a month, making it a popular place for residents and visitors to stroll, walk their dogs, fly kites, or take photographs of the beach and ocean below. Developers would pay tens of millions for the Land, because it would be a prime site for several condominium buildings with ocean views. Tests have also shown that valuable mineral deposits lie just below the surface of the Land. Until the recession of 2009, State X had preferred to retain the Land in its natural state for public use.

Budget cuts in 2010–11, however, compelled State X to find every possible source of revenue, leading to its decision to lease the Land to a mineral extraction firm (Mineral Corp.) for two years, as one of many such measures. Several provisions of the contract between State X and Mineral Corp. (the Lease) are summarized below:

- State X will transfer to Mineral Corp. the rights to occupy and extract minerals below the surface of each of four defined acres of the Land during the calendar years 2011 and 2012, with the occupation and extraction rights limited to one designated acre every six months and allowing public use of the unoccupied acres.
- Mineral Corp. will pay State X $250,000 on January 1 and June 1 of each year of the lease, for a total payment of $1 million in lease and extraction fees.
- Immediately on completing extraction of each acre, Mineral Corp. will fill voids left on that acre, restore the topsoil, and seed the topsoil with wild grasses to guard against erosion and to permit a return to public use as soon as possible. If Mineral Corp. fails to restore any portion of the Land in this manner, it will be liable to State X for agreed-upon damages of $100,000 for each acre in which some portion is left unrestored, which the parties have estimated would be the maximum cost of restoration of an acre that had been deeply and broadly extracted.

By the end of May 2011, which was the end of Mineral Corp.'s extraction rights on the first acre of the Land, Mineral Corp. had paid its first fee of $250,000 and had completed its extraction of valuable minerals on the first acre of the Land. It announced, however, that it would not fill voids left by its extraction on the first acre, nor would it replace the topsoil. It explained that it was barely making a profit in its extraction of minerals from the first acre and that the cost of restoring that acre would cause it to operate at a loss. All agree that the actual cost of restoring the first acre, which had been extracted to moderate depth, is $50,000.

Mineral Corp. conceded that it was in breach of contract and is willing to pay damages based on the difference between the market value of the acre if restored and its value as left unrestored. That difference in value, however, is likely no more than $10,000 because the market value of the land is based on development for condos, and a developer likely would alter the land anyway, such as by excavating for parking garages, swimming pools, and foundations for the condos.

State X is very unhappy with Mineral Corp.'s actions and position. The first acre is unsightly and will be unsafe for pedestrians when it is returned to State X, because it has been left with pits and uneven grades. State X wants to prevent Mineral Corp. from leaving the other acres in a similar condition, even if it means kicking Mineral Corp. off the Land and foregoing further payments on the Lease. It also desires maximum available damages, partly so that it can hire a contractor to restore the first acre to an even grade with seeded topsoil. It does not seek specific enforcement of Mineral Corp.'s restoration obligations, because it no longer trusts Mineral Corp. to restore the Land as required by the Lease.

Discuss the rights and liabilities of the parties that are raised by these facts, including the options open to State X consistent with its interests. Discuss each issue in a separate IRAC, and argue both sides whenever feasible. You may assume that no statutes provide special rules for contracts with a governmental entity. Apply only general common law principles. Do not discuss an issue unless it is raised by the stated facts and are consistent with State X's stated interests.

If you run out of time near the end of the exam, you should consider using your last few minutes conveying the remainder of your analysis in outline form, using words and phrases rather than complete sentences.

Chapter 13

Rights of Contract Beneficiaries

I. Introduction

In most of the contractual relationships we have studied, two parties have undertaken obligations to perform directly to each other. In such cases, each party receives the benefit of the other's performance and typically is the only one who may enforce the other party's obligations.

In some cases, however, two parties create contract rights in a third party by entering the contract with the specific intent of providing benefits to the third party. Consider the following example:

> Andy promises to pay Arizona Life Insurance Co. a monthly premium in return for Arizona Life Insurance Co.'s promise to pay $100,000 upon Andy's death to any person Andy names as the "beneficiary." Andy names his child, Isabel, as the beneficiary of the life insurance policy.

This typical life insurance contract is an example of a "third party beneficiary contract." Although the insurer made its promise to Andy, the parties clearly intended to benefit Isabel and even specifically characterized her as the "beneficiary." As an "intended beneficiary," Isabel has a right to enforce the insurer's contractual obligation if it fails to pay her the promised benefits on Andy's death, even though she was not a party to the contract. *See* RESTATEMENT (SECOND) OF CONTRACTS § 304 (1981).

The distinguishing feature of a third party beneficiary contract is the creation of the third party's contractual rights **when the contract is formed** and not through later assignment of rights. In contrast, through *assignment*, one party transfers to a third person the right to receive the performance of the other party **after the contract is formed**. This chapter will describe the legal principles that govern contract beneficiaries. Chapter 14 explores the legal principles that apply to assignment of contractual rights and delegation of contractual duties.

As you work through this chapter, consider the following questions:

- How do the majority of courts determine whether a third party is an intended beneficiary as distinguished from an incidental beneficiary?
- How does the approach in Arizona compare to the majority approach?

- What are the rights of an intended beneficiary?
- How and when do the rights of an intended beneficiary vest?
- Against whom are the rights of an intended beneficiary enforceable?
- What defenses can the obligated party raise against a claim advanced by an intended beneficiary?

II. Creation, Vesting, and Enforcement of Third Party Rights

A. Distinguishing between Intended Beneficiaries and Incidental Beneficiaries

If the parties to a contract did not intend to benefit a third party, the third party will have no legal rights under the contract, even if the third party would derive some incidental benefits from one or more performances of the contract. An "incidental beneficiary" cannot enforce the contract if one of the parties to the contract fails to perform. *See* RESTATEMENT (SECOND) OF CONTRACTS § 302(2) (1981) (distinguishing between intended and incidental beneficiaries).

A third party is most clearly an intended beneficiary if the parties specifically and expressly stated an intention to benefit that party in the contract. In the majority of states, however, courts will recognize third party rights when more general contract language or other circumstances reflect the parties' intention to benefit the third party.

The second Restatement recognizes third party beneficiary status if "appropriate to effectuate the intention of the parties," and if (a) the promised performance will satisfy an obligation owed by the promisee to the beneficiary, or (b) "the circumstances" show an intention by the promisee to benefit the beneficiary. RESTATEMENT (SECOND) OF CONTRACTS § 302(1) (1981). Even when adopted by a court, however, the Restatement test leaves ample room for debate about precisely how the court should determine the intention to benefit a third party. *See* David M. Summers, *Third Party Beneficiaries and the Restatement (Second) of Contracts*, 67 CORNELL L. REV. 880, 887–99 (1982).

As you read the following case, pay attention to the standard used by the court in determining whether a third party had acquired the rights of an intended beneficiary. Who is the promisee, and who is the promisor? What is the promise that benefits third parties? Who are the third party beneficiaries of the contract? Must the third party be identified in the contract when it is formed? How clear is the expression of intent to benefit a third party in this case? Was a promise benefiting the third party made at all? What public policy interests appear to be served by the outcome in this case?

Wolfgang v. Mid-America Motor Sports

111 F.3d 1515 (10th Cir. 1997)

[footnotes and internal citations omitted; paragraphing modified from original]

[Wolfgang, a race car driver, sued several parties who had been involved in promoting and conducting a "media day" practice session at Lakeside Speedway in Kansas City, Kansas. During the practice race, Wolfgang's car hit a tire at the edge of the track and swerved out of control into a concrete retaining wall. He was knocked unconscious, and his car caught fire. Because firefighters at the track were inadequate in number and were not adequately trained or equipped, Wolfgang remained in his burning car for eight to ten minutes before he could be extricated. As a result, he suffered injuries that could have been prevented by proper firefighting precautions.

Wolfgang sued the speedway in tort. He sued the organizer of the event, World of Outlaws, for breach of contract, claiming that he was a third party beneficiary of a contract entered into between the speedway and the organizer. In that contract, the organizer had promised that it would ensure safe racing conditions, including adequate fire protection, during the practice race. The jury awarded damages of $1,215,000 against the defendants.

On appeal, the U.S. Court of Appeals for the Tenth Circuit affirmed the tort judgment against the speedway. It also affirmed judgment against the organizer, World of Outlaws, on the theory that Wolfgang was an intended beneficiary of the contract between the speedway and the organizer. The federal court is exercising diversity jurisdiction and so is applying state law, in this case Kansas law.]

Kelly, Circuit Judge.

¶1 World of Outlaws argues that … it is merely a sanctioning body for sprint car races, and that as such, it owed no duty to provide or ensure adequate fire protection for sprint car drivers. The district court ruled, however, that there was sufficient evidence to show that World of Outlaws owed a duty to Mr. Wolfgang to ensure safe racing conditions on the day of the crash.

¶2 Defendants Mid-America Motorsports and World of Outlaws contracted to stage sprint car races at Lakeside Speedway on April 4 and 5, 1992. They entered into a standard contract, written by World of Outlaws, which Mid-America Motorsports was not permitted to change or deviate from in any way. In the section detailing the services World of Outlaws would provide, paragraph 10 states: "Designated World of Outlaws officials shall have the right to cancel any event due to unsafe racing conditions." Mr. Wolfgang alleged that this provision created a contractual obligation on the part of World of Outlaws to ensure that racing conditions were safe, and that as a participating driver, he was a third party beneficiary to this provision in the contract.…

¶3 A person may sue for damages resulting from the breach of a contractual obligation, even though he was not a party to the contract and had no knowledge of it when made, if he was an intended beneficiary of that obligation. It is not necessary that the third party be identified in the contract or at the time of contracting in order to be an intended beneficiary.

¶4 In determining the intent of the contracting parties with respect to whether a third party is an intended beneficiary, we must apply the general rules for construction of contracts. The intention of the parties and the meaning of the contract are to be determined from the instrument itself where the terms are plain and unambiguous. However, we will consider evidence of the facts and circumstances surrounding its execution when the instrument is ambiguous on its face and requires aid to clarify its intent.

¶5 The contract between World of Outlaws and Mid-America Motorsports merely states that World of Outlaws officials "shall have the right to cancel any event due to unsafe racing conditions." As an initial matter we think it is unassailable that the adequacy of fire protection for drivers is contemplated in the phrase "unsafe racing conditions." Second, World of Outlaws officials—the contracting party—are not actually racing on the track during an event, so "unsafe racing conditions" can only reasonably refer to World of Outlaws member-drivers and the race-going public that may be trackside watching the race. Thus, the instrument could be construed as clearly and unambiguously expressing the parties' intent that "safe racing conditions" benefit drivers such as Mr. Wolfgang. It is certainly not a clear and unambiguous expression that the parties did not intend to benefit the race car drivers.

¶6 At best for Defendants' sake the contract is ambiguous. In that case we look to the evidence adduced at trial to determine if race car drivers were intended beneficiaries. In his trial testimony, Ted Johnson, President of World of Outlaws, admitted that paragraph 10 imposed on World of Outlaws an obligation to ensure safe racing conditions, and that the drivers were direct beneficiaries of that obligation. Mr. Johnson also acknowledged that the presence of adequate firefighting equipment was one of the requirements for a race track to be safe, and he admitted that World of Outlaws had a responsibility to its member drivers to bring them only to racetracks that had adequate firefighting capabilities. Mr. Johnson further testified that if a track did not have adequate firefighting capabilities as part of its safety equipment, World of Outlaws drivers would be unnecessarily exposed to excessive danger. Thus, whether we consider such extrinsic evidence to clarify this ambiguous contract provision, or construe the provision as a clear and unambiguous expression of the parties' intent, we reach the same conclusion: Mr. Wolfgang, as a World of Outlaws sprint car driver, was an intended beneficiary of the contract between World of Outlaws and Mid-America Motorsports....

¶7 We therefore hold that World of Outlaws owed a legal duty to its member-drivers to ensure that Lakeside Speedway had adequate fire protection on the day Mr. Wolfgang crashed....

As you read the next case, *Norton v. First Federal Savings*, consider whether the Arizona courts follow the Restatement test, which permits parties to establish that they are intended beneficiaries from circumstances appearing outside the text of the contract. Or are the Arizona courts more demanding?

As you study *Norton*, construct a chart that identifies:

- the plaintiff third parties, along with the contractual promise they seek to enforce;
- the promisor and promisee on the obligation that the third parties seek to enforce;
- the entity to whom the promisor directly owed its duty to pay if construction of off-site improvements is faulty or incomplete.

Norton v. First Federal Savings

128 Ariz. 176, 624 P2d 854 (1981)

Gordon, Justice:

¶ 1 Plaintiffs/appellants entered into agreements on July 21, 1974, to purchase from Clyde Hutcheson three subdivision lots in Pinecrest Terrace Unit Six in the City of Flagstaff. As required by city ordinance, Hutcheson had posted a performance bond on August 7, 1973, with First Federal Savings as surety, to guarantee construction of off-site improvements on these lots.

¶ 2 On November 29, 1977, plaintiffs amended their complaint to add defendant/appellee First Federal Savings as a party. On May 2, 1978, plaintiffs filed a second amended complaint, Counts Four and Five of which sought damages from First Federal Savings due to Hutcheson's failure to complete the off-site improvements. Count Four alleged that plaintiffs were entitled to recover damages under the performance bond because they were third-party beneficiaries of the contract whereby First Federal agreed with Hutcheson to post such a bond. On July 8, 1978, partial summary judgment was entered in favor of First Federal Savings as to Counts Four and Five of plaintiffs' second amended complaint. It is from this partial summary judgment that plaintiffs now appeal. We affirm.

¶ 3 The Arizona rule is that in order for a person to recover as a third-party beneficiary of a contract, an intention to benefit that person must be indicated in the contract itself, *Irwin v. Murphey*, 81 Ariz. 148, 302 P.2d 534 (1956); *Basurto v. Utah Construction & Mining Co.*, 15 Ariz. App. 35, 485 P.2d 859 (1971). The contemplated benefit must be both intentional and direct, *Irwin, supra, Treadway v. Western Cotton Oil Etc. Co.*, 40 Ariz. 125, 10 P.2d 371 (1932), and "it must definitely appear that the parties intend to recognize the third party as the primary party in interest," *Irwin, supra,* at 154, 302 P.2d at 538.

....

¶ 4 Plaintiffs have pointed to nothing in any contract between First Federal Savings and Hutcheson which demonstrates an intention to benefit them. Nor does any intent to benefit plaintiffs appear in the terms of the bond. Rather, it appears from the record that plaintiffs' real contention is that they should be allowed to recover as third-party beneficiaries of the bond because the city's purpose in requiring performance bonds such as this one was to benefit purchasers of subdivision lots.

¶ 5 We have said that in the case of a bond given in compliance with a statute, the statute constitutes a part of the bond. *Employer's Liability Assur. Corp. v. Lunt*, 82 Ariz. 320, 313 P.2d 393 (1957). Plaintiff claims that the bond under consideration here was given in compliance with City of Flagstaff Ordinance 689 as mandated by A.R.S. § 9-463.01 C(8). We see nothing in the language of either piece of legislation which indicates an intent to create rights in lot purchasers to recover damages from a surety company in the event off-site improvements are not completed in a timely fashion.

....

¶ 6 Going to the merits of the argument, ... we note that there is a vast difference between identifying the broad purpose of an entire statutory scheme and holding that, because of such broad purpose, a benefitted group gains rights in contracts to which they are not parties. Assuming that the purpose of A.R.S. § 9-463.01 may be to insure that municipal subdivision lot buyers are provided with adequately improved lots, it does not follow that those lot buyers can sue for damages as third-party beneficiaries of performance bonds which may be required under subsection C(8) of that statute.

....

¶ 7 Municipalities have their own separate and identifiable interests in requiring performance bonds such as that called for in Section III(B)(4)(b). If a subdivision developer failed to finish off-site improvements after selling the subdivision lots, any improvements completed thereafter would be accomplished by the city with city funds. Similarly, if the developer installed defective improvements and refused to correct the defects, any repairs or alterations would be undertaken by the city. Performance bonds which insure the proper completion of street, sewer and water utilities by subdivision developers protect the city from the necessity of spending its citizens' money to fulfill the developers' responsibilities.

¶ 8 The purpose of requiring a performance bond from a subdivision developer who sells unimproved lots would seem to be assurance that the required off-site improvements are completed. The bond posted here could be satisfied either by the developer's satisfactory construction of improvements or by payment to the City of Flagstaff of the predicted cost of that construction for the city's use in completing the improvements. Allowing private lot buyers to collect on the performance bond for damages they suffered due to untimely completion of improvements would frustrate the purpose of the bond by depleting the funds thereby provided for the city's construction of improvements.

¶ 9 It is obvious that plaintiffs also have an interest in having these improvements completed, but in the absence of wording in the statute and/or ordinance to the contrary, it would be unreasonable to conclude that protection of the City of Flagstaff's interests was not the primary purpose of the bond requirement.

¶ 10 We feel, therefore, that plaintiffs are third party beneficiaries of neither the performance bond nor a contract between First Federal Savings and Hutcheson to post such a bond. Therefore, the trial court was correct in granting summary judgment in favor of First Federal on Count Four of plaintiffs' second amended complaint.

As you analyze *Norton*, it might help to know that the common law does not readily recognize third party beneficiary rights when a contractor enters into a contract with government to provide services to the public. *See* Restatement (Second) of Contracts § 313 (1981). The elevated requirements for establishing third party rights in a government contract are discussed in some detail in the next case, *Martinez*. Although *Norton* presents a suit between private parties, consider whether the presence of an ordinance to protect a city's finances helps to justify its holding. On the other hand, the court's statement of the law and its citation to precedent seem to apply broadly to any contract between private parties, and not just one in which a contractual obligation is required by ordinance. *See, e.g., Nahom v. Blue Cross & Blue Shield of Ariz., Inc.*, 180 Ariz. 548, 551–52, 885 P.2d 1113, 1116–17 (Ct. App. 1994) (applying *Norton* standards to private contract).

In light of *Norton*, Arizona's Revised Jury Instructions require the intent to benefit a third party to appear from the "contract itself":

> To recover, (name of third party) must prove:
>
> 1. The parties intended that (name of third party) directly benefit from the contract;
>
> 2. The parties intended to recognize (name of third party) as the primary party in interest; and
>
> 3. The contract itself indicated an intent to benefit (name of third party) or a class of persons including (name of third party).

Revised Arizona Jury Instructions (Civil, 6th ed. 2018).

Arizona's approach leaves open questions about the specificity with which the contract must identify the requisite intent. Can the parties' intent to benefit third party race car drivers be gleaned from a contract clause stating a general obligation to "ensure safe racing conditions" as in the *Wolfgang* case? Or will an Arizona court require the contract to expressly identify the third parties or class of third parties, and expressly state the intention to benefit them? Is it simply a matter of finding a contract term that arguably reflects the requisite intent and then employing permissible means of contract interpretation, including extrinsic evidence? *See generally Nahom v. Blue Cross & Blue Shield of Ariz., Inc.*, 180 Ariz. 548, 551–52, 885 P.2d 1113, 1116–17 (Ct. App. 1994) (describing this approach but finding the requisite intention without relying on extrinsic evidence). For a similarly demanding approach on this issue in Texas, see *First Bank v. Brumitt*, 519 S.W.3d 95 (Tex. 2017).

The next case, *Martinez*, is an unpublished decision of a federal trial court, so it has no precedential value. Nonetheless, it reflects careful application of third party beneficiary standards and so invites synthesis with *Norton*. Is *Martinez* consistent with *Norton*?

Unlike in *Norton*, which implicated governmental interests in a private contract, the third-party beneficiary contract in *Martinez* is in fact a government contract, thus even more clearly requiring a strong showing before recognizing an individual as an intended beneficiary. Is the procedural posture in *Martinez* significant? Or was the outcome compelled by facts that can be proved as easily as they are pleaded?

Martinez v. Cenlar, FSB

No. CV-13-00589-TUC-CKJ (D. Ariz. Sept. 3, 2014)
[Not reported in F. Supp. 3d] [footnotes omitted]

Cindy K. Jorgenson, District Judge.

. . . .

I. Background

A. Facts

¶ 1 Plaintiff purchased a house in Tucson, Arizona on March 7, 2008. Doc. 11 at ¶ 7. In the spring of 2010, Plaintiff lost her job and began experiencing financial difficulties. *Id.* at ¶ 8. On August 9, 2010, Plaintiff received a Notice of Trustee Sale. *Id.* at ¶ 9. After negotiating with her lender, MeriWest Credit Union, the Trustee Sale was cancelled and her mortgage payments were temporarily reduced. *Id.* However, one year later in August 2011, the temporary modification of her mortgage payments expired and her payment was increased. *Id.* at ¶ 10.

¶ 2 Plaintiff made the first two mortgage payments after the expiration of the temporary loan modification; however, she was unable to continue making payments. *Id.* at ¶ 11. On August 26, 2011, Defendant, Plaintiff's loan servicer, signed a contract with the Arizona Department of Housing, which is responsible for running the Arizona Hardest Hit Fund ("HHF") program. *Id.* at ¶ 14. The contract provides that "[u]pon notification that a borrower has been conditionally approved for HHF, the Servicer shall not initiate the foreclosure process or, if the borrower is already in the foreclosure process, [shall delay] a foreclosure sale for 45 days, with any extensions by mutual consent of the Eligible Entity and the Servicer." *Id.* at ¶ 15.

¶ 3 In April 2012, Plaintiff received a foreclosure notice. *Id.* at ¶ 12. In response, Plaintiff applied for the HHF program for assistance with her mortgage. *Id.* She was approved for Underemployment Assistance through the HHF, which provides a maximum monthly assistance of $2,000 for a term of 24 months. *Id.* at ¶ 13. On June 26, 2012, Defendant received an "I" record from the Arizona Department of

Housing indicating their intent to provide payment assistance to Plaintiff through the HHF program. *Id.* at ¶¶ 16, 19.

¶ 4 On July 3, 2012, Plaintiff's house was sold at an auction without Plaintiff's knowledge. *Id.* at ¶ 21. On July 6, 2012, Defendant sent an objection to the Arizona Department of Housing regarding Plaintiff's HHF assistance because the house had been foreclosed on July 3, 2012. *Id.* at ¶ 22. The sale of Plaintiff's house was irreversible, and Plaintiff was forced to vacate her home in July 2012. *Id.* at ¶¶ 23, 26.

B. Procedural History

¶ 5 On July 3, 2013, Plaintiff filed a Complaint. (Doc. 1). On July 25, 2013, Defendant filed a Motion to Dismiss Plaintiff's Complaint Pursuant to Fed. R. Civ. P. 12(b)(6). (Doc. 7)....

....

II. Motion for Judgment on the Pleadings

A. Governing Standard

¶ 6 Fed. R. Civ. P. 12(c) provides that, "[a]fter the pleadings are closed—but early enough not to delay trial—a party may move for judgment on the pleadings." Dismissal through a motion for judgment on the pleadings is appropriate "'only if it is clear that no relief could be granted under any set of facts that could be proven consistent with the allegations.'" *McGlinchy v. Shell Chemical Co.*, 845 F.2d 802, 810 (9th Cir.1988) (quoting *Hishon v. King & Spalding*, 467 U.S. 69, 73 ... (1984)). Judgment on the pleadings is appropriate when the moving party establishes that there are no material issues of fact to resolve and it is entitled to judgment as a matter of law. *Hal Roach Studios, Inc. v. Richard Feiner & Co., Inc.*, 896 F.2d 1542, 1550 (9th Cir. 1989). "All allegations of fact of the opposing party are accepted as true." *Austad v. United States*, 386 F.2d 147, 149 (1967). Furthermore, all inferences reasonably drawn from the alleged facts must be construed in favor of the responding party. *General Conference Corp. of Seventh-Day Adventists v. Seventh Day Adventist Congregational Church*, 887 F.2d 228, 230 (9th Cir.1989). However, conclusory allegations are insufficient to defeat a motion for judgment on the pleadings. *McGlinchy*, 845 F.2d at 810.

¶ 7 The Court may consider any matter set forth in the complaint which is subject to judicial notice. *Outdoor Media Group, Inc. v. City of Beaumont*, 506 F.3d 896, 899 (9th Cir. 2007). The Court may take judicial notice of "matters of public record" outside the pleadings without converting a motion for judgment on the pleadings into a motion for summary judgment. Fed. R. Evid. 201;.... The Court also may consider a document that is attached and referred to in the complaint without converting the motion into a motion for summary judgment if its authenticity is not questioned. *Branch v. Tunnell*, 14 F.3d 449, 453–454 (9th Cir. 1994), *overruled on other grounds*, *Galbraith v. County of Santa Clara*, 307 F.3d 1119 (9th Cir. 2002).

B. Discussion

1. Breach of Contract

¶8 Defendant entered into a Servicer Participation Agreement (Agreement) with the Arizona Department of Housing on August 26, 2011, in which Defendant agreed to participate in the HHF program. (Doc. 11 at ¶31). The purpose of the HHF program is to assist unemployed homeowners to keep their homes by providing monetary assistance. (*Id.* at ¶¶32, 33.) According to Plaintiff, Defendant breached the Agreement when it failed to delay the foreclosure proceedings in accordance with the terms of the Agreement despite receiving prior notice that Plaintiff had been approved for assistance through the HHF program. *Id.* at ¶51.

¶9 Defendant argues that Plaintiff does not have standing to bring a breach-of-contract claim against Defendant for allegedly breaching its Agreement with the Arizona Department of Housing. Defendant explains that the HHF program was created under the Making Home Affordable Act, which was an Act created under the Emergency Economic Stabilization Act (EESA). *See* 12 U.S.C. §§5201–5261. Since the HHF is a program created under the EESA, there is no private right of action upon which Plaintiff can base her breach of contract claim and it should be dismissed. *See Miller v. Chase Home Finance, LLC*, 677 F.3d 1113, 1116–1117 (11th Cir. 2012).

¶10 Plaintiff admits that there is no express private right of action embodied in the Economic Emergency Stabilization Act or the Home Affordable Modification Program (HAMP). (Doc. 41 at 6.) *See Marks v. Bank of America, N.A.*, 2010 WL 2572988, *5–6 (D. Ariz. 2010) (the district court held that the mortgagor had no private right of action under HAMP).

¶11 However, Plaintiff argues that because she was approved for assistance through the HHF program and Defendant was so notified, and specific identifying information was provided to Defendant about Plaintiff, she was an intended third-party beneficiary to the Agreement between Defendant and the Arizona Department of Housing, which provided that upon receipt of notification of conditional approval, Defendant would not commence foreclosure proceedings for 45 days or if already in the foreclosure process would not conduct a sale for 45 days. Specifically, the Agreement provides:

> Upon notification that a borrower has been conditionally approved for HHF, the Servicer shall not initiate the foreclosure process or, if the borrower is already in the foreclosure process, conduct a foreclosure sale for 45 days, with any extensions by mutual consent of the Eligible Entity and the Servicer.

Doc. 11-1 at ¶3

¶12 Plaintiff is not a party to the Agreement between Defendant and the Arizona Department of Housing. Therefore, to have standing to sue for breach of this Agreement, Plaintiff must be an intended third-party beneficiary to the contract as opposed to an incidental beneficiary. *GECCMC 2005-C1 Plummer Street Office Ltd. Partnership v. JPMorgan Chase Bank, Nat. Ass'n*, 671 F.3d 1027, 1033 (9th Cir. 2012);

Klamath Water Users Protective Ass'n v. Patterson, 204 F.3d 1206 (9th Cir. 2000). The Ninth Circuit defines third party beneficiaries as:

> (1) Unless otherwise agreed between promisor and promisee, a beneficiary of a promise is an intended beneficiary if recognition of a right to performance in the beneficiary is appropriate to effectuate the intention of the parties and … (b) the circumstances indicate that the promisee intends to give the beneficiary the benefit of the promised performance.
>
> (2) An incidental beneficiary is a beneficiary who is not an intended beneficiary.

Klamath, 204 F.3d at 1211 (citing the Restatement (Second) of Contracts § 302 (1979)). "To sue as a third-party beneficiary of a contract, the third party must show that the contract reflects the express or implied intention of the parties to the contract to benefit the third party." *Klamath*, 204 F.3d at 1211. The mere fact that a third party may benefit under the contract does not confer a right to sue, "instead, the parties must have intended to benefit the third party." *Id.* "[T]to prove intended beneficiary status, 'the third party must show that the contract reflects the express or implied intention of the parties to the contract to benefit the third party.'" *GECCMC 2005-C1 Plummer Street Office Ltd. Partnership*, 671 F.3d at 1033 (quoting *Klamath Water Users Prof. Assoc.*, 204 F.3d at 1211.)

¶ 13 While the contract does not have to specifically name the third party and can specify a class of parties to benefit from the contract, "'parties that benefit from a government contract are generally assumed to be incidental beneficiaries,' rather than intended beneficiaries, and so 'may not enforce the contract absent a clear intent to the contrary.'" *GECCMC 2005-C1 Plummer Street Office Ltd. Partnership*, 671 F.3d at 1033 (quoting *Cnty. of Santa Clara v. Astra USA, Inc.*, 588 F.3d 1237, 1244 (9th Cir. 2009), *rev'd on other grounds by Astra USA, Inc. v. Santa Clara Cnty.*, 131 S. Ct. 1342 … (2011)).

> This clear intent hurdle is a high one. It is not satisfied by a contract's recitation of interested constituencies, vague, hortatory pronouncements, statements of purpose, explicit reference to a third party, or even a showing that the contract operates to the third parties' benefit and was entered into with them in mind, … Rather, we examine the precise language of the contract for a clear intent to rebut the presumption that the third parties are merely incidental beneficiaries.

GECCMC 2005-C1 Plummer Street Office Ltd. Partnership, 671 F.3d 1027, 1033–1034 (9th Cir. 2012) (internal quotations and citations omitted). "One way to ascertain such intent is to ask whether the beneficiary would be reasonable in relying on the promise as manifesting an intention to confer a right on him or her." *Klamath*, 204 F.3d at 1211 (citing Restatement (Second) of Contracts § 302(1)(b) cmt. d). In *Marks*, the district court found that the plaintiff mortgagor was not an intended beneficiary because the language of the contract did not show that the parties to the contract intended to grant qualified borrowers the right to enforce and that the lender was not required to grant or deny the loan, only to consider it, so the plaintiff mortgagor could not have reasonably believed that the defendant lender was obligated to modify her loan. 2010 WL 2572988, at *4.

¶ 14 In the present case, Plaintiff argues that because Defendant had a duty under the Agreement to postpone any foreclosure proceeding upon notification that a borrower had been approved for HHF funding and because the "I" record sent to Defendant by the Arizona Department of Housing specifically identified Plaintiff as the person who would receive payment assistance, the parties manifested a clear intent to confer on Plaintiff status as a third-party beneficiary of the Agreements. Further, Plaintiff argues that she reasonably relied on Defendant's promise in the Agreement to postpone the trustee sale of her home upon preliminary approval for HHF funding. Defendant asserted at oral argument that there was no proof it had ever received the "I" record.

¶ 15 The majority of the cases found by this Court that address third-party beneficiary claims related to contracts or agreements concerning programs created under the EESA or HAMP deal with a borrower attempting to enforce compliance with the terms of HAMP Service Provider Agreements. *See Edwards v. Aurora Loan Services, LLC*, 791 F. Supp. 2d 144, 152 (D.D.C. 2011) (listing cases in which district courts have addressed the question of whether eligible borrowers have standing to enforce the terms of HAMP Service Provider Agreements as third party beneficiaries and decided against the borrowers); *Marks v. Bank of America, N.A.*, 2010 WL 2572988 (D. Ariz. 2010). The central theme in the reasoning of these opinions is that the HAMP contracts do not contain any provisions demonstrating the parties' intent to make eligible borrowers third-party beneficiaries with enforceable rights and the HAMP contracts provided the lenders with significant discretion on whether to modify borrower's loans. This case is distinguishable, and Defendant has not presented any cases that address the specific situation applicable in this case.

¶ 16 This is a close question. On the one hand, the language of the contract contains nothing specifically identifying borrowers as intended beneficiaries. But it also contains no language limiting the benefits of the Agreement to the parties to the Agreement. *Compare Escobedo v. Country Wide Home Loans, Inc.*, 2009 WL 4981618, at *2 (S.D. Cal. Dec. 15, 2009) (the Agreement specified that it "shall inure to the benefit of ... the parties to the Agreement and their permitted successors-in-interest."). The Agreement here does, however, contain the clause requiring the lender to defer or delay any foreclosure proceedings upon receipt of a notification that a borrower has been conditionally approved for HHF. The Court finds that this clearly expresses an intent to benefit those borrowers for whom the lender receives notification of conditional approval for HHF. (*See* Doc. 11-1, ¶ 3). Unlike the other HAMP cases in which the lender was under no obligation to modify the borrower's loan, in this case, there was an express clause requiring the Defendant to delay the foreclosure sale at least 45 days. The Agreement provides no discretion to the Defendant regarding delay of foreclosure action 45 days after receiving notice that a borrower had been conditionally approved for HHF funding. Plaintiff—a borrower who received conditional approval for HHF and on whose behalf a notice was sent to Defendant prior to the foreclosure sale—is within the class of persons that is an intended beneficiary of the Agreement.

¶ 17 Based on the facts of this case and the particular Agreement at issue, the Court finds that Plaintiff has stated a plausible claim for breach of contract for failing to delay the foreclosure process 45 days after receiving notice that Plaintiff had been approved for HHF funding.

¶ 18 Further, the Court does not believe that a finding that Plaintiff has standing in this case would open the door to potentially millions of homeowners filing claims and notes that at oral argument, Defendant did not claim to have information of such an opening of the "floodgates." The Court's holding is limited to the specific language used in this Agreement and to those borrowers on whose behalf a lender received notice of conditional approval for HHF funding but after receiving such notice, the lender failed to delay a foreclosure sale for at least 45 days as required by the relevant contract.

Exercise 13.1—Finding an Intention to Benefit a Third Party

In each of the following cases, is a court likely to find that the third party is an intended beneficiary or only an incidental beneficiary without rights to enforce the contract? In any of the cases, does the outcome depend on whether you apply the Restatement test or the Arizona test as stated in *Norton*?

1. Payment to Contractor's Creditor

Homeowner agreed to pay Construction Co. $10,000 to construct a swimming pool. When entering the contract with Homeowner, Construction Co. owed money to Finance Co. on an unrelated loan. Homeowner and Construction Co. agreed in their contract that, rather than Homeowner paying Construction Co., Homeowner will pay the $10,000 for the construction of the swimming pool "directly to Finance Co." If Homeowner breaches this promise, and if Construction Co. does not seek to enforce the promise, does Finance Co. have a right to sue the Homeowner as a third party beneficiary?

2. Construction Delay

Light Rail Co. ("LRC") contracted with City to construct 10 miles of light rail lines within the City boundaries. A provision in the contract required LRC to notify businesses along the light rail of the construction schedule and of any anticipated delays or changes in the completion date. City and LRC agreed upon a contract completion date of August 10th. If LRC does not meet the completion date, and businesses along the light rail line suffer lost profits as a result, would the businesses have a right to sue LRC for damages as third party beneficiaries?

3. Safety Precautions

Diamond Mining Co. contracted with Dynamic Construction to expand its mine. The contract called for Dynamic to perform numerous safety measures, and to take "all necessary precautions for the protection and safety of employees on the job site." The contract also stated that Dynamic "shall save harmless and indemnify Diamond Mining Co. from and against any expense, loss or damage on account of any claim, demand or suit made by any person" who was injured in or around the construction area. Did the contract indicate an intention to benefit third persons? If so, was the benefit intentional and direct? What are the arguments for both sides? On similar facts, the Arizona Court of Appeals found that the contract was not intended to benefit employees. *Basurto v. Utah Const. & Min. Co.*, 485 P.2d 859, 15 Ariz. App. 35 (1971). Does *Norton* provide reasoning with which you can defend such a conclusion?

B. Vesting of Rights in a Contract Beneficiary

The original parties to a third party beneficiary contract might wish to modify their contract to change or eliminate the promises that were intended to benefit a third party beneficiary. If so, they should expressly reserve the power to change a duty to an intended beneficiary in the original contract. It is common in life insurance policies, for example, to reserve to the insured a power to change the insurers' duties to the beneficiary by substituting another beneficiary.

When the power to do so has not been reserved, a subsequent agreement to modify third party rights cannot effectively diminish or eliminate the third party rights created in the original contract once those rights have "vested." In the absence of any such reserved power, a third party beneficiary's rights will vest if any of the following occur:

(1) The terms of the contract creating the third party rights provide that the rights are vested or cannot be changed or,

(2) A third party beneficiary knows about the rights conferred upon her in the contract and materially changes her position by relying on such rights or,

(3) A third party beneficiary brings a lawsuit to enforce her rights as a beneficiary or,

(4) A third party beneficiary assents to being a third party beneficiary at the request of either party.

RESTATEMENT (SECOND) OF CONTRACTS § 311 (1981) ("Variation of a Duty to A Beneficiary").

Exercise 13.2 — Determining if Contract Beneficiary Rights Have Vested

Review the following example. Determine which, if any, of the above principles regarding vesting would apply.

Construction Co. owed $10,000 to Finance Co. on a loan obligation that has become due along with late charges. When Finance Co. demanded payment, Construction Co. explained that it did not have the funds but that it would soon enter into a contract to build a swimming pool for Homeowner for a fee of $10,500. Finance Co. then offered to cease asserting its claim against Construction Co., stating that Construction Co. could accept its offer by succeeding within one week in entering into the construction contract with Homeowner and by providing in the construction contract that Homeowner would pay the $10,500 fee for pool construction directly to Finance Co. as a third party beneficiary. Two days later, Construction Co. succeeded in entering into such a contract with Homeowner. When Finance Co. was informed of this agreement between Construction Co. and Homeowner, Finance Co. ceased efforts to collect the debt directly from Construction Co. Subsequently, Homeowner and Construction Co. agreed to modify the construction contract and to redirect the payment of the construction fee directly to Construction Co. rather than to Finance Co. Does Finance Co. still have enforceable rights under the construction contract?

Draft a provision for the original construction contract that eliminates the power of Homeowner and Construction Co. to modify or eliminate third party rights, regardless of whether any vesting event has taken place. Conversely, draft a provision that would effectively preserve their right to modify or eliminate Finance Co.'s third party rights, even in the face of circumstances that otherwise would cause the third party rights to vest.

C. Defenses to Actions Brought by a Third Party Beneficiary

If a third party beneficiary attempts to enforce the contract provision that creates rights for the beneficiary, the promisor can raise any defense the promisor would be able to raise against the promisee provided that the defense arises out of the contract.

Naimo v. LaFianza

146 N.J. Super. 362, 369 A.2d 987 (Ch. Div. 1976)

[footnotes and internal citations omitted; paragraphs renumbered from original]

Kentz, J.S.C.

¶ 1 Plaintiff, individually and as guardian Ad litem of Mario Bruno, Jr. (Bruno, Jr.), seeks specific performance of an oral agreement allegedly made by Mario Bruno (Bruno) to make a testamentary gift for the benefit of Bruno, Jr.

¶ 2 The controlling facts are not disputed. It appears from the evidence that plaintiff, while seeking employment in this country, met Bruno in 1949. He was the owner of the business enterprise where plaintiff became employed. On occasion Bruno would drive the plaintiff home from work, and in the summer of 1950 while his family was away on vacation he invited the plaintiff out for dinner. This was repeated several times thereafter and during the course of these meetings Bruno engaged in conversations about his wife and adopted child. He indicated that his reason for the dinner meetings with plaintiff was because he disliked eating alone and was lonesome. This relationship between plaintiff and Bruno continued and he then started buying her presents and showing other acts of kindness and affection. He lamented the fact that he was not able to have children with his wife and he frequently expressed his desire to have a child of his own. He asked plaintiff to have his child and she refused. Bruno kept repeating his desire to have a child and finally offered to support any child that might be born of plaintiff. As a further inducement he said he would get a divorce from his present wife and marry plaintiff. He also promised to leave money for the child upon his death. By this time the relationship between plaintiff and Bruno had grown into a close and amorous one. In view of this, and as a result of his promises on which she relied, plaintiff changed her mind and agreed to have a child with Bruno.

¶ 3 Plaintiff became pregnant in 1950. She miscarried after three months of pregnancy. She testified that she saw Bruno regularly on Saturday mornings and Wednesday afternoons and continued to have sexual relations on these occasions with him in an effort to produce a child for him. Plaintiff further testified that she did not have sexual relations with any other men during this period. Not until 1963 did the plaintiff become pregnant again. Thereafter, a child was born to her on February 11, 1964. As agreed between plaintiff and Bruno, the child was named Mario Bruno, Jr. Plaintiff was admitted into the hospital under the name of Mrs. Mario Bruno. During her hospital stay Bruno visited her every day, and upon her discharge brought her home with the baby. All expenses in connection with the pregnancy and delivery of the child were paid by Bruno.

¶ 4 After the birth of the child Bruno paid the sum of $60 a week for support and also paid plaintiff's rent. He continued to show his great affection and love for plaintiff and his son by visiting the home each day. As the child grew older Bruno gave much of his time and attention to his son and participated as a father in many of his activities. In addition to weekly support payments he bought many gifts for Bruno, Jr. on holidays and other special occasions. He also purchased clothes for his son when they were needed.

¶ 5 Plaintiff testified that Bruno was "crazy" about his son. Although Bruno never actually lived with plaintiff after the child was born, he spent much of his time with plaintiff and his son. He was a very dutiful and interested father. On various occasions he sent plaintiff and his son on summer vacations. It is abundantly clear that he had a very close and affectionate relationship with Bruno, Jr. There can be no doubt that Bruno was the father of this child.

¶ 6 Bruno died suddenly on October 5, 1975. He left a last will and testament which was duly admitted to probate. There was no provision made therein for the benefit of plaintiff or his son. Plaintiff contends that there was an agreement which should be enforced by specific performance. It is well established law that a person may bind himself by contract to make a particular will. Equally well established is the proposition that a third-party beneficiary is himself entitled to maintain a suit for specific performance of an agreement between third persons to provide for him by will. Similarly, it has been recognized that a promisee of an agreement for the benefit of a third-party donee has sufficient interest in the enforcement of the promise to entitle him to sue. However, such agreements must be subjected to close scrutiny.

¶7 Defendants maintain that even if there is a contract, it is illegal and unenforceable since it was made in consideration of the commission of a future illicit act of intercourse and adultery. It is well established that illegal contracts are unenforceable. However, whether a promise to make a testamentary gift to a future-born illegitimate child in return for illicit acts of intercourse and adultery is an illegal and unenforceable agreement is a question of first impression in this State. However, courts in other jurisdictions have answered this question affirmatively.

¶8 An agreement by a father to support his illegitimate child made after birth is enforceable. Such an agreement would not be tainted by the past illicit intercourse and adultery between the parties. Rather, it would be a recognition by the father of his moral and legal obligation pursuant to N.J.S.A. 9:16-2 to support his illegitimate child during his lifetime. However, this action is not brought for that purpose. The agreement sued upon here was made in part to induce plaintiff to engage in illicit intercourse and adultery with Bruno. Consequently, the agreement, at least in part, is in violation of a penal statute, N.J.S.A. 2A:88-1, and is against public policy. Therefore, the entire contract is illegal and unenforceable.

¶9 It may be argued that in today's society, with its changing mores and life styles, the conduct of the parties which led to the making of this contract is such that it should not taint the contract and make it unenforceable. It is significant to note that most of the changing law resulting from our modern-day social values and life styles deals with cases where both parties were unmarried. We cannot be unmindful of the fact that here one party was unmarried and the other was married. Despite our changing standards of morality, the family unit is an integral part of our society and must be preserved and maintained. We cannot countenance the relationship of a married man and his mistress or lover. The mere fact that one party desires to produce a child of his own, while a noble motive, does not justify the means to that end. Even though the act of adultery may be decriminalized by legislative enactment, public policy cannot tolerate illicit relationships of this kind and any agreements arising therefrom.

¶10 Plaintiff argues that even though a contract may be based upon the commission of an illegal act, such should not invalidate the contract with respect to the child as the third-party beneficiary. There is no merit to this argument. It is a general rule of law that one not a party to an illegal contract cannot derive any benefit therefrom even though it were made in his behalf.

....

¶11 The foundation of any right the third-party beneficiary may have is the promisee's contract. Therefore, any defense arising in connection with the validity of the contract is available to the promisor against the beneficiary. 2 Williston on Contracts (3 ed. 1959), §394 at 1063. The beneficiary, in attempting to take advantage of a contract made for him by another, must make it subject to all legal defenses and inherent equities arising out of the contract as between the parties thereto and must bear the burdens thereof. In this case defendants clearly are entitled to raise the defense of illegality against the enforcement of the agreement by the beneficiary child. The illegality of the consideration arising from the illicit act of intercourse and adultery by the promisee goes to the very heart of the agreement and renders it invalid in law and in equity. Any contract made in consideration of an act forbidden by law or against public policy is unenforceable and the illegality of the contract will constitute a good defense at law as well as in equity. Since the illegality of the consideration renders the contract invalid and unenforceable as between the immediate parties, a court of equity cannot allow the beneficiary to enforce it, for a third-party beneficiary can acquire no better right to enforce the contract than that held by the contracting parties. The conclusion follows that the enforceability of this agreement by the beneficiary child is barred in toto by the defense of illegality.

Exercise 13.3 — Determining Defenses Arising out of the Contract

1. The Homeowner's Payment

Review Exercise 13.2. Finance Co. sues Homeowner for Homeowner's failure to pay the $10,500 to Finance Co. as promised by the terms of the contract between Homeowner and Construction Co. As a defense, Homeowner claims that Construction Co. breached its obligation by installing a pump, filter, heating system, and tile that do not conform to the contract requirements. As an additional defense, Homeowner claims that Construction Co. caused damage to Homeowner's car when moving heavy equipment away from Homeowner's residence after it had completed its performance. Would either or both of Homeowner's defenses be allowable? Explain.

2. The Insurance Beneficiary

Andy's child and life insurance beneficiary, Isabel, sues the insurer for refusing to pay her the benefits due under the insurance policy at Andy's death. As a defense, the insurer asserts that Andy had failed to make the premium payments, which was an express condition to the promise of paying benefits to the beneficiary under the insurance policy. Would the insurer be able to raise this defense against Isabel, the third party beneficiary? Explain.

Suppose that Andy had paid his premiums as agreed, but Andy had materially misrepresented his medical condition when he had contracted for the policy? Explain your analysis.

D. Enforcement Action by the Promisee against the Promisor

We have discussed the right of an intended third party beneficiary to bring an enforcement action against the promisor. The issue now under consideration is whether the promisee has the right to bring an action against the promisor to enforce the promisor's promise to the third party in a third party beneficiary contract. As an example, suppose the promisor, an insurance company, fails or refuses carry out its promise to make a payment to the intended beneficiary. We have discussed the rights of an intended beneficiary to enforce the contract against the promisor. May the insured promisee (or the promisee's representative, if the agreement is for life insurance) also sue the insurer to enforce the insurer's promises to pay benefits to the beneficiary?

Because the promisee is a party to the contract, the promisee can bring an action for specific performance to compel the promisor to perform as promised in favor of the third party beneficiary. A more difficult question is presented if the promisee performs in favor of the third party in place of a breaching promisor, or otherwise sustains damages because of the promisor's failure to perform its obligations to the third party. Does the promisee then have a claim against the promisor for reimbursement of the promisee's costs of performance or for other damages? According to the next case, on what additional factor does the answer depend?

Smith v. Maescher

21 Cal. App. 4th 100, 26 Cal. Rptr. 2d 133 (1993)

Work, J.

¶1 Donald Maescher appeals an order requiring him to reimburse his former wife, Daphne Smith, for education expenses she advanced to their son Peter for his senior year of college. He contends their marital separation agreement defining his obligation to pay college expenses created a third party beneficiary contract for the breach of which only Peter could recover damages.... Finally, he asserts the court erred in awarding Smith $1,000 in attorney's fees. Because we conclude the law of third party beneficiary contracts gives a promisee only a remedy of specific performance and, at best, nominal damages in a case such as this involving a donee beneficiary, the court erred in awarding Smith the moneys voluntarily loaned Peter. As a result, it also erred in awarding attorney's fees to Smith.

....

¶2 Whether she may recover damages depends on whether Peter was an intended "creditor" or "donee" beneficiary. The former type of beneficiary receives payment from the promisor of a debt or other obligation owed the beneficiary by the promisee, whereas the latter type does not and essentially receives a "gift" in the form of the promisor's obligation to it. (Rest. 2d Contracts, § 302, com. b & com. c.) If a promisor does not pay the promisee's debt to the creditor beneficiary, then the promisee will remain liable to the beneficiary for the full amount of the debt and could directly suffer damages in this full amount. In contrast, if the promisor does not perform its obligation to the donee beneficiary, the promisee will not be liable to the beneficiary for such performance and presumably will suffer only nominal damages. In both cases, however, as we noted above, the promisee may have a right to enforce the contract by obtaining specific performance against the promisor. As the Restatement Second of Contracts, section 305, comment a, states:

> The promisee of a promise for the benefit of a beneficiary has the same right to performance as any other promisee, whether the promise is binding because part of a bargain, because of his reliance, or because of its formal characteristics. If the promisee has no economic interest in the performance, as in many cases involving gift promises, the ordinary remedy of damages for breach of contract is an inadequate remedy, since only nominal damages can be recovered. In such cases specific performance is commonly appropriate. *See* § 307. In the ordinary case of a promise to pay the promisee's debt, on the other hand, the promisee may suffer substantial damages as a result of breach by the promisor. So long as there is no conflict with rights of the beneficiary or the promisor, he is entitled to recover such damages. *See* § 310.

¶ 3 A promisee cannot recover damages which may be suffered by the intended third party beneficiary, although the promisee may sue for specific performance of the promisor's obligation. (Rest. 2d Contracts, § 307, com. b.) The Restatement Second of Contracts, section 307, comment d, is even more specific as to donee beneficiary situations, stating:

> Where the promisee intends to make a gift of the promised performance to the beneficiary, the beneficiary ordinarily has an economic interest in the performance but the promisee does not. Thus the promisee may suffer no damages as the result of breach by the promisor. In such cases the promisee's remedy in damages is not an adequate remedy ... and specific performance may be appropriate.... The court may of course so fashion its decree as to protect the interests of the promisee and beneficiary without unnecessary injury to the promisor or innocent third persons. *See* § 358.

¶ 4 Illustration 2 to section 307 of the Restatement Second of Contracts is informative:

> As part of a separation agreement B promises his wife A not to change the provision in B's will for C, their son. A dies and B changes his will to C's detriment, adding also a provision that C will forfeit any bequest if he questions the change before any tribunal. A's personal representative may sue for specific performance of B's promise.

¶ 5 We infer from the above illustration that the promisee (i.e., A or A's personal representative) has no cause of action for breach of contract damages. Neither California nor Massachusetts case law appears to have dealt with these specific issues, so we adopt and apply the principles set forth in the Restatement Second of Contracts.

Exercise 13.4 — Enforcement Actions by Promisee

1. Revisiting *Smith v. Maescher*

In *Smith v. Maescher*, assume that the mother was unable to pay for the college expenses and the child, rather than his mother, had brought suit against the father. If the child had tried to enforce his father's promise to pay for the child's educational expenses, after the father had made the promise to the mother in the separation agreement, would the analysis and result be different?

2. Revisiting the Life Insurance Contract

Andy promised to pay Life Insurance Co. a monthly premium in return for Life Insurance Co.'s promise to pay $100,000 on Andy's death to any person Andy named as the "beneficiary." Andy named his child, Isabel, as the beneficiary of the life insurance policy. If Life Insurance Co. fails to pay Isabel on Andy's death, can Andy's executor bring an action to compel Life Insurance Co. to perform its promise? If Andy's executor pays all or part of the promised insurance proceeds from the estate's assets, can Andy's executor sue Life Insurance Co. for reimbursement?

3. Revisiting the Pool Construction Contract

Homeowner agreed to pay Construction Co. $10,500 to construct a swimming pool. When entering the contract with Homeowner, Construction Co. owed $10,000 plus late charges to Finance Co. on an unrelated loan. Homeowner and Construction Co. agreed in their contract that Homeowner would pay the $10,500 construction fee directly to Finance Co. rather than to Construction Co. The swimming pool was completed according to the contract, but Homeowner failed to pay Finance Co. Which party or parties can sue Homeowner for breach of its obligation under the construction contract to pay $10,500 to Finance Co.?

III. Summary

- Third party beneficiary rights are established by the original parties to a contract at the time of contract formation, by providing that a third party will receive benefits under the contract.
- If the third party beneficiary is "intended," he or she can enforce third party rights under the contract. A third party is an intended beneficiary if the parties to the contract intended to give the beneficiary the right to enforce the contract.
- Most states will permit a fact-finder to infer an intention to benefit a third party, from all the circumstances and from general contract language. Some states, including Arizona, follow a stricter rule and require a clear expression in the contract that the parties intended to benefit a third party.
- A person who benefits from a contract, but who does not qualify as an intended beneficiary, is an incidental beneficiary and has no enforceable rights under the contract.

- Parties to a contract that creates third party beneficiary rights may reserve the right to modify or eliminate the promise made to an intended beneficiary.
- In the absence of a reservation of the right to change or eliminate the rights of an intended beneficiary the parties may still do so unless the intended beneficiary rights have vested.
- Vesting takes place in four ways:
  - (1) The terms of the contract creating the duty to the intended beneficiary provide that the rights immediately vest or cannot be modified;
  - (2) The intended beneficiary knows about the rights and materially changes her position by relying on such rights;
  - (3) An intended beneficiary sues to enforce her rights as a beneficiary; or
  - (4) The intended beneficiary assents to being a third party beneficiary at the request of either party.
- If a third party beneficiary attempts to enforce the contract provision for her benefit, the promisor can raise any defense the promisor would be able to raise against the promisee, provided that the defense arises out of the contract.
- If the intended beneficiary is a donee beneficiary, the promisee cannot bring an action in damages for the promisor's breach of obligations to the third party, but the promisee may bring an action for specific performance of the promisor's obligations to the third party. If the intended beneficiary is a creditor beneficiary, the promisee may bring an action for any damages that the promisee sustains due to the promisor's breach of the promisor's obligations to the third party.

Chapter 14

Assignment and Delegation

I. Introduction

As noted in the Introduction to Chapter 13, in contrast to the rights of a third party beneficiary, an assignment is accomplished by the transfer of contract rights *after* the contract is formed.

The phrase "assignment of a contract" generally refers to a party's transfer of both its rights and duties under the contract. *See* RESTATEMENT (SECOND) OF CONTRACTS § 328(1) (1981) (interpretation of assignment of "the contract"). When referring to a transfer of rights only, such as the right to receive money under a contract, the assignment should clearly state that only those rights are being assigned. When referring to a transfer of a duty or an obligation under a contract, such as subcontracting or delegating one or more of the obligations under a contract, the delegation should clearly identify the duties being delegated.

An assignment of contracts rights moves from the "assignor," who assigns the rights to the "assignee." A delegation of duties moves from the "delegator" to a "delegatee." As the one who assumed the duty or obligation under the contract, the delegator is also the "obligor" of that duty. The "obligee," on the other hand, is the person to whom the duty is owed and to whom the original obligor or its delegatee must perform.

This chapter will describe the legal principles that govern the assignment of contract rights and the delegation of contract duties. As you work through this chapter, consider the following questions:

- Does the assignment of contract rights differ from third party beneficiary contracts?
- Does the assignment of contract rights affect the rights and obligations of all parties?
- To what extent may an assignment of contract rights be limited by law, public policy, or the terms of a contract?
- In a suit brought by an assignee of contract rights against the obligor, to what extent can the obligor assert contract defenses that the obligor could have asserted against the original obligee?
- Does the delegation of contract duties affect the rights and obligations of the original parties? How does the delegation of contract duties differ from a novation?
- In what circumstances is a duty nondelegable? In what circumstances will the obligee effectively waive a prohibition on delegation?

II. Characteristics of Assignments of Contract Rights

Consider the following example:

> Construction Co. agreed to build a swimming pool for Homeowner for the total cost of $10,000, payable at agreed-upon stages of completion of the swimming pool. One week later, Construction Co. assigned to Finance Co. its right to receive payment under the contract with Homeowner, because Construction Co. owes $9,850 to Finance Co. on a separate loan.

The effects of this transaction are as follows:

- The assignment of the contract right to receive payment from Homeowner transferred ownership of that right from Construction Co. to Finance Co.
- The right to receive payments from Homeowner is not effective, however, until Homeowner receives notice of the assignment. Until Homeowner receives notice of the assignment, Homeowner has the right to make payments to Construction Co. as provided in the contract.
- Once the assignment is effective, Finance Co. then owns the right to receive any payments due under the contract from Homeowner, and Construction Co.'s right to receive those payments is extinguished.
- After Homeowner has received notice of the assignment, Homeowner is legally obligated to make payments due under the contract to Finance Co. If Homeowner continues to make payments to Construction Co., Homeowner runs the risk that Construction Co. will not forward the payment to Finance Co. If so, Homeowner would still owe the payment to Finance Co. The obligation of Construction Co. to build the swimming pool would be unaffected by the assignment.
- On the other hand, Construction Co.'s assignment of Homeowner's payments on the contract to Finance Co. does not by itself extinguish Construction Co.'s obligation to pay Finance Co. on the outstanding loan. Construction Co. remains liable on that loan until it or Homeowner has fully paid the loan obligation.
- To extinguish its obligation to Finance Co. on the loan, Construction Co. could arrange for a novation. In a novation, all parties would agree that Homeowner will be substituted for Construction Co. as the obligor on the loan and that Construction Co. will be released from its obligation to Finance Co. on the loan.

III. Limitations on Assignment of Contract Rights

A party to a contract may assign rights under the contract unless assignment is prohibited by statute, would violate public policy, is "validly precluded by contract," or would materially and adversely change the position of the other party to the contract. Restatement (Second) of Contracts § 317(2) (1981). For example, an Arizona statute regulating the retirement plans of elected officials prohibits assignment of contract rights: "benefits ... payable under the plan are not subject to ... alienation, sale, transfer, assignment, [or] pledge ... before actually being received by the person entitled to the benefit." Ariz. Rev. Stat. Ann. § 38-809 (2012).

A. Assignment Violates Public Policy

The following case deals with the issue of whether an assignment of rights violates public policy in Arizona. In the case, the defendant's insurance company denied the defendant's request for a defense and for coverage under his policy after the plaintiff sued the defendant for negligent operation of an automobile. The defendant entered into an agreement to assign to the plaintiff any and all claims he had against his insurance company for bad faith in failing to defend him; in return, the plaintiff promised not to execute any judgment obtained against the defendant. The court addressed the question of whether such an agreement between the plaintiff and defendant amounts to collusion against the insurance company, violating public policy.

Damron v. Sledge

105 Ariz.151 (1969)

McFarland, Justice:

¶ 1 Clyde and Eileen Damron, hereinafter referred to as plaintiffs, brought an action against Ples Sledge (hereinafter referred to as Defendant Sledge) and Perel Polk (hereinafter referred to as Defendant Polk) to recover damages for personal injuries "allegedly sustained as the result of an automobile collision wherein Defendant Sledge negligently and carelessly drove Defendant Polk's vehicle into plaintiffs' vehicle." From a written order of the trial court granting Defendant Polk's motion to dismiss plaintiffs' complaint, plaintiffs appeal.

¶ 2 Plaintiffs' complaint alleged that Defendant Sledge was negligent and that he was driving Defendant Polk's vehicle with her permission and acquiescence. Defendant Polk was represented by the attorney for National Union Insurance Company, which insured her car. Defendant Sledge's insurance company, State Farm, secured attorneys who answered for him.

¶ 3 According to statements made by the attorneys for the parties on the day of trial, no insurance coverage is available for the acts of Defendant Sledge under the policies involved in the instant case if in fact Defendant Sledge was driving without the permission of Defendant Polk. On the basis of their assumption that Defendant Sledge was driving without permission, neither insurance company believed that it had a duty to defend him.

¶ 4 Evidently for this reason the attorneys for Sledge's insurance company withdrew, and Sledge thereafter was represented by his own attorney. In the pre-trial stages, Sledge's attorney soon found that he was putting in time, and advancing costs, and was not going to be able to collect any fee. He therefore applied to the court for permission to withdraw, and this was refused. On two occasions he made a request to the attorney for Defendant Polk that the insurance company pay his attorney's fees.

¶ 5 On the date set for trial, various motions were discussed in the trial judge's chambers. During the course of the argument, the substance of telephone calls, letters and conversations between all of the parties and their attorneys (as understood by the attorneys) since the time of the accident were related to the court. In particular, the following occurrences were related:

(1) Plaintiffs' attorney executed a covenant not to execute against Defendant Sledge; and

(2) Plaintiffs gave a note to the attorney for Defendant Sledge in the sum of $2,000.00 as payment of his attorney's fees; and

(3) In consideration therefore, Defendant Sledge assigned to plaintiffs whatever claim he had against the insurance companies for bad faith in failing to defend.

¶ 6 We are presented with the question of the validity of the prejudgment assignment which is claimed to be collusive and fraudulent.

¶ 7 It is well established that a claim by an insured against his insurer for failure of the insurer to defend may be assigned to the injured party. *Hatfield v. State*, Okla. Cr., 325 P.2d 972; *Critz v. Farmers Insurance Group*, 230 Cal. App. 2d 788, 41 Cal. Rptr. 401, 12 A.L.R.3d 1142. The objection in the instant case arises because the assignment was completed before judgment was taken against the insured. This type of prejudgment assignment of a claim against an insurance company for failure to defend was exhaustively considered in the California case of *Critz v. Farmers Insurance Group, supra*. We believe the *Critz* case comes the closest to the procedure followed by the parties in the case now before us. The California Court approved of the procedure followed in *Critz*, stating:

> When the insurer breaches its obligation of good faith settlement, it exposes its policyholder to the sharp thrust of personal liability. At that point, there is an acute change in the relationship between policyholder and insurer. The change does not or should not affect the policyholder's obligation to appear as defendant and to testify to the truth. He need not indulge in financial masochism, however. Whatever may be his obligation to the carrier, it does not demand that he bare his breast to the continued danger of personal liability. By executing the assignment, he attempts only to shield himself from the danger to which the company has exposed him. He is doubtless less friendly to his insurer than he might otherwise have been. The absence of cordiality is attributable not to the assignment, but to his fear that the insurer has callously exposed him to extensive personal liability.

¶ 8 In holding that the prejudgment assignment and covenant not to execute upon the judgment did not impart a collusive character to the personal-injury suit, the California court stated as follows:

> To uphold an equitable assignment under such circumstances does not supply the injured party with a disproportionate or unfair advantage. In our opinion, the present assignment is not violative of public policy if in fact a bad faith rejection had already occurred. If, on the other hand, the carrier was not guilty of bad faith, the plaintiff-assignee will lose the lawsuit regardless of the public policy aspects of the assignment.

¶ 9 Accordingly, we hold that the assignment in the instant case was not ipso facto collusive.

The public policy exception to assignability is limited in scope. In Arizona, unliquidated claims are generally assignable, with the exception of claims for damages for personal injury. *Web v. Gittlen*, 217 Ariz. 363, 174 P.3d 275 (2008). As a specific example of the exception for personal injury claims, some states, including Arizona, prohibit the assignment of legal malpractice claims. *Botma v. Huser*, 202 Ariz. 14, 39 P.3d 538 (App. 2002). But even this exception is carefully limited. In *Gittlen*, the Arizona Supreme Court held that a claim for breach of fiduciary duty against an insurance agent for failing to advise the insureds fully about available insurance coverage was assignable to a judgment creditor of the insured. The Court distinguished this case from claims against lawyers for malpractice, stating that the cases prohibiting assignment of legal malpractice claims do so because of the "uniquely personal" relationship between attorney and client, which gives rise to a "fiduciary relation of the very highest character." *Botma*, 202 Ariz. at 17. In contrast, insurance agents generally are not fiduciaries, but instead owe only a duty of "reasonable care, skill and diligence" in dealing with clients. *Gittlen*, 217 Ariz. at 279.

B. Assignment Materially Changes the Other Party's Position

In the following case, a successor company sought both monetary and injunctive relief against an employee for violating a noncompetition agreement entered into with the original company. The employee moved to dismiss on the ground that he did not consent to the assignment of the rights and duties under his employment contract.

Sogeti v. Scariano

606 F. Supp. 2d 1080 (D. Ariz. 2009)

[footnotes and internal citations omitted; paragraphs renumbered from original]

Roslyn O. Silver, District Judge.

PROCEDURAL BACKGROUND

¶ 1 On July 2, 2008 Plaintiff Sogeti USA LLC filed a six-count amended complaint against multiple defendants, including Christian and Teresa Martinez, from whom

Plaintiff seeks monetary and injunctive relief.... The claims stem from the departure of several of Plaintiff's employees who began working for Plaintiff's competitor and who allegedly recruited other employees to do the same....

FACTUAL BACKGROUND

¶ 2 Christian Martinez ("Martinez") was originally employed by Software Architects, Inc. ("SARK") with whom he signed an employment agreement ("Agreement") containing a non-competition provision ("restrictive covenant"). Plaintiff was not a party to the Agreement and the Agreement is silent as to assignability. Martinez became Plaintiff's employee following Plaintiff's acquisition of SARK on March 1, 2007. Plaintiff alleges SARK's rights in the Agreement were assigned to Plaintiff as part of the acquisition.

¶ 3 Martinez voluntarily terminated employment with Plaintiff on March 14, 2008 and began working for Defendant Neudesic, LLC on March 17, 2008. Plaintiff alleges Martinez violated the restrictive covenant in the Agreement by working for Neudesic and recruiting Plaintiff's employees to do the same.

DISCUSSION

....

¶ 4 A federal court looks to the substantive law of the forum state when sitting in diversity. *Klaxon Co. v. Stentor Elec. Mfg. Co.*, 313 U.S. 487, 496, ... (1941). The parties do not challenge the applicability of Arizona law.

¶ 5 Defendants argue Plaintiff does not have standing to enforce the restrictive covenant because (1) Plaintiff was not a party to the Agreement and (2) the restrictive covenant was not validly assigned to Plaintiff. The parties stipulate Plaintiff was not a party to the Agreement. However, the question of assignment is disputed. Defendants argue the question of assignment is beyond factual dispute because, absent Martinez's express consent, no valid assignment occurred and Plaintiff, a non-party to the Agreement, is precluded from enforcing the restrictive covenant. The Court disagrees and finds Martinez's express consent is not required for a valid assignment.

¶ 6 Whether an employee's express consent is required before an employment contract containing a restrictive covenant can be assigned to a successor company employer is a question of first impression in Arizona.

¶ 7 Under Arizona law, contractual rights are generally assignable unless the assignment is precluded by the contract, is forbidden by public policy or materially alters the duties of the obligor. *Highland Vill. Partners, LLC, v. Bradbury & Stamm Constr. Co.*, 219 Ariz. 147, 195 P.3d 184, 187 (Ariz. Ct. App. 2008) (*quoting* Restatement 2d Contracts § 317(2) (1981)). Moreover, an obligor's assent is "not necessary to make an assignment effective." Restatement 2d Contracts § 323 cmt. a. Reasonable restrictive covenants in employment contracts are not excepted from this rule and are generally enforceable and assignable.... *Supplies for Indus. v. Christensen*, 135 Ariz. 107, 659 P.2d 660, 662 (Ariz. Ct. App. 1983) (an employment contract containing language consenting to assignability allows a successor company to enforce a restrictive covenant contained therein).

¶ 8 Defendants argue this question is settled by *Christensen,* which, according to Defendants, requires employee consent before a valid assignment of a restrictive covenant in an employment contract can be made to a successor company employer. However, *Christensen* stands for a narrower proposition, recognizing a successor company's right to enforce a validly assigned restrictive covenant, and is silent on the question of whether the employee's consent is required for a valid assignment.

¶ 9 In *Christensen,* the court had to determine whether an equitable assignment between the employer and a third party beneficiary occurred. Language in the defendant's employment contract consenting to the assignment helped show that between the employer and the third party beneficiary, there was "an intention on the one side to assign and an intention on the other to receive [consideration]." The court considered the employment contract, including the restrictive covenant, an assignable asset transferrable to a successor. While the employee in *Christensen* had consented to the assignment, the court of appeals did not address whether consent was *required* to validate the assignment. Consent was merely a fact helpful to the court's analysis, not a part of the announced rule of law. Because neither *Christensen* nor other Arizona cases settle this question, the Court looks to other jurisdictions to help resolve the issue.

¶ 10 Jurisdictions outside Arizona disagree on whether an employee must consent to the assignment of a restrictive covenant prior to enforcement by a successor company. *See, generally,* Annotation, *Enforceability, by Purchaser or Successor of Business, of Covenant Not to Compete Entered Into by Predecessor and its Employees,* 12 A.L.R. 5th 847 (1993).

Jurisdictions Requiring Express Consent

¶ 11 Some jurisdictions require express consent because a restrictive covenant contained in an employment agreement is "personal" to the employee. The jurisdictions do not explicitly define "personal" as used in this context. However, the term appears to refer to a contract in which the promisor (employee) agrees to limit a right so fundamental to his liberty that the law presumes the promisor only agreed to bind himself in that way because the promisor knows and trusts the identity of the promisee (employer). *E.g., Hess v. Gebhard & Co., Inc.,* 570 Pa. 148, 808 A.2d 912, 922 (2002) (describing employee restrictive covenants as "personal" because they are based on the "trust that [employer or employee] has in the other ... [t]he fact that an individual may have confidence in the character and personality of one employer does not mean that the employee would be willing to suffer a restraint on his employment for the benefit of a stranger to the original undertaking.")....

Jurisdictions Not Requiring Express Consent

¶ 12 Other jurisdictions support the enforcement of restrictive covenants in employment contracts by successor companies even when the contract is silent as to assignability. In these jurisdictions, contractual rights are generally assignable, the "personal" nature of an employment contract ends following termination, and restrictive covenants are scrutinized to ensure reasonableness in scope or duration....

Arizona Rule

¶ 13 Arizona law is most consistent with the jurisdictions that allow successor companies to enforce restrictive covenants, even when the contract is silent regarding assignability and the employee has not consented. Like those jurisdictions, Arizona law favors the enforcement and assignment of contractual rights, *Highland,* 195 P.3d at 187, does not disfavor restrictive covenants in employment agreements, *Fearnow,* 138 P.3d at 725, and allows such restrictive covenants to be assigned, *Christensen,* 659 P.2d at 661. Arizona courts treat restrictive covenants in employment agreements as assignable assets enforceable by successor companies, not as highly personalized arrangements, scrutinizing restrictive covenants for whether they are "unreasonable ... demonstrate bad faith, or contravene public policy." *Fearnow,* 138 P.3d at 725....

B. Assignability of Martinez's Agreement

¶ 14 Under Arizona law, a contract is presumed assignable unless:

> (a) the substitution of a right of the assignee for the right of the assignor would materially change the duty of the obligor, or materially increase the burden or risk imposed on him by his contract, or materially impair his chance of obtaining return performance, or materially reduce its value to him, or
>
> (b) the assignment is forbidden by statute or is otherwise inoperative on grounds of public policy, or
>
> (c) assignment is validly precluded by contract.

Highland, 195 P.3d at 187 (*quoting* Restatement 2d Contracts § 317(2)).

¶ 15 As discussed above, the Agreement is silent on the question of assignability and thus assignment is not "validly precluded." Restatement 2d Contracts § 317 cmt. f (defining valid preclusion as a "contractual prohibition"). Nor is the assignment "inoperative on grounds of public policy," as the Court has rejected Defendants' proposed rule of public policy....

C. Plaintiff's Standing

¶ 16 Generally, "only the parties ... to a contract may enforce it." *Lofts at Fillmore Condo. Assoc. v. Reliance Commercial Constr.,* 218 Ariz. 574, 190 P.3d 733, 734 (2008) (*quoting Treadway v. W. Cotton Oil & Ginning Co.,* 40 Ariz. 125, 10 P.2d 371, 375 (1932)). However, assignees have standing to enforce contractual rights assigned to them. *Highland,* 195 P.3d at 187. Because the Court must assume the Agreement was assigned to Plaintiff, it must also assume Plaintiff has standing to enforce the Agreement. *Lazy Y. Ranch Ltd.,* 546 F.3d at 588.

Accordingly,

IT IS ORDERED Defendants' Motion to Dismiss ... IS DENIED.

C. Contractual Prohibition of Assignment

In the following case, the contract prohibited assignment of the right to receive periodic payments. Note how each party sought to invoke "public policy" in arguing whether this contractual prohibition should be enforced.

Piasecki v. Liberty Life Assurance Co. of Boston

312 Ill. App. 3d 872, 728 N.E.2d 71 (2000)

Justice Lytton delivered the opinion of the court:

¶ 1 After Donald and Eileen Piasecki (decedents) died in a motor vehicle accident, the co-administrators of the decedents' estates entered into a structured settlement agreement with the original defendants, Nussbaum Trucking, Inc. and Charles Ward (defendants). Two of the decedents' sons, John and David Piasecki (Piaseckis), assigned their future payments under the settlement agreement to Stone Street Capital, Inc. in exchange for lump sum payments. The defendants' insurers objected. The trial court allowed the assignment. We reverse.

¶ 2 The co-administrators of the decedents' estates entered into a structured settlement agreement with the defendants arising out of a wrongful death claim. Under this agreement, the defendants would provide the decedents' three sons an initial lump sum payment, followed by a stream of quarterly future payments. The settlement barred the payees from assigning their interests in the future payments.

....

¶ 3 When construing a contract, a reviewing court must determine and effectuate the meaning of the plain and ordinary language of the parties' contract de novo. *Gray v. Mundelein College*, 296 Ill. App. 3d 795, 803, 231 Ill. Dec. 260, 695 N.E.2d 1379 (1998).

¶ 4 Paragraph 4 of the settlement agreement states, in relevant part:

> Plaintiffs [Piaseckis] acknowledge that the Periodic Payments cannot be accelerated, deferred, increased or decreased by the Plaintiffs or any Payee; nor shall the Plaintiffs or any Payee have the power to sell, mortgage, encumber, or [sic] any part thereof, by assignment or otherwise.

....

¶ 5 The Piaseckis contend that the antiassignment clause is unenforceable in Illinois because it is against public policy in that it conflicts with Restatement (Second) of Contracts § 317(2) (1981), which generally permits assignment of contractual rights.

¶ 6 The insurers respond that the trial court erred by failing to enforce the terms of the settlement agreement barring the assignment of the periodic payments. The insurers argue that section 317(2) of the Restatement precludes the assignment in this case because they might suffer adverse tax consequences when the future payments to the Piaseckis were accelerated.

¶7 Section 317(2) of the Restatement states that:

> A contractual right can be assigned unless (a) the substitution of a right of the assignee for the right of the assignor would materially change the duty of the obligor, or materially increase the burden or risk imposed on him by his contract, … or materially reduce its value to him, … or (c) assignment is validly precluded by contract.

Restatement (Second) of Contracts § 317(2) (1981).

¶8 In *Henderson v. Roadway Express*, 308 Ill. App. 3d 546, 242 Ill. Dec. 153, 720 N.E.2d 1108 (1999), the fourth district addressed the same issue confronting us here. The court found that although antiassignment provisions are narrowly construed, there are valid reasons to uphold them in the context of structured settlement agreements. The language in the contract mirrored section 130 of the Internal Revenue Code of 1986 (Code) (26 U.S.C. § 130 (1994)), which grants favorable tax treatment to assignees of liability under certain prescribed circumstances. *Henderson*, 308 Ill. App. 3d at 550–51, 242 Ill. Dec. 153, 720 N.E.2d at 1112. The inclusion of this language in the settlement indicated that the parties had bargained for the antiassignment provision and intended to benefit from the favorable tax treatment it provided. The court added that the likelihood of adverse tax consequences resulting from the assignment of the future payments was less important than "the fact that the parties implemented the antiassignment provisions with these concerns in mind." *Henderson*, 308 Ill. App. 3d at 550, 242 Ill. Dec. 153, 720 N.E.2d at 1113. Under those circumstances, the court refused to discard or waive the bargained-for provisions in the settlement agreement. [citations omitted]. We agree with this reasoning.…

….

¶9 The antiassignment clause of the structured settlement agreement should be enforced. We reverse the trial court's orders approving the assignment of the future periodic payments from the Piaseckis to Stone Street.

….

Reversed.

Breslin and Koehler, JJ., concur.

Interestingly, an assignment of rights prohibited by contract may nonetheless be effective, if the *only* impediment to assignment is the provision in the contract precluding assignment. In such a case, the assignor may be liable for damages for breaching its promise to refrain from assigning its contracts rights. Restatement (Second) of Contracts § 322(2)(b) (1981).

Exercise 14.1 — Contractual Prohibition of Assignment

1. Assignment of Right to Payment

Homeowner hired Construction Co. to build a swimming pool for a fee of $10,000. Homeowner and Construction Co. agreed to add a provision to their contract that specifically prohibits either party from assigning any rights or benefits under the contract without the written consent of the other. Without such consent, Construction Co. assigned its right to payments from Homeowner to Finance Co. to secure a personal loan owing to Finance Co. The assignment does not increase Homeowner's burden or risk. Neither the assignment nor the anti-assignment clause violates law or public policy. When Homeowner receives notice of the assignment, Homeowner objects. What legal advice would you give to Homeowner in this situation?

2. Assignment of Right to Construction Services

In the example above, Homeowner has decided against building the swimming pool it contracted for with Construction Co. Not wanting to be in breach of contract, Homeowner has decided to assign its rights under the contract with Construction Co. to a family member who would like to have an identical swimming pool built at her home, which has similar access to its backyard and which is located five miles further away from Construction Co. than is Homeowner's residence. Although the contract entered into between Homeowner and Construction Co. has no provision in it prohibiting the assignment of rights, Construction Co. objects and consults with you as its attorney. What legal advice would you give to Construction Co. concerning its obligations under the contract?

IV. Defenses to Actions Brought by the Assignee of Contract Rights

In Chapter 13, we learned that a third-party beneficiary's rights are generally subject to a defense that the promisor could raise against the promisee, provided that the defense arises out of the contract. The same principle applies as well to the rights of an assignee of contract rights.

Exercise 14.2 — Deductions from Payment to Assignee

Homeowner has hired Construction Co. to build a swimming pool for $10,000, and their contract contains no provision barring assignment of Homeowner's rights. After Homeowner received notice of Construction Co.'s assignment of its contract rights to Finance Co., Construction Co. failed to perform its obligation under the contract to clean up the worksite. Homeowner paid another company the reasonable sum of $500 to clean up the construction site. Homeowner also has a reasonable claim against Construction Co. stemming from an employee kicking Homeowner's dog, which led to $400 in veterinary expenses. Homeowner wants to deduct $900 from the pool construction fees that it pays to Finance Co. What legal advice would you give Homeowner?

V. Delegation of Duties

A. Overview: Delegation, Third Party Rights, and Novation

In addition to the transfer of contract rights, a party to a contract may wish to transfer duties or obligations. Unlike an assignment, however, where notice to the obligor is sufficient to complete the transfer of a contract right from the assignor to the assignee, the delegation of a duty does not result in a substitution of the delegatee for the obligor. The obligor remains liable for any breach. RESTATEMENT (SECOND) OF CONTRACTS § 318(3) (1981).

The obligor would be released from its obligation, and the delegatee substituted as the new and sole obligor, only if the obligee agreed to a "novation." In a novation, an obligee agrees to accept an agreement between the obligor and a delegatee to substitute the delegatee in place of the obligor and release the obligor from his duties under the contract. A novation is not inferred, however, merely from the fact that the obligee accepts performance by the delegatee. The obligee's intent to agree to a novation must be clear and definite. Generally, this is accomplished by a separate agreement between the obligee and obligor specifically substituting the delegatee as the new obligor for the original obligor under the contract.

Consider the following illustration:

> Homeowner agrees to pay Construction Co. $10,000 to construct a swimming pool. Construction Co. acts as a general contractor in the construction of the swimming pool. It subcontracts with other business entities for the various stages of work: an excavation company to dig and shape the pool, a plumbing company to install the plumbing, an electrician for the electrical work, and a resurfacing company for the plastering, installing of tile, and sealing of the swimming pool.

Depending on further circumstances or assumptions, the following conclusions may apply:

- Construction Co. is the obligor under the contract because of its obligation to construct the swimming pool. Homeowner is the obligee under the contract with the right to receive full performance from Construction Co. In separate contracts with others, Construction Co. has delegated its duties under its contract with Homeowner by sub-contracting with various business entities to provide the labor, materials, and services necessary to comply with its contract to construct the swimming pool. All of the sub-contractors are Construction Co.'s "delegatees" of work or services to be performed. Each delegatee owes its performance obligations to Construction Co.
- If any delegatee fails to perform, or performs improperly, Homeowner can enforce its contract only by suing Construction Co. Homeowner cannot bring a contract action against a delegatee (sub-contractor) of Construction Co. because the delegatee is not a party to Homeowner's contract with Construction Co.

- If, however, the sub-contract between Construction Co. and a delegatee reflects a clear mutual intent to benefit Homeowner, Homeowner could have a right to enforce the contract against that delegatee as a third party beneficiary. Even if this were to occur, however, Construction Co. would also remain liable under the contract with Homeowner for completion of the swimming pool in the absence of a novation.
- If Homeowner expressly agrees to substitute an entity other than Construction Co. for performance of one or more of Construction Co.'s duties under the contract, and Construction Co. agrees to such substitution, Construction Co. would be released from its obligations by novation. In such a case, Homeowner could enforce its contract rights only against the substituted entity.

B. Limitations on Delegation of Contract Duties

Duties cannot be delegated if prohibited by public policy or by the terms of the contract. *See* Restatement (Second) of Contracts § 318(1) (1981). Policy considerations generally restrict delegation of duties in fewer instances than they do assignment of rights.

An express or implied contractual prohibition will bar delegation of duties unless the obligee consents, thus waiving the contractual prohibition. If the contract does not specifically prohibit delegation of duties, the contract's reference to a particular party owing a duty will not be interpreted to bar delegation of that duty unless the obligee "has a substantial interest in having that person perform or control the acts promised." *Id.* § 318(2).

In the following cases, neither contract included a clause specifically barring delegation. Why did the court nonetheless find the duties to be nondelegable in each case? The first case below refers to assignment of *the contract* for the sale of ore, which includes transfer of both rights and duties to another party, but the main difficulty appears in the delegation of the duties. In the second case, if the dance studio's duties were nondelegable, why was the obligee nonetheless denied recovery?

Arkansas Valley Smelting Co. v. Belden Mining Co.

127 U.S. 379 (1888) (paragraphing added)

Mr. Justice Gray, after stating the facts as above, delivered the opinion of the court.

¶ 1 [Belden Mining entered into a contract with Billing & Eilers, in which Belden Mining would deliver ore to Billing & Eilers, and the latter would pay for it at a rate that depended on the parties' mutual evaluation of the content of the ore. When Billing & Eilers dissolved, it assigned its contract to G. Billing without objection by Belden Mining. However, Belden Mining refused to perform further and sought to cancel the contract when G. Billing assigned its rights and obligations under the contract to Arkansas Valley Smelting, which sued Belden Mining.] The vital question in the case, therefore, is whether the contract between [Belden Mining] and Billing & Eilers was assignable by the latter, under the circumstances stated in the complaint.

¶ 2 At the present day, no doubt, an agreement to pay money, or to deliver goods, may be assigned by the person to whom the money is to be paid or the goods are to be delivered, if there is nothing in the terms of the contract, … which manifests the intention of the parties that it shall not be assignable. But every one has a right to select and determine with whom he will contract, and cannot have another person thrust upon him without his consent.

¶ 3 In the familiar phrase of Lord Denman, "You have the right to the benefit you anticipate from the character, credit, and substance of the party with whom you contract." *Humble v. Hunter*, 12 Q. B. 310, 317;….

¶ 4 The contract here sued on was one by which the defendant agreed to deliver 10,000 tons of lead ore from its mines to Billing & Eilers at their smelting works. The ore was to be delivered at the rate of 50 tons a day, and it was expressly agreed that it should become the property of Billing & Eilers as soon as delivered. The price was not fixed by the contract, or payable upon the delivery of the ore. But, as often as a hundred tons of ore had been delivered, the ore was to be assayed by the parties or one of them, and, if they could not agree, by an umpire; and it was only after all this had been done, and according to the result of the assay, and the proportions of lead, silver, silica, and iron thereby proved to be in the ore, that the price was to be ascertained and paid. During the time that must elapse between the delivery of the ore and the ascertainment and payment of the price [Belden Mining] had no security for its payment, except in the character and solvency of Billing & Eilers.

¶ 5 [Belden Mining], therefore, could not be compelled to accept the liability of any other person or corporation as a substitute for the liability of those with whom it had contracted.… [Belden Minding was not obligated] to deliver ore to a stranger, to whom Billing had undertaken, without the defendant's consent, to assign the contract.…

¶ 6 … In short, [Arkansas Valley Smelting] undertakes to step into the shoes of Billing, and to substitute its liability for his. The defendant had a perfect right to decline to assent to this, and to refuse to recognize a party, with whom it had never contracted, as entitled to demand further deliveries of ore.

¶ 7 The cases cited in the careful brief of the plaintiff's counsel, as tending to support [the validity of the assignment], are distinguishable from the case at bar, and the principal ones may be classified as follows: First. Cases of agreements to sell and deliver goods for a fixed price, payable in cash on delivery, in which the owner would receive the price at the time of parting with his property, nothing further would remain to be done by the purchaser, and the rights of the seller could not be affected by the question whether the price was paid by the person with whom he originally contracted or by an assignee. *Sears v. Conover*, 42 N. Y. 113,....

....

¶ 8 .... Without considering whether all the cases cited were well decided, it is sufficient to say that none of them can control the decision of the present case.

Judgment affirmed.

Seale v. Bates

145 Colo. 430, 359 P.2d 356 (1961) (en banc)

Doyle, Justice.

¶ 1 [The Seales] were plaintiffs in an action against ... the Bates Dance Studio, Inc. and the Dance Studio of Denver, Inc. The Seales sought to recover $2,040, which had been paid to the Bates Dance Studio to defray the cost of 300 hours of dance instruction.... [These contracts] with the Bates Dance Studio had been assigned to the Dance Studio of Denver, doing business as Dale Dance Studio. It is alleged that the [Bates Dance Studio] refused to carry out [its] obligations and duties under the said contracts.

¶ 2 The Seales ... entered into ... a contract with the Bates Dance Studio whereby they undertook to take a total of 600 one-half hour lessons. These lessons were interrupted due to illness in the family and upon the Seales' resuming classes they were told that the remainder of the lessons would be given at the Dale Studio. They then went to the Dale Studio to discuss the situation and were there advised by one of the former Bates employees, who was then working for Dale, that the latter had assumed the obligations of the Bates contracts. The Seales were told that the "students and the instructors, the entire organization was transferred to the Dale Studios; that we would have the same instructors, the same instruction, a continuation of what we had had at Bates."

¶ 3 They proceeded to take lessons at Dale, but after some 30 one-half hours of instruction they became dissatisfied with the conditions. This dissatisfaction arose from the fact that the room was much smaller and more crowded and the music from another room interfered with the lessons. Each of the Seales did not have his or her own instructor, Mr. Seale being required to take his lessons from a male instructor; there were difficulties in getting appointments and on some occasions when appointments were made an instructor would not be available. Mr. and Mrs. Seale complained to the management of the Dale Studio, but the conditions did not improve.... Mr. and Mrs. Seale stopped taking lessons in May of 1957. The following August they complained to Mr. John Bates of the Bates Studio and demanded that he refund their money or make proper arrangements for completing their contract. Bates informed them that his school was then closed and that there was no money to reimburse them. At the trial, in answer to a question as to why he continued to take lessons at the Dale Studios, Seale explained "I kept hoping that somebody would get the thing arranged to where we could continue as had been promised."

¶ 4 John Bates testified that he spoke to the Seales ... in March of 1957 and explained that "in order to protect their lessons that I would have to make arrangements to have them taught somewhere else, and that I was negotiating with Dale Dance Studio to teach their lessons. And they didn't object to it at that time."

....

¶ 5 The cause was tried to the court and at the close of plaintiffs' testimony, which included cross-examination of Bates, the court dismissed the plaintiffs' claims and entered informal findings and conclusions, giving these reasons:

> ... The basis for dispositions as to the Bates and Dale Studios was the assent of the plaintiffs to the assumption by Dale of the obligations under the contracts; that this acceptance of Dale was apparent from the plaintiffs' conduct.... The court rejected [the Seales'] theory that [they] consented to the assignment on any kind of conditional basis....

¶ 6 In seeking reversal, plaintiffs assert that the trial court erred in: ... failing to hold that duties under these contracts were personal, therefore non-assignable.

....

¶ 7 ... The argument of plaintiffs that this was a personal service contract and therefore non-assignable without their consent is valid. *Arkansas Valley Smelting Co. v. Belden Mining Co.*, 127 U.S. 379.... This assignment did not result in release of the assignor. 4 Corbin, Contracts, 476 (1951). 1 Restatement, Contracts, § 160(4) (1932).

¶ 8 This, however, does not furnish a reason for holding that [the Seales] are now entitled to recover. On the contrary, there is evidence to support the trial court's finding and conclusion that the [Seales] accepted the assignment as such; they did not elect to rescind when it was brought to their attention that the contracts had been assigned to Dale Dance Studio. The undisputed evidence shows that they accepted the assignment and proceeded to take lessons from the Dale Dance Studio. This conduct is inconsistent with plaintiffs' present theory that they at all times objected to the assignment. Had they refused to receive instruction from Dale and had they taken the position that their contract was with Bates and no other, there would be substance to their present contention that this violation justified the rescission.

....

¶ 9 It follows that the only substantial breach of the contract apparent from a careful reading of the record here is the assignment to the Dale Dance Studio. Had plaintiffs refused to accept this, there would have been a remedy by rescission or perhaps in breach of contract and they could have recovered at least the unused portion of the consideration. Accordingly the trial court's finding and conclusion that the plaintiffs waived any rights which may have arisen from the assignment must be upheld. Plaintiffs' conduct in accepting the transfer to Dale was in effect a waiver of this breach, and the evidence does not undisputedly show that the consent thereto was in any way conditional.

....

The judgment is affirmed.

Exercise 14.3 — Questions on *Seale v. Bates*

Because the court found that Bates's duties were nondelegable, the Seales could have rejected the delegation and asserted their contract rights against Bates when the Seales first received notice of the delegation. Alternatively, the court suggested that they could have placed conditions on their consent to it. What conditions should they have placed on their consent? If their conditions were not satisfied by the delegatee's performance, what recourse would they have had?

Given, however, that the Seales unconditionally consented to the delegation, thus waiving objection, they could not sue Bates for damages for the delegation of what otherwise would have been a nondelegable duty. The court also found that Bates's delegation was the "only substantial breach of the contract." Does that mean that the record established that Dale Dance Studio fully performed its delegated duty, or at least that the Seales could not prove damages from any minor deficiencies in the performance? Suppose that the Seales had consented to the delegation but Dale Dance Studio repudiated or otherwise materially breached its delegated duties. What recourse would the Seales have? Against whom? Did they consent to a novation or no more than a delegation?

Why were Bates's duties nondelegable at the outset? In a case in which assignment of rights or delegation of duties would violate public policy, could the other party validate the assignment or delegation through consent or waiver?

C. Limitations on Delegation of Contract Duties under the UCC

UCC § 2-210 (2011) is generally consistent with the common law principles discussed above. The main difference for sales of goods is found in UCC § 2-210(2)(b), which provides that: (1) the acceptance of a delegation of duties by the delegatee constitutes a promise to perform those duties and (2) this promise is enforceable by either the delegator or the obligee.

VI. Summary

The distinguishing feature of an assignment from a third party beneficiary is that the transfer of contract rights takes place *after* the contract is formed.

- An assignment of rights is not effective against the obligor until the obligor receives notice of the assignment. Until such notice is received the obligor may perform in accordance with the original contract.
- A contractual right can be assigned unless: (1) it would cause a substantial hardship on the obligor, (2) is forbidden by statute or public policy, or (3) is validly precluded by the contract. If it is precluded only by the contract, a court will generally consider the assignment effective and allow recovery for damages for breach of promise to refrain from assignment.
- If a legal action is brought against an obligor under the contract by an assignee, the obligor can raise any defenses that the obligor could have raised against the assignor so long as the defenses arise out of the contract.
- If the obligor delegates duties under a contract, the obligor (and now, delegator) remains liable to the obligee for any breach of contract.
- If all parties agree, the delegatee could become the sole party liable to the obligee by a transaction called a novation. In a novation, the obligee agrees to accept the delegatee as a complete substitute for the obligor and releases the obligor from his duties under the contract.
- Under common law, the obligee cannot sue the delegatee for breach of contract unless the parties entered into a novation or unless the obligee can enforce the agreement between the obligor and the delegatee as a third party beneficiary.
- Under the UCC, however, a delegatee's acceptance of a delegation of duties in a sales contract gives rise to the delegatee's promise to perform, which is enforceable by either the delegator or the obligee.
- An obligor cannot delegate his duties of performance if delegation is prohibited by public policy or by the terms of the contract, or if the obligee has a substantial interest in having the obligor personally perform or control the acts promised.

Appendices

Appendix 1

Texas Business and Commerce Code

TITLE 1. UNIFORM COMMERCIAL CODE
CHAPTER 1. GENERAL PROVISIONS

SUBCHAPTER A. GENERAL PROVISIONS

Sec. 1.101. SHORT TITLES.

(a) This title may be cited as the Uniform Commercial Code.

(b) This chapter may be cited as Uniform Commercial Code—General Provisions.

Amended by Acts 2003, 78th Leg., ch. 542, Sec. 1, eff. Sept. 1, 2003.

Sec. 1.102. SCOPE OF CHAPTER.

This chapter applies to a transaction to the extent that it is governed by another chapter of this title.

Amended by Acts 2003, 78th Leg., ch. 542, Sec. 1, eff. Sept. 1, 2003.

Sec. 1.103. CONSTRUCTION OF TITLE TO PROMOTE ITS PURPOSES AND POLICIES; APPLICABILITY OF SUPPLEMENTAL PRINCIPLES OF LAW.

(a) This title must be liberally construed and applied to promote its underlying purposes and policies, which are:

(1) to simplify, clarify and modernize the law governing commercial transactions;

(2) to permit the continued expansion of commercial practices through custom, usage and agreement of the parties; and

(3) to make uniform the law among the various jurisdictions.

(b) Unless displaced by the particular provisions of this title, the principles of law and equity, including the law merchant and the law relative to capacity to contract, principal and agent, estoppel, fraud, misrepresentation, duress, coercion, mistake, bankruptcy, or other validating or invalidating cause shall supplement its provisions.

Amended by Acts 2003, 78th Leg., ch. 542, Sec. 1, eff. Sept. 1, 2003.

Sec. 1.104. CONSTRUCTION AGAINST IMPLIED REPEAL.

This title being a general act intended as a unified coverage of its subject matter, no part of it shall be deemed to be impliedly repealed by subsequent legislation if such construction can reasonably be avoided.

Amended by Acts 2003, 78th Leg., ch. 542, Sec. 1, eff. Sept. 1, 2003.

Sec. 1.105. SEVERABILITY.

If any provision or clause of this title or its application to any person or circumstance is held invalid, the invalidity does not affect other provisions or applications of this title which can be given effect without the invalid provision or application, and to this end the provisions of this title are severable.

Amended by Acts 2003, 78th Leg., ch. 542, Sec. 1, eff. Sept. 1, 2003.

Sec. 1.106. USE OF SINGULAR AND PLURAL; GENDER.

In this title, unless the statutory context otherwise requires:

(1) words in the singular number include the plural, and those in the plural include the singular; and

(2) words of any gender also refer to any other gender.

Amended by Acts 2003, 78th Leg., ch. 542, Sec. 1, eff. Sept. 1, 2003.

Sec. 1.107. SECTION CAPTIONS.

Section captions are parts of this title.

Amended by Acts 2003, 78th Leg., ch. 542, Sec. 1, eff. Sept. 1, 2003.

Sec. 1.108. RELATION TO ELECTRONIC SIGNATURES IN GLOBAL AND NATIONAL COMMERCE ACT.

This title modifies, limits, and supersedes the federal Electronic Signatures in Global and National Commerce Act (15 U.S.C. Section 7001 et seq.) but does not modify, limit, or supersede Section 101(c) of that Act (15 U.S.C. Section 7001(c)) or authorize electronic delivery of any of the notices described in Section 103(b) of that Act (15 U.S.C. Section 7003(b)).

Amended by Acts 2003, 78th Leg., ch. 542, Sec. 1, eff. Sept. 1, 2003.

SUBCHAPTER B. GENERAL DEFINITIONS AND PRINCIPLES OF INTERPRETATION

This section was amended by the 84th Legislature. Pending publication of the current statutes, see S.B. 1077, 84th Legislature, Regular Session, for amendments affecting this section.

Sec. 1.201. GENERAL DEFINITIONS.

(a) Unless the context otherwise requires, words or phrases defined in this section, or in the additional definitions contained in other chapters of this title that apply to particular chapters or parts thereof, have the meanings stated.

(b) Subject to definitions contained in other chapters of this title that apply to particular chapters or parts thereof:

(1) "Action," in the sense of a judicial proceeding, includes recoupment, counterclaim, set-off, suit in equity, and any other proceeding in which rights are determined.

(2) "Aggrieved party" means a party entitled to pursue a remedy.

(3) "Agreement," as distinguished from "contract," means the bargain of the parties in fact, as found in their language or inferred from other circumstances, including course of performance, course of dealing, or usage of trade as provided in Section 1.303.

. . . .

(10) "Conspicuous," with reference to a term, means so written, displayed, or presented that a reasonable person against which it is to operate ought to have noticed it. Whether a term is "conspicuous" or not is a decision for the court. Conspicuous terms include the following:

(A) a heading in capitals equal to or greater in size than the surrounding text, or in contrasting type, font, or color to the surrounding text of the same or lesser size; and

(B) language in the body of a record or display in larger type than the surrounding text, or in contrasting type, font, or color to the surrounding text of the same size, or set off from surrounding text of the same size by symbols or other marks that call attention to the language.

(11) "Consumer" means an individual who enters into a transaction primarily for personal, family, or household purposes.

(12) "Contract," as distinguished from "agreement," means the total legal obligation that results from the parties' agreement as determined by this title as supplemented by any other applicable laws.

. . . .

(15) "Delivery," with respect to an electronic document of title, means voluntary transfer of control, and with respect to an instrument, a tangible document of title, or chattel paper, means voluntary transfer of possession.

. . . .

(17) "Fault" means a default, breach, or wrongful act or omission.

(18) "Fungible goods" means:

(A) goods of which any unit, by nature or usage of trade, is the equivalent of any other like unit; or

(B) goods that by agreement are treated as equivalent.

(19) "Genuine" means free of forgery or counterfeiting.

(20) "Good faith," except as otherwise provided in Chapter 5, means honesty in fact and the observance of reasonable commercial standards of fair dealing.

. . . .

(26) "Party," as distinguished from "third party," means a person that has engaged in a transaction or made an agreement subject to this title.

(27) "Person" means an individual, corporation, business trust, estate, trust, partnership, limited liability company, association, joint venture, government, governmental subdivision, agency, or instrumentality, public corporation, or any other legal or commercial entity.

(28) "Present value" means the amount as of a date certain of one or more sums payable in the future, discounted to the date certain by use of either an interest rate specified by the parties if that rate is not manifestly unreasonable at the time the transaction is entered into or, if an interest rate is not so specified, a commercially reasonable rate that takes into account the facts and circumstances at the time the transaction is entered into.

(29) "Purchase" means taking by sale, lease, discount, negotiation, mortgage, pledge, lien, security interest, issue or reissue, gift, or any other voluntary transaction creating an interest in property.

(30) "Purchaser" means a person that takes by purchase.

(31) "Record" means information that is inscribed on a tangible medium or that is stored in an electronic or other medium and is retrievable in perceivable form.

(32) "Remedy" means any remedial right to which an aggrieved party is entitled with or without resort to a tribunal.

(33) "Representative" means a person empowered to act for another, including an agent, an officer of a corporation or association, and a trustee, executor, or administrator of an estate.

(34) "Right" includes remedy.

....

(36) "Send" in connection with a writing, record, or notice means:

(A) to deposit in the mail or deliver for transmission by any other usual means of communication with postage or cost of transmission provided for and properly addressed and, in the case of an instrument, to an address specified thereon or otherwise agreed, or if there be none to any address reasonable under the circumstances; or

(B) in any other way cause to be received any record or notice within the time at which it would have arrived if properly sent.

(37) "Signed" includes using any symbol executed or adopted with present intention to adopt or accept a writing.

(38) "State" means a State of the United States, the District of Columbia, Puerto Rico, the United States Virgin Islands, or any territory or insular possession subject to the jurisdiction of the United States.

(39) "Surety" includes a guarantor or other secondary obligor.

(40) "Term" means a portion of an agreement that relates to a particular matter.

(41) "Unauthorized signature" means a signature made without actual, implied, or apparent authority. The term includes a forgery.

(42) "Warehouse receipt" means a document of title issued by a person engaged in the business of storing goods for hire.

(43) "Writing" includes printing, typewriting, or any other intentional reduction to tangible form. "Written" has a corresponding meaning.

Acts 1967, 60th Leg., p. 2343, ch. 785, Sec. 1, eff. Sept. 1, 1967. [Other references to amendments omitted.] Amended by: Acts 2005, 79th Leg., Ch. 122 (S.B. 1593), Sec. 2, eff. September 1, 2005.

Sec. 1.202. NOTICE; KNOWLEDGE.

(a) Subject to Subsection (f), a person has "notice" of a fact if the person:

(1) has actual knowledge of it;

(2) has received a notice or notification of it; or

(3) from all the facts and circumstances known to the person at the time in question, has reason to know that it exists.

(b) "Knowledge" means actual knowledge. "Knows" has a corresponding meaning.

(c) "Discover," "learn," or words of similar import refer to knowledge rather than to reason to know.

(d) A person "notifies" or "gives" a notice or notification to another person by taking such steps as may be reasonably required to inform the other person in ordinary course, whether or not the other person actually comes to know of it.

(e) Subject to Subsection (f), a person "receives" a notice or notification when:

(1) it comes to that person's attention; or

(2) it is duly delivered in a form reasonable under the circumstances at the place of business through which the contract was made or at another location held out by that person as the place for receipt of such communications.

(f) Notice, knowledge, or a notice or notification received by an organization is effective for a particular transaction from the time it is brought to the attention of the individual conducting that transaction and, in any event, from the time it would have been brought to the individual's attention if the organization had exercised due diligence. An organization exercises due diligence if it maintains reasonable routines for communicating significant information to the person conducting the transaction and there is reasonable compliance with the routines. Due diligence does not require an individual acting for the organization to communicate information unless the communication is part of the individual's regular duties or the individual has reason to know of the transaction and that the transaction would be materially affected by the information.

Amended by Acts 2003, 78th Leg., ch. 542, Sec. 1, eff. Sept. 1, 2003.

....

Sec. 1.204. VALUE. Except as otherwise provided in Chapters 3, 4, and 5, a person gives value for rights if the person acquires them:

(1) in return for a binding commitment to extend credit or for the extension of immediately available credit, whether or not drawn upon and whether or not a charge-back is provided for in the event of difficulties in collection;

(2) as security for, or in total or partial satisfaction of, a preexisting claim;

(3) by accepting delivery under a preexisting contract for purchase; or

(4) in return for any consideration sufficient to support a simple contract.

Amended by Acts 2003, 78th Leg., ch. 542, Sec. 1, eff. Sept. 1, 2003.

Sec. 1.205. REASONABLE TIME; SEASONABLENESS.

(a) Whether a time for taking an action required by this title is reasonable depends on the nature, purpose, and circumstances of the action.

(b) An action is taken seasonably if it is taken at or within the time agreed or, if no time is agreed, at or within a reasonable time.

Amended by Acts 2003, 78th Leg., ch. 542, Sec. 1, eff. Sept. 1, 2003.

Sec. 1.206. PRESUMPTIONS. Whenever this title creates a "presumption" with respect to a fact, or provides that a fact is "presumed," the trier of fact must find the existence of the fact unless and until evidence is introduced that supports a finding of its nonexistence.

Amended by Acts 2003, 78th Leg., ch. 542, Sec. 1, eff. Sept. 1, 2003.

SUBCHAPTER C. TERRITORIAL APPLICABILITY AND GENERAL RULES

Sec. 1.301. TERRITORIAL APPLICATION OF THE TITLE; PARTIES' POWER TO CHOOSE APPLICABLE LAW.

(a) Except as provided hereafter in this section, when a transaction bears a reasonable relation to this state and also to another state or nation the parties may agree that the law either of this state or of such other state or nation shall govern their rights and duties. Failing such agreement this title applies to transactions bearing an appropriate relation to this state.

(b) Where one of the following provisions of this title specifies the applicable law, that provision governs and a contrary agreement is effective only to the extent permitted by the law (including the conflict of laws rules) so specified:

Rights of creditors against sold goods. Section 2.402.

Applicability of the chapter on Leases. Sections 2A.105 and 2A.106.

Applicability of the chapter on Bank Deposits and Collections. Section 4.102.

Governing law in the chapter on Funds Transfers. Section 4A.507.

Letters of Credit. Section 5.116.

Applicability of the chapter on Investment Securities. Section 8.110.

Law governing perfection, the effect of perfection or nonperfection, and the priority of security interests and agricultural liens. Sections 9.301-9.307.

(c) If a transaction that is subject to this title is a "qualified transaction," as defined in Section 271.001, then except as provided in Subsection (b) of this section, Chapter 271 governs the effect of an agreement by the parties that the law of a particular jurisdiction governs an issue relating to the transaction or that the law of a particular jurisdiction governs the interpretation or construction of an agreement relating to the transaction or a provision of the agreement.

Added by Acts 2003, 78th Leg., ch. 542, Sec. 1, eff. Sept. 1, 2003. Amended by: Acts 2007, 80th Leg., R.S., Ch. 885 (H.B. 2278), Sec. 2.02, eff. April 1, 2009.

Sec. 1.302. VARIATION BY AGREEMENT.

(a) Except as otherwise provided in Subsection (b) or elsewhere in this title, the effect of provisions of this title may be varied by agreement.

(b) The obligations of good faith, diligence, reasonableness, and care prescribed by this title may not be disclaimed by agreement. The parties, by agreement, may determine the standards by which the performance of those obligations is to be measured if those standards are not manifestly unreasonable. Whenever this title requires an action to be taken within a reasonable time, a time that is not manifestly unreasonable may be fixed by agreement.

(c) The presence in certain provisions of this title of the phrase "unless otherwise agreed," or words of similar import, does not imply that the effect of other provisions may not be varied by agreement under this section.

Added by Acts 2003, 78th Leg., ch. 542, Sec. 1, eff. Sept. 1, 2003.

Sec. 1.303. COURSE OF PERFORMANCE, COURSE OF DEALING, AND USAGE OF TRADE.

(a) A "course of performance" is a sequence of conduct between the parties to a particular transaction that exists if:

(1) the agreement of the parties with respect to the transaction involves repeated occasions for performance by a party; and

(2) the other party, with knowledge of the nature of the performance and opportunity for objection to it, accepts the performance or acquiesces in it without objection.

(b) A course of dealing is a sequence of conduct concerning previous transactions between the parties to a particular transaction that is fairly to be regarded as establishing a common basis of understanding for interpreting their expressions and other conduct.

(c) A "usage of trade" is any practice or method of dealing having such regularity of observance in a place, vocation, or trade as to justify an expectation that it will be observed with respect to the transaction in question. The existence and scope of such a usage must be proved as facts. If it is established that such a usage is embodied in a trade code or similar record, the interpretation of the record is a question of law.

(d) A course of performance or course of dealing between the parties or usage of trade in the vocation or trade in which they are engaged or of which they are or should be aware is relevant in ascertaining the meaning of the parties' agreement, may give particular meaning to specific terms of the agreement, and may supplement or qualify the terms of the agreement. A usage of trade applicable in the place in which part of the performance under the agreement is to occur may be so utilized as to that part of the performance.

(e) Except as otherwise provided in Subsection (f), the express terms of an agreement and any applicable course of performance, course of dealing, or usage of trade must be construed whenever reasonable as consistent with each other. If such a construction is unreasonable:

(1) express terms prevail over course of performance, course of dealing, and usage of trade;

(2) course of performance prevails over course of dealing and usage of trade; and

(3) course of dealing prevails over usage of trade.

(f) Subject to Section 2.209, a course of performance is relevant to show a waiver or modification of any term inconsistent with the course of performance.

(g) Evidence of a relevant usage of trade offered by one party is not admissible unless that party has given the other party notice that the court finds sufficient to prevent unfair surprise to the other party.

Added by Acts 2003, 78th Leg., ch. 542, Sec. 1, eff. Sept. 1, 2003.

Sec. 1.304. OBLIGATION OF GOOD FAITH.

Every contract or duty within this title imposes an obligation of good faith in its performance and enforcement.

Added by Acts 2003, 78th Leg., ch. 542, Sec. 1, eff. Sept. 1, 2003.

Sec. 1.305. REMEDIES TO BE LIBERALLY ADMINISTERED.

(a) The remedies provided by this title must be liberally administered to the end that the aggrieved party may be put in as good a position as if the other party had fully performed but neither consequential or special damages nor penal damages may be had except as specifically provided in this title or by other rule of law.

(b) Any right or obligation declared by this title is enforceable by action unless the provision declaring it specifies a different and limited effect.

Added by Acts 2003, 78th Leg., ch. 542, Sec. 1, eff. Sept. 1, 2003.

Sec. 1.306. WAIVER OF RENUNCIATION OF CLAIM OR RIGHT AFTER BREACH.

A claim or right arising out of an alleged breach may be discharged in whole or in part without consideration by agreement of the aggrieved party in an authenticated record.

Added by Acts 2003, 78th Leg., ch. 542, Sec. 1, eff. Sept. 1, 2003.

Sec. 1.307. PRIMA FACIE EVIDENCE BY THIRD-PARTY DOCUMENTS. A document in due form purporting to be a bill of lading, policy or certificate of insurance, official weigher's or inspector's certificate, consular invoice, or any other document authorized or required by the contract to be issued by a third party is prima facie evidence of its own authenticity and genuineness and of the facts stated in the document by the third party.

Added by Acts 2003, 78th Leg., ch. 542, Sec. 1, eff. Sept. 1, 2003.

Sec. 1.308. PERFORMANCE OR ACCEPTANCE UNDER RESERVATION OF RIGHTS.

(a) A party that with explicit reservation of rights performs or promises performance or assents to performance in a manner demanded or offered by the other party does not thereby prejudice the rights reserved. Such words as "without prejudice," "under protest," or the like are sufficient.

(b) Subsection (a) does not apply to an accord and satisfaction.

Added by Acts 2003, 78th Leg., ch. 542, Sec. 1, eff. Sept. 1, 2003.

Sec. 1.309. OPTION TO ACCELERATE AT WILL. A term providing that one party or that party's successor in interest may accelerate payment or performance or require collateral or additional collateral "at will" or when the party "deems itself insecure," or words of similar import, means that the party has power to do so only if that party in good faith believes that the prospect of payment or performance is impaired. The burden of establishing lack of good faith is on the party against which the power has been exercised.

Added by Acts 2003, 78th Leg., ch. 542, Sec. 1, eff. Sept. 1, 2003.

Sec. 1.310. SUBORDINATED OBLIGATIONS. An obligation may be issued as subordinated to performance of another obligation of the person obligated, or a creditor may subordinate its right to performance of an obligation by agreement with either the person obligated or another creditor of the person obligated. Subordination does not create a security interest as against either the common debtor or a subordinated creditor.

Added by Acts 2003, 78th Leg., ch. 542, Sec. 1, eff. Sept. 1, 2003.

CHAPTER 2. SALES

SUBCHAPTER A. SHORT TITLE, GENERAL CONSTRUCTION AND SUBJECT MATTER

Sec. 2.101. SHORT TITLE. This chapter may be cited as Uniform Commercial Code—Sales.

Acts 1967, 60th Leg., p. 2343, ch. 785, Sec. 1, eff. Sept. 1, 1967.

Sec. 2.102. SCOPE; CERTAIN SECURITY AND OTHER TRANSACTIONS EXCLUDED FROM THIS CHAPTER.

Unless the context otherwise requires, this chapter applies to transactions in goods; it does not apply to any transaction which although in the form of an unconditional contract to sell or present sale is intended to operate only as a security transaction nor does this chapter impair or repeal any statute regulating sales to consumers, farmers or other specified classes of buyers.

Acts 1967, 60th Leg., p. 2343, ch. 785, Sec. 1, eff. Sept. 1, 1967.

Sec. 2.103. DEFINITIONS AND INDEX OF DEFINITIONS.

(a) In this chapter unless the context otherwise requires

(1) "Buyer" means a person who buys or contracts to buy goods.

(2) Reserved.

(3) "Receipt" of goods means taking physical possession of them.

(4) "Seller" means a person who sells or contracts to sell goods.

(b) Other definitions applying to this chapter or to specified subchapters thereof, and the sections in which they appear are:

"Acceptance". Section 2.606.

"Banker's credit". Section 2.325.

"Between merchants". Section 2.104.

"Cancellation". Section 2.106(d).

"Commercial unit". Section 2.105.

"Confirmed credit". Section 2.325.

"Conforming to contract". Section 2.106.

"Contract for sale". Section 2.106.

"Cover". Section 2.712.

"Entrusting". Section 2.403.

"Financing agency". Section 2.104.

"Future goods". Section 2.105.

"Goods". Section 2.105.

"Identification". Section 2.501.

"Installment contract". Section 2.612.

"Letter of credit". Section 2.325.

"Lot". Section 2.105.

"Merchant". Section 2.104.

"Overseas". Section 2.323.

"Person in position of seller". Section 2.707.

"Present sale". Section 2.106.

"Sale". Section 2.106.

"Sale on approval". Section 2.326.

"Sale or return". Section 2.326.

"Termination". Section 2.106.

(c) The following definitions in other chapters apply to this chapter:

"Check". Section 3.104.

"Consignee". Section 7.102.

"Consignor". Section 7.102.

"Consumer goods". Section 9.102.

"Control". Section 7.106.

"Dishonor". Section 3.502.

"Draft". Section 3.104.

(d) In addition Chapter 1 contains general definitions and principles of construction and interpretation applicable throughout this chapter.

Acts 1967, 60th Leg., p. 2343, ch. 785, Sec. 1, eff. Sept. 1, 1967. Amended by Acts 1999, 76th Leg., ch. 414, Sec. 2.14, eff. July 1, 2001; Acts 2003, 78th Leg., ch. 542, Sec. 2, eff. Sept. 1, 2003. Amended by: Acts 2005, 79th Leg., Ch. 122 (S.B. 1593), Sec. 3, eff. September 1, 2005.

Sec. 2.104. DEFINITIONS: "MERCHANT"; "BETWEEN MERCHANTS"; "FINANCING AGENCY".

(a) "Merchant" means a person who deals in goods of the kind or otherwise by his occupation holds himself out as having knowledge or skill peculiar to the practices or goods involved in the transaction or to whom such knowledge or skill may be attributed by his employment of an agent or broker or other intermediary who by his occupation holds himself out as having such knowledge or skill.

(b) "Financing agency" means a bank, finance company or other person who in the ordinary course of business makes advances against goods or documents of title or who by arrangement with either the seller or the buyer intervenes in ordinary course to make or collect payment due or claimed under the contract for sale, as by purchasing or paying the seller's draft or making advances against it or by merely taking it for collection whether or not documents of title accompany or are associated with the draft. "Financing agency" includes also a bank or other person who similarly intervenes between persons who are in the position of seller and buyer in respect to the goods (Section 2.707).

(c) "Between merchants" means in any transaction with respect to which both parties are chargeable with the knowledge or skill of merchants.

Acts 1967, 60th Leg., p. 2343, ch. 785, Sec. 1, eff. Sept. 1, 1967. Amended by: Acts 2005, 79th Leg., Ch. 122 (S.B. 1593), Sec. 4, eff. September 1, 2005.

Sec. 2.105. DEFINITIONS: TRANSFERABILITY; "GOODS"; "FUTURE" GOODS; "LOT"; "COMMERCIAL UNIT".

(a) "Goods" means all things (including specially manufactured goods) which are movable at the time of identification to the contract for sale other than the money in which the price is to be paid, investment securities (Chapter 8) and things in action. "Goods" also includes the unborn young of animals and growing crops and other identified things attached to realty as described in the section on goods to be severed from realty (Section 2.107).

(b) Goods must be both existing and identified before any interest in them can pass. Goods which are not both existing and identified are "future" goods. A purported present sale of future goods or of any interest therein operates as a contract to sell.

(c) There may be a sale of a part interest in existing identified goods.

(d) An undivided share in an identified bulk of fungible goods is sufficiently identified to be sold although the quantity of the bulk is not determined. Any agreed proportion of such a bulk or any quantity thereof agreed upon by number, weight or other measure may to the extent of the seller's interest in the bulk be sold to the buyer who then becomes an owner in common.

(e) "Lot" means a parcel or a single article which is the subject matter of a separate sale or delivery, whether or not it is sufficient to perform the contract.

(f) "Commercial unit" means such a unit of goods as by commercial usage is a single whole for purposes of sale and division of which materially impairs its character or value on the market or in use. A commercial unit may be a single article (as a machine) or a set of articles (as a suite of furniture or an assortment of sizes) or a quantity (as a bale, gross, or carload) or any other unit treated in use or in the relevant market as a single whole.

Acts 1967, 60th Leg., p. 2343, ch. 785, Sec. 1, eff. Sept. 1, 1967.

Sec. 2.106. DEFINITIONS: "CONTRACT"; "AGREEMENT"; "CONTRACT FOR SALE"; "SALE"; "PRESENT SALE"; "CONFORMING" TO CONTRACT; "TERMINATION"; "CANCELLATION".

(a) In this chapter unless the context otherwise requires "contract" and "agreement" are limited to those relating to the present or future sale of goods. "Contract for sale" includes both a present sale of goods and a contract to sell goods at a future time. A "sale" consists in the passing of title from the seller to the buyer for a price (Section 2.401). A "present sale" means a sale which is accomplished by the making of the contract.

(b) Goods or conduct including any part of a performance are "conforming" or conform to the contract when they are in accordance with the obligations under the contract.

(c) "Termination" occurs when either party pursuant to a power created by agreement or law puts an end to the contract otherwise than for its breach. On "termination" all obligations which are still executory on both sides are discharged but any right based on prior breach or performance survives.

(d) "Cancellation" occurs when either party puts an end to the contract for breach by the other and its effect is the same as that of "termination" except that the cancelling party also retains any remedy for breach of the whole contract or any unperformed balance.

Acts 1967, 60th Leg., p. 2343, ch. 785, Sec. 1, eff. Sept. 1, 1967.

Sec. 2.107. GOODS TO BE SEVERED FROM REALTY: RECORDING.

(a) A contract for the sale of minerals or the like (including oil and gas) or a structure or its materials to be removed from realty is a contract for the sale of goods within this chapter if they are to be severed by the seller but until severance a purported present sale thereof which is not effective as a transfer of an interest in land is effective only as a contract to sell.

(b) A contract for the sale apart from the land of growing crops or other things attached to realty and capable of severance without material harm thereto but not described in Subsection (a) or of timber to be cut is a contract for the sale of goods within this chapter whether the subject matter is to be severed by the buyer or by the seller even though it forms part of the realty at the time of contracting, and the parties can by identification effect a present sale before severance.

(c) The provisions of this section are subject to any third party rights provided by the law relating to realty records, and the contract for sale may be executed and recorded as a document transferring an interest in land and shall then constitute notice to third parties of the buyer's rights under the contract for sale.

Acts 1967, 60th Leg., p. 2343, ch. 785, Sec. 1, eff. Sept. 1, 1967. Amended by Acts 1973, 63rd Leg., p. 998, ch. 400, Sec. 3, eff. Jan. 1, 1974.

SUBCHAPTER B. FORM, FORMATION AND READJUSTMENT OF CONTRACT

Sec. 2.201. FORMAL REQUIREMENTS; STATUTE OF FRAUDS.

(a) Except as otherwise provided in this section a contract for the sale of goods for the price of $500 or more is not enforceable by way of action or defense unless there is some writing sufficient to indicate that a contract for sale has been made between the parties and signed by the party against whom enforcement is sought or by his authorized agent or broker. A writing is not insufficient because it omits or incorrectly states a term agreed upon but the contract is not enforceable under this paragraph beyond the quantity of goods shown in such writing.

(b) Between merchants if within a reasonable time a writing in confirmation of the contract and sufficient against the sender is received and the party receiving it has reason to know its contents, it satisfies the requirements of Subsection (a) against such party unless written notice of objection to its contents is given within ten days after it is received.

(c) A contract which does not satisfy the requirements of Subsection (a) but which is valid in other respects is enforceable

(1) if the goods are to be specially manufactured for the buyer and are not suitable for sale to others in the ordinary course of the seller's business and the seller, before notice of repudiation is received and under circumstances which reasonably indicate that the goods are for the buyer, has made either a substantial beginning of their manufacture or commitments for their procurement; or

(2) if the party against whom enforcement is sought admits in his pleading, testimony or otherwise in court that a contract for sale was made, but the contract is not enforceable under this provision beyond the quantity of goods admitted; or

(3) with respect to goods for which payment has been made and accepted or which have been received and accepted (Section 2.606).

Acts 1967, 60th Leg., p. 2343, ch. 785, Sec. 1, eff. Sept. 1, 1967.

Sec. 2.202. FINAL WRITTEN EXPRESSION: PAROL OR EXTRINSIC EVIDENCE. Terms with respect to which the confirmatory memoranda of the parties agree or which are otherwise set forth in a writing intended by the parties as a final expression of their agreement with respect to such terms as are included therein may not be contradicted by evidence of any prior agreement or of a contemporaneous oral agreement but may be explained or supplemented

(1) by course of performance, course of dealing, or usage of trade (Section 1.303); and

(2) by evidence of consistent additional terms unless the court finds the writing to have been intended also as a complete and exclusive statement of the terms of the agreement.

Acts 1967, 60th Leg., p. 2343, ch. 785, Sec. 1, eff. Sept. 1, 1967. Amended by Acts 2003, 78th Leg., ch. 542, Sec. 3, eff. Sept. 1, 2003.

Sec. 2.203. SEALS INOPERATIVE. The affixing of a seal to a writing evidencing a contract for sale or an offer to buy or sell goods does not constitute the writing a sealed instrument and the law with respect to sealed instruments does not apply to such a contract or offer.

Acts 1967, 60th Leg., p. 2343, ch. 785, Sec. 1, eff. Sept. 1, 1967.

Sec. 2.204. FORMATION IN GENERAL.

(a) A contract for sale of goods may be made in any manner sufficient to show agreement, including conduct by both parties which recognizes the existence of such a contract.

(b) An agreement sufficient to constitute a contract for sale may be found even though the moment of its making is undetermined.

(c) Even though one or more terms are left open a contract for sale does not fail for indefiniteness if the parties have intended to make a contract and there is a reasonably certain basis for giving an appropriate remedy.

Acts 1967, 60th Leg., p. 2343, ch. 785, Sec. 1, eff. Sept. 1, 1967.

Sec. 2.205. FIRM OFFERS.

An offer by a merchant to buy or sell goods in a signed writing which by its terms gives assurance that it will be held open is not revocable, for lack of consideration, during the time stated or if no time is stated for a reasonable time, but in no event may such period of irrevocability exceed three months; but any such term of assurance on a form supplied by the offeree must be separately signed by the offeror.

Acts 1967, 60th Leg., p. 2343, ch. 785, Sec. 1, eff. Sept. 1, 1967.

Sec. 2.206. OFFER AND ACCEPTANCE IN FORMATION OF CONTRACT.

(a) Unless otherwise unambiguously indicated by the language or circumstances

(1) an offer to make a contract shall be construed as inviting acceptance in any manner and by any medium reasonable in the circumstances;

(2) an order or other offer to buy goods for prompt or current shipment shall be construed as inviting acceptance either by a prompt promise to ship or by the prompt or current shipment of conforming or non-conforming goods, but such a shipment of non-conforming goods does not constitute an acceptance if the seller seasonably notifies the buyer that the shipment is offered only as an accommodation to the buyer.

(b) Where the beginning of a requested performance is a reasonable mode of acceptance an offeror who is not notified of acceptance within a reasonable time may treat the offer as having lapsed before acceptance.

Acts 1967, 60th Leg., p. 2343, ch. 785, Sec. 1, eff. Sept. 1, 1967.

Sec. 2.207. ADDITIONAL TERMS IN ACCEPTANCE OR CONFIRMATION.

(a) A definite and seasonable expression of acceptance or a written confirmation which is sent within a reasonable time operates as an acceptance even though it states terms additional to or different from those offered or agreed upon, unless acceptance is expressly made conditional on assent to the additional or different terms.

(b) The additional terms are to be construed as proposals for addition to the contract. Between merchants such terms become part of the contract unless:

(1) the offer expressly limits acceptance to the terms of the offer;

(2) they materially alter it; or

(3) notification of objection to them has already been given or is given within a reasonable time after notice of them is received.

(c) Conduct by both parties which recognizes the existence of a contract is sufficient to establish a contract for sale although the writings of the parties do not otherwise establish a contract. In such case the terms of the particular contract consist of those terms on which the writings of the parties agree, together with any supplementary terms incorporated under any other provisions of this title.

Acts 1967, 60th Leg., p. 2343, ch. 785, Sec. 1, eff. Sept. 1, 1967.

Sec. 2.209. MODIFICATION, RESCISSION AND WAIVER.

(a) An agreement modifying a contract within this chapter needs no consideration to be binding.

(b) A signed agreement which excludes modification or rescission except by a signed writing cannot be otherwise modified or rescinded, but except as between merchants such a requirement on a form supplied by the merchant must be separately signed by the other party.

(c) The requirements of the statute of frauds section of this chapter (Section 2.201) must be satisfied if the contract as modified is within its provisions.

(d) Although an attempt at modification or rescission does not satisfy the requirements of Subsection (b) or (c) it can operate as a waiver.

(e) A party who has made a waiver affecting an executory portion of the contract may retract the waiver by reasonable notification received by the other party that strict performance will be required of any term waived, unless the retraction would be unjust in view of a material change of position in reliance on the waiver.

Acts 1967, 60th Leg., p. 2343, ch. 785, Sec. 1, eff. Sept. 1, 1967.

Sec. 2.210. DELEGATION OF PERFORMANCE; ASSIGNMENT OF RIGHTS.

(a) A party may perform his duty through a delegate unless otherwise agreed or unless the other party has a substantial interest in having his original promisor perform or control the acts required by the contract. No delegation of performance relieves the party delegating of any duty to perform or any liability for breach.

(b) Unless otherwise agreed all rights of either seller or buyer can be assigned except where the assignment would materially change the duty of the other party, or increase materially the burden or risk imposed on him by his contract, or impair materially his chance of obtaining return performance. A right to damages for breach of the whole contract or a right arising out of the assignor's due performance of his entire obligation can be assigned despite agreement otherwise.

(c) The creation, attachment, perfection, or enforcement of a security interest in the seller's interest under a contract is not a transfer that materially changes the duty of or increases materially the burden or risk imposed on the buyer or impairs materially the buyer's chance of obtaining return performance within the purview of Subsection (b) unless, and then only to the extent that, enforcement actually results in a delegation of material performance of the seller. Even in that event, the creation, attachment, perfection, and enforcement of the security interest remain effective, but (i) the seller is liable to the buyer for damages caused by the delegation to the extent that the damages could not reasonably be prevented by the buyer, and (ii) a court having jurisdiction may grant other appropriate relief, including cancellation of the contract for sale or an injunction against enforcement of the security interest or consummation of the enforcement.

(d) Unless the circumstances indicate the contrary a prohibition of assignment of "the contract" is to be construed as barring only the delegation to the assignee of the assignor's performance.

(e) An assignment of "the contract" or of "all my rights under the contract" or an assignment in similar general terms is an assignment of rights and unless the language or the circumstances (as in an assignment for security) indicate the contrary, it is a delegation of performance of the duties of the assignor and its acceptance by the assignee constitutes a promise by him to perform those duties. This promise is enforceable by either the assignor or the other party to the original contract.

(f) The other party may treat any assignment which delegates performance as creating reasonable grounds for insecurity and may without prejudice to his rights against the assignor demand assurances from the assignee (Section 2.609).

Acts 1967, 60th Leg., p. 2343, ch. 785, Sec. 1, eff. Sept. 1, 1967. Amended by Acts 1999, 76th Leg., ch. 414, Sec. 2.15, eff. July 1, 2001.

SUBCHAPTER C. GENERAL OBLIGATION AND CONSTRUCTION OF CONTRACT

Sec. 2.301. GENERAL OBLIGATIONS OF PARTIES. The obligation of the seller is to transfer and deliver and that of the buyer is to accept and pay in accordance with the contract.

Acts 1967, 60th Leg., p. 2343, ch. 785, Sec. 1, eff. Sept. 1, 1967.

Sec. 2.302. UNCONSCIONABLE CONTRACT OR CLAUSE.

(a) If the court as a matter of law finds the contract or any clause of the contract to have been unconscionable at the time it was made the court may refuse to enforce the contract, or it may enforce the remainder of the contract without the unconscionable clause, or it may so limit the application of any unconscionable clause as to avoid any unconscionable result.

(b) When it is claimed or appears to the court that the contract or any clause thereof may be unconscionable the parties shall be afforded a reasonable opportunity to present evidence as to its commercial setting, purpose and effect to aid the court in making the determination.

Acts 1967, 60th Leg., p. 2343, ch. 785, Sec. 1, eff. Sept. 1, 1967.

Sec. 2.303. ALLOCATION OR DIVISION OF RISKS. Where this chapter allocates a risk or a burden as between the parties "unless otherwise agreed", the agreement may not only shift the allocation but may also divide the risk or burden.

Acts 1967, 60th Leg., p. 2343, ch. 785, Sec. 1, eff. Sept. 1, 1967.

Sec. 2.304. PRICE PAYABLE IN MONEY, GOODS, REALTY, OR OTHERWISE.

(a) The price can be made payable in money or otherwise. If it is payable in whole or in part in goods each party is a seller of the goods which he is to transfer.

(b) Even though all or part of the price is payable in an interest in realty the transfer of the goods and the seller's obligations with reference to them are subject to this chapter, but not the transfer of the interest in realty or the transferor's obligations in connection therewith.

Acts 1967, 60th Leg., p. 2343, ch. 785, Sec. 1, eff. Sept. 1, 1967.

Sec. 2.305. OPEN PRICE TERM.

(a) The parties if they so intend can conclude a contract for sale even though the price is not settled. In such a case the price is a reasonable price at the time for delivery if

(1) nothing is said as to price; or

(2) the price is left to be agreed by the parties and they fail to agree; or

(3) the price is to be fixed in terms of some agreed market or other standard as set or recorded by a third person or agency and it is not so set or recorded.

(b) A price to be fixed by the seller or by the buyer means a price for him to fix in good faith.

(c) When a price left to be fixed otherwise than by agreement of the parties fails to be fixed through fault of one party the other may at his option treat the contract as cancelled or himself fix a reasonable price.

(d) Where, however, the parties intend not to be bound unless the price be fixed or agreed and it is not fixed or agreed there is no contract. In such a case the buyer must return any goods already received or if unable so to do must pay their reasonable value at the time of delivery and the seller must return any portion of the price paid on account.

Acts 1967, 60th Leg., p. 2343, ch. 785, Sec. 1, eff. Sept. 1, 1967.

Sec. 2.306. OUTPUT, REQUIREMENTS AND EXCLUSIVE DEALINGS.

(a) A term which measures the quantity by the output of the seller or the requirements of the buyer means such actual output or requirements as may occur in good faith, except that no quantity unreasonably disproportionate to any stated estimate or in the absence of a stated estimate to any normal or otherwise comparable prior output or requirements may be tendered or demanded.

(b) A lawful agreement by either the seller or the buyer for exclusive dealing in the kind of goods concerned imposes unless otherwise agreed an obligation by the seller to use best efforts to supply the goods and by the buyer to use best efforts to promote their sale.

Acts 1967, 60th Leg., p. 2343, ch. 785, Sec. 1, eff. Sept. 1, 1967.

Sec. 2.307. DELIVERY IN SINGLE LOT OR SEVERAL LOTS.

Unless otherwise agreed all goods called for by a contract for sale must be tendered in a single delivery and payment is due only on such tender but where the circumstances give either party the right to make or demand delivery in lots the price if it can be apportioned may be demanded for each lot.

Acts 1967, 60th Leg., p. 2343, ch. 785, Sec. 1, eff. Sept. 1, 1967.

Sec. 2.308. ABSENCE OF SPECIFIED PLACE FOR DELIVERY.

Unless otherwise agreed

(1) the place for delivery of goods is the seller's place of business or if he has none his residence; but

(2) in a contract for sale of identified goods which to the knowledge of the parties at the time of contracting are in some other place, that place is the place for their delivery; and

(3) documents of title may be delivered through customary banking channels.

Acts 1967, 60th Leg., p. 2343, ch. 785, Sec. 1, eff. Sept. 1, 1967.

Sec. 2.309. ABSENCE OF SPECIFIC TIME PROVISIONS; NOTICE OF TERMINATION.

(a) The time for shipment or delivery or any other action under a contract if not provided in this chapter or agreed upon shall be a reasonable time.

(b) Where the contract provides for successive performances but is indefinite in duration it is valid for a reasonable time but unless otherwise agreed may be terminated at any time by either party.

(c) Termination of a contract by one party except on the happening of an agreed event requires that reasonable notification be received by the other party and an agreement dispensing with notification is invalid if its operation would be unconscionable.

Acts 1967, 60th Leg., p. 2343, ch. 785, Sec. 1, eff. Sept. 1, 1967.

Sec. 2.310. OPEN TIME FOR PAYMENT OR RUNNING OF CREDIT; AUTHORITY TO SHIP UNDER RESERVATION.

Unless otherwise agreed

(1) payment is due at the time and place at which the buyer is to receive the goods even though the place of shipment is the place of delivery; and

(2) if the seller is authorized to send the goods he may ship them under reservation, and may tender the documents of title, but the buyer may inspect the goods after their arrival before payment is due unless such inspection is inconsistent with the terms of the contract (Section 2.513); and

(3) if delivery is authorized and made by way of documents of title otherwise than by Subdivision (2) then payment is due regardless of where the goods are to be received:

(A) at the time and place at which the buyer is to receive delivery of the tangible documents; or

(B) at the time the buyer is to receive delivery of the electronic documents and at the seller's place of business or if none, the seller's residence; and

(4) where the seller is required or authorized to ship the goods on credit the credit period runs from the time of shipment but post-dating the invoice or delaying its dispatch will correspondingly delay the starting of the credit period.

Acts 1967, 60th Leg., p. 2343, ch. 785, Sec. 1, eff. Sept. 1, 1967. Amended by: Acts 2005, 79th Leg., Ch. 122 (S.B. 1593), Sec. 5, eff. September 1, 2005.

Sec. 2.311. OPTIONS AND COOPERATION RESPECTING PERFORMANCE.

(a) An agreement for sale which is otherwise sufficiently definite (Subsection (c) of Section 2.204) to be a contract is not made invalid by the fact that it leaves particulars of performance to be specified by one of the parties. Any such specification must be made in good faith and within limits set by commercial reasonableness.

(b) Unless otherwise agreed specifications relating to assortment of the goods are at the buyer's option and except as otherwise provided in Subsections (a)(3) and (c) of Section 2.319 specifications or arrangements relating to shipment are at the seller's option.

(c) Where such specification would materially affect the other party's performance but is not seasonably made or where one party's cooperation is necessary to the agreed performance of the other but is not seasonably forthcoming, the other party in addition to all other remedies

(1) is excused for any resulting delay in his own performance; and

(2) may also either proceed to perform in any reasonable manner or after the time for a material part of his own performance treat the failure to specify or to cooperate as a breach by failure to deliver or accept the goods.

Acts 1967, 60th Leg., p. 2343, ch. 785, Sec. 1, eff. Sept. 1, 1967.

Sec. 2.312. WARRANTY OF TITLE AND AGAINST INFRINGEMENT; BUYER'S OBLIGATION AGAINST INFRINGEMENT.

(a) Subject to Subsection (b) there is in a contract for sale a warranty by the seller that

(1) the title conveyed shall be good, and its transfer rightful; and

(2) the goods shall be delivered free from any security interest or other lien or encumbrance of which the buyer at the time of contracting has no knowledge.

(b) A warranty under Subsection (a) will be excluded or modified only by specific language or by circumstances which give the buyer reason to know that the person selling does not claim title in himself or that he is purporting to sell only such right or title as he or a third person may have.

(c) Unless otherwise agreed a seller who is a merchant regularly dealing in goods of the kind warrants that the goods shall be delivered free of the rightful claim of any third person by way of infringement or the like but a buyer who furnishes specifications to the seller must hold the seller harmless against any such claim which arises out of compliance with the specifications.

Acts 1967, 60th Leg., p. 2343, ch. 785, Sec. 1, eff. Sept. 1, 1967.

Sec. 2.313. EXPRESS WARRANTIES BY AFFIRMATION, PROMISE, DESCRIPTION, SAMPLE.

(a) Express warranties by the seller are created as follows:

(1) Any affirmation of fact or promise made by the seller to the buyer which relates to the goods and becomes part of the basis of the bargain creates an express warranty that the goods shall conform to the affirmation or promise.

(2) Any description of the goods which is made part of the basis of the bargain creates an express warranty that the goods shall conform to the description.

(3) Any sample or model which is made part of the basis of the bargain creates an express warranty that the whole of the goods shall conform to the sample or model.

(b) It is not necessary to the creation of an express warranty that the seller use formal words such as "warrant" or "guarantee" or that he have a specific intention to make a warranty, but an affirmation merely of the value of the goods or a statement purporting to be merely the seller's opinion or commendation of the goods does not create a warranty.

Acts 1967, 60th Leg., p. 2343, ch. 785, Sec. 1, eff. Sept. 1, 1967.

Sec. 2.314. IMPLIED WARRANTY: MERCHANTABILITY; USAGE OF TRADE.

(a) Unless excluded or modified (Section 2.316), a warranty that the goods shall be merchantable is implied in a contract for their sale if the seller is a merchant with respect to goods of that kind. Under this section the serving for value of food or drink to be consumed either on the premises or elsewhere is a sale.

(b) Goods to be merchantable must be at least such as

(1) pass without objection in the trade under the contract description; and

(2) in the case of fungible goods, are of fair average quality within the description; and

(3) are fit for the ordinary purposes for which such goods are used; and

(4) run, within the variations permitted by the agreement, of even kind, quality and quantity within each unit and among all units involved; and

(5) are adequately contained, packaged, and labeled as the agreement may require; and

(6) conform to the promises or affirmations of fact made on the container or label if any.

(c) Unless excluded or modified (Section 2.316) other implied warranties may arise from course of dealing or usage of trade.

Acts 1967, 60th Leg., p. 2343, ch. 785, Sec. 1, eff. Sept. 1, 1967.

Sec. 2.315. IMPLIED WARRANTY: FITNESS FOR PARTICULAR PURPOSE.

Where the seller at the time of contracting has reason to know any particular purpose for which the goods are required and that the buyer is relying on the seller's skill or judgment to select or furnish suitable goods, there is unless excluded or modified under the next section an implied warranty that the goods shall be fit for such purpose.

Acts 1967, 60th Leg., p. 2343, ch. 785, Sec. 1, eff. Sept. 1, 1967.

Sec. 2.316. EXCLUSION OR MODIFICATION OF WARRANTIES.

(a) Words or conduct relevant to the creation of an express warranty and words or conduct tending to negate or limit warranty shall be construed wherever reasonable as consistent with each other; but subject to the provisions of this chapter on parol or extrinsic evidence (Section 2.202) negation or limitation is inoperative to the extent that such construction is unreasonable.

(b) Subject to Subsection (c), to exclude or modify the implied warranty of merchantability or any part of it the language must mention merchantability and in case of a writing must be conspicuous, and to exclude or modify any implied warranty of fitness the exclusion must be by a writing and conspicuous. Language to exclude all implied warranties of fitness is sufficient if it states, for example, that "There are no warranties which extend beyond the description on the face hereof."

(c) Notwithstanding Subsection (b)

(1) unless the circumstances indicate otherwise, all implied warranties are excluded by expressions like "as is", "with all faults" or other language which in common understanding calls the buyer's attention to the exclusion of warranties and makes plain that there is no implied warranty; and

(2) when the buyer before entering into the contract has examined the goods or the sample or model as fully as he desired or has refused to examine the goods there is no implied warranty with regard to defects which an examination ought in the circumstances to have revealed to him; and

(3) an implied warranty can also be excluded or modified by course of dealing or course of performance or usage of trade.

(d) Remedies for breach of warranty can be limited in accordance with the provisions of this chapter on liquidation or limitation of damages and on contractual modification of remedy (Sections 2.718 and 2.719).

(e) The implied warranties of merchantability and fitness shall not be applicable to the furnishing of human blood, blood plasma, or other human tissue or organs from a blood bank or reservoir of such other tissues or organs. Such blood, blood plasma or tissue or organs shall not for the purpose of this Title be considered commodities subject to sale or barter, but shall be considered as medical services.

(f) The implied warranties of merchantability and fitness do not apply to the sale or barter of livestock or its unborn young.

Acts 1967, 60th Leg., p. 2343, ch. 785, Sec. 1, eff. Sept. 1, 1967. Amended by Acts 1979, 66th Leg., p. 190, ch. 99, Sec. 1, eff. May 2, 1979.

Sec. 2.317. CUMULATION AND CONFLICT OF WARRANTIES EXPRESS OR IMPLIED.

Warranties whether express or implied shall be construed as consistent with each other and as cumulative, but if such construction is unreasonable the intention of the parties shall determine which warranty is dominant. In ascertaining that intention the following rules apply:

(1) Exact or technical specifications displace an inconsistent sample or model or general language of description.

(2) A sample from an existing bulk displaces inconsistent general language of description.

(3) Express warranties displace inconsistent implied warranties other than an implied warranty of fitness for a particular purpose.

Acts 1967, 60th Leg., p. 2343, ch. 785, Sec. 1, eff. Sept. 1, 1967.

Sec. 2.318. CHAPTER NEUTRAL ON QUESTION OF THIRD PARTY BENEFICIARIES OF WARRANTIES OF QUALITY AND ON NEED FOR PRIVITY OF CONTRACT.

This chapter does not provide whether anyone other than a buyer may take advantage of an express or implied warranty of quality made to the buyer or whether the buyer or anyone entitled to take advantage of a warranty made to the buyer may sue a third party other than the immediate seller for deficiencies in the quality of the goods. These matters are left to the courts for their determination.

Acts 1967, 60th Leg., p. 2343, ch. 785, Sec. 1, eff. Sept. 1, 1967.

Sec. 2.319. F.O.B. AND F.A.S. TERMS.

(a) Unless otherwise agreed the term F.O.B. (which means "free on board") at a named place, even though used only in connection with the stated price, is a delivery term under which

(1) when the term is F.O.B. the place of shipment, the seller must at that place ship the goods in the manner provided in this chapter (Section 2.504) and bear the expense and risk of putting them into the possession of the carrier; or

(2) when the term is F.O.B. the place of destination, the seller must at his own expense and risk transport the goods to that place and there tender delivery of them in the manner provided in this chapter (Section 2.503);

(3) when under either Subdivision (1) or (2) the term is also F.O.B. vessel, car or other vehicle, the seller must in addition at his own expense and risk load the goods on board. If the term is F.O.B. vessel the buyer must name the vessel and in an appropriate case the seller must comply with the provisions of this chapter on the form of bill of lading (Section 2.323).

(b) Unless otherwise agreed the term F.A.S. vessel (which means "free alongside") at a named port, even though used only in connection with the stated price, is a delivery term under which the seller must

(1) at his own expense and risk deliver the goods alongside the vessel in the manner usual in that port or on a dock designated and provided by the buyer; and

(2) obtain and tender a receipt for the goods in exchange for which the carrier is under a duty to issue a bill of lading.

(c) Unless otherwise agreed in any case falling within Subsection (a)(1) or (3) or Subsection (b) the buyer must seasonably give any needed instructions for making delivery, including when the term is F.A.S. or F.O.B. the loading berth of the vessel and in an appropriate case its name and sailing date. The seller may treat the failure of needed instructions as a failure of cooperation under this chapter (Section 2.311). He may also at his option move the goods in any reasonable manner preparatory to delivery or shipment.

(d) Under the term F.O.B. vessel or F.A.S. unless otherwise agreed the buyer must make payment against tender of the required documents and the seller may not tender nor the buyer demand delivery of the goods in substitution for the documents.

Acts 1967, 60th Leg., p. 2343, ch. 785, Sec. 1, eff. Sept. 1, 1967.

Sec. 2.320. C.I.F. AND C. & F. TERMS.

(a) The term C.I.F. means that the price includes in a lump sum the cost of the goods and the insurance and freight to the named destination. The term C. & F. or C.F. means that the price so includes cost and freight to the named destination.

(b) Unless otherwise agreed and even though used only in connection with the stated price and destination, the term C.I.F. destination or its equivalent requires the seller at his own expense and risk to

(1) put the goods into the possession of a carrier at the port for shipment and obtain a negotiable bill or bills of lading covering the entire transportation to the named destination; and

(2) load the goods and obtain a receipt from the carrier (which may be contained in the bill of lading) showing that the freight has been paid or provided for; and

(3) obtain a policy or certificate of insurance, including any war risk insurance, of a kind and on terms then current at the port of shipment in the usual amount,

in the currency of the contract, shown to cover the same goods covered by the bill of lading and providing for payment of loss to the order of the buyer or for the account of whom it may concern; but the seller may add to the price the amount of the premium for any such war risk insurance; and

(4) prepare an invoice of the goods and procure any other documents required to effect shipment or to comply with the contract; and

(5) forward and tender with commercial promptness all the documents in due form and with any indorsement necessary to perfect the buyer's rights.

(c) Unless otherwise agreed the term C. & F. or its equivalent has the same effect and imposes upon the seller the same obligations and risks as a C.I.F. term except the obligation as to insurance.

(d) Under the term C.I.F. or C. & F. unless otherwise agreed the buyer must make payment against tender of the required documents and the seller may not tender nor the buyer demand delivery of the goods in substitution for the documents.

Acts 1967, 60th Leg., p. 2343, ch. 785, Sec. 1, eff. Sept. 1, 1967.

....

Sec. 2.325. "LETTER OF CREDIT" TERM; "CONFIRMED CREDIT".

(a) Failure of the buyer seasonably to furnish an agreed letter of credit is a breach of the contract for sale.

(b) The delivery to seller of a proper letter of credit suspends the buyer's obligation to pay. If the letter of credit is dishonored, the seller may on seasonable notification to the buyer require payment directly from him.

(c) Unless otherwise agreed the term "letter of credit" or "banker's credit" in a contract for sale means an irrevocable credit issued by a financing agency of good repute and, where the shipment is overseas, of good international repute. The term "confirmed credit" means that the credit must also carry the direct obligation of such an agency which does business in the seller's financial market.

Acts 1967, 60th Leg., p. 2343, ch. 785, Sec. 1, eff. Sept. 1, 1967.

....

Sec. 2.328. SALE BY AUCTION.

(a) In a sale by auction if goods are put up in lots each lot is the subject of a separate sale.

(b) A sale by auction is complete when the auctioneer so announces by the fall of the hammer or in other customary manner. Where a bid is made while the hammer is falling in acceptance of a prior bid the auctioneer may in his discretion reopen the bidding or declare the goods sold under the bid on which the hammer was falling.

(c) Such a sale is with reserve unless the goods are in explicit terms put up without reserve. In an auction with reserve the auctioneer may withdraw the goods at any time until he announces completion of the sale. In an auction without reserve, after the auctioneer calls for bids on an article or lot, that article or lot cannot be withdrawn unless no bid is made within a reasonable time. In either case a bidder may retract his bid until the auctioneer's announcement of completion of the sale, but a bidder's retraction does not revive any previous bid.

(d) If the auctioneer knowingly receives a bid on the seller's behalf or the seller makes or procures such a bid, and notice has not been given that liberty for such bidding is reserved, the buyer may at his option avoid the sale or take the goods at the price of the last good faith bid prior to the completion of the sale. This subsection shall not apply to any bid at a forced sale.

Acts 1967, 60th Leg., p. 2343, ch. 785, Sec. 1, eff. Sept. 1, 1967.

SUBCHAPTER D. TITLE, CREDITORS AND GOOD FAITH PURCHASERS

Sec. 2.401. PASSING OF TITLE; RESERVATION FOR SECURITY; LIMITED APPLICATION OF THIS SECTION. Each provision of this chapter with regard to the rights, obligations and remedies of the seller, the buyer, purchasers or other third parties applies irrespective of title to the goods except where the provision refers to such title. Insofar as situations are not covered by the other provisions of this chapter and matters concerning title become material the following rules apply:

(a) Title to goods cannot pass under a contract for sale prior to their identification to the contract (Section 2.501), and unless otherwise explicitly agreed the buyer acquires by their identification a special property as limited by this title. Any retention or reservation by the seller of the title (property) in goods shipped or delivered to the buyer is limited in effect to a reservation of a security interest. Subject to these provisions and to the provisions of the chapter on Secured Transactions (Chapter 9), title to goods passes from the seller to the buyer in any manner and on any conditions explicitly agreed on by the parties.

(b) Unless otherwise explicitly agreed title passes to the buyer at the time and place at which the seller completes his performance with reference to the physical delivery of the goods, despite any reservation of a security interest and even though a document of title is to be delivered at a different time or place; and in particular and despite any reservation of a security interest by the bill of lading

(1) if the contract requires or authorizes the seller to send the goods to the buyer but does not require him to deliver them at destination, title passes to the buyer at the time and place of shipment; but

(2) if the contract requires delivery at destination, title passes on tender there.

(c) Unless otherwise explicitly agreed where delivery is to be made without moving the goods,

(1) if the seller is to deliver a tangible document of title, title passes at the time when and the place where he delivers such documents and if the seller is to deliver an electronic document of title, title passes when the seller delivers the document; or

(2) if the goods are at the time of contracting already identified and no documents are to be delivered, title passes at the time and place of contracting.

(d) A rejection or other refusal by the buyer to receive or retain the goods, whether or not justified, or a justified revocation of acceptance revests title to the goods in the seller. Such revesting occurs by operation of law and is not a "sale".

Acts 1967, 60th Leg., p. 2343, ch. 785, Sec. 1, eff. Sept. 1, 1967. Amended by: Acts 2005, 79th Leg., Ch. 122 (S.B. 1593), Sec. 6, eff. September 1, 2005.

Sec. 2.402. RIGHTS OF SELLER'S CREDITORS AGAINST SOLD GOODS.

(a) Except as provided in Subsections (b) and (c), rights of unsecured creditors of the seller with respect to goods which have been identified to a contract for sale are subject to the buyer's rights to recover the goods under this chapter (Sections 2.502 and 2.716).

(b) A creditor of the seller may treat a sale or an identification of goods to a contract for sale as void if as against him a retention of possession by the seller is fraudulent under any rule of law of the state where the goods are situated, except that retention of possession in good faith and current course of trade by a merchant-seller for a commercially reasonable time after a sale or identification is not fraudulent.

(c) Nothing in this chapter shall be deemed to impair the rights of creditors of the seller

(1) under the provisions of the chapter on Secured Transactions (Chapter 9); or

(2) where identification to the contract or delivery is made not in current course of trade but in satisfaction of or as security for a pre-existing claim for money, security or the like and is made under circumstances which under any rule of law of the state where the goods are situated would apart from this chapter constitute the transaction a fraudulent transfer or voidable preference.

Acts 1967, 60th Leg., p. 2343, ch. 785, Sec. 1, eff. Sept. 1, 1967.

Sec. 2.403. POWER TO TRANSFER; GOOD FAITH PURCHASE OF GOODS; "ENTRUSTING".

(a) A purchaser of goods acquires all title which his transferor had or had power to transfer except that a purchaser of a limited interest acquires rights only to the extent of the interest purchased. A person with voidable title has power to transfer a good title to a good faith purchaser for value. When goods have been delivered under a transaction of purchase the purchaser has such power even though

(1) the transferor was deceived as to the identity of the purchaser, or

(2) the delivery was in exchange for a check which is later dishonored, or

(3) it was agreed that the transaction was to be a "cash sale", or

(4) the delivery was procured through fraud punishable as larcenous under the criminal law.

(b) Any entrusting of possession of goods to a merchant who deals in goods of that kind gives him power to transfer all rights of the entruster to a buyer in ordinary course of business.

(c) "Entrusting" includes any delivery and any acquiescence in retention of possession regardless of any condition expressed between the parties to the delivery or acquiescence and regardless of whether the procurement of the entrusting or the possessor's disposition of the goods have been such as to be larcenous under the criminal law.

(d) The rights of other purchasers of goods and of lien creditors are governed by the chapters on Secured Transactions (Chapter 9) and Documents of Title (Chapter 7).

Acts 1967, 60th Leg., p. 2343, ch. 785, Sec. 1, eff. Sept. 1, 1967. Amended by Acts 1993, 73rd Leg., ch. 570, Sec. 3, eff. Sept. 1, 1993.

SUBCHAPTER E. PERFORMANCE

Sec. 2.501. INSURABLE INTEREST IN GOODS; MANNER OF IDENTIFICATION OF GOODS.

(a) The buyer obtains a special property and an insurable interest in goods by identification of existing goods as goods to which the contract refers even though the goods so identified are non-conforming and he has an option to return or reject them. Such identification can be made at any time and in any manner explicitly agreed to by the parties. In the absence of explicit agreement identification occurs

(1) when the contract is made if it is for the sale of goods already existing and identified;

(2) if the contract is for the sale of future goods other than those described in Subdivision (3), when goods are shipped, marked or otherwise designated by the seller as goods to which the contract refers;

(3) when the crops are planted or otherwise become growing crops or the young are conceived if the contract is for the sale of unborn young to be born within twelve months after contracting or for the sale of crops to be harvested within twelve months or the next normal harvest season after contracting whichever is longer.

(b) The seller retains an insurable interest in goods so long as title to or any security interest in the goods remains in him and where the identification is by the seller alone he may until default or insolvency or notification to the buyer that the identification is final substitute other goods for those identified.

(c) Nothing in this section impairs any insurable interest recognized under any other statute or rule of law.

Acts 1967, 60th Leg., p. 2343, ch. 785, Sec. 1, eff. Sept. 1, 1967.

Sec. 2.502. BUYER'S RIGHT TO GOODS ON SELLER'S REPUDIATION, FAILURE TO DELIVER, OR INSOLVENCY.

(a) Subject to Subsections (b) and (c) and even though the goods have not been shipped a buyer who has paid a part or all of the price of goods in which he has a special property under the provisions of the immediately preceding section may on making and keeping good a tender of any unpaid portion of their price recover them from the seller if:

(1) in the case of goods bought for personal, family, or household purposes, the seller repudiates or fails to deliver as required by the contract; or

(2) in all cases, the seller becomes insolvent within ten days after receipt of the first installment on their price.

(b) The buyer's right to recover the goods under Subsection (a)(1) vests upon acquisition of a special property, even if the seller had not then repudiated or failed to deliver.

(c) If the identification creating his special property has been made by the buyer he acquires the right to recover the goods only if they conform to the contract for sale.

Acts 1967, 60th Leg., p. 2343, ch. 785, Sec. 1, eff. Sept. 1, 1967. Amended by Acts 1999, 76th Leg., ch. 414, Sec. 2.17, eff. July 1, 2001.

Sec. 2.503. MANNER OF SELLER'S TENDER OF DELIVERY.

(a) Tender of delivery requires that the seller put and hold conforming goods at the buyer's disposition and give the buyer any notification reasonably necessary to enable him to take delivery. The manner, time and place for tender are determined by the agreement and this chapter, and in particular

(1) tender must be at a reasonable hour, and if it is of goods they must be kept available for the period reasonably necessary to enable the buyer to take possession; but

(2) unless otherwise agreed the buyer must furnish facilities reasonably suited to the receipt of the goods.

(b) Where the case is within the next section respecting shipment tender requires that the seller comply with its provisions.

(c) Where the seller is required to deliver at a particular destination tender requires that he comply with Subsection (a) and also in any appropriate case tender documents as described in Subsections (d) and (e) of this section.

(d) Where goods are in the possession of a bailee and are to be delivered without being moved

(1) tender requires that the seller either tender a negotiable document of title covering such goods or procure acknowledgment by the bailee of the buyer's right to possession of the goods; but

(2) tender to the buyer of a non-negotiable document of title or of a written direction to the bailee to deliver is sufficient tender unless the buyer seasonably objects, and receipt by the bailee of notification of the buyer's rights fixes those rights as against the bailee and all third persons; but risk of loss of the goods and of any failure by the bailee to honor the non-negotiable document of title or to obey the direction remains on the seller until the buyer has had a reasonable time to present the document or direction, and a refusal by the bailee to honor the document or to obey the direction defeats the tender.

(e) Where the contract requires the seller to deliver documents

(1) he must tender all such documents in correct form, except as provided in this chapter with respect to bills of lading in a set (Subsection (b) of Section 2.323); and

(2) tender through customary banking channels is sufficient and dishonor of a draft accompanying or associated with the documents constitutes non-acceptance or rejection.

Acts 1967, 60th Leg., p. 2343, ch. 785, Sec. 1, eff. Sept. 1, 1967. Amended by Acts 1983, 68th Leg., p. 1530, ch. 290, Sec. 1, eff. Aug. 29, 1983. Amended by: Acts 2005, 79th Leg., Ch. 122 (S.B. 1593), Sec. 7, eff. September 1, 2005.

Sec. 2.504. SHIPMENT BY SELLER.

Where the seller is required or authorized to send the goods to the buyer and the contract does not require him to deliver them at a particular destination, then unless otherwise agreed he must

(1) put the goods in the possession of such a carrier and make such a contract for their transportation as may be reasonable having regard to the nature of the goods and other circumstances of the case; and

(2) obtain and promptly deliver or tender in due form any document necessary to enable the buyer to obtain possession of the goods or otherwise required by the agreement or by usage of trade; and

(3) promptly notify the buyer of the shipment.

Failure to notify the buyer under Subdivision (3) or to make a proper contract under Subdivision (1) is a ground for rejection only if material delay or loss ensues.

Acts 1967, 60th Leg., p. 2343, ch. 785, Sec. 1, eff. Sept. 1, 1967.

Sec. 2.505. SELLER'S SHIPMENT UNDER RESERVATION.

(a) Where the seller has identified goods to the contract by or before shipment:

(1) his procurement of a negotiable bill of lading to his own order or otherwise reserves in him a security interest in the goods. His procurement of the bill to the order of a financing agency or of the buyer indicates in addition only the seller's expectation of transferring that interest to the person named.

(2) a non-negotiable bill of lading to himself or his nominee reserves possession of the goods as security but except in a case of conditional delivery (Subsection (b) of Section 2.507) a non-negotiable bill of lading naming the buyer as consignee reserves no security interest even though the seller retains possession or control of the bill of lading.

(b) When shipment by the seller with reservation of a security interest is in violation of the contract for sale it constitutes an improper contract for transportation within the preceding section but impairs neither the rights given to the buyer by shipment and identification of the goods to the contract nor the seller's powers as a holder of a negotiable document of title.

Acts 1967, 60th Leg., p. 2343, ch. 785, Sec. 1, eff. Sept. 1, 1967. Amended by: Acts 2005, 79th Leg., Ch. 122 (S.B. 1593), Sec. 8, eff. September 1, 2005.

. . . .

Sec. 2.507. EFFECT OF SELLER'S TENDER; DELIVERY ON CONDITION.

(a) Tender of delivery is a condition to the buyer's duty to accept the goods and, unless otherwise agreed, to his duty to pay for them. Tender entitles the seller to acceptance of the goods and to payment according to the contract.

(b) Where payment is due and demanded on the delivery to the buyer of goods or documents of title, his right as against the seller to retain or dispose of them is conditional upon his making the payment due.

Acts 1967, 60th Leg., p. 2343, ch. 785, Sec. 1, eff. Sept. 1, 1967.

Sec. 2.508. CURE BY SELLER OF IMPROPER TENDER OR DELIVERY; REPLACEMENT.

(a) Where any tender or delivery by the seller is rejected because non-conforming and the time for performance has not yet expired, the seller may seasonably notify the buyer of his intention to cure and may then within the contract time make a conforming delivery.

(b) Where the buyer rejects a non-conforming tender which the seller had reasonable grounds to believe would be acceptable with or without money allowance the seller may if he seasonably notifies the buyer have a further reasonable time to substitute a conforming tender.

Acts 1967, 60th Leg., p. 2343, ch. 785, Sec. 1, eff. Sept. 1, 1967.

Sec. 2.509. RISK OF LOSS IN THE ABSENCE OF BREACH.

(a) Where the contract requires or authorizes the seller to ship the goods by carrier

(1) if it does not require him to deliver them at a particular destination, the risk of loss passes to the buyer when the goods are duly delivered to the carrier even though the shipment is under reservation (Section 2.505); but

(2) if it does require him to deliver them at a particular destination and the goods are there duly tendered while in the possession of the carrier, the risk of loss passes to the buyer when the goods are there duly so tendered as to enable the buyer to take delivery.

(b) Where the goods are held by a bailee to be delivered without being moved, the risk of loss passes to the buyer

(1) on the buyer's receipt of possession or control of a negotiable document of title covering the goods; or

(2) on acknowledgment by the bailee of the buyer's right to possession of the goods; or

(3) after the buyer's receipt of possession or control of a non-negotiable document of title or other written direction to deliver, as provided in Subsection (d)(2) of Section 2.503.

(c) In any case not within Subsection (a) or (b), the risk of loss passes to the buyer on his receipt of the goods if the seller is a merchant; otherwise the risk passes to the buyer on tender of delivery.

(d) The provisions of this section are subject to contrary agreement of the parties and to the provisions of this chapter on sale on approval (Section 2.327) and on effect of breach on risk of loss (Section 2.510).

Acts 1967, 60th Leg., p. 2343, ch. 785, Sec. 1, eff. Sept. 1, 1967. Amended by Acts 1983, 68th Leg., p. 1531, ch. 290, Sec. 2, eff. Aug. 29, 1983. Amended by: Acts 2005, 79th Leg., Ch. 122 (S.B. 1593), Sec. 10, eff. September 1, 2005.

Sec. 2.510. EFFECT OF BREACH ON RISK OF LOSS.

(a) Where a tender or delivery of goods so fails to conform to the contract as to give a right of rejection the risk of their loss remains on the seller until cure or acceptance.

(b) Where the buyer rightfully revokes acceptance he may to the extent of any deficiency in his effective insurance coverage treat the risk of loss as having rested on the seller from the beginning.

(c) Where the buyer as to conforming goods already identified to the contract for sale repudiates or is otherwise in breach before risk of their loss has passed to him, the seller may to the extent of any deficiency in his effective insurance coverage treat the risk of loss as resting on the buyer for a commercially reasonable time.

Acts 1967, 60th Leg., p. 2343, ch. 785, Sec. 1, eff. Sept. 1, 1967.

Sec. 2.511. TENDER OF PAYMENT BY BUYER; PAYMENT BY CHECK.

(a) Unless otherwise agreed tender of payment is a condition to the seller's duty to tender and complete any delivery.

(b) Tender of payment is sufficient when made by any means or in any manner current in the ordinary course of business unless the seller demands payment in legal tender and gives any extension of time reasonably necessary to procure it.

(c) Subject to the provisions of this title on the effect of an instrument on an obligation (Section 3.802), payment by check is conditional and is defeated as between the parties by dishonor of the check on due presentment.

Acts 1967, 60th Leg., p. 2343, ch. 785, Sec. 1, eff. Sept. 1, 1967.

Sec. 2.512. PAYMENT BY BUYER BEFORE INSPECTION.

(a) Where the contract requires payment before inspection non-conformity of the goods does not excuse the buyer from so making payment unless

(1) the non-conformity appears without inspection; or

(2) despite tender of the required documents circumstances would justify injunction against honor under this title (Section 5.109(b)).

(b) Payment pursuant to Subsection (a) does not constitute an acceptance of goods or impair the buyer's right to inspect or any of his remedies.

Acts 1967, 60th Leg., p. 2343, ch. 785, Sec. 1, eff. Sept. 1, 1967. Amended by Acts 1999, 76th Leg., ch. 4, Sec. 3, eff. Sept. 1, 1999.

Sec. 2.513. BUYER'S RIGHT TO INSPECTION OF GOODS.

(a) Unless otherwise agreed and subject to Subsection (c), where goods are tendered or delivered or identified to the contract for sale, the buyer has a right before payment or acceptance to inspect them at any reasonable place and time and in any reasonable manner. When the seller is required or authorized to send the goods to the buyer, the inspection may be after their arrival.

(b) Expenses of inspection must be borne by the buyer but may be recovered from the seller if the goods do not conform and are rejected.

(c) Unless otherwise agreed and subject to the provisions of this chapter on C.I.F. contracts (Subsection (c) of Section 2.321), the buyer is not entitled to inspect the goods before payment of the price when the contract provides

(1) for delivery "C.O.D." or on other like terms; or

(2) for payment against documents of title, except where such payment is due only after the goods are to become available for inspection.

(d) A place or method of inspection fixed by the parties is presumed to be exclusive but unless otherwise expressly agreed it does not postpone identification or shift the place for delivery or for passing the risk of loss. If compliance becomes impossible, inspection shall be as provided in this section unless the place or method fixed was clearly intended as an indispensable condition failure of which avoids the contract.

Acts 1967, 60th Leg., p. 2343, ch. 785, Sec. 1, eff. Sept. 1, 1967.

Sec. 2.514. WHEN DOCUMENTS DELIVERABLE ON ACCEPTANCE; WHEN ON PAYMENT.

Unless otherwise agreed documents against which a draft is drawn are to be delivered to the drawee on acceptance of the draft if it is payable more than three days after presentment; otherwise, only on payment.

Acts 1967, 60th Leg., p. 2343, ch. 785, Sec. 1, eff. Sept. 1, 1967.

Sec. 2.515. PRESERVING EVIDENCE OF GOODS IN DISPUTE. In furtherance of the adjustment of any claim or dispute

(1) either party on reasonable notification to the other and for the purpose of ascertaining the facts and preserving evidence has the right to inspect, test and sample the goods including such of them as may be in the possession or control of the other; and

(2) the parties may agree to a third party inspection or survey to determine the conformity or condition of the goods and may agree that the findings shall be binding upon them in any subsequent litigation or adjustment.

Acts 1967, 60th Leg., p. 2343, ch. 785, Sec. 1, eff. Sept. 1, 1967.

SUBCHAPTER F. BREACH, REPUDIATION AND EXCUSE

Sec. 2.601. BUYER'S RIGHTS ON IMPROPER DELIVERY.

Subject to the provisions of this chapter on breach in installment contracts (Section 2.612) and unless otherwise agreed under the sections on contractual limitations of remedy (Sections 2.718 and 2.719), if the goods or the tender of delivery fail in any respect to conform to the contract, the buyer may

(1) reject the whole; or

(2) accept the whole; or

(3) accept any commercial unit or units and reject the rest.

Acts 1967, 60th Leg., p. 2343, ch. 785, Sec. 1, eff. Sept. 1, 1967.

Sec. 2.602. MANNER AND EFFECT OF RIGHTFUL REJECTION.

(a) Rejection of goods must be within a reasonable time after their delivery or tender. It is ineffective unless the buyer seasonably notifies the seller.

(b) Subject to the provisions of the two following sections on rejected goods (Sections 2.603 and 2.604),

(1) after rejection any exercise of ownership by the buyer with respect to any commercial unit is wrongful as against the seller; and

(2) if the buyer has before rejection taken physical possession of goods in which he does not have a security interest under the provisions of this chapter (Subsection (c) of Section 2.711), he is under a duty after rejection to hold them with reasonable care at the seller's disposition for a time sufficient to permit the seller to remove them; but

(3) the buyer has no further obligations with regard to goods rightfully rejected.

(c) The seller's rights with respect to goods wrongfully rejected are governed by the provisions of this chapter on Seller's remedies in general (Section 2.703).

Acts 1967, 60th Leg., p. 2343, ch. 785, Sec. 1, eff. Sept. 1, 1967.

Sec. 2.603. MERCHANT BUYER'S DUTIES AS TO RIGHTFULLY REJECTED GOODS.

(a) Subject to any security interest in the buyer (Subsection (c) of Section 2.711), when the seller has no agent or place of business at the market of rejection a merchant buyer is under a duty after rejection of goods in his possession or control to follow any reasonable instructions received from the seller with respect to the goods and in the absence of such instructions to make reasonable efforts to sell them for the seller's account if they are perishable or threaten to decline in value speedily. Instructions are not reasonable if on demand indemnity for expenses is not forthcoming.

(b) When the buyer sells goods under Subsection (a), he is entitled to reimbursement from the seller or out of the proceeds for reasonable expenses of caring for and selling them, and if the expenses include no selling commission then to such commission as is usual in the trade or if there is none to a reasonable sum not exceeding ten per cent on the gross proceeds.

(c) In complying with this section the buyer is held only to good faith and good faith conduct hereunder is neither acceptance nor conversion nor the basis of an action for damages.

Acts 1967, 60th Leg., p. 2343, ch. 785, Sec. 1, eff. Sept. 1, 1967.

Sec. 2.604. BUYER'S OPTIONS AS TO SALVAGE OF RIGHTFULLY REJECTED GOODS.

Subject to the provisions of the immediately preceding section on perishables if the seller gives no instructions within a reasonable time after notification of rejection the buyer may store the rejected goods for the seller's account or reship them to him or resell them for the seller's account with reimbursement as provided in the preceding section. Such action is not acceptance or conversion.

Acts 2005, 79th Leg., Ch. 122 (S.B. 1593), Sec. 11, eff. September 1, 2005.

Sec. 2.605. WAIVER OF BUYER'S OBJECTIONS BY FAILURE TO PARTICULARIZE.

(a) The buyer's failure to state in connection with rejection a particular defect which is ascertainable by reasonable inspection precludes him from relying on the unstated defect to justify rejection or to establish breach

(1) where the seller could have cured it if stated seasonably; or

(2) between merchants when the seller has after rejection made a request in writing for a full and final written statement of all defects on which the buyer proposes to rely.

(b) Payment against documents made without reservation of rights precludes recovery of the payment for defects apparent in the documents.

Acts 1967, 60th Leg., p. 2343, ch. 785, Sec. 1, eff. Sept. 1, 1967. Amended by: Acts 2005, 79th Leg., Ch. 122 (S.B. 1593), Sec. 11, eff. September 1, 2005.

Sec. 2.606. WHAT CONSTITUTES ACCEPTANCE OF GOODS.

(a) Acceptance of goods occurs when the buyer

(1) after a reasonable opportunity to inspect the goods signifies to the seller that the goods are conforming or that he will take or retain them in spite of their non-conformity; or

(2) fails to make an effective rejection (Subsection (a) of Section 2.602), but such acceptance does not occur until the buyer has had a reasonable opportunity to inspect them; or

(3) does any act inconsistent with the seller's ownership; but if such act is wrongful as against the seller it is an acceptance only if ratified by him.

(b) Acceptance of a part of any commercial unit is acceptance of that entire unit.

Acts 1967, 60th Leg., p. 2343, ch. 785, Sec. 1, eff. Sept. 1, 1967.

Sec. 2.607. EFFECT OF ACCEPTANCE; NOTICE OF BREACH; BURDEN OF ESTABLISHING BREACH AFTER ACCEPTANCE; NOTICE OF CLAIM OR LITIGATION TO PERSON ANSWERABLE OVER.

(a) The buyer must pay at the contract rate for any goods accepted.

(b) Acceptance of goods by the buyer precludes rejection of the goods accepted and if made with knowledge of a non-conformity cannot be revoked because of it unless the acceptance was on the reasonable assumption that the non-conformity would be seasonably cured but acceptance does not of itself impair any other remedy provided by this chapter for non-conformity.

(c) Where a tender has been accepted

(1) the buyer must within a reasonable time after he discovers or should have discovered any breach notify the seller of breach or be barred from any remedy; and

(2) if the claim is one for infringement or the like (Subsection (c) of Section 2.312) and the buyer is sued as a result of such a breach he must so notify the seller within a reasonable time after he receives notice of the litigation or be barred from any remedy over for liability established by the litigation.

(d) The burden is on the buyer to establish any breach with respect to the goods accepted.

(e) Where the buyer is sued for breach of a warranty or other obligation for which his seller is answerable over

(1) he may give his seller written notice of the litigation. If the notice states that the seller may come in and defend and that if the seller does not do so he will be bound in any action against him by his buyer by any determination of fact common to the two litigations, then unless the seller after seasonable receipt of the notice does come in and defend he is so bound.

(2) if the claim is one for infringement or the like (Subsection (c) of Section 2.312) the original seller may demand in writing that his buyer turn over to him control of the litigation including settlement or else be barred from any remedy over and if he also agrees to bear all expense and to satisfy any adverse judgment, then unless the buyer after seasonable receipt of the demand does turn over control the buyer is so barred.

(f) The provisions of Subsections (c), (d) and (e) apply to any obligation of a buyer to hold the seller harmless against infringement or the like (Subsection (c) of Section 2.312).

Acts 1967, 60th Leg., p. 2343, ch. 785, Sec. 1, eff. Sept. 1, 1967.

Sec. 2.608. REVOCATION OF ACCEPTANCE IN WHOLE OR IN PART.

(a) The buyer may revoke his acceptance of a lot or commercial unit whose non-conformity substantially impairs its value to him if he has accepted it

(1) on the reasonable assumption that its non-conformity would be cured and it has not been seasonably cured; or

(2) without discovery of such non-conformity if his acceptance was reasonably induced either by the difficulty of discovery before acceptance or by the seller's assurances.

(b) Revocation of acceptance must occur within a reasonable time after the buyer discovers or should have discovered the ground for it and before any substantial change in condition of the goods which is not caused by their own defects. It is not effective until the buyer notifies the seller of it.

(c) A buyer who so revokes has the same rights and duties with regard to the goods involved as if he had rejected them.

Acts 1967, 60th Leg., p. 2343, ch. 785, Sec. 1, eff. Sept. 1, 1967.

Sec. 2.609. RIGHT TO ADEQUATE ASSURANCE OF PERFORMANCE.

(a) A contract for sale imposes an obligation on each party that the other's expectation of receiving due performance will not be impaired. When reasonable grounds for insecurity arise with respect to the performance of either party the other may in writing demand adequate assurance of due performance and until he receives such assurance may if commercially reasonable suspend any performance for which he has not already received the agreed return.

(b) Between merchants the reasonableness of grounds for insecurity and the adequacy of any assurance offered shall be determined according to commercial standards.

(c) Acceptance of any improper delivery or payment does not prejudice the aggrieved party's right to demand adequate assurance of future performance.

(d) After receipt of a justified demand failure to provide within a reasonable time not exceeding thirty days such assurance of due performance as is adequate under the circumstances of the particular case is a repudiation of the contract.

Acts 1967, 60th Leg., p. 2343, ch. 785, Sec. 1, eff. Sept. 1, 1967.

Sec. 2.610. ANTICIPATORY REPUDIATION.

When either party repudiates the contract with respect to a performance not yet due the loss of which will substantially impair the value of the contract to the other, the aggrieved party may

(1) for a commercially reasonable time await performance by the repudiating party; or

(2) resort to any remedy for breach (Section 2.703 or Section 2.711), even though he has notified the repudiating party that he would await the latter's performance and has urged retraction; and

(3) in either case suspend his own performance or proceed in accordance with the provisions of this chapter on the seller's right to identify goods to the contract notwithstanding breach or to salvage unfinished goods (Section 2.704).

Acts 1967, 60th Leg., p. 2343, ch. 785, Sec. 1, eff. Sept. 1, 1967.

Sec. 2.611. RETRACTION OF ANTICIPATORY REPUDIATION.

(a) Until the repudiating party's next performance is due he can retract his repudiation unless the aggrieved party has since the repudiation cancelled or materially changed his position or otherwise indicated that he considers the repudiation final.

(b) Retraction may be by any method which clearly indicates to the aggrieved party that the repudiating party intends to perform, but must include any assurance justifiably demanded under the provisions of this chapter (Section 2.609).

(c) Retraction reinstates the repudiating party's rights under the contract with due excuse and allowance to the aggrieved party for any delay occasioned by the repudiation.

Acts 1967, 60th Leg., p. 2343, ch. 785, Sec. 1, eff. Sept. 1, 1967.

Sec. 2.612. "INSTALLMENT CONTRACT"; BREACH.

(a) An "installment contract" is one which requires or authorizes the delivery of goods in separate lots to be separately accepted, even though the contract contains a clause "each delivery is a separate contract" or its equivalent.

(b) The buyer may reject any installment which is non-conforming if the non-conformity substantially impairs the value of that installment and cannot be cured or if the non-conformity is a defect in the required documents; but if the non-conformity does not fall within Subsection (c) and the seller gives adequate assurance of its cure the buyer must accept that installment.

(c) Whenever non-conformity or default with respect to one or more installments substantially impairs the value of the whole contract there is a breach of the whole. But the aggrieved party reinstates the contract if he accepts a non-conforming installment without seasonably notifying of cancellation or if he brings an action with respect only to past installments or demands performance as to future installments.

Acts 1967, 60th Leg., p. 2343, ch. 785, Sec. 1, eff. Sept. 1, 1967.

Sec. 2.613. CASUALTY TO IDENTIFIED GOODS.

Where the contract requires for its performance goods identified when the contract is made, and the goods suffer casualty without fault of either party before the risk of loss passes to the buyer, or in a proper case under a "no arrival, no sale" term (Section 2.324) then

(1) if the loss is total the contract is avoided; and

(2) if the loss is partial or the goods have so deteriorated as no longer to conform to the contract the buyer may nevertheless demand inspection and at his option either treat the contract as avoided or accept the goods with due allowance from the contract price for the deterioration or the deficiency in quantity but without further right against the seller.

Acts 1967, 60th Leg., p. 2343, ch. 785, Sec. 1, eff. Sept. 1, 1967.

. . . .

Sec. 2.615. EXCUSE BY FAILURE OF PRESUPPOSED CONDITIONS.

Except so far as a seller may have assumed a greater obligation and subject to the preceding section on substituted performance:

(1) Delay in delivery or non-delivery in whole or in part by a seller who complies with Subdivisions (2) and (3) is not a breach of his duty under a contract for sale if performance as agreed has been made impracticable by the occurrence of a contingency the non-occurrence of which was a basic assumption on which the contract was made or by compliance in good faith with any applicable foreign or domestic governmental regulation or order whether or not it later proves to be invalid.

(2) Where the causes mentioned in Subdivision (1) affect only a part of the seller's capacity to perform, he must allocate production and deliveries among his customers but may at his option include regular customers not then under contract as well as his own requirements for further manufacture. He may so allocate in any manner which is fair and reasonable.

(3) The seller must notify the buyer seasonably that there will be delay or non-delivery and, when allocation is required under Subdivision (2), of the estimated quota thus made available for the buyer.

Acts 1967, 60th Leg., p. 2343, ch. 785, Sec. 1, eff. Sept. 1, 1967.

Sec. 2.616. PROCEDURE ON NOTICE CLAIMING EXCUSE.

(a) Where the buyer receives notification of a material or indefinite delay or an allocation justified under the preceding section he may by written notification to the seller as to any delivery concerned, and where the prospective deficiency substantially impairs the value of the whole contract under the provisions of this chapter relating to breach of installment contracts (Section 2.612), then also as to the whole,

(1) terminate and thereby discharge any unexecuted portion of the contract; or

(2) modify the contract by agreeing to take his available quota in substitution.

(b) If after receipt of such notification from the seller the buyer fails so to modify the contract within a reasonable time not exceeding thirty days the contract lapses with respect to any deliveries affected.

(c) The provisions of this section may not be negated by agreement except insofar as the seller has assumed a greater obligation under the preceding section.

Acts 1967, 60th Leg., p. 2343, ch. 785, Sec. 1, eff. Sept. 1, 1967.

SUBCHAPTER G. REMEDIES

Sec. 2.701. REMEDIES FOR BREACH OF COLLATERAL CONTRACTS NOT IMPAIRED. Remedies for breach of any obligation or promise collateral or ancillary to a contract for sale are not impaired by the provisions of this chapter.

Acts 1967, 60th Leg., p. 2343, ch. 785, Sec. 1, eff. Sept. 1, 1967.

Sec. 2.702. SELLER'S REMEDIES ON DISCOVERY OF BUYER'S INSOLVENCY.

(a) Where the seller discovers the buyer to be insolvent he may refuse delivery except for cash including payment for all goods theretofore delivered under the contract, and stop delivery under this chapter (Section 2.705).

(b) Where the seller discovers that the buyer has received goods on credit while insolvent he may reclaim the goods upon demand made within ten days after the receipt, but if misrepresentation of solvency has been made to the particular seller in writing within three months before delivery the ten day limitation does not apply. Except as provided in this subsection the seller may not base a right to reclaim goods on the buyer's fraudulent or innocent misrepresentation of solvency or of intent to pay.

(c) The seller's right to reclaim under Subsection (b) is subject to the rights of a buyer in ordinary course or other good faith purchaser or lien creditor under this chapter (Section 2.403). Successful reclamation of goods excludes all other remedies with respect to them.

Acts 1967, 60th Leg., p. 2343, ch. 785, Sec. 1, eff. Sept. 1, 1967.

Sec. 2.703. SELLER'S REMEDIES IN GENERAL.

Where the buyer wrongfully rejects or revokes acceptance of goods or fails to make a payment due on or before delivery or repudiates with respect to a part or the whole, then with respect to any goods directly affected and, if the breach is of the whole contract (Section 2.612), then also with respect to the whole undelivered balance, the aggrieved seller may

(1) withhold delivery of such goods;

(2) stop delivery by any bailee as hereafter provided (Section 2.705);

(3) proceed under the next section respecting goods still unidentified to the contract;

(4) resell and recover damages as hereafter provided (Section 2.706);

(5) recover damages for non-acceptance (Section 2.708) or in a proper case the price (Section 2.709);

(6) cancel.

Acts 1967, 60th Leg., p. 2343, ch. 785, Sec. 1, eff. Sept. 1, 1967.

....

Sec. 2.706. SELLER'S RESALE INCLUDING CONTRACT FOR RESALE.

(a) Under the conditions stated in Section 2.703 on seller's remedies, the seller may resell the goods concerned or the undelivered balance thereof. Where the resale is made in good faith and in a commercially reasonable manner the seller may recover the difference between the resale price and the contract price together with any incidental damages allowed under the provisions of this chapter (Section 2.710), but less expenses saved in consequence of the buyer's breach.

(b) ... [E]very aspect of the sale including the method, manner, time, place and terms must be commercially reasonable. The resale must be reasonably identified as referring to the broken contract, but it is not necessary that the goods be in existence ....

(c) Where the resale is at private sale the seller must give the buyer reasonable notification of his intention to resell.

(d) Where the resale is at public sale

(1) only identified goods can be sold except where there is a recognized market for a public sale of futures in goods of the kind; and

(2) it must be made at a usual place or market for public sale if one is reasonably available and except in the case of goods which are perishable or threaten to decline in value speedily the seller must give the buyer reasonable notice of the time and place of the resale; and

(3) if the goods are not to be within the view of those attending the sale the notification of sale must state the place where the goods are located and provide for their reasonable inspection by prospective bidders; and

(4) the seller may buy.

(e) A purchaser who buys in good faith at a resale takes the goods free of any rights of the original buyer even though the seller fails to comply with one or more of the requirements of this section.

(f) The seller is not accountable to the buyer for any profit made on any resale. A person in the position of a seller (Section 2.707) or a buyer who has rightfully rejected or justifiably revoked acceptance must account for any excess over the amount of his security interest, as hereinafter defined (Subsection (c) of Section 2.711).

Acts 1967, 60th Leg., p. 2343, ch. 785, Sec. 1, eff. Sept. 1, 1967.

....

Sec. 2.708. SELLER'S DAMAGES FOR NON-ACCEPTANCE OR REPUDIATION.

(a) Subject to Subsection (b) and to the provisions of this chapter with respect to proof of market price (Section 2.723), the measure of damages for non-acceptance or repudiation by the buyer is the difference between the market price at the time and place for tender and the unpaid contract price together with any incidental damages provided in this chapter (Section 2.710), but less expenses saved in consequence of the buyer's breach.

(b) If the measure of damages provided in Subsection (a) is inadequate to put the seller in as good a position as performance would have done then the measure of damages is the profit (including reasonable overhead) which the seller would have made from full performance by the buyer, together with any incidental damages provided in this chapter (Section 2.710), due allowance for costs reasonably incurred and due credit for payments or proceeds of resale.

Acts 1967, 60th Leg., p. 2343, ch. 785, Sec. 1, eff. Sept. 1, 1967.

Sec. 2.709. ACTION FOR THE PRICE.

(a) When the buyer fails to pay the price as it becomes due the seller may recover, together with any incidental damages under the next section, the price

(1) of goods accepted or of conforming goods lost or damaged within a commercially reasonable time after risk of their loss has passed to the buyer; and

(2) of goods identified to the contract if the seller is unable after reasonable effort to resell them at a reasonable price or the circumstances reasonably indicate that such effort will be unavailing.

(b) Where the seller sues for the price he must hold for the buyer any goods which have been identified to the contract and are still in his control except that if resale becomes possible he may resell them at any time prior to the collection of the judgment. The net proceeds of any such resale must be credited to the buyer and payment of the judgment entitles him to any goods not resold.

(c) After the buyer has wrongfully rejected or revoked acceptance of the goods or has failed to make a payment due or has repudiated (Section 2.610), a seller who is held not entitled to the price under this section shall nevertheless be awarded damages for nonacceptance under the preceding section.

Acts 1967, 60th Leg., p. 2343, ch. 785, Sec. 1, eff. Sept. 1, 1967.

Sec. 2.710. SELLER'S INCIDENTAL DAMAGES.

Incidental damages to an aggrieved seller include any commercially reasonable charges, expenses or commissions incurred in stopping delivery, in the transportation, care and custody of goods after the buyer's breach, in connection with return or resale of the goods or otherwise resulting from the breach.

Acts 1967, 60th Leg., p. 2343, ch. 785, Sec. 1, eff. Sept. 1, 1967.

Sec. 2.711. BUYER'S REMEDIES IN GENERAL; BUYER'S SECURITY INTEREST IN REJECTED GOODS.

(a) Where the seller fails to make delivery or repudiates or the buyer rightfully rejects or justifiably revokes acceptance then with respect to any goods involved, and with respect to the whole if the breach goes to the whole contract (Section 2.612), the buyer may cancel and whether or not he has done so may in addition to recovering so much of the price as has been paid

(1) "cover" and have damages under the next section as to all the goods affected whether or not they have been identified to the contract; or

(2) recover damages for non-delivery as provided in this chapter (Section 2.713).

(b) Where the seller fails to deliver or repudiates the buyer may also

(1) if the goods have been identified recover them as provided in this chapter (Section 2.502); or

(2) in a proper case obtain specific performance or replevy the goods as provided in this chapter (Section 2.716).

(c) On rightful rejection or justifiable revocation of acceptance a buyer has a security interest in goods in his possession or control for any payments made on their price and any expenses reasonably incurred in their inspection, receipt, transportation, care and custody and may hold such goods and resell them in like manner as an aggrieved seller (Section 2.706).

Acts 1967, 60th Leg., p. 2343, ch. 785, Sec. 1, eff. Sept. 1, 1967.

Sec. 2.712. "COVER"; BUYER'S PROCUREMENT OF SUBSTITUTE GOODS.

(a) After a breach within the preceding section the buyer may "cover" by making in good faith and without unreasonable delay any reasonable purchase of or contract to purchase goods in substitution for those due from the seller.

(b) The buyer may recover from the seller as damages the difference between the cost of cover and the contract price together with any incidental or consequential damages as hereinafter defined (Section 2.715), but less expenses saved in consequence of the seller's breach.

(c) Failure of the buyer to effect cover within this section does not bar him from any other remedy.

Acts 1967, 60th Leg., p. 2343, ch. 785, Sec. 1, eff. Sept. 1, 1967.

Sec. 2.713. BUYER'S DAMAGES FOR NON-DELIVERY OR REPUDIATION.

(a) Subject to the provisions of this chapter with respect to proof of market price (Section 2.723), the measure of damages for non-delivery or repudiation by the seller is the difference between the market price at the time when the buyer learned of the breach and the contract price together with any incidental and consequential damages provided in this chapter (Section 2.715), but less expenses saved in consequence of the seller's breach.

(b) Market price is to be determined as of the place for tender or, in cases of rejection after arrival or revocation of acceptance, as of the place of arrival.

Acts 1967, 60th Leg., p. 2343, ch. 785, Sec. 1, eff. Sept. 1, 1967.

Sec. 2.714. BUYER'S DAMAGES FOR BREACH IN REGARD TO ACCEPTED GOODS.

(a) Where the buyer has accepted goods and given notification (Subsection (c) of Section 2.607) he may recover as damages for any non-conformity of tender the loss resulting in the ordinary course of events from the seller's breach as determined in any manner which is reasonable.

(b) The measure of damages for breach of warranty is the difference at the time and place of acceptance between the value of the goods accepted and the value they would have had if they had been as warranted, unless special circumstances show proximate damages of a different amount.

(c) In a proper case any incidental and consequential damages under the next section may also be recovered.

Acts 1967, 60th Leg., p. 2343, ch. 785, Sec. 1, eff. Sept. 1, 1967.

Sec. 2.715. BUYER'S INCIDENTAL AND CONSEQUENTIAL DAMAGES.

(a) Incidental damages resulting from the seller's breach include expenses reasonably incurred in inspection, receipt, transportation and care and custody of goods rightfully rejected, any commercially reasonable charges, expenses or commissions in connection with effecting cover and any other reasonable expense incident to the delay or other breach.

(b) Consequential damages resulting from the seller's breach include

(1) any loss resulting from general or particular requirements and needs of which the seller at the time of contracting had reason to know and which could not reasonably be prevented by cover or otherwise; and

(2) injury to person or property proximately resulting from any breach of warranty.

Acts 1967, 60th Leg., p. 2343, ch. 785, Sec. 1, eff. Sept. 1, 1967.

Sec. 2.716. BUYER'S RIGHT TO SPECIFIC PERFORMANCE OR REPLEVIN.

(a) Specific performance may be decreed where the goods are unique or in other proper circumstances.

(b) The decree for specific performance may include such terms and conditions as to payment of the price, damages, or other relief as the court may deem just.

(c) The buyer has a right of replevin for goods identified to the contract if after reasonable effort he is unable to effect cover for such goods or the circumstances reasonably indicate that such effort will be unavailing....

Acts 1967, 60th Leg., p. 2343, ch. 785, Sec. 1, eff. Sept. 1, 1967. Amended by Acts 1999, 76th Leg., ch. 414, Sec. 2.18, eff. July 1, 2001.

Sec. 2.717. DEDUCTION OF DAMAGES FROM THE PRICE. The buyer on notifying the seller of his intention to do so may deduct all or any part of the damages resulting from any breach of the contract from any part of the price still due under the same contract.

Acts 1967, 60th Leg., p. 2343, ch. 785, Sec. 1, eff. Sept. 1, 1967.

Sec. 2.718. LIQUIDATION OR LIMITATION OF DAMAGES; DEPOSITS.

(a) Damages for breach by either party may be liquidated in the agreement but only at an amount which is reasonable in the light of the anticipated or actual harm caused by the breach, the difficulties of proof of loss, and the inconvenience or non-feasibility of otherwise obtaining an adequate remedy. A term fixing unreasonably large liquidated damages is void as a penalty.

....

Acts 1967, 60th Leg., p. 2343, ch. 785, Sec. 1, eff. Sept. 1, 1967.

Sec. 2.719. CONTRACTUAL MODIFICATION OR LIMITATION OF REMEDY.

(a) Subject to the provisions of Subsections (b) and (c) of this section and of the preceding section on liquidation and limitation of damages,

(1) the agreement may provide for remedies in addition to or in substitution for those provided in this chapter and may limit or alter the measure of damages recoverable under this chapter, as by limiting the buyer's remedies to return of the goods and repayment of the price or to repair and replacement of non-conforming goods or parts; and

(2) resort to a remedy as provided is optional unless the remedy is expressly agreed to be exclusive, in which case it is the sole remedy.

(b) Where circumstances cause an exclusive or limited remedy to fail of its essential purpose, remedy may be had as provided in this title.

(c) Consequential damages may be limited or excluded unless the limitation or exclusion is unconscionable. Limitation of consequential damages for injury to the person in the case of consumer goods is prima facie unconscionable but limitation of damages where the loss is commercial is not.

Acts 1967, 60th Leg., p. 2343, ch. 785, Sec. 1, eff. Sept. 1, 1967.

....

Sec. 2.721. REMEDIES FOR FRAUD.

Remedies for material misrepresentation or fraud include all remedies available under this chapter for non-fraudulent breach. Neither rescission or a claim for rescission of the contract for sale nor rejection or return of the goods shall bar or be deemed inconsistent with a claim for damages or other remedy.

Acts 1967, 60th Leg., p. 2343, ch. 785, Sec. 1, eff. Sept. 1, 1967.

Sec. 2.722. WHO CAN SUE THIRD PARTIES FOR INJURY TO GOODS.

Where a third party so deals with goods which have been identified to a contract for sale as to cause actionable injury to a party to that contract

(1) a right of action against the third party is in either party to the contract for sale who has title to or a security interest or a special property or an insurable interest in the goods; and if the goods have been destroyed or converted a right of action is also in the party who either bore the risk of loss under the contract for sale or has since the injury assumed that risk as against the other;

(2) if at the time of the injury the party plaintiff did not bear the risk of loss as against the other party to the contract for sale and there is no arrangement between them for disposition of the recovery, his suit or settlement is, subject to his own interest, as a fiduciary for the other party to the contract;

(3) either party may with the consent of the other sue for the benefit of whom it may concern.

Acts 1967, 60th Leg., p. 2343, ch. 785, Sec. 1, eff. Sept. 1, 1967.

Sec. 2.723. PROOF OF MARKET PRICE: TIME AND PLACE.

(a) If an action based on anticipatory repudiation comes to trial before the time for performance with respect to some or all of the goods, any damages based on market price (Section 2.708 or Section 2.713) shall be determined according to the price of such goods prevailing at the time when the aggrieved party learned of the repudiation.

(b) If evidence of a price prevailing at the times or places described in this chapter is not readily available the price prevailing within any reasonable time before or after the time described or at any other place which in commercial judgment or under usage of trade would serve as a reasonable substitute for the one described may be used, making any proper allowance for the cost of transporting the goods to or from such other place.

(c) Evidence of a relevant price prevailing at a time or place other than the one described in this chapter offered by one party is not admissible unless and until he has given the other party such notice as the court finds sufficient to prevent unfair surprise.

Acts 1967, 60th Leg., p. 2343, ch. 785, Sec. 1, eff. Sept. 1, 1967.

. . . .

Sec. 2.725. STATUTE OF LIMITATIONS IN CONTRACTS FOR SALE.

(a) An action for breach of any contract for sale must be commenced within four years after the cause of action has accrued. By the original agreement the parties may reduce the period of limitation to not less than one year but may not extend it.

(b) A cause of action accrues when the breach occurs, regardless of the aggrieved party's lack of knowledge of the breach. A breach of warranty occurs when tender of delivery is made, except that where a warranty explicitly extends to future performance of the goods and discovery of the breach must await the time of such performance the cause of action accrues when the breach is or should have been discovered.

(c) Where an action commenced within the time limited by Subsection (a) is so terminated as to leave available a remedy by another action for the same breach such other action may be commenced after the expiration of the time limited and within six months after the termination of the first action unless the termination resulted from voluntary discontinuance or from dismissal for failure or neglect to prosecute.

(d) This section does not alter the law on tolling of the statute of limitations nor does it apply to causes of action which have accrued before this title becomes effective.

Acts 1967, 60th Leg., p. 2343, ch. 785, Sec. 1, eff. Sept. 1, 1967.

Appendix 2

Sample Contracts

For Form Contracts for Musical Performance and Agency, see musiccontracts.com.

Sample Requirements Contract

I. PARTIES

The parties to this contract for the purchase and sale of sand are:

1. Sooner Sand Co. ("Seller"), a general partnership consisting of the general partners Harley T. Price and W. M. McMichael, and

2. Bassi Distributing Co. ("Buyer"), a joint venture of Bassi Trucking Co. and Hardcore Rock & Gravel, Inc.

II. RECITALS

1. Seller is engaged in the business of selling and shipping sand from Phoenix to various customers in the State of Arizona but has not developed markets outside of Arizona. Seller desires to supply sand wholesale to a distributor with customers outside the state.

2. Buyer has an established business in Phoenix selling and shipping sand to various customers in several states outside Arizona, including California, Nevada, Utah, and Colorado. Buyer desires a stable source of supply of sand for that business.

III. MUTUAL RIGHTS AND OBLIGATIONS

Seller and Buyer agree to the following bargained-for exchange:

1. *Supply.* For a period of five years from the date of formation of this contract, Seller will supply Buyer with all the sand that Buyer requires for Buyer's business of selling and shipping sand to customers outside the State of Arizona.

2. *Delivery.* Buyer will order sand as Buyer's requirements arise by sending a written purchase order to Seller. On receipt of such a purchase order, Seller will deliver the ordered sand within ten days to Buyer's facility at 1531 Range Road in Glendale, Arizona.

3. *Quality.* Seller warrants that the quality of the sand that is delivered to Buyer will be at least equal to that of sand of corresponding grades sold by other sand companies in the City of Phoenix, Arizona.

4. *Price.* For each ton of sand delivered, Buyer will pay Seller a sum equal to sixty percent (60%) of the market price per ton of concrete in the City of Phoenix at the time of Seller's delivery to Buyer.

5. *Term of Payment.* Seller may give an invoice to Buyer for sand on or after Seller delivers the sand to Buyer. Buyer will pay the full amount of such an invoice within thirty (30) days of its receipt of the invoice.

Signed:

_______________________________________ ____________

Seller—Authorized Agent for Sooner Sand Co. Date

_______________________________________ ____________

Buyer—Authorized Agent for Bassi Distributing Co. Date

Format for More Complex Agreement

REQUIREMENTS CONTRACT

This contract for the purchase and sale of sand (the Agreement) is entered into on ______________ by the following parties:

1. Seller—Sooner Sand Co., a general partnership consisting of Harley T. Price and W. M. McMichael, general partners, and
2. Buyer—Bassi Distributing Co., a joint venture of Bassi Trucking Co. and Hardcore Rock & Gravel, Inc.

RECITALS

1. Seller is engaged....
2. Buyer has an established....

MUTUAL RIGHTS AND OBLIGATIONS

Seller and Buyer agree to the following bargained-for exchange:

ARTICLE I
Definitions

1.1 *Grades of sand*—....

1.2 *Market price*—....

ARTICLE II
Supply of Sand

2.1 *Quantity*—....

2.2 *Quality*—....

2.3 *Delivery*—....

ARTICLE III
Payment

3.1 *Price*....

3.2 *Terms of Payment*—....

ARTICLE IV
Miscellaneous Provisions

4.1 *No Oral Modification*—....

4.2 *Prior Negotiations Superseded*—....

Arizona State University
SAMPLE BASIC CONTRACT

This sample contract illustrates the basic provisions and requirements of a contract and is intended to be used solely as a resource in negotiating or drafting a contract. This is not a contract "approved as to form" by the Office of General Counsel because no subject matter is described. Each subject matter has its own unique legal issues that should be addressed in a contract. Please contact the Office of General Counsel directly for advice in drafting specific contracts.

This Agreement is entered into between the ARIZONA BOARD OF REGENTS for and on behalf of ARIZONA STATE UNIVERSITY ("University") and "Contractor" as of the "Effective Date."

UNIVERSITY:	**CONTRACTOR:**
	______________________
By: ______________________	By: ______________________
Printed: ______________________	Printed: ______________________
Title: ______________________	Title: ______________________
Effective Date: ______________________	

RECITALS

[Use this section to describe the objective(s) of the parties and the understandings of both parties that form the basis for entering into this contract.]

A.

B.

C.

AGREEMENT TERMS

1. DURATION

The duration, or term, of this Agreement will begin on the "Effective Date" and end on the date below. This Agreement may be terminated earlier by either party upon ten (10) days prior written notice to the other party.

Month: ______________________ Day:________ Year: ________

2. CONTRACTOR'S OBLIGATIONS

2.1. **[Describe what, when, and how the contractor is to perform.]**

2.2. **[NOTE: Some activities may require a higher amount of insurance coverage. Always coordinate insurance requirements with Risk Management.]**

2.3. **Insurance.** Contractor, at its expense, agrees to procure and maintain during the term a policy of commercial general liability insurance in an amount of not less than one million dollars ($1,000,000), single limit, against claims for bodily injury, death and not less than one hundred thousand dollars ($100,000) for property damage occurring in connection with this agreement. This insurance must name the Arizona Board of Regents, ASU, and the State of Arizona as additional insureds as to acts or omissions of Contractor and its officers, employees, and agents. Contractor must provide ASU with a certificate evidencing this insurance coverage no later than the effective date of this Agreement.

3. UNIVERSITY'S OBLIGATIONS

[Use this section to outline the University's obligations.]

3.1.

3.2.

4. STATE OF ARIZONA PROVISIONS

4.1. **Nondiscrimination.** The parties agree to comply with all applicable state and federal laws, rules, regulations and executive orders governing equal employment opportunity, immigration, nondiscrimination, including the Americans with Disabilities Act, and affirmative action.

4.2. **Conflict of Interest.** This Agreement is subject to Section 38-511 of the Arizona Revised Statutes. This Agreement may be cancelled if any person significantly involved in initiating, negotiating, securing, drafting or creating this Agreement on behalf of University is, at any time while this Agreement or any extension thereof is in effect, an employee or agent of the other party to this Agreement in any capacity or a consultant to any other party with respect to the subject matter of this Agreement.

4.3. **Notice of Arbitration Statutes.** Pursuant to Section 12-1518 of the Arizona Revised Statutes, the parties acknowledge and agree, subject to the Arizona Board of Regents Policy 3-809, that they will be required to make use of mandatory arbitration of any legal action that is filed in the Arizona superior court concerning a controversy arising out of this Agreement if required by Section 12-133 of the Arizona Revised Statutes.

4.4. **Contractor's Records.** To the extent required by Section 35-214 of the Arizona Revised Statutes, Contractor agrees to retain all records relating to this Agreement. Contractor agrees to make those records available at all reasonable times for inspection and audit by University or the Auditor General of the State of Arizona during the term of this Agreement and for a period of five (5) years after the completion of this Agreement. The records shall be provided at Arizona State University, Tempe, Arizona, or another location designated by University upon reasonable notice to Contractor.

4.5. **Failure of Legislature to Appropriate.** If University's performance under this Agreement depends upon the appropriation of funds by the Arizona Legislature, and if the Legislature fails to appropriate the funds necessary for performance, then University may provide written notice of this to Contractor and cancel this Agreement without further obligation of University. Appropriation is a legislative act and is beyond the control of University.

4.6. **Weapons, Explosive Devices and Fireworks.** University prohibits the use, possession, display or storage of any weapon, explosive device or fireworks on all land and buildings owned, leased, or under the control of University or its affiliated or related entities, in all University residential facilities (whether managed by University or another entity), in all University vehicles, and at all University or University affiliate sponsored events and activities, except as provided in Section 12-781 of the Arizona Revised Statutes or unless written permission is given by the ASU Police Department (ASU PD). Notification by Contractor to all persons or entities who are employees, officers, subcontractors, consultants, agents, guests, invitees or licensees of Contractor ("Contractor Parties") of this policy is a condition and requirement of this Agreement. Contractor further agrees to enforce this contractual requirement against all Contractor Parties. ASU's policy may be accessed through the following Web page: http://www.asu.edu/aad/manuals/pdp/pdp201-05.html.

4.7. **Legal Worker Requirements.** As required by Arizona Revised Statutes Section 41-4401, ASU is prohibited after September 30, 2008 from awarding a contract to any contractor who fails, or whose subcontractors/subrecipients fail, to comply with Arizona Revised Statutes Section 23-214A. Contractor warrants that it complies fully with all applicable federal immigration laws and regulations that relate to its employees, that it shall, as applicable or required under Arizona Revised Statutes § 23-214A, verify, through the employment verification pilot program as jointly administered by the U.S. Department of Homeland Security and the Social Security Administration or any of its successor programs, the employment eligibility of each employee hired to work on this Agreement, and that it shall, as applicable or required under Arizona Revised Statutes § 23-214A, require its subcontractors and sub-subcontractors to provide the same warranties to Contractor.

A breach of the foregoing warranty shall be deemed a material breach of this Agreement. In addition to the legal rights and remedies available to ASU hereunder and under the common law, in the event of such a breach, ASU shall have the right to terminate this Agreement. Upon request, ASU shall have the right to inspect the papers of each contractor, subcontractor or any employee of either who performs work hereunder for the purpose of ensuring that the contractor or subcontractor is in compliance with the warranty set forth in this provision

4.8. **Prohibited Business Operations with Sudan and Iran.** As required by Arizona Revised Statutes Sections 35-391.06(A) and 35-393.06(B), the Contractor certifies to the University that the Contractor does not have scrutinized business operations (as defined in A.R.S. 35-391 and 35-393 respectively) in Sudan or Iran.

5. DEFAULT AND REMEDIES

5.1. **Default.** Any one of the following events shall be deemed to be an "Event of Default" hereunder.

5.1.1. Failure by either party to perform as specifically described herein.

5.1.2. A court having jurisdiction over any of the parties shall enter an order for relief in any involuntary case commenced against the applicable party as debtor under the Federal Bankruptcy Code or the entry of a court decree or order appointing a custodian, receiver, liquidator, assignee, trustee, or other similar official.

5.1.3. [**List any other events that are important and necessary for this contract, the failure of which should be a default.**]

5.2. Upon the occurrence of an "Event of Default," the non-defaulting party:(1) shall have all the remedies afforded by law and in equity;(2) shall have the right to terminate this Agreement;(3) [**List any other remedy that would be appropriate.**]

6. MISCELLANEOUS

6.1. Each party shall be responsible for its and its agents' negligence, actions and omissions.

6.2. Neither party shall have the right to assign this Agreement without the prior written consent of the other party.

6.3. This Agreement constitutes the entire agreement and understanding of the parties with respect to its subject matter. No prior or contemporaneous agreement or understanding will be effective. This Agreement shall be governed by the laws of Arizona, the courts of which state shall have jurisdiction over its subject matter.

6.4. Neither Contractor nor any personnel of Contractor will for any purpose be considered employees or agents of University. Contractor assumes full responsibility for the actions of Contractor's personnel, and is solely responsible for their supervision, daily direction and control, payment of salary (including withholding income taxes and social security), worker's compensation and disability benefits.

6.5. Contractor's work under this agreement is "work for hire" for purposes of the copyright laws of the United States and any foreign countries, and title to any subject copyright will vest with the University.

6.5.1. If for any reason the Work would not be considered a work made for hire under applicable law, by signing below Contractor sells, assigns, and transfers to University all rights and title to the copyright in the Work, related registrations and copyright applications, and any related renewals and extensions. This grant of rights and assignment extends to all works based upon, derived from, or incorporating the Work, to all income, royalties, damages, claims and payments payable now or later, to all causes of action, either in law or in equity for past, present, or future infringement based on the copyrights, and to all corresponding rights throughout the world.

6.5.2. If the Work is one to which the provisions of 17 U.S.C. 106A apply, by signing below the Author waives and appoints University to assert on the Contractor's behalf the Contractor's moral rights or any equivalent rights regarding the form or extent of any alteration to the Work (including removal or destruction) or the making of any derivative works based on the Work, including photographs, drawings or other visual reproductions of the Work, in any medium, for university purposes.

6.5.3. Contractor agrees to execute all papers and to perform other proper acts as University may deem necessary to secure these rights for University or its designee.

6.5.4. The individual signing on behalf of Contractor hereby represents and warrants that s/he is duly authorized to execute and deliver this Agreement on behalf of Contractor and that this Agreement is binding upon Contractor in accordance with its terms.

Participation Agreement

Arizona State University requires that individuals who are not ASU employees but use university equipment or resources, or collaborate on university research, agree to the following provisions.

Signed: ______________________________

Name: ______________________________

Date: ______________

1. I agree to be bound by the Arizona Board of Regents Intellectual Property Policy 6-908, a copy of which is available on-line at: http://www.azregents.edu/policy manual/default.aspx
2. While using ASU facilities or participating in collaborative ASU research, I also agree to be bound by applicable university policies, including those that relate directly to research. These policies are updated regularly and are available in the online RSP manual at: http://www.asu.edu/aad/manuals/rsp/index.html
3. I agree to disclose promptly to the Arizona Science and Technology Enterprises ("AzTE") any invention or discovery conceived, or first reduced to practice, as part of or related to my activities at ASU and to assign to AzTE and/or ASU all rights to any invention or discovery if that is required by ASU's obligations to external sponsors of research or by ASU policy. Additional information is available on-line at: http://www.azte.com
4. I understand that the terms of sponsored research agreements sometimes bind individual researchers. I understand that I need to ascertain whether, and to what extent, these agreements relate to me. I understand that I will be required to comply with these terms to participate in the research.
5. I also understand that ASU and ABOR policy and obligations to external sponsors may preclude my being able to retain intellectual property rights. I agree in those cases to assign my rights to AzTE and/or ASU, ABOR, or its designee.
6. I will cooperate fully, at no expense to me, with ASU, or its designee, in the evaluation and prosecution of patents, in the registration of copyrights, and in the preparation and execution of all related documents.
7. I am now under no obligation to any person, organization, or corporation with respect to any rights in inventions, discoveries, or copyrightable materials that are, or could reasonably be construed to be, in conflict with this Agreement.
8. I recognize that this Agreement is part of the terms of my appointment at ASU or the conditions for my use of ASU facilities or resources. The obligations in this

Agreement will continue after termination of my ASU appointment and after I am no longer using ASU facilities or resources.

9. Finally, this Agreement shall apply to all copyrightable materials created and to all inventions made, conceived, or first actually reduced to practice after the date this Agreement is signed, and it binds me, my estate, heirs, and assigns.

Top 10 Ethics Mistakes and How to Avoid Them

Mistake #6—Have a Fee Agreement (and Update It), by Russell Yurk

Printed in Maricopa Lawyer, August 2014, pg. 4

Most lawyers know that they need a fee agreement, but may not know what must be in a fee agreement, what they may include in a fee agreement, what can't be included in a fee agreement, and when they need to update fee agreements. Let's break this issue down into those four categories. For the most part, the requirements for fee agreements are found in ER 1.5.

So, what needs to be in a fee agreement? The first requirement might surprise some lawyers: the scope of the representation. ER 1.5(b). This requirement is important both for the lawyer and for the client. What is the fee for? Lawyers can be retained to perform very specific transactional work, pretrial litigation work, or for a consultation. Always include a description of the case, issue, or limited scope for which the client is retaining you.

The second important requirement is more fundamental: the basis or rate of the fee. Will the client pay a flat fee, an hourly rate, or a contingency fee? Regardless of the basis or type of fee, it must be described sufficiently in the fee agreement. A description of how expenses will be billed must also be included in the fee agreement. Using the appropriate name for the fee charged can be important because certain types of fees may require additional language in the fee agreement itself. *See* Ethics Op. 10-03.

For example, if the fee is considered "earned upon receipt" or "nonrefundable," the client must be advised that "the client may nevertheless discharge the lawyer at any time and in that event may be entitled to a refund of all or part of the fee ..." ER 1.5(d)(3). The fee to which a lawyer is entitled if he or she is discharged or withdraws is determined under a "reasonableness" standard. *See* ER 1.5(a).

The final requirement of a fee agreement is that it must be communicated to the client in writing, including any special "earned upon receipt" disclaimers. ER 1.5(b), (d)(3).

Now that we know what is *required* in a fee agreement, what else might you want to consider including? Depending on how you plan to staff the case, you might want to include fee-sharing arrangements, terms regarding the hiring of associated counsel or non-lawyer personnel (e.g., paralegals), or your role as local counsel. You can also specify client or lawyer obligations.

Lawyers might also consider including terms regarding billing, such as billing policies, third-party payors, advance payments (and how they will be applied to outstanding invoices), interest on unpaid balances, collection of unpaid invoices, or fee or malpractice arbitration agreements. Lawyers also are often well served by including a description of their document retention and/or document storage policies. This can eliminate confusion regarding availability of the client file following the representation.

Now that we've discussed mandatory and permissive fee agreement terms, what can't you put in a fee agreement? In general, lawyers can't use fee agreements to circumvent other laws or charge fees that exceed those allowed under the law. Nor can lawyers use fee agreements to secure a prospective waiver of conflicts of interest, ethics obligations, or an agreement to not report a lawyer to the State Bar. Lawyers also can't include a waiver of a client's right to discharge a lawyer's fees in bankruptcy.

Finally, lawyers need to be careful to update their clients when the basis or rate of fees or expenses changes during the representation. ER 1.5(b). The important thing to remember is to tell your clients about rate changes *before* the increased fees or expenses are actually incurred. What does that mean? If your hourly rate increases on January 1, 2015, notify your clients before January 1, 2015 even if an invoice will not issue until February. It is not enough to inform your client of increased hourly rates when the invoice is issued. The client needs to be aware of increased rates before you do the work at the higher rate.

Fee agreements are an oft-overlooked part of the practice of law. I strongly recommend that lawyers review their standard fee agreements on a regular basis and review each individual fee agreement to ensure its compliance with the Rules of Professional Conduct.

Complaint and Promise in *Kim v. Son*

Superior Court of California
County of Orange

Case Number : 06CC02419

Copy Request: 2298014

Request Type: Case Documents

Prepared for: ig

Number of documents: 1

Number of pages: 10

REICH RADCLIFFE LLP
Richard J. Radcliffe, SBN 156774
Marc G. Reich, SBN 159936
Beth S. Kuttler, SBN 195347
4675 MacArthur Court, Suite 550
Newport Beach, CA 92660
Telephone: (949) 975-0512

Attorneys for Plaintiff Jinsoo Kim

FILED
SUPERIOR COURT OF CALIFORNIA
COUNTY OF ORANGE
CENTRAL JUSTICE CENTER
JAN 23 2006
ALAN SLATER Clerk of the Court
By E. PERREAULT, Deputy

SUPERIOR COURT OF CALIFORNIA

COUNTY OF ORANGE, CENTRAL JUSTICE CENTER

UNLIMITED CIVIL JUISDICTION

JINSOO KIM, an individual, Plaintiff, v. STEPHEN SON, an individual; and DOES 1 through 25, inclusive, Defendants.	CASE NO. 06CC02419 .09 **COMPLAINT FOR DAMAGES FOR:** **(1) DEFAULT OF PROMISSORY NOTE;** **(2) MONEY HAD AND RECEIVED; and** **(3) FRAUD** JUDGE COREY S. CRAMIN DEPT. C8 [Amount in controversy exceeds $25,000]

01060005570 KIM
06CC02419 SON
UF UNLIMITED CVL FILING; 0 320.00
EP 52A01 01/23/2006 16:00 PAID CHK/

Plaintiff Jinsoo Kim hereby alleges in support of his Complaint as follows:

PARTIES

1. Plaintiff Jinsoo Kim ("Kim") is, and at all times herein mentioned was, an individual residing in the State of California.

2. Defendant Stephen Son ("Son") is, and at all times herein mentioned, was an individual, residing in the County of Orange, State of California, and within this judicial district.

3. Plaintiff is unaware of the true names and capacities of Defendants sued herein as DOES 1 through 25, inclusive, and therefore sues these Defendants by such fictitious names. Plaintiff will amend this complaint to allege their true names and capacities when ascertained. Plaintiff is informed and believes and thereon alleges that each of the fictitiously named Defendants is responsible in some manner for the occurrences herein alleged, and that Plaintiff's damages, as herein alleged, were proximately caused by their conduct.

4. Defendants at all times herein mentioned were the agent and employee of their co-defendants DOES 1 through 25, inclusive, and in doing the things hereinafter alleged was acting within the course and scope of such agency and with the permission and consent of their co-defendants.

JURISDICTION AND VENUE

5. Subject matter jurisdiction for this action rests in the Superior Court, Unlimited Jurisdiction, because this is an action for damages for default of a promissory note, and the amount in controversy exceeds $25,000.

6. Venue is proper in this judicial district because the promissory note/contract on which this Complaint is based was entered into and to be performed in the County of Orange, and Defendant Son resides in the County of Orange.

FIRST CAUSE OF ACTION

(Default of Promissory Note/Breach of Contract)

(Against All Defendants)

7. Plaintiff Kim realleges as if fully set forth herein all of the allegations contained in paragraphs 1 through 6, inclusive of this Complaint.

8. On or about October 29, 2004, for valuable consideration, Defendants made, executed, and delivered to Plaintiff Kim a promissory note. Attached hereto as Exhibit "A" is a true and correct copy of said promissory note, which is written in Korean and executed by Defendant Son.

9. By terms of the Note, Defendants represented, promised and agreed to pay Plaintiff, the principal sum of 170 million won, which was the equivalent of US$170,000.00.

10. Defendants materially breached the contract evidenced by the Note by failing to make any payment on the Note to Plaintiff, despite repeated demand therefor.

11. Plaintiffs have performed all covenants, conditions, and obligations on their part to be performed under the Note, except those that were excused by Defendants' breach of contract or waiver.

12. As a direct and proximate result of Defendants' material breaches of contract, Plaintiff has been damaged in the principal sum of US$170,000.00, plus interest at the legal rate, from the October 29, 2004.

SECOND CAUSE OF ACTION

(For Money Had and Received)

(Against All Defendants)

13. Plaintiff Kim realleges as if fully set forth herein all of the allegations contained in paragraphs 1 through 12, inclusive of this Complaint, to the extent consistent with this cause of action.

14. Within the past two (2) years, at Defendants' special instance and request, Plaintiff Kim delivered to Defendants the principal amount of 170 million won, which was the equivalent of US$170,000.00. As a result, Defendants became indebted to Plaintiff in the principal sum of US$170,000.00. Despite demand, Defendants have failed and refused to repay any part of this sum to Plaintiff.

16. There is now owing the principal sum of US$170,000.00 from Defendants to Plaintiff, plus legal interest from the date of default.

THIRD CAUSE OF ACTION

(Fraud)

(Against All Defendants)

17. Plaintiff Kim realleges as if fully set forth herein all of the allegations contained in paragraphs 1 through 16, inclusive of this Complaint, to the extent consistent with this cause of action.

18. Plaintiff is informed and believes and thereon alleges that when Defendant Son made the representations detailed above, he, in fact, did not intend to follow through on his representations. In addition, Plaintiff further represented that if Kim advanced 170 million won to Son that (1) Kim would own ten percent of a company called MJ, Inc., (2) that MJ, Inc.'s capitalization was 500 million won, (3) that Mr. Kim would own 40 % of a company called Netouch International Inc. and that (4) Mr. Kim would be paid US$5,000 per month from Netouch.

19. Defendant Son made these representations to induce Plaintiff into providing Son 170 million won (US$170,000.00).

20. In reasonable reliance on Defendant Son's representations, Plaintiff provided Defendant Son 170 million won or US$170,000.00.

21. Had Plaintiff known that Defendant Son was not going to pay Plaintiff the $170 million won or US$170,000.00, as promised, or that the other representations set forth in paragraph 18 were false, Plaintiff would not have provided Defendant Son any money.

22. As a direct and proximate cause of the Defendant Son's fraud, Plaintiff has suffered out of pocket damages of 170 million won or US$170,000.00, and other consequential damages which on information and belief are believed to be in a sum no less than $5,000,000.00.

23. Plaintiff is informed and believes and thereon alleges that Defendant Son's conduct was willful, wanton, oppressive, fraudulent, and malicious, and justifies the awarding of exemplary and punitive damages in an amount sufficient to punish Defendant Son and deter him and other from such conduct in the future.

PRAYER

WHEREFORE, Plaintiff Kim prays for judgment against Defendants, and each of them, as follows as follows:

ON THE FIRST AND SECOND CAUSES OF ACTION

1. That this Court award compensatory damages in the principal sum of $170,000.00;
2. That this Court award prejudgment interest at the legal rate;
3. That this Court award costs incurred herein the instant suit; and
4. That this Court award Plaintiff any other relief that may be deemed just and equitable.

ON THE THIRD CAUSE OF ACTION

1. That this Court award compensatory damages in an amount according to proof in an amount no less than $5,170,000.00;
2. That this Court award prejudgment interest at the legal rate;
3. That this Court award costs incurred herein the instant suit;

4. That this Court award punitive and exemplary dames; and

5. That this Court award Plaintiff any other relief that may be deemed just and equitable.

DATED: January 23, 2006

REICH RADCLIFFE LLP

By: Richard J. Radcliffe
Attorney for Plaintiff Jinsoo Kim

EXHIBIT

A

EXHIBIT A

S.S

김진수 ~~형~~님께서 손실을 보신
금액 약 1억 7천에 대하여
손 명수는 최선을 다하여
갚아 드릴것을 약속 합니다.

손명수 [illegible]
10-29-2004

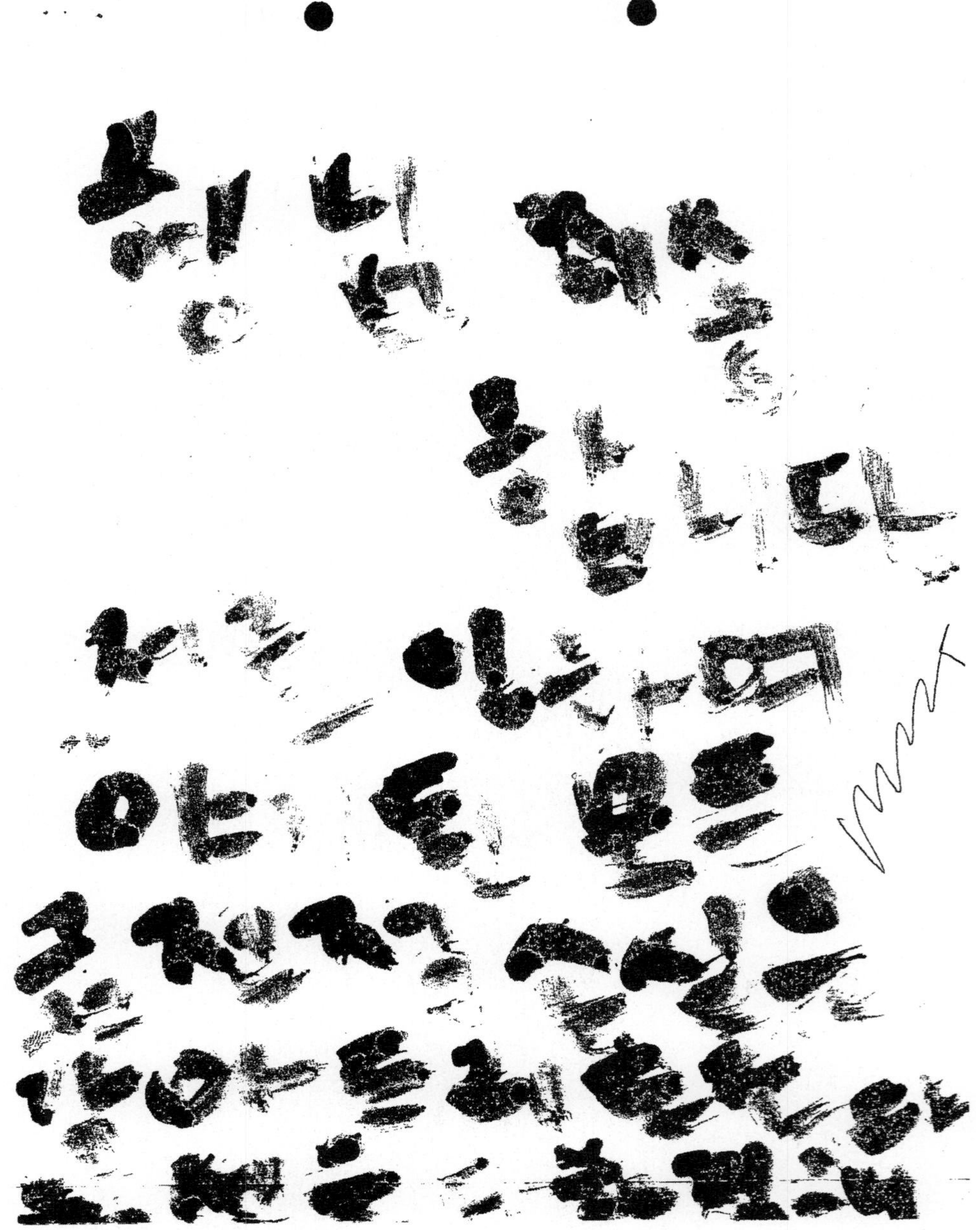

CM-010

ATTORNEY OR PARTY WITHOUT ATTORNEY (Name, State Bar number, and address):
Richard J. Radcliffe, SBN 156774
REICH RADCLIFFE LLP
4675 MacArthur Court, Suite 550; Newport Beach, CA 92660
TELEPHONE NO.: 949-975-0512 FAX NO.:
ATTORNEY FOR (Name): Plaintiff JINSOO KIM

FOR COURT USE ONLY

SUPERIOR COURT OF CALIFORNIA, COUNTY OF ORANGE
STREET ADDRESS: 700 Civic Center Drive West
MAILING ADDRESS:
CITY AND ZIP CODE: Santa Ana, CA 92702
BRANCH NAME: Central Justice Center

CASE NAME:
Kim v. Son

CIVIL CASE COVER SHEET
☑ **Unlimited** (Amount demanded exceeds $25,000) ☐ **Limited** (Amount demanded is $25,000 or less)

Complex Case Designation
☐ **Counter** ☐ **Joinder**
Filed with first appearance by defendant (Cal. Rules of Court, rule 1811)

CASE NUMBER: 06CC02419
JUDGE: JUDGE COREY S. CRAMIN
DEPT: DEPT. C8

Items 1–5 below must be completed (see instructions on page 2).

1. Check **one** box below for the case type that best describes this case:

Auto Tort
☐ Auto (22)
☐ Uninsured motorist (46)

Other PI/PD/WD (Personal Injury/Property Damage/Wrongful Death) Tort
☐ Asbestos (04)
☐ Product liability (24)
☐ Medical malpractice (45)
☐ Other PI/PD/WD (23)

Non-PI/PD/WD (Other) Tort
☐ Business tort/unfair business practice (07)
☐ Civil rights (08)
☐ Defamation (13)
☐ Fraud (16)
☐ Intellectual property (19)
☐ Professional negligence (25)
☐ Other non-PI/PD/WD tort (35)

Employment
☐ Wrongful termination (36)
☐ Other employment (15)

Contract
☐ Breach of contract/warranty (06)
☑ Collections (09)
☐ Insurance coverage (18)
☐ Other contract (37)

Real Property
☐ Eminent domain/Inverse condemnation (14)
☐ Wrongful eviction (33)
☐ Other real property (26)

Unlawful Detainer
☐ Commercial (31)
☐ Residential (32)
☐ Drugs (38)

Judicial Review
☐ Asset forfeiture (05)
☐ Petition re: arbitration award (11)
☐ Writ of mandate (02)
☐ Other judicial review (39)

Provisionally Complex Civil Litigation (Cal. Rules of Court, rules 1800–1812)
☐ Antitrust/Trade regulation (03)
☐ Construction defect (10)
☐ Mass tort (40)
☐ Securities litigation (28)
☐ Environmental/Toxic tort (30)
☐ Insurance coverage claims arising from the above listed provisionally complex case types (41)

Enforcement of Judgment
☐ Enforcement of judgment (20)

Miscellaneous Civil Complaint
☐ RICO (27)
☐ Other complaint (*not specified above*) (42)

Miscellaneous Civil Petition
☐ Partnership and corporate governance (21)
☐ Other petition (*not specified above*) (43)

2. This case ☐ is ☑ is not complex under rule 1800 of the California Rules of Court. If the case is complex, mark the factors requiring exceptional judicial management:
   a. ☐ Large number of separately represented parties
   b. ☐ Extensive motion practice raising difficult or novel issues that will be time-consuming to resolve
   c. ☐ Substantial amount of documentary evidence
   d. ☐ Large number of witnesses
   e. ☐ Coordination with related actions pending in one or more courts in other counties, states, or countries, or in a federal court
   f. ☐ Substantial postjudgment judicial supervision
3. Type of remedies sought (*check all that apply*):
   a. ☑ monetary b. ☐ nonmonetary; declaratory or injunctive relief c. ☑ punitive
4. Number of causes of action (*specify*):
5. This case ☐ is ☑ is not a class action suit.
6. If there are any known related cases, file and serve a notice of related case. (*You may use form CM-015.*)

Date: January 23, 2006
RICHARD J. RADCLIFFE
(TYPE OR PRINT NAME) ▶ [signature]
(SIGNATURE OF PARTY OR ATTORNEY FOR PARTY)

NOTICE
- Plaintiff must file this cover sheet with the first paper filed in the action or proceeding (except small claims cases or cases filed under the Probate Code, Family Code, or Welfare and Institutions Code). (Cal. Rules of Court, rule 201.8.) Failure to file may result in sanctions.
- File this cover sheet in addition to any cover sheet required by local court rule.
- If this case is complex under rule 1800 et seq. of the California Rules of Court, you must serve a copy of this cover sheet on **all** other parties to the action or proceeding.
- Unless this is a complex case, this cover sheet will be used for statistical purposes only.

Page 1 of 2

Form Adopted for Mandatory Use
Judicial Council of California
CM-010 [Rev. January 1, 2006]

CIVIL CASE COVER SHEET

Cal. Rules of Court, rules 201.8, 1800–1812;
Standards of Judicial Administration, § 19
www.courtinfo.ca.gov

American LegalNet, Inc.
www.USCourtForms.com

Appendix 3

Sample Answers to Practice Exam Questions

Exercise 2.17.1

Is the newspaper ad an offer?

[State your rule for offers, focusing on the circumstances in which a newspaper ad is an offer, and explaining why a typical ad is not.]

This ad arguably expresses commitment to sell a single, specifically described used car, because it refers to price, year, model, mileage, and condition. "Out it goes for $30,000" seems to express a current commitment to sell. Although it doesn't identify who can accept by saying "first-come, first-served," a reasonable person might interpret the final sentence, "Hurry, this will go fast!" as a statement that only the quickest response can accept, thus making it more plausible that the dealer was ready to commit. The offer is one to sell the car without financing, upgrades, or extras; those would require further negotiation, but Jana has not expressed an interest in additional features.

On the other hand, without clear identification of the single offeree who can claim the car, it would not be reasonable to read the ad as an offer to thousands of people who could each create a contract to buy the same car by arriving and expressing acceptance. American courts generally will not imply a term of "first-come, first-served" to make the ad more plausibly an offer to the first person to express assent, because they don't want to force people into contractual relations without a clear indication of commitment. For the same reason, a court would be hesitant to read too much into the exclamation, "Hurry, this will go fast!" This could just as well be interpreted as a means of attracting lots of buyers to come early and make their own offers to buy, thus keeping the price high. Moreover, the ad's references to upgrades, extras, and financing terms suggest that the dealer contemplates negotiation of further terms before an offer will be made.

On balance, [state your conclusion, but either conclusion is acceptable]

Under an objective theory of contracts, is Riley stuck with his unilateral mistake?

[Explain why the objective theory of contracts holds a party to his unilateral mistake in most states unless the other party caused the mistake or has notice of the mistake. A modern trend adds unconscionable injury as a ground for relief.]

Even though Riley subjectively intended to price the 2016 car at $50,000, he objectively communicated the $30,000 price advertised in the newspaper, committing a unilateral mistake through clerical error. Riley could argue that a 40% deviation from the market price put a knowledgeable buyer such as Jana on notice that the pricing is the product of a clerical error; indeed, she responded to the ad precisely because she recognized the advertised price as "quite substantially below market price." Moreover, in some states, Riley can argue that enforcing an agreement to sell the car for 3/5 of its value would cause a loss of $20,000 in this case, causing Riley to suffer unconscionable injury.

On the other hand, someone in Jana's position might simply interpret the advertised price as a great deal that Riley is using to generate publicity, as many vendors do. Jana might also have assumed that Riley acquired the 2016 model at a lower-than-market price, allowing him to use the car as a discounted item that would attract many buyers to his showroom. Moreover, even in a state that recognizes unconscionable injury as a ground for relief from unilateral mistake, a car dealer who has acquired at least two Jaguar cars, presumably as trade-ins from wealthy clients, likely can afford to absorb its mistake in this case without suffering unconscionable injury.

Conclusion: [state your conclusion, but either conclusion is fine]

Exercise 2.17.2

Unequivocal Expression of Acceptance prior to Signing Formal Document

[State rules in your own words about how acceptance must objectively and unambiguously convey assent to the terms of the offer and must not, for example, express a desire to delay acceptance until a different document can be signed.]

Dean can argue that he accepted Sophie's offer because he sent an email stating he was "approving" Sophie's proposal and "approve[s]" of all its terms, which a reasonable person would interpret as clear acceptance of her offer. His reference to putting the notes into a single document arguably reflects only a desire on his part to have a good, signed copy for convenience and evidentiary purposes, and not to delay the moment of commitment and contract formation. Also, his desire to "check it over" could convey no more than a quick check to ensure that the terms of their agreement have been correctly recorded in the formal written document. His statement in his email of his intentions to carry the business to new heights further conveys his view that the deal is closed and thus that he is currently accepting the offer.

On the other hand, Sophie can argue that Dean twice mentioned the need to put the notes into a single, "neat," "formal" document that both parties could sign. A reasonable person in Sophie's position would understand that Dean could be "approving" the current terms for inclusion in such a document, but that actual contract formation would not take place until both parties could review ("check over" in his words) all the terms in a single, neat, formal document without distracting notes scattered over four pages. Moreover, his reference to approving "all" terms on Sophie's notes may create some ambiguity over whether he is accepting just the terms that Sophie circled and offered, or whether further negotiations are required to sort that out.

Conclusion: [state your conclusion, but either conclusion is fine]

Acceptance by Authorized Mode

Sophie can argue that she required Dean to call her on her iPhone as the exclusive means of acceptance, because she said "you'll need to call me," and that Dean failed to accept in that required manner. Sending an email from his computer to her email account does not satisfy instructions to "call me on my iPhone" and "tell me that we have a deal." Sophie had scheduled a hectic morning in which she was "on the move" and therefore asked Dean to call her cell phone number. She may have required a phone conversation so that she could answer the phone while driving or use the opportunity to converse to clarify any ambiguities in Dean's response.

Dean can argue that Sophie's request that he call her on the iPhone was just a recommended means of acceptance and not a required one. By saying that Dean would "need" to call her, she was just telling him that she would be on the move and on her iPhone and that he would risk not reaching her if he didn't go through her iPhone. Sending her an email, which in fact did reach Sophie through her iPhone, perhaps was not as dependable as Sophie's recommended means, but it was a reasonable means of conveying acceptance. Alternatively, even if Sophie's statement should be interpreted as a required means of acceptance, a reasonable person could interpret "calling" her iPhone as meaning communicating through her iPhone in any way, including speaking, texting, or emailing.

Conclusion: [state your conclusion, but either conclusion is fine]

Exercise 3.10

Pre-Existing Duty Rule

[State the rule in your own words, including the general requirement of new consideration with reciprocal inducement on both sides of the modification, although some states allow for a one-sided modification if fair in light of unexpected circumstances.]

Jan can argue that the agreement is supported by consideration, because BB is giving new consideration in the form of setting aside time for possible media interviews, which could be quite valuable to the RR. Moreover, BB's is a more famous band than the one Bob booked in May, and its appearance thus is a more valuable "performance" that comes with great publicity. Alternatively, the courts might be amenable to a trend to allow a fair modification in light of unexpected circumstances, and the band's new-found fame—which comes to musicians only rarely—makes a 50% increase in the band's fee fair, as suggested by Bob's voluntarily offering it after speaking happily of his good fortune.

On the other hand, Bob can argue that BB's being available for possible media interviews is not a new performance but is routinely expected and was implicit in the original contract, as suggested by Jan's statement that he would "remind" the band members to make time for interviews. Moreover, even if Jan made a solid promise with his statement that he "can remind" the band members to save time for interviews, it's not clear that Bob is induced by such a promise: Bob responds that the show will put his club "in a national spotlight, interviews or not," and the inevitable publicity resulting from BB's performance is not the result of any new obligation assumed by BB. Also, although BB may be more famous in the minds of fans than when Bob booked it, it is still the same band, and Bob bargained for a band that was on the upswing and thus is entitled to one that has gained in fame and perfection since he booked it. If the jurisdiction follows the trend, Jan has a good argument for calling this a fair modification, even though it's one-sided, but Bob can argue that the band's new fame is not an unexpected change in circumstances; Bob bargained for a band that he knew was on the "upswing," and he was hoping for the band to gain in fame prior to the concert, something that even Jan acknowledged when he praised Bob for his ability to recognize talent "on the way up." Bob was also taking a risk that BB would fall out of style and not be worth the original contract fee.

On balance, I conclude that the band has not satisfied the traditional pre-existing duty rule but that a state following the trend would find that this is a fair modification in light of an unexpected change in circumstances. [This is just a sample conclusion; other conclusions are fine as well.]

Exercise 4.11.1

Liability for Unjust Enrichment:[1]

The unconscious victim could not communicate a promise to pay Reyes. Therefore, Reyes cannot recover on the basis of contract or promissory estoppel.[2]

Reyes likely will bring an action in quasi-contract for restitution of the reasonable value of the benefit that she conferred on the victim. To recover on this theory, she must prove that she unjustly enriched the victim.[3]

Enrichment is a measurable benefit. Reyes enriched the victim by rendering tangible first-aid services and summoning help, thus saving the victim's life.[4]

Reyes must prove that it would be unjust for the victim to retain the benefits of the first-aid services without compensating Reyes for them. Reyes could prove this by

1. This heading reflects the exam writer's decision to discuss issues of liability separately from those of remedies. Within the section addressing liability, the writer introduces and separately analyzes the elements of quasi-contract: (1) enrichment that is (2) unjust. She could have begun each of those analyses with a subsection heading, but good paragraphing appears to be a sufficient guide to organization within the two major sections, particularly because the facts raise no significant issue about enrichment.

2. This paragraph makes an introductory point about claims not in issue by stating the facts and conclusion and leaving the rules implicit. This paragraph could be omitted, but it might be good for an extra point or two because it explains how the student selected some issues for discussion and excluded others.

3. This paragraph identifies the main issue and states the applicable rule on the broadest, most general level.

4. This paragraph introduces a minor subissue, "enrichment," states the applicable rule, and reaches a conclusion on that subissue by applying the rule to the facts. Because this element of the claim is not seriously in doubt, it does not warrant fuller discussion. The brief discussion of this subissue serves primarily to introduce a more substantial issue in the next paragraph.

showing that she had some relationship with the victim that led Reyes reasonably to expect compensation. However, the courts ordinarily presume that emergency services at the scene of an accident are provided gratuitously. Reyes could overcome that presumption if she could show that she acted in a professional capacity when rendering the services or that the services she rendered were unusually burdensome or hazardous.

Reyes cannot establish any expectation of compensation based on her profession: She is a realtor and is not in the business of charging for medical services. She might have a better chance of rebutting the presumption of gratuitous emergency services by showing that her services were so burdensome that she expected compensation. After all, she engaged in the physically demanding task of cradling an accident victim in a moving car for 10 minutes while applying direct pressure to a severed artery. The physical and emotional distress of this event caused her to suffer exhaustion and distress for several hours. On the other hand, Reyes's actions posed little risk to her own safety, took relatively little time, and did not require special knowledge, skill, or training. Moreover, she likely would have felt distressed by the accident even if she had only witnessed the injury and had not acted to treat the victim.[5]

Although this is a close question, the facts suggest that Reyes could not reasonably have expected compensation for her emergency services. Therefore, I conclude that Reyes cannot recover.[6]

Remedies

Assuming that Reyes could prove a claim for quasi-contract, she would be entitled to restitution measured by the reasonable value of the benefit that she bestowed on the victim. The purpose of such relief would be to deny the unjust enrichment to the recipient of the benefit; therefore, whenever feasible, damages ought to be measured by the value that the recipient places on the benefit. If that is not feasible, a court may award damages based on the general market value of the benefit or, as a last resort, on the out-of-pocket costs incurred by the provider of the benefit.[7]

In this case, from the perspective of the victim, the value of the benefit bestowed by Reyes arguably is the value of the victim's life. A court would not use this value as the measure of the restitution, because it is relatively difficult to fix and because it is disproportionately greater than the effort expended by Reyes. Instead, the court probably would award the damages based on the general market value of Reyes's services. That measure is more nearly proportionate to Reyes's efforts, and it can

---

5. The preceding paragraph identifies a subissue and states the law applicable to that subissue. This paragraph reaches a conclusion on that subissue by applying the law to the facts. Notice how this paragraph argues both sides of the facts on this close question.

6. This paragraph states a conclusion on the entire issue of liability. A student undoubtedly could have received equal credit for reaching the opposite conclusion, so long as the student discussed all the facts and arguments. Indeed, notice how the next section assumes the opposite conclusion, for purposes of raising the issue of remedies.

7. This paragraph discusses the legal rules for computing damages.

easily be established by reference to the $600 fee that would have been charged by a paramedic. Alternatively, a court might award damages based on the actual costs incurred by Reyes, as measured by such things as inconvenience to Reyes and the cost of cleaning her jogging clothes. However, because the market-value remedy is more consistent with restitution, I conclude that a court would award $600 in damages if Reyes could establish a claim based on quasi-contract.[8]

Exercise 4.11.2

[Notice that quasi-contract is not in issue, because the essay question did not include facts suggesting any measurable benefit to Bradford; indeed, it specifically stated that Antillico's family did not provide any significant services or other benefits to Bradford. Notice also that Bradford had a motivation to make the promise, but that doesn't mean that he was induced by the prospect of Antillico moving to his land to make his promise; his motivation might simply have been a charitable desire to make a gift to a needy relative. The conclusion you reach is unimportant, so long as you spot the issues, summarize the law, analyze the facts (constructing arguments for both sides whenever possible), and reach some supportable conclusion.]

1. Consideration?

Bradford's promise to provide a house may be gratuitous and unenforceable for lack of consideration if he did not seek Antillico's presence in exchange for his promise, and thus did not satisfy the requirement of reciprocal inducement. Consideration generally requires a bargained-for exchange, which.... The parties act with reciprocal inducement if.... [state rules in your own words]

In this case, Bradford promised to provide a house, and Antillico responded by moving her household to that land, which could be a performance. However, it's not clear whether Antillico's doing so was an inducement for the Bradford's promise in the context of an exchange.

Bradford said that he would provide the place to stay "if you move your household to my estate." Because Bradford said he had more land than he could tend, and because the presence of the family might increase the likelihood that he would get help with his harvest, he might have sought the presence of Antillico's family in exchange for his promise, so that he could secure help. Moreover, Bradford stated his sense of a social obligation to be with Antillico and his sense of frustration that his work prevented him from traveling to her. Thus, he may have sought her move to his estate so that he could assess her welfare without leaving his harvest. Finally, he stated that he had no family and that Antillico and her family would be "most welcome" on his land, suggesting that he craved companionship and thus sought their presence in exchange for his promise. All these factors support an inference that the presence of Antillico and her family is an inducement for Bradford's promise.

---

8. This paragraph reaches a conclusion on the question of damages by applying the legal standards to the facts.

On the other hand, because Bradford could not move the house to her, his condition that she move to his estate ("if you move your household ...") is best interpreted as instructions about how she can collect the residence as a gift. This is especially true because this condition is stated immediately after Bradford wishes the best for Antillico and her family, expressing a charitable motivation that is consistent with a desire to make a gift. Moreover, in referring to having more land than he could tend, Bradford might have simply been reassuring Antillico that he could spare the land without any cost to himself, so that she could gracefully accept the gift. Similarly, his statement that he had no family could be a way of assuring Antillico that there was plenty of room for her family on his estate, again allowing her to gracefully accept the gift.

On balance, I conclude that....

2. Promissory Estoppel?

Even assuming that Bradford's promise was gratuitous and therefore not enforceable as part of a bargained-for exchange, Antillico's reliance might entitle her to relief under promissory estoppel.

For such relief, Antillico must prove that Bradford made a promise to her, that.... [state the general rule in your own words. Then add any necessary further information about the rule for each element, either here or just before the discussion of the facts of each element below.]

Reliance on a Promise—Bradford's letter states a promise to provide a house for Antillico until she can raise her children, and Antillico relied on that promise when she abandoned her land and moved to Bradford's property.

Foreseeability—Bradford should reasonably have expected Antillico to move, because he made it sound like such an attractive proposition. However, it's not clear that he reasonably should have expected Antillico to abandon her property without selling it, thus failing to secure her equity from it and ruining her credit. Indeed, Bradford's letter advises her to sell, and she failed to heed his advice.

Avoiding Injustice—Antillico might be the victim of an injustice, because she burned her bridges in reliance on Bradford's promise of a house and land; after once moving her household at some effort and expense, she now has no home to which to return and no means of securing one. On the other hand, Bradford had encouraged Antillico to sell her former house, suggesting that Antillico might be solely to blame for not having a house to which to return or the monetary equivalent.

I conclude that....

Exercise 5.8

[This requires an understanding of the rule of *Drennan* and the contrary ruling of *Baird*, both in Chapter 5. A good statement of the rule, which is fairly complicated, should start with the idea that promissory estoppel requires reliance on a promise, not an offer (which only *proposes* to give a promise in exchange for something else).]

Pathway gave notice of revocation before Contractor accepted, so Contractor can bind Pathway only if it has a legal basis for holding Pathway's offer open. Because Pathway's offer does not include an express promise not to revoke its bid, Contractor is relying only on an offer. True, reliance on an offer is sometimes justified, but normally only if the offer is for a unilateral contract, which necessarily requires reliance prior to acceptance. Reliance on an offer for a bilateral contract normally is not justified, because the offeree can create a binding contract with a return promise prior to any reliance.

One way to address this point is to ask whether the offer and the circumstances suggest that the parties must have intended the offer to be irrevocable for a period of time, so that the court can imply a promise not to revoke. According to the *Drennan* case, Contractor's dilemma justifies implying such a promise in Pathway's bid, even though that bid asks for a return promise as acceptance. Contractor necessarily must rely on the lowest bid on floor coverings by incorporating it into Contractor's own master bid, while awaiting word whether it has been awarded the master contract, all before accepting Pathway's bid. Just as in an offer for a unilateral contract, precontractual reliance by Contractor is necessary, justifying application of estoppel based on reliance on the offer, or on an implied promise not to revoke the offer.

On the other hand, contractors don't need this special protection as much as do offerees for unilateral contracts. Contractors have the bargaining power to supply the form on which sub-bids are made, and they can include provisions on bid forms that protect the Contractor's position. For example, the sub-bid form can include a promise by the subcontractor not to revoke its bid while the contractor is awaiting the award of the master contract (perhaps supported by a return promise to assess the bids in a certain way), or the bid form can include a provision allowing the contractor to accept the bid immediately (if it's the lowest bid) to create a sub-contract that is conditioned on the master contract being award to the contractor.

In my view, the *Drennan* view is [a good one] [not necessary to protect Contractor's interests.]

Exercise 6.12.1

Acceptance of Buyer's Written Offer

The machine parts are movable personal property; therefore, this is a "transaction in goods" governed by Article 2 of the UCC rather than common law principles (UCC §§ 2-102, 2-105). In contrast to the common law mirror-image rule, UCC § 2-207(1) recognizes a response to an offer as an acceptance, even if it contains additional or different terms, if it is a definite and "seasonable" expression of acceptance and if it does not expressly condition acceptance on the offeror's agreement to the additional or different terms. Such an express condition would make the response a rejection and counteroffer rather than an acceptance. A response is seasonable if sent within a time agreed or within a reasonable time (UCC § 1-204).

The question assumes that Buyer's purchase order is an offer. In the absence of Buyer's stating a time for acceptance, Seller's response time was clearly "seasonable," because Seller mailed it the same day as received, well within a reasonable time in a transaction calling for delivery within a month. Moreover, Seller appeared to definitely express acceptance with the phrase: "Your attached order is accepted,...." However, Seller then triggered the final proviso to UCC § 2-207(1) by expressing that Seller's acceptance was conditioned on Buyer's agreement to Seller's printed terms. Those printed terms include terms that were not in Buyer's offer, including terms relating to warranties and dispute resolution.

Consequently, because Seller insisted on Buyer's agreement to those additional terms, Seller's response is a rejection and counteroffer rather than an acceptance, even under the liberal provisions of § 2-207(1).

Contract Through Conduct

UCC § 2-207(3) governs conduct by the parties that arguably manifests their agreement if their forms fail to result in agreement under subsection 1. Subsection 3 states that if the writings do not establish a contract, the parties' conduct may nonetheless reflect a mutual intent to enter into a contract. The terms of such a contract by conduct will be those on which the writings agree, supplemented by "gap-filler" provisions of the UCC.

In this case, Seller's conduct of delivering the machine parts and Buyer's conduct of accepting delivery and paying for the goods constitute nearly every facet of performance and thus clearly reflect an intent to contract and the recognition of a contractual relationship. The contract of the parties will include the subject matter, quantity, price, and place of delivery on which the two forms of the parties agreed. The forms, however, did not agree on seller's requirement of private arbitration or disclaimer of warranties. Neither of these terms would become part of the agreement under § 2-207(3), because no gap-filler term of the UCC would require arbitration, and because UCC § 2-314 implies a warranty of merchantability in a sale of goods by a merchant of goods of that kind, unless the parties validly agree to disclaim it. Seller obviously is a merchant of these machine parts because it has a catalog listing these parts and their price, and thus "deals" in those goods under UCC § 2-104.

Consequently, the parties have a contract on the terms of Buyer's offer, and Buyer can assert his claim of breach of implied warranty in state court.

Exercise 6.12.2

Acceptance

In contrast to the common law mirror-image rule, UCC § 2-207(1) recognizes a response to an offer as an acceptance, even if it contains additional or different terms, if the response is a definite and "seasonable" expression of acceptance and if it does not expressly condition acceptance on the offeror's agreement to the additional or different terms. A response is seasonable if sent within a time agreed or within a reasonable time (UCC § 1-204).

The question assumes that Buyer's purchase form is an offer. In the absence of Buyer's stating a time for acceptance, Seller's response time was clearly "seasonable," because Seller mailed it the same day as received, well within a reasonable time in a transaction calling for delivery within a month. Moreover, Seller definitely expressed acceptance with the handwritten message: "Your attached order is accepted. Expect delivery within two weeks." Because Buyer's order was attached to Seller's response, the response refers unequivocally to the order. Moreover, the statement about delivery within two weeks is entirely consistent with a commitment by Seller to accept an offer that calls for delivery within a month.

Seller's acknowledgment form contained a term not found in Buyer's offer: a mandatory arbitration term. However, Seller did not condition its acceptance of Buyer's offer on Buyer's assent to Seller's additional printed term. Consequently, under the liberal terms of section 2-207(1), Seller's response is an acceptance despite its inclusion of an additional term. At this point, the acceptance is on the terms of Buyer's offer.

Terms of the Contract: Modification?

Section 2-207(2) states that the additional terms in the acceptance are "construed as proposals for addition to the contract." In other words, under the UCC, Seller's additional terms in the acknowledgment form implicitly state an offer to modify the contract that was just formed on Buyer's terms. Moreover, between merchants, this proposal to modify will automatically be viewed as accepted—even in the face of Buyer's silence—unless Buyer's offer precludes such additions, unless the additions would materially alter the terms of the original offer, or unless Buyer has already objected to such additions or does so within a reasonable time after receiving the acknowledgment form.

The mandatory arbitration clause appears to be an additional term, because the topic of dispute resolution was not addressed in Buyer's offer. Thus, it is a proposal to modify the contract that was formed on Buyer's offer. Because the question states that both parties are merchants, the terms will automatically be added to the contract unless at least one of the three exceptions of section 2-207(2) applies.

The first exception does not apply because Buyer's offer did not preclude addition to the contract. The second exception might exclude the proposed addition on the ground of material alteration. However, uncertainty in the definition and application of that test precludes the second exception as a basis for a clear answer.

The third exception, however, does clearly apply. Buyer's statement that "[w]e object to private mandatory arbitration" was sent by e-mail immediately upon receipt of the additional terms. The proposed addition to the contract would thus be excluded by objection under the third exception to subsection 2.

Conclusion

Under UCC § 2-207(1), the parties reached agreement through their forms on the terms of Buyer's offer, and that contract does not require mandatory arbitration because Seller's proposed additions to the contract were excluded under section 2-207(2) by Buyer's objections to them.

Exercise 8.4.4

Can Graham avoid the indemnity agreement on grounds of duress?

[Describe the standards for duress, leading to a defense or remedy of avoidance.]

Led Zeppelin could argue that Graham was not subjected to physical compulsion or even the threat of physical harm when he signed the release agreement. True, Led Zeppelin ("LZ") did state that it would refuse to take the stage if he did not sign, and a threat to repudiate an existing valid contract is viewed as an improper threat. However, courts will not readily assume that such an economic threat overcame Graham's free will; they will more likely assume that he signed voluntarily if he did not resist the threat. If Graham didn't like the terms of the indemnity agreement, he should have refused to sign, demanded performance of the musical performance contract, and sued for damages if LZ breached the contract by refusing to take the stage. After all, LZ would suffer its own loss of pay and reputation if it failed to perform.

Graham, on the other hand, could argue that LZ's improper threat left him no reasonable choice but to sign the agreement, against his will. Graham tried to call LZ's bluff by initially refusing to sign, but he discovered that the members of LZ were willing to carry out their threat, because they remained backstage after he initially refused to sign. At that point, Graham's only options were either to sign the indemnity agreement or cancel the remainder of the concert. If lost profits and other economic losses were the only consequence of canceling the concert, Graham could have recovered those losses in a lawsuit for breach of contract. The audience, however, was sufficiently rowdy that Graham could reasonably fear that canceling the show could result in violence, creating the risk of property damage and personal injury to fans. Public policy would encourage Graham to avoid such harm to the community. Moreover, canceling the show, with or without a violent reaction, could cause harm to Graham's reputation that would be difficult to calculate, prove, and recover in a damages action. He attempted unsuccessfully to resist the threat and then signed only when he had no other reasonable option.

[Conclusion?]

Is the Indemnity Agreement Supported by Consideration?

[State the pre-existing duty rule, and the consideration requirement of reciprocal inducement.]

Assuming that Graham cannot prove duress, he can argue that his promise to release the claim was not supported by consideration. LZ will argue that it exchanged its promise to perform an encore, a performance that was not part of its obligations under the first contract. Graham "liked" the idea of a guaranteed encore and so was at least partly induced by that promise to give his own; LZ, of course, was reciprocally induced by Graham's promise to indemnify LZ to promise its encore, because it aggressively advanced that exchange.

Graham, on the other hand, can argue that the promise to guarantee an encore was just a sham to create the false appearance of consideration. Although he might have paid a little extra for that promise in other circumstances, it was no inducement for him to sign the indemnity agreement, as evidenced by the fact that it was "inconsequential" when compared to his disdain for the indemnity promise. As argued earlier, Graham signed only to avoid the potentially catastrophic consequences of a canceled concert in front of thousands of impatient LZ fans.

[Conclusion?]

Exercise 8.8

Can Louis rescind for a material misrepresentation of fact during bargaining?

[State the rule, along with the premise that the possibility that another man was the father would have been material to Louis at the time of bargaining, because it presumably would have influenced whether he entered into a support contract, or how much support he would have agreed to provide.]

Misrepresentation?

[State rules about various kinds of misrepresentations, including half-truths, but not including simple non-disclosure except in the case of confidential relations.]

Hilda can argue that she stated no lies; everything she said was accurate. If Louis was curious about the possibility that another man could be the father, he should have asked. Hilda has no duty to educate him about everything she knows relating to the contract. Louis, however, will argue that Hilda engaged in a half-truth by addressing the topic of her pregnancy and her expectation that Louis provide support while failing to state that another man could be the father; the overall effect of these incomplete statements was to mislead Louis about a material fact.

Moreover, Louis could argue that their intimacy created a confidential relationship between them, so that he placed unusual trust in her. In such a relationship, he would not be expected to interrogate Hilda in a demeaning, aggressive way about other possible fathers. Moreover, he would not necessarily have access to information about whether she had been intimate with another man. In these circumstances, he should reasonably expect full disclosure from Hilda about all material facts prior to contracting. Hilda will counter that their physical intimacy did not translate into a lasting and meaningful relationship of trust; indeed, they seemed not to be in a meaningful relationship at all at the time of contracting.

On balance ... [conclusion about misrepresentation]

Justifiable Reliance?

Even if Hilda did engage in a form of misrepresentation of facts, she can argue that Louis did not justifiably rely on her implication that he was the only possible father. Arguably, he should have taken the precaution of taking the blood test prior to signing. Alternatively, prior to signing, he could simply have asked Hilda whether anyone else could be the father; she would then be forced either to tell the truth or to state a falsehood on which Louis would be justified in relying; even an evasive response would inform Louis of the need to make further inquiries. Louis can again fall back on his position that their intimate relationship made it unseemly for him to press Hilda in such a way, and that he was entitled to rely on her implications that he was the only possible father.

[Conclusion about justifiable reliance?]

[Conclusion about the entire claim?]

[For support for a duty to disclose in such a case, see *Jordan v. Knafel*, 378 Ill. App. 3d 219, 234, 880 N.E.2d 1061, 1073 (2007) (citing to Michelle Oberman, *Sex, Lies, and the Duty to Disclose*, 47 ARIZ. L. REV. 871 (2005)).]

Exercise 8.11

A. Mutual Mistake

In light of the lack of any evidence of illegality, duress, or misrepresentation, King's best chance for avoidance lies in a claim of mutual mistake, which requires proof that [State the rule in your own words.].

The parties did not discuss their assumptions about the amount of rock at the work site, so they did not express a shared assumption that turned out to be mistaken. However, they apparently both assumed that only a normal amount of rock would be found at the work site, because they were both genuinely "shocked" to discover the large boulders and sheets of rock. King's assumptions are further supported by his failure to conduct tests before signing the contract because large amounts of rock were so unusual in that area that he apparently did not suspect the possibility of such amounts. DD's CEO also stated later that he "too" had expected the excavation to be routine. Therefore, it appears that the parties shared a common misunderstanding about the material at the site at the time of contracting.

The fact about which the parties were mistaken may go to the essence of the contract, because it relates to a critical facet of King's obligation to excavate the site: the material that King must remove. Excavating the unusual amount of rock increases King's costs by 1/3, a substantial amount that causes him to sustain a loss rather than make a profit. On the other hand, any contracting job carries with it the risk of loss; moreover, King's burdens on any excavation always depend on the mix of materials that are encountered, and King certainly expected to encounter some rock. So the mistake relates only to relative amounts of expected materials of soil and rock at the site, which may not be a mistake that is sufficiently fundamental to the contract to justify rescission for an innocent mutual mistake. On balance, ... [Conclusion?]

Finally, even if King can establish a common mistake of fact that goes to a critically important matter, it's possible that the contract and other circumstances allocate the risk of such a mistake to him. Nothing in the contract specifically states that King must assume the risk of encountering unusual amounts of rock, and DD arguably is in as good a position as King to discover the nature of the excavation site. However, the contract requires King to remove "all soil, rock, and other material" at the site, thus arguably allocating to King the burden of removing whatever amount of any of those materials will be encountered. Moreover, since King is experienced in this kind of work, and since he had the right and ability to conduct tests, DD was not uniquely and exclusively in a position to gauge the risks before contracting. [Conclusion?]

B. Pre-Existing Duty Rule

If DD voluntarily agreed to modify the contract to allow greater time and pay to King, with nothing new provided in return, DD's new promises would not be supported by consideration, because King had a pre-existing duty to excavate the site. Although the UCC, which eliminates the consideration requirement for modifications in section 2-209, does not apply to this construction contract, a few states would not apply the common law pre-existing duty rule to this case, because they have abandoned the rule altogether or have abandoned it for written, signed modifications such as this one.

A few more courts, following a trend reflected in the Restatement Second, would enforce a one-sided modification if it is fair in light of unexpected circumstances. In such a state, the modification in this case would be a good candidate for enforcement, because DD's CEO has admitted that a modification was consistent with fairness, and because both parties were genuinely surprised by the unusual amount of rock, which dramatically increased King's costs.

Most courts, however, would not enforce this one-sided modification unless the parties had rescinded the first contract prior to the new agreement, or something new is promised by King in the modification. We have no evidence of an express rescission of the first contract before agreement to the second one. A few courts might imply a prior rescission from the very act of modification; however, that seems to be a fiction that should not earn widespread adoption. Moreover, the parties' attachment of the new agreement to the first contract, and its reference to the first contract, undermines an argument for implied rescission.

Because the modification refers to the first contract to describe King's excavation duties, King apparently has not agreed to add any new duties of that sort. However, because DD agreed to the modification after King mentioned his belief that the original contract was the product of a mutual mistake, King can argue that he surrendered a good-faith claim for avoidance (e.g., for mutual mistake) in exchange for the extra time and pay. By referring to the excavation duties of the original contract, the modification might be interpreted as providing that King was agreeing to drop any challenge to the validity of that contract and to embrace its duties. Moreover, although King has agreed only to excavate "all soil, rock, and other material" at the site, as he originally promised, he might be viewed as adding a new promise because he arguably has obligated himself to work for two additional weeks at the site and thus to devote his labor and equipment to the job for that longer period of time. DD can argue, however, that this element relates only to the maximum time allowed to King and not to any *requirement* that King devote any more time. In other words, DD can argue that this new term regarding timing has the sole effect of releasing King from a part of his obligations and not of adding to his obligations.

[Conclusion?]

Exercise 9.6

I. Public Policy Violation in the Non-Competition Clause

Courts will not enforce contracts that are illegal, including those that violate important public policies reflected in statutes or case law. Non-competition clauses raise competing policy concerns: [state the competing policies and resulting rule of reason in your own words].

Among other things, Lee's ability to raid BB's customers in one area of Phoenix shows that BB has legitimate business interests to protect. The reasonableness of its protection is best analyzed in the context of the three factors [that you would have] identified above:

Scope of Activities: In this case, the scope of activities affected is quite broad: "any capacity in the pest control trade." If read literally, this means that Lee would be prohibited from doing any work ranging from custodian to accountant to pension fund consultant in the industry. Such a broad restriction arguably goes beyond the kinds of jobs for which Lee developed some kind of competitive advantage by virtue of her work at BB. On the other hand, Lee has educational and experiential training in fields other than the pest control industry, such as in financial analysis, and thus could earn a living in another field. Moreover, she was indeed something of a "jack of all trades" at BB, working with inventory, sales, customer relations, billing, and even pesticide application in the field. These varied functions sufficiently exposed her to information and developed her expertise in the trade and her relations with customers and suppliers that she might take with her an unfair advantage relating to all aspects of the trade. In rebuttal, she could argue that BB was a new enterprise, so that she helped develop its information and expertise, rather than learned from it. On balance, [conclusion?]

Geographic Scope: To avoid further issues of public policy, a court might construe "Phoenix metropolitan area" narrowly to mean within Phoenix city limits. If so, the geographic scope of the clause is reasonable, because BB developed business within that area. On the other hand, the more common and natural interpretation of this phrase is the entire valley area, including the cities immediately surrounding the City of Phoenix. This is arguably unreasonable in scope, because BB had developed business and customer lists only within Phoenix City limits by the time Lee resigned. In rebuttal, BB could point out that it was poised to expand to surrounding cities and should be free to do so without competition from someone that it had trained. On this close question, ... [conclusion?]

Duration: Any competitive advantage gained by Lee from her work at BB would dissipate through the passage of time. In this case, the two-year duration of the restrictions is not outlandish and seems to reflect a good-faith effort to permit Lee to resume work in the industry after holding down another job for a suitable period. On the other hand, courts have often found that employers' interests are adequately protected by restrictions lasting no more than one year, sometimes no longer than six months. Similarly, the facts in our case show that any benefit to Lee in being exposed to BB's office procedures, clientele, and suppliers would have dissipated after about one year. Thus, the duration of the non-competition clause likely is overly broad.

In sum, the non-competition clause probably violates public policy in one or more respects.

II. Remedy for Violation of Public Policy

Traditionally, some courts [Describe the "all or nothing" approach in your own words.]

Because such clauses implicate competing public policies, however, some courts are willing to modify an unreasonable non-competition clause and to enforce it after limiting it to a reasonable restriction. The most liberal (or radical) version of this approach is simply to rewrite the contract for the parties. In this case, that would entail changing the duration of the clause to one year and perhaps limiting the geographic scope of the clause to the city of Phoenix (or to Phoenix and other cities to which to BB planned to expand in its second year of operation), and maybe to limit the restrictions to only those activities in which Lee had engaged at BB.

A less radical version of the modification approach is the "Blue-pencil rule," based on severance of provisions that violate public policy. [State the blue-pencil rule in your own words.] In this case, the court could strike out words and letters to change the duration of the restrictions from "a period of two years" to "a year." It would be even easier to strike out the words surrounding "Phoenix" to change "the Phoenix metropolitan area" to "Phoenix," which should effectively limit the scope to the City of Phoenix.

The activities restricted ("in any capacity in the pest control trade"), however, are not as easily edited with the blue pencil approach. They could be pared down to "in ... the pest control trade" to de-emphasize the comprehensiveness of the scope of activities, but this might remain problematic if the court has declined to find that Lee had a competitive advantage in every imaginable function in the industry.

Moreover, under either of the modification approaches, some courts would require an indication of the parties' intent to allow the court to modify the contract, or at least to sever unenforceable provisions and to enforce the remainder, and no contract clause to that effect is provided in this problem. Unless some other evidence of that intent is available, some courts would be reluctant to modify the contract and enforce it.

Exercise 9.11

Any purported agreement likely would be too indefinite to enforce because Dimmick never specified the amount of money that he would pay. Indeed, that missing term might prevent his statement from even amounting to an offer, or it might render his promise illusory if he was apparently retaining full discretion to determine whether to pay anything at all. Even assuming that the parties objectively expressed offer and acceptance to an exchange with apparent consideration, the Rowleys have strong defenses based on: (1) physical duress in the form of Dimmick's brandishing a knife as an improper threat and overcoming their free will, and (2) illegality in a bargain to pay the Rowleys to harbor a fugitive.

Exercise 9.12.1

As a matter of common law, courts will not enforce a contract if it contemplates a performance that violates law or the public policies that underlie the law. If an illegal clause is severable from the contract, then a court might strike out the illegal clause and enforce the remainder, particularly if the parties have signaled their consent to such severance. If an entire contract is illegal and unenforceable, however, the court usually will leave the parties as it found them, denying even restitution, except for discretion to grant relief if one party is less guilty of the illegality or would suffer a great forfeiture.

In this case, the contract that EE seeks to enforce contemplates the growing, processing, packaging, and wholesale of cannabis to a retailer for resale to the public for recreational use. State law, which is usually the focus of public policy analysis, is not offended by the activities of the parties. Indeed, these activities presumably are in line with public policy, because the state derives tax revenue from the activities (with which state services can be funded), and the legislature has apparently determined that the opportunity to use cannabis is not harmful to the state's population, even when not restricted to medical uses. Moreover, failure to enforce this contract could disrupt the entire cannabis industry in the state, and the state budget with it.

On the other hand, the activities contemplated in the contract—including both parties possessing large quantities of marijuana—still violate the letter of federal law, which law is supreme and thus applies in the states. Federal law has not been enforced in recent years, in a nod to allowing state experimentation, so EE can argue that this nonenforcement of federal law shows that state legalization of cannabis is consistent with federal law and policy. But it is difficult to negate federal public policy when the federal regulation is still on the books and enforcement is possible at any time, spurred by political developments. The statement by the new A.G. suggests that federal public policy still strongly opposes the activities of the parties, even if federal agents have not yet resumed enforcement. Moreover, a state court could very well exceed its proper authority if it dismisses the policies underlying a federal statute simply because the court believes that the statute is obsolete. Congress is the primary policy-making body for the federal government, and its enactments cannot be swept away by courts.

If the court determines that the contract is not enforceable for the full purchase price, EE could ask for restitution, which could be: (1) the reasonable wholesale value of the edibles sold by HH, and (2) return of the unsold edibles. However, it's not obvious that EE would qualify for an exception to the usual denial of restitution for performance of an illegal contract. It's unlikely that losing the revenue from this single delivery would work a great forfeiture on EE, which is described as having a booming business. On the other hand, in light of conflicting state and federal policies, the encouragement provided by state law and nonenforcement of federal law, and HH's questionable behavior of retaining the product and the partial sales proceeds without paying, a court might consider granting some restitution to EE out of fairness. A good compromise might be to order return of the unsold edibles while denying restitution of the revenue from the initial sales.

On balance, I conclude....

Exercise 9.12.2

Misrepresentation: Ada can try to remove the arbitration clause on the ground that Rick fraudulently added it to the contract. She could even ask for avoidance of the whole contract, because she has been paid for her past work and is now intent on getting damages under the discrimination statute.

Such relief requires proof of a misrepresentation of material fact on which the claimant justifiably relied. [Define the kinds of things that qualify as a misrepresentation.]

Facts on Half-Truth: In this case, Rick did not state a falsehood but technically told the truth when he answered Ada's query about the contract's conformance with negotiations by stating that the contract included "all the terms that you requested." On the other hand, he may be guilty of a half-truth by addressing the content of the contract without further disclosing the whole story: he had added some standard-form terms—including the arbitration clause—beyond the ones they had discussed over lunch. Rick's statement might nonetheless be defensible since he was so directly and accurately responding to a very specific question from Ada. On balance, a court likely would find....

Facts on Material Fact: Statements about the precise provisions in the contract are clearly ones of fact, as distinguished from "puffing" such as "this is a really sound and fair document." Rick might argue that the arbitration clause is not material, because it operates for and against both parties, replacing the court system as the means of dispute resolution, and because employees don't usually anticipate disputes but are more focused on the nature of the position and its compensation. Nonetheless, waiving the right to go to court is a substantial provision and could have affected negotiations. On balance, a court likely would find....

Facts on Justifiable Reliance: Even if Rick engaged in a form of misrepresentation, and even if we assume that Ada relied on Rick's pre-signing statement, Rick could argue that any reliance by Ada was unjustified: Ada could have easily read the contract before signing and discovered herself what it contained. After all, the contract was only four pages long, and even a quick glance at the general topics covered on the signature page would have revealed that it contained an arbitration clause. The traditional rule holds a party to the terms to which they manifest assent, regardless whether they took the time to read them. On the other hand, the equitable remedy of avoidance for misrepresentation provides the judge with some flexibility to be forgiving of such reliance on a misrepresentation if other elements of the claim are strongly established. Ada might have been lulled into placing unusual reliance on Rick because of the way in which he allowed her to choose among contract provisions over lunch. On balance,...

In light of all the factors relating to misrepresentation ... [Conclusion?]

Unconscionability: Even in the absence of a misrepresentation, the arbitration clause may be unenforceable if [In your own words, state the test for procedural and substantive unconscionability, and mention the minority approach of requiring only one branch to be established. After the U.S. Supreme Court's *AT&T* decision in 2011, which related to class action waivers, the FAA would not preclude a more general unconscionability challenge based on procedural problems and other kinds of substantive unconscionability, thus paving the way for an unconscionability analysis.]

Facts on Procedural Unconscionability: As the wealthy sole owner of the company, Rick normally would have much greater bargaining power than prospective or current employees. However, either he has decided not to exercise it to the maximum or Ada is a sufficiently superior candidate to have strong bargaining power, because Rick allowed Ada to have a hand in selecting the provisions of the contract. Moreover, the arbitration provision was not particularly hidden in the contract, but appeared in normal print on the signature page, where Ada could have easily read it, so it almost certainly was objectively conveyed to Ada and would not be excluded for lack of mutual assent. Nonetheless, Rick's possible half-truth at least might have caused Ada to relax her guard and to skip reading the contract, and—precisely because it was in the same font as other provisions—the arbitration clause was not particularly conspicuous and so did not stand out on the page. Moreover, the clause did not disclose the costs of arbitration, so Ada might not have fully understood its implications even if she had read it. Still, someone sophisticated enough to be hired as a sales manager probably would have the knowledge to understand the nature of arbitration and that it would not be cost-free. On balance, the arguments for procedural unconscionability are weak, but might amount to a minimal showing.

Facts on Substantive Unconscionability: The arbitration clause operates fairly equally for and against both parties, splitting the costs between them, and requiring both parties to submit all disputes to arbitration. Moreover, Ada's greater cost by far, either in arbitration or in court, is her attorney's fee, which she can recover under the statute if her claim is meritorious. On the other hand, Rick and SP are undoubtedly better able to pay their $6,000 share of the fee than is an unemployed worker who dug into her savings to hire her attorney; although that factor is mitigated by SP's own misfortunes in the economic downturn, it arguably suggests that the arbitration clause would be fairer if SP paid a larger share of the costs. Also, the majority of the arbitrators from ARB formerly represented employers when they practiced law, placing their objectivity in doubt. Finally, Rick included this clause in all his contracts for eight years, so SP and its attorneys could get to know these arbitrators and their arbitration styles in repeated disputes and hearings. In combination, these factors could make this part of the clause operate unfairly against Ada. Still, the arbitrators are professionals and presumably would try to apply their expertise objectively and neutrally. On balance,....

On the overall question of unconscionability, a court likely would ... [are the substantive problems sufficient to combine with a minimal showing of procedural problems to establish unconscionability?]

Violation of Public Policy: The state anti-discrimination statute has an unusual provision that takes important issues under the statute away from the judge on summary judgment and requires them to be decided by the jury in all cases. If this statute states a strong public policy for determination of those issues by a jury of peers, then it might violate public policy for the parties to contractually agree to litigate a claim under the statute before a panel of private arbitrators. On the other hand, three private arbitrators arguably are closer to a jury of peers than a single judge, so the statute's apparent policy is not strongly offended. Moreover, public policy generally favors arbitration, and any arbitration clause contemplates the waiver of a court trial and a jury. In this case, the waiver simply extends to a statutory claim that presents more jury questions than might otherwise be the case. On balance,....

[Other Premise: The statements by the parties just prior to signing the written agreement would not be excluded by the parol evidence rule if introduced for the purpose of showing that a contract or contract term should be avoided because misrepresentation, illegality, or unconscionability.]

Exercise 10.16.1

A. Entitlement to Payment

The court will attempt to determine the parties' intended meaning, reading the terms of the contract as a whole rather than focusing on any term in isolation. To avoid a forfeiture, courts will not lightly interpret a clause to be a condition, but will require clear language of condition, such as "if, but only if," or "on the condition that," or "in the event that." Moreover, in case of doubt about the parties' intentions, it will often construe an ambiguous contract term against the party who drafted it, because that party had the best opportunity to avoid the ambiguity. If a term states a condition, a court normally will require strict and complete satisfaction of the condition before the qualified duty arises, such as the holding in one case that qualifying for a bank loan at 8¾% did not satisfy a condition of qualifying for a bank loan at 8½%. If a clause does not state a condition, or if the condition is satisfied, any breach of a simple duty will permit the other party to cancel only for a material breach, which requires a substantial deprivation of expectations (not in issue in this case).

In this case, Owner has a good argument that it owes Contractor nothing. Section 2 of the contract uses clear words of condition: "but only in the event that." The clause preceding the language of condition states O's obligation to pay the landscaping fee: "Owner will pay a fee of $100,000 to Landscaper, ..." Thus, that payment obligation is subject to the condition. Accordingly, O's obligation to pay the fee arises only if the described event has occurred to the letter. The event described in the condition is completion of performance "as described in section 1," and section 1 requires completion of performance by December 3. Without any further evidence as to the meaning of "December 3," that deadline expires at the latest at midnight on December 3, and completion of performance by 6 a.m. on December 4 does not strictly satisfy the condition, and O's payment obligation does not arise. Remaining language of section 2 of the contract all assumes completion on December 3, because it contemplates payment on December 4 after an opportunity for inspection. But, if performance is not completed on December 3, everything else is moot because O's obligation to pay does not arise.

On the other hand, even though section 2 clearly uses words of condition, the obligation subject to the condition should be viewed as applying to both of the clauses preceding the language of condition in section 2, including the opening phrase "On December 4." Under this interpretation, if L does not meet the December 3 deadline, then O's obligation to pay on December 4 does not arise. But that would not exclude O's obligation to pay at some other time. The reference in section 2 to withholding payment until O has an opportunity to inspect and certify completion results in the following obligations: O must pay on December 4 if performance is completed on December 3; otherwise, O must pay after an opportunity to inspect and certify whenever L has completed performance. Because L completed performance only six hours late, with the delay occurring in the middle of the night prior to business hours, resulting in no damages at all to O, L would be in minor breach of section 1 (maybe we should say only a "nominal" or "technical" breach), so O would be obligated to pay the entire fee after certifying completion. Although this interpretation requires the condition to reach back to the beginning of section 2, despite the comma after "On December 4," it is consistent with the judicial inclination to avoid a forfeiture. Often courts avoid a forfeiture by interpreting a clause to state a duty rather than a condition, which is not feasible when the parties used the language "in the event that." Instead, the judicial tendency to avoid forfeiture could lead the court to interpret the clear condition to qualify only a narrow obligation—to pay on a certain date—rather than more broadly to qualify the obligation to pay at all.

Moreover, even if completion by December 3 was a condition of L ever getting paid, a court seeking to avoid a forfeiture might define December 3 loosely to mean any time prior to business hours on December 4, the first time that inspection presumably could take place, although that would require a more radical departure from a normal interpretation of the text on the face of the contract and from the usual rule of strict satisfaction of conditions.

On balance, I conclude....

B. Admission of Parol Evidence

The parol evidence rule will exclude testimony of an oral statement made prior to, or contemporaneous with, signing an integrated agreement if the statement contradicts any term in the integrated agreement. {Notice that—for purposes of this issue, the level of integration is irrelevant, although Q 2.A states that the LA is a completely integrated agreement.} Such testimony will be admitted for the purpose of explaining the meaning of a term in the agreement, rather than to contradict it. The testimony about prior oral statements regarding the deadline in the LA is classic parol evidence, so the remaining issue is whether that parol evidence would be viewed as explaining or contradicting a term in the contract.

1. Plain-meaning rule—Under a strong version of the plain-meaning rule—sometimes known as the four-corners rule—the judge will look only to the terms within the contract (perhaps supplemented by consulting a dictionary) to determine if a provision is ambiguous on its face. If it is ambiguous, the judge will admit parol evidence of a meaning to which the term is reasonably susceptible; otherwise, the judge will give the term the single plain meaning that is apparent from the judge's own linguistic training or the judge's consulting a dictionary, and the judge will exclude parol evidence of a different meaning.

In this case, section 1 of the LA clearly states L's deadline for completion as "December 3," which has a single plain meaning: the time for performance ends on or before midnight on December 3, and not at any time on December 4. It may be ambiguous whether "December 3" means till sundown on December 3, or the close of business hours, or midnight, but sometime in the morning of December 4 would not be within any ambiguity of "December 3," and would not be a definition found in a dictionary. A court applying the plain-meaning rule would regard such testimony as an attempt to contradict the term "December 3," rather than to explain its meaning.

Thus, a court applying a plain-meaning rule would not admit evidence that O and L orally agreed that "December 3" meant "December 3 and anytime prior to 8 a.m. on December 4."

2. Rejection of Plain-meaning rule—Some courts believe that a word or phrase has no plain meaning in the abstract, because its meaning depends on the context. These courts will give effect to an unusual meaning subjectively shared by the parties to the contract, even if it departs from any meaning held by most others in the population and thus if their meaning is not within any reasonable ambiguity of the contract term. Under this modern approach, the judge will consider the parol evidence prior to trial, and it will admit the evidence to the jury if the judge believes that the parties might plausibly have adopted that meaning of the contract, and will exclude the evidence only if the evidence fails a "laugh" test and thus is viewed as wholly irrelevant to the issue of interpretation, is viewed as an attempt to contradict the contract rather than explain its terms. If the parol evidence is admitted, the jury is still free to believe the testimony or reject it.

In this case, although "December 3" does not normally include the early morning hours of December 4, it is entirely plausible that the parties adopted that meaning because O likely would not care how late L worked prior to inspection; the only timing important to O was completion of the project prior to the earliest time he planned to inspect the work. He obviously would not be starting the next phase of construction at midnight at the end of December 3 if he didn't expect to inspect until the morning of December 4. The parties would have avoided litigation on this issue by simply changing "December 3" in section 1 to "prior to inspection by Owner at 8 a.m. on December 4," but their discussed meaning of December 3 as continuing through the night is not so implausible as to compel the conclusion that L is simply trying to contradict the contract.

Thus, a court that rejects the plain-meaning rule would permit the jury to hear evidence of the parties' discussion prior to signing, and will allow the jury to determine what meaning was intended by the parties.

Exercise 10.16.2

The sample below shows various ways that a student could score points within the best analytic frameworks, although no one student could be expected to convey all these points within the allotted time.

1. Liquidated Damages or Penalty Clause?

A clause stipulating damages is enforceable as liquidated damages if, at the time of contract formation, it represents a reasonable estimate of the damages that would be suffered if a breach later occurs, even if the actual damage turns out to be lesser or greater, or in some courts, even if damage is nonexistent. Courts will allow greater leeway in making this estimate if compensatory damages from the breach would be difficult to calculate and thus are uncertain. But stipulated damages that reflect an intention to award more than compensation for actual losses, to punish a party for breach, or to deter breach, constitute an unenforceable penalty clause, which violates public policy. A punitive intent can sometimes be inferred from stipulated damages that do not vary with the magnitude of breach or that greatly exceed a reasonable estimate of actual losses.

The stipulated damages in section III of the contract appear reasonable in light of the calibration between growing damages and increasing days of delay: they call for $3,000 in deductions from CC's fee for each day of delay, which would be the average daily loss for a delay of 20 days. Moreover, the stipulated damages are reasonable in that they are limited to the contract fee of $60,000, even though a delay of more than 20 days could cause losses exceeding that cap, and a delay of 30 days or more could cause very substantial losses. Although CC might complete the designated work with only five days' delay, in which case the losses could be avoided by paying a total of $10,000 for extra labor over 10 days, those costs are in the same general ballpark as the stipulated damages of $15,000 for that delay. The losses that G might ultimately suffer are uncertain, so the parties' estimate need not correspond perfectly with the damages expected for a given number of days of delay; a uniform imposition of average damages per day should suffice. In this case, the parties chose a middle ground: the cap at the upper end of delay makes up for minor overcompensation at the lower end.

On the other hand, according to CC's estimates, only the lower end of delay was expected by the parties. Even removal of the boulders might cause a delay of only about five days, which would cause a total of $10,000 in costs for extra work. The stipulated damages of $3,000/day over five days ($15,000) is 50% greater than actual estimated damages of $10,000, a difference that should be viewed as enough to discourage breach or punish CC. Moreover, as discussed in the next section, it is highly unlikely that the parties contemplated removal of those boulders at the time of contract formation; G developed that plan only after G realized that he no longer could cultivate grapes on the land. Therefore, the only delay the parties would have clearly contemplated at the time of contracting would be a slight weather delay, clearly within the five-day period of damages of only $1,000/day for 10 days = $10,000, suggesting that damages of $15,000 for five days of delay reflected a punitive intent.

Finally, the anticipated uncertainty in calculating actual losses does not justify allowing great leeway in estimating damages in this case. The greatest uncertainty in damages corresponds with a delay of beyond 30 days, which would delay planting for a year and cause uncertain lost profits. In contrast, the losses for a delay of five days or less, which the parties expected to be the maximum, are relatively certain, because the damage can be avoided completely by paying for extra work for 10 days. This certainty about losses for a short delay justifies a more demanding standard in assessing the reasonableness of the parties' estimation. Similarly, although reasonable liquidated damages are sometimes enforced even when no actual damages are suffered, their reasonableness should be subject to special scrutiny if, as in this case, any delay by CC could not possibly cause damage to G because his late testing shows that he ultimately has no reason to grade the land at all.

On balance, I conclude....

2. Breach of Duty of Good Faith

A duty of good faith and fair dealing in performance and enforcement is implied in every contract after its formation. Most relevant to our case, a party acts in bad faith by hindering the other party's performance, thus preventing him from enjoying the fruits of the contract. Even when a contract allocates discretion to a party, without any express limitation, the duty of good faith requires an inquiry into the reasonable expectations of the parties regarding the risks they assumed and thus the outer bounds of discretion that the parties must have intended. One way to determine whether an exercise of contractual discretion exceeds such bounds is to ask whether the parties would have agreed to it if they had discussed it during negotiations. The duty of good faith also is breached by some kinds of opportunistic behavior, such as when a party takes advantage of changed circumstances or a contract provision to achieve an unfair advantage at the expense of the other party, if in a manner inconsistent with the collaborative relationship of contracting parties.

G might not have violated any implied duty, because the contract gave him unusually great control over designating the land to be graded. The contract gave G more than just the right to approve CC's designation, and it went further even than giving G discretion to designate without any limitations; instead, it specifically permitted G to exercise "sole" discretion over that matter. The modifier "sole" suggests that G's discretion will not be questioned by anyone else except in extreme circumstances, thus expanding the range of choices that could be within the parties' reasonable expectations and the risks that CC assumed. Although CC would lose money with some designations by G, CC assumed that risk by agreeing to give G sole discretion, knowing that the land contained the hill of boulders. Moreover, although it would presumably constitute bad faith for G to make a designation solely to get out of the contract, without any other justification, getting rid of the hill of boulders in the northwest corner arguably was within G's contemplation for his final plan, because he was considering modifying his initial plan to designate land closer to the natural spring, and he was also concerned about the shade from the hill of boulders, which could be remedied by removing the hill and planting where the boulders stood. Thus, aside from the report about arsenic, he might have decided on the ninth day that removing the hill of boulders and grading the northwest corner was optimal for his purposes. True, on the ninth day, G had abandoned plans to grow grapes, so his designation was for purposes other than planting an optimal vineyard; still, his designation of the northwest corner arguably was within the risks assumed by CC when they entered into the contract.

Nonetheless, G probably violated the duty of good faith by designating the northwest corner of Terra for grading, requiring time-consuming removal of boulders, solely for the purpose of causing CC to withdraw from the contract so that G would not need to pay CC for grading the soil. G's preliminary plans for designating the 75% of Terra for grading excluded the northern portion containing the spring and the hill of boulders, and he changed that designation to include the hill of boulders only when he decided to abandon the grading contract after discovering the excessive levels of arsenic in the soil. Indeed, he opportunistically took advantage of his contractual discretion over the designation of land only after first considering buying his way out of the contract with CC. His designation ultimately was calculated to force CC to enter into a mutual rescission of the contract, because moving the boulders would cause CC to delay to the point of losing money because of the cost of performance and the stipulated damages clause.

Although G had great discretion over designation of land to be graded, the risks assumed by CC in that clause should be defined in light of other parts of the contract that state that the grading was for the purpose of preparing the land for growing grapes. That suggests that a designation for a purpose unrelated to growing grapes, simply to force CC to rescind, should be outside of G's permissible discretion. If G had proposed a contract clause that would require CC to remove the hill of boulders if G discovered a reason to abandon his plans for a vineyard, CC presumably would have rejected that idea under the contract's fee and deadline, because he would suffer a deduction of at least $15,000 from his $60,000 fee, and would spend at least $60,000 on completing the work. In that light, G acted in bad faith to hinder CC's performance and prevent CC from earning the full fruits of his contract with G.

On balance, I conclude....

3. G's Ground for Avoiding the Contract—Mutual Mistake of Fact

G can avoid the contract if, at the time of contracting, the parties shared a mutual but mistaken assumption of fact that formed the basis or essence of the contract, which requires a centrality to the bargain beyond the simple materiality required for misrepresentation. Even so, a party will not be entitled to avoidance if it assumed the risk of the mistake, which might be allocated by contract, industry standards, or that party's proceeding in conscious ignorance of the relevant facts.

G can argue that the parties shared an assumption of fact about the ideal nature of the soil, a fact that was central to the contract for preparing the soil for a vineyard, the only reason for G wanting to grade the soil. G selected CC largely for his experience with vineyards, and he joined with CC in inspecting the soil, which they both agreed had a sandy consistency and drainage that was ideal for cultivation of certain wine grapes. This shared assumption about the central basis of the contract was badly mistaken, because the soil turned out to be unsuitable for growing grapes, in light of the subsequent report from the lab about high arsenic levels.

CC can respond that the parties' shared assumption was not related to the essence of this contract for grading. Whether the soil had the best consistency and drainage for growing grapes might have been central to G's original decision to purchase the land for grape cultivation, but it's not clearly part of the basis of the contract with CC for grading the soil. For the contract with CC, it would be more central to the contract to reach some consensus about whether the ground was reasonably easy to grade or whether it contained too many boulders for removal. The parties' discussion of the suitability of the soil for growing grapes was a convenient confirmation of G's plans for planting vineyards, but it arguably does not undermine the basis for a contract to grade the land.

Moreover, at the time of contracting, G may have been certain about certain physical facets of the soil, but he was proceeding in conscious ignorance of the chemical content of the soil. The parties did not discuss anything about lack of toxins in the soil, and they could not test for that by running it through their hands, so they shared no assumptions about the chemical content of the soil. Indeed, G acknowledged that he was uncertain about the content of the soil at the chemical level because he sent a sample to a lab for analysis, something he could have done prior to contracting. Consequently, he should be viewed as assuming the risk of any mistake about the chemical content of the soil being suitable for growing grapes and thus in need of grading for vineyards (and, indeed, a lack of assumptions about chemical content undermines a finding of mistake in the first place). G could respond that he had no such conscious ignorance about the suitability of the soil for growing grapes, because CC's expertise with vineyards confirmed his certainty about the suitability of the soil, and because he submitted the sample to the lab solely to determine the best mix of fertilizers to maximize the nutrients of soil that was mutually assumed to be suitable. Even so, by custom or context, a court might charge a landowner and prospective grower with the responsibility for knowing of the risk of toxins in the soil and either testing for them prior to contracting or assuming that risk.

On balance, I conclude....

Analysis of the Exam

This essay exam required a lot of reading and thinking, as well as a fair amount of writing. Although it addressed only three issues and provided a prompt that pointed toward each issue, spotting the issues was a big part of the exam. Spotting the issue translated into identifying the best argument to reach a goal stated by the question. Understanding which argument would work best on the facts required a great deal of knowledge about the topics we studied, as well as a certain sense of judgment. That ability to identify a client's strongest argument, that sense of judgment, is something that you will develop further in law school and later in practice.

A simple example is presented by the third question. Because CC agreed that the soil was suitable for grapes, some students argued that G could avoid the contract for CC's unintentional misrepresentation of facts (or maybe material breach of warranty). That's not a terrible argument, and it earned some points, especially because some of its elements overlapped with mutual mistake. However, it's difficult to argue that G relied on a misstatement by CC, when it was G who first declared that the soil had the right consistency for growing grapes, and CC simply expressed agreement with that. It's much easier to argue that their agreement about the soil's suitability reflected a mutually shared assumption of fact that went to the essence of the bargain, thus making it easier for G to seek avoidance on the ground of mutual mistake. As you can see from the discussion above, the arguments and counter-arguments are fairly well balanced and would give the court a good deal to think about. The argument for avoidance on the basis of misrepresentation by CC, however, seemed to founder almost as soon as the fact analysis started.

A stronger example is provided by choosing unconscionability to attack G's designation of land, in response to the second question. Because unconscionability addresses unfairness in the contract and contracting process at the time of contract formation, some other doctrine, such as violation of good faith, is suitable for challenging G's behavior during performance. The only proper application of unconscionability to the facts would be a substantive challenge to the broad scope of the discretion clause on the face of the contract, but that's a very hard argument to make and even then it's extremely difficult to find any procedural unconscionability. In contrast, as discussed in this memo, the facts are well suited to a strong argument that C could reject G's designation of land because it represented bad faith by G during the performance of the contract; it parallels *Yakima* in that respect.

The best argument for CC in the first question should have been pretty clear: As soon as the question referred to the enforceability of a stipulated damages clause, along with lots of facts about how the clause operated, it should have stimulated thought about our covering just that issue on the final day of class.

Exercise 11.3.2

a. O should include an express condition that conditions her obligation to pay the bonus on completion by February 1, perhaps with an emphasis on the timing being critical. Example: "O will pay a bonus of $2,000 to C on the condition that C completes every detail of the painting required in this contract no later than precisely 5 p.m. on February 1."

b. Because the contract 10 years ago included only an exchange of mutual, unqualified promises, the painting contractor satisfied constructive conditions to his right to payment of the contract fee by substantially performing his duties. Therefore, although the painter was in minor breach, Owner was obligated to pay $1,500, while the contractor owed the Owner only the actual damages caused by missing a small portion of hard-to-see spots under the roofline. In the current contract, Owner should include an express condition that limits his promise to pay so that this obligation does not arise at all unless and until the contractor performs completely (rather than just substantially). A typical clause might look like the following: "Owner agrees to pay Contractor $1,500, but only if Contractor first completes every detail of the performance described in section 2 above." [Some students did a good job of making the condition even stronger by making Owner's duty to pay contingent on Owner's personal satisfaction with Contractor's full performance. A student might think of including a liquidated damages clause to address the difficulty of calculating the damages arising from a minor breach, but this would not address the specific dispute that Owner encountered 10 years ago regarding whether Owner could withhold all pay.]

Exercise 11.4.2

Did Padilla Substantially Perform or Did She Materially Breach?

Because of constructive conditions arising out of the dependency of mutual promises, [in your own words, summarize the rules of constructive conditions, substantial performance, and material breach, in an action for payment under the terms of the contract].

Padilla performed more than half of her obligations and produced notes that helped a substitute contractor finish the performance. Moreover, although she intentionally repudiated further obligations, she did so in response to a legitimate health concern and not out of spite or intent to injure. Still, she repudiated her obligations after finishing only 60% of her work, necessitating the hiring of a substitute on short notice, and she did not produce any of the final products: the brief and the oral argument.

If the contract is viewed as a whole, Padilla probably materially breached, allowing Lee to cancel his own obligations under that contract.

Is the Contract Divisible?

[In your own words, explain divisibility and how it could help Padilla.]

The contract calls for Padilla to perform five separate tasks and entitles her to an hourly fee. Thus, on its face the contract could be divided into five stages with consideration associated with the hours spent on each. Thus, Padilla could argue that she substantially performed the first three stages (studying the record, studying the opening brief, and performing research) and is entitled to the contract rate for her hours spent on those stages (minus damages owed to Lee because of Padilla's breach). Lee, on the other hand, could argue that the contract isn't clearly divided into parts, because no definite sum of money or hours was apportioned to each stage of work. More important, divisibility makes no sense in this case, because the work on the first three stages is of little benefit to Lee and his client without the final product of the brief and the oral argument. True, Padilla took copious notes during the first three stages, facilitating the substitute's work, but Padilla's departure still caused duplication of work.

[Conclusion?]

Can Padilla at Least Recover Restitution of the Value of the Benefit She Provided?

[You will be better prepared to discuss this issue after studying Chapter 12, and even then this goes beyond a satisfactory answer.]

[Explain the reluctance of courts to grant even restitution to a materially breaching party, but with some room for argument, based on all the facts.]

Restitution in this case might be measured, for example, by a reasonable hourly rate for the time saved because of Padilla's copious notes. That almost certainly would be less than the contract rate for Padilla's work, because her notes were less helpful to someone else than they would have been to Padilla herself had she completed the work. Moreover, some courts might deny all relief to Padilla because she intentionally repudiated. On the other hand, she quit the project not for arbitrary or spiteful reasons but to hasten her recovery from an illness.

[Conclusion?]

Exercise 11.10.1

A. Repudiation by EE?

A party can terminate an agreement if the other party repudiates its obligations by making a clear statement that it is unable or unwilling to perform according to the terms of the contract. The first party might choose to encourage the repudiating party to retract its repudiation, but it need not do so; it can cancel the contract and hire a substitute.

GC can argue that EE clearly stated that it would not perform unless GC changed the terms by granting EE more time and higher pay. EE's statement was a clear ultimatum because he said that such a change was "the only sensible solution," and that "we'll get the job done" after such a modification, suggesting that it would not perform under other circumstances. EE didn't leave room for GC to reject this proposal, because he seemed to tell GC to text back a single response, "yes," to confirm that he understood EE's message.

On the other hand, EE can argue that EE was only requesting a modification and was not insisting on a change. He stated that his proposal was the only "sensible" solution, not that it was the only possible course of action. Moreover, EE's asking for GC's confirmation should be interpreted as asking whether GC assented to the proposed change. When GC said, "No," EE would understand that its request had been rejected and that it would be bound to perform as dictated in the original contract, taking a loss. EE was strongly pressing for a modification, but even a strong plea to modify does not amount to the equivalent of "I will not perform unless you agree to these new terms."

I conclude....

B. Assurance of Performance

If a party has not received a repudiation but is reasonably insecure about the ability or willingness of the other party to perform, it should demand that the other party address that insecurity by providing adequate assurances of performance. If the other party fails to provide the assurance within a reasonable time, the first party can treat that failure as the equivalent of a repudiation in most courts. This procedure is codified in the UCC for sales of goods but likely will be adopted by most courts under common law as well.

In this case, it is subject to debate whether EE's statement amounts to a repudiation. Consequently, GC risks being the first materially breaching part if it cancels the contract and a court later determines that EE was simply asking about a possible modification. Accordingly, it would be much more prudent for GC to simply refuse EE's request and to demand assurance that EE will perform the contract as it stands. If EE refuses to do so, then GC will be on much better footing to cancel the contract, fire EE, and hire a substitute contractor. If EE provides the assurance, then GC should allow EE to proceed and should monitor the work closely.

Exercise 11.10.2

Anticipatory Breach by Repudiation

If BA has repudiated the wedding contract, then Rave could be in total anticipatory breach in November, permitting SJ to cancel, hire a replacement, and sue for breach of contract immediately, rather than waiting to see whether the band shows up on the due date for performance in February. Because a full repudiation puts a party in total breach prior to the performance date, a court will not lightly interpret a statement to be a repudiation.

In this case, BA never directly stated that Rave would not perform. In fact, he stated that he hoped that Rave could remain available and then denied that he had stated that Rave would cancel. He simply advised SJ to prepare for all eventualities, as might be the case if one anticipated that the band members could become unavailable because all were seriously injured in a car crash in February, for example.

On the other hand, a realistic interpretation of Agent's statements, in light of all the circumstances of Rave's new fame, would give SJ reason to doubt Rave's continuing commitment to the wedding. BA was not reassuring when he said that he didn't "exactly" say that Rave was canceling. Moreover, BA's statements that he "really hopes" that Rave will still perform for SJ, and that SJ should line up a replacement band to "cover all the bases," is tantamount to saying that Rave is not committed to playing and will perform at SJ's wedding only if they are not booked for another gig. If BA is placing a new condition on Rave's performance, stating a willingness or ability to perform only on different terms than originally agreed, that would amount to a repudiation of the contract.

On balance, I conclude....

Options

In the face of BA's ambiguous statements, SJ runs the risk of becoming the first materially breaching party if they treat BA's statements as a repudiation, cancel the contract, and hire a replacement. At the very least, SJ should seek to confirm Rave's repudiation before treating it as one, by making a formal demand for clarification. If SJ are lucky, Rave will provide them with a clear repudiation or a clear statement of intent to perform. If Rave is silent or still ambiguous in the face of such a demand, however, SJ would benefit from a court's adopting the UCC's position on demands for assurance.

Demand for Assurance

UCC § 2-609 has pioneered a doctrine that permits an insecure party to make a written demand of reassurance that the other party will perform; if such reassurance is not provided within a reasonable time not exceeding 30 days, the insecure party can treat that failure as a repudiation and assert its rights. This case is not for a sale of goods, but courts are likely to borrow some general form of this sensible rule and apply it to transactions governed by the common law, even if not adopting its every detail; it's just one step beyond the prudent practice of seeking clarification of ambiguous statements.

Because BA's comments are not unambiguously a repudiation, SJ should make a written demand for a statement of the band's continuing commitment, and for any supporting documentation needed for reassurance. Even if BA's statements are not a repudiation, they certainly are strong enough to give SJ a reasonable basis to feel insecure about Rave's continuing commitment to the contract. When confronted with a demand for reassurance, perhaps BA could convincingly and credibly retract his earlier ambiguous statements, or maybe he could produce a copy of a letter to a promoter, stating that the band was unavailable on Feb. 10 for concerts because of an unbreakable commitment to SJ's wedding reception. Absent some credible reassurance such as this, delivered within a reasonable time, SJ could treat the contract as breached prior to the wedding reception and could assert legal rights.

Assuming that BA had earlier repudiated, or if SJ secured the equivalent of repudiation after unsuccessfully demanding assurance of performance, SJ could waive their right to cancel the contract and could insist that Rave perform as promised. Rave might retract their repudiation (which they can do until SJ treats the repudiation as final or otherwise relies on it, such as by hiring another band). If Rave has clearly stated that it will not perform, however, SJ should not delay so long that they end up with no band at their wedding. At some point they should treat the repudiation as a total breach and should enforce their rights:

[The following discussion contemplates that you have studied Chapter 12.]

Specific Performance

SJ might momentarily consider suing for specific performance, requesting that the court order Rave to perform at their wedding. A court will grant such equitable relief only if the legal remedy of money damages is inadequate, and even then such relief lies within the discretion of the judge, who will not ordinarily compel complex or artistic personal services, which might require continuing court supervision.

Rave's talent and newfound fame probably make them sufficiently unique to satisfy the threshold requirement of inadequacy of the legal remedy of damages. A court, however, would almost certainly not force Rave to perform; that would implicate constitutional policies against involuntary servitude and might raise problems later of determining whether Rave complied with the court's order and really played with their usual energy and artistry. SJ could more easily secure a negative injunction prohibiting Rave from performing at a conflicting concert; that does not require Rave to perform, but it might put pressure on Rave to keep its commitment to SJ. However, such an action would amount to considerable expense to retain a band for a wedding reception, and it wouldn't guarantee that Rave would remain in the mood to perform with their artistry or that they would show up at all; it would just guarantee that Rave would not perform somewhere else that evening, which would not be valuable to a wedding couple. Moreover, a judge might be reluctant to prohibit a newly famous band from performing in a bigger forum, thus robbing a larger community of the opportunity to enjoy the band, along with the economic activity that would go with the bigger performance.

On balance, I conclude....

Money Damages

Mitigating and Suing for Damages: SJ will want to line up some band or DJ for its reception, rather than sitting around and waiting for Rave to show up or not, and risking a reception without a band. If they foolishly failed to mitigate damages in that way, they would not be able to recover the consequential losses of a ruined reception. So, SJ's damages will be their direct loss in value (the difference between the $8,000 contract price and the money needed to hire a band that is comparable to Rave with its newfound fame), plus an incidental costs of finding and contracting with a substitute band. SJ could recover this amount, but only if they could prove such foreseeable losses with reasonable certainty. SJ could prove Rave's newfound fame fairly easily through the Youtube hits and new offers for national concerts, but using that data to equate Rave with some other band of equal quality and charm might be speculative, and losses based on breach by a newly famous band might not have been foreseeable at the time of contracting. So, SJ might be limited to recovering the net cost of hiring a really good wedding band, rather than the cost of hiring a substitute famous concert band, which Rave has become.

Settlement: SJ could encourage Rave to decide by a certain date whether it will recommit to the wedding reception or take a more lucrative concert offer. If it does the latter, SJ could negotiate to voluntarily and mutually rescind the wedding reception contract, but only if Rave shares the increased earnings from a lucrative concert performance. For example, if Rave does land a conflicting concert for $40,000, and if it pays SJ $12,000 for a release/rescission, reducing its effective earnings to $28,000, Rave will still make $20,000 more than it had originally expected for that date ($28,000—

$8,000), and SJ will now have a total of $20,000 to hire a really terrific local or regional band or other special things for the reception ($8,000 originally set aside for the band plus $12,000 in settlement from Rave), and both parties will save litigation expenses.

Covering all Bases: If SJ wants to preserve the possibility that Rave will play, it will insist that Rave perform its contract but will ensure that it has music for the reception by contracting as well with a substitute band. To minimize its costs, it could condition performance of the second contract on Rave's failure to show up for set-up and sound check. The substitute band, however, likely wouldn't agree to such terms except for a minimum fee that was not subject to a condition, and to a premium fee if they do perform. A more prudent course along these lines would be to hire another band immediately, subject to the condition that the contract with Rave has been canceled no later than one month prior to the wedding.

Exercise 12.9.1

A. Entitlement to Payment

Substantial Performance and Material Breach—The contract does not expressly condition DD's obligation to pay KC on KC completing performance, but their promises are dependent so that KC's performance is a constructive condition of DD's duty to pay. KC can sue on the contract only if it has satisfied its constructive conditions to counter-performance by substantially performing its own obligations, thus committing only a minor breach rather than a material one.

KC breached, because it failed to clear all the specified growth by the contract due date. KC can argue, however, that its breach is only minor, and thus that it substantially performed the entire contract, because it cleared 80% of the growth—a very substantial portion—before the contract deadline. Moreover, KC stated its intention to return to complete the work when needs elsewhere were less urgent, so it has not repudiated any part of the contract; instead, its only breach is a delay in completing a small percentage of the work. Although KC's breach is intentional, motivated by a desire to earn more money, it will serve the public interest by efficiently reallocating KC's valuable resources to a more urgent need in the community. Moreover, allowing DD to cancel the contract would leave KC without compensation on the contract after completing nearly all the work, thus visiting a hardship on KC.

DD, on the other hand, can argue that she didn't get the substantial benefit of the promised performance, because any path of dry growth to her home could be sufficient to ignite a fire, including the 20% on the west side, a side that does not enjoy the added buffer of the swimming pool. Moreover, an assurance to complete the work later does little to reduce the magnitude of the breach; any delay creates increased risks during the fire season—especially when brush fires are burning at the other end of the canyon. In this situation, DD should be accorded the right to cancel the contract, avoid her own obligations to pay KC the contract rate, and hire a substitute contractor—or at least to suspend her performance until it becomes clear whether KC will complete work within a reasonable time.

Conclusion?

Divisibility—If KC can show that the contract is divisible into units of work for which units of consideration are allocated, and if DD would derive benefit from performance of some of those divisible units of work, then KC might be entitled to the contract rate for those units of work that it actually completed, although it would be liable for delay in completing other units.

In this case, KC can argue that the contract is divisible into square yards of mowing and clearing, because the contract quoted a price per square yard on its face, and because every square yard cleared reduced the fire hazard to some degree by allowing fire crews to concentrate on a smaller area around the house. DD can retort that the price per square yard was stated in the contract only to show how the total price was reached and not to suggest that the contract was divisible in any way. Moreover, DD derived meaningful benefit only through completion of the entire contract, because a brush fire that approached from any direction could burn around the property and could make its way close to the home through the path left uncleared by KC.

Conclusion?

B. Damages

Consequential Losses

KC may be liable for consequential losses caused by its breach, but only if the losses were a foreseeable consequence of breach at the time of contracting. It would be foreseeable if such losses would be a natural consequence of a failure to complete the work, or if they would arise from special circumstances made known to KC at the time of contracting.

DD can argue that the fire hazard of the dry growth near her home is obvious, especially to a contractor who apparently specializes in such work, because it was called to help with urgent clearing near the brush fire. The danger to her house was even more evident when KC left the job, because fire had already broken out at the other end of the canyon.

KC can argue that the loss of DD's home was not a foreseeable consequence of a brief delay in completing the contract by the contract deadline; such a loss was instead the result of unpredictable bad luck. He would argue, moreover, that the presence of the fire at the other end of the canyon should not be considered, because foreseeability should be tested as of the time of making the contract.

Conclusion?

Mitigation of Damages

Assuming that loss of the home would be viewed as a foreseeable loss, KC may escape liability for that loss if DD could have avoided that loss with a reasonable substitute transaction.

KC can argue that DD, who believed KC's breach to be material, should have canceled the contract and hired a substitute contractor to immediately clear the remaining growth. DD should have given priority to such an option in light of the presence of fire at the other end of the canyon. Such action almost certainly would have avoided the loss of the house, and DD could have recovered (or withheld) from KC the difference between the price agreed to be KC and that charged by the substitute contractor.

DD can argue that KC stated its intention of returning as soon as the urgency at the other end of the canyon had passed, so it was reasonable for her to opt to maintain the contract with KC and to wait for him to return to complete the work at the contract price, rather than pay another contractor double KC's contract rate. This approach was all the more reasonable in face of uncertainty about whether KC in fact materially breached and thus whether DD was legally entitled to cancel the contract.

Conclusion?

Exercise 12.9.2

Parol Evidence Rule

The alleged oral agreement to forbid the use of leaf blowers is not found in the written Landscaping Agreement ("LA"). The LA is a written integration of some sort, because it has been negotiated and signed by the parties in a way that reflects their intent to make it a statement of at least some of the terms of a final agreement. Under the parol evidence rule, therefore, Kiting can introduce evidence of the alleged oral agreement to forbid use of leaf blowers only if that is a collateral agreement, separate and independent from a completely integrated LA, or if it is a consistent supplemental term of a partially integrated LA, or if it is used to interpret a term in the LA.

The LA has no merger clause or other indication that it is a complete integration, so it arguably is only a partial integration, which means that it contains only some—but not all—of the terms of the parties' final agreement. DD could argue that the agreement should be regarded as a complete integration—one that completely and exclusively states all the terms of the parties' agreement on a certain subject matter—simply because the agreement looks complete: it is a formal, titled, written and signed document that describes the parties' duties in detail in 20 sections. The court in *Gianni* apparently found a complete integration on such a basis.

If the LA is a partially integrated agreement, then Kiting would be free to introduce the alleged oral agreement so long as it does not contradict the terms of the written LA. In this case, the alleged oral agreement appears not to contradict the written integration, because the written LA says nothing about equipment that may be used. Cruz can argue that the description of landscaping duties implicitly contemplates use of leaf blowers because the described grounds are so extensive and because leaf-blowers are customarily used for the kind of work that must be described in the LA (such as cleaning sidewalks); if so, an alleged oral agreement to the contrary arguably would conflict with the meaning of the written contract. On balance....

If the LA is a complete integration, then it will supersede even consistent additional terms within its subject matter. The LA does not address landscaping equipment, so Kiting could argue that the alleged oral agreement relates to a different subject matter in a separate transaction. Still, the LA describes CELS's landscaping maintenance duties in such detail that one would normally expect the parties to include a promise about not using leaf blowers in that written contract, if the parties agreed to it at all. Moreover, even Kiting's version of the conversation does not identify any separate consideration for Cruz's alleged oral promise, suggesting that even Kiting believed that Cruz's promise was exchanged for the fees in the written contract, which further supports the argument that the alleged oral agreement relates to the subject matter of the written LA. On balance, I conclude that Kiting cannot introduce evidence of the alleged oral agreement as a collateral agreement that is separate from the completely integrated LA.

Even if the written Landscaping Agreement is a completely integrated agreement, Kiting can introduce evidence of the alleged oral agreement if his purpose is simply to interpret some term that made it into the written contract. The written LA does state that CELS must maintain the landscaping "in keeping with the high standards at Shangrila." Kiting can argue that "high standards at Shangrila" include using methods that are consistent with the style and philosophy at Shangrila, and that the court should admit extrinsic evidence helping to explain these "high standards" and the methods that would be consistent with them. Testimony regarding the statement made by Kiting before signing would qualify as such admissible evidence relevant to interpretation. CELS, on the other hand, can argue that the plain meaning of "high standards," whether at Shangrila or elsewhere, relates to high quality in results and cannot convey any meaning relating to methods. The outcome of this argument very likely will turn on whether the court applies a traditional plain-meaning approach, especially one that limits the judge to the four corners of the contract, in which case it likely will decide that "high standards" is not susceptible of the meaning advanced by Kiting and that the extrinsic evidence is not admissible. Kiting will more likely win this argument if the court adopts the more progressive approach—one that allows the judge to initially consider the alleged conversation prior to signing—in deciding whether it's plausible that the parties might have used "high standards at Shangrila" to convey not only quality of results but also restrictions on methods of landscaping.

Material Breach

Kiting would be happier if he could cancel his contract with CELS and would be free to hire GTLC. There is no defect in contract formation, and Cruz has not repudiated or abandoned the contract as a whole. Thus, Kiting can cancel the contract only if Kiting can prove that the contract forbids use of gas-powered leaf blowers (see discussion above) and if CELS's breach or repudiation of that provision amounts to a material breach of the whole contract, which would constitute a failure of substantial performance by CELS and thus a failure to satisfy constructive conditions to Kiting's return obligations.

A breach of a construction contract is material depending on a number of factors, such as whether Kiting received the substantial benefit of the contract, whether Kiting will suffer a forfeiture or other prejudice if the contract is canceled, whether Kiting's interests can be protected by his maintaining the contract and retaining his claim for damages, and whether CELS acted in bad faith. CELS's breach may not reflect bad faith on his part if the obligation to exclude leaf blowers is recognized only as a close question of interpretation and if Cruz thought it wasn't part of the contract; however, it would be intentional if Cruz did expressly agree to it, as Kiting asserts, and if it's a term that supplements a partial integration.

Kiting arguably did not get the substantial benefit of the contract in light of the importance of serenity and harmony to him and the nature of Shangrila, as suggested by the habit of guests to avoid the leaf blowers when they are in operation, and considering that the leaf blowers are in operation somewhere on the grounds nearly every day. On the other hand, the leaf blowers are not used for long periods of time, and they don't seem to be having any negative effect on the success of the resort, which is fully booked.

The contract did not state how CELS would be paid; however, so long as it was paid periodically, such as monthly, CELS won't suffer any forfeiture if the contract is canceled; it will just cease working this job and cease earning further fees. Moreover, Kiting can argue that his interests can't be protected by maintaining the contract and retaining a claim for damages, because the problems of which he complains are not having an immediate economic impact; they are causing conflicts with his personal philosophy and may have a long-term effect on the popularity of the resort, but those are not damages that are easily proved or recovered. CELS can argue, however, that Kiting has not yet suffered any economic losses and that future performance by CELS without leaf blowers (assuming that Kiting proves such an obligation and CELS is forced to recognize it), will protect Kiting from any future losses.

On balance, ...

Remedies for Breach

If Kiting cannot cancel the contract, he can try to enforce the contract through specific performance, in which case a judge would order CELS to perform all the obligations, including the promise to refrain from using leaf blowers (assuming Kiting can prove that term). Specific performance is available, however, only if money damages are inadequate and even then it lies within the court's discretion. Kiting might be able to show that his legal remedy is inadequate because—although he and the resort are suffering injury—the injury is impossible to quantify in economic terms. It is highly unlikely, however, that a judge would order CELS to actually perform landscaping services in a manner that is unpopular with its employees. Such an order would be difficult to supervise and likely would cause friction within CELS's workforce and between the parties.

Whether or not Kiting can cancel the contract, it's unlikely that he can prove much in the way of recoverable damages, which usually are limited to economic losses and must be foreseeable and proved with reasonable certainty. His resort is not yet suffering any economic losses, and future losses due to CELS's breach are too speculative to prove. He might try to establish the resort's loss in value based on his personal valuation, considering his environmental sensibilities, and such a loss could be foreseeable in light of his pre-signing statement; however, that's a fairly progressive approach and would not be adopted by all courts.

In all but a few states, moreover, punitive damages are never awarded for even an intentional breach of contract, and damages for emotional distress generally are not awarded except in the unusual case of a contract that is designed to protect emotional security so that emotional distress is a foreseeable consequence of breach for reasons other than disappointment over pecuniary losses. If Kiting can introduce evidence of his pre-signing statements to Cruz, and prove the alleged oral agreement, he can argue that the contract was designed in part to ensure consistency with his philosophy of harmony and serenity and that use of gas-powered leaf blowers foreseeably would cause him distress. On the other hand, even if Kiting can show that the contract obligated CELS to refrain from using leaf blowers, it would not necessarily make the contract one designed to protect emotional security. The harm for breach of such an agreement could be measure solely by the extent to which it affected the popularity of the resort with guests.

In sum, Kiting's prospects for helpful judicial remedies are slim. Even if he proves a breach, he might be unable to prove substantial damages. Still, that would at least adjudicate the contents of the contract and might bring him an award of attorneys' fees in some states.

The best result for Kiting would be the ability to cancel the contract with CELS and hire GTLC, without expecting much or anything in damages for past breaches. However, even that self-help remedy is risky, because of the danger that a court might find that CELS did not breach the contract or that any breach was only minor. To play it safe, Kiting might want to negotiate with CELS to refrain from using leaf blowers in exchange for additional pay, or to buy out CELS's contract with a settlement agreement, leaving him free to hire GTLC.

Exercise 12.9.3

1. Grounds for Rescission or Non-Enforcement of Entire Lease

Unconscionability—The new Lease might be unconscionable, which in most states requires both procedural and substantive unconscionability. [Explain the rules in your own words] [note: unconscionability got a boost from the UCC, but it is widely recognized under common law for non-sales transactions, as evidenced by the arbitration-clause cases in our book that are set in transactions other than the sale of goods].

Procedural: The new Lease has one important element of procedural unconscionability—it is an adhesion contract, drafted entirely by Dell and not subject to change. This is illustrated by Dell responding "take it or leave it" and "my attorney won't let me change it" to Sato's demands that section 2 and 10 of the Lease be deleted. Moreover, because the signing occurred just before the noon opening of Sato's Sushi for the day, Sato presumably did not have time to haggle at length over the terms or to gather information important to the bargaining. Sato's complaints during signing showed that he was unhappy with some of the terms of the new Lease but viewed signing as better than the option of moving to a new location. Those circumstances clearly do not undermine consideration or amount to duress; however, they show that Dell has relatively great bargaining power and could dictate terms that Sato dislikes. The imbalance in bargaining power is accentuated by the fact that Dell apparently has consulted an attorney about the form lease, while Sato is reviewing the lease on his own and in a rush before the restaurant opens.

On the other hand, other common attributes of procedural unconscionability are absent. Sato was a successful, experienced businessman, whose restaurant was important to Dell, thus reducing the gap in bargaining power. None of the provisions was buried in fine print, the new Lease was only two pages long, and Sato noticed and understood the provisions to which he objected. Although Sato desired to remain in this successful location (because he had not learned yet of Gracy's closing), his first lease was ending, so he had the option of moving to another location rather than signing this lease.

Substantive: At the time of contracting, the new Lease arguably was lopsided against Sato, at least based on revenue for 2018, because clause 2—if applied to that year—would have resulted in the equivalent of total monthly rent of $2,000, $500 above market rents. Moreover, depending on how much business would be generated after 9 p.m., section 10 might force Sato to operate at a loss for those hours if his expenses exceeded revenue after 9 p.m. If so, this provision could cause Sato to lose net profits, while solely benefiting Dell, because Dell would be receiving a cut of the revenue without experiencing the corresponding expenses. At least, this provision presented that risk to Sato.

On the other hand, the base rent is $500 below the market rent, so that Dell is taking some risk that she would get only the market level or less if Sato's revenue plunged, something that Dell knew was a possibility when *Gracy's* folded. Indeed, in light of *Gracy's* departure (of which Dell was aware) if Dell wanted to maximize her income, she would have asked for maximum base rent rather than taking a risk with a percentage of revenue, on top of a base rent below market value. Moreover, although section 10 may give Dell substantial control over Sato's operating hours, it is triggered only when revenue falls to a stated level, and it might be viewed as a reasonable response to economic downturn, so that all of the businesses in the strip mall continue to bring business to each other late into the night.

Conclusion: I conclude that Sato can show fairly minimal procedural unconscionability, based on the adhesive nature of the new Lease. When added to substantive factors, I conclude....

Rescission for Misrepresentation [State the rule in your own words, taking care to define half-truth and possible grounds for requiring disclosure, and to mention the need for justifiable reliance, as well as flexibility in the equitable relief of rescission.]

Misrepresentation of Fact: Dell was refreshingly candid during the signing, sometimes admitting to greed ("I deserve a piece of this money machine."). He never made an affirmatively false statement, because it's true that Sato was making a good income at the time of the signing, that the location (near *Gracy's*) was a factor in the first-year profits, and that Dell undoubtedly "hoped" that Sato would continue to have success.

However, once Dell addressed the topics of revenue and location, he probably engaged in a misleading half-truth by failing to tell the whole story, including the fact—known to him—that *Gracy's* had declared bankruptcy and had announced that it soon would be closing. The cumulative effect of Dell's statements was to leave the impression that the location would continue to help Sato generate handsome revenue and profits.

Alternatively, although Dell wouldn't normally have a duty to affirmatively disclose material facts, he might have a duty to do so here if he knew that Sato was operating under a unilateral mistake regarding *Gracy's* or if Dell had a fiduciary duty to disclose material facts. Sato's reference to the good location might have given notice to Dell that Sato in fact mistakenly assumed that *Gracy's* would remain open, a mistake that Dell's statements might have advanced or at least did not dispel. Moreover, Dell and Sato were currently in a lease, so it's remotely possible that Dell's status as Sato's landlord created a fiduciary duty on her part to disclose information relevant to the success of Sato's business. On the other hand, Sato never specifically mentioned *Gracy's*, so Dell's duty to help Sato avoid a known mistake may not have been triggered. Moreover, Sato tried to protect his interests by discovering and demanding the deletion of two clauses, so he treated the bargaining as an arms-length transaction rather than one in which Dell had a special fiduciary duty to protect Sato's interests by disclosing all material facts. Moreover, it is not likely that many states would extend a statutory requirement of disclosure in *commercial lease* transactions, even if they require disclosure in sales of real estate (often limited to sales of dwellings).

Finally, Dell might have engaged in misrepresentation by active concealment by rushing the negotiations soon after disclosure of *Gracy's* bankruptcy, before Sato could discover that fact. However, simply acting quickly might not be enough to constitute actively preventing the other party from discovering information readily available in the media.

Materiality and Reliance: In light of Sato's statement acknowledging the importance of this "great location," and his statement that he couldn't "leave it" because it was a big hit "here," it appears that location was material to Sato's decision to sign the new Lease. Presumably, Sato realized that *Gracy's* was an important feature of that location and would have viewed the new Lease very differently had he known that *Gracy's* would be closing. Thus, one can fairly readily conclude that Sato relied on the implications of a material half-truth by Dell: that the location would remain unchanged in character.

Justifiable Reliance: On the other hand, Dell has a strong argument that Sato's reliance was not justified. *Gracy's* is situated nearby, and its bankruptcy had been reported in the local television news the previous evening and in print news that morning, making it difficult for the average person to avoid learning about it. This fact was even more easily available than the public zoning records in the *Kannavos* case.

Still, as in *Kannavos*, a court might find that the element of justified reliance should be relaxed a bit in light of the strong showing of a misleading half-truth. Because the court would be asked only to return the parties to precontractual status quo through rescission, it might excuse a busy business-owner for not learning about *Gracy's* announcement within the first 24 hours. After all, a busy restaurant owner presumably is not available to watch television during the dinner hour on a business day and might be too tired to read the paper before opening the next day.

Conclusion: On balance, I conclude....

[I did not view duress as a valid issue, because it requires an improper threat, and the class of improper threats clearly does not include the tough but permissible bargaining position of "take it or leave it." That quoted phrase means it's an adhesion contract, which is a huge red flag signaling the possibility of arguing unconscionability. It's precisely the absence of the rather extreme defense of duress that raises the issue of unconscionability, where a finding of procedural problems can rest on bargaining practices that are sharp but do not raise a plausible issue of duress (and then might combine with substantive unconscionability to warrant relief). Similarly, undue influence (relaxation of duress standards in light of a weakened condition or a special relationship) is not a fruitful defense because Sato was not in a weakened state and did not otherwise place unusual trust and confidence in Dell, as evidenced by his pointing out controversial clauses and demanding changes. His demands were futile, but that simply raises the problem of adhesion contract, which sets up the unconscionability argument. So, I generally did not give credit for arguing duress or undue influence, other than a point or two or three for explaining why these theories are not fruitful. If someone argued that the standards for duress ought to be relaxed to undue influence because Dell owed a fiduciary duty to Sato in her position as landlord in an existing lease, I gave a few points of credit for that; however, the landlord-tenant relationship is usually fairly adversarial (as this one seems to be), so it doesn't ordinarily lend itself to the kind of trust and confidence that might arise in a relationship such as attorney-client or similar kind of principal-agent relationship.]

2. *Indefiniteness* {which depends to some extent on Interpretation and Construction}

[This issue was a little more difficult to spot, but it did not count for as many points as did Q1.]

[State rule about requiring sufficient definiteness to define expectation interest; and secondarily about the parol evidence rule not applying to statements made during negotiations if offered to show the meaning of a term in the written contract, as well as interpretation and construction.]

Sato's obligation under section 10 to stay open until midnight is subject to the following vague condition: "if revenue ... will not otherwise adequately supplement the base rent." Since the parties disagree whether this condition has been met (Sato asserted that section 10 wasn't triggered), and because we have no evidence of helpful trade usage, a court arguably would have no objective basis for determining whether revenue was amounting to an "adequate supplement" to base rent. What's "adequate" could vary greatly depending on one's interests and perspectives.

On the other hand, the term "adequate" might be roughly equated with "reasonable," which courts and juries are frequently called upon to interpret and apply to specific facts. Perhaps a court could interpret "adequate supplement" to be a supplement to base rent that raises total rent for the year to the equivalent of market levels. Such an interpretation is supported by Dell's statement during negotiations that he wanted to "come away with at least the equivalent of market level rents," which would not be excluded by the parol evidence rule when used to explain the meaning of section 10. If so, the provision would be enforceable, because the obligation to stay open until midnight is perfectly clear and definite. At worst, "adequate" might mean what Dell assessed in good faith to be adequate in light of her economic needs, but that is less likely than a standard based on general reasonableness, because the clause does not refer to Dell's needs or views.

Reply: Dell's statement during negotiations that he "wants" at a minimum the equivalent of market rates for rent was an expression of general hope about Sato's business and was not clearly stated as a definition of section 10's trigger. Even if that interpretation is inconclusive, the court should resort to the rule of construction of construing a term against the drafter, Dell. In this case, that might mean resisting Dell's attempt to put a definite meaning on an otherwise uncertain term. Dell drafted the trigger for section 10 and should have written it more clearly if she wanted it to be enforceable.

Conclusion: ....

[Some students analyzed this as an issue of illusory promise. However, the clause didn't say anything like, "Sato will work extra hours if Sato feels like it." And it's not an illusory condition, because it doesn't even say anything like "Sato will work extra hours if Dell feels like it." The term "adequately supplement," although very arguably too indefinite to enforce, refers to something other than "if ... feels like it."]

3. Remedies

Specific Performance [Define this in your own words, explaining that it is both extraordinary (legal remedy must be inadequate) and discretionary]

Money damages arguably are inadequate because Sato's talents, vision, and restaurant are unique, and staying open until midnight will help to bring in increased revenue to a degree that would be difficult to prove, and would help the whole strip mall to be more vibrant at night. Moreover, after a year in operation, running the restaurant for a few extra hours could be viewed as a relatively mechanical, ministerial act, not like an opera singer's performance.

On the other hand, money damages would be perfectly adequate for bringing Dell's payments up to base rent plus an "adequate supplement," however that phrase was interpreted to trigger section 10. Moreover, a court would be reluctant to exercise its discretion to order Sato to labor late into the night, providing his personal touch on the cuisine and ambience, or that of a highly trained employee, with the court retaining jurisdiction to oversee its injunction. It might also withhold its discretion because of unclean hands and unfairness in the new Lease. Even if the lease is not unconscionable, and even if it is not subject to rescission for misrepresentation, Dell's selective statements about location, and her exercise of bargaining power to impose an adhesion contract with some terms that Sato found to be burdensome, might be enough to convince a court to leave Dell to its money damages.

As a last resort, Dell might be able to secure a negative injunction, enjoining Sato from opening his restaurant elsewhere, thus putting pressure on him to perform the contract terms of the new Lease. Such an injunction might overcome problems of affirmatively forcing Sato to engage in personal services; however, it would be no more likely to escape the court's discretionary decision to withhold equitable relief because of the adhesion contract and unfairness in the exchange.

Conclusion: ....

Substitutional Relief: Money Damages [state rules about proof with reasonable certainty in your own words]

Even if section 10's trigger is definite enough to enforce, so that Sato had an obligation to stay open until midnight during 2019, it will be difficult for Dell to prove her damages with reasonable certainty. Because Sato had never served customers between 9 p.m. and midnight at that location, it arguably would be completely speculative to assert that a certain amount of revenue would have been generated during that time (2% of which would be owed to Dell).

On the other hand, so long as Dell can prove that she would have suffered some loss, a court will provide some leeway in proof of the actual amount of damages, particularly because Sato's breach is the cause of the uncertainty in the lost revenue.

Even if nearly all people in the vicinity tend to finish dinner before 9 p.m., it is nearly certain that *Sato's Sushi* would have enjoyed the business of some customers after 9 p.m. Therefore, if section 10 is enforceable and was triggered, Dell should be free to advance some basis for determining the lost revenue. Perhaps a study of the relative amount of business enjoyed in the past by the coffee shop and the ice cream parlor after 9 p.m. could provide a basis to estimate the business that Sato's Sushi would have enjoyed during those hours.

In reply: Customer traffic at an ice cream parlor or coffee shop, both of which might be robust after the dinner hour, might not be a good indicator of the amount of business that a restaurant would enjoy when it mainly serves dinner fare. On the other hand, a sushi restaurant could adapt to later hours with drinks, late-night snacks, etc.

Conclusion: ....

Comments on General Exam Technique

The best fact analyses did the following:

1. They made factual assertions that were linked to an earlier stated element of the legal rule, as in: "Sato's reliance, however, might not have been justified, because he could have discovered prior to contracting that *Gracy's* was closing...." [This makes a factual assertion that relates to an earlier stated legal rule that rescission for misrepresentation generally requires justifiable reliance, which requires some diligence on the part of the person seeking rescission.].

2. The analysis supported the factual assertion, and any counter-arguments, with specific evidentiary facts and reasonable inferences from those facts, as in: "... might not have been justified, because he could have discovered prior to contracting that *Gracy's* was closing. The news about *Gracy's* impending closing had been reported on TV the night before and on the morning news. In light of the importance of the success of *Gracy's* to Sato's business, one might expect that Sato would be following such news more closely. On the other hand, Sato missed the news reports because of his busy schedule at the restaurant. He arguably did not lack diligence in failing to learn of *Gracy's* closing within less than 24 hours of the broadcasts, particularly when Dell was rushing him to sign in the minutes before the opening of the restaurant for the day."

A typical "issue-spotting" exam in law school, with lots of issues, probably doesn't permit this kind of fact analysis. However, I tried on this exam to give students enough time to develop factual arguments at or near this level.

Exercise 12.9.4

Contracts that call for an illegal performance generally are unenforceable. Indeed, to avoid participating in any way in illegality, a court generally will refuse even to grant restitution to a non-breaching party. These rules apply as well to contracts that violate the public policy of statutes or other laws, even if they do not violate the specific terms of the laws. In some cases, courts may relax the rules against restitution or even against enforcement if necessary to protect a party not equally at fault in the policy violation, or to avoid a default, or if policies conflict and are nearly evenly balanced toward enforcement or non-enforcement (such as in some cases of noncompetition agreements).

In this case, it is well known that Cloud is not being used as incense, but is being used as an alternative for marijuana. Indeed, this use is obviously within the contemplation of the contracting parties, because WPW is in the business of selling products that facilitate smoking. Although Cloud does not directly violate any laws at relevant times, it arguably violates the public policies underlying the state and federal statutes that currently prohibit the possession or sale of marijuana, because it is being used for the same purpose and with similar effect. Whatever are the evils of possession and sale of marijuana that prompted state and federal laws against it, those same evils are present in Cloud. Moreover, selling it for smoking purposes—while labeling it as incense—circumvents federal agency regulation of all smoking products.

On the other hand, Cloud does not currently violate any statutes, and is not even subject to any regulation when sold as incense. It is labeled as incense and includes a warning against human consumption; if consumers smoke it to get high, they are misusing the product in a way that is beyond the contracting parties' control. Indeed, the State AG has encouraged vendors to dispose of their remaining stocks, including by selling it, prior to January 1. Thus, the state officer in charge of enforcing state law has signaled that public policy is not offended by sales of Cloud prior to January 1. The sale of stocks of Cloud by Boomer Productions to WPW in November should be viewed as consistent with public policy at the time of contract formation and time for payment, and WPW should be obligated to pay. Alternatively, any violation of public policy should be viewed as minor, and a court should avoid a forfeiture suffered by Boomer Products by either enforcing WPW's obligation to pay $50,000 or by granting restitution of the normal wholesale market value of Cloud if that is less than $50,000.

Conclusion: ....

Exercise 12.9.5

Cancellation for Material Breach

State X's desire to prevent further breaches of the restoration obligation on the Land, and its willingness to give up further lease and extraction fees is consistent with cancellation of the lease. Under common law, it will be able to cancel the lease only if Mineral Corp. has materially breached the lease. [Divisibility is not in issue, because the breaching party is not seeking payment of the contract price, and State X is not looking to cancel just its obligations under the first acre, because it has already completed its obligations on that acre.] Relevant factors for material breach include whether State X received the substantial benefit of Mineral Corp.'s performance, whether State X can be adequately compensated with money damages for minor breach without giving it the right to cancel the whole contract, whether the breach was intentional or in bad faith, and whether Mineral Corp.'s breach so far is likely to recur and thus grow in magnitude.

Mineral Corp. can argue that State X has received all of its expected monetary benefit for the first six months, a lease payment of $250,000, while suffering only minor damages of no more than $10,000 in diminution in market value on that acre. A breach amounting in value to only 1/25 of the payment to State X should be viewed as minor. If the recession continues and State X is forced to sell to developers, it will retain $1 million dollars in lease fees, be able to sell the Land for almost entirely its value if restored, and can collect any diminution in value from Mineral Corp., which is willing to provide such compensation. Mineral Corp.'s breach should be viewed as minor, and its performance substantial, so that State X retains a claim for damages but cannot cancel the lease.

On the other hand, by failing to restore the first acre, Mineral Corp. intentionally withheld a contractual benefit highly valued by State X. The importance of restoration is evidenced by the liquidated damages clause tied directly to the explicit restoration obligation. Moreover, Mineral Corp. is undervaluing the loss of this contract right by referring only to the diminution in market value. State X has no desire to sell to developers, and it hopes that its lease will make such a sale unnecessary. Its loss in value should be measured by the cost to complete ($50,000) or maybe by the agreed-upon damages of $100,000. Moreover, Mineral Corp.'s willingness to breach on the first acre suggests that it will breach again, at least if other acres are no more profitable for it, and perhaps even if they are more profitable. State X should not be left to deal with even the temporary disruption and eyesore of an unrestored acre each six months, while it litigates Mineral Corp.'s obligation to pay more than the bare diminution in market value.

On balance, I conclude....

Liquidated Damages

Regardless whether State X can cancel the remainder of the Lease, it is entitled to damages for breach of the first acre. It can gain the most in damages by enforcing the liquidated damages clause in the Lease.

A court will enforce the parties' agreement on damages in the event of breach, but only if the agreed damages represent a reasonable estimate at the time of contracting of what the actual injury would be. Greater leeway is accorded to the parties in their estimate if they anticipate difficulty in ascertaining damages when a breach occurs, thus underscoring the justification for a liquidated damages clause. Some courts will also validate a damages clause that is reasonable in light of the damages that actually occur, regardless of the reasonableness at the time of contracting. Reasonableness is supported by a clause that calibrates liquidated damages to vary with the size of the breach.

Contractual damages that exceed a reasonable estimate of actual losses are viewed as penalties and are unenforceable as violations of public policy. If a damages clause is unenforceable, the victim of breach will recover those foreseeable damages it can actually prove with reasonable certainty.

In this case, the parties provided a reasonable estimate of the maximum damages that might result from failure to restore each of four acres, so they allowed for graduated damages, calibrated by the number acres left unrestored: $100,000/acre. Although the actual cost to complete restoration of the first acre is only $50,000, and the diminution in value is only $10,000, the damages clause should be enforceable because it was a reasonable estimate of actual possible losses at the time of contracting.

On the other hand, the damages clause was not finely calibrated to the anticipated losses caused by a breach, for two reasons: (1) it was based on an estimate of maximum injury that might result after extraction that was maximally deep and broad, and (2) the full contractual damages for an acre applied regardless of the portion of an acre left unrestored. Thus, the full $100,000 would be owed regardless of the amount of restoration work that was needed and left unperformed. Although reasonable liquidated damages can be awarded even when actual losses vary from the liquidated damages, the great discrepancy here between contractual damages and any measure of actual losses suggests that the parties never tried to come up with a reasonable estimate of actual losses. Instead, the damages clause appears to be a penalty designed to deter breach or to penalize Mineral Corp. if it did breach.

On balance, I conclude....

Damages Based on Proven Losses

If the contractual damages clause is unenforceable, State X will need to prove its losses with reasonable certainty. Its direct loss in value is the difference between the value of the first acre if restored as promised and the acre as returned to State X.

The costs to State X for any failure to restore the Land are foreseeable as flowing naturally from the breach; indeed, it is a form of direct loss rather than consequential damages. Moreover, there is no question about State X failing to mitigate its damages. The main issue is whether State X should be granted its diminution in market value, its cost to complete, or some other measure of damages. The cost to complete is an acceptable measure of loss value unless it is disproportionately high compared to other measures, or if it reflects economic waste.

Mineral Corp. will argue that the cost to complete ($50,000 to restore the first acre) is disproportionate to the measure based on diminution of market value, because it's at least five times greater. That reflects the waste associated with filling pits in the land and restoring topsoil if the State is forced by the recession to sell in two years, and a developer excavates and regrades for parking garages, foundations, swimming pools, and other amenities.

State X will argue that it is entitled to its cost to complete, because that allows it to most directly realize precisely the benefits of the contract, by allowing it to hire another contractor to restore the land as promised. Although that is at least five times the diminution in market value, the market value measure is inappropriate because State X has no desire to liquidate the Land and wants to retain it for public use, which is possible only if it is actually restored.

A few courts might consider a middle ground, awarding something like $30,000, which would not suffice to restore the first acre, but could represent the diminution in value to the State and its residents in not being able to use the land for recreation. Such a compromise measure might be appropriate if the court allows State X to cancel the lease so that the remaining three acres stays open for public use, thus limiting the loss of public use if the first acre is not completely restored.

[The question did not contain facts that supported an argument for mutual mistake of facts. By itself, Mineral Corp.'s disappointment about the profitability of the first acre establishes no more than the possibility it made a bad deal. I gave one or two points for students pointing out that the facts did not support such a claim, but I did not view it as a major issue warranting full discussion.]

Index